THE AURUM FILM ENCYCLOPEDIA
VOLUME ONE

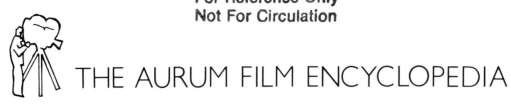

THE AURUM FILM ENCYCLOPEDIA

THE WESTERN

Phil Hardy

Illustrations by the Kobal Collection

AURUM PRESS

This book is dedicated to Joe,
the brightest star in my Western sky

Photographs from The Kobal Collection courtesy of Abkco; A. C. Lyles Productions; Adder Productions; Allied; Allied Artists; Allied Australian Films; Ambassador; Armada Productions; Ashton Productions; Avco; Batjac Productions; Bob Goldstein Productions; Brighton Pictures; Bryna; Charles B. Pierce Productions; Cherokee Productions; Cine Film; Cinema Centre Films; Circle Productions; Collier Young Associates; Columbia; Corona Films; Crossbow; Dargaud Films; Dino de Laurentiis Cinematografica; Dix International Pictures; DRM Productions; Eagle-Lion; Eagle's Wing Productions; E & R Productions; Edward Small; EK Corporation; Essanay; Fame Pictures; Fidelity; First Artist Productions; First National; Four Leaf; Fox; Geoffrey Productions; Globe Enterprises; Golden State; Grand National; Hecht-Lancaster; Hopalong Cassidy Productions; Howard Hughes Productions; Howco Productions; Huka Films; International; ITC Films; Jack Schwarz; Jaffilms; Jensen-Farley Pictures; Jolly Film; K-B Productions; Kingston Films; Kramer Co; Laurel; Lippert; Malpaso; Martin Mooney Productions; Martin Rankin Productions; Marvin Schwarz Productions; Mascot; MGM; Mirisch; Monogram; Monterey; National General; National Student Film Corporation; Palo Alto; Paramount; Partisan Productions; Pathe; PEA Cinematografica; Pearlberg-Seaton Productions; PRC; Pro-Artis Iberica; Producers Actors Corporation; Produzioni Europee Associate; Proteus Films; Rafran Cinematografica; Rank; Ranown Productions; Reliable; Republic; Rialto Film; RKO; Sancrosiap; Sanford Howard Productions; Santa Clara; Scott-Brown Productions; Security Pictures; Selznick Releasing Organization; Solar; Stockbridge; Sunset; TCF; Tiffany; Tobis-Rota; Triangle; United Artists; Universal; Vagabond; Walt Disney; Walter Wanger Productions; Warner Brothers; Wayne-Fellows; Windsor Pictures; WRG Productions; Zenith

Published by Aurum Press, 33 Museum Street, London WC1

ISBN 0 906053 57 9

Design by Robert Updegraff and Peter Matthews

Phototypeset by Bookworm Typesetting, Manchester
Printed in Belgium by Henri Proost & CIE PVBA

Acknowledgements

First and foremost I would like to thank Eric Mackenzie who researched this book. His diligence, commitment and enthusiasm went far beyond the call of duty. I would also like to thank all the staff of the British Film Institute's Information Library, whose unfailingly courteous assistance and response to the oddest (and sometimes silliest) queries helped me track down some of the historical curiosities included herein. They made my weeks at the Library far more pleasant than they might have been. Amongst the many people who helped in various ways are Anne Yelland, whose affability made the irksome bits and pieces of book production far less so; Roma Gibson, who knew where things were; Denis Gifford, who not only knew the name of the last on the left in the posse but could spell it as well; Michael Haggiag, who cracked the whip, as all publishers should; Carole James, who likes Westerns even less now but whose support was invaluable; David Meeker, who knew more than *Variety* about Herb Jeffries; and Paul Taylor, who reminded me of titles I might otherwise have missed.

I would also like to thank Ed Buscombe, Allen Eyles, Chris Frayling (twice), Colin McArthur, Tom Milne, Ted Reinhart, Richard Schickel, David Thomson and Robin Wood for their Top Tens and Gerald Peary, Dave Pirie and *Variety* for kindly allowing me to reprint material originally compiled by them.

Contents

Foreword   vii

Preface   viii

The Western in Perspective   ix

The Thirties: *The Rise and Rise of the B Western*   16

The Forties: *The Resurgence of the Genre*   102

The Fifties: *Indians and Psychopaths – A Genre Redefined*   186

The Sixties: *The Western Goes International*   272

The Seventies: *The Western in Transition*   320

The Eighties: *The Western Is Dead – Long Live the Western!*   356

All-Time Western Rental Champs   364

Most Successful Westerns: Inflation Adjusted   365

Biggest Money-Making Western Stars   366

Critics' Top Tens   367

Western Oscars   370

Selected Sound Westerns and Their Novel Sources   372

Select Bibliography   374

All Other Sound Westerns   375

Index   396

Notes on the Entries

Entries are arranged chronologically throughout the volume and alphabetically within each year. The definite and indefinite articles in both English and foreign titles have been disregarded in establishing alphabetical order.

The index gives the year under which all film titles having entries are to be found. Films that do not have an entry may be found, with brief credits, in Appendix 8.

The titles of all films which have their own entries are printed in bold throughout the book (except for a second reference to such a film in the same entry), with their date for ease of cross-referencing. All other films mentioned are printed in italics.

The running time of a film can vary considerably because different versions are often released in different territories. Accordingly, where such versions are known to be in circulation, the different lengths are listed in brackets after the original running time. All such lengths relate to theatrical screenings; on television, because of the medium's faster projection speed, a film will generally run (excluding commercial breaks), approximately four minutes per hundred shorter. Only films over 50 minutes in length are included.

Unless otherwise indicated all films are in colour and made in the United States of America.

For the purposes of this book the date of a film has been taken as the year of its release rather than its making. In the case of some films even this is open to debate, and many of the sources are inconsistent if not actively in dispute. In such cases I have opted for the date most often ascribed. Where the date is in doubt, you are advised to consult the index to find the year under which the title has been entered. Similarly, often films are given different titles for different markets. Accordingly, if a film seems to be missing, you are advised to consult the index to find out which title has been used here.

Although the credits have been exhaustively researched, inevitably some are missing. Most of these are producers' credits from the years prior to 1933. Before that date studio producers were not credited as such on individual films; in that year David O. Selznick joined MGM and his contract stipulated that he receive an on-screen credit for his productions. His first film to feature this was *Night Flight* (1933). All the other producers promptly followed suit.

Abbreviations and Explanation of Terms

| aka | also known as; used where a film has more than one title |
| orig | original; used where the English language title is not the original one |

Studios

AA	Allied Artists
COL	Columbia
FOX	Fox and (after 1935) Twentieth Century Fox
MGM	Metro Goldwyn Mayer
MON	Monogram
PAR	Paramount
PRC	Producer's Releasing Corporation
REP	Republic
RKO	RKO Radio
U	Universal
UA	United Artists
WB	Warner Brothers and (between 1967 and 1969) Warner Brothers-Seven Arts

b/w	black and white
sepia	Sepiatone
scope	all wide-screen anamorphic systems such as Cinemascope and Warnerscope except:
pv	Panavision
vv	Vistavision

Credits

d	director
p	producer
s	screenwriter
c	cinematographer
lp	leading players
co-	in collaboration

Foreword

The feature film has come of age. Today it is a respected art form with an impressive history of artistic achievement that dates back to the beginning of our century. At its best, it is comparable to the finest expressions of the older arts such as music, painting, dance, and literature, and can even be seen as a modern synthesis of these traditional forms. Yet it remains fundamentally a popular medium, an expensive entertainment dependant upon a vast public who registers approval by its attendance and can silently dictate its pleasures. Moreover, the enduring popularity of film is due less to its artistry than to the inherent magic of the silver screen with its unparalleled ability to transport audiences into a world apart, a complete self-contained universe of the imagination. No other medium of expression can claim to have manifested so thoroughly and variously what Carl Jung called our 'collective unconscious'. Throughout the past eighty or so years, the attitudes and customs, the fears and desires, the memories, hopes, and reflections of a great part of humanity have been faithfully recorded on celluloid. Taken as a whole, world cinema provides a more profound and accurate image of contemporary civilization than any social history could ever aspire to.

It is this dream universe, this cultural mirror, which *The Aurum Film Encyclopedia* has ambitiously attempted to chart in its nine-volume series covering the principal film categories or genres which have developed since the birth of the industry. These include The Western, Science Fiction, Horror, Comedy, Romance, War, Epics, Musicals and Thrillers. They are like major constellations in a hitherto poorly mapped firmament. While they cannot hope to cover every planet and star or even cluster of stars on the horizon, these volumes offer an important beginning. Each is complete in itself and can be used without reference to the others. Each offers a coherent theme in which particular films, located in their proper historical and cultural context, act like the myriad pieces of an enormous mosaic. Readers interested in the history of cinema can peruse the volumes for the larger, critical overview. Those who wish to refer solely to facts, have a wider compendium of source material than ever before.

No series of reference works on the cinema would be complete without a wealth of illustrations. Film is essentially a visual medium and without these pictures it would be impossible to convey the distinguishing elements of style, mood and atmosphere which mark different films as well as the different epochs in which they were made. We are extremely grateful to the Kobal Collection not only for granting us exclusive access to what is probably the finest archive of film photographs in the world, but also for their generous cooperation and support. Particular thanks must be given to John Kobal for his invaluable advice and to Simon Crocker and Alexandra Lascelles for their unstinting efforts in researching and assembling the available photographs, and, where necessary, acquiring new material. It has thus been possible to accompany with one or more film stills almost every entry which we felt required it, and to include historically significant and often rare photographs of famous stars or directors of a given era. The visual contribution to this series is far more than an embellishment; it is an integral part of the total mosaic whose value cannot be underestimated.

The Aurum Film Encyclopedia, although complete and authoritative enough to satisfy the most ardent film buff or professional, is aimed primarily at the general reader. Gone are the halcyon days when the whole family went out to the local cinema to see the Saturday night movie, whatever it might be. Departing rapidly too is the era of omnipotent TV network programmers who decide the evening's entertainment for an entire nation. With the advent of cable TV and video, the modern viewer is being given unprecedented choice and with it a new responsibility. The need to discriminate will continue to grow as future audiences are faced with an increasingly bewildering range of new and old products. We trust that *The Aurum Film Encyclopedia* will help to meet this need and be seen to have accomplished its purpose as a truly comprehensive and enduring reference guide to the fabulous world of film.

Michael Haggiag
Series Editor

Preface

At the time of writing, the Western stands in a peculiar position. Fewer and fewer are being made than at any point in the genre's history, and yet in the American video market B Westerns are the second most popular item. Hollywood's standard explanation of the genre's sudden dip in popularity is that people are bored with cowboys, but in recent years there has been a remarkable upsurge of writing devoted to the genre. The aim of this book is to document the Western's splendours, both consequential and inconsequential, and serve as a guide to the rugged terrain that is the Western.

What distinguishes this volume from others is its scope, which is truly encyclopedic, and its structure. The heart of the book is some 1,800 entries, arranged chronologically and alphabetically within each year, which are devoted to individual films. These entries range from fifty words to a thousand in a direct reflection of the film's interest and/or importance in the history of the Western. Each entry comprises fully researched credits (director, producer, writer, cinematographer and where possible a minimum of six leading players), a brief synopsis of the plot and informed critical comment on the film. Where relevant, cross reference is made to other movies. Thus it is possible to follow the career of important stars, directors and producers through the entries. A good example of this, and of how close knit a world the Western is, is the career of Harry Joe Brown, the director of numerous Ken Maynard B Westerns. After a stint as producer with Warners, he entered into independent production with Randolph Scott, in which capacity he hired Budd Boetticher to direct what turned out to be a classic series of B Westerns that culminated in **Comanche Station** (1960).

There are no silent films among the entries for two reasons. Because the Western was the most prolific genre in the history of Hollywood, space is at a premium. Moreover, at present, and for the foreseeable future, only a few silent Westerns are available for viewing and even less are commercially available. Accordingly, in a book intended as a viewing guide, it makes little sense to include them, especially when there are so many sound Westerns, films that will turn up on television, video and in the rental market, pressing for inclusion.

In addition to the entries the encyclopedia also contains numerous appendices. Of these the most important is Appendix 8 which lists, with brief credits, all the Westerns not given their own entry in the book, up to the end of 1982. Other appendices include a Critics' Top Ten, a ranking of Westerns by their rental earnings and a list of Oscars won by Westerns. Taken together, the appendices represent the most comprehensive statistical overview of the genre ever published.

Precisely because this is an encyclopedia of the Western rather than a personal view of the genre, I have cast my net wide when considering whether to include or exclude a title in the entries. My concern has not been 'Is it a Western in the strictest of senses?' but 'Has it developed from or does it contribute to the Western tradition in the broadest sense?'. Thus, I have included several Civil War films (but not *Gone With the Wind*, 1939); several films set in Colonial times and contemporary Westerns ranging from **Junior Bonner** (1972) and **Coogan's Bluff** (1968) to **Lonesome Cowboys** (1968) (but not Godard's *Le Vent d'Est* (1969) which, its title notwithstanding, owes little to the genre); and films about Western film-making such as **Hearts of the West** (1975). I have not included those films loosely called 'Indian', 'Japanese' or 'Brazilian' Westerns because, although they have adapted many of the conventions and traditions of the Western to local situations, those situations are so markedly different from the mainstream of the Western.

I have, of course, included Westerns made outside America. Thus, of all the entries, there are about a hundred devoted to the Italian Western. In my survey of this fascinating and controversial sub-genre I have relied heavily on Christopher Frayling's invaluable history of the phenomenon, *The Spaghetti Western*. Moreover, I have not restricted myself to Italian Westerns. Amongst the entries can be found German Westerns (of the thirties as well as of the sixties), a couple of British Westerns and even a Russian Western. Similarly I have included representative examples of that seventies' phenomenon, the sex Western, and the numerous cross-genre films like **Westworld** (1973) and **Billy the Kid vs. Dracula** (1965), where the Western elements are essential.

As part of the broad notion of the Western outlined above I have sought to include a substantial number of B Westerns. Too many accounts of the genre have restricted themselves to very narrow notions of the Western that have the films of John Ford at the centre and just at the edges admit the existence of, for example, Audie Murphy's fifties Westerns. Alternatively, writers have treated the world of the B Western, a world where the likes of Roy Rogers and Hopalong Cassidy are megastars, in splendid isolation. This view is understandable, since the two 'Westerns' influenced each other little, but when it comes to the actual films, despite their different perspectives (and budgets), both A and B Westerns clearly share so many characteristics that it is ridiculous to segregate the two. Accordingly, in this book at least, George O'Brien, the Three Mesquiteers and Smith Ballew ride the range in the company of John Wayne, Randolph Scott and James Stewart. Similarly, I have included a number of Western serials in the main body of the book. My concern when selecting serials or B Westerns has been to include not only the best, but also a judicious mix of those that are representative of their stars, those whose production circumstances are significant, those which are historically important and those which are accessible for viewing.

If A and B Westerns can sit side by side easily enough, however, to judge the series Westerns by the standards of the big budgeted A Westerns makes a nonsense of their inclusion. The production values of the Bs, their plots, direction and, usually, acting are, with few exceptions, vastly inferior to those evident in A Westerns. Moreover, to judge the Bs by the standards of the A Westerns would be to blind oneself to the charm, innocence and simplicity of the series Western at its best, in short to those qualities that have kept its memory alive for so long. Accordingly, my comments on the B Westerns are written from a different perspective and are relative, rather than directly comparable, to those appreciations of A Westerns. For my comments on the B Westerns included I have relied on extensive research in which I have been greatly aided by the maps of the sub-genre provided by Don Miller (in his intelligent and reliable study, *Hollywood Corral*), Jon Tuska (in his mammoth piece of research, *The Filming of the West*) and the anonymous reviewers of *Variety* and the *Motion Picture Herald*, of whom it must be said that though they rarely liked B Westerns they were quick to detect the minutest differences between them. With these as my guides I have sought to select the most interesting of the Bs, and so give a picture of the genre from both top and bottom. The result, I hope, is the most comprehensive guide in book form to the Western so far ever produced.

Happy Trails!

Phil Hardy
London 1983

The Western in Perspective

John Ford on location during the making of Stagecoach.

What's in a Name?

At a famous meeting, to identify himself as he rose to speak, one director said succinctly 'I'm John Ford, I make Westerns.' The deprecating nature of the remark is typical of Ford's easy confidence. Indeed the anecdote has become one of those most often told about him. Until recently, it has been a self-sufficient story; now there is a need to explain it. No director these days could, or would wish to, similarly identify himself. Quite simply, so few Westerns have been made recently that it is hard to talk of the genre except in the past tense. Similarly the days when so many stars were almost completely identified with the genre are long gone. W.S. Hart, John Wayne, Buck Jones, Tom Mix and Randolph Scott could also say, with John Ford, 'I make Westerns'. And it wasn't only stars who were identified with the genre: character actor Joseph Crehan donned whiskers and took up a cigar as part of his portrayal of President Ulysses Grant some fifty times in various Westerns, while Gabby Hayes was as much of a fixture in Westerns as the stars he supported.

If historical figures such as President Grant and other more romantic types like Buffalo Bill, Geronimo and Jesse James seemed perpetually to be playing second lead to Wayne, Mix and company as they criss-crossed the most recognizable landscape in cinema, the strong moral dimension to that landscape was at least as important as the stars. Perspectives may have changed as the Western evolved, but from the earliest days of the silent cinema to the present the idea of moral regeneration has remained one of the key elements in a story that has been told and retold countless times throughout the history of the genre. Figures as diverse as W.S. Hart, Harry Carey, John Wayne, Gary Cooper and Randolph Scott have been saved from themselves either by the love of a good woman or by a sense of mission. In so many of the Westerns' most famous scenes this moral dimension is an integral element of the drama: W.S. Hart setting fire to the town in *Hell's Hinges* (1916), Wayne gunning down the evil Plummer brothers in **Stagecoach** (1939) and William Holden leading the remainder of his gang to their deaths in **The Wild Bunch** (1969).

So strong is the contrast between the genre's triumphant past and the doldrums it currently finds itself in that one is inevitably led to the most obvious question: 'What is the Western?' It is not a new question. At every stage in the genre's evolution, it has been raised. In its crudest form it is seen in the bizarre debates about whether films like **Lonely Are the Brave** (1962) and **Hud** (1963) are Westerns or not, or whether there can be such a thing as the Italian Western. Though the Italian Western is now accepted as a significant part of the genre in the sixties and seventies, and Sergio Leone is thought by many to be one of the more interesting and influential makers of Westerns, when the sub-genre made its first appearance on the international market, the films, their success at the box office notwithstanding, were greeted with derision by most critics. Whatever the Western was, it was clearly assumed to be something that only Americans could make. This and other hidden assumptions about the genre need to be uncovered, if only to isolate the genre from the values ascribed to it. From this perspective it is worth having a look at a couple of attempted definitions of the Western.

In his classic essay 'The Westerner', Robert Warshow offers a thumbnail sketch of the Western and attempts to explain its enduring appeal. Warshow sees this as stemming primarily from the man with the gun at the centre of the genre. He is a man unconcerned with the realities of modern life and its constraints, a man who can act directly, if reluctantly, in support of values he believes in. Moreover, he acts with style. For Warshow, writing in 1954:

> Above all, the movies in which the Westerner plays out his role preserve for us the pleasures of a complete and self-contained drama – and one which still effortlessly crosses the boundaries which divide our culture – in a time when other, more consciously serious art forms are increasingly complex, uncertain and ill-defined.

In short, at a time when frustratingly complex issues like the Bomb, the Cold War, the House Un-American Activities Committee and Suez were being raised, the Western remained a simple, unchanging, clearcut world in which notions of Good and Evil could be balanced against each other in an easily recognizable fashion. Moreover, Good not only invariably triumphed but did so with style and grace. Warshow is concerned to distil the essence of the Western, to define the genre in terms of its essential elements. This becomes all the more obvious when he turns to the contemporary Western which he sees as confused either by a concern for 'social drama' or by attempts to aestheticize the genre. Warshow sees both these strands of the fifties Western as violating the 'Western form' and threatening the innocence of the genre. Thus, neither **High Noon** (1952) nor **Shane** (1953) are 'right'.

Shane: a fairy tale of a Western.

The first is a piece of 'vulgar anti-populism' which 'does not exist in the proper frame of the Western movie', while **Shane** is an attempt 'to freeze the Western myth once and for all' and accordingly the result is a film that is more 'fairy tale' than Western.

With the benefit of almost thirty years of hindsight, it is easy to counter some of Warshow's absolutist descriptions of the genre. To take just one example: 'The Westerner is *par excellence* a man of leisure. Even when he wears the badge of a marshal or, more rarely, owns a ranch, he appears to be unemployed' writes Warshow. Yet from **Will Penny** (1967) onwards there has been a new emphasis on work in the Western. The drudgery that is the life of the cowboy has been detailed in several films, like **Monte Walsh** (1970), as part of the process of de-romanticizing the cowboy. More importantly, Warshow's aims in writing his essay are clearer now. At a time when violence and complexity were intruding into the genre because the Western was reflecting its times more closely, Warshow was attempting to defend the Western's innocence, to save it from defilement. In this he was not alone.

In his influential essay, 'The Evolution of the Western', French film critic André Bazin takes a similar position. Calling **Shane** and **High Noon** 'Super-Westerns', Bazin compares them unfavourably to earlier Westerns for being self-conscious. Like Warshow, but even more explicitly, Bazin argues the merits of the Westerns of the forties, which he sees as the time of the classic Western. Bazin accepts developments in the genre – he warmly welcomes the first Westerns of Anthony Mann as building upon the tradition of **Stagecoach** (1939). But, in effect, what he and Warshow attempt is to define the genre, to pick out its essence, in such a way that their preferred films are the classics of the genre because they best exemplify the Western as defined by their criteria. George N. Fenin and William K. Everson in their book *The Western, From Silents to Seventies* proceed by a similarly self-referential route. Despite their chosen title, the authors clearly prefer the silent films of W.S. Hart above all others. Accordingly they develop 'realism' as the essential element of the genre, construct a 'realist tradition' which has Hart's films at its source and then value individual films by how closely they conform to that tradition. 'What is a Western?' is clearly a far more complex question than a simple matter of name. Similarly an 'essentialist' answer won't do, especially when the essence defined is either a defence of, or an attack on, the Western in a particular phase of its evolution.

America and History

A more useful starting point for a discussion of the Western and a probing of its identity or identities is American history. After all, the Western is fixed in time in a relatively straightforward way. Indeed Hollywood and the Western are part of the history of the West. When the genre first made its appearance on celluloid at the turn of the century, it might just as well have been called 'the Eastern'. Films like *Kit Carson* (1903) and Edwin S. Porter's far more famous *The Great Train Robbery* (1903) (which was neither the first Western nor the first narrative film, the legend surrounding it notwithstanding) were made in New Jersey. However, within ten years film production had gravitated to the West coast. The reasons for this were complex but high on the list was the Californian climate, which was first demonstrated in a series of two-reel Westerns made by Bronco Billy Anderson (who had a small part in *The Great Train Robbery*) for Colonel Selig.

The frontier had been declared closed and there was no more open range to settle but when the film-makers made their pioneer-like trek to California they found that the West was still alive, if only just. For the numerous cowboys who were being thrown off the range as the big ranches closed down, Hollywood, which quickly established itself as the movie capital, appeared just in time. Few of the cowboys who flocked there in search of work ever became stars but many of them found regular work and a few became well established as character actors. Several of the rodeo riders eventually did become stars, usually after working for a period as stuntmen. Notable examples were Tom Mix, Yakima Canutt and, much much later, Ben Johnson.

In an interview late in his life, Colonel Tim McCoy, who was born in 1891 in Saginaw, Michigan, spoke about this strange twilight period of the West:

> At the turn of the century, children could still dream. There were those who watched the fire wagons and wanted to be firemen and those who wanted to be policemen . . . I didn't want to be a fireman, nor a policeman . . . I wanted to be a cowboy.

And so, in 1907, after a week spent watching a Wild West show, McCoy quit college and headed for the West to become a cowboy. Thus, when Hollywood was founded it quickly became both the last real employer of cowboys and the inspiration of a new generation of kids who, unlike McCoy, couldn't become cowboys themselves.

Not surprisingly, since Westerns were to all intents and purposes contemporary films, silent Westerns made in Hollywood showed a great advance in realism over their Eastern counterparts. However, despite the presence in Hollywood of the likes of Wyatt Earp and Emmett Dalton as technical advisors, the scripts and acting styles remained firmly within the Wild West show and dime novel traditions. A thoroughgoing realism was occasionally attempted, as in *The Bank Robbery* (1908), but such films invariably fared badly at the box office. Nonetheless, *The Bank Robbery* remains a fascinating movie. It was made by the Oklahoma Mutoscene Company which was set up by Bill Tilghman and Al Jennings. Jennings was one of the last train robbers of note and Tilghman was the law officer who caught him! Their film which, it must be said, was crudely made, told the story of one of Jennings' attempted bank robberies and was shot on the actual Oklahoma locations. Jennings would soon follow Earp and others to Hollywood where, like them, he would help write the legend at the expense of reality. But *The Bank Robbery*, made before Hollywood had begun to streamline the Western, remains as a reminder of how close to reality the Western in fact was historically and how close it could attempt to get dramatically. The film represents a strand of film-making that would not re-enter the Western until the seventies. Ironically, at the time, what was seen as missing from *The Bank Robbery* was a sense of the West that actors like the athletic Tom Mix and W.S. Hart would exploit so melodramatically in their films.

Bronco Billy Anderson (left), the first Western star.

My Darling Clementine, *John Ford's poetic celebration of the coming of civilization to the old West.*

This is not to say that Westerns are to be valued purely in terms of their historical accuracy, but simply that the frontier, and, more particularly, the frontier between the Civil War and the turn of the century, forms the backdrop to most Westerns. The word 'most' is important. Films set in the Colonial period, like **Drums Along the Mohawk** (1939) and **Northwest Passage** (1940), and films set after 1900, like **Lonely Are the Brave** (1962) and **Westworld** (1973), clearly share enough important features of the genre and in some sense present themselves as Westerns to a degree that they can be usefully included in a broad notion of the genre. For though the period between 1860 and 1900, the years of America's headlong Westward expansion to the Pacific, provides the raw material of the Western, an equally important element is the idea of the frontier, of the West. It is to this idea that the above films direct themselves in various ways. This concept of the West is seen at its purest in films like *The Covered Wagon* (1923), the first epic Western, *The Iron Horse* (1924), **Dodge City** (1939), **My Darling Clementine** (1946), **Bend of the River** (1952) and **The Searchers** (1956), films which, in different ways, are explicitly about the idea of the West and the elements that go to make it up, like pioneering, making fertile what was desert, bringing law and order where there was only chaos, etc. The West, or at least the 'big themes' of the West are not necessarily present in all Westerns, but it is noticeable that even those series Westerns that are purely action-oriented were as often as not promoted by association with the idea of the West. To pick a few examples at random from Alan Barbour's compilation of ads for series Westerns, *Movie Ads of the Past*: Johnny Mack Brown's actioner, *The Law Comes to Gunsight* (1939) was advertised as taking place 'When Justice fought for its life on the ramparts of a bold and pioneering Nation!', and a Western which advertised its contents as 'A Beautiful Girl . . . A Murdered Brother . . . Stolen Gold' was entitled *Winning the West* (1931). Equally direct is the poster for Ken Maynard's *Come On Tarzan* (1932): 'A drama of men who ride with their stirrups long and their holsters handy . . . who deal across the top of the table . . . and shoot from the hip!' These posters and many like them invoke the idea of the West, associating the films they promote not merely with the years between 1860 and 1900 but, to borrow one of the copywriters' favourite phrases, with times 'when men were men . . .'.

However, this view of the West is only one of many. Just as the frontier can be celebrated as the place where men wore six-guns and were free to use them, so it can be described as a place where lynch law took the place of justice, food was scarce and culture non-existent. These different Wests have each made their mark on the Western, as a brief comparison between John Ford's **My Darling Clementine** and William Wellman's **The Ox-Bow Incident** (1943) makes clear. Ford's film deals with the moment when civilization reaches Tomb-

stone. Henry Fonda's Wyatt Earp is civilization's agent, the man who forgoes vengeance to become the representative of law and order. Similarly, the dance at the half-completed church, the scent Fonda wears to court Linda Darnell and Alan Mowbray's drunken Shakespearian actor all represent aspects of Tombstone's transition from a place of frontier savagery to an outpost of civilization. Wellman's film offers a sharp contrast to Ford's positive, not to say poetic, celebration of the civilizing of the West. Wellman and writer Lamar Trotti's frontier is one where fear and ignorance rule and where justice is trampled on in the search for a quick and easy solution to the problem posed by the three wandering cowboys who might have killed a local rancher. Even more damning is Wellman's indictment of the institutional representative, the Colonel, who is seen to act petulantly rather than with due consideration. The fact that Henry Fonda is the hero of both films makes the contrast between them all the more visible.

However, **My Darling Clementine** represents only a stage in Ford's evolving view of the West. His career from *The Iron Horse*, an innocent celebration of the winning of the West, to **Cheyenne Autumn** (1964), a bitter account of the bravery of the Cheyenne and their maltreatment by Ford's beloved Cavalry, reveals a dramatic shift in perspective. From the fifties onwards, Ford's Westerns increasingly question what he once celebrated, treating the arrival of civilization and law and order at the frontier in terms of the cost rather than of the achievement. The key films here are **The Searchers** and **The Man Who Shot Liberty Valance** (1962). Ford has explained the darkening mood of his films cryptically with the off-the-cuff remark, 'Maybe I'm growing old'. It should be emphasized however that Ford's change of attitude, though expressed in a uniquely Fordian way, is representative of, rather than at odds with, the general shift in the Western since the fifties.

This kind of reinterpretation of the West is significantly different from the changes in fashion that have periodically swept over the series Western although some of these changes have been direct if superficial responses to events outside the genre. In the early thirties when the crime melodrama and men with machines carried all before them, writers of Westerns quickly began writing city gangsters and machine guns into scripts which, otherwise, were entirely conventional. A common theme of these 'gangsters on the range' Westerns is the superiority of the Old West over the New East. Even more startling were the Nazi and Japanese sympathizers who took to the range in the early forties and had to be hunted down by Hollywood's series cowboy stars after America's entry into the Second World War.

Rather more interesting are the black Westerns that surfaced briefly in the thirties and again in the seventies. The first was **Harlem on the Prairie** (1937). Were it not for its all black cast the film would be just another independent quickie. The project was seen purely in novelty terms by producer Jed Buell, writer Fred Myton and director Sam Newfield, all veterans of series Westerns (like **Terror of Tiny Town**, 1938, which was made by the same team with a cast of midgets), but the success of **Harlem on the Prairie** with the black audiences, confirmed by the flurry of all-black Westerns that followed, marked the resurgence of the ghetto market. Black gangster films and musicals followed but, surprisingly, the Westerns were the most popular all-black features. Particularly interesting was the 'colour design' of most of the films. The hero, almost invariably played by Herb Jeffries, was light skinned, as was the heroine, while the comic support and villain were played by darker skinned actors in a literal version of the 'white hat for the hero, black hat for the villain' convention that still permeated the genre, at series level at any rate. Similarly the films aped the most successful form of series Western until then, the musical Western, while Jeffries, true to the tradition of series cowboy stars, took to ornamenting his car with bronzed horns and such like. The spate of the black-exploitation Westerns of the seventies was very different from that of the thirties in two important respects. Whereas the Westerns of the thirties were the product of the ghetto mentality, the black-exploitation films of the seventies were marketed to black and white alike and, ironically, are far surer of their blackness than the majority of their thirties counterparts.

What is notable about the Western since the fifties is that writers and directors have treated contemporary issues in Western form as a means of securing sufficient finance for their projects. The classic examples of this are the highly influential **Broken Arrow** (1950) and **High Noon** (1952). Both of these, and the numerous films that followed in the wake of each, are important because they introduced into the Western the sympathetic treatment of Indians and adult themes like civic responsibility. However, they didn't do this in a vacuum; they were examples of the 'liberal backlash' of the fifties, displaced into the Western in the same way that, in the seventies, the new Indian films like **Soldier Blue** (1970) were a displaced reaction to the Vietnam War.

Another indication of the Western's continual reinterpretation of the legend of the West is reflected in the way that the mythical last days of the frontier have been slowly pushed from around 1890 in the sixties to, by now, the years immediately prior to the outbreak of the First World War. Thus the classic example of mourning the dying frontier Western, **The Ballad of Cable Hogue** (1970), sees the man with the gun dying beneath the wheels of a motor car. This echoes the rather more mundane death of the Western's first 'last cowboy', Kirk Douglas, at the end of **Lonely Are the Brave** in which he is run over by a truck carrying a load of toilet pans, on the verge of reaching the border and freedom, like Jason Robards in the Peckinpah film.

Treading delicately through the maze of conflicting Wests, the place where men were men (or rather 'six foot two of Western rawhide'), the changing West of John Ford, the highly self-conscious West of the seventies, let alone the highly individual West of Sergio Leone and company, what should be clear is how flexible a genre the Western is. From this perspective it is not surprising that essentialist definitions, however illuminating they may be at the time, should fall by the wayside as the Western evolves.

Heroes and Villains

The raw material of the West is not merely America's westward expansion of the second half of the nineteenth century and the details of frontier life. A central element has always been the heroes and villains of the West, legendary characters from James Fenimore Cooper's Leatherstocking to Daniel Boone and from Deadwood Dick to Buffalo Bill, characters who from their beginnings were as much creatures of fiction as they were historical figures and vice versa. Cooper's Leatherstocking, the scout and first pioneer who led America into the forests and across the plains to the West – in *The Prairie*, Cooper describes him as having seen the Pacific – was a figure of myth. Cooper viewed his fictional hero with deep ambiguity. Henry Nash Smith in *Virgin Land*, his classic account of the West as myth, describes the first biographers of Daniel Boone as wrestling with the same problem as Cooper: 'which was the real Boone, the standard bearer of civilization and refinement or the child of nature who fled into the wilderness before the advance of the settlements?' Prophetically he concludes, 'the image of the Wild West Hero could serve either purpose.'

This is even more so in the case of the heroes who followed Leatherstocking and Boone. They weren't pioneers; the next significant Western heroes were the men with the guns – Buffalo Bill, Wild Bill Hickok, Billy the Kid, Wyatt Earp, Jesse James and company. These people were relatively unimportant in the overall history of the westward movement

and, accordingly, the literature that quickly surrounded them contained, for the most part, little reference to notions of the West or the pioneering spirit. Indeed by the 1890s the locale of the dime novel, in whose pages these heroes rode into legend, became largely insignificant; what mattered was the hero and the wholesale slaughter he was called upon to perform. The shift from the ambiguity with which Boone was viewed was significant. The frontier of the dime novel, even that of its most genteel practitioners, was blood red as heroes faced nature in the raw and the primitive savagery of the Red Man.

The legends soon took on lives of their own outside the dime novels: Deadwood Dick and his companions survived the death of the literature that gave them life. Moreover, because the Western hero was located in a particular time and place that was close enough to be accurately reported and far enough away to be shamelessly romanticized, a degree of self-consciousness entered the process and became part of the legend. Thus, in his own lifetime, Jesse James was treated both as a legend and as a real historical figure.

The most important of these legendary figures was William F. Cody, alias Buffalo Bill, the man Ned Buntline discovered in 1869 when he rode West in search of someone he could turn into a dime novel hero. Cody returned East with Buntline for publicity purposes and ended up playing himself on the stage. From then on, his career was consciously to make a spectacle of the Wild West, first on stage and then in the circus ring, while in print he 'chronicled' – ie had written for him – his life. Cody became Buffalo Bill to a degree that he and his role merged completely, as dime novel fiction and reality became inseparable. At times his letters suggest that his new role wore heavily upon him. Hence he wrote to his publisher, 'I am sorry to have to lie so outrageously in this yarn – if you think the revolver and the Bowie knife are used too freely, you may cut out a fatal shot or stab wherever you deem it wise.' At the end of his life he obviously felt trapped by his role: 'I do not want to die a showman. I grow tired of this show hero worship sometimes.' However, Cody continued with his role of *the* Wild West hero to the end of his life.

As Cody was glamorizing the West and popularizing it in Europe through his circus tours, some European travellers to the West were busy pointing out that the true character of the cowboy was being lost behind the glamour: he was becoming a legend.

> The cowboy has at the present time become a personage; maybe he is rapidly becoming a mythical one. Distance is doing for him what the lapse of time did for the heroes of antiquity. His admirers are investing him with all manner of romantic qualities; they descant upon his manifold virtues and his pardonable weaknesses as if he were a demi-god, and I have no doubt that before long there will be ample material for any philosophic enquirer who may wish to enlighten the world as to the cause of the cowboy myth.

The format of the Western, its conventions, stock characters, the function of Indians, the dude etc, derive from the legends of the West, the dime novel and Wild West shows. Similarly much of the Western's treatment of its heroes and villains can be traced back to the tensions between legend and reality that were implicit (and sometimes explicit) in the initial treatment of the heroes of the West. In short, the genre's literary origins reinforce the Western's flexibility by adding to its potential. Thus it is that Jesse James, and even more extraordinarily Billy the Kid, are both hero and villain. Indeed, in the case of Billy the Kid, it is the recurring theme of a long-running series starring Buster Crabbe as Billy and Al St John as his comic side-kick: Billy fights on the side of law and order but is thought to be an outlaw by all and sundry.

One way of writing a history of the Western would be to detail the changing views of its outlaw heroes. Butch Cassidy

Clockwise from top: *Heroes and Villains: W. S. Hart in* The Gunfighter; *a grinning outlaw from a Triangle silent; Roy Rogers clearing the name of Jesse James in* Days of Jesse James; *Bruce Cabot in the title role of* Wild Bill Hickock Rides; *the Daltons in* Jesse James versus the Daltons; *Henry Fonda in the title role in* The Return of Frank James *and Johnny Mack Brown as* Billy the Kid.

Clockwise: *More Heroes and Villains: John Sturges'* Gunfight at the O.K. Corral *and James Garner in* Hour of the Gun, *Sturges' second thought on the subject; Paul Newman and Robert Redford as* Butch Cassidy and the Sundance Kid*; Paul Newman in the title role in* Buffalo Bill and the Indians *and Stacy and James Keach as Frank and Jesse James in* The Long Riders.

made his appearance in forties Westerns as a devil and was slowly rehabilitated until, as impersonated by Paul Newman, he became a charming version of the last cowboy. Similarly, Wyatt Earp has oscillated between being presented as representative of law and order (**My Darling Clementine**) and maddened killer (**Hour of the Gun**, 1967). It is noticeable that, in the fifties, both hero and villain became more complex figures, far closer to each other than they had ever been presented in previous decades. Thus, in Boetticher's series of Westerns with Randolph Scott (which includes **The Tall T** (1957), **Ride Lonesome** (1959) and **Comanche Station** (1960)), the Scott figure actually inhabits the same moral landscape as his adversaries. Similarly, and more extremely, the hero of Anthony Mann's series of Westerns with James Stewart, which includes **Winchester '73** (1950), **Bend of the River** (1952) and **The Man from Laramie** (1955), feature a hero who is a psychopath for much of the picture (or in the director's own words, 'a man who could kill his brother').

It is not coincidental that such heroes arrived at a time when the positive values that lay behind the forties Western were being challenged. However, the legacy of those heroes was more problematic for the genre. Once the man with the gun was given a psychological dimension and confronted with problems that couldn't be solved by the speed of his draw, the simple appeal of the Western was thrown into doubt. Suddenly these were real men facing real issues, not creatures of make believe and fantasy like the Lone Ranger and company. In **My Darling Clementine**, his poeticizing not-

withstanding, Ford was able to insert his story into the 'Western form' (to use Warshow's phrase) without in any way deforming it. A few years later, the ending of Howard Hawks' **Red River** (1948), which saw John Wayne and Montgomery Clift *not* shooting it out, was much criticized for not being true to the verities of the genre. From the fifties onwards, more and more Westerns followed the line of **Red River** and in various ways deformed the genre, challenging its ossifying conventions. This evolution produced a richer form, but led to diminishing audiences, especially after the death of the B Western. From the sixties onwards, the Western has been a genre in search of heroes. Only very rarely have these heroes been like their uncomplicated brothers of earlier times. For the most part, they have been bemused observers of the pageant of the West (Dustin Hoffman in **Little Big Man**, 1970); self-personifications of the genre itself (John Wayne in **The Shootist**, 1976); men at the end of their tether (William Holden in **The Wild Bunch**, 1969) or unaware that their time is gone (Warren Beatty in **McCabe and Mrs Miller,** 1971).

It is against this background that the upsurge of wilderness and pioneering films (like **Jeremiah Johnson**, 1972 and **Heartland**, 1979) with their celebration of the beauty and ferocity of nature are to be understood. They, at least, provide heroes and heroines; they may be uncomplicated and their desires may be limited to a concern to survive but there is enough substance and variety already demonstrated in the sub-genre to make it clear that it is a far richer area than has been accepted as yet by most critics of the Western.

Hollywood and the Western

In Hollywood more Westerns have been made than any other kind of film. The economic importance of the Western to Hollywood in the thirties and forties cannot be overemphasized. One says *the* Western yet in fact there were two Westerns whose histories, for the most part, ran parallel to each other: the A Western and the series Western. The series Western was so called because its stars were contracted to make not an individual film but a series of films, usually six or eight. The first such Western star was 'Bronco Billy' Anderson. From 1910 onwards all Anderson's Essanay two-reelers featured him as Bronco Billy. Thus in one film the character might get married or be shot but at the start of the next he would once more be ready for action. The stories were discontinuous, the characters continuous.

Anderson was also the first cowboy producer-star. By the end of the twenties, Western production in Hollywood had become very specialized. Stars like Tom Mix and Ken Maynard made their own films for distribution by the major studios, which in turn had their own Western units churning out films by the week. The arrival of sound did little to change this production set-up. Although at first the majors were reluctant to invest in expensive sound equipment for their Western units, the speed with which the independents moved into the Western series market forced the majors to respond swiftly. By 1932, Western film production was higher than it had been at the end of the silent era. It was soon to ride even higher when Hollywood tried to offset the effects of the Depression by introducing double bills in a desperate attempt to boost sagging box-office receipts. Thus it was that, in the early thirties, a single cinema theatre could easily get through some 300 pictures a year. As the number of majors turning to double bills in all but their most prestigious theatres grew, so did the need for product to fill the lower half of those double bills. Faced with the winning combination of cheap costs and a ready market, production of series Westerns rocketed.

The classic example of this is Republic Studios. The studio was founded by Herbert J. Yates in 1935, as an act of desperation. Yates' Consolidated Film Laboratories processed over half the released footage in America and his biggest customers were the independent film companies of Hollywood's Poverty Row. When they faltered and the possibility of them defaulting on their debts was raised, Yates brought about the merger of several of them. Within two years Republic, as the resulting company was called, was making more films, albeit nearly all second features, than any other Hollywood studio. Needless to say, the staple diet of Republic's production lines was the series Western.

Herbert J. Yates, the founder of Republic, the studio that hitched its star to the series Western.

Republic's production values were high compared to those of the first independently produced sound series Westerns which were marked by inept cinematography and sound recording and speeded up action. Republic's experienced crews brought to a fine art many of the stock convention shots of the series Western – the running insert, the general use of camera trucks to intensify chases and the like. The series Westerns, especially the films of Gene Autry and Roy Rogers, were hugely profitable for the company, but despite Yates' many attempts, Republic never became a major studio and never found its way out of Poverty Row. Indeed it didn't long survive the death of the B Western and was sold in 1959. The studio's fate was mirrored by that of virtually every series star. The gap between the series Western and the A Western seemed unbridgeable; John Wayne was the only exception. Moreover, apart from Wayne (who only became a big box-office star after he quit series Westerns) and (very briefly) Gene Autry, no other series cowboy ever became a big box-office star. Indeed, during the heyday of the series Western, *Motion Picture Herald* ran a separate annual box-office poll for cowboy stars, a mark of their economic importance and their difference from other Hollywood stars (*see* Appendix 3).

Behind the scenes it was even more noticeable that once cinematographers, writers, producers and directors had accustomed themselves to the hectic pace of series production they invariably remained there. Amongst the few who escaped were Joseph H. Lewis and Gerd Oswald, who rose from the depths of second unit direction at Republic and Monogram respectively to the heights of the B Western in the fifties. But perhaps the most revealing demonstration of just how far apart were the series and A Western is the musical Western. This historical curiosity seemed to take over completely the series Western in the mid thirties, yet it hardly had any influence at all on the A Western. There were the occasional musical A Westerns, but none of the singing cowboy variety. Thus when Roy Rogers attempted the transition from series to film star in Raoul Walsh's **The Dark Command** (1940), he left his guitar behind.

Series Westerns did evolve. It is particularly noticeable that the role of women changed over the years, but in retrospect it is equally clear that such developments were marginal at best. Were it not for the fact that high production costs cut into profits after the Second World War and so hastened its decline, the signs are that the series Western might well have faded away on its own for lack of interest. Certainly it no longer catered for the interests of the fifties in the way that science fiction and horror films did. In a similar fashion the B Western soon followed its series cousin to the grave.

Thus, in 1960, the Western's position vis-à-vis Hollywood was radically different from what it had been before the Second World War. A change of a similar magnitude occurred in the years between 1960 and the present day. From one perspective these changes have left the Western less a genre and more a collection of films that just happen to be set in a particular time and place, yet from another these films are united by the modernist stance most of them adopt. All they lack is the automatic audience of their forebears, a lack that Hollywood itself is also facing.

The Western, then, has been dethroned; it is no longer the all-powerful genre that it was. Hollywood and audiences no longer seem interested in the last days of the frontier, which has resolutely remained the dominant theme of recent Westerns, even those set in the present day like **Rancho Deluxe** (1974). The Western's potential growth areas, the pioneering and wilderness films, might not prove to be as adaptable and flexible as they seem at present. Certainly without them it is hard to envisage the Western surviving in its present form. But then the history of the genre is one of rising from the grave, to which it has all too frequently been consigned, with the most unlikely of films.

The
1930s

The Rise and Rise of the B Western

In the thirties all trails led to Republic, the studio that raised itself by its own bootstraps through a wholesale commitment to the B Western. Up to 1935 and the formation of Republic it was, however, a fairly rocky road.

The decade opened decidedly inauspiciously for the Western. The last years of the silent cinema had brought a significant drop in the popularity of the Western, whose sexless and saintly characters were clearly out of step with the liberated twenties. The coming of sound only accelerated this decline in popularity. Moreover, the mechanical problems and the high costs associated with the bulky sound equipment made the major studios look with disfavour upon the genre.

Two films changed this view – **In Old Arizona,** and the independently produced **Overland Bound,** both of which were made in 1929. The former introduced music and sexuality (if not sex) to the genre and sparked off a short-lived wave of prestige Westerns (which included **Cimarron,** 1931, the only Western to date to win the Oscar for Best Picture). **Overland Bound** inspired the revival of the B Western, first from independent producers quick to notice a gap in the output of the major studios and then from the majors themselves.

Republic represented the culmination of these two strands in the development of the Western: the studio was formed to fill the lower half of the double bills that had become the norm in the course of the Depression, and its output is best represented by the image of the singing cowboy whose origins lie in the South of the Border Westerns of which **In Old Arizona** was the first. However, although the Republic formula for Westerns – action and/or music, production line scenarios and filming, and an efficient distribution system – quickly made the studio a giant on Poverty Row (and allowed its owner, Herbert Yates, to make the occasional prestige picture), like so many of the stars the studio created, it never achieved the respectability that Yates so desperately desired; nor would it survive the death of the double bill in the mid-fifties.

But in the thirties Republic reigned supreme, for the decade, more than any other, was the time of the B Western and its glorious inconsequentialities, of the Three Mesquiteers, Hopalong Cassidy and Gene Autry. Only in the forties was the Western to achieve respectability as major studios regularly committed big stars and budgets to the genre. Thus it was fitting that the thirties should end with the escape of John Wayne from the confines of the B Western, if not from Republic where he'd eventually taken refuge after the failure of his first Western of the decade, **The Big Trail** (1931).

Bride of the Desert

(TREM CARR PRODUCTIONS) b/w 57 min
An independently-produced quickie that borrows much of its plot from **In Old Arizona** (1929). Calhoun is the miner's wife being driven frantic by husband Mason when Laidlaw staggers into her log cabin (the film's only set) seeking refuge from a posse on his trail. She shelters him and their romance blossoms, to be legitimized in the final reel when it transpires that her husband is a killer. He is disposed of by Laidlaw after a lengthy fight. Stilted and melodramatic, its success pointed the way forward for other independents at a time when the major studios were worried about introducing the higher costs associated with sound into their series Westerns.

d Duke Worne p Trem Carr s Arthur Hoerl c Ernest Depew lp Alice Calhoun, LeRoy Mason, Ethan Laidlaw, Lum Chan, Walter Ackerman, Horace Carpenter

Courtin' Wildcats

(HOOT GIBSON PRODUCTIONS/U) b/w 58 min
Gibson's last outing in 1929 and, more significantly, his last part-talking film; henceforth his Westerns would be all-sound affairs. The plot is the usual piece of Gibson tomfoolery with him as the bookworm of a college boy sent West to be made a man of. He finds himself up against a two-gun heroine, Gilbert, accused of murdering a local rancher. First he clears her name and then romances her in his usual throw-away style.

d Jerome Storm p Hoot Gibson s Dudley McKenna c Harry Neumann lp Hoot Gibson, Eugenia Gilbert, Pete Morrison, Monte Montague, Harry Todd, John Oscar

In Old Arizona (FOX) b/w 95 min

The first major sound Western. Walsh had intended to star in as well as direct the film but he lost an eye in an accident. Baxter took over the role of the Cisco Kid and Cummings took a hand in the direction. One of the film's most notable features is its use of outdoor sound: Walsh's recordings of hoofbeats, gunshots and the sound of sizzling bacon helped persuade Hollywood that sound as well as speech could greatly aid the Western. The screenplay, though based on the O'Henry stories, owes much to Walsh's own silent films about the exploits of the battling Sergeants Flag and Quirt impersonated by Victor McLaglen and Edmund Lowe. Baxter is a dashing Cisco Kid, Lowe a wily Texas Ranger and Burgess the girl whose betrayal of Baxter nearly costs him his life.

The film was also significant for introducing music to the Western: the theme song, 'My Tonia', was a big hit for Nic Lucas. This in turn inspired Ken Maynard to experiment with music in his Universal Western series.

Baxter won an Oscar for his performance.

d Raoul Walsh, Irving Cummings s Tom Barry c Arthur Edeson lp Warner Baxter, Edmund Lowe, Dorothy Burgess, J. Farrell MacDonald, Fred Warren, Tom Santschi

Overland Bound (PRESIDIO PRODUCTIONS) b/w 58 min

This, the second sound Western and the first independently produced one, is a surprisingly well-staged film. Beebe's story is the old one of the railroad agent out to defraud ranchers (here widows, so melodramatically is the plot conceived) of their land. Perrin is the hero who discovers the truth at the last minute and stops the mother and her daughter, his love, serial queen Ray, from signing away their ranch. Actor Maloney directs with real vigour while his cast, who would make several pictures together for various independent companies, did their best with the crude but effective roles. More significantly, the film's success led to other independents flooding the market with quickie Westerns which in the main are better remembered as historical curiosities than for their quality.

Previous pages: The boom town of Osage from Cimarron, *the only Western to win the Oscar for best picture.*

Warner Baxter as the Cisco Kid and Edmund Lowe as the Texas Ranger on his trail in In Old Arizona, *the first major sound Western.*

Above: *Warner Baxter (left), Mona Maris and Antonio Moreno in* Romance of the Rio Grande.

Below: *Richard Arlen and Gary Cooper in* The Virginian, *the film that made 'Coop' a star.*

The film's major failing is its poor sound recording. Sadly Maloney's triumph was short-lived: he died of a heart attack a few days after the film opened to good reviews in New York.

d/p Leo Maloney *s* Ford Beebe *c* William Nobles
lp Wally Wales, Jack Perrin, Allene Ray, Leo Maloney, Lydia Knott, Joe Maloney

Romance of the Rio Grande (FOX) b/w 95 min

A well-staged piece of froth. Baxter, trapped South of the Border since the success of **In Old Arizona** (1929) in which he'd played the Cisco Kid (a part that would haunt him), is the ne'er-do-well long-lost grandson who returns just in time to put paid to Moreno's villainy and win Maris for himself. Duncan turns in a nice performance as a lady of the night, and Edeson's cinematography is magnificent.

d Alfred Santell *s* Marion Orth *c* Arthur Edeson
lp Warner Baxter, Mona Maris, Mary Duncan, Antonio Moreno, Robert Edeson, Merrill McCormack

Senor Americano

(KEN MAYNARD PRODUCTIONS) b/w 71 min
The best of Maynard's part-talking Westerns. The storyline is the hackneyed one of Maynard clearing California of crooks just prior to its annexation by the United States and romancing songstress Crawford by the bye. Efficiently mounted and neatly directed by Brown, a long-time associate of Maynard's, the film brought forth the naive view (hope ?) from trade reviewers that sound might possibly either kill off the series Western (because with sound they were a far costlier proposition) or so raise their standards that they couldn't be considered series films.

d Harry Joe Brown *p* Ken Maynard *s* Bennett Cohen
c Ted McCord *lp* Ken Maynard, Kathryn Crawford, Frank Yaconelli, J.P. McGowan, Frank Beal, Gino Corrado

The Virginian (PAR) b/w 90 min

The best known version of Owen Wister's famous novel *The Virginian* is verbose, slow and unlikely. Significantly, though the Virginian's retort to the evil Trampas (here Huston), 'When you call me that Smile' has passed into folklore, Wister's almost obsessive concern with capital punishment, seen in Cooper as the Virginian leading a search party for his friend (Arlen) even though he knows a hanging will result, is glossed over in most accounts of his work. W.S. Hart, who acted in the stage version of the novel in 1907, was highly critical of Wister's preference for abstract notions of justice over loyalty which, in W.S. Hart's eyes, would have stopped the Virginian leading the posse to Arlen.

Cooper, drawling beautifully, courtesy of Scott's dialogue coaching, is the mythic cowboy and Huston the evil Trampas under whose sway Arlen falls. Having led the posse to Arlen after he'd turned to rustling, Cooper then hunts down Huston before marrying Brian. The film's slowness is a direct result of the new slower pace sound brought to the cinema.

d Victor Fleming *p* Louis D. Lighton *s* Edward E. Paramore Jnr, Howard Estabrook *c* J. Roy Hunt *lp* Gary Cooper, Walter Huston, Richard Arlen, Mary Brian, Eugene Pallette, Randolph Scott

The Wagon Master

(KEN MAYNARD PRODUCTIONS) b/w 70 min
Maynard's first part-talkie and the first Western to emphasize music (something future Maynard outings would continue to do), this was also its star's first film for Universal. The plot has whip-snapping Santschi trying to prevent Maynard leading a wagon train to its destination. The novelty of sound is stressed throughout the film, from saloon girls clapping every punch Maynard lands to the crack of Santschi's whip. Brown, who would quit directing in 1934 to concentrate on producing (in which capacity he would be associated with a

marvellous series of Westerns directed by Budd Boetticher and starring Randolph Scott in the fifties) directs efficiently.

Footage from the film would re-appear in Maynard's Mascot serial, **Mystery Mountain** (1934) and more bizarrely in Buck Jones' serial, **The Miracle Rider** (1935).

d Harry Joe Brown *p* Ken Maynard *s* Marion Jackson *c* Ted McCord *lp* Ken Maynard, Edith Roberts, Tom Santschi, Jackie Hanlon, Al Ferguson, Frank Rice

1930

The Arizona Kid (FOX) b/w 88 min

Baxter's third outing South of the Border in less than a year, this pale reflection of **In Old Arizona** (1929) was heavily promoted by Fox as a sequel to the earlier film. He plays the Arizona Kid (rather than the Cisco Kid) hiding out from the law in Utah and living on the proceeds, not of earlier robberies, but of the sale of gold from his private goldmine. Maris is the heroine and von Eltz (cast for his resemblance to Edmund Lowe, Baxter's co-star in the earlier film) is the villain who steals the gold from Baxter. Santell directs vigorously, but the shadow of the earlier and far superior film looms over the proceedings.

d Alfred Santell *s* Ralph Brock *c* Glen MacWilliams *lp* Warner Baxter, Carole Lombard, Mona Maris, Theodore von Eltz, Hank Mann, Wilfred Lucas

The Bad Man (FIRST NATIONAL) b/w 77 min

A lacklustre Western, *The Bad Man* is a straightforward remake of the 1923 silent with Huston in the title role. The fault lies not in Huston's interpretation of the role of Pancho Lopez but in Estabrook's script which simply rehashes the melodramatics of the silent version as Huston, having settled matters with Blackmer's villain, accepts his death at the hands of the Texas Rangers with equanimity. Director Badger is best remembered for his work on *It* (1927). The film was subsequently remade as *West of Shanghai* (1937).

d Clarence Badger *s* Howard Estabrook *c* John Seitz *lp* Walter Huston, Dorothy Revier, Sidney Blackmer, Guinn Williams, James Rennie, Arthur Stone

The Big Trail

(FOX) b/w widescreen (70mm) 158(125) min

An epic in the tradition of *The Covered Wagon* (1923) and *The Iron Horse* (1924), *The Big Trail* was a surprising box office failure. Wayne, recommended to Walsh (who had intended to play the part himself before he lost an eye) by Ford, is more than adequate in the lead. However, soon after he was dropped by Fox and spent the thirties working on Poverty Row until Ford revived his flagging career with **Stagecoach** (1939). The film neatly unites a standard revenge plot (Wayne hunting for his father's murderer) with the story of the first wagon train's laborious progress along the Oregon Trail. The sequences of the wagons fording rivers and being manhandled up mountains and the action sequences are both realistic and visually breathtaking, but the interior scenes, as was the case with many early talkies, are spoilt by the genteel and overly theatrical speech patterns demanded by the film's dialogue director, Lumsden Hare.

German and Spanish versions (*Horizontes Huevos*) with different leading players were released by Fox in 1931.

d Raoul Walsh *s* Jack Peabody, Marie Boyle, Florence Postal, Fred Sersen *c* Lucien Andriot, Arthur Edeson *lp* John Wayne, Marguerite Churchill, Ward Bond, Tyrone Power Snr

Billy the Kid *aka* The Highwayman Rides

(MGM) widescreen b/w 90 min

Shot on location in the Lincoln County area of New Mexico where Billy (Brown) lived, and made with the technical advice of W.S. Hart, *Billy The Kid* is undeniably faithful to the look

of the old West, despite its big budget and romantic plot. Beery is a dignified Pat Garrett and Johnson is the woman he allows Brown to escape with when he has him cornered. Brown's explanation of his philosophy of life, 'I am a rebel', makes him very much a Vidor hero but the difficulties of making close-ups in the widescreen process made it impossible for Vidor to express fully the emotional tensions of his hero. Reputedly Brown, whose last prestige picture this was before he was relegated to the glories of Poverty Row, used William Bonney's actual guns during the film.

d King Vidor *s* Wanda Tuchock, Laurence Stallings, Charles MacArthur *c* Gordon Avil *lp* Johnny Mack Brown, Wallace Beery, Kay Johnson, Wyndham Standing, Karl Dane, Roscoe Ates

Warner Baxter and Carole Lombard exchange meaningful glances under the watchful eyes of Theodore von Eltz in The Arizona Kid.

John Wayne and Marguerite Churchill in a scene from The Big Trail, *the film that promised to make Wayne a star but in fact almost ended his career when it failed at the box office.*

Far right: *Richard Arlen and Fay Wray in a publicity still for Border Legion.*

Border Legion (PAR) b/w 68 min
The first sound version of Zane Grey's often-filmed novel sees Wray as the much-threatened heroine, Arlen as the man she loves and Holt as the good natured outlaw who sacrifices himself for her. The film's creaky, theatrical plot, stilted direction and use of stock footage betray the movie's silent-cinema origins.

d Otto Brower, Edwin H. Knopf *s* Percy Heath, Edward E. Paramore *c* Mark Stengler *lp* Richard Arlen, Jack Holt, Fay Wray, Eugene Pallette, Syd Saylor, Stanley Fields

Border Romance (TIFFANY) b/w 66 min
Thorpe's first sound feature, this Tiffany quickie was one of the several Westerns made in the early thirties that attempted

to cash in on the romance and action that the success of **In Old Arizona** (1929) had firmly associated with Mexico in audiences' minds. Terry is the gringo on the run from the law and Armida the señorita he falls for and rescues time and time again from rustlers. Glendon is the murderer Terry kills winning himself a pardon for doing so.

d Richard Thorpe *p* Lester F. Scott *s* Jack Natteford *c* Harry Zech *lp* Armida, Don Terry, J. Frank Glendon, Marjorie Kane, Victor Potel, Wesley Barry

The Concentratin' Kid
(HOOT GIBSON PRODUCTIONS/U) b/w 57 min
Gibson's final film for Universal, and one of his funniest. He's the Bar Q cowboy who falls in love with radio songstress Crawford and vows he'll marry her. On his return from town to woo her he finds that Mason has rustled the Bar Q cattle and kidnapped Crawford who's been brought to the range to serenade the cowboys. He rescues both.

Gibson's penchant for comedy and his self-indulgent attitude to his scripts sadly too often masked his considerable abilities. This skill was also obscured as increasingly sound Westerns lost the oddness that had characterized many of the best silents and the genre became more and more inflexible and the films more and more streamlined.

Johnny Mack Brown (centre) from King Vidor's Billy the Kid *in a scene that looks as though it could have been shot by John Ford.*

Far right: Courtship Hoot Gibson style: Gibson romances Kathryn Crawford in The Concentratin' Kid.

d Arthur Rosson *p* Hoot Gibson *s* Harold Tarshis
c Harry Neumann *lp* Hoot Gibson, Kathryn Crawford,
Duke Lee, Robert Homans, James Mason

The Fighting Legion (U) b/w 75 min

An important transitional B Western. Of all the silent cowboy
stars who learned to talk after the coming of sound, Maynard
was the first to be interested in the idea of music and singing
as well as talking and sound effects. In this, his last
part-sound part-silent movie, he features a singing trio, the
Hook Brothers. This film also sees Rice as Maynard's
side-kick for the first time.

Cohen and Mason's script, which has Maynard seeking
revenge for the murder of his Texas Ranger brother, opts for a
more dramatic tone than was usual. Thus, instead of an
action-packed climax, we watch the killer, Adams, deteriorate
as he waits and waits for Maynard to shoot it out at midnight.
Dwan is the girl Maynard kisses at the fade.

d Harry Joe Brown *p* Ken Maynard *s* Bennett Cohen,
Lesley Mason *c* Ted McCord *lp* Ken Maynard, Dorothy
Dwan, Frank Rice, Charles Whittaker, Ernie Adams, Harry
Todd

The Girl of the Golden West

(FIRST NATIONAL) b/w 81 min

The first sound version of David Belasco's famous play – so
famous in its time that Puccini made an opera of it in 1910.
First National hired Harding from Pathe for the part of the
girl who falls in love with a gallant outlaw and saves his life by
playing cards with the sheriff and winning. As part of her
contract, her husband, Bannister, was also hired, but in the
role of the sheriff, not the outlaw who was played by Rennie.
The film is virtually a transcription of the play, but without its
melodramatic power. Such were the limitations of the early
talkie, the film is wooden and stilted.

d John Francis Dillon *p* Robert North *s* Waldemar
Young *c* Sol Polito *lp* Ann Harding, James Rennie, Harry
Bannister, J. Farrell MacDonald, George Cooper, Arthur
Stone

Headin' North (TREM CARR PRODUCTIONS) b/w 60 min

An oddity, to say the least, *Headin' North* is interesting in part
because it demonstrates the pervasiveness of music in the
Western. After a lenghty fistfight for openers, Steele is
sought on a made-up charge and has to spend most of the film
disguised (with Murdock) as half of an English dance-hall
team, singing (well actually, miming) and dancing his way
closer to the truth, before catching the villains in another
lengthy fight. Steele is clearly out of his depth in both the part
and the 'funny clothes' (as heroine Luddy succinctly calls his
dude garb).

d/s J.P. McCarthy *p* Trem Carr *c* Archie Stout *lp* Bob
Steele, Barbara Luddy, Perry Murdock, Walter Shumway,
Eddie Dunn, Fred Burns

Hell's Heroes (U) b/w 66 min

The first sound version of Peter B. Kyne's much filmed
sentimental novel, *The Three Godfathers*. Bickford, Hatton
and Kohler are the outlaws who find a woman about to give
birth in the midst of a desert sandstorm and sacrifice
themselves to save the child. Wyler's direction is far more
detached than that of Ford who made both a silent and sound
version of the novel. Less static than most early talkies – it
was Wyler and Universal's first all sound outdoor film – it
remains impressive for its realistic treatment which gives
depth to an otherwise slight story.

d William Wyler *p* Carl Laemmle *s* Tom Reed *c* George
Robinson *lp* Charles Bickford, Raymond Hatton, Fred
Kohler, Fritzi Ridgeway, Maria Alba, Buck Connors

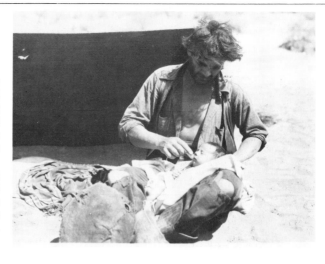

*Charles Bickford gives
his last drops of water to
the newborn baby in
Hell's Heroes.*

The Indians Are Coming (U) b/w 12 chaps

The first serial to have a Broadway opening, *The Indians Are
Coming*, which was released in both silent and sound versions,
is an historically important Western. Its success – produced
for $160,000, it reportedly grossed over $1 million within a
year – was further proof that sound Westerns could be
profitable at all levels. It also marked a transition from the
more melodramatic aspects of Westerns of the silent era to an
almost nostalgic account of the glories of the old West, as in
the long wagon-train journey with McCoy and Ray perpetually attacked by Indians. The film ended the career of silent star
Ray: her squeaky voice was in complete contrast to her
inviting blue eyes.

d/p Henry MacRae *s* George H. Plympton *lp* Allene Ray,
'Colonel' Tim McCoy, Francis Ford, Charles Royal, Edmund
Cobb, Bud Osborne

Last of the Duanes (FOX) b/w 58 min

Last of the Duanes was amongst the group of series Westerns,
mostly remakes of Tom Mix silents from the twenties, that
Fox made in 1930-31 with the intention of making O'Brien a
Western star. Henceforth O'Brien, who had previously

*Director John Francis
Dillon on the set of* The
Girl of the Golden
West *with his leading
players, James Rennie
and Ann Harding.*

Colonel Tim McCoy, eyes glinting, bides his time during one of the numerous Indian attacks in The Indians Are Coming.

George O'Brien and Myrna Loy in a studio portrait from Last of the Duanes. *By 1936 Loy had become Hollywood's number one female box-office star and the epitome of sophistication, but O'Brien, though a fine actor, from the early thirties made mostly series Westerns.*

Richard Arlen, best remembered for his starring roles in Wings *(1927) and* The Virginian *(1930), is watched by a pensive Mary Brian in* The Light of Western Stars.

worked with directors as diverse as Ford, Murnau and Hawks in all kinds of roles, would only appear in Westerns. Based on a Zane Grey novel the plot has O'Brien rescuing Brown from outlaw McGrail, being romanced by McGrail's wife, Loy, before finally handing McGrail over to the Texas Rangers. The action was interspersed with songs.

A Spanish language version, *Ultimo de Los Vargos* was simultaneously made by David Howard (the regular director of O'Brien's Fox Westerns) starring George Lewis and Luana Alcaniz.

d Alfred L. Werker *p* Edward Butcher, Harold B. Lipsitz *s* Ernest Pascal *c* Daniel Clark *lp* George O'Brien, Lucille Browne, Myrna Loy, Walter McGrail, Nat Pendleton, Lloyd Ingraham

The Light of Western Stars (PAR) b/w 70 min
Paramount's first sound Zane Grey Western, this features Arlen as the cowboy who has to fight Toomey and Kohler for Brian. Efficiently directed by serial regulars, Brower and Knopf, it was overseen by Sherman who was later to bring the phenomenally successful Hopalong Cassidy series to Paramount. Sherman remade the story yet again for Paramount in 1940 with Victor Jory in the lead.

d Otto Brower, Edwin H. Knopf *p* Harry Sherman *s* Grover Jones, William Slavens McNutt *c* Charles Lang *lp* Richard Arlen, Mary Brian, Regis Toomey, Fred Kohler, Syd Saylor, George Chandler

The Lone Rider
(BEVERLY PRODUCTIONS/COL) b/w 61 min
The first of Jones' all-talking Westerns for Columbia after the expiry of his silent contract with Fox, this sees him as an outlaw turned defender of law and order – he's the leader of

the local Vigilante Committee – whose past is revealed by outlaw Woods. After a period of being chased by both Woods and the Committee, Jones brings Woods to justice and wins the heart of Reynolds. Jones' command of the sound medium, at a time when many silent stars were failing, began his climb back to dominance in the Western field which culminated in his becoming the top-grossing Western star in 1934, far surpassing his popularity at the peak of his silent success.

d Louis King p Sol Lesser s Forrest Sheldon c Ted McCord lp Buck Jones, Vera Reynolds, Harry Woods, George Pearce

The Lone Star Ranger (FOX) b/w 64 min
O'Brien is the outlaw turned Texas Ranger in an effort to win himself a pardon after he's fallen for Carol's girl from the East in this, the first all-talking series Western. O'Brien had been a featured actor in silent films since his appearance in John Ford's *The Iron Horse* (1924) – and would make his last film appearance forty years later in that director's last Western, **Cheyenne Autumn** (1964) – but after this, his first series entry, he would ride the range as a mega star of series Westerns.

d/p A.F. Erickson s Seton Miller c Daniel Clark
lp George O'Brien, Sue Carol, Russell Simpson, Elizabeth Patterson, Richard Alexander, Bob Fleming

The Lonesome Trail (G.A. DURLAM) b/w 66 min
Another independent quickie, *Lonesome Trail* made it clear that though the singing cowboy was still a few years away, by mid-1930, the musical Western was a commonplace. Mix and Canutt are the villains after Faire and newcomer Delaney, in his only starring role, the hero.

d Bruce Mitchell p/s G.A. Durlam c Paul H. Allen
lp Charles Delaney, Art Mix, Yakima Canutt, Virginia Brown Faire, Ben Corbett, Lafe McKee

Men without Law
(BEVERLY PRODUCTIONS/COL) b/w 65 min
One of Jones' funnier outings, this begins at the Front during the First World War with Jones befriending the brother of Geraghty before his death. On his return to the range he seeks out Geraghty and outlaw Woods whose gang his own brother has joined. He rescues Geraghty from Woods' schemes to steal her and her father's extensive lands and ends Woods' days after a lengthy fight.

d Louis King p Sol Lesser s Dorothy Howell c Ted McCord lp Buck Jones, Carmelita Geraghty, Tom Carr, Harry Woods, Fred Burns, Lafe McKee

Montana Moon (MGM) b/w 90 min
One of the best of the numerous operettas roughly transposed to the cinema immediately after the advent of sound. Unlike a film like *Song of the West* (1930) whose makers refused to acknowledge they were making a Western (of sorts), rather than filming a stage musical, St Clair and writer Farnham liberally splattered their film with Western cliches as part of the process of opening out the stage play it was based on. Set in a fantasy world where ranchers wear tuxedos and buy modernistic furniture for their ranch houses, the film follows Crawford, as the Easterner on the run from her rich but stuffy daddy, who marries a calloused cowhand, Brown, in his last role before **Billy the Kid** (1930) would make him a huge star. At first, egged on by Cortez as the city slicker who comes between them, things go badly but, as ever, true love eventually triumphs.

d/p Malcolm St Clair s Joe Farnham c William Daniels
lp Johnny Mack Brown, Joan Crawford, Cliff Edwards, Ricardo Cortez, Dorothy Sebastian, Lloyd Ingraham

Mountain Justice aka Kettle Creek (U) b/w 74 min
Maynard's first legitimate talkie – previous entries were only part sound – *Mountain Justice* is notable for both the number of songs it has, thus prefiguring the era of the Singing Cowboy, and the high quality of the stunt work, done by Maynard himself. The climax has Maynard chasing Bates on a buckboard that all but collapses and then leaping from it onto a moving train and fighting Bates. Equally significantly, the script is based on Maynard's own ideas. In a few years' time Maynard was to be the B Western's only writer/director/producer (in all but name), sadly to his own detriment.

d/co-p Harry Joe Brown co-p Ken Maynard s Bennett Cohen c Ted McCord lp Ken Maynard, Kathryn Crawford, Fred Burns, Otis Harlan, Les Bates, Pee Wee Holmes

The Mounted Stranger
(HOOT GIBSON PRODUCTIONS/U) b/w 66 min
For the first of his all-talking Universal series of films, Gibson remained true to his silent image of the unglamorous cowpoke

Buck Jones and Harry Woods, one of seriesdom's most capable villains, prepare to fight it out in The Lone Rider.

Joan Crawford and Ricardo Cortez dancing Eastern-style in Montana Moon.

Kathryn Crawford comes between Ken Maynard (left) and Les Bates in Mountain Justice.

Hoot Gibson retains his unglamorous silent image in The Mounted Stranger, *a remake of his 1924 classic,* The Ridin' Kid from Powder River.

who, in marked contrast to Ken Maynard, was likely to wear his gun, if he wore one, stuffed in his boot. The film, a remake of his 1924 silent, saw Gibson out to revenge his father's murder and rescue Lorraine from Burns. The revenge plot, already a staple ingredient of the genre, usually indicates an action-packed film, but here the dramatics are defused by Gibson's nonchalance and the odd twists and turns of the plot. The film is also notable for containing what surely must be the first parody of the all-singing Western when Gibson, Williams, Ford and others offer their raucous version of campfire harmonizing.

d/s Arthur Rosson   *p* Hoot Gibson   *c* Harry Neumann
lp Hoot Gibson, Louise Lorraine, Francis Ford, Fred Burns, Pee Wee Williams, James Corey

Near the Rainbow's End   (TIFFANY)   b/w   58 min
Steele's first sound Western. The plot is the familiar one of rustlers causing hostilities between cattlemen and sheepmen for their own purposes and cattle rancher's son, Steele, putting an end to Ferguson's rustling days and bringing peace

to the valley by marrying sheepman's daughter, Lorraine. The fights, as usual in Steele's films, are particularly ferocious. A new element from McGowan, who had directed Steele's 1929 silent series for Syndicate, is the comic touch which Steele would try out briefly before discarding it in favour of unalloyed action.

d J.P. McGowan   *p* Trem Carr   *s* Sally Winters   *c* Hap Depew   *lp* Bob Steele, Louise Lorraine, Al Ferguson, Lafe McKee, Al Hewston, Hank Bell

Only the Brave   (PAR)   b/w   67 min
This weak melodrama sees Cooper as a disappointed lover volunteering for spy duty during the Civil War. Given false papers, he is instructed to head South and get captured. There he falls for Brian and makes an enemy of Holmes who also loves her. He is finally caught but the Confederates have been deceived by his false battle plans. The Union detachment wins the battle and rescues him just in time to smooth the path of true love. Script and direction are plodding.

d Frank Tuttle   *s* Edward E. Paramore Jnr, Agnes Brand Leahy   *c* Harry Fischbeck   *lp* Gary Cooper, Mary Brian, Phillips Holmes, James Neill, Morgan Farley, Guy Oliver

Parade of the West
(KEN MAYNARD PRODUCTIONS)   b/w   66 min
Maynard is the medicine showman who joins the circus as a bronco daredevil rider only to lose his nerve after a fall and return to the quiet backwaters of the medicine show. There he recovers in time to save the life of Hanlon's kid and wins the heart of McConnell. Much padded with stock footage of bronco riding and trick roping and listlessly directed by Brown, the film doesn't fulfill the promise of Maynard's earlier part-talkies.

d Harry Joe Brown   *p* Ken Maynard   *s* Leslie Mason
c Ted McCord   *lp* Ken Maynard, Gladys McConnell, Jackie Hanlon, Otis Harlan, Frank Rice, Fred Burns

Phantom of the Desert
(WEBB DOUGLAS PRODUCTIONS)   b/w   58 min
One of the several independently produced quickies Perrin made which secured him the title of the first regular series cowboy star of the sound era, but at the cost of his career, so ineptly made are most of them, with the exception of his first **Overland Bound** (1929). Trade reviewers, seeking something to praise, directed their comments to the performance of Perrin's horse, Starlight, who at one point eats a Wanted poster for himself and Perrin; a common sorrow was that he hadn't eaten the script.

d/co-p Harry Webb   *co-p* F.E. Douglas   *s* Carl Krusada   *c* William Nobles   *lp* Jack Perrin, Eve Novak, Josef Swickard, Ben Corbett, Edward Earle, Robert Walker

Ridin' Law   (BILTMORE PRODUCTIONS)   b/w   63 min
Perrin is the hero out to revenge the murder of his father, Canutt the villain and Borden the Mexican heroine whose accent keeps slipping. The film's significance lies purely in its existence: at a time when the major studios were only reluctantly making sound Westerns (or in the case of Universal, demanding that their stars contribute to the increased costs that sound recording meant), the independents were flocking to make them. Some are good; others, like this, celebrated their cheapness and lack of imagination in every frame. But they were made.

d/co-p Harry S. Webb   *co-p* F. E. Douglas   *s* Carl Krusada   *c* William Nobles   *lp* Jack Perrin, Yakima Canutt, Rene Borden, Jack Mowers, Ben Corbett, Fern Emmett

River's End   (WB)   b/w   75 min
Bickford is on fine form in the double role of the mountie and

the man he's after in this melodramatic Western all too slackly directed by Curtiz. The trouble with this remake of the 1922 silent is the common one that afflicted many early sound Westerns, the unsuitability of silent plotlines for the increased realism that sound brought to the cinema. Kenyon's unlikely script, based on a story by James Oliver Curwood, features the innocent Bickford posing as a dead mountie. Knapp is the girl who falls for him and MacDonald the villain.

d Michael Curtiz   *s* Charles Kenyon   *c* Bob Kurrle
lp Charles Bickford, Evalyn Knapp, J. Farrell MacDonald, Zasu Pitts, Walter McGrail, David Torrance

Roaring Ranch
(HOOT GIBSON PRODUCTIONS/U)   b/w   68 min
This is the first of a pair of films Gibson made with Eilers for Universal. But, though Eilers was briefly the love of his life and the romantic interest of the film, in typical Gibson fashion the movie's (melo)dramatics centre around his attempts to protect his land, a breezy baby – whose nappy he even changes at one point – and a mischievous child from the machinations of Oakman who wants his oil-rich ranch. The plot was subsequently rehashed for one of Ken Maynard's lacklustre Columbia outings, *Heir to Trouble* (1935).

d/s B. Reeves Eason   *p* Hoot Gibson   *c* Harry Neumann
lp Hoot Gibson, Sally Eilers, Wheeler Oakman, Bobby Nelson, Leo White, Frank Clark

Song of the Caballero
(KEN MAYNARD PRODUCTIONS)   b/w   73 min
This outing sees Maynard further increasing the musical content of his films and at one point even joining in on a song. Set in the days of old California, which in effect means swords and Spanish garb rather than stetsons and six guns, the plot

features Maynard as the defender of right and romancer of Hill. Full of Maynard's seemingly impossible horse stunts and put together at breakneck pace by Brown, it is one of Maynard's better early series outings.

d Harry Joe Brown   *p* Ken Maynard   *s* Bennett Cohen
c Ted McCord   *lp* Ken Maynard, Doris Hill, Francis Ford, Frank Rice, William Irving, Evelyn Sherman

Sons of the Saddle   (U)   b/w   76 min
The last of Maynard's first series for Universal saw him pitted against a villainous Ford with Rice once more his side-kick. By now Maynard was so keen on singing that he'd signed a record contract with Columbia Records. Universal were less impressed. Having discovered that the extra cost of sound recording made B Westerns unprofitable they dispensed with the services of both Maynard and Hoot Gibson and closed down their series department. The split with Universal was disastrous for Maynard, not least because it severed his relationship with producer and friend Brown who went to RKO rather than follow Maynard to the wilderness of Tiffany Studios.

d Harry Joe Brown   *p* Ken Maynard   *s* Bennett Cohen
c Ted McCord   *lp* Ken Maynard, Doris Hill, Francis Ford, Joe Girard, Harry Todd, Frank Rice

The Spoilers   (PAR)   b/w   86 min
Produced as a vehicle for Cooper, this is the first sound version of Rex Beach's often filmed novel. Cooper is the miner who foils Boyd's schemes to swindle other miners of their claims with the help of Ingraham's crooked judge. Johnson is the judge's niece who falls for Cooper and Compson the dance-hall queen he forsakes for her. The film's most talked about sequence is the lengthy fistfight between

Betty Compson as the dance-hall queen cast aside by Gary Cooper in The Spoilers.

Hoot Gibson and a terrified Indian in Spurs.

Cooper and Boyd for which the original combatants in the first silent version of 1914, William Farnum and Tom Santschi, were the technical advisers.

d/p Edwin Carewe   *s* Bartlett Cormack   *c* Harry Fishbeck
lp Gary Cooper, Kay Johnson, Betty Compson, William Boyd, Lloyd Ingraham, James Kirkwood

Spurs   (HOOT GIBSON PRODUCTIONS/U)   b/w   60 min

The best of Gibson's Universal films, this has stunning location cinematography from Neumann and a more actionful plot than usual. Gibson is the cowboy who first beats Morrison in the rodeo ring and then with his fists as he puts paid to his rustling plans and wins Wright and a pair of silver spurs for himself. The plot has fewer deviations than usual, a 'kids in peril' sub-plot notwithstanding. A fine series Western.

d/s B. Reeves Eason   *p* Hoot Gibson   *c* Harry Neumann
lp Hoot Gibson, Helen Wright, Pete Morrison, Robert Homans, Frank Clark, Buddy Hunter

The Texan   (PAR)   b/w   79 min

A picturesque version of the O'Henry short story, stronger on atmosphere than action. Cooper is the swaggering bandit who accepts Apfel's proposition to pretend to be the long lost son of Dunn in order to cheat an inheritance out of her. Only he falls instead for the charms of his 'cousin' (Wray in her third picture with Cooper). The melodramatic end has Marcus, as

James Marcus and Gary Cooper in a publicity shot for The Texan.

the sheriff who's been traiing Cooper, agreeing to Apfel's dead body being labelled as Cooper's, so leaving Wray and Cooper free to marry.

Paramount remade the film in 1939 as **The Llano Kid** with Tito Guizar in the Cooper role.

d John Cromwell   *s* Daniel N. Rubin   *c* Victor Milner
lp Gary Cooper, Fay Wray, Oscar Apfel, Emma Dunn, James Marcus, Donald Reed

Trailin' Trouble

(HOOT GIBSON PRODUCTIONS/U)   b/w   58 min

With the Hooter, as Gibson was affectionately known, in a business suit for most of the picture rather than his usual unruly denims, *Trailin' Trouble* is the oddest of his amiable series of films for Universal. The script has him and Morrison vying for the affections of Quimby and Gibson being branded a thief after he is robbed of the money he got for selling Quimby's father's cattle in Kansas City. Toy, the Chinese girl he's rescued in Kansas City, saves the day when she returns the money. A delightful picture.

d Arthur Rosson   *p* Hoot Gibson   *s* Harold Tarshis
c Harry Neumann   *lp* Hoot Gibson, Margaret Quimby, Pete Morrison, Olive Young, Ming Toy, William McCall

The Hooter, as Hoot Gibson was affectionately known, displays one of his Trigger Tricks.

Trigger Tricks

(HOOT GIBSON PRODUCTIONS/U)   b/w   61 min

Issued almost on the day of Gibson's disastrous marriage to his co-star, Eilers, *Trigger Tricks* is the funniest of Gibson's films for Universal. The end has Homans' gang held at bay by a Victrola recording while Gibson chases the gangleader. The plot is the archetypal revenge one with Gibson out to discover his brother's murderer. Eilers is the sheep rancher he helps along the way.

d/s B. Reeves Eason   *p* Hoot Gibson   *c* Harry Neumann
lp Hoot Gibson, Sally Eilers, Neal Hart, Robert Homans, Pete Morrison, Monte Montague

Under a Texas Moon   (WB)   b/w   82 min

A romantic adventure. Fay, who found working with Curtiz as difficult as Errol Flynn later would, is the Mexican bandido who criss-crosses the border caught between the charms of Loy and Torres. Beery provides the swagger and Kohler the deep-dyed villainy.

d Michael Curtiz   *s* Gordon Rigby   *c* Bill Rees   *lp* Frank Fay, Raquel Torres, Myrna Loy, Noah Beery Snr, George E. Stone, Fred Kohler

Under Texas Skies   (SYNDICATE)   b/w   65(57) min

One of the series Westerns Custer made for W. Ray Johnston's Syndicate Pictures, the independent company (with John R. Freuler's Big 4 Productions) that was the most active in the Western field in the early thirties. Custer is the official star but also featured are the equally famous Chandler and Cody, Syndicate's policy being to make one all-star series in which the leads changed from film to film. Custer is the mysterious cowboy – in fact a secret serviceman on the track of horse thieves – who foils Chandler's attempts to defraud an orphaned girl of her money. The plot is complicated by Chandler's impersonating an army officer he and the gang of horse thieves have captured. Custer wins through to get the

girl, Kingston, and free his friend, Cody. The movie is cheaply made but effective.

d J.P. McGowan *p* W. Ray Johnston *s* G.A. Durlam *c* Otto Himm *lp* Bob Custer, Natalie Kingston, Bill Cody, Lane Chandler, Tom London, Bob Roper

Way Out West (MGM) b/w 71 min
The first spoof Western of the sound era. Haines is the comic hero, a Western tenderfoot but an experienced trickster who does his cardsharping on cowboys, after being kicked out of the circus, only to have them force him to work off the $200 he cheated them out of. Saved by the love of Hyams, he in turn saves her from a sandstorm. Structured around Haines' smart-aleck comic persona, the film was just the first of many to use the West as a novelty backdrop for its star.

d Fred Niblo *s* Alfred Block, Ralph Spence, Joe Farnham *c* Henry Sharp *lp* William Haines, Leila Hyams, Polly Moran, Cliff Edwards, Vera Marsh, Charles Middleton

The Avenger
(BEVERLY PRODUCTIONS/COL) b/w 65 min
The last and best of Jones' Columbia Westerns produced by Lesser – henceforth they would be produced in house – this is a much-fictionalized account of the oft-filmed life of Joaquin Murrieta. It is imaginatively directed by Neill, a director better known for his superior Sherlock Holmes series of the forties, and brilliantly lit by Tetzlaff and Van Enger. The Townley-Morgan script sees Jones avenging the death of his brother, Fix, not as was usual his wife, and meting out justice to those responsible. As such it is a more domestic account of Murietta who is generally treated as the scourge of all gringos.

As an indication of the way things were to develop, the film opens with a dubbed Jones serenading Revier. Although the actual Townley-Morgan screenplay was only remade once (by Lambert Hillyer as *Vengeance of the West* starring Wild Bill Elliott, in 1942), the Murrieta story was to be the basis of numerous later films, of which **Robin Hood of El Dorado** (1936) was just the first.

Buck Jones as Joaquin Murrieta and Dorothy Revier as his wife in The Avenger, *the first sound version of the Murrieta story.*

d Roy William Neill *p* Sol Lesser *s* George Morgan, Jack Townley *c* Teddy Tetzlaff, Charles Van Enger *lp* Buck Jones, Edward Piel, Dorothy Revier, Otto Hoffman, Paul Fix, Slim Whitaker

Battling with Buffalo Bill (U) b/w 12 chaps
This was made by Universal to capitalize quickly on the phenomenal success of **The Indians Are Coming** (1930). However, although it is a superior serial, it did not match the success of the earlier chapter play in commercial terms. A major reason for its success is the second unit direction and stunting of Yakima Canutt. Canutt had starred in several early independent Westerns. Though he continued to act, usually as a villain, from 1931 he was to be found more frequently either behind the camera or doubling for the star.

Tyler was Universal's all-purpose serial hero in the thirties and would later achieve lasting serial fame as the impersonator of both Captain Marvel and the Phantom, in the forties. Here he's Buffalo Bill and the dependable Ford is the villainous gambler intent on creating an Indian war to frighten off the townspeople on whose lands he's discovered gold. Needless to say, after numerous cliffhangers and exciting stunts, Tyler foils Ford and manages to get the Cheyenne to smoke the peace pipe. Brown is the fragile heroine and Desmond is Ford's henchman.

d Ray Taylor *p* Henry MacRae *s* George Plympton, Ella O'Neill *lp* Tom Tyler, Rex Bell, William Desmond, Francis Ford, Yakima Canutt, Bud Osborne, Lucille Brown

Far left: William Haines as the breezy tenderfoot in the first spoof sound Western, Way Out West, *one of the last films he made before retiring from acting.*

Border Law (COL) b/w 63 min
One of Jones' best outings for Columbia in which he's the Texas Ranger granted leave of absence to go after Mason and his gang who shot and killed his brother in a hold-up. He masquerades as an outlaw and is befriended by Mason whom he finally puts paid to after a lengthy fistfight amidst the craggy mountains of New Mexico. Jones' phlegmatic approach to acting and the realistic action are even more appealing in contrast to the melodramatics and fantastical action sequences of contemporary series Westerns.

Ken Maynard remade the film as *Whistling Dan* (1932) and Jones himself remade it as **The Fighting Ranger** (1934).

d Louis King *p* Irving Briskin *s* Stuart Anthony *c* L.W. O'Connell *lp* Buck Jones, Lupita Tovar, James Mason, Frank Rice, Don Chapman, Glenn Strange

Cavalier of the West (ARTCLASS) b/w 75 min
One of Carey's few starring sound Westerns, this is an ineptly put together independent quickie. He's the army captain forced to declare martial law when the town's deputies turn against their sheriff. McCarthy directs whimsically, permitting his cast to fire endless blanks at each other. Carey, seen at his best in Cahn's magisterial **Law and Order** (1932), gives a solid performance.

d/co-s J.P. McCarthy *p* Louis Weiss *co-s* Harry P. Christ *c* Frank Kessock *lp* Harry Carey, Carmen LaRoux, George Hayes, Kane Richmond, Maston Williams, Theodore Adams

Warner Baxter as O'Henry's romantic bad man serenades Conchita Montenegro in The Cisco Kid.

Cimarron (RKO) b/w 131 min
The most successful Western epic of the early sound era, *Cimarron* includes a spectacular land rush sequence that compares favourably to the most famous land rush sequence ever in W.S. Hart's silent *Tumbleweeds* (1925). Adapted from Edna Ferber's 1930 novel, the film tells the story of the opening up of the Oklahoma Territory and its fight for statehood in the years 1890-1915, through the lives of Dix's pioneer and his entrepreneur wife, Dunne, who finishes what he starts when wanderlust reclaims him. The success of the film led to RKO re-instating their recently axed Western series. Though Ruggles' spirited direction seems dated now, the outdoor scenes still remain impressive.

Below: Richard Dix and Irene Dunne en route to the Oklahoma land rush in Cimarron.

The film won Oscars for best film, best adaptation and set decoration.

d Wesley Ruggles *p* William Le Baron *s* Howard Estabrook *c* Edward Cronjager *lp* Richard Dix, Irene Dunne, Estelle Taylor, Nance O'Neil, Roscoe Ates, Stanley Fields

The Cisco Kid (FOX) b/w 60 min
Baxter, who had won an Oscar for his portrayal of the Cisco Kid in **In Old Arizona** (1929), repeated the role here as did Lowe, playing the Texas Ranger determined to get his man. Lane is the damsel in distress whom Baxter's Robin Hood-like outlaw saves by a bank robbery. The best indication of the script's romanticism is that, in marked contrast to the silent versions of O'Henry's story, this (and later adventures of the Cisco Kid) sees the hero ride off into the sunset rather than swinging from a hangman's rope. Nonetheless, Baxter's charming and surprisingly complex interpretation overcomes the naiveties of the plot.

Baxter was to play the part again in **The Return of the Cisco Kid** (1939).

d Irving Cummings *s* Alfred A. Cohn *c* Barney McGill *lp* Warner Baxter, Edmund Lowe, Nora Lane, Conchita Montenegro, Chris-Pin Martin, Charles Stevens

Clearing the Range (ALLIED) b/w 61 min
Gibson's first Western for independent producer Hoffman and the last of his films with his wife, Eilers, who, after the release of her own starring vehicle, *Bad Girl* (1931) a few weeks later, (temporarily) became a far bigger star than her soon-to-be ex-husband. The plot mirrors this complicated relationship a little too closely with Gibson, as a ruse, acting as a coward and a weakling by day and thus incurring the wrath of Eilers, while at night he goes after the rustlers. Brower's direction is forceful and the production values better that what was to follow.

The film was quickly remade by Gibson as *The Dude Bandit* (1933).

d Otto Brower *p* M.H. Hoffman Jnr *s* Jack Natteford *c* Ernest Miller *lp* Hoot Gibson, Sally Eilers, Hooper Atchley, George Mendoza, Edward Piel, Edward Hearn

The Deadline (COL) b/w 65 min
Probably the best of Jones' series Westerns for Columbia, in great part because of its sober storyline. He's the man paroled from prison for a killing he didn't do who's determined to find the man responsible. On his return home, the townspeople ostracize him with the exception of his former sweetheart, Sayers, her little brother Ernest and, most surprising of all, her banker father, LeSaint, possibly the kindest banker ever

to appear in a thirties Western. Jones finds the killer and foils a bank robbery. Hillyer directs with an eye on atmosphere rather than melodrama.

d/s Lambert Hillyer *p* Irving Briskin *c* Byron Haskins *lp* Buck Jones, Loretta Sayers, George Ernest, Robert Ellis, Raymond Nye, Jack Curtis, Edward LeSaint

Desert Vengeance (COL) b/w 59 min

Co-starring Bedford, W.S. Hart's leading lady in *Tumbleweeds* (1925), *Desert Vengeance* is one of Jones' lesser Columbia outings. He's the outlaw leader, a role that would be unthinkable in a few years, and she's the adventuress who tries to trick him and is put to hard labour by Jones when she fails. But, after an attack by a rival outlaw band on Jones' hide-out leaves them the only survivors, they start a new life together.

d Louis King *p* Irving Briskin *s* Stuart Anthony *c* Ted McCord *lp* Buck Jones, Barbara Bedford, Buck Connors, Pee Wee Holmes, Slim Whitaker, Douglas Gilmore

Fighting Caravans *aka* Blazing Arrows
(PAR) b/w 91 min

A disappointing prestige Western in the mould of *Covered Wagon* (1923) despite being theoretically based on Zane Grey's 1929 novel. The complicated plot has wagon scout Cooper falling in love with Damita to whom he's been 'married' by friends to save him from prison. Kohler is the evil trader in league with the Indians. Footage shot but not used in the film was subsequently put to use in **Wagon Wheels** (1934).

d Otto Brower, David Burton *s* Edward E. Paramore Jnr, Keene Thompson, Agnes Brand Leahy *c* Lee Garmes, Henry Gerrard *lp* Gary Cooper, Lily Damita, Ernest Torrence, Fred Kohler, Tully Marshall, Syd Saylor

God's Country and the Man
(SYNDICATE) b/w 59 min

The last of Tyler's Westerns for Syndicate before the company changed its name to Monogram, this snappy picture sees him taking on six men with his fists and later ten with his guns and living to tell the tale. The plot is the old one of the government agent posing as a baddie to get outlaw Bridge. The twist is that the girl he falls for while in outlaw disguise is also a government agent who rejects him until she knows his true identity.

d/p J.P. McCarthy *s* Wellyn Totman *c* Archie Stout *lp* Tom Tyler, Betty Mack, George Hayes, Ted Adams, Al Bridge, Gordon DeMain

Gun Smoke (PAR) b/w 64 min

Boyd, soon to achieve lasting fame as Hopalong Cassidy, is the gun-crazy mobster who tries to muscle in on the range only to be soundly defeated by Arlen in this influential Western that set in motion a brief trend towards machine-guns-versus-six-guns gangster Westerns. Sloman's direction is flat and the script strangely undramatic – even Boyd's gunning down of men is baldly presented – to the detriment of the unusual storyline. Similarly Arlen and Brian's romance is only sketched in. Boyd puts in a fine performance.

d Edward Sloman *s* Grover Jones, William McNutt *c* Archie Stout *lp* Richard Arlen, Mary Brian, William Boyd, Eugene Pallette, Louise Fazenda, Charles Winninger

Hard Hombre (ALLIED) b/w 65 min

Whereas Gibson's earlier outings for Allied had been more action oriented, from *Hard Hombre* onwards, the films return to the style of the idiosyncratic and sentimental screenplays of his Universal days. Here, he's a would-be tough guy who repeatedly comes to his mother's aid. Brower directs easeful-

ly, creating spaces for Gibson's sly comic routines and the result is a cut above Gibson's other Allied outings.

d Otto Brower *p* M.H. Hoffman Jnr *s* Jack Natteford *c* Harry Neumann *lp* Hoot Gibson, Lina Basquette, Mathilde Comont, Jesse Arnold, Glenn Strange, Robert Burns

I Take This Woman (PAR) b/w 72 min

Lombard replaced Fay Wray to good effect in this intriguing Western that has an uncanny resemblance to Clint Eastwood's **Bronco Billy** (1980). She's the spoiled heiress who throws over the bland Vail for Cooper's ranch foreman. She doesn't really love Cooper but when Daddy disinherits her and she has to live with Cooper she starts to fall for his lethargic charms. Essentially a melodrama, down to the climax which has her return to him while he's unconscious after a fall in the course of his circus cowboy act, the film gains a lot from Lombard and Cooper's contrasting acting styles.

d Marion Gering *s* Vincent Lawrence *c* Victor Milner *lp* Carole Lombard, Gary Cooper, Helen Ware, Lester Vail, Charles Trowbridge, Syd Saylor

Gary Cooper as the rugged Westerner and Carole Lombard as the spoilt little rich girl who falls for him in I Take This Woman.

Below: *Eugene Pallette (left), Louise Fazenda and Charles Winninger in* Gun Smoke.

In Old Cheyenne (SONO ART/WORLD WIDE) b/w 60 min
One of Lease's few starring Westerns, this is more memorable for Woods' grinning villainy and Burbridge's screenplay, which features a fiery stallion innocently helping rustler Woods by running off with all the mares, after first untying the ropes to the coral, and taking them to his secret mountain hideout! Lease fights well but romances more hesitantly.

d Stuart Paton *p* Cliff Broughton *s* Betty Burbridge *c* William Nobles *lp* Rex Lease, Dorothy Gulliver, Harry Woods, Jay Hunt, Harry Todd

Lightning Warrior (MAS) b/w 12 chaps
Rin Tin Tin's finest hour, *Lightning Warrior* was the wonder dog's last film and Mascot's best serial. Rinty was over 13 years old when the chapter play was made and for most of the action sequences doubles were used (including a stuffed wolf dog for at least one of the breathtaking leaps). The superior action sequences and human stunting were the responsibility

Below: Rin Tin Tin in his prime.

of Yakima Canutt who joined Mascot as the head of the company's second unit in 1931 and henceforth would spend more time behind the camera than in front of it.

The complex plot features Brownlee as the mysterious wolfman who, with his band of white men dressed as Indians (a Western serial favourite), is trying to scare off a group of miners and settlers and so claim for himself the rich seam of gold only he knows about. Brent, youngster Darro and Rin Tin Tin join forces to end Brownlee's reign of terror. Hale is the plucky heroine.

d Armand Schaefer, Benjamin Kline *p* Nat Levine *s* Wyndham Gittens, Ford Beebe, Colbert Clark *c* Ernest Miller, William C. Nobles, Tom Galligan *lp* Rin Tin Tin, Frankie Darro, George Brent, Georgia Hale, Yakima Canutt, Kermit Maynard, Bob Kortman, Frank Brownlee

The Montana Kid (MON) b/w 64 min
This indifferent series Western is one of the several Cody and Shuford made as Bill and Ben. Shuford co-stars as the child whose father has been shot and whom Cody looks after. Thorne is the villain responsible for stealing Shuford's ranch and killing his father who Cody does melodramatic battle with and Hill the romantic interest.

Far right: William Boyd (right), soon to achieve lasting fame as Hopalong Cassidy, J. Farrell MacDonald and Helen Twelvetrees in The Painted Desert.

d Harry Fraser *p* Trem Carr *s* G.A. Durlam *c* Archie Stout *lp* Bill Cody, Doris Hill, Andy Shuford, W.L. Thorne, John Elliott, Paul Panzer

Near the Trail's End (TIFFANY) b/w 55 min
Steele's last picture for Tiffany before moving a little up Poverty Row to World Wide where the budgets were fractionally bigger. This outing sees him as the newly appointed marshal romancing Shockley as he rids his domain of a band of stagecoach robbers. Producer/director Carr, who would move with his star to World Wide, is less concerned with budgetary matters than he would be later as a producer. The result is a pleasant series Western.

d/p Trem Carr *s* G.A. Durlam *c* Archie Stout *lp* Bob Steele, Marion Shockley, Jay Morley, Si Jenks, Hooper Atchley, Fred Burns

The One Way Trail (COL) b/w 60 min
A superior series entry from McCoy who, though he was probably the fastest on the draw of all screen cowboys, opted for an austere image rather than the flashy gun-twirling image of so many cowboy stars. He was the man who could never be shaken off once he was on your trail. Plympton's screenplay is more thoughtfully constructed than usual with McCoy on the trail of Ferguson (who acts a shade too melodramatically). Ferguson's crime is to shoot McCoy's brother after being caught cheating at cards. Hill is the active heroine the unshy McCoy wooes.

d Ray Taylor *p* Irving Briskin *s* George Plympton *c* John Hickson *lp* Tim McCoy, Polly Ann Young, Doris Hill, Al Ferguson, Bud Osborne, Slim Whitaker

The Painted Desert (PATHE) b/w 80 min
One of the few Westerns Boyd made before assuming the mantle of Hopalong Cassidy, *The Painted Desert* is also interesting for the early performance of Gable as the villain. A superior production, it is one of the few A grade Westerns of the early thirties that isn't an epic. Boyd is the infant rescued by one-time partners Farnum and MacDonald who, in his maturity, settles the feud between them over water rights and marries MacDonald's daughter, Twelvetrees. Synder's desert landscapes give the film a much-praised austere beauty that helps rescue it from the sentimental dialogue and melodramatic plot.

d/co-s Howard Higgin   *p* E.B. Derr   *co-s* Tom Buckingham
c Ed Synder   *lp* William Boyd, Helen Twelvetrees,
William Farnum, Clark Gable, J. Farrell MacDonald,
Wade Boteler

Range Feud   (COL)   b/w   64 min

A routine Jones series entry. Wayne, in his first Western since
his disastrous debut as a leading man in **The Big Trail** (1930),
is the innocent cowhand and foster brother to Jones' sheriff,
accused of murdering a local rancher who's the father of the
girl he loves, Fleming. Woods is the villain of the piece,
unmasked just as the noose is slipped around Wayne's neck.

d D. Ross Lederman   *p* Irving Briskin   *s* Milton Krims
c Ben Kline   *lp* Buck Jones, John Wayne, Susan Fleming,
Harry Woods, Edward J. LeSaint, William Walling

Red Fork Range   (BIG 4)   b/w   59 min

One of the number of films made by Wales, who like Jack
Perrin was a victim of the sheer awfulness of most of the
independent sound quickies, before he changed his name to
Hal Taliaferro and became a character actor in the late
thirties. Here he wins a stagecoach race and rescues his girl,
Mix, from the clutches of villains Osborne and Lyons who are
masquerading as Indians.

d/s Alvin Neitz (Alan James)   *p* John R. Freuler   *c* William
Nobles   *lp* Wally Wales, Ruth Mix, Al Ferguson, Bud
Osborne, Cliff Lyons, Lafe McKee

Riders of the Purple Sage   (FOX)   b/w   58 min

A superior series entry, this Zane Grey remake features
O'Brien in the role essayed in silent films first by William
Farnum and then Tom Mix. McFadden, by all accounts a
poor director in general, and cinematographer Schneiderman

*Lupe Velez whose
performance as the
Indian maid, Naturich,
is the best thing in De
Mille's third version of*
The Squaw Man, *the
film with which he
began his directorial
career.*

combined to produce a beautiful-looking film, especially in
the scenes staged in the mountains, that is full of inventive
camerawork. Beery is the crooked judge and O'Brien the
Texas Ranger who exposes him and saves Churchill. In the
most romantic of endings, the lovers on the run take refuge in
a canyon and block the only entrance, thus creating their own
private paradise.

O'Brien, like Mix before him, immediately made a sequel,
The Rainbow Trail (1932).

*Elliott Dexter and Jack
Holt in De Mille's 1918
version of* The Squaw
Man.

A dispute over a friendly game of cards in Sunrise Trail.

d Hamilton McFadden *s* John F. Goodrich, Philip Klein, Barry Connors *c* George Schneiderman *lp* George O'Brien, Noah Beery, Marguerite Churchill, Yvonne Pelletier, Frank McGlynn, Stanley Fields

Son of the Plains (SYNDICATE) b/w 59 min

Another of Custer's Syndicate quickies, this features him as a deputy sheriff on the trail of the Polka Dot Kid (Hearn) who's kidnapped the father of Phillips, Custer's loved one. Thrown together, Stout's fine cinematography notwithstanding, the film, like many of Syndicate's Westerns, has a crude charm about it that is appealing.

d/s R.N. Bradbury *p* W. Ray Johnson *c* Archie Stout *lp* Bob Custer, Doris Phillips, Al St John, Edward Hearn, J.P. McGowan, Gordon DeMain

The Squaw Man aka The White Man
(MGM) b/w 106 min

De Mille's third version of the film with which he made his directorial debut in 1914 marked the end of his short-term production pact with MGM. The first version, like the first version of the oft-filmed *The Spoilers* (1914), had been a significant milestone in the history of both the Western and Hollywood; this version, made when De Mille's career was in crisis, was both a commercial and critical failure.

Baxter is the English Lord who heads West after being blamed for thievery performed by his cousin, whose wife (Boardman) he loves. In America he meets and rescues an Indian maid, Velez (whose spirited performance is the best thing in the film), marries her and sires a child by her, only to return to England, his title and Boardman after a series of melodramatic upsets.

d/p Cecil B. De Mille *s* Lucien Hubbard, Lenore Coffee *c* Harold Rosson *lp* Warner Baxter, Lupe Velez, Eleanor Boardman, Paul Cavanagh, Charles Bickford, Raymond Hatton

Sundown Trail (RKO-PATHE) b/w 56 min

The first of Keene's 12-strong series Westerns for RKO which, with **Come On Danger** (1932), was released under the Pathe banner prior to that company's being incorporated into RKO. Snappily directed by Hill, the story features Keene as the foreman willed, with the ranch, to Easterner Shilling by her father. At first she's disdainful of the West and hostile to Keene but when, with assistance from friendly outlaw Stuart, he saves her from crooked cattle dealers, she soon collapses in his arms.

Keene's RKO series is unique in one thing: it had more changes taking place behind the camera than any other, and five different producers worked on the 12 films.

d/s Robert Hill *p* Fred Allen *c* Ted McCord *lp* Tom Keene, Marion Shilling, Nick Stuart, Hooper Atchley, Louise Beavers, Stanley Blystone

Sunrise Trail (TIFFANY) b/w 65 min

This is one of the best of Steele's early talkies for Tiffany. He plays the deputy who goes undercover as a baddie to catch a band of rustlers and falls for Mehaffey's barmaid along the way. Steele's small stature made the fistfights, which always feature heavily in McCarthy's films, look odd at times, giving his undoubted athleticism a surrealistic edge as he downs swarthies who are towering above him one minute and on the floor the next.

d J.P. McCarthy *p* Trem Carr *s* Wellyn Totman *c* Archie Stout *lp* Bob Steele, Blanche Mehaffey, Jack Clifford, Eddie Dunn, Fred Burns, Dick Alexander

The Texas Ranger
(BEVERLY PRODUCTIONS/COL) b/w 61 min

This is one of the best of Jones' series Westerns for Columbia.

"The Sunrise T...

Geraghty (sister of producer/director Maurice and Gerald who wrote many of Roy Rogers' screenplays) is the girl forced off her land who turns to banditry to get even. Jones is the Texas Ranger sent after her who, after gaining her confidence, discards his identity as an outlaw and with her assistance rounds up the real outlaws. A fine film, energetically directed by Lederman with Jones in fine comic form. A very similar plot was used for **Come On Danger** (1932).

d D. Ross Lederman *p* Sol Lesser *s* Forrest Sheldon *c* Teddy Tetzlaff *lp* Buck Jones, Carmelita Geraghty, Harry Woods, Ed Brady, Harry Todd, Nelson McDowell

West of Cheyenne (SYNDICATE) b/w 56 min

Tyler's first film for Syndicate, which within a year would evolve into Monogram, *West of Cheyenne* is an indifferent revenge Western with its star on the trail of the men who murdered his father. To do so he poses as a bandit and joins the gang of Woods' snarling villain. Webb directs in a workmanlike fashion but the script is too hackneyed to keep one's attention for long.

d/p Harry S. Webb *s* Bennett Cohen, Oliver Drake *c* William Nobles *lp* Tom Tyler, Josephine Hill, Harry Woods, Robert Walker, Ben Corbett, Fern Emmett

Westward Bound (SYNDICATE) b/w 60 min

One of Syndicate's better quickie Westerns. Bill is the senator's son sent West, with his chauffeur, Roosevelt, to take care of him, after he's gotten himself involved in a publicity incident at a speakeasy, rescuing Ray from fake crooks. Once West, he and Roosevelt are mistaken for cattle rustlers, prove their innocence and once again rescue Ray, this time from real crooks led by Canutt. Webb directs efficiently, the story is unusual and the sound recording equipment better than that normally used – one result of this is that the harshness of Ray's voice is shown up. The result is a superior Western quickie.

d/co-p Harry Webb *co-p* F.E. Douglas *s* Carl Krusada *c* William Nobles *lp* Buffalo Bill Jnr, Buddy Roosevelt, Allene Ray, Yakima Canutt, Ben Corbett, Tom London

Wild Horse (ALLIED) b/w 77 min

Once claimed by Gibson to be his favourite sound picture, presumably because most of it is devoted to Mutt, his faithful Palomino horse, *Wild Horse* reveals just how out of touch 'the Hooter' was with developments in the B Western brought about by sound. With sound came the streamlining of drama and narrative, in place of the rambling, idiosyncratic films that were Gibson's trademark. Thus, though the action which deals with the capture of Mutt is striking, Gibson's attempts at drama are woefully inadequate; it is as though Gibson is incapable of keeping a straight face. Stepin Fetchit provides the comic relief.

d Richard Thorpe, Sidney Algier *p* M.H. Hoffman Jnr *s* Jack Natteford *c* Ernest Miller *lp* Hoot Gibson, Alberta Vaughn, Stepin Fetchit, Neal Hart, Edmund Cobb, Glenn Strange

Yankee Don *aka* Daredevil Dick

(CAPITOL FILM EXCHANGE) b/w 61 min
Another South-of-the-Border Western, a testament of the lasting influence of **In Old Arizona** (1929), this independent quickie sees Talmadge as the Bowery desperado who is hired by a bunch of outlaws to help capture a Mexican ranch for them. He switches sides, influenced by his falling in love with the Don's daughter, Tovar, and the rest of the picture consists of Talmadge and his Mexican cowboys standing off wave after wave of attacks from the outlaws. The film is one of Talmadge's last (the coming of sound having highlighted his guttural German accent) before he turned to second unit direction, in which capacity he was responsible for some of the scenes in **How the West Was Won** (1962).

d Noel Mason *p* Richard Talmadge *s* Frances Jackson *lp* Richard Talmadge, Lupita Tovar, Julian Rivero, Sam Appel, Gayne Whitman, Victor Stanford

The Big Stampede (WB) b/w 54 min

Wayne's second Western for Warners was yet another remake of a Ken Maynard silent, *Land Beyond the Law* (1927) which Warners would use again under the same title for a Dick Foran quickie in 1936. Beery is as imposing as ever as the scowling villain who kills the sheriff so he can rustle cattle to his heart's content and Wayne is the new sheriff who puts paid to his plans. Alberni provides the comic relief as an outlaw Wayne befriends and persuades to join him. The climactic stampede consists of footage from the silent version. Churchill, here playing the governor of New Mexico, was later to play the banker in **Stagecoach** (1939), the film that was finally to make Wayne a star.

d Tenny Wright *p* Leon Schlesinger *s* Kurt Kempler *c* Ted McCord *lp* John Wayne, Noah Beery, Mae Madison, Luis Alberni, Berton Churchill, Paul Hurst

Border Devils (ARTCLASS) b/w 65 min

Carey is the man who breaks out of jail in order to prove himself innocent of the charges laid against him in this

Hoot Gibson and friend catch up with a horse thief in Wild Horse.

engaging series Western. A touch of mystery is added by the head villain being a Chinaman seen only as a shadow on a wall until the last reel. Smith is the heavy, Collins the girl and Hayes, as he would be for the next three decades, the comic relief. Christ's screenplay is basic but Nigh's direction is pleasant enough.

d William Nigh *p* Louis Weiss *s* Harry C. Christ (Harry Fraser) *c* William Dietz *lp* Harry Carey, Kathleen Collins, Al Smith, George Hayes, Niles Welch, Ray Gallager

Broadway to Cheyenne (MON) b/w 62 min

The best of Bell's six-strong series for Monogram, this is another mobsters-on-the-range picture in the tradition of **Gun Smoke** (1931). The plot sees a gang of Broadway mobsters head for open country when New York becomes too hot for them only to find detective Bell, recuperating from the bullet wounds they've given him. Bell, who spent most of his time with Monogram heading West as a boxing champ, detective or whatever, is an athletic but limited performer, able to handle the riding and fighting scenes but unsure in lengthy dialogue exchanges.

d/co-s Harry Fraser *p* Trem Carr *co-s* Wellyn Totman *lp* Rex Bell, Marceline Day, Mathew Betz, George Hayes, Robert Ellis, Huntley Gordon

Come On Danger (RKO) b/w 60 min

A first rate Keene Western. Haydon is the girl forced into outlawry as the only way to protect her land from villain Ellis and Keene the Texas Ranger who swears to bring her in after his brother dies in the attempt. Keene's affability and Haydon's superior acting stand out from Cohen's melodramatic script which features a hidden valley as the hideout of Haydon and her fellow vigilantes. Hill's direction is at its best in the dramatic fistfight between Ellis, Keene and Lackteen at the movie's end. The film was remade unofficially as **Renegade Ranger** (1939) and officially under the same title in 1942 and as **Oklahoma Raiders** (1944).

d Robert Hill *s* Bennett Cohen *c* Nick Musuraca *lp* Tom Keene, Julie Haydon, Roscoe Ates, Robert Ellis, Wade Boteler, Frank Lackteen

Far left: Tom Keene *and* Julie Haydon, *one of the sound Western's first female outlaws, in* Come On Danger.

The Conquerors (RKO) b/w 88 min

RKO's follow-up to **Cimarron** (1931), based on a story by that film's writer and with Dix repeating his role as the empire builder with a touch of wanderlust and Harding, then billed as 'RKO's first lady of the cinema' in the Irene Dunne role.

Tom Mix, 'Hero of a Million Boys', and Claudia Dell in a publicity shot for his first talkie, Destry Rides Again.

Daring Danger (COL) b/w 57 min

A conventional and below-average series outing from McCoy. This time he's after Alexander who, in the film's opening fight, nearly kills kim. When he finally catches up with him, Alexander is involved with a bunch of rustlers so McCoy goes after them too. Lederman directs with little conviction and too much emphasis on mindless chases.

The screenplay is based on a story by William Colt MacDonald whose later stories would give birth to the Three Mesquiteers, the first and most significant of all the trio series Westerns.

d D. Ross Lederman *p* Irving Briskin *s* Michael Trevelyan *c* Benjamin Kline *lp* Tim McCoy, Alberta Vaughn, Dick Alexander, Wallace MacDonald, Robert Ellis, Edmund Cobb

Destry Rides Again *aka* **Justice Rides Again**

(U) b/w 61 (55) min

Mix's first sound feature. In 1929, he quit the movies and was only tempted back by Universal's offer of $10,000 a week for a series of six $100,000-budgeted features over which the fifty-year-old star would have casting and script control as well as the right to use his favourite cameraman, Clark. The plot of Max Brand's bestseller which features a hero revenging himself on the twelve jurors who'd unjustly sent him to jail was rejigged to make Mix's enemies a collection of crooked witnesses and Pitts, as a temperance worker berating a bartender, was written in to give the film a comic start. Dell provides the romantic interest and Mix's horse, Tony – or rather doubles for the horse! – the animal heroics.

d Ben Stoloff *p* Stanley Bergerman *s* Isadore Bernstein, Robert Keith, Richard Schayer *c* Daniel B. Clark *lp* Tom Mix, Zasu Pitts, Claudia Dell, Stanley Fields, Francis Ford, Edward Piel Snr

End of the Trail (COL) b/w 61 min

This is one of the most extraordinary of series Westerns. Made with a bigger budget than normal and with McCoy for once almost completely in control of the project from start to finish, the film is the **Broken Arrow** (1950) of its era. It has some of the vices of that film but, nonetheless, is a welcome counterblast to the 'only good Indian is a dead Indian' philosophy that supported so many early sound Westerns, such as the phenomenally successful **The Indians Are Coming** (1930).

McCoy plays an officer sympathetic to the Indian cause whose court-martial is engineered by fellow officer Oakman, the man responsible for selling guns to Indians, the crime that McCoy is charged with. The complex plot has McCoy stripped of all friends, including his foster son (Albright) and best friend (Boteler) who die on him – an unusual event in a Western, series or otherwise – before he himself is senselessly

The only significant difference between the two films was locale: **Cimarron** is set in Oklahoma, *The Conquerors* in Nebraska. The film's best moments, pressaging the bleak atmosphere of Wellman's later **The Ox-Bow Incident** (1943), are the lynching episodes. Otherwise, despite an ending which sees Dix's grandson (also played by Dix) joining Wellman's beloved Lafayette Escadrille, the film has little of Wellman's sardonic vision in it.

d William Wellman *p* David O. Selznick *s* Robert Lord *c* Edward Cronjager *lp* Richard Dix, Ann Harding, Edna May Oliver, Guy Kibee

Cowboy Counsellor (ALLIED) b/w 62 min

The best of Gibson's films for Allied. Gibson is the law-book salesman who clears Gilman of the stage robbery Rutherford has framed him for and Mannors is Gilman's sister who goes to Gibson for help. Much of the straight comedy is provided by Robbins, leaving Gibson free to indulge in his more idiosyncratic ideas, like having the plot resolution depend on an accident. Sadly, however, in the streamlined world of the B Western in the sound era Gibson's comic versatility and mixing of sentimentality with something approaching surrealism seems merely old fashioned.

d George Melford *p* M.H. Hoffman Jnr *s* Jack Natteford *c* Tom Galligan, Harry Neumann *lp* Hoot Gibson, Sheila Mannors, Skeeter Bill Robbins, Fred Gilman, Jack Rutherford, Bobby Nelson

Far right: Hoot Gibson as the law-book salesman turned lawyer defends Fred Gilman (left) and wins the approval of Sheila Mannors in the process in Cowboy Counsellor.

killed at the precise moment when he has saved the fragile peace that exists between red and whiteman and cleared himself of the false charges laid against him. At least, that's how McCoy, director Lederman and writer Anthony shot the ending; Columbia had cold feet and had an extra scene shot showing McCoy 'recovered' from his wounds to replace the one in which both red and white pay their respects to the dead soldier.

However, the false ending doesn't undo the effect of the many scenes of Indian life, some of which feature authentic sign language and which treat the redman as a man of culture. The film was shot entirely on location in Lander, Wyoming, mostly on the Arapaho reservation there. Ironically, its major impact on the Western was as the source for much of the stock footage of Indians for many years. McCoy, though he would never be in a position to control a similar film, jumped at the chance to play the officer who makes peace with the Sioux in Sam Fuller's **Run of the Arrow** (1957), a film whose central character is similarly, though for very different reasons, caught between two cultures. This is an important Western.

d D. Ross Lederman   *p* Irving Briskin   *s* Stuart Anthony   *c* Benjamin Kline   *lp* Tim McCoy, Luana Walters, Wheeler Oakman, Wally Albright, Wade Boteler, Lafe McKee

Galloping Thru (MON) b/w 58 min
This is the best of Tyler's series Westerns for Monogram. Ex-editor Nosler directs Totman's penny-plain screenplay about Tyler seeking revenge for the murder of his father with some finesse. The result is an all-action film but with more thoughtful camera angles and more dramatically staged confrontations than had been in evidence in Tyler's earlier outings for the studio. Bridge is the villain, Mack the girl and Blystone the friend who stands aside when his loved one declares herself for Tyler.

d Lloyd Nosler   *p* Trem Carr   *s* Wellyn Totman   *c* Archie Stout   *lp* Tom Tyler, Betty Mack, Al Bridge, Stanley Blystone, Si Jenks, John Elliott

The Gay Caballero (FOX) b/w 60 min
This is one of the better films O'Brien made during his productive stay with Fox. He's the footballer whose ranch is stolen and McLaglen is the bandit of the title. Like so many of the 'South of the Border' Westerns that were made in the early thirties in an attempt to repeat the success of **In Old Arizona** (1929), the movie is overly melodramatic. Werker's direction is only average, giving little indication of the string of impressive Westerns he was to end his career with in the fifties, beginning with **The Last Posse** (1953) and finishing with **At Gunpoint** (1955).

d Alfred Werker   *p* Edmund Grainger   *s* Barry Connors, Philip Klein   *c* George Schneiderman   *lp* George O'Brien, Victor McLaglen, Linda Watkins, Weldon Heyburn, Conchita Montenegro, Willard Robertson

Haunted Gold (WB) b/w 58 min
The best of Wayne's series of six Westerns for Warner Brothers. Buffington's action-packed screenplay has Wayne and Terry fighting off bandits who claim title to an abandoned mine, which, to complicate matters further, is haunted by a mysteriously cloaked figure, 'The Phantom'. Wright also directed Wayne in one of his best Republic Westerns, **Winds of the Wasteland** (1936).

d Mack V. Wright   *p* Leon Schlesinger   *s* Adele Buffington   *c* Nick Musuraca   *lp* John Wayne, Sheila Terry, Harry Woods, Erville Alderson, Slim Whitaker, Martha Mattox

Hell Fire Austin (TIFFANY) b/w 70 min
The last of Maynard's Westerns for the independent Tiffany

Ivy Merton, Ken Maynard and Tarzan in Hell Fire Austin, *the best of Maynard's films for Tiffany.*

Studios and one of the last films made by that company before its slide into bankruptcy, *Hell Fire Austin* has the look, if not quite the budget, of Maynard's earlier Universal series. Maynard's horsemanship is well displayed by a script which sees him (and LeMayne) come to the rescue of rancher Merton by winning a horse race despite the many attempts by loanshark Pendleton to stop him crossing the finishing line. Needless to say the horse is Tarzan.

d Forrest Sheldon   *p* Phil Goldstone   *s* Betty Burbridge   *c* Ted McCord, Joe Novak   *lp* Ken Maynard, Ivy Merton, Jack Perrin, Charles LeMayne, Nat Pendleton, Lafe McKee

Heritage of the Desert (PAR) b/w 60 min
The first of Paramount's remakes of their silent series of films based on stories by Zane Grey, this film gave Scott his first starring role, fittingly in a Western, the genre he was to be so closely associated with for three decades. His natural acting style won him praise from the critics, even though the screenplay, betraying its silent origins, is more than a trifle melodramatic.

Blane is the orphaned heroine, saved from the clutches of Landau's rustler by surveyor Scott. But though the plot is

Below: John Wayne (centre) and Sheila Terry temporarily in the hands of bandits in Haunted Gold.

Russell Hopton, Raymond Hatton and Walter Huston (left to right) in Law and Order, *one of the forgotten classics of the early sound era.*

action-packed, Hathaway concentrates on the growing love between Blane and Scott, giving it a gentleness unusual in Westerns of the period. Parts of the picture were shot on the town set used for the making of the 1929 version of **The Virginian**.

d Henry Hathaway *p* Harold Hurley *s* Harold Shumate, Frank Partos *c* Archie Stout *lp* Randolph Scott, Sally Blane, Guinn Williams, Vince Barnett, J. Farrell MacDonald, David Landau

Hidden Gold (U) b/w 60 min

A late outing for Mix, the Greatest Cowboy of them all, *Hidden Gold* features him in jailbird guise trying to get the confidence of three outlaws and then the location of the cash they've stolen. Rosson's direction is routine, only rising to the occasion when Mix enters a prizefight. The climactic forest fire in which two of the outlaws perish is certainly a tame affair.

d Arthur Rosson *p* Carl Laemmle Jnr *s* Jack Natteford, James Mulhauser *c* Dan Clark *lp* Tom Mix, Judith Barrie, Raymond Hatton, Eddie Gribbon, Donald Kirke, Willis Clark

Below: *Tom Mix and Mickey Rooney as cowboy and king respectively in the Ruritanian fantasy,* My Pal, the King.

Law and Order (U) b/w 70 min

Universal's first serious Western and Cahn's directorial debut, *Law and Order* is an historically important film. It is a fictionalized account of the cleaning up of Tombstone with Huston in the Wyatt Earp role and Carey as the Doc Halliday figure. Huston (Walter's son) and Reed's adaptation of W.R. Burnett's savage novel (which treated its characters more like gangsters than cowboys) centres on the endless killings that are the price of law and order. This feeling of despair culminates in Huston's being forced to hang a dumbwitted farmer (Devine), who had accidentally killed someone, in Tombstone's first legal execution. The austere tone, the traditional O.K. Corral gunfight notwithstanding, is all the more impressive considering the cheerful vacuity of most Westerns being made at the time.

The film was remade in 1940 and 1953.

d Edward Cahn *s* John Huston, Tom Reed *c* Jackson Rose *lp* Walter Huston, Harry Carey, Raymond Hatton, Andy Devine, Harry Woods, Walter Brennan

My Pal, the King (U) b/w 74 min

A film, as they say, for children of all ages. Rooney is the boy king of Ruritania who is befriended by Mix, and educated by him into the true ways of the Westerner. The film features extensive sequences of Mix's Wild West Show and a marvellously melodramatic plot, complete with a dungeon rapidly filling with water that Mix rescues Rooney from in the nick of time. Holmes is the power behind the throne who wants the throne for himself.

The film's real significance lay in its demonstration of the flexibility of the genre, which in a few years would be further proved by the even more improbable and even more successful **The Phantom Empire** (1935).

d Kurt Neumann *p* Carl Laemmle Jnr *s* Jack Natteford, Tom Crizer *c* Dan Clark *lp* Tom Mix, Mickey Rooney, Stuart Holmes, Noel Francis, Paul Hurst, Jim Thorpe

Mystery Ranch *aka* The Killer (FOX) b/w 56 min

Another superior O'Brien picture graced with atmospheric cinematography from August, a regular cameraman for both W.S. Hart and John Ford. Middleton is the villain, holding Parker captive until she agrees to marry him and so give him control of her extensive lands, who is foiled by hard-riding O'Brien. Howard directs with his usual panache and O'Brien gives a measured performance.

d David Howard *p* Sol Wurtzel *s* Al Cohn *c* Joseph August *lp* George O'Brien, Cecilia Parker, Charles Middleton, Roy Stewart, Charles Stevens, Forrest Harvey

The Night Rider (ARTCLASS) b/w 72 min

One of the number of lacklustre movies Carey made for producer Weiss. Production values are virtually nonexistent, particularly in the sound recording department and the film seems to have been thrown together rather than directed. Needless to say, the series did little for Carey, either careerwise or financially – he had to sue for his $5,000 salary. Here he impersonates a hooded rider, Kortman, in order to catch him. Hayes and Julian Rivero lend a little assistance.

d William Nigh *p* Louis Weiss *s* Harry P. Christ (Harry Fraser) *c* James Diamond *lp* Harry Carey, Eleanor Fair, George Hayes, Bob Kortman, Julian Rivero, Jack Weatherby

Outlaw Justice (MAJESTIC) b/w 61 min

This was the first of Hoxie's six sound Westerns, all of which are amateurish in concept and execution. Hoxie's voice didn't record well and after a few more independent sound quickies he quit pictures for the Wild West Shows. Here he's the man posing as a bandit to trap King. Martin, in one of his first roles, is the Mexican side-kick, a role he would make his own in innumerable series outings, and Gulliver the girl. Way down the cast list, where he was generally to be found, was Kermit, brother of Ken, Maynard.

Hoxie had a brother, Al, who was also a luckless Hollywood cowboy.

d Armand Schaefer *p* Larry Darmour *s* Oliver Drake
c William Nobles *lp* Jack Hoxie, Dorothy Gulliver, Charles King, Chris-Pin Martin, Kermit Maynard, Jack Rockwell

The Rainbow Trail (FOX) b/w 60 min
This sequel to **Riders of the Purple Sage** (1931) with O'Brien once more taking the role played by Tom Mix in the silent version is hard to follow unless you've seen the earlier film. O'Brien, in his usual good athletic form, plays the nephew of the character he played in *Riders of the Purple Sage* setting out in search of the whereabouts of himself (!?). Silent film actor Hearn takes over O'Brien's old role as the man trapped in a lost canyon and Parker (later of the Andy Hardy series) is the heroine. Thorne, his face half masked to cover a terrible disfigurement, is an effective villain but the film's greatest asset is Clark's photography of the Grand Canyon and the fast-paced direction of Howard, for whom the film marked the beginning of a lengthy association with O'Brien.

d David Howard *s* Barry Connors, Philip Klein *c* Daniel Clark *lp* George O'Brien, Cecilia Parker, Edward Hearn, W.L. Thorne, Roscoe Ates, James Kirkwood

Ride Him Cowboy *aka* The Hawk (WB) b/w 56 min
The first of Wayne's six-film season of films for Warners, *Ride Him Cowboy* is a remake of the Ken Maynard silent, *The Unknown Cavalier* (1926). The movie also introduces Duke (the horse that was to partner Wayne for the series) who is saved, tamed and ridden by Wayne as he tracks down the killer, the Hawk (Hagney) responsible for a string of bank robberies and who tried to have the horse destroyed in the first place. Harlan, reprising the role he played in the earlier version, is the crotchety judge and Hall, Wayne's girl. Allen's fast-paced direction makes this a superior series Western.

d Fred Allen *p* Leon Schlesinger *s* Scott Mason *c* Ted McCord *lp* John Wayne, Ruth Hall, Frank Hagney, Otis Harlan, Henry B. Wathall, Harry Gribbon

Rider of Death Valley (U) b/w 78 min
By common agreement Mix's finest sound film, *Rider of Death Valley* has the benefit of an unusually thoughtful script by Cunningham made convincing by Mix and Kohler's outstanding performances as the hero and villain and Clark's bleak location cinematography. Wilson is the Easterner who heads West to take over the mine, hidden deep in the desert, that she's inherited from her murdered brother. Kohler and Stanley are the men after it and Mix, with considerable help from Tony, his horse, the man who tries to protect the mine's hidden location. The superior production values, overseen by Mix, are evidenced in details like a runaway team of horses that actually look as though they are out of control and, most striking of all, the look of the cast when they're stranded without water in the desert.

d Albert Rogell *p* Carl Laemmle Jnr *s* Jack Cunningham *c* Dan Clark *lp* Tom Mix, Lois Wilson, Fred Kohler, Forrest Stanley, Willard Robertson, Edmund Cobb

Riders of the Desert
(SONO ART/WORLD WIDE) b/w 59 min
An entertaining Steele series outing with an exciting and lengthy gun battle on the cliffs for a climax. Bradbury (Steele's father) directs with his usual commitment to action rather than comprehensibility (or plausibility). Steele is the college student who helps foil a stagecoach robbery during one vacation and helps catch the man responsible (Hayes) who breaks out of jail in search of the buried loot, during his next vacation. Messinger is the comely heroine.

d Robert N. Bradbury *p* Trem Carr *s* Wellyn Totman *c* Archie Stout *lp* Bob Steele, Gertrude Messinger, George Hayes, Al St John, Greg Whitespear, Horace B. Carpenter

Tom Mix revives Lois Wilson while his horse Tony looks on in Rider of Death Valley, *one of his more realistic films.*

Ridin' for Justice (COL) b/w 61 min
Another pleasant outing from Jones, billed Charles 'Buck' Jones, which he preferred for a while, with the star in a more comic mood than normal. He's the bronco rider who hits it off with the ladies, including the sheriff's wife, Doran, but not the sheriff. Shumate's complicated plot sees Jones and Doran mixed up in a murder and on the run from the law until Jones proves the sheriff to be the guilty party.

d D. Ross Lederman *p* Irving Briskin *s* Harold Shumate *c* Benjamin Kline *lp* Buck Jones, Mary Doran, Russell Simpson, Walter Miller, Bob McKenzie, Lafe McKee

The Riding Tornado (COL) b/w 64 min
A superior McCoy series entry in which he's a bronco buster who takes a job on Grey's ranch, falls in love with her and sorts out the rustlers led by foreman Oakman, but only after Grey has been kidnapped and rescued. If the story is routine, McCoy's intense performance, seen at its best in the

game-of-poker sequence where Lederman's facial studies make the game very dramatic, and the action-packed climax are well above average.

d D. Ross Lederman *p* Irving Briskin *s* Kurt Kempler *c* Benjamin Kline *lp* Tim McCoy, Shirley Grey, Wheeler Oakman, Lafe McKee, Wallace MacDonald, Art Mix

South of the Rio Grande (COL) b/w 61 min
The influence of **In Old Arizona** (1929) (which was further increased after Warner Baxter reprised his role in **The Cisco Kid,** 1931) sent Jones South of the Border for this interesting series Western. He's the Mexican Army captain (in dress only; wisely he sticks with his own accent) on the trail of McCullough and adventuress Maris, who makes the best of her unsympathetic role. Fix repeats his role from **The Avenger** (1931) as Jones' weak-willed brother. The film includes footage from an earlier Jones outing, **Men without Law** (1930).

d Lambert Hillyer *p* Irving Briskin *s* Milton Krims *c* Benjamin Kline *lp* Buck Jones, Mona Maris, Philo McCullough, Paul Fix, Doris Hill, Charles Stevens

Joe E. Brown complete with gun, grin and Ginger Rogers in The Tenderfoot.

The Tenderfoot (FIRST NATIONAL) b/w 70 min
Joe E. Brown is the Texas cowboy who comes to New York and avoids being fleeced by all and sundry in this surprisingly listless comedy. Rogers is the girl he falls for and has to rescue when racketeers kidnap her after the show which the pair mount has been a huge success. Less ambiguously than Clint Eastwood, who more than thirty years later would confront the seamy side of New York in **Coogan's Bluff** (1968), Brown demonstrates that the Big Apple has no fears for one Texas born.

The film was remade in 1937 as *Dance Charlie Dance* and in 1940 as *An Angel from Texas* with Eddie Albert in the Brown role. Neither version was any closer to George S. Kaufman's witty play, *The Butter and Egg Man,* on which all three films were based.

d Ray Enright *p* Brian Foy *s* Arthur Caesar, Monty Banks, Earl Baldwin *c* Gregg Toland *lp* Joe E. Brown, Ginger Rogers, Lew Cody, Alan Lane, Ralph Ince, George Chandler

Texas Bad Man (U) b/w 63 min
Directed by Laemmle (no relation to the founder of Universal) at a spanking pace, this was Mix's follow-up to the well-received **Rider of Death Valley** (1932). Kohler is the villain once more, this time an outlaw whose gang is infiltrated by Mix's Texas Ranger posing as a baddie. Clark's cinematography is again sparkling, but Cunningham's screenplay is at best routine.

d Edward Laemmle *p* Carl Laemmle Jnr *s* Jack Cunningham *c* Dan Clark *lp* Tom Mix, Lucille Powers, Fred Kohler, Edward J. LeSaint, Willard Robertson, Bud Osborne

Texas Cyclone (COL) b/w 63 min
One of the earliest sound movies to use the look-alike plot that was to become a cliche of the B Western, *Texas Cyclone* stars McCoy as Pecos Grant, the stranger who arrives in town and is greeted as an old friend, thought dead, even by Grey, the wife of the man he looks like. Oakman, as ever, is the villain of the piece and way down the credits is one John Wayne coming to the end of his brief and disastrous stay at Columbia.

d D. Ross Lederman *p* Irving Briskin *s* Randall Faye *c* Ben Kline *lp* Tim McCoy, Shirley Grey, Wheeler Oakman, James Farley, Walter Brennan

Texas Tornado (MARCEY PRODUCTIONS) b/w 53 min
One of the better of the series of eight Westerns Chandler made for independent producer Kent. Chandler, probably best remembered as one of the five masked men who wasn't the Lone Ranger in Republic's 1938 serial of that title, was a better actor than this film suggests. Sadly, like so many independent productions of the very early thirties, the presence of writer/director Drake notwithstanding, the production values are limited. Here, Chandler is a Texas Ranger fighting gangsters trying to take over the prairie by putting their machine guns to use rustling cattle in a plot reminiscent of **Gun Smoke** (1931). Hill is the heroine and Canutt the heavy.

d/s Oliver Drake *p* Willis Kent *c* James Diamond *lp* Lane Chandler, Doris Hill, Yakima Canutt, Ben Corbett, Robert Gale, Fred Burns

Tombstone Canyon (KBS PRODUCTIONS) b/w 62 min
Directed by James (who under his original name of Alvin J. Neitz had directed numerous silent Westerns) at a breakneck speed and featuring the masked and bemantled villain so beloved of serialdom, this is one of Maynard's most entertaining series Westerns. Parker is the unusually active heroine who helps Maynard and his horse Tarzan as they travel the range searching for the phantom killer.

d Alan James *p* Burt Kelly, Sam Bischoff, William Saal *s* Claude Rister *c* Ted McCord *lp* Ken Maynard, Cecilia Parker, Lafe McKee, Sheldon Lewis, George Chesebro, Edward Piel Snr

Two Fisted Law (COL) b/w 64 min
Based on a story by William Colt McDonald, *Two Fisted Law* is as energetic a McCoy series Western as the title suggests. Oakman is the villain who cheats McCoy out of his ranch by first lending him money and then rustling his cattle so he can't repay it. Though MacDonald and Wayne, as the two ranch hands McCoy has to pay off, are only present for part of the picture, the story would seem to be the genesis of the trio Westerns that McDonald perfected with his Three Mesquiteers stories (in which Wayne would, briefly, star).

d D. Ross Lederman *p* Irving Briskin *s* Kurt Kempler *c* Benjamin Kline *lp* Tim McCoy, Alice Day, Wheeler Oakman, Wallace MacDonald, John Wayne, Walter Brennan

The Vanishing Frontier (PAR) b/w 65 min
One of a number of films Brown made during his limbo period after MGM decided to build Clark Gable, rather than him, into a star because **Billy the Kid** (1930) did only

moderate business. Brown's considerable acting abilities, which were to be sadly wasted in most of his series Westerns, are well put to use here as he essays a Maurice Chevalier-like interpretation of a piano-playing Spanish Robin Hood. Knapp is the romantic interest. Sadly, both the screenplay and direction are too leaden to raise the over familiar material.

d Phil Rosen *p* Sam Jaffe *s* Stuart Anthony *c* James S. Brown *lp* Johnny Mack Brown, Evalyn Knapp, Zasu Pitts, Raymond Hatton, Ben Alexander, J. Farrell MacDonald

Wild Horse Mesa (PAR) b/w 65 min
This remake by Hathaway of the 1925 silent is amongst the best of Paramount's Zane Grey series, silent and sound. It was filmed in the same locations as the silent version with Scott (who'd been given his big break by Hathaway when the director chose him to star in the first of Paramount's remakes of their Zane Grey silents, **Heritage of the Desert,** 1932) in the Jack Holt role and Kohler in the part played by Noah Beery.

Kohler is the horse trapper using barbed wire to catch wild stallions, Blane the girl and Scott the hero who rescues her and stops Kohler but is unable to prevent him being trampled to death by a wild stallion. Hathaway uses footage from the silent version, but, unlike that film's director, George B. Seitz, who'd concentrated on spectacular action, he emphasizes the character relationships, capturing a delicacy of emotion rare in series Westerns.

d Henry Hathaway *p* Harold Hurley *s* Frank Clark, Harold Shumate *c* Arthur Todd *lp* Randolph Scott, Sally Blane, Fred Kohler, George Hayes, James Bush, Jim Thorpe

Without Honors (ARTCLASS) b/w 66 min
The best of the Westerns Carey made for Artclass, this beautifully photographed movie features Carey as a gambler turned Texas Ranger out to prove that his brother is innocent of the crimes laid at his door and discover his killers. Along the way he breaks up a smuggling combine and romances Busch. Gowland is fine as the gang leader but it is Linden's deftly chosen angles and the fresh locations that lift this film above the average.

d William Nigh *p* Louis Weiss *s* Harry P. Christ (Harry Fraser), Lee Sage *c* Edward Linden *lp* Harry Carey, Mae Busch, Gibson Gowland, George Hayes, Lafe McKee, Tom London

1933

Crossfire (RKO) b/w 55 min
Another gangster/Western hybrid in the tradition of **Gun Smoke** (1931), this was the last of Keene's series films for RKO. He's the prospector who does his bit for President and Country in the First World War and who, on his return, finds one friend murdered and the other one falsely accused of the crime. The real villains are Chicago gangsters, complete with

Ken Maynard (left) in danger in The Fiddlin' Buckaroo.

machine guns, imported by Phillips. With help from Kennedy, Keene shows that Western ways are best and rounds up the gangsters and wins the heart of Furness.

d Otto Brower *p* David O. Selznick *s* Tom McNamara *c* Nick Musuraca *lp* Tom Keene, Betty Furness, Edward Phillips, Edgar Kennedy, Lafe McKee, Murdock McQuarrie

Drum Taps (KBS PRODUCTIONS) b/w 61 min
Odd though it may seem, the Boy Scouts are frequently featured in Westerns – another example is **Tex Rides with the Boy Scouts** (1938). It's as though the American Scout movement was seen as continuing the Western tradition in some way. Here the 107th troop of Los Angeles co-star with Maynard and help him drive landgrabbers from the range. At one moment, in a marvellously conceived piece of wishfulfilment, the scouts are mistaken for a troop of armed regular soldiers by Bridge's bandits. Maynard's brother Kermit, who regularly stunted for him, is featured down the cast list.

d J.P. McGowan *p* Burt Kelly, Sam Bischoff, William Saal *s* Alan James *c* Jack Young *lp* Ken Maynard, Dorothy Dix, Al Bridge, Kermit Maynard, Hooper Atchley, Slim Whitaker

Fargo Express (KBS PRODUCTIONS) b/w 61 min
This is a particularly silly Maynard series Western. He's in love with Mack whose younger brother, Fix, is falsely accused of robbing the stage, having been identified by his distinctive horse. Maynard captures a similar looking wild horse and repeats the robbery in an attempt to clear Fix who is still in jail. The result is a juvenile outing with plenty of action but little else to recommend it.

d Alan James *p* Burt Kelly, Sam Bischoff, William Saal *s* Earle Snell *c* Ted McCord *lp* Ken Maynard, Helen Mack, Paul Fix, Roy Stewart, William Desmond, Jack Rockwell

The Fiddlin' Buckaroo (U) b/w 65 min
One of several movies he directed himself, this otherwise routine Maynard series outing is notable for the high proportion of music that Maynard indulges himself with. He plays Fiddlin' (a fiddler and ventriloquist), a secret service agent on the trail of Kohler. He is mistakenly arrested following the looting of a township by Kohler. Shea is the passive heroine kidnapped by Kohler and rescued serial fashion by Maynard.

Far left: Crossfire: *one of the several gangster/ Western hybrids in which six guns did battle with machine guns in the West.*

d/p Ken Maynard *s* Nate Gatzert *c* Ted McCord *lp* Ken Maynard, Gloria Shea, Fred Kohler, Al Bridge, Bob Kortman, Slim Whitaker

The Fighting Parson (ALLIED) b/w 70 min

Gibson has the title role as the man mistaken for a preacher by a community expecting one to conduct a revival meeting. Ever willing to oblige, Gibson accepts the role thrust upon him. The plot makes a welcome change from the one where the hero pretends to be a baddie but, despite Gibson's evident enjoyment in the role, the storyline proves to be too restrictive. A landslide sequence is well done but otherwise the slack production values show up the material.

d/s Harry Fraser *p* M.H. Hoffman Jnr *c* Harry Neumann *lp* Hoot Gibson, Marceline Day, Robert Frazer, Charles King, Stanley Blystone, Frank Nelson

The Fugitive (MON) b/w 56 min

Another of Bell's half Eastern, half Western series for Monogram, this outing has him as a secret agent on the trail of mail robbers who goes to jail so he can join the gang. Kortman is his informant and Parker the heroine. Fraser directs with verve but the routine feel of the project is apparent to all concerned.

d/s Harry Fraser *p* Paul Malvern, Trem Carr *c* Archie Stout *lp* Rex Bell, Cecilia Parker, George Hayes, Bob Kortman, Tom London, Earl Dwire

John Wayne (left) in The Man from Monterey.

Galloping Romeo (MON) b/w 60 min

Featuring one of Steele's rare attempts at Hoot Gibson-type humour, this is a lacklustre series outing. Steele's virtues were of the athletic order and he had no feel for the light-touch comedy required. Thus Hayes, as his companion and fellow good-outlaw, steals the picture from Steele. The film also saw producers Carr and Malvern using footage from previous Steele outings as 'flashbacks' to help pad out the length and cut down on costs. This was to be the fate of most series as they approached their dotage.

d R.N. Bradbury *p* Trem Carr, Paul Malvern *s* Harry O. Jones (Harry Fraser) *c* Archie Stout *lp* Bob Steele, Doris Hill, George Hayes, Frank Ball, Lafe McKee, Earl Dwire

The Man from Monterey (WB) b/w 57 min

A swashbuckler set in Old California, this was Wayne's last series Western for Warners and the company's last for several years. Reed is the villain, trying to dispossess a Spanish landowner, McKee, of his (Spanish landgrant) lands and Wayne is the man who persuades McKee to register the land and supports his advice with surprisingly elegant derring-do and swordsmanship. Hall, Wayne's love in his first film for Warners, repeats her role. A pleasant film.

d Mack V. Wright *p* Leon Schlesinger *s* Lesley Mason *c* Ted McCord *lp* John Wayne, Ruth Hall, Donald Reed, Lafayette McKee, Luis Alberni, Francis Ford

Man of the Forest (PAR) b/w 62 min

This is a superior Paramount Zane Grey outing. Much revised from the original novel which was filmed in 1921 and 1926, Cunningham and Shumate's screenplay features Scott as the hero who kidnaps Hillie in order that Beery won't harm her only to have Beery frame him for the murder of Hillie's father, Carey. Hathaway directs with real feeling for the characters, but the melodramatic origins of the film – still present, as in the scene where Scott's pet lion helps him escape from jail – are difficult to overcome.

d Henry Hathaway *p* Harold Hurley *s* Harold Shumate, Jack Cunningham *c* Ben Reynolds *lp* Randolph Scott, Harry Carey, Buster Crabbe, Verna Hillie, Noah Beery, Guinn Williams

The Mysterious Rider *aka* The Fighting Phantom

(PAR) b/w 59 min

One of Paramount's Zane Grey budget Western series, *The Mysterious Rider* is a routine actioner. Taylor takes the title role as the avenger, Pichel is the man who tries to swindle homesteaders out of the money they've paid for their land and Patrick is the girl Taylor romances, and wins against the odds.

d Fred Allen *p* Harold Hurley *s* Harvey Gates, Robert N. Lee *c* Archie Stout *lp* Kent Taylor, Lona Andre, Gail Patrick, Irving Pichel, Warren Hymer, Berton Churchill

Operator 13 *aka* Spy 13 (MGM) b/w 86 min

A lavish Civil War melodrama, most memorable for the glowing notices Davies, unusually, received. She's the actress turned spy for the Union and Cooper's the Southern patriot who falls for her and finally saves her life after an elaborate game of bluff and double bluff. Disguised as an Octoroon servant – thus gaining the opportunity to 'act' that garnered her such plaudits – Davies inveigles her way into the household of Jeb Stuart (Dumbrille) only to meet and be smitten by Cooper. The film is remarkably similar, Boleslawski's imaginative direction apart, to **Only the Brave** (1930) which also stars Cooper.

d Richard Boleslawski *p* Lucien Hubbard *s* Harry Thew, Zelda Sears, Eve Greene *c* George Folsey *lp* Marion Davies, Gary Cooper, Jean Parker, Douglass Dumbrille, Ted Healy, Katharine Alexander

The Ranger's Code (MON) b/w 59 min
A decidedly routine entry for Steele, this series Western sees
him torn between arresting and letting go the brother of his
sweetheart, Hill. Duty wins out, of course, after which he sets
out to prove the brother to be innocent. Slackly directed by
Bradbury (Steele's father) and with nondescript production
values the entry suggested that the series was ailing, as indeed
it was. Hayes who alternated between comic and villain for
the series, here is a grinning villain.

d Robert N. Bradbury *p* Trem Carr *s* Harry O. Jones
(Harry Fraser) *c* Archie Stout *lp* Bob Steele, Doris Hill,
George Hayes, George Nash, Ernie Adams, Hal Price

Riders of Destiny (MON/LONE STAR) b/w 58 min
The first of sixteen films Wayne made for Monogram.
Produced by Malvern, under the auspices of his Lone Star
Productions, they are amongst the best-known thirties B
Westerns so often have they been packaged on TV as part of
John Wayne seasons. Written and directed by Bradbury, the
father of Wayne's boyhood friend, Bob Steele, the film
features Wayne as Singin' Sandy, an undercover government
agent sent to investigate claims by farmers that Taylor and
henchman Canutt are stealing their water. Malvern's original
idea was for Wayne to warble as he shot down the villains, but
Wayne (who according to different sources either sang himself
or was dubbed, possibly by Smith Ballew) refused.

Beyond Wayne's vocalizing, the film is memorable for the
fight between Wayne and Canutt as the 'dog heavy' (so called
because, in a wonderful example of genre conventions, to
establish his role as the heavy who did the dirty work, he
kicks a dog early in the movie). Previously, fights had been
highly stagey: together Wayne and stuntman Canutt developed a fight scene that with carefully chosen camera angles
and sharp editing looked far more realistic, even though the
punches were as wide of their mark as ever.

Bradbury's confident direction and Stout's fine cinematography give the production a glossy look that belies its tiny
$10,000 budget.

d/s Robert North Bradbury *p* Paul Malvern *c* Archie
Stout *lp* John Wayne, Cecilia Parker, George 'Gabby'
Hayes, Forrest Taylor, Yakima Canutt, Al St John

Robber's Roost (FOX) b/w 64 min
Boasting a fine cast – O'Sullivan as the heroine and Owen as
the villain – and some typical O'Brien moments, such as his
blinking when he fires his gun, this is a charming outing from
seriesdom's most adaptable cowboy star. It also boasts the
first Western script of Nichols, one of John Ford's closest
collaborators in the thirties and forties and the writer of
Ford's classic Western, **Stagecoach** (1939). But King's
direction and the overly sentimental Zane Grey material it was
based on prove too much for either O'Brien or Nichols.
O'Brien is the innocent man suspected of being a rustler and
O'Sullivan the heroine who believes in him and is forever
being rescued by him.

d Louis King *p* Sol Lesser *s* Dudley Nichols *c* George
Schneiderman *lp* George O'Brien, Maureen O'Sullivan,
Reginald Owen, Frank Rice, William Pawley, Ted Oliver

Sagebrush Trail (MON/LONE STAR) b/w 58 min
Wayne's second Western for Monogram is an altogether
quieter effort than his debut for the company which saw him
as Singin' Sandy. But, if the plot is routine – Wayne, wrongly
imprisoned on a murder charge escapes from jail and joins a
gang of outlaws in the hope of discovering the real killer –
Canutt's stunts are as inventive as ever. One has him doubling
for Wayne and hiding from his pursuers under water. Shubert
is the girl and Chandler the man Wayne finally unmasks as the
killer. Schaefer's direction is studied, as befits someone soon
to become a series producer.

Above: *John Wayne as Singin' Sandy in* Riders of Destiny.

Mary Pickford and Leslie Howard in Frank Borzage's frontier melodrama, Secrets.

Ken Maynard and Charles King in Strawberry Roan.

Scarlet River (RKO) b/w 57 min

Shumate's literate script features a Hollywood movie company on location making a Western and Keene's Hollywood cowboy coming to the rescue of Wilson's pretty rancher when Atchley tries to steal her ranch from her. Wittily directed by Brower, who makes the most of the filming of a film situation, and endowed with superior production values by Selznick, the film is one of Keene's very best Westerns. Ates supplies the comedy while Joel McCrea, Myrna Loy and others make fleeting guest appearances at the beginning.

d Otto Brower *p* David O. Selznick *s* Harold Shumate *c* Nick Musuraca *lp* Tom Keene, Dorothy Wilson, Hooper Atchley, Roscoe Ates, Creighton Chaney (Lon Chaney Jnr), Edgar Kennedy

Secrets (MARY PICKFORD PRODUCTIONS/UA) b/w 90 min

Pickford's last film, *Secrets* is a typical Borzage melodrama about the ability of love to triumph over circumstances. Pickford and Howard elope to the West where, after building up a cattle empire, Howard is championed for Governor only to have his political hopes dashed when his affair with Lloyd is discovered. Whereupon Pickford forgives him and they resume their happy life. Though the scenes of frontier life are unusually realistic for a melodrama, Borzage's romantic sensibility found the genre too inflexible for the film to be wholly successful.

d Frank Borzage *s* Frances Marion, Salisbury Field, Leonard Praskins *c* Ray June *lp* Mary Pickford, Leslie Howard, C. Aubrey Smith, Doris Lloyd, Alan Sears, Mona Maris

Somewhere in Sonora (WB) b/w 57 min

The first of the many films Wayne and Fix were to make together, *Somewhere in Sonora* also makes use of a staple B Western plot: the hero joining a gang of outlaws and outwitting them. Falsely accused of cheating at a rodeo, Wayne heads for Mexico where he stumbles on a plan to rob Lewis's silver mine. His success at stopping the robbers wins him the hand of Fay. A routine Western.

d Mack V. Wright *p* Leon Schlesinger *s* Joe Roach *c* Ted McCord *lp* John Wayne, Paul Fix, Ralph Lewis, Ann Fay, Shirley Palmer, Henry B. Wathall

Strawberry Roan (U) b/w 59 min

One of the most popular of Maynard's Universal series Westerns, in part because it has a song, much featured in the film, to go with it. The story is the timeless one of man and horse with Maynard as the bronco buster determined to show that he hasn't yet met his match. King, who would later concentrate on villainy, here shows his comic side while Hall provides the romance.

When Maynard was down on his luck, Gene Autry, who'd made his first film appearances in Maynard films, bought the rights to the story from him. Though the resulting 1947 film had the same title, the stories were only marginally related.

d Alan James *p* Ken Maynard *s* Nate Gatzert *c* Ted McCord *lp* Ken Maynard, Ruth Hall, Charles King, Frank Yaconelli, Harold Goodwin, Ben Corbett

The Telegraph Trail (WB) b/w 55 min

The least interesting of Wayne's series Westerns for Warners. The film is simply too melodramatic and old fashioned to be believable, and was even when first shown. Wayne is the army scout who volunteers to complete the stringing of the telegraph across the plains and Canutt, Wayne's most regular adversary in the thirties, the man who leads the Indians in revolt. Smith is the evil trader who stirs them up and Day the girl Wayne romances. Much of the action footage comes from *The Red Raiders* (1926).

d Tenny Wright *p* Leon Schlesinger *s* Kurt Kempler *c* Ted McCord *lp* John Wayne, Marceline Day, Frank McHugh, Yakima Canutt, Lafe McKee, Albert J. Smith

The Thrill Hunter (COL) b/w 60 min

One of the last of cinematographer Tetzlaff's series Westerns before moving on to bigger films at Paramount and then to directing in 1941, this is one of the most entertaining, and certainly the oddest, of Jones' Westerns for Columbia. He's the cowboy whose tall stories secure him the attention of a movie company on location. They are so impressed they let him demonstrate his supposed talents. The result is numerous wrecked racing cars – a real life passion of Jones' – and airplanes. Sacked and disconsolate, he then does the impossible to win the heart of Revier. A farce in the tradition of Baron Munchausen.

d George Seitz *p* Irving Briskin *s* Harry O. Hoyt *c* Ted Tetzlaff *lp* Buck Jones, Dorothy Revier, Arthur Rankin, Robert Ellis, Frank LaRue, Edward J. LeSaint

The Thundering Herd (PAR) b/w 62 min

The Thundering Herd is one of the best of Paramount's Zane Grey quickies. Scott is the buffalo hunter who falls in love with Allen, daughter of outlaw Beery who ferments trouble between the hunters and Indians. Hathaway's simple and dramatic presentation of events created a sense of romantic grandeur that belied the film's small budget. Even the generous use of stock footage from William K. Howard's 1925 silent version – notably the stampede of wagons across a frozen lake – doesn't disturb the mood of the film.

d Henry Hathaway *p* Harold Hurley *s* Jack Cunningham, Mary Flannery *c* Ben Reynolds *lp* Randolph Scott, Judith Allen, Buster Crabbe, Noah Beery, Harry Carey, Barton MacLane

To the Last Man (PAR) b/w 70 min

Another impressive Zane Grey Western with Scott, in the lead, now developing the austere assurance that was to be his defining characteristic, this film also features the debut of Shirley Temple and a 'tastefully photographed' nude swimming sequence. The story is the tired one of an ancient family feud that breaks out once more when one family turns to cattle rustling. Scott is the son in love with Ralston, Crabbe

his younger brother and MacLane the villain of the piece. Hathaway directs his impressive cast with elan.

d Henry Hathaway *p* Harold Hurley *s* Jack Cunningham
c Ben Reynolds *lp* Randolph Scott, Esther Ralston,
Noah Beery, Shirley Temple, Larry Crabbe, Barton MacLane

The Trail Drive (U) b/w 60 min

One of the best looking of Maynard's series Westerns thanks to the cinematographer McCord who responds to the simplicity of director James' story with a set of epic images that give the film the feel of a silent Western. The shots of the cattle both stampeding and grazing their way along the trail are quite stunning. Maynard is the strong hero and Kortman the rustling villain.

d/s Alan James *p* Ken Maynard *c* Ted McCord
lp Ken Maynard, Cecilia Parker, Bob Kortman, Wally Wales,
Ben Corbett, Lafe McKee

1934

Belle of the Nineties (PAR) b/w 75(70) min

West and Pryor are the night-club entertainer and prizefighter who find love and endless troubles in this entertaining frontier musical of a Western. The film was West's first to suffer from serious censorship troubles, troubles that would plague her subsequent films. However, though the censor curtailed the sexual suggestiveness, the film was still an enormous box-office success.

It was the last screen appearance by Brown (playing second lead to West) in a film by a major for some time. After completing the movie, he joined Bob Steele at Supreme Pictures and began in earnest his climb to success in seriesdom.

d Leo McCarey *p* William Le Baron *s* Mae West *c* Karl
Struss *lp* Mae West, Roger Pryor, Johnny Mack Brown,
John Miljan, Duke Ellington, Harry Woods

Blue Steel (MON/LONE STAR) b/w 54 min

Canutt's stunting and his appearance as the Polka Dot Bandit (!) are the best things in this otherwise routine Wayne series Western. Wayne is the marshal, gone undercover as so often, on the trail of bandits who in turn are trying to buy up a town at knock-down prices that is above a rich gold seam. Hayes is the tobacco-chewing, beard-scratching, perpetually puzzled sheriff and Hunt the charming but inept heroine.

d/s Robert N. Bradbury *p* Paul Malvern *c* Archie Stout
lp John Wayne, Eleanor Hunt, George Hayes, Edward Peil,
Yakima Canutt, George Cleveland

The Dude Ranger

(ATHERTON PRODUCTIONS) b/w 65 min
The first of O'Brien's films for Lesser's Atherton Productions

which were distributed, as before, by Fox. Whereas his earlier Fox films stressed action, henceforth the stories would stress character. Here he's the Easterner who inherits cattle rustling along with the ranch left him. He first suspects the father of the girl he falls for, Hervey, but quickly cottons on that Mason is the guilty party. In place of guns blazing all the while, Cline puts Good's scenic cinematography to good use and gives a sense of ranch life rare in the series Westerns.

d Edward F. Cline *p* Sol Lesser *s* Barry Barringer
c Frank B. Good *lp* George O'Brien, Irene Hervey,
Syd Saylor, LeRoy Mason, Lafe McKee, Henry Hall

The Fighting Ranger (COL) b/w 60 min

A remake of Jones' own **Border Law** (1931) with Jones, assisted by Rice once more, as the Ranger given leave of absence to track down the killer of his brother. The practice of remaking one's own films every couple of years or so was prevalent in the early thirties; it was as though stars and producers really believed that there were only ten Western stories and it was a waste of time confecting new wrinkles when the public would happily accept the same stories time and time again. This remake has the added bonus of Seitz's gripping direction and a strong cast that features Bond, Revier and LaRue amongst others.

d George B. Seitz *p* Irving Briskin *s* Harry O. Hoyt
c Sid Wagner *lp* Buck Jones, Dorothy Revier, Frank
Rice, Ward Bond, Frank LaRue, Bud Osborne

*Far left: The young
Randolph Scott is
caught unawares in* To
the Last Man.

Mae West as the Belle
of the Nineties; *although censored, the
film was an enormous
box-office success.*

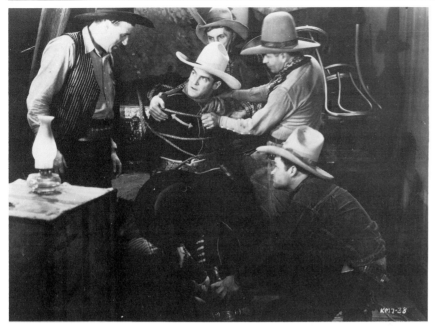

Ken Maynard tied up in In Old Santa Fé which was directed by David Howard while on loan from Fox to Mascot and completed by editor Joseph Kane when Howard's short term contract ran out towards the end of the film.

The Fighting Trooper (AMBASSADOR) b/w 61 min
The first sound film starring Maynard who, after a brief day of silent stardom, had been eclipsed by the meteoric rise of his brother Ken and the first sound Mountie series. 'Suggested' by a story by James Oliver Curwood who, after Zane Grey and Peter B. Kyne, was the most saleable writer in the Western genre, the film features Maynard as a tenderfoot Mountie out to avenge the murder of a colleague which he does by posing as a trapper. Maynard, who did all his own, often very dangerous, stunts, is superb as a man of action but less convincing romancing Worth. Mason is a spirited villain.

d Ray Taylor *p* Maurice Conn *s* Forrest Sheldon
c Edgar Lyons *lp* Kermit Maynard, Barbara Worth, LeRoy Mason, George Chesebro, Charles King, Lafe McKee

Frontier Marshal (FOX) b/w 66 min
The first sound version of Stuart N. Lake's novel *Wyatt Earp, Frontier Marshal* which also formed the basis of Ford's famous interpretation of the Earp legend, **My Darling Clementine** (1946) as well as a less famous remake in 1939 by Allan Dwan. It was produced independently by Lessor with a four-week shooting schedule, as opposed to the usual eight-day schedules of 'in house' productions, and released by Fox who had temporarily ceased making Western series. O'Brien is Michael Wyatt (*sic*), cleaning up Tombstone, being romanced by saloon girl Gillette and romancing Bentley. Seiler directs in full melodramatic style.

d Lew Seiler *p* Sol Lessor *s* William Counselman, Stuart Anthony *c* Robert Planck *lp* George O'Brien, Irene Bentley, Ruth Gillette, Ward Bond, George E. Stone, Alan Edwards

Honor of the Range (U) b/w 61 min
Heavily influenced by Mae West's *She Done Him Wrong* (1933) which Maynard had seen and liked, this odd movie sees Maynard in the double roles of sheriff and his twin evil brother, a plot device Maynard was especially fond of. The storyline calls for Maynard to spend much of the picture impersonating an English song and dance man (like Bob Steele before him in **Headin' North**, 1930) while he tracks down his twin who's absconded with his true love to Kohler's mountain hideout. The film is fantastical to say the least, with mountains exploding and horses opening doors, but the outstanding sequence is a highly realistic rooftop fight between Maynard and Kohler, expertly mounted and photographed by James.

d Alan James *p* Ken Maynard *s* Nate Gatzert *c* Ted McCord *lp* Ken Maynard, Cecilia Parker, Fred Kohler, Jack Rockwell, Al Bridge, Wally Wales

In Old Santa Fé (MASCOT) b/w 64 min
Maynard's one and only feature for Mascot, *In Old Santa Fé* is an interesting film, partly for its cast which boasts the first screen appearance of radio cowboy Gene Autry and his side-kick Smiley Burnette. Superior to both the Universal series that preceded it and the Columbia outings that followed, *In Old Santa Fé* features Maynard being framed for murder after losing his horse Tarzan in a crooked race. Set around a dude ranch, it was tightly controlled by producer Levine, who of all B producers was most successful in following the oldest of Hollywood's adages, 'shoot the money'.

d David Howard *p* Nat Levine *s* Colbert Clark, James Gruen *c* Ernest Miller, William Nobles *lp* Ken Maynard, Evalyn Knapp, George Hayes, Gene Autry, Lester 'Smiley' Burnette, H.B. Warner

The Last Round Up (PAR) b/w 61 min
Scott and Fritchie are the lovers, Kohler the rustler who lusts after her and Blue the outlaw who sacrifices his life for them, in this routine remake of Zane Grey's novel *Border Legion*. Stock footage from the silent version and **Border Legion** (1930) were used to spice up the action.

d Henry Hathaway *p* Harold Hurley *s* Jack Cunningham *c* Archie Stout *lp* Randolph Scott, Barbara Fritchie, Fred Kohler, Monte Blue, Fuzzy Knight, Charles Middleton

Lawless Frontier (MON/LONE STAR) b/w 59 min
Another Wayne outing that sees him on the trail of the murderers of his parents. Hayes is the oldtimer he rescues along the way, Terry the girl he falls for and Whitlock the halfbreed outlaw. Script and direction are routine and production values meagre but the commitment of all concerned is appealing.

d/s Robert N. Bradbury *p* Paul Malvern *c* Archie Stout *lp* John Wayne, Sheila Terry, George Hayes, Lloyd Whitlock, Yakima Canutt

The Lucky Texan (LONE STAR) b/w 56 min
This Western saw Hayes for the first time play the comic side-kick role that he was to make his own for some twenty years. Wayne is the two-fisted Easterner who goes West to join his father's partner, Hayes, in a mining operation. Whitlock and Canutt are the claimjumpers. The finale, a lengthy chase involving a model-T Ford, a railroad handcar and horses is doubly interesting for its mixture of comedy (courtesy of Hayes) and thrills.

Far right: The young John Wayne takes the young Ward Bond prisoner in The Lucky Texan.

d/s Robert N. Bradbury   p Paul Malvern   c Archie Stout
lp John Wayne, Barbara Sheldon, Lloyd Whitlock, George
Hayes, Yakima Canutt, Jack Rockwell

The Man from Hell
(MARCEY PRODUCTIONS)   b/w   58 min
This is one of the short-lived series of Westerns one-time
football star Russell made for Kent's Marcey Productions.
The strong cast, which includes Kohler as chief villain,
Canutt as a heavy and Hayes, notwithstanding, Kent's meagre
budgets and the inept direction of Collins, who in the late
forties would be one of the mainstays of the series Western,
results in an inferior film. Russell is the lawman posing as a
baddie to expose the town's mayor, Kohler, as the leader of a
gang of outlaws.

d Lew Collins   p Willis Kent   s Melville Shyer   c William
Nobles   lp Reb Russell, Fred Kohler, George Hayes,
Yakima Canutt, Slim Whitaker, Charles French

The Man from Utah   (MON/LONE STAR)   b/w   55 min
This indifferent series Western is set against a rodeo
background. It opens, as do so many of Wayne's Lone Star
films, with a fistfight that ends this time with an invitation to
Wayne to become the town's sheriff. Instead he heads off for
the local rodeo where he wins a horse race, after Canutt has
tried to fix it by putting a poisoned dart under his saddle, and
then sorts out the baddies.

d Robert N. Bradbury   p Paul Malvern   s Lindsley
Parsons   c Archie Stout   lp John Wayne, Polly Ann Young,
George Hayes, Yakima Canutt, Lafe McKee, George
Cleveland

The Man Trailer   (COL)   b/w   59 min
Jones' last Columbia outing, The Man Trailer is a remake of
his first Western for the company The Lone Rider (1930),
itself a remake of the silent W.S. Hart film, The Return of
Draw Egan (1916), also directed by Hillyer. Jones is the
innocent man on the run who foils a stagecoach robbery and
wins the heart of Parker. Appointed sheriff of a nearby town
he captures the outlaw threatening to reveal his past. Hillyer's
sombre direction, Jones' restrained performance and the adult
storyline combine to raise the film well above the average
series Western.

d/s Lambert Hillyer   p Irving Briskin   c Benjamin Kline
lp Buck Jones, Cecilia Parker, Arthur Vinton, Clarence
Geldert, Steve Clark, Charles West

Mystery Mountain   (MASCOT)   b/w   12 chaps
Maynard's only serial, Mystery Mountain is a loose remake of
Mascot's earlier serial, Hurricane Express (1932) with
Maynard in the John Wayne role. Cobb is the Rattler intent
on stopping the completion of a railroad and who, thanks to a
collection of rubber masks, can assume the identity of anyone
in the cast.

The serial clearly marked Maynard's declining drawing-
power. More significantly, his attitude during its making,
which veered from completely rewriting the scenario to
drunken, loutish behaviour, resulted in his losing the lead in
The Phantom Empire (1935) to Autry who (with Burnette)
has a minor, non-singing, role in this chapter play.

d B. Reeves Eason, Otto Brower   p Nat Levine   s Bennett
Cohen, Armand Schaefer   c Ernest Miller, William Nobles
lp Ken Maynard, Edmund Cobb, Verna Hillie, Lafe McKee,
Al Bridge, Syd Saylor

'Neath Arizona Skies   (MON/LONE STAR)   b/w   52 min
A routine Wayne series outing. This time the identity switch
plot is worked not on the look-alike basis but on an exchange
of clothes. Wayne, guardian to Ricketts who is heir to oil-rich
land, is set upon by bandits, his clothes exchanged for those of

a wanted killer, and left for dead. The handsomely mounted
climax features a lengthy fistfight between Wayne and Canutt
in mid river.

d Harry Fraser   p Paul Malvern   s Burl Tuttle   c Archie
Stout   lp John Wayne, Sheila Terry, Shirley Ricketts
(Shirley Jane Rickey), George Hayes, Yakima Canutt, Jay
Wilsey (Buffalo Bill Jnr)

Randy Rides Alone   (MON/LONE STAR)   b/w   53 min
The most intriguing of Wayne's Lone Star Westerns. The
movie opens with Wayne riding into a deserted town,
dismounting, heading for the saloon guided by a tinkling
piano, entering and finding inside, instead of smiling people,
a mechanical player piano and a bar room full of corpses.
From here on, though Parsons' plot becomes more routine,
the mystery of the film's beginning remains a powerful one
until the end when Hayes is revealed as the villain of the
piece, hiding his true identity under the disguise of Matt the
Mute.

The film, with The Man from Utah (1934), is also notable
for containing one of the few sequences of Wayne 'singing' –
his voice being dubbed by Smith Ballew according to most
sources – since his Monogram debut in the bizarre Riders of
Destiny (1933).

d Harry Fraser   p Paul Malvern   s Lindsley Parsons
c Archie Stout   lp John Wayne, Alberta Vaughn, George
Hayes, Yakima Canutt, Earl Dwire, Tex Phelps

The Red Rider   (U)   b/w   15 chaps
Jones' second serial for Universal, The Red Rider saw a
significant cutback in production values. The plot has Jones
as a one-time sheriff who abandons his job in his quest to
prove the innocence of his deputy, Withers, who is accused of
murder. Where Republic's serials were fast and furious,
Universal's were so cliched that distributors complained
about the company's over-reliance on the ending of chapters
with Buck and his white horse leaping from the cliffs into
water far below. In the final episode Jones unmasks Miller as
the murderer and rescues Maxwell from him. A routine affair.

d Lew Landers   p Milton Gatzert   s George Plympton, Vin
Moore, Ella O'Neill, Basil Bickey   lp Buck Jones, Grant
Withers, Marion Shilling, Walter Miller, Edmund Cobb, Bud
Osborne

Rocky Rhodes   (U)   b/w   64 min
An intriguing film, this was the first series Western Jones,
still billing himself as Charles 'Buck' Jones, made for
Universal. Beginning with newsreel footage of the Chicago
stockyard fire, the film quickly moves Westward, thus
allowing Jones to save Terry and sort out Arizona landgrab-

*Buck Rogers carries
Sheila Terry to safety in*
Rocky Rhodes.

A surreal moment from Smoking Guns, one of the most bizarre series Westerns.

bers led by Miller's suave villain. Assistance for Jones is provided by Fields as the gruff humorous criminal type, in a clear imitation of Wallace Beery. The direction is by Raboch, the art director of *Ben Hur* (1925), whose work was supervised by Jones.

d Al Raboch *p* Buck Jones *s* Edward Churchill *c* Ted McCord *lp* Buck Jones, Sheila Terry, Walter Miller, Stanley Fields, Paul Fix, Bud Osborne

Smoking Guns (U) b/w 62 min
Written by Maynard himself, so he could charge his crocodile hunting trips, of which he generally made home movies, to expenses, this was a disastrous film for its star. Intended as a parody – at one point a character shoots himself rather than have Maynard amputate his leg with a red hot poker – Maynard casts himself as the victim of a frame-up for a murder charge. He takes over the identity of the Ranger sent into the jungle to get him after the Ranger dies from a crocodile bite (despite his not looking in the least like him) and rescues his father, held prisoner for several years, from

The poster for Viva Villa!

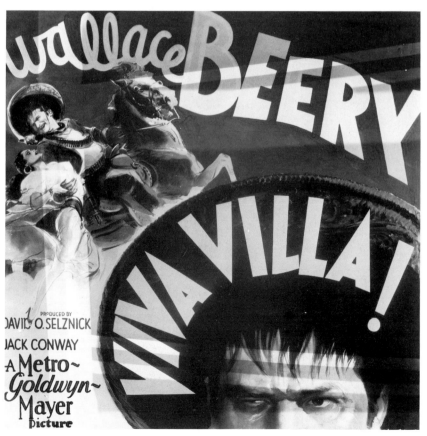

villains on his return to civilization. If the film is bad, its reception by Universal was even worse for Maynard. They demanded he remake it; he refused and quit the company for the wilderness of independent production, but without his own production unit to safeguard him from the budget-cutting wiles of indie producers.

d Alan James *p* Ken Maynard *s* Nate Gatzert *c* Ted McCord *lp* Ken Maynard, Gloria Shea, Bob Kortman, Jack Rockwell, Slim Whitaker, Wally Wales

The Star Packer (MON/LONE STAR) b/w 60 min
The last of Wayne's first series of Westerns for Monogram, *The Star Packer* unusually boasts Canutt, the regular heavy in the series, as a friendly Indian, Yak. The improbable plot features a tunnel under the town's mainstreet, complete with a phoney tree as the entrance/exit, constructed for the use of the Shadow who, of course, is one of the town's leading citizens, Hayes. Wayne is the stranger who exposes Hayes and his gang. The elaborately staged climax suggests that Trem Carr, Monogram's head, had considerably upped the budget on the series from the original figure of $5,000 to $8,000 per entry.

d/s Robert N. Bradbury *p* Paul Malvern *c* Archie Stout *lp* John Wayne, Verna Hillie, George Hayes, Yakima Canutt, Earl Dwire, Ed Parker

Thunder over Texas (BEACON) b/w 61 min
Based on a story by Ulmer's wife (Shirley Castle) and directed pseudonymously by him to prevent Universal from discovering that he was working elsewhere, this is the first Western directed by Ulmer. Disjointed and sentimental – at one point a child teaches grizzled cowboys to pray – it looks to be the inverse of the doom-laden films the director is best remembered for. Williams and schoolteacher Shilling are the couple who look after a young girl when her father is murdered by banker Peyton.

This was the first of Williams' six strong series for Beacon Productions. After his brief spell as a star, Williams and his simpleton's grin became one of the genre's most active supporting players.

Ulmer made only one other Western, the magnificent **The Naked Dawn** (1955).

d John Warner (Edgar G. Ulmer) *p* Max Alexander, Arthur Alexander *s* Eddie Granemann *c* Harry Forbes *lp* Guinn 'Big Boy' Williams, Marion Shilling, Helen Westcott, Ben Corbett, Claude Peyton, Victor Potel

The Trail Beyond (MON/LONE STAR) b/w 55 min
A superior series Western let down by Parsons' indifferent script. Based on a popular novel *The Wolf Hunters*, filmed previously under that title in 1926 and to be filmed later with Parsons producing but not writing in 1949, *The Trail Beyond* was the first Monogram Wayne Western to have its origins outside the company's script department. The increased budget was further reflected in the greater amount of location shooting and the presence of the Beerys as support for Wayne. Stout rose to the occasion, producing some stunning land-scapes amidst the sun-strewn forest. The script, however, with Wayne hunting for a missing girl, helping Beery Jnr and finding a gold mine as well as putting paid to the plans of Frazer's villain, is even more melodramatic than usual.

d Robert N. Bradbury *p* Paul Malvern *s* Lindsley Parsons *c* Archie Stout *lp* John Wayne, Noah Beery, Noah Beery Jnr, Verna Hillie, Robert Frazer, Iris Lancaster

Viva Villa! (MGM) b/w 115 min
A lively, much fictionalized and (surprisingly for the period) violent account of the career of the revolutionary and the founding of the Republic of Mexico. One of MGM's biggest

successes, it has a dash and verve that few of the company's Westerns possess. Beery gives a democratic interpretation of the title role, manhandling Wray into reluctant submission and furiously criss-crossing Mexico in search of the Federales. Although Conway got sole directorial credit, all the material shot on location in Mexico was directed by Howard Hawks. The sequences featuring Lee Tracy had to be re-shot with Erwin after a drunk Tracy had watered a military parade passing below his hotel balcony!

d Jack Conway *p* David O. Selznick *s* Ben Hecht
c James Wong Howe, Charles G. Clarke *lp* Wallace Beery, Fay Wray, Leo Carrillo, Stuart Erwin, Donald Cook, George E. Stone

Wagon Wheels (PAR) b/w 56 min
A remake of **Fighting Caravans** (1931) which starred Gary Cooper and was based on the Zane Grey story of the same title, this Scott outing has the added advantage of including background material shot for the Cooper film but not used in it. Scott is the scout guiding a wagon train to Oregon and Blue the half caste in the pay of speculators who tries to impede the progress of the wagon train by fermenting an Indian uprising. Patrick is the young widow Scott falls for.

d Charles Barton *p* Harold Hurley *s* Jack Cunningham, Charles Logan, Carl A. Buss *c* William Mellor
lp Randolph Scott, Gail Patrick, Billie Lee, Raymond Hatton, Monte Blue, Leila Bennett

West of the Divide (MON/LONE STAR) b/w 54 min
This is generally regarded as being amongst the best of Wayne's Lone Star Western series. It makes use of two of the most often-used plot ideas: a man seeking revenge for the murder of his father and going underground as an outlaw to achieve it. Wayne, whose confidence in his acting had clearly much improved since his Columbia days, takes the role seriously and this brings the plotline to life. Whitlock is the outlaw leader and murderer with whom Wayne has a splendid fistfight. The film is a remake of the Tom Tyler Western, *Partners of the Trail* (1931).

Richard Dix (right) rescues Martha Sleeper (centre), dressed as a boy, in West of the Pecos.

d/s Robert N. Bradbury *p* Paul Malvern *c* Archie Stout
lp John Wayne, Virginia Brown Faire, Lloyd Whitlock, George Hayes, Yakima Canutt, Lafe McKee

West of the Pecos (RKO) b/w 68 min
A superior Western, this is the first and best of Dix's for RKO. Based on a Zane Grey story set in Texas just after the Civil War, it features Sleeper as the girl who masquerades as a boy (and whose secret Dix keeps after he's rescued her from the River Pecos) and Dix, the star of **Cimarron** (1931), as the man determined to bring law and order back to Texas. An odd sequence has Alba flirting with Sleeper thinking her a boy; clearly intended to amuse, the sequence, especially when compared to Dix's 'restraint' throughout the film, seems peculiar to modern eyes. Kohler is the lively villain of the piece.

d Phil Rosen *p* Cliff Reid *s* Milton Krims, John Twist *c* James Van Trees, Russell Metty *lp* Richard Dix, Martha Sleeper, Maria Alba, Fred Kohler, Samuel S. Hinds, George Cooper

John Wayne in West of the Divide.

Top: *A bandaged Richard Dix as the marshal and Preston Foster as the reformed outlaw who helps him clean up Silver City in* The Arizonian.

Annie Oakley (RKO) b/w 90 min

The first Western made by Stanwyck, who unusually amongst actresses was to return to the genre time and time again, generally giving her roles a toughness few others could match. *Annie Oakley* is an efficient, if historically inaccurate, biopic. Stanwyck is in fine form as the tomboy sharpshooter who romances fellow sharpshooter Foster and is in turn romanced, unsuccessfully, by Douglas, the manager of Buffalo Bill's Wild West Show.

d George Stevens *p* Cliff Reid *s* Joel Sayre, John Twist *c* J. Roy Hunt *lp* Barbara Stanwyck, Preston Foster, Melvyn Douglas, Moroni Olson, Andy Clyde, Margaret Armstrong

William Boyd, an unusually elegant Hopalong Cassidy, holds a group of assorted bad men at bay in Bar 20 Rides Again.

The Arizonian (RKO) b/w 75 min

The strong cast and an original screenplay by Nichols (who won an Oscar for one of his other screenplays that year, *The Informer*) notwithstanding, this is at best a routine Western. Its budget was considerably higher than that of the average series Western but neither Nichols nor Vidor make much of their opportunity. Dix is the reforming marshal of Silver City, Calhern the slinky villain, Foster the outlaw redeemed by contract with Dix's moral certitude and Grahame the heroine who sets everybody's heart beating a little faster.

d Charles Vidor *p* Cliff Reid *s* Dudley Nichols *c* Harold Wenstrom *lp* Richard Dix, Preston Foster, Louis Calhern, Margot Grahame, James Bush, Bob Kortman

Below: *Barbara Stanwyck in her first Western, as the sharpshooting* Annie Oakley.

Bar 20 Rides Again (PAR) b/w 65 min

Although this, the third Hopalong Cassidy Western, was badly received by the trade, it proved to be the most popular of the first season of films devoted to the character and

pointed the way forward, not the least in the Hayes character being called Windy for the first time. Worth is the marvellous snuff-taking cattle rustler of a villain who dreams of an empire in the West and keeps a bust of Napoleon on his mantelpiece – thus anticipating Jeff Chandler in **The Jayhawkers** (1959) by some 20 years. More importantly, the film sees the refinement of the-Bar-20-riders-to-the-rescue sequence in which, beautifully edited by Edward Schroeder, we see the Bar 20 cowboys saddle up, mount their horses and ride to the rescue. Rapidly cut with carefully chosen angles by Stout, the sequence became the *sina qua non* of the series for several years, intensifying the drama of the pitched battle that inevitably followed.

d Howard Bretherton *p* Harry Sherman *s* Gerald Geraghty, Doris Schroeder *c* Archie Stout *lp* William Boyd, Jimmy Ellison, George Hayes, Harry Worth, Jean Rouveral, Al St John

Between Men (SUPREME) b/w 60 min

Another of Brown's independently-made series Westerns, with a script by Bradbury that looks to have been written with his son, Bob Steele (who was also contracted to Hackel) in mind. Brown is the son who searches for his father, Farnum, who believes him to be dead and Marion is the rejected granddaughter of his benefactor. Efficiently mounted and capably directed, the film's major failing is Longenecker's spotty cinematography and the slim budget.

d/s Robert N. Bradbury *p* A.W. Hackel *c* Bert Longenecker *lp* Johnny Mack Brown, William Farnum, Beth Marion, Earl Dwire, Lloyd Ingraham, Bud Osborne

Branded a Coward (SUPREME) b/w 57 min

One of the earliest of Brown's series Westerns for Hackel, this film is badly let down by Nobles' poor cinematography and

Snell's weak development of an interesting story. The film opens in flashback – an unusual device for a series Western – that explains why the otherwise brave Brown is reduced to jelly when under fire – he saw his parents gunned down. Thereafter, Snell's script quickly leaves **Pursued** (1947) territory for simple heroics, only returning to matters psychological at the conclusion when the villain is revealed to be Brown's own brother. Seward is the woman and Saylor the comic relief.

d Sam Newfield *p* A.W. Hackel *s* Earle Snell *c* William Nobles *lp* Johnny Mack Brown, Billie Seward, Syd Saylor, Yakima Canutt, Lloyd Ingraham, Lee Shumway

Call of the Wild (FOX) b/w 81 min
Gable is the wild Yukon prospector and Young the married woman who falls for him, thinking her husband to be dead, as they search for gold in the frozen north. Fowler and Praskins' script, although it deviates considerably from Jack London's classic novel, has space for the wolf-dog that saves Gable. Ironically, though the lacklustre 1972 remake by Ken Annakin is more faithful to the novel, Wellman's direction retains the bleak vision of London's work.

d William Wellman *p* Darryl F. Zanuck *s* Gene Fowler, Leonard Praskins *c* Charles Rosher *lp* Clark Gable, Loretta Young, Jack Oakie, Frank Conroy, Sidney Toler, Syd Saylor

The Cowboy Millionaire (ATHERTON/FOX) b/w 65 min
The third of Lesser's independently produced O'Brien features and the first released by Twentieth Century Fox after the merger of Zanuck and Fox's companies. The script is unusual for an O'Brien vehicle: he's the chief cowboy at a dude ranch who English rose Bostock falls for. They part after the inevitable misunderstanding and, just as inevitably, O'Brien follows her to London and woos her back. More a gentle comedy than an actioneer.

d Edward F. Cline *p* Sol Lesser *s* George Waggner, Dan Jarrett *c* Frank B. Good *lp* George O'Brien, Evalyn Bostock, Edgar Kennedy, Alden Chase, Maude Allen, Dan Jarrett

The Crimson Trail (U) b/w 60 min
Bleifer, as the aptly named Loco, cackling and chuckling as he plots the destruction of the families of Jones and Young (the elder sister of Loretta) with assistance from Bond, is the undisputed star of this extraordinary series Western. The plot is rudimentary but the staccato action scenes, like a midnight raid on a ranch, and Bleifer's over-the-top vision of menace, are very powerful.

d Al Raboch *p* Buck Jones *s* Jack Natteford *c* John Hickson *lp* Buck Jones, Polly Ann Young, John Bleifer, Ward Bond, Bob Kortman, Bud Osborne

The Dawn Rider (MON/LONE STAR) b/w 56 min
Once again Wayne is hunting the killer of his father in this Bradbury-scripted Western. The plotline (often combined with the assumed identity ploy) was a favourite of Bradbury's who used it even more frequently when directing his son, Bob Steele, in his various Western series. Here Meadows is the culprit and Burns, his sister, the girl who nurses Wayne back to life after he's stopped a bullet.

d/s Robert N. Bradbury *p* Paul Malvern *c* Archie Stout *lp* John Wayne, Marion Burns, Yakima Canutt, Reed Howes, Denny Meadows (Dennis Moore), Bert Dillard

The Desert Trail (MON/LONE STAR) b/w 54 min
Another routine series entry. Wayne is the star rodeo rider who with his gambler friend and comic side-kick, Chandler, is suspected of robbing a bank. They head after Fix and

George O'Brien and an irate Evalyn Bostock in The Cowboy Millionaire.

Ferguson, whom they suspect, and get their men, even though Wayne falls for Kornman, Fix's sister. Lewis' direction is stilted.

d Cullen Lewis (Lew Collins) *p* Paul Malvern *s* Lindsley Parsons *c* Archie Stout *lp* John Wayne, Mary Kornman, Paul Fix, Eddie Chandler, Al Ferguson, Carmen LaRoux

The Eagle's Brood (PAR) b/w 59 min
The second of Sherman's Hopalong Cassidy series – this is a distinct improvement on the first. Bretherton's direction is pacier and the climactic cliff-top struggle between Boyd and Richards is well mounted. The plot has sheriff Boyd promise an outlaw who saves his life (Farnum) that he'll find his grandson. For this he's voted out of office and sets out after Richards who's kidnapped the child. Boyd and Ellison complement each other well and Hayes puts in a nifty performance as a cigarette-rolling barman, but it is the splendidly orchestrated action sequences, especially the climax with the Bar 20 cowboys coming to the rescue Seventh Cavalry-style, that made the film so popular.

Below: Ward Bond *(second from right) holds Buck Jones at gunpoint while the crazed John Bleifer taunts him in* The Crimson Trail.

d Howard Bretherton *p* Harry Sherman *s* Doris
Schroeder, Harrison Jacobs *c* Archie Stout *lp* William
Boyd, Jimmy Ellison, Addison Richards, William Farnum,
George Hayes, Dorothy Revier

Gallant Defender (COL) b/w 60 min
The first of Starrett's series Westerns for Columbia, the
studio he'd stay with for 132 films until 1952 and **The Kid
from Broken Gun**. Intended as a mere replacement for Tim
McCoy – he was even assigned Selman as a director because
he'd assisted Ross Lederman, McCoy's regular director –
Starrett was the last cowboy star to be developed by a studio
before the singing cowboy arrived on the scene and drastically
changed the genre. Here, set in the usual cattlemen versus
homesteaders context, Starrett is the man falsely accused of
murder who sets out to prove himself innocent and Woods,
the guilty party. Perry is the girl. Though advertized as being
derived from a Peter B. Kyne story, as the first few in the
series would be, the film and series were solely developed by
writer/director Beebe.

*Far right: Buck Jones
about to be laid low in*
The Ivory-Handled
Guns.

d David Selman *p* Harry Decker *s* Ford Beebe
c Benjamin Kline *lp* Charles Starrett, Joan Perry, Harry
Woods, George Chesebro, Edmund Cobb, Al Bridge

Gun Play *aka* **Lucky Boots** (BEACON) b/w 59 min
An adequate series Western, this is one of the six Williams,
better known as a Western character actor, made with himself
in the leading role, for Beacon Pictures. Oddly Yaconelli is
the comedy support thus denying Williams his strong suit,
humour, and forcing him to be the decisive man of action he
clearly wasn't. Here he defends an Easterner, newly arrived in
the West, from Mexican outlaws after treasure buried on her
ranch and wins her heart. Wales, in one of his last roles before
changing his name to Hal Taliaferro and extending his career
as a character actor, offers fine support.

d Al Herman *p* Arthur Alexander *s* William L. Nolte
c William Hyer *lp* Big Boy Williams, Marion Shilling,
Roger Williams, Frank Yaconelli, Wally Wales, Tom London

Home on the Range (PAR) b/w 55 min
This is a typical racetrack melodrama unsurely transferred to
the range. Coogan is the kid brother and jockey slated to ride
Scott's horse Midnight which, if it wins, will solve the
brothers' financial problems. Jagger is the leader of the crooks
who try everything from simple burglary to a forest fire to
stop the brothers and Brent is the songstress who quits Jagger
for Scott. The movie is a lacklustre semi-Western most
notable for the early appearance of Sheridan as a night-club
entertainer and Scott's growing assurance as a leading man.

*William Boyd as Hoppy
in* Hop-a-Long
Cassidy, *the first of the
series.*

d Arthur Jacobson *p* Harold Hurley *s* Harold Shumate
c William Mellor *lp* Randolph Scott, Ann Sheridan,
Dean Jagger, Jackie Coogan, Fuzzy Knight, Evelyn Brent

Hop-a-Long Cassidy *aka* **Hopalong Cassidy Enters**
(PAR) b/w 62 min
The first entry in one of the longest running Western series.
Independent producer Sherman secured the rights to Clarence E. Mulford's painstakingly researched novels about the
adventures of the Bar 20 ranch hands in which a tetchy,
grizzled, hard-drinking cowhand, Hoppy – the limp which
gave the character his name being soon discarded in the films
– played a leading role and then set about looking for a star.
Boyd, a one-time silent star, whose career had declined,
agreed to play the lead only if the role was rewritten to make
the character clean living. Briskly directed by Bretherton with
an exhilarating chase at the end when the Bar 20 hands ride to
the rescue (which was to become a staple feature of the series
and of most of Sherman's Western productions), the film
immediately clicked with the public. The plot has Boyd,
Ellison, as a young hothead, and McGlynn Jnr preventing a

range war. Hayes, who plays an oldtimer who is killed in the
course of the film, was resurrected for subsequent outings.
Sherman masterminded the first 50 pictures of the series,
before selling the rights to Boyd, and carefully maintained the
balance between Hoppy and the secondary characters which
made the series so distinctive.

d Howard Bretherton *p* Harry Sherman *s* Doris
Schroeder *c* Archie Stout *lp* William Boyd, Jimmy
Ellison, Paula Stone, Charles Middleton, Frank McGlynn
Jnr, George Hayes

The Ivory-Handled Guns (U) b/w 60 min
An impressive series Western, this is set against the background of a family feud between different sheepmen (rather
than cattlemen versus sheepmen) for a change. Neville's
revenge plot has a surprise ending with both Jones and Miller
shot and Jones being crippled as his father was when he and
Miller's father fought. Whereupon Taylor, who Jones would
use almost uninterruptedly until he (Taylor) joined Republic
in 1936, cuts to a shot of the pair of ivory-handled guns,
Miller's and Jones', side by side in a guncase and now
signifying the end of the feud. The film is clearly a mature
Western with aspirations that couldn't be fulfilled in a plot
that also features Silver, Jones' horse, untying heroine
Wynters.

d Ray Taylor *p* Buck Jones *s* John Neville *c* Allen
Thompson, Herbert Kirkpatrick *lp* Buck Jones, Charlotte
Wynters, Walter Miller, Carl Stockdale, Lafe McKee,
Charles King

Justice of the Range (COL) b/w 58 min

This is generally reckoned to be amongst the best of McCoy's
series Westerns. Unlike most other cowboy stars, McCoy's
films are not all Westerns; indeed he only returned to the
range fulltime when Jones quit Columbia to join Universal,
thus leaving the studio without a resident cowboy. Here he's
the cattle detective caught up in a range war and family feud
who gets to the truth through some fancy sleuthing. The
action is fast and furious and Bond makes an impressive
heavy.

d David Selman *p* Irving Briskin *s* Ford Beebe
c George Meehan *lp* Tim McCoy, Billie Seward, Ward
Bond, Guy Usher, Jack Rockwell, George Hayes

The Last of the Clintons (AJAX) b/w 60 min

A routine Carey series entry in which he's the cattle detective
on the track of Dwire's gang of rustlers. He gets help from
Potel's grizzled prospector who pops up to save him on several
occasions. Neither Fraser nor cameraman Cline are at their
best and the action bumbles rather than flows. However,
Carey, as relaxed as ever, remains a joy to behold.

d Harry Fraser *p* William Berke *s* Weston Edwards
c Robert Cline *lp* Harry Carey, Betty Mack, Earl Dwire,
Victor Potel, Lafe McKee, Slim Whitaker

The Lawless Range (REP) b/w 59 min

Although this was released as a Republic picture, it was made
as a Monogram picture. Accordingly, its budget and production values were meagre compared to Wayne's other Republic
releases. McGlynn is the banker rustling cattle so as to clear
the valley of settlers and give him free access to the gold mine
only he knows is there. Parsons' script features the angular
cave made famous by its many appearances in Monogram's
serials.

d Robert N. Bradbury *p* Trem Carr *s* Lindsley Parsons
c Archie Stout *lp* John Wayne, Sheila Mannors, Earl Dwire,
Frank McGlynn Jnr, Jack Curtis, Yakima Canutt

The Man from Guntown (PURITAN) b/w 61 min

A rugged, physical series Western from McCoy in which the
star defends Seward from the likes of Chesebro and Oakman,
who are amongst the gang trying to gyp her of the ranch she's
inherited. They even go so far as to frame her for the murder
of her brother, Lease, a one-time cowboy star, before McCoy
arrives on the scene. The unusual ending has McCoy, instead
of staying with Seward, riding off alone to purge himself of the
killings forced upon him.

d/co-s Ford Beebe *p* Nat Ross *co-s* Thomas H. Ince Jnr
c James Diamond *lp* Tim McCoy, Billie Seward, Wheeler
Oakman, George Chesebro, Rex Lease, Jack Clifford

The Miracle Rider (MAS) b/w 15 chaps

Mix's most commercially successful film entry – it garnered
over $1 million at the box office in less than a year – and the
one he is generally remembered for, *The Miracle Rider* is a less
than entrancing serial. Well aware of Mix's right wing views,
Levine tempted Mix away from his circus, which he had quit
Universal to form a year earlier, by offering the star the
chance to, in Mix's own words, 'return to the screen in a
picture which would set an example for kids to follow – one
with good old-fashioned virtues and Western Justice'.
However, Mascot put its money not into the serial's
production – it cost $80,000, of which half went on Mix's
salary – but on publicizing it. The result, especially when

compared to Republic's De Luxe offerings, is creaky and
thin. Mix is the Captain of the Texas Rangers who exposes
Middleton's attempts to mine valuable mineral deposits in
Indian Territory.

d Armand Schaefer, B. Reeves Eason *p* Nat Levine *s* John
Rathmell *c* Ernest Miller, William C. Nobles *lp* Tom
Mix, Joan Gale, Charles Middleton, Jason Robards Snr,
Edward Hearn, George Chesebro

Moonlight on the Prairie (WB) b/w 60 min

Foran's debut as a singing cowboy, *Moonlight on the Prairie*
was released a couple of months after **Tumbling Tumbleweeds** (1935), the film which made Gene Autry a star
overnight and established the figure of the singing cowboy as
an important element of the B Western. With his light opera
baritone, Foran, like John Wayne before him, was eased into
numerous remakes of Ken Maynard silents, before being
discarded by Warners (like Wayne again) after a couple of
seasons. As Nick Foran he'd been a chorus boy in Fox
musicals. Here he's an out of work rodeo star who brings a
cattle rustler to justice. Warners' strong production values
and Lederman's efficient direction result in a pleasant musical
outing. Down the cast list, as he was to be for many of the
series, is one Gordon Elliott who later as Wild Bill Elliott was
to be another B Western star.

d D. Ross Lederman *p* Bryan Foy *s* William Jacobs
c Fred Jackman Jnr *lp* Dick Foran, Sheila Mannors, George
E. Stone, Glenn Strange, Joe Sawyer, Robert Barratt

*Burly Dick Foran, one
of the first singing
cowboys, in* Moonlight
on the Prairie.

*Kermit, brother of Ken,
Maynard as the mountie
with Eleanor Hunt in*
Northern Frontier, *one
of the few occasions he
got top billing.*

Gene Autry amongst the oddities of the underground world of Murania in the serial The Phantom Empire, *which established Autry and singing as staple elements in the B Western.*

Nevada (PAR) b/w 58 min
Crabbe (soon to become Flash Gordon) playing the same role as Gary Cooper in the silent version of Zane Grey's novel, is the one-time badman who is trying to go straight. He saves Burke from rustlers and finally uncovers the identity of their chief, Blue. Routine and athletic.

d Charles Barton *p* Harold Hurley *s* Garnett Weston, Stuart Anthony *c* Archie Stout *lp* Buster Crabbe, Kathleen Burke, Monte Blue, Syd Saylor, Raymond Hatton, Stanley Andrews

The New Frontier (REP) b/w 59 min
Wayne's second Western for Republic. Once again he's on the track of the man who killed his father. Following his father's footsteps he takes the job of sheriff in the town where he had died. Richmond is the saloon-keeper villain who has a razor-edged brim to his black hat; Bridge is the good outlaw who with his gang comes to Wayne's aid and kills Richmond at the cost of his own life. Though much of the opening sequence is a mixture of stock footage of the Cherokee Strip land rush and footage from Ken Maynard's silent, *The Red Raiders* (1927), the climax, in which Wayne and Bridge burn down a town, testifies to the substantial budgets Republic devoted to the Wayne Westerns.

d Carl Pierson *p* Paul Malvern *s* Robert Emmett (Tansey) *c* Gus Peterson *lp* John Wayne, Muriel Evans, Warner Richmond, Al Bridge, Mary MacLaren, Glenn Strange

Northern Frontier (AMBASSADOR) b/w 57 min
Maynard's second outing as a mountie for Conn's Ambassador Pictures, this is a significant improvement on his first, **The Fighting Trooper** (1934). Barrington enlivens the James Oliver Curwood story that 'inspired' his script by introducing gangsters and machine guns into the peaceful world of counterfeiting North of the Border. Hunt is the heroine and Mason the villain whose gang mountie Maynard infiltrates. The film's editor, John English, was soon to achieve fame with William Witney as 'King of the Serials'.

d Sam Newfield *p* Maurice Conn *s* Barry Barringer *c* Edgar Lyons *lp* Kermit Maynard, Eleanor Hunt, LeRoy Mason, Charles King, Lafe McKee, Tyrone Power Jnr

Paradise Canyon (MON) b/w 52 min
Wayne's last official Monogram film. He plays John Wyatt (the same name as the character he plays in his first Republic release, **Westward Ho**, 1935), a government agent on the track of counterfeiters working on the Mexican-American border. Canutt is the villain and Burns the love interest. Ex-editor Pierson's direction is no more than average and Parsons' and Emmett's script, with its bandits and their cave headquarters, seems more geared to the adolescent delights of the serial than the (only slightly) more adult world of the B Western.

d Carl Pierson *p* Paul Malvern *s* Lindsley Parsons, Robert Tansey (Emmett) *c* Archie Stout *lp* John Wayne, Marion Burns, Earle Hodgins, Yakima Canutt, Reed Howes, Perry Murdock

The Phantom Empire (MASCOT) b/w 12 chaps
Clearly based on James Churchward's series of 'factual' books about the lost continent of Lemuria, or Mu as he called it, that began with *The Lost Continent of Mu* (1926), this bizarre concoction of science fiction and the Western gave birth to that strangest of creatures, the singing cowboy in all his glory. Ken Maynard had originally been slated for the lead, but after his conduct during the making of **Mystery Mountain** (1934) he lost the role to the young Autry.

Playing himself, as he henceforth would always do, Autry is the dude cowboy who runs a radio station from his ranch with himself as its singing star. A gang of crooks covet his radium mine and, while being pursued by Autry, they stumble upon the entrance to Murania, an underground civilization far in advance of ours but riven by similar tensions which are exacerbated by exposure to mankind. Both the crooks and Autry and his helpers are captured by the Muranians and their slave robots and only escape when conflict breaks out between the Muranians themselves, after Oakman's High Chancellor seeks Christie's throne for himself, which leads to the destruction of Murania.

Reviews attacked the mixing of science fiction and the Western (which would be soon repeated in **Ghost Patrol**, 1936), Autry's wooden performance and a dramatic structure which had Autry forever rushing back to his radio ranch to sing his songs. But the public, and especially the rural public, lapped it up. Indeed, though future story backgrounds would be less excessive, the serial established the basic Autry persona which he would maintain with only minor variations until his last film, **Last of the Pony Riders** (1953). This was what critic Jon Tuska has neatly called 'The Autry Phantasy', in which the star is essentially a creature of fable, able to overcome the worst of dangers with a soothing song, his dandified country outfit protecting him as if it were armour, a man who wears his guns with an indifference that is threatening. In short a creature of legend, disdainful of the messy realities in which most cowboy stars are enmeshed; Charles Starrett might have been the Durango Kid and William Boyd Hopalong Cassidy, but Gene Autry was Gene Autry, no less.

The serial, which was edited down and re-issued as a feature in 1940 under the title, *Men with Steel Faces*, features Autry singing 'Silver Haired Daddy of Mine', his first million seller and the song (which he co-wrote) most closely associated with him.

d Otto Brower, B. Reeves Eason *p* Nat Levine *s* John Rathmell, Armand Schaefer *c* Ernest Miller, William Nobles *lp* Gene Autry, Wheeler Oakman, Frankie Darro, Betsy King Ross, Warner Richmond, Smiley Burnette, Dorothy Christie

Powdersmoke Range (RKO) b/w 71 min
Billed as 'the Barnum and Bailey of Westerns', *Powdersmoke Range* undeniably had, to quote from RKO's poster again, 'the

'greatest round-up of Western stars ever', even if they were all B feature stars. It wasn't the first film to feature William Colt MacDonald's characters, the Three Mesquiteers – that was *Law of the 45s* (1935) – but it was its success that led to the series being taken up, though not by RKO but by Republic whose Nat Levine had earlier had the foresight to buy up the rights to the characters.

MacDonald, a one-time member of Columbia's script department, published the first of his Mesquiteer novels in 1935 with immediate success. Basically using the Dumas characters in Western settings, the novels, few of which formed the basis for any of the films, are notable for their complex plotting. In *Powdersmoke Range* Carey is Tucson Smith, Gibson Stony Brooke and Williams (who'd played Tucson in *Law of the 45s*) Lullaby Joslin. Steele is the outlaw they befriend and who in return helps them defend their 3M ranch against Hardy and his hired gunmen (including Tyler). The stilted direction of Fox and the inconsequential script by Buffington didn't match the smoothness of RKO's publicity machine which, capitalizing on the film's strong cast, secured it saturation bookings and hence substantial profits. What the film clearly demonstrated was the attractiveness of a trio of 'big' stars in a Western. Thus the series was quickly put into production by Republic as the ideal complement to the studio's John Wayne and Gene Autry series.

d Wallace Fox *p* Cliff Reid *s* Adele Buffington *c* Harold Wenstrom *lp* Harry Carey, Hoot Gibson, Guinn 'Big Boy' Williams, Bob Steele, Tom Tyler, Sam Hardy

Rainbow Valley (MON) b/w 52 min
Unusually all six featured supporting players from **Texas Terror** (1935), the previous entry in Wayne's Monogram series, re-appear here in similar roles in this routine outing. Parsons' storyline has Wayne as an undercover agent whose cover is literally blown sky high – there's a lot of dynamite-action in the film – when he tries to protect men building a road in gold-mine territory. Buffalo Bill Jnr is the gunman Wayne outdraws and Mason the prominent citizen in league with the bandits.

d Robert N. Bradbury *p* Paul Malvern *s* Lindsley Parsons *c* William Hyer *lp* John Wayne, Lucille Browne, LeRoy Mason, George Hayes, Buffalo Bill Jnr, Lafe McKee

Rainbow's End (FIRST DIVISION) b/w 60 min
With **Sunset Range** (1935), Gibson's other film for First Division, the company to which producer M.H. Hoffman sold his contract, *Rainbow's End* is the best of Gibson's Westerns of the mid-thirties. The plot is the by now hackneyed one of gangsters making inroads into the contemporary West and being foiled at the last minute by old-fashioned Western heroics. But the script is loose enough for Gibson to indulge in the humorous asides he so loved. Gale, to whom Gibson was romantically inclined in real life, is the brave little lady he rescues.

d Norman Spencer *s* Rollo Ward *c* Gilbert Warrenton *lp* Hoot Gibson, June Gale, Buddy Roosevelt, Oscar Apfel, Warner Richmond, Ada Ince

Rocky Mountain Mystery (PAR) b/w 63 min
A solid piece of entertainment, this is essentially a comic murder mystery set in the West. Sale is the comic deputy unable to discover who's murdering people at a radium mine who turns to Scott for help. A sub-plot features Fung as a Chinaman involved in a plot to gain a share in a will. Sheridan supports Scott well in one of her first starring roles.

d Charles Barton *p* Harold Hurley *s* Edward E. Paramore Jnr, Ethel Doherty *c* Archie Stout *lp* Randolph Scott, Charles (Chic) Sale, Willie Fung, Ann Sheridan, Kathleen Burke, George Marion Snr

Charles Laughton as the gentleman's gentleman stranded in the Far West in Ruggles of Red Gap.

Buck Jones gets the drop on two baddies in Stone of Silver Creek.

Ruggles of Red Gap (PAR) b/w 90 min

Laughton is the very English butler of the title who is won from his English lord by an uncouth nouveau riche rancher (Charles Ruggles) in a poker game. Transported to Red Gap, a frontier town populated by brash goldminers and the like, so lordly is Laughton's manner that he is taken for a member of the aristocracy and alternately pandered to and treated with Republican disdain. In the film's best remembered sequence, Laughton deflects this inverted snobbery with a moving (if actorly) rendition of Lincoln's Gettysburg Address which marks his commitment to democratic manners and the frontiersmen's acceptance of him.

The brunt of the story has Laughton both serving the social ambitions of Ruggles and his wife, Boland, escaping the life of service – he opens his own restaurant – and facilitating the romance of Young. What is most notable about the film, however, is the gentleness of the confrontation of East and West. Where most East/West clashes leave the characters involved imprisoned in their roles, McCarey's actors quickly shed the rigidity of their roles as they bathe in the light of his sympathetic camera. The result is a funny and genuinely moving comic Western.

The film was remade as a vehicle for Bob Hope under the title of **Fancy Pants** (1950).

d Leo McCarey *p* Arthur Hornblow Jnr *s* Walter DeLeon, Harlan Thompson *c* Alfred Gilks *lp* Charles Laughton, Mary Boland, Charles Ruggles, Zasu Pitts, Roland Young, James Burke

Rustler's Paradise (AJAX) b/w 61 min

One of the six series Westerns Carey made for producer Berke, this is a run-of-the-mill film, Carey's fine performance notwithstanding. He plays a man embittered and grown old by his desire for revenge who, when he finally catches the man responsible (Cobb's El Diablo), is given a second chance of happiness when it transpires that Cobb's daughter is really his own. Carey gives the role real depth but Fraser's rough and ready direction and the screenplay's crudity conspire against him.

d Harry Fraser *p* William Berke *s* Weston Edwards *c* Robert Cline *lp* Harry Carey, Edmund Cobb, Gertrude Messinger, Carmen Bailey, Slim Whitaker, Chief Thundercloud

The Singing Vagabond (REP) b/w 55 min

An actionful entry in the Autry series, this is the second to feature Rutherford as his leading lady. Autry is the shy hero and Burnette the bumbling side-kick who causes more problems than the villains, Richmond and the ferocious looking Sears, a feature that would become *de rigueur* as the series progressed. Here the villains prey on a wagon train and kidnap runaway Rutherford, but to no avail.

d Carl Pierson *p* Armand Schaefer *s* Oliver Drake, Betty Burbridge *c* William Nobles *lp* Gene Autry, Smiley Burnette, Ann Rutherford, Allan Sears, Warner Richmond, Frank LaRue, Champion

Stone of Silver Creek (U) b/w 61 min

An unusually witty series entry that reverses the W.S. Hart formula of a bad man transformed into a good one through the love of a good woman and a lot of sermons. Jones is the proprietor of the local gambling hall who befriends Francis' young preacher, and plays Cupid to him and Shilling. In return Francis helps solve the mystery of who's been stealing gold from Jones.

d Nick Grinde *p* Buck Jones *s* Earle Snell *c* Ted McCord *lp* Buck Jones, Noel Francis, Murdock McQuarrie, Marion Shilling, Peggy Campbell

Sunset Range (FIRST DIVISION) b/w 60 min

This is the first of a pair of Westerns Gibson made for First Division. He's the foreman who comes to the rescue of Doran whose brother is a gangster and uses her trunk as a deposit box for stolen money. Routinely made and suffering from strong competition – Western production doubled between 1934 and 1935 reaching a peak of some 150 films – the film was helped, like many other series films, by a contest tie-in with a toothpaste manufacturer.

d Ray McCarey *s* Paul Schofield *c* Gilbert Warrenton *lp* Hoot Gibson, Mary Doran, James C. Eagles, Walter McGrail, John Elliott, Eddie Lee

Texas Terror (LONE STAR) b/w 58 min

Routine fare. Wayne is the sheriff who quits peacekeeping for prospecting when he thinks he's responsible for the death of his best friend. A few coincidences later he discovers, after rescuing the dead man's sister, Brown, that Mason was responsible.

d/s Robert N. Bradbury *p* Paul Malvern *c* Archie Stout *lp* John Wayne, Lucille Brown, LeRoy Mason, George Hayes, Buffalo Bill Jnr, Yakima Canutt

Thunder Mountain (ATHERTON/FOX) b/w 68 min

This feature from Lesser's Atherton Productions sees O'Brien as a prospector in the North West who is double-crossed by a scheming saloon keeper. Fritchie is the romantic interest but director Howard's emphasis is less on romance or action (O'Brien fighting to get his claim back) than on the scenic delights of the tall timber country. Jarrett and Swift's script has loose origins in a Zane Grey story.

d David Howard *p* Sol Lesser *s* Dan Jarrett, Don Swift *c* Frank B. Good *lp* George O'Brien, Barbara Fritchie, Frances Grant, Morgan Wallace, George Hayes, Edward J. LeSaint

Toll of the Desert (COMMONDORE) b/w 60 min

A lacklustre, not to say shoddy, independent quickie Western, this stars Kohler Jnr, son of one of the genre's most menacing villains. The two occasionally appeared together and this is a film that would have benefited from this as Kohler Jnr, in the plot, is on the trail of his father, a notorious outlaw. That said, the father is played with some conviction by Williams who captures the mixed emotions he has on meeting his son and lawman neatly enough. The movie's real weakness is Kohler Jnr whose breathtaking stunts are little compensation in a script that emphasizes character and dialogue. Poor production does little to help.

d/p William Berke *s* Miller Easton *c* Robert Cline
lp Fred Kohler Jnr, Betty Mack, Roger Williams, Tom London, Earl Dwire, Ted Adams

Tumbling Tumbleweeds (REP) b/w 57 min
This, Autry's first film as a star, was also the directorial feature debut of ex-editor Kane. Equally significantly, Beebe's story gives Burnette a far more prominent role as Autry's side-kick than he has in his earlier outings with him – the duo had been together since the beginning of Autry's career as a radio cowboy. The film is transitional; the musical numbers even being integrated into the plot in a way that no later Autry film would essay. Autry is clearly still inexperienced, as both an actor and horse rider, but the concentration of songs – the film features six – and the film's willingness to abbreviate, let alone interrupt, the narrative pointed the way forward. Beebe's screenplay has Autry and Burnette catch the murderer of Autry's estranged father and so clear Browne.

d Joseph Kane *p* Nat Levine *s* Ford Beebe *c* Ernest Miller *lp* Gene Autry, Smiley Burnette, Lucille Brown, Norma Taylor, George Hayes, Edward Hearn, Champion

Under the Pampas Moon (FOX) b/w 78 min
Carrying a bolas rather than a lariat, Baxter suffered through this variant of the Cisco Kid role he'd played so well in **In Old Arizona** (1929) and in which Fox tried to typecast him throughout the thirties. Set in Argentina, it features Baxter as the gaucho who goes to Buenos Aires in search of his stolen horse. The film also features one of the earliest appearances of Hayworth under her first stage name of Rita Cansino.

d James Tinling *p* B.G. De Sylva *s* Ernest Pascal, Bradley King *c* Chester Lyons *lp* Warner Baxter, Rita Cansino, Ketti Gallian, Jack LaRue, J. Carroll Naish, John Miljan

Wagon Trail (AJAX) b/w 55 min
One of Carey's better sound Westerns courtesy of Cline's superior cinematography. Carey had been a giant of a cowboy star in the silent days but after he broke with John Ford he was never quite so successful again and, sadly, in the sound era he was not given substantial parts, with few exceptions, such as the marvellous **Law and Order** (1932). Here he's the sheriff who loses his job when his son, apprehended for a stagecoach robbery, breaks jail. Dwire is the gambler (and local outlaw chief) who takes Carey's place. The climax sees Dwire shoot himself rather than face the angry townspeople after Carey has exposed his villainy.

d Harry Fraser *p* William Berke *s* Monroe Talbot *c* Robert Cline *lp* Harry Carey, Gertrude Messinger, Earl Dwire, Edward Norris, Chuck Morrison, Chief Thundercloud

Wanderer of the Wasteland (PAR) b/w 62 min
A slow-moving remake of the 1923 Zane Grey novel. Ellis is the prospector who saves mining engineer Jagger who's on the run because he thinks he's killed his brother. Patrick is the girl Jagger loves who convinces him to submit to the law, whereupon he discovers that his brother isn't dead.

d Otho Lovering *p* Harold Hurley *s* Stuart Anthony *c* Ben Rynolds *lp* Dean Jagger, Gail Patrick, Buster Crabbe, Edward Ellis, Raymond Hatton, Fuzzy Knight

Western Courage (COL) b/w 61 min
The second and best of the seven films Bennet made with Maynard after the star quit Universal. Maynard is the foreman of a dude ranch who gets involved with Mitchell's poor little spoilt rich kid. Bond is the villain and Keefe a

Above: *Gene Autry with gun in* Tumbling Tumbleweeds.

A lobby card for Under the Pampas Moon, *which transports Warner Baxter to Argentina.*

Ken Maynard astride Tarzan reading (and probably rewriting) his lines for Western Courage *under the watchful eyes of director Spencer G. Bennet.*

fortune hunter who also courts Mitchell. Snappily directed by Bennet who was experimenting with breaking action down into single shots – Maynard punching empty air, then cut to a shot of the villain pulling his head back – the fight scenes have an added impact that make up for Darmour's penny pinching six-day shooting schedule.

d Spencer G. Bennet *p* Larry Darmour *s* Nate Gatzert *c* Herbert Kirkpatrick *lp* Ken Maynard, Geneva Mitchell, Ward Bond, Cornelius Keefe, Charles K. French

George O'Brien (centre) in the gentle comedy, Whispering Smith Speaks.

Westward Ho (REP) b/w 60 min
Begun under the banner of Monogram Pictures but released as a Republic Production after Herbert Yates had brought off the merger of Monogram, Mascot, Majestic and Liberty Pictures to form Republic, *Westward Ho* sees Wayne yet again searching for the murderers of his parents who this time have taken his younger brother captive as well. Wayne is the leader of an unlikely group who call themselves 'The Singing Riders' and McGlynn is the film's worthy villain. But it's director Bradbury and cinematographer Stout who lift an otherwise routine outing. Wayne's singing voice, as usual, was dubbed.

d Robert N. Bradbury *p* Paul Malvern *s* Lindsley Parsons, Robert Emmett (Tansey), Harry Friedman *c* Archie Stout *lp* John Wayne, Sheila Mannors, Frank McGlynn Jnr, Jack Curtis, Yakima Canutt, Bradley Metcalf

Whispering Smith Speaks (FOX) b/w 65 min
Another gentle comic Western from O'Brien. This time out he's the son of the railroad president working his way through the railway business. Ware is the girl he meets as a track walker who is unaware that the land she's offering for sale to the company is valuable. As with most of Lesser's productions the supporting cast are not Western series regulars.

d David Howard *p* Sol Lesser *s* Dan Jarrett, Don Swift *c* Frank B. Good *lp* George O'Brien, Irene Ware, Kenneth Thompson, Maude Allen, Spencer Charters, Vic Potel

Far right: The publicity poster for The Big Show.

1936

Arizona Mahoney (PAR) b/w 58 min
A failed attempt at a comedy in Western setting. Cook is the circus man – he makes his entrance towed by an elephant – and Cummings his partner. In between jokes they settle the hash of rustlers Kohler and Miljan.

d James Hogan *p* A.M. Botsford *s* Robert Yost, Stuart Anthony *c* George Clemens *lp* Larry 'Buster' Crabbe, June Martel, Robert Cummings, Joe Cook, Fred Kohler, John Miljan

The Big Show (REP) b/w 70 min
The first of Autry's series Westerns to benefit from special location shooting. Autry has two roles, a temperamental cowboy and his stuntman double who takes over from him when he misses a personal appearance at the Texas Centennial celebrations in Dallas. The comedy involves the two girls (Payne and Hughes) Autry is engaged to in his dual role, while the music is supplied by the Western Swing of the Light Crust Doughboys (the group Bob Wills had first made his name with) and the Sons of the Pioneers, amongst whose members was one Leonard Slye who later, as Roy Rogers, would be Autry's only real competition in the singing cowboy

stakes. In Autry's next film, the lacklustre *The Old Corral* (1936), Rogers and Autry would have a brief fistfight which Rogers, then called Dick Weston, would lose.

d Mack V. Wright *p* Nat Levine *s* Dorrell McGowan, Stuart McGowan *c* William Nobles, Edgar Lyon *lp* Gene Autry, Smiley Burnette, Kay Hughes, Sally Payne, William Newell, Max Terhune, Champion

The Bold Caballero (REP) 69 min
Livingston, then Republic's busiest leading man, was the sound cinema's first Zorro, the masked champion of justice here fighting against a false murder charge and unjust taxation in Old California. The film, one of Republic's earliest essays in colour production, was very successful and led to a number of sequels, the most notable of which is MGM's prestige production, **The Mark of Zorro** (1941).

d/s Wells Root *p* Nat Levine *c* Alvin Wyckoff *lp* Robert Livingston, Heather Angel, Sig Rumann, Robert Warwick, Charles Stevens, Slim Whitaker

The Boss Rider of Gun Creek (U) b/w 65 min
Selander's second Western as director with Jones, this series outing features Jones in a dual role and finally clearing his

name by impersonating his double. Unusually, Evans, as the girl in love with Jones, is aware of the impersonation. Equally strangely, Guihan's screenplay limits most of the action to the corral where Jones breaks broncos for Evans.

d Lesley Selander *p* Buck Jones *s* Frances Guihan
c Allen Thompson, Herbert Kirkpatrick *lp* Buck Jones, Muriel Evans, Harvey Clark, Lee Phelps, Tom Chatterton, Joseph Swickard

The California Mail (WB) b/w 60 min
This time out Foran is a pony-express rider who with his horse, Smokey, wins a mail contract against crooked opposition. Perry is the girl who succumbs to his warbling and Farley the villain. Compared to earlier entries in the series, the production values show a marked decline, as if Warners, having established the series, were now content to let it chug along in low gear.

d Noel Smith *p* Bryan Foy *s* Harold Buckley, Roy Chanslor *c* Fred Jackman Jnr *lp* Dick Foran, Linda Perry, Edmund Cobb, Tom Brower, James Farley, Glenn Strange

The Cattle Thief (COL) b/w 50 min
A routine series entry from Maynard, capably but not very imaginatively directed by Bennet, the action sequences apart. Maynard is the cattle detective who masquerades as a peddlar by day and a masked rider by night in a role clearly intended for juvenile audiences. Bond is the slippery villain and victim of Maynard's fists in a long fight. Mitchell is the girl.

d Spencer G. Bennet *p* Larry Darmour *s* Nate Gatzert
c Herbert Kirkpatrick *lp* Ken Maynard, Geneva Mitchell, Ward Bond, Roger Williams, Glenn Strange, Jack King

Code of the Range (COL) b/w 55 min
Another traditional series Western from Starrett who regularly got good reviews for his films which still bore the legend 'from a story by Peter B. Kyne' although they were entirely the work of writer Beebe. The plot features Starrett helping open the range to sheepmen and as a result having his mortgage foreclosed and being accused of murder by Smith and his henchman, Caven. Blake is the weak heroine.

d C.C. Coleman Jnr *p* Peter B. Kyne *s* Ford Beebe
c George Meehan *lp* Charles Starrett, Mary Blake, Albert J. Smith, Allan Caven, Edmund Cobb, George Chesebro

The Cowboy and the Kid (U) b/w 58 min
Based on a story by Jones himself, and by all accounts largely written by him, this is a misguided attempt to emphasize atmosphere and character at the expense of action, especially in view of the sentimental nature of the material which is far closer to that of the silent rather than the sound period. Jones is the cowboy trying to rear a kid, Burrud, and Revier is the overly melodramatic schoolteacher he falls for. Worth, as the villain, has little to do.

d Ray Taylor *p* Buck Jones *s* Frances Guihan *c* Allen Thompson, Herbert Kirkpatrick *lp* Buck Jones, Billy Burrud, Dorothy Revier, Harry Worth, Lafe McKee, Bob McKenzie

Daniel Boone (RKO) b/w 77 min
For this, the first of O'Brien's series of Westerns for RKO, Hirliman, who'd taken over the production of O'Brien's features from Sol Lesser, cut down on the comedy and gave his star a bigger budget and better script than he had previously. Carradine, in a similar role to that he'd later play in **Drums Along the Mohawk** (1939), is typically oily as the trader selling rifles to the Indians. But it is O'Brien, at his muscular best, in the role of the scout leading a band of settlers to Kentucky in 1775 and then masterminding their

defence of the settlement against an Indian attack, who is the picture's undisputed star.

d David Howard *p* George A. Hirliman *s* Daniel Jarrett
c Frank Good *lp* George O'Brien, Heather Angel, John Carradine, Ralph Forbes, George Regas, Harry Cording

Desert Gold (PAR) b/w 58 min
This is the only sound version of Zane Grey's much-filmed melodramatic novel. Hunt has the role of the girl who is kidnapped by bandits, rescued by an Indian (Crabbe), survives a sandstorm and is finally rescued by her fiancé, Keene. Though it is a quickie, using stock footage from the 1926 silent version, the sturdy cast and Hogan's action-packed direction result in an above-average supporting feature.

d James Hogan *p* Harold Hurley *s* Stuart Anthony, Robert Yost *c* George Clemens *lp* Buster Crabbe, Robert Cummings, Marsha Hunt, Tom Keene, Leif Erickson, Raymond Hatton

Desert Phantom
(SUPREME/WILLIAM STEINER) b/w 60 min
A pleasant actioner. Hackett and King are the villains, this time out to cheat Mannors of her ranch until mysterious stranger Brown appears to romance and defend her. As usual Brown dominated the movie which was a remake of Harry Carey's **The Night Rider** (1932). Luby's direction is surprisingly loose for an ex-editor.

Above: Marion Weldon as the much threatened heroine of Dodge City Trail.

George O'Brien declares his love for Heather Angel in Daniel Boone.

Top: *Benny Baker as the Eastern ranch owner in* Drift Fence.

d S. Roy Luby   *p* A.W. Hackel   *s* Earle Snell   *c* Bert Longenecker   *lp* Johnny Mack Brown, Sheila Mannors, Ted Adams, Karl Hackett, Charles King, Hal Price

Dodge City Trail (COL) b/w 62 min

The first of Starrett's series Westerns to feature musical interludes (from Grayson), *Dodge City Trail* also had a bigger budget and longer running time than usual. The plot has Starrett rescue Weldon from kidnappers only to discover that the gangleader, Hicks, is her father and his prospective father-in-law. In the time-honoured tradition of B movies, Hicks dies, after his reformation to pay for his past sins.

d C.C. Coleman Jnr   *p* Peter B. Kyne   *s* Harold Shumate   *c* George Cooper   *lp* Charles Starrett, Donald Grayson, Marion Weldon, Russell Hicks, Si Jenks, Al Bridge

Drift Fence (PAR) b/w 56 min

Another of Paramount's superior economy Zane Grey adaptations, this stars Keene as the veteran wrangler who helps Easterner Baker first run the ranch he inherits and then defend it against cattle baron, Andrews. Crabbe, soon to be shot to fame as Flash Gordon, has a small role as a vacillating young rancher. A mark of the film's success is the good location photography and an unusual lack of stock footage.

d Otho Lovering   *p* Harold Hurley   *s* Robert Yost, Stuart Anthony   *c* Virgil Miller   *lp* Larry 'Buster' Crabbe, Katherine De Mille, Tom Keene, Benny Baker, Leif Erickson, Stanley Andrews

The Emperor of California aka Der Kaiser von Kalifornien

(TOBIS-ROTA/LUIS TRENKER FILM; GER)   b/w   97 min

Unlike James Cruze's version of the complicated story of Johann Sutter, **Sutter's Gold** (1936), which at least is fairly accurate, Trenker's film is a lengthy exercise in wish-fulfilment. Thus, the debates as to whether Sutter (played by Trenker himself) was a benign or despotic figure are omitted from the film and he is treated as a tragic hero whose dreams of empire are shattered by the rough democracy of the Forty Niners as they literally trample his agrarian hopes underfoot in their (illegal) search for gold. The film's nationalist strain made it a great success in Germany, which in turn sparked off a series of similar Westerns, **Sergeant Berry** (1938), *Gold in New Frisco* (1939), both of which, strangely, had titles in English, and, most importantly, **Water for Canitoga**, originally *Wasser für Canitoga* (1939).

Guinn Williams (left) and Jack Holt admire Louise Henry in End of the Trail.

Below: Mob rule in Luis Trenker's The Emperor of California, *the first significant European Western.*

d/p/s Luis Trenker   *c* Albert Benitz, Heinz von Jaworsky   *lp* Luis Trenker, Viktoria von Ballasko, Else Aulinger, Bernhard Minetti, Paul Verhoeven, Walter Franck

End of the Trail (COL) b/w 70 min

Set against the background of returning soldiers from the Spanish-American war, this is an unusually thoughtful series Western. Holt is the ne'er-do-well who can't find a job on his discharge and turns (briefly) to rustling. Williams is his boyhood friend forced to go after him when Holt avenges the death of his loved one's (Henry's) brother. It is directed by Kenton, better known for his work with Sennett and Abbott and Costello, who also takes the part of President Roosevelt in the Cuban war sequence. Holt and Williams perform a bizarre duet to comic effect, but it is the sombre tone of the film's end, with Holt walking to the gallows leaving his best friend and his girlfriend behind, both heartbroken, that is most memorable.

d Erle C. Kenton   *p* Irving Briskin   *s* Harold Shumate   *c* John Stumar   *lp* Jack Holt, Guinn Williams, Louise Henry, Douglass Dumbrille, George McKay, Gene Morgan

Fast Bullets (RELIABLE) b/w 57 min

A surprisingly elegant-looking piece of trash, courtesy of Goodfriend's cinematography and Gordon and Krusada's clumsy screenplay. Essentially a mobster-on-the-range pic, it features Tyler as the Ranger in search of Bridge's band of contraband runners with Lease (added to the cast on the principle that two mini stars are better than one when script and production values are slimmer than slim) as the young Ranger who wins his spurs. Nearing is the girl they rescue. The best bit in the film is the sequence where the Rangers use dummies on horseback to decoy the outlaws.

d Henri Samuels (Harry S. Webb) *p* Bernard B. Ray
s Carl Krusada, Rose Gordon *c* Pliny Goodfriend
lp Tom Tyler, Rex Lease, Al Bridge, Margaret Nearing,
Slim Whitaker, Charles King

Ghost Patrol (PURITAN) b/w 60 min
The most interesting, if not the best, of the ten Westerns
McCoy made for Puritan Pictures for $4,000 a film, *Ghost
Patrol* is a science-fiction Western. Heavily influenced by the
success of **The Phantom Empire** (1935), it is based on an
original story by Mascot script editor, Wyndham Gittens.
Ingraham is the inventor of a super ray that causes internal
combustion engines to stop working. He is held captive by
villains Miller and Oakman who use the invention to bring
down mail planes with typical lack of imagination. McCoy is
the G Man, equally at home behind the controls of a plane as
in the saddle of a horse, who investigates the 'crashes' and
brings the villains to justice. The direction, by the prolific
Newfield, is efficient, and the science fiction elements seem
no more out of place in the Western than Roy Rogers' jeeps.

d Sam Newfield *p* Sigmund Neufeld, Leslie Simmonds
s Wyndham Gittens *c* Jack Greenhalgh *lp* Tim McCoy,
Claudia Dell, Lloyd Ingraham, Walter Miller, Wheeler
Oakman, Dick Curtis

Ghost Town (COMMONDORE) b/w 60 min
Carey gives his usual dignified performance but neither
Fraser's badly-paced direction nor Edwards' screenplay give
him much to work with. The plot has him arrested for the
murder of an old friend and breaking out of jail to prove his
innocence.

d Harry Fraser *p* William Berke *s* Weston Edwards
c Robert Cline *lp* Harry Carey, Ruth Findlay, Jane
Novak, David Sharpe, Lee Shumway, Earl Dwire

The Glory Trail (CRESCENT) b/w 65 min
A routine Keene entry, let down by poor playing from the
supporting actors, especially Barclay as the heroine. Keene is
the scout who helps protect a government roadbuilding team
from Indian attacks. Long is the histrionic villain of the piece.

d Lynn Shores *p* E.B. Derr *s* John T. Neville *c* Arthur
Martinelli *lp* Tom Keene, Joan Barclay, Walter Long,
James Bush, E.H. Calvert, Frank Melton

Heart of the West (PAR) b/w 60 min
Hoppy and Ellison help restore Gabriel's ranch to its former
glory and put paid to Blackmer's rustling in this superior
series entry. The well-staged climax sees Hoppy divert a herd
of stampeding cattle with carefully positioned charges of
dynamite.

d Howard Bretherton *p* Harry Sherman *s* Doris Schroeder
c Archie Stout *lp* William Boyd, Jimmy Ellison,
George Hayes, Lynn Gabriel, Sidney Blackmer, Fred Kohler

Hopalong Cassidy Returns (PAR) b/w 71 min
The first of the series to be directed by Watt who for a long
time had been Lewis Milestone's assistant and who gives the
film an edge of violence that borders on the sadistic with its
opening showing an invalid crashing to his doom bound and
gagged. The film also introduced Morris who would soon
become Morris Ankrum and be one of Boyd's most regular
opponents. The end is almost worthy of Sam Fuller, so
powerful is it, with Brent, the dance-hall operator and brain
behind the outlaw gang, being gunned down by her henchman Morris, who in turn is cold-bloodedly shot by Boyd at
point blank range, not just once but twice.

d Nate Watt *p* Harry Sherman *s* Harrison Jacobs
c Archie Stout *lp* William Boyd, George Hayes, Evelyn
Brent, Stephen Morris (Morris Ankrum), Gail Sheridan,
Grant Richards

Idaho Kid (COLONY) b/w 69 min
Bell's good looks notwithstanding, this is a dismal outing
marred by cheap production values and shoddy direction
from Hill. The storyline has Bell trying to get his feuding
father and foster father to make peace with each other.
However, Bell's limited thespian abilities, especially when
compared to Dwire's growling presence, and Hill's undramatic handling of the material make a nonsense of Plympton's
script.

d Robert Hill *p* Arthur Alexander *s* George Plympton
c Robert Cline *lp* Rex Bell, Marion Shilling, David Sharpe,
Earl Dwire, Lane Chandler, Charles King

King of the Pecos (REP) b/w 54 min
One of the best of the many B Westerns Wayne made for
Republic. The plot once again has Wayne seeking revenge for
the murder of his parents, with the twist that this time he
knows who did it – Kendall, now the ruler of a million-acre
empire. Wayne is a law student who first tries to stop Kendall
from rustling cattle by legal means but finally has to form the
local ranchers into a vigilante group and take the law into his
own hands. Kane's fast-paced direction and Marta's fine
cinematography make the budget seem far bigger than it was.
The editor is Joseph H. Lewis, just beginning his two year
stay with Republic as editor and second unit director. He was

Far left: *Tom Tyler
menaced by Al Bridge
and cronies in* Fast
Bullets.

*Randolph Scott as
Hawkeye the white
hunter in one of the
many versions of James
Fenimore Cooper's
classic* The Last of the
Mohicans.

later to become a major B director with films like **The Halliday Brand** (1956) and **Terror in a Texas Town** (1958).

d Joseph Kane *p* Paul Malvern *s* Bernard McConville, Dorrell McGowan, Stuart McGowan *c* Jack Marta
lp John Wayne, Muriel Evans, Cy Kendall, Jack Clifford, Frank Glendon, Yakima Canutt

King of the Royal Mounted
(FOX) b/w 70(61) min

After George O'Brien left producer Lesser for George Hirliman and RKO, Lesser remained based at Fox turning out Westerns styled for, if not starring, O'Brien. *King of the Royal Mounted* is a case in point. Kent in the title role protects Keith when she claims the mine left her by her father. McGlynn is the crooked lawyer out to cheat her. The character of Sergeant King, which was later to spawn two William Witney directed serials, *King of the Royal Mounted* (1940) and **King of the Mounties** (1942), is based on the comic strip creation that in turn has its origins in a Zane Grey story.

d Howard Bretherton *p* Sol Lesser *s* Earle Snell
c Herman Neumann *lp* Robert Kent, Rosalind Keith, Jack Luden, Alan Dinehart, Frank McGlynn, Grady Sutton

Last of the Mohicans (UA) b/w 91 min

A robust version of Fenimore Cooper's classic novel. Scott, as amiable as ever, is Hawkeye the white hunter and Barrat his faithful Indian guide, Chingachgook. Set at the time of the French-Indian Wars, the plot revolves around sisters Barnes and Angel who are in love respectively with Scott and Reed's Indian brave, Uncas.

Director Seitz was responsible for the 1924 serial *Leatherstocking* which was a conflation of material from *Last of the Mohicans* and *The Deerslayer*.

Columbia produced an inferior remake of the film under the title of *Last of the Redmen* in 1947 starring Jon Hall and Buster Crabbe.

d George B. Seitz *p* Edward Small *s* Philip Dunne, John Balderston, Paul Perez, Daniel Moore *c* Robert Planck
lp Randolph Scott, Binnie Barnes, Heather Angel, Robert Barrat, Bruce Cabot, Philip Reed

The Last Outlaw (RKO) b/w 62 min

This marvellous B feature is loosely based on John Ford's screenplay for the 1919 two-reeler he made for Universal. Carey, in the role originally played by Gibson, is the ageing outlaw – called 'Pop' by his friends to their amusement and his chagrin – who, on his release from jail, is confronted by the evils of civilization, in this case, racketeers on the range. Gibson and hoodlum Tyler vie for the affections of Carey's daughter, Callahan. Cabanne's easy-going direction and Carey's evident delight in the part of the leathery but lovable old rascal combine to produce what is probably Carey's finest sound picture. Singing cowboy Fred Scott provides the musical interludes.

Ford planned to remake the story yet again with Carey once more in the lead but Carey died in 1947 before the project got underway.

d Christy Cabanne *p* Robert Sisk *s* John Twist, Jack Townley *c* Jack MacKenzie *lp* Harry Carey, Hoot Gibson, Tom Tyler, Margaret Callahan, Frank Jenks, Fred Scott

Law and Lead (COLONY) b/w 60 min

Bell, probably still better known for his whirlwind courtship and marriage to 'It' girl Clara Bow, was one of the most active of Westerns stars in the early thirties until the rise and rise of the singing cowboy curtailed his career. This outing sees him confronting a masked bandit who's masquerading as a reformed outlaw. Wood, daughter of the villain, Dwire, is the girl.

d Robert Hill *p* Arthur Alexander, Max Alexander
s Basil Dickey *lp* Rex Bell, Harley Wood, Wally Wales, Earl Dwire, Lane Chandler, Karl Hackett

Harry Carey (second from right) surveys an overdressed Hoot Gibson in the dry comedy The Last Outlaw.

The Lawless Nineties (REP) b/w 55 min

This was the first of a trio of Wayne Westerns for Republic to be directed by Kane. All the films were made on location at Lone Pine. Wayne is a government agent sent to Wyoming to ensure that there is no corruption during the referendum for affiliation with the Union and for statehood. Woods is the leading citizen who is also the leader of the terrorists who are trying to keep Wyoming out of the Union. Hayes, minus his beard, is the pompous editor and Rutherford his comely daughter. Kane's direction is surprisingly tame.

d Joseph Kane *p* Paul Malvern *s* Joseph Poland
c William Nobles *lp* John Wayne, Ann Rutherford, George Hayes, Harry Woods, Lane Chandler, Charles King

The Lonely Trail (REP) b/w 58 min

A routine B Western. Wayne is the Northerner appointed by the Governor of Texas to clear the State of corrupt carpetbaggers who has to overcome prejudice against him and opposition from Kendall. Rutherford is the girl he romances.

d Joseph Kane *p* Nat Levine *s* Bernard McConville, Jack Natteford *c* William Nobles *lp* John Wayne, Ann Rutherford, Cy Kendall, Bob Kortman, Fred Toones, Yakima Canutt

The Mysterious Avenger (COL) b/w 53 min

This is the second of Starrett's long-running series Westerns for Columbia, and, like the first in the series, **Gallant Defender** (1935), it is a traditional, safe film with the added box-office bonus of the name of Peter B. Kyne (one of the few

Charles Starrett and Joan Perry in The Mysterious Avenger.

Below: *Jean Arthur as Calamity Jane and John Miljan as General Custer in De Mille's epic* The Plainsman.

'Western' writers to mean anything to cinema audiences) as the ostensible source of Beebe's script. Starrett is the Texas Ranger called in to investigate rustling which one cattleman claims is being masterminded by his (Starrett's) father. Needless to say, both ranchers, McKee and LeSaint are innocent and the villain is the dependable Oakman.

d David Selman *p* Harry Decker *s* Ford Beebe *c* George Meehan *lp* Charles Starrett, Joan Perry, Wheeler Oakman, Edward J. LeSaint, Lafe McKee, Hal Price

The Oregon Trail (REP) b/w 59 min
A Republic quickie, *The Oregon Trail* was a virtual remake of **The Big Trail** (1930), the ill-fated film that gave Wayne his first starring role. Once more Wayne opens up the frontier and seeks the men who murdered his father. Rutherford is the romantic interest and Canutt, unusually present as a featured player, provides the stunts. After a couple more Republic quickie Westerns, Wayne signed up with producer Trem Carr to make six non-Westerns for Universal. The move was not a success – in great part because the films were even quicker than the Republic quickies Wayne was used to churning out – and within a couple of years Wayne was back at Republic.

d Scott Pembroke *p* Paul Malvern *s* Jack Natteford, Lindsley Parsons, Robert Emmett *c* Gus Peterson *lp* John Wayne, Ann Rutherford, Yakima Canutt, Frank Rice, Fern Emmett, Jack Rutherford

Phantom Patrol (AMBASSADOR) b/w 60 min
One of the worst of Maynard's short-lived series of Mountie films for producer Conn. The only wrinkle of interest is the bizarre plot which has Fix's villain impersonating an American detective-story writer at one point. Barclay is the dainty heroine rescued by Maynard.

d Charles Hutchison *p* Maurice Conn *s* Stephen Norris *c* Arthur Reed *lp* Kermit Maynard, Joan Barclay, Dick Curtis, Paul Fix, Harry Worth, George Cleveland

The Plainsman (PAR) b/w 115(113) min
Conceived and executed with all the brio typical of a De Mille epic – all the 64 pistols used in the film came from his personal collection – *The Plainsman*, for all its attention to petty historical detail – De Mille was insistent that the phrase 'Go West, young man' be correctly attributed to John B. Searle, the editor of *The Terra Haute Express* – plays fast and loose with history. Cooper is the austere Hickok, Ellison (a regular in the Hopalong Cassidy series, loaned to De Mille by 'Pops' Sherman) a boyish Buffalo Bill, Arthur a breezy Calamity Jane and Miljan a heroic Custer to whose defence all three come. Bickford is the smooth gun running villain. De Mille's well-practised abilities in handling big budgets, big casts and

big stories overcame the doggedly domestic drama of Cooper and Arthur's relationship. Slow moving and overly romantic by modern standards in its depiction of Westward expansion, *The Plainsman* remains an entertaining spectacle.

In 1966, Universal remade the movie as a vastly inferior telefilm.

d/p Cecil B. De Mille *s* Waldemar Young, Harold Lamb, Lynn Riggs *c* Victor Milner, George Robinson *lp* Gary Cooper, Jean Arthur, James Ellison, Charles Bickford, Porter Hall, John Miljan

Ramona (FOX) 90 min
A disappointing version of Helen Hunt Jackson's much-filmed novel. Young is the half breed who deserts her fiancé Taylor for Indian Chief's son Ameche and then suffers the prejudices of white homesteaders. Carradine is the farmer who kills Ameche when he 'borrows' a horse to ride for help for his sick daughter. King gave the project his customary religious feel but Trotti's insipid script and the casting of sophisticate Young as a plain Indian girl and Ameche as an Indian brave were too much to overcome. As so often in new versions of silent movies, the material needed drastically reshaping rather than simply remaking.

d Henry King *p* Sol M. Wurtzel *s* Lamar Trotti *c* William Skall, Chester Lyons *lp* Loretta Young, Don Ameche, Kent Taylor, John Carradine, Jane Darwell

Rebellion (CRESCENT) b/w 60 min
Featuring a rare screen appearance of President Zachary Taylor (Allan Cavan) who sends Keene to California to protect set-upon Mexicans after he's listened to the pleas made by Cansino on their behalf, this is a routine series entry. Keene does battle with the landgrabbing outlaws, wins Cansino and enough Mexican votes to be elected the first Governor of California.

d Lynn Shores *p* E.B. Derr *s* John T. Neville *c* Arthur Martinelli *lp* Tom Keene, Rita Cansino (Hayworth), Allan Cavan, Duncan Renaldo, William Royle, Jack Ingram

Red River Valley (REP) b/w 60 min
The fifth of Autry's series Westerns for Republic, this was made before the 'Autry Phantasy' had solidified and his films had become more and more inflexible. Chesebro and King are the villains out to stop the construction of a dam intended to alleviate a drought-parched valley. Autry, working under-cover as a ditch digger, foils them despite considerable 'assistance' from Burnette. The fights are still realistic and

Autry's singing the source of many a gibe from the villains, such as Chesebro's 'Sing your way out of that, ditch digger' as he holds him in an armlock before succumbing to Autry's persuasive fists.

d/p B. Reeves Eason   *s* Stuart McGowan, Dorrell McGowan
c William Nobles   *lp* Gene Autry, Smiley Burnette,
Frances Grant, George Chesebro, Charles King, Champion

Rhythm on the Range   (PAR) b/w 87 min

An indication of the growing popularity of the musical Western series, *Rhythm on the Range* is a big budget musical comedy of a Western. Crosby is the unlikely hired hand, singing bulls to sleep on the prairie and rescuing the boss's niece, Farmer, from bandits. Raye (in her first screen appearance) and Burns provide the hillbilly comedy relief.

Amongst the Sons of the Pioneers who appear in the film's big production number, 'I'm an old Cowhand', was one Len Slye, soon to become Dick Weston and thereafter achieve stardom as Roy Rogers.

Taurog subsequently reworked the film as a Dean Martin/ Jerry Lewis vehicle, **Pardners** (1956).

d Norman Taurog   *p* Benjamin Glazer   *s* John C. Moffit,
Sidney Salkow, Walter de Leon, Francis Martin   *c* Karl
Struss   *lp* Bing Crosby, Frances Farmer, Martha Raye, Bob
Burns, Samuel Hinds, George E. Stone

Roarin' Lead   (REP) b/w 57 min

A strangely pacifist Three Mesquiteers outing with flesh wounds and prison sentences rather than death, the title notwithstanding. Possibly because of this the film is decidedly routine. In between sorting out rustlers Chesebro and Hooper, Livingston romances one-time model Maple, leaving Corrigan and Terhune with little to do.

d Mack V. Wright, Sam Newfield   *p* Nat Levine   *s* Oliver
Drake, Jack Natteford   *c* William Nobles   *lp* Bob
Livingston, Ray Corrigan, Max Terhune, Christine Maple,
George Chesebro, Hooper Atchley

Robin Hood of El Dorado   (MGM) b/w 86 min

Co-written by Wellman and opera singer turned character actor Calleia from Walter Burns' biography of the Mexican bandit Joaquin Murrieta (Baxter), *Robin Hood of El Dorado*, as its title suggests, is a romantic but still powerful indictment of American injustice south of the Border. Baxter is the peon who refuses to quit his land when ordered to do so at the point of a gun by some men. He hunts down the men who then kill his wife, Margo, and so becomes a real life Zorro figure, harrying illegal American settlers in Southern California.

Made immediately before *A Star is Born* (1937) it has much of the bitter tone of that film.

d/co-s William A. Wellman   *p* John W. Considine Jnr
co-s Joseph Calleia, Malvin Levy   *c* Chester Lyons
lp Warner Baxter, Ann Loring, Bruce Cabot, J. Carrol Naish,
Edgar Kennedy, Margo

Far left: Bing Crosby and Frances Farmer in Rhythm on the Range, *an indication of the ever-growing popularity of the musical Western.*

Warner Baxter and members of his outlaw band are besieged by an avenging posse in William Wellman's biography of Joaquin Murrieta, Robin Hood of El Dorado.

Rose Marie *aka* **Indian Love Call** (MGM) b/w 113 min
The most commercially successful film by Eddy and MacDonald, *Rose Marie* was the team's second outing. Eddy is the mountie who gets his man and a woman, MacDonald. She is the opera-star sister of Stewart, the man Eddy's trailing. A mark of the film's popularity was that 'Indian Love Song', from the movie, was one of the few records to sell a million copies in the thirties. Van Dyke filmed mostly on location, which was highly unusual for a light operetta, thus giving the film the feel of a musical Western rather than an outdoor melodrama.

In 1954 Mervyn LeRoy made a stodgy, inferior remake with Ann Blyth and Howard Keel in the MacDonald and Eddy roles.

d W.S. Van Dyke   *p* Hunt Stromberg   *s* Frances Goodrich, Albert Hackett, Alice Duer Miller   *c* William Daniels
lp Jeanette MacDonald, Nelson Eddy, James Stewart, Alan Mowbray, David Niven, Allan Jones

Song of the Gringo (GRAND NATIONAL) b/w 62 min
The first Western to star Ritter, college graduate and historian who, ironically, of the three significant singing cowboys – the others being Gene Autry and Roy Rogers – most looked the part. Moreover his voice still stood for the Western long after his starring days were over, as he demonstrated when he recorded the theme song for **High Noon** (1952). Production values are minimal, but, with assistance from Knight, Ritter proved to be an immediate hit with audiences, as much for his fisticuffs as for his singing. He is the deputy sheriff on the trail of claim jumpers. As a bizarre touch ex-train robber Jennings, who also had a hand in the script and in teaching Ritter to draw in the course of the production, is a featured player as a judge.

d/co-s John P. McCarthy   *p* Edward Finney   *co-s* Robert Emmett (Tansey), Al Jennings   *c* Gus Peterson   *lp* Tex Ritter, Monte Blue, Fuzzy Knight, Joan Woodbury, Al Jennings, Warner Richmond

Song of the Saddle (WB) b/w 58 min
Foran's second Western for Warners and the first to see him billed as 'The Singing Kid'. The plot, as one would expect of a storyline that had already done service for Ken Maynard and John Wayne in earlier films, is predictable and formula ridden – a man on the trail of his father's murderers – but King's pacy direction, the strong cast and Foran's growing confidence in his horsemanship result in a better than average musical Western.

d Louis King   *p* Bryan Foy   *s* William Jacobs   *c* Dan Clark   *lp* Dick Foran, Alma Lloyd, Charles Middleton, Addison Richards, Eddie Shubert, Monte Montague

Sundown Saunders
(SUPREME/WILLIAM STEINER) b/w 59 min
Written and directed by Steele's father, Bradbury, this is one of the 52 Westerns Steele made for producer Hackel in less than five years. Steele wins a ranch in a horse race only to have Cassidy try and steal it from him. Dwire is the sheriff and Cotter the saccharine heroine. Bradbury's script, which has a few unusual twists, is far superior to his cost-paring direction.

d/s Robert N. Bradbury   *p* A.W. Hackel   *c* Bert Longenecker   *lp* Bob Steele, Catherine Cotter, Earl Dwire, Ed Cassidy, Milburn Morante, Charles King

Sunset of Power (U) b/w 66 min
Another of Jones' attempts at a more mature version of the series Western. Accordingly, the plot is more realistic (until the end) and the characters more rounded than the cyphers that inhabit most series films. Middleton is the hard cattleman determined that his daughter, Dix, will follow in his footsteps. In imitation of **Hop-a-Long Cassidy** (1935) – which, fantastical though it might seem nowadays, was far more realistic than most contemporary series Westerns – Jones has King and Corbett as his side-kicks, thus forming one of the Western's first, and most short-lived, trios.

d Ray Taylor   *p* Buck Jones   *s* Earle Snell   *c* Allen Thompson, Herbert Kirkpatrick   *lp* Buck Jones, Dorothy Dix, Charles Middleton, Charles King, Ben Corbett

Sutter's Gold (U) b/w 94 min
Originally to have been directed by Serge Eisenstein, this is the biography of John Sutter, the immigrant for whom the discovery of gold on his Californian land in 1849 marked the beginning of his downfall. The film cost Carl Laemmle the ownership of Universal when its spiralling costs forced him to sell his interests in the company. Howard Hawks briefly took over from Eisenstein, but Cruze, a director obviously happier in the silent cinema, shot the majority of the film's footage.

Arnold is more than adequate as the man whose dreams of a Californian empire are shattered by the mob fury that follows the 1849 gold rush, but the irredeemably sentimental script, complete with Barnes as a Russian Countess and object of Arnold's affections, the absence of star names and Cruze's intense direction, spelt disaster at the box office. Only the immense profits from *Showboat* (1936) saved Universal from bankruptcy.

d James Cruze *p* Edmund Grainger *s* Jack Kirkland, Walter Woods, George O'Neil *c* George Robinson
lp Edward Arnold, Lee Tracy, Binnie Barnes, Katherine Alexander, Harry Carey, Addison Richards

The Texas Rangers (PAR) b/w 95 min
Released in the year of Texas' Centennial celebrations, *The Texas Rangers* is a lively, if spotty Western. MacMurray and Oakie are the train robbers who join the Rangers and Nolan their onetime outlaw friend who becomes a famous bandit who they are sent after. Stevens' script is reputedly based on incidents drawn from the official records of the Rangers. But the comings and goings of the trio, with MacMurray refusing to go after Nolan, Oakie going and being shot, thus goading MacMurray into action at last, and so winning the hand of Parker, smack of fiction not fact, so smoothly do they proceed. Vidor's direction, especially of the action sequences, is as efficient as ever.

A routine sequel followed in 1940, **Texas Rangers Ride Again.**

d/p King Vidor *s* Louis Stevens *c* Edward Cronjager
lp Fred MacMurray, Jackie Oakie, Jean Parker, Lloyd Nolan, George Hayes, Fred Kohler

Three Godfathers *aka* **Miracle in the Sand**
(MGM) b/w 82 min
The second sound version of Peter B. Kyne's novel – the first was **Hell's Heroes** (1930) – *Three Godfathers* was directed by Boleslawski, the Polish born director better known for romantic costume dramas, such as *The Garden of Allah* (1936). Morris, Brennan and Stone are the three bank robbers who escape into the desert only to find an infant and its dying mother who they rescue at the cost of their freedom. The parable of the Three Wise Men behind Kyne's story – the town whose bank they rob is called New Jerusalem – is intensified by Boleslawski's melodramatic direction and Ruttenberg's fine camerawork.

d Richard Boleslawski *p* Joseph L. Mankevicz *s* Edward E. Paramore Jnr, Manuel Seff *c* Joseph Ruttenberg
lp Chester Morris, Lewis Stone, Walter Brennan, Robert Livingston, Sidney Toler, Victor Potel

Trail Dust (PAR) b/w 77 min
Hoppy leads a cattle drive and fights off would-be rustler Morris in this series entry which is fast paced despite its length. Ellison and Shipman provide the romance and Hayes the comedy, but Stout's superb outdoor cinematography is most impressive.

d Nate Watt *p* Harry Sherman *s* Al Martin *c* Archie Stout *lp* William Boyd, Jimmy Ellison, George Hayes, Gwynne Shipman, Stephen Morris, Al St John

The Trail of the Lonesome Pine (PAR) 102 min
The first outdoor film to be shot in the (then) new three colour Technicolor process. The resulting bright, crude, postcard images were attacked for being unrealistic and praised for their realistic qualities at one and the same time. The story, originally filmed by Cecil B. De Mille in 1916, is sentimental and slow moving. MacMurray is the railway engineer, Fonda and Bruce the feuding Blue Ridge Mountaineers whose lives are drastically changed by the coming of the railroad and Sidney the heroine.

The film made a star of Fonda who subsequently became the model for Al Capp's L'il Abner cartoon character.

d Henry Hathaway *p* Walter Wanger *s* Horace McCoy, Grover Jones, Harvey Thew *c* Howard Green *lp* Fred MacMurray, Henry Fonda, Sylvia Sidney, Nigel Bruce, Fuzzy Knight, Fred Stone

Trailin' West *aka* **On Secret Service** (WB) b/w 56 min
A routine Foran series entry. He's the singing secret agent sent by Lincoln to track down a band of renegades. Unlike other series, Foran's has no special feel to it. In great part this is because, though all the films were supervised by Foy and had a fairly firm stable of on-camera faces, director and writer changed with virtually every entry. Thus Smith was Foran's fourth director in five films.

d Noel Smith *p* Bryan Foy *s* Anthony Coldeway
c Sidney Hickox, Ted McCord *lp* Dick Foran, Paula Stone, Gordon (Bill) Elliott, Addison Richards, Eddie Shubert, Robert Barratt

The Traitor (PURITAN) b/w 56 min
McCoy's last film for Puritan and his last sortie in front of the cameras before a break of over a year due to a lawsuit, *The*

Above: Jackie Oakie (left) and Fred MacMurray (right) as the outlaws who join The Texas Rangers.

Walter Brennan, Chester Morris and Lewis Stone (left to right) with the infant they rescue at the cost of their own freedom in the most romantic version of Peter B. Kynes' much filmed story, Three Godfathers.

Traitor is routine fodder. The script has McCoy going undercover as a disgraced Texas Ranger, getting his man, Glendon, and then having to prove he was working undercover when the only man who knows is shot. Slow paced.

d Sam Newfield *p* Sigmund Neufeld, Leslie Simmonds
s Joseph O'Donnell *c* Jack Greenhalgh *lp* Tim McCoy,
Frances Grant, Wally Wales, J. Frank Glendon, Karl
Hackett, Jack Rockwell

Treachery Rides the Range (WB) b/w 56 min

One of the best of Foran's series of twelve Westerns for Warners. Jacobs' script has him on the trail of a couple of Buffalo hunters who are fermenting Indian troubles. Blue is the kindly Cavalry Colonel, Thorpe (whose tragic story was to be later filmed by Michael Curtiz: *Jim Thorpe, All-American*, 1951), the Indian Chief and Stone the heroine Foran romances. The songs are by Warner staff composers, M.K. Jerome and Jack Scholl.

d Frank McDonald *p* Bryan Foy *s* William Jacobs
c L.W. O'Connell *lp* Dick Foran, Paula Stone, Monte Blue,
Craig Reynolds, Jim Thorpe, Monte Montague

The Unknown Ranger (COL) b/w 57 min

The first of Allen's Texas Ranger series for Columbia, *The Unknown Ranger* sees him defeating the plans of cattle rustler Woods. The action, most of which centres on horses and includes a fight between a wild stallion and a horse, is fast and furious.

d Spencer G. Bennet *p* Larry Darmour *s* Nate Gatzert
c James S. Brown Jnr *lp* Bob Allen, Martha Tibbetts, Harry
Woods, Hal Taliaferro (Wally Wales), Robert (Buzz) Henry,
Edward Hearn

Wildcat Trooper (AMBASSADOR) b/w 60 min

The last, and one of the best, of the series of Mountie movies made by Ken Maynard's brother, Kermit, for producer Conn. Maynard's acting, as ever, is wooden but his superior riding and stunting together with Clifton's action-oriented direction give the film real pace. Bosworth is the seemingly kindly old medic who is really the evil genius of the piece, fermenting a feud between rival fur trappers so as to secure the furs for himself. Above average.

d Elmer Clifton *p* Maurice Conn *s* Joseph O'Donnell
c Arthur Reed *lp* Kermit Maynard, Hobart Bosworth,
Fuzzy Knight, Lois Wilde, Yakima Canutt, Jim Thorpe

Winds of the Wasteland (REP) b/w 57 min

The last of Wayne's first series of Westerns for RKO, *Winds of the Wasteland* saw the star re-united with Wright, the director of his earlier Warner Brothers' Westerns. A pleasant outing, it features Wayne and Chandler as the two friends who purchase a run-down stagecoach to compete for a government mail contract. Canutt is, as ever, the athletic villain out to stop them.

d Mack V. Wright *p* Nat Levine *s* Joseph Poland
c William Nobles *lp* John Wayne, Phyllis Fraser, Yakima
Canutt, Douglas Cosgrove, Lane Chandler, Bob Kortman

Yellow Dust (RKO) b/w 68 min

A flimsy Western with Dix as the innocent man accused of a series of stagecoach robberies and being forced to find the guilty men. The action is very slow, a direct result of Twist and Hume's inability to overcome their screenplay's stage origins. Stevens is the villain plotting to get Dix's gold mine and Hyams the songstress who wins Dix after rescuing his mine.

d Wallace Fox *p* Cliff Reid *s* Cyril Hume, John Twist
c Earl A. Wolcott *lp* Richard Dix, Leila Hyams, Onslow
Stevens, Andy Clyde, Ethan Laidlaw, Vic Potel

1937

Arizona Days (GRAND NATIONAL) b/w 57 min

Like many of Ritter's Grand National series Westerns this feature suffered badly from the company's minuscule budgets, generally around the $8-10,000 region. The plot has Ritter joining a travelling medicine show and foiling Taylor's nefarious plans. The direction by English, best known for his serial work with John Witney, is vigorous. The movie also includes a brief appearance from Ethelind Terry, a former musical comedy star.

d John English *p* Edward Finney *s* Sherman Lowe
c Gus Peterson *lp* Tex Ritter, Eleanor Stewart, Syd Saylor,
Ethelind Terry, William Faversham, Forrest Taylor

Arizona Gunfighter (REP) b/w 58 min

A minor series Western. Never known for his thespian skills, Steele was here required to act, rather than merely register the anger and grief supplied by Plympton's screenplay. Adams, in a role he made his own, is the outlaw turned baddie and Meehan the villain. The film was one of the last Steele made for producer Hackel.

d Sam Newfield *p* A.W. Hackel *s* George Plympton
c Robert Cline *lp* Bob Steele, Jean Carmen, Ted Adams,
Lew Meehan, Ernie Adams, Karl Hackett

The Bad Man of Brimstone (MGM) sepia 89 min

A superior Western. Beery is the outlaw who rescues his son (O'Keefe in his first major role) from a career of prizefighting. He directs his attention to the law, supports him through his studies and in the process reforms himself as well. If Beery's role is one he played many times, under the direction of Reuben he adds a dash of realism to his acting that makes the transformation more dramatic. Calleia and Stone are useful foils for the leads while Cabot makes a virile villain out of the character of Blackjack. The climax is particularly exciting with Beery, O'Keefe and company blazing away at Cabot with great glee.

Wallace Beery (centre) on the set of The Bad Man of Brimstone.

d J. Walter Reuben   *p* Harry Rapf   *s* Cyril Hume, Richard Maibaum   *c* Clyde De Vinna   *lp* Wallace Beery, Dennis O'Keefe, Joseph Calleia, Virginia Bruce, Lewis Stone, Bruce Cabot

Black Aces   (U)   b/w   59 min
This is one of the best of the films directed and produced by Jones. He's the shy, nervous cattleman taunted by everyone, especially the bandits masquerading as pillars of the community, to the consternation of heroine Linaker. But when they try to frame him for a series of murders, Jones throws off his mask of cowardice and sets about them. MacKaye and King are amongst the heavies.

d/p Buck Jones   *s* Frances Guihan   *c* Allen Thompson *lp* Buck Jones, Kay Linaker, Charles King, Bob Kortman, Fred MacKaye, William Lawrence

Blazing Sixes   (WB)   b/w   55 min
A flimsy musical Western. Foran is the government agent sent to stop a series of gold bullion robberies. He masquerades as an outlaw, joins the gang and so puts paid to Merton and his pencil thin moustache. McKinney provides the much-needed comic relief.

d Noel Smith   *p* Bryan Foy   *s* John T. Neville   *c* Ted McCord   *lp* Dick Foran, Helen Valkis, Myra McKinney, John Merton, Glenn Stange, Kenneth Harlan

Boothill Brigade   (REP)   b/w   56 min
A superior series entry, carefully constructed around its star, Brown, by Longenecker and Newfield who must have been the busiest cinematographer and director working in the Western field in 1937. Newfield keeps the dialogue to a minimum and Longenecker carefully chooses the right angles to give the fistfights the necessary realism. Plympton's screenplay has Brown protecting homesteaders from Cassidy and his men.

d Sam Newfield   *p* A.W. Hackel   *s* George Plympton *c* Bert Longenecker   *lp* Johnny Mack Brown, Claire Rochelle, Dick Curtis, Ed Cassidy, Horace Murphy, Frank LaRue

Border Phantom   (REP)   b/w   58 min
One of the best of Steele's series Westerns. Morita is the swaggering villain of the piece smuggling Chinese picture brides across the Mexican border. Ex-editor Luby reveals a sure comic touch that allows Barclay, one of the few side-kicks in B Westerns whose humour had a touch of sophistication, an opportunity to shine. Only Wood as the wooden heroine is disappointing.

d S. Roy Luby   *p* A.W. Hackel   *s* Fred Myton   *c* Jack Greenhalgh   *lp* Bob Steele, Harley Wood, Don Barclay, Karl Hackett, Miki Morita, Perry Murdock

Borderland   (PAR)   b/w   82 min
At 82 minutes this is the longest series Western ever. It also features the last appearance of Ellison as Johnny Nelson, the hothead and romantic lead of the Hopalong Cassidy series. The strong plot has Hoppy pretending to be an outlaw – and Boyd obviously enjoying himself drinking and being unkind to children! – and Morris the real outlaw pretending to be a half-wit.

d Nate Watt   *p* Harry Sherman   *s* Harrison Jacobs *c* Archie Stout   *lp* William Boyd, Jimmy Ellison, George Hayes, Karl Hackett, Stephen Morris (Morris Ankrum), George Chesebro

Born to the West *aka* **Hell Town**
(PAR)   b/w   59(50) min
Wayne's last B Western before he became a Mesquiteer, *Born to the West* is a decided cut above the series of pictures he'd

William Boyd in Borderland.

Above: *The child actor playing Bob Baker as a youngster rolling up his sleeves in preparation for battle, watched by an amused J. Farrell MacDonald, in* Courage of the West.

Dick Foran under arrest in The Devil's Saddle Legion.

just completed for Universal. He's the roving cowboy who arrives in town and promptly steals Brown's girlfriend, Hunt. However, after Wayne stops rustlers stealing Brown's cattle and Brown exposes the cardsharper who cheats Wayne of his money, the two become fast friends. The strong supporting cast includes Blue and, way down the cast list, Alan Ladd.

When the film was re-issued, to capitalize on Wayne and Ladd's subsequent success, footage of cattle drives and the like were spliced in at the beginning to make it longer.

d Charles Barton *s* Stuart Anthony, Robert Yost *c* J.D. Jennings *lp* John Wayne, Marsha Hunt, Johnny Mack Brown, Monte Blue, Syd Saylor, Earl Dwire

Boss of Lonely Valley (U) b/w 59 min
One of the worst of the 22 films Jones made for Universal. Miller and Phelps are the baddies who with fake papers obtain the property of deceased persons. Evans is the innocent and friend of Jones they try their tricks on after the death of her father. Jones and his horse Silver do their stuff, but neither Taylor's direction nor Guihan's screenplay have any wit or originality.

d Ray Taylor *p* Buck Jones *s* Frances Guihan *c* Allen Thompson, John Hickson *lp* Buck Jones, Muriel Evans, Walter Miller, Lee Phelps, Harvey Clark, Dickie Howard

The Californian *aka* The Gentleman from California
(PRINCIPAL/FOX) b/w 55 min
Cortez is the masked Robin Hood figure in this early imitation of Zorro who had debuted successfully a year earlier in Republic's **The Bold Caballero** (1936). Returning from Spain where he'd been educated, Cortez finds outlaws trying to deprive old Californian families (i.e. Spanish-Americans) of their lands immediately prior to the Civil War. With a bigger budget than most of Lesser's productions and an athletic swashbuckler in Cortez, the film is a cut above the average series Western.

d Gus Meins *p* Sol Lesser *s* Gilbert Wright, Gordon Newell *c* Harry Neumann *lp* Ricardo Cortez, Marjorie Weaver, Katherine De Mille, Nigel de Brulier, Morgan Wallace, Maurice Black

Cherokee Strip *aka* Strange Laws (WB) b/w 55 min
One of the last of Foran's series Westerns for Warners. In *Cherokee Strip* the studio began to use stock footage – here of the Oklahoma land rush – and to recycle old Ken Maynard scripts. Watson and Ward's plot has Smokey, Foran's horse, lamed by villains in an attempt to stake a claim on a particularly valuable stretch of land before the Oklahoma land rush. The movie also produced Foran's biggest ever hit record, the sentimental 'My Little Buckaroo'.

d Noel Smith *p* Bryan Foy *s* Joseph K. Watson, Luci Ward *c* Ted McCord *lp* Dick Foran, Jane Bryan, David Carlyle, Helen Valkis, Edmund Cobb, Glenn Strange

Come On Cowboys (REP) b/w 59 min
This formula ridden entry sees the Three Mesquiteers unmask a group of counterfeiters. Its circus background and Kane's direction barely distinguish it from other, equally routine, entries in the series.

d Joseph Kane *p* Sol C. Siegel *s* Betty Burbridge *c* Ernest Miller *lp* Bob Livingston, Ray Corrigan, Max Terhune, Maxine Doyle, Willie Fung, Yakima Canutt

Courage of the West (U) b/w 57 min
The first of Baker's short-lived series of musical Westerns for Universal. Baker, who was chosen over Dick Weston (soon to achieve fame as Roy Rogers) to replace Buck Jones when he quit the studio in 1937, could sing and in Lewis (here making his directorial debut) was fortunate to have a director with real visual flair. Sadly the formula ridden plots and penny pinching budgets soon put an end to the series. In this, the best entry, Baker is the child adopted by a special agent (MacDonald) who discovers that his real father (Woods) is an outlaw. Add to this a few plot complications, fine cinematography and Lewis' incisive direction and you have a superior B Western with musical interludes.

d Joseph H. Lewis *p* Paul Malvern *s* Norton S. Parker *c* Virgil Miller *lp* Bob Baker, Lois January, J. Farrell MacDonald, Fuzzy Knight, Harry Woods, Carl Stockdale

The Devil's Saddle Legion (WB) b/w 57 min
Routine fare, memorable only as choreographer Connolly's one foray into the Western. Foran is wrongfully imprisoned for the murder of his own father by a crooked sheriff. He escapes and with fellow outlaws forms a vigilante band to secure justice for all concerned. Nagel is the girl who loves him from afar.

d Bobby Connolly *p* Bryan Foy *s* Ed Earl Repp *c* Ted McCord *lp* Dick Foran, Anne Nagel, Willard Parker, Granville Owen, Carlyle Moore Jnr, Glenn Strange

Doomed at Sundown (REP) b/w 53 min
A superior Steele entry. His small stature, although it didn't impede the action in any way, made 'Battling Bob' a special favourite of juveniles. Here he plays a prankster of a son, suddenly thrust into adulthood by the death of his sheriff father. He sets out after the villains as a special deputy and soon brings in Richmond and Dwire. Hayes is, in the immortal words of *Variety*'s reviewer, 'the slightly kidnapped heroine'.

d Sam Newfield *p* A.W. Hackel *s* George Plympton
c Bert Longenecker *lp* Bob Steele, Lorraine Hayes (Laraine
Day), Warner Richmond, Earl Dwire, Dave Sharpe, Harold
Daniels

Forlorn River (PAR) b/w 56 min
In contrast to **Thunder Trail** (1937), scripted and directed by
the same team, this is a decidedly routine affair. Adapted
from the Zane Grey story of the same name, it stars Crabbe as
the daredevil hero on the trail of Stephen and his gang
responsible for the bank robbery that opens the film. Saylor is
Crabbe's perpetually hungry friend and Martel the very
wooden romantic interest. The best thing is Hallenberger's
bleak landscapes.

d Charles Barton *s* Stuart Anthony, Robert Yost *c* Harry
Hallenberger *lp* Larry 'Buster' Crabbe, June Martel,
Harvey Stephen, Syd Saylor, John Patterson, Chester
Conklin

Gambling Terror (REP) b/w 53 min
Despite poor production values which result in gaffes like the
fender of the camera car being visible at one point, this is a
better than average series Western. Brown is as nonchalant as
ever as the hero battling it out with would-be mobster Dwire
who's demanding protection money from local ranchers.

d Sam Newfield *p* A.W. Hackel *s* George Plympton, Fred
Myton *c* Bert Longenecker *lp* Johnny Mack Brown, Iris
Meredith, Charles King, Earl Dwire, Horace Murphy,
Dick Curtis

God's Country and the Man (MON) b/w 56 min
Keene is the hero, but it's King, playing a particularly nasty
villain, who steals the picture. The film also has superior
female support from Compson, as the dance-hall girl who
strikes it rich with a gold mine, and Henry, as the romantic
interest. Surprisingly, it's the action sequences, fistfights
apart, that let the movie down.

d/p R.N. Bradbury *s* Robert Emmett (Tansey) *c* Bert
Longenecker *lp* Tom Keene, Betty Compson, Charlotte
Henry, Charles King, Billy Bletcher, Eddie Parker

The Gun Ranger (REP) b/w 56 min
Despite its modern vigilante story – Steele is a Texas Ranger
who throws down his badge when the law lets a murderer off
and goes after him himself – this is a traditional series
Western. Indeed, perhaps it is most significant for featuring
no songs at a time when singing cowboys (as Steele himself
briefly and sadly became) were all the rage. Merton is the
villain out to gain control of Stewart's ranch.

d R.N. Bradbury *p* A.W. Hackel *s* George Plympton
c Bert Longenecker *lp* Bob Steele, Eleanor Stewart, John
Merton, Earl Dwire, Bud Buster, Frank Ball

Gunlords of Stirrup Basin (REP) b/w 53 min
A superior series entry. 'Battling Bob' Steele and Stanley are
the lovebirds caught in a feud between homesteaders and
cattlemen over water rights created by Hackett's shyster
lawyer. Despite the storyline, it's action rather than romance
that takes centre stage, courtesy of Newfield's uncluttered
direction.

d Sam Newfield *p* A.W. Hackel *s* George Plympton, Fred
Myton *c* Bert Longenecker *lp* Bob Steele, Louise Stanley,
Karl Hackett, Ernie Adams, Frank LaRue, Frank Ball

Gunsmoke Ranch (REP) b/w 56 min
A slow and routine Three Mesquiteers outing. Set amid the
floods of the Ohio and Mississippi Valleys in 1937, Drake's
screenplay features Harlan as a land thief and Thayer and
McKim as the juvenile leads. Oscar and Elmer, a couple of

unfunny hillbilly vaudevillians, join Terhune in providing the
comic relief. Even Corrigan and Livingston seem tired.

d Joseph Kane *p* Sol C. Siegel *s* Oliver Drake *c* Gus
Peterson *lp* Robert Livingston, Ray Corrigan, Max
Terhune, Kenneth Harlan, Julia Thayer (Jean Carmen),
Sammy McKim

Harlem on the Prairie *aka* **Bad Man of Harlem**
(ASSOCIATED FEATURES) b/w 55 min
The first Western to feature an all black cast, *Harlem on the
Prairie* stars Jeffries (a onetime vocalist with the Duke
Ellington Orchestra) as the singing cowboy. Set in modern
times, Myton's crude but effective script has Jeffries and
Harries (a weak heroine) searching for the gold hidden by her
father in his youth. Scripted and directed by veterans of the
genre, it is played entirely straight – Jeffries even rides a white
horse! – and was surprisingly successful in non-ethnic
theatres, grossing some $50,000 in its first year of distribu-
tion. Miller and Manton, an established black comic duo, do
their 'who's-a-skeered' routine in a dark cave and Sheffield is
the villain.

d Sam Newfield *p* Jed Buell *s* Fred Myton *c* William
Hyer *lp* Herbert Jeffries, F.E. Miller, Manton Morefield,
Connie Harries, Spencer Williams, Maceo Sheffield

Headin' East (COL) b/w 67 min
This superior Jones entry sees him heading for the big city
and sorting out the gangsters who have spoiled his father's
lettuce crop. The sprightly, well handled dialogue and the
witty confrontation of cowboy and gangster ways and Scott's
economic direction all contribute to making the film one of
Jones' best for some years.

d Ewing Scott *p* L.G. Leonard *s* Ethel La Blanche, Paul
Franklin *c* Allen Q. Thompson *lp* Buck Jones, Ruth
Coleman, Shemp Howard, Donald Douglas, Elaine Arden,
Earle Hodgins

*Buck Jones as the
cowboy who goes to the
big city in* Headin'
East.

Top: *Buck Jones as the stunt man in* Hollywood Round Up.

Below right: *Dick Foran 'the singing cowboy' pinioned in* Land Beyond the Law.

Below: *Ray Corrigan with Rita Hayworth in* Hit the Saddle.

Heart of the Rockies (REP) b/w 56 min
This, the first of the trio's 1937 season outings, sees the Three Mesquiteers accused of killing a bear they think has been raiding their stock. In fact Canutt and his rustlers are responsible, as becomes clear to the trio after much riding and fighting. Kane, directing the first of his Mesquiteer outings, keeps the action fast and furious.

d Joseph Kane *p* Sol C. Siegel *s* Jack Natteford, Oliver Drake *c* Jack Marta *lp* Bob Livingston, Ray Corrigan, Max Terhune, Yakima Canutt, Lynn Roberts, Hal Taliaferro (Wally Wales)

Hit the Saddle (REP) b/w 57 min
The presence of Hayworth (billed as Rita Cansino) in an early role enlivens this Three Mesquiteers outing. She is the girl who temporarily comes between Corrigan and Livingston. The strong plotline features McGowan as the boss of cattle rustlers who finally dies beneath the hooves of the killer horse he sets on Livingston. Famous stuntman (and later second unit director) Canutt is amongst the band of rustlers. The superb location photography in the Mojave desert compensates for the abundance of stock footage.

d Mack V. Wright *p* Nat Levine *s* Oliver Drake *c* Jack Marta *lp* Robert Livingston, Ray Corrigan, Max Terhune, Rita Cansino (Hayworth), Yakima Canutt, J.P. McGowan

Hollywood Round Up (COL) b/w 64 min
This is a superior Jones entry. He is the stunt stand-in for a

temperamental cowboy star (Withers) who takes a dislike to Jones when he discovers that he is romancing his leading lady, Twelvetrees. As well as revealing some of the simple camera trickery behind more common Western stunts, the film's Hollywood background makes the film appealing, especially when Hoffman and Shaff's script has Withers trying to claim the credit for foiling a bank robbery he got unintentionally involved in after Jones has sorted things out. Jones' reward, of course, is to be made the star of the cowboy series.

d Ewing Scott *p* L.G. Leonard *s* Joseph Hoffman, Monroe Shaff *c* Allen Q. Thompson *lp* Buck Jones, Helen Twelvetrees, Grant Withers, Shemp Howard, Dickie Jones, Edward Keane

Land Beyond the Law (WB) b/w 54 min
Directed with a rare gusto by Eason, this was probably the best of Foran's series outings for Warners. Woods is the rustling villain and Foran the rancher who becomes innocently involved. Eason, a serial regular and second unit director of action sequences for A features, such as *The Charge of the*

Light Brigade (1936), brings a speed and economy to the film rare in the musical Western of the time. But, though in 1937 Foran was voted fourth most popular Cowboy Star (after Gene Autry, William Boyd and Buck Jones), his days as a cowboy were limited. Rising star Morris was also featured in the movie.

d B. Reeves Eason *p* Bryan Foy *s* Luci Ward, Joseph K. Watson *c* L. W. O'Connell *lp* Dick Foran, Linda Perry, Wayne Morris, Harry Woods, Irene Franklin, Gordon Hart

Law for Tombstone (U) b/w 59 min

A minor Jones entry, notable only for being co-directed by its star. He's the special agent employed by the stagecoach line to halt a series of robberies. He quickly discovers that Twin Gun Jack (Hodgins) who is terrorizing Tombstone is responsible and with assistance from Doc Halliday (Clark) sets about restoring law and order to Tombstone.

co-d/p Buck Jones *co-d* B. Reeves Eason *s* Frances Guihan *c* Allen Thompson, John Hickson *lp* Buck Jones, Muriel Evans, Earle Hodgins, Harvey Clark, Carl Stockdale, Slim Whitaker

A Lawman Is Born (REP) b/w 58 min

A superior series Western. Brown and his regular villain, Richmond, are in fine form and director Newfield manages to get the supporting cast to do more than just chew the scenery for once. Similarly Plympton's script, though by no means particularly unusual – Brown foils rustling landgrabbers – is more realistic than normal with only the infinitely stocked guns of the hero to remind one of the movie's basic implausibilities. Meredith is the restrained heroine.

d Sam Newfield *p* A.W. Hackel *s* George Plympton *c* Bert Longenecker *lp* Johnny Mack Brown, Iris Meredith, Al St John, Warner Richmond, Dick Curtis, Charles King

Left Handed Law (U) b/w 63 min

A workmanlike series Western with Jones ridding a township of Fain and his gang. The plot is as cliched as they come but Selander's emphasis on action and Jones' dusty humour remain wonderfully enjoyable.

d Lesley Selander *p* Buck Jones *s* Frances Guihan *c* Allen Thompson, William Sickner *lp* Buck Jones, Noel Francis, Matty Fain, Frank LaRue, Lee Phelps, George Regas

Lightnin' Crandall (REP) b/w 60 min

Routine and overlong. Steele is the would-be pacifist of a gunman who finds himself in the middle of a range war. He falls for January, daughter of the besieged LaRue and helps them defend their property against Dwire and King's baddies.

d Sam Newfield *p* A.W. Hackel *s* Charles Francis Royal *c* Bert Longenecker *lp* Bob Steele, Lois January, Frank LaRue, Earl Dwire, Charles King, Horace Murphy

The Lost Ranch (VICTORY) b/w 56 min

One of Tyler's worst outings; in desperation he even sings. As usual he's the representative of the Cattleman's Protective Association, here on the trail of Taylor's gang of kidnappers who've taken to the hills with McKee as hostage. Martel is McKee's daughter who joins up with Tyler when it transpires they are both after Taylor. The direction by Katzman, Tyler's regular director during his brief stay with Victory Pictures, is indifferent.

d/p Sam Katzman *s* Basil Dickey *c* Bill Hyer *lp* Tom Tyler, Jeanne Martel, Forrest Taylor, Lafe McKee, Howard Bryant, Slim Whitaker

Moonlight on the Range (SPECTRUM) b/w 59 min

A solid musical Western. Scott is the baritone hero (and villain) on the trail of his double of a half-brother and being chased by the law who mistake him for his half-brother. The fistfight in which Scott reduces himself to a bloody pulp courtesy of the special effects department and the gun battle between the two are well directed by Newfield. January is the rather listless heroine and St John the comic side-kick who steals the show from Scott in several scenes, notably the jail escape.

d Sam Newfield *p* George Callaghan, Jed Buell *s* Fred Myton *c* Robert Cline *lp* Fred Scott, Al St John, Lois January, Dick Curtis, Frank LaRue, Ed Cassidy

Mystery of the Hooded Horsemen
(GRAND NATIONAL) b/w 60 min

Kelso's script for this bizarre Ritter entry is a clever variant on the masked hero ploy beloved of serialdom. The twist is that it

is the villain who is masked until the last reel. Here he leads a band of masked and becaped outlaws for good measure. Taylor's robust direction and King's wonderfully theatrical evil-doing make the film one of Ritter's best.

d Ray Taylor *p* Edward Finney *s* Edmund Kelso *c* Gus Peterson *lp* Tex Ritter, Iris Meredith, Horace Murphy, Charles King, Forrest Taylor, Lafe McKee

Johnny Mack Brown as the sheriff and Iris Meredith in her regular role of Western heroine in A Lawman Is Born.

The Old Wyoming Trail (COL) b/w 56 min

This is the first of Starrett's 1937-38 season of Westerns and sees the Sons of the Pioneers join Grayson in providing the musical interludes. The tired plot has villains trying to buy up land cheaply because they know a railroad is planned, but Curtis and Starrett's fistfights and Blangsted's to-the-point direction give it new life. Weeks, like so many sagebrush heroines, has little to do but stand and stare at the hero.

d Folmer Blangsted *p* Harry Decker *s* Ed Earl Repp *c* Allen G. Siegler *lp* Charles Starrett, Donald Grayson, Barbara Weeks, Dick Curtis, George Chesebro, Guy Usher

One Man Justice (COL) b/w 59 min

The last and possibly the best of the films director Barsha made with Starrett. Full of rugged action, from the street brawl that opens the film to the final gunfight, Perez's script has Starrett arrive in Mesa as the spitting image of a townsman, missing, believed dead for several years. Of course, Starrett is the townsman, with a touch of amnesia which clears up as he cleans up the town. Nice touches include Starrett at the end making the heavies walk out of town minus their guns and horses.

d Leon Barsha *p* Peter B. Kyne *s* Paul Perez *c* Allen G. Siegler *lp* Charles Starrett, Barbara Weeks, Hal Taliaferro (Wally Wales), Jack Clifford, Al Bridge, Dick Curtis

Below: Preston Foster as the gambler about to meet his maker and Van Heflin as the preacher in The Outcasts of Poker Flat.

The Outcasts of Poker Flat (RKO) b/w 68 min

Following the success of their reworking of **The Last Outlaw** (1936), producer Sisk, writer Twist and director Cabanne decided to remake John Ford's 1919 silent *The Outcasts of*

Poker Flat. In fact derived from two Bret Harte stories, *Outcasts* and *The Luck of Roaring Camp*, the film features Foster in the Harry Carey role of the gambler who after being cured of drunkenness by Heflin's preacher adopts a young boy and sacrifices himself for the child. His story, and stories of three others are told by the outcasts – they've been run out of town – while they shelter from a snowstorm in an isolated log cabin.

d Christy Cabanne *p* Robert Sisk *s* John Twist, Harry Segall *c* Robert De Grasse *lp* Preston Foster, Jean Muir, Van Heflin, Si Jenks, Monte Blue, Bradley Page

The Painted Stallion (REP) b/w 12 chaps

One of the most popular and unusual serials of all time. Witney, as editor, was promoted to co-director when Taylor fell behind schedule due to bad weather. So began the career of the man who was to direct or co-direct 24 of the 66 serials that Republic made between 1936 and 1955. Set in the 1820s, the chapter play tells the complicated story of a wagon train, led by Gibson, headed for Santa Fé with merchandise and accompanied by a US envoy, Corrigan, to open trade discussions with the new Governor of Santa Fé. The deposed Governor, Mason, and his henchman, Renaldo, attempt to kill Corrigan and destroy the wagon train. Eventually Corrigan with the help of, amongst others, Davy Crockett

Sheriff William Farnum (seated), Smiley Burnette complete with short wave radio, and Gene Autry in Public Cowboy No 1.

(Perrin), Jim Bowie (Taliaferro) and the young Kit Carson (McKim) put an end to Mason and Renaldo's plots, hatched as one would expect from a serial, deep in subterranean caves. But what is most striking about the serial is the role played by Thayer, The Rider. Reared by the Comanche and worshipped by them as a Goddess (because of her blonde hair) she devotes herself to preserving justice and in particular keeping the wagon train and Corrigan alive and out of trouble with her 'whistling arrows'. The unusual plotline, fine stunting from Yakima Canutt, a rousing score by Raoul Kraushaar and the splendid photography (of Utah) by Nobles all help to make *The Painted Stallion* a superior serial.

d William Witney, Ray Taylor, Alan James *p* J. Laurence Wickland *s* Barry Shipman, Winston Miller *c* William Nobles, Edgar Lyons *lp* Ray Corrigan, Hoot Gibson, Sammy McKim, Jack Perrin, Hal Taliaferro (Wally Wales), Julia Thayer, Duncan Renaldo, LeRoy Mason

Prairie Thunder (WB) b/w 54 min

The last of Foran's twelve-strong series of Westerns for Warners, *Prairie Thunder* is a remake of **The Telegraph Trail** (1933). Foran is the scout given the task of repairing the telegraph lines pulled down by hostile Indians under the influence of crooked traders. Canutt, repeating his role from the earlier film, is as athletic a villain as ever and Clancy a more active heroine than usual. Eason's pacy direction gives the production a verve than even the over-reliance on stock footage can't destroy.

d B. Reeves Eason *p* Bryan Foy *s* Ed Earl Repp *c* L.W. O'Connell *lp* Dick Foran, Ellen Clancy, Wilfred Lucas, Frank Orth, Yakima Canutt, Frank Ellis

Public Cowboy No 1 (REP) b/w 62 min

A perfect example of the streamlining process that Autry's Westerns represented, *Public Cowboy No 1* is set in the modern world with airplanes, short wave radios and refrigerator trucks but has a plot that makes it clear that blazin' six guns and horses are superior to such modern gimmicks, hence the song, 'The West Ain't what it Used to Be'. Silent star Farnum is the sheriff who calls in Autry and Burnette to solve the mystery of how local cattle are being rustled. Burnette soon tracks them down with his short wave radio and Autry sorts them out.

d Joseph Kane *p* Sol C. Siegel *s* Oliver Drake *c* Jack Marta *lp* Gene Autry, Smiley Burnette, Ann Rutherford, William Farnum, James C. Morton, Frank LaRue

Range Defenders (REP) b/w 56 min

One of the better of the Three Mesquiteers outings. Woods is the cattleman villain, trying to rid the range of sheep at all

costs with assistance from Canutt and Merton. Surprisingly, though the film's climax is a mass shoot out with all guns blazing, the mood of the movie for the most part is comic with Terhune given several opportunities to practise his ventriloquism and Corrigan and Livingston ribbing each other more than usual.

d Mack V. Wright *p* Sol C. Siegel *s* Joseph Poland *c* Jack Marta *lp* Bob Livingston, Ray Corrigan, Max Terhune, Harry Woods, Yakima Canutt, John Merton

Ranger Courage (COL) b/w 58 min
Routine. Allen is the Texas Ranger sent to defend a wagon train bearing a well-stocked strongbox through Indian territory, Kortman the outlaw and Miller the renegade Indian chief out to get the money. Script and direction are cliched in the extreme, but Allen, who was one of the few *actors* to become a sagebrush star, is as sprightly as ever.

d Spencer G. Bennet *p* Larry Darmour *s* Nate Gatzert *c* Arthur Reed *lp* Bob Allen, Martha Tibbetts, Walter Miller, Bob Kortman, Buzz Henry, Bud Osborne

The Rangers Step In (COL) b/w 58 min
The age-old range feud story is revived for this lacklustre Allen series entry. He's the Texas Ranger who resigns his commission because his superiors refuse to send him to keep the peace when a longstanding feud breaks out between his kin and Stewart's. Stewart, of course, is in love with Allen and between them they bring Merton and Ingraham, who've re-opened the feud by their rustling, to justice. Routine.

d Spencer G. Bennet *p* Larry Darmour *s* Jesse Duffy, Joseph Levering *c* James S. Brown Jnr *lp* Bob Allen, Eleanor Stewart, John Merton, Jack Ingraham, Hal Taliaferro (Wally Wales), Jay Wilsey (Buffalo Bill Jnr)

The Reckless Ranger (COL) b/w 56 min
This is one of the better of the generally lacklustre Texas Ranger series Allen made for Columbia. Here he comes to the aid of a sheepman after his sheepman brother has been murdered by cattleman Woods (who steals the picture with his chilling performance). One-time series Western star Perrin takes a second lead as Allen's assistant. Bennet's direction is routine but the script's sympathy for the sheepman makes the film unusual for the period.

d Spencer G. Bennet *p* Larry Darmour *s* Nate Gatzert *c* Bert Longenecker *lp* Bob Allen, Louise Small, Harry Woods, Jack Perrin, Lane Chandler, Bud Osborne

Renfrew of the Royal Mounted
(GRAND NATIONAL) b/w 57 min
The first of Grand National's Renfrew series, based on the books by Laurie York Erskine that had already produced a radio series. Interestingly, Renfrew is impersonated by an actor, Newill, better known on radio – he was a regular singer with the Burns and Allen show – than in films. The action-packed plot has Newill foiling counterfeiters and romancing and serenading Hughes. Newill is more than adequate but the slim production values, which fell further as the series continued, suggested it would be short-lived.

d/p Al Herman *s* Charles Logue *c* Francis Corley *lp* James Newill, Carol Hughes, William Royle, Herbert Corthell, Kenneth Harlan, Dickie Jones

Riders of the Dawn (MON) b/w 55 min
The first of Randall's short-lived series of singing Westerns. The older brother of Bob Livingston, Randall was never able to establish himself either in the public's eye or with Republic and his career never really took off, despite the big budget and the big plans his new studio, Monogram, had for him. Here he's a frontier marshal cleaning up a town run by baddie

Ray Corrigan captured by Indians in Riders of the Whistling Skull.

Richmond. The climax has hero and villain battling it out on a runaway stage and Richmond literally being killed by a bolt from the blue, a bolt of lightning. But the strong story and production values were let down by the inept recording and synching of Randall's songs.

d/p R.N. Bradbury *s* Robert Emmett (Tansey) *c* Bert Longenecker *lp* Jack Randall, Peggy Keyes, Warner Richmond, George Cooper, Earl Dwire, Yakima Canutt

Riders of the Rockies (GRAND NATIONAL) b/w 56 min
Ritter's seventh outing, this saw Pollard, who in the twenties had been the star's favourite silent comic, elevated to the status of comic side-kick. Emmett's script has Ritter turn rustler to catch King and his band of outlaws. His fight with King, who was Ritter's regular opponent – this was their eleventh fight – just as Yakima Canutt was John Wayne's, culminates in King's cheek being ripped open in, for the period, graphic detail. A superior series entry.

d R.N. Bradbury *p* Edward Finney *s* Robert Emmett (Tansey) *c* Gus Peterson *lp* Tex Ritter, Louise Stanley, Charles King, Snub Pollard, Horace Murphy, Yakima Canutt

Riders of the Whistling Skull (REP) b/w 54 min
Thought by many to be the best of the Three Mesquiteers series before John Wayne took over the Stony Brooke role, *Riders of the Whistling Skull* has an unusual plotline. A mystery Western, it features the trio as guides to an archaeological expedition to a lost Indian city guarded by a strange rock formation which produces eerie whistles as the wind passes through it. They find the lost city of Lukachakai, capture Williams and his gang who have been looting the city of its treasures and rescue a professor held prisoner by Williams. Emmett as a man-chasing spinster provides a nice comic complement to Terhune and his wooden dummy Elmer. But it was the cinematography, with the Indians as shadowy presences, and the well-staged action sequences, in which, for instance, Corrigan was bound to a rock with an avalanche imminent, that made the film so popular with audiences.

d Mack V. Wright *p* Nat Levine *s* Oliver Drake, John Rathmell *c* Jack Marta *lp* Bob Livingston, Ray Corrigan, Max Terhune, Mary Russell, Roger Williams, Fern Emmett

The Roaming Cowboy (SPECTRUM) b/w 56 min

A routine musical Western. Scott is the drifter of the title who, with comic assistance from St John, still building up the 'Fuzzy' characterization that he would play for nearly a quarter of a century, saves the local homesteaders from eviction and wins the hand of rancher's daughter, January.

d Robert Hill *p* Jed Buell *s* Fred Myton *c* William Hyer *lp* Fred Scott, Al St John, Lois January, Forrest Taylor, Roger Williams, George Chesebro

Roaring Six Guns (AMBASSADOR) b/w 57 min

Flint, the father of Maynard's fiancée, and his unscrupulous partner try and cheat Maynard out of the parcel of land he wants for setting up home in this slow series outing. Adapted from a story by James Oliver Curwood, the film's main failing is its melodramatic tone.

d J.P. McGowan *p* Maurice Conn *s* Arthur Everett *c* Jack Greenhalgh *lp* Kermit Maynard, Mary Hayes, Sam Flint, John Merton, Budd Buster, Robert Fiske

Romance of the Rockies (MON) b/w 53 min

An engaging series Western. Keene is the country doctor who settles the age-old water rights issue in spectacular fashion – he dynamites an underground stream to the surface – and romances one-time showgirl Wallace. Dwire is the slippery villain of the piece, all growls and guns. Bradbury's direction is solid, but nothing more.

d/p R. N. Bradbury *s* Robert Emmett (Tansey) *c* Bert Longenecker *lp* Tom Keene, Beryl Wallace, Earl Dwire, Don Orlando, Bill Cody Jnr, Franklyn Farnum

Rustler's Valley (PAR) b/w 60 min

The presence of Cobb as a baddie notwithstanding, this is a pretty scrappy Hopalong Cassidy entry. Cobb is the crooked lawyer putting pressure on Morris who's mortgaged his ranch to the hilt and Boyd the breezy foreman who clears everything up in a thrice. Only the cinematography of Harlan who had just been assigned to the series is at all distinguished.

d Nate Watt *p* Harry Sherman *s* Harry O. Hoyt *c* Russell Harlan *lp* William Boyd, George Hayes, Russell Hayden, Lee J. Cobb, Stephen Morris (Morris Ankrum), Muriel Evans

Secret Valley (PRINCIPAL/FOX) b/w 60 min

Grey is the society lady hiding from her husband who she discovers is a gangster on a ranch and Arlen the cowboy who comes to her rescue when he appears with his gang to take her back. A routine, melodramatic Western.

d Howard Bretherton *p* Sol Lesser *s* Paul Franklin, Dan Jarrett, Earle Snell *c* Charles Schoenbaum *lp* Richard Arlen, Virginia Grey, Jack Mulhall, Norman Willis, Syd Saylor, Russell Hicks

The Silver Trail

(RELIABLE/WILLIAM STEINER) b/w 58 min

Lease is the miner who finds his partner murdered and the record of their claim tampered with in this silly melodrama of a Western. With the help of a marshal posing as an idiot (!) he unmasks the culprit and wins the hand of Russell. Even the presence of Rin Tin Tin Jnr can't lift such material.

d/p Raymond Samuels (B.B. Ray) *c* Pliny Goodfriend *lp* Rex Lease, Mary Russell, Ed Cassidy, Steve Clark, Slim Whitaker, Oscar Gahan

Sing Cowboy Sing (GRAND NATIONAL) b/w 59 min

An amiable series movie with Ritter defending a covered wagon freightline from hoodlums trying to wrest the franchise for themselves. The emphasis is on humour throughout with Bradbury spending more time on the antics of Conklin, St John and McKenzie than the routine storyline. The film is also interesting as an example of how tightly knit a group the men making series Westerns could become. Thus Ritter and director Bradbury even collaborated on one of the film's songs, 'Twilight Reverie'.

d R.N. Bradbury *p* Edward Finney *s* Robert Emmett (Tansey) *c* Gus Peterson *lp* Tex Ritter, Louise Stanley, Al St John, Chester Conklin, Bob McKenzie, Charles King

The Singing Buckaroo (SPECTRUM) b/w 50 min

A routine musical Western. Scott wears the white hat and protects Vinton from a pair of hoodlums out to steal her money. The emphasis is on action with fights and rough riding well to the fore, the musical interludes notwithstanding. For the climax a mysterious Red Indian appears to help Scott free Vinton from her kidnappers. Primitive but pleasant.

d/s Tom Gibson *p* Jed Buell, George H. Callaghan *c* Robert Doran *lp* Fred Scott, William Faversham, Victoria Vinton, Cliff Nazarro, Howard Hill, Dick Curtis

Stars over Arizona (MON) b/w 62 min

Singing cowboy Randall and his partner, Murphy, are sent to Yuba City to clear up outlawry there in this routine series entry. Richmond puts in a telling appearance as the villain, but Monogram's lack of confidence in their new 'star', seen in the pinched budget, signalled the beginning of the end of the series.

d/p R.N. Bradbury *s* Robert Emmett (Tansey), Ernie Adams *c* Bert Longenecker *lp* Jack Randall, Kathleen Elliott, Horace Murphy, Warner Richmond, Hal Price, Earl Dwire

Texas Trail (PAR) b/w 60 min

A lively Hopalong Cassidy outing. Hoppy and his Bar 20 cowboys become virtual Rough Riders, rounding up horses for the US Army in the Spanish-American War. More realistic than previous series entries, and with plot and action shared by Allen and Hayden (less of a matinee idol than Jimmy Ellison whom he replaced) the result was a fine addition to a superior series.

d David Selman *p* Harry Sherman *s* Jack O'Donnell *c* Russell Harlan *lp* William Boyd, George Hayes, Russell Hayden, Robert Kortman, Karl Hackett, Judith Allen

Tex Ritter (right) and his regular villain, Charles King, in mid-fight in Riders of the Rockies.

Thunder Trail (PAR) b/w 58 min
An intelligent and well-made B Western. Roland and Craig are the brothers separated when Bickford kills their father, takes Craig and rears him as his own son. After a search of several years, Roland comes across Bickford terrorizing Blue and his daughter, Hunt. He defends them, wins Hunt in the process and secures his revenge. Script, acting and direction give the story a weight unusual in B features.

d Charles Barton s Robert Yost, Stuart Anthony c Karl Struss lp Gilbert Roland, James Craig, Charles Bickford, Marsha Hunt, Monte Blue, J. Carrol Naish

Trail of Vengeance (REP) b/w 58 min
One of the best of Brown's Republic outings, *Trail of Vengeance* sees its star, carrying the unlikely name of Dude Ramsey, pitted against Richmond in an effort to stop the range war in which his brother died. Both Brown and Richmond are well cast, giving their roles a rough-and-ready feel rare in series Westerns. Accordingly, Meredith as the romantic interest has little to do but look at Brown.

d Sam Newfield p A.W. Hackel s George Plympton, Fred Myton c Arthur Reed lp Johnny Mack Brown, Iris Meredith, Warner Richmond, Karl Hackett, Frank LaRue, Dick Curtis

Trapped (COL) b/w 56 min
The directional debut of ex-editor Barsha, this is a superior Starrett series entry. Opening with a bang (Starrett coming home to find his brother dying, victim of a gang of rustlers) and following his search for the rustlers, the film is faster paced than Starrett's previous entries. Sears is the depraved-looking heavy and Middlemass the villain, feigning paralysis from below the waist to better disguise his villainy. Stratford is the girl.

d Leon Barsha p Harry Decker s John Rathmell c Allen G. Seigler lp Charles Starrett, Alan Sears, Robert Middlemass, Peggy Stratford, Ed Piel, Jack Rockwell

The Trigger Trio (REP) b/w 60 min
Byrd substitutes for an injured Robert Livingston in this routine Three Mesquiteers entry notable only for being the feature film debut of serial specialist Witney. However, he was given little opportunity to indulge in the fanciful action sequences he so loved. The real star of the movie is Buck, a dog who leads the Mesquiteers in search of a killer and his cohorts who have been spreading foot and mouth disease throughout the locality.

d William Witney p Sol C. Siegel s Oliver Drake, Joseph Poland c Ernest Miller lp Ray Corrigan, Max Terhune, Ralph Byrd, Sandra Corday, Hal Taliaferro (Wally Wales), Robert Warwick

Yakima Canutt (left), series heavy, stuntman extraordinaire and occasional director, Rita Hayworth and Tex Ritter in Trouble in Texas.

Trouble in Texas (GRAND NATIONAL) b/w 53 min
The fourth and most heavily promoted of Ritter's series of twelve films for Edward Alperson's Grand National Pictures, *Trouble in Texas* co-starred Hayworth in the last film she made under the name of Rita Cansino. She is the undercover government agent assisting Ritter in his investigations into a series of mysterious robberies at rodeos. King and Canutt, needless to say, are the villains of the piece. Emmett's script is careful to leave enough space for Ritter to show his horsemanship and his prowess with his fists and to air his tonsils. The result was a fine series entry with a thunderous climactic ride that sees Ritter and Canutt in a runaway dynamite-laden buckboard.

d R.N. Bradbury p Edward Finney s Robert Emmett (Tansey) c Gus Peterson lp Tex Ritter, Rita Cansino (Hayworth), Earl Dwire, Yakima Canutt, Charles King, Dick Palmer

Two Fisted Sheriff (COL) b/w 60 min
One of Starrett's finest series Westerns. The plot has him defending killers from a lynch mob, in the course of which his friend (a suspected murderer), Lane, escapes thus bringing about Starrett's dismissal from his job. To reinstate himself and clear Lane he sets off after the baddies. The action is well-paced with a welter of fistfights leading up to the final showdown between Starrett and Sears, playing one of the first psychopaths to ride the range.

d Leon Barsha p Harry Decker s Paul Perez c Allen G. Seigler lp Charles Starrett, Barbara Weeks, Bruce Lane, Alan Sears, Walter Downing, Ernie Adams

Far left: A studio portrait of Charles Starrett, star of Trapped *and* Two Fisted Sheriff.

Barbara Weeks tells Charles Starrett she believes he's innocent in Two Fisted Sheriff.

Under Strange Flags (CRESCENT) b/w 64 min

Black is Pancho Villa in this routine adventure film. Keene, once a Western superstar now reduced to making quickies, comes to the assistance of Walters when the silver mine she owns is threatened by the Federales. With Villa's assistance, he puts paid to their would-be thievery and unmasks D'Arcy as a treacherous aide to Villa. Well acted, it suffers from the limited budgets that characterize E.B. Derr's productions.

d I.V. Willat *p* E.B. Derr *s* Mary Ireland *c* Arthur Martinelli *lp* Tom Keene, Maurice Black, Luana Walters, Roy D'Arcy, Budd Buster, Donald Reed

Above: *Laurel and Hardy in the classic* Way Out West.

Way Out West (MGM) b/w 65 min

One of the most enduring of Western spoofs, *Way Out West* is also one of Laurel and Hardy's finest feature films. The duo arrive at Brushwood Gulch with the deeds to their deceased partner's gold mine which they intend to give to his daughter. Lynne, the mistress of crooked saloon keeper Finlayson, successfully poses as the daughter and takes the deeds before the real daughter, Lawrence, appears. Around this strong but simple storyline, Laurel, the creative member of the partnership – and here acting as producer – and director Horne weave a number of marvellous diversions, ranging from the surreal (Stan's hat eating and finger lighting) to the musical (most notably the duo's rendering of 'Trail of the Lonesome Pine'). Forty years later, when a scratchy single of the song (on which Chill Wills dubbed Stan's voice) was released in Britain, it surprised everyone by hitting the Top Twenty.

d James W. Horne *p* Stan Laurel *s* Charles Rogers, Felix Adler, James Parrott *c* Art Lloyd, Walter Lundin *lp* Stan Laurel, Oliver Hardy, James Finlayson, Sharon Lynne, Stanley Fields, Rosina Lawrence

Wells Fargo (PAR) b/w 115 min

One of Paramount's big budget Westerns, this highly fictionalized account of the Wells Fargo Company features McCrea and his wife Dee. The role of the trail blazer was one of McCrea's first starring roles and sees his acting style, heavily influenced by W.S. Hart, even more austere than it would be later. The bulk of the film deals with his on-off marriage to Dee who supports the South when the Civil War breaks out and who McCrea thinks has tipped off the Confederates about gold shipments Wells Fargo is carrying for the Union. Paramount's production values are solid enough, though Lloyd wisely eschews any crowd scenes, but the material doesn't stretch to the 115 minutes' running time.

d/p Frank Lloyd *s* Paul Schoefield, Gerald Geraghty, Frederick Jackson *c* Theodor Sparkuhl *lp* Joel McCrea, Frances Dee, Bob Burns, Lloyd Nolan, Henry O'Neill, Ralph Morgan

Panning for gold in Wells Fargo.

Western Gold (PRINCIPAL/FOX) b/w 57 min
Ballew, Lesser's singing replacement for George O'Brien who'd quit him for George Hirliman and RKO, is ill served in this his first feature as a star. Snell and Barnes' script uses the tired device of a Union Officer (Ballew) sent West to find out how the Confederates are stopping the gold shipments from California. Ballew, better remembered as the man who reputedly dubbed John Wayne's voice in his Singin' Sandy outings, doesn't even get to kill the villain of the piece, Mason, so little action is there.

d Howard Bretherton *p* Sol Lesser *s* Forrest Barnes, Earle Snell *c* Herman Neumann *lp* Smith Ballew, Heather Angel, LeRoy Mason, Ben Alexander, Otis Harlan

Where Trails Divide (MON) b/w 60 min
An indifferent series Western. Keene is the undercover agent masquerading as a lawyer in order to catch a band of stagecoach robbers and Richmond the sly outlaw. Bradbury's tired direction and the lacklustre script by Robert Tansey (under his Emmett pseudonym) which has hardly a gunshot in it doesn't help matters. Only the end, with Richmond and his gang wandering the Mojave desert in search of water, finally to die of thirst, is memorable.

d/p R.N. Bradbury *s* Robert Emmett (Tansey) *c* Bert Longenecker *lp* Tom Keene, Eleanor Stewart, Warner Richmond, David Sharpe, Lorraine Randall, Steve Clark

Whistling Bullets (AMBASSADOR) b/w 57 min
A superior cheapie from indie producer Conn. Former editor and serial director, English enlivens the cliched story of the Texas Ranger, falsely imprisoned so he can break jail with an outlaw and locate his hidden loot, with his taut direction. Maynard's stunting is as capable as ever while Ingraham is a suitably nasty villain.

d John English *p* Maurice Conn *s* Joseph O'Donnell *c* Jack Greenhalgh *lp* Kermit Maynard, Harlene (Harley) Wood, Jack Ingraham, Karl Hackett, Maston Williams, Bruce Mitchell

Wild and Woolly (FOX) b/w 65 min
This is an amiable if unimaginative comic Western. Brennan is in fine form as the sheriff who, after years of failing to win office due to the chicanery of his political opponents, foils a bank robbery and wins the election. Werker directs neatly while Withers and Moore offer solid support.

At the end of his career, Werker returned to the Western and made a series of distinguished, although little known, genre films of which **The Last Posse** (1953) was the first.

d Alfred Werker *p* John Stone *s* Lynn Root, Frank Fenton *c* Harry Jackson *lp* Walter Brennan, Jane Withers, Pauline Moore, Douglas Fowley, Robert Wilcox, Lon Chaney Jnr

Wild Horse Rodeo (REP) b/w 55 min
Sherman's first film as a director, *Wild Horse Rodeo* is a better than average Three Mesquiteers entry. It's also notable for the musical sequence featuring Weston, soon to become famous as Roy Rogers. The plot has the trio following the rodeo circuit and the climax has Corrigan bringing down a plane, that's strafing our heroes, with a single shot from his pistol. Martel is the horse painter who gets romantically involved with Livingston.

John Carroll (left) and Helen Christian admiring the portrait of Carroll's father behind which lies the secret cave in which Carroll becomes the masked avenger in Zorro Rides Again.

d George Sherman   *p* Sol C. Siegel   *s* Betty Burbridge   *c* William Nobles   *lp* Bob Livingston, Ray Corrigan, Max Terhune, June Martel, Edmund Cobb, Dick Weston

Zorro Rides Again (REP) b/w 12 chaps

So successful was **The Bold Caballero** (1936) that Republic immediately revived the Zorro character for this fast and furious serial. Carroll is the derring-do hero, an idle dandy on first appearance with the full-length portrait of his father on his wall which swings back to reveal the black suit and horse on which he becomes Zorro the avenger. In this role he is impersonated for the most part by Canutt whose stunts were a key element in the serial's success. Renaldo who was later to assume the role of the Cisco Kid is the faithful side-kick. So pervasive was the influence of the musical Western at the time that Carroll even sings. In 1958, Republic released an edited down feature film of the serial.

d William Witney, John English   *p* Sol C. Siegel   *s* Morgan Cox, Ronald Davidson, John Rathmell, Barry Shipman, Franklyn Adreon   *c* William Nobles   *lp* John Carroll, Helen Christian, Duncan Renaldo, Reed Howes, Noah Beery, Yakima Canutt

1938

Billy the Kid Returns (REP) b/w 58 min

Rushed into production after Rogers' success with **Under Western Stars** (1938), in which he'd been a pseudo Gene Autry, this film sees Rogers replacing Johnny Mack Brown who'd quit Republic for Universal. Accordingly, though the film retains a strong musical content, it is far more action oriented. The plot sees Rogers as a Billy the Kid look-alike who, with comic assistance from Burnette, uses the resemblance to bring back law and order to Lincoln County after the outlaw's death.

d Joseph Kane   *p* Charles E. Ford   *s* Jack Natteford   *c* Ernest Miller   *lp* Roy Rogers, Smiley Burnette, Lynne Roberts, Morgan Wallace, Fred Kohler Snr, Trigger

Black Bandit (U) b/w 57 min

The first and probably the worst of the eight films which Waggner directed and scripted under his West pseudonym with Baker starring. The storyline has Baker as (good and bad) twins vying for the hand of Reynolds until the bad twin

reforms and saves his brother's life at the cost of his own. The production values, like the script, are dire, but somehow Baker manages to take his role seriously.

d George Waggner   *p* Paul Malvern   *s* Joseph West (George Waggner)   *c* Gus Peterson   *lp* Bob Baker, Marjorie Reynolds, Hal Taliaferro (Wally Wales), Forrest Taylor, Glenn Strange, Jack Rockwell

Border Wolves (U) b/w 57 min

Lewis' fine direction notwithstanding, this film marks a decline in Baker's series Westerns. The routine plot has him trying to clear his name and`romancing Moore. But neither the songs, which seem to be inserted on a one-every-ten-minutes basis rather than planned for, nor the script which looks as if much rewritten during filming, so often does it change tack, give Baker and Lewis anything substantial to work with. Subsequent Baker outings were to be similarly marred.

d Joseph H. Lewis   *p* Paul Malvern   *s* Norton S. Parker   *c* Harry Neumann   *lp* Bob Baker, Constance Moore, Fuzzy Knight, Dickie Jones, Glenn Strange, Dick Dorrell

California Frontier (CORONET/COL) b/w 54 min

Based on fact supposedly, this is yet another version of the story of the terrorizing of Spanish Californians by landgrabbers on the eve of the state's entry into the Union. Full of improbabilities, even more than was normal in the series Western, it is the last and worst of Jones' films for Coronet Productions. The plot has him as an undercover agent out to get the landgrabbers and engaging in fistfight after fistfight.

d Elmer Clifton   *p/co-s* Monroe Shaff   *co-s* Arthur Hoerl   *c* Edward Linden   *lp* Buck Jones, Carmen Bailey, Milburn Stone, Glenn Strange, Ernie Adams, Forrest Taylor

Call the Mesquiteers (REP) b/w 55 min

This time the trio are searching for silk thieves, but the emphasis is less on them than on McKim as the little boy who stumbles on the thieves hideout and his dog, Flash, a pale imitation of Rin Tin Tin. The film is routine.

d John English   *p* William Berke   *s* Luci Ward   *c* William Nobles   *lp* Bob Livingston, Ray Corrigan, Max Terhune, Lynn Roberts, Sammy McKim, Earle Hodgins

Cassidy of Bar 20 (PAR) b/w 56 min

The seventh in the Hoppy series, the only action series to maintain its production values without a singing hero. Here Hoppy comes to the rescue of old beau Lane when Fiske's cattle rustling gets too much for her. The action is well handled, particularly the climax with the Bar 20 cowboys riding to Hoppy's rescue like the Seventh Cavalry.

d Lesley Selander   *p* Harry Sherman   *s* Norman Houston   *c* Russell Harlan   *lp* William Boyd, Russell Hayden, Nora Lane, Robert Fiske, Frank Darien, John Elliott

Cattle Raiders (COL) b/w 61 min
While Starrett seeks to prove his innocence of the murder of a sheriff, Grayson, backed by the Sons of the Pioneers, warbles in sympathy. Curtis is the suitably menacing heavy, but the direction of Nelson, and Poland and Repp's loose screenplay blunt any interest there might have been in the story.

d Sam Nelson *p* Harry L. Decker *s* Joseph Poland, Ed Earl Repp *c* John Boyle *lp* Charles Starrett, Donald Grayson, Iris Meredith, Dick Curtis, Bob Nolan, Edmund Cobb

The Cowboy and the Lady
(SAM GOLDWYN PRODUCTION) b/w 91 min
This weak comedy, needing a more spirited leading lady to give it some fire, has Cooper as the rodeo star and Oberon as the bored daughter of a Presidential candidate who marries him for a lark. Cooper overdoes the drawling sincerity, especially when he lectures the effete Easterners on 'manly virtues' but his role is at least substantial unlike Oberon's which requires her to twist and turn every which way to follow a script that seems to have been much rewritten in the course of shooting. Only Toland's cinematography is distinguished.

d Henry C. Potter *p* Sam Goldwyn *s* S.N. Behrman, Sonya Levien *c* Gregg Toland *lp* Gary Cooper, Merle Oberon, Patsy Kelly, Walter Brennan, Fuzzy Knight

Cowboy from Brooklyn (WB) b/w 80 min
Powell is the cowboy of the title, a drifter who becomes a singing cowboy at a dude ranch and is made into a radio star by promoter O'Brien. Lane is the rancher's daughter who cures him of his fear of animals through a mixture of hypnosis and love. The film works best as a satire on the singing cowboy phenomenon with Powell and O'Brien clearly enjoying their roles.

d Lloyd Bacon *p* Lou Edelman *s* Earl Baldwin *c* Arthur Edeson *lp* Dick Powell, Pat O'Brien, Ronald Reagan, Dick Foran, Priscilla Lane, Ann Sheridan

Forbidden Valley (U) b/w 67 min
Beery is the kid reared on the timberline who goes to town in search of justice – his father has been murdered – and romance – he falls for poor little rich girl, Robinson, an actress better known for her serial work. Kohler is the villain of the piece and Gittens, another serial veteran, directs his own screenplay in the cheerfully uncluttered way that juvenile audiences found so appealing.

d/s Wyndham Gittens *p* Henry MacRae, Elmer Tambert *c* Elwood Bredeli *lp* Noah Beery Jnr, Frances Robinson, Robert Barrat, Fred Kohler Snr, Henry Hunter, James Foran

Above: *Gary Cooper and Merle Oberon as the spoilt little rich girl who falls for him in* The Cowboy and the Lady.

Frontier Scout
(FINE ARTS/GRAND NATIONAL) b/w 61 min
One time opera singer Houston essays the role of Wild Bill Hickok in this routine B Western. It opens with a bang, with Houston forcing Lee's surrender and ending the Civil War, but slows down considerably when it switches to the West where Houston ends Chase's cattle rustling. Newfield's direction is similarly slow. Marion is the damsel in distress and St John the bewhiskered comic relief.

d Sam Newfield *p* Franklyn Warner, Maurice Conn *s* Frances Guihan *c* Jack Greenhalgh *lp* George Houston, Al St John, Guy (Alden) Chase, Beth Marion, Dave O'Brien, Slim Whitaker

The Frontiersman (PAR) b/w 74 min
Another offbeat Hopalong Cassidy entry with Boyd helping schoolteacher Venable run a school on the range. The schoolboys in question were impersonated by the St Brendans Boys' Choir and accordingly Boyd and Venable are much serenaded. The action, saved until the end, has the Bar 20 cowboys riding in hot pursuit of Barcroft and his rustlers.

d Lesley Selander *p* Harry Sherman *s* Norman Houston, Harrison Jacobs *c* Russell Harlan *lp* William Boyd, George Hayes, Russell Hayden, Evelyn Venable, Roy Barcroft, William Duncan

The Girl of the Golden West (MGM) sepia 121 min
In 1938, David Belasco's often filmed play was resurrected for the last time in Hollywood as a starring vehicle for the singing

Dick Powell and Priscilla Lane in one of the many films to parody the singing cowboy phenomenon, Cowboy from Brooklyn.

Above: *Jeanette MacDonald, looking remarkably like Barbara Stanwyck, in* The Girl of the Golden West.

Gabby Hayes (left) best remembered as being Roy Rogers' constant companion, Olivia De Havilland and George Brent in Gold Is Where You Find It.

George O'Brien (left) and Frank O'Connor as marshal and minister respectively in Gun Law.

team of Eddy and MacDonald. He is the outlaw and she the girl who loves him and saves him by winning a card game with him as the stake against Pidgeon's sheriff, Eddy's rival in love. The original play is melodramatic in the extreme and writer Dawn's transformation of it into a light operetta and Eddy's overly genteel performance make it even more old fashioned. Even the songs, by Gus Kahn and Sigmund Romberg, couldn't help the film repeat the success Eddy and MacDonald had had with **Rose Marie** (1936).

d Robert Z. Leonard *p* William Anthony McGuire *s* Isabel Dawn *c* Oliver Marsh *lp* Jeanette MacDonald, Nelson Eddy, Walter Pidgeon, Buddy Ebsen

Gold Is Where You Find It (WB) 90 min
The first attempt by Curtiz and Buckner (here with assistance from Duff), who were to have phenomenal success with a string of Westerns beginning with **Dodge City** (1939), at a sprawling, would-be epic Western. The plot is simple but effective. Miners and ranchers fight it out when gold is discovered in California in 1849 and there's a landslide at the climax. But Polito's high-key early Technicolor cinematography and the strong cast notwithstanding, Curtiz seems unable to animate the film. However, it remains an interesting film, if only to compare with **Sutter's Gold** (1936) and **The Emperor of California** (1936).

d Michael Curtiz *p* Hal B. Wallis *s* Warren Duff, Robert Buckner *c* Sol Polito *lp* George Brent, Olivia DeHavilland, Claude Rains, Margaret Lindsay, John Litel, Tim Holt

The Great Adventures of Wild Bill Hickok
(COL) b/w 15 chaps
This is the serial that transported one moustachioed Gordon Elliott (who as a Warner Brothers contract player had played villain to Dick Foran in many of Foran's series Westerns beginning with **Moonlight on the Prairie**, 1935) to Western series stardom as the clean shaven 'Wild Bill' Elliott, a tag Columbia quickly stuck on him to identify him with the Hickok role that brought him success. Following the release of the chapter-play Columbia signed Elliott for a Western series to complement their Charles Starrett series.

Here, as Hickok, Elliott is the marshal of Abeline confronting the Phantom Raiders, who prey on the cattle being driven from Texas to Kansas. To do this better, he organizes a group of vigilantes, the Flaming Arrows, which includes youngsters Darro, Jones and McKim. Like many of the players, the script is childish, but Wright and Nelson's energetic direction papers over the story's flaws efficiently enough. Even more significantly, Columbia's promotion

department got behind the serial. The result was Columbia's first really successful serial outing and the real beginning of Elliott's career in the saddle.

d Mack V. Wright, Sam Nelson *p* Jack Fier *s* George Rosener, Charles Arthur Powell, George Arthur Durlam, Dallas Fitzgerald, Tom Gibson *c* George Meehan, Benjamin Kline *lp* Gordon Elliott (Bill Elliott), Monte Blue, Frankie Darro, Kermit Maynard, Sammy McKim, Carole Wayne, Dickie Jones

Gun Law (RKO) b/w 60 min
One of the best of O'Brien's RKO series Westerns. The plot is the familiar one of mistaken identity but O'Brien, doing his own stunts as usual and charming the camera with his cheek, handles the action with an ease few Western stars achieve. He's the marshal and O'Connor is the minister who together are determined to bring law and religion to the range. Whitley is the singing waiter while Bond supplies the villainy.

d David Howard *p* Bert Gilroy *s* Oliver Drake *c* Joseph August *lp* George O'Brien, Rita Oehmen, Frank O'Connor, Ward Bond, Ray Whitley, Paul Everton

Hawaiian Buckaroo (PRINCIPAL/FOX) b/w 62 min
The arrival of Taylor as director for this the first of Ballew's final trio of films brings a definite improvement to the short-lived series. Set in Hawaii, it features singing cowboy Ballew and his side-kick Burt starting a pineapple plantation but ending up saving snooty rancher Knapp from the treachery of foreman Woods. The locale and a script that calls for much more action than before result in an above average outing.

d Ray Taylor *p* Sol Lesser *s* Dan Jarrett *c* Allen Thompson *lp* Smith Ballew, Evalyn Knapp, Benny Burt, Pat O'Brien, Harry Woods, George Regas

Heroes of the Hills (REP) b/w 56 min
In this above average Three Mesquiteers outing the trio transform their ranch into a prison farm in the interests of penal reform and fall foul of a crooked contractor who's miffed because he wants to build the new prison they're demonstrating is unnecessary. Barcroft handles the villainy with his customary aplomb and Lawson swoons at Livingston at the appropriate moments. Bizarre.

d George Sherman *p* William Berke *s* Betty Burbridge, Stanley Roberts *c* Reggie Lanning *lp* Bob Livingston, Ray Corrigan, Max Terhune, Priscilla Lawson, Roy Barcroft, LeRoy Mason

In Early Arizona (COL) b/w 53 min
This is the first of Elliott's Westerns for Columbia made at the time when the company was desperately trying to find a second star to complement their Charles Starrett series after failing so disastrously with Jack Luden and Bob Allen. A fictionalized account of Wyatt Earp's cleaning up of Tombstone, it had a bigger budget than most films churned out by Darmour's unit at Columbia. But most of all it has Elliott who with his grim smile looked the part of a Western hero. Woods is the villain and King, for a change, is on the side of the law.

d Joseph Levering *p* Larry Darmour *s* Nate Gatzert *c* James S. Brown Jnr *lp* Bill Elliott, Dorothy Gulliver, Harry Woods, Charles King, Jack Ingram, Ed Cassidy

In Old Mexico (PAR) b/w 62 min
The loose sequel to **Borderland** (1937) verges on being a suspense film with its complicated detective plot that sees Hoppy unravelling a murder mystery while in Mexico. The film also marked the movie debut of Clayton, who was married to Hayden in real life, as the pert heroine. The production values as ever are superior for a series Western.

d Edward D. Venturini *p* Harry Sherman *s* Harrison Jacobs *c* Russell Harlan *lp* William Boyd, George Hayes, Russell Hayden, Jane Clayton, Glenn Strange, Al Garcia

Knight of the Plains
(SPECTRUM/STAN LAUREL PRODUCTIONS) b/w 57 min
The last of Stan Laurel's essays into production with Buell, *Knight of the Plains* features Merton as the villain, promoting a phoney land grant and almost causing a range feud between the homesteaders in residence and the new arrivals. But Scott sorts things out. As usual, Scott sings well and St John provides reliable comic support but Myton's storyline is too tired to inspire any of the principals to do anything but read their lines correctly.

d Sam Newfield *p* Jed Buell *s* Fred Myton *c* Mack Stengler *lp* Fred Scott, Al St John, John Merton, Marion Weldon, Frank LaRue, Lafe McKee

Land of Fighting Men (MON) b/w 53 min
Never one of the happiest of singing cowboys, Randall here grimaces his way through his musical numbers, only relaxing his face when the song is over. O'Donnell's script has Randall come to Brix's assistance in his fight against landgrabber Oakman only to be accused by Oakman of Brix's murder. Stanley is the attractive romantic interest.

d Alan James *p* Maurice Conn *s* Joseph O'Donnell *c* Robert Cline *lp* Jack Randall, Louise Stanley, Herman Brix (Bruce Bennett), Wheeler Oakman, Lane Chandler, Rex Lease

The Last Stand (U) b/w 56 min
This is the last of Baker's quartet of Lewis-directed Westerns. Though it lacks the production values of the earlier films in the series, Lewis and writers Parker and Hoyt overcame this by hard-paced direction and a script that is distinctively thrillerish. The basic plot is old hat, with Baker impersonating an outlaw as part of his search for his father's murderer but the speed with which Lewis and his writers twist the plot first this way and then that brings it to life. Similarly, Lewis, rather than merely carve out spaces for the trio of songs, places them so that they further the action. All in all, a triumph of craftsmanship over economy.

d Joseph H. Lewis *p* Trem Carr *s* Harry O. Hoyt, Norton S. Parker *c* Harry Neumann *lp* Bob Baker, Constance Moore, Fuzzy Knight, Earle Hodgins, Forrest Taylor, Glenn Strange

Law of the Plains (COL) b/w 58 min
One of the better of Starrett's Columbia entries, *Law of the Plains* is notable for the emphasis laid on the Sons of the Pioneers who replaced Donald Grayson. The plot is the old one of the evil banker (Warwick) pretending to have the interests of the community at heart while he secretly controls the outlaws who are terrorizing the local farmers. As an added twist Warwick is also passing himself off as Meredith's father.

d Sam Nelson *p* Harry Decker *s* Maurice Geraghty *c* Benjamin Kline *lp* Charles Starrett, Iris Meredith, Bob Nolan, Robert Warwick, Dick Curtis, George Chesebro

Law of the Texan
(CORONET PRODUCTIONS/COL) b/w 54 min
Once again Jones masquerades as an outlaw in his attempts to

Bob Baker (left) in The Last Stand.

bring in an outlaw gang who specialize in stealing silver bullion. Clifton's over-concentration on action at the expense of the, admittedly slight, story results in a film that abounds in fistfights but little else. Harlan is the villain and Fay the energetic heroine.

d Elmer Clifton *p/co-s* Monroe Shaff *co-s* Arthur Hoerl *c* Edward Linden *lp* Buck Jones, Dorothy Fay, Kenneth Harlan, Don Douglas, Forrest Taylor, Bob Kortman

The Law West of Tombstone (RKO) b/w 72 min

Holt's first Western, *The Law West of Tombstone* sees him supporting Carey (in his last RKO Western) who plays a Judge Roy Bean like confidence trickster. Holt is the local gunslinger, a Billy the Kid figure, in love with Brent, Carey's daughter. Basically a comedy, director Tryon encouraged Carey to embroider his role as the judicial rogue beyond belief. Screenwriters Twist and Young were similarly minded: not satisfied with having got Billy the Kid and Judge Roy Bean in the same plot, they also managed to make the Clantons the villains of the piece.

d Glenn Tryon *p* Cliff Reid *s* John Twist, Clarence Upson Young *c* J. Roy Hunt *lp* Harry Carey, Tim Holt, Evelyn Brent, Allan Lane, Ward Bond, Kermit Maynard

Harry Carey (centre) is chided by his daughter, Evelyn Brent, in his last film for RKO, The Law West of Tombstone.

Lawless Valley (RKO) b/w 59 min

Another top notch series outing from O'Brien. Released from jail, he's determined to find the outlaws who framed him and his dead father for a number of stagecoach robberies. With help from Miller he exposes lawmen Hodgins and Wills as being in league with outlaw Kohler. The neat plot and the twist of the two Kohlers playing father and son were appealing enough but it's O'Brien's rugged heroism, well captured by Howard, that makes the film so pleasing.

d David Howard *p* Bert Gilroy *s* Oliver Drake *c* Harry Wild *lp* George O'Brien, Kay Sutton, Walter Miller, Earle Hodgins, Chill Wills, Fred Kohler Snr, Fred Kohler Jnr

The Lone Ranger (REP) b/w 15 chaps

A landmark in the history of the serial, *The Lone Ranger*, released in a feature film format as *Hi Yo Silver* in 1940, was publicized by one of the oldest tricks in the book: the puzzle the viewer was set wasn't the serial's normal one of 'Who is the masked villain?', but 'What is the identity of the hero?'. Set in the years immediately after the Civil War, the plot featured five identically clad masked 'Lone Rangers' fighting Andrews and his army of bandits. As the weeks went by, one by one the heroes fell until in the last chapter Powell was revealed as *the* Lone Ranger.

The fast paced direction of Witney and English, by now the acknowledged kings of the serial, and Republic's attention to detail, such as the silver bullets moulded by the Lone Ranger

himself and the glistening revolvers with their pearl white handles, combine to produce a serial of mythic proportions.

d William Witney, John English *p* Sol C. Siegel *s* Barry Shipman, George Worthing Yates, Franklyn Adreon, Ronald Davidson, Lois Eby *c* William Nobles *lp* Lee Powell, Bruce Bennett, Stanley Andrews, George Montgomery, Chief Thundercloud, Lynn Roberts

The Man from Texas (MON) b/w 56 min

One of Ritter's best series entries. He's the railroad agent and Wood is the Shootin' Kid, a baddie Ritter persuades to go straight and help him sort out Barcroft who is trying to buy up valuable railroad land very cheaply, using terrorist tactics. LePicard's camerawork is a little primitive but Herman's no-nonsense direction emphasizes action to good effect as in the spectacular gun battle at the climax. Less ambitious than recent Ritter outings it was far more successful.

d Al Herman *p* Edward Finney *s* Robert Emmett (Tansey) *c* Marcel LePicard *lp* Tex Ritter, Ruth Rogers, Charles B. Wood, Roy Barcroft, Hal Price, Frank Wayne

The Mexicali Kid (MON) b/w 57 min

Barry has the title role, a strong indication that Randall's days as a cowboy star were numbered. Another sign was Monogram's assigning Tansey (who also wrote the screenplay under

his Emmett pseudonym) to produce. Yet another sign was the studio's decision that henceforth Randall wasn't to sing in his films. Considering all this it comes as some surprise to find the film is better than it could have been. Randall is the vengeance-seeking brother of a murdered bank cashier who rescues Barry in the desert, sets about reforming him, and with his help saves Stewart's ranch. The climax is a gun battle in a burning town with Barry dying for his past sins.

d Wallace Fox   *p/s* Robert Emmett (Tansey)   *c* Bert Longenecker   *lp* Jack Randall, Wesley Barry, Eleanor Stewart, Ed Cassidy, Bud Osborne, George Chesebro

The Mysterious Rider *aka* Mark of the Avenger
(PAR) b/w 74 min
Dumbrille, normally cast as a heavy, took over the lead from George Bancroft while the latter was in the middle of a financial dispute with producer Sherman for this remake of **The Mysterious Rider** (1933). The effect is to make his supposed treachery even more plausible, despite the presence of good guy Toler as his side-kick, but not to make the plot's twist, in which it is revealed that the crooked Hayden has tricked the homesteaders by signing their leases in invisible ink (!), any more believable.

d Lesley Selander   *p* Harry Sherman   *s* Maurice Geraghty
c Russell Harlan   *lp* Douglass Drumbrille, Russell Hayden, Sidney Toler, Charlotte Fields, Stanley Andrews, Monte Blue

The Old Barn Dance   (REP) b/w 60 min
It was his appearance in this, as Dick Weston, that gave Yates, Republic's owner, the idea of building up Rogers as a replacement singing cowboy for Autry who, after the picture's completion, refused to appear before the studio's cameras 'for contractual reasons' – i.e. he wanted more money which he certainly deserved since his films were keeping Republic alive.

The plot is decidedly fanciful with Autry, Burnette and company first selling horses to ranchers, then singing over the radio sponsored by the tractor outfit whose mechanical horses put them out of business and then finding the tractors malfunctioning and exposing the firm behind them as being run by crooks.

d Joseph Kane   *p* Sol C. Siegel   *s* Bernard McConville, Charles Francis Royal   *c* Ernest Miller   *lp* Gene Autry, Smiley Burnette, Helen Valkis, Sammy McKim, Ivan Miller, Dick Weston (Roy Rogers), Champion

Out West with the Hardys
(MGM) b/w 90(84) min
This routine entry in the Hardy family series, so beloved by Louis B. Mayer, sees America's first family taking a holiday on a dude ranch. Rooney, as Andy, gets his comeuppance from Weidler, Judge Hardy (Stone) saves a local rancher from a shyster lawyer and Marion (Parker) has an adolescent romance with Jones' ranch foreman.

d George B. Seitz   *p* J. J. Cohn   *s* Kay Van Riper, Agnes Christine Johnston, William Ludwig   *c* Lester White
lp Lewis Stone, Mickey Rooney, Virginia Weidler, Cecelia Parker, Fay Holden, Gordon Jones

Gene Autry, Smiley Burnette and assorted ranch hands in The Old Barn Dance.

Outlaws of Sonora   (REP) b/w 55 min
Routine fare. The plot twist has Livingston essay two roles, a Mesquiteer and an outlaw. Outlaw Livingston intercepts Mesquiteer Livingston on his way to collect some money and when the outlaw notices the similarities between them decides to collect the money himself. The confused identities lead to some confusion in the minds of Corrigan and Terhune but things are sorted out and the outlaws rounded up in a typically rip-roaring finale.

d George Sherman   *p* William Berke   *s* Betty Burbridge, Edmund Kelso   *c* William Nobles   *lp* Bob Livingston, Ray Corrigan, Max Terhune, Otis Harlan, George Chesebro, Frank LaRue

Overland Stage Raiders   (REP) b/w 58 min
Wayne's second outing as a Mesquiteer, *Overland Stage Raiders* is most memorable as being the last film of Brooks, the lustrous star of G.W. Pabst's masterpiece, *Pandora's Box* (1929). She plays Wayne's unlikely girfriend. The overland stage of the title turns out to be a Greyhound bus (!) and the plot has Wayne, Corrigan and Terhune shipping gold by air and fighting would-be hijackers.

d George Sherman   *p* William Berke   *s* Luci Ward
c William Nobles   *lp* John Wayne, Louise Brooks, Ray Corrigan, Max Terhune, Frank LaRue, Yakima Canutt

The Painted Desert   (RKO) b/w 59 min
A routine remake of the 1931 film with O'Brien in the William Boyd role. The plot was extensively revised to confront O'Brien and Day as partners in a tungsten mine with Kohler as a corrupt mining agent and William V. Mong as a corrupt banker who attempt to jump the claim. Much of the action footage, notably the magnificent explosion at the mine, was taken from the earlier film. Ray Whitley and his Prairie Musicians, better known for their twenty minute musical shorts, provide the musical interludes that slow the action down.

John Wayne (centre), Louise Brooks, sadly without those famous bangs, and Ray Corrigan in Overland Stage Raiders.

d David Howard p Bert Gilroy s John Rathmell, Oliver Drake c Harry Wild lp George O'Brien, Laraine Day, Fred Kohler, Ray Whitley, Stanley Fields, William V. Mong

The Painted Trail (MON) b/w 50 min

A solid Keene outing, this film re-united its star with director Hill with whom he'd worked extensively before. Tansey's script (written under his Emmett pseudonym) is routine with Keene as the undercover agent on the track of smugglers Mason and Long who are working the Mexican-American border. Keene is as athletic as ever and Stewart a rather passive heroine. The climax has Keene and Long shooting it out across the border line, one on each side.

d Robert Hill p/s Robert Emmett (Tansey) c Bert Longenecker lp Tom Keene, Eleanor Stewart, LeRoy Mason, Walter Long, Forrest Taylor, Bud Osborne

Pals of the Saddle (REP) b/w 55 min

Wayne's first outing as a Mesquiteer – he replaced Bob Livingston – *Pals of the Saddle*, like so many of the Three Mesquiteers films, is set in modern times. The complicated plot features Corrigan and Terhune trying to find out what's happened to Wayne's Stony Brooke who has stumbled on a plan by enemy agents to smuggle a chemical, Monium (out of which poison gas can be made) to Mexico and sell it to foreign interests. Needless to say the Mesquiteers save the day and secret agent McKay.

d George Sherman p William Berke s Betty Burbridge, Stanley Roberts c Reggie Lanning lp John Wayne, Ray Corrigan, Max Terhune, Doreen McKay, Josef Forte, George Douglas

John Wayne in difficulties in Pals of the Saddle.

Panamint's Bad Man (PRINCIPAL/FOX) b/w 60 min

The final outing for singing cowboy Ballew. An orchestra leader and singer, Ballew was discovered by producer Lesser after his appearance as a cowboy in Paramount's *Palm Springs* (1936). But though Ballew looked a little like Gary Cooper, his wooden acting and the inferior scripts limited the series to five titles. *Panamint's Bad Man* has a strong supporting cast with Beery as the scowling, mustache-twirling outlaw leader whose gang Ballew infiltrates, Fields as the baddie who does the right thing and Daw as the object of Ballew's affections and songs.

d Ray Taylor p Sol Lesser s Luci Ward, Charles A. Powell c Allen Thompson lp Smith Ballew, Evelyn Daw, Noah Beery, Stanley Fields, Harry Woods, Pat O'Brien

Partners of the Plains (PAR) b/w 68 min

This superior Hopalong Cassidy series entry is as much a testament to Sherman's abilities as a producer as anything else. Unlike many series Westerns which are populated by types rather than actors, whose plots are routine to the point of cliche and were given minuscule budgets, Sherman always looked for new names and consistently refused to cut corners. This outing features Gaze as a spoiled English lady who inherits a ranch and has to be taught 'proper Western ways' by ranch foreman Boyd. Bridge is the local badman and Warburton, as Gaze's British fiancé, is as ill at ease on the range as she.

d Lesley Selander p Harry Sherman s Harrison Jacobs c Russell Harlan lp William Boyd, Harvey Clark, Gwen Gaze, Al Bridge, John Warburton, Russell Hayden

Phantom Gold (COL) b/w 56 min

Luden was Columbia's third-string Western star and as such got only the smallest of budgets. This is one of the best of his short-lived series for the company and sees him battling against a band of outlaws led by Whitaker who are using a ghost town as their hideout. Gatzert's screenplay is snappy and full of bizarre complications: at one point Whitaker salts a gold mine to conjure up people to rob only to pick a real gold mine as the site of his false one! But the concentration of the trade reviews on Tiffany the dog didn't bode well for the series.

d Joseph Levering p Larry Darmour s Nate Gatzert c James S. Brown Jnr lp Jack Luden, Beth Marion, Charles Whitaker, Hal Taliaferro (Wally Wales), Barry Downing, Jack Ingram

The Phantom Ranger (MON) b/w 54 min

A serviceable McCoy series entry. The script's many dialogue weaknesses are soon lost in the action, as McCoy dons outlaw guise to hunt down a band of counterfeiters led by Hackett and King. At the same time he romances Kaaren, herself masquerading as a dance-hall entertainer while she searches for her father, an engineer kidnapped by the baddies.

d Sam Newfield p Maurice Conn s Joseph O'Donnell c Jack Greenhalgh lp Tim McCoy, Karl Hackett, Charles King, Suzanne Kaaren, John St Polis, Tom London

Prairie Moon (REP) b/w 58 min

An indifferent Autry entry in which Republic's increased budget is hardly visible. Autry promises a dying gangster to look after his three kids. Predictably when they arrive on the ranch they are young toughs and street urchins, but equally predictably Autry and Burnette drag the good out of them with the result that they help Autry and company put paid to a bunch of local cattle rustlers.

d Ralph Staub p Harry Grey s Betty Burbridge, Stanley Roberts c William Nobles lp Gene Autry, Smiley Burnette, Shirley Deane, Tommy Ryan, Walter Tetley

Pride of the West (PAR) b/w 56 min

A superior Hopalong Cassidy entry with Boyd out to get the mysterious outlaw leader who is responsible for a string of stagecoach robberies. Watt gives the storyline a number of unexpected twists that add real tension while Selander's vigorous direction produces some memorable fistfights. Field is the romantic interest and onetime silent screen star Harlan, the villain.

d Lesley Selander p Harry Sherman s Nate Watt c Russell Harlan lp William Boyd, George Hayes, Russell Hayden, Kenneth Harlan, Earle Hodgins, Charlotte Field

1938

The Purple Vigilantes (REP) b/w 58 min
A strong Three Mesquiteers entry, this was the second to be
directed by Sherman who was to become a regular on the
series. Burbridge and Drake's witty plot has the Mesquiteers
on the trail of purple-hooded vigilantes who, after clearing up
a town, start using their disguises to line their own pockets.
Unlike recent entries which had too often been bogged down
in comedy, Sherman wisely emphasizes the strong plotline
and action sequences. Thus even the romance between
Livingston and Barclay is no more than sketched in.

d George Sherman p Sol C. Siegel s Betty Burbridge,
Oliver Drake lp Bob Livingston, Ray Corrigan, Max
Terhune, Joan Barclay, Jack Perrin, Earle Hodgins

The Ranger's Roundup
(SPECTRUM/STAN LAUREL PRODUCTIONS) b/w 55 min
The first of Stan Laurel's brief forays into production outside
of his work with Oliver Hardy, this Buell-produced film was
officially billed as a Stan Laurel Production. Sadly Laurel's
appearance on the scene seems to have been entirely a matter
of finance: the film is no different from Scott's previous
outings. Scott is an undercover singing ranger putting paid to
Hackett's outlaw gang which is run under the cover of a
medicine show.

d Sam Newfield p Jed Buell s George Plympton
c William Hyer lp Fred Scott, Al St John, Christine
McIntyre, Karl Hackett, Earle Hodgins, Steve Ryan

Rawhide (PRINCIPAL/FOX) b/w 58 min
Featuring a tight script by Jarrett, George O'Brien's old
writer, and an engaging performance by baseball star Gehrig
as the rancher being threatened by McKee and assorted
heavies, Rawhide is the best of singing cowboy Ballew's
short-lived Fox series. Ballew is the lawyer in love with the
sister of Gehrig who organizes the ranchers.

d Ray Taylor p Sol Lesser s Dan Jarrett, Jack Natteford
c Allen Thompson lp Smith Ballew, Lou Gehrig, Lafe
McKee, Evalyn Knapp, Arthur Loft

Red River Range (REP) b/w 56 min
Of all the Three Mesquiteers films, the eight starring Wayne
as Stony Brooke are the best known and most popular. This,
his fourth, sees the trio appointed special deputies to stop
cattle rustling and Wayne pretending to be an outlaw. The
pace is slower than earlier entries in the series with comedy to
the fore (notably in the performance by Moran) on the dude
ranch that the outlaws are using as cover.

d George Sherman p William Berke s Stanley Roberts,
Betty Burbridge, Luci Ward c Jack Marta lp John
Wayne, Ray Corrigan, Max Terhune, Polly Moran, Kirby
Grant, Sammy McKim

The Renegade Ranger (RKO) b/w 60 min
Hayworth, bringing a bigger budget than normal as well as
her charm, is the girl unjustly accused of murder who

Top: *Max Terhune,
Bob Livingston and
Ray Corrigan (left to
right) one of the better
known of the ever-
changing line ups that
comprised the Three
Mesquiteers in The
Purple Vigilantes.*

*Battlin' Bob Baker, yet
another Western series
star who was forced to
take up his guitar and
sing, in The Singing
Outlaw.*

becomes a female Robin Hood organizing homesteaders into
vigilante groups to fight off rustlers and crooked politicians in
this excellent series entry. O'Brien handles the action with his
usual nonchalance as the Texas Ranger assigned to bring her
in while Holt is in equally fine form as the Ranger who quits
the service to go to Hayworth's assistance. Royale is the villain
and Whitley provides the musical interludes. Drake's script is
an unofficial remake of a Tom Keene Western, **Come On
Danger** (1932) which would be officially remade under the
same title in 1942 by RKO.

d David Howard p Bert Gilroy s Oliver Drake c Harry
Wild lp George O'Brien, Rita Hayworth, Tim Holt, Ray
Whitley, William Royale, Lucio Villegas

Ride 'Em Cowgirl
(CORONADO/GRAND NATIONAL) b/w 52 min
The first, and best, of Page's trio of Westerns for Grand
National featuring her as a singing cowgirl. The only actress
ever given the lead or principal part in a series Western, Page
is supported by Frome in the odd role of the attendant male
love interest who also does the fighting. Page was a pretty
singer and convincing horse rider, but sadly the formula of the
series Western was too rigid to accommodate a female hero. In
this entry she steals the $5,000 her father was cheated of, is
declared an outlaw and wins a horse race before exposing
Girard as the real culprit (and a silver smuggler as well) with
help from Frome and Barnett. An engaging curiosity.

d Samuel Diege p Arthur Dreifuss s Arthur Hoerl
c Mack Stengler lp Dorothy Page, Milton Frome, Vince
Barnett, Lynne Mayberry, Joseph Girard, Frank Ellis

Rio Grande aka Rio Grande Stampede
(COL) b/w 58 min
A minor Starrett outing notable for Ballard's superior
cinematography and Doran as the heroine, a role Meredith

*Tim Holt, Rita
Hayworth and George
O'Brien in The
Renegade Ranger.*

Hans Albers as the flamboyant Chicago detective who heads West in Sergeant Berry, *one of the earliest European Westerns.*

had fulfilled in previous Starrett outings. The screenplay has him leading the Sons of the Pioneers against Curtis who has designs on Doran's ranch.

d Sam Nelson   *p* Harry Decker   *s* Charles Francis Royal *c* Lucien Ballard   *lp* Charles Starrett, Ann Doran, Bob Nolan, Dick Curtis, Hal Taliaferro (Wally Wales)

Rollin' Plains   (GRAND NATIONAL)   b/w   57 min
Ritter's previous entry, *Frontier Town* (1938) relied fairly extensively on stock footage of rodeo events; *Rollin' Plains* goes one further: the whole of the last reel is lifted from an early Ritter film, **Sing Cowboy Sing** (1937). Finney's drastic solutions to what were clearly pressing economic problems offered the strongest possible indications that Ritter's days at Grand National were numbered. The trouble wasn't Ritter, who was as successful as ever, but Grand National itself which was nearing financial collapse after an ill-advised venture into big budget film-making.

Parsons and Kelso's script features Ritter as a drifter trying to bring peace between those most traditional of Western enemies, cowmen and sheepmen. After one more film, Finney, who had Ritter under personal contract, and his star quit Grand National for Monogram and bigger budgets.

d Al Herman   *p* Edward Finney   *s* Lindsley Parsons, Edmund Kelso   *c* Francis Corby   *lp* Tex Ritter, Hobart Bosworth, Snub Pollard, Horace Murphy, Harriet Bennett, Charles King

Santa Fé Stampede   (REP)   b/w   58 min
Silent screen star Farnum is the prospector who invites the Mesquiteers, who grubstaked him, to share the profits when he finds gold in this intriguing entry in the series. Once they arrive the trio get involved with a crooked politician, Mason, who is using the law to his own advantage. Sherman's direction is routine but Lanning's cinematography is superb and the script by Ward and Burbridge has a couple of unusual touches, such as the death of two children – an unheard of thing in a B Western – when a runaway buckboard crashes.

d George Sherman   *p* William Berke   *s* Luci Ward, Betty Burbridge   *c* Reggie Lanning   *lp* John Wayne, Ray Corrigan, Max Terhune, William Farnum, LeRoy Mason, Charles King

Sergeant Berry   (TOBIS FILMKUNST; GER)   b/w   113 min
This German Western is constructed as a showcase for the flamboyant Albers. The result is a decidedly European film, especially in its vulgar humour: at one point Albers even runs around naked. The hackneyed plot features Albers as the detective of the title and master of disguise who heads West to settle the hash of a band of Mexican smugglers and at the same time pursue von Bukovics. Shot on location in the Italian desert (rather than in Spain where the Italian-German co-productions of the sixties were filmed), the movie is highly theatrical.

The characters are little but clichés, from their gaily coloured bandanas to their '*carambas*' which are exclaimed at every opportunity, but Albers' performance as the all-powerful hero, despite the broad humour of the film, places him firmly within the Dr Mabuse tradition so strong in German fiction.

d Herbert Selpin   *p* Hans Albers   *s* Walter Wasserman, C. H. Diller   *c* Franz Koch   *lp* Hans Albers, Roni von Bukovics, Peter Vob, Gerda Hochst, Alexander Engel, Herbert Hubner

The Singing Outlaw   (U)   b/w   56 min
The second of Baker's outings as a singing cowboy in notable for Miller's exceptional camera work and Lewis' emphatic direction. The routine plot has Baker, as Scrap Gordon, come across a 'singing outlaw' and a US marshal fighting to the death and assuming the identity of the marshal. Before he can re-assert his own identity, he has to round up a bunch of rustlers, led by the ubiquitous Woods, and succumb to the charms of rancher's daughter Barclay.

d Joseph H. Lewis   *p* Paul Malvern   *s* Harry O. Hoyt *c* Virgil Miller   *lp* Bob Baker, Joan Barclay, Harry Woods, Fuzzy Knight, Carl Stockdale, LeRoy Mason

Song of the Buckaroo   (MON)   b/w   58 min
One of Ritter's best movies during his three-year stay with Monogram. Rathmell's script has Tex running for mayor and cleaning out a gang of crooks who are trying to fix the election. Model Falkenberg is a glamorous leading lady and Herman's direction, if a little slow, gives a touch of sophistication to Murphy and Pollard's cornpoke antics.

d Al Herman   *p* Edward Finney   *s* John Rathmell *c* Francis Corby   *lp* Tex Ritter, Jinx Falkenberg, Horace Murphy, Snub Pollard, Charles King, Frank LaRue

Songs and Bullets
(SPECTRUM/STAN LAUREL PRODUCTIONS)   b/w   58 min
The second of Stan Laurel's essays into production, *Songs and Bullets*, its fine title notwithstanding, is badly let down by Newfield's penny-plain direction. Moreover, since Scott sings rather better than he throws a punch, the action is on the primitive side. O'Donnell and Plympton's screenplay has him stop an outburst of cattle rustling and put paid to villains King and Hackett.

d Sam Newfield   *p* Jed Buell   *s* Joseph O'Donnell, George Plympton   *c* Mack Stengler   *lp* Fred Scott, Al St John, Alice Ardell, Charles King, Karl Hackett, Frank LaRue

Terror of Tiny Town   (COL)   b/w   62 min
Another novelty film from producer Buell who a year earlier had had the idea for the first all-black Western, **Harlem on the Prairie** (1937) the success of which led to a (short-lived) series of blaxploitation Westerns. Those films are notable for the way they religiously follow the (white) conventions of the genre. The gimmick in the case of *Terror in Tiny Town* is its cast of some 60 midgets, but otherwise the film is played as straight as possible. The plot is certainly 'traditional': Little Billy is the baddie who incites a feud between two families in

the hopes of taking over their lands and Curtis is the all-in-white hero who finally foils his plan. Krebs is the bar room songstress in love with Little Billy and Moray the maiden Curtis romances.

At the time, the movie was seen as just another novelty item; half-a-century later when most series Westerns look odd enough without gimmicks, the film seems cruel. Unlike Todd Browning's *Freaks* (1932) which treated its cast of abnormal actors with compassion, Newfield's film pretends that they're normal people and invites us to smirk at a cast dwarfed by the hitching posts they tie their Shetland ponies to. The film was moderately successful and a sequel announced, but not made.

d Sam Newfield *p* Jed Buell *s* Fred Myton *c* Mack Stengler *lp* Billy Curtis, Little Billy, Nita Krebs, Yvonne Moray, Johnny Bembury, Billy Platt

Tex Rides with the Boy Scouts
(GRAND NATIONAL) b/w 57 min
Producer Finney noticed that Ritter's last outing, the juvenile-oriented **The Mystery of the Hooded Horsemen** (1937) had been a big hit with audiences. Accordingly, he had Kelso quickly rewrite the next script to include a juvenile angle. This was the result, a modern Western in which Tex is helped by the scouts, whose virtues are extolled in a specially prepared prologue, to catch King's band of gold robbers. In between fighting King, Ritter serenades Reynolds.

d Ray Taylor *p* Edward Finney *s* Edmund Kelso *c* Gus Peterson *lp* Tex Ritter, Marjorie Reynolds, Snub Pollard, Charles King, Horace Murphy, Edward Cassidy

The Texans (PAR) b/w 92 min
A prestige Paramount production, this remake of the 1924 silent, *North of '36'*, is a clumsy epic about the opening of the Chisholm Trail, the formation of the Ku Klux Klan and the impact of the arrival of the transcontinental railroad on the frontier. Scott is the trail boss who gets his 10,000 strong herd to the Kansas rail head after all sorts of dangers and Brennan, in a role he was to make his own (notably in **Red River,** 1948) is the crusty trail cook.

d James Hogan *p* Lucien Hubbard *s* Bertram Milhauser, Paul Sloane, William Wister Haines *c* Theodor Sparkuhl *lp* Joan Bennett, Randolph Scott, Walter Brennan, May Robson, Raymond Hatton, Robert Cummings

Under Western Stars (REP) b/w 65 min
Fittingly directed by Kane who'd secured Rogers his screen test at Republic and was to direct 42 films with 'The King of the Cowboys', this was Roger's first starring film. Rogers was chosen by Republic's owner, Herbert J. Yates, to be built into a second-string singing cowboy as part of a bargaining tactic to threaten Gene Autry, Republic's quarrelsome star singing

cowboy. But, though the company lavished great care on the production and even gave Rogers Autry's side-kick, Burnette, as a co-star, it was surprised by the rapturous reception the film received from reviewers – ranging from the trades to the *New York Times* – and public alike. The good review in the *New York Times*, a paper not known for its fondness of series Westerns was most surprising: its critic, Bosley Crowther enthused, 'Republic has discovered...a new Playboy of the Western world in the sombrero'd person of Roy Rogers who has a drawl like Gary Cooper, a smile like Shirley Temple and a voice like Tito Guizar'.

The topical plot features Rogers as a singing Congressman elected to Washington on a free water platform to save a dust bowl area. This he does, proving his case by showing

Above: *A scene from* Terror of Tiny Town, *surely the most gimmick-ridden series Western ever.*

Far left: *Tex Ritter at the campfire in* Tex Rides with the Boy Scouts.

Randolph Scott and Joan Bennett in her only Western, The Texans, a prestige Paramount production.

Above: *Roy Rogers as the singing congressman in* Under Western Stars, *his first starring film.*

Far right: *Claire Trevor and John Wayne as early Pennsylvania settlers and lovers in* Allegheny Uprising.

Washington society a dust bowl documentary and so securing a flood control bill. The film is remarkably similar to (and shared screenwriter credits with) Gene Autry's **Rovin' Tumbleweeds** (1939).

d Joseph Kane *p* Sol C. Siegel *s* Dorrell McGowan, Stuart McGowan, Betty Burbridge *c* Jack Marta *lp* Roy Rogers, Smiley Burnette, Carol Hughes, Guy Usher, Tom Chatterton, Kenneth Harlan, Trigger

Utah Trail (GRAND NATIONAL) b/w 56 min

Ritter himself supplied the original idea for this his last film for the soon-to-be bankrupt Grand National: cattle rustlers who escape on a train that literally disappears. The effect works on screen but Finney's penny-pinching budget and the presence of five songs left little space for the fisticuffs that Ritter's fans demanded.

d Al Herman *p* Edward Finney *s* Edmund Kelso *p* Tex Ritter, Horace Murphy, Snub Pollard, Karl Hackett, Charles King, Edward Cassidy

Valley of the Giants (WB) 79 min

A weak Warners production-line movie. Morris is the lumberman fighting lumber pirates and winning the hand of Trevor in the process. Keighley's direction is efficient, but empty, just as Miller's screenplay, based on a novel by the

Wayne Morris and Donald Crisp in Valley of the Giants.

prolific Peter B. Kyne, who supplied the original story for the often filmed *Three Godfathers*, is solid and unimaginative.

d William Keighley *p* Lou Edelman *s* Seton I. Miller, Michael Fessier *c* Sol Polito *lp* Wayne Morris, Claire Trevor, Frank McHugh, Alan Hale, Donald Crisp, Charles Bickford

West of Cheyenne (COL) b/w 59 min

In this minor Starrett series outing the Sons of the Pioneers take up so much of the action that it seems as though they, rather than Starrett, are the stars. Accordingly there's fewer fights than usual and the plot, about cattle rustling, is much compressed. Altogether a puzzling film, made even more so by Nelson's hit and miss direction.

d Sam Nelson *p* Harry Decker *s* Ed Earl Repp *c* Benjamin Kline *lp* Charles Starrett, Iris Meredith, Bob Nolan, Dick Curtis, Edward LeSaint, Pat Brady

Where the Buffalo Roam (MON) b/w 61 min

A lacklustre series entry. Ritter co-stars with grainy library footage of buffalo and King, as usual the villain of the piece, is here needlessly overhunting buffalo. Murphy and Pollard, soon to be replaced by Arkansas Slim Andrews, are the comic relief.

d Al Herman *p* Edward Finney *s* Robert Emmett (Tansey) *c* Francis Corby *lp* Tex Ritter, Horace Murphy, Snub Pollard, Dorothy Short, Charles King, Richard Alexander

1939

Allegheny Uprising *aka* Allegheny Frontier
aka The First Rebel (RKO) b/w 81 min

Released at the same time as **Drums Along the Mohawk** (1939) which is set in the same period, *Allegheny Uprising* is notable for RKO's swift re-pairing of Wayne and Trevor on the heels of their immense success in **Stagecoach** (1939). An

unpretentious Western about the pre-Revolutionary-War years, it features Wayne as the frontiersman who smashes Donlevy's illicit trade in liquor with the Indians, Trevor as the girl who follows him through thick and thin and Sanders as a tyrannical British officer. Musuraca's expressionistic lighting and Seiter's efficient direction give a necessary punch to Wolfson's somewhat stilted script.

d William A. Seiter *p* Pandro S. Berman *s* P. J. Wolfson *c* Nicholas Musuraca *lp* John Wayne, Claire Trevor, Brian Donlevy, George Sanders, Chill Wills, Robert Barrat

Arizona Legion (RKO) b/w 58 min
An exciting series entry. O'Brien is the ranger masquerading
as a baddie as part of a plan to clean up the Arizona Territory.
Drake's screenplay is routine but O'Brien's athletic prowess
and charm give the story the necessary lift. A subplot has him
competing with Moore for the hand of Johnson. Wills, as
comic support, plays the appropriately named Whopper
whose tall stories are as strong as Gabby Hayes'.

d David Howard *p* Bert Gilroy *s* Oliver Drake *c* Harry
Wild *lp* George O'Brien, Lorraine Johnson (Day), Chill
Wills, Carlyle Moore Jnr, Harry Cording, Lafe McKee

The Arizona Wildcat (FOX) b/w 69 min
Withers is the teenage tearaway of the title in this comedy
Western. With her foster father, Carrillo, she puts paid to the
plans of Woods and his gold robbers. Andriot's cinematography is better than either the script, or Withers' mischief,
deserve.

d Herbert I. Leeds *p* John Stone *s* Barry Trivers, Jerry
Cady *c* Lucien Andriot *lp* Jane Withers, Leo Carrillo,
Pauline Moore, William Henry, Henry Wilcoxon, Harry
Woods

Bad Lands (RKO) b/w 70 min
An intriguing B Western, *Bad Lands* is a variant of *The Lost
Patrol* (1934) with Barrat as the sheriff who leads a posse into
the desert after marauding Indians and watches them being
killed one by one. Unusually Beery is cast in an unsympathetic role and Ford and Williams offer strong support. Landers'
forceful direction is occasionally let down by Redman's weak
cinematography.

d Lew Landers *p* Robert Sisk *s* Clarence Upson Young
c Frank Redman *lp* Robert Barrat, Noah Beery Jnr, Guinn
(Big Boy) Williams, Francis Ford, Andy Clyde, Jack (John)
Payne

The Bronze Buckaroo
(HOLLYWOOD PRODUCTIONS) b/w 57 min
After the success of **Harlem on the Prairie** (1937), producer
Kahn formed Hollywood Productions with the express
purpose of making all-black films. All would be Westerns.
The first, starring Jeffries who had the lead in **Harlem on the
Prairie** (1937), was *The Bronze Buckaroo*. With his side-kick,
Jeffries sets out on the trail of the murderers of Young's
father. The climax is a lengthy and highly improbable gun
battle between Jeffries and Brooks. The film is 'colour
designed', with the blacker actors playing villains to the
light-skinned singing hero.

d/p/s Richard Kahn *c* Roland Price *lp* Herbert Jeffries,
Artie Young, Rellie Hardin, Spencer Williams, Clarence
Brooks, F.E. Miller

*Johnny Mack Brown
(left) on the trail of secret
agents in* Chip of the
Flying U.

Chip of the Flying U (U) b/w 55 min
Brown's third Universal Western of the year, *Chip of the
Flying U* shows a marked decline in production values for all
the company's initial trumpeting that the series would be 'the
most expensive Western schedule since the days of Buck
Jones'. The plot is a tired rehash of one of Tom Mix's best
silents, with Brown as the ranch foreman accused of
murdering a banker who clears himself by revealing, in a
modern plot twist, that the real culprits are foreign agents
dealing in munitions. Brown's partner in the series, Baker,
quit in 1940 to be replaced by petite Nell O'Day as a cowgirl
auxiliary. Knight provides the weary comedy.

d Ralph Staub *s* Larry Rhine, Andrew Bennison
c William Sickner *lp* Johnny Mack Brown, Bob Baker,
Fuzzy Knight, Doris Weston, Karl Hackett, Forrest Taylor

Crashin' Thru (MON) b/w 65 min
Announced by Grand National and finally released by
Monogram after that company had gone bankrupt, this weak
outing signalled the end of the Renfrew of the Mounties
series. Stone is the American gangster hoping to hijack a
shipment of gold bullion with the help of his sister, Carmen,
who is foiled by Newill's singing mountie.

d Elmer Clifton *p* Philip N. Krasna *s* Sherman Lowe
c Edward Linden *lp* James Newill, Jean Carmen, Milburn
Stone, Warren Hull, Iron Eyes Cody, Roy Barcroft

Days of Jesse James (REP) b/w 63 min
Barry, who would achieve Western stardom with the addition
of the soubriquet 'Red' for **Adventures of Red Ryder** (1940) a
year later, is Jesse James and Rogers is the man who proves he
didn't rob the Northfield bank, in this confused Western.
The villains, as one would expect, are crooked bank officials.
Nonetheless, despite Snell's clumsy plot, the film is a distinct
improvement on the star's recent outings.

d/p Joseph Kane *s* Earle Snell *c* Reggie Lanning *lp* Roy
Rogers, George Hayes, Donald Barry, Pauline Moore, Harry
Woods, Arthur Loft, Trigger

Desperate Trails (U) b/w 58 min
Brown's first feature for Universal is a fanciful actioneer that
augured well for his projected series. The plot is routine with
Brown after rustlers and Robinson, but the strong production
values and the direction of Ray, who had been in control of
some of Brown's Supreme releases, give the film a real punch.

*Roy Rogers (left),
Gabby Hayes (with
money) and Don 'Red'
Barry in* Days of Jesse
James.

Henry Fonda and Claudette Colbert in John Ford's Drums Along the Mohawk.

Only Baker, once a series star in his own right, seemed unsure of what was expected of him.

d/p Albert Ray   *s* Andrew Bennison   *c* Jerry Ash
lp Johnny Mack Brown, Bob Baker, Fuzzy Knight, Frances Robinson, Bill Cody Jnr, Ed Cassidy

Destry Rides Again (U) b/w 94 min

This film has even less resemblance to Max Brand's novel than the 1932 version. Producer Pasternak had the idea of resurrecting the role that had made Dietrich famous, the bar room singer of *The Blue Angel* (1930), in an effort to revive her then flagging career. A Western seemed a likely setting and Universal owned the rights to *Destry Rides Again*. The new script which deftly mocks many of the Western's conventions features Stewart as a gunless, milk-drinking deputy sheriff, Donlevy as the crooked gambler wrestling for control of the town and Dietrich as Frenchy, Donlevy's girl who falls for Stewart and finally dies to save his life. Dietrich steals the picture, whether fighting Una Merkel, in the film's most famous sequence, singing ('See What the Boys in the Backroom Will Have') or just wisecracking, aided by Marshall's relaxed direction and Stewart's charming support.

Below: Marlene Dietrich holds a gun on James Stewart's milk drinking sheriff in the most famous version of Destry Rides Again, *the film that resurrected Dietrich's flagging career.*

d George Marshall   *p* Joe Pasternak   *s* Felix Jackson, Henry Myers, Gertrude Purcell   *c* Hal Mohr   *lp* Marlene Dietrich, James Stewart, Charles Winninger, Mischa Auer, Brian Donlevy, Una Merkel

Dodge City (WB) 104 min

The most successful of the historical Westerns made by Warners in the late thirties and early forties, *Dodge City* is a sprawling epic with Flynn, in fine swashbuckling form, taming the West and De Havilland. Very loosely based on the exploits of Wyatt Earp, it makes an interesting comparison with Ford's version of the Earp legend, **My Darling Clementine** (1946). Both films deal with the coming of law and order to the frontier. But where for Ford this is represented by a series of cultural rituals (Shakespeare, perfume, the dance and the church) overlaying the almost Biblical confrontation of the Clantons and the Earps, for Curtiz and screenwriter Buckner 'Civilization' means organization: the railroad, gangsterism, the press. Ford looks on with mixed feelings, Curtiz with an eye to the urban future. Yet ironically, the soft early Technicolor images of cinema-

Alan Hale and Errol Flynn in Dodge City, *the most successful of the series of prestige Westerns made by Warners in the late thirties and forties.*

tographer Polito, the stirring music of Max Steiner and Curtiz's emphatic direction (at its best in the big set-piece scenes) give the film an innocence and charm that belie its plot.

d Michael Curtiz   *p* Robert Lord   *s* Robert Buckner   *c* Sol Polito, Ray Rennahan   *lp* Errol Flynn, Olivia De Havilland, Ann Sheridan, Bruce Cabot, Alan Hale, John Litel

Down the Wyoming Trail (MON) b/w 56 min

A camera breakdown which resulted in the unusual snowy locations looking like murky process-shots put paid to Finney's hopes of making this a special entry in his slim budgeted Ritter series. King and Ingraham are the rustlers, stampeding herds of wild elk into ranchers' stocks until Ritter puts paid to their plans. The end is unusual: King commits suicide in the snow.

d Al Herman   *p* Edward Finney   *s* Peter Dixon, Roger Merton   *c* Marcel LePicard   *lp* Tex Ritter, Mary Brodel, Charles King, Jack Ingraham, Horace Murphy, Frank LaRue

Drums Along the Mohawk (FOX) 103 min

Ford's first colour feature is both one of his prettiest looking and most commercially successful films. Fonda and Colbert are the couple who just before the outbreak of the War of Independence join a group of settlers in the Mohawk Valley and withstand assorted frontier hardships and British engineered Indian attacks, as they come to see themselves as Americans rather than colonials. The film's episodic structure and its extensive details of frontier life betray its origins in Walter Edmond's best-selling novel, as does the presence of Colbert – not the kind of actress Ford liked working with – in the role of the Easterner complaining about the privations of frontier life. But, if the film isn't one of Ford's best, in sequences like Fonda's race for help in the early morning while being pursued by Indians, Ford and cinematographer

Glennon create breathtakingly beautiful images. Similarly Oliver's daunting matriarch is a wholly Fordian character.

Footage from the film was used in **Buffalo Bill** (1944) and *Mohawk* (1956).

d John Ford *p* Raymond Griffith *s* Lamar Trotti, Sonya Levien *c* Bert Glennon, Ray Rennahan *lp* Claudette Colbert, Henry Fonda, Edna May Oliver, John Carradine, Eddie Collins, Doris Bowdon

The Fighting Gringo (RKO) b/w 59 min

A taut actioneer in the best tradition of O'Brien's series Westerns. O'Brien leads a band of socially minded gunmen who clear up a murder and cement Mexican-American relations at the same time by wooing Tovar. Howard directs briskly.

d David Howard *p* Bert Gilroy *s* Oliver Drake *c* Harry Wild *lp* George O'Brien, Lupita Tovar, Glenn Strange, Slim Whitaker, LeRoy Mason, Chris-Pin Martin

Frontier Marshal (FOX) b/w 71 min

Dwan's first sound Western is a remake of Lew Seiler's **Frontier Marshal** (1934). It is particularly interesting for the similarities it has to John Ford's **My Darling Clementine** (1946), which also derives from Stuart N. Lake's novel, *Wyatt Earp, Frontier Marshal*. Several incidents from the Dwan film are repeated in Ford's – Charles Stevens even repeats his role as the drunken Indian! – but the mood and tone of the films are entirely different. Ford's Earp brings civilization to Tombstone, Dwan's far more innocent hero (Scott) brings only law and order. Similarly, Dwan's direction is more direct and to the point than Ford's. Romero is a slick Doc Halliday who loses his girl to Scott.

d Allan Dwan *p* Sol M. Wurtzel *s* Sam Hellman *c* Charles G. Clarke *lp* Randolph Scott, Cesar Romero, Nancy Kelly, John Carradine, Ward Bond, Lon Chaney Jnr

Frontiers of '49 (COL) b/w 54 min

The second of Elliott's Westerns for Columbia, like his first, is loosely based on fact. The plot is the familiar one of the Spanish land grant problem. King is the head of a syndicate practising legal robbery and Elliott is the Cavalry captain sent to clear things up. The film is routine – coaxing a famous review out of *Variety*, 'So-so b.o., no mo' – but it helped establish Elliott who was to become one of the greats of the B Western.

d Joseph Levering *p* Larry Darmour *s* Nate Gatzert *c* James S. Brown Jnr *lp* Bill Elliott, Charles King, Luana DeAlcaniz, Hal Taliaferro (Wally Wales), Slim Whitaker, Bud Osborne

Harlem Rides the Range

(HOLLYWOOD PICTURES) b/w 58 min

The second of producer Kahn's trio of Black Westerns – the

others being **The Bronze Buckaroo** (1939) and *The Two Gun Man from Harlem* (1940). Co-written by black actors Williams and Miller (who contributed additional dialogue to the first all-black Western, **Harlem on the Prairie,** 1937) the plot features Jeffries putting an end to Brooks' attempt to steal a radium mine from Young. By all accounts, a routine film, it is historically important, less for the light it throws on black aspirations than for the inflexibility of the genre it reveals. For, though it was written by blacks, the film aped white Westerns totally and was far removed from black interests. Only in the cool style, usually associated with the villain in the traditional Western, paraded by Jeffries is there any sense of blackness. What was even more amazing was the penchant Jeffries developed, again in mimicry of other Western stars, for ornamenting his car with bronze Western motifs.

d/p Richard Kahn *s* Spencer Williams Jnr, F.E. Miller *c* Roland Price, Clark Ramsey *lp* Herbert Jeffrey (Jeffries), Lucius Brooks, Artie Young, F.E. Miller, Spencer Williams, Clarence Brooks

Heritage of the Desert (PAR) b/w 74 min

The third and best version of Zane Grey's novel. Unlike Henry Hathaway in his 1932 film, Selander keeps the action back until the end. The result is a terrific climax, like those producer Sherman generally produced for his Hopalong Cassidy series. Woods is the Eastern lawyer who heads West to inspect his mine holdings and discovers that his manager, Gordon, has been cheating him steadily over the years. Rescued by rancher Barrat, he falls for the rancher's daughter, Venable, and finally leads a posse, guns ablazing, in pursuit of Gordon. Toler, better remembered as Charlie Chan, is on hand to provide the comic support.

d Lesley Selander *p* Harry Sherman *s* Norman Houston, Harrison Jacobs *c* Russell Harlan *lp* Donald Woods, C. Henry Gordon, Robert Barrat, Evelyn Venable, Russell Hayden, Sidney Toler

In Old Monterey (REP) b/w 74 min

It was Republic's practice with both their Roy Rogers and Autry series to give bigger budgets and extra guest stars to two of the twelve features they made each year and sell them

Bob Livingston (left) as the Lone Ranger in Kansas Terrors, *a Three Mesquiteer outing which, its title notwithstanding, was set in the Caribbean.*

as specials. Despite the extra money spent on it, this, the last Autry feature to be directed by Kane, is only a routine outing. The main point of interest in the film lies in its revealing that even Autry's fantastical world could be influenced by real life events, in this case America's preparations for war. Thus Autry is the army attaché assigned to buy out-of-the-way land for use as a practice bombing range. Hale and his cohorts are the Un-American types trying to make a quick buck buying land and selling it to the army at inflated prices.

d Joseph Kane   *p* Armand Schaefer   *s* Gerald Geraghty, Dorrell McGowan, Stuart McGowan   *c* Ernest Miller
lp Gene Autry, Smiley Burnette, June Storey, George Hayes, The Hoosier Hot Shots, Sarie and Sallie, Jonathan Hale, Champion

Jesse James   (FOX)   105 min
The first of a cycle of glamourized biographies of Western badmen that was a feature of the early forties. Johnson's script has Donlevy force Power (Jesse) and Fonda (Frank) into Robin Hood-like outlawry as they fight for their ranch against crooked railroad agent Meek. Scott is the sympathetic sheriff, John Carradine the treacherous Bob Ford who shoots Jesse in the back and Hull the newspaper editor who publicizes and then defends the gang's exploits. Even more marked than the distortion of history that Johnson's script represents are the soft, lyrical Technicolor images provided by cinematographer Barnes that seem to bathe the brothers in saintly haloes.

Below: A scene from Jesse James, *the commercial success of which gave new impetus to the Western and inspired a slew of glamourized biographies of outlaws.*

So successful was the film at the box office that Fox immediately started a sequel, **The Return of Frank James** (1940).

d Henry King   *p* Darryl Zanuck   *s* Nunnally Johnson
c George Barnes, W.H. Greene   *lp* Tyrone Power, Henry Fonda, Randolph Scott, Nancy Kelly, Henry Hull, Brian Donlevy, Donald Meek

Kansas Terrors   (REP)   b/w   57 min
An oddity in the Three Mesquiteers series. This film introduces Renaldo to the trio, sees Livingston return to the role of Stony Brooke and Grey replace Berke as producer. Set on a small Caribbean island to which Livingston and Hatton deliver a herd of horses, the plot sees the duo aiding Renaldo and his band of rebels in their struggle against the island's cruel ruler, Douglas. At the end of the film, Renaldo quits the island to join the duo. The film's oddest moments come when Livingston, who'd just completed the serial, **The Lone Ranger Rides Again** (1939), briefly reprises the part, white horse and all.

d George Sherman   *p* Harry Grey   *s* Jack Natteford, Betty Burbridge   *c* Ernest Miller   *lp* Bob Livingston, Raymond Hatton, Duncan Renaldo, George Douglas, Jacqueline Wells (Julie Bishop), Yakima Canutt

The Law Comes to Texas   (COL)   b/w   58 min
The best of the four films starring Elliott produced by Darmour. Elliott is the rugged lawyer who gives up his legal studies to help bring an end to the lawlessness plaguing Texas. To this end he becomes a state trooper and works undercover, with help from King (on the side of the angels for once) to expose outlaw Whitaker and Osborne's crooked judge. The climax is a massed shoot-out spiritedly mounted by Levering.

d Joseph Levering   *p* Larry Darmour   *s* Nate Gatzert
c James S. Brown Jnr   *lp* Bill Elliott, Charles King, Slim Whitaker, Bud Osborne, Veda Ann Borg, Lane Chandler

Law of the Pampas   (PAR)   b/w   74 min
The first of Hoppy's outings after Gabby Hayes left for the second and last time. The novel plot has Boyd and Hayden delivering a herd of cattle in South America and falling foul of Blackmer's villain. Toler, better known for his impersonation of Charlie Chan, briefly replaced Hayes but the emphasis is on action rather than comedy with an extended bar room brawl as the centrepiece of the movie.

d Nate Watt   *p* Harry Sherman   *s* Harrison Jacobs
c Russell Harlan   *lp* William Boyd, Russell Hayden, Sidney Blackmer, Sidney Toler, Steffi Duna, Glenn Strange

Let Freedom Ring   (MGM)   b/w   100(85) min
Climaxing with a rousing rendition of 'The Star Spangled Banner' this hokey story of pioneering days features Eddy as a crusading lawyer cleaning up his frontier hometown and sabotaging the crooked dealings of the local railroad heads. The strong cast and Hecht's energetic script (a celebration of American democracy at work) makes light of Conway's stiff direction. Bruce provides the romantic interest.

d Jack Conway *p* Harry Rapf *s* Ben Hecht *c* Sidney Wagner *lp* Nelson Eddy, Virginia Bruce, Victor McLaglen, Lionel Barrymore, Edward Arnold, Guy Kibbee

The Llano Kid (PAR) b/w 70 min
Conceived as a vehicle for Mexican singing star Guizar (who typically wasn't allowed to sing (!)) in the hope of cashing in on the current craze for Cisco Kid movies, *The Llano Kid* is a pleasant B Western, but no more. In the title role Guizar gleefully impersonates the legendary kissing bandit who gets involved with a plot by Mowbray and Sondergaard to defraud a Mexican innocent, Clayton (whose Kansas accent is distinctly out of place). The film is a loose remake of John Cromwell's **The Texan** (1930) which stars Gary Cooper as the Llano Kid.

d Edward Venturini *p* Harry Sherman *s* Wanda Tuchock *c* Russell Harlan *lp* Tito Guizar, Gale Sondergaard, Alan Mowbray, Jane Clayton, Chris-Pin Martin, Glenn Strange

The Lone Ranger Rides Again (REP) b/w 15 chaps
Compared to the original **The Lone Ranger** (1938), this sequel is at best a routine outing. Livingston, fresh from the role of Zorro, replaced Lee Powell as the Lone Ranger and was granted the additional assistance of Renaldo (as Juan Vasquez) as well as Chief Thundercloud's Tonto. The plot sees Livingston (ever so slowly) bringing peace to the range. Livingston wasn't the only substitute: Powell's horse, Silver King, was renamed Silver Chief for Livingston. More significantly, its whiteness helped spread the pervasive B Western theory, that white was quickest and best.

d William Witney, John English *p/co-s* Robert Beche *co-s* Barry Shipman, Franklyn Adreon, Ronald Davidson, Sol Shor *c* William Nobles *lp* Robert Livingston, Chief Thundercloud, Duncan Renaldo, Bart Dolan, Rex Lease, Glenn Strange

Lone Star Pioneers (COL) b/w 56 min
The third of Elliott's Darmour-produced Westerns for Columbia. Its favourable reception both with the critics and at the box-office led Columbia to take over production of the series directly. Set in Texas after the Civil War, Gatzert's plot has Elliott working as an undercover government agent on the track of looters King and Whitaker who are holding a rancher and his daughter captive on their own ranch to provide themselves with a hideout.

d Joseph Levering *p* Larry Darmour *s* Nate Gatzert *c* James S. Brown Jnr *lp* Bill Elliott, Charles Whitaker, Charles King, Dorothy Gulliver, Jack Ingram, Frank LaRue

The Marshal of Mesa City (RKO) b/w 63 min
Undoubtedly one of the best O'Brien series Westerns. He's the former marshal pressganged into the service of the community to squeeze a band of range terrorists from office who enlists baddie Brandon as his deputy to the chagrin of Ingraham and company who originally imported Brandon to gun down O'Brien. Howard, so familiar with his star because of their long association, handles the action with ease. The heroine, Vale, despite having been a Paramount starlet as Dorothy Howe, was billed as the winner of the second of RKO's 'Gateway to Hollywood' talent contests so assiduously promoted by the company.

d David Howard *p* Bert Gilroy *s* Jack Lait Jnr *c* Harry Wild *lp* George O'Brien, Virginia Vale, Henry Brandon, Lloyd Ingraham, Harry Cording, Slim Whitaker

Mexicali Rose (REP) b/w 58 min
This series outing gives one a fair idea of just how fantastical Autry's films had become. In one scene he is tied up beside a campfire by a Mexican bandit, Beery (clearly down on his luck) and his men. On discovering that Beery's favourite hobby is collecting Gene Autry records, he is first freed when he offers to sing about Robin Hood and then wins Beery's undying affection because after the bandit's recording of 'Mexicali Rose' breaks in mid-song, Autry continues (with full orchestral backing, despite being in the middle of the prairie). The plot has Autry and Burnette protecting Farnum, who runs a mission for poor Mexican children, from swindlers after the mission's oil-rich land.

d George Sherman *p* Harry Grey *s* Gerald Geraghty *c* William Nobles *lp* Gene Autry, Smiley Burnette, Noah Beery, Luana Walters, William Farnum, LeRoy Mason, Champion

New Frontier *aka* **Frontier Horizon** (REP) b/w 57 min
Wayne's final outing as a Mesquiteer, *New Frontier* was held back by Republic to cash in on the star's new popularity after the huge success of **Stagecoach** (1939). Although both script and direction are routine, the plot itself tweaks two of the main strands of thought much celebrated in the pre-Second World War Western. The valley where the trio's ranch is located is to be flooded to make a reservoir for the use of a nearby city. The settlers protest and lose on the grounds of the greatest good for the greatest number. Then when the settlers discover that the valley they are being moved to isn't

The poster for New Frontier, *John Wayne's last outing as a Mesquiteer.*

irrigated as promised, the Mesquiteers lead them in a successful attack on the crooked dam builders and secure promises of irrigation from the authorities. The film thus ends with the city folk getting their reservoir and the settlers, after they've fought for it, getting better land than they gave up.

Needless to say, this parable about the need for a judicious mix of belief in the common good and self-help is clothed in a fair measure of exciting action. The young settler girl who eyes Wayne, Isley, was later to achieve stardom as Jennifer Jones.

d George Sherman *p* William Berke *s* Betty Burbridge, Luci Ward *c* Reggie Lanning *lp* John Wayne, Ray Corrigan, Raymond Hatton, Phylis Isley (Jennifer Jones), Eddy Waller, LeRoy Mason

The Night Riders (REP) b/w 58 min
The Night Riders is the first of Wayne's second batch of four Three Mesquiteers features made when his career was at rock bottom. After two years of disastrous freelancing, in an attempt to get away from Westerns, Wayne's new contract with Republic saw his salary drop from $24,000 to $16,000. When the film was released, however, Wayne fresh from his triumph in **Stagecoach** (1939) was a star. Shot in five days, *Night Riders* is a quickie and shows it. Moreover, in place of the usual action-packed plot, *Night Riders* sees the trio moving close to Zorro territory. A fake Spanish nobleman dispossesses the Mesquiteers of their 3M ranch and so 'forces' them to adopt the masked and caped personae of Los Copqueros to expose him. Maynard is on hand as a friendly sheriff, Tyler as a baddie and Sayles puts in an appearance as President Garfield.

d George Sherman *p* William Berke *s* Betty Burbridge, Stanley Roberts *c* Jack Marta *lp* John Wayne, Ray Corrigan, Max Terhune, Kermit Maynard, Tom Tyler, Francis Sayles

Oklahoma Frontier (U) b/w 58 min
Brown's second Universal feature is a marked improvement on his first, thanks in part to the killing off of Baker halfway through the movie. Beebe's scripting is as good as his directing which stresses action all the way as former marshal Brown puts paid to Kortman's plans to grab the best land when Oklahoma is opened for homesteading. A further surprise comes at the film's conclusion which sees Brown marry heroine Gwynne. The musical interludes are supplied by the Texas Rangers.

Johnny Mack Brown in The Oregon Trail.

Below: Ward Bond *(left),* James Cagney *(centre) and Humphrey Bogart (right) make an unlikely trio of gunmen in* The Oklahoma Kid.

d/s Ford Beebe *p* Albert Ray *c* Jerome Ash *lp* Johnny Mack Brown, Bob Baker, Fuzzy Knight, Bob Kortman, Anne Gwynne, Charles King

The Oklahoma Kid (WB) b/w 85(80) min
The best thing about this big budget Western is Howe's luminous cinematography. As a novelty, Cagney and Bogart were taken from the urban jungle they normally prowled and set down in the wide open spaces of the Cherokee Strip of the 1890s. The move was hardly a success: Bogart looks uncomfortable as the all-in-black villain and Cagney, who even sings a couple of numbers, is equally ill at ease as the Robin Hood figure out to revenge the murder of his crusading father and to put an end to Bogart's land grabbing schemes. The film's best moments are mostly comic, notably Cagney blowing smoke from his pistol as he guns villains down.

d Lloyd Bacon *p* Samuel Bischoff *s* Warren Duff, Robert Buckner, Edward E. Paramore *c* James Wong Howe *lp* James Cagney, Humphrey Bogart, Rosemary Lane, Donald Crisp, Charles Middleton, Ward Bond

The Oregon Trail (U) b/w 15 chaps
Bearing little relation to either the Republic film of 1936 or Universal's 1923 serial, this serial features Brown as the scout hired by the government to stop outlaws and Indians attacking a wagon train heading West. For once in a Brown serial, the heroine, Stanley, isn't called 'Lucy'. With this one exception the serial is routine.

d Ford Beebe, Saul A. Goodkind *p* Henry MacRae *s* George Plympton, Basil Dickey, Edmund Kelso, W.W. Watson *c* Jerry Ash *lp* Johnny Mack Brown, Louise Stanley, Fuzzy Knight, Roy Barcroft, Lane Chandler, Charles King

Overland with Kit Carson (COL) b/w 15 chaps
This is Columbia's most successful serial. Though the idea of a whiteman leading a bunch of renegade Indians against settlers wasn't new and the script is loosely constructed at best, Nelson and Deming's rough and ready direction and Bardette's almost demonic performance as the villain, Pegleg, make for a genuinely exciting serial. Bardette is the fur trader who dreams of an empire in the West and who, in his disguise as Pegleg, rides at the head of a troop of black-cloaked

horsemen to terrorize settlers into submitting to his rule. The story owes more than a touch to **Lightning Warrior** (1931), of which cinematographer Kline had been the co-director, and would be remade as **Blazing the Overland Trail** (1956).

The serial helped consolidate the success Elliott had had with his first Columbia outing, **The Great Adventures of Wild Bill Hickok** (1938) and prepared the way for his first series of Westerns for the company.

d Sam Nelson, Norman Deming *p* Jack Fier *s* Morgan Cox, J.W. Cody, Ned Dandy *c* Benjamine Kline *lp* Bill Elliott, Iris Meredith, Richard Fiske, Bobby Clark, Hal Taliaferro (Wally Wales), Trevor Bardette

Racketeers of the Range (RKO) b/w 62 min
A superior O'Brien series entry set in the present. He's the rancher who leads other ranchers against Fiske whose meat packing combine takes to rustling their cattle in an effort to force the price of beef down. O'Brien's stunting is as delightful as ever – the climax sees him leaping from horseback to a speeding train in medium close-up – and Reynolds is a personable enough heroine.

d Ross Lederman *p* Bert Gilroy *s* Oliver Drake *c* Harry Wild *lp* George O'Brien, Chill Wills, Robert Fiske, Marjorie Reynolds, Ray Whitley, Monte Montague

The Return of the Cisco Kid (FOX) b/w 70 min
A sequel to **The Cisco Kid** (1931), for which Baxter had reprised the role he'd played so well in **In Old Arizona** (1929). Though it lacked the prestige and budget of earlier entries, the movie was so successful commercially that Fox speedily got a series underway devoted to the character, with Romero, a side-kick in this film, as the Cisco Kid.

Sperling's amiable script for this outing has Baxter on holiday (!) from derring-do, falling for Bari, helping her in her struggle with crooked lawyer Barrat and then sending his rival for Bari's affections, Richmond, into a trap before changing his mind at the last minute and re-uniting the lovers. Martin provides the comic relief.

d Herbert I. Leeds *p* Kenneth MacGowan *s* Milton Sperling *c* Charles Clarke *lp* Warner Baxter, Lynn Bari, Cesar Romero, Robert Barrat, Kane Richmond, Chris-Pin Martin

Riders of the Frontier (MON) b/w 58 min
This series entry once again sees Finney trying to stretch a small budget too far. The result is a cheap looking film that even Bennet's fast paced direction can't save. The plot features Ritter in disguise as an outlaw to trap crooked ranch foreman Barcroft. After it the series went rapidly downhill.

d Spencer Bennet *p* Edward Finney *s* Jesse Duffy, Joseph Levering *c* Marcel LePicard *lp* Tex Ritter, Jack Rutherford, Roy Barcroft, Hal Taliaferro (Wally Wales), Jean Joyce, Marin Sais

Romance of the Redwoods (COL) b/w 61 min
Bickford is the lumberjack who loses out to city slicker Oliver in their battle for the hand of Parker and then is suspected of Oliver's murder when he dies in suspicious circumstances. Basically a melodrama with its cast in work shirts rather than tuxes, it's badly let down by Simmons' slow-moving screenplay and Vidor's erratic direction which makes even the forest fire of the climax seem pretty tame.

d Charles Vidor *s* Michael Simmons *c* Allen G. Siegler *lp* Charles Bickford, Jean Parker, Gordon Oliver, Alan Bridges, Lloyd Hughes, Don Beddoe

Rough Riders' Roundup (REP) b/w 58 min
This is another serviceable series entry from Rogers. Cast more in the action than musical mould, Natteford's script features Rogers and other Rough Riders joining together to rid the range of Meeker's outlaw band. It was the first of Rogers' films to be produced and directed by Kane and the first to feature soon-to-become Mesquiteer Hatton as comic support. Made well before Republic would promote Rogers as 'King of the Cowboys' and try to fix his screen persona in aspic, it demonstrates how flexible and uncharismatic a figure Rogers actually is.

d/p Joseph Kane *s* Jack Natteford *c* Jack Marta *lp* Roy Rogers, Mary Hart, Raymond Hatton, Eddie Acuff, William Pawley, George Meeker, Trigger

Rovin' Tumbleweeds aka Washington Cowboy
(REP) b/w 62 min
Badly received and slackly made, this is nonetheless an interesting Autry outing. Clearly heavily influenced by Frank Capra's *Mr Smith Goes to Washington* (1939) – its working title was *Washington Cowboy* – the film features Autry as a singing Congressman trying to speed up the passage of a flood control bill that is being stalled by a crooked politician seeking to make a huge land-sale profit after he has bought up land and the bill is passed. The little-man-versus-the-political-machine theme fitted both Autry's image and the political beliefs of Republic's owner, Herbert Yates. But, sadly, Sherman was

Far left: *Cesar Romero (left) and Warner Baxter (centre) south of the border in* The Return of the Cisco Kid.

Gene Autry as a singing congressman, a role Roy Rogers essayed in Under Western Stars *(1938), with Mary Carlisle in* Rovin' Tumbleweeds.

no Capra and Autry no James Stewart. The result is a curiosity, but no more.

d George Sherman *p* William Berke *s* Betty Burbridge, Dorrell McGowan, Stuart McGowan *c* William Nobles *lp* Gene Autry, Smiley Burnette, Mary Carlisle, Douglass Dumbrille, William Farnum, Jack Ingram, Champion

The Singing Cowgirl

(CORONADO/GRAND NATIONAL) b/w 59 min
The last of Page's short-lived series of musical Westerns. Richmond and crooked lawyer Price are the villains, trying to swindle a youngster out of his ranch which they think has gold on it. Page, who with O'Brien puts a stop to the swindle, rides, sings and acts well enough but the mere fact of her being the 'hero' created problems that were insurmountable in 1939.

d Samuel Diege *p* George Hirliman *s* Arthur Hoerl *c* Mack Stengler *lp* Dorothy Page, Warner Richmond, Stanley Price, David O'Brien, Vince Barnett, Ed Piel

Six Gun Rhythm

(ARCADIA/GRAND NATIONAL) b/w 55 min
The only Western by Fletcher, a singing radio cowboy who played guitar left-handed. As if that in itself wasn't unusual, the plot has him as a pro. footballer transplanted to Texas on his father's death. However, the film's minuscule budget belied the ballyhoo Grand National made. Howes is the rustler, Barclay the seasoned romantic interest and Peters the side-kick who gets his laughs with acrobatics rather than tall stories.

d/p Sam Newfield *s* Fred Myton *c* Art Reed *lp* Tex Fletcher, Joan Barclay, Reed Howes, Ralph Peters, Ted Adams, Slim Hacker

South of the Border (REP) b/w 71 min

The success of this routine Autry entry that firmly committed its star to the war effort (even though the United States had not yet committed itself), with Autry and Burnette sent to Mexico to put down a potential revolution fermented by foreign agents with their eyes on Mexico's large deposits, gave the original singing cowboy's career an unexpected lift that led immediately to bigger budgets. Soon, however, the action would be so reduced by musical numbers that even *Variety* would ask of Autry's films: 'What kind of Western is this?'

d George Sherman *p* William Berke *s* Betty Burbridge, Gerald Geraghty *c* William Nobles *lp* Gene Autry, Smiley Burnette, June Storey, Mary Lee, Duncan Renaldo, William Farnum, Champion

Stagecoach

(WALTER WANGER PRODUCTIONS) b/w 96 min
In many ways *Stagecoach*, Ford's first Western for 13 years, is the most significant sound Western ever. It was Ford's first film in Monument Valley (which he was to make his own preserve in over a quarter of a century of film-making there), his first to feature the Seventh Cavalry, the film that rescued Wayne from the doldrums of the B Western and so began what surely must rank as the most creative relationship between an actor and a director in the history of the cinema, and it was the film that gave such an impetus to the genre that it must be called the first modern Western.

The view of Monument Valley, the place John Ford would make his own preserve over a quarter century of film-making, in Stagecoach.

Based on an Ernest Haycox story that is clearly influenced by de Maupassant's tale, *'Boule de suif'*, the greatness of *Stagecoach* lies less in its literary qualities and more in what Andrew Sarris, in a moment of wonderful insight, called Ford's 'Double Image; alternating between close-ups of emotional intimacy and long shots of epic involvement, thus capturing both the twitches of life and the silhouettes of legend'. Wayne is the Ringo Kid – introduced in a thrilling tracking shot that starts with him posed statue-like, twirling his rifle, and ends on a pensive close-up – seeking vengeance for the murder of his father and brother. Trevor is the whore with all the virtues of a mother and Mitchell the drunkard and philosopher of a doctor. All the characters reveal their true nature in the course of the journey to Lordsburg. Social outcasts all, they reveal an innate nobility by their actions that shames the snobbery of Platt's pregnant 'lady', Carradine's romantic cynic of a gambler and Churchill's crooked banker. But it is Wayne, the escaped convict, who is the hero: he saves the passengers and achieves his personal revenge.

Thus, though the film functions for much of the time as a sort of travelling *Grand Hotel* (1932), in the final sequence, after the stage and its passengers have reached safety, in the shadows of Lordsburg Ford devotes the whole of his cinematic skill to romanticizing and making heroic Wayne's beautiful innocence. His success is perhaps best caught by a brief quotation from Walker Percy's novel *The Moviegoer* whose alienated hero only comes alive in the cinema: 'Other people treasure memorable moments in their lives.... What I remember is the time John Wayne killed three men with a carbine as he was falling to the dusty street in *Stagecoach,* and the time the kitten found Orson Welles in the doorway in *The Third Man.*'

Wayne's gallantry wins him not only Trevor but his freedom, as the sheriff 'forgets' to re-arrest him, instead sending the pair into the wilderness where they'll be 'saved from the blessings of civilization' and in the passing years be slowly transformed by Ford into the more complex characters at the centres of **The Searchers** (1956) and *Seven Women* (1966) respectively. A magnificent film.

d John Ford   *p* Walter Wanger   *s* Dudley Nichols   *c* Bert Glennon   *lp* John Wayne, Claire Trevor, John Carradine, Thomas Mitchell, Andy Devine, Louise Platt, Berton Churchill

Stand Up and Fight (MGM) b/w 99(95) min
A brawling, stagecoach versus railroad, Western with Beery and Taylor as the feuding pair. Taylor is the bankrupt Maryland aristo who throws in his lot with the railroad folk and Beery the colourful manager of Rice's stagecoach line. Bickford is the real villain of the piece, but most of the action, including two lengthy fistfights, is devoted to Taylor and Beery's rowdy antagonism. An enjoyable but empty piece of entertainment.

d W.S. Van Dyke   *p* Mervyn LeRoy   *s* James M. Cain, Jane Murfin, Harvey Ferguson   *c* Leonard Smith   *lp* Wallace Beery, Robert Taylor, Florence Rice, Charles Bickford, Barton MacLane, John Qualen

Sunset Trail (PAR) b/w 60 min
Beautifully photographed by Harlan (whose cloud formations won great praise from the *Variety* reviewer) this is one of the best Hopalong Cassidy outings. Houston's comic screenplay gives Boyd the opportunity to impersonate an Eastern dude, to his evident enjoyment, in the course of his search for Fiske and his gang who've murdered Wynters' father. Selander's direction is efficient, if routine.

d Lesley Selander   *p* Harry Sherman   *s* Norman Houston   *c* Russell Harlan   *lp* William Boyd, George Hayes, Russell Hayden, Charlotte Wynters, Robert Fiske, Glenn Strange

William Boyd impersonating a dude cowboy, complete with bow tie, to the evident delight of Russell Hayden (left) and Gabby Hayes (right), from Sunset Trail.

Taming of the West (COL) b/w 55 min
The first of Elliott's series Westerns for Columbia to be actually produced in house, *Taming of the West* saw a considerable hike in its budget. By now it was clear that Elliott's appeal lay in his abilities with his fists rather than his charm and accordingly he was dubbed Wild Bill and given no-nonsense plots. This one features Curtis as a cattle rustler and Meredith, for so long Charles Starrett's beau in his series Westerns, as his heroine.

Below: *Wallace Beery (standing) and Robert Taylor in the middle of the climactic fistfight from* Stand Up and Fight.

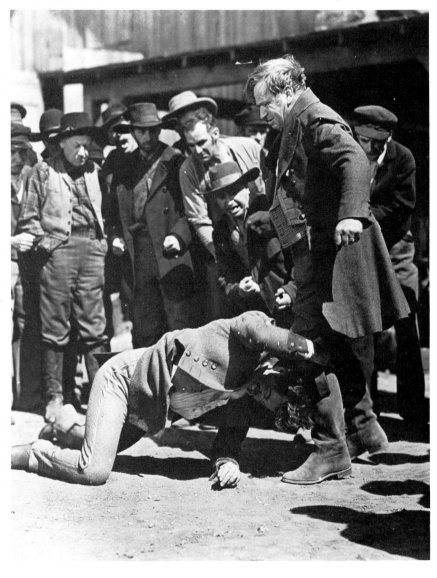

Above: *Ray Corrigan, Max Terhune (centre), in his last outing as a Mesquiteer, and John Wayne in* Three Texas Steers.

d Norman Deming *p* Leon Barsha *s* Charles Francis Royal, Robert Lee Johnson *c* George Meehan *lp* Bill Elliott, Iris Meredith, Dick Curtis, Dub Taylor, Don Beddoe, Charles King

Texas Stampede (COL) b/w 57 min

Photographed by Ballard to give it the look of a film with a far bigger budget, *Texas Stampede* is an unusual series Western. Starrett rides a white horse and wears a white hat, but there's no villain to speak of, only Kohler as a cattle baron out to stop sheep grazing on his range. But even he learns the error of his ways in the final reel. Meredith is the heroine and the Sons of the Pioneers provide the musical interludes.

d Sam Nelson *p* Harry Decker *s* Charles Francis Royal *c* Lucien Ballard *lp* Charles Starrett, Iris Meredith, Fred Kohler Jnr, Bob Nolan, Ray Bennett, Edmund Cobb

Three Texas Steers *aka* Danger Rides the Range (REP) b/w 59 min

One of the funniest of the Three Mesquiteers' outings. The budget seems suddenly bigger because the opening scenes of fire running amok at the circus run by the heroine, Landis, are borrowed from *Circus Girl* (1937). Graves is the villain trying to run down the circus so Landis will sell him her ranch on which he plans to build a dam (!?). The trio first save her life and then the ranch when Terhune, in his last film in the series, wins the necessary money in a comic trotting race after the trio have set upon Graves and his cronies in a lengthy fistfight.

d George Sherman *p* William Berke *s* Betty Burbridge, Stanley Roberts *c* Ernest Miller *lp* John Wayne, Ray Corrigan, Max Terhune, Carole Landis, Ralph Graves, Roscoe Ates

Trigger Pals (CINEMART/GRAND NATIONAL) b/w 60 min

Jarrett's only Western. Despite sterling support from Powell (Republic's Lone Ranger) who got most of the attention in the trade reviews, the film was a complete failure at the box office and no more of the planned series was made. Adams is the rustler who tries to frame Jarrett and Faye the dude who falls for Adams' glib tongue. Finally Powell and Jarrett, who looks uncomfortable on horseback and is in bad voice, find the rustler's underground hideout and expose it to the light of day with a little dynamite.

d Sam Newfield *p* Phil Krasne *s* George Plympton *c* Jack Greenhalgh *lp* Art Jarrett, Lee Powell, Dorothy Faye, Ted Adams, Al St John, Charles King

Trouble in Sundown (RKO) b/w 60 min

O'Brien, probably the best scrapper in series Westerns, here fights three heavies, including Bond, to a bloody pulp in one long sequence in this amiable series Western. Drake's plot has Kendall trying to legally steal ranches by calling in their mortgages after robbing the bank of the money they've deposited there. Wills supplies the comedy and Keith the wistful looks at O'Brien.

d David Howard *p* Bert Gilroy *s* Oliver Drake, Dorrell McGowan, Stuart McGowan *c* Harry Wild *lp* George O'Brien, Ward Bond, Cy Kendall, Rosalind Keith, Chill Wills, Earl Dwire

Union Pacific (PAR) b/w 133 min

Reputedly, having decided to do a Western about the railroad, De Mille tossed a coin to decide whether to make the story about the Union Pacific or the Santa Fé Railroad. McCrea is the overseer on the job of building the first transcontinental railroad and Donlevy the gambler determined to stop him. Stanwyck is the athletic heroine, leaping

A scene from Union Pacific, *one of Cecil B. De Mille's many versions of the winning of the West.*

on and off boxcars with the best of them. Though the script betrays the fact that it is the work of many hands and the film contains directorial contributions from James Hogan and Arthur Rossen (who worked on it when De Mille fell ill), De Mille's emphatic and graceless style reigns over all. Joseph Crehan portrays Ulysses S. Grant. This was the 41st time he had put on the presidential whiskers and puffed an overlong cigar.

d/p Cecil B. De Mille s Walter De Leon, C. Gardner Sullivan, Jesse Lasky Jnr c Victor Milner, Dewey Wrigley lp Barbara Stanwyck, Joel McCrea, Akim Tamiroff, Robert Preston, Brian Donlevy, Anthony Quinn

Wall Street Cowboy (REP) b/w 66 min

Although, in the main, Rogers stuck to historical Westerns before the forties, like Gene Autry he occasionally travelled to the present and the East. This is a case in point. A Wall Street syndicate learns that Rogers' ranch is rich in molybdenum and attempts to foreclose on it when he has difficulty meeting his mortgage repayments. With assistance from Hatton and Hayes, who was fast making himself an indispensable part of the Rogers entourage, the syndicate is foiled. Badly received, the film demonstrates just how insubstantial the Rogers persona was without the support of either music or action.

d/p Joseph Kane s Gerald Geraghty, Norman Hall c Jack Marta lp Roy Rogers, George Hayes, Raymond Hatton, Ann Baldwin, Jack Ingram, Trigger

Water for Canitoga orig Wasser für Canitoga

(BAVARIA-FILMKUNST; GER) b/w 109 min
Similar in theme to Luis Trenker's **The Emperor of California** (**Der Kaiser von Kalifornien**, 1936), this pioneering epic stars Albers as the leader of a group of settlers trying to secure a steady supply of water for their mining community. Like Sutter in Trenker's film, Albers dies a martyr's death after his fellow settlers turn against him and his American employers refuse him the extra funds necessary to complete the pipeline. The result is an unsatisfactory film, the real significance of which lies in its celebration of the indomitable Aryan spirit.

d Herbert Selpin s Emil Burri, Peter Francke c Franz Koch, Josef Illig lp Hans Albers, Charlotte Susa, Hilde Sessak, Peter Voss, Josef Sieber, Andrews Engelman

Water Rustlers

(CORONADO/GRAND NATIONAL) b/w 54 min
The second Western starring singing cowgirl Page, *Water Rustlers* is vastly inferior to her first outing, **Ride 'Em Cowgirl**

Gabby Hayes (centre) with Roy Rogers as the Wall Street Cowboy.

Raymond Hatton, John Wayne and Ray Corrigan as the Three Mesquiteers in Wyoming Outlaw.

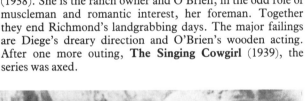

Reed Hadley as Zorro in Zorro's Fighting Legion *about to discover that the villainous Don Del Oro is missing from his suit of armour.*

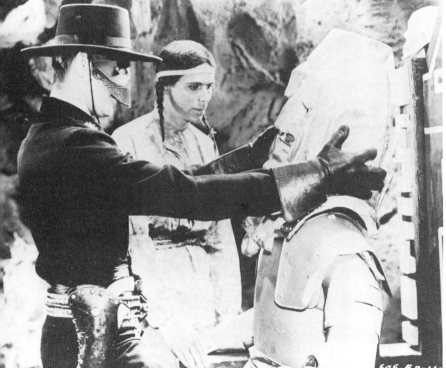

(1938). She is the ranch owner and O'Brien, in the odd role of muscleman and romantic interest, her foreman. Together they end Richmond's landgrabbing days. The major failings are Diege's dreary direction and O'Brien's wooden acting. After one more outing, **The Singing Cowgirl** (1939), the series was axed.

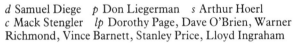

d Samuel Diege   p Don Liegerman   s Arthur Hoerl
c Mack Stengler   lp Dorothy Page, Dave O'Brien, Warner Richmond, Vince Barnett, Stanley Price, Lloyd Ingraham

Wyoming Outlaw   (REP)   b/w   62 min
Wyoming Outlaw is based on an actual incident about a would-be modern Robin Hood of a desperado who was finally killed by a small town gas-station attendant. The role of the outlaw launched Barry's career as a Western star. In the movie Wayne makes his penultimate Three Mesquiteers outing. The main body of the plot features the trio (with Hatton replacing Max Terhune) fighting a dishonest politician who was selling jobs to out-of-work cowboys. Elmo Lincoln, the screen's first Tarzan, has a small part as a lawman.

d George Sherman   p William Berke   s Betty Burbridge, Jack Natteford   c Reggie Lanning   lp John Wayne, Ray Corrigan, Raymond Hatton, Don 'Red' Barry, Adele Pearce, Charles Middleton

Zorro's Fighting Legion   (REP)   b/w   12 chaps
For Witney and English's second serial outing with Zorro (and their fourth serial of the year!) Hadley took over the title role from John Carroll. His opponent, in typical Republic serial style, is a similarly masked villain, 'Don Del Oro', who poses as a Yaqui God in order to steal gold from terrified Indians to finance his plans of empire building in the Old West. The absence of Yakima Canutt as stuntman means a slowing down of the action, but in compensation there is Lanning's textured cinematography.

d William Witney, John English   p Hiram S. Brown Jnr
s Ronald Davidson, Franklyn Adreon, Morgan Cox, Sol Shor, Barney Sarecky   c Reggie Lanning   lp Reed Hadley, Sheila Darcey, Leander de Cordova, Edmund Cobb, John Merton, Charles King

The 1940s

The Resurgence of the Genre

The most significant Western of 1939 was undoubtedly **Stagecoach**. But although John Ford's triumphant return to the Western gave the genre a short-lived respectability, its impact was little compared to that of Henry King's **Jesse James** (1939). The huge success of that film inspired a number of glamorized biographies of outlaws from the major studios which, with Warner's Errol Flynn Westerns and De Mille's epics, gave the Western a new-found profitability. More importantly these films, many of them in colour, reintroduced 'big themes', such as the Winning of the West, to the genre. Above all they celebrated Americanness. In their own way they were part of the general response to the Second World War in America, with the nation both looking inward and celebrating the fight for freedom in Europe and the Far East.

The B Western reacted most directly to the war, sending its series heroes to search out the Nazis and their sympathizers who took to the range in numerous films like **Cowboy Commandos** (1943). In general, though, the B Western in the forties seemed to exist out of time. Its heroes and plots looked back to those of the thirties. Only in its renewed emphasis on violence, seen most clearly in the radical shift in the films of Roy Rogers from ballads to extended gory fistfights (and ballads), was the B Western at one with the times. As the decade progressed the mood of optimism and confidence evaporated as suddenly as it had come. Whereas a few years earlier, outlaws had been glamorized, the means by which the frontier was tamed were now questioned in a number of films from **The Ox-Bow Incident** (1943) onwards. Moreover, by the end of the decade the influence of psychology and *film noir* began to throw their shadows over the genre. The classic example of this is **Pursued** (1947), but even if one looks at Howard Hawk's **Red River** (1948) which has the appearance of a simple cattle-drive Western (and is often celebrated as such), the tone of the film is clearly far removed from the easy optimism and heroics of a film like De Mille's **Union Pacific** (1939).

Thus it was that the Western reached the brink of the fifties in an uncharacteristic mood of introspection. Equally significantly, the end of the forties saw the first transmission of series Westerns on television when in 1948 the Hopalong Cassidy Westerns were sold to the new medium. This began television's long-lived affair with the Western that was to have many repercussions both on the Western itself and on Hollywood.

Adventures of Red Ryder (REP) b/w 12 chaps
This serial, derived from the Fred Harman newspaper strip, marked the first appearance of the Red Ryder character who was to become a regular in Republic's Western series throughout the forties. Barry as the athletic hero took the soubriquet 'Red' to further stress his identity with the role of the frontier tamer here out to thwart crooked banker Worth's attempts to defraud a group of ranchers whose land, unknown to them, is wanted for a projected railway. Beery provides suitably laconic comic support and Cook is the enthusiastic Indian boy helper.

d William Witney, John English *p* Hiram S. Brown Jnr *s* Ronald Davidson, Franklyn Adreon, Sol Sohr, Barney Sarecky, Norman S. Hall *c* William Nobles *lp* Don 'Red' Barry, Noah Beery, Tommy Cook, Harry Worth, Maude Pierce Allen, Hal Taliaferro (Wally Wales)

Arizona (COL) b/w 127 min
A would-be epic in the style of the director's own **Cimarron** (1931), *Arizona* is more memorable for the thousands of feet of stock footage it provided for other films. For this tale of the development of Arizona, Columbia reconstructed Tucson as the mud-adobe town it had been, while Ruggles created set-pieces in the style of De Mille, if not Griffith. In one, the town's inhabitants watch the Union troops setting light to everything in their wake, as they withdraw. But the result is just another dull big-picture. Holden, in the role intended for Gary Cooper, does well in his first Western, as the young cowboy for whom Arthur falls and who protects her struggling freight-line against villains William and Hall, but the film is simply too slow for its 127 minutes.

d/p Wesley Ruggles *s* Claude Binyon *c* Joseph Walker, Harry Hollenberger, Fayte Brown *lp* Jean Arthur, William Holden, Warren William, Porter Hall, Paul Harvey, George Chandler

Beyond the Sacremento *aka* **Power of Justice**
(COL) b/w 58 min
Routine fare. Elliott in his Wild Bill Hickok persona saves the townspeople of Lodestone from Page and LaRue when they attempt the launch of a phoney bond issue. A nice touch

Previous pages: *Action series style: Johnny Mack Brown gets his man in* The Lone Star Trail.

Jack Benny, in costume for Buck Benny Rides Again, *complete with cowgirl chorus.*

William Holden, Jean Arthur and the adobe walls of Tucson on which producer/director Wesley Ruggles spent most of the budget of Arizona.

has Elliott not only beat up their minions but denounce the pair in a front page story, set overnight, in LaRue's own paper. Keyes is the demure heroine. The action is fast, furious and undistinguished.

d Lambert Hillyer *p* Leon Barsha *s* Luci Ward *c* George Meehan *lp* Bill Elliott, Evelyn Keyes, Dub Taylor, Frank LaRue, Bradley Page, Don Beddoe

Blazing Six Shooters (COL) b/w 61 min
A superior entry from Starrett courtesy of Lewis's hard-edged direction. For once Curtis and Meredith, in their usual roles of villain and heroine respectively, don't look as though they've said their lines countless times before (which, of course, they had). The unlikely plot has Curtis trying to gain control of two ranches near the place where he has discovered silver. The Sons of the Pioneers provide the musical interludes.

d Joseph H. Lewis *p* Irving Briskin *s* Paul Franklin *c* George Meehan *lp* Charles Starrett, Iris Meredith, Dick Curtis, Bob Nolan, Al Bridge, George Cleveland

The Border Legion *aka* West of the Badlands
(REP) b/w 58 min
For this streamlined version of Zane Grey's much filmed novel the role of the good-natured outlaw who sacrifices himself to save a pair of lovers was tailored to suit Rogers. In the same year Rogers and Hayes made the most notable of their infrequent forays out of the Western and low budget movies when they took supporting roles in Raoul Walsh's **The Dark Command**, 1940.

d/p Joseph Kane *s* Olive Cooper, Louis Stevens *c* Jack Marta *lp* Roy Rogers, George 'Gabby' Hayes, Carol Hughes, Joe Sawyer, Hal Taliaferro, Fred Burns

Brigham Young (FOX) b/w 114 min
An inaccurate and plodding biography of Brigham Young (Jagger) who led the Mormons on the long trek to Utah after the death of Joseph Smith (Price) and the onset of fierce religious persecution. Power and Darnell are the young

Far right: Dean Jagger as the Mormon pioneer Brigham Young.

pioneer lovers. Trotti's script is one-dimensional but Hathaway's brusque direction and the special effects, notably the attack on the Mormon farmlands by locusts, are fine.

d Henry Hathaway *p* Kenneth MacGowan *s* Lamar Trotti *c* Arthur Miller *lp* Tyrone Power, Linda Darnell, Dean Jagger, Brian Donlevy, Jane Darwell, Vincent Price, Mary Astor

Buck Benny Rides Again (PAR) b/w 82 min
Benny is the would-be cowboy constantly getting himself into trouble in this wholesale transposition of his radio show (complete with supporting cast) to celluloid. The result is an amusing lightweight comedy.

d/p Mark Sandrich *s* William Morrow, Edmund Beloin *c* Charles Lang *lp* Jack Benny, Ellen Drew, Andy Devine, Phil Harris, Eddie (Rochester) Anderson, Virginia Dale

1940

Bullet Code (RKO) b/w 58 min

A pleasant actioner with O'Brien and supposed talent contest winner Vale giving spirited performances as the ranch owner and damsel in distress respectively. Woods is the cattle baron terrorizing Vale and her father. Howard directs with an ease that comes from his long association with O'Brien.

d David Howard *p* Bert Gilroy *s* Doris Schroeder *c* Harry Wild *lp* George O'Brien, Virginia Vale, Slim Whitaker, Harry Woods, Robert Stanton (Kirby Grant), William Haade

The Cisco Kid and the Lady (FOX) b/w 74 min

Virtually a reprise of the plot of **The Return of the Cisco Kid** (1939) with the addition of a girl who really loves Cisco (Romero), *The Cisco Kid and the Lady* is the first of Fox's six strong series devoted to the character. The movie is well titled, indicating that the centre of interest of the film – indeed of the series – would be Romero's love life. Weaver is the girl Romero moons over, Montgomery the man she loves and Barrat the crooked sheriff. Routine.

d Herbert Leeds *p* John Stone *s* Frances Hyland *c* Barney McGill *lp* Cesar Romero, Marjorie Weaver, Chris-Pin Martin, George Montgomery, Robert Barrat, Ward Bond

Covered Wagon Days (REP) b/w 56 min

Strictly routine fare, this is one of the seven Three Mesquiteer outings to feature Renaldo as the third member of the trio. Here they come to the rescue of his brother, framed for a murder by Merton and Howes when he stumbles on their silver smuggling operation.

d George Sherman *p* Harry Grey *s* Earle Snell *c* William Nobles *lp* Robert Livingston, Raymond Hatton, Duncan Renaldo, John Merton, Reed Howes, Kay Griffith

The Dark Command (REP) b/w 94 min

With a budget of three-quarters of a million dollars, *The Dark Command* was the most expensive and most successful film of Republic's early years. Set in Kansas in 1859 as the political tension between the states was growing, it features Pidgeon as Cantrill (presumably intended to be Quantrill) who organizes a guerilla band to raid the surrounding country, supposedly acting on behalf of the Confederacy. Wayne is the marshal who tracks him down, but only after Pidgeon and his men have burnt down the town of Lawrence in a spectacular scene. Trevor is the girl caught between the two men and Rogers, oddly effective outside the small world of the Western series, her trigger-happy younger brother. Walsh's direction is efficient but surprisingly anonymous.

The most famous scene of the film, the leap by four men and a team of horses off a bluff into a lake was filmed by Joseph Kane's second unit with Yakima Canutt and Cliff Lyons doubling for Wayne and Hayes. It was subsequent attempts by other, less careful second unit directors and stuntmen to mimic this that directly led to the formation of the Society for the Prevention of Cruelty to Animals.

d Raoul Walsh *p* Sol C. Siegel *s* Grover Jones, Lionel Houser, F. Hugh Herbert *c* Jack Marta *lp* John Wayne, Claire Trevor, Walter Pidgeon, Roy Rogers, George 'Gabby' Hayes, Porter Hall

The Durango Kid (COL) b/w 60 min

'Masked in mystery 'till he unmasks his father's killers! The terror of cattle thieves, the idol of thrill lovers', so ran the ad campaign for Starrett's first outing as the Durango Kid, a role he was to have phenomenal success with when he resurrected it as his series character in 1945. Here Starrett is the gun-fanning Robin Hood of the West saving homesteaders from MacDonald's rustlers. Walters replaced Meredith who had been Starrett's beau for too long.

Above: *Roy Rogers, in one of the few films he made outside the world of series Westerns, Walter Pidgeon and John Wayne (left to right) in* The Dark Command, *the biggest of Republic's early productions.*

Cesar Romero, whose interpretation of the role of the Cisco Kid was more athletic than romantic, in The Gay Caballero.

The Marx Brothers and Diana Lewis in a publicity shot for Go West.

Go West (MGM) b/w 80 min

The film begins promisingly with Groucho attempting to fleece Chico and Harpo of the ten dollars he needs to make up the price of a railway ticket and being completely outsmarted. But, once the brothers reach the West, in comparison with classics like *A Night at the Opera* (1935), the comedy is pretty thin until the final Keystone Cops-like chase in which they demolish a train in pursuit of the villains. The script which has the brothers attempting to retrieve stolen land deeds from Barrat was to have been written by Bert Kalamar and Harry Ruby who provided the team with *Duck Soup* (1933) and *Horse Feathers* (1932).

d Edward Buzzell *p* Jack Cummings *s* Irving Brecher *c* Leonard Smith *lp* the Marx Brothers (Groucho, Harpo and Chico), Robert Barrat, John Carroll, Diana Lewis

Heroes of the Saddle (REP) b/w 59 min

A flimsy story that only keeps one's attention courtesy of Witney's lively direction. A contemporary tale, it centres on the attempts of the Mesquiteers to adopt the orphan (Parsons) of a friend, and the red tape they run into. The reason, of course, is skullduggery at the orphanage which is only settled when Livingston puts things to rights. Nonetheless the film has a wistful edge to it, somehow suggesting that the Mesquiteers' easy going ways couldn't long survive 'the blessings of civilization'.

d William Witney *p* Harry Grey *s* Jack Natteford *c* William Nobles *lp* Robert Livingston, Raymond Hatton, Duncan Renaldo, Patsy Lee Parsons, Reed Howes, Kermit Maynard

d Lambert Hillyer *p* Jack Fier *s* Paul Franklin *c* John Stumar *lp* Charles Starrett, Luana Walters, Bob Nolan, Kenneth MacDonald, Forrest Taylor, Frank LaRue

Frontier Crusader (PRC) b/w 62 min

One of the first films released by Producers Distributing Corporation under its new (and more familiar) name of Producers Releasing Corporation, PRC, this is the second of seven to feature McCoy and to be directed by Sam Newfield under his Stewart identity. Far better than McCoy's recent work, it stars the Colonel in stern mood up against Merton, Hackett and company who are trying to prevent a mining company uncover a rich vein of gold.

d Peter Stewart (Sam Newfield) *p* Sigmund Neufeld *s* William Lively *c* Jack Greenhalgh *lp* Tim McCoy, Karl Hackett, John Merton, Dorothy Short, Forrest Taylor, Hal Price

The Gay Caballero (FOX) b/w 57 min

The best, and shortest, of Fox's short-lived Cisco Kid series. The plot has less time for romance and director Brower was a veteran of action Westerns. An extra twist has Beecher as the female crook who is not content to try and cheat Ryan out of her land but does it in the name of the Cisco Kid. The result is a film whose hero (Romero) is less dashing than O'Henry's original but far more at home in the world of the B Western.

d Otto Brower *p* Walter Morosco, Ralph Dietrich *s* Albert Duffy, John Larkin *c* Edward Cronjager *lp* Cesar Romero, Sheila Ryan, Robert Sterling, Chris-Pin Martin, Janet Beecher, Edmund McDonald

Geronimo (PAR) b/w 89 min

With a script that meticulously transfers the Indian world of *The Lives of a Bengal Lancer* (1935) to the West and with lashings of stock footage from **The Plainsman**, **The Texas Rangers** (both 1936) and **Wells Fargo** (1937) amongst others, *Geronimo* was a surprising hit for Paramount. The bulk of the film concerns Foster's attempts to stop the inevitable Indian war. Lockhart is the gun runner, and Chief Thundercloud, in an all too brief appearance, takes the title role.

Far right: *Jon Hall (centre) in the title role with Ward Bond in* Kit Carson, *a Poverty Row epic.*

d/s P.H. Sloane *c* Henry Sharp *lp* Preston Foster, Ellen Drew, Andy Devine, William Henry, Chief Thundercloud, Gene Lockhart

Kit Carson (UA) b/w 97 min

A flimsy but entertaining addition to the Kit Carson legend. Hall is Carson, helping defend the Freemont expedition to California from marauding Indians while competing with Freemont (Andrews) for the affections of Bari. Seitz, known as the serial king for his work with Pearl White in the twenties, borrowed De Mille's famous bathtub sequence to spice up the action at one point.

d George B. Seitz *p* Edward Small *s* George Bruce *c* John Mescall, Robert Pittack *lp* Jon Hall, Lynn Bari, Dana Andrews, Ward Bond, Clayton Moore, Raymond Hatton

Knights of the Range (PAR) b/w 68 min

Hayden, abandoning his role of Lucky in the Sherman-produced Hopalong Cassidy series, takes the lead in this better-than-average Zane Grey outing from Paramount. He plays the youth tempted into cattle rustling who gives it up

just in time to save Parker and her father. Ankrum is the rustler, Jory the crooked lawyer, while Harlan provides the memorable scenic cinematography. The Kings Men provide the less memorable musical interludes.

d Lesley Selander *p* Harry Sherman *s* Norman Houston *c* Russell Harlan *lp* Russell Hayden, Victor Jory, Jean Parker, Britt Wood, Morris Ankrum, J. Farrell MacDonald

Law and Order (U) b/w 57 min
This loose remake of W.R. Burnett's novel *Saint Johnson* which formed the basis of Edward L. Cahn's superb 1932 film (as well as, bizarre as it must seem, being the source of Brown's 1937 serial, *Wild West Days*) is an easy going actioneer. Brown is the retired marshal forced to pick up his guns again when trouble breaks out. Knight offers his usual inept assistance.

d Ray Taylor *p* Joseph Sanford *s* Sherman Lowe, Victor McLeod *c* Jerome Ash *lp* Johnny Mack Brown, Fuzzy Knight, Nell O'Day, James Craig, Charles King, Kermit Maynard

The Light of Western Stars (PAR) b/w 67 min
Another of Paramount's Zane Grey series, this is a remake of the 1930 film that had been Sherman's first job as a producer for the company. Houston's screenplay which follows the original story closely is a little old fashioned with its confrontation of East (Sayers) and West (Jory) in which the East naturally succumbs to the West when Sayers heads West to prevent an East-West marriage only to fall for Jory. Selander's direction is far too leisurely.

d Lesley Selander *p* Harry Sherman *s* Norman Houston *c* Russell Harlan *lp* Russell Hayden, Victor Jory, Jo Ann Sayers, Noah Beery Jnr, Tom Tyler, Alan Ladd

The Man from Dakota *aka* Arouse and Beware
(MGM) b/w 75 min
A better title for this amiable Beery vehicle might have been *The Lady from Moscow*, so strange is Del Rio's introduction into the film as the Russian emigré who meets up with Beery and Howard, who are Union soldiers escaping from a Confederate prison. As usual Beery is the oafish bull of a

soldier and, as usual, he turns out to be a hero at the end, thus allowing Howard to recapture important Union documents and so redeem his black past and win Del Rio. Fenton directs anonymously.

d Leslie Fenton *p* Edward Chodorov *s* Laurence Stallings *c* Ray June *lp* Wallace Beery, John Howard, Dolores Del Rio, Donald Meek, Addison Richards, William Haade

The Man from Tumbleweeds (COL) b/w 59 min
In this fast-paced series entry Elliott forms a band of rangers from inhabitants of the state penitentiary to rid Gaslight of Bennett and his cronies. Lewis's direction sidesteps the awkwardnesses of Royal's gimmicky script by concentrating on the action. The result is an engaging, if minor, film from a director who was later to produce two of the the most striking B Westerns of the fifties, **The Halliday Brand** (1957) and **Terror in a Texas Town** (1958).

d Joseph H. Lewis *p* Leon Barsha *s* Charles Francis Royal *c* George Meehan *lp* Bill Elliott, Iris Meredith, Dub Taylor, Raphael Bennett, Edward LeSaint, Francis Walker

The Mark of Zorro (FOX) b/w 94 min
One of the most elegant of all swashbucklers and undeniably the best of the many Zorro movies. Its success rests less on its big budget and stars than in Mamoulian's intelligent direction. He cleverly gives equal weight to the action, best exemplified in the marvellous climatic duel between Rathbone's icy villain and Power (doubled by Albert, son of technical director Fred Cavens), and the romantic liaison of Power, in his role of the foppish aristo, and Darnell's shimmering beauty of a Governor's daughter. Though Power is not as athletic as Douglas Fairbanks' silent Zorro, or even

Above: *Tyrone Power, the most elegant Zorro of all, tests the sharpness of his rapier in* The Mark of Zorro.

Wallace Beery (left) and John Howard as the feuding Union soldiers in The Man from Dakota.

My Little Chickadee (U) b/w 83 min

Perhaps the oddest of Western satires, *My Little Chickadee* teams West and Fields as competing con artists. Fields is the vulnerable one of the two. Tricked into marriage by West when she sees his bag full of (counterfeit) money, he then tries to win her affections while she romances Calleia's masked bandit. More stilted than **Destry Rides Again** (1939), it satirizes Western conventions to greater effect with the help of such B Western stalwarts as Foran, Fuzzy Knight and Si Jenks. The film's climax has Fields borrow the immortal line, 'Come up and see me some time' from West and make the sentiment wholly his own with the addition of 'in Philadelphia'.

d Edward Cline *p* Lester Cowan *s* Mae West, W.C. Fields *c* Joseph Valentine *lp* Mae West, W.C. Fields, Joseph Calleia, Dick Foran, Fuzzy Knight, Si Jenks

North West Mounted Police (PAR) 125 min

A stilted and much fictionalized account of the Riel Indian Rebellion in Canada in the 1880s. Mountie Foster and Texas

Above: *W. C. Fields getting himself into yet another fine mess with Mae West in* My Little Chickadee.

Yakima Canutt in **Zorro Rides Again** (1937), Mamoulian is so adept at suggesting continuous movement by a series of brief shots and sudden darting camera movements that it hardly matters. This means that the result is a superb, and very funny, film.

It was unsuccessfully remade as a telefilm with Frank Langella in the title role, in 1974.

d Rouben Mamoulian *p* Raymond Griffith *s* Garret Ford, Bess Meredith *c* Arthur Miller *lp* Tyrone Power, Linda Darnell, Basil Rathbone, Eugene Pallette, J. Edward Bromberg, Gale Sondergaard

Paulette Goddard and Preston Foster in De Mille's melodramatic account of the Riel Indian Rebellion, North West Mounted Police.

Melody Ranch (REP) b/w 80 min

This film, which features Miller, Durante and Vague, was clearly an attempt by Republic to further broaden Autry's appeal. It was advertised as a musical rather than a Western and in Santley had a director more at home on the sound stages of the musical than on the range. But, though Autry would later guest in **Shooting High** (1940), Fox's musical extravaganza, and though he was only tenuously connected to the mainstream of the Western, he proved to be a fish out of water in non-Western films and henceforth restricted himself to specials, like **In Old Monterey** (1939), when he wanted to *further* emphasize the musical content of his films.

The title comes from Autry's radio show which, for the film, has Durante as announcer. Moffitt and Herbert's screenplay has Autry invited to return to Torpedo to be honorary sheriff only to discover that he has to do the job properly when gangsters, led by MacLane, try and send him packing.

For one sequence, John Wayne, rather than Ted Mapes, Autry's usual double, substitutes for Autry.

Far right: Jimmy Durante, Gene Autry and Ann Miller in Melody Ranch, *a musical rather than a musical Western.*

d Joseph Santley *p* Sol C. Siegel *s* Jack Moffitt, F. Hugh Herbert *c* Joseph August *lp* Gene Autry, Jimmy Durante, Ann Miller, Barton MacLane, Barbara Jo Allen (Vera Vague), George 'Gabby' Hayes, Champion

Ranger Cooper, in Canada on the trail of murderer Bancroft, who it transpires is behind the rebellion, combine to put down the rebellion while competing for the affections of Carroll. Milner's spectacular early colour photography displays Canada's landscape to perfection but plot and direction too often sink to the level of melodrama. Staunch courage and lofty aims win a mite too inevitably over cunning treachery.

d/p Cecil B. De Mille   *s* Alan LeMay, Jesse Lasky Jnr, C. Gardner Sullivan   *c* Victor Milner, W. Howard Green
lp Gary Cooper, Madeleine Carroll, Paulette Goddard, Preston Foster, George Bancroft, Robert Preston

Northwest Passage (MGM) 126 min

Intended as the first of a two-part film (the second part of which was never made as Tracy refused to work with Vidor again) this fictionalized account of the expedition of Roger's Rangers into Canada in 1760 to punish an Indian tribe that had been raiding the colonists is notable for its harsh view of nature. Like Samuel Fuller's *Merrill's Marauders* (1962), the film stresses the effort involved in the trek which leaves the men emaciated savages with one even succumbing to cannibalism at one stage.

The Rangers are led by Tracy whose earthy yet eloquent leadership is first frowned on by Young's map-maker who travels with them and matures in the course of the journey.

d King Vidor   *p* Hunt Stromberg   *s* Lawrence Stallings, Talbot Jennings   *c* Sidney Wagner, William V. Skall
lp Spencer Tracy, Robert Young, Walter Brennan, Lumsden Hare, Ruth Hussey, Nat Pendleton

One Man's Law (REP) b/w 57 min

With *One Man's Law*, Sherman, who'd directed Barry's debut for Republic, **Wyoming Outlaw** (1939) in the Three Mesquiteer series, was made producer of the company's brand new Western series. Barry plays the drifting cowboy who picks up the sheriff's badge and rids a town of its riffraff so it can win a railroad spur and economic independence. Taylor, another newcomer to Westerns, provides the comedy and Waldo the romantic interest. Way down the cast list was Rex Lease, a one-time series star himself.

d/p George Sherman   *s* Bennett Cohen, Jack Natteford
c Reggie Lanning   *lp* Donald Barry, Janet Waldo, Dub Taylor, George Cleveland, Edmund Cobb, Carleton Young

A gaunt Spencer Tracy in Northwest Passage.

Pioneers of the Frontier *aka* The Anchor

(COL) b/w 58 min
Winters, who reverted to her real name of Dorothy Comingore for her role as Kane's wife in *Citizen Kane* (1941), is the lively heroine of this action-packed Elliott entry. Curtis is the villain whose land grabbing activities Elliott in his Wild Bill Saunders guise puts to an end.

d Sam Nelson   *p* Leon Barsha   *s* Fred Myton   *c* George Meehan   *lp* Bill Elliott, Linda Winters (Dorothy Comingore), Dick Curtis, Dub Taylor, Carl Stockdale, Lafe McKee

Ragtime Cowboy Joe (U) b/w 58 min

The second of O'Day's films with Brown. Unusually for a girl in Westerns, O'Day does more than smile at the hero and canter side-saddle to meet him. Here she helps Brown (who eventually falls for the charms of Merrick) take on property speculator Curtis. The action is well presented with Barcroft clearly relishing his villainous role.

d Ray Taylor   *p* Joseph Sanford   *s* Sherman Lowe
c Jerome Ash   *lp* Johnny Mack Brown, Fuzzy Knight, Nell O'Day, Marilyn (Lynn) Merrick, Dick Curtis, Roy Barcroft

The Range Busters (MON) b/w 56 min

The first of the Range Busters series that was closely modelled on the Three Mesquiteers series of which both Corrigan and Terhune (who even brought his dummy Elmer to the new series) had been long-standing members. Efficiently directed by Luby, who would be in control of all 16 of the series, it also has a strong screenplay from Rathmell that cleverly balances old-fashioned mystery – who is the phantom? – with action. LaRue is the seemingly kind doctor who advises calling the Range Busters in to investigate the murder of Walters' father and who is finally exposed by the trio as the guilty party.

d S. Roy Luby   *p* George W. Weeks   *s* John Rathmell
c Edward Linden   *lp* Ray Corrigan, John King, Max Terhune, LeRoy Mason, Luana Walters, Frank LaRue

Below: *Ray Corrigan and the villainous Frank LaRue in the first of yet another trio Western series,* The Range Busters.

Henry Fonda (right) in The Return of Frank James, *Fox's quickly mounted sequel to the hugely successful* Jesse James *(1939).*

Rangers of Fortune (PAR) b/w 80 min
Clearly intended as the first in yet another series about a trio of trouble-shooting drifters, this above-average B Western strangely had no sequels at all. MacMurray is the renegade Army officer, Roland the 'happy-go-lucky' Mexican and Dekker the ex-prizefighter. They all discover a town run by hoodlums and quickly set matters to rights. MacMurray's easy-going acting in the capable hands of Wood, whose presence assured the film superior production values, suggests the rumpled charm he brought to his major roles when he finally quit the Western in the mid-fifties.

d Sam Wood *p* Dale Van Every *s* Frank Butler
c Theodor Sparkuhl *lp* Fred MacMurray, Gilbert Roland, Albert Dekker, Patricia Morison, Dick Foran, Betty Brewer

The Return of Frank James (FOX) 92 min
Lang's first Western and his first colour film is a sequel to the enormously successful **Jesse James** (1939). Though Fonda, Hull and Carradine repeat their roles from the earlier film, the mood of the two is entirely different. Where Henry King's film is romantic, lush even, Lang's, despite the revenge theme which occurs so often in his work as the force behind the narrative, is almost a sentimental celebration of the Old West. Tierney is the newspaperwoman who falls for Fonda's Frank James and urges him to give up his quest for revenge on Carradine's Bob Ford. The result is a slow-moving and strangely anonymous looking film.

d Fritz Lang *p* Darryl F. Zanuck *s* Sam Hellman
c George Barnes, William V. Skall *lp* Henry Fonda, Gene Tierney, Jackie Cooper, Henry Hull, John Carradine, Donald Meek

The Return of Wild Bill (COL) b/w 60 min
Although his fancy tracking shots and odd angles can't disguise the impoverished budget of this Elliott series Western, Lewis' edgy direction is absolutely the best thing about this film. The film's major point of interest is Walters as the sister of Lloyd's baddie. She gives a spirited performance and dies a splendid death at the end. The plot-line has Elliott returning home to find his father dying and then tracking down the men responsible.

d Joseph H. Lewis *p* Leon Barsha *s* Robert Lee Johnson, Fred Myton *c* George Meehan *lp* Bill Elliott, Iris Meredith, Luana Walters, George Lloyd, Frank LaRue, Edward J. LeSaint

Ride, Tenderfoot, Ride (REP) b/w 66 min
Routine fare, this is as representative an Autry film as one could hope to find. He's the shy cowboy who falls heir to a meat-packing company and incurs the wrath of Storey, who runs a rival company, after an unfortunate misunderstanding. The officers of that company try to run Autry out of business but are foiled by the bizarre combination of Autry, Burnette and the precocious Lee, sister of Storey. This is a silly but very successful film.

d Frank McDonald *p* William Berke *s* Winston Miller *c* Jack Marta *lp* Gene Autry, Smiley Burnette, June Storey, Mary Lee, Forbes Murray, Joe McGuinn, Champion

River's End (WB) b/w 69 min
The third version of James Oliver Curwood's novel first filmed in 1922. Morgan is the man framed for murder who takes the identity of the mountie trailing him when the

mountie dies. He's able to do this because by wonderful coincidence they look alike. He then tracks down the real murderer. Earl is the woman who falls for Morgan. A slight film but superior to Curtiz's 1930 version.

d Ray Enright   *p* William Jacobs   *s* Barry Trivers, Bertram Milhauser   *c* Arthur L. Todd   *lp* Dennis Morgan, Elizabeth Earl, George Tobias, Victor Jory, James Stephenson, Edward Pawley

Santa Fé Trail   (WB)   b/w   110 min
A solemn, highly inaccurate biography of the early years of Confederate General Jeb Stuart, *Santa Fé Trail* is the third Western Flynn made with director Curtiz and writer Buckner. Flynn and Reagan (as Custer, a role Flynn himself would play the next year in **They Died with Their Boots On,** 1941) are the West Point graduates sent to put an end to the activities of Massey's John Brown and who compete for the affections of De Havilland's tomboyish Kit Carson Halliday. Curtiz and Buckner's usual flamboyant approach to history was much more subdued by the studio's concern to deal impartially with Brown's controversial raid on Harper's Ferry so as not to affect the film's chances in the South. The result is a would-be romantic Western whose perspective is limiting rather than liberating.

d Michael Curtiz   *p* Robert Fellows   *s* Robert Buckner   *c* Sol Polito   *lp* Errol Flynn, Olivia De Havilland, Raymond Massey, Ronald Reagan, Alan Hale, Van Heflin

Shooting High   (FOX)   b/w   65 min
Autry's first film away from Republic, the first feature in which he didn't play himself and the movie that brought forth Bosley Crowther's famous comment on the singing cowboy: 'Mr Autry has a unique way of projecting moods. He does not change expression; he just changes cowboy suits.'

A spoof about Hollywood and film-making, the plot concerns a film company in town to make a film about Autry's famous grandfather. The company hires Autry as a stand-in for the actor chosen to play the part, Lowery. But Autry proves himself to be a real hero by foiling a bank robbery and so gets the main part. A subplot features Withers, Fox's mischievous version of Shirley Temple, scaring Lowery out of town and Weaver as the girl Autry loves. Crowther's remarks were fair comment. Outside his normal world with its well-known supporting props and characters, Autry is very wooden.

d Alfred E. Green   *p* John Stone   *s* Lou Breslow, Owen Francis   *c* Ernest Palmer   *lp* Gene Autry, Jane Withers, Marjorie Weaver, Robert Lowery, Charles Middleton, Tom London

The Showdown   (PAR)   b/w   65 min
Including an extended poker sequence in which Hoppy outwits a crooked dealer, this is one of the better of Boyd's outings as Hopalong Cassidy after the arrival of vaudevillian veteran Wood in place of Gabby Hayes. A contemporary film, it sets Boyd and Hayden against a gang of horse thieves led by Ankrum in the unlikely guise of a 'European Baron'. Kermit, brother of Ken, Maynard and a one-time series star himself, has a featured role.

d Howard Bretherton   *p* Harry Sherman   *s* Harold Kusel, Daniel Kusel   *c* Russell Harlan   *lp* William Boyd, Russell Hayden, Britt Wood, Morris Ankrum, Jane (Jan) Clayton

Stage to Chino   (RKO)   b/w   58 min
Generally regarded as the best of O'Brien's RKO Westerns, *Stage to Chino* sees its star as an undercover postal agent sent West to ensure that the mail gets through. Vale is the pretty stagecoach-line owner and Barcroft the baddie employed by her cheating uncle to drive her out of business who meets his match in O'Brien. Cavanaugh as the timid travelling saleman,

Errol Flynn romancing Olivia De Havilland yet again in Santa Fé Trail, *one of the least successful of Warners' big budget Westerns.*

a direct descendant of Donald Meek's role in **Stagecoach** (1939), provides the comedy. Killy directs effortlessly, seaming together character, comedy and action without any of the awkward pauses that mar so many series Westerns.

d Edward Killy   *p* Bert Gilroy   *s* Morton Grant, Arthur V. Jones   *c* J. Roy Hunt   *lp* George O'Brien, Virginia Vale, Roy Barcroft, Hobart Cavanaugh, Carl Stockdale, William Haade

Texas Rangers Ride Again   (PAR)   b/w   67 min
A routine sequel to King Vidor's 1936 movie, **The Texas Rangers.** Howard and Crawford are the Rangers who turn up incognito at Robson's ranch to investigate the mysterious disappearance of her cattle and Miljan and ranch foreman Quinn, the culprits. Hogan's direction is flat while McCoy and Lipman's script uneasily juggles its modern and traditional elements, cars, radio receivers, six guns and horses.

Below: *Gene Autry with Jane Withers in a publicity photo for* Shooting High.

Andy Clyde (left), William Boyd (centre) and Esther Estrella in Three Men from Texas, *one of the best of Hopalong Cassidy's series Westerns.*

Anthony Quinn (seated) as the grinning villain with Broderick Crawford (extreme right) and John Howard (right), the puzzled undercover lawmen in the uninspired Texas Rangers Ride Again.

the clowning of Clyde, in the role of California Carson, to the series. The script by Parker is tough to the point of killing off Hayden's love interest, Estrella, early on in the story and Selander's direction is fast and furious. The plot features Hoppy and company putting paid to Ankrum's plans to gain complete control of the Mexican Border territory by driving people off their ranches. The superior musical score is by Victor Young.

d Lesley Selander   *p* Harry Sherman   *s* Norton S. Parker *c* Russell Harlan   *lp* William Boyd, Russell Hayden, Andy Clyde, Esther Estrella, Morris Ankrum, Morgan Wallace

Trail of the Vigilantes   (U)   b/w   75 min
Tone is the undercover man from the East sent to put an end to rustler activities of William who is being perpetually rescued by Crawford and his side-kick Devine in this lightweight but amiable tongue-in-cheek Western directed in his usual unassuming style by veteran Dwan. Mischa Auer, Paul Fix, and Moran, as the film's romantic interest, are among the strong supporting cast.

d/p Allan Dwan   *s* Harold Shumate   *c* Joseph Valentine, Milton Krasner   *lp* Franchot Tone, Broderick Crawford, Peggy Moran, Andy Devine, Warren William, Mischa Auer, Paul Fix, Porter Hall

Trailin' Double Trouble   (MON)   b/w   56 min
The second in the Range Busters series and a good indication of the rocky roads ahead. The script is offbeat (as many would be) with the trio kidnapping and looking after a baby in the interests of fair play, but the action is lacklustre. Barcroft is the villain trying to use the power of attorney that comes with the guardianship of the baby to secure himself a fortune. Conway is the heroine.

d S. Roy Luby   *p* George W. Weeks   *s* Oliver Drake *c* Edward Linden   *lp* Ray Corrigan, John King, Max Terhune, Lita Conway, Roy Barcroft, Tom London

Triple Justice   (RKO)   b/w   66 min
In this his last Western until the end of the war, O'Brien signed off by marrying the heroine Vale, after sorting out bank robbers Fix, Strange and McTaggart with his customary athleticism. Even the running inserts of the horse chase are done with a touch of class: Howard has the horses running at an angle to the camera truck so as not to smother them with the truck's dust. A superior film.

d David Howard   *p* Bert Gilroy   *s* Arthur V. Jones, Morton Grant   *c* J. Roy Hunt   *lp* George O'Brien, Virginia Vale, Peggy Shannon, Paul Fix, Glenn Strange, Bud McTaggart

The Tulsa Kid   (REP)   b/w   57 min
The presence of Beery as Barry's gunman of a foster father more than compensates for the insipid vocalizing of Wakely in this superior series entry. The climax, well handled by Sherman who was to direct 17 of the first 18 of Barry's outings for Republic, has Beery and Barry facing up to each other but unable to shoot. The plot features Barry, as the lawman of the title, cleaning up Wild River and Beery as the gunman hired to put an end to him by outlaw Douglas.

d/p George Sherman   *s* Oliver Drake, Anthony Coldeway *c* John MacBurnie   *lp* Donald Barry, Luana Walters, Noah Beery, Jimmy Wakely, George Douglas, David Durand

Twenty Mule Team   (MGM)   b/w   84 min
Beery and Carrillo are the borax miners and Fowley the villain who tries to steal their claim in this robust oater. Baxter, in her screen debut, is the daughter of saloon owner Rambeau (who was briefly Beery's regular partner in the forties before Marjorie Main supplanted her) and the object of Fowley's romantic interests.

d James Hogan   *p* Edward T. Lowe   *s* William R. Lipman, Horace McCoy   *c* Archie Stout   *lp* Ellen Drew, John Howard, May Robson, Broderick Crawford, Anthony Quinn, John Miljan

Texas Stagecoach   (COL)   b/w   59 min
Another edgy series Western from Lewis who in *Gun Crazy* (1949) (one of the most delirious of B features ever) was to celebrate his days with Starrett, Bob Baker and Wild Bill Elliott by dressing Peggy Cummins in Annie Oakley costume. Myton's screenplay features Curtis as the heavy working for MacDonald's scheming banker who is intent on bankrupting a stagecoach line. Unusually Starrett and Curtis don't have an extended brawl at the film's climax.

d Joseph H. Lewis   *p* Leon Barsha   *s* Fred Myton *c* George Meehan   *lp* Charles Starrett, Iris Meredith, Dick Curtis, Kenneth MacDonald, Bob Nolan, Edward J. LeSaint

Three Men from Texas   (PAR)   b/w   70 min
One of the finest – indeed thought by many to be the best – of the Hopalong Cassidy series, *Three Men from Texas* introduces

d Richard Thorpe *p* J. Walter Ruben *s* Cyril Hume, E.E.
Paramore, Richard Maibaum *c* Clyde DeVinna
lp Wallace Beery, Leo Carrillo, Marjorie Rambeau, Anne
Baxter, Noah Beery Jnr, Douglas Fowley

Two Fisted Rangers (COL) b/w 62 min
The arrival of Lewis as director saw a marked improvement in
Starrett's series Westerns which had been going steadily
downhill under Sam Nelson. Myton's screenplay is routine
with Starrett seeking revenge for the murder of his sheriff
brother but the action as captured by Lewis' tracking camera
sparkled. The Sons of the Pioneers provide the music and
Meredith the romance, as usual.

d Joseph H. Lewis *p* Leon Barsha *s* Fred Myton
c George Meehan *lp* Charles Starrett, Iris Meredith, Bob
Nolan, Hal Taliaferro (Wally Wales), Dick Curtis, Kenneth
MacDonald

Under Texas Skies (REP) b/w 57 min
This outing sees a much changed line-up for the Three
Mesquiteers. Davis makes his first appearance, replacing
Raymond Hatton, and Steele replaces Duncan Renaldo, thus
leaving Livingston (who was soon to quit) as the only original
Mesquiteer. Sadly it wasn't a change for the better. The tired
storyline has Livingston returning home to find his father
dead and Steele framed for the murder by Brandon's crooked
sheriff.

d George Sherman *p* Harry Grey *s* Anthony Coldeway,
Betty Burbridge *c* William Nobles *lp* Robert
Livingston, Bob Steele, Rufe Davis, Lois Ranson,
Henry Brandon, Rex Lease

Virginia City (WB) b/w 121 min
An inferior follow-up to the very successful **Dodge City**
(1939). Made by virtually the same team, it lacks the élan and
bite of the earlier movie. Flynn is the Union officer sent West
to stop shipments of gold to the Confederacy by Scott who has
to team up with him to fight off Bogart's highly unlikely
Mexican bandit complete with a wonderfully wavering accent.

Hopkins is the saloon singer and undercover agent for the
Confederacy.

By all accounts, though Flynn and Curtiz maintained their
traditionally uneasy working relationship, neither Bogart nor
Hopkins had any confidence in either the project or Curtiz
and made the director's life very difficult.

d Michael Curtiz *p* Robert Fellows *s* Robert Buckner
c Sol Polito *lp* Errol Flynn, Miriam Hopkins, Randolph
Scott, Humphrey Bogart, Alan Hale, Guinn 'Big Boy'
Williams

Above: *Randolph Scott
(left) and Errol Flynn as
the Confederate and
Union officers who join
forces to fight off
Humphrey Bogart's
Mexican bandit in
Virginia City.*

*Walter Brennan
declaring his love for
Lillie Langtry and
winning himself an
Oscar in the process in*
The Westerner.

Viva Cisco Kid (FOX) b/w 70 min
Badly received by the critics but lapped up by the series Western addicts because it foreswore romance in favour of action, this is the second of Romero's outings as the Cisco Kid. Clarke's fine cinematography makes the best of the unusual locations. The climax, more suited to a serial than a feature, but not the less exciting for that, has Romero and Rogers trapped in a sealed tunnel by Fields' villain and blasting their way to freedom.

d Norman Foster *p* Sol M. Wurtzel *s* Samuel G. Engel, Hal Long *c* Charles Clarke *lp* Cesar Romero, Jean Rogers, Chris-Pin Martin, Stanley Fields, Minor Watson, Harold Goodwin

Wagon Train (RKO) b/w 62 min
RKO's replacement for George O'Brien when he quit the studio after **Triple Justice** (1940) was Holt. The salary saving – Holt received only a third of O'Brien's fee – notwithstanding, the studio slashed the film's budget and the result was a series that nearly died before it got off the ground. Holt's inexperience didn't help matters either. Here he's out to get the man who murdered his father and running a wagon freight line to isolated pioneer settlements. O'Driscoll is the heroine he saves from marriage to McTaggart's son.

d Edward Killy *p* Lee Marcus *s* Morton Grant
c Harry Wild *lp* Tim Holt, Ray Whitley, Emmett Lynn, Martha O'Driscoll, Bud McTaggart, Carl Stockdale

Wagons Westward (REP) b/w 70 min
One of Republic's periodic big budget Westerns, *Wagons Westward* is noticable for Jones being cast against type as a cold-blooded evil sheriff but little else. Morris plays twin brothers, one good, one bad. He impersonates his worse half to capture Williams and Fowley only to have dance-hall girl Louise mistake him for his brother and demand the marriage she's been promised. Munson, his true love, stands by with teeth clenched.

d Lew Landers *p* Armand Schaefer *s* Harrison Jacobs, Joseph M. March *c* Ernest Miller *lp* Chester Morris, Anita Louise, Buck Jones, Guinn Williams, Douglas Fowley, Ona Munson

When the Daltons Rode: Broderick Crawford as Bob Dalton takes a swipe at Edgar Dearing's sheriff while his brothers, played by Frank Albertson (Emmett), Stuart Erwin (Ben) and Brian Donlevy (Grat) and Randolph Scott's lawyer look on.

West of Abilene *aka* **The Showdown**
(COL) b/w 58 min
The only Western directed by Cedar, this is an agreeable series entry. Starrett and his brother, Bennett, stake claims 'West of Abilene' only to have Beddoe try and run them off. Pawley is magnificent as the hired gun Starrett strikes up an edgy friendship with but finally has to kill in a dramatic gunfight. Another unusual aspect is the heroine being romanced by Bennett rather than the hero.

d Ralph Cedar *p* Leon Barsha *s* Paul Franklin *c* George Meehan *lp* Charles Starrett, Marjorie Cooley, Bruce Bennett, Don Beddoe, William Pawley, Bob Nolan

The Westerner (UA) b/w 100 min
The Westerner is a prestigious Western distinguished by Toland's magnificent camerawork and Brennan's Oscar winning performance as Judge Roy Bean. Cooper is the drifter who escapes hanging in the judge's courtroom by claiming friendship with Bond's Lillie Langtry and who eventually puts an end to Brennan's reign of terror 'West of the Pecos'. Whereas John Houston, in **The Life and Times of Judge Roy Bean** (1972), looking at Bean from a modern perspective, sees him as an out of time representative of the 'Old West' who ended his days fighting oilmen, Busch and Swerling's script sees Bean as a ruthless despot who tries to stop settlers from homesteading his range. The film's famous climax has Brennan alone in a theatre awaiting a performance by Lillie Langtry and the curtain rising to reveal Cooper, guns at the ready, on stage. The film also marked the screen debuts of Dana Andrews and Forrest Tucker.

d William Wyler *p* Samuel Goldwyn *s* Jo Swerling, Niven Busch *c* Gregg Toland, Archie Stout *lp* Gary Cooper, Walter Brennan, Doris Davenport, Chill Wills, Lillian Bond, Fred Stone, Paul Hurst

When the Daltons Rode (U) b/w 80 min
An enjoyable, and highly fictionalized history of the Daltons which ends with their failed attempts at a double bank raid in Coffeyville. This is one of the better of the several romantic biographies of Western badmen that followed the huge success of **Jesse James** (1939). Crawford, Donlevy, Erwin and Albertson as the Dalton brothers embark on a life of crime when the railroad tries to steal their farm and later switch to robbing banks. Scott is the young lawyer who befriends them, but it is Marshall's emphatic direction that pleads their case best. The movie features one of the trickiest stunts ever to be attempted on film: men on horseback jumping from a moving train and then riding off down an incline.

d/p George Marshall *s* Harold Shumate *c* Hal Mohr
lp Randolph Scott, Kay Francis, Brian Donlevy, Broderick Crawford, Stuart Erwin, Frank Albertson

Wildcat of Tucson (COL) b/w 59 min
An indifferent series entry for Elliott, distinguished only by his final exciting showdown with MacDonald. Surprisingly, since Elliott had developed his own distinctive form of fistfighting, there isn't a real brawl in the film. The story has Elliott searching for his younger brother who's become involved in claim jumping.

d Lambert Hillyer *p* Leon Barsha *s* Fred Myton
c George Meehan *lp* Bill Elliott, Evelyn Young, Stanley Brown, Dub Taylor, Kenneth MacDonald, Edmund Cobb

Wyoming *aka* **Bad Man of Wyoming**
(MGM) b/w 89 min
The first of numerous films Beery and Main were to make together, this slick Thorpe-directed opus sees them establish the roles of edgy, hostile lovers which they would later refine. Beery is the Missouri outlaw who joins the side of law and order and sets off after one-time buddy, Carrillo.

d Richard Thorpe *p* Milton Bren *s* Jack Jevne, Hugo Butler *c* Clyde DeVinna *lp* Wallace Beery, Leo Carrillo, Ann Rutherford, Marjorie Main, Lee Bowman, Henry Travers

Young Bill Hickok (REP) b/w 59 min
This is another lacklustre 'historical' entry in Rogers' series of Westerns with its star in the title role and Payne as Calamity Jane. Together they foil Taliaferro and Blue's plans to carve out an empire for themselves in the American West with their guerilla band. It is efficiently, but not very imaginatively, mounted by producer/director Kane.

d/p Joseph Kane *s* Norton S. Parker, Olive Cooper *c* William Nobles *lp* Roy Rogers, George Hayes, John Miljan, Sally Payne, Monte Blue, Hal Taliaferro, Trigger

1941

Across the Sierras (COL) b/w 59 min
Once again Elliott as Wild Bill Hickok expresses the desire to be a peaceable man before belting the living daylights out of a string of heavies. Here his adversary is Curtis, the man he put in jail years before, just released and seeking vengeance. An unusual plot twist has Elliott victorious over Curtis but rejected by Walters who can't abide a man carrying a gun.

d D. Ross Lederman *p* Leon Barsha *s* Paul Franklin *c* George Meehan *lp* Bill Elliott, Richard Fiske, Luana Walters, Dub Taylor, Dick Curtis, LeRoy Mason

Arizona Bound (MON) b/w 57 min
The first of Jones, Hatton and McCoy's Rough Rider series. The screenplay, by veteran Buffington (who would script all eight) under her Bowers pseudonym, keeps from the audience the fact that its lead trio are a team until the very end, even though the film's pre-publicity made this clear. Jones is called in to clear up Mesa City and with help from McCoy (working undercover as a gun-carrying parson) and Hatton he exposes Moore and saves the stagecoach franchise for Walters.

d Spencer G. Bennett *p* Scott R. Dunlap *s* Jess Bowers (Adele Buffington) *c* Harry Neumann *lp* Buck Jones, Tim McCoy, Raymond Hatton, Dennis Moore, Luana Walters, Slim Whitaker

Arizona Cyclone (U) b/w 59 min
The first and best of the three Brown films Lewis was to direct for the star's 1941/42 season. Brown runs the local freight line and falls foul of Curtis who wants to muscle in on the act. Lowe's screenplay is routine but Lewis' adventurous

direction, which even presents the action from unusual angles, gives the whole project a lift. Adams provides the romantic interest.

d Joseph H. Lewis *p* Will Cowan *s* Sherman Lowe *c* Charles Van Enger *lp* Johnny Mack Brown, Fuzzy Knight, Dick Curtis, Kathryn Adams, Nell O'Day, Kermit Maynard

Back in the Saddle (REP) b/w 73 min
Surprisingly, in view of the drift of recent Autry's away from action, this is an action-packed outing. Autry is the young rancher who finds copper on his land and sparks off a boom that excites the interest of villain Norris. Wells is the heroine and Lee, in her penultimate outing with Autry, the precocious teenager.

d Lew Landers *p* Harry Grey *s* Richard Murphy, Jesse Lasky Jnr *c* Ernest Miller *lp* Gene Autry, Smiley Burnette, Mary Lee, Edward Norris, Jacqueline Wells, Addison Richards, Champion

The Bad Man (MGM) b/w 70 min
Beery is the blustering border bandit (almost a parody of Pancho Villa whom he played so well in **Viva Villa**, 1934) in this routine remake of Porter Emerson Browne's melodrama. He plays Robin Hood to Reagan and his wheelchair-ridden grandfather, Barrymore (who rants almost as much as Beery growls in their scenes together) when they fall behind on the mortgage payments on their ranch. Day is Reagan's childhood love and Conway the man she has mistakenly married. Thorpe's direction is routine.

d Richard Thorpe *p* J. Walter Ruben *s* Wells Root *c* Clyde De Vinna *lp* Wallace Beery, Lionel Barrymore, Laraine Day, Ronald Reagan, Tom Conway, Chill Wills

Bad Men of Missouri (WB) b/w 74 min
Out of the many glamourized biographies of outlaws that followed the enormous success of Henry King's **Jesse James** (1939). The subject this time is the Younger Brothers, impersonated here by Morgan, Morris and Kennedy, whose outlawry is explained as a Robin Hood response to Northern carpetbaggers and their vulture-like descent on the defeated South. Wyman supplies the romance, Jory the dyed-in-the-

Wallace Beery as the former Missouri outlaw turned lawman with outlaw friend Leo Carrillo in Wyoming.

Below: *Buck Jones, Tim McCoy and Raymond Hatton in* Arizona Bound, *the first of the Rough Riders series.*

Top: *Wallace Beery with his arms around Laraine Day and Ronald Reagan on the set of* The Bad Man.

wool villainy. Grayson's script and Enright's fast-paced direction are as entertaining as they are mindless.

d Ray Enright *p* Harlan Thompson *s* Charles Grayson
c Arthur L. Todd *lp* Dennis Morgan, Jane Wyman, Wayne Morris, Arthur Kennedy, Victor Jory, Alan Baxter

The Badlands of Dakota (U) b/w 74 min
Slickly directed by Green and capably acted by a strong cast, this is a better than average Western. Set at the time of the Dakota Gold Rush of 1876, the plot features Stack and Crawford as the brothers, one a sheriff, the other an outlaw, and historical figures like Custer (Richards), Hickok (Dix) and Calamity Jane (Farmer). Though Stack and Rutherford, the girl over whom he and Crawford quarrel, are the nominal stars, Farmer, as the gutsy Calamity Jane, and the blustering Crawford have the better parts. Indeed, Farmer's shooting of Crawford, the man she loves, at the end is the emotional highpoint of the film.

d Alfred E. Green *p* George Waggner *s* Gerald Geraghty *c* Stanley Cortez *lp* Robert Stack, Ann Rutherford, Richard Dix, Addison Richards, Broderick Crawford, Frances Farmer

Belle Starr (FOX) 87 min
Tierney is Belle, the Southern aristo who turns gunfighter and marries Confederate guerilla-leader Scott to continue the fight against carpetbagger Yankees in this romantic but stilted

The poster for Belle Starr.

Right: *Dennis Morgan, Wayne Morris and Arthur Kennedy (left to right) as the Younger Brothers in* Bad Men of Missouri.

biopic. It would be better and certainly more impassioned had it been scripted by Niven Busch from a story by Trotti, rather than otherwise, as it is. Similarly, although Tierney doesn't look too embarrassed with a gun in her hand, it wasn't until the like of Peggie Castle and Beverly Garland took up arms in **Oklahoma Woman** (1956) and **Gunslinger** (1956) respectively, that the full potential of a woman gunslinger would be explored.

d Irving Cummings *p* Kenneth MacGowan *s* Lamar Trotti *c* Ernest Palmer, Rory Rennahan *lp* Randolph Scott, Gene Tierney, Dana Andrews, John Sheppard, Elizabeth Patterson, Chill Wills

Billy the Kid (MGM) 95 min
This prestige production saw the legend rewritten to make Garrett (Donlevy) and Billy childhood friends. The striking

outdoor colour photography, Fowler's literate, albeit romantic, script and Taylor (all in black) as the outlaw are the best things in an otherwise pedestrian film.

d David Miller   *p* Irving Asher   *s* Gene Fowler
c Leonard Smith, William V. Skall   *lp* Robert Taylor, Brian Donlevy, Ian Hunter, Mary Howard, Gene Lockhart, Lon Chaney Jnr

Border Vigilantes   (PAR)   b/w   62 min
The directorial debut of Abrahams, a former assistant and editor on many of Sherman's productions, this is a better than average outing for Hoppy who in his recent films had become more and more a sort of Robin Hood of the range. Here he comes to the aid of a mining community terrorized by Jory and Ankrum, in a screenplay that has more gunplay than usual.

d Derwin Abrahams   *p* Harry Sherman   *s* J. Benton Cheney   *c* Russell Harlan   *lp* William Boyd, Russell Hayden, Andy Clyde, Victor Jory, Morris Ankrum, Frances Gifford

The Cowboy and the Blonde   (FOX)   b/w   68 min
A 'Taming of the Shrew' comedy set in Hollywood. Montgomery is the rodeo cowboy who's a success in Hollywood until the temperamental Hughes causes difficulties in both his professional and personal life. The end has Montgomery putting Hughes in her place after making her fall in love with him. A routine series entry.

d Ray McCarey   *p* Ralph Dietrich, Walter Morosco   *s* Walter Bullock   *c* Charles Clarke   *lp* Mary Beth Hughes, George Montgomery, Alan Mowbray, Fuzzy Knight, Robert Conway, John Miljan

Desert Bandit   (REP)   b/w   56 min
Barry gives a good performance, despite his anger at being forced to sport a false 'Red Ryder' hairpiece, and the presence of Sherman as producer/director guarantees strong production values. Sadly the script by Cohen and Gibbons is as hackneyed as they come: Barry is the Texas Ranger who goes undercover to catch a band of gun smugglers and the dishonest sheriff in cahoots with them.

d/p George Sherman   *s* Eliot Gibbons, Bennett Cohen   *c* William Nobles   *lp* Don Barry, Lynn Merrick, William Haade, James Gilette, Charles King, Dick Wessell

Doomed Caravan   (PAR)   b/w   62 min
One of the best of the high-quality Hopalong Cassidy series. Boyd is the frontier Samaritan who protects Gombell's wagon train from Ankrum and Bardette who are planning to take over the world, starting with her wagon franchise. McCulley and Chase's screenplay is routine but cinematographer Harlan makes the best of the unusual Californian Sierra locations.

d Lesley Selander   *p* Harry Sherman   *s* Johnston McCulley, J. Benton Chase   *c* Russell Harlan   *lp* William Boyd, Russell Hayden, Andy Clyde, Minna Gombell, Morris Ankrum, Trevor Bardette

Down Mexico Way   (REP)   b/w   77 min
The second outing as director of Santley, a man better known for his musicals and comedies, like his first, **Melody Ranch** (1940), this is a decidedly livelier Autry film than the ones in between, which, though they have more action-oriented plots, have little actual action. Here Autry and Burnette, his faithful comic, head South of the Border in search of the con men who've fleeced the good citizens of Sage City (Sage City, indeed?). McKenzie is the heroine and Renaldo, Fix and Blackmer are amongst the strong support.

d Joseph Santley   *p* Harry Grey   *s* Olive Cooper, Albert Duffy   *c* Jack Marta   *lp* Gene Autry, Smiley Burnette, Fay McKenzie, Sidney Blackmer, Duncan Renaldo, Paul Fix, Champion

Robert Taylor, all in black, in the title role of David Miller's slow-moving Billy the Kid.

The Dude Cowboy   (RKO)   b/w   59 min
Grant's fine screenplay and Howard's taut direction make this one of Holt's best series Westerns. He's a secret service agent on the track of counterfeiters operating out of a Nevada dude ranch and using a gambling casino to spread the money. The usual all-guns-blazing climax is handled with aplomb by Howard who situates it way out in the desert around an abandoned mine. Ingraham is the villain.

d David Howard   *p* Bert Gilroy   *s* Morton Grant   *c* Harry Wild   *lp* Tim Holt, Marjorie Reynolds, Ray Whitley, Lee 'Lasses' White, Lloyd Ingraham, Glenn Strange

Go West Young Lady   (COL)   b/w   70 min
A would-be farce of a Western that doesn't come off because Strayer and his writers can't decide just what it is about the West(ern) that they want to poke fun at. More significantly, it

The Cowboy and the Blonde: *Mary Beth Hughes is the blonde and George Montgomery the Hollywood cowboy.*

William Boyd, Russell Hayden and Andy Clyde (left to right) in In Old Colorado.

was the first of several Westerns to feature Bob Wills (and his Texas Playboys) who, unlike any of the other regular singing musicians appearing in Westerns, was a major star of country music. His subsequent films would feature his small 'big band' but for *Go West Young Lady* he assembled his biggest ever band on celluloid, a twenty-strong orchestra including French horns and oboes. Sadly he never recorded with such a band. The film's simple plot features Ford as the marshal and Singleton, the tomboy Easterner, and Miller, the dance-hall queen, as the two girls who fight over him.

d Frank R. Strayer *p* Robert Sparks *s* Richard Flournoy, Karen DeWolf *c* Henry Freulich *lp* Penny Singleton, Glenn Ford, Ann Miller, Charlie Ruggles, Onslow Stevens, Bob Wills

Gunman from Bodie (MON) b/w 62 min
The second and, according to many, the best of the Rough Rider series. Jones is the gunman on the run, McCoy the marshal and Hatton the cook who together foil the plans of Frazer to clear all the homesteaders out of the valley. A sub-plot has Jones finding and caring for a baby. It was shot back to back with the first of the series, **Arizona Bound** (1941) which explains why it shares so many scenes (and costumes) with that film.

d Spencer G. Bennett *p* Scott R. Dunlap *s* Jess Bowers (Adele Buffington) *c* Harry Neumann *lp* Buck Jones, Tim McCoy, Raymond Hatton, Robert Frazer, Christine McIntyre, Frank LaRue

Honky Tonk (MGM) b/w 105 min
A glossy MGM Western, all froth and little substance but not the less entertaining for that. The first pairing of Gable and Turner, *Honky Tonk* features him as the con man setting out to make his fortune in a boom time and her as the Eastern girl who marries and then tames him. Trevor is the dance-hall girl with the heart of gold whom Gables leaves behind and Dekker the villain of the piece. An indication of how close the film is to a soap opera is that Gable's 'moral regeneration' begins when Turner has a miscarriage. Efficiently directed by Conway, the film is as much a tribute to the MGM production department as to its sparring leads.

d Jack Conway *p* Pandro S. Berman *s* Marguerite Roberts, John Sanford *c* Harold Rossen *lp* Clark Gable, Lana Turner, Frank Morgan, Claire Trevor, Albert Dekker, Chill Wills

In Old Colorado (PAR) b/w 66 min
Another superior Hopalong Cassidy entry, this is the first to be directed by Bretherton on his return to the series. Ankrum is the outlaw who exploits a feud between local ranchers over water rights, hoping to grab their lands after they've killed each other off. Harlan's cinematography is even better than usual and Bretherton produces a rousing climax with all the parties blazing away at each other.

d Howard Bretherton *p* Harry Sherman *s* J. Benton Cheney, Norton S. Parker, Russell Hayden *c* Russell Harlan *lp* William Boyd, Russell Hayden, Andy Clyde, Margaret Hayes, Morris Ankrum, Cliff Nazarro

Jesse James at Bay (REP) b/w 56 min
So sure were Republic of their star's clean image that they cast Rogers as Jesse James in this efficient actioner. Barcroft, Rogers' favourite villain, leads a landgrabbing outfit working for the railroad that is trying to steal the land of Missouri homesteaders. In a distinctly Robin Hood interpretation of Jesse James, Rogers engages upon a series of train robberies to help the settlers continue their fight against the railroad magnate.

The film was Rogers' last actionful entry for some time; soon he was to be firmly entombed in musical numbers.

d/p Joseph Kane *s* James R. Webb *c* William Nobles *lp* Roy Rogers, George Hayes, Sally Payne, Pierre Watkin, Gale Storm, Roy Barcroft, Trigger

Below: Clark Gable as the confidence trickster about to be tarred and feathered in Honky Tonk.

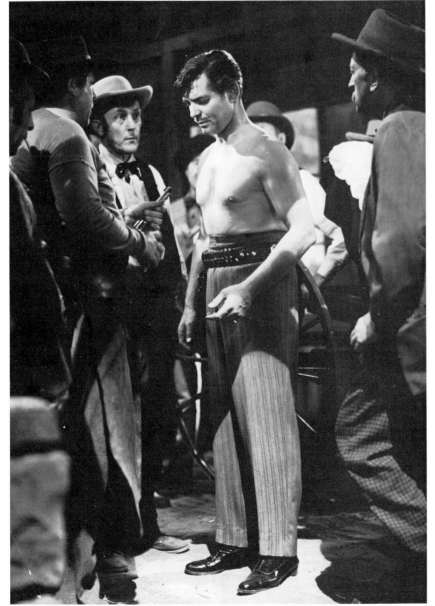

Kansas Cyclone (REP) b/w 58 min

A superior series Western. Barry is the marshal who adopts the disguise of a geologist in order to catch bandits who have been robbing Wells Fargo. Drake and Schroeder's screenplay is deft and to the point and Sherman directs with verve, but it is Barry and heroine Merrick (who introduces a higher degree of sexuality than normal in series Westerns) who make the pic so appealing. Taylor is the outlaw.

d/p George Sherman   s Oliver Drake, Doris Schroeder
c William Nobles   lp Don Barry, Lynn Merrick, William Haade, Forrest Taylor, Harry Worth, Yakima Canutt

The King of Dodge City (COL) b/w 63 min

The first and best of Ritter and Elliott's eight-strong co-starring series for Columbia. It was written by Geraghty to what has been called 'the Drake formula', so named after Oliver Drake who first used it consistently in his scripts for the Three Mesquiteers series. The formula is simple: Elliott and Ritter work separately on the same problem until the climax when they unite to save one or the other and catch the villain. This story has them cleaning up Dodge City and features a rousing gun-blazing climax.

d Lambert Hillyer   p Leon Barsha   s Gerald Geraghty
c Benjamin Kline   lp Bill Elliott, Tex Ritter, Judith Linden, Dub Taylor, Edmund Cobb, George Chesebro

King of the Texas Rangers (REP) b/w 12 chaps

Surely the most surreal of Republic's serials, this modern-day Western features one-time footballer and would-be series star, Baugh, as the man who throws up a brilliant career to join the Texas Rangers, and so legally avenge the death of his father, and Renaldo, as his Mexican counterpart, on the trail of Axis spies. Much trimmed by the Hays office who thought its violence too vivid, the chapter play has Baugh and Renaldo

outwitting a legion of spies whose secret headquarters is a Zeppelin hovering over Texas (!?) from which they set oilfields alight, destroy railroads and the like. The result is a silly, but hugely enjoyable chapter play, in small doses.

d William Witney, John English   p Hiram S. Brown Jnr
s Ronald Davidson, Norman S. Hall, Joseph Poland, Joseph O'Donnell, William Lively   c Reggie Lanning
lp Sammy Baugh, Duncan Renaldo, Neil Hamilton, Pauline Moore, Charles Trowbridge, Herbert Rawlinson

Lady from Cheyenne (U) b/w 87 min

Gambler Arnold and Quaker Young do battle in this entertaining history of the Women's Suffrage Movement in Wyoming, which, it is suggested, got off the ground because without the vote women couldn't sit on juries and therefore couldn't convict racketeers and gamblers like Arnold. The screenplay is clearly intended to be droll and Lloyd directs with an eye to the humorous but the plot's complexities bog everybody down.

d/p Frank Lloyd   s Kathryn Scola, Warren Duff   c Milton Krasner   lp Loretta Young, Robert Preston, Edward Arnold, Frank Craven, Gladys George, Stanley Fields

Sally Payne holds Roy Rogers as Jesse at gunpoint while Gale Storm and Gabby Hayes look on in Republic's Jesse James at Bay.

Loretta Young, a suffragette in Lady from Cheyenne but just a woman in real life: here, on the set of the film, she toasts marshmallows with co-star Robert Preston.

Last of the Duanes (FOX) b/w 57 min

This Zane Grey remake was quickly put into production by Fox as a sequel to **Riders of the Purple Sage** (1941) in which Montgomery had been a huge hit. For this film he took the role (previously essayed by Tom Mix and George O'Brien in 1930) of the man on the run out to clear his name. This he does, as well as rescue Arden from a band of outlaws. William Farnum who had the lead in the first ever version of Grey's novel, has a small part as a Texas Ranger.

d James Tinling   p Sol M. Wurtzel   s Irving Cummings Jnr, William Conselman Jnr   c Charles Clark   lp George Montgomery, Lynne Roberts, Eve Arden, Francis Ford, George E. Stone, Harry Woods

Law of the Range (U) b/w 59 min

A slow-moving outing with Brown trying to bring an end to his family's long-standing feud with O'Day's family and to find out who murdered O'Day's father. Bridges is the outlaw responsible, but it's O'Day (a spirited performance) and Morley, as the rancher's daughter, who take up most of

George Montgomery and Eve Arden in Last of the Duanes.

Philip Terry (left) and Charlie Ruggles as reverend and mayor respectively in The Parson of Panamint.

Brown's time. The film is a remake of Buck Jones' **The Ivory Handled Gun** (1935), also directed by Taylor.

d Ray Taylor *p* Will Cowan *s* Sherman Lowe *c* Charles Van Enger *lp* Johnny Mack Brown, Fuzzy Knight, Nell O'Day, Al Bridges, Charles King, Elaine Morley

The Medico of Painted Springs *aka* Doctor's Alibi
(COL) b/w 58 min

The first of Starrett's trio of Westerns in which he plays Dr Steven Monroe, a travelling doctor straightening trouble as well as bones as he journeys through the West. Here, officially in town to examine recruits for the Rough Riders, he sorts out some trouble between cattlemen and sheepmen. Needless to say, Oakman is the villain, while the Simp-Phonies provide both musical and comic relief. The picture's main failing is Miller and Gittens' dialogue which has Starrett oscillate between being a brash cowboy and a mild-mannered medico.

d Lambert Hillyer *p* Jack Fier *s* Winston Miller, Wyndham Gittens *c* Benjamin Kline *lp* Charles Starrett, Terry Walker, Bud Osborne, Richard Fiske, Ray Bennett, Wheeler Oakman

North from the Lone Star (COL) b/w 58 min

Featuring a rousing bar-room brawl from seriesdom's most 'peaceable man', this is a routine entry in Elliott's Wild Bill Hickok series. He takes on the job of marshal to clear the frontier of Fiske and his cronies, Loft and Roper. Fay and Rochelle are the ladies who fight over Elliott to no avail.

d Lambert Hillyer *p* Leon Barsha *s* Charles Francis Royal *c* Benjamin Kline *lp* Bill Elliott, Richard Fiske, Dorothy Fay, Arthur Loft, Jack Roper, Claire Rochelle

Outlaws of the Desert (PAR) b/w 66 min

Hoppy with Clyde and King (the replacement for Russell Hayden who joined Charles Starrett in his Columbia series) in tow heads for Arabia to buy some horses for the Government and gets involved in a kidnapping plot. Renaldo, who'd just quit being a Mesquiteer, is the desert prince and Deste the siren and queen of his harem. With **Secrets of the Wasteland** (1941) it sees the series looking for novelty for its own sake, a sure indication that the end was in sight for Hoppy and the Bar 20 cowboys.

d Howard Bretherton *p* Harry Sherman *s* J. Benton Cheney, Bernard McConville *c* Russell Harlan *lp* William Boyd, Brad King, Andy Clyde, Luci Deste, Duncan Renaldo, Jean Phillips

Outlaws of the Panhandle (COL) b/w 59 min

Routine fare. The plot has a group of ranchers trying to build a railroad spur so as to be able to ship their cattle to market without fear of rustlers. Willis is the outlaw trying to prevent them by serenading the workmen with wine, women and song. Starrett and his never-ending supply of bullets make sure the line is completed.

d Sam Nelson *p* Jack Fier *s* Paul Franklin *c* George Meehan *lp* Charles Starrett, Frances Robinson, Bob Nolan, Richard Fiske, Ray Teal, Norman Willis

The Parson of Panamint (PAR) b/w 84 min

Adapted from the *Saturday Evening Post* story by Peter B. Kyne, better known as the author of the short story filmed variously as **Three Godfathers** (1936,1948) and **Hell's Heroes** (1930), *The Parson of Panamint* is an equally melodramatic mix of sentimentality and irony. Told in flashback by Ruggles, the one-time mayor of the ill-fated town of Panamint, it features newcomer Terry as the two fisted Reverend who attempts to reform the rough-and-ready gold-mining town only to be swept away with most of the townspeople when the river overflows and turns the prosperous outpost into a ghost town. Terry is suitably brash as the athletic defender of God and Ruggles equally laconic as the storyteller. Drew provides the romantic interest.

d William McGaan *p* Harry Sherman *s* Harold Shumate, Adrian Scott *c* Russell Harlan *lp* Charlie Ruggles, Ellen Drew, Phillip Terry, Joseph Schildkraut, Porter Hall, Paul Hurst

The Phantom Cowboy (REP) b/w 56 min
Marx's 'El Lobo' is the hooded defender of justice who gets wounded and hands on his mask and cape to Barry in this slackly scripted but energetically directed outing. Stone and Lease are the baddies out to drive homesteaders off the properties left them in the will of Stone's boss.

d/p George Sherman *s* Doris Schroeder *c* Reggie Lanning *lp* Don Barry, Virginia Carroll, Milburn Stone, Neyle Marx, Rex Lease, Bud Osborne

Pirates on Horseback (PAR) b/w 69 min
In fact there are no pirates, on or off horseback; instead, there's Ankrum as a gambling czar attempting to defraud Stewart of ownership of a lost mine. Hoppy and Hayden, with comic assistance from Clyde, have first to find the mine and then save it. A fine fistfight between Ankrum and Boyd is the showpiece of the pic.

d Lesley Selander *p* Harry Sherman *s* Ethel La Blanche, J. Benton Cheney *c* Russell Harlan *lp* William Boyd, Russell Hayden, Andy Clyde, Eleanor Stewart, Morris Ankrum, William Haade

Prairie Stranger (COL) b/w 68 min
The third and last of Starrett's series outing as Doctor Monroe. The lack of action inherent in the idea of a cowboy

Above: *Mary Howard and George Montgomery as the lovers in one of the several versions of* Riders of the Purple Sage.

doctor and legal problems over Columbia's rights to the stories of James L. Rubel, on which the films were based, were the stated reasons for ending the series. Here Starrett and Edwards lose all their paying clients to an Eastern doctor and so turn to cowboying. When a disease spreads through the herd Starrett cures the cows and catches the culprits.

d Lambert Hillyer *p* William Berke *s* Winston Miller *c* Benjamin Kline *lp* Charles Starrett, Cliff Edwards, Frank LaRue, Edmund Cobb, Patti McCarty, Forbes Murray

Red River Valley (REP) b/w 62 min
Not to be confused with Gene Autry's 1936 release of the same title, this film sees the Sons of the Pioneers, the group Rogers (as Leonard Slye) had earlier helped form, join Rogers on a regular basis. Naturally the musical content is accordingly raised but Kane keeps the action well to the fore with Rogers laying down his guitar to do battle with Bardette who stole the $182,000 that Rogers has persuaded local ranchers to raise towards the cost of a reservoir. Along the way Rogers wins the affections of Storm. Soon, however, music would overwhelm action, even supplanting it as the climax of a Rogers' outing.

d/p Joseph Kane *s* Malcolm Stuart Boylin *c* Jack Marta *lp* Roy Rogers, George Hayes, Sally Payne, Trevor Bardette, Gale Storm, Robert Homans, Trigger

Ride on Vaquero (FOX) b/w 64 min
The last of Fox's Cisco Kid series, *Ride on Vaquero* has Romero on the trail of kidnappers and Hughes as the dance-hall girl he romances in between fistfights. The series, though never that enthusiastically received, was successful enough for Fox to want to continue. But when Romero went into the armed services, they couldn't find a suitable contract replacement and so the series lapsed until Monogram revived the character with **The Cisco Kid Returns** (1945).

d Herbert I. Leeds *p* Sol M. Wurtzel *s* Samuel G. Engel *c* Lucien Andriot *lp* Cesar Romero, Mary Beth Hughes, Chris-Pin Martin, Robert Lowery, Ben Carter, William Demarest

Russell Hayden (left) and William Boyd with Eleanor Stewart in Pirates on Horseback.

Riders of Death Valley (U) b/w 15 chaps

The first million-dollar serial production, though, ironically with Universal spending so much on the cast and publicity, the serial had even more stock footage than usual, including a sandstorm lifted from *Flash Gordon's Trip to Mars* (1938). The riders of the title are Jones, Carrillo (who provides the comic relief with his 'Listen, I theenk I hear footprints...' patter), Beery, Williams and Strange who help break up a group of land-grabbers who have killed miner Foran's partner. Taylor and Beebe cut whatever corners they can: thus Rod Cameron visibly doubles for Jones, even in non-action shots to save time.

The film was the last Jones made before his death in 1942.

d Ford Beebe, Ray Taylor *p* Henry McRae *s* Sherman Lowe, George Plympton, Basil Dickey, Jack Connell *lp* Dick Foran, Leo Carrillo, Buck Jones, Charles Bickford, Lon Chaney Jnr, Noah Beery Jnr, Jeanne Kelly, Guinn 'Big Boy' Williams, Glenn Strange

Riders of the Purple Sage (FOX) b/w 56 min

Montgomery, in one of the few B features he made before stardom, is in fine romantic vein as the Texas Ranger on the trail of a crooked lawyer turned judge in this often-filmed Zane Grey story. The ending has Montgomery and Howard blocking the only entrance (and exit) to the canyon they take refuge in. By 1941, Grey's melodramatic plot was creaking considerably though Bruckner and Metzler's script papered over the implausibilities as neatly as possible.

d James Tinling *p* Sol M. Wurtzel *s* William Bruckner, Robert Metzler *c* Lucien Andriot *lp* George Montgomery, Mary Howard, Robert Barrat, Lynne Roberts, Kane Richmond, LeRoy Mason

Ridin' on a Rainbow (REP) b/w 79 min

This lacklustre Autry outing, set mostly on a showboat, is one of the most musical and least action-packed of the series. Lee, who upstages Autry for most of the picture, is the would-be teenage singing star and Byron Foulger her wayward father who helps robbers steal the money Autry has just persuaded to deposit in the local bank. What action there is, as was usual with the musical Autrys, takes place all at once at the end when Autry and Burnette shoot it out with the outlaws after a spirited chase.

d Lew Landers *p* Harry Grey *s* Bradford Ropes, Doris Malloy *c* William Nobles *lp* Gene Autry, Smiley Burnette, Mary Lee, Ed Cassidy, Forrest Taylor, Tom London

Road Agent aka Texas Road Agent (U) b/w 60 min

Yet another trio Western with Foran, who had had his own series as a singing cowboy for Warners earlier in 1935–37, in the lead. He, Carillo and Devine are wrongly imprisoned, suspected of a bank robbery, and then let go to prove their innocence. They infiltrate the real villains, steal back the gold bullion and rescue Gwynne along the way. The result is an enjoyable, minor B Western.

d Charles Lamont *p* Ben Pivar *s* Morgan Cox, Arthur Strawn *c* Jerome Ash *lp* Dick Foran, Leo Carrillo, Andy Devine, Anne Gwynne, Richard Davies, Morris Ankrum

Robbers of the Range (RKO) b/w 61 min

Made just prior to his securing the part of the spoiled son in *The Magnificent Ambersons* (1942), this is the best of Holt's early Westerns. The plot is the standard one about the coming of the railroad and a crooked land agent, but Holt, with strong support from Mason's baddie and Wild's superior cinematography, brings a freshness to it that is appealing. Vale, the regular heroine in George O'Brien's films, whom Holt replaced, re-assumed her usual role with this film.

d Edward Killy *p* Bert Kilroy *s* Morton Grant, Arthur V. Jones *c* Harry Wild *lp* Tim Holt, Virginia Vale, Ray Whitley, LeRoy Mason, Frank LaRue, Emmett Lynn

The Round Up (PAR) b/w 90 min

An overlong and over-melodramatic remake of the 1920 silent of the same title. Dix is the rancher Morison marries believing Foster, whom she loved, to be dead. He returns on the wedding day to plague their happiness before dying in the last reel. Selander, normally an economic and tidy director, is clearly in over his head and only seems happy directing the humorous scenes with Cowan.

d Lesley Selander *p* Harry Sherman *s* Harold Shumate *c* Russell Harlan *lp* Richard Dix, Patricia Morison, Preston Foster, Don Wilson, Jerome Cowan, Morris Ankrum

The Royal Mounted Patrol aka Giants A'Fire (COL) b/w 59 min

Starrett is joined by Bridges and Hayden (fresh from his role as Lucky Jenkins in the Hopalong Cassidy series) for this superior Mountie outing. Curtis is the lumberman who causes a forest fire and kills Bridges, and one-time model McKay is the sister over whom Starrett and Hayden quarrel. Down the cast list is Kermit Maynard who once starred in his own Mountie series. Though there's nothing very fancy about the pic, Lewis' deft direction and the strong cast make it well above average.

d Joseph H. Lewis *p* Will Cowan *s* Sherman Lowe *c* George Meehan *lp* Charles Starrett, Russell Hayden, Lloyd Bridges, Donald Curtis, Wanda McKay, Ted Adams

Saddlemates (REP) b/w 56 min

Routine fare. The Mesquiteers join the army as scouts to help trail renegade Indian chief Lynn who, in fact, is masquerading as an Indian interpreter for the army! The climax has a wagon train encircled by Indians and the Cavalry arriving just in the nick of time. Storm is the commandant's daughter with eyes for Livingston.

d Les Orlebeck *p* Louis Gray *s* Albert Demond, Herbert Dalmas *c* William Nobles *lp* Robert Livingston, Bob Steele, Rufe Davis, Gale Storm, George Lynn, Glenn Strange

Richard Dix (left) and Preston Foster vie for the affections of Patricia Morison in The Round Up.

Secrets of the Wasteland (PAR) b/w 66 min
This wonderfully far-fetched Hopalong Cassidy outing sees Hoppy protecting a group of Chinese against landgrabbers and helping them settle in a fertile California Valley – a neat variant on the 'Spanish Land Grant' plot. The film also marks the arrival of King as the young pardner after Russell Hayden's departure from the series. The series started to go downhill after this entry.

d Derwin Abrahams *p* Harry Sherman *s* Gerald Geraghty *c* Russell Harlan *lp* William Boyd, Andy Clyde, Brad King, Barbara Britton, Douglas Fowley, Keith Richards

The Shepherd of the Hills (PAR) 98 min
A sentimental, rural idyll of a Western. Wayne is the inarticulate young moonshiner whose love for Field is overshadowed by his hatred of his father (Carey) for leaving his mother and himself at an early age. Carey, who had a good reason to go, returns and reveals himself to Wayne who, after beginning a shooting match he can't finish, is reconciled to him. Bond is the charmingly oafish villain of the piece. The film's offbeat story and its depiction of rural life result in a pleasing, if cloying movie.

d Henry Hathaway *p* Jack Moss *s* Grover Jones, Stuart Anthony *c* Charles Lang, W. Howard Greene *lp* John Wayne, Betty Field, Harry Carey, Ward Bond, Beulah Bondi, James Barton

Six Gun Gold (RKO) b/w 57 min
One of the better of Holt's series Westerns. The bizarre opening has Holt visiting his brother and pretending to be frightened when he meets Mason posing as him. Eventually with assistance from Whitley and White, Holt unmasks Mason and after a lengthy gun battle frees his captive brother. A subsidiary plot has Holt leading a wagonload of gold, attacked by Mason, to safety.

d David Howard *p* Bert Gilroy *s* Norton S. Parker *c* Harry Wild *lp* Tim Holt, Ray Whitley, LeRoy Mason, Lee White, Jan Clayton, Lane Chandler

The Son of Davy Crockett (COL) b/w 59 min
This series outing sees Elliott forsaking his Wild Bill Hickok persona in favour of impersonating a number of other historical figures. Here he's Crockett's son, delegated by President Grant to help secure Texas' vote for inclusion in the Union. MacDonald is the outlaw with different plans. The script mistakenly stresses dialogue rather than action.

d/s Lambert Hillyer *p* Leon Barsha *c* Benjamin Kline *lp* Bill Elliott, Iris Meredith, Dub Taylor, Kenneth MacDonald, Richard Fiske, Donald Curtis

Texas (COL) sepia 94 min
Holden and Ford are the happy-go-lucky scoundrels who, after a series of scrapes with the law end up on different sides, Ford settling down to work on a ranch and Holden joining Buchanan's gang. Trevor is the heroine undecided between the two. Although the film is a minor one, its easy charm and dry humour, deftly handled by Marshall, belie its small budget and make it one of Columbia's better forties Westerns.

d George Marshall *p* Sam Bischoff *s* Horace McCoy, Lewis Meltzer, Michael Blankfort *c* George Meehan *lp* William Holden, Glenn Ford, Claire Trevor, George Bancroft, Edgar Buchanan, Don Beddoe

They Died with Their Boots On
(WB) b/w 140 min
Classic Walsh. Though *They Died with Their Boots On* might seem to prove Andrew Sarris' famous description of Walsh ('If the heroes of Ford are sustained by tradition, and the heroes of Hawks by professionalism, the heroes of Walsh are

sustained by nothing more than a feeling for adventure'), a close look at the film explodes that view. Walsh and writer Klein heavily romanticize both Flynn's Custer – making him pro-Indian for example – and the battle of the Little Big Horn. But if the film is historically inaccurate, Walsh's depiction of his hero as rootless, scared of domesticity and fearful for his masculinity is highly original. The film marked the last time De Havilland would co-star with Flynn.

d Raoul Walsh *p* Robert Fellows *s* Wally Klein, Aeneas MacKenzie *c* Bert Glennon *lp* Errol Flynn, Olivia De Havilland, Arthur Kennedy, Charles Grapewin, Anthony Quinn, Gene Lockhart

Thunder over the Prairie (COL) b/w 61 min
This outing introduced Edwards, a correspondence school doctor!, as Starrett's comic side-kick for his Doctor Monroe pics. The script is far superior to the first in the series, **The Medico of Painted Springs** (1941), concentrating as it does more on action and less on the bedside-manner aspect of doctoring. Starrett clears a fellow medical student of cattle-rustling charges and exposes contractors using Indians as slave labour. Hillyer's direction is plain but efficient.

Harry Carey, at the table, observed by Marjorie Main, James Barton and Betty Field (left to right) in the idyllic The Shepherd of the Hills.

Errol Flynn as Custer at the Little Big Horn in They Died with Their Boots On.

Preston Foster (left), Frances Gifford as the dainty heroine, and Richard Dix in American Empire.

d Lambert Hillyer   *p* William Berke   *s* Betty Burbridge   *c* Benjamin Kline   *lp* Charles Starrett, Eileen O'Hearn, Cliff Edwards, Stanley Brown, Donald Curtis, Jack Rockwell

Two Gun Sheriff (REP) b/w 56 min
Once again it's the twins plot with Barry in the dual role. His bad half kidnaps his good half, a sheriff, and impersonates him while planning a robbery only to see the light, egged on by his mother (Sais) who is torn between her love for both her sons. Badly received at the time, in retrospect Barry's ability to be a less than pure hero marked a significant shift of emphasis in the development of the hero in the Western.

d/p George Sherman   *s* Doris Schroeder, Bennett Cohen   *c* William Nobles   *lp* Don Barry, Lynn Merrick, Marin Sais, Jay Novello, Fred Kohler Jnr, Lupita Tovar

Western Union (FOX) 94 min
An epic in the mould of **The Plainsman** (1936), this is a far better film than Lang's first Western, **The Return of Frank James** (1940). Scott is the former outlaw who scouts for the Western Union company while their telegraph line is being completed and fights off his evil brother, MacLane, who is trying to prevent the line being finished. Beautifully photographed by Cronjager in a manner that avoids the flatness of colour so often the mark of early Technicolor, the film has the fatalistic inflection of so many of Lang's films. Accordingly, the climax with Scott dying a redeemed man at the hand of his brother (who is then quickly dispatched by Young) is less cliche and more the result of destiny. The film is also significant as being the first time producer Brown and Scott, who in the fifties were to team up to great effect, worked together.

Below: *Barton MacLane guns down Randolph Scott in* Western Union.

d Fritz Lang   *p* Harry Joe Brown   *s* Robert Carson   *c* Edward Cronjager   *lp* Robert Young, Randolph Scott, Dean Jagger, John Carradine, Barton MacLane, Virginia Gilmore

Wide Open Town (PAR) b/w 78 min
One of the longest ever series Westerns and one of the best of Hopalong Cassidy's outings. On the trail of rustlers, Hoppy and the Bar 20 cowboys arrive at the town run by Brent, the mastermind behind Jory's outlaw gang. Boyd is elected sheriff, cleans up the town and finds the missing cattle. A predictable enough plot, but Boyd, Brent and, in particular, Jory bring real conviction to their parts and, with Selander's snappy direction, the result is a superior series entry.

d Lesley Selander   *p* Harry Sherman   *s* Harrison Jacobs, J. Benton Cheney   *c* Sherman A. Rose   *lp* William Boyd, Russell Hayden, Evelyn Brent, Victor Jory, Andy Clyde, Morris Ankrum

1942

American Empire *aka* **My Son Alone**
(UA) b/w 82 min
In this routine movie made at the end of his career, Dix builds a vast cattle empire in Texas after the Civil War, despite the activities of Mexican rustlers and his erstwhile partner Foster. A romantic rather than realistic tale of frontier life, it comes complete with square and jutting jaws, odd scraps of frontier lore and a dainty heroine.

d William McGann   *p* Dick Dickson   *s* J. Robert Bren, J. Gladys Atwater, Ben Grauman Kohn   *c* Russell Harlan   *lp* Richard Dix, Preston Foster, Frances Gifford, Guinn 'Big Boy' Williams, Leo Carrillo, Jack LaRue

Arizona Terrors (REP) b/w 56 min
One of the best of Barry's series Westerns for Republic. Writers Cavan and Schroeder engineer an unlikely meeting between President McKinley and Barry by having him jump aboard the presidential train while escaping from outlaws. A further twist has the president commission Barry in secret to sort out Hadley's fake Spanish Land Grant, with which he's trying to oust homesteaders. This Barry does by going under-ground as an outlaw, but the President is assassinated before he can prove Barry to be innocent. Add to this Sherman's efficient direction and the result is a snappy series Western.

d/p George Sherman   *s* Doris Schroeder, Taylor Cavan   *c* Ernest Miller   *lp* Don Barry, Lynn Merrick, Reed Hadley, Al St John, Rex Lease, John Maxwell

Bells of Capistrano (REP) b/w 73 min
This was Autry's last film before he went into the army to spend the next four years away from Republic's cameras. The

film also features the last appearance of Strauch, as Tadpole to Burnette's Frog, who'd been a regular (replacing Mary Lee's precocious teenager) in recent Autry pictures. The unlikely screenplay has Autry putting an end to Conway and his nefarious tricks to put his girlfriend, Grey, out of business. Lanning, who'd recently joined the production team as cinematographer, gives the film a much needed sparkle.

d William Morgan *p* Harry Grey *s* Lawrence Kimple
c Reggie Lanning *lp* Gene Autry, Smiley Burnette, Virginia Grey, Lucien Littlefield, Morgan Conway, Joe Strauch Jnr, Champion

Below the Border (MON) b/w 57 min

Another formula-ridden entry in the Rough Riders series. Jones poses as a bandit and McCoy as a cattle buyer who put paid to Barcroft's rustling activities in Border City. As ever Jones and McCoy worked so well together, leaving the dependable Hatton to take care of the comedy chores, that the hackneyed script, by Adele Buffington (who scripted all eight of the Rough Riders series under the pseudonym of Bowers), is only the slightest of embarrassments.

d Howard Bretherton *p* Scott R. Dunlap *s* Jess Bowers (Adele Buffington) *c* Harry Neumann *lp* Buck Jones, Tim McCoy, Raymond Hatton, Linda Brent, Roy Barcroft, Charles King

Billy the Kid Trapped (PRC) b/w 59 min

A routine Billy the Kid series entry with Crabbe as athletic as ever in the title role and St John, who played the same role in both the Billy the Kid series and the Lone Rider series, as funny as ever. Here the pair are rescued from hanging by outlaws who need their assistance. A few gunfights and fistfights later, the outlaws are behind bars and justice reigns supreme again, until the next outing when once more Billy will be falsely accused of yet another crime. Ingram as the chief baddie has the best part.

d Sherman Scott (Sam Newfield) *p* Sigmund Neufeld
s Oliver Drake *c* Jack Greenhalgh *lp* Buster Crabbe, Al St John, Bud McTaggart, Anne Jeffreys, Jack Ingram, Glenn Strange

Boss of Hangtown Mesa (U) b/w 58 min

The last of Lewis' outings with Brown, this is a routine series Western. Farnum and Prosser are the crooks out to stop the completion of a telegraph line and Deverell is the girl determined to get the line through at all costs, especially after her uncle is murdered. Lease, a one-time star of his own series of Westerns, has the role of the ornery but hard-working foreman. Brown, who has fewer fights than normal, provides the necessary protection.

d Joseph H. Lewis *p/s* Oliver Drake *c* Charles Van Enger
lp Johnny Mack Brown, Fuzzy Knight, Helen Deverell, William Farnum, Hugh Prosser, Rex Lease

Call of the Canyon (REP) b/w 71 min

This Autry entry features another of Cooper's inventive plots. Local ranchers are being taken advantage of by the local agent of a meat-packing firm who is also defrauding the meat company. Autry goes to the city in search of the company's owner, while back at the Melody Ranch an airplane causes a cattle stampede. All comes out well when Hall turns up as the scenery-chewing fairy godfather to fix the broadcast of his protégé, Terry, who's hired the ranch for recording purposes. It transpires that Hall is also the owner of the meat-packing company. Santley directs this farago of nonsense with real economy.

d Joseph Santley *p* Harry Grey *s* Olive Cooper *c* Reggie Lanning *lp* Gene Autry, Smiley Burnette, Ruth Terry, Thurston Hall, Joe Strauch Jnr, Cliff Nazarro

Come On Danger (RKO) b/w 58 min

Holt and Whitley, fresh from supporting roles in the unofficial remake of **Come On Danger** (1932), **The Renegade Ranger** (1938), take the leads with Neal in this efficient but anonymous remake. As the script is virtually the same scene by scene in all versions, comparison between the three is revealing. Rita Hayworth (billed as Rita Cansino) in the 1938 version is by far the most appealing, and active, heroine, but Holt runs O'Brien a close second as a hero.

d Edward Killy *p* Bert Gilroy *s* Norton S. Parker
c Harry Wild *lp* Tim Holt, Frances Neal, Ray Whitley, Lee 'Lasses' White, Karl Hackett, Bud McTaggart

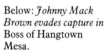

Al St John (left) and Buster Crabbe (centre) temporarily behind bars in Billy the Kid Trapped.

Below: *Johnny Mack Brown evades capture in* Boss of Hangtown Mesa.

Above: *Thurston Hall, Ruth Terry, Dorothy Kent and Joe Strauch (left to right) anxiously await the arrival of Gene Autry in* Call of the Canyon.

Cowboy Serenade (REP) b/w 66 min
This outing, directed by ex-editor Morgan, is one of the better of Autry's series Westerns, despite Cooper's hackneyed screenplay. He's trying to break a gambling ring and finds his task complicated by the fact that the head of the ring is the father of his girl (McKenzie in one of her numerous films with Autry). She, of course, is sure that Autry is wrong and starts her own investigation only to find Richards is indeed guilty, whereupon he kindly dies so as not to cause any further complications.

d William Morgan *p* Harry Grey *s* Olive Cooper
c Jack Marta *lp* Gene Autry, Smiley Burnette, Fay McKenzie, Cecil Cunningham, Addison Richards, Randy Brooks, Champion

Dawn on the Great Divide (MON) b/w 63 min
This was Jones' last movie, released just after he died in a fire on November 28, 1942. McCoy, the third member of the Rough Riders team, had been placed on the active service list so producer Dunlap substituted him with Bell, a one-time cowboy star. To make up for this change he gave the film a bigger budget than usual. The result, despite Bell's ineptness at handling either his lines or a gun, is a better-than-average Western, but nothing compared to earlier entries in the Rough Rider series. Bowers' script has Jones as a scout for a wagon train carrying supplies for settlers and the railroad. With assistance from Bell and Hatton, he puts an end to the evil doings of Woods and company.

d Howard Bretherton *p* Scott R. Dunlap *s* Jess Bowers (Adele Buffington) *c* Harry Neumann *lp* Buck Jones, Raymond Hatton, Rex Bell, Mona Barrie, Harry Woods, Robert Frazer

Deep in the Heart of Texas (U) b/w 62 min
The first of the seven Westerns Brown and Ritter co-starred in at Universal. Unlike Bob Baker, Brown's previous co-star, Ritter wasn't content to merely provide the musical interludes (that as often as not was left to Wakely and (usually dubbed) Jennifer, sister of Tim Holt) and demanded he be fully integrated into the plot. Moreover, with some five years of practice slugging it out with Charles King, Ritter was almost as capable as Brown in the action department. Norton's script has Brown returning home after the Civil War to discover that his father, Farnum, is the head of a gang of landgrabbers.

A studio portrait of Buck Jones who, sadly, died just before the release of Dawn on the Great Divide.

d Elmer Clifton *p* Oliver Drake *s* Grace Norton
c Harry Neumann *lp* Johnny Mack Brown, Tex Ritter, Fuzzy Knight, Jennifer Holt, William Farnum, Jimmy Wakely Trio

Down Rio Grande Way (COL) b/w 57 min
Featuring almost non-stop action – Starrett and Hayden appear in no less than six different fights in the course of the film – *Down Rio Grande Way* takes for its plot a moment in the early history of Texas as it trembled on the brink of joining the Union. Clark leads the faction trying to keep Texas out of the Union and whose trickery is foiled by Starrett and Hayden. Berke's direction is decidedly penny-plain.

d William Berke *p* Jack Fier *s* Paul Franklin *c* George Meehan *lp* Charles Starrett, Russell Hayden, Britt Wood, Davidson Clark, Edmund Cobb, Rose Ann Stevens

Down Texas Way (MON) b/w 57 min
A routine Rough Riders series outing. This time Jones and McCoy come to the rescue of Hatton who has been framed for the murder of his best friend. They then round up mobsters Woods, Strange and company who are the guilty ones.

d Howard Bretherton *p* Scott R. Dunlap *s* Jess Bowers (Adele Buffington) *c* Harry Neumann *lp* Buck Jones, Tim McCoy, Raymond Hatton, Luana Walters, Harry Woods, Glenn Strange

Ghost Town Law (MON) b/w 62 min
The most unusual of the Rough Riders series, *Ghost Town Law* mixes mystery and suspense with the trio's usual fast-paced action. King and his henchmen make their hideout in a dilapidated mansion and systematically slaughter anyone who comes near. After they've killed two marshals, the Riders go after them. Although the opening sequences, with hooded horsemen riding to and fro mostly at night, are a shade murky, Bretherton, who was to be in control of the remainder of the series, directs with his usual ease.

d Howard Bretherton *p* Scott R. Dunlap *s* Jess Bowers
(Adele Buffington) *c* Harry Neumann *lp* Buck Jones,
Tim McCoy, Raymond Hatton, Charles King, Virginia
Carpenter, Ben Corbett

The Great Man's Lady (PAR) b/w 90 min
Made in the same year as **American Empire** (1942), which
took for its hero a cattle baron (Preston Foster) whose trials
and tribulations it charted, *The Great Man's Lady*, as its title
suggests, examines the power behind the throne of a city
builder. McCrea is the frontiersman who, after building a city
in the wilderness, falls out with his wife, Stanwyck, when his
desire for the coming of the railway leads him to the brink of
allowing the railroad company, rather than the townspeople,
to dominate the town. Wellman handles the shifting relationship between Stanwyck and McCrea well, but the plot, a
hand-me-down version of **Cimarron** (1931), is too episodic –
and is made even more so through being structured via
flashbacks – to be anything more than an epical melodrama.

d/p William Wellman *s* W.L. River *c* William C.
Mellor *lp* Barbara Stanwyck, Joel McCrea, Brian Donlevy,
Katherine Stevens, Thurston Hall, Lloyd Corrigan

Heart of the Golden West (REP) b/w 65 min
In 1942, Autry quit Republic for the army and Rogers' budget
rose accordingly now that he was the only singing cowboy on
the studio's books. More significantly, as if in an attempt to
make a Gene Autry out of Rogers, the money was mostly
spent on the film's musical production numbers. Republic's
boss, Herbert J. Yates, had seen the just-opened stage show
Oklahoma and had been greatly impressed by it. Henceforth,
Republic's singing cowboys were to become more and more
stage-bound. A further aspect of the build-up being given to
Rogers was his being given two side-kicks, Burnette being
available now that Autry was in the services.
   The modern-day plot, which has Rogers exposing a greedy
trucking company executive who has been cheating ranchers,
is thrilling rather than action-packed.

d/p Joseph Kane *s* Earl Felton *c* Jack Marta
lp Roy Rogers, Smiley Burnette, George Hayes, Ruth Terry,
Bob Nolan and the Sons of the Pioneers, Trigger

In Old California (REP) b/w 88 min
This minor Western saw Republic paring down the film's
budget as if the presence of Wayne, after **Stagecoach** (1939) a
huge star, alone would be enough to sell the movie. He's the
pharmacist, Barnes is the dance-hall queen and Dekker is the
crooked politician whose activities complicate their affair.
Dekker, who receives protection money from local ranchers,
substitutes poison for one of Wayne's tonics when the
pharmacist tries to rouse the ranchers against him. A man dies

and Wayne is about to be lynched when he's given the
opportunity to prove himself by defeating the epidemic that
breaks out in the gold mines. McGann directs unimaginatively.

d William McGann *p* Robert North *s* Gertrude Purcell,
Frances Hyland *c* Jack Marta *lp* John Wayne, Binnie
Barnes, Albert Dekker, Helen Parrish, Patsy Kelly, Edgar
Kennedy

King of the Mounties (REP) b/w 12 chaps
In 1940, Republic released *King of the Royal Mounted*, a serial
devoted to the patriotic exploits of Sergeant King (Lane).
Though the impact of the chapter play was much reduced by
the villains not being clearly identified as Germans (which
they were), because America was still at peace, it was a
resounding success. Hence this sequel in which, America now
being at war, the enemies are clearly identified as agents of

*Above: Barbara
Stanwyck, pioneer and
The Great Man's
Lady.*

*Smiley Burnette (left) in
his first film with Gabby
Hayes (centre) and Roy
Rogers, Heart of the
Golden West.*

Above: *Tim Holt examines the books in* Land of the Open Range.

Allan Lane as King of the Mounties, *one of the most patriotic serials ever.*

Germany, Japan and Italy helping to prepare for an Axis invasion of Canada by bombing it from an undetectable plane. An inventor who comes up with a new kind of plane detector is killed, leaving Lane to protect the detector and rescue the inventor's daughter, Drake, when she's kidnapped by the enemy...

All thrilling stuff and above all *patriotic*, as Republic made clear in its promotion of the chapter play: 'Unscrupulous plans for western world conquest are shattered to bits when the hordes of yellow-bellied rats come to grips with the courage and cunning of Canada's Mounted Police!'. Witney, directing on his own for a change, produced a stylish piece of nonsense, hindered only by the budgetary economies that war brought: to take just one example, blanks were rationed.

d William Witney *p* W.J. O'Sullivan *s* Taylor Cavan, Ronald Davidson, William Lively, Joseph O'Donnell, Joseph Poland *c* Bud Thackery *lp* Allan Lane, Gilbert Emery, Russell Hicks, Peggy Drake, Douglass Dumbrille, Duncan Renaldo

Land of the Open Range (RKO) b/w 60 min
This film begins intriguingly with a (crooked) lawyer reading a will giving a crook's lands to participants in a homestead race limited to crooks who've spent at least two years in jail. However, it soon becomes just a routine Holt outing. He's given the job of making sure that each jailbird, including a benign Barcroft, gets his fair share and that the lawyer is denied his for his attempted cheating. White provides the comedy, Whitley the songs.

d Edward Killy *p* Bert Gilroy *s* Morton Grant *c* Harry Wild *lp* Tim Holt, Ray Whitley, Janet Waldo, Lee White, Roy Barcroft, Frank Ellis

Lawless Plainsmen (COL) b/w 59 min
This is Berke's debut as director of the Starrett-Hayden series that he'd earlier worked on as a producer. It is noticeable that, henceforth, economy would be name of the game and sequences would only be re-shot if there was a major gaffe – and a microphone left in picture wasn't a major gaffe! The plot features Starrett helping protect a wagon train from Indian attacks until the Seventh Cavalry appear. A routine series Western.

d William Berke *p* Jack Fier *s* Luci Ward *c* Benjamin Kline lp Charles Starrett, Russell Hayden, Cliff Edwards, Luana Walters, Frank LaRue, Ray Bennett

Little Joe the Wrangler (U) b/w 64 min
The second of Brown and Ritter's short-lived series together sees them tracking down a band of outlaws stealing gold shipments. Collins' direction is pacy and Strange provides a welcome air of malevolence as the chief baddie. Interestingly, in contrast to the normal practice of writing a song to go with the film's title, all the series are named after a song.

d Lewis Collins *p* Oliver Drake *s* Sherman Lowe *c* William Sickner *lp* Johnny Mack Brown, Tex Ritter, Fuzzy Knight, Jennifer Holt, Hal Taliaferro (Wally Wales), Glenn Strange

Lone Star Ranger (FOX) b/w 58(54) min
Kimbrough, a football star who briefly turned actor, is the star of this wishy washy remake of George O'Brien's 1929 film of the same title. Loosely based on a Zane Grey novel, it features Kimbrough in the title role working to prevent Hale and Farnum grabbing vast acres of Texas for themselves by driving would-be settlers away. Stone impresses most as the insurance agent who teams up with Kimbrough. A mediocre film.

d James Tinling *p* Sol M. Wurtzel *s* William Conselman Jnr, George Kane, Irving Cummings Jnr *c* Lucien Andriot *lp* John Kimbrough, Sheila Ryan, Jonathan Hale, William Farnum, George E. Stone, Truman Bradley

Man from Cheyenne (REP) b/w 60 min
Made just after Rogers had changed his name from Leonard Slye to Roy Rogers by deed poll, this is a routine outing. He's the government agent on the trail of modern rustlers led by Eastern girl Carver. She first charms information out of unsuspecting ranchers and then relieves them of their cattle. Her motive is equally odd: she wants to get enough money together to go back East and live in style amongst the Beautiful People. Her punishment, after Rogers has got wise

to her and restored the cattle to their rightful owners, is to be left with the very angry duo of Payne and Storm, who drag her to jail by her hair.

d/p Joseph Kane   *s* Winston Miller   *c* Reggie Lanning
lp Roy Rogers, George Hayes, Sally Payne, Lynn Carver, William Haade, Gale Storm, Trigger

Men of Texas *aka* **Men of Destiny**   (U)   b/w   87 min
Robert Stack is the journalist and Carrillo the photographer, sent to report on what's happening in Texas just after the Civil War, in this oddity which sets out to prove that the pen is indeed mightier than the sword. Crawford is the Confederate who refuses to accept defeat and gathers around him a rebel band and Gwynne the Southern girl who melts Stack's icy Northern heart. Producer Waggner gave the film the production values he so regularly denied to the series Westerns he oversaw. An entertaining, minor film.

d Ray Enright   *p* George Waggner   *s* Harold Shumate
c Milton Krasner   *lp* Robert Stack, Broderick Crawford, Jackie Cooper, Leo Carrillo, Anne Gwynne, Jane Darwell

The Old Chisholm Trail   (U)   b/w   61 min
A scrappy B feature. Brown and Ritter come to the assistance of cattlemen on the Chisholm Trail by re-opening a locked water hole in this routine entry in their short-lived series together. Barcroft adds a touch of class as the villain of the piece. Knight provides the comedy and Wakely the music, Ritter confining himself to the title song.

d/s Elmer Clifton   *p* Oliver Drake   *c* William Sickner
lp Johnny Mack Brown, Tex Ritter, Fuzzy Knight, Jennifer Holt, Roy Barcroft, Jimmy Wakely Trio

Outlaws of Pine Ridge   (REP)   b/w   56 min
A simple but well-made series Western enlivened by Thackery's fine cinematography and the hard-edged direction of Witney at the helm of one of the first of many series Westerns. Beery is the man standing for Governor who needs the protection of Barry, looking more pinch-faced than ever, to save him from his double-dealing opponent. The fights are more violent than ever before – the film opens with a body being hurled through a saloon window – as one might expect from Witney, an action specialist.

d William Witney   *p* Eddy White   *s* Norman S. Hall
c Bud Thackery   *lp* Don Barry, Lynn Merrick, Noah Beery, Emmett Lynn, Clayton Moore, Forrest Taylor

A dramatic moment from Men of Texas, *one of the more interesting movies set in the immediate aftermath of the Civil War.*

Pierre of the Plains   (MGM)   b/w   66 min
A bristling melodrama set in North-West Canada, this was the last production of Selwyn, who'd written and starred in the original stage play in 1907 and later, with his brother, formed Goldwyn Pictures which would eventually give MGM its middle name. That said, Seitz's direction makes this an historical curiosity but nothing more. Cabot is the trapper whose seemingly endless string of adventures threaten his romance with innkeeper Hussey.

d George B. Seitz   *p* Edgar Selwyn   *s* Lawrence Kimble, Bertram Millhauser   *c* Charles Rosher   *lp* John Carroll, Ruth Hussey, Bruce Cabot, Phil Brown, Reginald Owen, Henry Travers

Ride 'Em Cowboy   (U)   b/w   86 min
Abbott and Costello are the New York hot-dog vendors tricked into going West to a dude ranch in this, one of the duo's better films. Brown is the ranch foreman, Gwynne the girl and Foran the unlikely visiting Western writer. An even more unlikely Ella Fitzgerald is on hand to sing 'A Tisket, a Tasket'. The film should not be confused with either John Wayne's 1932 or Buck Jones' 1936 film of the same title.

d Arthur Lubin   *p* Alex Gottlieb   *s* True Boardman, John Grant   *c* John Boyle   *lp* Bud Abbott, Lou Costello, Dick Foran, Anne Gwynne, Johnny Mack Brown, Douglass Dumbrille

Riders of the Northland   (COL)   b/w   58 min
The first series Western to reflect the fact that America was at war, *Riders of the Northland* sees Starrett and Hayden as Texas Rangers sent to Alaska to ferret out Nazi spies and sympathizers who are refuelling German subs and building a secret airfield. Sutton is the head Nazi patrolling his domain behind a very menacing string of barbed wire.

d William Berke   *p* Jack Fier   *s* Paul Franklin
c Benjamin Kline   *lp* Charles Starrett, Russell Hayden, Cliff Edwards, Paul Sutton, Lloyd Bridges, Shirley Patterson

Riders of the West   (MON)   b/w   58 min
Another below-par Rough Riders entry with far less action than in their previous outing, **Down Texas Way** (1942). The plot is the hackneyed one of cattle rustlers, led by Woods, trying to bankrupt local ranchers so as to get their land

Bruce Cabot holds a gun on Phil Brown (centre) in Pierre of the Plains.

Joe Brown as the dude in the hilarious Shut My Big Mouth.

Randolph Scott and Marlene Dietrich in the third version of The Spoilers.

Far right: Johnny Mack Brown mixing it with LeRoy Mason in The Silver Bullet.

cheaply. The Riders soon put a stop to that. Bretherton's direction is aimless and Neumann's cinematography surprisingly spotty.

d Howard Bretherton *p* Scott R. Dunlap *s* Jess Bowers (Adele Buffington) *c* Harry Neumann *lp* Buck Jones, Tim McCoy, Raymond Hatton, Harry Woods, Sarah Padden, Dennis Moore

Shut My Big Mouth (COL) b/w 71 min
This Western spoof is the best of Brown's films for Columbia. He is the Eastern dude elected sheriff who outwits Jory's black villain. For much of the film Brown appears in drag to the obvious bewilderment of Jory. The effect, as milked by director Barton, is hilarious. Amongst Jory's gang are Tucker and Bridges.

d Charles Barton *p* Robert Sparks *s* Oliver Drake, Karen DeWolf, Francis Martin *c* Henry Freulich *lp* Joe E. Brown, Adele Mara, Lloyd Bridges, Forrest Tucker, Don Beddoe, Victor Jory

Una Signora Dell'Ovest (SCALERA FILM; IT) b/w 88 min
Fittingly, the first feature-length Italian Western was a loose adaptation of Puccini's 1910 opera, *Girl of the Golden West*, itself an adaption from David Belaco's much filmed stage play of the same title.

Filmed against cardboard sets, Koch's melodrama tells the story of Cortese's dance-hall queen whose lover is killed by Simon, who also frames Brazzi, her new lover. She's at first consoled by Simon but when the truth comes out rushes to Brazzi only to find him happily married. Its success inspired the making of the only other significant Italian Western, **Il Fanciullo del West** (1943), before the arrival of the Spaghetti Western in the sixties.

d/co-s Carlo Koch *p* Franco Magli *co-s* Lotte Reiniger *c* Ubaldo Arata *lp* Michael Simon, Isa Pola, Rossano Brazzi, Valentina Cortese, Renzo Merusi, Carlo Duse

The Silver Bullet (U) b/w 56 min
A superior series Western. Brown carries the silver bullet of the title, dug out of his own back. He's on the trail of the man who shot him and killed his father and he discovers him still up to his old tricks. Lewis' direction is as edgy as ever, making the most of every confrontation whether it be in the desert or on the main street of town, as in the final shoot-out between Mason and Brown, thought by many to be one of the best in seriesdom.

d Joseph H. Lewis *p* Oliver Drake *s* Elizabeth Beecher *c* Charles Van Enger *lp* Johnny Mack Brown, Fuzzy Knight, Jennifer Holt, William Farnum, LeRoy Mason, Rex Lease

The Spoilers (U) b/w 87 min
William Farnum, star of the original 1914 silent version and technical advisor to the 1930 version, has a supporting role in this, the third, re-make of Rex Beach's novel. The plot was revamped to accommodate Dietrich, once again a star after **Destry Rides Again** (1939). Wayne is the mine owner and Scott the crooked gold commissioner determined to swindle miners out of their claims. Dietrich as the dance-hall queen fights for her man and wins him, but, once again, it is the elaborately staged fistfight between Wayne and Scott that is the film's highlight. Enright's direction is unfussy and to the point.

d Ray Enright *p* Frank Lloyd *s* Lawrence Hazard, Tom Reed *c* Milton Krasner *lp* Marlene Dietrich, Randolph Scott, John Wayne, Margaret Lindsay, Harry Carey, Richard Barthelmess

Stagecoach Buckaroo (U) b/w 58 min
A superior Brown series Western. Rawlinson is the outlaw leader whose attacks on the stagecoach line run by O'Day lead to Brown heading after him. A truly bizarre sequence has Knight and two others foiling an attempt on the stage in women's clothes.

d Ray Taylor *p* Will Cowan *s* Al Martin *c* Jerome Ash *lp* Johnny Mack Brown, Fuzzy Knight, Nell O'Day, Herbert Rawlinson, Glenn Strange, Kermit Maynard

Texas to Bataan (MON) b/w 56 min

In this, the first film of Tansey's brief sojourn with the ever-changing Range Busters, the trio (now King, Terhune and Sharp) escort some horses to the Philippines and expose a Filipino cook as a Japanese spy. Interesting, like **Riders of the Northland** (1942), as an example of how adaptable the genre is. The listless production values suggested the end was in sight for the series.

d Robert Tansey *p* George W. Weeks *s* Arthur Hoerl
c Robert Cline *lp* John King, David Sharpe, Max Terhune, Marjorie Manners, Budd Buster, Frank Ellis

Tombstone *aka* Tombstone, the Town too Tough to Die (PAR) b/w 79 min

Another film version of the cleaning-up of the West's most famous frontier town. However, unlike **Law and Order** (1932), **Frontier Marshal** (1939) or **My Darling Clementine** (1946), this version has no point of view of any significance. LeVino and Paramore construct a neat enough story about the conflict between the Earps and the Clantons. Dix as Earp (in his biggest role since **Cimarron,** 1931), Jory (Ike Clanton) and Buchanan (Curly Bill), to name only the most obvious, take the chances their parts offer, but the film remains oddly lifeless. Harlan's cinematography, especially in the night scenes, is fine but McGann's direction is too even paced to cause excitement.

d William McGann *p* Harry Sherman *s* Albert Shelby LeVino, Edward E. Paramore *c* Russell Harlan
lp Richard Dix, Kent Taylor, Victor Jory, Edgar Buchanan, Frances Gifford, Don Castle

Undercover Man (UA) b/w 68 min

Announced by Paramount but released by United Artists, *Undercover Man* is a weak entry in the Hopalong Cassidy stakes. Kirby replaces Brad King in the role first essayed by James Ellison in 1935, while Cheney's script features a bandido criss-crossing the border and robbing from Mexican and American alike, so causing ill-feeling between the two nations. Selander directs with the verve he brought to all twenty-nine of his pictures with Boyd but the hackneyed plot and weak cast result in an inferior outing.

d Lesley Selander *p* Harry Sherman *s* J. Benton Cheney
c Russell Harlan *lp* William Boyd, Andy Clyde, Jay Kirby, Chris-Pin Martin, Antonio Moreno, Earle Hodgins

Above: *Frances Gifford and Richard Dix in* Tombstone.

The Valley of Hunted Men (REP) b/w 60 min

An escaped Nazi assumes the identity of a nephew of a German refugee from Hitler, who has perfected a method of extracting rubber from culebra plants. He is finally exposed by a suspicious Three Mesquiteers (now Steele, Tyler and Dodd) who get the real nephew's mother to the scene just in time after a lot of horse chases. Much of the footage is stock but the combination of DeMond and Grant's extraordinary screenplay and English's vigorous direction of the action set-pieces makes the film one of the more appealing of the late films of the trio.

d John English *p* Louis Gray *s* Albert DeMond, Morton Grant *c* Bud Thackery *lp* Bob Steele, Tom Tyler, Jimmie Dodd, Anna Marie Stewart, Budd Buster, Hal Price

Valley of the Sun (RKO) b/w 79 min

Craig is the government agent who doubles as a renegade Indian, Jagger the corrupt Indian agent and the unlikely Ball the restaurant owner they both have designs on in this pedestrian Western. Heavily promoted by RKO, as the biggest outdoor Western since **Cimarron** (1931), it is surprisingly domestic considering the claims. Veteran actor Tyler appears as a vicious Geronimo and silent comics St John and Conklin have featured roles.

d George Marshall *p* Graham Baker *s* Horace McCoy
c Harry Wild *lp* Lucille Ball, James Craig, Sir Cedric Hardwicke, Dean Jagger, Tom Tyler, Al St John, Chester Conklin

West of the Law (MON) b/w 60 min

McCoy and Hatton pose as minister and undertaker respectively to back up Jones in this superior Rough Riders entry. Barcroft, as ever, is the villain, this time masquerading as the town's leading citizen while he hijacks gold shipments. The script, by veteran Adele Buffington (under the pseudonym of Bowers) is as formula-ridden as ever with Jones' lengthy pauses as he chews his gum a typically unnecessary piece of characterization. But under the watchful eye of Dunlap, whose idea the pairing of Jones and McCoy had been, and Bretherton, whose direction is as punchy as ever, the series did very well in the popularity stakes.

d Howard Bretherton *p* Scott R. Dunlap *s* Jess Bowers (Adele Buffington) *c* Harry Neumann *lp* Buck Jones, Tim McCoy, Raymond Hatton, Roy Barcroft, Evelyn Cook, Milburn Morante

Bruce Cabot with his gun on Ward Bond (back to the camera) and his accomplices in Wild Bill Hickock Rides.

Wild Bill Hickock Rides (WB) b/w 82 min

Another of Warner's entertaining small budget Westerns. Cabot takes the title role while a decidedly out-of-place Bennett is the dance-hall queen he romances. Bond is the villain trying to oust homesteaders as part of his criminal dreams of empire. It is all very routine, from the staged fights to the awkward script, but Enright presided over it all with an unassuming modesty that allowed the company's production values to sparkle. Fittingly, he was rewarded with bigger budgets and stars when he quit Warners for Universal after the film.

d Ray Enright   p Edmund Grainger   s Charles Grayston, Paul Gerald Smith, Raymond Schrock   c Ted McCord   lp Bruce Cabot, Constance Bennett, Ward Bond, Warren William, Betty Brewer, Frank Wilcox

1943

Apache Trail (MGM) b/w 66 min

One of director Thorpe's better efforts, this B Western stars Nolan, and Withers, a would-be series star who never quite made it, who are desperately trying to put down an Apache uprising caused by the theft of a ceremonial peace pipe. Geraghty's screenplay is based on an Ernest Haycox short story. MGM remade the film in 1952 as **Apache War Smoke**.

d Richard Thorpe   p Samuel Marx   s Maurice Geraghty   c Sidney Wagner   lp Lloyd Nolan, Donna Reed, Grant Withers, Fuzzy Knight, Chill Wills, Ray Teal

Arizona Trail (U) b/w 56 min

A better-than-average Ritter entry with the star in a role originally intended for Johnny Mack Brown before he quit Universal for Monogram and Moore taking the role intended for Ritter. Moore and Ritter are step brothers who put aside

Lloyd Nolan and Donna Reed in a publicity still for Apache Trail.

their differences to help Alderson defend his ranch from would-be landgrabber Ingram. The music is supplied by Johnny Bond and his Red River Valley Boys.

d Vernon Keays   p Oliver Drake   s William Lively   c William Sickner   lp Tex Ritter, Fuzzy Knight, Dennis Moore, Erville Alderson, Jack Ingram, Johnny Bond

The Avenging Rider (RKO) b/w 55 min

A routine Holt entry in which, seemingly unaffected by a bullet wound in one arm, he takes on the villain in a lengthy fistfight and emerges victorious. The plot is the cliched one about a dead partner and a mine up for grabs, given a fresh twist by having Holt and Edwards spend a fair amount of time breaking out of jail.

d Sam Nelson   p Bert Gilroy   s Morton Grant, Harry O. Hoyt   c Jack Lockert   lp Tim Holt, Cliff Edwards, Ann Summers, Davison Clark, Karl Hackett, Earle Hodgins

Bar 20 (UA) b/w 54 min

A film whose credits are the most interesting thing about it. It was co-written by Wilson who was later to be blacklisted for political reasons, co-stars Reeves who was later to be television's Superman, Farnum who was the daughter of veteran cowboy star Dustin Farnum and features Mitchum in his first good-guy role. Jory is the stagecoach-robbing bandit who Boyd puts out of business in an over-complicated plot.

d Lesley Selander   p Harry Sherman   s Morton Grant, Norman Houston, Michael Wilson   c Russell Harlan   lp William Boyd, Andy Clyde, George Reeves, Dustine Farnum, Bob Mitchum, Victor Jory

Beyond the Last Frontier (REP) b/w 57 min

The fact that Burnette, his supposed side-kick, got most of the attention in the trade reviews of this, his first starring series Western, suggested that Dew's days as a star would be short lived. Moreover what attention Burnette didn't bag went to Mitchum as the reformed baddie. Dew plays the unlikely character of a lawman called John Paul Revere. Nonetheless, Dew's failings apart, the film has a delightful plot in which two spies chase each other. Dew is the ranger masquerading as an outlaw to get the goods on Woods and Mitchum is another spy who infiltrates the ranger camp and at the climax risks his life to save Burnette.

d Howard Bretherton   p Louis Gray   s John K. Butler, Morton Grant   c Bud Thackery   lp Eddie Dew, Smiley Burnette, Harry Woods, Bob Mitchum, Kermit Maynard, Lorraine Miller

Black Hills Express (REP) b/w 56 min

The first of Barry's films with Vernon as comic relief and one of the best of Barry's series Westerns. Myton and Hall's intelligent script has Barry suspected of a string of stagecoach robberies and unmasking the real villains, the sheriff and the local banker. English, best known for his work on innumerable serials, provides the fast-paced direction.

d John English   p Eddy White   s Norman Hall, Fred Myton   c Ernest Miller   lp Don Barry, Wally Vernon, Ariel Heath, LeRoy Mason, Jack Rockwell, Bob Kortman

Blazing Guns (MON) b/w 55 min

The first of the Trail Blazer series to be directed by Tansey, *Blazing Guns* was a cheap movie, and looks it. Wearing his producer's hat Tansey had a firm policy of no retakes unless *absolutely* necessary. Accordingly, the fight sequences which required careful preparation and safety shots are jerky and patchy to a degree that even Gibson's joshing couldn't explain away. LePicard's cinematography is similarly murky. Nonetheless, the time-honoured plot, which has Gibson and

Maynard getting a bunch of ex-cons to help them clean up a lawless town, is lively enough.

d/p Robert Tansey *s* Frances Kavanaugh *c* Marcel LePicard *lp* Ken Maynard, Hoot Gibson, Kay Forrester, LeRoy Mason, Charles King, Lloyd Ingraham

Border Buckaroos (PRC) b/w 60 min
A routine Texas Ranger entry from PRC, only of interest because it is directed by veteran writer/producer Drake. The much-recycled screenplay has O'Brien, Newill and Wilkerson putting paid to King, Ingraham and company's plans to take over a ranch with valuable mineral deposits.

d/s Oliver Drake *p* Alfred Stern, Arthur Alexander *c* Ira Morgan *lp* Dave O'Brien, Jim Newill, Guy Wilkerson, Charles King, Jack Ingraham, Christine McIntyre

Border Patrol (UA) b/w 66 min
Mitchum's acting debut, *Border Patrol* is also one of the four in the Hopalong Cassidy series to be written by Wilson. He was later to achieve notoriety for being blacklisted and had his name actually removed from the credits of **Friendly Persuasion** (1956) and *The Bridge on the River Kwai* (1957). The plot certainly has an unusual edge to it: Simpson (to whom Mitchum was an uncredited henchman) is a ruthless silvermine owner using Mexicans as slave labour and Boyd is the Texas Ranger who ends his reign of terror.

d Lesley Selander *p* Harry Sherman *s* Michael Wilson *c* Russell Harlan *lp* William Boyd, Andy Clyde, Russell Simpson, Duncan Renaldo, Claudia Drake, Bob Mitchum

Calling Wild Bill Elliott (REP) b/w 55 min
Reputedly the first sound movie to incorporate its star's name into its title, *Calling Wild Bill Elliott* marks the star's first outing with Republic. Hayes, transferred by the studio from its Roy Rogers series, is the braggard who boasts of his friendship with Wild Bill only to have Elliott appear in person. Thereafter the plot twists and turns, rather like the movie's wicked Governor, Heyes, until Elliott, with interference from Hayes, puts Heyes behind bars. Bennet's direction is fast paced and the script has more than enough brawls and chases.

d Spencer Bennet *p* Harry Grey *s* Anthony Coldeway *c* Ernest Miller *lp* Bill Elliott, George Hayes, Anne Jeffreys, Herbert Heyes, Roy Barcroft, Fred Kohler Jnr

Colt Comrades (UA) b/w 67 min
An interesting series Western. The script, by Wilson who was later to be blacklisted as a member of the Communist Party, is routine but Selander's direction is energetic enough. Jory, once again, is the villain who refuses to supply the local ranchers with water until Boyd and Clyde, drilling for oil, find some. Mitchum, who was soon to leave the series that had given him his start in motion pictures, has a small role as a

Wild Bill Elliott, Anne Jeffreys and youngster in Calling Wild Bill Elliott.

henchman of Jory's. Another series regular also bound for (a rather more limited) success is Reeves, later to become television's Superman.

d Lesley Selander *p* Harry Sherman *s* Michael Wilson *c* Russell Harlan *lp* William Boyd, Andy Clyde, Victor Jory, Bob Mitchum, George Reeves, Earle Hodgins

Cowboy Commandos (MON) b/w 55 min
One of the last of the Range Busters series Westerns, this deliciously titled outing sadly doesn't live up to its name. Beecher's script has the trio tracking down Nazi agents who are sabotaging shipments of magnesite -- 'a valuable secret ore'. As played by Merton and Buster the saboteurs are so evil that they belong in serialdom. As a final dig at the Nazis Johnny Bond sings, 'I'll Get the Fuhrer, Sure as Shootin''.

d S. Roy Luby *p* George W. Weeks *s* Elizabeth Beecher *c* Edward Kull *lp* Ray Corrigan, Dennis Moore, Max Terhune, Budd Buster, John Merton, Johnny Bond

Cowboy in the Clouds (COL) b/w 54 min
The first of cinematographer Kline's Starrett series Westerns as a director. Kline had directed serials for Mascot but was best known as Columbia's series cameraman, and as such was a regular on the Starrett Westerns. As the title suggests, the novelty storyline heavily features flying. The patriotically inspired Civilian Air Patrol is being hindered by cattlemen who think the scheme hairbrained until Starrett uses a CAP plane to rescue a prominent rancher's daughter, Duncan, from a forest fire and catch a murderer. Kline's direction emphasizes action, a feature that would increase in his subsequent outings.

d Benjamin Kline *p* Jack Fier *s* Elizabeth Beecher *c* George Meehan *lp* Charles Starrett, Dub Taylor, Julie Duncan, Jimmy Wakely, Charles King, Lane Chandler

Daredevils of the West (REP) b/w 12 chaps
Reputedly the most action-packed of all Western serials, this Republic chapter play features series star Lane as the defender of Aldridge's stage line against villain Frazer. He plans to take over the line and so tries to stop Aldridge and her father finishing a road, that will win them a government

A scene from Cowboy Commandos, *one of the many series Westerns to pit its heroes, here the Range Busters, against the Nazis after America entered the Second World War.*

Far right: Larry Parks, Wanda McKaye, Jean Parker and Bruce Kellogg (left to right) in the title role of Deerslayer, *a film that has its origins in James Fenimore Cooper's classic novel but is best remembered for being the most inept production ever to be released under Republic's banner.*

contract, on time. To do this he employs renegade Indians to prey on the construction crew. The script is very rough and ready but English's frenetic direction and Howard Lydecker's miniatures (the key to many of Republic's outstanding special effects) combine to give the chapter play a welcome feel of non-stop action. In particular, the constant threats to the life of Aldridge, Princess of the serials to Linda Sterling's Queen, are entertainingly staged.

d John English *p* W.J. O'Sullivan *s* Ronald Davidson, Basil Dickey, Joseph O'Donnell, Joseph Poland, William Lively *c* Bud Thackery *lp* Allan Lane, Kay Aldridge, Eddie Acuff, William Haade, Robert Frazer, Rex Lease

Days of Old Cheyenne (REP) b/w 56 min
Barry is the drifter speedily elevated to Governor of the Territory with background assistance from Haade who plans to profit from Barry's political innocence. Clifton's direction wisely glosses over the plot's more unbelievable aspects, stressing incident rather than story, as in the climactic gunfight between Barry and Haade. Lynn provides the turgid humour.

d Elmer Clifton *p* Eddy White *s* Norman S. Hall *c* Reggie Lanning *lp* Don Barry, Lynn Merrick, William Haade, Emmett Lynn, Herbert Rawlinson, Charles Miller

Dead Man's Gulch (REP) b/w 56 min
This is one of Barry's best Republic outings. Serial ace English directs at a breakneck pace and the interesting plot features McTaggart as a one-time friend of Barry's who's gone wrong and is helping a gaggle of mobsters in their attempts to keep their freightline monopoly.

d John English *p* Eddy White *s* Norman S. Hall, Robert Williams *c* Ernest Miller *lp* Don Barry, Lynn Merrick, Clancy Cooper, Bud McTaggart, Rex Lease, Emmett Lynn

Robert Mitchum (right) in his acting debut as henchman to Russell Simpson (centre) with William Boyd in Border Patrol.

Death Rides the Plains (PRC) b/w 55 min
A routine series entry. Bennett is the crook with the novel idea of luring prospective buyers to his ranch and then murdering them for the purchase price, in O'Donnell's

intriguing script. But the performances, excepting St John's, are so leaden and Newfield's direction so uneven that it's hard to take the story seriously. Kermit Maynard, brother of Ken and briefly a series star himself, has a small part down the cast list.

d Sam Newfield *p* Sigmund Neufeld *s* Joseph O'Donnell *c* Robert Cline *lp* Bob Livingston, Al St John, Ray Bennett, Nica Doret, Karl Hackett, Kermit Maynard

Death Valley Rangers (MON) b/w 59 min
This Trail Blazers outing sees Steele joining Gibson and Maynard to make the duo a trio, the most favoured format of series Westerns. Tansey's direction reduces the plot to virtual non-stop action as the trio confront stagecoach robbers King and Harlan. The film opens with Steele turning outlaw so as to join the gang and ends with a lengthy gun-battle between all concerned. Brent supplies the (much abbreviated) romantic interest.

d/p/co-s Robert Tansey *co-s* Frances Kavanaugh, Elizabeth Beecher *c* Edward Kull *lp* Ken Maynard, Hoot Gibson, Bob Steele, Kenneth Harlan, Charles King, Linda Brent

Deerslayer (REP) b/w 67 min
An independent production released through Republic, *Deerslayer* is probably the most inept film ever to be distributed under the company's aegis. The action is even more improbable than that in the cheapest of serials and the direction absent minded. A cult film.

Fox's 1957 version with Lex Barker, Rita Moreno and Forrest Tucker is only slightly better.

d Lew Landers *p/co-s* E.B. Derr *co-s* P.S. Harrison *c* Arthur Martinelli *lp* Bruce Kellogg, Larry Parks, Jean Parker, Yvonne De Carlo

The Desperadoes (COL) 85 min
Columbia's first colour film. Scott is the sheriff, Ford his outlaw friend and Keyes the girl who persuades him to go straight. Buchanan makes the most of his role as the smooth-talking postmaster and brains behind a gang of outlaws. He tries to frame Ford for a bank robbery. Vidor's

Il Fanciullo del West (SCALERA FILM; IT) b/w 82 min
Promoted as *Romeo and Juliet* in a Western setting, this Italian Western utilizes the plot of feuding frontier families, a regular plot in series Westerns. Grasso is the outsider who unmasks one of the frontier patriarchs as an outlaw who is using the feud to his own ends.

Though the film was a commercial failure, it was praised for various inventive touches – a machine that catapulted men into the air, for example – and for its parodying of the Hollywood Western. Elements like these were to be crucial to the success of the Spaghetti Western of the sixties.

d/co-s Giorgio Ferroni *p* Giulio Fabris *co-s* Vittorio Metz, Vincenzo Rovi, Gian Paolo Callegari *c* Sergio Pesce *lp* Giovanni Grasso, Nino Pavese, Adriana Sivieri, Egisto Olivieri, Tino Scotti, Nada Fiorelli

Fighting Frontier (RKO) b/w 57 min
A better-than-average outing from Holt. Cheney and Parker's script takes the ploy of posing as an outlaw further than usual with Holt imprisoned and nearly lynched at one point. Hillyer's direction stresses comedy almost as much as action. Nonetheless, the war-time economies which affected series production drastically – even blanks were rationed! – were beginning to show.

d Lambert Hillyer *p* Bert Gilroy *s* J. Benton Cheney, Norton S. Parker *c* Jack Greenhalgh *lp* Tim Holt, Cliff Edwards, Ann Summers, Eddie Dew, Slim Whitaker, Bud Osborne

Frontier Badman (U) b/w 80 min
An efficient B feature with a strong supporting cast. Paige and Beery are the cattlemen who survive the rigours of the Chisholm Trail only to find a syndicate run by Gomez and his hired killers, including a sadistic Chaney, denying them the fruit of their labours. Singing star Tex Ritter and silent screen star William Farnum are on hand to help settle matters.

d/p Ford Beebe *s* Gerald Geraghty, Morgan Cox *c* William Sickner *lp* Diana Barrymore, Robert Paige, Noah Beery Jnr, Andy Devine, Thomas Gomez, Lon Chaney Jnr

Diana Barrymore as the card dealer of the Red Bull Saloon in Frontier Badman.

Guinn Williams, Glenn Ford, Evelyn Keyes, Randolph Scott and director Charles Vidor (left to right) relaxing on the set of The Desperadoes.

direction is energetic and Davey and Meehan cope with the problems of colour easily enough in the exterior sequences, though the interiors feature some strange colour effects.

d Charles Vidor *p* Harry Joe Brown *s* Robert Carson *c* George Meehan, Allen M. Davey *lp* Randolph Scott, Glenn Ford, Claire Trevor, Edgar Buchanan, Evelyn Keyes, Guinn Williams

False Colors (UA) b/w 65 min
A minor series entry, this sees Rogers, the son of Will, take over the role of the juvenile side-kick inaugurated by Jimmy Ellison in 1935. Dumbrille is the villain, killing off the heirs to a large ranch-spread to secure control of local water rights. Mitchum returns to the series once more as a heavy, and in a magical moment is jailed by Barcroft, a sheriff for once. Like all the other Hopalong Cassidy Westerns in which he appears it was later re-released with Mitchum's name above Boyd's.

d George Archainbaud *p* Harry Sherman *s* Bennett Cohen *c* Russell Harlan *lp* William Boyd, Andy Clyde, Jimmy Rogers, Douglass Dumbrille, Bob Mitchum, Roy Barcroft

Hoppy Serves a Writ (UA) b/w 67 min

The last Hopalong Cassidy series film to be based on an original story by Clarence Mulford, creator of the series, and the first to feature Mitchum, who had made his debut in the series with a walk-on part in **Border Patrol** (1943), in a substantial part. Also the first to be directed by Archainbaud, it shows a marked improvement on the earlier United Artists' entries in Sherman's long-running series. Boyd is the sheriff, Jory the villain he has to tempt back into Texas before he can serve his writ and Mitchum a minor baddie. A simple and effective series Western.

d George Archainbaud *p* Harry Sherman *s* Gerald Geraghty *c* Russell Harlan *lp* William Boyd, Andy Clyde, Jay Kirby, Victor Jory, Bob Mitchum, George Reeves

Idaho (REP) b/w 70 min

This is a significant film in the Rogers canon. Earlier outings, especially since Gene Autry had quit Republic for the army, had seen the musical content grow; this film sees the arrival of the musical spectacle as an essential ingredient. Henceforth at the conclusion of the story the Rogers films would feature a staged musical celebration and their star would begin to outdo Autry in grotesque costumary (especially after the advent of Trucolour). Chanslor and Cooper's screenplay features Rogers as a state ranger who comes to the rescue of a judge, Shannon, who is trying to clear the range of Munson's gambling emporium so that the youth of America can grow up in an untainted atmosphere.

The film was Kane's last as producer on the Rogers series.

d/p Joseph Kane *s* Roy Chanslor, Olive Cooper *c* Reggie Lanning *lp* Roy Rogers, Smiley Burnette, Bob Nolan and the Sons of the Pioneers, Virginia Grey, Harry J. Shannon, Ona Munson, Trigger

In Old Oklahoma *aka* War of the Wildcats

(REP) b/w 102 min

Wayne and Dekker are the battling oilmen in this Republic oater. Dekker wants to drill for oil on Indian land but the Indians give the contract to their friend Wayne with the proviso that he beat a deadline or lose the deal to Dekker. Further confusing matters is schoolmistress Scott who fluctuates between the two. But the best things in the film are the action sequences, notably the convoy of oil-filled wagons

dashing across the prairie through a bushfire. Dale Evans, who in a year's time was to become a fixture in Roy Rogers movies, has a featured part.

d Albert S. Rogell *p* Robert North *s* Ethel Hill, Eleanor Griffin *c* Jack Marta *lp* John Wayne, Martha Scott, Albert Dekker, George Hayes, Harry Woods, Grant Withers

The Kansan (UA) b/w 79 min

The first of Sherman's package of three small A-budgeted Westerns for United Artists, *The Kansan* stars Dix as the roaming cowboy who settles in a Kansas town and cleans it up, even though it means taking on Dekker. Jory, sympathetically cast for a change, is the man who steps aside when Wyatt, the woman he loves, declares herself in love with Dix. Archainbaud's deft direction and Harlan's superior cinematography lift an otherwise routine project.

d George Archainbaud *p* Harry Sherman *s* Harold Shumate *c* Russell Harlan *lp* Richard Dix, Jane Wyatt, Victor Jory, Albert Dekker, Robert Armstrong, Glenn Strange

King of the Cowboys (REP) b/w 67 min

With the release of this film, Republic began their heavy promotion of Rogers who'd just made the cover of *Life* magazine as 'King of the Cowboys', which henceforth became his 'official' title. Along with the extensive promotion came another significant upping of the films' budgets and a strong patriotic slant to the storylines. Cooper and Cheney's plot features Rogers as a rodeo star/government agent on the trail of saboteurs led by Mohr, who are blowing up government

warehouses. In the course of his investigations ploys like code words uttered during spiritualist performances, devices one would associate with serialdom rather than feature films, are brought to bear. The flag-waving climax has a wounded Rogers disarming a bomb while under fire from the saboteurs and so saving a troop of American soldiers.

d Joseph Kane *p* Harry Grey *s* Olive Cooper, J. Benton Cheney *c* Reggie Lanning *lp* Roy Rogers, Smiley Burnette, Peggy Moran, Bob Nolan and the Sons of the Pioneers, Gerald Mohr, Dorothea Kent, Trigger

A Lady Takes a Chance (RKO) b/w 86 min
Produced by Arthur's husband, *A Lady Takes a Chance* is a gentle comedy Western. She's the bored Easterner who sets off on a '14 Breathless Days in the West' coach tour and meets rodeo rider Wayne when he literally falls into her lap. He introduces her to the 'real West' – brawling and gambling – and she falls for him and then sets about marrying him. Garson Kanin's uncredited involvement in the script guarantees a degree of wit but Seiter's flat direction and the film's impoverished production values are insurmountable, even by Arthur's grin.

d William Seiter *p* Frank Ross *s* Robert Ardrey, Garson Kanin *c* Frank Redman *lp* John Wayne, Jean Arthur, Charles Winninger, Phil Silvers, Mary Field, Don Costello

Law of the Northwest (COL) b/w 57 min
Once again Starrett, now minus Hayden who'd gone on to star in his own series at Columbia, is in Mountie uniform and once again he takes on the Nazis, attempting to block the completion of a vital supply route for the Allies in the north-west region of Canada. Hunnicutt, taking over the comedy role from Cliff Edwards, is in fine form, as is Curtis, as ever the villain of the piece.

d William Berke *p* Jack Fier *s* Luci Ward *c* Benjamin Kline *lp* Charles Starrett, Arthur Hunnicutt, Shirley Patterson, Don Curtis, Stanley Brown, Davidson Clark

The Law Rides Again (MON) b/w 59 min
The second in Monogram's Trail Blazers series, put together by the company after the death of Buck Jones had brought an end to their successful Rough Riders series. LaRue is the bandit used by a rather lethargic Gibson and Maynard to expose crooked Indian agent Harlan, who offers as melodramatic interpretation of his role as ever. LePicard's cinematography, which seems very primitive for 1943, probably as a result of Tansey's economizing, lets the film down badly.

d Alan James *p* Robert Tansey *s* Frances Kavanaugh *c* Marcel LePicard *lp* Ken Maynard, Hoot Gibson, Betty Miles, Jack LaRue, Kenneth Harlan, Chief Thundercloud

The Leather Burners (UA) b/w 58 min
A peculiar series Western. Jory is the rustler baron Boyd suspects and goes to work for only to be framed, with Clyde, for a murder he didn't commit. Larson is the youngster whose sleuthing proves them innocent. It's here that the plot takes a bizarre twist when it's revealed that Jory, in league with a crazed mine owner, Givot, has turned a mine into a huge underground cattle pen. An underground stampede and a blazing gun battle later the rustlers are exposed. Mitchum, in his third outing with Hoppy, has a small role.

d Joseph E. Henabery *p* Harry Sherman *s* Jo Pagano *c* Russell Harlan *lp* William Boyd, Andy Clyde, Victor Jory, Bobby Larson, George Givot, Bob Mitchum

The Lone Star Trail (U) b/w 58 min
The last and undoubtedly the best of Brown and Ritter's co-starring Westerns for Universal. Brown is the man framed for robbery who, when he's pardoned, sets out to find the real villains. Taylor's direction is economic and forceful. A big plus is the film's finest sequence, a lengthy, realistic scrap between Brown and Mitchum that leaves Mitchum on the floor and Brown bruised and bloodied.

d Ray Taylor *p/s* Oliver Drake *c* William Sickner *lp* Johnny Mack Brown, Tex Ritter, Fuzzy Knight, Jennifer Holt, Jack Ingram, Bob Mitchum

Man from Music Mountain (REP) b/w 71 min
This film sees Rogers in effect playing himself, as Gene Autry had done from the beginning of his career. In a plot reminiscent of Autry's **Melody Ranch** (1940), Rogers is the famous radio country singer who, on his return to his home

Rodeo rider John Wayne attempts to lassoo Jean Arthur during the filming of A Lady Takes a Chance.

Right: A sultry Jane Russell in Howard Hughes' voyeuristic epic, The Outlaw.

Below: Johnny Mack Brown (centre) and a bruised Robert Mitchum after their furious fistfight that is the climax of The Lone Star Trail.

town, is appointed deputy sheriff and finds himself in the middle of a sheepmen-v-cattlemen feud stirred up by Kelly and his gang. He succeeds with several minutes to spare during which he and the cast mount an impromptu miniature musical, by now the standard end to a Roy Rogers Western.

d Joseph Kane *p* Harry Grey *s* Bradford Ropes, J. Benton Cheney *c* William Bradford *lp* Roy Rogers, Ruth Terry, Paul Kelly, Ann Gillis, George Cleveland, Pat Brady, Trigger

The Outlaw

(HOWARD HUGHES PRODUCTIONS) b/w 126(117) min
One of the most (in)famous Westerns of all time. Like Selznick whose **Duel in the Sun** (1946) is an equally erotic (though not as sadistic) film, Hughes was an obsessive film-maker. Similarly, Hawks, the original director, quit the film for precisely the same reasons as King Vidor was later to quit *Duel in the Sun*. The plot, by Furthman, a regular collaborator of Hawks', has Buetel as Billy the Kid and Huston as Doc Halliday quarrelling over Russell and being trailed by Mitchell's Pat Garrett. But the film's centre of interest, certainly the key element in its promotion, was ex-dentist's receptionist Russell and her bust, made even more prominent by Hughes' specially designed cantilevered brassière – 'What are the two reasons for Jane Russell's rise to stardom?' ran one ad campaign.

Yet ironically, Hughes, in his depiction of Russell's Mexican spitfire, stresses that she is unimportant except as the possessor of large breasts for the viewer to ogle. At one point in the film, Huston and Buetel argue whether Russell or a horse should be the winnings in a card game they've just finished: they decide on a horse as being more valuable! Hughes' obsession aside, the film is memorable as one of Hawks' buddy movies, with Buetel and Mitchell as friends, despite being on opposite sides of the law.

co-d/p Howard Hughes *co-d* Howard Hawks *s* Jules Furthman *c* Gregg Toland *lp* Jack Buetel, Jane Russell, Thomas Mitchell, Walter Huston, Joe Sawyer, Mimi Aguglia

The Ox-Bow Incident *aka* Strange Incident

(FOX) b/w 75 min
A landmark Western. Often attacked for being solemn, serious and deadly dull – James Agee suggested it suffers from 'rigor artis' – Wellman's bleak film remains as impressive as ever. Based on Walter Van Tillberg Clark's novel it tells the story of three cowboys (Andrews, Quinn and Ford) who after a rough-and-ready trial are lynched for cattle rustling on the flimsiest of circumstantial evidence. After the real rustlers have been caught, back in town, Fonda, an unwilling party to the lynching, reads out loud Andrews' poignant last letter to his wife to the assembled members of the posse and shames them into protestations of doing the right thing in future.

The film marked a significant re-interpretation of the West and its assorted myths. Before the spirit of the West had been seen as essentially optimistic and its heroes as men of action. In *The Ox-Bow Incident* Wellman and Trotti depict a West in which meanness and suspicion are dominant and characters (the film has no hero as such) have a deeper psychological dimension than is normal. This feeling, oddly enough, is further re-inforced by the decision of Darryl F. Zanuck, who clearly had no faith in the project, to shoot all the exteriors on studio sets. Combined with Miller's dark, slightly expressionistic photography the result is a feeling of unreality that enhances the psychological dimension of the film. The climax is undeniably sentimental, but the members of the posse are delineated with a sharpness that still impresses: bartender Paul Hurst as the goader of the posse's fury, Frank Conroy as the fake Confederate Colonel more concerned with his son's pacificism (and what that might entail) than justice, Darwell as a rancher with no sympathy in her heart and Fonda and Morgan as ineffectual doubters cast in the role of observers.

Though the film's thoroughgoing pessimism would not re-appear in the Western for some time, the psychological emphasis of Trotti's script had an immediate impact on the development of the genre.

d William Wellman *p/s* Lamar Trotti *c* Arthur Miller *lp* Henry Fonda, Dana Andrews, Anthony Quinn, Henry Morgan, Jane Darwell, Francis Ford

Raiders of San Joaquin (U) b/w 60 min
A modern Western. Hall is the powerful, cynical landbaron building up his empire by cheating people out of their land in this complicated B feature. Brown and Ritter sort things out with comic assistance from Knight who by this time was a surprisingly effective comic.

d Lewis Collins *p* Oliver Drake *s* Elmer Clifton, Morgan Cox *c* William Sickner *lp* Johnny Mack Brown, Tex Ritter, Fuzzy Knight, Jennifer Holt, Henry Hall, Joseph Bernard

Riders of the Deadline (UA) b/w 70 min
Mitchum's last B Western as a villain, *Riders of the Deadline* has a complicated plot in which Boyd lets smuggler Warde use the Bar 20 as a hideout so as to catch the Mr Big of the organization, who, naturally, turns out to be the town's

Above: *Dana Andrews, Francis Ford and Anthony Quinn about to be hung in William Wellman's scathing indictment of the frontier spirit,* The Ox-Bow Incident.

A concerned William Boyd and Frances Woodward in Riders of the Deadline.

banker, Halligan. It is noticeable that, whereas previous Hopalong Cassidy outings had always been reviewed by the critics as superior series Westerns, this, like other recent ones, only got 'ho hum' reviews of the type, 'same people, same troubles, same end'.

d Lesley Selander *p* Harry Sherman *s* Bennett Cohen *c* Russell Harlan *lp* William Boyd, Andy Clyde, Tony Ward (Anthony Warde), Bob Mitchum, William Halligan, Earle Hodgins

Riding High *aka* Melody Inn (PAR) 88 min
A dull musical Western. Burlesque queen Lamour is miner Moore's daughter. She returns to the West where she puts on a show at a dude ranch for the benefit of local ranchers. Powell is the mining engineer who romances her and puts an end to a gang of counterfeiters.

d George Marshall *p* Fred Kohlmar *s* Walter de Leon, Arthur Phillips, Art Arthur *c* Karl Struss, Harry Hallenberger *lp* Dorothy Lamour, Dick Powell, Victor Moore, Rod Cameron, Lane Chandler, Gil Lamb

Silver City Raiders (COL) b/w 55 min
One of the eight-strong series of Westerns Hayden made for Columbia that features Wills and his Texas Playboys in supporting roles. Repp's screenplay has Ingram as an unscrupulous landgrabber playing a variant of the Spanish Land Grant trick on Hayden and his fellow ranchers to little avail. Carroll is the dapper heroine, but it's Wills and the Playboys with their marvellous Western Swing that steal the show.

d William Berke *p* Leon Barsha *s* Ed Earl Repp *c* Benjamin Kline *lp* Russell Hayden, Dub Taylor, Bob Wills, Jack Ingram, Alma Carroll, Edmund Cobb

Silver Spurs (REP) b/w 65 min
One of Rogers' action-packed entries, the second half of this outing features almost non-stop stunting from Yakima Canutt (as Rogers). The crude but effective screenplay has Carradine – whose mere presence is a mark of how big Rogers' budgets had become – as the villain trying to dupe Cowan out of his oil-rich land and using anything from drink to mail-order brides to get his way. Brooks is the lively heroine and Lanning photographs the action, especially the climactic chase, with real élan.

Roy Rogers astride Trigger with Smiley Burnette in Silver Spurs, *one of the most action packed of Rogers' outings.*

d Joseph Kane *p* Harry Grey *s* John K. Butler, J. Benton Cheney *c* Reggie Lanning *lp* Roy Rogers, Smiley Burnette, John Carradine, Phyllis Brooks, Jerome Cowan, Joyce Compton, Trigger

Tenting Tonight on the Old Camp Ground
(U) b/w 59 min
One of the best of the Brown-Ritter series Westerns. The two join forces to help Holt win a stagecoach mail contract by protecting the new road it requires from the outlaws trying to sabotage it. Collins' direction is brusque and Beecher's screenplay has some nice touches. Chandler as Duke Merrick is a suitably regal villain.

d Lewis Collins *p* Oliver Drake *s* Elizabeth Beecher *c* William Sickner *lp* Johnny Mack Brown, Tex Ritter, Fuzzy Knight, Jennifer Holt, Lane Chandler, Rex Lease

Wagon Tracks West (REP) b/w 55 min
This is an oddity. Tyler is the crooked medicine-man and Frazer the crooked Indian agent exposed by Elliott and Hayes when an old friend of theirs, Vallin, an Indian fresh from medical school, is shunned by his fellow Indians when he returns to the reservation. Barcroft puts in an appearance as a heavy. The screenplay doesn't live up to its creator's name.

d Howard Bretherton *p* Louis Gray *s* William Lively *c* Reggie Lanning *lp* Bill Elliott, George Hayes, Tom Tyler, Robert Frazer, Rick Vallin, Roy Barcroft

Wild Horse Rustlers (PRC) b/w 58 min
Another series Western that pits its heroes, St John and Livingston, newly arrived in the role of the Lone Rider, against the Nazis. The bizarre plot features Chandler as twins, a loyal 100% American and a ... Nazi agent 'trying to sabotage the Army's horse procurement plan', to quote the publicity booklet. With help from St John, Livingston puts an end to Chandler and Price's plans. Newfield's direction is adequate.

d Sam Newfield *p* Sigmund Neufeld *s* Joe O'Donnell *c* Robert Cline *lp* Bob Livingston, Al St John, Lane Chandler, Stanley Price, Linda Johnson, Frank Ellis

1944

Arizona Whirlwind (MON) b/w 59 min
The last of Maynard's films with the Trail Blazers. He quit because he was dissatisfied with the wholesale economies producer Tansey was making which did indeed make the films amongst the crudest of series Westerns. King and Hackett are the diamond smugglers.

d/p Robert Tansey *s* Frances Kavanaugh *c* Edward Kull *lp* Ken Maynard, Hoot Gibson, Bob Steele, Charles King, Karl Hackett, Myrna Dell

Barbary Coast Gent (MGM) b/w 87 min
The first of many Westerns from Del Ruth, this was the best of Beery's later films. He's the con-man who, when he's run out of California, heads for the Nevada gold fields where, with help from Barnes, he reforms and turns Robin Hood to put paid to the thievery of Carradine and Ankrum. The rousing climax has him led to jail with brass band accompaniment.

d Roy Del Ruth *p* Orville O. Dull *s* William R. Lipman, Grant Garrett, Harry Ruskin *c* Charles Salerno *lp* Wallace Beery, Binnie Barnes, John Carradine, Morris Ankrum, Bruce Kellogg, Chill Wills

Beneath Western Skies (REP) b/w 56 min
In 1943 Republic had tried to make Eddie Dew a series star as John Paul Revere but had dropped him when the villains got better reviews than he. However, they continued the series character with Livingston for a few more films. This was Livingston's second outing in the role, abbreviated to Johnny

1944

Revere. DeMond and Williams' complicated screenplay has Livingston suffering from amnesia and being told by baddies that he's one of them and accepting it as gospel fact until another knock on the head sets his mind to rights.

d Spencer Bennet *p* Louis Gray *s* Albert DeMond, Bob Williams *c* Ernest Miller *lp* Robert Livingston, Smiley Burnette, Effie Laird, LeRoy Mason, Jack Ingram, Budd Buster

The Big Bonanza (REP) b/w 69 min

Arlen is the Cavalry officer unjustly courtmartialled for cowardice who, on his return home, discovers that his boyhood pal has turned bad and is now terrorizing the town. Indeed he's so bad that at one point he even attempts the murder of his own brother, Driscoll, who is the sole witness to a murder he's committed. Frazee is the dance-hall queen who switches sides when she falls for Arlen.

d George Archainbaud *p* Eddy White *s* Dorrell McGowan, Stuart McGowan, Paul Gangelin *c* Reggie Lanning *lp* Richard Arlen, Robert Livingston, Bobby Driscoll, Jane Frazee, George Hayes, Lynne Roberts, Charles King

Buffalo Bill (FOX) 90 min

One of the two films made by Wellman for Fox as part of the deal to direct **The Ox-Bow Incident** (1943), *Buffalo Bill* is a sentimental biography of the scout and hunter turned Wild West showman. McCrea, practising the quiet confidence that was to become his trademark, is competent as the buckskin-fringed hero, but the script allowed him to do little but glower his dislike for Washington politicians and show his prowess on horseback. Amongst the strong supporting cast Mitchell (as Ned Buntline), Blackmer (a frontier interpretation of Theodore Roosevelt) and O'Hara (McCrea's wife) stand out.

Above: *Thomas Mitchell as Ned Buntline, the journalist who was to make Bill Cody into the stuff of dreams by the mere addition of the tag 'Buffalo' with his subject, Joel McCrea, and Maureen O'Hara.*

d William Wellman *p* Harry Sherman *s* Aeneas MacKenzie, Clements Ripley, Cecile Kramer *c* Leon Shamroy *lp* Joel McCrea, Maureen O'Hara, Thomas Mitchell, Linda Darnell, Edgar Buchanan, Sidney Blackmer

The Cowboy and the Senorita (REP) b/w 78 min

This was Rogers' first film with Evans, who was to appear in twenty films in a row with him and finally marry him in 1947. She was a versatile workhorse of a singer-cum-dancer whose maternal sexuality complemented Rogers' oddly boyish charm. She's the senorita of the title, Ysobel Martinez, whose cousin, Lee, is left a gold mine that Hubbard tries to seize. Rogers and Williams (still parading the simple smile that was his trademark) foil Hubbard. This is an historically interesting, rather than important, series Western.

d Joseph Kane *p* Harry Grey *s* Gordon Kahn *c* Reggie Lanning *lp* Roy Rogers, Mary Lee, Dale Evans, John Hubbard, Guinn 'Big Boy' Williams, Fuzzy Knight, Trigger

Cowboy Canteen (COL) b/w 72 min

A series Western version of *Hollywood Canteen* (1944) with Starrett as the rancher in army uniform who finds that romance and patriotism mix well, especially if helped along by a number of cowboy personalities. Notable for one of the few film appearances of country singer Ray Acuff, at his prime, the film also features musical interludes by Ritter, Rogers and the Mills Brothers (!) in place of the more usual gun battles of Starrett's series outings. The film gives a fair indication of the strength of the Western – imagine a film called *Detective Canteen* – a genre whose characters were so well established that even Terhune, who does his ventriloquist act here, had his own fan club!

d Lew Landers *p* Jack Fier *s* Paul Gangelin *c* George Meehan *lp* Charles Starrett, Jane Frazee, Tex Ritter, Dub Taylor, Guinn Williams, Max Terhune

The Drifter (PRC) b/w 62 min

Crabbe, finally liberated from his role as Billy the Kid, has the role of outlaw and hero in this routine PRC Western. As the hero he's a Robin Hood figure, riding the range to help others while as a baddie he is a bank robber trading on the good reputation of his other half. Parker is the girl who falls for him and gets understandably confused by the different identities.

d Sam Newfield *p* Sigmund Neufeld *s* Patricia Harper *c* Robert Cline *lp* Buster Crabbe, Al St John, Carol Parker, Kermit Maynard, Jack Ingram, George Chesebro

Roy Rogers (right), Mary Lee and Guinn Williams, one of the Westerns most recognizable character actors, in The Cowboy and the Senorita.

The Mills Brothers with their barbershop harmonies and satin dungarees in Cowboy Canteen, *a testament to the genre's flexibility if ever there was one.*

Paul Hurst (left), Robert Mitchum and Frances Langford in Girl Rush, *a frontier musical.*

Forty Thieves (UA) b/w 60 min

The last of Sherman's Hopalong Cassidy series. When Hoppy returned to the screen in 1946, it would be under the wing of Boyd's own production company. Here he's the sheriff who is defeated, when he runs for re-election, by Alyn who all the baddies support because he's weak. When the bad elements, led by Dumbrille, take command Hoppy decides enough is enough and sets about running them out of town. Whereupon Dumbrille summons 40 gunmen to town to kill him. The climax is justly famous, if fantastical to say the least. Boyd faces the 40 gunmen and not only survives, but drives them from town!

d Lesley Selander *p* Harry Sherman *s* Michael Wilson, Bernie Kamins *c* Russell Harlan *lp* William Boyd, Andy Clyde, Kirk Alyn, Douglass Dumbrille, Jimmy Rogers, Louise Currie

Buster Crabbe, with Carol Parker as the girl who loves him through thick and thin, in The Drifter.

Girl Rush (RKO) b/w 65 min

A frontier musical featuring RKO's short-lived rivals to Abbott and Costello, Brown and Carney. They're the vaudeville artists stranded amidst the California Gold Rush who turn to prospecting and then gambling in an attempt to keep their troupe together. Mitchum, beginning his long stint with RKO and billed as Robert (rather than Bob), is the young miner who tries, unsuccessfully, to keep them on the straight and narrow. This is a robust B feature.

d Gordon Douglas *p* John Auer *s* Robert E. Kent *c* Nicholas Musuraca *lp* Wally Brown, Alan Carney, Robert Mitchum, Frances Langford, Paul Hurst

Hands Across the Border (REP) b/w 73 min

Another of Rogers' musical extravaganzas, this has the usual double climax of those films, first a dramatic resolution of the story and then a miniature musical revue. Centring on Trigger, Rogers' famous Palomino horse, the plot has Rogers helping Terry, who joins him in several duets, raise horses for the army and find the man responsible for the murder of her father.

Several of the songs are by Hoagy Carmichael.

d Joseph Kane *p* Harry Grey *s* Bradford Ropes, J. Benton Cheney *c* Reggie Lanning *lp* Roy Rogers, Ruth Terry, Guinn 'Big Boy' Williams, Onslow Stevens, Mary Treen, Roy Barcroft, Trigger

The Last Horseman (COL) b/w 60 min

The last of Hayden's Columbia series Westerns to feature Bob Wills and his Texas Playboys. The plot is a real mishmash, with Hayden as the ranch foreman robbed of the $12,000 he got for the sale of a herd of cattle that he was delivering to his boss. Finally, with enthusiastic support from Wills who liked to join in the action whenever possible, he retrieves the money after spending a large part of the picture disguised as a woman.

d William Berke *p* Leon Barsha *s* Ed Earl Repp *c* George Meehan *lp* Russell Hayden, Dub Taylor, Bob Wills, Ann Savage, Frank LaRue, Forrest Taylor

Nevada (RKO) b/w 62 min

Mitchum, who'd first appeared as an extra and then graduated to being a heavy in Hopalong Cassidy series Westerns, was chosen by RKO to replace Tim Holt as the studio's cowboy star when Holt joined the Military Service. This Zane Grey remake has Mitchum in the role of a cowboy trying to go straight, a part first essayed by Gary Cooper in the original silent film of 1927. Williams provides the comic relief, Martin the vocalizing and Jeffreys the romantic interest.

d Edward Killy p Herman Schlom s Norman Houston
c Harry Wild lp Robert Mitchum, Anne Jeffreys, Guinn 'Big Boy' Williams, Richard Martin, Nancy Gates, Harry Woods

Oklahoma Raiders (U) b/w 57 min

Ritter's last film for Universal – indeed his last significant film – this is a loose remake of the much-filmed **Come On Danger** (1932, 1942). Ritter and Knight, sent to buy horses for the Cavalry, stumble on the villainy of Ingram and Eldridge and masked vigilante Jennifer, sister of Tim, Holt, who rather grandly calls herself El Vengador. Collins' direction is forceful and Holt proves a charming foil to Ritter's *basso profundo*. The film, like many forties Westerns in which horses figure prominently, includes substantial footage from *King of the Stallions* (1942).

d Lewis Collins p Oliver Drake s Betty Burbridge
c William Sickner lp Tex Ritter, Fuzzy Knight, Jennifer Holt, Jack Ingram, George Eldridge, Dennis Moore

Outlaw Trail (MON) b/w 53 min

Chief Thundercloud made his debut in this Trail Blazers outing, replacing Ken Maynard who quit after **Arizona Whirlwind** (1944). Kavanaugh's interesting plot has Kendall as Honest John slowly getting the rest of the town in his debt – he even prints his own money – until the Trail Blazers come to town. The production values are primitive, as was usually the case with Tansey's productions, but his direction, with his almost gleeful celebration of the most unlikely circumstances, is simply charming.

d/p Robert Tansey s Frances Kavanaugh c Edward Kull
lp Hoot Gibson, Bob Steele, Chief Thundercloud, Cy Kendall, Jennifer Holt, Charles King

Partners of the Trail (MON) b/w 57 min

One of the few of Brown's Monogram series Westerns not written by Adele Buffington (using her Jess Bowers pseudonym) and one of the most distinctive. Young's

screenplay is slow-moving but purposive and Brown seems, for the first time, happy on the Monogram lot where he was to remain for many years. Ingraham is the chief villain and McIntyre the lady of the piece.

d Lambert Hillyer p Scott R. Dunlap s Frank Young
c Harry Neumann lp Johnny Mack Brown, Raymond Hatton, Christine McIntyre, Jack Ingram, Lloyd Ingraham, Craig Woods

Range Law (MON) b/w 57 min

This routine outing has Brown and Hatton sorting out landgrabbers who try to swindle local ranchers out of their land in order to get the valuable silver deposits they know are there. Hillyer's direction is sprightly, but the script by Young is hackneyed and slow moving.

d Lambert Hillyer p Charles J. Bigelow s Frank H. Young c Harry Neumann lp Johnny Mack Brown, Raymond Hatton, Sarah Padden, Lloyd Ingraham, Bud Osborne, Jack Ingram

The San Antonio Kid (REP) b/w 59 min

A routine series Western. Elliott, in his Red Ryder guise, puts paid to Mason and Strange's plan to drive off the ranchers whose lands they know to be oil rich. Renaldo is the Kid of the title, hired by Strange to kill Elliott but deciding to team up with him.

d Howard Bretherton p Stephen Auer s Norman S. Hall c William Bradford lp Bill Elliott, Glenn Strange, LeRoy Mason, Duncan Renaldo, Alice Fleming, Linda Stirling

San Fernando Valley (REP) b/w 74 min

This is the first of the three films serial ace English would make with Rogers and the first not to be directed by Joseph Kane who had guided the singing cowboy's career over 42 films from the beginning. The film also sees Rogers receive his first screen kiss, albeit in a dream sequence, ironically from Porter rather than Evans. English directs the few action sequences neatly enough and the film was a resounding success in the market place, but in retrospect English was clearly unsure how to handle the lavish production numbers. Similarly the script, which features Rogers as the man brought in to clean up the valley of the title and falling foul of Evans, is well thumbed rather than original.

Tex Ritter with Jennifer Holt in Oklahoma Raiders, *his last series Western of note.*

Johnny Mack Brown (with rifle) listens to Jack Ingram's tale of rustling in Partners of the Trail.

Above: *Roy Rogers with Dale Evans, by now his most regular heroine and soon to be his wife, in* San Fernando Valley.

Far right: *Bob Crosby as the Broadway cowboy singing star reluctantly sworn in as sheriff in* The Singing Sheriff, *yet another would-be spoof Western.*

Ward Bond sends John Wayne flying – usually it was the other way round – in the best of their fistfights in Tall in the Saddle.

Sundown Valley   (COL)   b/w   55 min

This is one of Starrett's several series Westerns directed by Kline who had made some serials for Mascot but was better known as a cinematographer, in which capacity he'd worked on all Columbia's series Westerns. Kline's promotion was clearly, at least in part, intended as an economy move, as the decreased budgets demonstrated. His response to lack of funds, like that of producer/director Robert Tansey, was to emphasize the action at all costs, including comprehension of the plot. This time, however, the plot is bizarrely interesting with Starrett and Taylor (the long-time side-kick of Wild Bill Elliott, here replacing Arthur Hunnicutt) ridding the range of Nazis (who included Oakman amongst their number), who are trying to halt production at the gunsight plant where Starrett is manager.

d Benjamin Kline   *p* Jack Fier   *s* Luci Ward
c George Meehan   *lp* Charles Starrett, Bud Taylor, Jimmy Wakely, Wheeler Oakman, Jeanne Bates, Jack Ingram

Tall in the Saddle   (RKO)   b/w   87 min

Co-scripted by Fix, a regular actor in Wayne pictures, *Tall in the Saddle* is memorable for Raines' tempestuous performance as the independent woman who romances Wayne with a

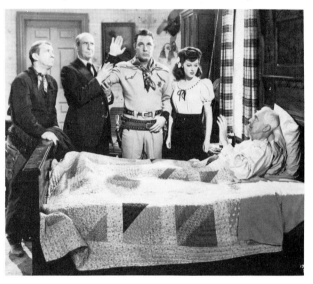

mixture of aggression – at one point she fires a pistol at him ! – and sultry sensuality that prefigures the relationship of Angie Dickinson and Wayne in **Rio Bravo** (1959). The complicated plot concerns Bond's attempts to first wrest control of Long's ranch and then frame Wayne for murder when he discovers Bond's plans. Although the script's complexities seem more suited to a serial, Marin's spirited direction, the two lengthy fistfights and Raines' performance result in an engaging movie.

d Edwin L. Marin   *p* Robert Fellows   *s* Michael Hogan, Paul Fix   *c* Robert De Grasse   *lp* John Wayne, Ella Raines, Ward Bond, Audrey Long, George Hayes, Raymond Hatton

The Singing Sheriff   (U)   b/w   63 min

This is an unorthodox B Western. The strange plot has Crosby, singing-cowboy star of a Broadway show, discovering that helping a friend out means becoming sheriff when the real sheriff is incapacitated. More by accident than design he succeeds in rounding up Sawyer's posse of bandits with comic assistance from Knight. Clearly intended as a satire on things Western, it works best as a straight comedy.

d Leslie Goodwins   *p* Bernard W. Burton   *s* Henry Blankford, Eugene Conrad   *c* Charles Van Enger
lp Bob Crosby, Fay McKenzie, Joe Sawyer, Fuzzy Knight, Samuel S. Hinds, Andrew Tombes

d John English   *p* Edward J. White   *s* Dorrell McGowan, Stuart McGowan   *c* William Bradford   *lp* Roy Rogers, Dale Evans, Jean Porter, Andrew Tombes, Charles Smith, Edward Gargan, Trigger

Westward Bound   (MON)   b/w   59 min

Looking as though it were completed in hours rather than days, this is a decidedly rough entry in the Trail Blazers series, the kind of film that got the dreaded tag line in *Variety* 'Par for this type of film'. Woods and Hackett are the villains of the piece, trying to drive ranchers off their property but falling foul of the Trail Blazers. The climax, much of which is 'borrowed footage', has Gibson dynamiting Woods and company into submission.

d/p Robert Tansey   *s* Frances Kavanaugh   *c* Marcel LePicard   *lp* Ken Maynard, Hoot Gibson, Bob Steele, Betty Miles, Harry Woods, Karl Hackett

Zorro's Black Whip (REP) b/w 12 chaps

Strangely Zorro himself doesn't appear in this late entry in the Zorro canon. His place is taken by Stirling as a masked female avenger who is ably assisted by Lewis, normally cast as a heavy. Stirling who made six serials in the late forties, is energetic enough but despite strong second-unit direction by Yakima Canutt the serial's poor production values showed Republic's growing lack of faith in swordplay in Old California.

d Spencer Bennet, Wallace Grissell p Ronald Davidson
s Basil Dickey, Jesse Duffy, Grant Nelson, Joseph Poland
c Bud Thackery lp George J. Lewis, Linda Stirling, Lucien Littlefield, Hal Taliaferro, John Merton, Forrest Taylor

1945

Along Came Jones (INTERNATIONAL) b/w 90 min

Produced by its star who specially commissioned a script from Johnson that makes fun of his languid, naive screen persona, *Along Came Jones* is a minor comic Western. Mistaken for killer Duryea, Cooper, who can't even draw a gun properly, becomes the centre of interest to those hunting for Duryea's treasure. Eventually he even wins Duryea's girlfriend, Young (who gives a deliciously knowing performance). However, the plot complications are too mechanical and don't allow the pair to develop a relationship. Routine.

d Stuart Heisler p Gary Cooper s Nunnally Johnson
c Milton Krasner lp Gary Cooper, Loretta Young, Dan Duryea, William Demarest, Frank Sully, Russell Simpson

Bells of Rosarita (REP) b/w 68 min

This absurd film is the work of director McDonald, who made some eleven films with Rogers. Rogers and Bob Nolan, of the Sons of the Pioneers, play themselves (Republic Western stars) making a movie on location at the circus left Evans by her father that Withers is trying to cheat her out of. Rogers is soon wise to Withers' tricks and, in a surreal moment calls on his fellow (Republic) cowboy stars, Wild Bill Elliott, Allan Lane, Don Barry, Sunset Carson and Bob Livingston – and their various steeds, Thunder, Feather, Cyclone, Silver and Shamrock, respectively – to help him round up Withers and company. The gimmick is one Republic would regularly repeat in their various series.

d Frank McDonald p Edward J. White s Jack Townley
c Ernest Miller lp Roy Rogers, George Hayes, Dale Evans, Adele Mara, Grant Withers, Roy Barcroft, the Sons of the Pioneers, Trigger

The Cherokee Flash (REP) b/w 55 min

Barcroft, in a sympathetic role after playing innumerable baddies, makes this late entry in Republic's short-run Sunset Carson series more interesting than most. Writer/producer Cohen's script features Carson as Barcroft's foster son to whom the aging outlaw goes for help when members of his old gang try to stop him going straight. With comic assistance from London, Carson and Barcroft put the gang away, thus allowing a smiling Barcroft to retire in peace.

d Thomas Carr p/co-s Bennett Cohen co-s Betty Burbridge
c Reggie Lanning lp Sunset Carson, Linda Stirling, Tom London, Roy Barcroft, John Merton, Bud Geary

The Cisco Kid Returns (MON) b/w 64 min

The first of Renaldo's trio of Cisco Kid films for Monogram after Romero quit to go into the Navy. Burbridge's traditional screenplay has the Kid rescuing a young child from the dastardly arms of Pryor and then having to prove that he hasn't kidnapped the child. It all ends well enough, but with such plots the series looked to be in a very shaky situation. Garralaga is Pancho and Callejo the romantic interest.

d John P. McCarthy p Philip Krasne s Betty Burbridge
c Harry Neumann lp Duncan Renaldo, Roger Pryor, Martin Garralaga, Cecilia Callejo, Bud Osborne, Anthony Warde

Dakota (REP) b/w 82 min

One of the many Republic films to star Ralston (wife of Herbert J. Yates, the studio's owner), *Dakota* was nearly never made when Wayne refused to work with her. He finally reluctantly gave way (as he was to on subsequent occasions). The constant battles on the set are reflected in the sluggish and erratic pace of the film. Not surprisingly, most of the film's best scenes are directed by Yakima Canutt's second unit. Wayne and Ralston play the young couple who stumble across Bond and Mazurki and their plans to buy up land along the route of a planned railway outside of Fargo. The film's cliched plot was adapted by Howard Estabrook, writer of **Cimarron** (1931), from a story by Carl Foreman (who was later to write **High Noon**, 1952). For Kane the film's stormy production circumstances were nonetheless infinitely preferable to the treadmill of the Roy Rogers and Gene Autry series Westerns he had been churning out by the dozen.

Above: *John Wayne as the unwelcome guest in* Dakota.

d/p Joseph Kane *s* Lawrence Hazard *c* Jack Marta
lp John Wayne, Vera Ralston, Ward Bond, Walter Brennan, Mike Mazurki, Paul Fix

The Daltons Ride Again (U) b/w 72 min
A Universal quickie made in sixteen days, this rehash of **When the Daltons Rode** (1940) is a perky oater. Curtis, Taylor, Chaney Jnr and Beery Jnr are stonefaced as the brothers spreading devastation throughout Kansas before meeting their end in the course of an attempted bank robbery in Coffeyville. A fast, efficient and anonymous Western.

d Ray Taylor *p* Howard Welsch *s* Roy Chanslor, Paul Gangelin *c* Charles Van Enger *lp* Alan Curtis, Kent Taylor, Lon Chaney Jnr, Noah Beery Jnr, Martha O'Driscoll, Douglass Dumbrille

Above right: *Alan Curtis, Lon Chaney, Kent Taylor and Noah Beery Jnr (left to right) as Emmett, Grat, Bob and Ben Dalton in* The Daltons Ride Again.

Flame of the Barbary Coast (REP) b/w 91 min
Released to tie in with the celebrations for Republic's tenth anniversary, *Flame of the Barbary Coast* is the first major big budget feature directed by Kane, veteran of Roy Rogers series Westerns. His fluid camerawork, best seen in the superb tracking shots around Schildkraut's gambling emporium, proves he could rise to the occasion. Sadly Chase's script is confused and neither Wayne nor Dvorak seem really interested in their parts. He's the wandering cowboy who falls for her, after she's helped him win a fortune at San Francisco's gambling tables and who vows revenge on Schildkraut who wins the fortune back by cheating at cards.

Ann Dvorak and John Wayne in Flame of the Barbary Coast.

After a brief stay in Montana, where he learns to play cards from veteran gambler Frawley, he returns to San Francisco, wins another fortune and opens his own gambling saloon with Dvorak as resident songbird, only to have the roof literally fall in on him in the form of the 1906 San Francisco earthquake. After scrabbling through the ruins the pair recuperate in the clean untainted air of Montana. The contrast between working the land and spinning a roulette wheel is one Chase would use to much greater effect in his script for **Bend of the River** (1952).

d/p Joseph Kane *s* Borden Chase *c* Robert De Grasse
lp John Wayne, Ann Dvorak, Joseph Schildkraut, William Frawley, Virginia Grey, Paul Fix

Flaming Frontier *aka* Flame of the West
(MON) b/w 70 min
Thought by many to be Brown's best Western, this prestige production stars Brown not as his series character, Nevada John McKenzie, but as a pacifist doctor. Considered a coward by the townspeople because he won't oppose the local outlaws, Brown is finally goaded into action by the murder of the sheriff (an unusually restrained performance from Dumbrille). Hillyer, who made silents with W.S. Hart, directs with a sombre grace. The musical interludes are supplied by Pee Wee King (the composer of 'Tennessee Waltz' and one of the few important country music stars, as opposed to Hollywood stars, to appear in Westerns).

d Lambert Hillyer *p* Scott R. Dunlap *s* Adele Buffington
c Harry Neumann *lp* Johnny Mack Brown, Raymond
Hatton, Douglass Dumbrille, Joan Woodbury, Harry Woods,
Lynne Carver

Frontier Gal *aka* **The Bride Wasn't Willing** (U) 84 min
A broad comedy in the mould of **Destry Rides Again** (1939),
but without that film's deft touch. Cameron and De Carlo (in
roles originally intended for Jon Hall and Maria Montez) are
the feuding lovers, he an outlaw, she a saloon singer, who
marry at gunpoint and are finally reconciled by their
five-year-old daughter after Cameron has spent the interven-
ing years in jail. The film helped establish De Carlo as a star.

d Charles Lamont *p/s* Michael Fessier, Ernest Pagano
c George Robinson, Charles P. Boyle *lp* Yvonne De Carlo,
Rod Cameron, Andy Devine, Fuzzy Knight, Rex Lease, Jack
Ingram

In Old New Mexico (MON) b/w 62 min
This is generally considered to be the best of Renaldo's trio of
Cisco Kid movies for Monogram. Kenyon is the girl falsely
accused of murder. So the good Samaritan of the range
kidnaps her to save her life and sets out to prove her innocent.

d Phil Rosen *p* Philip Krasne *s* Betty Burbridge
c Arthur Martinelli *lp* Duncan Renaldo, Gwen Kenyon,
Martin Garralaga, Norman Willis, Lee White, Bud Osborne

The Lost Trail (MON) b/w 53 min
Though it opens well, with Brown stopping a runaway
stagecoach and discovering its driver dead, killed in a bullion
robbery by MacDonald's men, the plot is the hackneyed one
of rivalry for the stagecoach-line franchise that Holt has and
MacDonald wants. Brown was still an athletic hero, handling
fist- and gunfights with ease, but henceforth trade reviewers
would harp on his growing paunch rather than his punch.

d Lambert Hillyer *p* Charles J. Bigelow *s* Jess Bowers
(Adele Buffington) *c* Marcel LePicard *lp* Johnny Mack
Brown, Raymond Hatton, Jennifer Holt, Kenneth
MacDonald, Riley Hill, Frank LaRue

The Navajo Kid (PRC) b/w 59 min
Steele is the adopted Indian on the trail of the killer of his
foster father in this routine series Western, one of the last
Steele was to star in. The plot, seemingly entirely constructed
around coincidence, has Steele, after he's had his revenge,
arrested by the sheriff who it rapidly turns out, is his real
father. King's son, Charles King Jnr, has a minor role and
Saylor provides the comedy.

d/s Harry Fraser *p* Arthur Alexander *c* Jack Greenhalgh
lp Bob Steele, Syd Saylor, Edward Cassidy, Caren Marsh,
Charles King, Bud Osborne

*Rod Cameron and
Yvonne De Carlo as the
feuding lovers in*
Frontier Gal.

Oregon Trail (REP) b/w 55 min
Carson's third solo outing for Republic, *Oregon Trail* is a
remake of a much-filmed title (eg 1936, 1939), invigorated by
the action-packed direction of Carr. Also of interest is the fact
that the film features Carr's mother, a one-time silent screen
star, Mary Carr, in a supporting role. The plot has Carson
helping wagons roll westward and putting an end to Duncan's
plans of Empire.

d Thomas Carr *p* Bennett Cohen *s* Betty Burbridge
c Bud Thackery *lp* Sunset Carson, Peggy Stewart, Frank
Jaquet, Si Jenks, Keene Duncan, John Merton

San Antonio (WB) 111 min
Neither Max Steiner's rousing score nor the uncredited
directorial assistance of Raoul Walsh can raise this Western
from the leaden depths Butler consigns it to. Perhaps if
Buckner had scripted it, as he did **Dodge City** (1939), rather
than produced it, the result might have been more than a tired
formula star Western. Set against the backdrop of ranchers
fighting off mysterious rustlers, LeMay and Burnett's screenplay makes Flynn the wandering cowboy who falls foul of
crooked saloon keeper Francen as they vie for the affections of
singer Smith. Glennon's lustrous cinematography, especially
in the final shoot-out at the deserted Alamo, is the best thing
in the film.

d David Butler *p* Robert Buckner *s* Alan LeMay, W.R.
Burnett *c* Bert Glennon *lp* Errol Flynn, Alexis Smith,
S.Z. Sakall, Victor Francen, Tom Tyler, Monte Blue

Santa Fé Saddlemates (REP) b/w 56 min
Although his baby face and high-pitched voice were real
disadvantages for a would-be Western star, Sunset Carson was
given a two year run by Republic in the mid forties. The
plots, like this one which has Sunset as a government agent

*The villainous Victor
Francen surrounded by
his henchmen in* San
Antonio.

Top: *Bud Geary and Linda Stirling, Republic's best remembered B feature heroine, in danger in Santa Fé Saddlemates.*

Eddie Dean with Jennifer Holt in the first of his shortlived Western series, Song of Old Wyoming.

Below: *Ingrid Bergman and John Warburton watched by an impassive Flora Robson in Saratoga Trunk.*

working under cover as an outlaw on the trail of smugglers helped by reporter Stirling, are always routine, but the action is invariably fast and furious. This one begins with three fistfights in swift succession. The film also marks the beginning of Carson's association with director Carr who would be in control of his next ten pictures.

d/p Thomas Carr *s* Bennett Cohen *c* William Bradford
lp Sunset Carson, Linda Stirling, Roy Barcroft, Olin Howlin, Rex Lease, Bud Geary

Saratoga Trunk (WB) b/w 135 min
Made by Bergman and Cooper immediately after *For Whom the Bell Tolls* (1943), but not released for a couple of years, *Saratoga Trunk* is a tiresome melodrama. She is the beautiful fortune-hunter and he's the lanky cowboy who helps build a railroad spur for millionaire Warburton whom Bergman finally foresakes for Cooper. Robinson's script lacks any subtlety, moreover the material is far too slight for the 135 minutes lavished on it. Director Wood reportedly shot 600,000 feet of film to get a 15,000 foot feature. Only Robson as Bergman's loyal mulatto servant makes anything of her part.

d Sam Wood *p* Hal B. Wallis *s* Casey Robinson *c* Ernest Haller *lp* Gary Cooper, Ingrid Bergman, Flora Robson, John Warburton, Jerry Austin, Florence Bates

Song of Old Wyoming (PRC) 65 min
This was the first of Dean's ill-fated PRC series intended to make him a star. But even though there was little competition around, 1945 being the beginning of the end of the series

Western, Dean was rapidly eclipsed by one of the film's featured players, LaRue, soon to find fame as Lash LaRue. LaRue plays Cheyenne, the all-in-black gunman with a snarl for a voice, who reforms just in time to die at the end of the movie. Dean is the singing hero, imported by the villains to sabotage an old lady's ranch and turning out to be her long-lost son. Kavanaugh's plot is decidedly routine. The film was made in Cinecolor, a cheap colour process best remembered for inspiring Kenneth Tynan's witty clerihew:

> I can't bear films in sepia
> Except about once every leap-year
> And about those in Cinecolor,
> I'm even cynicaller

d/p Robert Emmett (Tansey) *s* Frances Kavanaugh
c Marcel LePicard *lp* Eddie Dean, Jennifer Holt, Sarah Padden, Al LaRue, Emmett Lynn, John Carpenter

South of the Rio Grande (MON) b/w 62 min
Renaldo and Garralaga are Cisco and Pancho in this lacklustre series outing. They expose the chicanery of Lewis, the corrupt district military officer whose racket is killing ranchers on the pretext of their being rustlers and then 'impounding' their cattle. Posing as the district supervisor, Renaldo leads a posse of local ranchers against Lewis' outlaw band.

d Lambert Hillyer *p* Philip N. Krasne *s* Victor
Hammond, Ralph Bettinson *c* William Sickner *lp* Duncan
Renaldo, Martin Garralaga, Armida, George J. Lewis, Lillian
Molieri, Francis McDonald

Sunset in El Dorado (REP) b/w 65 min
Another musical rather than actionful film from Rogers, this
outing has the advantage of a carefully constructed, unusual
plot. A bored Evans quits her job to visit the ghost town of El
Dorado where her grandmother was a famous, not to say
notorious, dance-hall queen, Kansas Kate. She meets Rogers,
Hayes and all the principal characters in an extended dream
sequence that features her as Kansas Kate. The film's success
intensified the drift away from action in Rogers films.

d John McDonald *p* Louis Gray *s* John K. Butler
c William Bradford *lp* Roy Rogers, George Hayes, Dale
Evans, Hardie Albright, Margaret Dumont, Roy Barcroft,
Trigger

Utah (REP) b/w 78 min
English's last, and best, film with Rogers, *Utah* features
Evans as the Eastern musical comedy star who heads West to
sell the ranch she's never seen to help keep her musical show
running. Rogers is the ranch foreman and Hayes, making a
welcome return to the series, is the fellow rancher. Together
they combine to prevent her doing such a foolish thing.
Stewart, Browning and Loyd are the three showgirls Evans
brings West with her.

d John English *p* Donald H. Brown *s* Jack Townley, John
K. Butler *c* William Bradford *lp* Roy Rogers, George
Hayes, Dale Evans, Peggy Stewart, Beverly Loyd, Jill
Browning, Trigger

Wanderer of the Wasteland (RKO) b/w 67 min
Bearing no relation to either Zane Grey's original novel or to
earlier films of the same title, *Wanderer of the Wasteland*
features Warren in his debut as the unluckiest ever of series
heroes. He is bested in his every encounter with the villains,
only surviving courtesy of Martin and Chips Rafferty. Long
provides the romantic interest. Co-director Grissell had
served a lengthy apprenticeship as an editor of series
Westerns.

d Edward Killy, Wallace Grissell *p* Herman Schlom
s Norman Houston *c* Harry Wild *lp* James Warren,
Audrey Long, Richard Martin, Robert Barrat, Harry Woods,
Jason Robards Snr

West of the Pecos (RKO) b/w 66 min
A remake of the 1934 film with Richard Dix, this was one of
RKO's better Zane Grey outings. Mitchum, who received his
best reviews hitherto, is the happy-go-lucky cowpoke for
whom debutante Hale falls. A slight complication has her
disguised as a boy for most of the picture. Woods is the outlaw
Mitchum and his side-kick, Martin, tangle with.

d Edward Killy *p* Herman Schlom *s* Norman Houston
c Harry Wild *lp* Robert Mitchum, Barbara Hale, Richard
Martin, Thurston Hall, Harry Woods, Bill Williams

1946

Abilene Town (UA) b/w 89 min
Clearly constructed in the mould of **Dodge City** (1939), this is
an entertaining account of the early days of the town at the
end of the Chisholm Trail. Against a background of cattlemen
versus homesteaders, Shumate's tight script tells the story of
Scott's cleaning-up of Abilene, routing out the corrupt
cattlemen and calming down the homesteaders led by a
hot-tempered Bridges. An unusual twist has Scott at the end
forsaking the 'nice' girl, Fleming, for dance-hall queen
Dvorak. Buchanan provides one of his droll cameos as the
sheriff who'd rather drink than fight.

Above: *Duncan
Renaldo serenading
Armida in* South of the
Rio Grande.

*Roy Rogers, fists flying,
in* Utah.

Robert Mitchum in
West of the Pecos, *the
film which drew
Mitchum his best
reviews so far.*

Lloyd Bridges, as the romantic youngster, declares his love for Rhonda Fleming in Abilene Town.

Far right: Brian Donlevy (left) and Dana Andrews, the friendly rivals for the affections of Susan Hayward, in Canyon Passage.

Randolph Scott confronted by a table full of gunmen, Gabby Hayes, William Moss, James Warren, Phil Warren and Steve Brodie (left to right) in Badman's Territory.

d Edwin L. Marin *p* Jules Levey *s* Harold Shumate
c Archie Stout *lp* Randolph Scott, Ann Dvorak, Lloyd Bridges, Rhonda Fleming, Edgar Buchanan, Howard Freeman

Bad Bascomb (MGM) b/w 112 min
The highlight of this sentimental Western (about a bankrobber (Beery) who, when hiding out in a Mormon wagon train, is charmed by O'Brien's spunky moppet) is O'Brien helping fend off an Indian attack with a pea shooter! Beery is oafishly charming, Main suitably gruff as O'Brien's grandmother and Naish momentarily threatening as Beery's suave and unrepentant ex-partner who fails to persuade him to steal the Mormons' gold.

d S. Sylvan Simon *p* Orville O. Dull *s* William Lipman, Grant Garrett *c* Charles Schoenbaum *lp* Wallace Beery, Margaret O'Brien, Marjorie Main, J. Carrol Naish, Marshall Thompson, Russell Simpson

Badman's Territory (RKO) b/w 97 min
In the early forties Universal began grouping numbers of monsters in individual horror films to stimulate declining attendances. The move was successful. In a similar attempt to enliven their B Westerns, in *Badman's Territory* RKO set Scott against the James Gang, the Daltons, Sam Bass and Belle Starr as he helps bring the Oklahoma Territory into the Union. The number of featured parts necessarily make for an episodic structure but Whelan's spirited direction lifts the material well above the rut of the routine.

d Tim Whelan *p* Nat Holt *s* Jack Natteford, Luci Ward, Clarence Upson Young, Bess Taffel *c* Robert De Grasse
lp Randolph Scott, Ann Richards, George 'Gabby' Hayes, Chief Thundercloud, Tom Tyler, Steve Brodie

California (PAR) 99 min
Milland is the soldier of fortune, Stanwyck the gambler and Coulouris the former slave trader attempting to turn California into an independent empire who is foiled by Fitzgerald's blarney and Milland's guns. The story is hackneyed and the script slow moving but Farrow's enthusiatic direction brings the best out of his cast, especially Milland with whom he worked quite frequently.

d John Farrow *p* Seton I. Miller *s* Frank Butler, Theodore Strauss *c* Ray Rennahan *lp* Ray Milland, Barbara Stanwyck, Barry Fitzgerald, George Coulouris, Anthony Quinn

Canyon Passage (U) 99(92) min
Tourneur's reputation is largely based on his horror films, however his Westerns, of which this is his first, are of considerable interest. Set in the Oregon Territory in 1854, it features Andrews as the scout turned general-store owner who has to fully settle down and Donlevy as an equally unsettled banker – he uses his depositors' money to fund his poker playing – in friendly rivalry for Hayward. Bond is the brutish rather than menacing outlaw and Carmichael the wandering minstrel and friend of all. He sings 'Ole Buttermilk Sky'. The limpid colour photography of Cronjager and the gentle pace of the film mirror the sense of drifting that lies at the heart of this unusual Western.

d Jacques Tourneur   *p* Walter Wanger   *s* Ernest Pascal
c Edward Cronjager   *lp* Dana Andrews, Brian Donlevy,
Susan Hayward, Hoagy Carmichael, Ward Bond, Andy
Devine

The Caravan Trail   (PRC)   57 min
The third of Dean's short-lived series of musical Westerns,
this is enlivened by the return of LaRue who had made his
debut as a character in the first of the series, **Song of Old
Wyoming** (1945). Dean takes the job of marshal with the idea
of revenging the murder of a friend and restoring to
homesteaders land stolen from them by Taylor and King.
LaRue, now firmly on the side of law and order, gives solid
support.

d/p Robert Emmett (Tansey)   *s* Frances Kavanaugh
c Marcel LePicard   *lp* Eddie Dean, Emmett Lynn, Al
LaRue, Jean Carlin, Charles King, Forrest Taylor

Colorado Serenade   (PRC)   70 min
An indifferent series Western in which Ates replaces Emmett
Lynn as singing cowboy Dean's stuttering side-kick and
Sharpe takes over the role vacated by Al LaRue. Here he's an
undercover government agent and his athleticism makes
Dean, the film's official star, look pallid by comparison.
Shackelford's cinematography is far superior to that of Marcel
LePicard, the usual cameraman of the series. King turns in a
neat comic performance as a deputy.

d/p Robert Emmett (Tansey)   *s* Frances Kavanaugh
c Robert Shakelford   *lp* Eddie Dean, Roscoe Ates, Charles
King, Mary Kenyon, Forrest Taylor, David Sharpe

Drifting Along   (MON)   b/w   60 min
An oddity in Brown's series Westerns. It opens with him
crooning the title song (dubbed, of course) under the credits
and later in the picture he watches Ballew serenading heroine,
Carver. The experiment of setting Brown against a musical
context was continued for one more film, *Under Nevada Skies*
(1946) and then scrapped. Buffington's plot is the hackneyed
one of cattle rustlers trying to bankrupt Carver so they can
take over her ranch.

d Derwin Abrahams   *p* Scott R. Dunlap   *s* Adele
Buffington   *c* Harry Neumann   *lp* Johnny Mack Brown,
Lynne Carver, Raymond Hatton, Smith Ballew, Douglas
Fowley, Milburn Morante

Duel in the Sun
(SELZNICK RELEASING ORGANIZATION)   138 min
Affectionately known as 'Lust in the Dust' nowadays but
greeted as a moral outrage at the time, *Duel in the Sun* is the
most commercially successful Western ever made. Just as
Gone With the Wind (1939) was to be seen as a hymn of praise

to Selznick's first wife, Irene, so *Duel in the Sun* is an
impassioned, ambiguous and extravagant deification of his
second wife, Jones. Significantly, though Niven Busch's
tempestuous novel ended happily, Selznick's script has
half-caste Jones and Peck dying in each other's arms after
shooting each other to death in one of Hollywood's most
excessive sequences ever.

The dynastic plot features Peck and Cotten as Cain and
Abel brothers fighting over Jones and against their crippled
father, Barrymore, who sees his million-acre private empire of
a ranch threatened by the coming of the railroad. But it is
Jones' demented performance as the girl torn between good
and evil and succumbing to her passions, Vidor's sultry
direction and Selznick's manic energy (which kept the project
alive when several times it seemed to be on the point of
extinction) that are the keys to the film's success.

Vidor only directed a little over half of the actual footage
used, finally quitting over Selznick's continual demand of
re-takes to further eroticize Jones. Directors as diverse as
William Dieterle, William Cameron Menzies, Joseph Von
Sternberg (as lighting consultant for Jones' scenes) and
Selznick himself worked on the film; and second unit
directors, B. Reeves Easton and Otto Brower, were in charge
of several major scenes. Nonetheless, the film is recognizable
as a Vidor film: if the vision is Selznick's it is Vidor who
articulates the theme of unreconciled passions to such
powerful effect.

d King Vidor   *p/co-s* David O. Selznick   *co-s* Oliver H.P.
Garrett   *c* Lee Garmes, Hal Rossen, Ray Rennahan
lp Jennifer Jones, Gregory Peck, Joseph Cotten, Lionel
Barrymore, Lillian Gish, Walter Huston

The Harvey Girls   (MGM)   101 min
One of the numerous 'How the West Was Civilized' movies,
this lightweight musical features Garland, Lansbury and
Charisse, among others, as the waitresses of Fred Harvey's
railway station restaurants who follow the railway West. The
slim story provides a convenient hook for a series of
semi-lavish MGM production numbers in which the Wild West
becomes little but a painted backcloth to an MGM sound stage.

*Johnny Mack Brown
(right) manhandles
Douglas Fowley under
the watchful gaze of
Lynne Carver in
Drifting Along.*

*Walter Huston tries to
preach the devil out of
Jennifer Jones with
assistance from Lillian
Gish in David O.
Selznick's epic* Duel in
the Sun.

Henry Fonda as the bringer of civilization to the frontier in John Ford's My Darling Clementine.

John Hodiak (left) and Angela Lansbury (right) look on as Judy Garland tries her hand as a gunslinger in The Harvey Girls.

Crabbe, a regular serial hero, never graduated to major roles despite promising work in Paramount's Zane Grey series, while St John, a distant relative of Fatty Arbuckle and like him a silent comic, had the distinction of being the only comic side-kick to play the same role, Fuzzy Q. Jones, in two concurrent series, the Lone Rider with George Houston and Billy the Kid with Crabbe. This outing, by no means one of the best in the series, sees Crabbe and St John foiling a plot by Brent to substitute a bad assay report on a mine for the real one and so buy the mine for a pittance.

d Sam Newfield *p* Sigmund Neufeld *s* Elmer Clifton
c Jack Greenhalgh *lp* Buster Crabbe, Al St John, Mady Lawrence, Ray Brent, Harry Hall, Steve Darrell

The Man from Rainbow Valley (REP) 56 min
A fine entry in Hale's short-lived series of Magnacolor (later Trucolor) Westerns for Republic, directed, like the first in the series, *Home on the Range* (1946), by Springsteen. Burbridge's Saturday-matinee-oriented script has Hale hunting down a wild rodeo horse which has been stolen from a strip cartoonist's ranch. The horse is needed to help publicize the cartoon for which he's the model. Springsteen, finding his feet as a Western director, directs efficiently and energetically.

d Robert Springsteen *p* Louis Gray *s* Betty Burbridge
c Bud Thackery *lp* Monte Hale, Adrian Booth, Jo Ann Marlowe, Emmett Lynn, Tom London, Ferris Taylor

My Darling Clementine (FOX) b/w 96 min
Like many Hollywood directors Ford's claims for his films are very modest. For him the key thing about *My Darling Clementine* is its authenticity: 'I knew Wyatt Earp ... and he told me about the fight at the O.K. Corral. So in *My Darling Clementine* we did it exactly the way it had been.' For viewers, however, the film's greatness (and enjoyability) rests not in the accuracy of the final shoot-out but in the orchestrated series of incidents – the drunken Shakesperian actor, Earp's visit to the barber, the dance in the unfinished church, etc – which give added significance to the final confrontation.

The film wholeheartedly celebrates the coming of law and order and civilization to the West in the form of Fonda's Earp, the cowboy who gives up his nomadic existence and notions of personal vengeance to rid Tombstone of the anarchic Clantons. As such it is best seen alongside **The Man Who Shot Liberty Valance** (1962) in which Ford reflects

Nonetheless, the film was surprisingly successful, earning some $4.5 million at the box office and winning Harry Warren and Johnny Mercer an Oscar for the best original song of 1946 with 'On the Atchison, Topeka and the Santa Fé'.

d George Sidney *p* Arthur Freed *s* Edmund Beloin, Nathaniel Curtis *c* George Folsey *lp* Judy Garland, Ray Bolger, John Hodiak, Preston Foster, Angela Lansbury, Cyd Charisse

In Old Sacramento *aka* Flame of Sacramento
(REP) b/w 89 min
Kane's third remake of his own short story, 'Diamond Carlisle' and the first starring role for Elliott who dropped the soubriquet 'Wild Bill' as a mark of his graduating to A pictures. Elliott is Spanish Jack, a masked bandit with a way with the ladies who finally dies in the arms of songstress Moore. He made the change from series to A grade productions effortlessly but refused to move outside of the genre. Kane's direction is action-packed, as ever.

d/p Joseph Kane *s* Frances Hyland *c* Jack Marta
lp Bill Elliott, Constance Moore, Hank Daniels, Eugene Pallette, Jack LaRue, Hal Taliaferro (Wally Wales)

Lightning Raiders (PRC) b/w 61 min
One of the last of the 36 Crabbe-St John Westerns made by PRC between 1941 and 1946. All were directed by Newfield who was so prolific a director that between 1941 and 1943 he used the pseudonyms of Peter Stewart and Sherman Scott for his PRC work.

more sombrely on the same subject. For its treatment of Wyatt Earp it is interesting to compare it to Allan Dwan's similar but far less reflective **Frontier Marshal** (1939) and Edward L. Cahn's bleak **Law and Order** (1932).

The film was Ford's last as a contract director for Fox, the company he'd worked for since 1921.

d John Ford *p/co-s* Samuel G. Engel *co-s* Winston Miller
c Joseph P. MacDonald *lp* Henry Fonda, Linda Darnell, Victor Mature, Walter Brennan, Tim Holt, Ward Bond, Alan Mowbray

My Pal Trigger (REP) b/w 79 min
Rogers' own favourite amongst his movies, this is his most successful and, by general agreement, one of his very best. Remarkably similar in plot to **The Strawberry Roan** (1948), primarily because Autry 'borrowed' the plot of the Rogers film to spite Republic which he'd just quit for Columbia, the film features Rogers trying to mate his mare with Hayes' stallion and being accused of killing the stallion when Holt, who's trying to do the same thing, accidentally kills the horse. While Rogers is in jail the mare's foal grows into Trigger who helps Rogers clear his name and save Hayes' ranch when Rogers is finally released. Lyrically directed by McDonald with unusual and atmospheric camera angles supplied by Bradford, the series' regular cameraman, and well acted by the principals – unlike Autry, Rogers could act – the film has an innocence that remains charming to the present day.

d Frank McDonald *p* Armand Schaefer *s* Jack Townley, John K. Butler *c* William Bradford *lp* Roy Rogers, George Hayes, Dale Evans, Jack Holt, LeRoy Mason, Roy Barcroft, Trigger

Out California Way (REP) 67 min
A bizarrely entertaining movie, this was the third of Hale's series Westerns for Republic. Set in a mythical movie studio, Burbridge's script features Hale and Dehner as the quarrelling leading actors. A sub-plot has Blake (lately Little Beaver in the Red Ryder series who was to return in triumph to the Western in the title role of **Tell Them Willie Boy Is Here**, 1969), trying to get a part for his educated horse, Pardner, in an upcoming Western. Wittily directed by Selander and featuring walk-on cameos from Roy Rogers, Trigger, Don Barry, Allen Lane and Dale Evans to give a touch of realism to its movie background, it is one of Hale's best Westerns. The only trouble is the awful Trucolor process which, like PRC's Cinecolor is gaudy and cheap and has a tendency to over emphasize orange and green.

d Lesley Selander *p* Louis Gray *s* Betty Burbridge
c Bud Thackery *lp* Monte Hale, John Dehner, Bobby Blake, Adrian Booth, Tom London, Edward Keane

Andy Clyde, in his best role ever, Gail Patrick, Vera Ralston and Bill Elliott in The Plainsman and the Lady.

The Plainsman and the Lady (REP) b/w 87 min
In Old Sacramento (1946), Elliott's first A production for Republic, did well so the company put him in another prestige Western with Kane once more in control. A handsomely-mounted production, it features Elliott as the wealthy cattleman determined to set up a Pony Express business and Schildkraut as the stagecoach owner determined to stop him. Barry, like Elliott a series regular, gives a nice performance as the all-in-black gunman Elliott has to go up against while Ralston, the wife of Republic's boss Herbert J. Yates, is better than usual as the heroine. Similarly Clyde, freed from his usual role as William Boyd's mindless side-kick, takes the opportunity to turn in a good performance as Elliott's friend. With Kane's camera as mobile as ever, the result is a fluffy outdoor spectacle with little rhyme or reason but nonetheless hugely entertaining for what it is.

d/p Joseph Kane *s* Richard Wormser *c* Reggie Lanning
lp William Elliott, Vera Ralston, Joseph Schildkraut, Donald Barry, Andy Clyde, Gail Patrick

Renegades (COL) 88 min
Renegades' unusual plotline has Keyes briefly foresake medico Parker for the excitement of life with Parks, a member of an outlaw family headed by Buchanan that includes Bannon and Tucker amongst its members. Carefully photographed in colour, then still an unusual feature of B Westerns, by Snyder and energetically directed by Sherman, the film, though closer to series Westerns in budgetary terms than it might look is eons away from them in outlook as is clear from Columbia's ad campaign: 'The red-blooded story of a red haired girl'.

d George Sherman *p* Michel Kraike *s* Melvin Levy, Francis Edward Faragoh *c* William Snyder *lp* Evelyn Keyes, Willard Parker, Larry Parks, Edgar Buchanan, Jim Bannon, Forrest Tucker

Roll on Texas Moon (REP) b/w 67 min
The first of the 27 Rogers films to be directed by Witney, better known for his serial work with John English (who directed a few Rogers outing himself, but made far more Gene Autry Westerns). Witney, once dubbed the Sam Peckinpah of

Roy Rogers in My Pal Trigger, *his personal favourite of all his movies.*

the thirties and forties for the violence of his movies, quickly changed the direction of Rogers' movies, emphasizing action and stunts at the expense of music and gaudy costumes and vastly quickening the pace of the films. This, however, like his first few films, is routine – Witney had only directed a few features before and clearly needed practice. Rogers is the troubleshooter who puts a stop to a cattlemen-versus-sheepmen range war.

d William Witney *p* Edward J. White *s* Paul Gangelin, Mauri Grashin *c* William Bradford *lp* Roy Rogers, George Hayes, Dale Evans, Dennis Hoey, Bob Nolan and the Sons of the Pioneers, Trigger

Romance of the West (PRC) 58 min

The second of Dean's short-lived PRC series that is best remembered for giving birth to the Lash LaRue character. LaRue isn't in this film and it's the worse for it. Dean, though he could sing, is wooden in front of the camera and Tansey (using his Emmett pseudonym) and writer Kavanaugh seem determined to cut as many corners as possible in order to save the money spent on using colour. The plot features Dean as an Indian scout keeping the peace on the range and Taylor as the baddie trying to ferment an Indian war so as to grab land rich in silver for himself.

d/p Robert Emmett (Tansey) *s* Frances Kavanaugh *c* Marcel LePicard *lp* Eddie Dean, Joan Barton, Emmett Lynn, Forrest Taylor, Chief Thundercloud, Stanley Price

Sioux City Sue (REP) b/w 69 min

Cooper's almost surreal plot has Roberts stumble on Autry and persuade him to go to Hollywood in search of fame. This he does, only to discover that what Hollywood wants of him is to provide the voice for an animated donkey! He quits of course when he discovers the trick only to return as the star of *Sioux City Sue* when the producers hear him sing. In between doing all this, Autry has time to foil outlaws who blow up a dam as part of a rustling scheme. The movie was Autry's first after the Second World War.

d Frank McDonald *p* Armand Schaefer *s* Olive Cooper *c* Reggie Lanning *lp* Gene Autry, Lynne Roberts, Sterling Holloway, Richard Lane, LeRoy Mason, Tris Coffin

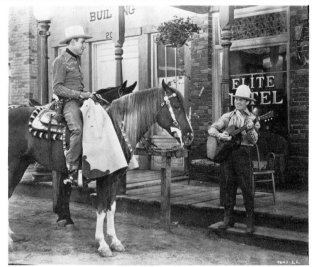

Sunset Pass (RKO) b/w 59 min

A remake of Henry Hathaway's 1933 film, this version of the Zane Grey story features Warren as the railway police officer on the trail of robbers. Simply scripted and efficiently directed it lacks only a charismatic pair of leads to remove it from the also-ran category.

d William Berke *p* Herman Schlom *s* Norman Huston *c* Frank Redman *lp* James Warren, Nan Leslie, Jane Greer, Harry Woods, Steve Brodie, John Laurenz

Terrors on Horseback (PRC) b/w 55 min

One of the last of the 36-strong Western series Crabbe and St John made for PRC together and one of their better efforts. Milton's screenplay opens promisingly with the duo discovering a stagecoach full of corpses and eventually discovering why the passengers were massacred. Add to that the complete absence of any love interest, Greenhalgh's exciting photography, the horse chases and some fine fistfights and the result is a surprisingly successful series outing.

d Sam Newfield *p* Sigmund Neufeld *s* George Milton *c* Jack Greenhalgh *lp* Buster Crabbe, Al St John, Henry Hall, Kermit Maynard, Karl Hackett, George Chesebro

The Virginian (PAR) 90 min

A routine remake of Victor Fleming's much over-praised 1929 movie. McCrea is the Virginian, Tufts the friend he brings to justice and Donlevy the evil Trampas who makes a rustler out of Tufts. McCrea is more believable than Gary Cooper in the role of Owen Wister's stoic cowboy, but in 1946, the plotline was too hackneyed and thin to impress.

The appeal of the title *The Virginian* was such, however, that in 1962 a teleseries was created around the character with James Drury in the title role and Doug McClure as Trampas, now a friend of the Virginian. The series ran until 1970.

d Stuart Gilmore *p* Paul Jones *s* Frances Goodrich, Albert Hackett *c* Harry Hallenberger *lp* Joel McCrea, Brian Donlevy, Sonny Tufts, Barbara Britton, Al Bridge, Martin Garralaga

West of the Alamo (MON) b/w 58 min
One of the undistinguished series of musical Westerns starring Wakely, a one-time support to both Don 'Red' Barry and Charles Starrett. Wakely, who has little charisma, is out of place in the hero's role. Here, with White as comic support, he exposes bank president Ingram as the man behind a prairie crime-wave and so clears Clive who is suspected of the bank robberies.

d/p Oliver Drake *s* Louise Rousseau *c* Harry Neumann
lp Jimmy Wakely, Lee White, Ray Whitley, Jack Ingram, Iris Clive, Budd Buster

Wild West (PRC) 73 min
The last of Dean's series Westerns for PRC to be made in Cinecolor (the company's cheap and gaudy version of Technicolor), *Wild West* sees LaRue return to the series to handle the more athletic bits of action. He, Dean and comic support Ates are the trio of Texas Rangers who assist in the laying of telegraph lines. In one of the oddest moves ever, in 1948 Tansey recut the film to lose some 15 minutes and re-issued it as *Prairie Outlaw* in black and white to better trade reviews than this received.

d/p Robert Emmett (Tansey) *s* Frances Kavanaugh *c* Fred Jackman Jnr *lp* Eddie Dean, Roscoe Ates, Al LaRue, Robert Henry, Sarah Padden, Warner Richmond

Lash LaRue (centre), once tagged the poor man's Bogart, and Eddie Dean, the nominal star of Wild West.

Along the Oregon Trail (REP) b/w 64 min
Hale is the protégé of Kit Carson who guides a party of explorers, who are mapping out the Oregon Trail, into the interior. He comes across Moore (later to be famous as television's Lone Ranger) planning a private empire in the West and fermenting Indian troubles to keep pioneers put. An amiable enough series entry.

Below: Harry Carey (left), John Ford's oldest collaborator, with John Wayne, his most regular, and Gail Russell in the leisurely Angel and the Badman.

A wounded John Carroll assisted by Catherine McLeod in the fascinating The Fabulous Texan.

Jane Wyman (centre) and Dennis Morgan in Cheyenne.

d R.G. Springsteen *p* Melville Tucker *s* Earle Snell
c Alfred S. Keller *lp* Monte Hale, Adrian Booth, Max
Terhune, Clayton Moore, Roy Barcroft, LeRoy Mason

Angel and the Badman (REP) b/w 100 min

Badly received at the time, this genteel, leisurely Western has
aged far better than many of it's action-packed contempor-
aries. Its plot, with Wayne as the outlaw who puts up his guns
when he falls in love with the daughter (Russell) of a Quaker
family who give him refuge, is reminiscent of several of the
silent Westerns made by John Ford and Harry Carey, present
here as the kindly marshal who befriends Wayne. It is the first
film produced by Wayne, then king of the Republic lot, and
the only one directed by Grant who as Wayne's regular
rewrite man was presumably unable to resist the star's
tendency to speechify when producing (or directing) himself.

d/s James Edward Grant *p* John Wayne *c* Archie Stout
lp John Wayne, Gail Russell, Harry Carey, Bruce Cabot,
Irene Rich, Paul Hurst

Belle Starr's Daughter
(ALSON PRODUCTIONS/FOX) b/w 85 min

A routine sequel to **Belle Starr** (1941) with Roman in the title
role. Burnett's screenplay features Montgomery as the
marshal Roman mistakenly believes killed her famous outlaw
mother. Cameron is the outlaw leader who briefly persuades
her to join his gang before Montgomery shows her the error of
her ways. Selander's direction is robust.

d Lesley Selander *p* Edward L. Alperson *s* W.R. Burnett
c William Sickner *lp* George Montgomery, Rod Cameron,
Ruth Roman, Wallace Ford, Charles Kemper, William
Phipps

Bells of San Angelo (REP) 78 min

This was the first Rogers film to be scripted by Nibley
(husband of serial-queen Linda Sterling) and the first of the
'violent' Rogers films in which bloody noses were the least one
expected from a fistfight. Attacked at the time by many for
this, the film marks a welcome change of direction for Rogers.
Witney's strong camera angles and fast pacing give the action
a pleasing toughness while Rogers, to everyone's surprise,
proves to be adept with his fists. Here he's a border
investigator who, with help from Western novelist Evans (in
her last film with Rogers before their marriage), rounds up a
group of smugglers. McGuire is the villain who, with

assistance from Sharpe and others, at one point beats Rogers
senseless, as if to emphasize just how far Witney and Nibley
were willing to take the 'new' Rogers. Devine, in his first film
with Rogers, provides the comedy.

d William Witney *p* Edward J. White *s* Sloan Nibley
c Jack Marta *lp* Roy Rogers, Dale Evans, Andy Devine,
John McGuire, Olaf Hytten, David Sharpe, Trigger

Bowery Buckaroos (MON) b/w 66 min

This Western satire sees the Bowery Boys transplanted from
the sidewalks of New York to the open range of the West.
One of the better entries in their long running series of 48
films over two decades that began with *Dead End* (1937), it
pokes fun at Western stereotypes in the marvellously crude
manner that typifies their humour – 'I'm going out to
prosecute for gold'. The slim plot features the boys clearing
Gorcey of a murder charge and retrieving Briggs' goldmine
after Norman has swindled her out of it.

d William Beaudine *p* Jan Grippo *s* Tim Ryan, Edmond
Seward *c* Marcel LePicard *lp* Leo Gorcey, Huntz Hall,
Billy Jordan, Julie Briggs, Bernard Gorcey, Jack Norman
(Norman Willis)

Buffalo Bill Rides Again (JACK SCHWARZ) b/w 70 min

A lightweight B Western directed with an unsure touch by
Ray. Sarecky and Gilbert's screenplay resurrects the 'who's
been fermenting Indian trouble ?' question and sends Arlen's
Buffalo Bill into the wilds to discover a syndicate using the
threat of an Indian War to drive ranchers off their oil-rich
lands. Holt offers pleasant support.

d Bernard B. Ray *p* Jack Schwarz *s* Barney Sarecky, Fran
Gilbert *c* Robert Cline *lp* Richard Arlen, Jennifer Holt,
Lee Shumway, Edmund Cobb, Ted Adams, Edward Cassidy

Cheyenne (WB) b/w 100 min

The least of Walsh's many Westerns. Bennett is the doggerel-
spouting outlaw leader, with a penchant for strong boxes,
known as 'The Poet'. Wyman is his unlikely wife and
Morgan, the gambler turned lawman who joins his gang to
stop him and ends up stealing his wife. Despite the strong
supporting cast of Warner's regulars, which includes Ken-

nedy as the Sundance Kid and the likes of Bob Steele and Tom Tyler, and Hickox's classic cinematography the film is little more than routine, its sensibilities being too literary for the robust Walsh.

Stock shots from it would later re-appear in the director's own **Colorado Territory** (1949).

d Raoul Walsh   *p* Robert Buckner   *s* Alan LeMay, Thames Williamson   *c* Sid Hickox   *lp* Dennis Morgan, Jane Wyman, Bruce Bennett, Alan Hale, Arthur Kennedy

Cheyenne Takes Over   (PRC)   b/w   58 min
For a change, this Lash LaRue outing has a mystery- rather than action-based plot. Accordingly, LaRue's bullwhip remains sheathed (as it were) and his prowess as a sleuth is called upon to expose the fact that Chesebro isn't who he claims to be, but a murderer impersonating his victim. Matters are made much easier by having Gates turn up as an eyewitness to the act. This is a smooth, but rather silly outing.

d Ray Taylor   *p* Jerry Thomas   *s* Arthur E. Orloff
c Ernest Miller   *lp* Lash LaRue, Al St John, Nancy Gates, George Chesebro, Lee Morgan, John Merton

The Fabulous Texan   (REP)   b/w   95 min
An opulent-looking film by Republic's standards, this is one of Elliott's series of A features, all Westerns, for the studio. Though he never quite escaped the tag of being a star of B and series Westerns and was undoubtedly less talented than Randolph Scott or Joel McCrea, the actors he is usually compared with, he brought an element of introspection to his Republic A features that was impressive. The film also has the advantage of an intriguing plot by Hazard and McCoy. Elliott and Carroll are Confederate officers who, on their return to Texas after the Civil War, find it transformed into a despotic state, in short into the kind of police state the American Right imagined Eastern European states to be, ruled by Dekker.

Dekker's 'police' kill Elliott's father and Elliott becomes a freedom fighter, leading a crusade against Dekker while Carroll turns bank robber before coming to the assistance of Elliott, by now a Federal Marshal, and finally dying to save him. It's hard to overemphasize the parallels between the immediate post-war situation and the film's plot but the result is a fascinating, if erratic, film.

Director Ludwig also made the equally hysterical *Big Jim McLain* (1952), in which John Wayne, as a special agent for the House Un-American Activities Committee, goes commie hunting in Hawaii.

d Edward Ludwig   *p* Edmund Grainger   *s* Lawrence Hazard, Horace McCoy   *c* Reggie Lanning   *lp* William (Bill) Elliott, John Carroll, Albert Dekker, Catherine McLeod, Andy Devine, Jim Davis

The Gunfighters   (COL)   87 min
It was the success of this film that led producer Brown and Scott to form a production company of their own to make a series of medium-budget Westerns that in the mid-fifties blossomed when director Budd Boetticher joined the team and they began making films of the quality of **The Tall T** (1957) and **Ride Lonesome** (1959). Ironically, *The Gunfighters* itself is a decidedly routine affair. Scott is the tight-lipped hero who, though he's foresworn the six gun, takes down his holster just one more time when he finds his friend murdered. Withers is the crooked deputy, Cabot the evil cattle baron Scott must take on and Hart and Britton the cattle baron's daughters (good and bad respectively) he must choose between.

d George Waggner   *p* Harry Joe Brown   *s* Alan LeMay
c Fred Jackman Jnr   *lp* Randolph Scott, Barbara Britton, Grant Withers, Dorothy Hart, Bruce Cabot, Forrest Tucker

Hoppy's Holiday
(HOPALONG CASSIDY PRODUCTIONS)   b/w   60 min
This is one of the twelve Hopalong Cassidy films made by Boyd's own production company after he bought the rights when Harry Sherman stopped the series in 1944. Compared to the earlier films it's routine, lacking the production values Sherman insisted on when he was in control. The plot contrasts the new and old West, a favourite storyline of series Westerns, with horseless carriages and bank robbers being defeated by the Bar 20 cowboys, thus demonstrating the physical and moral superiority of the Old West.

Randolph Scott with his co-stars of The Gunfighters, *Barbara Britton (left) and Dorothy Hart.*

Gilbert Roland (left) in his last outing as the Cisco Kid, King of the Bandits.

Gene Autry with Jean Heather in The Last Round-up, *Autry's first picture for Columbia.*

William Boyd, now producer as well as star of the Hopalong Cassidy series, gives orders to Andy Clyde and Rand Brooks while Dorinda Clifton (left) and Mary Newton look on in The Marauders.

output. Indeed the film is probably the perfect example of what critic Jon Tuska has called 'The Autry Phantasy'. Set in 1947, the film features Autry trying to re-locate a tribe of Indians so an aqueduct can be built on their (barren) land, dealing with a minor Indian uprising and a cattle stampede and making a television broadcast. Heather is the heroine and Morgan the heavy. Fittingly, for a man for whom time spent in front of the camera was time spent away from the phone and business deals, Autry spends most of the picture negotiating between various parties. Most of the action is courtesy of library footage from **Arizona** (1940).

d John English *p* Armand Schaefer *s* Jack Townley, Earle Snell *c* William Bradford *lp* Gene Autry, Jean Heather, Ralph Morgan, Carol Thurston, Mark Daniels, Bobby Blake, Champion

Law of the Lash (PRC) b/w 53 min
This is one of the better Lash LaRue entries. Nolte's screenplay has a few psychological twists to it that come as a surprise in a series Western. Lash is the undercover marshal who unites with prospector St John to rid a town of a bunch of outlaws. Although Lash's bullwhip never found favour with trade reviewers – 'strictly for the minor kid trade', ran one review – he was a firm favourite with the Saturday matinee audience.

d Ray Taylor *p* Jerry Thomas *s* William L. Nolte *c* Robert Cline *lp* Lash LaRue, Al St John, Mary Scott, Charles King, Slim Whitaker, Lee Roberts

The Lone Hand Texan *aka* The Cheat
(COL) b/w 54 min
A routine entry from Starrett as the Durango Kid, in which he's confronted with a female villain, Newton, out to steal oil-rich land. Fred Sears, who was to become a regular B director in the fifties (when he would add F as a middle initial in a bid for extra distinction) has a featured part.

d Ray Nazarro *p* Colbert Clark *s* Ed Earl Repp *c* George F. Kelley *lp* Charles Starrett, Smiley Burnette, Mary Newton, George Russell, George Chesebro, Robert Stevens

The Marauders
(HOPALONG CASSIDY PRODUCTIONS) b/w 63 min
This is a high point in the generally inferior Hopalong Cassidy Westerns that were produced by Boyd's own production company after he'd bought the rights from Harry Sherman. Belden's screenplay, which features Boyd doing as much sleuthing as fistfighting, has Hoppy stopping a band of outlaws, responsible for a string of murders, from the ultimate crime of tearing down a church in a ghost town in their search for oil. Wolfe makes a nice sanctimonious heavy masquerading as a deacon and Archainbaud directs efficiently.

d George Archainbaud *p* Lewis J. Rachmil *s* J. Benton Cheney, Bennett Cohen, Ande Lamb *c* Mack Stengler *lp* William Boyd, Andy Clyde, Rand Brooks, Mary Ware, Jeff Corey, Andrew Tombes

King of the Bandits (MON) b/w 66 min
The last of Roland's outings as the Cisco Kid and one of the most effusive – he was credited with 'additional dialogue'. He is in search of Warde who's pulling off stagecoach robberies in his name. Greene provides the romantic interest and Martin makes a welcome return as Pancho.

d Christy Cabanne *p* Jeffrey Bernerd *s* Bennett Cohen *c* William Sickner *lp* Gilbert Roland, Angela Greene, Chris-Pin Martin, Anthony Warde, Laura Treadwell, Boyd Irwin

The Last Days of Boot Hill (COL) b/w 56 min
With only 15 minutes of new footage and a running time of some 56 minutes, *The Last Days of Boot Hill* is a production triumph for Clark and writer Hall, who created a flashback story to explain the vast amounts of old footage, mostly from *Both Barrels Blazin'* (1945). The plot has Starrett searching for loot buried by Bridge and adopting his Durango persona to sort out baddie Free. Virtually all Starrett's subsequent outings would include old footage, but never so extensively.

d Ray Nazarro *p* Colbert Clark *s* Norman S. Hall *c* George F. Kelly *lp* Charles Starrett, Smiley Burnette, Virginia Hunter, Bill Free, Alan Bridge, Bob Wilke

The Last Round-up
(GENE AUTRY PRODUCTIONS/COL) b/w 76 min
This, Autry's first for Columbia, the studio he joined after quitting Republic over money matters, was the star's own favourite amongst his pictures. Produced by Autry's own production company, many of whose employees, like director English, producer Schaefer and cameraman Bradford, as well as several of the technical staff, Autry had brought with him from Republic, the film is in keeping with his Republic

d George Archainbaud   *p* Lewis J. Rachmil   *s* Charles Belden   *c* Mack Stengler   *lp* William Boyd, Andy Clyde, Rand Brooks, Ian Wolfe, Harry Cording, Earle Hodgins

The Marshal of Cripple Creek (REP) b/w 58 min

This was the last of Lane's outings as Red Ryder and the last Republic outing for the character. Efficiently, if anonymously, directed by Springsteen, its slim budget and meagre production values, compared to earlier entries in the series, signalled the end. Snell's tired screenplay features Lane unmasking the outlaw genius regularly stealing gold shipments from a Colorado mining town. Only Bardette as a reformed outlaw makes much of his part.

d R.G. Springsteen   *p* Sidney Picker   *s* Earle Snell
c William Bradford   *lp* Allan Lane, Bobby Blake, Martha Wentworth, Trevor Bardette, Roy Barcroft, Tom London

Michigan Kid (U) 69 min

One of Hall's few Westerns, this Cinecolor outing is much helped by cameraman Miller's careful exclusion of pure reds and greens from the prairie. McLaglen is the surprisingly meek-mannered outlaw, Johnson the athletic damsel-in-distress and Devine, for once cast against type, is the mean outlaw. The primitive screenplay has Hall fall foul of McLaglen when he foils his attempted stage robbery and then having to catch him before McLaglen catches him.

d Ray Taylor   *p* Howard Welsch   *s* Roy Chanslor   *c* Virgil Miller   *lp* Jon Hall, Rita Johnson, Victor McLaglen, Andy Devine, Milburn Stone, Ray Teal

Northwest Outpost (REP) 91 min

Dwan transforms what could have been a turgid melodrama (Cavalry officer Eddy rescuing a young Russian girl, Massey, held captive by her husband in a Russian outpost in California) into a delightful if lightweight film by the simple act of poking fun at Eddy and his material. Accordingly, in the manner of too many series singing cowboys, Eddy is frequently caught open mouthed with a song on the soundtrack (as well as in his heart) as he gallops to the rescue.

d/p Allan Dwan   *s* Elizabeth Meehan, Richard Sale
c Reggie Lanning   *lp* Nelson Eddy, Ilona Massey, Joseph Schildkraut, Elsa Lanchester, Hugo Haas, Rich Valin

On the Old Spanish Trail (REP) 75 min

A whimsical rather than actionful outing from Rogers, set in modern times. Guizar, a huge draw South of the Border, is the Mexican Robin Hood who teams up with Rogers to put an end to McGraw's villainy. But, if the plot is fanciful, Rogers' grotesque costumes are gone, replaced by simple denims which soon Rogers was to regularly get grubby not to mention bloody under Witney's direction.

A scene from The Prairie, *one of the many films to have its origins in the classic pioneering novels of James Fenimore Cooper.*

d William Witney   *p* Edward J. White   *s* Sloan Nibley
c Jack Marta   *lp* Roy Rogers, Tito Guizar, Jane Frazee, Andy Devine, Estelita Rodriguez, Charles McGraw, Trigger

Oregon Trail Scouts (REP) b/w 58 min

A routine Red Ryder entry with Lane in the role just vacated by 'Wild Bill' Elliott (who'd replaced Don 'Red' Barry) and Wentworth replacing Alyce Flemming as the Duchess. Snell's screenplay sees Lane and Barcroft at odds with each other in Indian country. Barcroft wants the fur trading rights Lane has negotiated for himself with the Indians and kidnaps the chief's son as a bargaining counter.

d R.G. Springsteen   *p* Sidney Picker   *s* Earle Snell
c Alfred Keller   *lp* Allan Lane, Bobby Blake, Martha Wentworth, Roy Barcroft, Edmund Cobb, Earle Hodgins

Pioneer Justice (PRC) b/w 56 min

Generally regarded as the best of LaRue's PRC films, *Pioneer Justice* sees Lash, with assistance from St John, rescuing Holt from the attentions of Ingram, who sees himself as a sort of Napoleon of the plains, and his gang of cut throats. LaRue handles the bullwhip with confidence and snarls just enough to remind us of his origins as a baddie in **Song of Old Wyoming** (1945).

d Ray Taylor   *p* Jerry Thomas   *s* Adrian Page   *c* Ernest Miller   *lp* Lash LaRue, Al St John, Jennifer Holt, Jack Ingram, William Fawcett, Slim Whitaker

Pirates of Monterey (U-INTERNATIONAL) 77 min

A stilted actioneer set in Old California when the area belonged to Mexico. Cameron is the soldier of fortune who takes a wagon train full of the latest model of rifles and survives ambushes, treachery and much swordplay before reaching his goal, the open arms of Montez. Looking far better than it deserves courtesy of Mohr's handsome cinematography, the script and direction suffer from primitive notions of drama.

d Alfred Werker   *p* Paul Malvern   *s* Sam Hellman, Margaret Buell Wilder   *c* Hal Mohr   *lp* Maria Montez, Rod Cameron, Mikhail Rasumny, Gilbert Roland, Philip Reed, Gale Sondergaard

Lash LaRue (right), Jennifer Holt and Al St John, all series stalwarts, held at gunpoint in Pioneer Justice.

Veronica Lake between Preston Foster (left) and Joel McCrea in Ramrod.

The Prairie (ZENITH) b/w 66 min

A slow-moving, low-budget version of James Fenimore Cooper's epic novel about a wagon train voyaging into the newly opened Louisiana Purchase Territory. Wisbar dwells less on the problems of hostile Indians and more on the natural hazards faced by patriarch Evans and his clan. Baxter is the army cartographer who appears regularly at the most vital moments and Aubert the sole survivor of an Indian raid who threatens to divide Evans' clan. The film is well intentioned, but not well made nor well received.

d Frank Wisbar *p* George Moskov *s* Arthur St Claire *c* James S. Brown Jnr *lp* Lenore Aubert, Alan Baxter, Charles Evans, Jay Silverheels, Russ Vincent, Jack Mitchum

Prairie Express (MON) b/w 55 min

This is a decidedly routine entry in Brown's Monogram series of Westerns with Hatton in support. The plot is the old one of the villain (Ruhl) knowing the railroad is coming and trying to scare people into selling their ranches to him for a pittance. Brown, oddly enough with hardly any assistance from Hatton, sorts matters out.

d Lambert Hillyer *p* Barney Sarecky *s* Anthony Coldeway, J. Benton Cheney *c* William Sickner *lp* Johnny Mack Brown, Raymond Hatton, William Ruhl, Virginia Belmont, Marshall Reed, Frank LaRue

Pursued (WB) b/w 101 min

One of the blackest Westerns ever made. Produced when psychoanalysis was at its most influential in Hollywood, *Pursued* remains an *action* movie, albeit a static one with Mitchum haunted by a childhood trauma and repeatedly surrounded by bewildering, dangerous happenings, the cause and meaning of which he never quite understands. Told in flashback as Mitchum desperately tries to unscramble the far

Robert Mitchum and Teresa Wright in a publicity still for Raoul Walsh's classic Pursued.

past and his childhood memories of jangling spurs in order to explain the immediate past and so clear his name, *Pursued* has a beautifully interlocked double structure in which the events and forces that Mitchum sees as controlling his life only lose their power when Mitchum starts to seek the truth rather than merely react to events. Thus the first half of the movie sees Mitchum, adopted by Anderson, quarrelling with his half brother, going off to war (on the toss of a coin), losing his half of the ranch (on another toss of a coin) and then winning a fortune on a further toss of a coin. But from the moment Mitchum justifiably kills his 'brother' (Rodney) and Wright sets her cap at him with the idea of revenging her brother's death by marrying him and hating him, Mitchum is forced to consider what lies behind the hostility Anderson and Jagger have to him. Slowly he begins to act rather than react.

The film's tension is the sum of Walsh's tendency to romantic tragedy, writer Busch's fatalism, Howe's sombre shadowy photography and the contrast between Mitchum's hulking, brooding, intense style of acting and Wright's more open and enthusiastic performance. A classic Western.

d Raoul Walsh *p* Milton Sperling *s* Niven Busch *c* James Wong Howe *lp* Robert Mitchum, Teresa Wright, Judith Anderson, Dean Jagger, John Rodney, Alan Hale

Ramrod (HARRY SHERMAN PICTURES) b/w 94 min

McCrea gives a fine performance in the title role in this superior Western, the first of several he was to make with director De Toth, but it is Lake as the thin-lipped, embittered daughter who most impresses. The complex screenplay features Lake as the strong-willed girl who forms her own gang when the man she loves is shamed by his friend, the villainous Foster. The two gangs then go on the rampage, despite McCrea's attempts to keep the peace. After a score of deaths, McCrea takes on Foster and kills him before scooping up the wholesome Whelan and riding off. De Toth's strong sense of evil informs the film from its bewildering beginning to the end, intensifying our sense of the characters not being in control of themselves.

d Andre De Toth *p* Harry Sherman *s* Jack Moffitt, Graham Baker, Cecile Kramer *c* Russell Harlan *lp* Joel McCrea, Veronica Lake, Preston Foster, Arleen Whelan, Charlie Ruggles, Lloyd Bridges

Robin Hood of Texas (REP) b/w 71 min

Autry's last film for Republic, the studio he'd had a tempestuous relationship with since 1935 and **Tumbling Tumbleweeds,** this is far better than his recent outings for the studio. On his return after the war, it seemed that Autry had put more into his fights with Republic's head, Herbert

Yates, than into his films. The story is interestingly poised between being a detective and Western one with Autry blamed for a bank robbery and having to catch the real culprit. Selander's efficient direction and Autry's evident enjoyment result in a superior series entry.

d Lesley Selander *p* Sidney Picker *s* John K. Butler, Earle Snell *c* William Bradford *lp* Gene Autry, Lynne Roberts, Sterling Holloway, Adele Mara, James Cardwell, John Kellogg, Champion

Rustlers of Devil's Canyon (REP) b/w 58 min
Efficiently directed with the odd bravura touch by Springsteen and featuring a clever storyline from Snell, this is a superior entry in the Red Ryder series. Lane returns home after the Spanish-American War to discover rustlers, homesteaders and ranchers in a three-cornered fight for control of the territory. He exposes Space's kindly old doctor as the rustler's leader and secures peace between the cattlemen and farmers with the maximum of action and the minimum of talk.

d R.G. Springsteen *p* Sidney Picker *s* Earle Snell
c William Bradford *lp* Allan Lane, Bobby Blake, Martha Wentworth, Arthur Space, Peggy Stewart, Roy Barcroft

The Sea of Grass (MGM) b/w 131 min
Shot for the most part in the studio, to Kazan's evident distaste, this epic Western stars Tracy as the tough rancher and Hepburn as his equally strong-willed wife. The grass of the title is the farming land under threat from barbed wire. Walker is the son who goes to the bad for lack of parental guidance.

d Elia Kazan *p* Pandro S. Berman *s* Marguerite Roberts, Vincent Lawrence *c* Harry Stradling *lp* Spencer Tracy, Katharine Hepburn, Melvyn Douglas, Phyllis Thaxter, Robert Walker, Harry Carey

Gene Autry in Robin Hood of Texas, *his last film for Republic.*

Son of Zorro (REP) b/w 13 chaps
Set in the post-Civil War period, rather than Old California, this tired serial stars Turner as a cowboy who resurrects the Zorro character to fight the good fight against corruption in the far West. After one more entry, **Ghost of Zorro** (1949), Republic finally gave up on the character who had served them so well. The character, however, did not fade away so quietly, as the following list of titles make clear:
   Zorro (Disney TV series, 1959)
   Zorro (1961, Spain)
   Zorro the Avenger (1963, Spain)
   Zorro and the Three Musketeers aka *March of the Three Musketeers* (1963, Italy)

Katharine Hepburn between Edgar Buchanan (left) and Spencer Tracy, confronted with the rigours of frontier cooking in The Sea of Grass.

George Turner, behind bars, as the cowboy who resurrects the Zorro character in Son of Zorro.

Texas grasshoppers tall enough to pick their teeth with barbed wire. Scott is Bat Masterson, lawman and would-be reporter, Ryan the good capitalist investing in farmers and Brodie the gambler and would-be cattle baron. Inevitably Ryan and Brodie come into conflict and just as inevitably Scott sorts things out. Jeffreys is the saloon singer caught between the two men and Meredith the straightlaced object of Ryan's affection who's perpetually threatening to return to the East.

d Ray Enright *p* Nat Holt *s* Norman Houston, Gene Lewis *c* Roy Hunt *lp* Randolph Scott, Robert Ryan, Anne Jeffreys, George 'Gabby' Hayes, Steve Brodie, Madge Meredith

Unconquered (PAR) 147 min
Another of De Mille's overwrought epics about the making of America. Goddard is the indentured English slave sent to the colonies where she suffers the indignities of an Indian torture stake, going over rapids and one of De Mille's infamous bath tub sequences before becoming an American and being swept into the hands of Cooper's waiting Virginia militiaman. Around them the standard Indians-versus-the-colonists plot is

Zorro-v-Maciste aka *Samson and the Slave Queen* (1963, Italy)
Three Swords of Zorro (1964, Italy)
Behind the Mask of Zorro (1964, Italy)
The Erotic Adventures of Zorro (1972)
   This last, a piece of soft porn, wasn't the end of the trail for Zorro. The saga continued with **Zorro the Gay Blade** (1981).

d Spencer Bennet, Fred C. Brannon *p* Ronald Davidson *s* Franklyn Adreon, Basil Dickey, Jesse Duffy, Sol Shor *c* Bud Thackery *lp* George Turner, Peggy Stewart, Roy Barcroft, Edward Cassidy, Edmund Cobb, Charles King

Springtime in the Sierras (REP) 75 min
This is one of the best of the early Witney-directed Rogers series Westerns. Bachelor is the evil villainess and Barcroft her grinning heavy who tries to throw Rogers into a meat freezer. The plot is slight. Bachelor heads a gang shooting game out of season, but the fights are ferocious and the pace fast. Frazee replaces Dale Evans as the heroine.

d William Witney *p* Edward J. White *s* Sloan Nibley *c* Jack Marta *lp* Roy Rogers, Jane Frazee, Andy Devine, Stephanie Bachelor, Hal Landon, Roy Barcroft, Trigger

Thunder Mountain (RKO) b/w 60 min
A (very) loose remake of the George O'Brien film of 1935, this is an energetic re-working of Zane Grey's novel. Holt is the son returning home from college to discover an old family feud resurrected by villains trying to scare both farmers off their land on which the government wants to build a dam. A few coincidences and right hooks later, Woods and Powers (better known as Tom Keene) are exposed and the two families are united through Holt and Hyer's romance. Robards supplies a neat cameo as a drunk attorney.

d Lew Landers *p* Herman Schlom *s* Norman Houston *c* Jack MacKenzie *lp* Tim Holt, Martha Hyer, Richard Powers (Tom Keene), Harry Woods, Jason Robards Snr, Steve Brodie

Trail Street (RKO) b/w 84 min
An unassuming Western that outlines a few of the contours of the genre to perfection. Set in the town of Liberal, it features Farmers versus Cattlemen, wilderness versus cultivated land, East versus West, democratic versus individualist action and is punctuated by Gabby Hayes' tall stories about the likes of

The unassuming Robert Ryan in Trail Street.

pumped out with cannon, fire and dynamite. Da Silva is the evil trader and Karloff (who learnt the Seneca dialect and played his part in a brace covered by a loincloth and a few narrow strips of fur following an accident!) the wise Indian chief. But for all the on-screen excitement and De Mille's emphasis on his $5 million worth of production values, the film is flat and listless.

d/p Cecil B. De Mille *s* Charles Bennett, Frederic M. Frank, Jesse Lasky Jnr *c* Ray Rennahan *lp* Gary Cooper, Paulette Goddard, Howard Da Silva, Boris Karloff, Cecil Kellaway, Ward Bond

Under Colorado Skies (REP) 65 min
A superior Hale entry with strong direction from Springsteen, now billing himself R.G. as he would henceforth. Haade is the villain, leader of a band of outlaws whom Hale, a medical student working part time in a bank, is accused of being in league with. Several gunfights later the truth is out – the inside man was the brother of Hale's fiancée, Booth – and Haade is behind bars. The routine story is enlivened by lively direction and acting.

d R.G. Springsteen *p* Melville Tucker *s* Louise Rousseau *c* Alfred S. Keller *lp* Monte Hale, Adrian Booth, Paul Hurst, William Haade, John Alvin, LeRoy Mason

Under the Tonto Rim (RKO) b/w 61 min
Although it carries the same title as the silent movie and 1933 sound version, Houston's script bears no relation to either film. Holt is the stagecoach-line owner whose stage is robbed and who sets out to catch the outlaws with the assistance of Martin. Powers (Tom Keene with a new name) is the outlaw leader and Leslie his sister and apple of Holt's eye. The film's strong plot, RKO's strong support which ensured scenic locations, superior running inserts and good stunting and Landers' stylish direction make it Holt's best movie for RKO.

d Lew Landers *p* Herman Schlom *s* Norman Houston *c* J. Roy Hunt *lp* Tim Holt, Nan Leslie, Richard Martin, Richard Powers, Jason Robards Snr, Lex Barker

Vigilantes of Boom Town (REP) b/w 56 min
Probably the best of Lane's seven outings as Red Ryder for Republic under the control of Springsteen who'd graduated to directing after a lengthy apprenticeship at the company. Snell's fanciful script has Lane trying to prevent a bank robbery planned to coincide with the staging of the Fitzimmons-Corbett world championship fight, which Stewart, as the fiery heroine, is trying to prevent taking place. Barcroft is the heavy.

Bill Elliott and Albert Dekker at the conclusion of their climactic fistfight in Wyoming.

d R.G. Springsteen *p* Sidney Picker *s* Earle Snell *c* Alfred Keller *lp* Allan Lane, Bobby Blake, Martha Wentworth, Roy Barcroft, Peggy Stewart, John Dehner

The Vigilantes Return (U) b/w 67 min
An effective, modest actioner in which Holt is the undercover representative of law and order sent to expose Wilcox, owner of the local saloon and gambling hall, as an outlaw leader. Lindsay is his old flame, in business with Wilcox, who comes to his aid when he's framed for murder. Efficiently directed by Taylor the film includes an early appearance of Jack Lambert, who, in the fifties, was to become a major Western heavy.

d Ray Taylor *p* Howard Welsch *s* Roy Chanslor *c* Virgil Miller *lp* Jon Hall, Margaret Lindsay, Andy Devine, Robert Wilcox, Lane Chandler, Paula Drew

West to Glory (PRC) b/w 61 min
Routine fare, this is a loose remake of *Border Bandits* (1946) with Dean trying to prevent the theft of valuable jewels from a Mexican rancher. It is surprisingly slow for a film by Taylor, with more romance than action.

d Ray Taylor *p* Jerry Thomas *s* Elmer Clifton, Robert Churchill *c* Milford Anderson *lp* Eddie Dean, Roscoe Ates, Delores Castle, Gregg Barton, Zon Murray, Alex Montoya

White Stallion *aka* Harmony Trail
(WALT MATTOX PRODUCTIONS) b/w 54 min
One of the black and white pictures Dean was relegated to after his much touted debut for PRC, **Song of Old Wyoming** (1945) in glorious (and gaudy) Cinecolor. Maynard, who'd quit *The Trail Blazers* and Terhune join him and, in an unusual twist, all use their own names. King supplies the villainy as a bank robber while Roman is the (much abbreviated) romantic interest, a role she was to perform in so many Westerns.

d Robert Emmett (Tansey) *p* Walt Mattox *s* Frances Kavanaugh *c* Edward Kull *lp* Ken Maynard, Eddie Dean, Max Terhune, Charles King, Ruth Roman, Glenn Strange

The Wild Frontier (REP) b/w 59 min
Lane's first film for Republic after the demise of his Red Ryder series sees him using his own name, suddenly the in-thing for cowboy stars. Ford directs the routine plot about a son succeeding his father as sheriff and getting the men

Singing Cowboy Monte Hale, who was given his own series when Gene Autry quit Republic, in Under Colorado Skies.

Gabby Hayes shows Randolph Scott the evidence of sabotage in Albuquerque.

responsible for his death with unusual intensity. Similarly Holt's being cast against type made the ploy of the baddie hiding under a mask of goodness believable for once.

d Philip Ford *p* Gordon Kay *s* Albert DeMond *c* Alfred S. Keller *lp* Allan Lane, Jack Holt, Eddy Waller, Pierre Watkin, Roy Barcroft, Budd Buster

Wild Horse Mesa (RKO) b/w 60 min
This routine fare is loosely based on a Zane Grey story. Houston's screenplay has Holt and Robards searching for the hiding place of the 2,000 strong herd of wild horses and capturing Woods' murderer in the process. Slower than most Westerns of the period and with pictorial values emphasized over action, the film fades towards the end as though director Grissell's imagination simply gave out.

d Wallace Grissell *p* Herman Schlom *s* Norman Houston *c* Frank Redman *lp* Tim Holt, Nan Leslie, Jason Robards Snr, Richard Martin, Harry Woods, Richard Powers (Tom Keene)

Wyoming (REP) b/w 84 min
Beautifully lit by Alton with a vividness that was unusual for the period – only the shots of Ralston were made with the traditional (and flattering) gauze filter demanded by most leading ladies – and energetically directed by Kane, this is one of Elliott's best prestige Westerns. He rises from pioneer to cattle baron until Dekker publicizes the Homestead Act to encourage homesteading on the range so fermenting a cattlemen versus farmers range war that allows him to rustle away until there are no cows to come home. The lengthy fistfight between Elliott and Dekker over Grey is comparable to the one that is the high point of all three versions of **The Spoilers** (1930, 1942, 1956), especially the 1942 version.

The film was the last for Republic by Hayes. A further point of interest is that Kane's own daughter played the younger Ralston.

d/p Joseph Kane *s* Lawrence Hazard, Gerald Geraghty *c* John Alton *lp* William Elliott, Vera Ralston, Louise Kane, George Hayes, Albert Dekker, Virginia Grey

1948

Jeffrey Lynn (left) with Dan Duryea as the affable villains and heroes of Black Bart.

Adventures in Silverado *aka* Above All Laws
(COL) b/w 75 min
Made in the same year as the director's impressive **Thunderhoof** (1948), this is an interesting low-budget Western. The unusual script is based on a 'true' story by Robert Louis

Stevenson, *Silverado Squatters* and tells of a stagecoach driver (Bishop) who captures a hooded highwayman, 'The Monk' (Tucker) and so clears himself of suspicion. Stevenson himself figures in the movie as a passenger on the stage. Karlson directs incisively.

d Phil Karlson *p* Ted Richmond, Robert Cohn, *s* Kenneth Gamet, Tom Kilpatrick, Joe Pagano *c* Henry Freulich *lp* William Bishop, Gloria Henry, Edgar Buchanan, Forrest Tucker, Irving Bacon, Fred Sears

Albuquerque *aka* Silver City (PAR) 90 min
Scott is the nephew of town tyrant, Cleveland, who turns on his uncle and the crooked sheriff (Chaney) to help a small wagon-train line that Cleveland is trying to close down in this superior Pine-Thomas production. Smoothly scripted by Lewis and Young, with Scott making the central character a believable one (rather than the series superhuman), the production is only marred by Enright's spotty direction which slows the action down too frequently.

d Ray Enright *p* William Pine, William Thomas *s* Gene Lewis, Clarence Upson Young *c* Fred Jackman Jnr *lp* Randolph Scott, Barbara Britton, George Hayes, George Cleveland, Lon Chaney Jnr, Russell Hayden

Arizona Rangers (RKO) b/w 63 min
One of the best of Holt's series of Westerns for RKO, *Arizona Rangers* co-stars him with his father Jack. In an odd reflection of the social upsets that followed the Second World War, Holt is the unsettled youngster who, on his discharge from Roosevelt's Rough Riders, can't settle down. He refuses to run the family farm and joins the Arizona Rangers instead, whereupon Holt Snr, as the father, turns his back on his son. Holt sorts out outlaw Brodie, whose much mistreated wife, Leslie, falls in love with him, and eventually son and father are reconciled. Holt's cheeful athleticism and RKO's superior production values mean that the result is an engaging movie.

d John Rawlins *p* Herman Schlom *s* Norman Houston *c* J. Roy Hunt *lp* Tim Holt, Jack Holt, Nan Leslie, Richard Martin, Steve Brodie, Paul Hurst

Black Bart (U-INTERNATIONAL) 80 min
A marvellous-looking film, this was the first released for Goldstein's Universal-International Pictures. Moreover, with villains for heroes who die for their sins without a thought of reforming, *Black Bart*'s script marked a decisive shift of attitudes in the Western. Duryea and Lynn are the rogues first seen about to meet their maker on the end of a rope who, on being rescued by Kilbride, return to thievery with an

Robert Mitchum as the lonely gunman in the atmospheric Blood on the Moon.

abandon and humour that makes the film very different from other Westerns of the day. De Carlo decorates the story as an aggressive rather than romantic interest. The result is hugely enjoyable.

d George Sherman *p* Leonard Goldstein *s* Luci Ward, Jack Natteford, William Bowers *c* Irving Glassberg *lp* Yvonne De Carlo, Dan Duryea, Jeffrey Lynn, Percy Kilbride, Lloyd Gough, John McIntyre

Blood on the Moon (RKO) b/w 88 min
Wise and cinematographer Musuraca's previous work together on horror films, like the classic *Curse of the Cat People* (1944), can be clearly seen in this shadow-filled, taut Western. The plot is the traditional one of the gunman (a brooding Mitchum) who switches sides to defend a rancher (Bel Geddes) against his one-time friend and mentor (Preston). Wise's direction and the locales (mostly indoors) give the material a strong psychological dimension.

d Robert Wise *p* Theron Warth *s* Lillie Hayward *c* Nicholas Musuraca *lp* Robert Mitchum, Barbara Bel Geddes, Robert Preston, Walter Brennan, Tom Tyler, Harry Carey Jnr

The Bold Frontiersman (REP) b/w 60 min
A fast-moving Lane outing with an old-fashioned emphasis on action and stunts. Barcroft is the villain after the money local ranchers in a drought area have raised to build a dam. Ford directs crisply and Miller's cinematography is sparkling.

d Philip Ford *p* Gordon Kay *s* Bob Williams *c* Ernest Miller *lp* Allan Lane, Eddy Waller, Roy Barcroft, Fred Graham, Francis McDonald, Edmund Cobb

Carson City Raiders (REP) b/w 60 min
A snappy series Western with Lane, more flamboyant than usual, as the express company agent who rids Carson City of the crooks led by the town's banker, Reicher. Canutt's direction is fast paced and, as one would expect from an ex-stunt man and second unit director, the stunts and action sequences are superbly orchestrated. Indeed, the emphasis on stunts is unusual for the period, with even Black Jack, Lane's horse, getting in on the act and warning its master of an ambush.

Allan 'Rocky' Lane gets the drop on the baddies in the action-packed Carson City Raiders, *one of the few films to be directed by Yakima Canutt.*

Randolph Scott and Marguerite Chapman in Coroner Creek, *the first film made by Scott and producer Harry Joe Brown's own production company.*

d Yakima Canutt *p* Gordon Kay *s* Earle Snell
c William Bradford *lp* Allan Lane, Eddy Waller, Frank Reicher, Beverly Jons, Edmund Cobb, Bob Wilke

Coroner Creek

(PRODUCERS-ACTORS CORPORATION) 90 min

The first film made by Scott and producer Brown after they had formed their Producers-Actors production company, *Coroner Creek* is a solid Western. The opening is of particular interest, considering the direction Scott and Brown would take with their splendid series of Westerns directed by Budd Boetticher in the fifties that culminated in **Ride Lonesome** (1959) and **Comanche Station** (1960). In the opening, Scott's intended wife is attacked in a raid on a stagecoach by Indians and kills herself. So, for the first of many times, Scott sets off to revenge the death of his 'wife'. The search brings him to Coroner Creek and Macready who has made a respectable citizen out of himself with money stolen from the stagecoach. After a lengthy and violent fistfight with Tucker, in the course of which each treads on the trigger finger of the other on purpose, Scott is about to take his revenge on Macready when the villain falls on the knife Scott's fiancée killed herself with. Enright's direction is tough, emphasizing the violence of the action and the steadfastness of Scott in equal measure. This is a significant Western.

d Ray Enright *p* Harry Joe Brown *s* Kenneth Gamet
c Fred H. Jackman *lp* Randolph Scott, Marguerite Chapman, George Macready, Forrest Tucker, Edgar Buchanan, Sally Eilers

The Dead Don't Dream

(HOPALONG CASSIDY PRODUCTIONS) b/w 62 min

As the magnificent title of this Hopalong Cassidy entry suggests, *The Dead Don't Dream* is a thriller in Western setting. Hoppy is set the problem of finding out why three men were killed in a hotel room. Concentrating on murky atmospherics – night chases through mine shafts – rather than the massed action that characterizes the Harry Sherman-produced films, this, the penultimate outing in the 66-strong series, is only routine and unworthy of its title.

d George Archainbaud *p* Lewis J. Rachmil *s* Francis Rosenwald *c* Mack Stengler *lp* William Boyd, Andy Clyde, Rand Brooks, Francis McDonald, John Parrish, Leonard Penn

Eddie Albert and an exasperated Gale Storm surrounded by Indians in The Dude Goes West.

The Dude Goes West (AA) b/w 87 min

An enjoyable spoof Western with Albert in fine form as the gunsmith who travels to Arsenic City to sell his wares and Storm as the girl he meets who's trying to find out who killed her father. Gleason, MacLane (as the outlaw leader) and Roland turn in sprightly performances mocking Western conventions and stereotypes with obvious delight. The score by Dmitri Tiomkin and Struss' bold cinematography give the film a fittingly brash air.

d Kurt Neumann *p* Frank King, Maurice King
s Richard Sale, Mary Loos *c* Karl Struss *lp* Eddie Albert, Gale Storm, James Gleason, Gilbert Roland, Barton MacLane, Tom Tyler

Eyes of Texas (REP) 70 min

Witney directs this impressive Rogers outing at his usual breakneck speed. Though Bryant is a melodramatic villain, the tone is noticeably grimmer than one would expect with Bryant using a pack of trained killer-dogs for his murders, committed as part of his attempt to obtain valuable ranch land. Barcroft is the amiable heavy who finally gets his comeuppance from Rogers after a lengthy and bloody fistfight.

d William Witney *p* Edward J. White *s* Sloan Nibley
c Jack Marta *lp* Roy Rogers, Lynne Roberts, Andy Devine, Nana Bryant, Roy Barcroft, Danny Morton, Trigger

Fort Apache (RKO) b/w 127 min

A masterpiece. Behind the assured dramatics of Nugent's script and Ford's leisurely re-moulding of the Custer myth lies a complex and entertaining Western.

For Ford, the Cavalry is a microcosm of an idealized America, a democractic community of equals unified, despite previous loyalties (to the Confederacy, to Ireland...) and military hierachy, by isolation and a common purpose, the defence of the frontier. In this, the first of a loose trilogy of films devoted to the Cavalry (that continues with **She Wore a Yellow Ribbon,** 1949 and **Rio Grande,** 1950), Ford examines the divisive effects of the arrival of a new commander, Fonda, on the men of a lonely outpost. A demoted officer, Fonda rigidly follows the rule book, despite having no experience of fighting Indians. He is contrasted to his second-in-command, Wayne, a 'team player' who finally covers up Fonda's blunder and makes a gallant hero out of him for the sake of the Cavalry. Equally important in the movie is Ford and Nugent's articulation of the social life of the fort which Fonda also disrupts. His social rigidity – he even dances stiffly – prevents him from becoming a real member of the community of Fort Apache. In Ford's eyes this is as damming as his military

Below: *Charles Bickford as the marshal questions Martin Garralaga about the whereabouts of outlaw Joel McCrea in* Four Faces West.

failings. The film ends in defeat, as in *They Were Expendable* (1945), a film it closely resembles, but Ford's vision, especially in the idealized domestic scenes, is wholly positive.

d/co-p John Ford *co-p* Merian C. Cooper *s* Frank S. Nugent *c* Archie Stout *lp* John Wayne, Henry Fonda, Shirley Temple, Ward Bond, Victor MacLaglen, John Agar, George O'Brien

Four Faces West *aka* They Passed This Way
(UA) b/w 90 min
This unusually sensitive Western stars the husband and wife team of McCrea and Dee. It is the last sagebrush production of 'Pops' Sherman, best known as the man who brought Hopalong Cassidy to the screen. McCrea is the gentle outlaw, who turns to banditry to save his father's ranch and is only caught because he goes out of his way to help a Mexican family struck down with illness. Bickford is the honest lawman reluctantly on his trail. A box-office failure, probably due to its lack of action, it has survived better than most. Harlan's evocative camerawork is particularly noteworthy.

d Alfred E. Green *p* Harry Sherman *s* Graham Baker *c* Russell Harlan *lp* Joel McCrea, Charles Bickford, Frances Dee, Joseph Calleia, Forrest Taylor, Martin Garralaga

Fury at Furnace Creek (FOX) b/w 88 min
A superior B feature. Mature and Langan are the sons determined to prove their father, the commander of a lonely cavalry outpost, acted correctly and was not responsible for the fort's destruction in an Indian attack. In doing so they expose a plot by Dekker to buy up Cavalry land rich in mineral deposits for a pittance. Script and direction give the production a stylish edge.

The ever swarthy Victor Mature (left) confronts Albert Dekker in Fury at Furnace Creek.

d Bruce Humberstone p Fred Kohlmar s Charles G. Booth c Harry Jackson lp Victor Mature, Coleen Gray, Glenn Langan, Albert Dekker, Reginald Gardiner

The Gallant Legion (REP) b/w 88 min
Elliott is the Texas Ranger and Booth the journalist who together foil a plot by Schildkraut to disband the Rangers and then split Texas into several sections rather than have the territory be absorbed into the Union as a single state. The script is wooden and Kane directs at best efficiently but the strong supporting cast, a Barcroft-Woods, if not quite an A-Z of featured Western players, make the film essential viewing for nostalgia buffs.

d/p Joseph Kane s Gerald Adams c Jack Marta lp William (Bill) Elliott, Adrian Booth, Joseph Schildkraut, Bruce Cabot, Andy Devine, Grant Withers, Adele Mara, Hal Taliaferro, Harry Woods, Roy Barcroft, Bud Osborne, Jack Ingram, George Chesebro, Rex Lease, Kermit Maynard, Fred Kohler

The Gay Ranchero (REP) 72 min
This is another modern Western from Rogers. Despite the slight, not to say absurd plot – Rogers and Guizar on horseback capturing a gang sabotaging planes in an attempt to gain control of an airport South of the Border – the action is strong, even bloody at times. A regular leitmotif of the films, under Witney's direction, is a lengthy sequence in which Rogers is cruelly beaten up. Here the beating looks even more lurid being in Trucolor, Republic's pinch-penny version of Technicolor.

d William Witney p Edward J. White s Sloan Nibley c Jack Marta lp Roy Rogers, Tito Guizar, Jane Frazee, Andy Devine, Estelita Rodriguez, George Meeker, Trigger

Grand Canyon Trail (REP) 67 min
This routine series entry sees the Riders of the Purple Sage replace the Sons of the Pioneers. Rogers is the hard-up owner of a run-down silver mine and ex-Mesquiteer Livingston the mining engineer who tries to swindle him, knowing the mine to be rich in silver. Played as much for comedy as thrills – hence Devine takes part in the fistfights – the film is nonetheless paced at Witney's usual breakneck speed. It is

A dramatic moment from Indian Agent, *one of Tim Holt's best series outings.*

written by Geraghty whose sister Carmelita was the heroine of several early Buck Rogers sound Westerns, notably **Men Without Law** (1930).

d William Witney p Edward J. White s Gerald Geraghty c Reggie Lanning lp Roy Rogers, Jane Frazee, Andy Devine, Robert Livingston, Roy Barcroft, Charles Coleman, Trigger

Guns of Hate (RKO) b/w 62 min
Holt and Martin, accused of the murder of Robards for his map giving the location of a fabulously rich mine, set out to prove that in fact Brodie and Barrett (who both give superb performances) are responsible. This is a rather aimless series Western slipped in by RKO amidst its Holt/Zane Grey series.

d Lesley Selander p Herman Schlom s Norman Houston, Ed Earl Repp c George E. Diskant lp Tim Holt, Nan Leslie, Richard Martin, Jason Robards Snr, Tony Barrett, Steve Brodie

Indian Agent (RKO) b/w 63 min
One of the absolute best of Holt's series Westerns, featuring a strong cast that includes Woods and Powers as the villains, Beery as the Indian chief and a superior screenplay by Houston. Woods and Indian agent Powers attempt to divert food from the reservation to the gold fields (a plot device that was to serve Borden Chase in similar circumstances for **Bend of the River,** 1952) whereupon the Indians grow restless. Holt and Martin stop the food thievery, in the nick of time preventing an Indian uprising. Selander directs efficiently.

d Lesley Selander p Herman Schlom s Norman Houston c J. Roy Hunt lp Tim Holt, Noah Beery Jnr, Richard Powers (Tom Keene), Harry Woods, Richard Martin, Nan Leslie

The Kissing Bandit (MGM) 102 min
A silly variant on the Zorro theme with Sinatra as the shy young man who inherits his father's role as masked highwayman and ladies' man in Old California. Grayson is the lady who returns him to the straight and narrow. The film's best

moments are provided by Charisse, Miller and Montalban in the production number 'Dance of Fury' added by MGM as an afterthought.

d Laslo Benedek   *p* Joe Pasternak   *s* Isobel Lennart, John Briard Harding   *c* Robert Surtees   *lp* Frank Sinatra, Kathryn Grayson, J. Carrol Naish, Cyd Charisse, Ricardo Montalban, Ann Miller

Last of the Wild Horses

(LIPPERT/SCREEN GUILD)   sepia   84 min
This is one of the few films directed by theatre owner and quickie producer Lippert. Ellison and Hadley are the opponents in this overlong but nevertheless engrossing story of rivalry on the range that has the added twist of playing its climax over the opening credits as a strange anticipatory effect. Hadley is the crook who frames Ellison for the murder of Dumbrille.

d Robert L. Lippert   *p* Carl Hittleman   *s* Jack Harvey *c* Benjamin Kline   *lp* James Ellison, Mary Beth Hughes, Reed Hadley, Jane Frazee, Douglass Dumbrille

The Man from Colorado   (COL)   99 min

This movie is an interesting failure. Based on an original story by Borden Chase, it features Ford as an army officer transformed into a sadistic killer by his experiences in the Civil War. He is struggling against his growing insanity when he's appointed a Federal Judge with the power of life and death over others. Holden, as Ford's former adjutant, takes the job of marshal in a desperate attempt to ameliorate his evil-doing. Obviously a reflection of the problems faced by the soldiers returning from the Second World War, the psychological dimension (which secured the film bad reviews at the time) is handled awkwardly by Levin and his writers. The climax has Holden, forced into outlawry by the reign of terror Ford imposes, finally uniting the townspeople against Ford. Drew is Ford's wife who quits him for Holden when she discovers what Ford has become.

d Henry Levin   *p* Jules Schermer   *s* Robert D. Andrews, Ben Maddow   *c* William Snyder   *lp* Glenn Ford, William Holden, Ellen Drew, Ray Collins, Edgar Buchanan, James Millican

Mark of the Lash

(WESTERN ADVENTURE/SCREEN GUILD)   b/w   60 min
The ancient 'water rights' plotline surfaces yet again in this late entry in producer Ormond's Lash LaRue series. LaRue, much improved in handling both his bull whip and his fists since his 1947 debut, takes on Reed who has dammed the river in an attempt to deprive local ranchers of water and so drive them away. To do this LaRue takes the identity of a dead land investigator, killed by Reed and his men.

d Ray Taylor   *p/co-s* Ron Ormond   *co-s* Ira Webb *lp* Lash LaRue, Al St John, Suzi Crandall, Marshall Reed, John Cason, Jimmy Martin

Marshal of Amarillo   (REP)   b/w   60 min

One of the better of Lane's series Westerns, *Marshal of Amarillo* opens well with Lane's comic side-kick, Waller, experiencing odd happenings at a deserted way station (which is an outlaws' hideout) and ends even more successfully with Lane driving a stage in pursuit of chief villain Moore, also driving a stage. Fast paced and exciting.

d Philip Ford   *p* Gordon Kay   *s* Bob Williams *c* John MacBurnie   *lp* Allan Lane, Eddy Waller, Mildred Coles, Clayton Moore, Roy Barcroft, Trevor Bardette

The Paleface   (PAR)   91 min

Written by Tashlin as a satire on Owen Wister's novel *The Virginian* but directed by McLeod as an out and out farce, *The Paleface* co-stars Hope and Russell. She is Calamity Jane, an

Frank Sinatra in costume for the lacklustre The Kissing Bandit.

Glenn Ford as the army officer turned psychopath by his experiences in the Civil War in the interesting The Man from Colorado.

Bob Hope and friends in The Paleface.

Phantom Valley (COL) b/w 53 min
One of the slacker of Starrett's Durango series, this is essentially a mystery tale set in the West. Starrett is the marshal trying to prevent a range war breaking out and wondering which of the several likely candidates is behind it. Hunter, ungallantly shot in the back by Starrett at the end, is the surprise choice of villain but the sleuthing that leads to her unmasking is ponderously slow.

Way down the cast is one Fred Sears who was to become Starrett's regular director within a year beginning with **Desert Vigilante** (1949).

d Ray Nazarro *p* Colbert Clark *s* J. Benton Cheney *c* George F. Kelley *lp* Charles Starrett, Smiley Burnette, Virginia Hunter, Sam Flint, Zon Murray, Joel Friedkin

The Plunderers (REP) 87 min
This was Kane's first film in colour and one of the most successful of Republic's prestige Westerns of the forties. Opening with Cameron murdering a sheriff (a trick to get him in the gang) which still surprises today, the film has all the pace one would expect of a Kane movie. In addition there's strong characterization from the likes of Ford, Fix and Cleveland as well as Tucker as the heavy and Holmes as the evil genius. Massey and Booth are the girls who love Cameron and Tucker respectively.

d/p Joseph Kane *s* Gerald Geraghty, Gerald Adams *c* Jack Marta *lp* Rod Cameron, Ilona Massey, Paul Fix, Francis Ford, George Cleveland, Forrest Tucker, Taylor Holmes, Adrian Booth

undercover government agent, and he 'Painless' Potter, the incompetent dentist she marries to provide herself with a cover. The combination of Hope, Russell and slapstick proved irresistible at the box office and a sequel soon followed, **Son of Paleface** (1952). For Russell, who'd previously been presented in movies solely as a sex-object, most notably in **The Outlaw** (1943), the role allowed her to expand her repertoire and become the 'good hearted, well stacked, goodtime girl' whose business-like competence was to become a feature of many adventure films during the fifties.

The plot has the pair putting an end to gun trading with the Indians. 'Buttons and Bows', the film's featured song, won an Oscar for best song.

d Norman Z. McLeod *p* Robert L. Welch *s* Edmund Hartman, Frank Tashlin *c* Ray Rennahan *lp* Bob Hope, Jane Russell, Robert Armstrong, Iris Adrian, Robert Watson, Jack Searle

Panhandle (AA) sepia 85 min
The first of actor Edwards' forays into production, this and **Stampede** (1949) won him praise as an inventive and literate writer/producer of B films. Cameron is the gunman who has to buckle on his guns just one more time to avenge the murder of his brother by Hadley who has ambitions to run the territory as his personal empire. Gwynne is Hadley's lively secretary (a job that defies description in the Western) who Cameron chooses, after disposing of Hadley in a well-mounted gunfight, over the sweet but stand-offish Downs. Edwards puts in a neat performance as Hadley's top heavy. Selander, who was so fond of the subject that he would remake it in 1966 as *The Texan*, directs with purpose and the result is a superior B feature.

Though Edwards made his name as a comedy director (he was responsible for the Pink Panther films, amongst others), he would make a triumphant return to the genre with **Wild Rovers** (1971), a quarter of a century later.

Rod Cameron in a publicity still from Panhandle in which he plays the gunman forced to buckle on his guns just one more time.

d Lesley Selander *p/s* John C. Champion, Blake Edwards *c* Harry Neumann *lp* Rod Cameron, Cathy Downs, Reed Hadley, Anne Gwynne, Blake Edwards, Francis McDonald

Rachel and the Stranger (RKO) b/w 93 min

A leisurely told tale of frontier love, *Rachel and the Stranger*'s gentle, unassuming virtues are clearer in retrospect than they seemed at the time. Holden is the homesteader who buys a bondswoman, Young, to cook and help raise his son after his wife, to whom he is still deeply attached, has died and Mitchum is his Romeo of a friend who romances her. The predictable result is that Holden, who has previously paid Young no attention, becomes appreciative of her. Mitchum, who clearly enjoyed his role, sings several songs in his odd but fetching manner. The film was rush-released by RKO to capitalize on Mitchum's sudden notoriety after his arrest for possession of marijuana.

d Norman Foster *p* Richard H. Berger *s* Waldo Salt
c Maury Gertsman *lp* Loretta Young, William Holden, Robert Mitchum, Gary Gray, Tom Tully, Frank Ferguson

The Red Pony (REP) 89 min

Scripted by Steinbeck from his own novel, this is a sincere, well-meaning and rather dull movie. Mitchum plays the handyman and substitute father to Miles whose parents, Strudwick and Loy (who gives the film's best performance), are having difficulties. Calhern has the plum role of the grandfather living in dreams of the good old pioneer days. Cinematographer Gaudio outdid himself on his last movie to produce lovingly-textured colour images. Aaron Copeland wrote one of his rare movie scores for the film.

The film was remade as an inferior television film in 1972, by Robert Totten.

d/p Lewis Milestone *s* John Steinbeck *c* Tony Gaudio
lp Myrna Loy, Robert Mitchum, Louis Calhern, Shepperd Strudwick, Peter Miles, Beau Bridges

Red River (MONTEREY) b/w 125(112) min

A seminal Western, as much for Wayne's performance, which drew the response from John Ford of 'I didn't know the sonofabitch could act!', as for Hawks' magisterial direction. Wayne is the ruthless rancher, Thomas Dunson, determined to get his huge herd of Texas cattle to market and to have his revenge on his adopted son (Clift, in his screen debut) who, rebelling against Wayne's growing authoritarianism, takes the cattle to Abeline 'his way'. Interestingly, rather than integrate the development of Wayne and Clift's edgy relationship within the sprawling epic tale of the opening of the Chisholm Trail, Hawks alternates between his two stories. He outlines the grandeur of the hazards of the journey – it's the most beautiful looking of Hawks' films – in one and dwells on the obsessive qualities necessary to accomplish such a task in the other, and only unites the two strands of his plot in the climax at Abeline. Accordingly, more than any other of Hawks' movies, it is a film of moments, Wayne parting from Gray, the

bleak funeral in the desert, Wayne's fight with Dru (who, unlike Gray, refuses to be separated from the man she loves) and the marvellous, and controversial, final confrontation between Wayne and Clift. Chase's novel has the Ireland character fatally wound Wayne; the film ends with Wayne, wounded by Ireland, shooting his guns at Clift to no avail – Clift refuses to fire back – and the pair of them, after a boisterous brawl and emotional telling-off by Dru, being reconciled. The ending has been attacked as a compromise that makes a nonsense of Wayne's character as a man who sees things through to the bitter end, and certainly it seems out of kilter with the thrust of Chase's script; indeed Hawks even shot an alternative ending with Wayne firing at Clift and nicking his ears. All that one can say of the ending as used is that it works.

The importance of the film to Wayne is perhaps best indicated by the fact that he wore the Red River D belt from that film in all his subsequent movies for Hawks and in any other Western where it was appropriate.

d/p Howard Hawks *s* Borden Chase, Charles Schnee
c Russell Harlan *lp* John Wayne, Montgomery Clift, Joanne Dru, Walter Brennan, Coleen Gray, John Ireland

Return of the Badmen (RKO) b/w 90 min

Scott is the retired marshal forced to take up his guns again when Ryan (as the Sundance Kid) unites a gaggle of badmen, including the Youngers, Daltons, and Billy the Kid, to terrorize the Oklahoma territory. Ryan's edginess and Scott's air of assured competence complement each other well and, despite the showier roles of Brodie (Cole Younger) and Armstrong (Wild Bill Doolin'), they are always at the centre of the film. This is a superior RKO star Western.

d Ray Enright *p* Nat Holt *s* Charles O'Neal, Jack Natteford, Luci Ward *c* J. Roy Hunt *lp* Randolph Scott, Robert Ryan, Anne Jeffreys, George Hayes, Steve Brodie, Robert Armstrong

The Return of Wildfire (CRESTWOOD) 80 min

One of the best of the several Westerns to feature horses that were made in the late forties and sporadically thereafter. Most are 'animal Westerns' with children in support, but this is a

Robert Mitchum and Loretta Young at work on Rachel and the Stranger.

Robert Mitchum as the cowboy, Peter Miles as the youngster and Louis Calhern as the grandfather in The Red Pony.

full-blooded horse opera with Hadley as the villain trying to corner the wild-horse market and turning to murder in his efforts. Arlen is the wrangler who comes to the aid of Hughes and Morison and takes Hadley on. The film also features a spectacular fight between two wild stallions, dramatically filmed by Taylor.

d Ray Taylor *p/co-s* Carl K. Hittleman *co-s* Betty Burbridge *c* Ernest Miller *lp* Richard Arlen, Patricia Morison, Mary Beth Hughes, Reed Hadley, James Millican, Chris-Pin Martin

Silver River (WB) b/w 110 min
The last film Flynn and Walsh made together, *Silver River* has far less of the dash and gusto that marks their earlier collaborations. The first half with Flynn heading West after the Civil War and becoming a silver magnate by pulling strings and marrying Sheridan after sending her first husband (Bruce Bennett) to his death, is cast in the mould of **They Died with Their Boots On** (1941). But the second half which sees Flynn rebelling against the system of political corruption he helped create is much darker. Badly received at the time, primarily because Flynn is cast so unsympathetically, its combination of jauntiness and darkness remains oddly powerful to this day.

d Raoul Walsh *p* Owen Crump *s* Harriet Frank Jnr, Stephen Longstreet *c* Sid Hickox *lp* Errol Flynn, Ann Sheridan, Thomas Mitchell, Barton MacLane, Monte Blue, Alan Bridge

Above: *Ann Sheridan and Errol Flynn, cast unsympathetically for a change, in* Silver River.

John Wayne, resolutely turning away from death, branding the first cow with the Red River D brand while Walter Brennan and Micky Kuhn (as the young Montgomery Clift) look on at the beginning of Red River.

Silver Trails (MON) b/w 53 min

A modest Wakely series entry notable for being the last film of a director whose career stretched back to 1913 and the film that introduced Whip Wilson, who like Lash LaRue and Sunset Carson sported a bullwhip as his distinctive mark. Wilson would soon have his own series and Wakely be without his. Cheney's screenplay features Meeker as the outlaw boss trying to create a range war for his own interests and Larson as the girl Wakely romances.

d Christy Cabanne   *p* Louis Gray   *s* J. Benton Cheney
c Harry Neumann   *lp* Jimmy Wakely, Dub Taylor, Whip Wilson, George Meeker, Christine Larson, Robert Strange

Six Gun Law (COL) b/w 54 min

This is a modest Starrett entry in his Durango Kid series. Forced by Prosser to replace the sheriff he's deluded into thinking he has killed, Starrett uses his masked identity – which made stunting for him so easy – to foil the schemes and robberies of Prosser's gang. Amusingly scripted by Shipman and efficiently directed by Nazarro, it only stumbles when the action ceases.

d Ray Nazarro   *p* Colbert Clark   *s* Barry Shipman
c George F. Kelley   *lp* Charles Starrett, Smiley Burnette, Nancy Saunders, Hugh Prosser, George Chesebro, Bob Wilke

Sons of Adventure (REP) b/w 60 min

Directed by ex-stuntman Canutt, this is one of the more realistic, in atmosphere if not in plot, of the behind-the-scenes-in-Hollywood movies. A Western hero is killed on the set and stuntman Hayden, a veteran of innumerable series Westerns, sets out to find out who is responsible, clearing the name of his old buddy, Jones, along the way. Roberts is charming as a Western stunt girl and Barcroft, Chandler and Withers turn in knowing performances.

d Yakima Canutt   *p/co-s* Franklin Adreon   *co-s* Sol Shur
c John MacBurnie   *lp* Lynne Roberts, Ross Hayden, Gordon Jones, Grant Withers, George Chandler, Roy Barcroft

A Southern Yankee *aka* My Hero (MGM) b/w 90 min

An uneven comedy set amidst the Civil War with Skelton unwittingly impersonating a Confederate spy, the Spider, and falling for Dahl's come-hither-inclined Southern Belle. Though the laughs in Tugend's screenplay (which owes more than a little to the Gary Cooper vehicle, **Operator 13**, 1933) are few and far between, some of the jokes are very funny. One such sees Skelton walking between enemy lines with two flags, showing one to the Confederate side and the other to the Union side.

d Edward Sedgwick   *p* Paul Jones   *s* Harry Tugend   *c* Ray June   *lp* Red Skelton, Brian Donlevy, Arlene Dahl, George Coulouris, Lloyd Gough, John Ireland

Station West (RKO) b/w 92 min

An unusual and intriguing Western, ruggedly directed with a humorous 'tough guy' script by Fenton and Miller and an excellent cast to deliver the one-liners. Powell, as the investigator looking into suspicious deaths at a Western fort and Greer as the villainess, prowl nicely around each other while the likes of Moorehead, Burr and Brodie give firm support. Powell and Williams also feature in a terrific fight.

d Sidney Lanfield   *p* Robert Sparks   *s* Frank Fenton, Winston Miller   *c* Harry Wild   *lp* Dick Powell, Jane Greer, Agnes Moorehead, Raymond Burr, Steve Brodie, Guinn Williams

The Strawberry Roan

(GENE AUTRY PRODUCTIONS/COL)   76 min

Autry's first film in colour (well Cinecolor), this remake of the Ken Maynard film of 1933 was a huge hit despite its close resemblance to Roy Rogers' **My Pal Trigger** (1946). Both films feature their stars' horses, Champion in this case, and have Holt as the villain. Directed at a fast pace by English who, with William Witney, was responsible for the best Republic serials, Cummins and Yost's screenplay features Holt wanting to shoot the wild horse Autry and his cowboys capture after it's responsible for injuring his son, Jones. All is finally resolved when Jones relearns to ride on . . . the strawberry roan.

The film introduced Buttram, who subsequently would become Autry's regular side-kick, in a small role.

d John English   *p* Armand Schaefer   *s* Dwight Cummins, Dorothy Yost   *c* Fred H. Jackman   *lp* Gene Autry, Gloria Henry, Jack Holt, Dick Jones, Pat Buttram, Rufe Davis, Champion

Sundown Riders (FILM ENTERPRISES)   56 min

The first of the few films made in 16mm for commercial distribution to the growing 16mm market. Shot in eight days on Kodachrome, with a professional crew and cast, and costing some $30,000, which was less than the average cost of a black and white series Western, it looked to be a promising business proposition. But, though a series of six was planned

Ross Hayden (centre) as the Hollywood stuntman in trouble in Sons of Adventure.

Harry Carey Jnr, John Wayne and Pedro Armendariz in Three Godfathers, *the film John Ford dedicated to his mentor, Harry Carey.*

Walter Huston (left), Humphrey Bogart (centre) and Tim Holt (right) in The Treasure of the Sierra Madre.

relations between the cast of three change considerably as Bishop vies with Foster for Stuart.

The film is one of the most ambitious B Westerns ever, part allegory and part psychological drama. Bishop and, in particular, Stuart's acting is hardly Shakespearian, but Smith's clever script and Karlson's tight direction are superb.

d Phil Karlson   *p* Ted Richmond   *s* Hal Smith   *c* Henry Freulich   *lp* Preston Foster, Mary Stuart, William Bishop, Thunderhoof

The Treasure of the Sierra Madre   (WB) b/w 126 min
Bogart, Holt, Huston and Bennett are the impoverished prospectors turned into near-animals by greed and lust for gold in this impressive film. The acting and script are melodramatic but Huston's direction, which alternates close-ups of his actors with almost formal three shots, is clinically masterful. The film is based on a story by B. Traven, the mysterious German exile as well known for keeping his identity secret as for his novels. It secured Oscars for both Walter and John Huston, the only time a father and son have won Oscars for the same film.

d/s John Huston   *p* Henry Blanke   *c* Ted McCord
lp Humphrey Bogart, Walter Huston, Tim Holt, John Huston, Bruce Bennett, Barton MacLane

Two Guys from Texas   (WB)   b/w   86 min
Carson and Morgan are the vaudevillians who end up on a dude ranch in this amiable spoof Western. The witty script, co-written by Diamond who is better known for his work with

and announced, no more films followed, presumably because the domestic/institutional 16mm market was not quite as large as it seemed. (MGM's much publicized plan to distribute 16mm films throughout the world soon went the same way.)

The idea was Wade's who, with Kirby and cinematographer Stensvold, had a share in the profits, thus anticipating by two years the first significant profit-sharing contract, James Stewart's for **Winchester '73** (1950). All the ballyhoo notwithstanding, the film is routine. Wade and two alumni of the currently defunct Hopalong Cassidy series, Kirby and Clyde, put paid to an outlaw gang.

d Lambert Hillyer   *p* H.V. George   *s* Rodney J. Graham
c Alan Stensvold   *lp* Andy Clyde, Jay Kirby, Russell Wade, Evelyn Finley, Jack Ingram, Bud Osborne

Three Godfathers   (MGM)   106 min
Ford's own remake of *Marked Men* (1919), *Three Godfathers* is best remembered by Ford aficionados for its opening dedication to Harry Carey, the star of the earlier film and one of his most regular collaborators: 'To the memory of Harry Carey – Bright star of the early Western Sky.' In Ford's hands, the parable of the three wise men (the three bank robbers, Wayne, Carey Jnr and Armendariz) who deliver the Christ child they find in the desert safely to (New) Jerusalem (at the cost of their freedom which is so stressed in Richard Boleslavski's 1936 version) is less significant than that of the prodigal son (here Wayne). But, interesting though the film is, Ford's religiosity leads him to dawdle over the ritualistic details of his plot at the expense of character credibility. The result is minor Ford, of interest for the light it throws on major films like **The Searchers** (1956) rather than for itself.

d/co-p John Ford   *co-p* Merian C. Cooper   *s* Laurence Stallings, Frank S. Nugent   *c* Winton Hoch   *lp* John Wayne, Pedro Armendariz, Harry Carey Jnr, Ward Bond, Mildred Natwick, Ben Johnson

Thunderhoof   (COL)   b/w   77 min
A remarkable B Western. Foster is the middle-aged rancher, Stuart his young wife and Bishop the tearaway of an adopted son who all set off for the wilds of Mexico in search of Thunderhoof, a magnificent wild black and white stallion. Foster breaks a leg but they still catch the stallion and commence the arduous journey back in the course of which

Red Skelton as A Southern Yankee.

Billy Wilder, more than compensates for Butler's leaden direction. Edwards, a Western regular, and Malone are the girls they fall for and Tucker the gangster they drive off the range. Julie Styne and Sammy Cahn's forgettable song typifies the movie's aspirations: 'I Wanna be a Cowboy in the Movies'.

d David Butler *p* Alex Gottlieb *s* I.A.L. Diamond, Allen Boretz *c* Arthur Edeson *lp* Dennis Morgan, Jack Carson, Dorothy Malone, Penny Edwards, Forrest Tucker, Monte Blue

The Untamed Breed (COL) 79 min
One of the few starring vehicles created for Tufts before his career went into decline in the fifties and his very name brought titters, *The Untamed Breed* is an undistingushed Western. He plays the ambitious rancher who wants to improve Texas cattle by introducing them to his Bramha bull and falls foul of his fellow ranchers. Reed's screenplay is of the sort Wayne could, and did, sleepwalk through in the sixties and seventies, but such a relaxed notion of acting wasn't valued in the fifties and, accordingly, Tufts and Bishop look strained trying to follow the episodic plot as the prize bull destroys all and sundry. Only Buchanan and, surprisingly, Britton, seem able to just get on with it.

d Charles Lamont *p* Harry Joe Brown *s* Tom Reed *c* Charles Lawton Jnr *lp* Sonny Tufts, Barbara Britton, George Hayes, William Bishop, Edgar Buchanan, George E. Stone

Whispering Smith (PAR) 88 min
One of the dozen or so films directed by actor Fenton, most of which were Westerns, this is a solid actioner with Ladd in the role first essayed by W.S. Hart. He is the railway detective who has to set off in pursuit of the man (Preston) who married the girl he loves and who has turned railroad robber and joined Crisp's gang. The opening is particularly effective, with Ladd's horse being shot out from under him by a member of Crisp's gang. Fenton manages to keep a fast pace going throughout the whole film.

d Leslie Fenton *p* Mel Epstein *s* Frank Butler, Karl Lamb *c* Ray Rennahan *lp* Alan Ladd, Robert Preston, Brenda Marshall, Donald Crisp, William Demarest, Ray Teal

Yellow Sky (FOX) b/w 98 min
A bleak, stylish Western, memorable for MacDonald's compelling black and white cinematography. Peck and Widmark are the leaders of a seven-strong gang of bank robbers that heads into the desert after their latest robbery and stumbles upon the salt flats of a ghost town, a crazy prospector, Barton, and his tomboy daughter, Baxter. Loosely based on *The Tempest*, the movie is similar in tone to Wellman and Trotti's other Western together, **The Ox-Bow Incident** (1943), although it is a far more conventional movie, with Peck defending Baxter against Widmark's grinning advances.

In 1967, Robert D. Webb remade the film as *The Jackals*, setting the story in South Africa.

d William Wellman *p/s* Lamar Trotti *c* Joe MacDonald *lp* Gregory Peck, Richard Widmark, Anne Baxter, Henry Morgan, James Barton, Paul Hurst, John Russell

Donald Crisp (left) as the outlaw leader and Alan Ladd (centre) as the railway detective Whispering Smith.

1949

Bad Men of Tombstone (AA) b/w 75 min
An unusual and historically significant Western that, like **Black Bart** (1948) left its badmen/heroes dead in the dirt without a thought of reformation in their heads and with little romanticization on their behalf by writer Yordan. Sullivan is the gunman-lover, Reynolds his willing mistress and Crawford the outlaw leader who finally leads his men to their deaths on Tombstone's mainstreet. Even Sullivan's attempt to go straight with Reynolds is only cursorily dealt with.

d Kurt Neumann *p* Maurice King, Frank King *s* Philip Yordan, Arthur Strawn *c* Russell Harlan *lp* Barry Sullivan, Marjorie Reynolds, Broderick Crawford, Fortunio Bonanova, Guinn Williams, Harry Cording

The Beautiful Blonde from Bashful Bend
(FOX) 77 min
A delightful farce. Grable is the saloon singer who hides out as a school-teacher when the pot shot she takes at her wayward lover, Romero, ends up in the rear end of a judge. Made with the same brash, anarchic energy that characterizes Sturges' better-known films (*Sullivan's Travels, Palm Beach Story*, both 1942) it only lacks the cutting edge of their social criticism. Nonetheless, this frenetic satire on all things Western, is far better than its reputation might suggest. Vallee, wonderfully out of place in the West, is Grable's new suitor but there's no doubt that Grable is the real star.

John Russell threatens Anne Baxter in William Wellman's Yellow Sky.

d/p/s Preston Sturges   *c* Harry Jackson   *lp* Betty Grable, Cesar Romero, Rudy Vallee, Sterling Holloway, Frank Herbert, Alan Bridge

The Big Sombrero
(GENE AUTRY PRODUCTIONS/COL)   77 min
After **The Strawberry Roan** (1948), this was Autry's only colour outing. His biggest musical for several years – it features no less than nine songs – it opens with an impoverished Autry pawning his guitar, but not before serenading the pawnbroker. In Mexico he mounts a fiesta at the ranch of Verdugo and stops her marriage to Dunne who is only after her extensive lands. McDonald, who'd directed many of Roy Rogers' musical works at Republic, handles the direction with some distinction.

d Frank McDonald   *p* Armand Schaefer   *s* Olive Cooper *c* William Bradford   *lp* Gene Autry, Elena Verdugo, Stephen Dunne, George J. Lewis, Vera Marshe, William Edmunds, Champion

Brimstone   (REP)   b/w   90 min
Cameron and Brennan, as marshal and outlaw respectively, romp through this briskly directed prestige Western from Republic. Brennan is the cattle rancher who turns to crime in a desperate attempt to bankrupt homesteaders who invade the open range in the rambling Williams screenplay. Cameron, whose role is by no means as juicy as that of Brennan, does well as the marshal but Kane seems more interested in matters of production than direction.

d/p Joseph Kane   *s* Thames Williams   *c* Jack Marta *lp* Rod Cameron, Adrian Booth, Walter Brennan, Forrest Tucker, Jim Davis, Guinn Williams

Brothers in the Saddle   (RKO)   b/w   60 min
Another superior Holt entry with Brodie as the brother Holt must ride to the rescue of. Though the number of continuity slips indicate that the budget was being cut rather than raised, Selander's artless, efficient direction, Houston's workmanlike screenplay and the fact that the series was still being made by a tight group of people, results in a taut little Western. An intriguing twist, which explains Brodie's casting, is having him go loco, when Holt doesn't rescue him in time, and turn into a villain, guns blazing and a sneer on his lips, before dying at the hands of Holt.

d Lesley Selander   *p* Herman Schlom   *s* Norman Houston *c* J. Roy Hunt   *lp* Tim Holt, Richard Martin, Steve Brodie, Virginia Cox, Richard Powers (Tom Keene), Stanley Andrews

Calamity Jane and Sam Bass
(U-INTERNATIONAL)   85 min
Sam Bass gets his usual whitewash in this beautiful-looking but slow-moving Western. He is portrayed by Duff as a wronged man forced into crime. Geraghty and Levy's screenplay is a touch moralistic for the period with Duff dying committing his last crime while De Carlo, the girl who loved him and fought by his side, looks on.

d George Sherman   *p* Leonard Goldstein   *s* Maurice Geraghty, Melvin Levy   *c* Irving Glassberg   *lp* Yvonne De Carlo, Howard Duff, Dorothy Hart, Willard Parker, Lloyd Bridges, Milburn Stone

Canadian Pacific (FOX) 95 min

A romantic, not to say inaccurate, account of the building of the Canadian Pacific Railroad. Scott is the line surveyor and Jory the man who leads the trappers in opposition to the railroad and tries to ferment Indian troubles, to no avail. Wyatt is the object of Scott's affections. Although script and direction are anonymous, the location cinematography of Jackman makes the film easy on the eye.

d Edwin L. Marin *p* Nat Holt *s* Jack DeWitt, Kenneth Gamet *c* Fred Jackman Jnr *lp* Randolph Scott, Jane Wyatt, Nancy Olsen, Victor Jory, J. Carrol Naish, Robert Barratt

Colorado Territory (WB) b/w 94 min

A classic Western, this bleak reworking of Walsh's own superb gangster film, *High Sierra* (1941), substitutes McCrea's weary desperation for Bogie's laconic interpretation of the bandit who wants to go straight but signs up for 'just one more job'. Cinematographer Hickox piles on the black – to give the film the look of a *film noir* – and writers Twist and North create a fitting atmosphere of doom around McCrea and Mayo as the tragic lovers, but it is Walsh whose direction brings this darkly romantic Western to life. The bravura treatment of landscape is particularly impressive, especially in the confrontation where the ant-size humans meet their malevolent destiny amid barren mountains. The final shot, an optical zoom of McCrea's death, is magnificent.

d Raoul Walsh *p* Anthony Veiller *s* John Twist, Edmund H. North *c* Sid Hickox *lp* Joel McCrea, Virginia Mayo, Dorothy Malone, Henry Hull, John Archer, Harry Woods

The Cowboy and the Indians (COL) b/w 68 min

This is an interesting film made just before **Broken Arrow** and **Devil's Doorway** (both 1950), which unleashed vast numbers of Indian Westerns, most of them sympathetic to Indians. This modern series outing sees Autry in step with, if not in advance of, the times as he comes to the defence of Indians being bilked by an unscrupulous Indian agent and exonerates Silverheels' articulate, educated Indian. However, there is one significant difference between Autry's vision of

white-red relationships and that of Delmer Daves and Anthony Mann. Where their films offer a radical (for Hollywood) re-interpretation of history and interrogate the spectre of racism, Autry offers only a song and vacuous vows of eternal friendship. Autry's Indian pictures are wholly within the series Western tradition which sees the Indian as savage or victim in vivid black and white.

d John English *p* Armand Schaefer *s* Dwight Cummins, Dorothy Yost *c* William Bradford *lp* Gene Autry, Sheila Ryan, Frank Richards, Hank Patterson, Jay Silverheels, Clayton Moore, Champion

Daughter of the West

(MARTIN MOONEY PRODUCTIONS/FILM CLASSICS) 77 min

An unusual Western set in a Navajo reservation in the 1880s, it features Vickers as the convent-educated daughter of Ramona who is unaware of her birthright until she falls for educated Indian, Reed. Together they stop the schemes of Indian agent Woods to obtain for himself valuable mineral rights that rightly belong to the tribe. But more important than the jerky plot is the journey of discovery of her Indianness that Vickers makes.

d Harold Daniels *p* Martin Mooney *s* Irwin R. Franklyn, Raymond L. Schrock *c* Henry Sharp *lp* Martha Vickers, Philip Reed, Donald Woods, Marion Carney, Anthony Barr, William Farnum

Desert Vigilante (COL) b/w 56 min

This is the first film as a director by Sears who was to become one of the most prolific of B directors in the fifties. Slower paced than recent Starretts (and certainly slower than subsequent efforts by Sears would be), it features Starrett as a Federal marshal on the trail of Coffin's band of smugglers. Wakely joins Starrett to provide the musical interludes.

d Fred F. Sears *p* Colbert Clark *s* Earle Snell *c* Rex Wimpey *lp* Charles Starrett, Smiley Burnette, Peggy Stewart, Tristram Coffin, George Chesebro, Jimmy Wakely

The Doolins of Oklahoma *aka* The Great Manhunt

(PRODUCERS-ACTORS CORPORATION) b/w 90 min

A routine film from Scott and Brown's own production company in which Scott is Bill Doolin who takes up his guns

Gene Autry with two of his young fans on the set of The Cowboy and the Indians.

Virginia Mayo and Joel McCrea as the star-crossed lovers in Colorado Territory.

Above: *Martha Vickers (left) as the convent educated Indian who rediscovers her Indianness in* Daughter of the West.

Jim Bannon (left), one of several actors to play Red Ryder, in The Fighting Redhead.

Bottom: *Vera Ralston, Oliver Hardy, in one of his rare appearances without Stan Laurel, and John Wayne in* The Fighting Kentuckian.

when his close friends the Daltons are massacred. Douglas directs with some style but the plot, which seeks to romanticize Scott as the leader of five lead-spewing gunmen, is too old fashioned, especially in comparison to films like **Black Bart** (1948) and **Bad Men of Tombstone** (1949). Only Lawton's stunning cinematography is at all modern.

d Gordon Douglas *p* Harry Joe Brown *s* Kenneth Gamet
c Charles Lawton Jnr *lp* Randolph Scott, George Macready, Louise Allbritton, John Ireland, Noah Beery Jnr, Virginia Huston

Down Dakota Way (REP) 67 min

A well-mounted Rogers series outing. Rogers is the stranger who arrives in town to find his friend, the local vet, murdered and Barcroft, Rogers' most regular villain, the guilty party who needs the vet out of the way so he can sell his diseased cattle to meat-packers. The film is co-written by Nibley who became the series' story editor, after Witney's arrival as director, and with him radically changed the development of the Rogers persona, giving the films a more violent and (in the context of the series Western) 'realistic' edge.

d William Witney *p* Edward J. White *s* John K. Butler, Sloan Nibley *c* Reggie Lanning *lp* Roy Rogers, Dale Evans, Pat Brady, Monte Montana, Elizabeth Risdon, Roy Barcroft, Trigger

The Fighting Kentuckian (REP) b/w 100 min

This routine outing cast a reluctant Wayne with Ralston (the wife of Republic boss, Herbert J. Yates) for the second time. He's the bluff trapper romancing her upper-class French exile in the Alabama of the 1820s and having to foil the landgrabbing plans of his rival, Howard, before he can win her hand. Produced by Wayne himself, it features Hardy, in a rare appearance without his partner Stan Laurel. Garmes' superb deep-focus cinematography compensates for Waggner's indifferent direction.

d/s George Waggner *p* John Wayne *c* Lee Garmes
lp John Wayne, Vera Ralston, Philip Dorn, Oliver Hardy, John Howard, Marie Windsor

Fighting Man of the Plains (FOX) 94 min

A solid, if unimaginative actioneer. Scott is the ex-Quantrill Raider turned gunfighter turned lawman who clears up the town of Lanyard with the assistance of Robertson's Jesse James. Jory is the villain of the piece.

d Edwin L. Marin *p* Nat Holt *s* Frank Gruber
c Fred Jackman Jnr *lp* Randolph Scott, Bill Williams, Victor Jory, Jane Nigh, Dale Robertson, Douglas Kennedy

The Fighting Redhead (EAGLE-LION) 55 min

This is the last of Bannon's short-lived Red Ryder series for Eagle-Lion. Hart is the rustler and Stewart the tomboy daughter of one of his victims who vows to avenge her murdered father but is getting nowhere until Bannon arrives on the scene. Collins' direction is lacklustre and anonymous and the result is a mediocre Western, even by Eagle-Lion standards.

d Lewis D. Collins *p* Jerry Thomas *s* Paul Franklin, Jerry Thomas *c* Gilbert Warrenton *lp* Jim Bannon, Emmett Lynn, Marin Sais, Peggy Stewart, John Hart, Forrest Taylor

The Gal Who Took the West

(U-INTERNATIONAL) 84 min
A would-be satire on Westerns, this mediocre film is best remembered for Daniels' handsome cinematography. Bowers and Brodney's screenplay tells the story, in flashback, of the legendary O'Hara family and of the lengthy feud between

Russell and Brady over De Carlo's Eastern songbird. Far from poking fun at frontier Westerns, the first half of the film is indistinguishable from such movies.

d Frederick de Cordova *p* Robert Arthur *s* William Bowers, Oscar Brodney *c* William Daniels *lp* Yvonne De Carlo, Charles Coburn, Scott Brady, John Russell, James Millican, Myrna Dell

Ghost of Zorro (REP) b/w 12 chaps

Moore, who was later to find lasting fame as TV's Lone Ranger, is the engineer descendant of Zorro in this routine serial. This time he's fighting scheming businessmen trying to stop the completion of a telegraph line. Barcroft is the swarthy heavy. The serial, Republic's last fling with Zorro and which as usual was re-edited for release as a feature, is fondly remembered by fans for its over-reliance on Moore's ability to swiftly regain consciousness and roll away from a falling object in a fraction of a second and so survive until the next episode.

d Fred C. Brannon *p* Franklyn Adreon *s* Roy Cole, William Lively, Sol Shor *c* John MacBurnie *lp* Clayton Moore, Roy Barcroft, Pamela Blake, George Chesebro, Charles King, I. Stanford Jolley

The Golden Stallion (REP) 67 min

Trigger is the real star of this highly improbable Rogers entry scripted by series veteran Nibley. The plot features diamond smuggling across the Mexican Border with the gems hidden in a specially designed horse-shoe worn by a tame Palomino mare that criss-crosses over the border at will with a herd of wild horses. When Rogers captures the herd, Trigger falls for the mare and then kills one of the smugglers when she is mistreated. To save his horse Rogers takes the blame and ends up in jail where he remains until Trigger Jnr (!) exposes the smugglers. Although it was not as well received as **My Pal Trigger** (1946), the first and best Rogers entry devoted to Trigger, the equine action made for a pleasant change from the musical-dominated films made before Witney and Nibley took control of the series.

d William Witney *p* Edward J. White *s* Sloan Nibley *c* Jack Marta *lp* Roy Rogers, Dale Evans, Estelita Rodriguez, Pat Brady, Douglas Evans, Frank Fenton, Trigger

Horsemen of the Sierras (COL) b/w 56 min

The second directorial effort of Sears, an actor who'd appeared way down the cast list in several Starrett Westerns before graduating to dialogue coach and then fully fledged director with **Desert Vigilante** (1949). A marked improvement on his first film, it sees him bringing fresh camera angles to the Durango Kid series. Nonetheless the plot is routine with Starrett ending a range feud manufactured by the combatants so as to scare the surrounding ranchers off their oil-rich land. The strong supporting cast includes O'Mahoney

Clayton Moore (with mask) in Republic's last Zorro outing, Ghost of Zorro.

(soon to be a B Western star himself) who was also Starrett's stunt double.

d Fred F. Sears *p* Colbert Clark *s* Barry Shipman *c* Fayte Browne *lp* Charles Starrett, Smiley Burnette, Jock O'Mahoney, Lois Hall, John Dehner, Jason Robards Snr

I Shot Jesse James (LIPPERT) b/w 81 min

For his directorial debut, Fuller produced not only a stylistic tour de force but also totally transformed the James legend, ripping away its traditional props to make it a tragedy of misplaced love. Ireland as Bob Ford, 'the dirty little coward who shot Mr Howard', kills Hadley's Jesse James to get the pardon that will allow him to marry his childhood sweetheart, Britton, only to have her reject him. Told in jarring close-ups that strip the characters down to elemental emotions, it is, with the director's own **Forty Guns** (1957) amongst the most delirious of Westerns.

d/s Samuel Fuller *p* Robert L. Lippert, Carl Hittleman *c* Ernest Miller *lp* John Ireland, Barbara Britton, Reed Hadley, Preston Foster, Tom Tyler, Byron Foulger

The Last Bandit (REP) 80 min

A fast-paced remake by Kane of his own 1941 non-Western outing, *The Last Bandit* is one of Elliott's few big budget features. He and Tucker are brothers who end up on different sides of the law when Tucker robs the train Elliott is guarding. Booth is Tucker's scheming girlfriend who reforms when she falls for Elliott and with whom he suffers several uncomfortable love scenes; Elliott is far better at athletic heroics than the love-making the script calls for.

d/p Joseph Kane *s* Thomas Williamson *c* Jack Marta *lp* William (Bill) Elliott, Andy Devine, Jack Holt, Forrest Tucker, Adrian Booth, Grant Withers

Law of the Golden West (REP) b/w 60 min

One of the best of Hale's series Westerns, this is cleverly constructed to exploit some of Republic's 'excess' footage from bigger budgeted productions. Hale, no longer singing in

Charles Starrett (with mask) as the Durango Kid in Horsemen of the Sierras.

Above: *John Ireland as Bob Ford and Preston Foster in Sam Fuller's delirious* I Shot Jesse James.

his films, plays Buffalo Bill as a young man seeking the murderer of his father on the Kansas-Missouri border just prior to the Civil War. He uncovers a plot by Holland and chief villain Barcroft to carve themselves an empire in the West. Ford, a regular with the series, directs with real verve.

d Philip Ford *p* Melville Tucker *s* Norman S. Hall *c* Ernest Miller *lp* Monte Hale, Paul Hurst, Gail Davis, John Holland, Roy Barcroft, Lane Bradford

Glenn Ford and Ida Lupino as the schemers who seek control of the legendary Lost Dutchman Mine in Lust for Gold.

Loaded Pistols
(GENE AUTRY PRODUCTIONS/COL) b/w 77 min
Another surprisingly actionful outing from Autry graced with the hard-riding Britton as the heroine and spiritedly directed by English who'd quit Republic to get out of serial production. Cummins and Yost's screenplay has Autry investigate a case of murder while he's hiding the youngster accused. Wills handles the comic chores.

d John English *p* Armand Schaefer *s* Dwight Cummins, Dorothy Yost *c* William Bradford *lp* Gene Autry, Barbara Britton, Chill Wills, Jack Holt, Russell Arms, Robert Shayne, Champion

Below: A quintessential Western scene from Massacre River.

Look Out Sister
(ASCOR PICTURES/R.M. SAVANI PRODUCTIONS) b/w 64 min
Louis Jordan singing 'Caldonia' in a Western ! ? It could only happen in a dream, which is precisely how this fascinating all-black Western is structured. Though the film was clearly made on a shoestring, Gordon's screenplay is ambitious: while asleep Jordan dreams he's on a dude ranch and so the action begins with Jordan and company breaking up their broad satire of Western ways with 11 marvellous numbers. Hawley is the villain and Harbin the love interest for whom 'Two Gun' Jordan rescues her ranch from foreclosure by Hawley. Unlike earlier all-black Westerns such as **Harlem on the Prairie** (1937), *Look Out Sister* has more of the cool, jivetalking aspect of black culture, as one would expect from Jordan. Similarly, its participants are clearly less in awe of the Western. A fascinating film.

d Bud Pollard *p* Berle Adams *s* John E. Gordon *c* Carl Berger *lp* Louis Jordan, Monte Hawley, Suzette Harbin, Glenn Allen, Jack Clisby, Tommy Southern

Lust for Gold (COL) sepia 90 min
An oddity. The film is based on the true story of the lost location of the legendary Lost Dutchman Goldmine. Structured around a flashback of the double dealings of Ford, Lupino and husband Young as they plot against each other for control of the fabled mine, this sepia-hued adventure follows Ford's grandson, Prince, as he tries to rediscover the mine. Simon, who replaced George Marshall as director at the last minute, so simplifies the complex plot that Barry Storm, on whose novel the film is based and after whom the Prince character is called, sued for misrepresentation.

d/p S. Sylvan Simon *s* Ted Sherdeman, Richard English *c* Archie Stout *lp* Ida Lupino, Glenn Ford, Gig Young, William Prince, Edgar Buchanan, Will Geer

Massacre River (WINDSOR PICTURES) sepia 75 min
Madison's second outing in Western garb, clothes he was to become very familiar with in the course of his lengthy career, this inept actioneer sees Calhoun and him as a pair of army officers in love with the same woman, Downs. However, it is Brodie, as the menacing gambler, who steals the film, especially as the action scenes of the Indians going on the warpath are so weakly done.

d John Rawlins *p* Julian Lesser, Frank Melford *s* Louis Stevens *c* Jack MacKenzie *lp* Guy Madison, Rory Calhoun, Carole Mathews, Steve Brodie, Cathy Downs, Johnny Sands

Outlaw Country (WESTERN ADVENTURE) b/w 76 min
This is one of the best, and surprisingly the longest, of the Lash LaRue series. Swiftly paced by Taylor – it's almost non-stop action – it features the time-honoured 'twins' plot

with LaRue as a Federal Marshal and a notorious counterfeiter who eventually changes sides to help bring in White's band of outlaws.

d Ray Taylor *p/co-s* Ron Ormond *co-s* Ira Webb
c Ernest Miller *lp* Lash LaRue, Al St John, Nancy Saunders, Dan White, House Peters Jnr, Ted Adams

Pioneer Marshal (REP) b/w 60 min
Routine fare. Hale is the marshal in disguise who arrives at an outlaws' refuge on the trail of embezzler Healey and decides to bring to justice the suave O'Flynn who runs the refuge and charges his guests a percentage of their takings, as well. The film is unimaginatively directed by Ford with an eye that seems more on the budget than the action. Barcroft chips in with a chilling performance as a killer.

d Philip Ford *p* Melville Tucker *s* Bob Williams *c* John MacBurnie *lp* Monte Hale, Nan Leslie, Paul Hurst, Roy Barcroft, Myron Healey, Damian O'Flynn

Powder River Rustlers (REP) b/w 60 min
This is one of the best of Lane's series Westerns for Republic. He and Waller, his tall-story-telling side-kick, prevent McDonald, the town's tailor (!), from stealing the $50,000 bond the town has raised to bring the railroad there, but only after Lane's been falsely accused of murder and theft himself. The climactic fight between McDonald and Lane, with McDonald plunging a pair of scissors into Lane, is magnificently staged.

d Philip Ford *p* Gordon Kay *s* Richard Wormser *c* John MacBurnie *lp* Allan Lane, Eddy Waller, Francis McDonald, Roy Barcroft, Gerry Ganzer, Cliff Clark

Range Land (MON) b/w 56 min
One of the better of the 22 series Westerns Wilson made for Monogram. Buffington's script, which has Wilson become an outlaw to catch a gang of bandits, was hardly original but it has the advantage of being well laid out. Similarly Clyde gives the same kind of solid support he once gave William Boyd in the Hopalong Cassidy series. Penn is the villain of the piece.

d Lamber Hillyer *p* Eddie Davis *s* Adele Buffington *c* Harry Neumann *lp* Whip Wilson, Andy Clyde, Leonard Penn, Kermit Maynard, Reed Howes, Keene Duncan

Ranger of Cherokee Strip (REP) b/w 60 min
In this, one of the best of his series outings, Hale is the Ranger who, with the Cherokee Indian (Kennedy) he's supposed to bring to justice, frustrates the plans of Barcroft and his fellow cattlemen, who are trying to squeeze the Indians out of land granted them by Washington. They also discover Kennedy to be innocent of the murder he's accused of after being framed by the cattlemen. In fact the weak-willed Meeker did the killing. Ford handles the action at a fast and furious pace while Williams' screenplay confirmed that, even in the B and series Westerns, the fifties was to be the decade of the Indian Western.

d Philip Ford *p* Melville Tucker *s* Bob Williams *c* Ellis W. Carter *lp* Monte Hale, Paul Hurst, Douglas Kennedy, Roy Barcroft, George Meeker, Alice Talton

Red Desert (LIPPERT) b/w 60 min
A diverting mystery co-written by Ullman whose one stylistic trait was his penchant for writing thrillers in Western guise. Barry is the government agent assigned to track down an outlaw (Foulger) who's stolen gold bullion. Beebe directs efficiently and Miller's camerawork suggests a bigger budget than could have been available.

d Ford Beebe *p/co-s* Ron Ormond *co-s* Daniel B. Ullman *c* Ernest Miller *lp* Donald Barry, Tom Neal, Jack Holt, Byron Foulger, Margia Dean, Tom London

Riders in the Sky
(GENE AUTRY PRODUCTIONS/COL) b/w 69 min
Named after the song, this Autry outing is notable for the renewed emphasis on action it suggests and for its star's far less ostentatious outfits than usual. The plot sets Autry against ex-Mesquiteer Livingston as the gambler and town boss who makes the mistake of trying to frame a friend of Autry's for murder. Writer Geraghty was the brother of director/producer Maurice, and of Carmelita who'd appeared in several of Buck Jones' series Westerns.

d John English *p* Armand Schaefer *s* Gerald Geraghty *c* William Bradford *lp* Gene Autry, Gloria Henry, Pat Buttram, Mary Beth Hughes, Robert Livingston, Steve Darrell, Champion

Rim of the Canyon
(GENE AUTRY PRODUCTIONS/COL) b/w 70 min
This actioneer from Autry is doubly interesting: for only the second time, the first being **Shooting High** (1940), Autry plays someone other than himself; his father (as well as himself), while the film's baddie is Mahoney who would eventually replace Ted Mapes as Autry's own stunt double.

Allan 'Rocky' Lane, one of seriesdom's most athletic heroes, in Powder River Rustlers.

The pinch-faced Don 'Red' Barry, star of Red Desert.

Above: *Monte Hale (left) in a scene from* Ranger of Cherokee Strip.

The plot has Autry Jnr on the track of $30,000 that three thieves, who were captured by Autry Snr (Autry with a mustache) some twenty years ago, are now out to retrieve. The impressive ghost-town locations are well captured by cinematographer Bradford while English's aggressive direction, especially of the lengthy Autry-Mahoney fight, gives the film a tougher edge than normal.

d John English *p* Armand Schaefer *s* John K. Butler *c* William Bradford *lp* Gene Autry, Nan Leslie, Thurston Hall, Clem Bevans, Walter Sande, Jock (O')Mahoney, Champion

Far right: *Robert Sterling, Claude Jarman Jnr and John Ireland, guns at the ready, in* Roughshod.

Roll Thunder Roll (EQUITY) 60 min
The second of the four-strong ill-fated Red Ryder series Westerns to star Bannon in the title role, this is an unmitigated disaster, attempting to mix mystery and action to

Gene Autry and the bespectacled Nan Leslie in Rim of the Canyon.

no purpose. Jolley is the would-be humorous Mexican Robin Hood who gets in the way of Bannon's pursuit of Strange.

d Lewis D. Collins *p* Jerry Thomas *s* Paul Franklin *c* Gilbert Warrenton *lp* Jim Bannon, I. Stanford Jolley, Glenn Strange, Emmett Lynn, Marin Sais, Nancy Gates

Roughshod (RKO) b/w 88 min
Sterling and Jarman are the brothers, travelling to California with a herd of thoroughbred horses and a bevy of dance-hall girls, who meet up with escaped convict Ireland in this entertaining B Western. Purposely avoiding the endless chases – more often than not over the same patch of ground – that characterize the series Western, director Robson here concentrates on drama and character with Grahame and Ireland coming out particularly well.

d Mark Robson *p* Richard H. Berger *s* Geoffrey Homes *c* Joseph F. Biroc *lp* Robert Sterling, Claude Jarman Jnr, Gloria Grahame, John Ireland, Jeff Donnell, Jeff Corey

Rustlers (RKO) b/w 61 min
Another steady entry from Holt, this Natteford and Ward screenplay has him once again in pursuit of Brodie. He's the mastermind behind a novel rustling scheme: he sells back the cattle he's rustled, ready to be rustled again. It is energetically directed and acted.

d Lesley Selander *p* Herbert Schlom *s* Jack Natteford, Luci Ward *c* J. Roy Hunt *lp* Jim Holt, Martha Hyer, Richard Martin, Steve Brodie, Francis McDonald, Addison Richards

She Wore a Yellow Ribbon (RKO) 103 min
In complete contrast to **Fort Apache** (1948) which treats the disaster of Custer's defeat as a moment of glorious, albeit wrong-headed heroism, *She Wore a Yellow Ribbon* is a success story. But that success is filtered through the haunting colours of Hoch's intensely melancholic cinematography (for which he won a deserved Oscar). This mood is prepared for by the film's spoken introduction: 'Custer is dead and around the bloody guidons of the Seventh Cavalry lie the 212 officers and men he led.' Moreover, whereas **Fort Apache** is peopled by young ambitious officers, men at the beginning of their careers, the characters of *She Wore a Yellow Ribbon* are in the autumn of their lives, looking back to the past and fearful of a future outside the Cavalry. Wayne's journey to the Indian encampment in search of peace has some of the grandeur of his five-year journey in **The Searchers** (1956) but whereas the thrust of that film is tragic and analytic, that of *She Wore a Yellow Ribbon* is melancholic and full of reverie. Fittingly, its key moments are of communication with the dead and the past, Wayne talking to his wife in her grave, Mildred Natwick watching the men march out and wondering how many will

die and Cliff Lyons as 'Trooper Smith', an ex-Confederate General, dying amidst alien corn. Indeed Wayne's victory is not so much his stopping the outbreak of an Indian war but side-stepping his exile from the Arcadian community of the Cavalry.

d/co-p John Ford   *co-p* Merian C. Cooper   *s* Frank S. Nugent, Laurence Stallings   *c* Winton Hoch   *lp* John Wayne, Joanne Dru, John Agar, Ben Johnson, Harry Carey Jnr, Victor McLaglen

Sheriff of Wichita   (REP)   b/w   60 min
An entertaining series entry from Lane, memorable for being the first of his films to feature a headlong jump towards the camera in an effort to escape an adversary. Future entries would regularly feature this jump, making it more and more elaborate – through glass, into water, etc. – and dangerous. Williams' plot has Lane in the title role on the trail of a five-year-old army payroll robbery by Barcroft and Bardette. Springsteen directs with a firm eye on the action.

d R.G. Springsteen   *p* Gordon Kay   *s* Bob Williams   *c* John MacBurnie   *lp* Allan Lane, Eddy Waller, Roy Barcroft, Trevor Bardette, Clayton Moore, Lyn Wilde

South of St Louis   (WB)   b/w   88 min
As might have been expected, Enright's first film on his return to Warners was a Western. This one features McCrea (who gives a fine performance), Scott and Kennedy as the brawling ranchers seeking revenge on Jory and his Union guerrillas who maliciously burnt down their ranches at the start of the Civil War. Alexis Smith and Malone are the ladies. A modest, entertaining Western.

d Ray Enright   *p* Milton Sperling   *s* Zachary Gold, James R. Webb   *c* Karl Freund   *lp* Joel McCrea, Alexis Smith, Zachary Scott, Dorothy Malone, Douglas Kennedy, Victor Jory

Stallion Canyon   (KANAB/ASTOR)   72 min
This is one of the few Westerns to star Curtis and the first by Kanab Pictures, named after the place they were made. Curtis, who sings and grins better than he rides is the hero who, with his horse Thundercloud, foils rustlers Taylor and Adams, but it is the locations, new to series Westerns, that get most of cinematographer McCluskey's attention.

d Harry Fraser   *s* Hy Heath   *c* Jack McCluskey   *lp* Ken Curtis, Carolina Cotton, Forrest Taylor, Ted Adams, Shug Fisher, Billy Hammond

Below: Rod Cameron and Gale Storm in the Blake Edwards scripted Stampede.

Stampede (AA) sepia 78 min

Praised for its realistic portrayal of ranch life, *Stampede* features Cameron and Castle as the feuding cattle barons and a paunchy-looking Brown as the sheriff whose job it is to pacify the brothers and catch the crooks who've cheated settlers of their water rights. Selander's direction is as robust as ever but the script, only the second by Edwards who was later to emerge as a significant writer/director in the sixties, is decidedly routine. Edwards also appears in the film in a bit part.

d Lesley Selander *p/s* John C. Champion, Blake Edwards *c* Harry Neumann *lp* Rod Cameron, Gale Storm, Johnny Mack Brown, Don Castle, Don Curtis, John Miljan

Streets of Laredo (PAR) 92 min

This remake of **The Texas Rangers** (1936) with Holden, Bendix and Carey in the roles originated by Fred MacMurray, Jackie Oakie and Lloyd Nolan, is particularly interesting for the change in emphasis between the two versions. The plots are virtually the same: two former outlaws join the Texas Rangers and go after a former fellow-outlaw who has become a famous bandit. But where the first version represents an epic tribute to progress, in its celebration of the pacifying of Indians which brought peace to the frontier and literally transformed outlaws into lawmen, the 1949 version is stripped of its historical context. Being merely the story of three individuals, the Indians of the 1936 film are missing from this version.

William Bishop and Ella Raines (centre) with Edgar Buchanan and John Ireland (back centre) in a studio portrait for The Walking Hills.

d Leslie Fenton *p* Robert Fellows *s* Charles Marquis Warren *c* Ray Rennahan *lp* William Holden, William Bendix, Macdonald Carey, Mona Freeman, Ray Teal, Clem Bevins

Trail's End (MON) b/w 57 min

This is one of the lesser Brown series entries made when the series was clearly on its last legs. Terhune, taking over the lighter moments from Hatton – briefly both had supported Brown – re-activates his old Alibi character from his Three Mesquiteer days. Brown defends Morley and her ranch from outlaws after the gold they know is on her land.

d Lambert Hillyer *p* Barney Sarecky *s* J. Benton Cheney *c* Harry Neumann *lp* Johnny Mack Brown, Max Terhune, Kay Morley, Myron Healey, Douglas Evans, George Chesebro

The Walking Hills (COL) b/w 78 min

Similar in theme to **The Treasure of the Sierra Madre** (1948), *The Walking Hills* was the first of director Sturges' many Westerns. Scott, Buchanan, Kennedy, Raines and Ireland are amongst the party searching for a wagon train of gold buried years ago in Death Valley. Lawton's expressive camerawork and Sturges' taut direction make the most of LeMay's simple storyline. Scott takes the acting honours as the escaped killer who 'does the right thing' when gold lust grips the party.

d John Sturges *p* Harry Joe Bown *s* Alan LeMay *c* Charles Lawton *lp* Randolph Scott, Ella Raines, William Bishop, Edgar Buchanan, Arthur Kennedy, John Ireland

Western Renegades (MON) b/w 56 min

A breezy Brown outing in which he foils Prosser's attempts to take over a town before getting bogged down in the plot complications of a dance-hall girl pretending to be the long-lost mother of a couple of kids. Brown is the marshal, looking far fatter than he did a decade before but still able to mix it as well as ever.

d Wallace Fox *p* Eddie Davis *s* Adele Buffington *c* Harry Neumann *lp* Johnny Mack Brown, Max Terhune, Jane Adams, Hugh Prosser, Myron Healey, Marshall Reed

The Wyoming Bandit (REP) b/w 60 min

A pleasant series outing from Lane. Webster's inventive screenplay features Bardette, who gives a memorable performance as the outlaw who joins the side of law and order to help get the men who shot his son. Lane, after the same men, impersonates a bandit and eventually exposes Kilian's saddle-maker as the outlaw chief. Ford directs as efficiently as ever.

d Philip Ford *p* Gordon Kay *s* M. Coates Webster *c* John MacBurnie *lp* Allan Lane, Eddy Waller, Trevor Bardette, Victor Kilian, Rand Brooks, Bob Wilke

The Younger Brothers (WB) b/w 77 min

One of several films devoted to the career of the Younger brothers who after Jesse James and Billy the Kid must have had their story told more than any other outlaw by Hollywood. This version features all four Youngers (Morris, who played a Younger earlier in **Bad Men of Missouri**, 1941, Bennett, Hutton and Brown) and their attempts to stay out of trouble for two weeks and so keep their freedom. Brooks is the good girl, Paige the temptress and Hale and Tyler the outlaws who get the brothers innocently involved in a bank robbery. Marin's direction is economic if hardly forceful.

d Edwin L. Marin *p* Saul Elkins *s* Edna Anhalt *c* William Snyder *lp* Wayne Morris, Bruce Bennett, Geraldine Brooks, Robert Hutton, James Brown, Alan Hale, Tom Tyler, Janis Paige

The 1950s

Indians and Psychopaths – A Genre Redefined

The two most influential (and imitated) Westerns of the fifties were undoubtedly **Broken Arrow** (1950) and **High Noon** (1952). The former inaugurated a cycle of Indian Westerns which treated Indians and their culture sympathetically (if, for the most part, patronizingly), while the latter was the first of an informal series in which social issues such as civic responsibility were raised in a rather self-conscious fashion. Both films reflected a growing, and general, unease with their times that formed the backdrop to many of the decade's finest films. It was this that made the fifties Western more complex and interesting. In contrast to the easy optimism of the early forties and the resigned disillusionment of the seventies and beyond, the Western in the fifties was at its most flexible and open.

It is not surprising therefore that the decade witnessed a marvellous blossoming of the genre, with directors Boetticher, Ford and Mann working at their peak and the likes of Daves, Dwan, Fuller, Hawks, Lang, Penn, Ray, Sturges, Tourneur and Walsh producing individual masterpieces. Of these, Boetticher and Mann, who produced their best work in the Western, are particularly interesting. They approached the genre from opposite ends – Boetticher from the perspective of the B Western, whose conventions he effortlessly twisted to make supple what could so easily have been brittle in other hands. Mann on the other hand took for his starting point the A Western and its 'big themes', but in place of Errol Flynn effortlessly taming the frontier there was James Stewart as a man at odds with himself, caught in the grip of obsessions he was only dimly aware of, and living in an extremely dangerous world.

That the Western could accommodate such drastic revisions of its conventions and themes and of the assumptions about America they supported, testifies to the vitality of the genre. A vivid demonstration of this can be seen in the large number of fifties Westerns to deal with troubled adolescents and stern patriarchs: even the legendary Jesse James could be reinterpreted in terms of adolescent frustrations in **The True Story of Jesse James** (1957). But though writers and directors could make adolescents the subject of Westerns they failed to make them the audience, as they had been in earlier decades. Viewed from the drive-in what was notable about the fifties was the rise of science fiction (and later horror) films which took the place of the Western. Far more worrying at the time, however, was the competition from TV. Despite the flurry of widescreen and 3-D movies and the renewed emphasis on the cinema, the fifties saw a steadily growing audience. Ironically a lot of those stay-at-homes were watching Westerns, be they series Westerns which effortlessly made the production jump to TV or adult programmes like *Gunsmoke*, which was closely modelled on *High Noon*.

In retrospect the fifties was a traumatic period for the genre, though this was masked at the time by the consistently high quality of Westerns and their box office success. The death of the series Western and the slow decline of the B Western which culminated in the closure of Republic in 1958 meant that the genre which had for so long supported so many Hollywood studios lost its economic *raison d'être*. Henceforth, the Western would merely be just one genre amongst many, and soon it would not even belong exclusively to America.

Across the Badlands (COL) b/w 55 min
A superior series entry from Starrett whose recent outings had been less than impressive. Sears' direction is capable, especially in the action scenes where Mahoney does Starrett's stunts, and Shipman's script is as fantastical as ever. This time both as Durango and as a deputy sheriff Starrett helps map out a new railroad line when surveyors meet opposition from a township sure it will be bankrupt if the line doesn't come through their town.

d Fred F. Sears *p* Colbert Clark *s* Barry Shipman
c Fayte Brown *lp* Charles Starrett, Smiley Burnette, Helen Mowery, Stanley Andrews, Bob Wilke, Jock (O')Mahoney

Ambush (MGM) b/w 89 min
The last picture of director Wood and the first as producer of Deutsch, *Ambush* is a very routine Western. Taylor is the frontier scout who romances Dahl and rescues her sister from the Apache and Bruce Cowling the villain. Action and script are robust enough, but, in comparison with Taylor's other Western of 1950, **Devil's Doorway,** the film is hopelessly old fashioned, though contemporary reviewers, who concentrated their attention and comments on Dahl's tight frontier dresses and plunging decolletage, clearly thought otherwise.

d Sam Wood *p* Armand Deutsch *s* Marguerite Roberts
c Harold Lipstein *lp* Robert Taylor, John Hodiak, Arlene Dahl, Don Taylor, Bruce Cowling, John McIntire

Annie Get Your Gun (MGM) 107 min
A surprisingly successful, but nonetheless stage-bound musical considering its producer and subject, the life and times of Annie Oakley the famous sharp shooter and Wild West Show star. The film was originally to have starred Judy Garland (who 'fell ill') and be directed by first Busby Berkeley and then Charles Walters. Considering the production difficulties, Hutton's acrobatic and enthusiastic performance as the raw hillbilly who tries to charm Keel's Wild West showman is more than competent. Songs include 'Doin' What Comes Natur'lly' (in a bowdlerized version) and 'There's No Business Like Showbusiness'.

Previous pages: *The neurotic fifties: Paul Newman in* The Left Handed Gun.

John McIntire (left) and a grizzled Robert Taylor as frontier scouts in Ambush.

Above: *The Indian dance number from Annie Get Your Gun.*

Far right: *Barbara Britton as the* Bandit Queen, *yet another tale of Old California.*

d George Sidney   *p* Arthur Freed   *s* Sidney Sheldon
c Charles Rosher   *lp* Betty Hutton, Howard Keel, Louis Calhern, J. Carroll Naish, Edward Arnold, Keenan Wynn

The Arizona Cowboy   (REP)   b/w   67 min
This is the first of Allen's series Westerns for Republic as a crooning cowboy. A former radio and recording star, Allen would last for some 31 films until 1953 before finally hanging up his stetson and becoming a singer-narrator for Walt Disney. Not as athletic as Ritter but with a charm and an Arizona drawl that lives up to his nickname of 'Arizona', Allen needs more support than he gets from Jones or Springsteen, whose direction is oddly quiet. The routine screenplay has Allen out to prove his father innocent of theft. Barcroft is the engaging villain.

d R.G. Springsteen   *p* Franklin Adreon   *s* Bradford Ropes
c William Bradford   *lp* Rex Allen, Gordon Jones, Roy Barcroft, Teala Loring, Edmund Cobb, Chris-Pin Martin

Bandit Queen   (LIPPERT)   b/w   70 min
Set in the days of Old California, this preposterous piece of fantasy features Britton in the title role as the woman who, like Batman, turns masked avenger when she witnesses the

Vincent Price (centre), and Ellen Drew with the map of the barony in Samuel Fuller's masterpiece of the pulp imagination, The Baron of Arizona.

murder of her parents and in conjunction with Joaquin Murietta (Reed) rids the territory of Parker and MacLane. Britton snaps her whip well and Reed is a capable assistant but West and Lesser's screenplay cuts too many corners to keep the smiles on its audience's faces.

d/p William Berke   *s* Victor West, Budd Lesser   *c* Ernest Miller   *lp* Barbara Britton, Willard Parker, Philip Reed, Barton MacLane, John Merton, Jack Ingram

The Baron of Arizona   (LIPPERT)   b/w   93 min
In Fuller's second film the twin concerns of **Forty Guns** (1957), love and responsibility, are joined in a single relationship. Price, who works as a clerk in the land office sets about systematically forging evidence to the effect that Drew, an orphan whom he marries, is the last of the Peralta family and heir to the stretch of land commonly called Arizona. By the small print, as it were, Price attempts to create his own barony. He does not commit forgery for money: after he has 'repossessed' Arizona, even though he knows that the American government is still uncertain as to the legality of his claims, he refuses a $25 million settlement for it. He seeks recognition as the just and lawful Baron of Arizona. Nor does

his forgery involve a mere sleight of hand: he spends years in a Spanish monastery to alter its records and even carves his name on the land and then falsifies a trail to his 'claim stake'. Of all Fuller's heroes, Price comes closest to the achievement of an alternative source of allegiance and identity. Unlike Rod Steiger in **Run of the Arrow** (1957), who can only flee from the hated victorious Union at the end of the Civil War, Price creates his own country to be lord and master of.

Even the extensive use of stock footage can't diminish the grandeur of Price's dream or the power of Fuller's emotionally charged direction. A minor, if unlikely sounding, masterpiece and a triumph of the pulp imagination.

The film is (very loosely) based on fact.

d/s Samuel Fuller   *p* Carl K. Hittleman   *c* James Wong Howe   *lp* Vincent Price, Ellen Drew, Beulah Bondi, Vladimir Sokoloff, Reed Hadley, Robert Barrat

Barricade   (WB)   b/w   75 min
A would-be prestige production let down by its writer and director. Massey is the sadistic miner who runs his mine at the point of a gun, Clark the outlaw who finally beats him to death in a bloody brawl when all else fails and Roman, the girl whose near death sparks off their fight. Massey catches the coldbloodedness necessary to make him believable as the tyrant of the gold mining camp, but Godfrey is unable to inspire his other actors similarly. Sackheim's script is obviously closely influenced by Jack London's oft-filmed novel, *The Sea Wolf*.

d Peter Godfrey   *p* Saul Elkins   *s* William Sackheim
c Carl Guthrie   *lp* Dane Clark, Raymond Massey, Ruth Roman, Robert Douglas, Morgan Farley, Walter Coy

Bells of Coronado (REP) 67 min

In this contemporary outing Rogers settles the hash of would-be uranium smugglers as an insurance agent (!?) on the trail of Withers and his band of foreign agents. However, although Nibley's plot is fantastical, the action, as overseen by Witney, is fast and furious. The well-staged climax has Rogers catch the baddies just as they're about to load the ore on a plane bound for foreign parts.

d William Witney p Edward J. White s Sloan Nibley c John MacBurnie lp Roy Rogers, Dale Evans, Pat Brady, Grant Withers, Leo Cleary, Clifton Young, Trigger

Beyond the Purple Hills

(GENE AUTRY PRODUCTIONS/COL) sepia 69 min

This otherwise routine outing sees Buttram, who'd had a small part in **The Strawberry Roan** (1948), elevated to the role of side-kick and marks the debut of Champion Jnr. As part of the shift to a plainer view of the West, rather than the fanciful extravaganza that earlier films had presented, the musical numbers are reduced to two and Autry is dressed a shade more realistically. The plot has O'Brien (later to become television's Wyatt Earp) falsely accused of murdering his father and Autry proving his innocence and catching the culprit, the town's banker who's been stealing from the dead man's estate.

d John English p Armand Schaefer s Norman S. Hall c William Bradford lp Gene Autry, Pat Buttram, Jo Dennison, Don Beddoe, James Millican, Hugh O'Brien, Champion

Border Outlaws aka The Phantom Horseman

(JACK SCHWARZ) b/w 59 min

This is the second of Cooley's ill-fated couple of films for Schwarz. Whereas in the **The Silver Bandit** (1950) Cooley had the limelight to himself, here the action is taken care of by Edwards leaving Cooley as the dude ranch manager, to handle the music, which he does with aplomb; he was after all a major figure in the development of Western Swing music. Ex-stuntman Talmadge directs uneasily, seemingly only happy in the action sequences. The plot features Edwards after a group of outlaws led by a mysterious masked horseman.

d/co-p Richard Talmadge co-p Jack Schwarz s Arthur Hoerl lp Spade Cooley, Maria Hart, Bill Edwards, Bill Kennedy, Bud Osborne, George Slocum

Broken Arrow (FOX) 93 min

With the lesser-known **Devil's Doorway** (1950), *Broken Arrow* marked the beginning of a cycle of Indian Westerns that either took Indians like Cochise (here Chandler in the first of his many Indian roles) as their heroes or treated Indian problems seriously and sympathetically. Stewart is the Cavalry scout who lives with the Apache and prevents the outbreak of an Indian war. Later films would lay the blame for the scandalous treatment of the Indians firmly at the door of the Indian Bureau and Washington business interests but in the fifties, as here, it was renegades and crooked traders who stood in for these rapacious interests. Similarly, though the marriage between Stewart and Paget's Indian maid and the depiction of Indian life as cultured rather than primitive was seen as daring at the time, Paget is required to die in the last reel and Stewart to return to civilization. The film spawned the TV series *Broken Arrow* (1956–58).

d Delmer Daves p Julian Blaustein s Michael Blankfort c Ernest Palmer lp James Stewart, Jeff Chandler, Debra Paget, Arthur Hunnicutt, Will Geer, Basil Ruysdael

California Passage (REP) b/w 90 min

A prestige Republic Western featuring Tucker and Davis (who turns out to have a sideline in stealing bullion) as the saloon partners and rivals for the love of Mara. Kane directs at his usual faster-than-fast pace, keeping the screenplay by Grant, a writer with a tendency to go on and on, trim and taut. The result is an action-packed, entertaining film made even more so by Kane's florid camera movements.

d/p Joseph Kane s James Edward Grant c John MacBurnie lp Forrest Tucker, Jim Davis, Adele Mara, Paul Fix, Estelita Rodriguez, Alan Bridge

The Caribou Trail (FOX) 81 min

Actually shot in Colorado, this tale of British Columbia features Scott as the prospector who finally quits searching for gold for ranching and Jory as the territory's badman. Marin's direction is routine as is Gruber's screenplay, but Scott's resoluteness and Jackman's handling of the much improved Cinecolor process have their moments.

Jeff Chandler (left) as Cochise and James Stewart, about to become a blood brother to the Apache, in Broken Arrow, the Western whose success brought about a radical shift in the genre's treatment of Indians.

Leo McMahon, Randolph Scott and Bill Steele in Colt .45.

Ray Milland as the Southern gentleman hero in John Farrow's energetic Copper Canyon.

d Edwin L. Marin *p* Nat Holt *s* Frank Gruber *c* Fred Jackman Jnr *lp* Randolph Scott, George Hayes, Victor Jory, Douglas Kennedy, Karin Booth, Jim Davis

Colt .45 (WB) 74 min

A pleasing actioneer, *Colt .45* was one of the most successful Westerns of the year. Randolph Scott is the gunsalesman whose distinctive long barrelled colt .45s are stolen by Zachary Scott and used in a series of robberies. Determined to regain the guns, Randolph sets off in search of Zachary. Blackburn's screenplay is plain but efficient and Marin's direction forceful, but it is the charm of Randolph Scott, his ungainly romancing of Roman notwithstanding, that carries the film.

d Edwin L. Marin *p* Saul Elkins *s* Thomas Blackburn *c* Wilfred M. Cline *lp* Randolph Scott, Zachary Scott, Ruth Roman, Lloyd Bridges, Alan Hale, Ian MacDonald

Comanche Territory (U-INTERNATIONAL) 76 min

Carey is a surprisingly sophisticated Jim Bowie in this overblown Indian Western. O'Hara and Drake are the sister and brother villains out to mine silver on Indian land and who Carey foils by romancing the headstrong O'Hara and turning her against her brother who's growing more evil by the minute. The finale has O'Hara and the 7th Cavalry bringing a wagon-load of rifles to the Indians so they can beat off Drake and his silver-hungry gang.

d George Sherman *p* Leonard Goldstein *s* Oscar Brodney, Lewis Meltzer *c* Maury Gertsman *lp* Maureen O'Hara, Macdonald Carey, Will Geer, Charles Drake, Glenn Strange, Edmund Cobb

Copper Canyon (PAR) 83 min

The intriguing screenplay by pulp writer turned Hollywood hack, Latimer, features Lamarr and Carey ruthlessly trying to gain control of copper mines out West by playing on Union-Confederate antagonisms just after the Civil War. Milland is the Southern dandy who comes to the miners' defence and proves yet again that a boudoir is as fine a place for diplomacy as any. Farrow's direction is as fluid as ever, especially in the final gundown between Carey and Milland.

d John Farrow *p* Mel Epstein *s* Jonathan Latimer *c* Charles B. Lang Jnr *lp* Ray Milland, Hedy Lamarr, Macdonald Carey, Mona Freeman, Harry Carey Jnr, Frank Faylen

Macdonald Carey (left) as Jim Bowie, complete with knife, in Comanche Territory.

Crooked River (LIPPERT) b/w 55 min

The last of the six-strong series of films Hayden and Ellison made for Lippert Pictures, a series that had been announced with a loud fanfare only to have all the pictures in it be shot 'back to back' within a month! As if that isn't enough, this film is even padded out with Bob Steele library footage. The cliche-ridden script has Ellison on the trail of the villains who've murdered his parents. Carr directs slackly.

d Thomas Carr *p/co-s* Ron Ormond *co-s* Maurice Tombragel *c* Ernest Miller *lp* Jimmy Ellison, Russell Hayden, Fuzzy Knight, Raymond Hatton, Betty (Julie) Adams, Tom Tyler

Curtain Call at Cactus Creek

(U-INTERNATIONAL) 86 min

Though it lacks the easy charm of George Cukor's delightful **Heller in Pink Tights** (1960), this is an engaging account of the travails of a theatrical troupe out West. O'Connor is the stagehand desperate for a part and Brennan the grumpy bandit chief he captures singlehandedly. Price and Arden, as a pair of washed-up thespians, contribute neat cameos while Dimsdale's screenplay neatly details the Victoriana of theatrical life that later directors would make so much off.

d Charles Lamont   *p* Robert Arthur   *s* Howard Dimsdale
c Russell Metty   *lp* Donald O'Connor, Gale Storm,
Vincent Price, Walter Brennan, Eve Arden, Rex Lease

Dakota Lil   (FOX)   88 min
An Alperson quickie directed with his usual verve by
Selander. Montgomery is the secret service agent sent West to
uncover a gang of counterfeiters and Windsor the dance-hall
girl who falls for him and helps sort out Cameron and his
bandits.

d Lesley Selander   *p* Edward L. Alperson   *s* Maurice
Geraghty   *c* Jack Greenhalgh   *lp* George Montgomery,
Marie Windsor, Rod Cameron, John Emery, Wallace Ford,
Jack Lambert

Dallas   (WB)   94 min
An attempt by Warners to rekindle the dwindling flame of the
brawling, town-taming big budget Westerns they'd been so
successful with, after **Dodge City** (1939), throughout the
forties. Twist's script and Heisler's direction are more spirited
than that of either Robert Buckner or Michael Curtiz, who
were jointly responsible for **Dodge City**. But in the year of
Winchester '73 and **Broken Arrow**, the idea behind *Dallas*
was simply out of date. Cooper is the renegade Confederate
Colonel who masquerades as a frontier marshal in order to
clean up Dallas and so gain a pardon. Roman is the romantic
interest and Cochran, Massey and Hadley the no-good
Marlowe brothers, bizarrely first-named William, Cullen and
Bryant respectively.

d Stuart Heisler   *p* Anthony Veiller   *s* John Twist
c Ernest Haller   *lp* Gary Cooper, Ruth Roman, Steve
Cochran, Raymond Massey, Reed Hadley, Leif Erickson

Donald O'Connor and Gale Storm in the engaging Curtain Call *at Cactus Creek.*

Devil's Doorway   (MGM)   b/w   84 min
Made before, but held back until after the successful release of
Broken Arrow (1950), so worried were MGM, *Devil's Doorway*
is a far harder-hitting Indian Western than Daves' film. Taylor
is the educated Indian who though he has fought for the
Union in the Civil War, and won a Congressional Medal of
Honour, is judged unable to own and farm his ancestral lands.
Egged on by Calhern's crooked gambler people homestead the
land and Taylor leads his tribe in its defence, using not Indian
strategy but the military tactics taught him by the officers now
confronting him. What makes the film so impressive is
Trosper's articulate script and Mann's handling of the theme
of identity – the major theme of Mann's series of classic
Westerns in the fifties – with Taylor caught – literally, his
dress alternates between that of Indian and white man –
between the conflicting identities and loyalties of Indian and
American. The bleak ending, which pressages that of *El Cid*
(1961), has Taylor dying in order to prevent the massacre of
his tribe.
  The film also marked the final collaboration of Mann and
cinematographer Alton, who contributed greatly to the forties
thrillers with which Mann made his name in Hollywood.

d Anthony Mann   *p* Nicholas Nayfack   *s* Guy Trosper
c John Alton   *lp* Robert Taylor, Louis Calhern, Paula
Raymond, Marshall Thompson, James Mitchell, Edgar
Buchanan

The Eagle and the Hawk   (PAR)   104 min
Howe's dazzling cinematography is the real star of this
pleasant actioneer from producers Pine and Thomas. Payne
and O'Keefe are the pair of Americans sent into Mexico to try
and stop a planned attack on Texas fermented by agents of
Napoleon III in 1863. Fleming is the wife of the chief plotter,
Clark, who falls for Payne. Foster directs his own script
energetically, taking special pleasure in placing Payne in great
danger.

d/co-s Lewis R. Foster   *p* William H. Pine, William Thomas
co-s Geoffrey Homes   *c* James Wong Howe   *lp* John Payne,
Rhonda Fleming, Dennis O'Keefe, Fred Clark, Thomas
Gomez, Walter Reed

Gary Cooper as the counterfeit marshal and town tamer in Dallas.

Fancy Pants (PAR) 92 min

An inferior, but nonetheless occasionally funny remake of Leo McCarey's classic **Ruggles of Red Gap** (1935). Hope has the Charles Laughton role as a butler (here an actor masquerading as a gentleman's gentleman) who accompanies Ball's wildcat – she lassoes straying boyfriends – to her frontier home.

d George Marshall *p* Robert Welch *s* Edmund Hartman, Robert O'Brien *c* Charles Lang Jnr *lp* Bob Hope, Lucille Ball, Bruce Cabot, Eric Blore, Jack Kirkwood, John Anderson

The Furies (PAR) b/w 109 min

The most ambitious, and the least successful, of the three Westerns Mann made in 1950. Based on a novel by Niven Busch, author of *Duel in the Sun*, the story is one of dynastic struggles, with Greek Tragedy and Freudian overtones strongly to the fore. Huston, in his last film, is the cattle baron who rejects the advice of his tomboy daughter, Stanwyck, marries socialite Anderson, and then lets his ranch go to seed. Stanwyck and gambler Corey, also spurned by Huston, unite to force Huston into bankruptcy and repossess the ranch. Mann's *noir*ish direction and Milner's brooding interiors and harsh location shooting bring Schnee's limp script to life but Corey is no match for Stanwyck at her most aggressive – at one point she stabs Anderson in the eye.

d Anthony Mann *p* Hal B. Wallis *s* Charles Schnee *c* Victor Milner *lp* Barbara Stanwyck, Walter Huston, Wendell Corey, Judith Anderson, Gilbert Roland, Thomas Gomez

The Gunfighter (FOX) b/w 84 min

A seminal Western. *The Gunfighter* introduces a new theme to the genre, that of an ageing gunfighter (Peck) trying to live down his reputation and re-enter normal life but being railroaded into a final gunfight by a gun-happy, glory-seeking

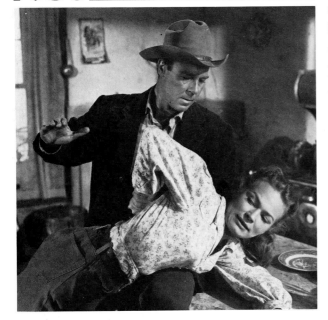

youngster (Homeier). Based on a story by veteran director Andre De Toth, Bowers and Sellers' bleak script is enhanced by Miller's stark, sombre photography and King's restrained direction. But the centre of the film is Peck's magisterial performance, his every action indicating his prowess with guns and his desperation at being forever forced to use them. The film forms a midpoint between **My Darling Clementine** (1946) which sees the transformation of Wyatt Earp into a solid citizen and Sam Peckinpah's more worried accounts of a 'civilized' West that has no place for old-fashioned heroes.

d Henry King   *p* Nunnally Johnson   *s* William Bowers, William Sellers   *c* Arthur Miller   *lp* Gregory Peck, Millard Mitchell, Karl Malden, Richard Jaeckel, Helen Westcott, Skip Homeier

Gunmen of Abilene (REP) b/w 60 min
This is a superior entry in Lane's long-running series for Republic, despite its old-fashioned plot device of a seam of gold running along the main street of Abilene as the reason Barcroft and company are trying to scare the townspeople away. Lane, as so often, goes underground (literally in this case) to expose the culprit and restore law and order.

d Fred C. Brannon   *p* Gordon Kay   *s* M. Coates Webster   *c* Ellis W. Carter   *lp* Allan Lane, Eddy Waller, Roy Barcroft, Donna Hamilton, Peter Brocco, George Chesebro

High Lonesome
(LEMAY-TEMPLETON/EAGLE LION)   81 min
LeMay's only film as a director and the second for the production company he briefly formed with producer Templeton, *High Lonesome* is an unusual Western. Elam and Kashner are the sons returned as if from the dead to wipe out all their enemies and Barrymore is their patsy. Although LeMay lets the story ramble overmuch, the superior location cinematography of Greene and the strong cast result in an above average production. Nonetheless, LeMay's real claim to fame remains the novel from which John Ford fashioned **The Searchers** (1956).

d/s Alan LeMay   *p* George Templeton   *c* W. Howard Greene   *lp* John Barrymore Jnr, Jack Elam, Chill Wills, Lois Butler, John Archer, Dave Kashner

Hoedown (COL) b/w 64 min
A slick and silly B Western, this was the first to feature Mahoney as its star and also includes one of Arnold's rare screen appearances. Shipman's fantastical plot has Mahoney

as a cowboy actor fired by his studio and stumbling on bank robbers who are hiding out at Arnold's 'singing' dude ranch. The film's limited budget makes one think that perhaps it was seeing it being made that left 'Colonel' Tom Parker (then Arnold's manager and soon to be Elvis Presley's) with the disregard for movies he so obviously showed while masterminding Presley's subsequent Hollywood career.

d Ray Nazarro   *p* Colbert Clark   *s* Barry Shipman   *c* Fayte Browne   *lp* Jock (O')Mahoney, Eddy Arnold, Jeff Donnell, Guinn Williams, Carolina Cotton, Fred Sears

Hostile Country (LIPPERT) b/w 60 min
The second of Ellison and Hayden's outings as the Irish Cowboys for Lippert Pictures, this stressed comedy far more than the first, **West of the Brazos** (1950). The films, made on the back of the pair's new-found audience on television, where their Hopalong Cassidy films were getting their first showing, were modestly budgeted but interesting. Here the duo set off to visit a relative and discover a range war in progress and their relative missing. Carr directs with economy at the forefront of his mind.

d Thomas Carr   *p/co-s* Ron Ormond   *co-s* Maurice Tombragel   *c* Ernest Miller   *lp* Jimmy Ellison, Russell Hayden, Fuzzy Knight, Raymond Hatton, Betty (Julie) Adams, Tom Tyler

I Killed Geronimo (JACK SCHWARZ) b/w 62 min
As the title suggests, this is a glib Indian Western. Ellison is the army captain who worms his way into the trust of a gang of gunrunners led by Adams and bags their main client, Geronimo (Chief Thundercloud) into the bargain. One-time singing cowboy star Ballew gives Ellison good support as a fellow officer but neither Hoffman's direction nor Neumann's screenplay give the actors many opportunities.

d John Hoffman   *p* Jack Schwarz   *s* Sam Neumann, Nat Tanchuck   *lp* James Ellison, Virginia Herrick, Ted Adams, Chief Thundercloud, Smith Ballew, Dennis Moore

I Shot Billy the Kid (LIPPERT) b/w 57 min
The second and best of Barry's short season of four Westerns for Lippert, this is yet another rehash of the Billy the Kid story with Barry as a much whitewashed William Bonney. A routine affair, it is efficiently mounted and directed by Berke without being imaginative in the least.

John Barrymore Jnr and Lois Butler in a scene from High Lonesome.

Brenda Marshall and George Montgomery in the colonial Western, The Iroquois Trail.

Audie Murphy, soon to become a stalwart of the B Western, with Gale Storm in The Kid from Texas.

d/p William Berke   *s* Orville Hampton   *c* Ernest Miller
lp Don Barry, Robert Lowery, Wally Vernon, Tom Neal, Judith Allen, John Merton

Indian Territory

(GENE AUTRY PRODUCTIONS/COL)   sepia   70 min
Like **The Last Round Up** (1947), this film borrows library footage from Wesley Ruggles' **Arizona** (1940) for many of its action sequences. Set just after the Civil War, Hall's screenplay features Autry as a Cavalry officer sympathetic to Indians who, with assistance from Buttram and later Grant, exposes former Austrian army officer Van Zandt and Collins as the men responsible for fermenting Indian trouble. Once again the film has only two songs which was the regulation number for the less fantastical Autry outings. Davis is the heroine.

d John English   *p* Armand Schaefer   *s* Norman S. Hall
c William Bradford   *lp* Gene Autry, Pat Buttram, Gail Davis, Kirby Grant, James Griffith, Pat Collins, Philip Van Zandt, Champion

The Iroquois Trail *aka* The Tomahawk Trail

(EDWARD SMALL)   b/w   85 min
This is a weak Western set in colonial times. Karlson's direction is emphatic enough but Schayer's script is too meandering. Montgomery is the scout who helps the British in their struggle with the French for control of the settlement in a plot full of double-dealing and villainy. Blue and Leonard are the Indian guides, one on the side of the British, the other a renegade double-crossing the British in favour of the French.

d Phil Karlson   *p* Bernard Small   *s* Richard Schayer
c Henry Freulich   *lp* George Montgomery, Brenda Marshall, Glenn Langan, Monte Blue, Sheldon Leonard, Reginald Denny

Martha Hyer in a scene from The Kangaroo Kid, *one of several Westerns set in Australia.*

The Kangaroo Kid

(ALLIED AUSTRALIAN FILMS; AUS)   b/w   72 min
An intriguing American-Australian co-production featuring an Australian supporting cast and locations and four American leads, as well as an American director, editor and cinematographer. Mahoney is the cop sent to the Australian goldfields of the 1880s to bring back crooked lawyer Dumbrille and finding himself in familiar surroundings as stagecoach hold-ups and gold-mine robberies take place at regular intervals. Harlan makes the most of the spectacular Australian scenery, but nonetheless, the film is more significant for the co-production possibilities it suggested than for anything else. Selander and Harlan might have been so efficient that they brought the film in under budget but the film was a failure in Australia where audiences saw it for the piece of cultural exploitation it was. It fared hardly better in America.

d Lesley Selander   *p* Howard C. Brown   *s* Sherman Lowe
c Russell Harlan   *lp* Jock (O')Mahoney, Douglass Dumbrille, Veda Ann Borg, Guy Doleman, Alec Kellaway, Martha Hyer

Kansas Raiders   (U-INTERNATIONAL)   80 min

Jesse James (Murphy) and Quantrill (Donlevy) ride again in this routine oater that pours so much whitewash over its central characters that they have hardly enough guts to be heroes, let alone badmen. The plot also features the Younger Brothers (Best and Martin) and Kit Dalton (Tony Curtis in an early featured role) joining Quantrill to get their education in action before graduating to outlawry on their own. The best things about the film are Enright's direction of the infamous sacking of Lawrence and Murphy's considered performance as the man who idolizes Quantrill but is beset by doubts about him.

d Ray Enright   *p* Ted Richmond   *s* Robert L. Richards
c Irving Glassberg   *lp* Audie Murphy, Brian Donlevy, James Best, Dewey Martin, Marguerite Chapman

The Kid from Texas *aka* Texas Kid, Outlaw

(U-INTERNATIONAL)   78 min
One of Murphy's first starring roles in the genre he was to dominate well into the sixties when he remained the only star regularly making low-budget Westerns. Here he plays Billy the Kid. Interestingly, the screenplay vacillates about Billy, first treating him sympathetically as someone who tries to lay down his gun and then simply watching him gun men down.

d Kurt Neumann   *p* Paul Short   *s* Robert Hardy Andrews, Karl Lamb   *c* Charles Van Enger   *lp* Audie Murphy, Gale Storm, Albert Dekker, Shepperd Strudwick, Will Geer, Ray Teal

Lightning Guns *aka* **Taking Sides** (COL) b/w 55 min
This is one of the best of Starrett's late series Westerns. Sears directs energetically and Mahoney, Starrett's stuntman for several years, has a meaty role on the side of law and order. Arthur's screenplay has Starrett stumbling on a range war and help track down the killers who frame his friend, Dearing, when he opposes a dam.

d Fred Sears *p* Colbert Clark *s* Victor Arthur *c* Fayte Browne *lp* Charles Starrett, Smiley Burnette, Gloria Henry, Jock (O')Mahoney, Edgar Dearing, George Chesebro

Montana (WB) 76 min
One of Flynn's last Hollywood films before his disastrous foray into production, *Montana*, like **Rocky Mountain** (1950) is a lacklustre attempt by all concerned to recapture the heady days of Warner's big, big Westerns of the forties, many of which starred Flynn. The script has a little of the empire-building feel of **Lone Star** (1952), also co-written by Chase. The tired performances and slack direction make a nonsense of the frontier spirit everybody talks about.

Flynn is the sheepman who invades Montana, the domain of cattle ranchers Smith and Kennedy. Freund's tasteful cinematography is the best thing about the film.

d Ray Enright *p* William Jacobs *s* James R. Webb, Borden Chase, Charles O'Neal *c* Karl Freund *lp* Errol Flynn, Alexis Smith, Douglas Kennedy, Ian MacDonald, Monte Blue, S.Z. Sakall

Mule Train
(GENE AUTRY PRODUCTIONS/COL) sepia 69 min
This is loosely based on the song that gave Frankie Laine his third million-selling disc in 1949. The practice of structuring a film around a popular song, which was a common one in the musical Western, would continue after the death of the singing cowboy only sporadically with films like **The Legend of Tom Dooley** (1959).

Livingston is the villainous freight shipper and claim jumper who eyes the natural cement claim of a friend of Autry when the contract for the supply of cement for the construction of a dam nearby is open for bids.

The film was selected by the Museum of Modern Art in New York to represent Autry in its film collection.

d John English *p* Armand Schaefer *s* Gerald Geraghty *c* William Bradford *lp* Gene Autry, Pat Buttram, Sheila Ryan, Robert Livingston, Frank Jaquet, Vince Barnett, Champion

The Nevadan *aka* **The Man from Nevada**
(COL) 81 min
A minor Scott Western. He's the undercover marshal on the trail of Tucker and $25,000, who meets up with rancher Macready, who also wants the loot, and Malone whom he romances. George and Slavin clearly enjoyed twisting the characters this way then that as Tucker and Scott unite against Macready before squaring off against each other for the final showdown. To some extent they anticipate the characters who would populate Burt Kennedy's superb screenplays for Scott's classic Westerns of the fifties. Lawton's cinematography is luscious and Douglas' direction punchy.

d Gordon Douglas *p* Harry Joe Brown *s* George W. George, George F. Slavin *c* Charles Lawton Jnr *lp* Randolph Scott, Dorothy Malone, Forrest Tucker, George Macready, Frank Faylen, Jock (O')Mahoney

North of the Great Divide (REP) 67 min
Barcroft is the villain in this below average Rogers entry. He opens a salmon cannery on the American-Canadian border and by overfishing causes the local Indians, dependent on salmon for food, to turn to thievery. Rogers as a representative of the Department of Indian Affairs sorts out matters. This silly plot isn't helped by Republic's cost-cutting production which sees Edwards replacing Dale Evans, just as earlier the Riders of the Purple Sage and Jones take over the chores of the Sons of the Pioneers and Gabby Hayes.

d William Witney *p* Edward J. White *s* Eric Taylor *c* Jack Marta *lp* Roy Rogers, Penny Edwards, Gordon Jones, Roy Barcroft, the Riders of the Purple Sage

Outlaws of Texas (MON) b/w 56 min
Badly received at the time for being 'all talk and little action', in retrospect this is one of the more interesting of the generally routine Whip Wilson series Westerns. Written by Ullman, who on the demise of the series Western graduated to television where he eventually became the producer and story editor of *Laramie* as well as writing for other Western teleseries, the picture features Coates as an outlaw leader and Wilson as the marshal who tries to infiltrate her gang. But, if the storyline is routine, the twists and turns of Ullman's screenplay as presented by director Carr were decidedly novel. The film also features Clyde as Wilson's side-kick for the last time.

d Thomas Carr *p* Vincent M. Fennelly *s* Dan Ullman *c* Gilbert Warrenton *lp* Whip Wilson, Andy Clyde, Phyllis Coates, Terry Frost, Tommy Farrell, Zon Murray

Gloria Henry, Charles Starrett (left) and Jock Mahoney (extreme right), who was once Starrett's double and was to become a series star in his own right, in Lightning Guns.

Randolph Scott with Dorothy Malone, who made several Westerns in the fifties, in The Nevadan.

John Ireland as the Jesse James lookalike in The Return of Jesse James.

of the five rings which together form the key to the whereabouts of ... and Starrett and villain Dearing racing each other to the solution. Burnette, as the comic detective, has more to do than usual while Starrett in his Durango guise rides hither and thither at speed.

d Fred F. Sears *p* Colbert Clark *s* Barry Shipman
c Fayte Browne *lp* Charles Starrett, Smiley Burnette, Edgar Dearing, Kay Buckley, Billy Kimbley, Lee Morgan

The Return of Jesse James (LIPPERT) b/w 73 min

Ireland, in his first starring role, is the outlaw who joins Hull in running the remnants of the James gang and who, because of his resemblance to Jesse, gives rise to the legend that Jesse has risen from the grave. Hadley, who'd played Jesse in **I Shot Jesse James** (1949), is Frank, the respectable citizen who has to bring Ireland in. Hilton, making his debut behind the megaphone, directs efficiently.

d Arthur Hilton *p* Carl K. Hittleman *s* Jack Natteford
c Karl Struss *lp* John Ireland, Ann Dvorak, Henry Hull, Reed Hadley, Hugh O'Brian, Carleton Young

Return of the Frontiersman (WB) 74 min

A pleasant actioneer. Anhalt's complex plot sees sheriff's son MacRae imprisoned for a murder he didn't commit, breaking jail and unmasking the real villain, Calhoun, with assistance from London, cast as she often is in Westerns as the woman in the background. The direction by Bare, who subsequently worked mostly in television, is penny plain.

d Richard Bare *p* Saul Elkins *s* Edna Anhalt *c* Peverell Marley *lp* Gordon MacRae, Jack Holt, Rory Calhoun, Julie London, Fred Clark, Edwin Rand

Rider from Tucson (RKO) b/w 60 min

Niftily directed by Selander, this is an engaging Holt outing. Repp's screenplay has Holt and Martin invited to a wedding and finding the groom besieged by claimjumpers out to steal his goldmine and his bride-to-be kidnapped. Borg and Reed have the plum roles as the claimjumpers.

d Lesley Selander *p* Herman Schlom *s* Ed Earl Repp
c Nicholas Musuraca *lp* Tim Holt, Richard Martin, Marshall Reed, Veda Ann Borg, Douglas Fowley, Harry Tyler

The Outriders (MGM) 93 min

In this routine Western McCrea is as jaunty as ever as the escaped Confederate who gets unwillingly involved with Quantrill's Raiders and a plot to hijack a wagon train of silver bullion before love sets him to rights. Most of the film's sparkle lies in its production values. Two minor points of interest are the presence of silent screen heart-throb Novarro in one of his few speaking roles and the script by Ravetch, his first Western. Later, with his wife Harriet Frank, he was to write **Hombre** (1967) and **Hud** (1963) for director Martin Ritt.

d Roy Rowland *p* Richard Goldstone *s* Irving Ravetch
c Charles Schoenbaum *lp* Joel McCrea, Arlene Dahl, Barry Sullivan, Ramon Novarro, Claude Jarman Jnr, Jeff Corey

Raiders of Tomahawk Creek (COL) b/w 55 min

This is an entertaining Starrett series Western directed with real zest by Sears. Shipman's screenplay features the old ploy

Charles Starrett (left) as the Durango Kid with Smiley Burnette in Raiders of Tomahawk Creek, *one of the numerous series Westerns to employ the map torn into five pieces plot.*

Rio Grande (REP) b/w 105 min

Together with **Fort Apache** (1948) and **She Wore a Yellow Ribbon** (1949), *Rio Grande* forms a loose trilogy about Ford's beloved 7th Cavalry. A wistful, intimate evocation of the immediate aftermath of the Civil War, shown in the broken marriage of Wayne and O'Hara, *Rio Grande* suggests the reconciliation of North and South through individual action against a common military enemy – the troop chase a band of Apache over the border into Mexico – and the rapprochement of Wayne and O'Hara. However, Ford fails to integrate the songs of the Sons of the Pioneers, regulars in Roy Rogers Westerns. The songs stress continuity and tradition but their performances have an exhibitionist quality that is alien to the best of Ford's work. The result is a film that has something of the feel of *The Sun Shines Bright* (1953) but little of that film's majesty. Similarly, Wayne and O'Hara's on-off relationship lacks the spark that animates *The Quiet Man* (1952). But, if *Rio Grande* is a minor work, it offers, especially in the scenes devoted to the minor characters (Johnson, Carey Jnr and McLaglen as the wonderfully oafish Sergeant Quincannon), a wealth of Fordian moments.

d/co-p John Ford *co-p* Merian C. Cooper *s* James Kevin McGuinness *c* Bert Glennon *lp* John Wayne, Maureen O'Hara, Ben Johnson, Harry Carey Jnr, Victor McLaglen, Chill Wills

Rock Island Trail (REP) b/w 90 min

Part of Republic's continuing informal series about the Westward expansion of America, *Rock Island Trail* tells the story of Tucker's attempts to push his rails West of the Mississippi and of how he runs into Cabot's crooked riverboat operator, a lack of money and marauding Indians. Banker's daughter Mara supplies the money and Tucker's fists put paid to Cabot in a splendidly staged fistfight in a tavern where they 'duel' with mops laden with boiling soup. More interesting still is the solution to the Indian problem which has a friendly tribe (the daughter of which, Booth, is in love with Tucker) come to the railroad's rescue à la Seventh Cavalry. Ironically, despite Republic's extensive promotion, the film did poorly at the box office.

d Joseph Kane *p* Herbert J. Yates *s* James Edward Grant *c* Jack Marta *lp* Forrest Tucker, Adele Mara, Bruce Cabot, Adrian Booth, Chill Wills, Roy Barcroft

Rocky Mountain (WB) b/w 83 min

Flynn's last Western, *Rocky Mountain*, its unusual tragic ending which sees Flynn and his men wiped out by the Indians aside, is a routine affair. Based on a real incident, it features Flynn as the leader of an assorted group of renegades trying to carve out a Californian outpost for the Confederacy. They rescue a girl (Wymore, later to become Flynn's third wife) from Indians and capture a Union patrol led by her fiancee, Forbes, but later perish when they try and hold off an Indian attack after letting Wymore and Forbes go free. Cast in the mould of earlier Warners' epic Westerns like **Dodge City** (1939) and **San Antonio** (1945) the film only served to show how old fashioned the style was in 1950.

John Wayne grieving for the past in John Ford's Rio Grande.

A publicity still for Errol Flynn's last Western, Rocky Mountain.

d William Keighley   *p* William Jacobs   *s* Winston Miller, Alan LeMay   *c* Ted McCord   *lp* Errol Flynn, Patrice Wymore, Guinn Williams, Scott Forbes, Dick Jones, Slim Pickens

Saddle Tramp (U-INTERNATIONAL)   77 min

McCrea is the roaming cowboy suddenly saddled with four young boys in this appealing, sentimental tale in which McCrea's abilities to steal food – the rancher he goes to work for doesn't like children – are as important as his prowess with a gun. Fregonese's direction is equal to the job of moving from kids to rustlers, but it's McCrea and his easy-going charm that makes the film so appealing.

d Hugo Fregonese   *p* Leonard Goldstein   *s* Harold Shumate   *c* Charles P. Boyle   *lp* Joel McCrea, Wanda Hendrix, John Russell, John McIntyre, Russell Simpson, Ed Begley

Short Grass (AA)   b/w   82 min

This entertaining range war Western pits Brown and Cameron against Ankrum's ambitious rancher. Brown is the marshal and Cameron the drifter pushed off his land by Ankrum when he returns after five years. Cameron also discovers that his girlfriend is married to a drunkard. Blackburn's taut script (from his own novel) is particularly good in its details. Thus few of the characters involved are the gunmen who populate series Westerns, most are just working cowboys forced to use their guns. The climax, a running street battle, is particularly effective.

d Lesley Selander   *p* Scott R. Dunlap   *s* Tom W. Blackburn   *c* Harry Neumann   *lp* Rod Cameron, Cathy Downs, Johnny Mack Brown, Morris Ankrum, Alan Hale Jnr, Harry Woods

The Showdown (REP)   b/w   86 min

Like many of Republic's B Westerns of this period, this was shot on sound stages with back-projection and process-work standing in for the big blue yonder once so much a part of the Western. Nonetheless, like *Hellfire* (1949), also scripted by the McGowans, this was a fitting end to Elliott's long stay with Republic. The interesting script has Elliott on the trail of the murderer of his brother and joining a wagon train knowing that one of the men is the guilty one. In an attempt to find out which one, he pushes men and cattle beyond their natural endurance. Brennan, cast against type as the quiet and

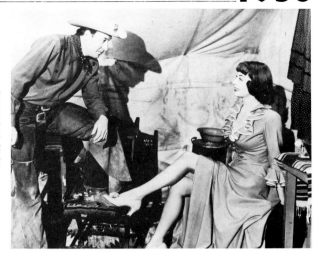

friendly man who is finally gored to death, is the guilty one and Windsor is the saloon keeper who buys an interest in the herd and travels with it. The direction is as eloquent as the screenplay and Elliott plays his forceful role to the hilt.

d/s Dorrell McGowan, Stuart McGowan   *p* William J. O'Sullivan   *c* Reggie Lanning   *lp* Bill Elliott, Walter Brennan, Marie Windsor, Henry (Harry) Morgan, Jim Davis, Leif Erickson

Sierra (U-INTERNATIONAL)   83 min

A slow-moving B Western enlivened by Metty's lush Technicolor images. Murphy, still lacking in confidence as an actor, is with his father, Jagger, holed up in the hills when Hendrix's unlikely lawyer stumbles into their lair and decides to prove them innocent of the crimes that have caused them to flee to the hills. Ives, as the singing prospector, contributes a solid performance but the uneasiness of the principals and Green's unimaginative direction prove to be insurmountable problems.

d Alfred E. Green   *p* Michel Kraike   *s* Edna Anhalt   *c* Russell Metty   *lp* Audie Murphy, Wanda Hendrix, Dean Jagger, Burl Ives, Anthony (Tony) Curtis, Jack Ingram

The Silver Bandit (RAYMOND FRIEDGEN)   b/w   54 min

This is the first of Cooley's inept starring Westerns. The self-styled King of Western Swing, Cooley, who like Bob Wills and Pee Wee King had provided musical support for Charles Starrett in his series Westerns, is a minor but engaging musician and a terrible actor. He isn't helped by the anonymous cinematographer of this quickie whose work is so blurry it's sometimes hard to distinguish who's who. The soundtrack is similarly mutilated. Clifton's pseudonymously written script has Cooley as a dude capturing the Silver Bandit of the title. The musical interludes are the most significant aspect of the horrendous production.

d Elmer Clifton   *p* J.R. Camomille   *s* Elmer S. Pond (Elmer Clifton)   *lp* Spade Cooley, Bob Gilbert, Virginia Jackson, Richard Elliott, Billy Dix, Jene Gray

Stars in My Crown (MGM)   b/w   89 min

Best known for his films of the supernatural, *Cat People* (1942) and *Night of the Demon* (1957) and his magnificent *film noir, Out of the Past* (1947), Tourneur's world is one where reason is forever under attack from either superstition (the supernatural) or obsessive behaviour. From this perspective, *Stars in My Crown* is the exception that proves the rule. The film depicts a life in which the rational and the supernatural are in equilibrium, in short an idealized community. It is the story of one year in the life of a small Southern community that weathers the storms of illness, the KKK and superstition thanks to the gunslinging rationalism of McCrea's parson.

d Jacques Tourneur *p* William H. Wright *s* Margaret Fitts *c* Charles Schoenbaum *lp* Joel McCrea, Ellen Drew, Dean Stockwell, Alan Hale, James Mitchell, Lewis Stone

Storm Over Wyoming (RKO) b/w 60 min

Holt and a much improved Martin stumble into yet another range war when they interrupt a lynching in this cattlemen-versus-sheepmen Western. Nash is the pretty heroine who gets more of the action than normal and Underwood the dance-hall girl who pops up in the most surprising situations to help Holt and Martin out. Smoothly directed by Selander, the project only needs a better script to be an above average series entry.

d Lesley Selander *p* Herman Schlom *s* Ed Earl Repp *c* J. Roy Hunt *lp* Tim Holt, Richard Martin, Noreen Nash, Betty Underwood, Richard Powers (Tom Keene), Kenneth MacDonald

The Sundowners *aka* Thunder in the Dust

(LEMAY-TEMPLETON/EAGLE LION) 83 min

Preston and Sterling are the brothers battling with each other for domination of the range in this rugged Western. Elam (who starred in the Templeman produced, LeMay directed **High Lonesome**, 1950) puts in a neat performance as a weak husband but, Hoch's glorious cinematography notwithstanding, the weak acting and erratic direction of Templeton fail to impress.

d/co-p George Templeton *co-p/s* Alan LeMay *c* Winton C. Hoch *lp* Robert Preston, John Barrymore Jnr, Robert Sterling, Jack Elam, Chill Wills, Cathy Downs

Texas Dynamo (COL) b/w 54 min

A dull affair, of interest only because Shipman managed to give Starrett three roles to play! He's Steve Drake and the Durango Kid as usual, but, after being framed for murder, he adopts yet another identity, as a gunman, in order to get in with the crooks to supposedly help catch himself (as Durango). Dehner contributes a telling piece of villainy and way down the cast is Fred Sears, who, when he wasn't directing, was only too willing to return to acting to help pay for his supper.

d Ray Nazarro *p* Colbert Clark *s* Barry Shipman *c* Fayte Browne *lp* Charles Starrett, Smiley Burnette, Lois Hall, Fred Sears, John Dehner, Jock (O')Mahoney

A Ticket to Tomahawk (FOX) b/w 91 min

An enjoyable spoof Western. Director Sale reworks the old stagecoach versus the railroad theme to great comic effect. Calhoun is the stagecoach owner trying bandits, Indians and even a theatrical touring company in a desperate attempt to stop sharp-shooting Baxter and travelling salesman Dailey getting the railway to the Colorado finishing line on time. Marilyn Monroe has a small part as a chorus girl in the theatrical troupe.

d/co-s Richard Sale *p* Robert Bassler *co-s* Mary Loos *c* Harry Jackson *lp* Dan Dailey, Anne Baxter, Rory Calhoun, Walter Brennan, Arthur Hunnicutt, Charles Kemper

Dan Dailey and his chorus girls, including Marilyn Monroe (extreme right), in A Ticket to Tomahawk.

Trail of Robin Hood (REP) 67 min

This is one of the most surreal of series Westerns, and all the more charming for it. Holt is the retired screen cowboy raising and selling Christmas trees at cost price to the poor, who falls on hard times when a commercial Christmas-tree outfit try to prevent him harvesting and transporting his trees to market. Rogers rides to the rescue and, in a variant of the guest-star climax used so often by Republic, as well as cowboy heroes like Rex Allen, Allan 'Rocky' Lane, Monte Hale, Kermit Maynard, Tom Keene, Ray Corrigan and William Farnum appearing, there also comes George Chesebro, who is automatically cold-shouldered by the cowboy stars until he announces, 'I'm George Chesebro and I've been a villain in Jack Holt's movies for twenty years, now I'd like to be on the right side for a change.' Fittingly, one of the songs is 'Everyday is Christmas Day in the West'.

d William Witney *p* Edward J. White *s* Gerald Geraghty *c* John MacBurnie *lp* Roy Rogers, Penny Edwards, Gordon Jones, Jack Holt, Emory Parnell, Clifton Young, Trigger

Two Flags West (FOX) b/w 92 min

An ambitious, energetic Western constructed in the mould of John Ford's **Fort Apache** (1948). Cotten leads a group of Confederate prisoners to help fight Indians in New Mexico under the command of Chandler who in addition to lusting after his sister-in-law, Darnell, hates Rebels almost as much as Indians. Chandler kills an Indian chief, so triggering off an Indian uprising which Cotten and his men put down after Chandler's death. Robinson's script unites two of the main concerns of the fifties Western – an interest in the psychology of the film's characters and a sympathetic attitude to Indians. And if the plot is too melodramatic and Chandler's acting too one-dimensional for the movie to be wholly successful, Wise's seriousness is compelling.

Rex Allen astride Koko (left) greets Roy Rogers astride Trigger in surely the most surreal series Western ever, Trail of Robin Hood.

Jeff Chandler, with eyepatch, inspects the Confederate prisoners led by Joseph Cotten (standing) in the ambitious Two Flags West.

Ward Bond (extreme left), as the most worldly religious leader ever, invites Ruth Clifford to dance while Ben Johnson (left), Joanne Dru, Alan Mowbray (seated) and Francis Ford (director John's brother) look encouragingly on in Wagonmaster, Ford's most luminous Western.

d Robert Wise *p/s* Casey Robinson *c* Leon Shamroy
lp Joseph Cotten, Linda Darnell, Jeff Chandler, Cornel Wilde, Dale Roberston, Arthur Hunnicutt

Under Mexicali Stars (REP) b/w 67 min
One of the best of Allen's 51 series Western outings for Republic. Williams' fanciful plot has him as a singing US Treasury agent breaking up a gang of smugglers who are using a helicopter to get stolen gold refined across the border.

Ebsen, who gives a fine performance, replaced Fuzzy Knight to become Allen's fourth side-kick in the series. Barcroft is the swaggering villain and Blair directs vigorously and economically.

d George Blair *p* Melville Tucker *s* Bob Williams *c* John MacBurnie *lp* Rex Allen, Dorothy Patrick, Roy Barcroft, Buddy Ebsen, Walter Coy, Frank Ferguson

The Vanishing Westerner (REP) b/w 60 min
Extravagantly scripted by Williams – it features a sheriff who comes from England and masquerades as his titled twin brother and a deputy whose girlfriend wants him to quit his dangerous job – this is a superior Hale series Western. If the plot is complicated by the likes of blanks and Britishers, Ford's direction is action-packed. Murder and robbery make regular appearances as Hale struggles to prove his innocence of the murder Space and Barcroft try to pin on him. This is an exciting series Western.

d Philip Ford *p* Melville Tucker *s* Bob Williams *c* Ellis W. Carter *lp* Monte Hale, Paul Hurst, Roy Barcroft, Aline Towne, Dick Curtis, Arthur Space

Wagonmaster (ARGOSY PICTURES/RKO) b/w 86 min
Once described as 'an intimate epic' and several times named by Ford as his favourite film – perhaps because he wrote the original story and his son co-wrote the script – *Wagonmaster* is surely its director's most optimistic and uncomplicated Western. The reasons are equally straightforward, the film's heroes, the Mormons whom Johnson and Carey lead to the promised land, are pioneers, settlers, innocents and in Johnson and Bond they have the most prudent and pragmatic defenders a community could wish for.

Episodically constructed, the film tells the story of a group of Mormons who are kidnapped by Kemper and his malevolent brood of outlaws and finally set free by Johnson. The storyline is slim but the details of the movie are resonant with meaning: Bond's worldly religious leader, Mowbray and Clifford's hammy aging nomadic actors, Dru's spiritedness and most of all the fairy-tale like vistas of the wagons as they

roll ever onward to the promised land. Johnson in particular as the drifter who, with Carey's hot-head, guides the Mormons through the desert, gives a marvellous, dignified performance. This is a great film.

d/co-p John Ford *co-p* Merian C. Cooper *s* Frank S. Nugent, Patrick Ford *c* Bert Glennon *lp* Ben Johnson, Harry Carey Jnr, Ward Bond, Charles Kemper, Joanne Dru, Alan Mowbray, Ruth Clifford

West of the Brazos (LIPPERT) b/w 58 min
The first of the six films Hopalong Cassidy protégés Ellison and Hayden made 'back-to-back' for Lippert Pictures. Made with identical casts over a period of a month and released one by one throughout 1950-51, the films had the lowest of low budgets, despite producer Ormond's trumpeting about five-year contracts and the like. Ellison and Hayden, as Shamrock and Lucky, are the 'Irish Cowboys' who find Cason's Cyclone Kid posing as the heir to the ranch left to them because he knows that there is oil on the land. Carr's direction and the screenplay are erratic, but the cast project a sense of enjoyment that is endearing, if unbelievable.

d Thomas Carr *p/co-s* Ron Ormond *co-s* Maurice Tombragel *c* Ernest Miller *lp* Jimmy Ellison, Russell Hayden, Raymond Hatton, Fuzzy Knight, Betty (Julie) Adams, John Cason

West of Wyoming (MON) b/w 57 min
This is a tired Brown entry with its beefy star as a government agent foiling plans by cattlemen to frighten off homesteaders. Andrews makes a fine cattle baron and Moore an evil-looking heavy, but, though Brown could still swing his punches with the best of them, both plot and direction are simply too old fashioned.

d Wallace Fox *p* Eddie Davis *s* Adele Buffington *c* Harry Neumann *lp* Johnny Mack Brown, Gail Davis, Dennis Moore, Stanley Andrews, Milburn Morante, Myron Healey

Western Pacific Agent (LIPPERT) b/w 65 min
A minor but interesting B Western from Lippert. The film has a traditional plot with Taylor as the agent of the title on the trail of murderer and robber Knox. But Newfield's

direction is infected with the violence that was definitely making its way into the genre: thus Knox is a crazed killer and the film's opening stresses not the robbery but the double murder he commits in the process.

d Sam Newfield *p* Sigmund Neufeld *s* Fred Myton *c* Ernest Miller *lp* Kent Taylor, Sheila Ryan, Mickey Knox, Robert Lowery, Morris Carnovsky, Frank Richards

Winchester '73 (U) b/w 92 min
Mann's first film with Stewart (with whom he was to make a series of classic Westerns), *Winchester '73* offers the clearest example of Mann's use of the revenge plot. Hero and villain (McNally) are brothers who were taught to shoot by their father. After McNally murders his father, Stewart seeks revenge to prove himself worthy of his father's name, symbolized by the perfect Winchester Stewart wins in a shooting contest and McNally steals from him. So begins the long chase to one of the most neurotic shoot-outs in the history of the Western, after which a purified Stewart is claimed by Winters. Duryea appears as an even more pathological gunman while McIntire, J.C. Flippen and Will Geer appear as assorted father figures. A great Western.

The movie was remade as an inferior telefilm in 1967 with Duryea this time cast as a friend of the hero, Tom Tryon.

d Anthony Mann *p* Aaron Rosenberg *s* Robert L. Richards, Borden Chase *c* William Daniels *lp* James Stewart, Shelley Winters, Dan Duryea, Stephen McNally, Millard Mitchell, John McIntire

Wyoming Mail (U-INTERNATIONAL) 87 min
A solid, dull Universal Western with McNally as the postal engineer who poses as a bank robber to help catch a band of train robbers whose activities are threatening to lose the Wyoming Railroad its mail franchise. Smith is the good/bad girl who foresakes inside-man Roberts for McNally and saves his life. DaSilva is a breathy villain and Metty provides the lustrous cinematography, but to no avail for the film lacks any energy.

d Reginald LeBorg *p* Aubrey Schenck *s* Harry Essex, Leonard Lee *c* Russell Metty *lp* Stephen McNally, Alexis Smith, Roy Roberts, Howard DaSilva, Ed Begley, James Arness

Julie Adams and James Ellison in West of the Brazos, *one of the shortlived series Ellison co-starred in with fellow Hopalong Cassidy protégé, Russell Hayden.*

Will Geer (centre) tosses up the target coin for James Stewart (left) while his murderer brother Stephen McNally looks on, in the shooting match for the perfect Winchester at the start of Winchester '73.

1951

Across the Wide Missouri (MGM) 78 min

Savagely cut after it was previewed, this is perhaps the most ambitious of Wellman's Westerns. Where **The Ox-Bow Incident** (1943) stressed the meanness, stupidity and fragility of frontier civilization, *Across the Wide Missouri* centres on the natural, idyllic state that was Colorado in the 1820s and the ease with which Gable's two-fisted trapper could get on with Marques' Blackfoot maiden. But it's a paradise that is threatened with extinction as white civilization moves deeper and deeeper into the fur country. The theme isn't a new one, it was introduced into American literature by James Fenimore Cooper, but whereas the films of his novels rarely dwell on the majesty of the wilderness that his heroes move through, Wellman's film addresses itself particularly to this. The result is an impressive film that alternates between lyricism and bitterness as astonishing landscapes are bloodied and a seemingly perfect life-style destroyed.

d William Wellman *p* Robert Sisk *s* Talbot Jennings
c William C. Mellor *lp* Clark Gable, Ricardo Montalban, John Hodiak, Adolphe Menjou, Maria Elena Marques

Al Jennings of Oklahoma (COL) 79 min

Based on Jennings' own autobiography, Bricker's screenplay carefully changes the emphasis from the redemption of Duryea's Jennings to the reasons for his life of crime. The reason, for 1951, was a topical one: war. Accordingly, Duryea is a product of the Civil War – he's even seen crying as a baby when Union troops ransack the family home – forced into crime by the breakdown of the social order around him. With his brother, Foran (a one-time singing cowboy), he turns to crime when falsely accused of murder before, having paid for his sins, returning to the Bar, his first profession. Nazarro directs with his usual eye for action.

One-time bankrobber Jennings, who became a regular actor in Westerns, is the man who taught Tex Ritter how to handle a gun in **Song of the Gringo** (1936).

d Ray Nazarro *p* Rudolph C. Flothow *s* George Bricker
c W. Howard Greene *lp* Dan Duryea, Gale Storm, Dick Foran, Gloria Henry, Guinn Williams, Stanley Andrews

Along the Great Divide (WB) 88 min

A bleak revenge movie. Douglas, in his first Western, is the marshal beset by guilt – he thinks he caused the death of his father, also a marshal – who brings in father-figure Brennan, suspected of killing Ankrum's son. In the course of their journey across the desert the pair are attacked by Ankrum and his sons (who want to hang Brennan immediately) and by Brennan's tomboy daughter who mounts her own rescue attempt. The result is a story full of shifting allegiances in which the journey to Santa Loma and justice is also a journey back into the past. Although the script, particularly at the denouement, lacks the cutting edge of, say, **Pursued** (1947), the spectacular desert locations and the strong performances, from Mayo and Douglas especially, give a resonance to the mood of romantic tragedy that Walsh creates.

d Raoul Walsh *p* Anthony Veiller *s* Walter Doniger, Lewis Meltzer *c* Sid Hickox *lp* Kirk Douglas, Walter Brennan, Virginia Mayo, John Agar, Morris Ankrum, Ray Teal

Apache Drums (U-INTERNATIONAL) 75 min

The last film to be produced by Lewton, best known for horror films like *Cat People* (1942), *Apache Drums* is a worthwhile Western. Moreover, Fregonese's direction makes interesting nods towards the play of light and dark that characterizes Lewton's earlier films, especially in the lengthy sequence where the townspeople take refuge in a church in an attempt to wait out an Indian attack. Chandler's over-loquacious screenplay features McNally as the gambler who fails to convince the town that threw him out that the Indians really are coming.

d Hugo Fregonese *p* Val Lewton *s* David Chandler
c Charles P. Boyle *lp* Stephen McNally, Coleen Gray, Willard Parker, Arthur Shields, James Griffith, James Best

Arizona Manhunt (REP) b/w 60 min

This, the penultimate in Republic's last and least Western series starring juveniles Chapin and Janssen, is memorable only for the company's attempt to gain publicity by calling its stars, 'The Rough-Ridin' Kids'. It was to no avail. Here the duo win over an outlaw's daughter to the side of law and order and so catch the gang. Lively's screenplay certainly doesn't live up to its author's name.

d Fred C. Brannon *p* Rudy Ralston *s* William Lively
c John MacBurnie *lp* Michael Chapin, Eilene Janssen,
James Bell, Roy Barcroft, Lucille Barkley, Stuart Randall

The Battle at Apache Pass (U-INTERNATIONAL) 85 min
A lacklustre actioneer in which Chandler impersonates
Cochise for the second time – he played the Indian Chief in
Broken Arrow (1950) – and unites with Lund's Cavalry
officer to drive off Geronimo (Jay Silverheels) and crooked
Indian-affairs representative, Cowling. The Indians are presented in some depth but the plot is far too melodramatic,
clearly being foisted upon the characters rather than emerging
from them.

d George Sherman *p* Leonard Goldstein *s* Gerald Drayson
Adams *c* Charles P. Boyle *lp* John Lund, Jeff Chandler,
Jay Silverheels, Bruce Cowling, Jack Elam, Susan Cabot

Best of the Badmen (RKO) 84 min
Another portmanteau piece of outlawry featuring the James
and Younger brothers and assorted badmen. Ryan is the
Confederate guerilla forced into outlawry by Preston's greed,
who, with other outlaws, starts a vendetta against Preston's
multifarious banking and railroad interests and steals his wife,
Trevor, to boot. Essentially an innocent adventure yarn, its
contemporary relevance suddenly becomes apparent when
former Quantrill Rider Brennan ponders on why he was
decorated a few years ago for the same thing as he is doing
now but now has a price on his head. The film also features a
much changed Buetel (as Bob Younger) in his first screen role
since **The Outlaw** (1943).

d William D. Russell *p* Herman Schlom *s* Robert Hardy
Andrews, John Twist *c* Edward Cronjager *lp* Robert Ryan,
Claire Trevor, Jack Buetel, Robert Preston, Walter Brennan,
Bruce Cabot

Branded (PAR) b/w 95 min
The first Western as director of one-time cinematographer
Mate, *Branded* features a literate script from Boehm and
Hume and an icy performance from Ladd in the central role.
He's the no-gooder out to steal a fortune by pretending to be
the long-lost (kidnapped at five) son of a cattle baron,
Bickford. He then falls for his 'sister', Freeman, and decides
to get back the real son from Calleia's bandit. Atmospheric
rather than action-packed, the film treats the question of
identity intelligently and Ladd gives a fine performance, even
remaining convincing when he turns out to be the hero after
all.

d Rudolph Mate *p* Mel Epstein *s* Sidney Boehm, Cyril
Hume *c* Charles B. Lang Jnr *lp* Alan Ladd, Mona
Freeman, Charles Bickford, Joseph Calleia, Robert Keith,
Milburn Stone

Buckaroo Sheriff of Texas (REP) b/w 60 min
The first of Republic's four-strong series of Westerns with
juveniles, Chapin and Janssen, as the leads, or as *Variety*
dubbed the series, 'moppet oaters'. The problem with the
films is twofold: the central characters and the lack of action.
Orloff's plot has Chapin, grandson of a sheriff, and Janssen
foil Coffin, who seizes land locally while Chapin's father is
away at the Civil War.

d Philip Ford *p* Rudy Ralston *s* Arthur E. Orloff *c* John
MacBurnie *lp* Michael Chapin, Eilene Janssen, Tristram
Coffin, James Bell, Hugh O'Brian, William Haade

Callaway Went Thataway *aka* **The Star Said No**
(MGM) b/w 81 min
Keel is the washed-up drunk of a cowboy star whose career is
given a sudden fillip when his old movies become popular on
television. Like **Slim Carter** (1957), a spoof on the Hopalong

Cassidy saga, the comedy of the situation is much enlivened
by the performances of MacMurray and McGuire as the
fast-talking (self) promoters. Clark Gable, Robert Taylor and
Elizabeth Taylor are amongst the guest stars who lend a touch
of Hollywood authenticity to the proceedings.

The film is particularly revealing as an indication of both
the power of television and of its hunger for film material.
(The film was made just after Republic began to sell its back
catalogue of series Westerns to television and so helping to
create the demand for Westerns on TV that was to last for a
couple of decades.)

Frank and Panama together show themselves to be far more
at home in the world of light comedy – indeed too at home,
the film needs a touch of acid – than Panama was on his own
in the world of the action Western, as evident by his lacklustre
handling of **The Jayhawkers** (1959).

d/p/s Melvin Frank, Norman Panama *c* Ray June *lp* Fred
MacMurray, Howard Keel, Dorothy McGuire, Jesse White,
Stan Freberg, Douglas Kennedy

Joel McCrea as the tough trail boss and Dean Stockwell as the poor little rich kid in Cattle Drive.

Cattle Drive (U-INTERNATIONAL) 77 min
An unusual, worthwhile juvenile Western, far superior to
Republic's short-lived series with Michael Chapin and Eilene
Janssen. Stockwell is the little snob of a rich kid brought
down to earth when, left alone in the desert by mistake, he
joins a cattle drive to get back to civilization. McCrea is the
tough but fair trail boss who earns Stockwell's respect. Shot in
Death Valley and looking fresher than most B Westerns for
the change from the usual locations, it is well paced by
Neumann. A nice touch is McCrea pulling out a photo of his
real wife (Francis Dee with whom he'd acted in several
Westerns) when he shows Stockwell a picture of the girl
waiting for him at the end of the trail.

d Kurt Neumann *p* Aaron Rosenberg *s* Jack Natteford,
Lillie Hayward *c* Maury Gertsman *lp* Joel McCrea, Dean
Stockwell, Chill Wills, Leon Ames, Bob Steele, Howard
Petrie

Cattle Queen *aka* **Queen of the West**
(JACK SCHWARZ) b/w 69 min
Hart has the title role in this, one of the few Westerns to have
a woman as lead. However, Tansey's cost-cutting production,
which used a much thumbed script, and his erratic direction
drain the film of much of its interest. She's the whip-cracking

rancher and Smith is her foreman. Together, with assistance from a bunch of paroled outlaws, they clean up their town and prevent Gardette thwarting the sale of her cattle through a faked disease.

d/s Robert Tansey *p* Jack Schwarz *c* Elmer Dyer
lp Maria Hart, Drake Smith, William Fawcett, Robert Gardette, John Carpenter, Edward Clark

Cavalry Scout (MON) 78 min
Like so many of Ullman's scripts, this is basically a thriller set in the West with Cameron desperately racing against time to get proof that Millican in a gunrunner before Millican can deliver a pair of gatling guns to the Indians. Cameron, growing more confident with every film, makes an energetic hero and Millican a devious villain while Selander gets as much suspense as possible from his material.

d Lesley Selander *p* Walter Mirisch *s* Dan Ullman
c Harry Neumann *lp* Rod Cameron, Audrey Long, James Millican, Jim Davis, James Arness, Rory Mallison

Cave of Outlaws (U-INTERNATIONAL) 75 min
This is one of the several Westerns made by Castle, who was one of the first producer-directors to capitalize on the horror boom of the mid-fifties that coincided with the death of the B Western. Carey is the outlaw released from jail who returns to the scene of the crime, the Carsbad Caverns, to search for his lost loot and is followed by detective Buchanan and villain Jory. Glassberg makes the best of the unusual locations while Castle skims over the implausibilities in the plot.

d William Castle *p* Leonard Goldstein *s* Elizabeth Wilson
c Irving Glassberg *lp* Macdonald Carey, Alexis Smith, Edgar Buchanan, Victor Jory, Hugh O'Brian, Charles Horvarth

Colorado Ambush (MON) b/w 51 min
Written by Healey, who appropriated the best role, of the heavy, for himself, this is one of the best of the late, and generally indifferent, Brown series outings. He's the undercover agent on the trail of a band of outlaws who specialize in robbing payroll messengers. The well-staged climax features a gun battle between Brown, a sheriff and the gang's inside man, Farrell (who's gone straight after the gang's murdered his father) against Healey and an acerbic McIntyre. Collins directs with the evident enjoyment of one who likes plenty of action.

d Lewis Collins *p* Vincent M. Fennelly *s* Myron Healey
c Gilbert Warrenton *lp* Johnny Mack Brown, Myron Healey, Lois Hall, Tommy Farrell, Christie McIntyre, Lee Roberts

Distant Drums (UNITED STATES PICTURES/WB) 101 min
This is a loose remake of Walsh's own *Objective Burma* (1945) with the Everglades and the Seminole taking the place of Burma and the Japanese. Cooper is Captain Wyatt who leads a punitive expedition against a group of gun runners in Florida and then has to make his way back under constant threat from the Seminole. Walsh unites the diverse elements in Rackin and Busch's script in the character of backwoodsman Cooper, reluctant but natural leader and woman hater. The group's flight back through the Everglades, with Aldon whom they've rescued from the gun runners, is superbly orchestrated by Walsh and cinematographer Hickox. The finale is a marvellous underwater knife-fight between Cooper and the Seminole Indian chief, but the emphasis of the film is less on simple action and more on Cooper's education back into humanity by Aldon.

d Raoul Walsh *p* Milton Sperling *s* Niven Busch, Martin Rackin *c* Sid Hickox *lp* Gary Cooper, Mari Aldon, Richard Webb, Ray Teal, Arthur Hunnicutt, Clancy Cooper

Drums in the Deep South (KING BROTHERS) 87 min
Directed by one of America's most influential art directors – he received an Oscar for his work on *Gone With the Wind* (1939) – this is a mediocre film, poised confusedly between the romance of a *Gone With the Wind* and an action picture. Madison is the Union soldier with Southern friends, Stevens and Craig, whom he eventually meets in battle. Payton as Stevens' wife provides the romance element and the espionage sub-plot.

d William Cameron Menzies *p* Maurice King, Frank King
s Philip Yordon, Sidney Harmon *c* Lionel Lindon
lp James Craig, Barbara Payton, Guy Madison, Craig Stevens, Barton MacLane, Tom Fadden

Fort Defiance (VENTURA) 81 min
Johnson's magnificent performance and Cortez's bravura cinematography make this a superior B Western. Johnson is seeking Clark, whose desertion in the middle of a Civil War skirmish led to Johnson's company being wiped out, who finds Graves, Clark's blinded younger brother. Add to this Navajos on the warpath and yet another revenger seeking the

destruction of Clark's whole family and the result is a complex, action-filled film.

d John Rawlins *p* Frank Melford *s* Louis Lantz
c Stanley Cortez *lp* Dane Clark, Ben Johnson, Peter Graves, Tracey Roberts, George Cleveland, Dennis Moore

Fort Savage Raiders (COL) b/w 54 min
Directed energetically by Nazarro, this Starrett outing has the added (cult) bonus of one of the last appearances of director Sears in front of the camera. Shipman's unusual screenplay features Dehner as a mentally deranged army officer who escapes from military prison and leads a group of his prison-mates on a campaign of terror before Starrett tracks him down. Dehner, who brings a real depth to his role, and Shipman's intriguing script give the movie some of the edge of the superior **The Man from Colorado** (1948).

d Ray Nazarro *p* Colbert Clark *s* Barry Shipman
c Henry Freulich *lp* Charles Starrett, Smiley Burnette, John Dehner, Fred Sears, Trevor Bardette, Peter Thompson

Fort Worth (WB) 80 min
Scott is the gunman who lays down his guns and picks up the pen as a reforming newspaper editor to oppose Brian's plans to buy up the territory and who has to reluctantly put his guns back on when Brian is joined by a group of renegades. Twist's superior script is efficiently, if anonymously, directed by Marin.

d Edwin L. Marin *p* Anthony Veiller *s* John Twist *c* Sid Hickox *lp* Randolph Scott, David Brian, Phyllis Thaxter, Dick Jones, Ray Teal, Bob Steele

The Great Missouri Raid (PAR) 83 min
An intriguing retelling of the oft-told tale of the early days of Frank (Corey) and Jesse (Carey) James with the Younger clan thrown in for good measure. Bond is the vengeful brother of a Union soldier who Corey and Carey mistakenly kill and who pushes them into full-time outlawry. But the stress in Gruber's literate screenplay is less on explaining the James boys' actions than on watching them rush to their ends.

d Gordon Douglas *p* Nat Holt *s* Frank Gruber *c* Ray Rennahan *lp* Wendell Corey, MacDonald Carey, Ellen Drew, Ward Bond, Edgar Buchanan, Tom Tyler

The Groom Wore Spurs (FIDELITY) b/w 80 min
A jerky but mildly enjoyable satire on the life of a Hollywood cowboy. Carson is the cowboy star who's a coward when the camera's not on him and Rogers is the legal eagle who rescues him, marries him and finally makes a man out of him after much clowning about. A silly sub-plot has Carson framed for murder and the pair of them trailing the real villains along the dry gulches and across the prairies of Hollywood.

d Richard Whorf *p* Howard Welsch *s* Robert Carson, Robert Libott, Frank Burt *c* Peverell Marley *lp* Ginger Rogers, Jack Carson, Joan Davis, Stanley Ridges, James Brown, John Litel

Heart of the Rockies (REP) b/w 67 min
As the series Western journeyed further and further into the fifties, it looked and felt increasingly out of time. As the market for them slipped so did their budgets. Rogers, with Gene Autry, of course, was one of the few stars whose films maintained the high production values they'd begun with. Here, under Witney's aggressive direction, Rogers is in charge of the construction of a road across land owned by Morgan who, fearful people will find out how he acquired the land, attempts to sabotage the project. Needless to say, he fails. Edwards is the heroine, replacing Dale Evans who'd retired in 1950.

d William Witney *p* Edward J. White *s* Eric Taylor
c Reggie Lanning *lp* Roy Rogers, Penny Edwards, Gordon Jones, Ralph Morgan, Fred Graham, Mira McKinney, Trigger

King of the Bullwhip
(WESTERN ADVENTURE) b/w 60 min
The first of Ormond's Lash LaRue Westerns to be distributed by Realart, and, like so many series firsts, one of the best. Ormond has the credits played over the climactic fight, a trick he was particularly fond of, to create a greater sense of excitement at the beginning of the film. However, Lewis and Webb's screenplay swiftly flags after the novel idea of having a bandit pretend to be Lash, so Lash can go undercover (complete with his whip). Moore is the bank clerk turned gold-bullion robber.

d/p Ron Ormond *s* Jack Lewis, Ira Webb *c* Ernest Miller
lp Lash LaRue, Al St John, Jack Holt, Dennis Moore, Tom Neal, Anne Gwynne

The Lady from Texas (U-INTERNATIONAL) 77 min
An amiable, if rather sentimental, Western in which Duff is the drifter who, egged on by Freeman, comes to the aid of Hull when Stevens tries to browbeat the old lady into selling her ranch to him at a knockdown price and tries to get her

John Ireland (left) and Lloyd Bridges as the quarrelling officers trying to warn Custer of impending doom in Little Big Horn.

Far left: Jack Carson and Ginger Rogers in a publicity still for The Groom Wore Spurs, yet another comic exposé of the life of a Hollywood cowboy.

certified as part of the process. The court scenes, which include the reading of a letter from Lincoln, are very stagey but the strong performances of Duff, Hull and Freeman and one-time actor Pevney's sensitive direction are compelling.

d Joseph Pevney *p* Leonard Goldstein *s* Gerald Drayson Adams, Connie Lee Bennett *c* Charles P. Boyle *lp* Howard Duff, Mona Freeman, Josephine Hull, Craig Stevens, Ed Begley, Chris-Pin Martin

The Last Outpost (PAR) 88 min

Reagan and Bennett are the brothers, Confederate and Unionist respectively, in conflict over gold shipments from Arizona. Bennett has orders to facilitate their passage for the Union cause, Reagan to halt them. Indian troubles force the two of them, and their men, to join together to protect the surrounding settlers. Fleming is the romantic interest.

The film is a good example of the work of producers Pine and Thomas who made B features for Paramount throughout the forties and in the fifties briefly scaled the heights to double A features. It's routine but rugged. Reagan rode his own horse, Tarbaby, in the film.

d Lewis R. Foster *p* William H. Pine, William C. Thomas *s* Geoffrey Homes, George Worthing Yates, Winston Miller *c* Loyal Griggs *lp* Ronald Reagan, Rhonda Fleming, Bruce Bennett, Noah Beery Jnr, Bill Williams, Peter Hanson

Little Big Horn *aka* The Fighting Seventh
(LIPPERT) b/w 86 min

The directorial debut of Warren, a Western novelist turned scriptwriter who, in the sixties, was to find his niche as a producer in television, *Little Big Horn* was Lippert's biggest budgeted film hitherto. The film's hook, reputedly derived from a real incident, is the attempt by a small contingent of Cavalry to get through hostile Indian territory to warn Custer of the ambush planned by the Sioux. Accordingly the suspense comes from watching the patrol slowly but surely cut down until none are left while the antagonism between Bridges and Ireland (whom Bridges thinks has stolen his wife from him) provides the human drama.

Randolph Scott in the unlikely role of ladies man with Joan Leslie in Man in the Saddle.

d/s Charles Marquis Warren *p* Carl K. Hittleman *c* Ernest Miller *lp* Lloyd Bridges, Marie Windsor, John Ireland, Reed Hadley, Jim Davis, Hugh O'Brian

The Longhorn (MON) sepia 70 min

The first script by Ullman who, in the fifties, was to write some of the more interesting series Westerns. Elliott, noticeably a more realistic figure than before, is the cattleman who, with Healey, heads up a trail drive of Hereford cattle to cross-breed with his Texas longhorns. The details of the trail drive are neatly handled by Collins, even if the turnabout, when Healey is revealed to be in league with the rustlers, is far too melodramatic in view of what goes before.

d Lewis Collins *p* Vincent M. Fennelly *s* Dan Ullman *c* Ernest Miller *lp* Bill Elliott, Myron Healey, Phyllis Coates, John Hart, Marshall Reed, William Fawcett

Man in the Saddle
(PRODUCERS-ACTORS CORPORATION) 87 min

Memorable for its superb night-time photography and an extended brawl between Scott and Russell, this is one of De Toth's best Westerns. Gamet's strong plot has Knox attempting to run Scott off the range after Leslie, Scott's one-time fiancée, decides to marry him rather than Scott. Scott takes to the hills with schoolteacher Drew and, after being forced into a gunfight by Russell, emerges to do battle with Knox. Scott, his demeanour expressing his growing authority, is simply marvellous, providing De Toth with a gaunt visage for his camera to probe.

d Andre De Toth *p* Harry Joe Brown *s* Kenneth Gamet *c* Charles Lawton Jnr *lp* Randolph Scott, Joan Leslie, John Russell, Alexander Knox, Ellen Drew, Guinn Williams

Mark of the Renegade (U-INTERNATIONAL) b/w 81min

Montalban is the seeming renegade of the title. He teams up with Tobias' evil pirate who plans to sack Los Angeles (!) and falls foul of Roland who dreams of a Californian Empire before being forced to court Charisse as daughter of the leader of the Republic of California. If the plot is confusing, especially when Montalban reveals himself to be an agent of the Republic of Mexico sent to protect Mexico's interests, Fregonese's direction is crystal clear: action and spectacle at any cost. And to a great extent, he's successful, producing a superbly orchestrated piece of candy floss.

d Hugo Fregonese *p* Jack Cross *s* Louis Solomon, Robert Hardy Andrews *c* Charles P. Boyle *lp* Ricardo Montalban, Cyd Charisse, Gilbert Roland, J. Carroll Naish, Antonio Moreno, George Tobias

My Brother the Outlaw *aka* My Outlaw Brother
(BENEDICT BOGEAUS PRODUCTIONS) b/w 82 min

This is a mediocre juvenile outing that wastes its assets on a silly story. Rooney, out of place in the West, is travelling to see his brother, Stack, when he links up with ranger Preston and discovers that Stack is a bandit. There follows a would-be thrill-a-minute series of incidents before Preston and Rooney finally get the upper hand and send Stack, who gives a very mechanical performance, to jail. The film was shot in and around Mexico City.

d Elliott Nugent *p* Benedict Bogeaus *s* Gene Fowler Jnr *c* Jose Ortiz Ramos *lp* Mickey Rooney, Wanda Hendrix, Robert Stack, Robert Preston, Carlos Muzquiz, Jose Tervay

Night Riders of Montana (REP) b/w 60 min

With the help of his faithful steed, Black Jack, Lane routs the rustling plans of Space (here masking his outlawry under the guise of the town's gunsmith) and Barcroft, still managing that frightening grin when called for. Healey is the hot head of a red herring and Barrett the comely romantic interest.

Brannon directs persuasively, promising more action than he ever delivers.

d Fred C. Brannon *p* Gordon Kay *s* M. Coates Webster
c Jack MacBurnie *lp* Allan Lane, Chubby Johnson, Arthur Space, Roy Barcroft, Myron Healey, Claudia Barrett

Only the Valiant (WB) 105 min
In this intelligent Western, Peck is the fierce disciplinarian who nearly drives his men to mutiny in the course of their attempt to recapture the fort that commands a mountain pass from Indians after an uprising. The literate script is based on a novel by Charles Marquis Warren who briefly turned director in the fifties before finding himself a comfortable niche in television as an executive producer on series such as *Gunsmoke* and *Rawhide*.

d Gordon Douglas *p* William Cagney *s* Edmund H. North, Harry Brown *c* Lionel Lindon *lp* Gregory Peck, Barbara Payton, Ward Bond, Gig Young, Lon Chaney Jnr, Neville Brand

Pals of the Golden West (REP) b/w 68 min
Rogers' last series Western – he would subsequently make only guest appearances and star in one last film, the intriguing **MacKintosh and T.J.** (1975) – this is only a routine entry. The real villain of the piece is foot and mouth disease (a recurring motif in Rogers' films) which Barcroft and Caruso are bringing into the States with diseased cattle. Rogers is the border offical responsible for keeping America pure and fighting a sandstorm into the bargain. Fittingly, Evans, Rogers' regular companion on and off screen, returned to the series for the final entry of a series that, despite its fall in popularity in recent years, had, uniquely amongst Western series, maintained its production values to the end.

d William Witney *p* Edward J. White *s* Albert DeMond, Eric Taylor *c* Jack Marta *lp* Roy Rogers, Dale Evans, Estelita Rodriguez, Pinky Lee, Roy Barcroft, Anthony Caruso, Trigger

Passage West *aka* High Venture (PAR) 80 min
Photographed in glowing colour by Griggs, this is a decidedly off-beat Western. O'Keefe is the two-fisted parson leading a wagon train West and Payne the leader of a group of escaped convicts who take shelter with the wagon train and force it forward at a dangerous speed to avoid their recapture. On their arrival in the Western territories, the convicts, impressed by the ways of the religious settlers, stay on to help out until gold is discovered and Payne has to fight his fellow convicts and then blow up the gold mine (and himself) to prevent their reverting to type. Foster's direction is slow

moving like his screenplay, but Paramount's huge publicity campaign made the film a surprise box-office success.

d/s Lewis R. Foster *p* William Pine, William Thomas *c* Loyal Griggs *lp* John Payne, Dennis O'Keefe, Arleen Whelan, Frank Faylen, Mary Anderson, Peter Hanson

Prairie Round Up (COL) b/w 53 min
Possibly Sears' best film with Starrett, *Prairie Round Up* sees its director confident enough to choose unusual camera angles for the action sequences. The plot has former Texas Ranger Starrett murdering his alter ego, the Durango Kid, and then breaking jail as part of a complicated ploy to unmask Fenton, who just happens to be planning his own cattle empire in the West.

d Fred F. Sears *p* Colbert Clark *s* Joseph O'Donnell *c* Fayte Browne *lp* Charles Starrett, Smiley Burnette, Mary Castle, Frank Fenton, Lane Chandler, Forrest Taylor

Raton Pass *aka* Canyon Pass (WB) b/w 84 min
Morgan and Neal are the married combatants in this odd movie. She swindles him out of his half share in their empire of a cattle ranch and then hires a band of outlaws to help her keep it. Morgan responds by uniting the surrounding homesteaders, threatened with eviction by Neal, into a vigilante group and recovering his ranch. In the process he picks up a new wife, Hart. An energetic little Western.

d Edwin L. Marin *p* Saul Elkins *s* Tom W. Blackburn, James R. Webb *c* Wilfrid M. Cline *lp* Dennis Morgan, Patricia Neal, Steve Cochran, Scott Forbes, Dorothy Hart, Basil Ruysdael

Rawhide *aka* Desperate Siege (FOX) b/w 86 min
Hathaway's first Western for some twenty years, *Rawhide* is a suspenseful actioneer. Marlowe and Elam are particularly good as the escaped convicts lying in wait at a stagecoach way station for a shipment of gold who terrorize unexpected arrivals Hayward and Power. As much a thriller as a Western (hence Elam's sadistic interpretation of his role) the film demonstates Nichols' uneasiness with the violent mores of the post-war Western. Hathaway's direction is simple and direct.

The Red Badge of Courage, *John Huston's dramatic but unromantic view of the Civil War.*

Far left: *Estelita Rodriguez (left) and Dale Evans with Roy Rogers in his last series outing,* Pals of the Golden West.

Denver and Rio Grande, *1952*

The Outlaw, *1943*

Joel McCrea and Maureen O'Hara in Buffalo Bill, *1944*

Howard Keel in Annie Get Your Gun, *1950*

Joan Crawford in Johnny Guitar, *1954*

Clark Gable and Jane Russell in The Tall Men, *1955*

John Wayne leading The Horse Soldiers, *1959*

Richard Widmark and George Matthews in The Last Wagon, *1956*

The Magnificent Seven, *1960*

The Alamo, *1960*

John Wayne and Henry Morgan in How the West Was Won, *1962*

Clint Eastwood in For a Fistful of Dollars, *1964*

Nathaniel Narcisco and Gregory Peck in Stalking Moon, *1968*

Gary Cooper in Garden of Evil, *1954*

Dana Andrews in Town Tamer, *1965*

Jane Fonda in Cat Ballou, *1965*

John Wayne, Robert Mitchum and Arthur Hunnicutt, in El Dorado, *1967*

Steve McQueen in Nevada Smith, *1966*

Return of the Seven, *1966*

Paul Newman in Hombre, *1967*

John Wayne, Kirk Douglas and Howard Keel in War Wagon, *1967*

Terence Stamp in Blue, *1968*

Richard Harris in A Man Called Horse, *1970*

Marilyn Monroe in River of No Return, *1954*

Paul Newman and Robert Redford in Butch Cassidy and the Sundance Kid, *1969*

Richard Widmark and victim in Death of a Gunfighter, *1969*

John Wayne and Rock Hudson in The Undefeated, *1969*

True Grit, *1969*

Little Big Man, *1970*

Candice Bergen and Gene Hackman in The Hunting Party, *1971*

John Wayne with The Cowboys, *1971*

Jeff Bridges in Bad Company, *1972*

John Wayne in Chisum, *1970*

James Coburn in A Fistful of Dynamite, *1971*

Robert Redford and Will Geer in Jeremiah Johnson, *1972*

Michael J. Pollard in Dirty Little Billy, *1972*

Lucky Luke, *1971*

Yul Brynner and Richard Benjamin in Westworld, *1973*

John Wayne and Lauren Bacall in The Shootist, *1976*

Pat Garrett and Billy the Kid, *1973*

Goldie Hawn in The Duchess and the Dirtwater Fox, *1976*

John Travolta in Urban Cowboy, *1980*

Robert Redford in The Electric Horseman, *1979*

d Henry Hathaway *p* Samuel G. Engel *s* Dudley Nichols *c* Milton Krasner *lp* Tyrone Power, Susan Hayward, Hugh Marlowe, Jack Elam, Dean Jagger, Edgar Buchanan

The Red Badge of Courage (MGM) b/w 69 min

Huston's film is an arty, self-conscious adaption of Stephen Crane's classic novella about a young soldier (Murphy) caught in the midst of the Civil War who runs away from his first battle. The film was pointedly antipathetic to the emotional climate of America in the early fifties, and not surprisingly Huston encountered a series of problems with MGM, who wanted a more positive, upbeat film. These problems are catalogued in awesome detail in Lilian Ross' *Picture*, a classic account of the process of film-making.

d/s John Huston *p* Gottfried Reinhardt *c* Harold Rosson *lp* Audie Murphy, Bill Mauldin, Douglas Dick, Royal Dano, John Dierkes, Andy Devine, Arthur Hunnicutt

Red Mountain (PAR) 84 min

This is one of the last films photographed by Lang for Paramount before he went freelance in 1952. The plot is the standard 'War in the West' version of the Civil War with Ladd as the Confederate and Kennedy a neutral. Together they foil the plans of Ireland's Quantrill to build himself an empire in the West. The climax is a brutal, no holds barred, gunfight well staged by Dieterle. Brand and Carey do well as heavies.

d William Dieterle *p* Hal B. Wallis *s* John Meredyth Lucas, George F. Slavin, George W. George *c* Charles B. Lang Jnr *lp* Alan Ladd, Lizabeth Scott, John Ireland, Arthur Kennedy, Jeff Carey, Neville Brand

The Redhead and the Cowboy (PAR) b/w 83 min

Fleming and Ford have the title roles in this enjoyable minor Western. Set at the time of the Civil War, Latimer and O'Brien's script features Fleming as the Confederate spy and Ford as the cowboy who needs her as a witness to prove that he's innocent of the murder charge laid against him. O'Brien is the Union agent trying to break the Confederate spy network and protect the shipment of gold the Confederates

Alan Ladd and Lizabeth Scott as the lovers in Red Mountain.

are after. Smartly directed by Fenton, whose last film it was, and well acted by its principals, it is an entertaining, if lightweight, film.

d Leslie Fenton *p* Irving Asher *s* Jonathan Latimer, Liam O'Brien *c* Daniel Fapp *lp* Glenn Ford, Edmond O'Brien, Rhonda Fleming, Morris Ankrum, Alan Reed, Ray Teal

Ridin' the Outlaw Trail (COL) b/w 56 min

Another superior Starrett series Western, this sees its star, in the dual role of a Texas Ranger and masked mysterio, the Durango Kid, on the trail of Morgan and the $20,000 in gold coins he's stolen. Pee Wee King offers solid musical support while Burnette, as an inept blacksmith, handles the comedy chores. Neatly scripted and directed, the film is a good representative example of the series Western in the early fifties.

d Fred F. Sears *p* Colbert Clark *s* Victor Arthur *c* Fayte Browne *lp* Charles Starrett, Smiley Burnette, Pee Wee King, Sunny Vickers, Jim Bannon, Lee Morgan

Rodeo King and the Senorita (REP) b/w 67 min

A remake of Roy Rogers' **My Pal Trigger** (1946) with Allen's horse, Koko, in the Trigger role and the pair of them exposing the crooked partner who's trying to bankrupt a travelling Wild West Show that has been left to DeSimone. Allen, serenading all in sight, lets the film's mawkish moments pass over him like water off a duck's back, though director Ford is unable to make the material seem fresh for any length of time.

d Philip Ford *p* Melville Tucker *s* John K. Butler *c* Walter Strenge *lp* Rex Allen, Mary Ellen Kay, Bonnie DeSimone, Buddy Ebsen, Roy Barcroft, Tristram Coffin

Saddle Legion (RKO) b/w 61 min

A routine series outing enlivened by the presence of Malone as a doctor who gives the film a touch of class way above Schlom's budget. Also of interest is the presence of Livingston, one of the original Three Mesquiteers, as a heavy. The plot features Holt and Martin putting an end to a rustling set-up with a new twist: a crooked cattle inspector who condemns the herd of cattle about to be rustled. So when the cattle of the good folk who've given Holt a job are condemned as having the dreaded black leg....

d Lesley Selander *p* Herman Schlom *s* Ed Earl Repp *c* J. Roy Hunt *lp* Tim Holt, Dorothy Malone, Richard Martin, Robert Livingston, James Rush, Bob Wilke

Santa Fé (PRODUCERS-ACTORS CORPORATION) 89 min

A cut-down version of **Union Pacific** (1939), this is one of the last films to be directed by Pichel. Produced by Scott and Brown's own company it features Scott as the Confederate who heads West, to escape the ignominy of defeat, with a trio of brothers who turn on him when he decides to throw in his lot with the Santa Fé Railroad. Roberts is the villain and Mahoney, fresh from stunting for Charles Starrett, his athletic henchman. Although it lacks the easy bitter-sweet charm of the later Scott-Brown productions, Scott's grim visage and Gamet's tight screenplay have their enjoyable moments.

d Irving Pichel *p* Harry Joe Brown *s* Kenneth Gamet *c* Charles Lawton Jnr *lp* Randolph Scott, Roy Roberts, Jock (O')Mahoney, Janis Carter, Jerome Courtland, Peter Thompson

Silver City (PAR) 90 min

O'Brien is the mining expert reduced to near penury by Arlen's vindictiveness who finds redemption in the arms of De Carlo. She and her father, Buchanan, seek assistance from O'Brien when they run foul of Fitzgerald and his gunslinger, Moore. Haskin directs briskly, unusually giving O'Brien and

De Carlo's romance as much attention as the fistfights and dynamite explosions that punctuate the film.

d Byron Haskin *p* Nat Holt *s* Frank Gruber *c* Ray Rennahan *lp* Edmond O'Brien, Yvonne De Carlo, Richard Arlen, Edgar Buchanan, Barry Fitzgerald, Michael Moore

Silver City Bonanza (REP) b/w 67 min

This amiable series outing features Ebsen for the second time as Allen's comic side-kick. Williams' screenplay, as fantastical as ever, utilizes a blind man's dog which helps track down the murderer of its master, a lengthy underwater scrap and a haunted ranch. Kennedy is the villain, trying to drive Kay off her ranch so as to be able to collect the silver he knows to be at the bottom of her lake (!) and being foiled at the last minute by Allen and Ebsen.

d George Blair *p* Melville Tucker *s* Bob Williams *c* John MacBurnie *lp* Rex Allen, Buddy Ebsen, Mary Ellen Kay, Bill Kennedy, Alix Ebsen, Clem Bevins

Stage to Tucson *aka* Lost Stage Valley (COL) 82 min

This routine oater is enlivened by Lawton's superior cinematography. Despite the presence of other hands, the screenplay has all the marks of a Williams' original with its bizarre premise that the Confederacy are stealing Arizona stagecoaches to break the Union's Western supply lines. Cameron and Morris are the Union agents sent to put a stop to it, who expose Roberts as the ringleader masking his money-grabbing schemes under the cloak of being a Southern sympathizer. Murphy directs efficiently.

d Ralph Murphy *p* Harry Joe Brown *s* Bob Williams, Frank Burt, Robert Libott *c* Charles Lawton Jnr *lp* Rod Cameron, Wayne Morris, Kay Buckley, Roy Roberts, Carl Benton Reid, Douglas Fowley

Sugarfoot *aka* Swirl of Glory (WB) 80 min

Scott and Massey are the old enemies who meet up in Arizona in this routine oater. Scott's the ex-rebel officer hoping to start anew as a rancher only to find that Massey has sewn up the town and all the available land. Inevitably they come into conflict. Jergens stands by. Hughes' script, based on the novel by Clarence Buddington Kelland, inspired the teleseries, *Sugarfoot*.

d Edwin L. Marin *p* Saul Elkins *s* Russell Hughes *c* Wilfrid M. Cline *lp* Randolph Scott, Adele Jergens, Raymond Massey, Robert Warwick, Hugh Sanders, Arthur Hunnicutt

Texas Lawmen (FRONTIER PICTURES/MON) b/w 54 min

This is another good late entry in Brown's series Westerns. Based on an original story by actor Myron Healey (who'd scripted **Colorado Ambush,** 1951 for Brown), Holland's screenplay centres on the conflict of loyalties faced by Ellison as the son of a bandit turned sheriff asked by Brown to help bring in his own father. Collins' direction is taut and to the point, made even more so by the absence of female characters.

d Lewis Collins *p* Vincent M. Fennelly *s* Joseph Holland *c* Ernest Miller *lp* Johnny Mack Brown, Jimmy Ellison, I. Stanford Jolley, Marshall Reed, Lee Roberts, Terry Frost

The Texas Rangers (COL) 74 min

Schayer's decidedly pulp 'history' of the formation of the Texas Rangers sees Montgomery, as an ex-convict, leading the Rangers against a massed band of outlaws led by Bishop's Sam Bass and seeking MacDonald's Sundance Kid who framed him. Karlson, a director whose concern for authenticity often shows itself in strange ways – for *The Phenix City Story* (1955), which was based on an actual murder case, he had John McIntyre wear the actual clothes of the murdered man – gives the outlaws in MacDonald's gang the names of

George Montgomery as the outlaw turned lawman in Phil Karlson's The Texas Rangers.

real-life bandits from Texas' early days. But, though his direction is equally tough-minded, it can't overcome Schayer's novelettish screenplay. Nonetheless this is a superior B picture.

d Phil Karlson *p* Edward Small *s* Richard Schayer *c* Ellis W. Carter *lp* George Montgomery, Gale Storm, William Bishop, Ian MacDonald, Noah Beery Jnr, John Dehner

Thunder in God's Country (REP) b/w 67 min

This pleasant series outing sees Allen and his new comic side-kick, Ebsen, in a contemporary setting. Allen is the roving Western artist (!) who foils gambler MacDonald's plans to take control of Hidden Valley and transform it into a new Las Vegas, with a percentage of every bet going to him. Another modern touch is the faked tape recording which MacDonald and his political cronies use to try and swing the election they have to win before they can put their plan into operation. Needless to say, the old virtues win out and Hidden Valley is saved from its intended fate as a slotmachine paradise.

d George Blair *p* Melville Tucker *s* Arthur E. Orloff *c* John MacBurnie *lp* Rex Allen, Mary Ellen Kay, Buddy Ebsen, Ian MacDonald, Paul Harvey, Frank Ferguson

Tomahawk (U-INTERNATIONAL) 82 min

Clearly influenced by **Broken Arrow** (1950), *Tomahawk* nonetheless remains essentially an actioneer with the Cavalry and the Sioux once more at war following the Fetterman Massacre. Crooked traders and sadistic Cavalry officers (here Nicol) are given as the cause of the Sioux uprising, but from there on it's pure action with the Sioux finally falling to the rapid-action, breech-loading rifles used against them for the first time. Heflin is the scout who fails to prevent the war and De Carlo the actress he somewhat lackadaisically romances.

d George Sherman *p* Leonard Goldstein *s* Silvia Richards, Maurice Geraghty *c* Charles P. Boyle *lp* Van Heflin, Yvonne De Carlo, Preston Foster, Alex Nicol, Rock Hudson, Jack Oakie

Vengeance Valley (MGM) 83 min

Lancaster is the ranch foreman who covers up for his wayward foster-brother, Walker, son of cattleman Collins, in this slow-moving character study. Ravetch's script is purposeful and well-intentioned, though it lacks the rigour and

Far right: *Kirk Douglas as the land speculator in* The Big Trees.

economy of his work on **Hud** (1963) and **Hombre** (1967), but Thorpe's direction is far too slack. As a result, especially since Walker's fate is obvious from the beginning, there is no tension in the film.

d Richard Thorpe   *p* Nicholas Nayfack   *s* Irving Ravetch *c* George Folsey   *lp* Burt Lancaster, Robert Walker, Joanne Dru, Ray Collins, John Ireland, Sally Forrest

Warpath (PAR)   95 min
Gruber's screenplay neatly crosses the revenge plot – O'Brien on the trail of the three men who murdered his fiancée – with the story of the attempt by a group of people to warn Custer of the ambush the Sioux have planned for him. Haskin's direction is decidedly pulpish but the acting, particularly by Carey as the troop commander and Tucker as the murderer-turned-Cavalryman, is solid enough and cinematographer Rennahan brings real excitement to the clashes between the Indians and the Cavalry.

d Byron Haskin   *p* Nat Holt   *s* Frank Gruber   *c* Ray Rennahan   *lp* Edmond O'Brien, Dean Jagger, Forrest Tucker, Harry Carey Jnr, James Millican, Paul Fix

1952

Apache War Smoke (MGM)   b/w   67 min
This is an indifferent remake of **Apache Trail** (1943). Horton, who a few years later was to achieve lasting western fame as a scout on the *Wagon Train* teleseries, is the manager of a way station where the passengers of a stagecoach await an Indian raid. He refuses to defuse the situation by handing over Roland, suspected of killing Indians. The irony inherent in the Ernest Haycox story the film is based on is rather lost in Kress' stolid direction but Alton's cinematography, especially of the Indian attack and the desertscapes, is superb.

d Harold Kress   *p* Hayes Goetz   *s* Jerry Davis   *c* John Alton   *lp* Gilbert Roland, Glenda Farrell, Robert Horton, Henry (Harry) Morgan, Myron Healey, Gene Lockhart

Bend of the River *aka* **Where the River Bends** (U)   91 min
Bend of the River is Mann's most satisfying Western. The script interweaves the story of Stewart's desperate search for a

James Stewart in manic mood knifes Jack Lambert in Anthony Mann's classic Bend of the River.

new identity for himself with the epic struggle of a group of pioneers to reach their chosen Eden. The movie is scripted by Chase in an old-fashioned manner with heavy reliance on cliches ('one bad apple destroys the rest of the barrel' etc), and simple contrasts between farming and mining the land and incongruous cameos like that of Fetchit. Its greatness stems from Mann's transformation of the naive into the elemental.

For the pioneers the natural obstacles they encounter are just that, natural obstacles; for Stewart they have a private significance as the milestones on his personal route to redemption. Like Kennedy, his brother under the skin, he is a former outlaw who wants to go straight. But where Kennedy freely admits his past, Stewart hides his (and the scar, the result of a near hanging that signifies it). It is only when Kennedy turns against the pioneers and tries to sell the food promised them to miners who have discovered gold and leaves Stewart to die when he (Stewart) objects, that Stewart is able to recover his suppressed abilities and use them legitimately in defence of the settlers and his prospective new life.

Left to die on the top of Mount Hood, Stewart seems to become almost an avenging spirit of Nature as, armed with only his desire for revenge, he follows the departing wagon train of food and single-handedly saves the pioneer's winter provisions before symbolically being washed clean of his past in the Snake River that sweeps Kennedy to his doom.

Bend of the River fully justifies the description of Mann as the Virgil of the West made by several French critics; his camera offers a majestic panorama of mountains and forest that represents both the promised land and the obstacles, interior as well as exterior, facing would-be travellers to the West. A magnificent film.

d Anthony Mann   *p* Aaron Rosenberg   *s* Borden Chase *c* Irving Glassberg   *lp* James Stewart, Arthur Kennedy, Rock Hudson, Jay C. Flippen, Julia Adams, Stepin Fetchit

The Big Sky
(WINCHESTER PRODUCTIONS)   b/w   140(122) min
An inferior companion piece to **Red River** (1948), *The Big Sky* also features a long trek, by fur trappers up the Missouri River to unexplored territory, in the 1830s, and the maturing of a youth, Martin. Douglas is the happy-go-lucky trapper whom Martin models himself on, seeing in him the elder brother killed in his youth. But their relationship lacks the depth and complexity of that between John Wayne and Montgomery Clift in the earlier film. Thus, ironically for a director not noted for his 'beautiful' images, the film's best sequences are of the hauling of the keelboat up the river by hand. The triangular relationship of Douglas, Threatt and Martin is always subservient to the adventure story, the homosexual implications in Douglas and Martin's friendship notwithstanding.

d/p Howard Hawks   *s* Dudley Nichols   *c* Russell Harlan *lp* Kirk Douglas, Dewey Martin, Elizabeth Threatt, Arthur Hunnicutt, Hank Worden, Jim Davis

The Big Trees (WB) 89 min

Made by Douglas for no salary in exchange for the termination of his contract with Warners, *The Big Trees* features him as the con man who turns out to be a likeable rogue. He's the land speculator who intends to use a legal loophole to shift a group of religious settlers and so gain their land and its valuable timber. He's set on by one-time partner, Buchanan, a rival schemer, Archer and his ex-girlfriend, Wymore, before he sees the light and helps the settlers fight for what is theirs. Routine and rather soggy.

d Felix Feist *p* Louis F. Edelman *s* John Twist, James R. Webb *c* Bert Glennon *lp* Kirk Douglas, Eve Miller, Patrice Wymore, Edgar Buchanan, John Archer, Alan Hale Jnr

Black Hills Ambush (REP) b/w 54 min

Barcroft as the villain and Lane as the hero almost make one believe that this film was made a decade earlier, so innocent is it compared to other Westerns of the fifties. Lane is the marshal and Barcroft the leader of a gang driving Waller into bankruptcy while Hall is on hand as a gunman waiting to be reformed. Keller directs efficiently, if anonymously.

d/p Harry Keller *s* M. Coates Webster, Ronald Davidson *c* Bud Thackery *lp* Allan Lane, Eddy Waller, Roy Barcroft, Michael Hall, Leslye Banning, Edward Cassidy

Brave Warrior (COL) 73 min

A lacklustre Indian Western from veteran quickie producer Katzman, one of the last of the independent producers to desert the Western. Set just prior to the war of 1812, Kent's script features Hall as the government agent trying to find out who is turning the Indians' thoughts to rebellion. Silverheels (soon to become Tonto) is the good Indian and Ansara the villain of the piece.

d Spencer G. Bennet *p* Sam Katzman *s* Robert E. Kent *c* William V. Skall *lp* Jon Hall, Christine Larson, Jay Silverheels, Michael Ansara, Harry Cording, George Eldridge

Bronco Buster (U-INTERNATIONAL) 80 min

The first of the films of Boetticher to win real praise, *Bronco Buster* has an ease about it that prefigures the majestic

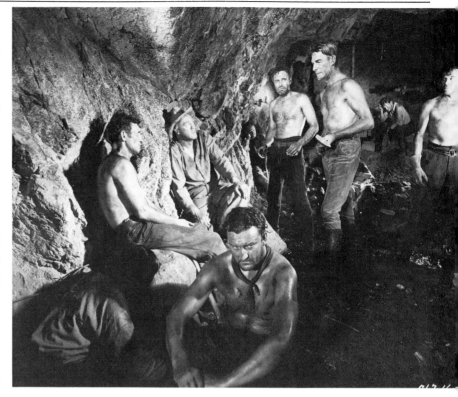

Randolph Scott (centre) helping to extend the railroad to Carson City.

Westerns he was to make with Randolph Scott later in the decade. Even the rivalry between the Lund and Brady characters, as they compete in the ring and out of it for the hand of Holden, prefigures that between Scott and the series of amiable villains Boetticher confronts him with in classic films like **Ride Lonesome** (1959) and **Comanche Station** (1960). Lund is quietly effective in the Scott role while Brady is more hammy as the 'villain'. Real-life rodeo stars Casey Tibbs, Pete Crump, Bill Williams and Jerry Ambler supply strong support. But in Boetticher's hands it is less the actuality of the rodeo that matters than its closeness to the bullring and the metaphor of the closed circle that is so powerfully present in Boetticher's movies. The result is an assured film.

d Budd Boetticher *p* Ted Richmond *s* Horace McCoy, Lillie Hayward *c* Clifford Stine *lp* John Lund, Scott Brady, Joyce Holden

Buffalo Bill in Tomahawk Territory

(JACK SCHWARZ) b/w 66 min

A real quickie in which Moore, later to achieve greater fame as television's Lone Ranger, is Buffalo Bill trying to deliver a herd of cattle to the Sioux to end an Indian uprising that Hubbard and his gang are trying to prolong so as to have the Indians driven out of their own lands which are rich in gold. The film makes extensive use of stock footage and dialogue.

d/co-p B.B. Ray *co-p* Edward Finney *s* Sam Neumann, Nat Tanchuck *c* Elmer Dyer *lp* Clayton Moore, Slim Andrews, Tom Hubbard, Rodd Redwing, Chief Thundercloud, Sharon Dexter

Bugles in the Afternoon (WB) 85 min

Routine. Brown and Homes' script features Milland as the cavalry officer victimized by his commanding officer, Marlowe, who is jealous of Carter's affections for Milland. He's demoted, but not dispirited and performs heroically at Little Big Horn. Rowland's direction is fast and furious. Writer Harry Brown should not be confused with producer/writer Harry Joe Brown who had worked in the genre since silent days and is best remembered for his series of Westerns with Budd Boetticher and Randolph Scott in the sixties.

Ray Milland and Helena Carter in Bugles in the Afternoon.

d Roy Rowland   *p* William Cagney   *s* Geoffrey Homes, Harry Brown   *c* Wilfrid M. Cline   *lp* Ray Milland, Helena Carter, Hugh Marlowe, Forrest Tucker, Barton MacLane, George Reeves

The Bushwackers *aka* The Rebel
(JACK BRODER PRODUCTIONS)   b/w   70 min
This was the directorial debut (and only Western) of Amateau, a former radio writer and second-unit director who, in the sixties, moved on to television. Chaney is the land baron and Ireland the gunman who has vowed never to use his guns again but buckles them on one more time when Malone's reforming newspaper editor of a father is brutally gunned down by Chaney's men. Amateau directs a touch amateurishly, but Ireland, in his first leading role, gives a nice gruff performance.

d/co-s Rod Amateau   *p* Larry Finley   *co-s* Thomas Gries
c John MacBurnie   *lp* John Ireland, Wayne Morris, Lon Chaney Jnr, Dorothy Malone, Jack Elam, Lawrence Tierney

California Conquest   (COL)   79 min
A quick reaction to the ever decreasing temperatures of the Cold War, this Katzman quickie posited California poised between joining the US and Russia in an attempt to end its subservience to Mexico. Ever so loosely based on fact, Kent's screenplay has Dehner as the wealthy landowner who seeks union with Russia and needs guns to stage a revolt. Wilde and Wright find the missing guns, stolen on his instructions, and so foil his ambitions. A silly piece of Cold-War mongering, but an engaging enough swashbuckling tale of 'Old California'.

d Lew Landers   *p* Sam Katzman   *s* Robert E. Kent
c Ellis W. Carter   *lp* Cornel Wilde, Teresa Wright, John Dehner, Alfonso Bedoya, Lisa Ferraday, Eugene Iglesias

Captive of Billy the Kid   (REP)   b/w   54 min
This is one of Lane's best series Westerns. Writers Webster and Wormser resurrect the treasure map plot (here giving the location of Billy the Kid's stolen wealth). The five pieces are given to friends, one of whom, Withers, wants everything for himself until Lane's cattle detective stops him. Brannon directs suspensefully and Barcroft sneers his way joyfully through the role of chief heavy.

Below: *Audie Murphy as* The Cimarron Kid *with Beverly Tyler.*

d Fred C. Brannon   *p* Harry Keller   *s* M. Coates Webster, Richard Wormser   *c* John MacBurnie   *lp* Allan Lane, Penny Edwards, Grant Withers, Roy Barcroft, Clem Bevins, Mauritz Hugo

Carson City   (WB)   87 min
One of the several Scott Westerns directed by De Toth, *Carson City* was the first film made in Warnercolor (Eastmancolor by another name). Though he had success in other genres (notably with *House of Wax*, 1953 and *Monkey on My Back*, 1957) De Toth's most consistent work was in the Western where his lyrical photography of nature could be given full rein. This film, co-scripted by Nibley, a veteran of Roy Rogers movies, sees Scott in charge of laying the railroad track between Virginia and Carson City. Massey is the cold-eyed villain and Norman the girl who falls for Scott.

d Andre De Toth   *p* David Weisbart   *s* Sloan Nibley, Winston Miller   *c* John Boyle   *lp* Randolph Scott, Lucille Norman, Raymond Massey, Richard Webb, James Millican, Larry Keating

Cattle Town   (WB)   b/w   71 min
A quickie, *Cattle Town* re-united director Smith and producer Foy who had previously worked together in the thirties on Dick Foran's musical Westerns. The screenplay by Blackburn, which features Morgan as the man sent by the Governor of Texas to sort out conflict between ranchers and homesteaders just after the Civil War, seems to be of a similar vintage. Teal is the villain and Moreno and Blake the girls who compete for Morgan's affections.

d Noel Smith   *p* Bryan Foy   *s* Tom Blackburn   *c* Ted McCord   *lp* Dennis Morgan, Philip Carey, Rita Moreno, Amanda Blake, Ray Teal, Charles Meredith

The Cimarron Kid   (U-INTERNATIONAL)   84 min
Although Stevens' screenplay is hardly demanding, Boetticher and Murphy, who gives a surprisingly confident performance, do what they can. The pair would work together much more creatively in Murphy's last film, **A Time for Dying**, 1969. Murphy is the innocent forced into crime by past associations who briefly unites the remnants of the Dalton gang before giving himself up to Erickson's marshal in preparation for a life of domesticity with Tyler. This is a minor, but entertaining, film.

d Budd Boetticher   *p* Ted Richmond   *s* Louis Stevens
c Charles P. Boyle   *lp* Audie Murphy, Yvette Dugay, Beverly Tyler, Leif Erickson, Noah Beery Jnr, John Hudson

Colorado Sundown   (REP)   b/w   67 min
This film saw Allen's budget much reduced from earlier outings as Republic retrenched following the loss of Roy Rogers. Accordingly the amount of stock footage began to grow and grow, testing the ingenuity of regular writers such as Milton Raison and here Taylor and Lively. The plot has Allen helping a friend claim his inheritance which is also claimed by an evil brother-and-sister team, Vincent and Graham. Witney directs as forcefully as his budget allows while Pickens, who replaces Buddy Ebsen, handles the comedy chores more than capably.

d William Witney   *p* Edward J. White   *s* Eric Taylor, William Lively   *c* John MacBurnie   *lp* Rex Allen, June Vincent, Fred Graham, Slim Pickens, Mary Ellen Kay, John Daheim

Cripple Creek   (RESOLUTE)   78 min
An unassuming actioneer set in gold rush days. Montgomery and Courtland are the government agents who go undercover as outlaws to investigate a gold robbery and smuggling operation. Montgomery gives a tough performance as does Egan in one of his first featured roles as the agent who's

unmasked and shot. Dehner is the villain and Bishop his boss. Well paced by Nazarro, the film seems shorter than its 78 minutes.

d Ray Nazarro *p* Edward Small *s* Richard Schayer *c* William V. Skall *lp* George Montgomery, Karin Booth, Jerome Courtland, Richard Egan, John Dehner, William Bishop

Denver and Rio Grande (PAR) 89 min

A railway Western that tells of the competition between the Denver and the Rio Grande, and the Canyon City and San Juan lines to cross the Rockies first. O'Brien, standing in for the D & RG and Hayden for the CC & SJ, battle it out, Hayden cheating to no avail. Amongst the highlights is a real train crash with engines and carriages fashioned from old D & RG rolling stock which Haskin directs with obvious delight. Nonetheless the film's ambitions are firmly circumscribed by the ambiance of the B movie.

d Byron Haskin *p* Nat Holt *s* Frank Gruber *c* Ray Rennahan *lp* Edmond O'Brien, Sterling Hayden, Dean Jagger, Laura Elliott, Lyle Bettger, Zasu Pitts

Desert Passage (RKO) b/w 60 min

This is the last of Holt's series Westerns for RKO. Houston's clever script features a flock of thieves, including Dehner, McDonald and Moore trying to outwit each other and trying to discover where Reed hid the money he stole. Holt and Martin, who run a bankrupt stageline, are drawn in to help ensure that the money goes to Dixon, daughter of the banker it was stolen from. The movie is a fitting end to a fine Western series.

d Lesley Selander *p* Herman Schlom *s* Norman Houston *c* J. Roy Hunt *lp* Tim Holt, Richard Martin, Joan Dixon, Clayton Moore, Francis McDonald, John Dehner, Walter Reed

The Duel at Silver Creek (U-INTERNATIONAL) 77 min

A highly implausible, but nonetheless enjoyable, Western, padded out with a prologue and pointless chases, that is made to look far better than it is thanks to Glassberg's crystal-clear cinematography and Siegel's fast narrative pace. Domergue and Mohr are the claimjumpers and Murphy, whose father they've killed, the fast-gun on their trail who McNally makes his deputy sheriff. The action is fast and furious, but it is the

Randolph Scott as the amiable Confederate guerilla in Roy Huggins' impressive Hangman's Knot.

often humorous contrast between Domergue and Cabot (who mistakenly loves McNally who mistakenly loves Domergue) which is forever being pointed out by Murphy (who acts as the teacher figure so common in Siegel's films) that lies at the heart of the movie. A minor, but entertaining Western.

d Don Siegel *p* Leonard Goldstein *s* Gerald Drayson Adams, Joseph Hoffman *c* Irving Glassberg *lp* Audie Murphy, Faith Domergue, Gerald Mohr, Stephen McNally, Susan Cabot, Lee Marvin

Flaming Feather (PAR) 78 min

Jory is the mysterious outlaw who leads a band of renegade Indians and who is sought by rancher Hayden and Cavalry officer Tucker in this strong Western firmly directed by Enright. Rush, in one of her first featured roles, is good as the girl who feels duty-bound to marry Jory, in his guise of a local rancher, because he saved her life years ago. MacDonald is the evil grinning gunman.

d Ray Enright *p* Nat Holt *s* Gerald Drayson Adams *c* Ray Rennahan *lp* Sterling Hayden, Forrest Tucker, Victor Jory, Barbara Rush, Ian MacDonald, Edgar Buchanan

The Half-Breed (RKO) 81 min

Hadley is the man determined to drive the Indians off their land so he can mine the gold he's sure is there in this silly Western that has marshal MacLane, gambler Young and Buetel (in the title role) puzzle through 80 minutes or so wondering who's behind it all. Not that this bothered contemporary reviewers who concentrated their attention and comments on Carter's costume. Gilmore directs forcefully but the plot by veterans Shumate and Wormser is too dog-eared to surprise.

d Stuart Gilmore *p* Herman Schlom *s* Harold Shumate, Richard Wormser *c* William V. Skall *lp* Robert Young, Janis Carter, Jack Buetel, Reed Hadley, Barton MacLane, Porter Hall

Hangman's Knot
(PRODUCERS-ACTORS CORPORATION) 84 min

This is the only film directed by Huggins who was later to achieve lasting fame as the creator of the *Maverick* teleseries (1957-62) and the even better *Rockford Files* (1974-80). Huggins' wry humour is perfectly matched by Scott's austerity and the resulting film was a resounding success.

Far left: Alan Ladd as Jim Bowie, all American hunter, gambler, land speculator and finally hero in The Iron Mistress.

Presumably Huggins, who soon after went into television as a producer on *Cheyenne,* wanted the greater control that came with producing and writing rather than directing. His plot has Scott as the Confederate officer who hijacks a Union gold shipment only to learn that the Civil War is over. Before Scott and his men can decide what to do they are besieged by outlaws in an isolated way station (a favourite location of producers Brown and Scott who would use it to great effect in their cycle of Westerns directed by Budd Boetticher). Huggins directs with intelligence, centring his mobile camera on the violence to a surprising extent. Marvin is threatening in one of his earliest featured roles as the killer amongst Scott's men. The result is a fascinating film, making one wonder what would have happened if Huggins had gone on to direct the films that Budd Boetticher in fact directed with Scott.

d/s Roy Huggins *p* Harry Joe Brown *c* Charles Lawton Jnr *lp* Randolph Scott, Donna Reed, Claude Jarman Jnr, Lee Marvin, Guinn Williams, Richard Denning

Hellgate (COMMANDER FILMS) b/w 87 min
An efficiently made Western, this reworking of John Ford's *The Prisoner of Shark Island* (1936) stars Hayden as the innocent man found guilty of spying during the Civil War and imprisoned in New Mexico's notorious Hellgate Prison. He gets involved in a prison break and then wins himself a pardon by helping stem an epidemic that breaks out in the prison.

d/s Charles Marquis Warren *p* John C. Champion *c* Ernest Miller *lp* Sterling Hayden, Joan Leslie, Ward Bond, James Arness, Sheb Wooley, Timothy Carey

High Noon (UA) b/w 85 min
A much argued about Western. Howard Hawks, who made **Rio Bravo** (1959) in response to Zinnemann's film, dismissed it for its unrealistic central premise – that a marshal should require assistance and that the population of Hadleyville would cower before four gunmen – while others have celebrated it as an attack on America's growing silent majority. What is unusual is Foreman's device of making screen time correspond to real time as a means of intensifying the drama of Cooper's lone marshal waiting for the train that will bring the man he sent to prison to town seeking vengeance. This intensity is further heightened by producer Kramer's re-editing of the material, after a disastrous preview, to include inserts of Cooper's anguished face and close-ups of clocks remorselessly ticking out the passage of time. In retrospect the film has a certain obviousness about it, as for instance in the ploy of Kelly as the Quaker wife finally deserting her principles of non-violence to come to Cooper's aid, that defuses the power of any 'message' Foreman might have intended.

d Fred Zinnemann *p* Stanley Kramer *s* Carl Foreman *c* Floyd Crosby *lp* Gary Cooper, Thomas Mitchell, Grace Kelly, Lloyd Bridges, Katy Jurado, Lee Van Cleef

Horizons West (U-INTERNATIONAL) 81 min
Ryan and Hudson are the half brothers who go different ways after the Civil War in this ambitious but deeply flawed Boetticher Western. Ryan, who has come to like the danger that goes with war, plans an empire in the West, knowing he'll have to step outside the law to achieve it and eventually confronts his brother who's resumed his quiet life as a rancher. Both actors give strong performances but Stevens' script, unlike those Burt Kennedy would later provide for Boetticher, is too crude.

d Budd Boetticher *p* Albert J. Cohen *s* Louis Stevens *c* Charles P. Boyle *lp* Robert Ryan, Julia Adams, Rock Hudson, John McIntire, Raymond Burr, Dennis Weaver

The Iron Mistress (WB) 110 min
Ladd is a stoic Jim Bowie in this routine biopic about the inventor of the famous double-edged knife. Webb's screenplay has him embittered after rejection by an unworthy Mayo, turn gambler and land speculator before heading into the backwoods. Finally he is redeemed by the love of Kirk, daughter of the Governor of Texas, en route to a hero's death at the Alamo.

d Gordon Douglas *p* Henry Blanke *s* James R. Webb *c* John Seitz *lp* Alan Ladd, Virginia Mayo, Joseph Calleia, Phyllis Kirk, Douglas Dick, Anthony Caruso

Kangaroo (FOX) 84 min
An Australian Western with kangaroos substituting for cows and Aborigines for Indians but otherwise as traditional as they come. Lawford and Boone are crooks trying to swindle Currie out of his ranch and Rafferty the 'mountie' on their trail. The ending has Lawford, who's fallen for Currie's daughter, O'Hara, give himself up knowing that she'll wait for him. Script and direction are routine but the Australian outback looks magnificent and Boone is as enchantingly cruel as ever.

d Lewis Milestone *p* Robert Bassler *s* Harry Kleiner *c* Charles G. Clark *lp* Maureen O'Hara, Peter Lawford, Finlay Currie, Richard Boone, Chips Rafferty

Kansas Territory (MON) sepia 65 min
Another intriguing Ullman-scripted, Collins-directed Western starring Elliott; it is one of the most adult of B Westerns of the period. Elliott returns to Kansas intent on revenging the death of his brother only to discover that his brother was a killer and deserves to die. Collins directs tautly and cinematographer Miller gives the film a distinguished look.

d Lewis Collins *p* Vincent M. Fennelly *s* Dan Ullman *c* Ernest Miller *lp* Bill Elliott, Peggy Stewart, House Peters Jnr, Fuzzy Knight, Lane Bradford, Stanley Andrews

The Kid from Broken Gun (COL) b/w 56 min
This was the last of Starrett's long-running series of Westerns for Columbia in which he'd played the same character for some seven years. Fittingly, although it isn't a particularly good outing, it is scripted by Shipman and directed by Sears who'd been in control of the best of his films in the previous three years. Padded with too much stock footage, Repp and Shipman's complicated screenplay, told in flashback, has Starrett save Mahoney from a charge of murder and expose his lawyer, Stevens, as the guilty party. It is a typically fantastical Shipman and Repp screenplay, though sadly Sears'

Gary Cooper as the embattled marshal in High Noon, *with* Broken Arrow *the most influential Western of the fifties.*

direction lacks the energy he'd given to earlier outings with Starrett.

d Fred F. Sears *p* Colbert Clark *s* Ed Earl Repp, Barry Shipman *c* Fayte Browne *lp* Charles Starrett, Smiley Burnette, Jack (Jock) Mahoney, Angela Stevens, Myron Healey, Tristram Coffin

Laramie Mountains (COL) b/w 54 min

One of the last of Starrett's series Westerns, *Laramie Mountains* is well below the average outing. In his dual role of Indian agent and Durango Kid, Starrett is sent to keep the peace between whitemen and redmen that two Indian scouts, who know that there is gold on the Indians' lands, are trying to disturb. The film was one of the first to feature Mahoney as Mahoney rather than O'Mahoney; now all he had to do was change his first name to Jock and he would quickly become a Western teleseries star as Range Rider (1951-53), Yancy Derringer (1958-59) before becoming Tarzan. Director Sears also has a small part.

d Ray Nazarro *p* Colbert Clark *s* Barry Shipman *c* Fayte Browne *lp* Charles Starrett, Smiley Burnette, Jack (Jock) Mahoney, Fred Sears, Marshall Reed, Bob Wilke

The Lawless Breed (U) 83 min

Walsh neatly transforms this (highly inaccurate) biography of John Wesley Hardin (Hudson) into a bleak portrait of a pathetic criminal life that is more an accident than anything else. It is told in flashback, which has the effect of making Hudson's life seem even more bizarrely fatalistic, as he tries to prevent history repeating itself with his son. The contrast between Hudson's evident desires for domesticity and his forced life as a criminal, a recurrent theme in Walsh, is elegantly plotted. Walsh directs in his classical, rather than animated, style, giving the film a strangely formal look.

d Raoul Walsh *p* William Alland *s* Bernard Gordon *c* Irving Glassberg, William Fritszche *lp* Rock Hudson, Julia Adams, Mary Castle, John McIntire, Hugh O'Brian, Dennis Weaver

The Lion and the Horse (WB) 83 min

Cochran is the horse-loving cowboy and Wild Fire the horse he tracks down after, unbeknown to him, it's sold to a

travelling rodeo in this mediocre film. The title comes from an extended fight between the horse and a wild lion. The film was the first to be released in Warnercolor (Eastmancolor).

d Louis King *p* Bryan Foy *s* Crane Wilbur *c* Edwin Du Par *lp* Steve Cochran, Ray Teal, Bob Steele, Harry Antrim, George O'Hanlon, Lane Chandler

Rock Hudson, as John Wesley Hardin, leaves jail at the beginning of The Lawless Breed.

Lone Star (MGM) b/w 94 min

Featuring one of Chase's most 'patriotic' scripts – he was a co-founder of the Motion Picture Alliance for the Preservation of American Ideals – *Lone Star* lacks the violent edge that makes his screenplays so powerful when directed by the likes of Anthony Mann or Howard Hawks. Accordingly, although the storyline of *Lone Star*, which follows the creation of Texas (rather than the separate country that Barrymore and Crawford are plotting for), is interesting for the light it throws on his scripts for **Bend of the River** (1952) and **The Far Country** (1955), Sherman's insipid direction renders that interest academic. This is despite a boisterous performance by Gable as the cattle baron whose help Andrew Jackson enlists to stop Texas being made a separate country.

d Vincent Sherman *p* Z. Wayne Griffin *s* Borden Chase *c* Harold Rosson *lp* Clark Gable, Ava Gardner, Broderick Crawford, Lionel Barrymore, Beulah Bondi, Ed Begley

The Lusty Men (RKO) b/w 113 min

This is one of the best contemporary Westerns ever. It features equally fine performances from Mitchum, as the perplexed ex-rodeo rider who desperately wants to settle down, and Hayward, as the woman effortlessly domesticating the caravan life-style of the rodeo circuit but having difficulty with Kennedy, who is still caught between the desire for responsibility and the adolescent desire to impress. Mitchum, playing against type to suggest brooding depths rather than sleepy-eyed nonchalance, is the one-time rodeo star who helps get Kennedy started but is unable to make a man out of him and who finally and tragically dies in the rodeo ring, a star once more. Ray's direction constantly contrasts Hayward and Mitchum's desire for security and domesticity with the transient life of the rodeo, where the wind seems forever to be

Clark Gable and Ava Gardner in Lone Star.

whipping around as a mad reminder of the rolling prairie, and is simply marvellous. It makes the rather simple antagonisms of McCoy and Dortort's literate script visual.

d Nicholas Ray   *p* Jerry Wald, Norman Krasna   *s* Horace McCoy, David Dortort   *c* Lee Garmes   *lp* Susan Hayward, Robert Mitchum, Arthur Kennedy, Arthur Hunnicutt, Lane Chandler, Glenn Strange

The Maverick (SILVERMINE/AA) sepia 71 min
The first of Carr's trio of Westerns with Elliott. He's the Cavalry officer who, with Healey and Bray, sets out to deliver a couple of gunmen responsible for starting a range war to justice and escort Coates and her aunt home. Theil's screenplay is over-loquacious until Healey reverts to type and goes over to the gunmen's side. A lengthy gun battle is required before Coates and Elliott are free to follow their own devices.

d Thomas Carr   *p* Vincent M. Fennelly   *s* Sid Theil
c Ernest Miller   *lp* Bill Elliott, Phyllis Coates, Myron Healey, Robert Bray, Robert Wilke, Richard Reeves

Montana Belle (RKO) 81 min
Russell as Belle Starr quite overwhelms the masculine world of the Western in this engaging, if minor, film. She quits the Daltons to go into business as a bankrobber with Lambert and Tucker. The central section of the film has her romancing saloon keeper Brent as part of a ploy to deprive him of $50,000 before being killed by the Daltons, led by Teal, when they catch up with her. The film was completed several years before its release by Republic and bought from that company by Howard Hughes, who had Russell under contract, for RKO. Russell's spirited interpretation of Belle Starr is probably the best committed to the screen.

d Allan Dwan   *p* Howard Welsch   *s* Horace McCoy, Norman S. Hall   *c* Jack Marta   *lp* Jane Russell, George Brent, Forrest Tucker, Jack Lambert, Ray Teal, Scott Brady

Navajo (BARTLETT-FOSTER) b/w 70 min
This highly unusual Western was shot for the most part on a Navajo reservation with Navajos acting out the simple story concocted by Bartlett. It features magnificent cinematography by Miller (that won him the praise of being 'art house worthy' from *Variety*). *Navajo* offers a bitter-sweet account of the confrontation of white and Indian culture. Teller is the

Below: *Forrest Tucker, Scott Brady and Jane Russell, as Belle Starr, hold up a bank in* Montana Belle.

Navajo boy who rejects the whiteman's school, and producer Bartlett – the only trained actor to appear in the film – is the school instructor who takes off after him when he runs away. In many ways, despite its sentimental conclusion, it remains a far truer depiction of Indian life and mores than the far better-known **Tell Them Willie Boy Is Here** (1969).

d/s Norman Foster   *p* Hall Bartlett   *c* Virgil E. Miller
lp Francis Kee Teller, Hall Bartlett, John Mitchell, Mrs Teller, Billy Draper

Night Raiders (MON) b/w 51 min
This is routine fare from Whip Wilson. Here, with Farrell, he's presented with the bizarre occurrence of local ranchers being subject to night raids in the course of which nothing is stolen, though the ranches are ransacked. The explanation is a missing $15,000 that Reed's sheriff appropriated for himself when he recovered it from a train robbery that saloon keeper Frost went to jail for. But even with solid direction and superior cinematography the Wilson persona seems too thin and too close an imitation of Lash LaRue (which of course it was) to excite.

d Howard Bretherton   *p* Vincent M. Fennelly   *s* Maurice Tombragel   *c* Ernest Miller   *lp* Whip Wilson, Fuzzy Knight, Lois Hall, Tommy Farrell, Marshall Reed, Terry Frost

Old Oklahoma Plains (REP) b/w 60 min
Clearly scripted so extensive use could be made of footage from Republic's *Army Girl* (1938), this Allen series Western sees its hero helping the army clear the range of cattle for rather belated tank trials in 1926. Barcroft is the leader of the stockmen fearful of the loss of the army as a regular customer for their horses who tries to sabotage the tests. A bizarre highlight of the film is a race between a tank and a troop of Cavalry. Witney directs with his old verve, but the writing was clearly on the wall and soon Allen would go the way of Charles Starrett and Tim Holt, who all rode the range for the last time as series stars in 1952.

d William Witney   *p* Edward J. White   *s* Milton Raison
c John MacBurnie   *lp* Rex Allen, Slim Pickens, Roy Barcroft, Elaine Edwards, John Crawford, Russell Hicks

The Old West
(GENE AUTRY PRODUCTIONS/COL) b/w 60 min
Though the Autry series had changed in the last few years to maximize their appeal to a rapidly changing film market that had just brought about the end of Roy Rogers' series, this film reflected Autry's declining drawing-power in the most drastic fashion possible: a cut in running time to 60 minutes and an even bigger cut in the budget. Here he befriends a preacher trying to save Saddlerock from the evil Talbot who is also seeking to get Autry's contract to supply horses to the stagecoach line company. The film also marked the arrival of Archainbaud on the series. He would be Autry's director until the end. A lacklustre film.

d George Archainbaud   *p* Armand Schaefer   *s* Gerald Geraghty   *c* William Bradford   *lp* Gene Autry, Pat Buttram, Gail Davis, Lyle Talbot, Syd Saylor, Champion

The Outcasts of Poker Flat (FOX) b/w 81(80) min
An inferior remake of Christy Cabanne's 1937 film (itself a remake of the John Ford silent). Saloon singer Hopkins, gambler Robertson, prostitute Baxter and killer Mitchell are the snowbound group who reminisce about their pasts. However, whereas in Bret Harte's story they are real characters and earlier film versions had been successful because they were character studies rather than simple shoot-em-ups, Newman's version sees the characters reduced to cliches.

d Joseph M. Newman   *p* Julian Blaustein   *s* Edmund H. North   *c* Joseph La Shelle   *lp* Anne Baxter, Dale Robertson, Miriam Hopkins, Cameron Mitchell, Craig Hill, Barbara Bates

Outlaw Women   (HOWCO PRODUCTIONS)   75 min

Co-directed by producer Ormond and Newfield, presumably for reasons of economy and speed, this is a quickie with a difference. The difference is that gambling queen Windsor with her 'dance and gun' girls control the town of Las Mujeres. Rober is the gambler turned marshal who finally pacifies Windsor. In a witty conclusion, the town is still run by the girls, now as wives. Hart, who'd had the lead in the earlier **Cattle Queen** (1951), is the 'heavy'. Ormond and Newfield glide easily over the obstacles of implausibility set them by Hampton's screenplay by their unswerving commitment to action and novelty.

d/p Samuel Newfield, Ron Ormond   *s* Orville Hampton
c Ellis W. Carter   *lp* Marie Windsor, Richard Rober, Maria Hart, Allan Nixon, Jackie Coogan, Brad Johnson

Pony Soldier   (FOX)   82 min

Power is the mountie in this pedestrian actioneer that uses stock footage from William Wellman's **Buffalo Bill** (1944) for its climactic fight between the Cavalry and Indians. Horton is the escaped convict who kills Cree Indian Mitchell and so starts the Indian uprising and Edwards the girl Power rescues. Newman's direction is tired but Higgins' script has its moments.

d Joseph M. Newman   *p* Samuel G. Engel   *s* John C. Higgins   *c* Harry Jackson   *lp* Tyrone Power, Cameron Mitchell, Thomas Gomez, Robert Horton, Penny Edwards, Anthony Numkena

The Raiders   (U-INTERNATIONAL)   80 min

Conte is the leader of a small group of miners and homesteaders who stand up to Ankrum's landgrabbers with assistance from Martin. Conte, an actor closely associated with the dark, rain-splattered streets of the crime movie, adapts himself well to the mores of the Western, certainly far better than Lindfors, who is miscast as a Mexican beauty. Selander handles his odd cast with his usual verve, clearly glad to be back with the big screen after a stint of directing Russell Hayden's Western teleseries, *Cowboy G-Men*.

d Lesley Selander   *p* William Alland   *s* Polly James, Lillie Hayward   *c* Carl Guthrie   *lp* Richard Conte, Richard Martin, Morris Ankrum, Viveca Lindfors, Barbara Britton, Dennis Weaver

Rancho Notorious   (FIDELITY PICTURES/RKO)   89 min

Compromised by constant disagreement between Lang and Dietrich during shooting and constrained by a budget from Howard Hughes which restricted Lang to cheap studio sets, *Rancho Notorious* is nonetheless one of the most extraordinary and expressionistic Westerns ever made. The first Western to use a ballad as a major integral motif, it is a key film in the Lang canon. The film's overriding sense of artificiality works in its favour, making its tale of 'hate, murder and revenge', to quote the song, all the more haunting and fatalistic.

Kennedy is the good man who vows vengeance on the outlaws who kill his bride-to-be. He sets out to find Chuckaluck, an outlaws' hideout run by Dietrich's legendary Altar Keane. When he finally gets there, Dietrich falls in love with him, thinking him to be a good man, at the very moment his obsession with revenge is directly leading to the destruction of her and Ferrer's private Eden. The end of the film thus has him destroying her happiness just as his was destroyed in the film's opening minutes.

This is one of the great Westerns.

Gambling queen Marie Windsor (centre) with two of her 'gun girls' in Outlaw Women.

d Fritz Lang   *p* Howard Welsch   *s* Daniel Taradash   *c* Hal Mohr   *lp* Marlene Dietrich, Arthur Kennedy, Mel Ferrer, William Frawley, Jack Elam, Gloria Henry

Return of the Texan   (FOX)   b/w   88 min

An intriguing contemporary Western with a strong cast and script. Robertson is the widower who returns to his run-down Texas farm with his kids and father, Brennan. Daves is very successful at showing Robertson's obsession with the past and his dead wife that is finally broken by Dru, sister of Boone, the man Robertson goes to work for. An unassuming and unexpectedly quiet Western for the fifties.

d Delmer Daves   *p* Frank P. Rosenberg   *s* Dudley Nichols   *c* Lucien Ballard   *lp* Dale Robertson, Joanne Dru, Walter Brennan, Richard Boone, Tom Tully, Robert Horton

Ride the Man Down   (REP)   90 min

In this a workmanlike Western from Kane, Cameron is the ranch foreman trying to keep a cattle empire together after his boss dies. He's opposed by Tucker who's romancing the fiery Raines, heir to the ranch, and also by a jealous neighbour, Donlevy. The movie is less flamboyantly directed than one would imagine from Kane, possibly because the script is too talky. Marta's Trucolor cinematography shows the process to be much improved since its inception.

d/p Joseph Kane   *s* Mary McCall Jnr   *c* Jack Marta
lp Brian Donlevy, Rod Cameron, Forrest Tucker, Ella Raines, Barbara Britton, Chill Wills

Road Agent   (RKO)   b/w   60 min

A mediocre Holt series Western from the last season of his RKO contract. Holt had had great success in major motion pictures like *The Magnificent Ambersons* (1942) and **The Treasure of the Sierra Madre** (1948) but never graduated to a career in A pictures. Here he is as athletic a hero as ever but RKO's lack of confidence in both series Westerns and Holt results in a ridiculous plot and meagre production values. Having refused to pay a toll, Holt and Martin discover that the toll road is part of Hugo's plan to break the local ranchers and buy their property for peanuts. They dress in Robin Hood outfits and put paid to Hugo's schemes. Even Selander's direction is tired.

d Lesley Selander   *p* Herman Schlom   *s* Norman Houston
c J. Roy Hunt   *lp* Tim Holt, Richard Martin, Noreen Nash, Mauritz Hugo, Dorothy Patrick, Tom Tyler

Far right: *Charlton Heston is* The Savage.

Rodeo (MON) 70 min

This is a family film from Beaudine, a veteran of numerous Bowery Boys and East Side Kids comedies. Nigh takes on the management of a rodeo in settlement of a bad debt and is romanced by bronc rider Archer. Ford is the garrulous old wrangler whose accident is a near disaster for all concerned. Knight, Healey and Jolley give strong support.

d William Beaudine   *p* Walter Mirisch   *c* Charles R. Marion   *c* Harry Neumann   *lp* Jane Nigh, John Archer, Wallace Ford, Fuzzy Knight, Myron Healey, I. Stanford Jolley

Rose of Cimarron (ALCO/FOX) 74 min

Buetel and Powers are the marshal and Indian-reared avenging daughter on the trail of a band of outlaws who killed Powers' Indian parents in this Alperson quickie. Keller's direction has more bite than usual and Steele, star of so many B Westerns, gives the unlikely hero and heroine solid support. Nonetheless the film marks a sad decline from Buetel's debut, **The Outlaw** (1943).

d Harry Keller   *p* Edward L. Alperson   *s* Maurice Geraghty   *c* Karl Struss   *lp* Jack Buetel, Mala Powers, Bill Williams, Jim Davis, Dick Curtis, Bob Steele

The Savage (PAR) 95 min

A lacklustre Indian Western. Heston is the orphan brought up as a Sioux who rediscovers civilization and rejects it only to have his tribe reject him as a white man. Heston's performance is fine but the turgid script offers few of the characters any depth. The one exception is Stone's philosopher of a Cavalryman.

d George Marshall   *p* Mel Epstein   *s* Sydney Boehm   *c* John F. Seitz   *lp* Charlton Heston, Susan Morrow, Peter Hanson, Joan Taylor, Milburn Stone, Frank Richards

Sky Full of Moon (MGM) b/w 73 min

A gentle comedy. Carpenter is the cowboy who arrives in Las Vegas to compete in a rodeo and wins the heart of a shady showgirl, Sterling. Full of charm and directed with fluent ease by ex-actor Foster, it failed to click at the box office.

d/s Norman Foster   *p* Sidney Franklin Jnr   *c* Ray June   *lp* Carleton Carpenter, Jan Sterling, Keenan Wynn, Emmett Lynn, Douglass Dumbrille, Elaine Stewart

Arthur Kennedy (left), Marlene Dietrich as the object of everybody's desires, and Mel Ferrer in Fritz Lang's magnificent Rancho Notorious.

Son of Paleface (PAR) 95 min

Even better than the original **The Paleface** (1948), in *Son of Paleface* Hope is the Harvard graduate and nincompoop who travels West to claim the treasure left him by his prospector father. Russell is the outlaw he falls in love with and who has to perpetually rescue him. Tashlin had been a cartoonist and the style of the film is very much that of a series of animated cartoons. Rogers, cast as a government agent on Russell's trail, and Trigger are also on hand to add a touch of knowingness to the comedy.

d/co-s Frank Tashlin   *p/co-s* Robert L. Welch   *co-s* Joseph Quillan   *c* Harry J. Wild   *lp* Jane Russell, Bob Hope, Roy Rogers, Trigger, Douglass Dumbrille, Lloyd Corrigan

Springfield Rifle (WB) 93 min

De Toth's taut direction and Warren and Davis' economical screenplay (based on a story by Sloan Nibley, a veteran of dozens of Roy Rogers' scripts) bring new life to the story of the man who pretends he's an outlaw in order to catch a gang. This time Cooper is the Union officer cashiered to better infiltrate a band of Confederates who are rustling shipments of horses during the Civil War. The emphasis on treachery and spying, intensified by having Cooper, in his first film since **High Noon** (1952), as the hero, is in marked contrast to the simpler heroics of earlier Westerns. They either avoid such plots, or when they use them, skirt around the issues they raise. Here Thaxter as Cooper's wife is bewildered by his activities, believing him to be really cashiered, while Cooper at one point has to cold-bloodedly cause the death of a fellow outlaw. Like *High Noon*, but far more modestly, *Springfield Rifle* sees the Western responding to changes in American life.

d Andre De Toth   *p* Louis F. Edelman   *s* Charles Marquis Warren, Frank Davis   *c* Edwin Du Par   *lp* Gary Cooper, Phyllis Thaxter, David Brian, Paul Kelly, Lon Chaney Jnr, Guinn Williams

Target (RKO) b/w 61 min

Holt's penultimate series Western, *Target* is directed by editor Gilmore. Holt and his side-kick, Martin, come to the aid of girl marshal Douglas who is after Reed's crooked railroad agent. The plot is pretty much standard – Reed's after the local rancher's lands so he can sell it at exorbitant profit to the railroad – but Gilmore's economical direction makes it seem fresh enough.

d Stuart Gilmore *p* Herman Schlom *s* Norman Houston
c J. Roy Hunt *lp* Tim Holt, Richard Martin, Linda Douglas, Walter Reed, Harry Harvey, Lane Bradford

Toughest Man in Arizona (REP) 90 min
This is the second of singing bandleader Monroe's musical Westerns. This time out, he's a marshal travelling back to Tombstone with survivors of an Indian attack and Jory is the man who sold the Indians the guns. Jory, of course, escapes and has to be recaptured to the accompaniment of much gunfire. Buchanan provides a neat piece of supporting acting as a sheriff and Springsteen directs in his usual rugged manner.

d R.G. Springsteen *p* Sidney Picker *s* John K. Butler
c Reggie Lanning *lp* Vaughn Monroe, Joan Leslie, Victor Jory, Edgar Buchanan, Harry Morgan, Jean Parker

The Treasure of Lost Canyon
(U-INTERNATIONAL) 81 min
Powell, in his return to pictures after a three-year lay-off, plays a kindly medic who befriends an orphan in this ill-conceived film based on a Robert Louis Stevenson story. At the heart of the plot lies a treasure chest which Powell and Hull seek, Powell on behalf of the orphan (Ivo), Hull on his own behalf. Metty's dramatic camerawork is the best thing about this very spotty film.

d Ted Tetzlaff *p* Leonard Goldstein *s* Brainerd Duffield, Emerson Crocker *c* Russell Metty *lp* William Powell, Julia Adams, Henry Hull, Jimmy Ivo, Charles Drake, Chubby Johnson

Untamed Frontier (U-INTERNATIONAL) 75 min
A lacklustre piece of packaging, this was the first of many indifferent films that Cotten (like his mentor Orson Welles) would lend his name to all over the world in the course of the next three decades. Winters is the woman married to Brady to

A publicity still for Westward the Women. *Robert Taylor is the misogynist scout and Denise Darcel (first right) the girl who tames him.*

prevent her giving evidence against him who falls for Cotten who in turn exposes Brady when he turns to rustling his (Cotten's) father's cattle. Fregonese directs as though he gave up when he read the script.

d Hugo Fregonese *p* Leonard Goldstein *s* Gerald Drayson Adams, John Bagni, Gwen Bagni *c* Charles P. Boyle
lp Joseph Cotten, Shelley Winters, Scott Brady, Antonio Moreno, Lee Van Cleef, Fess Parker

Viva Zapata! (FOX) b/w 113 min
This is the most interesting version of Hollywood's view of the Mexican Revolution, if only because it is the only one to deal (in its own fashion) with the ideas as well as the events of the revolution. The first script, written by Lester Cole, specifically portrayed Zapata as a socialist revolutionary. MGM were prepared to shoot this until Cole was subpoenaed by the House Un-American Activities Committee. The direct association of Zapata (via Cole) with Communism led MGM to pass on the project to Fox where Kazan and Steinbeck took particular care to make the central character, in Kazan's own words, 'a man of individual conscience'. This was made even more pointed by the casting of Brando in the central role, thus making the film a star vehicle. As if that wasn't enough, Steinbeck and Kazan then falsified history by contrasting an illiterate Zapata with a Communist intellectual (Wiseman).

At the same time, ironically enough, Kazan was going to great lengths to give the film the look of reality. He based the visual style of the picture on the Casasola photographs (five books of photographs of the events of the revolution by two Mexican photographers), though the film was actually shot in Texas because the Mexican government objected to the script. Accordingly, the film for the most part avoids the comic opera vision of Mexico beloved by Hollywood. Nonetheless, it is the film's trenchantly anti-Communist line that remains the most significant aspect of the project. The film's credits are written as if they were slogans but the movie that follows is the epitome of romantic liberalism, with Brando's Zapata as a champion of the people who is finally betrayed (like Jesse James and King Arthur before him) by a friend.

Quinn, who plays Zapata's loutish brother, won an Oscar as best supporting actor for his performance.

d Elia Kazan *p* Darryl F. Zanuck *s* John Steinbeck *c* Joe MacDonald *lp* Marlon Brando, Jean Peters, Anthony Quinn, Joseph Wiseman, Arnold Moss, Lou Gilbert, Alan Reed

Gene Tierney and Rory Calhoun in Way of a Gaucho.

Waco (MON) sepia 68 min

This is an interesting Elliott B Western. Elliott had been built up into a star by Republic before the studio's retrenchment forced him to work elsewhere and in his 11 Westerns for Monogram he seemed determined to make serious rather than series Westerns. Hence the strong tone of realism he introduced into the films. Here Ullman's script has him as an outlaw, cussing and drinking in a way that would be inconceivable in seriesdom, hired to clean up a town and asked to stay on as sheriff afterwards. Fierro is the mean killer and Jolley an outlaw friend.

d Lewis Collins p Vincent M. Fennelly s Dan Ullman
c Ernest Miller lp Bill Elliott, Pamela Blake, I. Stanford Jolley, Rand Brooks, Stanley Andrews, Paul Fierro

Wagons West (MON) 70 min

A routine Western starring Cameron who, though only ever a minor motion-picture star, became a major star in the gossip papers in 1960 when he divorced his second wife to marry her mother. Here, Ullman's unusually slack script casts him as a wagonmaster set the task of protecting his wagon train from marauding Indians and watching out for gunrunner Ferguson. Beebe directs aggressively but is unable to lift the material.

d Ford Beebe p Vincent M. Fennelly s Dan Ullman
c Harry Neumann lp Rod Cameron, Noah Beery Jnr, Frank Ferguson, Peggie Castle, Michael Chapin, Henry Brandon

Way of a Gaucho (FOX) 91 min

Calhoun is the gaucho of the title who flees to the outback rather than suffer the coming of civilization in this Argentinian Western. When he organizes an outlaw gang to hold back the railroad policeman, Boone is sent into the interior after him. Finally Calhoun bends to the ways of progress and wins Tierney as his prize. Tourneur's direction invests Dunne's script with a dignity that deepens its resonances. In one marvellous moment, in the middle of the pampas, Calhoun stands on his horse to see if anyone is near. It's an example of the visual delights and economy of Tourneur's direction.

Below: Cyd Charisse and Stewart Granger in The Wild North.

d Jacques Tourneur p/s Philip Dunne c Harry Jackson
lp Rory Calhoun, Gene Tierney, Richard Boone, Hugh Marlowe, Everett Sloan

Westward the Women (MGM) b/w 118 min

Taylor is the misogynist scout hired to lead a wagon train of 150 women to their waiting mail-order husbands in California. The women prove along the way that they are as capable pioneers as men in this original Western based on a story by Frank Capra of all people. Darcel is the fiery French girl who tames Taylor while Emerson, Lonergan and Henry Nakamura (as the Japanese cook) provide the laughs. But what gives the film power is less its offbeat storyline than the rigour with which Wellman puts his unusual cast through the cliches of the wagon train sub-genre of the Western, with the ladies manhandling their wagons over mountains, withstanding Indian attacks, illness, etc. The film's climax which sees the women, not the men, choosing their partners in the promised land of California, neatly sums up the rights they've won by their rite of passage.

d William A. Wellman p Dore Schary s Charles Schnee
c William Mellor lp Robert Taylor, Denise Darcel, John McIntire, Hope Emerson, Marilyn Erskine, Lenore Lonergan

Wild Horse Ambush (REP) b/w 54 min

The last entry in Chapin and Janssen's short-lived juvenile Westerns, this is as bad as the other three films in the series. Here the juvenile duo help sheriff Bell and Mexican police officer Avonde, operating undercover as a bandit, break a gang of counterfeiters who are smuggling their counterfeit money into America by gluing the notes under the manes of horses (!). Barcroft is the chief heavy.

d Fred C. Brannon p Rudy Ralston s William Lively
c John MacBurnie lp Michael Chapin, Eilene Janssen, James Bell, Richard Avonde, Roy Barcroft, Julian Rivero

The Wild North (MGM) 97 min

The first film in Ansacolor (a single negative colour stock developed by Ansco and Metro), this is an otherwise routine mountie film. Granger is the trapper falsely charged with murder and Corey the mountie sent after him. But, despite the abundance of natural hazards, ranging from blizzards to wolves, Marton's elaboration of the trek back is decidedly plodding. Charisse, in a small role as Granger's girlfriend, steals the film, which is reputedly based on a case in the files of the Royal Canadian Mounted Police.

d Andrew Marton p Stephen Ames s Frank Fenton
c Robert Surtees lp Stewart Granger, Wendell Corey, Cyd Charisse, Howard Petrie, Morgan Farley, Ray Teal

1953 _____

Ambush at Tomahawk Gap (COL) 73 min

One of the number of Westerns made by 'the American Vadim', Derek, an actor and later director known best for his wives, two of whom were Ursula Andress and Bo Derek. Lang's story has Derek, Hodiak, Teal and Brian released from jail and on the trail of their ex-partner and the money they stole. What is most noticeable about the film is Sears' grim direction which emphasizes violent fights and deaths – a man hit by a flaming arrow, for example – in a way that would have been unthinkable a few years earlier.

d Fred F. Sears p Wallace MacDonald s David Lang
c Henry Freulich lp John Hodiak, John Derek, David Brian, Ray Teal, Maria Elena Marques, John Doucette

Arena (MGM) 83 min

A soap-opera version of Nicholas Ray's marvellous **The Lusty Men** (1952), this was originally shown in 3-D. Young is the rodeo star whose marriage to Hagen has collapsed, Lawrence his mistress and Van Cleef (who gives the film's best performance) his washed-up partner whose death precipitates Young's coming to his senses. Fleischer is unable to do much with Bloom's melodramatic script but Vogel's cinematography, especially the rodeo scenes filmed at the Tucson Rodeo, is quite stunning. The film was unofficially remade as **The Honkers** (1971).

d Richard Fleischer   *p* Arthur M. Loew Jnr   *s* Harold Jack Bloom   *c* Paul C. Vogel   *lp* Gig Young, Jean Hagen, Polly Bergen, Henry Morgan, Lee Van Cleef, Barbara Lawrence

Arrowhead (PAR) 105 min
Based on incidents in the life of Indian scout, Al Seiber, *Arrowhead* was made using many of the same sets and actors as the vastly inferior **The Savage** (1952). Heston is the swaggering, evil-grinning chief of scouts for the Cavalry, fighting the Apache in the far West who is relieved of his commission because of his highly individualistic, not to mention illiberal actions. Palance is Toriano, the Apache chief who intends to stop the transportation of his tribesmen to reservations in Florida. Warren's emphatic direction makes the most of this slim story.

d/s Charles Marquis Warren   *p* Nat Holt   *c* Ray Rennahan
lp Charlton Heston, Jack Palance, Katy Jurado, Brian Keith, Milburn Stone, Lewis Martin

Calamity Jane (WB) 101 min
A frenetic musical. Closely patterned on **Annie Get Your Gun** (1950), though less stagebound and with a more wholesome star in Day, *Calamity Jane* follows the lengthy wooing of Keel's Wild Bill Hickok by tomboy Day. The plot offers Day and Keel ample opportunity to dress in the clothes of the opposite sex to comic and sometimes disturbing effect while Cline's garnish colours make the most of the theatrical sets. Butler's animated direction is well suited to the material.

Paul Francis Webster and Sammy Fain got an Oscar for 'Secret Love' as the best song of 1953. A year later, her recording of the song garnered Day her sixth million-selling record.

d David Butler   *p* William Jacobs   *s* James O'Hanlon
c Wilfrid M. Cline   *lp* Doris Day, Howard Keel, Allyn McLerie, Philip Carey, Dick Wesson, Paul Harvey

Doris Day on the Deadwood Stage in Calamity Jane.

The Charge at Feather River (WB) 96 min
An impressive Western, *The Charge at Feather River* survives the special effects like tomahawks and arrows flying straight at the audience – that came with the 3-D format – thanks to Douglas' strong direction and the evocative cinematography of Marley. Madison leads the platoon of guardhouse cavalrymen and rescues Miles and Westcott. Undoubtedly the best of the rash of 3-D Westerns of the mid fifties, and certainly the most commercially successful: it was the largest grossing Western of the year.

d Gordon Douglas   *p* David Weisbart   *s* James R. Webb
c Peverell Marley   *lp* Guy Madison, Frank Lovejoy, Helen Westcott, Vera Miles, Dick Wesson, Lane Chandler

Conquest of Cochise (COL) 70 min
Hodiak takes over the role of Cochise from Jeff Chandler in this routine Indian Western. Lewis and Scott's melodramatic script, which features both a love affair between Hodiak and a Spanish aristocrat, Page, and the Gadsen Purchase, is simply too silly for words. Stack is the Cavalry officer sent to protect America's new citizens from a threatened Comanche uprising. Castle directs as if in his sleep.

d William Castle   *p* Sam Katzman   *s* Arthur Lewis, DeVallon Scott   *c* Henry Freulich   *lp* John Hodiak, Robert Stack, Joy Page, Rico Alaniz, Fortunio Bonanova, Edward Colemans

Cow Country (AA) b/w 82 min
A slow-moving film, scripted by veteran Buffington and directed far too respectfully by Selander. It has far too much talk and not enough action, especially for 1953. Barrat is the rancher who O'Brien saves when banker MacLane tries to bankrupt him with help from rustler Lowery. Castle is the flashy saloon singer and Westcott the nice girl O'Brien saves from Lowery.

d Lesley Selander   *p* Scott R. Dunlap   *s* Adele Buffington
c Harry Neumann   *lp* Edmond O'Brien, Robert Barrat, Barton MacLane, Robert Lowery, Peggie Castle, Helen Westcott

Far left: Jack Palance as the Indian chief in Arrowhead.

Devil's Canyon (RKO) 92 min

Another grim Western from Werker, notable for the realism of its depiction of life in the Arizona State Penitentiary at the turn of the century. McNally is the psychotic killer seeking revenge on Robertson, also imprisoned, while Mayo is the girl working in the prison dispensary to help McNally to escape who switches sides at the last minute. In all essentials a prison-break movie in Western costume, it survives the imposition of 3-D thanks to Musuraca's low-key lighting effects.

d Alfred Werker p Edmund Grainger s Frederick Hazlitt Brennan c Nicholas Musuraca lp Virginia Mayo, Dale Robertson, Stephen McNally, Arthur Hunnicutt, Robert Keith, Jay C. Flippen

El Paso Stampede (REP) b/w 54 min

The last of Lane's series Westerns for Republic after six years with the studio, *El Paso Stampede* is a decidedly minor film. The strength of Lane's pictures is their scripts, but Orloff's final screenplay is a sad let-down. Lane is the marshal sent to stop rustlers who are rustling valuable cattle intended to feed US troops in their fight against Spain, and Chase is the outlaw masquerading as the town dentist. In short, a conventional old-fashioned Western.

d Harry Keller p Rudy Ralston s Arthur Orloff c John MacBurnie lp Allan Lane, Eddy Waller, Phyllis Coates, Stephen Chase, Roy Barcroft, Edward Clark

Escape from Fort Bravo (MGM) 98 min

Based on a story by veteran actor Michael Pate whose Indians and heavies grace many a B Western, *Escape from Fort Bravo* is a modest and effective film. The scenes of the Indians' attack on the fort are particularly good. The carefully chosen compositions reveal a real flair for the dramatic handling of complicated action that was to serve Sturges well in **Gunfight at the O.K. Corral** (1957). Holden is the tough Cavalry captain who heads off into Indian territory to recapture escaped Confederate prisoners and Parker the *femme fatale* who masterminds the escape.

William Holden and Eleanor Parker in Escape from Fort Bravo.

d John Sturges p Nicholas Nayfack s Frank Fenton c Robert Surtees lp William Holden, Eleanor Parker, John Forsythe, William Demarest, John Lupton, Richard Anderson

Fort Ti (COL) 73 min

Set in Colonial days and featuring the flaming arrows and missiles of all descriptions that go with 3-D, this is a routine actioneer. Montgomery flexes his muscles to some effect but Kent's screenplay, which sees a bunch of Colonial irregulars dislodge a fort of French troops, is somewhat befuddled, except when it settles on the curvacious Vohs and Fowler.

The film was the first to be shown on British television in full 3-D in December, 1982.

d William Castle p Sam Katzman s Robert E. Kent c Lester H. White, Lothrop B. Worth lp George Montgomery, Joan Vohs, Phyllis Fowler, Irving Bacon, Howard Petrie, Ben Astar

Goldtown Ghost Raiders

(GENE AUTRY PRODUCTIONS/COL) sepia 57 min

This odd Autry series Western features him as a circuit judge trying a murder in a mining town and being faced with the guilty party telling him he can't be tried because he's already served time for killing the murdered man. The two men, Pyle and Doucette, were swindlers and one was convicted of murdering the other, though in reality the supposed victim survived, waiting to be killed by his assassin on his release from jail. The film is bizarrely plotted, but less interestingly filmed.

d George Archainbaud p Armand Schaefer s Gerald Geraghty c William Bradford lp Gene Autry, Smiley Burnette, Gail Davis, Kirk Riley, Denver Pyle, John Doucette, Champion

Gun Fury (COL) 83(80) min

An interesting film, this is deformed by the peculiar performance of Hudson. He and his bride, Reed, are travelling West when Carey (who steals the picture as the demented villain) and his gang abduct Reed, whereupon Hudson gives chase. The script and Walsh's strong direction have a gaunt logic, with Carey as the psychopath and Hudson resisting all temptations to become one in the course of the chase. Finally he discards his previous ideas of non-involvement to become a man of action in defence of ideals he sees threatened by Carey. However, Hudson's flamboyant performance is completely out of kilter with the role.

Marvin turns in a neat performance as one of Carey's gang of outlaws.

d Raoul Walsh p Lewis J. Rachmil s Roy Huggins, Irving Wallace c Lester H. White lp Rock Hudson, Donna Reed, Phil Carey, Lee Marvin, Neville Brand, Leo Gordon

Hannah Lee *aka* Outlaw Territory (BRODER) 71 min

The only film directed (and produced) by Ireland (in tandem with cinematographer Garmes), this is an interesting 3-D Western. Carey is the hired killer brought in to rid the range of homesteaders at $800 a family and Ireland the marshal who catches up with him. Dru (Ireland's wife in real life) is the saloon operator who falls for Carey but backs off when she discovers he's a killer. However, Garmes and Ireland's direction is too erratic to convince. It's as though the technical problems of shooting in 3-D were too weighty for the novice directors to leave them with enough time to think of anything else.

d/p John Ireland, Leo Garmes s MacKinlay Kantor, Rip Von Ronkle c Leo Garmes lp Joanne Dru, MacDonald Carey, John Ireland, Stuart Randall, Frank Ferguson, Peter Ireland

Hondo (WAYNE-FELLOWS) 93 min

A superior Western. The screenplay by Wayne's regular writer, Grant, is clearly influenced by **Shane** (1953) but the look of the film is entirely Fordian with many of the exteriors looking like tests for **The Searchers** (1956). One reason for this was Ford's presence during filming. Wayne is the despatch-rider who rescues Page and her son, deserted by husband, Gordon, from Apaches marauding her lonely homestead on the fringes of the New Mexico desert. The sympathetic, almost matter-of-fact, treatment of the Indians is remarkable; even more remarkable is the psychological depth of the Wayne character. The film, originally released in 3-D, was Wayne's first major success as a producer.

The story was remade as a telefilm in 1967.

d John Farrow *p* Robert Fellows *s* James Edward Grant *c* Robert Burks, Archie Stout *lp* John Wayne, Geraldine Page, Ward Bond, Michael Pate, Leo Gordon, James Arness

Kansas Pacific (AA) 73 min

Hayden is the Army engineer sent to speed up the work on completion of the Kansas Pacific Railroad which is being slowed down by Confederate sympathizers, just prior to the outbreak of the Civil War. Ullman's script is well constructed while Nazarro and Neumann show off Wanger's budget (a bigger one than either of them was used to) in the time-honoured tradition of 'shooting the money'.

d Ray Nazarro *p* Walter Wanger *s* Dan Ullman *c* Harry Neumann *lp* Sterling Hayden, Eve Miller, Barton MacLane, Douglas Fowley, Myron Healey, Clayton Moore

Last of the Comanches *aka* The Sabre and the Arrow

(COL) 85 min

Crawford leads a group of survivors from an Indian raid a hundred miles through hostile territory to safety in this routine Western. De Toth handles the action and the desert well enough but there is little suspense, even when they shelter in an abandoned Mission and the Indians prepare to attack. More interesting is the contrast between Crawford's tough sergeant and the genteel humanism of Hale which is entirely modern in feel.

d Andre De Toth *p* Buddy Adler *s* Kenneth Gamet *c* Charles Lawton Jnr *lp* Broderick Crawford, Barbara Hale, Johnny Stewart, Lloyd Bridges, Mickey Shaughnessy, George Mathews

Last of the Pony Riders

(GENE AUTRY PRODUCTIONS/COL) sepia 58 min

This is the last of Autry's series Westerns. Henceforth, he would devote himself to television, where his Flying A Productions' logo would be regularly seen, and his multifa-

Geraldine Page pulls a gun on John Wayne in Hondo.

rious business interests which made him one of Hollywood's richest men. Fittingly, the first and longest-lived singing cowboy is re-united with Burnette, with whom he'd begun his long screen career, for his final outing. The plot has the deadly duo resisting attempts by Downey's unscrupulous banker to steal their mail franchise. Like most of Autry's films for Columbia it is efficiently made and hopelessly old fashioned.

d George Archainbaud *p* Armand Schaefer *s* Ruth Woodman *c* William Bradford *lp* Gene Autry, Smiley Burnette, Kathleen Case, Dick Jones, John Downey, Howard Wright, Champion

The Last Posse (COL) b/w 73 min

An interesting film. Gamet and Bennett's ambitious screenplay contrasts the empty rhetoric of a Founder's Day speech with the actions of a posse of upstanding citizens who 'steal' the money they rescue from rancher Homeier and his associates who have stolen it from Bickford's cattle baron. Crawford is the once heroic sheriff turned drunkard and Derek is Bickford's son who is called on to set things to rights and, as it were, blot out the past. He does this with great élan, courtesy of Werker's forceful direction and Guffey's superb cinematography.

d Alfred Werker *p* Harry Joe Brown *s* Seymour Lee Bennett, Connie Lee Bennett, Kenneth Gamet *c* Burnett Guffey *lp* Broderick Crawford, John Derek, Charles Bickford, Skip Homeier, Wanda Hendrix, Henry Hull

Law and Order (U) b/w 80 min

Reagan is the frontier marshal who wants to hang up his guns in this tired remake of Edward L. Cahn's superior 1932 film. It retains the plot of the original version, unlike the Johnny Mack Brown remake in 1940, but lacks the incisiveness and dramatic density of the original. Malone is the romantic interest.

d Nathan Juran *p* John W. Rogers *s* John Bagni, Gwen Bagni, D.D. Beauchamp *c* Clifford Stine *lp* Ronald Reagan, Dorothy Malone, Alex Nicol, Preston Foster, Dennis Weaver, Chubby Johnson

The Man Behind the Gun (WB) 82 min

A routine oater. Scott is the undercover agent sent to California to quell separatist intrigue in Los Angeles who falls for the charms of school-mistress Wymore. Twist's old-fashioned script (based on a story by Robert Buckner) is handled in a workmanlike fashion by Feist.

Far left: Sheriff Broderick Crawford collapses, surrounded by Brick Sullivan, Warner Anderson, Tom Powers, John Derek and Eddy Waller (left to right) in The Last Posse.

Far right: Barbara Stanwyck as the sheriff with Fred MacMurray, the rustler she's after, in The Moonlighter.

d Felix Feist *p* Robert Sisk *s* John Twist *c* Bert Glennon *lp* Randolph Scott, Patrice Wymore, Dick Wesson, Philip Carey, Morris Ankrum, Roy Roberts

The Man from the Alamo (U-INTERNATIONAL) 79 min

A superior B Western from Boetticher. Ford is the man chosen to escape and warn Texas families of the impending defeat at the Alamo and who is branded a coward by all and Jory is the renegade who, with his gang, is terrorizing people posing as Mexican soldiers. The script is too direct for Boetticher to indulge in the games that typify his best work but the action sequences, such as Ford's protecting a wagon train from Jory, are amongst the most impressive Boetticher has ever filmed. One reason for this is Metty's fine cinematography.

d Budd Boetticher *p* Aaron Rosenberg *s* Steve Fisher, D.D. Beauchamp *c* Russell Metty *lp* Glenn Ford, Julia Adams, Victor Jory, Chill Wills, Hugh O'Brian, Jeanne Cooper

The Marshal of Cedar Rock (REP) b/w 54 min

Directed by Keller, who was to take over the production of the last few of Lane's series Westerns, this outing sees Lane and his horse, Black Jack, fighting yet another crooked railroad agent, Barcroft, who is trying to buy up land cheaply. Barcroft swaggers nicely when unmasked and huffs and puffs to perfection in his guise of respectable citizen. Coates is the love interest.

d Harry Keller *p* Rudy Ralston *s* Albert DeMond *c* John MacBurnie *lp* Allan Lane, Roy Barcroft, Eddy Waller, Phyllis Coates, Bill Henry, Kenneth MacDonald

The Marshal's Daughter (UA) b/w 71 min

The presence of Gibson, in his first film for nearly a decade, as the marshal and cameos from the likes of Brown and Wakely notwithstanding, this is a silly novelty Western. Television's Anders – 'Ah love those wide open spaces' – takes the title role and with limited assistance from Gibson tracks down and shoots outlaw Duncan in between songs. Producer Murray gives himself a comic role and Tex Ritter sings the title song.

d William Berke *p* Ken Murray *s* Bob Duncan *c* Jack MacKenzie *lp* Hoot Gibson, Laurie Anders, Johnny Mack Brown, Jimmy Wakely, Bob Duncan, Forrest Taylor

The Moonlighter (WB) 77 min

A peculiar film. MacMurray is the rustler who escapes from jail as he's about to be lynched and swears vengeance on the

James Stewart gives the most hysterical of performances in Anthony Mann's magisterial The Naked Spur.

mob who string up a hobo by mistake for him. He turns bank robber and his ex-girlfriend, Stanwyck, is deputized and given the job of bringing him in. Bond, Elam and Ankrum offer solid support but, sadly, Busch's tough script is let down by Rowland's listless direction.

d Roy Rowland *p* Joseph Bernhard *s* Niven Busch *c* Bert Glennon *lp* Barbara Stanwyck, Fred MacMurray, Ward Bond, Morris Ankrum, Jack Elam, William Ching

The Naked Spur (MGM) 91 min

This is an extraordinary Western. On the surface a simple bring-the-body-back-dead-or-alive type of film with Stewart as the bounty hunter and Ryan as the body, *The Naked Spur* is soon transformed into the most extreme of revenge films through Stewart's hysterical performance and Mann's intensely physical direction which uses landscape as a correlative for the conflicting drives of the Stewart character. From the film's opening with Meeker's cynical derring-do as he helps Stewart's supposed sheriff capture Ryan through the journey back, with Ryan taunting and dividing his uneasy guards, to the final climactic battle between Ryan and the wounded Stewart, Mann relentlessly strips the characters of their self-justifications and self-deceptions until they stand naked.

Stewart here is the most neurotic of Mann's heroes, trying to buy back his farm and lost innocence with a succession of dead bodies until Leigh saves him from himself.

d Anthony Mann *p* William H. Wright *s* Sam Rolfe, Harold Jack Bloom *c* William Mellor *lp* James Stewart, Robert Ryan, Janet Leigh, Ralph Meeker, Millard Mitchell

The Nebraskan (COL) 68 min

An indifferent 3-D Western, full of 'pelt and burn' effects but little else. The only real point of interest is the odd cast which features Carey (television's Philip Marlowe) and Van Cleef, in one of his first roles, as a cold-blooded killer and deserter who's clearly modelled himself on Richard Widmark in *Kiss of Death* (1947). Lang and Berkeley's script has Carey and company pinned down by Indians and threatened by dissension from within led by Van Cleef. Sears' direction is lacklustre.

d Fred Sears *p* Wallace MacDonald *s* David Lang, Martin Berkeley *c* Henry Freulich *lp* Phil Carey, Roberta Haynes, Lee Van Cleef, Wallace Ford, Richard Webb, Dennis Weaver

The Pathfinder (COL) 78 min

Very loosely based on James Fenimore Cooper's classic novel of the same title, this Katzman-produced film stars Montgomery in the title role. With assistance from Carter and Silverheels (always the side-kick, never the star, here as

Chingachgook), he exposes French plans to gain control of the Great Lakes. Lester is the British officer who leads the 'Cavalry' to the rescue when Carter and Montgomery are set in front of a firing squad by the French.

d Sidney Salkow   *p* Sam Katzman   *s* Robert E. Kent
c Henry Freulich   *lp* George Montgomery, Helena Carter, Jay Silverheels, Bruce Lester, Walter Kingsford, Rodd Redwing

Pony Express   (PAR)   101 min

A pedestrian story about the opening of the mail route to the West. A subplot has Heston as Buffalo Bill putting an end to Moore's plans to split California from the Union with assistance from Tucker's Wild Bill Hickok and Sterling. Fleming gives a typically robust performance that complements Heston's virile interpretation of his role but Hopper's unimaginative direction makes the film's 101 minutes seem excessive.

The film was a loose remake of James Cruze's silent *Pony Express* (1925).

d Jerry Hopper   *p* Nat Holt   *s* Charles Marquis Warren
c Ray Rennahan   *lp* Charlton Heston, Rhonda Fleming, Jan Sterling, Forrest Tucker, Michael Moore, Henry Brandon

Powder River   (FOX)   78 min

A taut town Western. Calhoun is the marshal searching for a murderer and Mitchell the doctor who befriends him before it transpires that he is the killer. In an unusual touch, Mitchell dies from the brain tumour that made him quit medicine just as he outdraws Calhoun. Minor but enjoyable.

d Louis King   *p* Andre Hakim   *s* Geoffrey Homes
c Edward Cronjager   *lp* Rory Calhoun, Corinne Calvet, Cameron Mitchell, Penny Edwards, Carl Betz, John Dehner

The Redhead from Wyoming

(U-INTERNATIONAL)   80 min

O'Hara is the dance-hall queen Bishop plans to use as his 'fall guy' in his crooked attempts to get himself elected Governor of Wyoming in this glorious-looking but rather dull Western. Nicol is the sheriff who first imprisons O'Hara for cattle rustling and murder and then helps prove her innocence. The

film's major failing is that neither Bishop nor Nicol are strong enough to stand up to O'Hara's overpowering screen presence.

d Lee Sholem   *p* Leonard Goldstein   *s* Polly James, Herb Meadow   *c* Winton C. Hoch   *lp* Maureen O'Hara, Alex Nicol, William Bishop, Robert Strauss, Jeanne Cooper, Dennis Weaver

Ride Vaquero!   (MGM)   89 min

Quinn, clearly aping Wallace Beery's many swaggering Mexican bandits, gives a wonderfully exuberant performance as the demented, ruthless bandido whose territory is invaded in this spirited Western. Keel and Gardner are the settlers who refuse to be budged, despite having their ranch burnt down around them and Taylor, Quinn's half-brother and advisor, is the man who can't decide what to do. Inevitably the movie ends with Taylor and Quinn killing each other in a shoot-out.

d John Farrow   *p* Stephen Ames   *s* Frank Fenton
c Robert Surtees   *lp* Robert Taylor, Ava Gardner, Howard Keel, Anthony Quinn, Jack Elam, Rex Lease

San Antone   (REP)   b/w   90 min

Another spotty Western from Kane, once Republic's most dependable house director. Set at the time of the Civil War, Fisher's overwrought plot features Cameron as the rancher and Tucker as the psychopathic Confederate officer-turned-bandit whom Cameron swears revenge on after he's imprisoned and murdered his father. Kane directs the action sequences energetically enough, but, like his cast, he seems at sea in the explanatory scenes that come in between. Whelan gives an almost operatic performance as Tucker's girlfriend, but more beguiling, if equally odd, is the harmonizing trio of Carey, Steele and Lilburn who perform the film's title song.

d/p Joseph Kane   *s* Steve Fisher   *c* Bud Thackery   *lp* Rod Cameron, Forrest Tucker, Arleen Whelan, Harry Carey Jnr, Bob Steele, James Lilburn

Above: Arleen Whelan and Rod Cameron in the indifferent San Antone.

Anthony Quinn as the bandido in Ride Vaquero!

Alan Ladd shows Brandon De Wilde how to wear a gun to the horror of Jean Arthur in Shane, *a fairy tale of a Western.*

Below: Anthony Quinn as the Indian chief with Rock Hudson in Seminole.

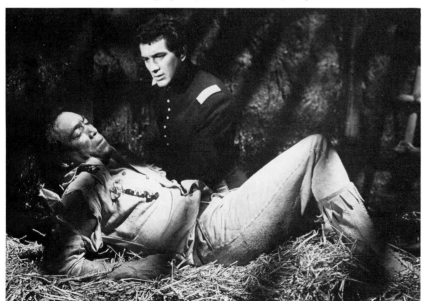

Seminole (U) 86 min

A minor Western. Hudson is the West Pointer and Quinn the Seminole Indian Chief who circle each other warily in the swamps in search of peace between red and white man and Hale the girl they both love. The 'surprise' attack on the Seminole led by Hudson's Indian-hating superior, Carlson, which wittily ends with the Cavalry surrounded in the middle of the swamp by the Indians they can't find, is an indication of what Boetticher and cinematographer Metty could do when the script didn't get in their way.

d Budd Boetticher *p* Howard Christie *s* Charles K. Peck Jnr *c* Russell Metty *lp* Rock Hudson, Barbara Hale, Anthony Quinn, Richard Carlson, Hugh O'Brian

Shane (PAR) 118 min

Ladd is the mysterious stranger who accepts work at Arthur and Heflin's homestead and subsequently helps them when Meyer's cattle baron tries to clear the fertile valley of all homesteaders in this classic Western. Once celebrated for its realism, in retrospect, *Shane*, with its snow-capped vistas, De Wilde's arch innocence, Ladd's archetypal white-fringed, buckskin-suited hero and Palance's demoniac villain, is clearly a Western that yearns for the mythic, almost indeed for the innocent verities of Hopalong Cassidy, Roy Rogers, *et al*. The mud-covered town and Elisha Cook's three-foot backward jump when Palance's bullet slams into his body testify to Stevens' realistic approach to Jack Shaefer's novel but the feel of the stately movie, with its genre types (farmer, gunman, cattle baron...) rather than rounded characters, is entirely mythical. Significantly, unlike Gregory Peck's aging gunslinger, who can find no good use for his guns, in **The Gunfighter** (1950), Ladd can ride off into the mountains, his name echoing around him, like a guardian angel who's done his task. Indeed Ladd's Shane is like no cowboy the cinema had ever seen before; the film's few infelicities lie in the suggested love-hate relationship between Arthur and Ladd which gives Ladd the human emotions that as an idealized figure on film he cannot have.

In short the film is less an exploration of such Western cliches as 'A man's gotta do what a man's gotta do', than a mature version of 'Heigh Ho Silver'.

d/p George Stevens *s* A.B. Guthrie Jnr *c* Loyal Griggs *lp* Alan Ladd, Jean Arthur, Van Heflin, Brandon De Wilde, Ben Johnson, Emile Meyer, Jack Palance

Son of Belle Starr (AA) 70 min

Not to be confused with **Belle Starr's Daughter** (1947), this engaging low-budget quickie stars Larsen as the youngster forced into outlawry by his mother's reputation and crooked sheriff Healey. Drake and Castle are the girlfriends, bad and

good respectively. Beauchamp and Raynor's screenplay weaves a neat circle, with Larsen trying to prove his innocence and dying just as he's in a position to do so.

d Frank McDonald p Peter Scully s D.D. Beauchamp, William Raynor c Harry Neumann lp Keith Larsen, Dona Drake, Peggie Castle, Myron Healey, Regis Toomey, Robert Keys

The Stand at Apache River
(U-INTERNATIONAL) 77 min
This is routine fare. McNally is the sheriff who, with a motley band that includes a prisoner (Johnson), a dissatisfied wife (Greene) and an intended fiancée (Adams), must make a stand at the Apache River way station against Barrier's Indian band. Kelly and O'Brian contribute neat cameos but both direction and script are too predictable to sustain one's interest.

d Lee Sholem p William Alland s Arthur Ross c Charles P. Boyle lp Stephen McNally, Julia Adams, Russell Johnson, Jaclynne Greene, Edgar Barrier, Jack Kelly, Hugh O'Brian

Star of Texas (WESTWOOD/AA) b/w 68 min
The first entry in what is generally regarded as the last Western series. Morris was simply given the scripts intended for Wild Bill Elliott who had moved over to work under Monogram's more prestigious Allied Artists banner. Ullman's script, a straightforward imitation of 'Dragnet's' documentary style, has Morris on the trail of a bunch of crooks led by Fix and going undercover to nab them. Carr directs in his usual frantic style and the result is a far better film than Morris' first outing as a Western hero, *Desert Pursuit* (1952).

d Thomas Carr p Vincent M. Fennelly s Dan Ullman c Ernest Miller lp Wayne Morris, Paul Fix, Robert Bice, Frank Ferguson, Rick Vallin, Jack Larson

The Stranger Wore a Gun (COL) 83 min
Another of the slew of 3-D films, or 'depthies' as they were called in the trade, that appeared around this time. Scott is the Quantrill Raider who can't shake his reputation but decides to go straight when he sees that Macready's plans will soon bankrupt Weldon's stageline. After playing on the rivalry between Macready and Mexican bandido, Bedoya, he finally shoots Macready in a superb gun battle in a blazing saloon before riding off to Texas with Trevor. De Toth directs vigorously with an eye to more than the 'pelt and burn' philosophy that dominates so many 3-D pics. Marvin and Borgnine seize their opportunities as the featured villains.

d Andre De Toth p Harry Joe Brown s Kenneth Gamet c Lester H. White lp Randolph Scott, Claire Trevor, George Macready, Joan Weldon, Alfonso Bedoya, Lee Marvin, Ernest Borgnine

Take Me to Town (U) 80 min
This is a delightful film, rendered all the more so by Sirk's deft touch. Sheridan is the saloon songbird Vermillion O'Toole, who hides out in the backwoods as the minder of preacher Hayden's children and decides she would make them a good mother and him a good wife. She proves herself by driving off an old lover, killing a bear and raising money to build a church by putting on a musical show. Metty's cinematography is simply lustrous, fitting Sirk's own description of the film perfectly: 'A little lyrical poem to the American Western past'.

d Douglas Sirk p Leonard Goldstein, Ross Hunter s Richard Morris c Russell Metty lp Ann Sheridan, Sterling Hayden, Philip Reed, Phyllis Stanley, Larry Gates, Lane Chandler

The Tall Texan (LIPPERT) b/w 82 min
The directorial debut of editor Williams who'd just won an Oscar for his work on **High Noon** (1952), this is an intriguing little film. Essentially a character study, it features Bridges (an escaped murderer), Cobb and Windsor amongst a small group of gold seekers who are set upon by Indians when they start mining in Indian territory. Roecca's script sags a little at times, but Williams' direction (and hard-edged editing) pack a punch that belies his lack of success as a director, excluding his one memorable documentary, *Cowboy* (1954).

d Elmo Williams p T.J. Wood, Robert L. Lippert Jnr s Samuel Roecca c Joseph Biroc lp Lloyd Bridges, Lee J. Cobb, Marie Windsor, Luther Adler, Syd Saylor, George Steel

Far left: *Dona Drake and Keith Larsen as the weak willed* Son of Belle Starr.

Ernest Borgnine and the young Lee Marvin hold Randolph Scott at gunpoint in The Stranger Wore a Gun.

Another man is picked off in War Paint.

Texas Bad Man (WESTWOOD/AA) b/w 62 min

This pleasant outing from Morris is one of the last series Westerns ever made. He's the sheriff bedevilled by a crooked father who, with the help of a trio of gunmen, is after the gold bullion from the local mine. Collins directs energetically, but the screenplay by Poland lacks the dramatic edge that Daniel Ullman produced so regularly in his scripts for Morris.

d Lewis Collins *p* Vincent M. Fennelly *s* Joseph F. Poland *c* Gilbert Warrenton *lp* Wayne Morris, Frank Ferguson, Elaine Riley, Sheb Wooley, Denver Pyle, Myron Healey

Thunder Over the Plains (WB) 82 min

An amiable actioneer with Scott as the reluctant Texan sent by his superiors to protect carpetbaggers and crooks from the wrath of the men they are cheating. De Toth directs in his usual telling manner, especially after the action hots up when patriotic leader McGraw is framed by Barker and his henchmen.

d Andre De Toth *p* David Weisbart *s* Russell Hughes *c* Bert Glennon *lp* Randolph Scott, Lex Barker, Phyllis Kirk, Charles McGraw, Henry Hull, Elisha Cook Jnr

Topeka (AA) b/w 69 min

One of the first, and best, of Elliott's final Western series, *Topeka* is best remembered for its exuberant use of the crane shot by director Carr and cinematographer Miller which gives the film a strange sense of delirium. The film is also notable for its realism and for the casting of Elliott as an outlaw hired as sheriff to rid a small town of more outlaws. He hires his old gang to help and is then tempted to take over the town but is redeemed by the love of Coates and sets about cleaning up the town again.

d Thomas Carr *p* Vincent M. Fennelly *s* Milton M. Raison *c* Ernest Miller *lp* Bill Elliott, Phyllis Coates, John James, Fuzzy Knight, Rick Vallin, Denver Pyle

Vanquished (PAR) 84 min

A mild actioneer from Pine and Thomas, now making double A features after years of producing low-budget quickies and series films. Routinely scripted and even more routinely directed, it features Payne as the Southerner who returns home after the Civil War to find carpetbagger Bettger ruling the roost with assistance from Parker's corrupt official. Payne is unable to do anything with his flat role.

Far right: Joan Leslie as The Woman They Almost Lynched.

d Edward Ludwig *p* William H. Pine, William C. Thomas *s* Winston Miller, Frank Moss, Lewis R. Foster *c* Lionel Lindon *lp* John Payne, Jan Sterling, Coleen Gray, Lyle Bettger, Willard Parker, Roy Gordon

War Paint (K-B PRODUCTIONS) 89 min

Filmed entirely on location in Death Valley, this is the best of veteran director Selander's later films. Stack, trying to get a peace treaty to an Indian chief on time, leads a small Cavalry patrol through Death Valley and is menaced from within and without. Doucette and Wilke in particular give strong supporting performances.

d Lesley Selander *p* Howard W. Koch *s* Richard Alan Simmons, Martin Berkeley *c* Gordon Avil *lp* Robert Stack, Joan Taylor, John Doucette, Robert Wilke, Peter Graves, Keith Larsen

Wings of the Hawk (U-INTERNATIONAL) 81 min

At the time of its release this film was seen as one of the best films ever made in 3-D, because it didn't shout 3-D at its audiences. Shown 'flat' *Wings of the Hawk* remains a likeable, if minor, movie. Set against the background of the Mexican Revolution, it features Heflin as the dispossessed miner who joins a revolutionary group led by Adams. Though the swashbuckling screenplay hardly engages Boetticher's attention in the way that Burt Kennedy's script for **Seven Men from Now** (1956), his next film, would, he and cinematographer Stine worked closely together to great effect, making this the most visually appealing of the director's early films.

d Budd Boetticher *p* Aaron Rosenberg *s* James E. Moser *c* Clifford Stine *lp* Van Heflin, Julia Adams, Abbe Lane, George Dolenz, Antonio Moreno, Noah Beery Jnr

The Woman They Almost Lynched

(REP) b/w 90 min

This is another of Dwan's delicious Western parodies. Leslie is the Eastern girl who inherits a saloon used by Charles and Kate McCoy Quantrill (Donlevy and Totter). She takes them on, even buckling on a gun to confront Totter, only to be arrested by the townspeople as a Union spy before being rescued by Lund.

Fisher's script, which includes cameos by the James and Younger brothers and a couple of songs, is gloriously nonsensical while Dwan effortlessly charms us into complicity with his mockery of the genre.

d/p Allan Dwan *s* Steve Fisher *c* Reggie Lanning *lp* Joan Leslie, John Lund, Brian Donlevy, Audrey Totter, James Brown, Jim Davis

Apache (UA) 91 min

A hard-hitting Indian Western from Webb, who was later to script **Cheyenne Autumn** (1964) for Ford, *Apache* stars Lancaster as one of Geronimo's (one-time matinee idol, Blue) braves who refuses to surrender. Unlike the Indian Westerns that preceded it, *Apache* features an active central character and makes its points by disciplined observation of the one-man war against the US Cavalry waged by Lancaster and by Webb's clever reversal in the script which forces us to see the excesses of white civilization from the Indian's point of view. Aldrich's direction, with its fluid travelling shots, is marvellously assured. But sadly the film is flawed by the ending forced upon Hecht and Lancaster by UA. They had wanted Lancaster to be pointlessly shot by the Cavalry after he had begun to cultivate the land and turn his thoughts to peace under the influence of Peters. Instead the end is wildly optimistic.

d Robert Aldrich *p* Harold Hecht *s* James R. Webb
c Ernest Laszlo *lp* Burt Lancaster, Jean Peters, John McIntire, Charles Bronson, Monte Blue, John Dehner

Arrow in the Dust (AA) 80 min

Hayden is the deserter who has to impersonate an officer to lead a wagon train to safety in this routine outing. The story is rather aimless and made odder by the glaring mismatch of the footage from *New Mexico* (1951), inserted to beef up the action sequences. Under Hayden's guidance the wagon train gets through, Owen, a would-be gunrunner, gets his just deserts and Gray gets to wait for Hayden, sentenced to the briefest term of imprisonment for his desertion.

d Lesley Selander *p* Hayes Goetz *s* Don Martin *c* Ellis W. Carter *lp* Sterling Hayden, Coleen Gray, Keith Larsen, Tudor Owen, Lee Van Cleef, Jimmy Wakely

Battle of Rogue River (COL) 71 min

Montgomery is the officer sent to the Rogue River fort to strengthen discipline only to find Denning trying to ferment a rebellion against him and Granger trying to start an Indian war. As if that isn't enough, Evans is the leader of a syndicate of crooked businessmen who are trying to secure Oregon's mineral wealth for themselves.

d William Castle *p* Sam Katzman *s* Douglas Heyes *c* Henry Freulich *lp* George Montgomery, Richard Denning, Martha Hyer, Michael Granger, Charles Evans, John Crawford

Burt Lancaster takes pity on Jean Peters in Apache, *the most hard hitting Indian Western of the fifties.*

Bitter Creek (WESTWOOD/AA) b/w 74 min

One of the best of Elliott's Westerns. Waggner's screenplay uses the revenge plot to great effect and Carr's tight, yet playful direction – he was clearly still practising his crane shots – is a cut above the average. Garland, in an early Western performance, is marvellous as a younger version of Barbara Stanwyck, playing the female lead with a touch of hardness that is unusual. She's the girl who believes in Young who is himself suspected by Elliott of being responsible for the death of his brother. Carr advances the drama emphatically, giving his players plenty of opportunity to develop their characters as well as pushing the story remorselessly forward to the inevitable confrontation between Young and Elliott.

d Thomas Carr *p* Vincent M. Fennelly *s* George Waggner *c* Ernest Miller *lp* Bill Elliott, Carleton Young, Beverly Garland, Claude Akins, Earle Hodgins, Forrest Taylor

The Black Dakotas (COL) 65 min

Buffum and Scott's unusual screenplay has Confederate Merrill impersonate the emissary sent by President Lincoln to make a peace treaty with the Sioux, and so release Union troops for the Civil War. Merrill, of course, wants an Indian war to tie up Union troops and to secure the Sioux's gold for his own pocket. Nazarro handles the action sequences well but, as so often in B Westerns, the dialogue scenes fall oddly flat. Hendrix provides the romantic interest.

d Ray Nazarro *p* Wallace MacDonald *s* Ray Buffum, DeVallon Scott *c* Ellis W. Carter *lp* Gary Merrill, Wanda Hendrix, John Bromfield, Noah Beery Jnr, Jay Silverheels, Clayton Moore

Black Horse Canyon (U-INTERNATIONAL) 82 min

A pleasant horse-opera of a Western, the horse in question being a wild black stallion that Blanchard, helped by McCrea, and Vye want for stock-rearing purposes. Homes' dialogue is realistic, the action natural and Hibbs' direction superior. McCrea in particular is at his ease in the film's domestic environment.

d Jesse Hibbs *p* John W. Rogers *s* Geoffrey Homes *c* George Robinson *lp* Joel McCrea, Mari Blanchard, Murvyn Vye, Irving Bacon, Ewing Mitchell, John Pickard

Border River (U-INTERNATIONAL) 81 min

This is an entertaining Western, set against the background of the Civil War. Sackheim and Stevens' screenplay features McCrea as the Confederate officer seeking arms in Mexico

Far left: *Bill Elliott (left) and Carleton Young prepare to fight it out to the horror of Beverly Garland in* Bitter Creek. *Behind them on the right is the young Claude Akins.*

with gold bullion stolen from a Union payroll. Various would-be predators circle him and try and steal the bullion but McCrea, with assistance from De Carlo, foils them all including Armendariz and his German advisor, Triesault.

d George Sherman *p* Albert J. Cohen *s* William Sackheim, Louis Stevens *c* Irving Glassberg *lp* Joel McCrea, Yvonne De Carlo, Pedro Armendariz, Ivan Triesault, Howard Petrie, Lane Chandler

The Bounty Hunter (TRANSCONA/WB) 79 min
Scott, in the title role, uses all the tight-lipped charm at his disposal as he trails train robbers Petrie, Windsor and Taylor who, to give the plot a twist, are masquerading as respectable citizens. De Toth's direction is as imaginative and forceful as ever.

d Andre De Toth *p* Sam Bischoff *s* Winston Miller *c* Edwin DuPar *lp* Randolph Scott, Marie Windsor, Howard Petrie, Dub Taylor, Dolores Dorn, Ernest Borgnine

The Boy from Oklahoma (WB) 88 min
Routine fare. Rogers, who had just starred in a biography of his father Will, *The Story of Will Rogers* (1952) for Curtiz, is the law student who abandons his books to become sheriff of Bluerock. A gentle, if self-consciously charming, comedy, it is at its best when Rogers is well to the fore, either romancing Olson or enquiring into the murder of her father. Caruso is the villain.

d Michael Curtiz *p* David Weisbart *s* Frank Davis, Winston Miller *c* Robert Burks *lp* Will Rogers Jnr, Nancy Olson, Lon Chaney Jnr, Anthony Caruso, Wallace Ford, Slim Pickens

Broken Lance (FOX) scope 96 min
A Western remake of Joseph L. Mankievicz's *House of Strangers* (1950), *Broken Lance*, like **Duel in the Sun** (1946), takes for its subject the squabbles of a family and their troubled cattle empire. Tracy is the over-reaching father forced to divide up his ranch amongst his sons, and Wagner and Widmark the brothers fighting over their birthright. McDonald's sharp cinematography and the superb ensemble-acting are highlighted by Dmytryk's edgy direction that creates an atmosphere in which violence is never far away.

d Edward Dmytryk *p* Sol C. Siegel *s* Richard Murphy *c* Joseph McDonald *lp* Spencer Tracy, Robert Wagner, Jean Peters, Richard Widmark, Katy Jurado, Hugh O'Brian

Ronald Reagan as the government agent with Barbara Stanwyck in Allan Dwan's charming Cattle Queen of Montana.

Cattle Queen of Montana (RKO) 88 min
Perhaps the most uncomplicated of America's classic directors, Dwan made a series of films in the fifties for producer Bogeaus that allowed him a degree of flexibility he'd been unused to since the silent days. *Cattle Queen of Montana*, the tale of Stanwyck's struggles to hold on to the property of her murdered father, is beautifully lit by cinematographer Alton, the great unsung Hollywood cameraman. It evokes a world of easeful innocence far removed from the cynicism and violence that was the norm in the Western of the fifties. Reagan is the mysterious gunman (and government undercover agent) who comes to Stanwyck's rescue, puts paid to outlaw Evans' plans for a cattle empire and prevents the outbreak of an Indian war.

Stanwyck, who did all her own stunts, so impressed the Blackfeet Indians hired as extras that they made her a blood sister and gave her the Indian name of Princess Many Victories.

d Allan Dwan *p* Benedict Bogeaus *s* Robert Blees, Howard Estabrook *c* John Alton *lp* Barbara Stanwyck, Ronald Reagan, Gene Evans, Jack Elam, Anthony Caruso, Myron Healey

The Command (WB) scope 88 min
An interesting movie, *The Command* was Warner's first film in cinemascope. Hughes' script is based on a novel by James Warner Bellah as adapted by Samuel Fuller, a writer/director whose concerns are partly reflected in the film, especially in the role of the gruff sergeant played by Whitmore. Madison is the liberal doctor suddenly elevated to the command of a cavalry unit escorting a wagon train through hostile Indian territory. As a doctor, he's used to healing; suddenly he finds he must shed blood to preserve life and be educated in the realities of war by Whitmore. Weldon is the girl he loves. The script's concern with Madison's liberal dilemma is unusual and thought-provoking, but Butler's direction (especially in comparison to Fuller's direction of his own scripts) is leaden.

d David Butler *p* David Weisbart *s* Russell Hughes, Samuel Fuller *c* Wilfrid M. Cline *lp* Guy Madison, Joan Weldon, James Whitmore, Carl Benton Reid, Ray Teal, Harvey Lembeck

The Desperado (SILVERMINE/AA) b/w 81 min
A tightly-plotted Western thriller with a strong performance from Lydon in support of Morris. Lydon is the young Texan on the run from the carpetbaggers' 'State Police' who teams up with a wanted killer, Morris, to end Barnes' reign of terror in Texas. Homes' screenplay sketches in the background with emphatic brevity so leaving the players and director Carr free from the need to explain matters. The result is a superior low-budget Western.

d Thomas Carr *p* Vincent M. Fennelly *s* Geoffrey Homes *c* Joseph M. Novac *lp* Wayne Morris, James Lydon, Rayford Barnes, Beverly Garland, Lee Van Cleef, Roy Barcroft

Drum Beat (WB) scope 111 min
In this intriguing Indian Western, Daves, who in **Broken Arrow** (1950) had examined white/Indian relations from the point of view of the redman, looks at them from the perspective of the settlers. Based on his own research, it tells the story of the forging of peace with the Modoc. Ladd is the Indian Fighter who has argued against making peace with the Modoc because he distrusts their chief, Captain Jack (Bronson in his first major role) and who is asked to try and keep the peace after the Indians break out of their reservation. He successfully pacifies both the Indians and the settlers and brings a lasting peace to the battle-scarred Oregon-California border. Daves' landscape photography is as majestic as ever.

231

d/s Delmer Daves   p Alan Ladd   c J. Peverell Marley
lp Alan Ladd, Audrey Dalton, Charles Bronson, Marisa
Pavan, Robert Keith, Elisha Cook Jnr

Drums Across the River (U-INTERNATIONAL)   78 min
Juran's swift-paced direction glosses over the many inconsistencies in Butler and Roman's story-packed plot. Bettger is the villain, trying to create an Indian war so that the Utes will be moved on and he can mine the gold only he knows lies beneath their land, and Murphy is the man he tries to frame for a stagecoach robbery. With assistance from his dad (a crusty performance from Brennan), Murphy soon puts an end to Bettger's plans. The strong supporting cast includes veterans Steele, Ankrum and Silverheels.

d Nathan Juran   p Melville Tucker   s John K. Butler,
Lawrence Roman   c Harold Lipstein   lp Audie Murphy,
Lyle Bettger, Walter Brennan, Bob Steele, Morris Ankrum,
Jay Silverheels

The Forty-Niners (AA)   b/w   71 min
One of the very last of Elliott's programme Westerns. Ullman's screenplay is so influenced by thrillers it even has a voice-over narration. However, the plot construction isn't as tight as one would expect from the Ullman-Carr partnership: once Elliott, on the trail of three killers in California in 1849, reaches the town where they're hiding, the film drifts aimlessly. Morgan, as the cardsharp Elliott tags along with, steals the picture. Doucette and Bradford as two of the killers die convincingly.

d Thomas Carr   p Vincent M. Fennelly   s Dan Ullman
c Ernest Miller   lp Bill Elliott, Virginia Grey, Henry (Harry)
Morgan, John Doucette, Lane Bradford, Denver Pyle

Garden of Evil (FOX)   scope   100 min
A dull, meandering film from Hathaway with Cooper, Widmark and Mitchell as the adventurers hired by Hayward to escort her through hostile Indian country back to a gold mine, situated in sacred ground, where her husband has been trapped by a cave-in. They get there easily enough, but on the way back distrust, sown by greed for gold and Indians, cuts its way through the group until only Cooper and Hayward are left.

d Henry Hathaway   p Charles Brackett   s Frank Fenton
c Milton Krasner, Jorge Stahl Jnr   lp Gary Cooper, Susan
Hayward, Richard Widmark, Cameron Mitchell, Hugh
Marlowe, Rita Moreno

Jesse James versus the Daltons (COL)   65 min
In typical exploitation-picture fashion, Kent's script bears little relation to the title that veteran quickie producer Katzman slapped on the movie. King is the young gunman who thinks he might be Jesse James' son and sets off in search of his legendary father, joining the Daltons in the hope of finding him quicker. Put as baldly as that the plot is interesting, but dressed up by Castle the result is a mediocre film. It was originally shown in 3-D.

d William Castle   p Sam Katzman   s Robert E. Kent
c Lester White   lp Brett King, Barbara Lawrence, James
Griffith, Bill Phillips, John Cliff, Rory Mallison

Jesse James' Women (UA)   83 min
A mediocre Western, only notable for being the only film its star, Barry, ever directed. Beauchamp's script has Barry as Jesse James holed up in a small Mississippi town and romancing a clutch of women (Castle, Baron, Rhed and Brueck) before heading back to Missouri. Understandably trade reviewers concentrated on the low-cut gowns of the cast rather than the low-budget action scenes which are often ludicrous, as in the case of the fight between Castle and

Peggie Castle as the female gunslinger in the mediocre Jesse James' Women, *the only film directed by series star Don 'Red' Barry.*

Brueck. Barry's stilted direction isn't helped by Peach's fuzzy cinematography.

d Donald Barry   p Lloyd Royal, T.V. Garraway
s D.D. Beauchamp   c Ken Peach   lp Don Barry, Jack
Buetel, Peggie Castle, Lita Baron, Joyce Rhed, Betty Brueck

Johnny Guitar (REP)   110 min
Lyrical, baroque and giddy in a way few Westerns are, *Johnny Guitar* is a masterpiece. Yordan's trance-like dialogue, Hayden and, in particular, Crawford's mannered performances (as they endlessly torment each other, testing their love), Stradling's garish, almost surreal, Trucolor lighting and James Sullivan's wonderful sets are all contributing factors but it's Ray's grandiose, neurotic direction that brings these elements to life and makes the film so powerful. Crawford, dressed in black for much of the film, is the ambitious hostess who builds a successful gambling saloon on land wanted by the railroad and who romances Brady, an outlaw and the one-time lover of McCambridge's envious cattle-queen. Hayden, Crawford's old flame re-appears and becomes her protector when McCambridge and Bond stir up the townspeople against her. Reduced to such basics, the plot seems too cliched for even a series Western – the outlaws even have a 'secret entrance' to their hideout through a waterfall ! – but Ray (and his willing accomplice Crawford) transform the material to give it the delirious intensity that François Truffaut mentioned in his review of the film when it first was shown in France: 'Never trust appearances. Beauty and profundity are not always found in the "obvious" traditional places; a Trucolor Western from humble Republic can throb with the passion of *l'amour fou* or whisper with an evening delicacy.'

d Nicholas Ray   p Herbert J. Yates   s Philip Yordan
c Harry Stradling   lp Joan Crawford, Sterling Hayden,
Mercedes McCambridge, Scott Brady, Ward Bond, Ernest
Borgnine

Jubilee Trail (REP)   103 min
Another of Republic's showcases for Ralston, wife of the studio's owner, Herbert J. Yates, *Jubilee Trail* is an overlong, flamboyant, historical, would-be epic. Ralston is the dance-

hall queen who teaches Easterner Leslie the tricks of frontier life in the course of a wagon-train journey to California while romancing Tucker's grizzled trader at the same time. Kane and Marta, his regular cinematographer, handle the unusually big budget with their usual efficiency.

d/p Joseph Kane *s* Bruce Manning *c* Jack Marta *lp* Vera Ralston, Joan Leslie, Forrest Tucker, John Russell, Jack Elam, Jim Davis

The Law versus Billy the Kid (COL) 73 min
This is yet another account of the short and violent life of William Bonney, here impersonated by Brady. Once again, he's forced into a life of crime and once again his friend sheriff Pat Garrett, must go after him. Castle, to his credit, speeds through the explanations and concentrates on the action. St John is the girl Brady loves and kills for.

d William Castle *p* Sam Katzman *s* John T. Williams *c* Henry Freulich *lp* Scott Brady, Betta St John, James Griffith, Alan Hale Jnr, Paul Cavanaugh, William Phillips

The Lawless Rider
(ROYAL WEST PRODUCTIONS/UA) b/w 62 min
The last film directed by former rodeo star and ace second-unit director, Canutt, who in 1966 was given a special Oscar for 'creating the profession of stuntman as it exists today'. Scripted by Carpenter, who also has the leading role as

Joan Crawford as the gunslinger and much much more in the marvellous Johnny Guitar.

the marshal who goes undercover, the plot is routine but Canutt's direction brings a touch of authenticity to the action scenes that raises the film well above the average. Heroine Bascom is a trick-rope rodeo champ and so is able to come to Carpenter's aid at the film's climax. Although Canutt directed no more films he continued to work as a second-unit director for many years.

This is undoubtedly the best film made by producer/actor/writer Carpenter's independent productions – his other claim to fame, **I Killed Wild Bill Hickok,** 1956, is a better title than film. Carpenter, who is not to be confused with the director of *Halloween* (1978), was unusual in that, unlike most other producers of quickies in the fifties, he made mostly Westerns rather than jump on the more profitable horror/science fiction bandwagons.

d Yakima Canutt *p/s* John Carpenter *c* William C. Thompson *lp* John Carpenter, Rose Bascom, Frankie Darro, Douglass Dumbrille, Bud Osborne, Tap Canutt

The Outcast (REP) 90 min
One of Witney's last pictures for Republic, the studio he served for so long, *The Outcast* is an action-packed Western. Derek is rarely seen without a gun or the reins of a horse in his hands. Davis is the crooked uncle who cheats Derek out of the ranch that's rightfully his and Evans and McLeod are the girls Derek romances in between fighting for his rights. One-time series star Steele is effective as one of the gunmen Derek hires to help him.

d William Witney *p* William J. O'Sullivan *s* John K. Butler, Richard Wormser *c* Reggie Lanning *lp* John Derek, Joan Evans, Jim Davis, Catherine McLeod, Bob Steele, Harry Carey Jnr

Overland Pacific (RELIANCE) 73 min
This is a smooth B Western. Mahoney and director Sears were old friends from the days when both acted (and Mahoney stunted) in Charles Starrett's *Durango* series Westerns. Mahoney is the gently spoken railroad detective sent to discover what's delaying the laying of track and finding out that it's Bishop who wants the railroad to pass through his land. Mahoney is an athletic hero as always but the Color Corporation of America's version of Technicolor is rather too murky to be that enjoyable.

d Fred F. Sears *p* Edward Small *s* J. Robert Bren, Gladys Atwater, Martin Goldsmith *c* Lester White *lp* Jack (Jock) Mahoney, Peggie Castle, Adele Jergens, William Bishop, Walter Sande, Chubby Johnson

Passion (RKO) b/w 84 min
Wilde is the athletic vacquero bent on avenging the murder of his parents and reclaiming his lands in this amiable romp through California's early history from the dependable Dwan. Burr is the sweaty villain and De Carlo the statuesque heroine. In contrast to most Westerns of the fifties, the film embodies a charmingly innocent world view in which right will always triumph.

d Allan Dwan *p* Benedict Bogeaus *s* Joseph Leytes, Beatrice A. Dresher, Howard Estabrook *c* John Alton *lp* Cornel Wilde, Yvonne De Carlo, Rodolfo Acosta, Raymond Burr, Lon Chaney Jnr, Anthony Caruso

The Raid (FOX) 83 min
This fine Western is based on a little-known incident of the Civil War. Boehm's screenplay features Heflin as the Confederate officer who, after escaping to Canada from a Union prison camp with several of his men, plans to take over and sack a town just across the Canadian border in retribution for Northern raids into the South. Marvin is the fiery officer who nearly gives the game away, Boone the one-armed Union

veteran and Bancroft the war widow Heflin boards with while studying the lay-out of the town. Fregonese directs suspensefully, much aided by Ballard's brooding cinematography.

d Hugo Fregonese *p* Robert L. Jacks *s* Sidney Boehm *c* Lucien Ballard *lp* Van Heflin, Anne Bancroft, Richard Boone, Lee Marvin, Peter Graves, Paul Cavanaugh

Rails into Laramie (U-INTERNATIONAL) 81 min
Another lively Western from director Hibbs. Here Payne is the hero assigned to put an end to Duryea and his gang who are preventing the completion of the railroad to Laramie. A bizarre sub-plot has Blanchard organizing an all-female jury to convict the charming Duryea, but it is Hibbs' energetic and imaginative direction that lifts the material above the average. Rex Allen, whose own series of Westerns had just ended, sings the title song, yet another indication of how influential **High Noon** (1952) was.

d Jesse Hibbs *p* Ted Richmond *s* D.D. Beauchamp, Joseph Hoffman *c* Maury Gertsman *lp* John Payne, Dan Duryea, Mari Blanchard, Lee Van Cleef, Barton MacLane, Harry Shannon

Ride Clear of Diabolo (U-INTERNATIONAL) 81 min
In this well-plotted, cleverly directed Western, Murphy is the son out to avenge the murder of his father and kid brother and Duryea, the colourful gunman who comes to his assistance. Birch and Pullen are the guilty men, sheriff and lawyer respectively. Hibbs directs his cast with confidence and, thanks to Glassberg's fine cinematography, produces a stunning-looking B Western.

d Jesse Hibbs *p* John W. Rogers *s* George Zuckerman *c* Irving Glassberg *lp* Audie Murphy, Dan Duryea, Susan Cabot, Paul Birch, William Pullen, Jack Elam

Riding Shotgun (WB) 75 min
A lively budget film. Scott is the stagecoach guard accused of complicity in a hold-up who sets out after the outlaws to prove his innocence. Both Blackburn's script and De Toth's forceful and imaginative direction bring an extra lease of life to the cliched story. Morris is the baddie, Weldon the girl and, down the cast list, Charles Bronson puts in an appearance as a heavy.

d Andre De Toth *p* Ted Sherdeman *s* Tom Blackburn *c* Bert Glennon *lp* Randolph Scott, Wayne Morris, Joan Weldon, Joe Sawyer, James Millican, Charles Buchinsky (Bronson)

River of No Return (FOX) scope 90 min
Preminger's only Western tells the story of the growing respect and then love for each other of a saloon singer, Monroe, and a farmer, Mitchum, in the course of an enforced river journey together after gambler Calhoun steals Mitchum's horse and leaves him without supplies in Indian territory. It is shot with the typical 'objectivity' we have come to associate with Preminger. Accordingly, without any special pleading or point-making in either the film's script or images – there are few reaction shots for example – the movie's outcome has the *appearance* of being wholly logical rather than merely a plot resolution. Mitchum and Monroe are marvellous together.

d Otto Preminger *p* Stanley Rubin *s* Frank Fenton *c* Joseph LaShelle *lp* Robert Mitchum, Marilyn Monroe, Rory Calhoun, Tommy Rettig, Don Beddoe, John Doucette

Saskatchewan *aka* **O'Rourke of the Royal Mounted** (U) 87 min
This is the least interesting of Walsh's Westerns of the fifties. Beautifully photographed by Seitz on location near Banff, the film features Ladd as the Mountie reared by Indians romancing saloon girl Winters and tracking down Sioux Indians who, after their victory over Custer at the Little Big Horn, have gone north to try and incite Canadian Indians to follow their example.

d Raoul Walsh *p* Aaron Rosenberg *s* Gil Doud *c* John Seitz *lp* Alan Ladd, Shelley Winters, Robert Douglas, J. Carrol Naish, Hugh O'Brian, Jay Silverheels

Seven Brides for Seven Brothers (MGM) scope 104 min
A lusty musical, directed with verve by Donen and choreographed to perfection by Michael Kidd, this is undeniably the best musical Western. Even the painted sets and idealized bucolic charm of the setting work to the film's benefit. Keel is the elder brother who takes himself a wife, Powell, and so sets in motion the carrying-off of six townswomen by his uncouth younger brothers. At first much distressed, after a winter spent in isolation with the brothers during which they and Powell educate them into cultivated ways, the women elect to remain, to the chagrin of their one-time beaus. Keel and Tamblyn in particular are effervescent. The result is a delightful film, even if its central idea (that women want to be abducted) is highly dubious.

d Stanley Donen *p* Jack Cummings *s* Frances Goodrich, Albert Hackett *c* George Folsey *lp* Howard Keel, Jane Powell, Jeff Richards, Russ Tamblyn, Howard Petrie, Tommy Rall

The Siege at Red River (PANORAMIC PRODUCTIONS/FOX) 86 min
A routine Western given added punch by Mate's forceful direction. Johnson is the Confederate officer smuggling gatling guns back to Confederate lines and Boone the renegade who steals them to sell to the Shawnee. The final battle between the Cavalry and Indians, like that of **Pony Soldier** (1952), is lifted, virtually intact from **Buffalo Bill** (1944). Dru is the Union nurse who falls for Johnson.

d Rudolph Mate *p* Leonard Goldstein *s* Sydney Boehm *c* Edward Cronjager *lp* Van Johnson, Joanne Dru, Richard Boone, Milburn Stone, Jeff Morrow, Craig Hill

Silver Lode (RKO) 80 min
Made as a quickie for producer Bogeaus, *Silver Lode* is one of Dwan's unqualified masterpieces. From a simple story of

Robert Mitchum as the farmer and Marilyn Monroe as the saloon singer he tames with Tommy Rettig in River of No Return.

Seven Brides for Seven Brothers, undeniably the best musical Western.

revenge – Payne is wrongfully accused of murder on his wedding day and becomes the object of a manhunt led by Duryea as he tries to clear his name – Dwan produces the most succinct anti-McCarthy tract ever made in Hollywood and a delirious film about memory, visualized in repeated images seen in different contexts.

d Allan Dwan   *p* Benedict Bogeaus   *s* Karen De Wolfe
c John Alton   *lp* John Payne, Dan Duryea, Lizabeth Scott, Dolores Moran, Emile Meyer, Harry Carey Jnr

Sitting Bull   (UA)   105 min
The most accurate depiction of the events that led up to the Battle of the Little Big Horn. Kennedy is the Indian-hating Custer and Robertson the friend of the Indians whose life Naish's Sitting Bull saves by petitioning President Grant after he has been court-martialled for befriending the enemy and trying to prevent the massacre of the Little Big Horn. The film's accuracy is presumably to be credited to Iron Eyes Cody who, as well as playing Crazy Horse, was the film's technical advisor.

d/co-s Sidney Salkow   *p* W.R. Frank   *co-s* Jack DeWitt
c Charles Van Enger   *lp* Dale Robertson, Mary Murphy, J. Carrol Naish, Iron Eyes Cody, Douglas Kennedy, John Litel

Southwest Passage *aka* Camels West
(EDWARD SMALL)   82 min
Camels and 3-D are the gimmicks of this amiable B Western. Cameron is the scout charting a new trail to California who is determined to prove that camels can be put to practical use in the West and Ireland is the bank robber who joins him to evade the law. Dru (Ireland's wife in real life) plays his girl and Dehner the member of the expedition who wants the loot the now reformed Ireland intends to return. Other hazards include Indians and a water shortage.

d Ray Nazarro   *p* Edward Small   *s* Harry Essex   *c* Sam Leavitt   *lp* John Ireland, Joanne Dru, Rod Cameron, Guinn Williams, John Dehner, Morris Ankrum

Taza Son of Cochise   (U)   77 min
Perhaps the oddest of the cycle of Indian films of the fifties, this movie by Sirk, a director better known for his melodramas than his Westerns, follows the career of Taza (Hudson) caught between the US Cavalry and his war-mongering brother in his search for peace. The film has been attacked as being hopelessly compromised and for Hudson's performance; at the same time it has been celebrated, especially in France, for its lyrical tone and its feel for Indian life. Originally shot in 3-D (which explains some of the gimmicky

shots) the film, like the director's *Sign of the Pagan* (1954), lacks the clear, powerful narrative line that characterizes the director's best work.

Jeff Chandler has a cameo as the dying Cochise, a role he virtually made his own.

d Douglas Sirk   *p* Ross Hunter   *s* George Zuckerman
c Russell Metty   *lp* Rock Hudson, Barbara Rush, Gregg Palmer, Morris Ankrum, Bart Roberts, Gene Iglesias

They Rode West   (COL)   84 min
In this slackly scripted but strongly directed film, Francis is the doctor in a lonely fort who causes bad feelings amongst his fellow officers when he starts treating an epidemic on a Kiowa reservation. When an Indian war threatens to break out, Francis' medical abilities prevent it and he wins his fellow officers' respect. Reed and Carey make the best of their one-dimensional characters.

d Phil Karlson   *p* Lewis J. Rachmil   *s* DeVallon Scott, Frank Nugent   *c* Charles Lawton Jnr   *lp* Robert Francis, Donna Reed, Phil Carey, Onslow Stevens, May Wynn, Roy Roberts

Three Hours to Kill   (COL)   77 min
Another superior Western from Werker, one of the most interesting (and uncelebrated) directors working in the Western genre in the early fifties. His films, **The Last Posse, Devil's Canyon** (both 1953) and **At Gunpoint** (1955), all share a concern for individuals sacrificed by the societies they work for. Though, here, the script suffers from being the work of many hands, the film and its unremitting bleak vision are unmistakably Werker's.

Andrews is the stagecoach driver accused of killing his one-time fiancée's brother. He's briefly 'hung' by a drunken posse before his innocence is proved. He turns roving gunfighter and later, still embittered, returns to find the real killer who, ironically, turns out to be the only man in town to have treated him sympathetically. The story is handled in an adult fashion with townspeople clearly the equals of the hysterical lynch mob of **The Ox-Bow Incident** (1943). Influenced, like *At Gunpoint*, by **High Noon** (1952) it has a bitter edge to it that *High Noon* lacks.

d Alfred Werker   *p* Harry Joe Brown   *s* Richard Alan Simmons, Roy Huggins, Maxwell Shane   *c* Charles Lawton Jnr   *lp* Dana Andrews, Donna Reed, Dianne Foster, Stephen Elliott, Richard Coogan, Lawrence Hugo

Track of the Cat   (WB)   scope   102 min
An ambitious Western. Bezzerides' script, based on a novel by Walter Van Tillberg Clark (one of whose other books had earlier been filmed by Wellman – **The Ox-Bow Incident,** 1943), neatly balances a hunt for a cougar, which is never seen, with the family drama taking place inside a snow-bound

Northern California farmhouse. The feeling of despair and gloom that hangs over the film has brought comparisons with Eugene O'Neill (and even Poe), but Wellman's analysis of his characters is less psychological and more moral than that suggests. Mitchum (a superb performance) and Hunter who wants to marry a neighbour's daughter, Lynn, are the warring brothers, Wright the strong-willed daughter, Tonge the weak father and Bondi the ramrod of a matriarch.

Clothier's stylized cinematography in which the primary colours were bleached out, giving the resulting colour images the look and feel of black and white, is very effective.

d William Wellman *p* John Wayne, Robert Fellows *s* A.I. Bezzerides *c* William H. Clothier *lp* Robert Mitchum, Teresa Wright, Diana Lynn, Tab Hunter, Philip Tonge, Beulah Bondi

Two Guns and a Badge (AA) b/w 69 min

Generally regarded as the last series Western ever made, this Morris vehicle features him as an ex-convict mistaken for a sheriff who comes up against rancher and rustler Barcroft. Garland as Barcroft's daughter provides the romantic interest. Routine, but efficiently put together, its timeless simplicities contrasted strongly with the psychological, violent and self-conscious Westerns then being made.

d Lewis D. Collins *p* Vincent Fennelly *s* Dan Ullman *c* Joseph Novac *lp* Wayne Morris, Morris Ankrum, Beverly Garland, Roy Barcroft, William Phipps, Bob Wilke

Vera Cruz

(HECHT-HILL-LANCASTER PRODUCTIONS/UA) scope 94 min
Disliked by the critics when it was released because of its cynicism, *Vera Cruz* is in many ways the forerunner of **The Wild Bunch** (1969). Moreover its amoral adventures and the

Apache Woman: *Joan Taylor as the halfbreed and one of the many creatures from the depths to feature in the work of Roger Corman.*

plot of double- and double-double-cross prefigure the direction the Italian Western was to take a decade later; it certainly was an influence on Sergio Leone. Its plot is simple: two adventurers in Mexico in the aftermath of the Civil War, Lancaster and Cooper, try to out double-cross each other over a hoard of gold. 'How do I know I can trust you?' ask the heroes of each other at regular intervals before Aldrich answers for them by reversing the 'good guy always wins' convention, and having Cooper only win by becoming a killer. Lancaster is marvellous as the perpetually smiling villain.

Oddly enough though Tony Martin's singing of the title theme was cut from the film, it was still released by RCA to tie in with the film.

d Robert Aldrich *p* James Hill *s* Roland Kibbee, James R. Webb *c* Ernest Laszlo *lp* Gary Cooper, Burt Lancaster, Denise Darcel, Cesar Romero, Sarita Montiel, Jack Elam

Apache Ambush (COL) b/w 68 min

Opening with Lincoln, in conciliatory mood just before his assassination, sending a mixed group of Union and Confederate soldiers to drive a herd of cattle from Texas to market in the North, this is an interesting film. Once in Texas, Williams and Harvey find a box of repeating rifles to be the centre of interest for Indians, renegade Confederates and even Mexicans, who are hoping to win back Texas. A splendid gun battle against Apaches and Mexicans ends the ruggedly directed film. Former series stars Ritter and Corrigan have featured roles.

d Fred F. Sears *p* Wallace MacDonald *s* David Lang *c* Fred Jackman Jnr *lp* Bill Williams, Don Harvey, Tex Ritter, Ray Corrigan, Richard Jaeckel, Movita

Apache Woman (GOLDEN STATE) 69 min

Corman's second Western to be distributed by the American Releasing Corporation (soon to become AIP and enter film production), *Apache Woman* deals with racial prejudice like

Far left: *Burt Lancaster (centre) with Gary Cooper (right) in* Vera Cruz, *one of the important influences on the Italian Western.*

the director's better known (but less successful) *The Intruder* (1962). Rusoff's plot is firmly traditional, with Bridges sent to investigate a series of robberies supposedly being done by a tribe of peaceful Apache. But Corman's primitive, confrontatory directorial style is far more modern. Taylor is the half breed Bridges falls for and Fuller her brother and the mastermind behind the thefts.

d/p Roger Corman   *s* Lou Rusoff   *c* Floyd Crosby
lp Lloyd Bridges, Joan Taylor, Lance Fuller, Paul Birch, Jonathan Hale, Morgan Jones

At Gunpoint (AA) scope 81 min
This is virtually a remake of **High Noon** (1952) which, with **Broken Arrow** (1950), was the most influential and imitated Western of the fifties. MacMurray is the storekeeper who accidentally kills a bank robber with a lucky shot. First he is celebrated as a local hero by his fellow townspeople and then deserted by them when they learn that he can't shoot and remember that the robbers have threatened reprisals. They even go so far as to boycott his store when he won't quit Plainview until his steadfastness and the constant support given to him by local doctor Brennan win them round and they see the error of their ways. Whereupon they help him deal with the outlaws when they return. Ullman sermonizes a little too often but Werker and his actors, especially MacMurray and Malone, as his wife, give the story some real conviction.

d Alfred Werker   *p* Vincent M. Fennelly   *s* Daniel B. Ullman   *c* Ellsworth Fredericks   *lp* Fred MacMurray, Dorothy Malone, Walter Brennan, Skip Homeier, Frank Ferguson, Tommy Rettig

Bad Day at Black Rock (MGM) scope 81 min
A modern Western whose liberal sentiments won it favourable comparisons with **High Noon** (1952). Tracy is the one-armed

Spencer Tracy as the one-armed bearer of retribution in the stylish Bad Day at Black Rock.

stranger who unleashes his fury on the inhabitants of Black Rock when he discovers that the father of the Japanese-American, who saved his life in the war and to whom he wants to present the son's posthumously-won medal, was murdered by the townspeople on the outbreak of the war when they got 'patriotic drunk'. What gives the film its force is Sturges' bold, thrillerish, direction, which uses the scope screen to dramatic effect, and the army of heavies (including Marvin at his most loutish) who give a real air of menace to Kaufman's literate screenplay. A mark of the film's impact was the speed with which the title phrase passed into American slang usage.

d John Sturges   *p* Dore Schary   *s* Millard Kaufman
c William C. Mellor   *lp* Spencer Tracy, Robert Ryan, Ernest Borgnine, Anne Francis, Lee Marvin, Walter Brennan

Canyon Crossroads
(JOYCE-WERKER PRODUCTIONS/UA) b/w 83 min
This unusual low-budget modern Western shot on location in Utah, re-united Basehart (who gives a marvellous performance) with Werker, the director (with an uncredited Anthony Mann) of Basehart's first starring film, *He Walked by Night* (1947). For the greater part of his career Werker's work was routine and nondescript, but the Westerns he made in the fifties at the end of his career (notably **The Last Posse**, 1953 and **At Gunpoint**, 1955) are distinctive for their sober realism and bitter edge. In essence, the film is a claim-jumping Western with helicopters and uranium replacing mules and gold, but the feel is intensely claustrophobic. This is an intriguing film.

d Alfred Werker   *p* William Joyce   *s* Emmett Murphy, Leonard Heideman   *c* Gordon Avil   *lp* Richard Basehart, Phyllis Kirk, Stephen Elliott, Russell Collins, Richard Hale, Alan Wells

Chief Crazy Horse *aka* **Valley of Fury** (U) 86 min
Its sympathetic treatment of the Indians notwithstanding, *Chief Crazy Horse* is one of the weaker films in the fifties cycle of Indian films. Mature gives a lacklustre performance as the Indian chief convinced he can inflict a terrible defeat on the white man if only he can unite the tribes behind him. He does so at the Little Big Horn, only to die at the hands of Danton, cast in the unlikely role of the renegade half-caste, Little Big Man. Sherman's direction is wholly anonymous.

d George Sherman   *p* William Alland   *s* Gerald Drayson Adams, Franklin Coen   *c* Harold Lipstein   *lp* Victor Mature, Suzan Ball, John Lund, Ray Danton, Keith Larsen, Dennis Weaver

Davy Crockett, King of the Wild Frontier
(BUENA VISTA) 93 min
Originally shown as a three-part serial in the *Disneyland* television series, this romantic biography became one of Buena Vista's most commercially successful live-action films when it was released theatrically. A mark of its success was the coonskin-cap craze it started. The film tells the story of Crockett's rise as a frontier hero, his adventures in Congress and his heroic death at the Alamo. Parker's cheerful interpretation of the title role (originally intended for Ebsen who subsequently took the supporting role of the journalist who publicizes Crockett's exploits) is perfectly matched by Foster's energetic direction.

d Norman Foster   *p* Bill Walsh   *s* Tom Blackburn
c Charles Boyle   *lp* Fess Parker, Buddy Ebsen, Hans Conreid, Basil Ruysdael, William Bakewell, Ken Tobey

Destry (U) 95 min
A lacklustre remake by Marshall of his earlier classic **Destry Rides Again** (1939) with Murphy and Blanchard in the roles originated by James Stewart and Marlene Dietrich. Though it

retains the plot of the earlier film, it omits the cheerful excess that made it such a success. The best things in the movie are the cameos from stalwarts such as Buchanan, Mitchell and Ford.

d George Marshall *p* Stanley Rubin *s* Edmund H. North, D.D. Beauchamp *c* George Robinson *lp* Audie Murphy, Mari Blanchard, Lyle Bettger, Thomas Mitchell, Edgar Buchanan, Wallace Ford

The Far Country (U) 97 min

In Mann's hands the Western cliche of the hero as a man with a painful past is given renewed life through the intensity Stewart (the star of most of Mann's Westerns) brings to the role and the parable-like nature of Chase's scripts. Similarly, the ancient drama of good versus evil is given an unusual edge by Mann's conception of the hero as essentially malevolent and the villain (here McIntire) as being cheerful to the point of affability. While the formal perfection of *The Far Country*, the director's last collaboration with writer Chase, which sees a reluctant Stewart finally rescuing the emerging community of Dawson and ridding it of McIntire's tyrannical rule, somewhat blurs these interior issues, Mann's foreboding use of landscape is ample compensation.

d Anthony Mann *p* Aaron Rosenberg *s* Borden Chase *c* William Daniels *lp* James Stewart, Ruth Roman, Walter Brennan, John McIntire, Jay C. Flippen, Steve Brodie

The Far Horizons (PAR) vv 108 min

A flabby, highly inaccurate account of Lewis and Clark's famous expedition of 1803 into the interior, clearly inspired by Howard Hawks' far superior **The Big Sky** (1952). MacMurray is Lewis, Heston Clark and Reed their Indian guide who falls for Heston and so causes the expedition leaders to fall out with each other. Mate's direction is routine and Fapp's cinematography suggests a bigger budget than was clearly available, but North and Miller's script is too stodgy and talkative for its subject.

d Rudolph Mate *p* William H. Pine, William C. Thomas *s* Winston Miller, Edmund H. North *c* Daniel L. Fapp *lp* Fred MacMurray, Charlton Heston, Donna Reed, Barbara Hale, William Demarest, Alan Reed

Five Guns West (PALO ALTO) 79 min

This surprisingly ambitious Western was the first film directed by Corman and the second to be partly funded by of the American Releasing Corporation which within a year would become AIP. Basically a variant of *The Dirty Dozen* (1967) story, it features Lund as the Confederate officer leading a group of prisoners in search of a shipment of Union gold and a traitor, Ingram. At a way station the prisoners, who include Connors (later to become a television star after he changed his first name to Mike) and Birch, turn on Lund and try to rape Malone before Lund can beat them off. Crudely directed, the film's significance rests more on its being made as a Western than anything else. Had Corman and AIP come on the scene a couple of years later, the film would have been a science-fiction or horror film, genres more directly attuned to the drive-in sensibilities of the growing youth market AIP would aim its product at. As it is, *Five Guns West* and the other three Westerns Corman made for AIP form the bridge between the Poverty Row of the thirties (when Republic was formed) and the Poverty Row of the fifties (when Republic died).

d/p Roger Corman *s* R. Wright Campbell *c* Floyd Crosby *lp* John Lund, Dorothy Malone, Jack Ingram, Touch (Mike) Connors, Paul Birch, Jonathan Haze

The Gun That Won the West (COL) 71 min

A Katzman quickie with stock footage from a variety of sources and a plot to match. Morgan and Denning are the

scouts who lead the Cavalry and a party of engineers along the Bozeman trail, building a string of forts to protect the crews who will be building a new railraod. Beyond that, there's little rhyme or reason as Castle desperately tries to accommodate his actors and locations to those of the stock footage.

John Lund (right) and Mike Connors (centre) in Five Guns West, *Roger Corman's directorial debut.*

d William Castle *p* Sam Katzman *s* James R. Gordon *c* Henry Freulich *lp* Dennis Morgan, Paula Raymond, Richard Denning, Robert Bice, Chris O'Brien, Michael Morgan

The Indian Fighter (BRYNA/UA) scope 88 min

A superior Indian Western. Probably best remembered for Martinelli's bathing scenes which brought nudity, if not sexuality, to the mainstream Western, *The Indian Fighter*, its title notwithstanding, is for the most part a paean to the closeness to nature of the Indian. The rather elaborate plot concerns Douglas' attempts as a scout to forge a peace treaty with the Sioux that will let a wagon train through their territory on its way to Oregon. Landers is the war-crazed Indian and Chaney and Matthau the settlers turned secret miners of Indian gold. It is noticable that De Toth handles the action scenes briskly, so much so that even the covered wagons are pulled at a trot rather than a walk by their horses, and that he dwells on the developing relationship between Douglas and Martinelli's Indian Maid and matters of Indian culture.

Diana Douglas who plays the settler girl who sets her cap at Douglas is his ex-wife.

d Andre De Toth *p* William Schorr *s* Frank Davis, Ben Hecht *c* Wilfrid M. Cline *lp* Kirk Douglas, Elsa Martinelli, Walter Matthau, Lon Chaney Jnr, Elisha Cook Jnr, Harry Landers

Far right: *Victor Mature as the Noble Savage with Anne Bancroft in* The Last Frontier.

The Kentuckian (HECHT-LANCASTER) scope 104 min

The only film directed by Lancaster, whose production company with Hecht produced several notable films of the fifties, this is a slow-moving Western. Lancaster, in the title role, is the man who sets off for the promised land of Texas with his young son, MacDonald, only to get caught up in a feud that runs back generations. Foster is the bondswoman who they free in return for rescuing them and Matthau is the vengeful family enemy. Lancaster directs tentatively, emphasizing character and relationships at the expense of plot. The lengthy sequence in which the unarmed Lancaster is bull-whipped by Matthau was much trimmed for distribution outside America.

d Burt Lancaster *p* Harold Hecht *s* A.B. Guthrie Jnr *c* Ernest Laszlo *lp* Burt Lancaster, Dianne Foster, Ronald MacDonald, Walter Matthau, John Carradine, John McIntire

The Last Command (REP) 110 min

Republic's own version of the battle of the Alamo, made by the company to spite John Wayne – whose long-planned film, **The Alamo** would not appear until 1960 – after he'd left the company rather than film the story, a project close to his heart, with Republic producing. Duff's screenplay plays fast and loose with the facts in usual Hollywood fashion. Hayden, as Bowie, is a personal friend of Naish's Santa Anna who counsels moderation when other Texas settlers argue for a rebellion against Mexico. But he ends up leading a small group, including Crockett (Hunnicutt), in a fight to the death in the Alamo.

d/p Frank Lloyd *s* Warren Duff *c* Jack Marta *lp* Sterling Hayden, Anna Maria Alberghetti, J. Carrol Naish, Arthur Hunnicutt, Ernest Borgnine, Richard Carlson

The Last Frontier (COL) scope 97 min

Mann's oddest Western, dominated by his moving camera which tracks and cranes, virtually at will through the dark – much of the film was shot at night – *The Last Frontier* documents the 'civilizing' of a 'Noble Savage'. Mature is the bearish, comically naive trapper who becomes obsessed with the idea of wearing cavalry uniform. At first, he seems to make the transformation effortlessly, winning the affections of Bancroft and saving the fort from an Indian attack which Preston's martinet of a colonel causes. But, despite the film's upbeat ending, with Mature in cavalry uniform saluting the flag, the film's second half details Mature's emasculation by the contradictory rules of civilized life.

Burt Lancaster (left) and Walter Matthau in the infamous bullwhip scene from The Kentuckian.

d Anthony Mann *p* William Fadiman *s* Philip Yordan, Russell S. Hughes *c* William Mellor *lp* Victor Mature, James Whitmore, Robert Preston, Guy Madison, Anne Bancroft, Pat Hogan

Last of the Desperadoes (ASSOCIATED) b/w 71 min

This is a modest, old-fashioned Western. Hampton's equally traditional script has Craig as Pat Garrett killing Billy the Kid at the beginning and then taking on the remaining members of his gang (including veterans such as Steele and MacLane) who come after him. The modern twist is the lack of support the townspeople give their sheriff after the gang have killed several innocent people. These killings result in Craig (who gives a fine measured performance) moving on and changing his name briefly before once more pinning on his star.

d Sam Newfield *p* Sigmund Neufeld *s* Orville Hampton *c* Eddie Linden *lp* James Craig, Jim Davis, Barton MacLane, Bob Steele, Margia Dean, Myrna Dell

Lawless Street

(PRODUCERS-ACTORS CORPORATION) scope b/w 78 min

A superior Western which Lewis directs with real flair. Intriguingly Gamet's script edges Scott closer to the character he was to play so well in the series of Westerns he was to make with Budd Boetticher commencing with **Seven Men from Now** (1956). Scott is a town tamer whose dedication to his job and an abstract notion of justice have cost him his wife, Lansbury. The end sees him hanging up his guns and re-united with Lansbury – an option unavailable in the Boetticher films in which the wife is generally dead – but only after cleaning up the town of Medicine Bend. Pate is the likeable gunman hired to try and stop Scott by villains Anderson and Emery.

d Joseph H. Lewis *p* Harry Joe Brown *s* Kenneth Gamet *c* Ray Rennahan *lp* Randolph Scott, Angela Lansbury, Michael Pate, Warner Anderson, John Emery, Jean Parker

A Man Alone (REP) 96 min

The directorial debut of Milland, this is a superior and highly unusual Western. Milland is the lone gunman who, having witnessed the honest businessmen of the town rob the bank, takes refuge in the cellar of the town's sheriff, Bond. There he makes friends with Bond's daughter, Murphy, and the unlikely duo set out to expose the corrupt burghers of the town, starting with Bond who's been in the robbers' pay. Thus he clears his name.

The sheriff's speech in defence of his past actions, after he's joined the side of the angels, where he compares the hopes that the West represented to settlers with the old reality of frontier life, is all the more pointed by being delivered by one of the genre's moral-authority figures. Equally bitter is

Milland's stated reason for settling in the town with Murphy: the next one will probably be just as bad.

Milland's direction is fittingly static for such a townbound tale.

d Ray Milland *p* Herbert J. Yates *s* John Tucker Battle
c Lionel Lindon *lp* Ray Milland, Mary Murphy, Ward Bond, Raymond Burr, Lee Van Cleef, Alan Hale Jnr

The Man from Bitter Ridge (U-INTERNATIONAL) 80 min
This snappy Western was the first to directed by Arnold, a master of low-budget science-fiction quickies in the fifties. Barker is the investigator sent to find out who's responsible for a series of stagecoach hold-ups. McNally is the sheepman he first suspects and Dehner the aspiring politician with a trio of gunmen at his beck and call who is the guilty party. Arnold directs furiously, piling on the action while Metty gives the film the look of a movie with twice the budget.

d Jack Arnold *p* Howard Pine *s* Lawrence Roman
c Russell Metty *lp* Lex Barker, Mara Corday, Stephen McNally, John Dehner, Trevor Bardette, Myron Healey

The Man from Laramie (COL) scope 101 min
With **Man of the West** (1958), this is Mann's most ambitious Western. At the time of his death, Mann had been planning a Western version of *King Lear* to be called *The King*. *The Man from Laramie*, co-scripted by Yordan who earlier had written a modern version of *Macbeth*, *Joe Macbeth* (1955) and accordingly was sympathetic to such a transposition, is in many ways a rough sketch for that film. Crisp is the cattle baron (going blind, like Gloucester) pre-occupied with who will inherit his empire, Nicol his psychopath of a son and Kennedy the rational son, adopted to keep Nicol in order. Into this seething morass rides Stewart in search of the man responsible for selling the guns to the Indians who slaughtered the Cavalry detachment led by his younger brother.

Stewart's entry into this private world (which finally meshes with his own when Kennedy is revealed to be the gunrunner) is typically violent. His wagon is burnt, his horses stolen and his life only spared when Kennedy stops Nicol killing him. Nicol's punishment of Stewart for meddling, later in the film, is even more violent, recalling the scene in **Bend of the River** where Stewart is left to die at the top of Mount Hood: in the middle of an arid plain, at point blank range Nicol shoots Stewart in the hand, as if castrating him, in one of the most brutal scenes in the American Western.

Stewart's continued presence, signalling his refusal to give up his mission, forces the evil that lies at the heart of Crisp's empire into the open. First Crisp is murdered by his son – the ritual of the return of his horse bearing his dead body anticipating the similar sequence in **The Tin Star** (1957) – and then Kennedy kills Nicol in a further attempt to prevent the dark secret getting out and finally Stewart kills Kennedy in a climactic gun battle amongst the rocks.

If the film is a flawed work, primarily because the emphasis is on the corrupt Waggoman family, rather than on Stewart, it remains a marvellous example of what Mann could do with the Western and contains some of the best sequences Mann ever filmed.

The movie marked the last collaboration of Mann and Stewart, a creative partnership that matched that of Randolph Scott and Budd Boetticher, if not of John Wayne and John Ford.

d Anthony Mann *p* William Goetz *s* Philip Yordan, Frank Burt *c* Charles Lang *lp* James Stewart, Arthur Kennedy, Donald Crisp, Alex Nicol, Cathy O'Donnell, Jack Elam

Man with the Gun *aka* **Deadly Peacemaker**
(UA) b/w 83 min
Writer Wilson's directorial debut, this is a bleak Western. Mitchum is the professional gunman who cleans up Sheridan

City in an attempt to win back his estranged wife, Sterling, only to have the town complain that he's been excessive after he's burnt down the saloon where the lawless elements gather. Mitchum plays the role with the sense of a man compelled – he saw his father gunned down – but who is also weary of his mercenary career. Wilson directs incisively, using humour as well as drama to explore his central character. The film was the maiden production of Goldwyn Jnr, son of Sam.

d/co-s Richard Wilson *p* Samuel Goldwyn Jnr *co-s* N.B. Stone Jnr *c* Lee Garmes *lp* Robert Mitchum, Jan Sterling, Karen Sharpe, Henry Hull, Emile Meyer, Angie Dickinson

Man without a Star (U) 89 min
Another sweaty Western, full of sexual tension from King Vidor, the director of **Duel in the Sun** (1946). Douglas is the drifter who is temporarily seduced by rancher Crain into settling down and working for her. But when she starts expanding her herd and local homesteaders put up barbed wire to protect their grazing lands, he quits and leads the local ranchers against her, despite his hatred of barbed wire, the symbol to Douglas of the closing of the West, before once more heading Westward. Trevor is the dance-hall hostess with the proverbial heart of gold and Boone Douglas' sadistic replacement.

The centre of the film is the love-hate relationship between the feisty, broody Douglas and the scheming Crain. So sure was Vidor of his ability to create sexual tension in the film that he took time out to mercilessly poke fun at C.B. De Mille's much loved 'bathtub' scenes with their prudish sexuality. A subsidiary theme is Douglas' education of the young cowboy Campbell, who tags along after him, and which harkens back to Vidor's earlier masterwork, *The Champ* (1931).

Above: James Stewart, eyes ablaze and with vengeance in his heart in Anthony Mann's magnificent The Man from Laramie.

Universal later remade the film as **A Man Called Gannon** (1968).

d King Vidor *p* Aaron Rosenberg *s* Borden Chase, D.D. Beauchamp *c* Russel Metty *lp* Kirk Douglas, Jeanne Crain, Claire Trevor, William Campbell, Richard Boone, Jay C. Flippen

Many Rivers to Cross (MGM) scope 94 min

An enjoyable farce of a frontier romance, Kentucky, 1798 style, with Parker as the girl determined to win Taylor's hand in marriage as well as his love and McLaglen, in fine knockabout form, as her oafish father. Rowland's direction is inventive but it is the script, co-written by Trosper who also scripted the much darker **Devil's Doorway** (1950) for Taylor, that is the key to the film's success, blending as it does humour with drama at every stage. Thus, even in the final fight where Taylor rescues Parker from an Indian attacker, Parker continually gets in the way of Taylor's would-be heroics.

d Roy Rowland *p* Jack Cummings *s* Harry Brown, Guy Trosper *c* John Seitz *lp* Robert Taylor, Eleanor Parker, Victor McLaglen, Russ Tamblyn, James Arness, Alan Hale Jnr

Masterson of Kansas (COL) 73 min

A real bang, bang Western with Montgomery in the title role, supported by Griffith (Doc Holliday) and Cowling (Wyatt Earp), sharpshooting his way through Kansas and preventing an Indian war. Castle directs emphasizing action above all else, as if sure the script won't make sense if the audience has time to think about it. Henry is the villain.

d William Castle *p* Sam Katzman *s* Douglas Heyes *c* Henry Freulich *lp* George Montgomery, Nancy Gates, James Griffith, Bruce Cowling, William Henry, Jay Silverheels

Arthur Kennedy as the swaggering bandido in Edgar Ulmer's masterly The Naked Dawn.

The Naked Dawn (U-INTERNATIONAL) 82 min

Made for peanuts in Mexico, this is one of Ulmer's greatest films. A fatalist's essay on greed and steamy atmospherics, it features a trio of weak-willed characters: Kennedy as the

bandido who hires Iglesias to help him retrieve money from a robbery and St John as Iglesias' wife. Soon Iglesias covets all the money while his wife plots to run off with Kennedy. Then in an unusually optimistic ending for Ulmer, Kennedy dies so that the Mexican couple might find happiness together. The film's greatness lies in the way Ulmer's camera relentlessly shows the characters trapped by choices they barely understand.

Though he was a veteran of Poverty Row, Ulmer surprisingly made only one other Western, the pseudonymously directed **Thunder Over Texas** (1934).

d Edgar G. Ulmer *p* James O. Radford *s* Nina Schneider, Herman Schneider *c* Frederick Gately *lp* Arthur Kennedy, Betta St John, Eugene Iglesias, Charlita, Roy Engel

Oklahoma (MAGNA) Todd-AO 145 (143) min

As a stage play Richard Rogers and Oscar Hammerstein II's *Oklahoma* was revolutionary, as a film it was merely extremely successful, grossing some $7 million within a year of its release in North America. MacRae is the cowboy, Jones his loved one and Steiger, a clever piece of casting, the evil man who attempts to come between them. Grahame, in another piece of surprising casting, is marvellous as the girl who 'can't say no', but Zinnemann's direction is flat and slow paced. Songs include 'Surrey with the Fringe on Top', 'Oh What a Beautiful Morning' and 'Oklahoma'.

d Fred Zinnemann *p* Arthur Hornblow Jnr *s* Sonya Levien, William Ludwig *c* Robert Surtees *lp* Gordon MacRae, Gloria Grahame, Shirley Jones, Rod Steiger, Eddie Albert, Roy Barcroft

Rage at Dawn (RKO) 87 min

This is one of the last films made by Whelan, an American director who made his name in Britain before returning to Hollywood at the outbreak of the second World War where he found himself making action pictures rather than the comedies he was known for. McCoy's gritty script has Scott as an undercover agent on the trail of the Reno Brothers (impersonated by Tucker, Healey and Naish) and romancing their sister, Powers. The action sequences are very well done but the film ends anti-climactically, but powerfully, with the brothers being lynched after they've been caught by Scott and the townspeople they've held sway over for so long.

d Tim Whelan *p* Nat Holt *s* Horace McCoy *c* Ray Rennahan *lp* Randolph Scott, Forrest Tucker, Mala Powers, J. Carrol Naish, Myron Healey, Edgar Buchanan

The Road to Denver (REP) 90 min

An amiable Western, directed with his old verve by Kane. Payne and Homeier are the brothers who end up battling each other when Payne joins Middleton in setting up a stagecoach line to Denver and Homeier joins Cobb, head of the local band of outlaws. Clyde, one-time side-kick to William Boyd's Hopalong Cassidy, and Cleef, making a name for himself as a heavy with a malevolent squint, are amongst the supporting cast.

d Joseph Kane *p* Herbert J. Yates *s* Horace McCoy, Allen Rivkin *c* Reggie Lanning *lp* John Payne, Lee J. Cobb, Skip Homeier, Ray Middleton, Andy Clyde, Lee Van Cleef

Run for Cover

(PINE-THOMAS PRODUCTIONS/PAR) vv 93 min

This is a curious but important film. The original story upon which Miller's script is based is by the writing team of Irving Ravetch and Harriet Frank and has the same allegorical feel, that strains towards the mythic, of films like **Hud** (1963) and **Hombre** (1967) which they scripted. Similarly, the generational conflict and the violent path of Cagney and Derek's journey to self-knowledge echoes the themes of Ray's undisputed masterpieces, **Johnny Guitar** (1954) and *Rebel Without a Cause* (1955).

Cagney (looking a little out of place in Western costume) is the older man who, in company with Derek, is mistaken for a train robber. Derek is shot and crippled by the posse and out of guilt the townspeople make Cagney their sheriff and Derek his deputy. Despite his doubts about Derek, Cagney blinds himself to his faults so keen is he to make of him the son he never had. So, ironically, he forces Derek down a disastrous path to self-knowledge, which begins symbolically enough with Derek smashing their father and son image in a mirror with the chair Cagney forced him to practice walking with. The end, after Derek has rebelled against his 'father' and Cagney has been forced to kill his 'son', sees Cagney form a partnership of equals with Lindfors. The film is marvellously directed by Ray who catches both the repressions of his characters and the violence necessary to break through them.

d Nicholas Ray   *p* William H. Pine, William C. Thomas
s Winston Miller   *c* Daniel Fapp   *lp* James Cagney, Viveca Lindfors, John Derek, Grant Withers, Ernest Borgnine, Ray Teal

Santa Fé Passage   (REP)   90 min
Witney's last Western for Republic, the studio where he'd worked for so long, this is a rugged actioneer. Payne is the scout ostracized by all because he's thought to have betrayed a wagon train to Apaches. Cameron, cast as an unsympathetic character for once, is the man who hires him to guide a wagon-train load of guns through hostile Indian territory and Domergue the Indian maid romanced by both men. Payne proves himself to be innocent of all the charges. Cameron, who turns out to be the villain, redeems himself by staying behind so Domergue and Payne can escape together.

d William Witney   *p* Sidney Picker   *s* Lillie Hayward
c Bud Thackery   *lp* John Payne, Faith Domergue, Rod Cameron, Slim Pickens, Anthony Caruso, Irene Tedrow

Seven Angry Men   (AA)   b/w   90 min
This is an intense biography of Abolitionist John Brown (Massey). In contrast to **Santa Fé Trail** (1940) (in which Massey also portrayed Brown), that softened its view of Brown so as not to 'distress' Southerners (and so cut into the film's market), Ullman's script follows the facts remarkably closely. Massey is the rugged, domineering father who, with his six sons, turns to more and more extreme action in his attempts to end slavery in the South. Accordingly Brown is shown neither as a hero nor is his fanaticism softened to make him more palatable. Only Hunter and Paget's romance seems out of place.

d Charles Marquis Warren   *p* Vincent M. Fennelly
s Daniel B. Ullman   *c* Ellsworth Fredericks   *lp* Raymond Massey, Jeffrey Hunter, Larry Pennel, Debra Paget, Leo Gordon, Dennis Weaver

Shotgun   (AA)   b/w   81 min
Co-scripted by Calhoun, who'd hoped to star in it before Allied Artists picked the project up, this is a better than average Western. Fredericks' cinematography is superb, Selander directs efficiently and the script is well constructed. Hayden is the deputy on the trail of Prescott, who's blown a marshal in half with his shotgun. He's joined by bounty hunter Scott and De Carlo whom he rescues from marauding Indians. The climactic shotgun battle between Prescott and Hayden is exciting, even if the outcome is predictable.

d Lesley Selander   *p* John C. Champion   *s* Clark E. Reynolds, Rory Calhoun   *c* Ellsworth Fredericks
lp Sterling Hayden, Yvonne De Carlo, Zachary Scott, Guy Prescott, Robert Wilke, Lane Chandler

The Silver Star   (LIPPERT)   b/w   73 min
In this strange movie, producer Lyon is the man elected sheriff against his wishes who refuses to buckle on his gunbelt – he doesn't believe in killing – and hides when three gunmen hired by Chaney (whom he beat for the job) come looking for him. Director Bartlett has the role of one of the killers and Buchanan is the retired marshal who finally shames Lyon into action by buckling on his guns. Clearly modelled on **High Noon** (1952), the film sadly fails because neither the action nor the script can keep the tensions inherent in the idea bubbling away for the duration of the film.

d/co-s Richard Bartlett   *p* Earle Lyon   *co-s* Ian MacDonald
c Guy Roe   *lp* Edgar Buchanan, Marie Windsor, Earle Lyon, Lon Chaney Jnr, Richard Bartlett, Morris Ankrum

Smoke Signal   (U-INTERNATIONAL)   88 min
A nice looking but rather aimless Western in which Slavin and George's screenplay follows the attempts of a small Cavalry patrol to evade an Indian war party on their trail by way of uncharted river rapids. Shot in and around the Grand Canyon the picture looks good but Andrews and an uncomfortable looking Laurie as the romantic leads and Reason, Stone and Wilke have little to do but get on each other's nerves as the journey proceeds.

d Jerry Hopper *p* Howard Christie *s* George S. Slavin, George W. George *c* Clifford Stine *lp* Dana Andrews, Piper Laurie, Rex Reason, Milburn Stone, Bob Wilke, William Talman

Stranger on Horseback (UA) 66 min

A companion piece to the director's **Stars in My Crown** (1950). As in the earlier film, which also starred McCrea, it is its hero's commitment to what he does that ensures the rule of reason and law, here civil law as opposed to the spiritual law of *Stars in My Crown*. He's a circuit judge who backs up his tomes with his guns and so makes sure that the son (McCarthy) of a powerful cattle baron (McIntire) is tried and convicted for the murder he commits and that the rule of public rather than private law returns to the range. Miroslava is the tempestuous niece, who turns against McIntire's patriarch and helps McCrea and Meyer, the spineless sheriff re-awakened to a sense of duty by McCrea. A fine Western.

d Jacques Tourneur *p* Robert Goldstein *s* Herb Meadow, Don Martin *c* Ray Rennahan *lp* Joel McCrea, Miroslava, John McIntire, Kevin McCarthy, Emile Meyer, John Carradine

Tall Man Riding (WB) 83 min

Scott is the obsessional hero in this taut little movie. He returns home to discover that gambler Barrat has double-crossed his way into a cattle barony. Malone is Barrat's daughter who finally melts Scott's heart so the two become allies. Selander directs efficiently, if unimaginatively.

d Lesley Selander *p* David Weisbart *s* Joseph Hoffman *c* Wilfrid M. Cline *lp* Randolph Scott, Dorothy Malone, Robert Barrat, Peggie Castle, John Dehner, Lane Chandler

The Tall Men (FOX) scope 122 min

Set against the epic journey of a cattle drive from Texas to Montana, *The Tall Men* tells the story of the competition between Gable and Ryan for the love of Russell. Ryan offers her position and wealth – he dreams of owning Montana – while Gable 'dreams small', offering her only love and a homestead in Prairie Dog Creek. Ryan is the aggressive Walsh hero, second cousin to *White Heat*'s James Cagney – 'Made it Ma, made it to the Top of the World' – and Gable the mature Walsh hero, a man who knows himself and therefore doesn't need to be continually testing himself. Equally significant is Russell's role. She is no prize to be given to the best man; rather she deflates the bravado of the one and the wealth of the other. Needless to say, it is she who chooses.

Clark Gable (left) mourns his brother with Jane Russell and Robert Ryan in Raoul Walsh's classic The Tall Men.

The film is also notable for two scenes which are characteristic of Walsh. The first has Gable and brother pass a couple of corpses strung up from a tree: 'Must be getting near civilization,' says Gable to Mitchell. The other is the extended sequence in which Russell and Gable spend the night in a shack cuddling together to keep warm in a fashion which has a mature but nonetheless playful sexuality about it, far removed from the infantilism of **The Outlaw** (1943). A magnificent film.

d Raoul Walsh *p* William A. Bacher, William B. Hawks *s* Sydney Boehm, Frank Nugent *c* Leo Tover *lp* Clark Gable, Jane Russell, Robert Ryan, Cameron Mitchell, Harry Shannon, Emile Meyer

Ten Wanted Men (SCOTT-BROWN/COL) 80 min

A rare Western from Humberstone, a veteran B director, who specialized in detective stories and musicals, this is a routine affair. Made by Scott's own production company, the film follows his attempts to bring law and order to the vast section of the Arizona Territory that he controls. Boone, who gives another of his fine mannered performances, is a lesser landowner who prefers the private rule of law, his law, and is willing to support his case with guns. Gamet's less than convincing screenplay is based on a story by Irving Ravetch and Harriet Frank Jnr, writers better known for their scripts for **Hombre** (1967) and **Hud** (1963).

d Bruce Humberstone *p* Harry Joe Bown *s* Kenneth Gamet *c* Wilfrid M. Cline *lp* Randolph Scott, Jocelyn Brando, Richard Boone, Alfonso Bedoya, Lee Van Cleef, Dennis Weaver

Tennessee's Partner (RKO) 86 min

Dwan's own favourite of the ten pictures he made for producer Bogeaus. Payne is the gambler in the gold-mining town of Sandy Bar, Reagan the cowpoke who saves his life and for whom, in return, Payne decides to prove that Gray, Reagan's fiancée, is a gold-digger. Fleming, who runs a saloon aptly called 'The Marriage Market', is Payne's understanding girlfriend. The complicated plot has its origins in a Brete Harte story. Alton's cinematography is simply lustrous and Dwan's direction has that melodramatic serenity that characterizes his handling of **Cattle Queen of Montana** (1954).

d Allan Dwan *p* Benedict Bogeaus *s* Milton Krims, D.D. Beauchamp, Graham Baker, Teddi Sherman *c* John Alton *lp* John Payne, Ronald Reagan, Rhonda Fleming, Coleen Gray, Angie Dickinson, Leo Gordon

Texas Lady (RKO) scope 86 min

The last film made by Whelan, an American who made his reputation in comedy and in Britain, this is a mediocre Western featuring Colbert as the crusading newspaperwoman and Sullivan as the gambler who falls for her. The title song gave Les Paul and Mary Ford one of their many hits.

d Tim Whelan *p* Nat Holt *s* Horace McCoy *c* Ray Rennahan *lp* Claudette Colbert, Barry Sullivan, Gregory Walcott, Ray Collins, Walter Sande, James Bell

Timberjack (REP) 94 min

Carmichael, as saloon owner Ralston's pianist, is the best thing in this tired actioner. Brian and Hayden are the lumberjack enemies and Ralston is the woman in the middle. Brian makes a convincing enough villain, but Hayden is unusually restrained while Ralston, as ever, is only adequate as the supposedly fiery saloon singer. Kane directs with little confidence from a script that was, by all accounts, re-written day by day.

d Joseph Kane *p* Herbert J. Yates *s* Allen Rivkin *c* Jack Marta *lp* Sterling Hayden, Vera Ralston, David Brian, Adolphe Menjou, Hoagy Carmichael, Chill Wills

Top Gun (FAME PICTURES) b/w 73 min

Hayden takes the title role in this pleasant minor Western which sees him ostracized by the townspeople he tries to help because he's a gunman. Obviously influenced by **High Noon** (1952) which introduced the theme of the lonely man of integrity contrasted with the cowardly townspeople to the genre, *Top Gun* is too predictable to be more than routine. Dehner is the baddie Hayden takes on and Booth, in another bow to *High Noon*, is the girlfriend who saves the hero's life by taking up a gun when he's about to be killed.

d Ray Nazarro *p* Edward Small *s* Richard Schayer, Steve Fisher *c* Lester White *lp* Sterling Hayden, William Bishop, John Dehner, Karen Booth, James Millican, Rod Taylor

The Treasure of Pancho Villa

(RKO) scope 96 min

This is an oddity. Busch's screenplay, which is far too talkative for the production, is also treated with too much respect by Sherman. Beginning with a flashback, a frequent device of Busch's but one that still seems fresh (if a little out of place) in the Western, the film follows Calhoun and Roland on their journey to the climax which sees them fighting off Federales who are after the gold intended for Villa. Eventually they dynamite the Federales, the gold and themselves to death.

d George Sherman *p* Edmund Grainger *s* Niven Busch *c* William Snyder *lp* Rory Calhoun, Shelley Winters, Gilbert Roland, Joseph Calleia, Fanny Schiller, Tony Carvajal

The Vanishing American (REP) b/w 90 min

A journeyman remake of George B. Seitz's controversial silent film that depicted 'the adjustment of the Indian' to the advance of the white man into his territory. For the most part a sentimental film, its prologue (which showed race succeeding race and came complete with a quotation from Herbert Spenser on the survival of the fittest) came close to claiming absolute superiority for the white race.

Kane's remake has none of this context; instead he concentrates on the action plot which features Brady as the young Indian out to stop land grabbers from taking his land and Totter as the romantic interest. Routine.

d Joseph Kane *p* Herbert J. Yates *s* Alan LeMay *c* John L. Russell *lp* Scott Brady, Audrey Totter, Forrest Tucker, Gene Lockhart, Jim Davis, Lee Van Cleef

The Violent Men aka Rough Company

(COL) scope 96 min

This is a hand-me-down version of **Jubal** (1956) with Robinson as the wheelchair-bound cattle baron, Stanwyck as his two-timing wife and Keith as her lover. Ford is the squatter who stands fast against Robinson's dreams of empire but it's the domestic drama that takes pride of place with Keith a superb villain and Stanwyck a blowzy mistress. A steamy but, oddly, insubstantial film.

d Rudolph Mate *p* Lewis J. Rachmil *s* Harry Kleiner *c* Burnett Guffey, W. Howard Greene *lp* Edward G. Robinson, Barbara Stanwyck, Brian Keith, Glenn Ford, Richard Jaeckel, Dianne Foster

White Feather (FOX) scope 102 (100) min

An intelligent, well-meaning, Indian Western severely marred by Webb's nondescript direction. Daves' script is very much in the tradition of his earlier **Broken Arrow** (1950). Lund is the Cavalry officer in charge of the resettlement of the Plains Indians and Wagner the surveyor who falls for an Indian maid (Paget, in the role she played in *Broken Arrow*) who's engaged to a young buck, Hunter, who is a friend of Wagner's. The peace treaty is saved when Wagner fights Hunter and O'Brian in single combat. Ballard's cinematography was (deservedly) much praised at the time.

d Robert Webb *p* Robert L. Jacks *s* Leo Townsend, Delmer Daves *c* Lucien Ballard *lp* Robert Wagner, John Lund, Debra Paget, Jeffrey Hunter, Noah Beery Jnr, Hugh O'Brian

Wichita (AA) scope 81 min

A superior Western in which McCrea is Wyatt Earp (whose biographer Stuart N. Lake was the film's technical advisor) given the task of cleaning up the railhead cow town by the town's elders. Ford and Bridges give him strong support as the villains he comes up against while Tourneur's direction is simple and stylish and Ullman's script action-packed.

d Jacques Tourneur *p* Walter Mirisch *s* Daniel B. Ullman *c* Harold Lipstein *lp* Joel McCrea, Vera Miles, Lloyd Bridges, Wallace Ford, Edgar Buchanan, Peter Graves

Sterling Hayden (right) and William Bishop in Top Gun.

Below: Robert Wagner as the surveyor enters Indian territory in the indifferent White Feather.

Hugh O'Brian, guns ablaze, in Gerd Oswald's exuberant The Brass Legend.

Wyoming Renegades (COL) 73 min
A rugged Western directed at breakneck speed by Sears. Carey is the badman trying to go straight with the aid of Hyer and Evans' outlaw leader Butch Cassidy. The film's climax has the ladies of the town lying in wait to ambush Evans and his men after the men of the town have fled. Energetically directed, this sequence is amongst the best ever in a B Western. One of the minor villains is Aaron Spelling, who in 1960 was to launch himself to fame as the producer of television's *Zane Grey Theatre* and later to achieve even greater fame when, in association with Leonard Goldberg, he had the idea for *Charlie's Angels*.

d Fred F. Sears *p* Wallace MacDonald *s* David Lang
c Lester H. White *lp* Phil Carey, Martha Hyer, Gene Evans, Douglas Kennedy, Don Beddoe

1956

Backlash (U) 84 min
An unusual and interesting Western, less for Sturges' oddly anodyne direction than for Chase's superior script. Mining areas he had developed with great success in the Westerns he wrote for Anthony Mann (**Winchester '73**, 1950, **Bend of the River**, 1952 and **The Far Country**, 1955), the plot features Widmark searching for the father he never knew and finding a man who sold out his partners to the Indians for a fortune in gold. The comparison with *Winchester '73* is particularly interesting: whereas in that film a son proves himself worthy of his father's name, here, after showing himself (unbeknown to himself) to be like his father, he then struggles to prove himself superior to his father. Widmark's travelling companion is Reed.

d John Sturges *p* Aaron Rosenberg *s* Borden Chase
c Irving Glassberg *lp* Richard Widmark, Donna Reed, John McIntire, Barton MacLane, William Campbell, Harry Morgan

Bandido! (UA) scope 92 min
Mitchum and Scott are the Americans who go South of the Border and end up in different camps in this lacklustre Mexican Revolution film. Roland is the revolutionary bandido and Thiess is Scott's wife, whom Mitchum finds almost as attractive as the shipment of arms he has. Felton's would-be

tongue-in-cheek script however is too low on humour and Michum's roguery is too confected for the enterprise to be taken seriously. Like his other film situated at the time of the Mexican Revolution, **Villa Rides** (1968), it's just another adventure yarn.

d Richard Fleischer *p* Robert L. Jacks *s* Earl Felton
c Ernest Laszlo *lp* Robert Mitchum, Zachary Scott, Gilbert Roland, Ursula Thiess, Henry Brandon, Douglas Fowley

The Black Whip (REGALFILMS/FOX) b/w scope 77 min
Made by independent producer Lippert's Regal Films for Fox, this bizarre quickie stars Marlowe as the meek-mannered guy who suddenly turns hero. He's the manager of a way station who defends a quartet of *femmes fatales*, Dickinson, Gray, Mara and Schuyler, who have been stranded when their coach is attacked by a band of outlaws. Richards is the whip-snapping outlaw leader. The presence of Dickinson helps edge this otherwise routine movie towards cult status.

d Charles Marquis Warren *p* Robert Stabler *s* Orville Hampton *c* Joseph Biroc *lp* Hugh Marlowe, Coleen Gray, Paul Richards, Angie Dickinson, Adele Mara, Dorothy Schuyler

Blackjack Ketchum, Desperado (COL) b/w 76 min
Another tale of a gunman trying to live down his reputation as a fast gun and forced to buckle on his gunbelt one more time before he can settle down. The second film as director by Bellamy (who was to become a prolific teleseries director), it is a well constructed and realistically fashioned Western, if a little predictable in parts. Jory is the cattle baron who tries to take over a peaceful valley and Mahoney the girl Duff romances more vigorously than is usual in Westerns.

d Earl Bellamy *p* Sam Katzman *s* Luci Ward, Jack Natteford *c* Fred Jackman Jnr *lp* Howard Duff, Victor Jory, Maggie Mahoney, Angela Stevens, Martin Garralaga, David Orrick

Blazing the Overland Trail (COL) b/w 15 chaps
This is notable only as being the last serial made. The script, by veteran Plympton (who'd written his first serial in 1931) with uncredited assistance from producer Katzman, was carefully fashioned so that virtually all the action sequences could be culled from **Overland with Kit Carson** (1939), Columbia's most successful serial. To facilitate this, in a trick common in the cheapo, cheapo world of serialdom, Roberts and Moore are dressed in costumes identical to those worn by Bill Elliott and Richard Fiske in the earlier serial.

Barton is the leader of the Black Raiders who dreams of an empire in the West but is foiled by Moore and Roberts. The direction by Bennett, serialdom's most prolific director – 52 of his 105 features are serials! – is slack, as one would expect since he was simply shooting linking material for footage that was nearly twenty years old.

d Spencer Gordon Bennett *p* Sam Katzman *s* George Plympton *c* Ira H. Morgan *lp* Lee Roberts, Dennis Moore, Norma Brooks, Gregg Barton, Kermit Maynard, Al Ferguson

The Brass Legend (UA) b/w 79 min
A marvellous Western from Oswald, a director who brought an intensity and fluidity to the B Western that seems impossible given the five- to seven-day shooting schedule it and the equally impressive **Fury at Showdown** (1957) shared. Burr and O'Brian are the baddie and peace officer respectively set on collision course when O'Brian captures Burr only to have him escape. The action is breathtaking – the climax has Burr and O'Brian racing towards each other on horseback, guns drawn – but it is Oswald's assertive camera, creating a jail break in one long take, for instance, that one remembers.

d Gerd Oswald *p* Herman Cohen *s* Don Martin
c Charles Van Enger *lp* Hugh O'Brian, Nancy Gates,
Raymond Burr, Reba Tassell, Donald MacDonald, Robert
Burton

The Broken Star (BEL-AIR) b/w 82 min
A modest actioneer. Scripted by Higgins, a writer best known
for his interesting screenplays for Anthony Mann's B thrillers
(made before he graduated to the Western and big budgets)
Railroaded and *T Men* (both 1947) and *Border Incident* (1949),
this is very similar in tone to those films. Duff is the lawman
gone wrong and Williams his fellow officer who must go after
him when he murders a rancher for gold. Selander directs
erratically, clearly unsympathetic to the script and its edgy
violence.

d Lesley Selander *p* Howard W. Koch *s* John C. Higgins
c William Margulies *lp* Howard Duff, Bill Williams, Lita
Baron, Douglas Fowley, Addison Richards, Henry Calvin

The Burning Hills (WB) scope 94 min
One of the several scripts Wallace wrote before he became
such a successful popular novelist that films were based on his
novels rather than him having to write screenplays, *The
Burning Hills* is an impressive revenge Western. Hunter is the
cowboy seeking revenge for the murder of his brother who is
forced to take to the hills himself with Wood's senorita when
the murderers set out after him. Homeier is chillingly
blood-thirsty as the son of grizzled cattle baron Teal. Strongly
reminiscent of **Hondo** (1953) in both theme and style, the
film's emphasis on youth announced a minor trend that future
Westerns would follow with a vengeance.

d Stuart Heisler *p* Richard Whorf *s* Irving Wallace
c Ted McCord *lp* Tab Hunter, Natalie Wood, Skip
Homeier, Ray Teal, Earl Holliman, Claude Akins

Canyon River (AA) scope 80 min
This is a minor actioneer. Ullman's talkative screenplay
features rancher Montgomery driving a herd of Hereford
cattle from Oregon to Texas to crossbreed them with his
Longhorns and Henderson as the trail cook he romances.
Graves is the foreman who first plans to help Sande steal the

cattle but then changes his mind and dies saving the herd for
Montgomery.

d Harmon Jones *p* Richard Heermance *s* Daniel B.
Ullman *c* Ellsworth Fredericks *lp* George Montgomery,
Peter Graves, Marcia Henderson, Richard Eyer, Walter
Sande, Alan Hale

Dakota Incident (REP) 88 min
An indifferent film, enlivened by the imaginative cinema-
tography of Haller who won an Oscar for his lighting of *Gone
With the Wind* (1939). Bank robber Robertson, lady of the
night Darnell and politico Bond are amongst the group of
people pinned down in a Dakota gully by a marauding band of
Indians. One by one they die until only Robertson and
Darnell are left alive, redeemed by their experiences.

d Lewis R. Foster *p* Michael Baird *s* Frederic Louis Fox
c Ernest Haller *lp* Linda Darnell, Dale Robertson, Ward
Bond, John Lund, Regis Toomey, Skip Homeier

The Fastest Gun Alive (MGM) b/w 92 min
Gilroy's script for this taut little Western had already formed
the basis of a teleplay, but, to eveyone's surprise, the film
turned out to be one of MGM's better grossers of that year.
Ford is the mild-mannered storekeeper trying to live down his
father's past as an expert gunman but who is forced to buckle
on his dad's gunbelt and prove he's a man. Crain is his patient
wife, Tamblyn the youngster who comes to town and
Crawford the baddie who taunts Ford with his father's name.

d/co-s Russell Rouse *p* Clarence Greene *co-s* Frank D.
Gilroy *c* George Folsey *lp* Glenn Ford, Jeanne Crain,
Broderick Crawford, Russ Tamblyn, Leif Erickson, Noah
Beery Jnr

The First Texan (AA) scope 82 min
A rather earnest and much glamourized biography of Sam
Houston. McCrea's performance as the lawyer turned hero is
simply too respectful and Haskin's direction is equally quiet.
The plot is the common one of the hero who does all he can to
resist the heroic role others thrust upon him until the very last
minute. Accordingly, McCrea spends most of the picture
trying to keep out of the fight to free Texas from Mexican
domination, until he's ordered to act by President Jackson.

d Byron Haskin *p* Walter Mirisch *s* Daniel B.
Ullman *c* Wilfrid Cline *lp* Joel McCrea, Felicia Farr, Jeff
Morrow, Wallace Ford, Abraham Sofaer, Jody McCrea

A scene from Great Day
in the Morning, *one of
the many Civil War
Westerns of the fifties.*

*Far left: Gary Cooper
and Dorothy McGuire
as the Quakers forced to
question their beliefs
when they become
embroiled in the Civil
War in* Friendly
Persuasion.

The First Travelling Saleslady (RKO) 92 min

Eastwood's first and RKO's last, this is a plodding would-be comedy constructed around a rather appealing idea. Rogers is the corset designer who heads West to peddle her wares with her secretary, Channing, when a Broadway show is closed because of a number featuring her corsets and little else. Lubin's direction is tedious and, though Channing and Rogers triumph over their weak material, the film can't sustain its slim beginnings.

d/p Arthur Lubin *s* Devery Freeman, Stephen Longstreet
c William Snyder *lp* Ginger Rogers, Carol Channing, Barry Nelson, James Arness, Clint Eastwood, Frank Wilcox

Flesh and the Spur (AIP) 80 min

The only Western, other than the four Roger Corman made for the company, produced by AIP. The script, co-written by Griffith, a Corman regular, is interesting but the direction by Cahn, who in the fifties and sixties made low-budget quickie after quickie, shows a sad decline from the majesty of his first Western, **Law and Order** (1932). Agar is the youngster seeking the murderer of his twin brother who teams up with Connors only to find out that he is the killer. The film is of historical interest only.

d Edward L. Cahn *p* Alex Gordon *s* Charles B. Griffith, Mark Hanna *c* Frederick E. West *lp* John Agar, Marla English, Touch (Mike) Connors, Raymond Hatton, Maria Monay, Kermit Maynard

Friendly Persuasion (AA) scope 140 min

This portrait of a Quaker family forced to question its beliefs by the outbreak of the Civil War is a good example of a worthy (rather than enjoyable) film. Perkins is the son, sure of his principles but worried that they might be an excuse for cowardice and Cooper his equally troubled father. Ironically for a film so concerned with principles, on its release screenwriter Wilson's name was omitted because Allied Artists exercised their 'right to deny credit to a writer revealed to be a member of the Communist party or one who refused to answer charges of Communist affiliation'.

d/co-p William Wyler *co-p* Robert Wyler *s* Michael Wilson *c* Ellsworth Fredericks *lp* Gary Cooper, Dorothy McGuire, Marjorie Main, Anthony Perkins, Richard Eyer, Robert Middleton

Fury at Gunsight Pass (COL) b/w 68 min

Lang's complex script and Sears' punchy direction make this B Western a decided cut above the average. Brian and Brand are the outlaws who try to double-cross each other in the course of a bank robbery only to lose the money. Whereupon, with their gang, they hold the whole town of Gunsight hostage until the money, hidden by their inside man, is found. Individual scenes, such as the meeting Brand holds in the

middle of the main street during a sand storm at which the outlaws threaten to kill a townsperson an hour until the missing money is found, are quite superb, though inflections towards **High Noon** (1952) seem grafted on rather than to grow naturally from the script. Long is the banker's son determined to rescue his father's good name and save the town that turned its collective back on him.

d Fred F. Sears *p* Wallace MacDonald *s* David Lang
c Fred Jackson *lp* David Brian, Neville Brand, Richard Long, Lisa Davis, Frank Fenton, Morris Ankrum

Giant (WB) 201 (197) min

Co-scripted by Moffat who successfully turned *King Lear* into a Western screenplay, *The King*, on commission from Anthony Mann just prior to the director's death, this is an epic family saga of a Western. Hudson and Dean are the rival Texas cattle barons and Taylor the Easterner who marries Hudson and befriends Dean (in the role originally intended for Alan Ladd). However, Edna Ferber's sprawling novel doesn't compress easily and its simmering tensions are hardly well served by Stevens' almost placid direction. But, in comparison to **The Big Country** (1958) which attempts a hysterical tone from start to finish, the film has an appealing classicism about it.

d/co-p George Stevens *co-p* Henry Ginsberg *s* Fred Guiol, Ivan Moffat *c* Edwin DePar, William C. Mellors
lp Rock Hudson, Elizabeth Taylor, James Dean, Mercedes McCambridge, Carroll Baker, Dennis Hopper, Sal Mineo

Great Day in the Morning (RKO) scope 92 min

An atmospheric Western. Set in the Colorado Territory just prior to the outbreak of the Civil War, Samuels' literate screenplay follows the tensions that arise when Northern and Southern partisans stir up the gold hungry prospectors and the townspeople of Denver, hungry for statehood. Neatly titled *L'Or et L'Amour* by the French, it features Stack as the hero torn between Mayo and Roman and undecided as to where his larger loyalties lie. Tourneur's direction is stronger on detail than action.

d Jacques Tourneur *p* Edmund Grainger *s* Lesser Samuels *c* William Snyder *lp* Virginia Mayo, Rogert Stack, Ruth Roman, Alex Nicol, Raymond Burr, Leo Gordon

Gun Brothers (GRAND PRODUCTIONS) b/w 79 min

Crabbe, in one of his last starring roles, returns home to find his brother, Brand, a bandit leader and sets out to catch him. A complicating wrinkle is Ansara, one-time henchman to Brand, setting up in business for himself. Salkow handles the action well, especially the climax when Brand dies at his brother's side when they take on Ansara.

d Sidney Salkow *s* Gerald Drayson Adams, Richard Schayer *c* Kenneth Peach *lp* Buster Crabbe, Ann Robinson, Neville Brand, Michael Ansara, Roy Barcroft, Slim Pickens

Gun the Man Down (UA) b/w 78 min

The directorial debut of McLaglen who was to be the director most closely associated with the genre in the sixties and seventies. The son of Victor McLaglen, he worked briefly as an assistant to Budd Boetticher and John Ford, whose style he has often, but rarely successfully, tried to imitate, usually with the assistance of Clothier, a regular cameraman to both directors. A further point of interest is the script by Kennedy, a regular writer for Boetticher, who would also become a director closely associated with the genre.

Arness is the man deserted by his companions in the middle of a bank robbery who, on his release from jail, sets out after them. When he finds them, rather than gunning them down, he decides to play a waiting game in an attempt to give them a taste of the imprisonment he suffered. Dickinson and Wilke

James Dean in Giant.

give solid performances as two of the gang, as do Meyer and Carey as representatives of the law. This is an enjoyable and significant Western.

d Andrew V. McLaglen *p* Robert E. Morrison *s* Burt Kennedy *c* William Clothier *lp* James Arness, Angie Dickinson, Robert Wilke, Emile Meyer, Harry Carey Jnr, Don Megowan

The Gunslinger

(AMERICAN RELEASING CORP/SANTA CLARA) 71 min
Featuring Garland and Haze, who were to become Corman regulars, this is the most extreme and daring of Corman's Westerns. Garland is the wife of the marshal, who takes over his job when he's killed and who comes up against Haze, a gunman hired by Hayes to drive homesteaders off land she wants to buy cheaply. A bizarre complication has Haze fall for Garland, kill Hayes (who ordered him to kill Garland) and finally be shot by Garland who is torn between love and duty. The primitive drama of the film, which parallels that, in intensity, if not achievement, of Samuel Fuller's **Forty Guns** (1957), is further exaggerated by the film being shot ankle deep in mud. But if the film is more uneven than many other B Westerns, Corman's aspirations make it simply entrancing.

d/p Roger Corman *s* Mark Hanna, Charles B. Griffith *c* Fred West *lp* John Ireland, Beverly Garland, Allison Hayes, Jonathan Haze, Martin Kingsley, Richard Miller

Hidden Guns (REP) b/w 66 min

An interesting failure of a Western. Bennett is the gambler arrested by a father and son sheriff and deputy team, Arlen, and country singer Young in his only Western. They then have to prove him guilty of murder and survive the attempts, orchestrated by Bennett, made on their lives by the likes of gunman Carradine. One of the intriguing devices director Gannaway uses is a choral group that comments on and develops the action. The gunfights and lengthy fistfight are equally well handled.

d/p/co-s Al Gannaway *co-s* Sam Roeca *c* Clark Ramsey *lp* Richard Arlen, Bruce Bennett, Faron Young, John Carradine, Angie Dickinson, Lloyd Corrigan

I Killed Wild Bill Hickok

(WHEELER COMPANY PRODUCTIONS) b/w 63 min
Written and produced by and starring Carpenter (under the name of John Forbes) this is a far better title than a film. Featuring a lot of stock footage, the film simply makes Hickok (Brown) an old-fashioned baddie who's cheating the government in a horse deal with no explanation as to why such a revered figure should turn villain and gives Carpenter the job of killing him. Talmadge directs with little belief in the project.

d Richard Talmadge *p/s* John Carpenter *c* Virgil Miller *lp* John Forbes (Carpenter), Tom Brown, Helen Westcott, Frank Carpenter, I. Stanford Jolley, Virginia Gibson

Johnny Concho (UA/KENT) b/w 84 min

An oddity. Sinatra, whose company produced the movie, plays the coward who lords it over Cripple Creek by virtue of his brother's prowess with a gun. When the brother is killed and another gunfighter, Conrad, takes his place, Sinatra first runs away, only to return, after building up his courage with help from Kirk, for the inevitable confrontation. McGuire, who co-wrote **Bad Day at Black Rock** (1955) directs laboriously. Conrad's exuberant performance is the best thing in the film.

d/co-s Don McGuire *p* Henry Sanicola, Frank Sinatra *co-s* David P. Harmon *c* William Mellor *lp* Frank Sinatra, Keenan Wynn, William Conrad, Phyllis Kirk, Wallace Ford, Howard Petrie

Jubal (COL) scope 101 min

A gripping Western. Ford, rejected by his mother who wanted him, and not his father, to drown, is befriended by Borgnine and offered a place in what seems to be a happy home, but quickly turns out to be a sexual hothouse. French, Borgnine's promiscuous wife, is attracted to Ford and flirts with him rather than her old flame, the coldblooded Steiger – 'He don't like nobody – not even himself'. Steiger, playing his role with a steady whine, turns in a fierce performance as a Western Iago who finally prompts Borgnine into a fatal gunbattle with Ford. Then Steiger eggs the posse on to lynch Ford after raping and beating up French. With her dying breath, French saves Ford and sets up the inevitable final confrontation between him and Steiger. Daves presents the characters forcefully, his swooping camera creating a sense of boxed-in tensions and sense of depth unusual in a Western.

d/co-s Delmer Daves *p* William Fadiman *co-s* Russell S. Hughes *c* Charles Lawton Jnr *lp* Glenn Ford, Ernest Borgnine, Rod Steiger, Valerie French, Charles Bronson, Jack Elam

The King and Four Queens

(UA/RUSS-FIELD-GABCO PRODUCTIONS) scope 84 min
Like so many of Walsh's later films, this austere Western mocks its hero. Gable is the weary conman out to convince the widows of four outlaw brothers that he was a member of the gang and therefore has a right to a share in the loot the husbands hid somewhere in the vicinity of the decaying farm inhabited by their mother, Van Fleet, and the wives. Full of sexual innuendo with Gable trying to charm and divide the widows and being foiled every step of the way by Van Fleet's iron-clad matriarch, the film delights in Gable's slow realization that it is he who is being manipulated. Beneath its joky surface one senses a bitter film in which the humiliation of the male hero is taken even further than in **The Sheriff of Fractured Jaw** (1959).

d Raoul Walsh *p* David Hempstead *s* Margaret Fitts, Richard Alan Simmons *c* Lucien Ballard *lp* Clark Gable, Eleanor Parker, Jean Willes, Barbara Nichols, Jo Van Fleet, Jay C. Flippen

The Last Hunt (MGM) scope 108 (103) min

One of the last films made under Schary's troubled reign as head of production at MGM, *The Last Hunt* was first eagerly promoted by him and then mutilated when it became clear

An example of Delmer Daves' camera style with its strong sense of depth from Jubal.

Clayton Moore (right) and Jay Silverheels, the best remembered Lone Ranger and Tonto respectively in The Lone Ranger, *a children's classic.*

the serial character into a swashbuckling character with great success. The result is a charmingly innocent Western with Moore, and his TV side-kick Silverheels as Tonto, preventing an Indian war and unmasking Bettger's plans to mine silver in Indian territory. Moore's wooden interpretation, with or without his mask, strangely doesn't in any way limit the film's appeal. A masterpiece of children's cinema.

So successful was the film that United Artists immediately prepared a sequel, **The Lone Ranger and the Lost City of Gold** (1958).

d Stuart Heisler *p* Willis Goldbeck *s* Herb Meadow
c Edwin DuPar *lp* Clayton Moore, Jay Silverheels, Lyle Bettger, Robert Wilke, Bonita Granville, Lane Chandler

The Man from Del Rio (UA) b/w 82 min

An offbeat Western. Quinn is the tormented Mexican gunfighter trying to drown his past in drink, who is made sheriff of a small town after fending off a group of even drunker gunmen who are harassing the good folk of the town. Having celebrated his redemption with a new suit of clothes and a new spirit to match, he discovers that as a Mexican he's not good enough to mix socially with the men whose life and property he is employed to protect. In a drunken brawl he breaks his wrist but still faces down Whitney when he tries to take over the town. Carr's screenplay makes its points incisively.

d Harry Horner *p* Robert L. Jacks *s* Richard Carr
c Stanley Cortez *lp* Anthony Quinn, Katy Jurado, Peter Whitney, John Larch, Douglas Fowley, Guinn Williams

Massacre (FOX) 76 min

A routine Western, its chilling climax notwithstanding. Clark is the government agent on the trail of gunrunners inciting Yaqui Indians. After destroying the smugglers' cache of arms Clark and the gunrunners are massacred by the Indians. The film was shot in Mexico with Roth as the romantic interest.

d Louis King *p* Robert L. Lippert Jnr *s* D.D. Beauchamp
c Gilbert Warrenton *lp* Dane Clark, James Craig, Marta Roth, Jamie Fernandez, Ferrusquilla, Miguel Torruco

The Maverick Queen (REP) scope 92 min

Kane's last big budget film for Republic, this was the studio's first film in its own anamorphic (wide-screen) process, Naturama. Theoretically based on a Zane Grey story that was 'completed by his son Romer from notes after the author's death' (an indication of the publicity value put upon Zane Grey's name), the film features Stanwyck in the title role and Sullivan as the Pinkerton agent who poses as a bandit to break up the Wild Bunch gang. A contrast between it and **Butch**

that Brooks' savage indictment of the wasteful slaughter of the buffalo spelt disaster at the box office. Taylor is the Indian-hating hunter intent on destroying the herds of buffalo because, 'One less buffalo means one less Indian' and Granger is his companion who falls in love with Paget's Indian maiden. The lengthy sequence in which the hunters massacre a herd of bison is chilling, as is the final confrontation between Granger and Taylor which has the latter freezing to death while waiting to ambush Granger. Harlan's low-key photography captures beautifully the bleak tone of Brooks' script and direction.

d/s Richard Brooks *p* Dore Schary *c* Russell Harlan
lp Robert Taylor, Stewart Granger, Lloyd Nolan, Debra Paget, Russ Tamblyn, Constance Ford

The Last Wagon (FOX) scope 99 min

Before Daves lost his way in the sixties, he produced a string of interesting Westerns. Of these, *The Last Wagon*, though not his most famous – **Broken Arrow** (1950) fits that bill – is the best. Widmark is the trapper who, after brutally revenging the murder of his Indian wife and children, leads a wagon train of virtual racists to salvation before being acquitted of the 'murders' and left free to start life anew with Farr, the one member of the wagon train to show him any decency. Widmark's journey of self-knowledge is an intensely physical one (at one point he is even 'crucified') like that of James Stewart in Anthony Mann's classic fifties Westerns.

d/co-s Delmer Daves *p* William B. Hawks *co-s* James Edward Grant, Gwen Bagni Gielgud *c* Wilfrid Cline *lp* Richard Widmark, Felicia Farr, Nick Adams, Timothy Carey, Tom Rettig, James Drury

The Lone Ranger (WB) 86 min

Moore, television's Lone Ranger for over a decade, secured the lead when Warners decided to resurrect the character on film in 1956. Heisler and writer Meadow opted to transform

Far right: Richard Widmark 'crucified' in The Last Wagon.

Cassidy and the Sundance Kid (1969) is revealing. Where the later film simply uses the character names as hooks on which to hang a story of innocent outlawry, *Maverick Queen* is full of romantic pathos and explanations. Thus, its Sundance (Brady) is a rat and Stanwyck's outlaw queen must not only die but die in love with a good man (Sullivan) rather than a bad one (Brady). Indeed she even dies to save Sullivan when the real Cole Younger, the outlaw whose identity Sullivan has borrowed, appears on the scene. An interesting period piece.

d/p Joseph Kane   *s* Kenneth Gamet, DeVallon Scott
c Jack Marta   *lp* Barbara Stanwyck, Barry Sullivan, Scott Brady, Mary Murphy, Wallace Ford, Jim Davis

Oklahoma Woman   (SUNSET)   b/w   scope   73 min
With the demented **The Gunslinger** (1956), this is the most assured of Corman's quartet of Westerns. Like so many of Corman's movies, the film centres on a dominating woman. Thus the climax has Downs forcing a pistol-packing Castle to confess and so secure the freedom of Denning, the man she loves. Denning's role is paralleled by that of Connors as the crazed gunman who loves Castle.

d/p Roger Corman   *s* Lou Rusoff   *c* Fred West   *lp* Richard Denning, Peggie Castle, Cathy Downs, Tudor Owen, Touch (Mike) Connors, Jonathan Haze

Pardners   (PAR)   vv   88 (82) min
The penultimate Martin and Lewis film and the best of the duo's efforts with Taurog, *Pardners* is a remake of the director's own **Rhythm on the Range** (1936). The plot of the earlier film is largely retained with the original Bing Crosby role being split between Martin and Lewis, Martin singing the cows to sleep and Lewis accidentally cleaning up the West. The presence of B stars, Steele, Elam and Van Cleef, give extra spice to the film.

d Norman Taurog   *p* Paul Jones   *s* Sidney Sheldon
c Daniel Fapp   *lp* Dean Martin, Jerry Lewis, Agnes Moorehead, Bob Steele, Jack Elam, Lee Van Cleef

The Peacemaker   (UA)   b/w   82 min
The directorial debut of Post, who would later become Clint Eastwood's unofficial tutor in the ways of film direction during the star's stay with the *Rawhide* teleseries and would be rewarded with big-budget films to direct like **Hang 'Em High** (1968), when Eastwood returned to America as a mega star. Mitchell is the gunman turned parson who finds he has to bring the law to the range before he can spread the good word and Merlin is the gunman brought in by Patterson to fan the flames of range war.

d Ted Post   *p* Hal R. Makelim   *s* Hal Richards, Jay Ingram
c Lester Schorr   *lp* James Mitchell, Jan Merlin, Herbert Patterson, Rosemarie Bowe, Jess Barker, Hugh Sanders

The Proud Ones   (FOX)   scope   94 min
A solid, thoughtful Western. Ryan is the marshal faced with Hunter, whose father he killed in the course of his duty, and Middleton who's scheming to turn the town wide open. The script's inflections in the direction of **High Noon** (1952) are unnecessary and cumbersome but Ryan gives real weight to the role of the uncompromising marshal. Mayo, Brennan and O'Connell give their usual sterling support.

d Robert D. Webb   *p* Robert L. Jacks   *s* Edmund North, Joseph Petracca   *c* Lucien Ballard   *lp* Robert Ryan, Virginia Mayo, Jeffrey Hunter, Robert Middleton, Walter Brennan, Arthur O'Connell

Ramsbottom Rides Again
(JACK HILTON PRODUCTIONS; GB)   b/w   92 min
English publican Askey inherits a ranch in Canada and on his arrival there discovers what remains of the Old West. The result is ruggedly proletarian farce decorated by Sabrina and with James as the unlikely villain (a role he was to repeat in the equally bizarre **Carry On Cowboy**, 1966). Listlessly directed by Baxter, it is only of curiosity value as a foreigner's view of the West that in fact reveals more about the humour of its country of origin than about the Western.

d/p/co-s John Baxter   *co-s* Basil Thomas   *c* Arthur Grant
lp Arthur Askey, Sidney James, Betty Marsden, Glenn Melvyn, Shani Wallis, Sabrina

The Rawhide Years   (U)   85 min
Curtis is the riverboat gambler, charged with a murder he didn't commit, who has to use his quick wits to save himself from both the law and baddies in this amiable Western. Kennedy is the cheerful villain (a role he specialized in during the fifties, notably in **Bend of the River**, 1952 and **The Man from Laramie**, 1957 for Anthony Mann) and Van Eyck the cold, smooth baddie. Mate directs, as energetically as ever, a plot in which confusion reigns supreme.

d Rudolph Mate   *p* Stanley Rubin   *s* Earl Felton, Robert Presnell Jnr, D.D. Beauchamp   *c* Irving Glassberg
lp Tony Curtis, Colleen Miller, Arthur Kennedy, Peter Van Eyck, William Demarest, Chubby Jones

Rebel in Town   (BEL-AIR)   b/w   78 min
An impressive B Western, this is strong on character and atmosphere. Naish is the Confederate patriarch one of whose sons accidentally kills the little boy of Payne and Roman. They seek revenge while Naish and his sons, including Smith as an instinctive killer, and Johnson and Cooper, who want to do the right thing but don't know what it is, ponder what to do. Werker, whose Westerns are far superior to his other films, directs Arnold's literate script with evident relish.

d Alfred Werker   *p* Howard W. Koch   *s* Danny Arnold
c Gordon Avil   *lp* John Payne, J. Carrol Naish, Ruth Roman, Ben Johnson, Ben Cooper, John Smith

Red Sundown   (U-INTERNATIONAL)   81 min
In this intriguing B Western, Calhoun is the gunman trying to abandon life with the gun, following the death of an old friend. But after a spell of punching cattle, he has to buckle on

Peggie Castle as the mud splattered gunslinger in Oklahoma Woman, *the best of Roger Corman's quartet of Westerns.*

John Wayne leads the settlers at the start of his long quest in John Ford's masterpiece, The Searchers.

his gunbelt again, this time supporting it with a star, to prevent a range war. Middleton is the greedy landowner who dreams of a cattle empire and Hyer the sheriff's daughter who persuades him it's the cause a gun is put to that matters. Arnold directs briskly.

d Jack Arnold *p* Albert Zugsmith *s* Martin Berkeley *c* William Snyder *lp* Rory Calhoun, Martha Hyer, Dean Jagger, Robert Middleton, James Millican, Trevor Bardette

The Searchers (WB) vv 119 min

Ford's masterpiece. Wayne is the nomad who returns home briefly, only to have that home destroyed in an Indian attack, his loved ones massacred and Wood, his niece and daughter that could have been, taken captive. He sets off on an impossible five-year search for her with the idea of killing her and her captor, Brandon's Indian Chief, Scar, who has defiled her. Wayne is accompanied by Hunter, a half-breed and adopted brother who hopes to prevent Wayne from fulfilling his grim promise. Finally after Wayne has twice lost the trail and Worden's Shakesperian Fool has twice pointed the wanderers in the right direction for the promise of the home and a rocking chair by the fire, Wayne finds Wood but is unable to kill her. So he brings her home. But if in so doing he is purged of his all-consuming bitterness, at the end of his journey, there is neither a rocking chair by the fire nor a waiting woman for him. Once the trio return, after Wood has been publicly readmitted into the family, in one of Ford's most memorable sequences, Wayne seems momentarily about to enter the house but steps aside that Hunter and Miles might enter. He remains in the doorway as the camera retreats into the comfort of the home until the door is closed, leaving Wayne outside to 'wander forever between the winds'.

What makes *The Searchers* so successful – and it was one of the most commercially successful Westerns of the fifties – is Ford's confident handling of such complex material, his ability to mix frontier slapstick (Worden, and Bond's Reverend Captain Clayton), mythic landscapes (the film contains some of the most striking location footage of the fifties) and character exploration with telling economy. At the heart of the film lies Ford's incisive disassociation of Wayne's motives for action (which lie wholly in the past and are clearly neurotic) with the results of that action (the restoration of home). Unlike earlier Ford heroes, Wayne is not part of the Westward March of Civilization; rather, like Brandon, he is an embodiment of the primitive forces that must be squashed before the foundations of civilization can be properly laid and the desert transformed into a garden. Thus, whereas for Wayne there is no rest at the completion of his quest, for Hunter the quest is merely the preparation for domesticity and marriage with Miles.

The film's sombre themes and its unexpected density, which surprised contemporary reviewers, are the culmination

Far right: Lee Marvin (left) as the chilling killer in Seven Men from Now, *the movie that marked the beginning of the partnership of producer Harry Joe Brown, star Randolph Scott and director Budd Boetticher, one of the most creative partnerships in the history of the Western.*

of Ford's deepening sense of the paradoxes that his central characters contain from **Stagecoach** (1939) onwards. But, if the action of *The Searchers* is essentially interior, its greatness lies in its fulfilling Ford's statement made just before he started shooting the film: 'I should like to do a tragedy, the most serious in the world, that turned into the ridiculous.'

d John Ford *p* Merian C. Cooper, C.V. Whitney *s* Frank S. Nugent *c* Winton C. Hoch *lp* John Wayne, Jeffrey Hunter, Vera Miles, Ward Bond, Natalie Wood, Henry Brandon, Hank Worden

Seven Men from Now (BATJAC/WB) 78 min

A marvellous movie, *Seven Men from Now* marked the beginning of the partnership of Scott, Kennedy (whose first script this is) and director Boetticher who, together with producer Harry Joe Brown, were to make a series of classic Westerns in the fifties. Scott is the man on the trail of the outlaws who killed his wife in a robbery. In the desert he meets up with a married couple, Russell and Reed, and two of the outlaws, Larch and Marvin (who gives a chilling performance) who are after the gold Reed is secretly carrying. After an Indian attack Scott kills Marvin, who dies with a smile of disbelief on his lips, and heads off with Russell.

In the later films, the possibility of starting over again that Russell represents is either absent or only available to the people Scott befriends. Similarly, in the later films the villains are not as black as Marvin. What *Seven Men from Now* has in common with the rest of the informal series is Kennedy's real wit, Boetticher's stark, yet deeply comic, direction and Scott. Like many Hollywood stars, Scott had been playing the same role for a quarter of a century, a smiling, affable, yet slightly austere man. Suddenly, as the lines on his face tightened, as his speech became increasingly clipped and he grew to look even more like W.S. Hart, Scott was frightening, a man who cultivated the past at the expense of the present. It was a role he, Kennedy and Boetticher found wonderfully resonant, pushing it first this way, then that, until by the time of **Ride Lonesome** (1959) and **Comanche Station** (1960) they were producing leisurely, almost effortless, masterpieces.

d Budd Boetticher *p* Andrew V. McLaglen, Robert E. Morrison *s* Burt Kennedy *c* William H. Clothier *lp* Randolph Scott, Gail Russell, Lee Marvin, Walter Reed, John Larch, Donald Barry

Seventh Cavalry
(PRODUCERS-ACTORS CORPORATION) 75 min

This is an oddly static Western from Lewis, a director best remembered for his unusual camera angles and mobile camera. Scott is the officer accused of cowardice for not being present at the battle of Little Big Horn who volunteers to head a burial detail to recover the bodies of the dead. The film is scarred by a script that takes itself too seriously and yet stoops to engineering an end through having the Indians scared of Custer's horse. Hale is the girl who believes in Scott.

d Joseph H. Lewis   *p* Harry Joe Brown   *s* Peter Packer
c Ray Rennahan   *lp* Randolph Scott, Barbara Hale, Jay C. Flippen, Harry Carey Jnr, Donald Curtis, Frank Wilcox

The Spoilers (U) 84 (82) min
This routine remake of Rex Beach's often-filmed novel follows the plot of the 1942 version rather than the 1930 version. Baxter takes over Marlene Dietrich's role as the dance-hall entertainer, Chandler slips into John Wayne's shoes and Calhoun is the crooked official who steals a miner's title deeds. Danton as a menacing gunman brings a touch of mania to an otherwise flat film.

d Jesse Hibbs   *p* Ross Hunter   *s* Oscar Brodney, Charles Hoffman   *c* Maury Gertsman   *lp* Anne Baxter, Jeff Chandler, Rory Calhoun, Ray Danton, Barbara Britten, John McIntire

Stagecoach to Fury (FOX) b/w scope 75 min
Decidedly routine. Tucker is the Cavalry captain who organizes his fellow stagecoach passengers when they run into a bunch of Mexican outlaws who are trying to hijack a gold shipment at a way station. As an extra twist, while they wait for death, flashbacks establish the characters' fears. The script is based on that for **Rawhide** (1951).

d William Claxton   *p* Earle Lyon   *s* Eric Norden   *c* Walter Strenge   *lp* Forrest Tucker, Mari Blanchard, Wallace Ford, Margia Dean, Rodolfo Hoyos, Paul Fix

Star in the Dust (U-INTERNATIONAL) 80 min
A superior B Western, this is one of the best of a number of Westerns that set lawmen against the people they were elected to protect. All the action takes place between sun-up and sundown as sheriff Agar ponders what to do. There's a killer due to be hanged at sundown but the cattlemen have imported gunmen to frighten the farmers who have come to town in strength to make sure that the man hangs. Erickson is the banker and true villain of the piece and the legendary Van Doren his niece and the fiancée of Agar. Director Haas, making his directorial debut here, is better known as the writer and producer of Frank Borzage's wonderful *Moonrise* (1949).

d Charles Haas   *p* Albert Zugsmith   *s* Oscar Brodney
c John L. Russell Jnr   *lp* John Agar, Richard Boone, Leif Erickson, Mamie Van Doren, Coleen Gray, James Gleason

Strange Lady in Town (WB) scope 118 min
Garson, in the title role, is the lady doctor who arrives at Santa Fé in 1879 and has to fight against social prejudice and male bigotry before she gets to practice medicine. Andrews is the doctor who romances her, Mitchell her gunslinger of a brother, while amongst her patients are Billy the Kid (Adams), Lew Wallace and Geronimo. LeRoy's direction is heavy-handed and Butler's script too cute by far, but Garson and Andrews make a likeable pair and Rosson's cinematography makes the most of the Tucson locations.

d/p Mervyn LeRoy   *s* Frank Butler   *c* Harold Rosson
lp Greer Garson, Dana Andrews, Cameron Mitchell, Lois Smith, Nick Adams, Bob Wilke

Tribute to a Badman (MGM) scope 95 min
Beautifully photographed (on location in Colorado) by Surtees, this is an intriguing little Western. Cagney, replacing Spencer Tracy who walked off the picture because of disagreements with director Wise, is the gruff cattle baron and Papas the woman he courts. Essentially a domestic Western, despite the presence of Morrow, Dano and Van Cleef as rustlers, it follows the ups and downs of Cagney and Papas' tempestuous relationship, taking time out to depict, with some accuracy, life in the old West.

d Robert Wise   *p* Sam Zimbalist   *s* Michael Blankfort
c Robert Surtees   *lp* James Cagney, Don Dubbins, Irene Papas, Vic Morrow, Royal Dano, Lee Van Cleef

Two Gun Lady (ASSOCIATED) b/w 70 min
Castle takes the title role, in this taut little revenge Western, as the girl who comes to town looking for the murderers of her parents. Unusually (but quite aptly) the heavies are played by members of the production staff, Lyon (executive producer), MacDonald (associate producer) and writer Jolley. Talman is the marshal who helps and romances Castle. The film is far better than Bartlett and Lyon's previous outing, **The Silver Star** (1955).

d/p Richard H. Bartlett   *s* Norman Jolley   *c* Guy Roe
lp Peggie Castle, William Talman, Earle Lyon, Ian MacDonald, Norman Jolley, Marie Windsor

Walk the Proud Land (U-INTERNATIONAL) scope 88 min
A leisurely Western, this tells the true story of John Philip Clum, the Indian agent at the San Carlos Apache reservation. It fails because it overstresses the domestic problems of Clum (Murphy) and his young wife (Crowley) rather than concentrating on his unique relationship with the Apache which resulted in his being able to persuade Geronimo (Silverheels in the role for the third time) to surrender. Drake is the kindly Cavalry officer who helps.

d Jesse Hibbs   *p* Aaron Rosenberg   *s* Gil Doud, Jack Sher
c Harold Lipstein   *lp* Audie Murphy, Anne Bancroft, Pat Crowley, Charles Drake, Jay Silverheels, Morris Ankrum

Westward Ho the Wagons (DISNEY) 90 min
One of the last films of the prolific Beaudine, this is a family Western for the Disney studio enlivened by a thrilling Indian battle staged by the equally prolific Yakima Canutt. Parker, fresh from his triumph in **Davy Crockett, King of the Wild Frontier** (1955), his first film for Disney, is the scout and medico who wins the Sioux's friendship when he ministers to the chief's son. Amiable and old-fashioned.

d William Beaudine   *p* Bill Walsh   *s* Tom Blackburn
c Charles Boyle   *lp* Fess Parker, Jeff York, Kathleen Crowley, Sebastian Cabot, George Reeves, Karen Pendleton

Far left: Randolph Scott as the obsessive hero of Budd Boetticher's Decision at Sundown.

James Cagney as the gruff cattle baron and Irene Papas as the woman he courts in the intriguing Tribute to a Badman.

1957

Apache Warrior (FOX) b/w scope 74 min

A real curiosity. Williams, a celebrated editor – he won an Oscar for his editing of **High Noon** (1952) – and later a studio executive at Twentieth Century Fox, is best remembered in Western circles for his fine, if over romantic, 1954 documentary, *Cowboy. Apache Warrior*, one of his few features as director, stars Larsen as the Indian scout of the title who helps round up Apaches for the Cavalry after the defeat of Geronimo and who gets caught in the complications of white man's law. Davis is the white scout sent after him who lets him go when he catches up with him. The story is supposedly based on fact.

d Elmo Williams *p* Plato Skouras *s* Carroll Young, Kurt Neumann, Eric Norden *c* John M. Nickolaus Jnr
lp Keith Larsen, Jim Davis, Rodolfo Acosta, Eugenia Paul, John Milijan, Damian O'Flynn

Badlands of Montana (FOX) b/w scope 75 min

Ullman, who scripted most of the Wayne Morris Monogram films of the early fifties (generally regarded as the last official B Western series), here returned to his old ploy of writing a gangster film in the form of a Western. Reason is the battling DA (in fact sheriff) cleaning up his town and disposing of a gang of hoods. As with most B crime sagas, it's the criminals, here Meyer and his daughter Garland (before she falls for Reason), who get the best lines and scenes, at least until the end.

d/p/s Daniel B. Ullman *c* Frederick Gately *lp* Rex Reason, Margia Dean, Beverly Garland, Keith Larsen, Robert Cunningham, Emile Meyer

The Big Land *aka* Stampeded (WB) 93 min

Routine fare. Ladd is the man of vision who unites the Texas cattlemen and farmers to build a railroad spur and so bring their markets nearer to home and bypass Caruso's cattle buyer who cheats them. Mayo is the love interest.

d Gordon Douglas *p* George C. Bertholon *s* David Dortort, Martin Rackin *c* John Seitz *lp* Alan Ladd, Virginia Mayo, Edmond O'Brien, Anthony Caruso, Julie Bishop, John Qualen

Black Patch (MONTGOMERY PRODUCTIONS/WB) 83 min

An offbeat Western. Scripted by Gordon who also takes the role of the friend turned bankrobber that marshal Montgomery is accused of murdering for the money, *Black Patch* is directed with verve by Miner, a protégé of Robert Aldrich. Pittman contributes a distinctly modern interpretation of his role as the distraught teenager who faces up to Montgomery at the climax.

d/p Allen H. Miner *s* Leo Gordon *c* Edward Colman
lp George Montgomery, Diane Brewster, Tom Pittman, Leo Gordon, Lynn Cartwright, Strother Martin

Copper Sky (REGAL FILMS) scope b/w 77 min

This is an odd Western. Norden's screenplay has for its start a striking, if not wholly original, premise: a jailbird, Morrow, and a prim schoolteacher, Gray, as the sole survivors of an Indian massacre of an entire township, trying to reach safety through hostile territory. They start off hating each other but end up in each other's arms. The film's major fault is Warren's inability to contextualize and Westernize the script's many borrowings from *The African Queen* (1952).

d Charles Marquis Warren *p* Robert Stabler *s* Eric Norden *c* Brydon Baker *lp* Jeff Morrow, Coleen Gray, Paul Brinegar, Strother Martin, John Pickard, Jack M. Lomas

The Dalton Girls (BEL-AIR) b/w 71 min

An energetic little film that works because it follows its initial premise (four daughters turning to banditry for a living when their outlaw father is killed) to its logical conclusion. Thus one girl, Davis, is an instinctive killer, two want to settle down (Edwards and George) and Anders, as the sisters' leader, wonders what to do. Russell is the gambler who romances Edwards and Hinton the detective on their trail. Needless to say, the film ends tragically with all but Edwards dead.

d Reginald Le Borg *p* Howard W. Koch *s* Maurice Tombragel *c* Carl E. Guthrie *lp* Merry Anders, Lisa Davis, Penny Edwards, Sue George, John Russell, Ed Hinton

Decision at Sundown

(SCOTT-BROWN PRODUCTIONS) 77 min
Though the plot and direction are full of the comic touches one expects from Boetticher, the mood of *Decision at Sundown* is darker than that of any other of his Westerns. Scott arrives in town intent on revenging himself on Carrol whom he holds responsible for his wife's death, only to find out that it was his wife and not Carrol who was to blame. When he still demands revenge, French, Carrol's bride-to-be, shoots Carrol in the shoulder to prevent him being murdered by Scott in 'fair play'.

Scott's obsession, which for a time makes him totally deranged, and unlike the grim-faced, bitter, lonely men he usually plays for Boetticher, suggests the (superior) performances James Stewart gave in Anthony Mann's Westerns.

d Budd Boetticher *p* Harry Joe Brown *s* Charles Lang *c* Burnett Guffey *lp* Randolph Scott, John Carrol, Karen Steele, John Archer, Noah Beery Jnr, Valerie French

The Deerslayer (FOX) scope 76 min

A quickie that has its origins somewhere in Fenimore Cooper's often-filmed classic. Set in pre-Colonial times, it features Flippen as the scalp-hunting trader and Barker as the frontier scout of the title who comes to the rescue of Flippen and his daughters, Moreno and O'Donnell, when the Hurons demand the return of the scalps Flippen has taken. Inept, but not as inept as Lew Landers' 1943 version of the novel.

d/p/co-s Kurt Neumann *co-s* Carroll Young *c* Karl Struss *lp* Lex Barker, Rita Moreno, Forrest Tucker, Cathy O'Donnell, Jay C. Flippen, Carlos Rivas

The Domino Kid (RORVIC PRODUCTIONS) b/w 74 min

The first of Calhoun's independent productions, this is a serviceable revenge Western. Calhoun plays the son who, on his return from the Civil War, sets off in search of the five outlaws who gunned down his father and ran off with his cattle. A sub-plot features Duggan as a moneylender trying to steal Calhoun's ranch from under him. Nazarro, a veteran of series Westerns, directs with an eye to the action.

d Ray Nazarro *p* Rory Calhoun, Victor M. Orsatti *s* Kenneth Gamet *c* Irving Lippman *lp* Rory Calhoun, Kristine Miller, Andrew Duggan, Peter Whitney, Roy Barcroft, Ray Corrigan

Dragoon Wells Massacre (AA) scope 88 min

A beautiful looking actioneer courtesy of Clothier's magnificent location cinematography. O'Keefe leads a party through hostile Indian territory that contains a killer, Sullivan, and an entertainer, Jurado, amongst others. Douglas' screenplay is fairly predictable but Schuster's beefy direction and the cast produce a mildly entertaining movie.

d Harold Schuster *p* Lindsley Parsons *s* Warren Douglas *c* William Clothier *lp* Barry Sullivan, Dennis O'Keefe, Mona Freeman, Katy Jurado, Jack Elam, Sebastian Cabot

Drango (EARLMAR PRODUCTIONS) b/w 92 min

Made by Chandler's own production company, *Drango* is an intriguing film. Set in the reconstruction period immediately after the Civil War, Bartlett's screenplay features Chandler as the new military Governor of Georgia which has just been ravished by Sherman's march to the sea, a campaign he took part in. Howard (the son of Leslie Howard) is the leader of a group trying to continue the struggle against the Union and Dru the daughter of a Union sympathizer Chandler can't stop a mob from lynching. The direction of Bartlett and Bricken is uneven but Howe's cinematography is wonderfully fluent.

co-d/p/s Hall Bartlett *co-d* Jules Bricken *c* James Wong Howe *lp* Jeff Chandler, Joanne Dru, Julie London, Ronald Howard, Donald Crisp, Morris Ankrum

Duel at Apache Wells (REP) scope b/w 70 min

An amiable film from veteran Kane. Cooper is the son who, on his return home, finds his father's ranch threatened by Davis, a rustler turned rancher who fences in the only water hole in the vicinity. A duel between Cooper and Davis settles matters once Steele, as Davis' henchman, has failed to gun Cooper.

d/p Joseph Kane *s* Bob Williams *c* Jack Marta *lp* Anna Marie Alberghetti, Ben Cooper, Jim Davis, Harry Shannon, Bob Steele, Ian MacDonald

Forty Guns (GLOBE ENTERPRISES) scope b/w 80 min

This is an even more extreme film than **I Shot Jesse James** (1949). In the earlier film, the narrative line was clearly visible, in this the narrative structure is so brutally handled that on the level of plot the film is almost incomprehensible. This stylistic hysteria exactly mirrors its subject, the love of Sullivan for Stanwyck whose brother, Ericson kills Sullivan's brother (Barry) and forces Sullivan (who has not killed a man for ten years) to kill him. Fuller intended the film to end with Ericson holding Stanwyck in front of him as a shield, taunting Sullivan to shoot and being surprised when Sullivan calmly shot and killed first Stanwyck and then him. In the released version this is altered and Stanwyck is only wounded, but the effect is the same. Ericson dies crying 'I'm killed Mr Bonnell, I'm killed' and Sullivan walks past the bodies saying coldly 'Get a doctor, she'll live.' The film then closes with Sullivan leaving town and Stanwyck running after him, but their coming together is irrelevant.

The violence of Stanwyck and Sullivan's relationship is contrasted with the ease of that of Barry and Brent, celebrated in one of Fuller's most famous shots, of Brent through a gun barrel that tracks into a close-up of her and then cuts to her and Barry kissing, that Jean Luc Godard imitated in his first film, *A Bout de Souffle* (1960). It is this, the film's stylistic hysteria, that is its most notable feature: the sudden cuts from long shots of Stanwyck at the head of a table at which sit some forty gunmen to huge isolating close-ups of Sullivan and, most impressive of all, the famous 'walk' of Sullivan, seen mostly in rapidly cut close-ups of eyes and feet, as he bears down on a nervous gunman whom he defeats as much by moral authority as physical superiority.

The film's reception remains the quintessential example of the contrasting attitudes to Hollywood of American and European critics: in America it was (and mostly still is) roundly condemned for its tattiness; in Europe it was wildly praised for its primitive vigour.

d/p/s Samuel Fuller *c* Joseph Biroc *lp* Barbara Stanwyck, Barry Sullivan, Dean Jagger, Gene Barry, Eve Brent, Hank Worden, John Ericson

Fury at Showdown

(BOB GOLDSTEIN PRODUCTIONS) b/w 75 min
A stylistic tour de force and undoubtedly Oswald's best film,

John Ericson tries to shield himself with his sister, Barbara Stanwyck, to no avail in the climactic moment of Sam Fuller's extravagant Forty Guns.

Below: *An example of the studied formalism of Gerd Oswald's masterpiece,* Fury at Showdown. *John Derek (centre) is the gunman trying to go straight.*

Audie Murphy preparing his troops for an Indian attack in The Guns of Fort Petticoat.

Fury at Showdown has a formal excellence that belies its five-day shooting schedule and shames many a bigger budgeted movie. Derek is the soured gunman trying to go straight, Adams his ebullient, trusting younger brother trying to help him and Clarke the crooked attorney lusting for revenge – it was his brother whom Derek shot in a fair fight. Clarke first tries to swindle Derek out of the family ranch and then sets his hired gunman, Smith, on to him, after killing Adams. Plot and characterization are stark. Oswald's direction is even starker as his camera gazes impassively at the characters trapped in the net of his gaze amidst sets shorn of the normal bits and pieces of decor. Rarely has economy been put to such a positive use. The conclusion has Derek shoot Smith and ensure Clarke is turned over to the law before relaxing in the arms of Craig who has spent the entire film wondering whether she loves him.

d Gerd Oswald *p* John Beck *s* Jason James *c* Joseph La Shelle *lp* John Derek, John Smith, Nick Adams, Gage Clarke, Carolyn Craig, Robert E. Griffin

Gun for a Coward (U-INTERNATIONAL) scope 88 min
One of the few films made by Biberman as director, an actor turned acting coach who once taught Marilyn Monroe and Tony Curtis. Hunter is considered a coward by his older brothers Stockwell and MacMurray because of his distaste for violence (and because he's been smothered by his mother, Hutchinson). Stockwell is the tearaway and MacMurray the sober brother who loses Rule to Hunter. The film's major point of interest, beyond being part of the cycle of 'youth' Westerns, is the contrasting acting styles of its principals, especially between MacMurray, and Stockwell's James Dean-inspired histrionics.

d Abner Biberman *p* William Alland *s* R. Wright Campbell *c* George Robinson *lp* Fred MacMurray, Jeffrey Hunter, Janice Rule, Dean Stockwell, Josephine Hutchinson, Chill Wills

Gun Glory (MGM) scope 89 min
Granger is the gunman who, after a three-year absence, returns home to find his wife dead and his son (played by director Rowland's own son) and the townspeople resentful of him. All changes when the town is threatened by Johnson and his gang. Granger protects the town, thus proving to the people that violence has to be met by violence, at least

sometimes, an unusual moral to come from writer Ludwig who was better known for his scripts for the Hardy Family series. Routine fare.

d Roy Rowland *p* Nicholas Nayfack *s* William Ludwig *c* Harold J. Marzorati *lp* Stewart Granger, Rhonda Fleming, Chill Wills, Steve Rowland, Arch Johnson, James Gregory

Gunfight at the O.K. Corral (PAR) VV 122 min
An enormously influential film. Its great success at a time when less Westerns were being made helped reshape Hollywood's attitude to the genre with the result that by the sixties big budget Westerns were the norm and B features just a memory. Sturges and Uris' concentration on the climactic gunfight itself (which lasts some six minutes of screen time) has the unfortunate result of making its participants – Douglas as Doc Holliday, Lancaster as Wyatt Earp and Bettger as the leader of the Clanton clan – mere cyphers, let alone historical figures. The result is an impressive but oddly disjointed Western that for all its pyrotechnics seems flat.

Sturges later made a bitter and much better sequel, **Hour of the Gun** (1967).

d John Sturges *p* Hal B. Wallis *s* Leon Uris *c* Charles Lang Jnr *lp* Burt Lancaster, Kirk Douglas, Rhonda Fleming, John Ireland, Jo Van Fleet, Lyle Bettger

The Guns of Fort Petticoat (U-INTERNATIONAL) 82 min
Murphy's first independent production, despite the presence of Brown as producer and Marshall as director is a routine affair. Doniger's screenplay is unable to make the most of the simple but effective idea behind William Harrison's original story: Murphy and a group of women holding off an Indian attack. Murphy is the liberal officer who rebels rather than go through with the Sand Creek Massacre and returns to Texas to defend the unprotected women he knows the Indians will seek their revenge on.

d George Marshall *p* Harry Joe Brown *s* Walter Doniger *c* Ray Rennahan *lp* Audie Murphy, Kathryn Grant, Hope Emerson, Jeff Donnell, Jeanette Nolan, Ray Teal

Gunsight Ridge (UA) b/w 85 min
McCrea is the undercover agent and Stevens the outlaw masquerading as a mine owner in this routine film. Richards

is the sheriff killed by Stevens when he grows suspicious of Stevens and Weldon the sheriff's daughter who wins McCrea after he's pinned on the sheriff's badge. Laszlo's beautiful cinematography is wasted by Lyon's lacklustre direction.

d Francis D. Lyon   *p* Robert Bassler   *s* Talbot and Elizabeth Jennings   *c* Ernest Laszlo   *lp* Joel McCrea, Mark Stevens, Joan Weldon, Addison Richards, Darlene Fields, Jody McCrea

The Halliday Brand
(COLLIER YOUNG ASSOCIATES)   b/w   77 min
A marvellous film. Bond is the domineering patriarch of a sheriff and Cotten the son who must stand up to him to achieve his own identity. Eventually when Bond refuses to stop a lynch mob out to string up a half-breed, Cotten rebels against his father and is branded an outlaw. The intensity of Lewis' direction can be judged from the fact that the final confrontation sees a dying Bond still trying to kill his son but collapsing before he can pull the trigger. This is undoubtedly the most powerful of Lewis' Westerns in the fifties.

d Joseph H. Lewis   *p* Collier Young   *s* George W. George, George S. Slavin   *c* Ray Rennahan   *lp* Joseph Cotten, Ward Bond, Viveca Lindfors, Betsy Blair, Glenn Strange, Jay C. Flippen

The Hard Man   (ROMSON PRODUCTIONS)   80 min
Madison is the too-quick-on-the-trigger Texas Ranger who resigns to become a deputy sheriff and immediately becomes involved in a range war with Greene (and an affair with Greene's wife, French). But, though the film makes token bows towards modernity, the film is essentially an old-fashioned Western. Accordingly, French seems out of place, her character being both too rounded and too unsympathetic.

d George Sherman   *p* Helen Ainsworth   *s* Leo Katcher   *c* Henry Freulich   *lp* Guy Madison, Valerie French, Lorne Greene, Robert Burton, Trevor Bardette, Myron Healey

The Hired Gun   (RORVIC)   b/w   scope   63 min
Independently produced by Calhoun and his agent, this odd Western sees him as the professional gunman hired to track down and bring back escaped murderess Francis. Convinced

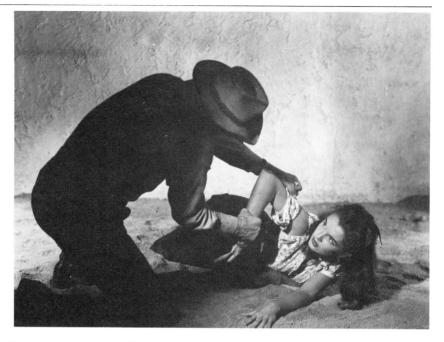

by her protestations of innocence when he captures her, Calhoun sets out to find the guilty men. Nazarro directs efficiently if anonymously, as one would expect from a series veteran.

Luana Patten under attack in the thrillerish Joe Dakota.

d Ray Nazarro   *p* Rory Calhoun, Victor M. Orsatti   *s* David Lang, Buckley Angell   *c* Harold J. Marzorati   *lp* Rory Calhoun, Anne Francis, Vince Edwards, Chuck Connors, John Litel, Guinn Williams

The Iron Sheriff   (GRAND PRODUCTIONS)   b/w   73 min
Lester's clever script has Hayden as the sheriff who first supplies the evidence that convicts his son, Hickman, of murder and then disproves it and tracks down the guilty party, Donovan, in time to save his son's life. Dehner, as the silver-tongued lawyer who pleads for Hickman, has the best role. An interesting feature of the film is its tone which uses a suspense gimmick – the question of whether Hayden will bring Donovan in like a good sheriff or will kill him in a cold-blooded manner as he threatens to do.

d George Marshall   *p* Harry Joe Brown   *s* Seeleg Lester   *c* Kenneth Peach   *lp* Sterling Hayden, Constance Ford, Darryl Hickman, King Donovan, John Dehner, Kent Taylor

Joe Dakota   (U-INTERNATIONAL)   79 min
Clearly influenced by **Bad Day at Black Rock** (1955), this intelligently scripted film stars Mahoney as the Cavalry officer who comes looking for an old Indian who was his scout. McGraw is the villain who organized the lynch mob that hanged the Indian in order to gain possession of his oil-rich land and Patten the girl who helps Mahoney. Though the film lacks the vigour of *Bad Day at Black Rock* with its attacks on racism and civic cowardice, it remains an unusually thoughtful movie.

d Richard Bartlett   *p* Howard Christie   *s* William Talman, Norman Jolley   *c* George Robinson   *lp* Jock Mahoney, Luana Patten, Charles McGraw, Claude Akins, Lee Van Cleef, Anthony Caruso

Last of the Badmen   (AA)   scope   80 min
This is a silly but enjoyable minor Western. Ullman and Chantler's script has Kennedy's gang of outlaws springing wanted men from jail, using them in robberies and, when the price on their heads has risen high enough, turning them in, or shooting them for the bounty. Montgomery is the Chicago

Far left: Ward Bond as the stern father and slack sheriff in The Halliday Brand.

detective masquerading as a badman who manages to put the gang out of business before the price on his head rises too high.

d Paul Landres *p* Vincent M. Fennelly *s* Daniel B. Ullman, David Chantler *c* Ellsworth Fredericks *lp* George Montgomery, Keith Larsen, Douglas Kennedy, James Best, Addison Richards, Meg Randall

The Lonely Man (PAR) vv 87 min

This is an interesting minor Western. In contrast to most of the father-son Westerns of the fifties that emphasize the adolescent (usually trying to overcome the dead weight of the past), this centres as much on the father, Palance, as on the son, Perkins in one of his few Western outings. Palance is the reformed outlaw who returns home to make his peace with his son who hates him for deserting his mother. As such it's a harsher, more psychologically complex version of **The Shepherd of the Hills** (1941); but with an equally sentimental ending. Perkins and Palance act well together and Brand and Van Cleef are suitably threatening as Palance's old cronies who come seeking vengeance.

d Henry Levin *p* Pat Duggan *s* Harry Essex *c* Lionel Lindon *lp* Jack Palance, Anthony Perkins, Elaine Aiken, Neville Brand, Lee Van Cleef, Elisha Cook Jnr

Man in the Shadow *aka* Pay the Devil
(U-INTERNATIONAL) b/w scope 80 min

An intriguing contemporary Western in which Welles, in his only ever Western, is the cattle baron who rules the range and Chandler is the newly appointed sheriff who crosses him when he investigates the death of one of Welles' Mexican ranch hands. Chandler refuses to drop the case, even when local citizens press him and Welles has two of his hands drag him through the town from the back of a pick-up. Finally Chandler demonstates that foreman Larch is guilty of the murder. Welles, as ever, dominates the film, overbalancing its structure by his sheer presence, transforming an intended allegory about Fascism and corruption into an exercise in acting technique.

d Jack Arnold *p* Albert Zugsmith *s* Gene L. Coon *c* Arthur E. Arling *lp* Jeff Chandler, Orson Welles, Colleen Miller, John Larch, Joe Schneider, Leo Gordon

Night Passage (U-INTERNATIONAL) technirama 90 min

This is the film that Anthony Mann was scheduled to direct but backed out of at the last minute because he thought Chase's script was too weak. Against all advice Stewart

James Craig (left) and William Talman vie for the support of the townspeople in The Persuader, *one of the first Westerns made specifically for the Midwest Bible Belt market.*

continued with Neilson replacing Mann as director. Stewart's reason for making the film was that he played the accordion in it and was keen to show off his musical as well as acting abilities. The result is a Chase-Stewart Western that lacks the intensity of **Winchester '73** (1950), in short, that lacks Mann as director to enliven its tale of two brothers, one bad, one good. Where Mann reduces Chase's explanations to ellipses, Neilson structures his film around them. The plot has Stewart working for the railroad and Murphy trying to rob it. Neilson worked mostly for Disney subsequently.

d James Neilson *p* Aaron Rosenberg *s* Borden Chase *c* William Daniels *lp* James Stewart, Audie Murphy, Dan Duryea, Dianne Foster, Elaine Stewart, Brandon de Wilde

The Oklahoman (AA) scope 81 min

A low-budget epic with McCrea in fine form as the medico whose practice grows with the state of Oklahoma. Dexter and Dick are the brother cattle barons who run the territory and whose paths he crosses. Ullman handles the growing enmity between then well while Lyon mounts an exciting climactic gunfight that leaves McCrea wounded and Dexter dead.

d Francis D. Lyon *p* Walter Mirisch *s* Daniel B. Ullman *c* Carl Guthrie *lp* Joel McCrea, Barbara Hale, Brad Dexter, Douglas Dick, Gloria Talbott, Anthony Caruso

The Parson and the Outlaw
(CHARLES B. ROGERS PRODUCTIONS) 71 min

A throwback to Westerns of a decade earlier in looks and style, this film is directed and co-scripted by Drake, a veteran who'd written for Tom Mix, George O'Brien and Johnny Mack Brown amongst others. In the company of Westerns like **Forty Guns, The Tall T** and **The Tin Star** (all 1957), *The Parson and the Outlaw* looks as old-fashioned as it sounds. Billy the Kid (Dexter) is the hero, trying to forget his past as a gunman but forced back into outlawry when his friend the local parson is murdered. Tufts is the villain.

d/co-s Oliver Drake *p* Robert Gilbert, Charles Rogers *co-s* John Mantley *c* Clark Ramsey *lp* Anthony Dexter, Sonny Tufts, Marie Windsor, Charles Rogers, Robert Lowery, Bob Steele

Pawnee (REP) 80 min

This is a mediocre Indian Western. Montgomery is the adopted (white) son of a Pawnee chief who takes the job of scout to a wagon train on the Oregon Trail 'to learn the ways of the white man' – the dialogue is that cliched. Horvath is his rival who briefly wrests control of the tribe from him and leads them against the wagon train from which Montgomery has been banished as a treacherous renegade. The climax has Montgomery bringing the Seventh Cavalry to sort matters out, after which, naturally, he rejects his Pawnee love, Austin, for his white one, Albright.

d/co-s George Waggner *p* Jack J. Gross, Philip N. Krasne *co-s* Louis Vittes, Endre Bohem *c* Hal McAlpin *lp* George Montgomery, Bill Williams, Lola Albright, Charles Horvath, Charlotte Austin, Raymond Hatton

The Persuader (WORLD-WIDE/AA) b/w 72 min

A religious Western in which Talman is the preacher who arrives in town to discover his brother murdered because he tried to resist Craig (who runs the town) and Hickman the son bent on revenge. Kenyon's script has Talman's preaching turn the cowed townspeople into strong civic-minded citizens who force Craig to quit town, after they've built a church. The film's box-office success led to other producers creating Westerns specifically for the Bible Belt market.

d/p Dick Ross *s* Curtis Kenyon *c* Ralph Woolsey *lp* William Talman, James Craig, Darryl Hickman, Kristine Miller, Georgia Lee, Gregory Walcott

Quantez (U-INTERNATIONAL) scope 80 min
An oddly listless film. Well-mounted and handsomely photographed, the script is too meandering to overcome the routine
plot which has Larch and his outlaw gang trapped in a ghost
town by an Apache war party. After far too much discussion,
Gavin and Malone survive, courtesy of MacMurray's tired
gunman. Barton, as the peddler who gets caught up with
them (and sings the title song), has the best part.

d Harry Keller *p* Gordon Kay *s* R. Wright Campbell
c Carl E. Guthrie *lp* Fred MacMurray, Dorothy Malone,
James Barton, John Larch, John Gavin, Sydney Chaplin

The Quiet Gun (REGAL FILMS) scope b/w 77 min
Tucker, in the title role, is the sheriff who has to confront the
people of the town who turn into a mob when egged on by
Brown and Van Cleef in this interesting film. The pair have
framed rancher Davis hoping to take over his spread when
he's been lynched. Claxton directs amiably.

d William Claxton *p* Earle Lyon *s* Eric Norden
c John Mescall *lp* Forrest Tucker, Mara Corday, Jim Davis,
Lee Van Cleef, Tom Brown, Kathleen Crowley

The Restless Breed (FOX) 86 (81) min
For his last Western, veteran director Dwan transforms
Fisher's crude revenge plot into a gentle comedy. Brady is the
son of a government agent out to revenge his father's death,
Davis the outlaw leader who inhabits a Mexican-American
border town and Bancroft the girl who gets her man. Made on
a miniuscule budget, the film has an austerity and formality
about it that few films achieve. As a delightful touch (and a
throwback to the days of silent cinema) Dwan has the
characters appear to be perpetually eavesdropping on each
other. A marvellous film.
The music is by the producer's son, Edward Alperson Jnr.

d Allan Dwan *p* Edward L. Alperson *s* Steve Fisher
c John W. Boyle *lp* Scott Brady, Anne Bancroft, Jim
Davis, Jay C. Flippen, Rhys Williams, Leo Gordon

Revolt at Fort Laramie
(BEL-AIR PRODUCTIONS) 73 min
A routine film from Selander without any of the style that
made his series Westerns so charming. Dennis' script features
a Cavalry fort divided by the outbreak of the Civil War until
Palmer's Union troops and Dehner's Confederates are re-
united by the common enemy: Indians. A further complication is the $50,000 in gold, eyed by the Confederate troops,
that Little's Red Cloud demands to sign a peace treaty.

d Lesley Selander *p* Howard W. Koch *s* Robert C. Dennis
c William Margulies *lp* John Dehner, Gregg Palmer,
Frances Helm, Don Gordon, Eddie Little, Robert Keys

Ride a Violent Mile (FOX) b/w scope 80 min
A routine quickie enlivened by Warren's economic direction.
Edwards is the Union agent posing as a dance-hall girl in an
attempt to prevent the Confederates trading cattle for military
assistance with Mexico. Agar is her boyfriend and helper.
Together they stampede the cattle and the Confederate plans.

d Charles Marquis Warren *p* Robert Stabler *s* Eric
Norden *c* Brydon Baker *lp* John Agar, Penny Edwards,
John Pickard, Bing Russell, Richard Shannon, Charles Gray

The Ride Back
(UA-THE ASSOCIATES AND ALDRICH COMPANY) b/w 79 min
This unusual Western features producer Conrad as the
lawman taking Quinn back to Texas to face a murder trial.
The four-day journey becomes a test of character of each with
Quinn's blustering insolence crumbling and Conrad begin-
ning to doubt his captive's guilt. After Conrad is wounded in
an Indian attack, Quinn escapes and then returns to help him

and the young girl they've picked up along the way back to
safety, even though it means facing a murder trial. The film,
Miner's directorial debut, was supervised by Robert Aldrich.

d Allen H. Miner *p* William Conrad *s* Anthony Ellis
c Joseph Biroc *lp* William Conrad, Anthony Quinn, Lita
Milan, George Trevino, Victor Millan, Joe Dominguez

Ride Out for Revenge
(BRYNA PRODUCTIONS) b/w 78 min
With the series Western dead and 'adult/serious' Westerns
doing big business at the box office, the mid-fifties saw a
number of low-budget would-be 'adult' Westerns. This is
one. Producer Retchin's screenplay operates on the simple
principle of inversion. Thus the Indians are heroic and the
Cavalry (in the main) drunken and cowardly. In particular,
Bridges is the corrupt officer in charge of the enforced move
of the Cheyenne from their ancestral home and Calhoun the
scout who tries to alleviate the Indians' troubles which
intensify when gold is found on the land intended to be their
new reservation. Unlike John Ford's **Cheyenne Autumn**
(1964) which fails because it is too general, *Ride Out for
Revenge* fails because it is too melodramatic but it is
nonetheless interesting.

d Bernard Girard *p/s* Norman Retchin *c* Floyd Crosby
lp Rory Calhoun, Gloria Grahame, Lloyd Bridges, Joanne
Gilbert, Vince Edwards, John Merrick

Run of the Arrow (GLOBE ENTERPRISES) scope 85 min
Fuller's cinema, as has been said so many times, is one of
primitive emotions and visceral paradoxes. *Run of the Arrow*,
his most accessible film, demonstrates this in its very
structure. Thus the film begins and ends with Steiger
shooting the same bullet at the same man (Meeker) and the
plot has him become a Sioux, rather than accept the defeat of
the South by the North, before being forced, with the Sioux,
to become an American. The result is Fuller's most compelling treatment of (national) identity as the film remorselessly
works through the implications of national allegiance.
The film's sympathetic treatment of the Indians, who are
seen as, above all, cultured rather than primitive – in a
wonderful joke Flippen explains that, although he could have
become a chief in his tribe, he quit to drift because he
'couldn't stand the politics' – explains the presence of McCoy
in his first Western for some fifteen years as the army officer
who signs the peace treaty with the Sioux. In 1932 McCoy
made **End of the Trail,** a film which dealt with remarkably
similar themes.
Montiel was dubbed by Angie Dickinson.

*Rod Steiger (centre) as
the Southerner who
attempts to become a
Sioux but finally
becomes an American in
Sam Fuller's* Run of
the Arrow.

d/p/s Samuel Fuller c Joseph Biroc lp Rod Steiger, Brian Keith, Ralph Meeker, Sarita Montiel, Tim McCoy, Jay C. Flippen

Shoot Out at Medicine Bend (WB) 87 min

The presence of Garner (in one of his first roles) and Dickinson enlivens this otherwise routine offering. Scott is the Cavalry officer on the trail of the men who sold his brother's outfit faulty ammunition and so caused their death at the hands of the Sioux. The plot looks back to that of **The Man from Laramie** (1955) but Beauchamp and Battle's screenplay and Bare's direction pale beside the majesty of that film.

d Richard L. Bare p Richard Whorf s John Tucker Battle, D.D. Beauchamp c Carl Guthrie lp Randolph Scott, James Craig, Angie Dickinson, James Garner, Gordon Jones

Sierra Stranger (COL) b/w 74 min

A decidedly minor problem Western that borrows its theme from Nicholas Ray's **Run for Cover** (1955) but treats it far more crudely. Duff is the Samaritan who rescues and befriends Kemmer only to discover, when he robs a stage and turns on him, that he's bad through and through. Former singing star Foran has a small role as the only other character who believes in Kemmer. Sholem directs awkwardly.

d Lee Sholem p Norman T. Herman s Richard J. Dorso c Sam Leavitt lp Howard Duff, Gloria McGhee, Dick Foran, Ed Kemmer, John Hoyt, Barton MacLane

Slim Carter (U-INTERNATIONAL) 82 min

An amusing spoof on Hollywood and the Western in which Mahoney is the egotistical cowboy transformed into a star by his first film and Adams the press agent who discovered him and is given the job of nursing him along when the studio discovers just how selfish he is. Hovey is the child who wins a month's stay with the star as a contest prize and quickly humanizes him. Johnson, as a stuntman, and Moore, as the sex symbol Mahoney briefly romances, offer sterling support.

The story, which is very similar to that of **Callaway Went Thataway** (1951), was very loosely based on the career of William Boyd for whom David Bramson, who wrote the original script with his wife, Mary McCall Jnr, had worked in the thirties.

d Richard Bartlett p Howie Horwitz s Montgomery Pittman c Ellis W. Carter lp Jock Mahoney, Julie Adams, Tim Hovey, Ben Johnson, Joanna Moore, Maggie Mahoney

The Tall Stranger (MIRISCH) scope 81 min

Briskly directed by Carr, who'd made some interesting Westerns with Bill Elliott earlier, this is an old-fashioned Western, its 'Damms' and 'Hells' notwithstanding. McCrea is the wounded Union officer who tries to mediate when a wagon train of Confederates homestead the range ruled by his half-brother Kelley. Ansara, as a bandit using the region, provides a sub-plot. McCrea projects his usual air of amiable authority and Mayo is the active heroine.

d Thomas Carr p Walter Mirisch, Richard Heermance s Christopher Knopf c Wilfrid Cline lp Joel McCrea, Virginia Mayo, Barry Kelley, Michael Ansara, Leo Gordon, Ray Teal

The Tall T (COL) 77 min

A marvellous Western, *The Tall T* contrasts a phlegmatic, world-weary (and slightly puritanical) hero, Scott, with a flamboyant yet desperately lonely, homestead-yearning villain, Boone, and effortlessly moves from comedy – the opening is virtually a parody of **Shane** (1953) – to violence and on to tragedy. The bleakest of Boetticher's Westerns, it relentlessly moves towards the final gunfight that both hero and villain try to avoid before admitting from their various perspectives that 'some things a man can't ride around'. The end, however, is no vindication of Scott, but rather a sad reminder of the inevitable roles that Scott and Boone have chosen to imprison themselves within. Homeier and Silva provide sharply etched performances as the young gunmen, the one aping Boone, the other desperate for affection from anybody.

d Budd Boetticher p Harry Joe Brown s Burt Kennedy c Charles Lawton Jnr lp Randolph Scott, Richard Boone, Maureen O'Sullivan, Skip Homeier, Henry Silva, Arthur Hunnicutt

3:10 to Yuma (COL) b/w 92 min

A rancher, Heflin, agrees to take a captured outlaw, Ford, whose gang promise to free him, to Yuma and the marshal for a reward which exactly matches the price he has to pay for water supplies to his drought-stricken land. Acknowledged as a classic Western, the formal perfection of *3.10 to Yuma* – close-ups alternating with crane shots, a psychological drama indoors alternating with the natural drama of the parched land waiting for the coming of water – defuses the uneasy contrast between Ford's amiable, but deadly, scoundrel and Heflin's distress at his failing ranch and the failure of those around him to take their social responsibilities at all seriously. An impressive but somewhat cold film.

d Delmer Daves *p* David Heilweil *s* Halsted Welles
c Charles Lawton Jnr *lp* Glenn Ford, Van Heflin, Felicia Farr, Leora Dana, Henry Jones, Richard Jaeckel

Three Violent People (PAR) vv 100 (98) min
Mate's nonchalant direction and Heston's obvious delight at playing a 'bastard' immediately after impersonating Moses for Cecil B. De Mille in *The Ten Commandments* (1956) give some substance to Grant's slim story that has Heston and Tryon as strong-willed brothers quarrelling while their ranch is threatened by carpetbagging landgrabbers. A further complication is Baxter's past as a prostitute prior to her marriage to Heston. Roland is in fine form as the ranch foreman.

d Rudolph Mate *p* Hugh Brown *s* James Edward Grant
c Loyal Griggs *lp* Charlton Heston, Anne Baxter, Gilbert Roland, Tom Tryon, Forrest Tucker, Barton MacLane

The Tin Star
(A PEARLBERG-SEATON PRODUCTION) b/w vv 93 min
Although it isn't one of Mann's best Westerns, *The Tin Star* is nevertheless an intriguing study in character development. Perkins is the young sheriff taught how to use his anger constructively by bounty hunter and ex-sheriff Fonda. The film's formal qualitites – it begins and ends with the same shot and the sheriff's window is often used by Mann and cinematographer Griggs as a screen within a screen – the theme of apprenticeship, the town-bound setting and the presence of Fonda rather than James Stewart as the hero, has the effect of limiting, almost repressing the emotional intensity one associates with Mann's characters. Only in the final showdown between Perkins and Brand and the sequence detailing the return of the doctor's buggy, with McIntire dead in it, does Mann invest his images with that intensity.

d Anthony Mann *p* William Pearlberg, George Seaton
s Dudley Nichols *c* Loyal Griggs *lp* Henry Fonda, Anthony Perkins, Neville Brand, John McIntire, Lee Van Cleef, Betsy Palmer

Trooper Hook (UA) b/w 81 min
Badly received by the critics because it touched the twin nerves of sexuality and racism, *Trooper Hook* is a significant Western, marred only by a too talkative screenplay. McCrea is

Henry Fonda is the bounty hunter in Anthony Mann's The Tin Star.

the Cavalry sergeant detailed to take Stanwyck who, after her capture by the Indians, has been living with Acosta's chief, back to her husband, Dehner. She refuses to leave her Indian child behind, Acosta doesn't want her to go and Dehner doesn't want her back. Though the film never reaches the level of hysteria about miscegenation which is a feature of John Ford's **Two Rode Together** (1961), Warren neatly and powerfully forces his characters to confront their previously unexamined attitudes. Only the climax which has Acosta and Dehner conveniently kill each other off, seems out of place. Tex Ritter sings the title song.

d/co-s Charles Marquis Warren *p* Sol Baer Fielding
co-s David Victor, Herbert Little Jnr *c* Ellsworth Fredericks *lp* Joel McCrea, Barbara Stanwyck, Rodolfo Acosta, John Dehner, Earl Holliman, Edward Andrews

The True Story of Jesse James
(FOX) scope 93 min
Though the credits read, 'based on a screenplay by Nunnally Johnson', Newman's script and Ray's direction offer a radically different interpretation of Jesse James to Henry King and Johnson's romantic view expressed in **Jesse James** (1939). The actual story is little changed, but whereas the earlier film had the James Brothers turn to outlawry as a reaction to the arrival of Northern carpetbaggers in the defeated South, Ray sees Jesse and Frank as disaffected teenagers caught in a hostile world. Wagner and Hunter are Jesse and Frank, betrayed first when they are shot at as they surrender under a white flag and then refused work in a Unionist outpost in the South because of their Southern sympathies. They turn to bankrobbing as a way out of their predicament only to become trapped by the excitement which quickly turns to frustration when they realize you just can't stop being a bank robber. From this perspective, the film is in marked contrast to Ray's *Rebel Without a Cause* (1955) whose adolescent heroes become mature adults through caring for each other; in *The True Story of Jesse James*, Jesse merely apes the values of the adult world he despises because it has excluded him. Lange is the girl he marries and with whom he briefly settles down to domestic bliss.

Far left: Robert Wagner (centre) as the rebellious Southern youth on his way to becoming Jesse James in Nick Ray's interpretation of the legend, The True Story of Jesse James.

d Nicholas Ray   *p* Herbert B. Swope Jnr   *s* Walter Newman
c Joe MacDonald   *lp* Robert Wagner, Jeffrey Hunter, Hope
Lange, Agnes Moorehead, Alan Hale, John Carradine

Utah Blaine (COL) b/w 75 min

Another of the many low-budget Westerns derived from the
novels of Louis L'Amour, in the fifties. Sears directs in his
usual fast-paced, rugged style, finding odd angles to film the
action from, but the screenplay is too predictable to excite.
Calhoun, in the title role, is the cowboy who rescues a man
from a lynching and so wins a half share in a ranch that Teal
and his gang lay claim to. With assistance from Baer (and his
six guns) and Langton (and his shotgun), Calhoun cuts Teal
down to size. This film and others, notably **Shotgun** (1955),
saw the beginning of a marked shift in the weaponry of the
genre that reached its climax in the Italian Western.

d Fred F. Sears   *p* Sam Katzman   *s* Robert E. Kent, James
B. Gordon   *c* Benjamin Kline   *lp* Rory Calhoun, Susan
Cummings, Max Baer, Ray Teal, Paul Langton, Jack Ingram

War Drums (BEL-AIR PRODUCTIONS) 75 min

This is an unimaginative Indian Western. Although *War
Drums* is sympathetic to Indians it is constructed in such a
melodramatic fashion as to be ridiculous. Barker is famed
Indian Chief Mangas Colorados, pushed into war by whites
who break the treaty they've signed with him and Johnson the
whiteman who allows him (and his warrior bride, Taylor) to
lead his people back to the hills at the end rather than be
settled on a reservation.

d Reginald LeBorg   *p* Howard W. Koch   *s* Gerald Drayson
Adams   *c* William Margulies   *lp* Lex Barker, Ben Johnson,
Joan Taylor, Larry Chance, Richard Cutting, James Parnell

1958

Ambush at Cimarron Pass (FOX) b/w scope 73 min

This was Eastwood's second Western, the first being **Star in
the Dust** (1956), and first major part before his role as Rowdy
Yates in the *Rawhide* teleseries which brought him a
modicum of fame and security. Brady is the Cavalry sergeant
transporting a prisoner across Apache territory who meets a
group of rebels. Together they fight off the Apache and after a
seven-day walk reach the fort, but not before Brady and
Eastwood have fought over Dean. Later Eastwood would

*Charlton Heston as the
big man in* The Big
Country.

summarily dismiss the film as 'the lousiest Western ever
made'.

d Jodie Copelan   *p* Herbert E. Mendelson   *s* Richard G.
Taylor, John K. Butler   *c* John M. Nickolaus Jnr
lp Scott Brady, Margia Dean, Clint Eastwood, Irving Bacon,
Frank Gerstle, Dirk London

The Badlanders (ARCOLA PICTURES) scope 85 min

Routine fare, considering it's directed by Daves. Borgnine
and Ladd are the uneasy conspirators planning a gold
robbery, and determined to outsmart each other, in turn of
the century Arizona. Virtually a remake of *The Asphalt Jungle*
(1950), it even features Caruso who has a small role in the
earlier film.

d Delmer Daves   *p* Aaron Rosenberg   *s* Richard Collins
c John Seitz   *lp* Alan Ladd, Ernest Borgnine, Katy Jurado,
Anthony Caruso, Kent Smith, Claire Kelly

Badman's Country (PEERLESS/WB) b/w 68 min

Montgomery as Pat Garrett enlists the aid of Wyatt Earp
(Crabbe), Buffalo Bill (Atterbury) and Bat Masterson (Ankrum) for a final showdown with Brand's Butch Cassidy (a
minor outlaw whose day of glory would come later) in this
bizarre Western. Hampton's script treats history in a cavalier
fashion that is matched by Sears' exuberant direction. The
result is a film which is hard to dislike.

d Fred F. Sears   *p* Robert E. Kent   *s* Orville Hampton
c Benjamin H. Kline   *lp* George Montgomery, Buster
Crabbe, Morris Ankrum, Neville Brand, Karin Booth,
Malcolm Atterbury

The Big Country (UA/WORLDWIDE) 163 min

A large-scale family feud of a Western with Bickford and Ives
as the patriarchs competing for the water rights owned by
Simmons' schoolmarm. Co-producer Peck is the sea captain
who arrives to marry Bickford's daughter, Baker, and Heston
(who gives a superb performance) the vicious ranch foreman
with whom he quarrels immediately. Intended by Wyler and
his troop of writers (which included an uncredited Jessamyn
West) as an epic with emotions to match Planer's magisterial
landscapes, the movie is surprisingly tame, excepting the
lengthy fight between Peck and Heston which ends with the
pair of them on their knees in the dust. Nevertheless it was a
considerable commercial success, grossing over $4 million in
its first year of release in Northern America.

d/co-p William Wyler   *co-p* Gregory Peck   *s* James R.
Webb, Sy Bartlett, Robert Wilder   *c* Franz Planer
lp Gregory Peck, Jean Simmons, Charlton Heston, Carroll
Baker, Burl Ives, Charles Bickford

Blood Arrow (EMIRAU) scope b/w 76 min

Coates is the Mormon girl transporting smallpox serum
through hostile Blackfoot territory to try and save the lives of
a community suffering the ravages of the disease. Brady is the
gunfighter, Richards is the gambler and Haggerty amongst
those who accompany her. Warren, once noted for the
authenticity of his Westerns, here directs in the throwaway
style of recent outings like **Cattle Empire** (1958). It was to be
his last film as director for over a decade, during which time
he worked extensively in television.

d Charles Marquis Warren   *p* Robert Stabler   *s* Fred
Freiberger   *c* Fleet Southcott   *lp* Scott Brady, Phyllis
Coates, Paul Richards, Don Haggerty, Rocky Shahan

The Bravados (TCR) scope 98 min

A routine, would-be prestige Western. Peck, whose earlier
collaboration with director King produced the magnificent
The Gunfighter (1950), is the lonely embittered stranger on
the trail of the four men he believes raped and murdered his

wife. When the men escape hanging (for another murder), Peck sets after them and kills them one by one until the last one, Silva, persuades him that they weren't responsible for his wife's death. Peck briefly contemplates his moral collapse before returning to Collins, whose performance as his girlfriend is marred by her bad horsemanship, for consolation. Yordan's script is similar in tone and structure to his work for Anthony Mann, notably **The Man from Laramie** (1955), but both King's direction and Peck's acting lack the intensity needed to animate it.

d Henry King   *p* Herbert B. Swope Jnr   *s* Philip Yordan
c Leon Shamroy   *lp* Gregory Peck, Joan Collins, Stephen Boyd, Albert Salmi, Henry Silva, Lee Van Cleef

Buchanan Rides Alone

(SCOTT-BROWN PRODUCTIONS)   77 min
Saddled with a character that was derived from an established series of novels (the 'Buchanan' novels) and is 'happy-go-lucky' rather than the grim-visaged persona Scott usually adopted, Boetticher and writer Lang wisely opted to produce a tongue-in-cheek farce. Accordingly, Scott, clearly stretched by the novelty of the situation, is shunted around by the plot never quite understanding why the other characters are acting as they do.

Arriving in Agrytown, a place so corrupt even the brothers of the ruling Agry family are trying to double-cross each other, Scott is promptly put in jail with Rojas, whose brutal murder halfway through the film is decidedly out of place. The end, with Scott holding off assorted heavies interested only in the money bag, is a marvellous example of greed visualized. Accordingly, it's fitting that Scott should leave the corpse-strewn town to Stevens, whose steadfast loyalty to the corrupt Avery is a mark of heroism in a film so full of treachery. This is a witty, minor film.

d Budd Boetticher   *p* Harry Joe Brown   *s* Charles Lang
c Lucien Ballard   *lp* Randolph Scott, Craig Stevens, Barry Kelley, Tol Avery, Manuel Rojas, Peter Whitney

Bullwhip   (AA)   scope   80 min

An intriguing minor film, made all the more so by being scripted by Buffington, veteran of so many series Westerns. Madison is the man about to be hanged for a murder he didn't commit who is freed on condition he marries Fleming and then forgets all about her. She is part Cheyenne and wields the bullwhip of the title. She plans on being the richest fur trader in the West and needs the marriage to own property in her own right. Though the 'Taming of the Squaw' comedy is rather too farcical to work, the action, as Madison confronts killer Griffith amidst the soft autumnal colours provided by Martin, is well done.

d Harmon Jones   *p* William F. Broidy   *s* Adele Buffington
c John J. Martin   *lp* Guy Madison, Rhonda Fleming, James Griffith, Don Beddoe, Peter Adams, Dan Sheridan

Cattle Empire   (FOX)   scope   83 min

This otherwise routine Western is given a real sense of authority by the simple presence of McCrea in the lead role. He's the trail boss who, on his release from prison, hires as cowboys a number of the townspeople who had him imprisoned when his men shot up their town. In the course of the long arduous cattle drive they discover why the men shot their town up and McCrea tempers his desire to perpetually humiliate them. The script is based on a story by Daniel B. Ullman, the most intriguing of B Western specialists in the fifties.

d Charles Marquis Warren   *p* Robert Stabler   *s* Endre Bohem, Eric Norden   *c* Brydon Baker   *lp* Joel McCrea, Gloria Talbott, Don Haggerty, Phyllis Coates, Bing Russell, Paul Brinegar

Cole Younger, Gunfighter   (AA)   scope   78 min

One of the few Westerns written by Mainwaring, a writer better known for thrillers (*Out of the Past*, 1947) and gangster films (*Baby-Face Nelson*, 1957), this is an engaging, if somewhat confusing, film. Merlin and Best are the youngsters in love with the same girl, Dalton, and Lovejoy is the handsome Cole Younger who comes to Best's assistance in spectacular fashion – he holds up a courtroom! – after Merlin has falsely accused Best of murder. Springsteen directs with his usual verve.

d R.G. Springsteen   *p* Ben Schwalb   *s* Daniel Mainwaring
c Harry Neumann   *lp* Frank Lovejoy, James Best, Jan Merlin, Abby Dalton, Frank Ferguson, Myron Healey

Cowboy   (COL)   92 min

Loosely based on Frank Harris' *My Reminiscences as a Cowboy*, *Cowboy* stars an unlikely Lemmon as the tenderfoot hotel clerk who learns the arts of self-sufficiency and comradeship in the course of a 2,000-mile cattle drive under the tutelage of Ford's stern cattle boss. An atmospheric and episodic film, which, despite writer North's desperate attempts to fashion a conventional dramatic narrative from his material, has an understandably romantic edge.

The film is not to be confused with Elmo Williams' 1954 documentary about the everyday life of a cowboy, also called *Cowboy*.

Dennis Hopper (left), who was eventually to make his name both as Hollywood's resident anarchist and as a director of distinction, with Don Murray in From Hell to Texas.

Far left: James Best (left) as yet another fifties adolescent who goes astray in Cole Younger, Gunfighter.

d Delmer Daves   *p* Julian Blaustein   *s* Edmund H. North
c Charles Lawton Jnr   *lp* Jack Lemmon, Glenn Ford, Brian
Donlevy, Anna Kashfi, Dick York, Richard Jaeckel

Day of the Bad Man

(U-INTERNATIONAL)   scope   81 min
MacMurray is the judge about to pass sentence on a convicted
killer when four of his old gang, led by Middleton and
Homeier, ride into town to set him free. Soon the townspeople, including Ericson's sheriff, want to set the killer free but
MacMurray sticks to his guns and, in a tense fight with
minimal assistance from Buchanan, he kills the baddies and so
wins back Weldon. The sight of townspeople cowed into
submission by gun-toting baddies was, in 1958, as familiar as
the unmasking scene, in which the town's banker is revealed
to be the villain, was in 1938. Routine fare.

d Harry Keller   *p* Gordon Kay   *s* Lawrence Roman
c Irving Glassberg   *lp* Fred MacMurray, Joan Weldon,
Robert Middleton, Skip Homeier, John Ericson, Edgar
Buchanan

Escape from Red Rock

(REGAL FILMS)   b/w   scope   75 min
Donlevy is the nominal star of this pleasant actioneer but
Murray, as the youngster who briefly becomes an outlaw to
save his brother, has the biggest part. Murray heads into
Indian territory with Janssen where they find and rescue a
baby and fight off an Indian attack. Donlevy is his usual
authoritarian self with the twist that, like Flippen, he melts at
the sight of a baby.

d/s Edward Bernds   *p* Bernard Glasser   *c* Brydon Baker
lp Brian Donlevy, Eilene Janssen, Gary Murray, Jay C.
Flippen, Richard Healey, William Phipps

The Fiend Who Walked the West

(FOX)   b/w   scope   103 min
Evans, in the role that made Richard Widmark's name, is the
psychopath in this loose remake of *Kiss of Death* (1947). The
essentially decent O'Brian tells him about a cache of buried
money when they are in jail together. On his release, Evans

Robert Evans (right) as
The Fiend Who
Walked the West.

kills O'Brian's partner to get the money and then kidnaps and
torments O'Brian's wife, Cristal. O'Brian is set free, and in a
final confrontation kills Evans. The movie was much criticized at the time for its brutality and violence.

d Gordon Douglas   *p* Herbert B. Swope Jnr   *s* Harry
Brown, Philip Yordan   *c* Joe MacDonald   *lp* Hugh
O'Brian, Robert Evans, Dolores Michaels, Linda Cristal,
Stephen McNally, June Blair

Fort Bowie   (UA)   b/w   80 min

This is an indifferent Cavalry-versus-Indian actioneer with
the predictable sub-plot of a superior officer (Taylor) who
thinks his wife (Harrison) is having an affair with a
subordinate officer (Johnson). The movie begins well with a
well-staged massacre of a group of Apache about to surrender
and ends interestingly with the Cavalry storming their own
fort after the Apache have captured it, but it's a long slog from
beginning to end. Johnson gives his role real dignity.

d Howard W. Koch   *p* Aubrey Schenck   *s* Maurice
Tombragel   *c* Carl E. Guthrie   *lp* Ben Johnson, Jan
Harrison, Kent Taylor, Jana Davi, Larry Chance, J. Ian
Douglas

Fort Dobbs   (WB)   90 min

This slack Western is notable for being one of the first
attempts to make a film star out of a television star, Walker, of
the *Cheyenne* teleseries. The complicated plot sees Walker,
wanted on a murder charge, rescue a widow from the
Comanche (as Randolph Scott would later do at the beginning
of the Kennedy-scripted **Comanche Station,** 1960) and then
successfully masterminding the defence of Fort Dobbs, and
so clearing his name.

d Gordon Douglas   *p* Martin Rackin   *s* Burt Kennedy,
George W. George   *c* William Clothier   *lp* Clint Walker,
Virginia Mayo, Brian Keith, Richard Eyer, Russ Conway,
Michael Dante

Fort Massacre

(MIRISCH COMPANY/UA)   scope   80 min
McCrea is the tough Indian-hating top sergeant who tries to
lead the remnants of a Cavalry troop back to the fort through
hostile Indian land, only to lead them into another ambush.
Newman's direction is slack but the acting of McCrea, Tucker
and especially Russell is strong.

d Joseph M. Newman   *p* Walter M. Mirisch   *s* Martin N.
Goldsmith   *c* Carl Guthrie   *lp* Joel McCrea, Forrest
Tucker, Susan Cabot, Anthony Caruso, John Russell, Denver
Pyle

From Hell to Texas *aka* Manhunt

(FOX)   scope   100 min
A lively Western. Murray is the man on the run after
accidentally killing a man, pursued by a vengeful father,
Armstrong, and his remaining sons. Wills is the sympathetic
rancher and Varsi his tomboy daughter who falls for Murray.
Hathaway's direction is rumbustious and uncomplicated but
it is producer Buckner's ambitious, parable-like script that is
the most interesting feature of the film. The final confrontation between Murray and Hopper, which ends not in death
but with Armstrong calling off the vendetta, is particularly
well done.

d Henry Hathaway   *p/co-s* Robert Buckner   *co-s* Wendell
Mayes   *c* Wilfrid M. Cline   *lp* Don Murray, Diane Varsi,
Chill Wills, Dennis Hopper, R.G. Armstrong, Harry Carey
Jnr

Gun Fever   (UA)   b/w   81 min

Directed and co-scripted by its star, this is a mediocre film.
Stevens plays the fast-gun of a miner seeking Saxon's

renegade who murdered his father. A minor point of interest is that it was one of the earliest modern Westerns to be shot in two versions, American and foreign, with the foreign version containing an extended nude-bathing sequence featuring the heroine, Davi. The days of the sex Western were not far ahead.

d/co-s Mark Stevens *p* Harry Jackson, Sam Weston *co-s* Stanley H. Silverman *c* Charles Van Enger *lp* Mark Stevens, Aaron Saxon, John Lupton, Jana Davi, Larry Storch, Jerry Barclay

Gunman's Walk (COL) scope 97 min

One of the most interesting of the Westerns of the fifties that centre on the conflict between a father and a son. Heflin is the patriarch and Hunter the son who tries to outdo his father, the man who brought law and order to the range with his own guns, and turns killer. Whereupon Heflin, never flinching from his biblical sense of morality, guns him down. Nugent's screenplay is a little facile, making Heflin and Hunter cyphers rather than characters but Karlson, remorselessly pushing the film to its inevitable climax, directs impressively. Darren is the second son who, left to his own devices, has no need to prove himself to Heflin.

d Phil Karlson *p* Fred Kohlmar *s* Frank Nugent *c* Charles Lawton Jnr *lp* Van Heflin, Tab Hunter, Kathryn Grant, James Darren, Ray Teal, Mickey Shaughnessy

The Last of the Fast Guns

(U-INTERNATIONAL) scope 82 min

Mahoney is the hired gun of the title, searching for the brother (Franz) of industrialist Reid in this enterprising film. Working against Mahoney are gunmen in the pay of Reid's crooked partner who is out to steal the business from under the brothers. Largely photographed in the mountain region of New Mexico, the film looks far better than its traditional action plot might suggest. Another asset is Roland as the grinning, double-crossing villain of the piece.

d George Sherman *p* Howard Christie *s* David P. Harmon *c* Alex Phillips *lp* Jock Mahoney, Eduard Franz, Carl Benton Reid, Gilbert Roland, Linda Cristal, Lorne Greene

The Law and Jake Wade (MGM) scope 86 min

Often celebrated for the beautiful colour photography of Surtees, much of the credit for the success of *The Law and Jake Wade* must go to Bowers for his wonderfully laconic script. The movie is a witty and deeply ironic account of Sheriff Taylor's attempts to remain an ex-bandit in the face of much counter-persuasion from Widmark, the outlaw and one-time friend he rescues from a hanging to his cost. The result is one of the few of director Sturges' films to create a gradual (and lasting) tension, rather than the episodic dramatics of a film like **The Magnificent Seven** (1960).

d John Sturges *p* William Hawks *s* William Bowers *c* Robert Surtees *lp* Robert Taylor, Richard Widmark, Patricia Owens, Robert Middleton, Henry Silva, DeForest Kelley

The Left Handed Gun (WB) b/w 102 min

Penn's first feature film. He had already directed Gore Vidal's teleplay (on which Stevens' script is based) in 1955 with Newman in the lead. Both film and TV versions marked a radical transformation of the legend of Billy the Kid. Where previously he had been either the incarnation of evil or a romantic hero, in Penn's film he appears as an illiterate and introspective victim of his circumstances who actually believes the purple prose that newspapers write about him. Penn also changed the relationship between Billy (Newman) and Pat Garrett (Dehner) making Dehner a threatening father-figure unlike the gentle Keith-Johnston, whose murder and Billy's excessive revenge for it, sets Billy outside the law.

Penn's camerwork is equally inventive, seeming to only just catch the characters before they dart out of frame and giving the film a liveliness that surprises to this day.

d Arthur Penn *p* Fred Coe *s* Leslie Stevens *c* J. Peverell Marley *lp* Paul Newman, John Dehner, Hurd Hatfield, James Best, Colin Keith-Johnston, Lita Milan

The Lone Ranger and the Lost City of Gold

(UA) 80 min

A lacklustre sequel to **The Lone Ranger** (1956). Television's Lone Ranger and Tonto (Moore and Silverheels) repeat their roles in this tired account of outlaw Kennedy's attempts to discover, and profit from, a lost Indian gold – surely it should have been silver! – mine. Subsequently Moore and Silverheels were to reprise the parts that made them famous in in-person performances and on TV commercials until they were stopped by a series of injunctions.

d Lesley Selander *p* Sherman A. Harris *s* Robert Schaefer, Eric Freiwald *c* Kenneth Peach *lp* Clayton Moore, Jay Silverheels, Douglas Kennedy, Charles Watts, Noreen Nash, Ralph Moody

Man from God's Country (AA) scope 72 min

Montgomery is the sheriff who retires because his fellow townspeople want a quieter town and who travels to Sundown, a town that certainly needs his skills. There he persuades Peters, an old friend, to quit the side of town tyrant Wilcox, and join him in cleaning up Sundown. Landres directs at breakneck speed, as if to keep the audience's attention off the ponderous screenplay supplied by veteran Waggner.

d Paul Landres *p* Scott R. Dunlap *s* George Waggner *c* Harry Neumann *lp* George Montgomery, Randy Stuart, James Griffith, Frank Wilcox, House Peters Jnr, Susan Cummings

Man of the West

(ASHTON PRODUCTIONS) scope 95 min

This is Mann's most ambitious Western. Its hero is not Cooper, though it's he who sits statue-like astride his horse to form a backdrop to the film's main titles, but Cobb's demented patriarch. At the start Cooper seems to be a solid enough, if overly cautious, citizen but from the moment the

The poster for The Left Handed Gun, *which treats Billy the Kid as yet another disturbed teenager.*

Above: *A demented Gary Cooper savages Jack Lord in Anthony Mann's marvellous* Man of the West.

malevolent Cobb enters the story and claims Cooper as the favourite son he once was – 'Do you remember Uvalde...eleven thousand dollars...you held him, I took off the top of his head' – Cooper must live through his past and finally kill the evil father as the price of the re-assertion of his identity.

Cobb's performance as the evil Doc Tobin, who lives mostly in the past (where Lassoo, whose bank he plans to rob now that Cooper is back in the gang, is a thriving town and not the ghost town it is in actuality) is wonderfully overblown, matching Mann's Shakesperian concept of his characters. Similarly Dano, as the mute idiot (granted speech, one desperate elongated howl, only at the moment of his death), Lord as the hulking heavy of a brother and Dehner as the rational brother, looking after Cobb and wary that Cooper is only pretending to have returned home, give assured performances as members of the horrific family that Cooper once called his own.

In contrast to the Westerns he made with James Stewart which (their emotional intensity notwithstanding) hugged close to the contours of the genre, *Man of the West* is a far more desperate film. Cooper must kill his father or become him; no other options are available. Accordingly the film's style is more visceral and less formal. The result is Mann's most powerful film, a movie whose characters are stripped of all but their elemental natures. Unlike **Bend of the River** (1952), which ties its hero to the land and the opportunities it offers him (mining or farming), the landscape of *Man of the West* is just that, landscape, a stage on which Mann mounts the almost biblical confrontation of Cooper and Cobb that ends with the maddened father forcing his son to shoot him, taunting him to the very end: 'You've lost the appetite for it'.

d Anthony Mann   *p* Walter Mirisch   *s* Reginald Rose
c Ernest Haller   *lp* Gary Cooper, Lee J. Cobb, Julie London, Jack Lord, John Dehner, Royal Dano

Once upon a Horse

(U-INTERNATIONAL)   b/w   scope   85 min
A would-be Western farce starring Rowan and Martin who, in the sixties, were to become cult figures following the phenomenal international success of their television show *Rowan and Martin's Laugh In*. Here, they are the luckless cowboys perpetually trying to decide whether to go straight or turn to outlawry and failing to make a living either way. The plot is episodic, allowing more space for jokes than story, but, considering the low budget, Kanter's trick effects work well enough. Hyer and Talbot are the women, Erickson the heavier-than-heavy heavy and Keene, Maynard, Steele and Livingston themselves as members of a highly disorganized posse.

d/p/s Hal Kanter   *c* Arthur E. Arling   *lp* Dan Rowan, Dick Martin, Martha Hyer, Nina Talbot, Leif Erickson, Tom Keene, Bob Livingston, Kermit Maynard, Bob Steele

The Proud Rebel   (MGM)   103 min

This is a family Western, most notable for the superb cinematography of McCord, a veteran of countless series Westerns before his elevation to A features by Warners in the late forties. Ladd is the father travelling the country after the Civil War in search of a doctor to cure his son's dumbness (caused by 'the trauma of war') who, à la **Shane** (1953) becomes involved in De Havilland's struggle against Jagger's land baron. The result is a trite movie, made more so by the son's well timed rediscovery of the power of speech.

d Michael Curtiz   *p* Sam Goldwyn Jnr   *s* Joseph Petracca, Lillie Hayward   *c* Ted McCord   *lp* Alan Ladd, Dean Jagger, Olivia De Havilland, David Ladd, Dean Stanton, John Carradine

Quantrill's Raiders   (AA)   scope   71 min

A no-nonsense quickie that re-writes history in a marvellously carefree manner (Quantrill dies in the course of the raid upon St Lawrence, Kansas for example) always in the interest of action. Gordon is the snarling Quantrill, using the Civil War to settle old scores, and Cochran the Confederate officer detailed to help him plan the raid on the Union ammunition dump in St Lawrence who then has to switch sides when the ammo is moved and Quantrill refuses to give up the raid.

d Edward Bernds   *p* Ben Schwalb   *s* Polly James
c William Whitley   *lp* Steve Cochran, Diane Brewster, Leo Gordon, Gale Robbins, Myron Healey, Glenn Strange

Saddle the Wind   (MGM)   scope   84 min

Cassavetes' Method-style acting brings a real touch of freneticism to the character of the trigger-happy younger brother of retired gunman Taylor in this static Western that delays the inevitable confrontation between the brothers far too long. The best moments are the drawn-out killings of McGraw (a fine cameo) and Dano by Cassavetes. London is the saloon singer seeking security and torn between the two brothers. Writer Serling is best known for his TV plays (*Requiem for a Heavyweight*) and series (*The Twilight Zone*).

d Robert Parrish   *p* Armand Deutsch   *s* Rod Serling
c George J. Folsey   *lp* Robert Taylor, John Cassavetes, Julie London, Donald Crisp, Charles McGraw, Royal Dano

The Sheepman   (MGM)   scope   91 (85) min

Ford is the sheepman of the title determined to settle in cattle country in this comic Western from the director of **Destry Rides Again** (1939). MacLaine gives a perky performance as the girl Ford steals from Nielson but it is Buchanan who steals the film with his gloriously comic interpretation of his role as the local windbag. The film's major fault is its obviousness once Ford has demonstrated his toughness by asking for a glass of milk in the saloon immediately on his arrival.

1958

d George Marshall p Edmund Grainger s James Edward Grant, William Bowers c Robert Bronner lp Glenn Ford, Shirley MacLaine, Leslie Nielson, Edgar Buchanan, Mickey Shaughnessy, Slim Pickens

Showdown at Boot Hill (FOX) b/w scope 71 min
The best film of B director Fowler, better known as the director of such horror movies as *I Was a Teenage Werewolf* (1956) and *I Married a Monster from Outer Space* (1959). Bronson is the soul-searching marshal who discovers that the man he killed, trying to bring in, is known as a desperate criminal in one part of the state but is well respected in another. Indeed, the townspeople refuse to identify the corpse as a means of denying Bronson his bounty. This turn of events, and the presence of Matthews, gives Bronson time to reflect on his job. The result is a superior B Western.

d Gene Fowler Jnr p Harold E. Knox s Louis Vittes c John M. Nickolaus Jnr lp Charles Bronson, Robert Hutton, John Carradine, Carole Matthews, Paul Maxey, Thomas B. Henry

Sierra Baron (FOX) scope 80 min
A dreary Spanish land-grant Western. Brodie is the land speculator who tries to dispossess Jason of his huge tract of land and imports gunman Keith from Texas to back up his legal double-crossings with force. The grateful members of a wagon train he's given assistance to come to Jason's aid and Keith falls for his sister, Gam, and quickly changes sides before dying.

d James B. Clark p Plato A. Skouras s Houston Branch c Alex Phillips lp Brian Keith, Rick Jason, Rita Gam, Steve Brodie, Mala Powers, Lee Morgan

Terror in a Texas Town (UA) b/w 80 min
The most celebrated of Lewis' low-budget Westerns, if only for its highly unusual climax which sees Hayden face up to gunslinger Young with a harpoon, and kill him. More impressive though, than this witty gimmick, is Lewis' orchestration of the hackneyed plot, which has Cabot buying up oil-rich land for a pittance and murdering those who won't sell, including Hayden's father, with slow, fluid, formal camera movements that break down the drama into ritualisti-

Burl Ives (centre) as the evil patriarch in Day of the Outlaw.

cally conceived individual playlets. Thus if Hayden's Swede, home from the sea, searching for his father's killer and finally uniting the town against Cabot, seems to combine too many elements to work as a character, Millan's Mexican farmer and Young's gunman are marvellously conceived characters. All in black, Young rasps out his code of conduct which demands he perform his duties as a gunman, even though his abilities are sadly impaired, to his mistress who is threatening to leave him and to Cabot's breezily evil town tyrant. The final confrontation may be theatrical, but from Young's point of view, the main street of every town is his theatre. A triumph of form over content.

d Joseph H. Lewis p Frank N. Seltzer s Ben L. Perry c Ray Rennahan lp Sterling Hayden, Sebastian Cabot, Carol Kelly, Victor Millan, Ned Young, Eugene Martin

Villa! (FOX) scope 72 min
A minor, and wholly inaccurate, entry in the list of films devoted to Pancho Villa. Vittes' script has Villa as a playboy who discovers social reform when he witnesses government excess in response to the peons' requests for minimal reforms. Romero is his sadistic lieutenant and Dean (who wrote her own songs) the American saloon singer and mistress he abandons when he joins the revolution. Keith comes out of the film best as the American gun runner who supplies him with arms.

d James B. Clark p Plato Skouras s Louis Vittes c Alex Phillips lp Brian Keith, Cesar Romero, Margia Dean, Rosenda Monteros, Carlos Muzquiz, Elisa Loti

1959

Alias Jesse James (HOPE ENTERPRISES) 92 min
Corey is Jesse James and Hope the naive insurance salesman who sells him a policy and is then sent West to protect him in this silly but pleasant enough comedy. When Corey has the idea of killing Hope (who looks like him) for the insurance money and running off to California with Fleming, every Hollywood cowboy and cowgirl worth his six gun comes to Hope's rescue. Among them are Hugh O'Brian (as Wyatt Earp), Ward Bond (Major Seth Adams), James Arness (Matt Dillon), Fess Parker (Davy Crockett), Gail Davis (Annie Oakley), James Garner (Brett Maverick), Jay Silverheels (Tonto) and as themselves Roy Rogers, Gary Cooper and Gene Autry.

Far left: Glenn Ford (centre) is The Sheepman.

266

d Norman McLeod *p* Jack Hope *s* D.D. Beauchamp, William Bowers *c* Lionel Lindon *lp* Bob Hope, Rhonda Fleming, Wendell Corey, Jim Davis, Gloria Talbot, Will Wright

Curse of the Undead (U) b/w 79 min

This is a crude mixing of the Horror and Western genres. Pate is the mysterious gunslinger with vampirish intentions towards Crowley, and Fleming the preacher confronted with a bevy of unusually toothy ladies of the night. The climax has Fleming kill Pate by shooting him with a bullet on which he has carved a cross. Like other similar films, **Billy the Kid vs. Dracula** (1965) and **Jesse James Meets Frankenstein's Daughter** (1966), the gimmick soon palls.

d/co-s Edward Dein *p* Joseph Gershenson *co-s* Mildred Dein *c* Ellis Carter *lp* Eric Fleming, Kathleen Crowley, John Hoyt, Michael Pate, Bruce Gordon, Edward Binns

Day of the Outlaw (SECURITY PICTURES) b/w 96 min

A splendid B Western. Ives is the brutish outlaw leader on the run from the Cavalry who with his gang, takes over an isolated community and Ryan is the tough rancher who finally forsakes his isolationism to make a stand against him. Both actors are magnificent but it is De Toth's cold direction and Harlan's austere black and white cinematography, made even bleaker by the snow that covers everything, that gives the film its real distinction. The well-staged climax has Ryan and Ives shooting it out in a blizzard.

d Andre De Toth *p* Sidney Harmon *s* Philip Yordan *c* Russell Harlan *lp* Robert Ryan, Burl Ives, Tina Louise, Nehimiah Persoff, Jack Lambert, Alan Marshall

Escort West

(BATJAC ENTERPRISES/ROMINA) b/w scope 75 min
A serviceable B Western, co-scripted by actor Gordon (who has a small part in the film). Mature is the ex-Confederate officer who meets two sisters, the survivors of an Indian attack, in the course of his trek West with his daughter at the end of the Civil War and escorts them to safety. Full of action and well mounted by Lyon with Mature as gruff as can be, the film is a cut above the average Western.

Michael Pate with victim in Curse of the Undead, *one of several horror-Westerns of the fifties.*

d Francis D. Lyon *p* Robert E. Morrison, Nate H. Edwards *s* Leo Gordon, Fred Hartsook *c* William Clothier *lp* Victor Mature, Elaine Stewart, Faith Domergue, Harry Carey Jnr, Slim Pickens, Leo Gordon

Gunfight at Dodge City (MIRISCH/UA) scope 81 min

A routine film, this was intended by McCrea to be his last until Sam Peckinpah persuaded him and Randolph Scott out of retirement for **Ride the High Country** (1962). McCrea is Bat Masterson, a gambler elected sheriff of Dodge City to clean up the town. He even goes against his old gang but still falls foul of the local politicos. Ullman and Goldsmith's script has its moments but Newman's direction is as flat as ever.

d Joseph M. Newman *p* Walter Mirisch *s* Daniel B. Ullman, Martin M. Goldsmith *c* Carl Guthrie *lp* Joel McCrea, Julie Adams, John McIntire, Nancy Gates, Richard Anderson, Walter Coy

The Hanging Tree (WB) 106 min

A curiously slow-moving Western that takes its pace from Cooper's performance as the emotionally scarred gunman/doctor. Arriving at a Montana mining town he takes upon himself the physical education of the (temporarily) blinded Schell and the moral education of Piazza, so running up against the law of disorder represented by Malden and Scott (in his screen debut). Although Daves' formalist concerns too often blur the film's edges the result is nonetheless strangely moving.

d Delmer Daves *p* Martin Jurow, Richard Shepherd *s* Wendell Mayes, Halsted Welles *c* Ted McCord *lp* Gary Cooper, Maria Schell, Karl Malden, George C. Scott, Ben Piazza, Karl Swenson

The Hangman (PAR) b/w 86 min

Curtiz's tired direction doesn't much help this lacklustre Western, scripted by Nichols. Taylor is the marshal famed for always getting his man who decides not to take Lord in for his role in a hold-up years ago after discovering that Lord has rehabilitated himself and become a respected and useful citizen. Louise is Lord's old flame who wins Taylor for herself and Parker the sheriff who helps dissuade Taylor from his rigidly held views on law and order.

d Michael Curtiz *p* Frank Freeman Jnr *s* Dudley Nichols *c* Loyal Griggs *lp* Robert Taylor, Fess Parker, Jack Lord, Tina Louise, Gene Evans, Mickey Shaughnessy

The Horse Soldiers (UA/MIRISCH) 119 min

Minor Ford. Based on an actual incident at the time of the siege of Vicksburg, *The Horse Soldiers* features Wayne and Holden as the argumentative leaders of a Union Cavalry patrol sent on a mission to destroy the railway lines along which the Confederate troops are being supplied. The film's greatest moments, the Cavalry strung across the horizon and the cadets from the Confederate Military Academy marching helplessly against Wayne's troops, for all their visual delight, are purely rhetorical. The love-hate relationship between Wayne and Towers, the Southern lady travelling with the Union troops in the hope of sabotaging their plans, doesn't have the resonance of that between Wayne and Maureen O'Hara in **Rio Grande** (1950). Similarly, Ford is uneasy with the liberal sentiments Mahin has Holden mouth by the paragraph.

d John Ford *co-p* Martin Rackin *s/co-p* John Lee Mahin *c* William Clothier *lp* John Wayne, William Holden, Constance Towers, Althea Gibson, Hoot Gibson, Anna Lee

The Jayhawkers (PAR) vv 100 min

One of the several Westerns set against the background of the events just prior to the outbreak of the Civil War. Chandler is the Kansas-border raider who dreams of an empire on the plains of mid-America with himself as Napoleon. Parker is the man who thwarts that dream. Sadly Frank's direction is so flat and Parker so wooden a hero that Chandler's dreams are never given the opportunity to flow. Even the action sequences are stilted. That said, the film has a reputation of sorts in France, possibly because of the torrent of references to Napoleon.

d/co-p/co-s Melvin Frank *co-p* Norman Panama *co-s* Joseph Petracca, Frank Fenton, A.I. Bezzerides *c* Loyal Griggs *lp* Jeff Chandler, Fess Parker, Nicole Maurey, Henry Silva, Herbert Rudley, Leo Gordon

King of the Wild Stallions (AA) scope 76 min
Written by veteran serial director Beebe this is a charmingly innocent Western. Brewster is the rancher who needs the $500 Meyer's cattle baron is offering for the capture of the horse of the title, Hartleben her young son who's set on owning the horse for himself and Montgomery her foreman and suitor who sorts things out. Springsteen's direction is similarly old fashioned, relying for much of its effect on the sight of herds of wild horses. One of the best of the many 'boy and his horse' Westerns.

d R.G. Springsteen *p* Ben Schwalb *s* Ford Beebe *c* Carl Guthrie *lp* George Montgomery, Diane Brewster, Emile Meyer, Jerry Hartleben, Edgar Buchanan, Denver Pyle

The Last Train from Gun Hill
(PAR/BRYNA) vv 98 min
This film marks the stage in Sturges' career at which his previous interest in the psychological make-up of his characters changed to a concern with sketchy characters, each with their own foibles and quirks, but with little else beneath the surface. Accordingly, this tale about a marshal (Douglas) trying to take in the man (Holliman) who raped and murdered his wife who just happens to be the son of Douglas' oldest friend, Quinn, who just happens to try and stop Douglas getting his prisoner on the last train to prison, falls flat because the characters have no substance. Poe's screenplay is literate and Sturges' direction abounds in tension, in the manner of his **Gunfight at the O.K. Corral** (1957), but the drama is forced and hollow, albeit entertaining for the most part.

d John Sturges *p* Hal B. Wallis *s* James Poe *c* Charles Lang Jnr *lp* Kirk Douglas, Anthony Quinn, Earl Holliman, Brian Hutton, Carolyn Jones, Brad Dexter

The Legend of Tom Dooley (COL) b/w 79 min
This unusually sombre Western was based on the traditional folk song 'Tom Dooley' which was a surprise million seller for the Kingston Trio (who perform the song over the film's credits) when it was released as a single in 1958. Neither Post nor writer/producer Shpetner try to evade the song's tragic end which has Dooley (Landon) hung after he's been caught robbing a Union stagecoach not knowing that the Civil War is over. Rust offers fine support as another of the Confederates on the run for murder.

d Ted Post *p/s* Stan Shpetner *c* Gilbert Warrenton *lp* Michael Landon, Jo Morrow, Jack Hogan, Richard Rust, Ken Lynch, Howard Wright

Lone Texan (FOX) b/w scope 70 min
This is an impressive low-budget Western. Parker, in the title role, is the man who fought for the Union and on his return finds the townspeople against him and his younger brother Williams and his cronies, as sheriff and deputies, terrorizing the town. Tightly scripted, and efficiently directed by Landres who, thanks to creative art direction by Edward Shiells, makes the most of his backlot Western street. The well-staged climax has the brothers confronting each other and Parker killing Williams when he thinks he's drawing on him. In fact Williams is drawing on a deputy about to shoot Parker in the back.

d Paul Landres *p* Jack Leewood *s* James Landis, Jack Thomas *c* Walter Strenge *lp* Willard Parker, Grant Williams, Audrey Dalton, Douglas Kennedy, June Blair, Dabbs Greer

Miracle of the Hills (FOX) b/w scope 73 min
This is one of a number of 'inspirational' Westerns made in the fifties with the Bible Belt in mind as the target audience. The miracle in question is the escape of three children from a mine flood when an earthquake unjams a safety door. As a direct result former prostitute Gerson, who controls the town's only source of livelihood, the mine, and has become a malevolent despot, has a change of heart and with Reason's rugged episcopal minister starts to reform the town. The plot, with obligatory stops along the way for the drunk to be cured and similar occurrences, is hammy but Landres directs with a stark realism that is both effective and unusual.

'You sure make fine coffee, Ma'am': Randolph Scott and Karen Steele in the middle of one of the many elliptical campfire conversations that punctuate the glorious Ride Lonesome.

Far left: Kirk Douglas in John Sturges' over-complicated The Last Train from Gun Hill.

d Paul Landres   *p* Richard E. Lyons (Earle Lyons)
s Charles Hoffman   *c* Floyd Crosby   *lp* Rex Reason, Betty
Lou Gerson, Theona Bryant, Gilbert Smith, Jay North, Gene
Roth

Money, Women and Guns

(U-INTERNATIONAL)   scope   80 min

Mahoney is the frontier detective hired to discover who killed
an old prospector and trace his heirs and Hunter the woman
he falls in love with in the course of the job. Pittman's script is
clever but Bartlett's direction is oddly listless and accordingly
the mystery unravels rather like a ball of wool instead of
dramatically. The film was one of cameraman Lathrop's first.
He's better known for his work on later movies like **Wild
Rovers** (1971).

d Richard Bartlett   *p* Howie Horowitz   *s* Montgomery
Pittman   *c* Philip Lathrop   *lp* Jock Mahoney, Kim Hunter,
Tim Hovey, Lon Chaney Jnr, Gene Evans, Jeffrey Stone

No Name on the Bullet   (U)   scope   77 min

Undoubtedly the best of Arnold's Westerns, this is a stylish if
slow-moving essay in paranoia in which the leading players
reveal all their guilty secrets, so sure are they that Murphy's
gunslinger has come to town to get them. Murphy, hiding his
boyish charms behind a becoming mustache and with a sneer
to match, makes a suprisingly effective gunman, while Drake
is suitably heroic as the town doctor who eventually faces up
to him. However, it is Murphy's victims who make the film so
memorable: Bissell who commits suicide when he can't buy
off Murphy, Stevens who tries to drink up enough courage to
face the gunman, and most effective of all Stelhi as the judge
and real object of Murphy's attentions who, though paralysed, tries to rise from his wheelchair to gun Murphy down.

d/co-p Jack Arnold   *co-p* Howard Christie   *s* Gene L. Coon
c Harold Lipstein   *lp* Audie Murphy, Joan Evans, Charles
Drake, R.G. Armstrong, Warren Stevens, Whit Bissell,
Edgar Stelhi

The Oregon Trail   (FOX)   scope   86 (82) min

MacMurray is the reporter sent to Oregon to investigate
Indian attacks on settlers in this lacklustre piece of budget-
film packaging that makes better use of stock footage than it
does of original footage. Shipman is the girl and Bishop
MacMurray's rival for her affections.

*Below: John Wayne
and Ricky Nelson burst
into action in* Rio
Bravo, *Howard
Hawks' classic Western.*

d/co-s Gene Fowler Jnr   *p* Richard Einfeld   *co-s* Louise
Vittes   *c* Kay Norton   *lp* Fred MacMurray, William
Bishop, Nina Shipman, Gloria Talbot, John Carradine,
Henry Hull

Ride Lonesome   (COL)   scope   74 (73) min

A magical Western. Kennedy's elegant script has lawman
Scott (looking more and more like W.S. Hart) and amiable
outlaws Roberts and Coburn competing for possession of
outlaw Best. Scott hopes Best will lead him to brother Van
Cleef who in the distant past murdered Scott's wife while
Roberts and Coburn, dreaming of a small ranch, are seeking
the pardon promised for Best's capture. The film is the most
optimistic of the several Westerns Boetticher made with Scott
in the fifties. At the end Scott foregoes his revenge and allows
Roberts and Coburn to collect their pardons and ride off with
Steele, who joins the group in the course of their journey.

Boetticher marvellously captures the shifting alliances
within the group as they discuss the day's journey across the
arid desert around the campfire each evening. His comic
touch twists the film's many ironies still deeper. With
Comanche Station (1960), the last Boetticher-Scott collaboration and an equally elegaic film, and Sam Peckinpah's
Ride the High Country (1962), it stands as the culmination of
the B Western and lasting proof of the suppleness of the genre
in the hands of a team of people who can exploit its
opportunities with intelligence and wit.

d/p Budd Boetticher   *s* Burt Kennedy   *c* Charles Lawton
Jnr   *lp* Randolph Scott, Karen Steele, Pernell Roberts,
James Best, Lee Van Cleef, James Coburn

Rio Bravo   (ARMADA PRODUCTIONS)   141 min

One of the great Westerns.

Rio Bravo was made by Hawks as a calculated rejoinder to
Fred Zinnemann's **High Noon** (1952), which featured Gary
Cooper desperately seeking help from the indifferent inhabitants of the town where he's the marshal. Hawks' film
features a sheriff (Wayne) shunning the help he clearly needs
unless it comes from fellow professionals. Thus the help
proffered by Martin, the drunk who redeems himself,
Brennan's quarrelsome mother hen, Nelson's young gunman
and Dickinson's professional gambler is refused by Wayne.
Moreover, where a Ford film, for example, is full of a flurry of
Western details, for Hawks the West is simply the stage on
which his characters (close to stereotypes, some of them)
move. Accordingly, there is no feel of the West in *Rio Bravo*;
in its place is a complex set of relationships as the squabbling
characters slowly form themselves into a 'family', even
celebrating their new-found unity of purpose in the firework
display of the final shoot-out.

The plot is simple. Wayne imprisons Akins to stand trial
for murder and his brother (Russell) and his gunmen isolate
the town and lay siege to the jail in an attempt to free him.
The fundamental irony of the movie, of course, is that,
though he doesn't ask for help, Wayne needs it as desperately
as Gary Cooper's marshal, and in the course of providing it,
Martin, Nelson and company force Wayne to question his
'isolationism'. Dickinson is particularly successful at this.
First she pokes fun at him in the famous scene where Wayne
models an enormous pair of red bloomers – 'Those things
have possibilities sheriff, but not on you' – then she proves
him wrong (she's not the cardsharp) and refuses to accept his
reproval for her chosen career. Similarly, Wayne helps
Martin, who has become a drunk since his girlfriend left him,
recover his dignity and self-respect, simply by needing his
assistance and allowing Martin to feel needed again. Nonetheless he remains isolated, he doesn't join in the sing song in the
jail, until he is fully humanized by Dickinson.

The majesty (and humour) of *Rio Bravo*, a film ostensibly
made to show that a sheriff doesn't need help, is that it shows
that independence, self-respect and dignity are essential but

mustn't get in the way of relationships. Hence, in a shift that would be intensified in **El Dorado** (1966) and **Rio Lobo** (1970), which with *Rio Bravo* form a loose trilogy, the film sees Hawks treating his characters less as a group and more as a family.

d/p Howard Hawks *s* Jules Furthman, Leigh Brackett *c* Russell Harlan *lp* John Wayne, Dean Martin, Ricky Nelson, Angie Dickinson, Walter Brennan, Claude Akins, John Russell

The Sheriff of Fractured Jaw
(FOX; GB) scope 103 min
One of the strangest of director Walsh's movies, *Sheriff of Fractured Jaw* seems, like *A Private Affair* (1959), to be an assault upon the masculinity he so often celebrated in earlier films. The plot, a cross between that of **The Paleface** (1948) and **Ruggles of Red Gap** (1935), sees More as an English gunsmith who goes West to sell his wares and successfully confronts his own cowardice and Mansfield's pneumatic charms. Shot in England, and looking like it, the film survives the unlikely pairing of More and Mansfield thanks to Walsh's taking the possibilities inherent in their role reversal beyond the merely comic. Certainly the film remains the oddest of comedy Westerns.

Mansfield's singing voice was dubbed by Connie Francis.

d Raoul Walsh *p* Daniel M. Angel *s* Arthur Dales *c* Otto Heller *lp* Kenneth More, Jayne Mansfield, Bruce Cabot, Robert Morley, Henry Hull, William Campbell

These Thousand Hills (FOX) scope 96 min
A superior Western. Murray is the ambitious cowboy who coldly sacrifices everything for his political ambitions. With a loan from dance-hall girl Remick, who loves him, he buys a ranch and then marries Owens, the niece of the local banker, Dekker. When in a posse in search of Whitman, an old friend, he does nothing to prevent his hanging when found. He is only forced into action when a fellow rancher, Egan, turns on Remick. Although the script is a little abstract at times, Fleischer is remarkably successful at suggesting Murray's computer-like calculations as he coldly plans his rise to the top.

d Richard Fleischer *p* David Weisbart *s* Alfred Hayes *c* Charles G. Clarke *lp* Don Murray, Richard Egan, Lee Remick, Patricia Owens, Albert Dekker, Stuart Whitman

Thunder in the Sun (PAR) 81 min
A tiresome Western, with Chandler as the scout leading a wagon train of rugged, independent Basques to the Nappa valley of California with their precious vines which are to be the start of the California wine industry. Amongst their number is Hayward, lumbered with a terrible 'Basque' accent that makes much of what she says unintelligible. She is the object of Chandler's affections, even though she's married. The best sequences are the strikingly photographed action scenes, notably the ambushing of the Indians by the mountain-climbing Basques.

Kenneth More looks elegantly on while Jayne Mansfield sorts things out in the bizarre The Sheriff of Fractured Jaw.

d/s Russell Rouse *p* Clarence Greene *c* Stanley Cortez *lp* Susan Hayward, Jeff Chandler, Jacques Bergerac, Blanche Yurka, Carl Esmond, Felix Locher

Warlock (FOX) scope 122 min

Dmytryk's masterpiece, this grand guignol Western stars Fonda and Quinn as the gunmen hired to clean up a town, Widmark as the seemingly impotent sheriff who attempts to stop their excesses and Malone as the woman out to revenge Quinn's killing of her fiancé. The result is a film of forever changing personal alliances and mounting hysteria that is only bettered by Nicholas Ray's **Johnny Guitar** (1954). The complex love-hate relationship between the club-footed Quinn (blond for the only time in his career) and Fonda is perhaps the most open depiction of homosexual love in the classic Western.

d/p Edward Dmytryk *s* Robert Alan Arthur *c* Joe MacDonald *lp* Richard Widmark, Henry Fonda, Anthony Quinn, Dorothy Malone, Dolores Michaels, Richard Arlen

Westbound (WB) 96 min

A minor Western from Boetticher, starring Scott but not written by Kennedy nor produced by Harry Joe Brown, as were Boetticher's masterpieces, **Ride Lonesome** (1959) and **Comanche Station** (1960). *Westbound*'s failings help demonstrate the importance of Ranown (the production company formed by Scott and Brown) and Kennedy to Boetticher. Where their input was entirely creative, to producer Blanke and writers Giler and LeVino, *Westbound* was clearly just another chore. Nonetheless, the film had its delights, especially in Steele's aggressive interpretation of her role. The plot features Scott re-establishing a stagecoach line to ship essential Californian gold to Union forces. Duggan is the villain and Steele (then Boetticher's wife) the heroine. Boetticher directs with style and raises the film above the average, but the story is simply too slight.

d Budd Boetticher *p* Henry Blanke *s* Berne Giler, Albert Shelby LeVino *c* J. Peverell Marley *lp* Randolph Scott, Virginia Mayo, Karen Steele, Andrew Duggan, Michael Dante, Michael Pate

The Wonderful Country (DRM PRODUCTIONS) 96 min

A deservedly much-praised Western, as much for Ardrey's complex script as for Parrish's assured direction. Mitchum, whose DRM Productions made the film, is the hired gun of petty Mexican tyrants (Armendariz and Mendoza). When he is disabled while gunrunning he recuperates on the Texas side of the border. A cynic, he becomes involved with London, the wife of the Mexicans' gunrunning partner, Merrill, only to be expelled from paradise (as he sees Texas) and sent back to the purgatory of Mexico. Ardrey's screenplay forcefully contrasts Armendariz, Mendoza and Merrill vying with each other for control of the land in which the Apache and Mexican peons peacefully live, with Mitchum's inner turmoil. Crosby and Phillips' cinematography is superb, amplifying Mitchum's relationship to the land as he struggles for redemption. The end is particularly well conceived with Mitchum symbolically laying down his gun beside his beloved dead horse and walking across the Rio Grande to the promised land of Texas.

d Robert Parrish *p* Chester Erskine *s* Robert Ardrey *c* Floyd Crosby, Alex Phillips *lp* Robert Mitchum, Julie London, Pedro Armendariz, Victor Mendoza, Gary Merrill, Jack Oakie

Yellowstone Kelly (WB) 91 min

One of the more interesting of Douglas' Westerns. Much of the credit for this must go to writer Kennedy (who would later recycle huge chunks of the script in his debut movie as director, **The Canadians**, 1961). Walker, star of the teleseries *Cheyenne*, is the fur trapper who prevents an Indian war and marries Indian maid, Martin. Reflecting the growing importance of television, the film features another TV star, Byrnes, in a supporting role.

d Gordon Douglas *s* Burt Kennedy *c* Carl Guthrie *lp* Clint Walker, Andra Martin, Edward Byrnes, John Russell, Warren Oates, Claude Akins

The Young Land (C.V. WHITNEY) 89 min

This is a lacklustre outing, more notable for its credits than anything else. Only cinematographers Sharp and Hoch, and Hopper, in one of his first featured roles, emerge from the project favourably. He's the American on trial for killing a Mexican in California in 1848. With him in the dock is American justice from the point of view of the largely Hispanic population of the newest state of the Union. However well intentioned the project was, neither Ford (son of John), as producer, nor Wayne (son of John), as hero, have the confidence to carry it off. Thus, for example, there are hardly any close-ups in the film and the action is forever being described rather than shown.

d Ted Tetzlaff *p* Patrick Ford *s* Norman Shannon Hall *c* Winton Hoch, Henry Sharp *lp* Pat Wayne, Yvonne Craig, Dennis Hopper, Dan O'Herlihy, Roberto de la Madrid, Ken Curtis

The 1960s

The Western Goes International

The sixties was the decade of the Italian Western. Westerns had been made in Europe since the days of the silent cinema. In Britain the River Thames had stood in for the Rio Grande and in France Gaston Modot starred in several charming Western farces long before the First World War. However, it wasn't until Clint Eastwood rode the range to such phenomenal international success as the Man with No Name in Sergio Leone's Dollar trilogy that a European sensibility dominated the Western.

Moreover, this Italian co-option of the Western came when the Hollywood version was in a perilous state. Significantly the major trend in America was the parody Western of the ilk of **Cat Ballou** (1965). The joky relationship to the genre of that film was seen in different ways in the works of McLaglen and Kennedy, the two directors most associated with the Western in the sixties (and seventies). McLaglen, with the capable assistance of John Wayne, produced a broad knockabout vision of the West, while Kennedy, at his best, opted for a more playful and engaging game with the Western's conventions and themes. The dominance of such attitudes hardly suggested a developing genre. Of course, there were notable exceptions: the elegiac (and violent) films of Peckinpah which culminated in the majestic **The Wild Bunch** (1969); the bitter, end-of-career statements of Ford, Hawks and Walsh; the bleak vision of Hellman as evinced in his pair of Poverty Row masterpieces, **The Shooting** and **Ride in the Whirlwind** (both 1966); and an intriguing string of contemporary Westerns like **Lonely Are the Brave** (1962) which bemoaned the vanishing West. But so many of the Hollywood Westerns of the sixties were tired examples of formula pictures. Some, like Audie Murphy's low-budget quickies were rehashes of plots that were hackneyed in the forties, and in the case of A. C. Lyles productions featured actors who were elderly in the forties as well. Similarly big-budget Westerns like the very successful **Butch Cassidy and the Sundance Kid** and **True Grit** (both 1969) were old-fashioned star vehicles, films constructed purely to show off their stars' talents.

Italian Westerns were also made to a formula – indeed they were almost literally a composite of the spy films and the sword and sandal epics that had preceded them: James Bond + Hercules = The Man with No Name. This formula quickly became as rigid as any in Hollywood, but it was a new and far more violent formula, and far more at one with the times. More importantly, simply because it was so different, the Italian Western forced a rethinking of attitudes to the West and the Western. That rethinking and the consequent reworking of the genre was to dominate the Western in the seventies.

The Alamo

(BATJAC PRODUCTIONS) Todd-AO 192 min

Planned for some ten years by Wayne and Grant, who'd scripted Wayne's first production, **Angel and the Badman** (1947), *The Alamo* is one of the most direct of Hollywood's epics. At times the film's patriotism is overwhelming – 'Republic... I like the sound of the word' begins Wayne's final speech as 7,000 Mexicans mass for the final assault on a tiny group of Texans, holding out to give Boone's Sam Houston time to raise an army – but the strong cast and the simple dramatics of the situation more than compensate for this. For his directorial debut, Wayne received uncredited help from John Ford whose stock company also figured strongly amongst the bit-parts and extras. Similarly, the very successful climactic sequence was the responsibility of second-unit director Cliff Lyons.

An alternative view of the events that constitute *The Alamo* can be found in *Seguin* (1982), a telefilm directed by Jesus Salvador Trevino. This tells the story of the Chicano defenders of the Alamo, Hispanics who chose Texas rather than Mexico. Part of a series about America's Chicanos, the telefilm caused much controversy when it was screened. Many thought it made the Chicanos the dupes of Sam Houston and traitors to their race.

d/p John Wayne *s* James Edward Grant *c* William Clothier *lp* John Wayne, Richard Widmark, Laurence Harvey, Richard Boone, Frankie Avalon, Linda Cristal

Cimarron (MGM) scope 147 min

Subject to great studio interference – Mann wanted to shoot on location but was forced to make the bulk of the film on studio sets – and much cut about, this remake of the 1931 classic attempts to explore the wanderlust of its central character. Accordingly the film is best viewed as the bridge between Mann's classic Westerns of the fifties and the epics he was to turn his hands to, where he would repeat this psychologizing to great effect, as in *El Cid* (1961). In *Cimarron*, however, such a psychological approach has the effect of distorting Edna Ferber's novel by concentrating almost exclusively on Ford, a man whose imagination can transform a kitchen table and utensils into a map of the Cherokee Strip landrush he is planning to enter. This unevenness in the film's structure is made even more evident by the cold persona Schell adopts as the wife who completes

Previous pages: *The comedy Western comes of age: James Garner and Jack Elam in* Support Your Local Sheriff.

The Alamo.

Above: *Randolph Scott and Nancy Gates as the woman he rescues from the Indians in Budd Boetticher's magisterial* Comanche Station.

Far right: Sophia Loren, temptress, actress and Heller in Pink Tights.

what Ford has started. Baxter and Tamblyn turn in fine performances as the lusty dancer Ford must leave and the young gunslinger he adopts as a memory of his earlier self. In an effort to save the film, Grainger hired Reggie Callow to direct additional scenes to clarify and soften the ambiguous relationship between Ford and Schell.

d Anthony Mann   *p* Edmund Grainger   *s* Arnold Schulman
c Robert L. Surtees   *lp* Glenn Ford, Maria Schell, Anne Baxter, Arthur O'Connell, Russ Tamblyn, Vic Morrow

Comanche Station

(RANOWN PRODUCTIONS)   scope   73 min
In this, the last in the series of films made with Scott throughout the fifties, Boetticher neatly balances his concerns with youth and age. He contrasts Scott's pointless ten-year search for his wife, kidnapped by Indians, which clearly marks him as a character obsessed with the past and with little time or ability to think about the future, with Homeier and Rust's adolescent gunmen, thinking and talking all the while about a future they will never share. Scott is emotionally dead; soon they will be literally dead.

Kennedy's deceptively casual script details Scott's escorting of Gates, a rancher's wife kidnapped by Indians, home and fending off Akins and his young gunmen, keen to claim the reward for rescuing her. Like Richard Boone before him, in the equally bleak **The Tall T** (1957), Akins is a likeable, if cynical, villain whose death at Scott's hands, after Scott has offered him a chance to escape, is a sad rather than joyful event. Just as Scott is trapped in his ridiculous quest, so Akins is trapped by his flamboyance, and must go for his gun. The

emotional centre of the film is the death of Rust and Homeier, which presages that of the youthful hero of **A Time for Dying** (1969) and marks Boetticher's return to pessimism, albeit much inflected with ironic humour, after the optimism of the glorious **Ride Lonesome** (1959).

d/p Budd Boetticher   *s* Burt Kennedy   *c* Charles Lawton Jnr   *lp* Randolph Scott, Claude Akins, Skip Homeier, Richard Rust, Nancy Gates, Rand Brooks

Flaming Star (FOX)   scope   101 (92) min
Written for Marlon Brando (by Johnson) and then rewritten (by Huffaker) for Presley, whose best film this undoubtedly is, *Flaming Star* is a late entry in the Indian Western stakes. Presley is the half-caste son of McIntire's marriage to Del Rio. Thus loyalties are divided between Indians and whites when the Kiowas go on the rampage. Despite the script's liberal pre-occupation with racial prejudice, Siegel's direction concentrates on the inevitability of violence in the situation, stressing not the causes but the consequences of the characters' descent into chaos.

d Don Siegel   *p* David Weisbart   *s* Nunnally Johnson, Clair Huffaker   *c* Charles G. Clarke   *lp* Elvis Presley, Barbara Eden, John McIntire, Dolores Del Rio, Steve Forrest, Rudolfo Acosta

Guns of the Timberland *aka* Stampede (WB)   91 min
Ladd and Roland are the logging partners who fall out with local ranchers when felling trees and then with each other over horse-trader Crain in this dreary Western. Even the film's climax, a raging forest fire, is a pretty tame affair. Co-writer and producer Spelling would later make his name in television production.

d Robert D. Webb   *p/co-s* Aaron Spelling   *co-s* Joseph Petracca   *c* John Seitz   *lp* Alan Ladd, Jeanne Crain, Gilbert Roland, Frankie Avalon, Lyle Bettger, Noah Beery Jnr

Hell Bent for Leather
(U-INTERNATIONAL)   scope   82 min
Murphy is the cowboy mistaken for a murderer and McNally the marshal who, knowing him to be innocent, plans on killing him to receive the credit of his capture. Farr is the girl Murphy kidnaps to make his escape. She comes to believe him to be innocent and that Merlin is the real murderer. Sherman directs in a dull workmanlike fashion from Knopf's routine screenplay.

d George Sherman   p Gordon Kay   s Christopher Knopf
c Clifford Stine   lp Audie Murphy, Stephen McNally,
Felicia Farr, Robert Middleton, Jan Merlin, Bob Steele

Heller in Pink Tights

(PONTI-GIROSI PRODUCTIONS/PAR)   100 min

Cukor's only Western, *Heller in Pink Tights* is a delightful romantic comedy, a study in Americana and one of the most charming of the director's many tributes to the acting profession. Loosely based on the career of Adah Isaacs Menken who brought culture and the footlights to the frontier in the 1860s, Nichols' script features Loren as the tempestuous leading lady of the Healy Dramatic Company. Though their shows amuse and titillate their audiences, they are nevertheless perpetually on the run from creditors. The plot concerns Forrest, a gunfighter who falls for Loren and briefly becomes the troupe's guardian much to the chagrin of Quinn who is also in love with Loren. But Cukor and Nichols devote most of their time to loving portraits of the social misfits that make up the troupe, Lowe's broken-down Shakesperian ham, O'Brien, struggling with her mother, Heckart, for acceptance as a woman rather than a child. This is a marvellous film.

d George Cukor   p Carlo Ponti, Marcello Girosi   s Dudley Nichols, Walter Bernstein   c Harold Lipstein   lp Sophia Loren, Anthony Quinn, Margaret O'Brien, Steve Forrest, Edmund Lowe, Eileen Heckart

The Magnificent Seven

(UA/MIRISCH)   pv   138 (126) min

A highly influential Western. In the process of adapting Kurosawa's classic film *Seven Samurai* (1952), Sturges and Roberts coarsened the interlocking concern with Samurai honour and social responsibility of the original. In its place they offered the theme of professionals coming together to defend a seemingly impossible cause as a means of exercising and narcissistically displaying their talents. This struck a deep chord with audiences throughout the world, especially in Italy where the total identification of a character with a specific talent, for example Coburn's skill at knife throwing, became a central element in 'Spaghetti Westerns'.

Brynner is the gunman who first recruits a motley crew of outcasts and then successfully leads them against Wallach's bandit chief, but it was the cameo performances, by Coburn, Bronson, Vaughn and above all McQueen with his dry humorous asides that made the film so successful. Similarly Sturges' direction successfully emphasizes the set pieces, which bring the individual characters to life at the expense of the narrative flow.

d/p John Sturges   s William Roberts   c Charles Lang Jnr
lp Yul Brynner, Eli Wallach, Steve McQueen, Horst Buchholz, James Coburn, Charles Bronson, Robert Vaughn

John Wayne (left) and Stewart Granger (centre) at the start of one of the many brawls in Henry Hathaway's rumbustious North to Alaska.

Noose for a Gunman   (UA) b/w   69 min

Another traditional Western from the team of producer Kent and director Cahn. Davis is the professional gunman as honest as the day is long and De Corsia the ogre of a gunman in cahoots with MacLane's land baron. The plot is complicated but Cahn directs simply and vigorously.

d Edward L. Cahn   p Robert E. Kent   s Robert B. Gordon
c Al Cline   lp Jim Davis, Ted De Corsia, Barton MacLane, Lyn Thomas, Harry Carey Jnr, Kermit Maynard

North to Alaska   (FOX)   scope   122 min

This a is hugely enjoyable movie. Conceived as a piece of old-fashioned adventure but given a broad comic touch by Hathaway, *North to Alaska* sees Wayne for the first time adopt the genial, bluff, hearty persona that he was to use for most of his subsequent Westerns, like **McLintock!** (1963) and **Big Jake** (1971). Rackin and Mahin's rumbustious script has Wayne and Granger as miners who hit gold in Alaska and brawl their way through the film's two hours for the love of Capucine. Wayne first romances her for Granger and then falls for her himself. Finally, in a sequence reminiscent of the end of *The Quiet Man* (1952), he stops her leaving Nome in a lengthy piece of public courting on the town's muddy mainstreet. Kovacs is the amiable con man out to steal their claim and Fabian Granger's younger brother. The riotous brawls, performed with great gusto by all concerned are amongst the biggest ever filmed in Hollywood.

d/p Henry Hathaway   s John Lee Mahin, Martin Rackin, Claude Binyon   c Leon Shamroy   lp John Wayne, Stewart Granger, Ernie Kovacs, Fabian, Capucine, Mickey Shaughnessy

Oklahoma Territory   (UA) b/w   67 min

Featuring a wonderfully contrived plot and a spirited performance from its star, Williams, *Oklahoma Territory* was one of the last films to be directed by Cahn who, after his first film, the memorable **Law and Order** (1932), declined to directing low-budget pics. Williams is the district attorney prosecuting Indian chief De Corsia for murder, getting him convicted and then freeing him because he knows he's innocent. The climax has him, guns drawn, force a Federal Judge to re-open the case and give an acquittal. Richards is the railway agent trying to ferment an Indian war so as to get

Far left: *The unsuspecting Robert Wilkie (right) about to be knifed by James Coburn in perhaps the best remembered scene from* The Magnificent Seven.

land for his railway and Talbott the unlikely Indian maid Williams romances. For children of all ages.

d Edward L. Cahn *p* Robert E. Kent *s* Orville Hampton *c* Walter Strenge *lp* Bill Williams, Ted De Corsia, Grant Richards, Gloria Talbott, Walter Sande, Walter Baldwin

One Foot in Hell (FOX) scope 90 min
An ambitious, off-beat Western. Ladd is the embittered citizen intent on wreaking his revenge on his fellow citizens for allowing his wife to die for the want of a few dollars for medicine. He becomes sheriff and plans to cripple the town financially by stealing the money from the bank after the annual cattle sale. Murray and gunslinger Cox join him, but when Murray falls for Michaels and decides to go straight he stops Ladd going through with the job. One-time editor Clark rises to the occasion.

d James B. Clark *p/co-s* Sydney Boehm *co-s* Aaron Spelling *c* William C. Mellor *lp* Alan Ladd, Don Murray, Dan O'Herlihy, Dolores Michaels, Barry Cox, Larry Gates

The Plunderers (AUGUST/AA) b/w 94 min
Often dismissed as *The Wild One* (1953) in period costume, this tale of four adolescents who terrorize a town in the Old West until a one-armed Civil War veteran, Chandler, stands up to them, is crisply directed by Pevney. It's also well acted, especially by Saxon as the tearaways' leader and Chandler who eschews his usual fixed grimace. However, Barbash's screenplay is too predictable to be wholly successful.

d Joseph Pevney *p* Lindsley Parsons *s* Bob Barbash *c* Sol Polito *lp* Jeff Chandler, John Saxon, Ray Stricklyn, Jay C. Flippen, Dolores Hart, Marsha Hunt

A handcuffed Woody Strode as the black cavalryman in John Ford's Sergeant Rutledge.

Sergeant Rutledge (WB) 111 min
A courtroom drama with Strode as the black Cavalryman accused of rape, *Sergeant Rutledge*, like **Cheyenne Autumn** (1964), is too schematic a film to be wholly successful. But if

the courtroom scenes with their parading of racial stereotypes and dramatic verbal duels are a shade too melodramatic, the flashback sequences of Strode in action give great resonance to his defence that his record as 'First Sergeant Braxton Rutledge, C Troop, Ninth United States Cavalry' (as Strode invariably identifies himself) rather than the circumstantial evidence should speak for him.

Accordingly, Ford evades the issue of Strode's colour, identifying him as a Cavalryman before anything else. Nonetheless, in sequences showing Strode singing 'Captain Buffalo', and riding across the Pecos River, the film gives Strode a new dignity as a blackman. As Strode himself recalled later: 'You never seen a negro come off a mountain like John Wayne before. I had the greatest Glory Hallelujah ride across the Pecos River...I carried the whole black race across that river.'

d John Ford *co-p/co-s* Willis Goldbeck *co-p* Patrick Ford *co-s* James Warner Bellah *c* Bert Glennon *lp* Jeffrey Hunter, Constance Towers, Woody Strode, Billie Burke, Carleton Young, Walter Reed

The Unforgiven (UA) pv 125 (120) min
A fascinating film. Beautifully shot in soft, natural colours by Planer, *The Unforgiven* is both a study of racism – Hepburn is suspected of being an Indian orphan – and a surprising paen to the settlers of the American West. Lancaster is marvellous as the patriarchal rancher as are Gish and Bickford in their supporting roles, but it is Murphy, in his best screen role, as Hepburn's bigoted 'brother' who steals the film. Like **The Searchers** (1956) it is based on a novel by Alan LeMay.

d John Huston *p* James Hill *s* Ben Maddow *c* Franz Planer *lp* Burt Lancaster, Audrey Hepburn, Audie Murphy, John Saxon, Charles Bickford, Lillian Gish

Walk Like a Dragon (PAR) b/w 95 min
A highly unusual and ambitious Western in which Lord is the arrogant rancher who frees a Chinese slave girl (McCarthy) at the San Francisco slavemarket in 1870 and brings her back home with Chinaman Shigeta, whose ambition is to become a gunfighter, in tow. Torme, as the all-in-black gunslinger, adds a distinctive touch of class to the proceedings. Writer/producer Clavell, who would become one of the most successful one-man bands of the seventies, directs somewhat earnestly, but the film's exposé of the workings of racism in a small cow town is neatly enough done. Griggs' harsh cinematography obscures the film's impoverished budget.

d/p/co-s James Clavell *co-s* Daniel Mainwaring *c* Loyal Griggs *lp* Jack Lord, James Shigeta, Nobu McCarthy, Mel Torme, Michael Pate, Donald Barry

Walk Tall (FOX) scope 60 min
One of the first of producer/director Dexter's quickies, *Walk Tall* is an undistinguished film. Parker is the lawman on the trail of Indian-hater and killer Taylor whom he must catch to prevent the Shoshone taking the warpath. The direction is leaden and the script's complications – a snakebite and Meadows' beautiful young girl – predictable, but Crosby, Roger Corman's regular cameraman, makes the San Bernadine locations look pretty.

d/p Maury Dexter *s* Joseph Fritz *c* Floyd Crosby *lp* Willard Parker, Joyce Meadows, Kent Taylor, Russ Bender, Ron Sable, Bill Mims

Young Jesse James (FOX) b/w scope 73 min
Stricklyn and Dix are Jesse and Frank in this unimaginative account of their early years. Meyer as Quantrill, Parker as Cole Younger and Anders as Belle Starr provide the back-up outlaw support. The script has Jesse join Quantrill after witnessing the hanging of his father and graduate to bank robbery despite an earnest desire to become a farmer.

d William Claxton p Jack Leewood s Orville H.
Hampton, Jerry Sackheim c Carl Berger lp Ray Stricklyn,
Willard Parker, Merry Anders, Robert Dix, Emile Meyer,
Jacklyn O'Donnell

1961

The Canadians (FOX) scope 85 min

Kennedy's directorial debut, *The Canadians* is undoubtedly
the most anonymous-looking of all the movies Kennedy has
been associated with. The script has none of the wit and
compression that mark his earlier scripts for Budd Boetticher,
such as **The Tall T** (1957), **Ride Lonesome** (1959) and
Comanche Station (1960), while his direction lacks the
breezy confidence of later work like **Support Your Local
Gunfighter** (1971). Since he'd directed before, for television,
one can only assume it was the cinemascope format, which
Fox had insisted on for nearly all its Westerns since the
mid-fifties, that he was uncomfortable with. The plot
concerns mountie Ryan trying to keep the peace on the
Canadian-American border while rancher Dehner massacres
Indians as they round up wild horses.

d/s Burt Kennedy p Herman E. Webber c Arthur
Ibbetson lp Robert Ryan, John Dehner, Torin Thatcher,
Burt Metcalfe, John Sutton, Jack Creley

The Comancheros (FOX) scope 107 min

Excluding his excesses of the seventies, *The Comancheros* sees
Wayne at his most tongue-in-cheek in the role of the Texas
Ranger on the trail of a Confederate renegade planning to set
up an empire in Mexico and unloose a horde of Winchester-
armed Indians against the Union in revenge of the Confederacy's defeat. The scenes at Persoff's half-built would-be
Southern Imperial mansion have a gaunt beauty about them,
but the tone of the film is best captured by the director of the
action sequences, Cliff Lyons, whose stuntmen fall over a
shade too perfectly. Whitman provides steady support as the
gambler whose unwilling help Wayne demands. Bob Steele
and Guinn 'Big Boy' Williams add cameos perfectly in
keeping with the cheerful mood of the film.

d Michael Curtiz p George Sherman s James Edward
Grant, Clair Huffaker c William H. Clothier lp John
Wayne, Stuart Whitman, Ina Balin, Nehemiah Persoff, Lee
Marvin, Pat Wayne

The Deadly Companions
(PATHE-AMERICAN-CAROUSEL) pv 90 min

The first film by Peckinpah and the first by its much touted
but short-lived production company, Pathe-American, *The
Deadly Companions* was, like so many of its director's films,
taken from him and recut against his wishes. Nonetheless, it
remains an individual work and is astonishingly assured for a
first film. The characters are all obsessives: O'Hara taking her

dead son to be buried in a ghost town in the middle of Apache
territory beside the father the inhabitants of Gil City refuse to
believe in and so free herself of the burden of the past;
Cochran the stylish gunfighter with eyes for O'Hara; Wills the
first of the shambling monsters who dominate Peckinpah's
later films; and Keith the would-be rational man, complete
with horrendous scar and powerless shooting arm determined
not to reduce himself to the animal level of Wills by taking his
revenge on the man who scalped him. Together all four
journey to their destination, passing such sights as Indians
drunkenly parodying their earlier stagecoach robbery, a
reflection of the uneasy, blurred relationship between Wills
and Keith in which one is never sure who is the savage, who is
the rational man and who is the pursuer. The superbly staged
stagecoach sequence is the first indication of how powerful a
revision of Western themes and images Peckinpah would
embark on. The film is flawed but its power is undiminished.

d Sam Peckinpah p Charles S. FitzSimons s A.S.
Fleischman c William H. Clothier lp Maureen O'Hara,
Brian Keith, Steve Cochran, Chill Wills, Strother Martin, Jim
O'Hara

Five Guns to Tombstone (UA) b/w 71 min

This is another of Kent and Cahn's traditional Westerns that
was clearly targeted at children. Brown is the retired gunman
turned government agent lured out of retirement by his
brother Karnes who ends the days of outlaw leader Coy. The
screenplay is crude but Cahn's stress on action and Gertsman's unostentatious cinematography are appealing.

*Far left: John Wayne
tries to restrain Lee
Marvin in Michael
Curtiz's* The
Comancheros.

*Maureen O'Hara in
Sam Peckinpah's
assured debut,* The
Deadly Companions.

Kirk Douglas and Carol Lynley, father and daughter on the verge of incest in Robert Aldrich's The Last Sunset.

Gold of the Seven Saints (WB) scope 88 min
Soon to become the suave star of *The Saint* teleseries, Moore is as believable as an Irish cowboy turned prospector transporting a load of gold bullion through the desert, as the Brackett-Freeman script is incisive. Fellow television star Walker is his partner, Roman, the girl they briefly quarrel over and Evans and Middleton are amongst the marauders enviously eyeing the gold. Douglas' direction is routine.

d Gordon Douglas *p/co-s* Leonard Freeman *co-s* Leigh Brackett *c* Joseph Biroc *lp* Clint Walker, Roger Moore, Leticia Roman, Robert Middleton, Gene Evans, Chill Wills

Gun Street (UA) b/w 67 min
The last Western to be directed by Cahn, who began his career with the coming of sound and, after making major films like **Law and Order** (1932), quickly plummeted to low-budget action movies, most of which were Westerns. Unlike many of the films he made for producer Kent – **Five Guns to Tombstone** (1961) and **Noose for a Gunman** (1960) for example – this isn't a traditional Western. Here, with writer Freedle, Cahn attempts a modern Western. Brown is the sheriff pursuing an escaped gunman and wondering if he can shoot his old friend, only to have the gunman expire of a bullet wound received earlier. Sadly, the results as performed by the weak cast, whose roles seem to have been created as a pale reflection of the world of the *Gunsmoke* teleseries, are decidedly uninteresting to watch. Even Cahn's direction is listless.

Far right: A scene from The Misfits, *one of the better contemporary Westerns of the sixties.*

d Edward L. Cahn *p* Robert E. Kent *s* Sam C. Freedle *c* Gilbert Warrenton *lp* James Brown, Jean Willes, John Clark, Ned Flory, John Pickard, Sandra Stone

The Last Rebel *orig* El Ultimo Rebelde
(HISPANO CONTINENTAL FILMS; MEX) 83 min
A Mexican version of the oft-filmed life of Joaquin Murrieta (Thompson), the peaceful prospector turned bandido and scourge of the Californian gringos after his wife was murdered by five miners. He organizes a huge outlaw band and, with the assistance of Acosta, kills hundreds of miners before dying at the hands of Fawcett and a whole bevy of Texas Rangers. Though the film is surprisingly low key, the extended sequences of Mexican peasants mourning for him, are more powerful than the more sentimental asides made by American films such as **Murrieta** (1965) or **Robin Hood of El Dorado** (1936).

d/p/co-s Miguel Contreras Torres *co-s* Manuel R. Ojeda *c* Jose Ortiz Ramos *lp* Carlos Thompson, Rodolfo Acosta, Charles Fawcett, Lee Morgan, Ariadne Welter

The Last Sunset (U) 112 min
This powerful essay in sexual neurosis is, oddly enough, the most lyrical of Aldrich's films. Douglas, whose philosophizing and blarney are matched by Laszlo's sensuous images, is the man frozen in adolescence beneath whose romantic charms lies a pathological concern with an ideal rather than a real world. He and Hudson, the marshal on his trail, with whom he enjoys a jokey relationship, join a cattle trek from Mexico to California headed up by his ex-wife, Malone and her daughter Lynley. In the course of the drive Malone and Hudson fall for each other. Lynley is similarly impressed by Douglas' dash and, in turn, he comes to worship her, after being rejected by her mother, only to find that she is truly the unattainable idealized woman, his own daughter. Unable to have her and having committed so much to the (idealized) relationship he commits suicide by drawing on Hudson with an empty gun.

d Robert Aldrich *p* Eugene Frenke, Edward Lewis *s* Dalton Trumbo *c* Ernest Laszlo *lp* Rock Hudson, Kirk Douglas, Dorothy Malone, Joseph Cotten, Carol Lynley, Jack Elam

The Misfits (UA) b/w 124 min
The last film by both Gable and Monroe, *The Misfits* was a box-office disaster. The script by Miller (then Mr Monroe) was attacked as being pretentious and for continually hammering at the message that there was no place for nonconformity in modern America. In retrospect, although both script and direction are over-explicit at times, the charges are unfounded. The heart of the film lies not in the characters' talk with each other but in the relationships they form. Gable is the aging cowboy, Monroe the jaded divorcee he meets and Clift the has-been rodeo performer whom Gable persuades to join him in rounding up 'misfits', horses too small for riding, which they intend to sell for dogfood. Together they form a society apart, united by their shared dissatisfactions with

279

modern America. The sequences devoted to the rounding-up of the stallions, with Clift and Gable alone against the horses – a sequence that was to become one of the cliches of the modern Western – are marvellous and Metty's camera gives the action a romantic glow. A far better and more complex film than the similarly themed **Lonely Are the Brave** (1962).

d John Huston *p* Frank E. Taylor *s* Arthur Miller
c Russell Metty *lp* Clark Gable, Marilyn Monroe, Montgomery Clift, Thelma Ritter, Eli Wallach, Kevin McCarthy

One-Eyed Jacks (PAR) vv 141 min
A unique Western. With characteristic bravado, Brando, after Stanley Kubrick quit as director, took control of every major aspect of the film, finally cutting some five hours of finished film to a mere two-and-a-half hours. Contrary to cynical expectations the result is riveting with Brando, playing against Malden, in the classic role of a terse outlaw who returns from the past to settle an unfinished score. Although the movie, which has an intensity of feeling rarely seen outside the work of King Vidor or Anthony Mann, can be seen as a forerunner of the 'modern' Westerns of Sam Peckinpah, it is far more than that. Brando's charismatic, albeit indulgent, acting and his symbolically inclined camera force extra meaning from Trosper and Willingham's complex story of revenge. Similarly, the film's main locale, the coast of Monterey, the edge of America (wonderfully photographed by Lang) gives the story an added dimension. But, above all, it is Brando and Malden's knowing father-son relationship that fuels the movie's tensions, giving Brando's planned seduction of Malden's daughter an almost Oedipal intensity. For all that, the film is undeniably flawed, as much by Brando's inability to handle narrative as by the studio's barbarous re-editing of the material to make the Brando character the film's hero and produce the statutory happy ending.

d Marlon Brando *p* Frank P. Rosenberg *s* Guy Trosper, Calder Willingham *c* Charles Lang Jnr *lp* Marlon Brando, Karl Malden, Pina Pellicer, Ben Johnson, Katy Jurado, Slim Pickens

Posse from Hell (U-INTERNATIONAL) 89 min
Shot on location around Mount Whitney, where many of the Hopalong Cassidy series Westerns had been made, this is a beautiful looking, but otherwise routine Western. Murphy is the gunman turned lawman who leads a posse after a quartet of killers. Coleman directs efficiently and the interesting cast includes Van Cleef and Morrow at their snarling best as two of the killers and Lampert as the girl they kidnap.

d Herbert Coleman *p* Gordon Kay *s* Clair Huffaker
c Clifford Stine *lp* Audie Murphy, John Saxon, Zohra Lampert, Vic Morrow, Lee Van Cleef, Robert Keith

The Second Time Around (FOX) scope 99 min
A family Western in which Reynolds takes the role that would seem to have been fashioned for Doris Day, as the widow who, faced with the problem of raising two children, first takes to cowboying and then gets herself elected sheriff of an Arizona township in 1911. Griffith and Forrest are the ranchers who vie for her affections. Sherman directs lightly enough but the film's sugary sentimentality is overwhelming.

d Vincent Sherman *p* Jack Cunningham *s* Oscar Saul, Cecil Van Heusen *c* Ellis W. Carter *lp* Debbie Reynolds, Steve Forrest, Andy Griffith, Juliet Prowse, Thelma Ritter, Timothy Carey

The Singer Not the Song (RANK; GB) scope 132 min
Bogarde was often ill-used in the course of his lengthy contract with the Rank organization. This novelettish Western is a prime example of that. He's the black-suited atheist of a bandido struggling with Mills' Oxbridge-accented priest for

control of a village. Their struggle is intensified by the homosexual interest Bogarde has in Mills who is also the object of the affections of local rancher's daughter Demongeot. Balchin's screenplay is literate, but Baker's direction is purple prose from start to finish.

d/p Roy Baker *s* Nigel Balchin *c* Otto Heller *lp* John Mills, Dirk Bogarde, Mylene Demongeot, John Bentley, Roger Delgado, Lee Montague

A Thunder of Drums (MGM) scope 97 min
Hamilton is the newly commissioned Cavalry officer, son of a former general, who gets roughly treated by Boone (a fine snarling performance), the commander of the isolated frontier outpost Hamilton's posted to. He finally proves himself worthy of his father's name when the Apache go on the rampage. Sadly, Bellah's script compares unfavourably with his stories that provided the basis for Ford's loose trilogy about the Cavalry, **Fort Apache** (1948), **She Wore a Yellow Ribbon** (1949) and **Rio Grande** (1950), even though it covers some of the same ground. Newman's direction is similarly routine. The film also features Chamberlain's debut movie performance.

d Joseph M. Newman *p* Robert J. Enders *s* James Warner Bellah *c* William Spencer *lp* Richard Boone, George Hamilton, Luana Patten, Richard Chamberlain, Charles Bronson, Slim Pickens

Two Rode Together
(FORD-SHPETNER PRODUCTIONS/COL) 109 min
Dismissed by Ford as a casual favour to Columbia's boss Harry Cohen, *Two Rode Together* repays careful attention. Stewart is the cynical marshal hired to repatriate the children of pioneers caught by the Comanche, and Widmark is the Cavalry officer who accompanies him. Gone is the idea of the clean frontier as a would-be garden as in **The Searchers** (1956) and earlier. Instead Ford offers viewers a nightmare vision of the frontier overrun by hysteria and hypocrisy, a frontier in which even the Indians are seen as primitive entrepreneurs.

d John Ford *p* Stan Shpetner *s* Frank Nugent *c* Charles Lawton Jnr *lp* James Stewart, Richard Widmark, Shirley Jones, Linda Cristal, Andy Devine, John McIntire

Above: *Marlon Brando's humiliation at the hands of his 'father', Karl Malden, in* One-Eyed Jacks, *Brando's only film as director to date.*

Kirk Douglas as the last cowboy in Lonely Are the Brave.

Geronimo (UA) pv 101 min
A badly miscast Connors is the much-idealized Geronimo in this version of the legend. Beginning with his surrender in 1883, it follows the mistreatment of Geronimo and his tribe by corrupt officials and businessmen to end bizarrely with Pyle, as a US Senator, riding to prevent the massacre of the Indians, when they finally threaten to rebel, by the Cavalry.

d/p Arnold Laven *s* Pat Fielder *c* Alex Philips *lp* Chuck Connors, Kamala Devi, Adam West, Ross Martin, Denver Pyle, Pat Conway

How the West Was Won
(MGM) cinerama 165 (162) min
A vast sprawling epic that chronicles the development of the West through the adventures of one family, *How the West Was Won* was the first feature film to use the Cinerama system, previously only used for travelogues. The three sequences directed by Hathaway are the most successful articulation of the adventure of America's westward expansion, but it is Ford's Civil War sequence that is the most interesting. The fifteen-minute sequence tells the story of a farm boy (Peppard) preventing the assassination of General U.S. Grant (Morgan) who is so horrified by the bloody rout of the Battle of Shiloh that he is contemplating quitting. The weaving of Peppard's puzzled coming-of-age and Morgan's (and by extension America's) fate is done with an economy that puts the rest of the film to shame. Typically Ford chooses a moment of near defeat, seen in the image of the river of blood and the massed graves that represent Shiloh, and a moment of desperation, to celebrate the (re)building of America.

John Mills falls beside Dirk Bogarde's homosexual gunman in Roy Ward Baker's bizarre The Singer Not the Song, *another step nearer to the demented excesses of the Italian Western.*

d Henry Hathaway (*The Rivers, The Plains, The Outlaws*), John Ford (*The Civil War*), George Marshall (*The Railroad*) *p* Bernard Smith *s* James R. Webb *c* William H. Daniels, Milton Krasner, Charles Lang Jnr, Joseph La Shelle *lp* Spencer Tracy (Narrator), Carroll Baker, Lee J. Cobb, Henry Fonda, Gregory Peck, George Peppard, James Stewart, John Wayne, Richard Widmark, Henry Morgan, Karl Malden

Lonely Are the Brave (U/JOEL) b/w pv 107 min
A self-consciously serious contemporary Western. Douglas is the embittered cowboy who breaks jail and heads for the hills. Matthau is the weary but sympathetic sheriff marshalling jeeps and helicopters to track Douglas down and finding that man and horse are still an unbeatable combination. The ending, with Douglas run over by a huge container truck carrying lavatories, is trite and obvious, as is Miller's strident direction. Nevertheless Trumbo's script, although it never achieves the mythic dimension it clearly aspires to, does successfully present Douglas as the last real cowboy, lost in the realities of the jet age.

d David Miller *p* Edward Lewis *s* Dalton Trumbo *c* Philip Lathrop *lp* Kirk Douglas, Gena Rowlands, Walter Matthau, George Kennedy, Michael Kane, Carroll O'Connor

The Man Who Shot Liberty Valance
(FORD PRODUCTIONS/PAR) b/w 122 min
This is a key work. More than any other, this film, with its extended treatment of the garden/civilization versus the wilderness/nature theme that is so central to Ford, articulates its director's sombre gainsaying of what once he had so gaily celebrated, most notably in **My Darling Clementine** (1946), whose credit sequence the later film cruelly mimics. The earlier film is, in the words of Andrew Sarris, full of 'poetic touches which...fluttered across the meanings and feelings of [Ford's] art'; the later film, in complete contrast, is an austere production, shot almost entirely on sound stages where 'the cactus was planted last night'.

In the movie, the promise of the sunlit present and the reservoir that will make the desert flower is bitterly undercut by the central flashback sequence in which it is revealed that this new West, modern America, only came into being at the expense of an old West, represented by the heroic figure of Wayne's Tom Doniphon, lying in state in his coffin and attended worshipfully by Ford (and a little testily by Stewart). The result is an even richer and more complex film than **The Searchers** (1956), a movie whose images echo down the years of Ford's career, and films with an even greater resonance than the simple (but intensely moving) image of the half-closed, closing door that ends *The Searchers*.

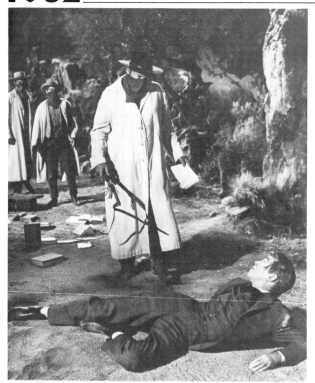

Stewart is the senator who makes his political name as the man who shot the ironically-named Liberty Valance (Marvin) and brought law and order to the territory. But it is Wayne who, unbeknown to Stewart at the time, really shot Marvin (who gives a chillingly evil performance of almost comic-strip proportions) and then faded back into the darkness and out of history. It is his story that Stewart tells the waiting newsmen, curious as to why a senator should attend the funeral of a nonentity. Stewart's law books and irrigation schemes have won, courtesy of Wayne's gun, at the cost to Wayne of losing his girl (Miles) to Stewart and his private garden back to the desert.

The film's sombre dignity is made the more so by Ford's even-handed treatment of his leading characters (if not his players; Wayne is granted the lustrous close-ups that symbolize heroism) as he watches both bend to the inevitability of the historical process.

The film's title song provided Gene Pitney with his second million-selling disc.

d John Ford *p/co-s* Willis Goldbeck *co-s* James Warner Bellah *c* William H. Clothier *lp* John Wayne, James Stewart, Vera Miles, Lee Marvin, Edmond O'Brien, Andy Devine

Ride the High Country *aka* Guns in the Afternoon
(MGM) scope 94 min

Peckinpah's most accomplished and most appealing film. Hugging close to the contour lines of the genre, it contrasts the embittered puritanism and idealism of McCrea with the worldly (but, needless to say, finally honourable) pragmatism of Scott. They play two ageing – but mythically ageless – gunmen who, like heroes of yore, set out, just once more, to do 'what a man's gotta do'. In short, an elegiac version of **The Wild Bunch** (1969). The duo, caught out of time in a world of horseless carriages and Chinese restaurants, accept the job of transporting gold from a mining camp back to town. For McCrea the commission is a means of regaining his self-respect, for Scott, who intends to steal the gold, a means of featherbedding his retirement. In the course of the journey, however, both men are forced to question their self images and values by the presence of Hartley, the girl they take to her miner fiancé (Drury) and whom they then have to take back

with them after witnessing the brutality of Drury and his brothers. The brothers pursue the group, forcing Scott and McCrea to forsake their differences in defence of the gold and Hartley. The end, with Scott and McCrea shooting it out, just like the old days, is simply marvellous.

Despite MGM's bad distribution, the film won immediate acclaim (and a prize at the Venice Film Festival). Even more than **The Deadly Companions** (1961) it sowed the seeds of concerns that were to culminate in Peckinpah's masterpieces, **The Wild Bunch** (1969) and **Pat Garrett and Billy the Kid** (1973).

d Sam Peckinpah *p* Richard E. Lyons *s* N.B. Stone Jnr *c* Lucien Ballard *lp* Randolph Scott, Joel McCrea, Marriette Hartley, Edgar Buchanan, James Drury, R.G. Armstrong

Sergeants Three (E-C) pv 112 min

A crude 'Westernization' of Rudyard Kipling's oft-filmed *Gunga Din* with Sinatra and his clan. Sinatra, Martin and Lawford take the parts, played by Cary Grant, Victor McLaglen and Douglas Fairbanks Jnr in the classic 1939 version, of the brawling sergeants sent to establish an outpost in an outlying prairie settlement. In a series of slapstick action sequences, they foil Silva's Indian attacks. Often funny, the film nonetheless becomes rapidly tiresome as it proceeds, lacking any perspective of its own.

d John Sturges *p* Howard W. Koch *s* W.R. Burnett *c* Winton H. Koch *lp* Frank Sinatra, Dean Martin, Sammy Davis Jnr, Peter Lawford, Henry Silva, Ruta Lee

Six Black Horses (U-INTERNATIONAL) 80 min

Scripted by Kennedy and directed by Keller, this is an interesting Western, if only for the light it throws on the question of who was the dominant influence in the Budd Boetticher-directed, Kennedy-scripted Westerns starring Randolph Scott. Here, Kennedy's script is full of jokes and similar in tone to his scripts for Boetticher (and, later for himself), but, though Murphy and Duryea as the reluctant opponents parallel Scott and the amiable villains of films like **The Tall T** (1957) and **Ride Lonesome** (1959), neither they nor Keller bring anything of their own to the roles.

O'Brien is the widow determined to have her revenge on Duryea for the murder of her husband. A minor, but

Far left: Lee Marvin as the bullwhip wielding spirit of anarchy tears up James Stewart's law books in John Ford's seminal The Man Who Shot Liberty Valance.

The wedding procession in Ride the High Country, *Sam Peckinpah's most assured Western.*

Lex Barker (left) and Pierre Brice as Winnetou in The Treasure of Silver Lake, the first of the Winnetou series of German-made Westerns.

engaging, film, made the more so by the presence of veterans Steele and Barcroft.

d Harry Keller p Gordon Kay s Burt Kennedy c Maury Gertsman lp Audie Murphy, Dan Duryea, Joan O'Brien, Roy Barcroft, Bob Steele, George Wallace

The Treasure of Silver Lake orig Der Schatz im Silbersee

(RIALTO FILM/JADRAN FILM; WG, YUG) scope 111 (80) min
The first of the Winnetou series of films based on the writings of Europe's most prolific pulp writer, Karl May. The films were phenomenally successful throughout Europe, making profits of around $2 million each, inspiring pop songs ('Der Win der Prairie') and a revival of interest in things Western, if not the American Western. More significantly they created the commercial and cultural context which produced the Italian Western. Badly dubbed and shorn of some 30 minutes when shown outside of Europe, this film remains a breezy, if inconsequential Western. Brice is Apache Chief Winnetou, who, with his friend, Old Shatterhand (Barker) finds himself in the middle of the oft used hidden-treasure, torn-map plot when he goes to the assistance of George and Dor. The finale is charming: first Lom is killed when he triggers a downpour of gold upon himself and then Winnetou leads a band of Indian braves to the rescue of the lovers.

d Harald Reinl p Horst Wendlandt s Harald G. Petersson c Ernst W. Kalinke lp Lex Barker, Pierre Brice, Gotz George, Herbert Lom, Karin Dor, Eddi Arent

Young Guns of Texas (FOX) scope 78 min

The young guns include James, son of Robert Mitchum and Jody, son of Joel McCrea while Alana, daughter of Alan Ladd is the romantic interest. That said, the cast list is the most interesting thing about this Western. Conway is the man on the trail of the outlaws who survives the Apache attack that kills them.

d/co-p Maury Dexter co-p Robert L. Lippert s Henry Cross c John Nickolaus Jnr lp James Mitchum, Jody McCrea, Alana Ladd, Chill Wills, Gary Conway, Robert Lowery

1963

Cattle King (MGM/MISSOURI PRODUCTIONS) 88 min

A routine MGM quickie, Cattle King was shot in under two weeks by veteran B director Garnett. Taylor, a rancher, crosses swords with Middleton's cattle speculator who wants to open the range to grazing which will bring him short term profits but finally result in the destruction of the grasslands

Far right: Robert Taylor in Cattle King.

that Taylor and his fellow ranchers depend on and are carefully conserving. Caulfield is the woman Taylor loves.

d Tay Garnett p Nat Holt s Thomas Thompson c William E. Snyder lp Robert Taylor, Joan Caulfield, Robert Middleton, Ray Teal, Robert Loggia, Larry Gates

Four for Texas (WB) 124 min

A disaster, all the more so in comparison with the director's **Apache** (1954) and **The Last Sunset** (1961). *Four for Texas* suffers from Aldrich's recurrent tendency to exaggerate in the name of satire when precision is required. It begins well enough with Sinatra and Martin, rival would-be looters of a stagecoach, gloriously pulling rabbit after rabbit out of their hats in attempts at one-upmanship, but soon descends to the level of having Ekberg and Andress in various degrees of *deshabille* for its would-be appeal. Buono is a wonderfully measured villain. The film includes one of the last screen appearances of the Three Stooges.

d/p/co-s Robert Aldrich co-s Teddi Sherman c Ernest Laszlo lp Frank Sinatra, Dean Martin, Anita Ekberg, Ursula Andress, Charles Bronson, Victor Buono

Gringo orig Duello nel Texas aka Gunfight at Red Sands

(TECISA FILM/JOLLY FILM; SP, IT) 95 (86) min
This is an interesting Italian Western, if only because it was one of the first (pre-dating Leone's transformation of the genre by a year) to forsake 'the Indian story' that dominated Continental Westerns of the early sixties. Though it's clearly a transitional film – its downtrodden Mexicans live in California, for example, and, even more interestingly, the plot has Harrison as the hero quitting the revolutionary war in Mexico to seek revenge on his foster father – and Blasco's direction is routine, it very successfully introduced the notion of an avenging stranger to the genre. What it lacks is the ritualistic orchestration of detail that made the Dollar films so unusual.

d/co-s Riccardo Blasco p/co-s Albert Band (Alfredo Antonini) c Jack Dalmas (Massimo Dallamano) lp Richard Harrison, Giacomo Rossi Stuart, Mikaela, Sara Lezana, Daniel Martin

The Gun Hawk (BERN-FIELD PRODUCTIONS) 92 min
In this contrived Western Calhoun is the dying gunslinger trying to reform a trigger-happy youth, Lauren. Calhoun is his usual quiet-spoken self and Wilke the evil, grinning villain, but Ludwig's direction, especially in the second half of the film, is far too slow. The bizarre climax has Calhoun, not wanting to die in bed, bullying the youngster, who he's been trying to get to put his guns down, into shooting him in a duel. Cameron is the sympathetic sheriff who watches over things.

d Edward Ludwig *p* Richard Bernstein *s* Jo Heims
c Paul C. Vogel *lp* Rory Calhoun, Rod Cameron, Ruta Lee, Rod Lauren, Robert J. (Bob) Wilke, John Litel

Gunfight at Comanche Creek (AA) pv 91 min
This remake of **Last of the Badmen** (1957) is a serviceable Murphy Western. This time he's a member of the National Detective agency sent to ferret out a gang whose trick is springing prisoners from jail and killing them when the reward money due on them after enough crimes have been committed under their name is high enough. Murphy goes undercover and from then on it's a race between him and his reward tag as to who'll get shot first, him or gangleader Cooper. The film is efficiently directed and straightforwardly acted by Murphy, by now the undisputed king of budget Westerns.

d Frank McDonald *p* Ben Schwalb *s* Edward Bernds
c Joseph Biroc *lp* Audie Murphy, Ben Cooper, Coleen Miller, DeForrest Kelley, Jan Merlin, John Hubbard

Hud (PAR/SALEM/DOVER) b/w pv 112 min
A superior contemporary Western. Howe's bleak black and white photography of the flat Texas plains, perfectly captures the spiritual desolation that lies at the heart of Ravetch and Frank's literate script. Newman is the irresponsible, sexually arrogant son and Douglas the equally uncompromising moralist of a father (a distant cinematic descendant of the Lionel Barrymore character in **Duel in the Sun,** 1946). De Wilde is the nephew who idolizes Newman and Neal the housekeeper who hopes to tame Newman. But as so often in Ritt's films, events swiftly push matters past a point of reconciliation. Thus, when the cattle contract foot and mouth

Keir Dullea as the spirited youngster for whom Buddy Ebsen (left) orders a Mail Order Bride.

disease and Douglas slaughters them, the barren open spaces become as claustrophobic as a prison cell, driving first Neal and then De Wilde away and leaving Newman, unmoved even by his father's death, to sit drinking beer in splendid isolation. Unlike *The Last Picture Show* (1971), which also derives from a Larry McMurtry novel but romanticizes the 'old West' far more, there is no resolution at the end of *Hud* because Newman, whose performance helped fix his screen image for some time, has no capacity for change.

Douglas won an Oscar as Best Supporting Actor and Neal as Best Actress.

d/co-p Martin Ritt *co-p/co-s* Irving Ravetch *co-s* Harriet Frank Jnr *c* James Wong Howe *lp* Paul Newman, Melvyn Douglas, Patricia Neal, Brandon De Wilde, John Ashley, Whit Bissell

Mail Order Bride *aka* **West of Montana**
(MGM) pv 85 min
Like Kennedy's later **The Rounders** (1965), this is another gentle comedy, a marked contrast to his later and far broader Westerns such as **Support Your Local Sheriff** (1968). Ebsen is the worried father who attempts (successfully by the end) to get his hell-raiser of a son, Dullea, to settle down by importing a bride, Nettleton. Oates, Windsor and Fix supply the strong supporting cast and Vogel the lyrical cinematography. A little diamond of a film.

d/s Burt Kennedy *p* Richard E. Lyons *c* Paul C. Vogel
lp Buddy Ebsen, Keir Dullea, Lois Nettleton, Warren Oates, Marie Windsor, Paul Fix

McLintock! (UA/BATJAC) pv 127 min
Wayne and O'Hara are the battling husband and wife in this extremely profitable comedy Western directed by Andrew (son of Victor) McLaglen and produced by Michael (son of John) Wayne. Clearly influenced by Ford's **Rio Grande** (1950) and *The Quiet Man* (1952), but lacking the depth of either film, it is a broad comedy with oceans of mud at its centre. The plot, which has Wayne ostensibly negotiating with Lowery's Governor on behalf of Indians, quickly devolves into a lengthy *Taming of the Shrew*-type slanging-match between Wayne and O'Hara. Patrick and Aissa Wayne have featured roles.

d Andrew V. McLaglen *p* Michael Wayne *s* James Edward Grant *c* William H. Clothier *lp* John Wayne, Maureen O'Hara, Yvonne De Carlo, Robert Lowery, Stefanie Powers, Chill Wills

Far left: Paul Newman is Hud.

Savage Sam (WALT DISNEY) 103 min

This is a lacklustre Western from the Disney studio. Keith is the leader of a posse of Texans who, with help from a hound called Savage Sam, trail an Apache war party that has kidnapped two of their children. Tokar directs listlessly with no feeling for either the kidnapped children or their family.

d Norman Tokar *p* Walt Disney *s* Fred Gipson, William Tunberg *c* Edward Colman *lp* Brian Keith, Tommy Kirk, Kevin Corcoran, Dewey Martin, Jeff York, Slim Pickens

Winnetou the Warrior *orig* Winnetou *aka* Apache Gold
(RIALTO FILM/JADRAN FILM/STE NOUVELLE DE CINEMA; WG, YUG, FR) scope 101 (89) min

The second and most interesting of Reinl's series of Westerns based on the stories of Europe's most prolific writer of Westerns, Karl May. Like **The Treasure of Silver Lake** (1962) it was badly cut and dubbed when shown outside Europe and as a result much of the bold romanticism of the film is lost. Brice's Apache chief Winnetou and Barker's railway investigator, Old Shatterhand, combine to foil Adorf's plan of running a railroad directly through Apache territory in Petersson's action-packed plot. Nonetheless, Reinl, taking his cue as much from James Fenimore Cooper as from May, goes out of the way to stress the fierce friendship that develops between the good whiteman and the noble savage, further ennobled by Kalinke's elaborate cinematography which is somewhat similar to Delmer Daves' in its treatment of landscape and use of the crane.

d Harald Reinl *p* Horst Wendlandt *s* Harald G. Petersson *c* Ernst W. Kalinke *lp* Lex Barker, Pierre Brice, Mario Adorf, Marie Versini, Ralf Wolter, Walter Barnes

1964

Advance to the Rear *aka* Company of Cowards
(MGM) pv 97 min

This genuinely witty comedy Western has a surprisingly strong anti-military tone to it. Set in the last days of the Civil War, it features Douglas and Ford as the officers in charge of Company Q, a Cavalry troop with an outstanding ability to foul up whatever task is entrusted to it. Nonetheless, despite preferring the attractions of harlots, Stevens and Blondell, to

any sort of hazardous duty, Douglas and Ford manage to capture a rebel spy and save a Union gold shipment. Marshall directs with obvious delight at the suppleness of Peeples and Bowers' screenplay.

d George Marshall *p* Ted Richmond *s* Samuel A. Peeples, William Bowers *c* Milton Krasner *lp* Glenn Ford, Stella Stevens, Melvyn Douglas, Jim Backus, Joan Blondell, Andrew Prine

Among Vultures *orig* Unter Geiern
(RIALTO FILM/ATLANTIS FILM/S.N.C./JADRAN FILM; WG, IT, FR, YUG) scope 102 (99) min

This Winnetou film sees Granger take the place of Lex Barker as the white blood-brother of the Apache chief. He plays a character called Old Surehand: 'Why are we all "old" – Old Shatterhand, Old Surehand?' once rhetorically asked a bemused Granger, who was to introduce a clear element of parody into the series, of a journalist. Sommer is the heroine in distress whose journey from Texas to Arizona forms the backbone of the storyline, and George is the outlaw, masquerading as an Indian, out to get her and her money belt. Brice and Granger between them prove the Shoshone innocent of the charges laid against them and capture the evil George. This is the least interesting of the series so far.

d Alfred Vohrer *p* Preben Philipsen *s* Eberhard Kleindorff, Johanna Sibelius *c* Karl Lob *lp* Stewart Granger, Pierre Brice, Elke Sommer, Gotz George, Walter Barnes, Renato Baldini

Apache Rifles (FOX) 93 min

One of the trio of Murphy Westerns Witney made in the mid-sixties, *Apache Rifles* has little of the verve that characterizes the serials he made with John English in the thirties and forties, or even the violence he brought to the 27 Roy Rogers films he made after the War. Smith's script casts Murphy as a man of peace trying to prevent another Indian war and to win the hand of Indian maiden Lawson.

d William Witney *p* Grant Whytock *s* Charles B. Smith *c* Arch R. Dalzell *lp* Audie Murphy, Michael Dante, Linda Lawson, L.Q. Jones, Ken Lynch, Joseph Vitale

Ballad of a Gunfighter
(BILL WARD PRODUCTIONS) 84 min

This independent production features country singer Robbins whose career, after his million-selling record 'El Paso' in 1959, was inextricably linked to the gunfighter ballad. He and Barron are the bandit friends who fall out over Redd.

Robbins' nervous performance belies his easy stage manner while Ward's slim budget was clearly stretched to near breaking point. This is a curiosity.

d/p/s Bill Ward *c* Brydon Baker *lp* Marty Robbins, Joyce Redd, Bob Barron, Nestor Paiva, Michael Davis, Charlie Aldrich

Buffalo Bill, Hero of the Far West *orig* Buffalo Bill, L'Eroe del Far West (FILMES/GLORIA FILM/FILMS CORONA; IT, WG, FR) scope 93 min

This is one of the earliest Italian Westerns, made before Sergio Leone reconstructed the sub-genre with his Dollar movies. Like Harald Reinl's German Westerns, it centres on matters Indian. Scott is Buffalo Bill, sent by President Grant, as his personal representative, to put an end to the rebellion of Brega's eager young Sioux chief. Hendriks is the evil gunrunner. The film is notable for being one of the first Italian Westerns to achieve international, rather than merely European, distribution.

d John W. Fordson (Mario Costa) *p* Solly Bianco *s* Nino Stresa, Luciano Martino *c* Jack Dalmas (Massimo Dallamano) *lp* Gordon Scott, Jan Hendriks, Mario Brega, Catherine Ribeiro, Mirko Ellis, Roldano Lupi

Bullet for a Badman

(GORDON KAY & ASSOCIATES) 80 min

This is one of the better of the series of low-budget Westerns Murphy made in the sixties. The unusual plot has him and McGavin fighting over Lee, once McGavin's wife and now Murphy's. This conflict is set against the backdrop of Murphy escorting McGavin and his stolen money back to town with a posse who've only got eyes for the money. Murphy, his staccato delivery much softened by now, is in good form and Springsteen directs vigorously.

d R.G. Springsteen *p* Gordon Kay *s* Mary Willingham, Willard Willingham *c* Joseph Biroc *lp* Audie Murphy, Darren McGavin, Ruta Lee, Skip Homeier, Alan Hale, Bob Steele

Cheyenne Autumn (WB) pv 170 (161) min

Ford's most ambitious Western, *Cheyenne Autumn* tells the story of the flight of 300 Cheyenne from an Oklahoma reservation to their ancestral lands in the Dakota mountains. But, if the journey is an epic one with the Indians surviving cavalry harassment as well as appalling natural hazards, the film is wooden and ponderous, for all the Fordian composi-

Clint Eastwood counts his earnings in A Fistful of Dollars, *his first outing as the 'Man With No Name' and the most influential Italian Western ever.*

tions and the marvellous, and much misunderstood, comic Dodge City interlude (intended as a satirical comment on the main story). Its failings are a reflection of both Ford's ill health and his inability to bring Indians to life with the roundedness and complexity he had been able to bring to his depiction of his beloved cavalry.

d John Ford *p* Bernard Smith *s* James R. Webb *c* William Clothier *lp* Richard Widmark, Carroll Baker, James Stewart, Edward G. Robinson, Karl Malden, Dolores Del Rio

A Distant Trumpet (WB) pv 115 min

Like Ford, Walsh re-assessed his attitude to Indians at the end of his career. An indication of this shift in *Distant Trumpet* (Walsh's last film and an ironic variant on the Custer story which he had earlier filmed with Errol Flynn, **They Died with Their Boots On**, 1941) is that the Indians speak their own (subtitled) language. Walsh's classic framing looks old fashioned, even in Panavision, and the film moves slowly but its argument, concerned with military tactics and honour, is wholly contemporary as is the handling of the romance between Donahue and Pleshette.

d Raoul Walsh *p* William H. Wright *s* John Twist *c* William Clothier *lp* Troy Donahue, Suzanne Pleshette, Diane McBain, James Gregory, William Reynolds, Claude Akins

A Fistful of Dollars *orig* Per un Pugno di Dollari

(JOLLY FILM/CONSTANTIN/OCEAN; IT, WG, SP) scope 100 (95) min

Eastwood's first ride into the mythical as the 'Man With No Name' – a persona he has since adopted and adapted for his own use in his own films – and the first of the stream of Italian Westerns that were to radically re-interpret the genre to achieve international success. Leone originally offered the main part to James Coburn and then to Charles Bronson but both demanded more than the $15,000 that was available. Eastwood, looking to expand his career beyond the *Rawhide* teleseries, took the part immediately it was offered. The script is a reworking of *Yojimbo* (1961) by Akira Kurosawa (whose *Seven Samurai*, 1954, had been the model for the **Magnificent Seven**, 1960).

Far left: The Cheyenne flee their reservation in Cheyenne Autumn.

Eastwood is the laconic, pancho-clad, cigar-chewing mercenary who, on finding a town ruled by two warring clans, offers his services to first one, then the other, until by the end of the movie he's gunned down both clans. Eastwood had a significant hand in shaping the dialogue, cutting much of his own and eliminating most of the European poeticisms of the original script and Volonte provides a striking villain, but it is Leone and his unflinching vision of violence who makes the film so striking.

The details of Leone's film, the baroque framing, the stretching of time, Ennio Morricone's music, and the emphasis on violence would soon become the cliches of the Italian Westerns that followed, but in Leone's hands they are the building blocks of what was (at that time) the bleakest view of the West ever put on celluloid.

d/co-s Sergio Leone   *p* Harry Colombo (Arrigo Colombo), George Papi (Giorgio Papi)   *co-s* Duccio Tessari   *c* Jack Dalmas (Massimo Dallamano)   *lp* Clint Eastwood, Marianne Koch, John Wells (Gian-Maria Volonte), Pepe Calvo, Wolfgang Lukschy, Sieghart Rupp

Right: *Yul Brynner as the Creole gunfighter who turns on his employers in* Invitation to a Gunfighter.

Last of the Renegades, *another Harald Reinl Winnetou Western.*

Invitation to a Gunfighter
(KRAMER CO/LARCOS PRODUCTIONS/HERMES PRODUCTIONS)
92 min
An intriguing off-beat Western with Brynner (in one of his best roles) as the dandyish Creole gunman who avenges his slave heritage by taking money from whites to kill other whites, usually correcting their pronunciation of his name (Jules Gaspard D'Estaing) before drawing his gun. He's imported into town to flush out Segal who's barricaded himself in the family home the venal Hingle had swindled him out of. However, when Brynner starts running amok, Hingle persuades Segal to help him rid the town of Brynner. Wilson's script, written with his wife, is sometimes too clever but his direction, as one might expect from someone who learnt his craft in the Mercury Theater and acted in most of Orson Welles' American films, is beautifully measured. This is a minor classic.

d/p/co-s Richard Wilson   *co-s* Elizabeth Wilson   *c* Joseph MacDonald   *lp* Yul Brynner, Janice Rule, Brad Dexter, George Segal, Pat Hingle, Strother Martin

Last of the Renegades *orig* Winnetou II
(RIALTO FILM/JADRAN FILM/ATLANTIS FILM/S.N.C.;
WG, YUG, IT, FR)   scope   93 min
Kinski and Steel are the wonderfully evil villains who are hungry for the oil they know to be beneath Indian lands and who are foiled by blood brothers Brice (as the Apache chief Winnetou) and Barker (as the old scout Shatterhand) in this entertaining European Western. As usual with the films derived from the stories of Karl May the line-up is noble savage plus scout versus renegade Indian plus renegade whiteman with Winnetou leading his braves, Seventh Cavalry style, to the rescue at the film's climax. An interesting addition to May's cast of types – May created types not characters – is Arent's Lord Castlepool. He's an English lord and therefore a gentleman and a fool and as such fitting comic relief for Winnetou. Shot, like the others in the series, at superb locations around Split in Yugoslavia and handsomely mounted by Reinl, *Last of the Renegades* shows how flexible a genre the Western is, when viewed through European eyes.

d Harald Reinl   *p* Wolfgang Kuhnlenz   *s* Harald G. Petersson   *c* Ernst W. Kalinke   *lp* Lex Barker, Pierre Brice, Anthony Steel, Karin Dor, Klaus Kinski, Mario Girotti, Eddie Arent

Law of the Lawless   (PAR)   scope   87 min
In the early sixties, Lyles, a one-time messenger boy at Paramount, had the idea of producing a series of B feature Westerns using veteran stars from the past. This is the first and best of the eleven-strong series. Robertson is the gunfighter turned judge who refuses to buckle his gunbelt on again despite severe provocation from Cabot, Agar, MacLane and others. De Carlo provides the love interest. Claxton's direction is pedestrian, but as the *New York Times* pointed out, the interest of the film lies elsewhere: 'a cast studded with familiar names makes this frontier outpost look like an old folks' home.'

d William F. Claxton   *p* A.C. Lyles   *s* Steve Fisher   *c* Lester Shorr   *lp* Dale Robertson, William Bendix, Yvonne De Carlo, Bruce Cabot, Barton MacLane, John Agar

The Man from Galveston   (WB)   b/w   57 min
This is the film on which the teleseries *Temple Houston* was based. Its production circumstances are more interesting than the film itself, revealing as they do the growing closeness of the cinema and TV in terms of production. Producer Webb, the creator of the *Dragnet* teleseries, was at the time head of Warners' TV division and director Conrad was an ex-radio actor turned actor/director best known for his (later) starring role *Cannon*. The film, intended as a pilot for the teleseries,

was released as a feature in an attempt to give the projected series more prestige.

Hunter is the young lawyer who defends Moore on a murder charge by solving the case in court à la Perry Mason. The strong supporting cast includes Coburn and Foster.

d William Conrad   *p* Jack Webb, Michael Meshekoff
s Dean Riesner, Michael Zagor   *c* Bert Glennon   *lp* Jeffrey Hunter, Preston Foster, James Coburn, Joanna Moore, Edward Andrews, Kevin Hagen

Minnesota Clay

(ULTRA/JAGUAR/FRANCO-LONDON; IT, SP, FR)   95 (89) min
The first Western of Corbucci, the most prolific director of Italian Westerns, this was made at the same time as Sergio Leone's **A Fistful of Dollars** (1964). It tells the story of a gunfighter who cleans up a town though he's going blind. Marred by Corbucci's inability to discipline himself, the film is nonetheless interesting for the different tack it took from Leone's. Despite its excesses, which were soon to be seen to even greater effect in **Django** (1966), it is clearly modelled on American Westerns.

d/co-s Sergio Corbucci   *p* Danilo Marciani   *co-s* Adriano Bolzoni   *c* Jose Fernandez Aguayo   *lp* Cameron Mitchell, George Riviere, Ethel Rojo, Antonio Casas, Fernando Sancho, Diana Martin

Old Shatterhand *aka* Apaches Last Battle *aka* Shatterhand

(CCC/AVALA FILM/CRITERION/SERENA; WG, YUG, FR, IT)
scope   122 (98) min
A superbly photographed piece of fluff which retains the contrast between the painted savage – the Comanche – and the

noble savage – the Apache, epitomized by Winnetou – so central to Karl May's original stories. But this contrast is only the basis of the film's plot which has Madison as an unsympathetic Cavalry officer fermenting trouble between the tribes so he can have his own Indian war. Accordingly without the supporting romantic rhetoric – and with the action made even more inconsequential by the crude cutting of some 20 minutes off the film when shown outside Europe – the movie is thin and banal.

d Hugo Fregonese   *p* Arthur Brauner   *s* Ladislas Fodor, Robert A. Stemmle   *c* Siegfried Hold   *lp* Lex Barker, Pierre Brice, Daliah Lavi, Guy Madison, Ralf Wolter, Bill Ramsey

The Outrage   (MGM) b/w pv 97 min
A remake of Kurosawa's *Rashomon* (1950) in a Western setting. Newman is the outlaw, Harvey the husband who is murdered and Bloom, repeating her role from the 1959 Broadway adaption, his wife. At a deserted station preacher Shatner is told the trio's story, from the differing perspective of each of the participants, in the course of an account of Newman's trial for raping Bloom and killing Harvey. Unlike Kurosawa's *Seven Samurai* (1954) which was neatly transposed into **The Magnificent Seven** (1960), this translation of the East to the West reduces the original's hard-edged enquiry into truth to little more than a 'thrice-told tale'. Newman, in particular, seems out of place as the swarthy bandit.

d Martin Ritt   *p* A. Ronald Lubin   *s* Michael Kanin
c James Wong Howe   *lp* Paul Newman, Laurence Harvey, Claire Bloom, Edward G. Robinson, William Shatner, Paul Fix

Rio Conchos   (FOX) scope 107 min
Writers Huffaker and Landon and director Douglas re-invigorate the old cliche of 'Who's selling rifles to the Apache?' in this spendidly entertaining Western. Boone is the obsessive on the trail of the rifles and O'Brien (who gives a marvellous performance) the equally obsessive Confederate Colonel who hopes to continue the Civil War by unleashing the Apache nation on the war-weary Union. The climax at O'Brien's half-completed head-quarters is magnificently staged, rising to operatic heights at moments. The movie, which is an informal remake of **The Comancheros** (1961), marked the acting debut of Brown.

Richard Boone, Stuart Whitman and Jim Brown (left to right) in trouble in Rio Conchos.

Far left: Paul Newman and Claire Bloom in The Outrage.

d Gordon Douglas *p* David Weisbart *s* Joseph Landon,
Clair Huffaker *c* Joe MacDonald *lp* Richard Boone,
Stuart Whitman, Tony Franciosa, Wende Wagner, Edmond
O'Brien, Jim Brown

Stage to Thunder Rock (PAR) scope 89 (82) min
An unassuming budget actioneer, *Stage to Thunder Rock* has
producer Lyles' usual quota of aging stars and character
actors amongst its cast. Sullivan is the sheriff who rests at a
lonely way station with his bankrobber prisoner (Taeger) and
has to fight off fellow peace officer Brady, who wants the
reward for himself and Taeger's father Wynn. The direction
by Claxton, who is probably better known for his TV work
(*Bonanza, High Chapparal* and *Little House on the Prairie*) is
adequate but the script's longueurs – especially if one
compares it to Burt Kennedy's similar script **Ride Lonesome**
(1959) – make the 89 or so minutes hard going.

d William F. Claxton *p* A.C. Lyles *s* Charles Wallace
c W. Wallace Kelly *lp* Barry Sullivan, Marilyn Maxwell,
Scott Brady, Ralph Taeger, John Agar, Keenan Wynn

1965

Arizona Colt
(LEONE FILM/ORPHEE PRODUCTIONS/ARTURO GONZALES;
IT, FR, SP) scope 104 min
In this routine Italian Western, Gemma is the desperado hero
who refuses to join Sancho's gang, even after Sancho frees
him from jail. Finally à la **The Magnificent Seven** (1960), he
helps defend the town of Blackstone against Sancho. In place
of the regular gimmicks of the sub-genre, director Lupo offers
frequent sex scenes.

Lon Chaney on the set of
Stage to Thunder
Rock, *one of the series
of A. C. Lyles
productions to feature
aging character actors
made during the sixties.*

d Michele Lupo *p* Elio Scardamaglia *s* Ernesto Gastaldi
c Guglielmo Maniori *lp* Giuliano Gemma, Fernando
Sancho, Nello Pazzafini, Corinne Marchand, Roberto
Camardiel, Rosalba Neri

Arizona Raiders (ADMIRAL PICTURES) scope 88 min
An odd Murphy Western in which the plot, despite modern
interpolations (like good Indians) is highly traditional with
Murphy and Cooper as reformed Quantrill's Raiders helping
Crabbe's Arizona Ranger hunt down former comrades turned
outlaws. The spirited direction by serial ace Witney is
similarly traditionally inclined. Dante makes a tough outlaw.

d William Witney *p* Grant Whytock *s* Alex Gottlieb,
Mary Willingham, Willard Willingham *c* Jacques
Marquette *lp* Audie Murphy, Ben Cooper, Buster Crabbe,
Michael Dante, Gloria Talbott, Red Morgan

Billy the Kid vs. Dracula
(CIRCLE PRODUCTIONS) 89 (73) min
Carradine gives a truly hammy performance as the Vampire
uncle of Plowman whom Courtney's Billy the Kid intends to
marry and settle down with. Carey and Barcroft are on hand
to give the lacklustre film a few touches of authority. Like
Jesse James Meets Frankenstein's Daughter (1966), also by
Beaudine, the film has achieved a certain cult status in recent
years.

d William Beaudine *p* Carroll Case *s* Carl K. Hittleman
c Lothrop Worth *lp* Chuck Courtney, John Carradine,
Melinda Plowman, Virginia Christine, Walter Janovitz,
Harry Carey Jnr, Roy Barcroft

The Bounty Killer
(PREMIERE PRODUCTIONS) scope 92 min
This is one of the last films directed by Bennet, a veteran of
series Westerns, many of the stars of which appear in this
movie, including Crabbe, Brown, Steele, Knight and Arlen.
But, despite the cast and script, co-written by Gordon (a
well-known Western character actor), the film is distinctly
modern in tone. Duryea is the mild man who wipes out an
outlaw gang (by a fluke) and becomes a bounty hunter. Then,
when his friend, Knight minus his beard, is killed, he turns
killer until finally he is killed himself by a youngster out to
make a name for himself. This twist is made even more
unusual by having the youngster played by an uncredited
Peter Duryea, Duryea's own son.

d Spencer G. Bennet *p* Alex Gordon *s* R. Alexander, Leo
Gordon *c* Frederick E. West *lp* Dan Duryea, Audrey
Dalton, Fuzzy Knight, Rod Cameron, Richard Arlen, Buster
Crabbe, Johnny Mack Brown, Bob Steele, Bronco Billy
Anderson

Cat Ballou (COL) 96 min
If **A Fistful of Dollars** (1964) was the most significant
Western of the sixties, *Cat Ballou* and **The Wild Bunch**
(1969) were the most significant Westerns of the decade to be
made in Hollywood. Both films offer radical re-interpreta-
tions of the Western hero. Peckinpah's is the more thoroughgoing and Silverstein's the more easygoing (and more directly
imitated), offering as it does a mix of comedy and heroism
that is far more traditional. It wasn't the first comedy Western
by any means, but its success – it grossed some $20 million
worldwide – revived that sub-genre.
  The plot is simple enough. Arriving home from the East in
the company of would-be outlaws, Callan and Hickman,
Fonda discovers her father living under threat of death unless
he sells his ranch to the Wolf City Development Corporation.
When he is killed by the silver-nosed Tim Strawn (Marvin),
Fonda sends for the famous Kid Sheleen, hero of the pulp
novel she read on her journey home. On his arrival, Sheleen
(Marvin again) turns out to be Strawn's brother and, more

significantly, a drunkard who literally can't hit a barn door at 20 paces. But when all seems lost, Marvin, like the heroes of old, shows himself able to regenerate himself and kill his brother while Fonda and company prove themselves more plucky than they imagine.

Although many of the jokes simply don't come off and Silverstein's direction lacks any subtlety, the script by Newman and Pierson (who, by all accounts, was the more influential of the two writers; certainly his work on the teleseries *Nichols* is in the same vein) despite occasional awkwardnesses, touches many of the basic aspects of the traditional Western. A good example of this is Fonda's utter bewilderment on reaching the legendary Hole-in-the-Wall, a refuge for outlaws, and discovering its inhabitants are men and women in their sixties and seventies who want to die peacefully.

But, all its other virtues notwithstanding, what makes the film such a success is Marvin's Oscar-winning performance as the saviour in filthy red underpants. The film is at its best when Marta's camera simply watches Marvin, drunkenly seeking support from a horse that seems as drunk as he is, or, Samurai-like, ceremonially preparing himself for battle.

In a witty linking device Nat 'King' Cole (whose last screen appearance this is) and Stubby Kaye sing 'The Ballad of Cat Ballou'.

d Eliot Silverstein *p* Harold Hecht *s* Walter Newman, Frank R. Pierson *c* Jack Marta *lp* Lee Marvin, Jane Fonda, Michael Callan, Dwayne Hickman, Tom Nardini, Arthur Hunnicutt

Deadwood '76

(FAIRWAY INTERNATIONAL) scope 97 min
This is a mediocre indie Western, its bitter and surprising ending notwithstanding. Written by its star, the complicated plot follows the fortunes of a youngster mistaken for Billy the Kid in the notorious town of Deadwood. Lester is his crooked salesman of a partner, Watters his unhinged father and Dix,

son of Richard (star of many Westerns in the thirties and forties) is Wild Bill Hickok. The film's production values are decidedly Poverty Row. It is of interest as an early example of the work of cinematographer Zsigmond. Best known for his work on **McCabe and Mrs Miller** (1971) and **Heaven's Gate** (1980), Zsigmond, after fleeing to America during the 1956 Hungarian Uprising, worked on a number of low-budget films in the sixties, including **Five Bloody Graves** and **The Gun Riders** (both 1969).

d James Landis *p* Nicholas Meriwether *s* Arch Hall Jnr *c* Vilmos (William) Zsigmond, Lewis Guinn *lp* Arch Hall Jnr, Jack Lester, Melissa Morgan, William Watters, Robert Dix, LaDonna Cottier

The Desperado Trail *orig* Winnetou III

(RIALTO FILM/JADRAN FILM; WG, YUG) scope 93 min
This routine European Western sees the complex romanticism of Karl May, upon whose stories it is based, reduced to the simplicity of good against evil. The good are Barker and Brice, the flinty frontierman and the noble savage, and the evil is Maricic, a land speculator. Even odder is the substitution of the more traditional Cavalry for the band of Indians May usually has arrive at the last minute. Although Winnetou dies in the last reel this was not the last film to feature the character.

d Harald Reinl *p* Horst Wendlandt *s* Harald G. Petersson, Joachim Bartsch *c* Ernst W. Kalinke *lp* Pierre Brice, Lex Barker, Ralf Wolter, Renato Baldini, Veljko Maricic, Sophie Hardy

For a Few Dollars More *orig* Per Qualche Dollari in Piu

(P.E.A./ARTURO GONZALES/CONSTANTIN FILM; IT, SP, WG) scope 130 (128) min
The second of Leone's Dollar trilogy, *For a Few Dollars More* is more complex than **A Fistful of Dollars** (1964). The presence of Van Cleef as the Major both tightens up the plot, by adding a revenge element to the chase, and provides a contrast to Eastwood's enthusiastic cynicism. Nevertheless the centre of the film remains Volonte's Indio, who is far more than merely the villain of the piece. In his monstrosity, a human reflection of the inhospitable land the characters pass over, he defines the edge of humanity, the point from which Eastwood and Van Cleef instinctively withdraw.

The details of the film were to be very influential: Van Cleef's extraordinary collection of arms introduced to the genre a strain of technological gadgetry and the mysterious flashbacks to the rape of Van Cleef's sister, for the first time gave a major Leone character a significant past and saw the beginnings of Leone's wholly individual use of flashbacks which reached its climax in **Once upon a Time in the West** (1968).

Far left: *Lee Marvin as the drunk Kid Sheleen in* Cat Ballou, *the film that signalled the revival of the comedy Western.*

Lee Van Cleef, in For a Few Dollars More, *with some of the gadgetry that would feature extensively in subsequent Italian Westerns.*

Above: *Richard Harris (left) as the hopeless romantic and Charlton Heston as the overreacher in Sam Peckinpah's mutilated masterpiece,* Major Dundee.

d/co-s Sergio Leone   *p* Alberto Grimaldi   *co-s* Luciano Vincenzoni   *c* Massimo Dallamano   *lp* Clint Eastwood, Lee Van Cleef, Gian-Maria Volonte, Klaus Kinski, Mario Brega, Mara Krup

The Glory Guys   (BRISTOL PICTURES)   pv   112 min

This interesting Western resembles John Ford's **Fort Apache** (1948) as well as Peckinpah's own **Major Dundee** (1965) in its plot – an ambitious commander sacrifices his men for his own personal glory – but is wholly dissimilar in tone. In Ford's film greater unity of purpose comes out of defeat; in Peckinpah's script, there is only death, and even the madness of Duggan, leading his men to destruction, is seen as just that, madness. The film's sub-plot features Tryon and Presnell vying for the attention of Berger who also appears in **Major Dundee**. Laven's direction is no more than routine but Howe's cinematography, especially the extended battle sequence, in which the Cavalry are decimated by the Indians, is superb.

d/co-p Arnold Laven   *co-p* Arthur Gardner, Jules Levy   *s* Sam Peckinpah   *c* James Wong Howe   *lp* Tom Tryon, Andrew Duggan, Harve Presnell, Senta Berger, James Caan, Slim Pickens

Gunfighters of Casa Grande

(MGM; SP)   scope   92 min

An oddity whose production circumstances are far more interesting than anything on the screen, *Gunfighters of Casa Grande* was, with the even drearier *Son of a Gunfighter* (1965), the last cinemascope film released by MGM. The pair were shot back to back in Spain with Welch overseeing both. Chase's script, his last, from his own novel, is unrecognizable as being by the man who wrote **Red River** (1948), **Winchester '73** (1950) and **Bend of the River** (1952). Nicol is the border raider who carries off a huge cattle theft only to be defeated in his attempts to double-cross his gang and the local ranchers. Director Rowland, as he often did, cast his son Steve in a supporting role.

d Roy Rowland   *p* Lester Welch   *s* Borden Chase, Patricia Chase   *c* Jose F. Aguayo, Manuel Merino   *lp* Alex Nicol, Jorge Mistral, Dick Bentley, Steve Rowland, Phil Posner, Mercedes Alonso

The Hallelujah Trail

(UA/MIRISCH/KAPPA)   pv   167 (156) min

A grossly-inflated and over-extended would-be comedy Western, notable only for the superb performance by Keith as the rabble-rouser and self-appointed guardian of the whisky Lancaster and his Cavalrymen are escorting to Denver and thirsty miners. Remick leads the band to temperance ladies who also appoint themselves guardians of the whisky. Although many of the jokes and situations are funny, the basic idea is far too slight to carry the ponderous story developed around it by writer Gay.

d/p John Sturges   *s* John Gay   *c* Robert Surtees   *lp* Burt Lancaster, Lee Remick, Brian Keith, Jim Hutton, Donald Pleasence, Martin Landau

The Last Tomahawk *orig* Der Letze Mohikaner

(INTERNATIONAL GERMANIA FILM/CINEPRODUZIONI ASSOCIATE/ P.C. BALCAZAR; WG, IT, SP)   scope   89 min

Although this was officially based on *The Last of the Mohicans*, as one might expect from Reinl, the director most closely associated with the Winnetou series of Westerns, the film owes much more to Karl May than James Fenimore Cooper. In common with all the Winnetou films, the movie is composed mosaic-like with narrative pace, rather than motivation, joining together the action set-pieces. Italian Western star De Teffe is Strongheart – the name change from Leatherstocking is perhaps the clearest indication of just how much Cooper's character is seen through the lens of May's far more intense romanticism. With assistance from Martin, as the last of the Mohicans, De Teffe saves the lives of Lange and his daughters. Surprisingly little is made of the inter-racial love of Martin and Dor; instead Reinl concentrates on the action sequences, the most notable of which is a splendid avalanche. Reinl subsequently made a two-part version of Wagner's *Der Ring des Nibelungen* (1966) which one reviewer neatly called 'a De Luxe edition of his Karl May Westerns'.

d Harald Reinl   *p* Franz Thierry   *s* Joachim Bartsch   *c* Ernst Kalinke, Francisco Marin   *lp* Anthony Steffens (Antonio De Teffe), Karin Dor, Dan Martin, Joachim Fuchsberger, Carl Lange, Marie France

Major Dundee   (COL)   pv   134 min

A magnificent broken-backed sprawling epic of a Western which, despite its mutilation by Columbia, remains a landmark in the genre. Heston is the Union officer who leads a mixed group of Confederate prisoners and thieves deep into Mexico on a punitive raid against the Apache. Harris is the Confederate rebel who assists him. At the centre of the film lies the uneasy relationship between the two, Heston the overreacher, a man wracked by past failures who sees the mission as a means to personal salvation and Harris the cashiered officer and hopeless romantic. In Mexico the group's fragile unity of purpose is nearly broken when Heston, blaming himself for a temporary setback, wallows in self-pity until Harris goads him back to action. Finally the Apache are defeated and the troop return, victorious but much depleted, to America.

In part the relationship between Heston and Harris is a development of that between Joel McCrea's moral rigidity and Randolph Scott's more flexible and realistic moral code in the magisterial **Ride the High Country** (1962) which was to be further developed in the far more violent **The Wild Bunch** (1969). But *Major Dundee* is the more ambitious of the three films with its historical sweep, its questioning of its characters' (and America's) sense of identity and its articulation of the obsessive drives of Heston and company.

d/co-s Sam Peckinpah   *p* Jerry Bresler   *co-s* Harry Julian Fink, Oscar Saul   *c* Sam Leavitt   *lp* Charlton Heston, Richard Harris, Jim Hutton, James Coburn, Senta Berger, Warren Oates

Murrieta *aka* **Joaquin Murrieta** *aka* **Vendetta**
(PRO-ARTIS IBERICA; SP)   108 min
This virtual remake of **Robin Hood of El Dorado** (1936) is
interesting as a transitional movie, being a move towards the
Italian Western on behalf of Hollywood. Sherman's direction
is traditional, but the subject – Hunter as the Mexican farmer
turned bandit seeking out the gold-hungry gringo prospectors
for the murder of his wife – and its treatment by writer
O'Hanlon marks a shift in attitudes to violence. Similarly,
where the earlier film had made its hero a Robin Hood figure
as a justification, here Hunter is a vengeful bandido and no
more. All the film lacks is a sense of excitement.

d George Sherman   *p* Jose Sainz de Vicuna   *s* James
O'Hanlon   *c* Miguel F. Mila   *lp* Jeffrey Hunter, Arthur
Kennedy, Diana Lorys, Sara Lezana, Roberto Camardiel,
Pedro Osinaga

The Outlaws Is Coming *aka* **Three Stooges Meet the
Gunslinger** (COL)   b/w   89 min
The last of the Three Stooges films and the best of their last
batch of movies for Columbia, *The Outlaws Is Coming* is a
genuinely funny, if primitive, spoof Western. The Stooges,
members of the Preservation of Wild Life Society, are sent
West to stop the slaughter of the buffalo. They run into
trouble when their plans conflict with those of outlaws trying
to ferment an Indian rising. The story is episodic but West
(later to be television's Batman) and Kovack make sympathetic leads and some of the jokes are very funny: a skunk named
Elvis, a fight between Annie Oakley and Belle Starr and, best
of all, a silly gunfight between the West's assorted gunmen
and lawmen.

d/p Norman Maurer   *s* Elwood Ullman   *c* Irving Lippman
lp The Three Stooges, Adam West, Nancy Kovack, Mort
Mills, Henry Gibson, Don Lamond

A Pistol for Ringo *orig* **Una Pistola per Ringo**
(P.C.M./BALCAZAR; IT, SP)   scope   99 min
Director Tessari is one of the many writers and directors who
graduated to the Western from the series of sword and sandal
mini-epics that dominated Italian film production in the early
sixties. Tessari (who, uncredited, co-wrote **A Fistful of
Dollars,** 1964, with Sergio Leone) borrows freely from
American directors, notably Hawks and Ford, on whom he
modelled his plot, if not his style. Accordingly, the film is less
episodic, more sophisticated and without the excessive
violence that characterizes so many Italian Westerns.

   Here Gemma is the adventurer (rather than mercenary)
who saves a family of Texas aristocrats from a vicious Mexican
bandit who is using their ranch as a hideout.

d/s Duccio Tessari   *p* Luciano Ercoli, Albert Pugliese
c Francisco Marin   *lp* Montgomery Wood (Guiliano
Gemma), Hally Hammond (Lorella de Luca), Fernando
Sancho, Antonio Casas, Nieves Navarro, Jorge Martin

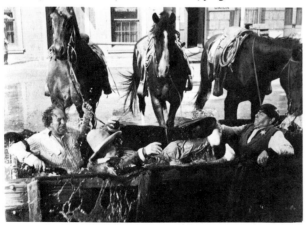

*Jeffrey Hunter vows
revenge in* Murrieta,
*one of the many versions
of the life of Joaquin
Murrieta.*

The Return of Ringo *orig* **Il Ritorno di Ringo**
(P.C. MEDITERRANEE/RIZZOLI FILM/P.C. BALCAZAR; IT, SP)
96 min
This is even better than Tessari's first Ringo film, **A Pistol for
Ringo** (1965). Gemma plays the man returning to his
home-town after the Civil War to find himself reported dead,
the town ruled by Sancho and his Mexican bandidos and his
family held captive. Tessari's ability to integrate the baroque
inventions of the Italian Western (a wrought-iron machinegun, a fortune teller watching a gunfight from a verandah and
Gemma's astonishing appearance at the centre of a sandstorm,
for example) into his tightly constructed story make his
movies unique amongst Italian Westerns. Gemma is also a
more believable character, not an invulnerable mercenary.
He's a frightened man fighting for his family.

d/co-s Duccio Tessari   *p* Alberto Pugliese, Tuciano Ercoli
co-s Fernando Di Leo   *c* Francisco Marin   *lp* Giuliano
Gemma, Fernando Sancho, Hally Hammond (Lorella de
Luca), Nieves Navarro, Antonio Casas, Pajarito

The Rounders (MGM)   pv   85 min
An eloquent, wry comedy about two modern cowboys, Fonda
and Ford, forever on the verge of settling down and never
quite making it. In this they're like the stubborn horse they
try to break, with hilarious results, several times in the course
of the film. Langdon and Holiday are the girls who
temporarily waylay them. Kennedy directs with a relaxed
assurance.

d/s Burt Kennedy   *p* Richard E. Lyons   *c* Paul C. Vogel
lp Glenn Ford, Henry Fonda, Sue Ann Langdon, Hope
Holiday, Chill Wills, Edgar Buchanan

Run Home Slow (JOSHUA PRODUCTIONS)   b/w   75 min
This nondescript Western is notable for being scored by
Frank Zappa, long before he was a well-known rock star, and
for the strange performance of McCambridge. The peculiar
plot features her and Scott, as the daughter and daughter-in-
law respectively, who go on a bank robbery spree with sons
Richards and Kent when their father dies. They blame the
local bank manager who wouldn't advance their father money
for medicine. Interestingly, the film pre-dates *Bonnie and
Clyde* (1967).

d/p Tim Sullivan *lp* Mercedes McCambridge, Linda Gaye
Scott, Allen Richards, Gary Kent
★ No other credits available

*The Three Stooges in
their last film,* The
Outlaws Is Coming.

Seven Guns for the MacGregors *orig* 7 Pistole per il MacGregor (PRODUZIONE D.S./JOLLY FILM/ESTELA FILM; IT, SP) scope 95 (90) min

A fine comedy Western from Giraldi, for which most of the deft parody sequences were written by Tessari who had earlier parodied both the sword and sandal epics and thriller cycles of the early sixties. The film tells the story of two unlikely elderly Scottish pioneers and their sons and their battle against a band of Mexican outlaws. Some of the jokes, like the running gag of the Scotsmen's meanness with ammunition, for example, are overplayed but the general tone of the film comes as a breath of fresh air at a time when the cliches of the Italian Western were being endlessly repeated following the success of **A Fistful of Dollars** (1964).

d Frank Grafield (Franco Giraldi) *p* Ted O'Darsa (Dario Sabatello) *s* Vincent Eagle (Enzo dell'Aquila), Fernando Lion (Fernando di'Leo), David Moreno, Duccio Tessari *c* Alejandro Ulloa *lp* Robert Woods, Manny Zarzo (Monolo Zarzo), Fernando Sancho, Jesus Puente, Max Dean (Massimo Righi), Peter Cross (Pierre Cressoy)

Shenandoah (U) 105 min

Shenandoah sees Stewart revive his thirties comedy persona and overlay it with the obsessive individualist of his films with Anthony Mann in the fifties. The result is the folksy patriarch determined to keep his family together in the midst of the Civil War. McLaglen's, cinematographer Clothier's and writer Barrett's constant references to Ford give the film the feel of a pastiche. Nonetheless, despite its excessive sentimentality, it remains one of McLaglen's best Westerns to date.

In 1974, it was (briefly) transformed into a Broadway musical.

d Andrew V. McLaglen *p* Robert Arthur *s* James Lee Barrett *c* William Clothier *lp* James Stewart, Rosemary Forsyth, Doug McClure, Glenn Corbett, Katharine Ross, Patrick Wayne

The Sons of Katie Elder (PAR) pv 122 min

Wayne, Martin, Anderson Jnr and Holliman are the battling sons in question who take on all comers in their attempts to restore their mother's good name in this undemanding actioneer. Hathaway breezes through the script's complexities only slowing down for regular bouts of, surprisingly violent,

action. Hopper turns in a chilling performance as the villain and James Gregory is successfully cast against type as his boss.

d Henry Hathaway *p* Hal B. Wallis *s* William H. Wright, Allan Weiss, Harry Essex *c* Lucien Ballard *lp* John Wayne, Dean Martin, Martha Hyer, Michael Anderson Jnr, Earl Holliman, Dennis Hopper

Town Tamer (A.C. LYLES PRODUCTIONS) scope 89 min

This is Selander's first film for producer Lyles and his best Western for years. Like all of Lyles' Westerns, the main fault is the pedestrian screenplay which features Andrews as the hired killer seeking revenge for the death of his wife at the hands of Bettger and Cabot. He finds them ensconced as sheriff and saloon owner respectively, from which positions they're bleeding the town dry. Thus Andrews can liberate the town as well as secure his revenge in a corpse-strewn finale. Jaeckel has a marvellous part as Bettger's sadistic deputy.

d Lesley Selander *p* A.C. Lyles *s* Frank Gruber *c* W. Wallace Kelley *lp* Dana Andrews, Bruce Cabot, Lyle Bettger, Richard Jaeckel, Pat O'Brien, Coleen Gray

Young Fury

(A.C. LYLES PRODUCTIONS) scope 80 min

This is routine fare. Nyby directs efficiently but the story, based on an 'idea' by producer Lyles, is too weak. Pierce is the adolescent gunman who, with a gang of juveniles, takes control of Dawson. Arlen is the ineffective sheriff and Mayo and Calhoun the troubled parents of Pierce who is finally reformed by his father. The central idea, the inverse of Lyles' usual productions which feature elderly actors rather than younger ones in substantial roles, is intriguing but, as developed by Fisher, it rapidly becomes a series of cliches.

d Christian Nyby *p* A.C. Lyles *s* Steve Fisher *c* Haskell Boggs *lp* Rory Calhoun, Virginia Mayo, Lon Chaney, Richard Arlen, Preston Pierce, John Agar

Alvarez Kelly (COL) pv 116 min

Reputedly based on actual events, this indifferent and confused Western stars Holden as a Mexican-Irish cattleman trying to play the North and South off against each other, selling cattle first to one side and then the other but getting caught between the two sides himself. Widmark is the one-eyed Confederate officer who swears vengeance when Holden helps his bride-to-be, Rule, to elope with another man. Their antagonism is the best thing in Coen and Arnold's flat screenplay.

d Edward Dmytryk *p* Sol C. Siegel *s* Franklin Coen, Elliott Arnold *c* Joseph MacDonald *lp* William Holden, Richard Widmark, Janice Rule, Patrick O'Neal, Victoria Shaw, Harry Carey Jnr

The Appaloosa *aka* Southwest to Sonora

(U) scope 98 min

For this Brando-vehicle Furie attempts to cash in on the atmosphere of **One-Eyed Jacks** (1961) but, despite some similarities of location and theme, the two films are worlds apart. *One-Eyed Jacks* is obsessive, *The Appaloosa* mannered. Accordingly, the simple story of Brando's attempts to re-capture a stolen horse and his dignity is broken into a myriad of intrusive details (teeth, reins, lone figures set against a landscape), a style which enhanced *The Ipcress File* (1965) but only confuses here. The result is a film which slowly but surely drains Brando of charisma.

d Sidney J. Furie *p* Alan Miller *s* James Bridge, Roland Kibbee *c* Russell Metty *lp* Marlon Brando, Anjanette Comer, John Saxon, Emilio Fernandez, Alex Montoya, Larry Mann

The Avenger *orig* Texas Addio

(B.R.C. PRODUZIONE FILM/ESTELA FILMS; IT, SP) scope 92 min

This Italian Western is cast more in the mould of the Hollywood Western than usual. Nero is the hero intent on revenging his father's death who gets his man only to discover that he's the father of his younger (half) brother, Kitosch. Baldi's direction is similarly Americanized with few of the ritual time-stretching sequences or balletic set-pieces one

expects from an Italian Western. Nero's laconic performance is, however, typically Italian.

d/co-s Ferdinando Baldi *p* Manolo Bolognini *co-s* Franco Rossette *c* Enzo Barboni *lp* Franco Nero, Cole Kitosch, Jose Suarez, Elisa Montes, Livio Lorenzon, Jose Guardiola

The Big Gundown *orig* La Resa dei Conti

(P.E.A./P.C. TULIO DEMICKELI; IT, SP) scope 105 (84) min

An important Italian Western, this was Van Cleef's first starring role after co-starring with Clint Eastwood in the last two Dollar films, and the first of a trio of Westerns to be directed by Sollima, all of which have a political edge to them. Van Cleef is the believer in law and order hired by Barnes' railroad tycoon to track down and capture Milian's Mexican bandido, ostensibly because of the rape of a white girl, but, in fact, to end his revolutionary agitation. In the course of the lengthy pursuit, the two men learn to respect each other's abilities and later Van Cleef learns from Barnes' treatment of Milian (which includes hunting him like an animal) that 'law and order' is a fiction, here being manipulated by Barnes to protect his vested economic interests.

The film is based on an original story by Franco Solinas, one of the most political and prolific of Italian screenwriters.

d/co-s Sergio Sollima *p* Alberto Grimaldi *co-s* Sergio Donati *c* Carlo Carlini *lp* Lee Van Cleef, Tomas Milian, Walter Barnes, Fernando Sancho, Nieves Navarro, Luisa Rivelli

A Big Hand for the Little Lady *aka* Big Deal at Dodge City (WB/EDEN PRODUCTIONS) 96 min

Fonda and Woodward lead an all-star cast that includes Robards, Meredith and Bickford (in his last screen role) in this adaptation of Carroll's original teleplay. Fonda is the ex-gambler on his way West who gatecrashes a high-stakes poker game against the wishes of his wife, Woodward, only to die of a heart attack in mid-game. His wife has to take his seat and hand. Taken slowly, with the actors given time to flesh out their roles and so make themselves deserving of the confidence trick Woodward and Fonda pull, the film is quite charming.

d/p Fielder Cook *s* Sidney Carroll *c* Lee Garmes *lp* Henry Fonda, Joanne Woodward, Jason Robards, Kevin McCarthy, Charles Bickford, Burgess Meredith

Far left: Marlon Brando in the mannered The Appaloosa.

Sidney Poitier (centre) with Bill Travers (left) and Dennis Weaver in Duel at Diablo *which examines racism within a cavalry troop with far more rigour than John Ford's* Sergeant Rutledge *(1960).*

Sid James (left) as the Rumpo Kid in the ridiculous Carry On Cowboy.

A Bullet for the General *orig* Quien Sabe?

(MGM; IT)   scope   135 (77) min

This is probably the best political Italian Western. Castel is the American mercenary, Volonte a bandido and budding revolutionary and Kinski his committed brother. Solinas and Laurani's allegorical screenplay has Volonte tempted from the path of revolution by Castel, who is using him as bait to help him fulfil his commission of killing a revolutionary hero. Much of the argument of the film is lost in the drastically cut version usually screened.

The climax is particularly fine, with Castel offering half the blood-money to Volonte only to have the man who once nursed him back to health kill him. Damiani's slow-paced direction is very effective.

d Damiano Damiani   *p* Bianco Manini   *s* Salvatore Laurani, Franco Solinas   *c* Toni Secchi   *lp* Gian-Maria Volonte, Lou Castel, Martine Beswick, Klaus Kinski, Jaime Fernandez, Andre Checchi

Carry On Cowboy

(ADDER PRODUCTIONS; GB)   b/w   95 min

The eleventh in the Carry On series, this was the only one to overrun its shooting schedule. Dale is the sanitary engineer mistakenly sent to clean up Stodge City who gets help from Douglas' sharp-shooting Calamity Jane on the trail of James' Rumpo Kid who killed her father. This is crudely made with few redeeming features.

d Gerald Thomas   *p* Peter Rogers   *s* Talbot Rothwell   *c* Alan Hume   *lp* Sidney James, Kenneth Williams, Jim Dale, Joan Sims, Angela Douglas, Bernard Bresslaw

Django

(B.R.C./TECISA; IT, SP)   95 min

With Sergio Leone's **A Fistful of Dollars** (1964), this is the most influential Italian Western, beginning as it did as a series that, including films retitled to cash in on the popularity of the Django character, lasted for well over thirty movies; and this from a film that was banned outright in several markets for its extreme violence. Corbucci directs the action, which mostly consists of the indestructible Django (Nero) shooting his way out of impossible odds, in his usual comic-strip style, mixing comedy and bizarre violence with an ease that is confusing.

Towing his coffin, in which he keeps his machinegun, behind him, Django arrives in a town in which the Ku Klux Klan and Mexican bandidos vie for power. Quickly drawn into the conflict which has virtually denuded the town of

menfolk, Django eliminates his opponents in a series of unlikely set-pieces that reach a crescendo of outrageous violence in the climactic battle in the cemetery with Django, his hands crushed by the KKK, resting his gun on a metal cross to steady it as he wreaks his revenge. Although, unlike the surrealistic violence of **Django Kill** (1967), Corbucci's violence is more exploitative, his rhetorical style creates a dreamlike mood which softens the film's brutality.

d/co-s Sergio Corbucci   *p* Manola Bolognini   *co-s* Bruno Corbucci, Franco Rossetti, Jose G. Maesso   *c* Enzo Barboni   *lp* Franco Nero, Eduardo Fajardo, Loredana Nusciak, Jose Bodalo, Angel Alvarez, Rafael Vaquero

Duel at Diablo   (UA)   103 min

An ambitious and confused Western, *Duel at Diablo* highlights its concern with racism with some of the bloodiest footage shot in the sixties prior to the director's own **Soldier Blue** (1970). The complex script essays an examination of the members of a Cavalry troop taking a wagon train of explosives to an isolated fort. Poitier is the black sergeant and Andersson the woman who, with her half-breed baby, is as badly mistreated as the Apache. Garner is the grim-faced scout with thoughts of revenge never far from his mind and Travers the weak-willed officer. Director Nelson has a bit part as Colonel Foster.

d/co-p Ralph Nelson   *co-p* Fred Engel   *s* Marvin H. Albert, Michael M. Grilikhes   *c* Charles F. Wheeler   *lp* James Garner, Sidney Poitier, Bibi Andersson, Bill Travers, John Hoyt, Dennis Weaver

Five Giants from Texas *orig* I Cinque della Vendetta

(MIRO CINEMATOGRAFICA/P.C. BALCAZAR; IT, SP)   101 min

A mundane Italian Western, notable only for the presence of Madison, one of the first American 'stars' to move to Europe. After appearing in a couple of Winnetou films, he crossed the Alps to Italy where he performed in the Sandokan series of films before returning to the Western with films like *Duel at Rio Bravo* (1965). Here he's the 'liberal American' resisting attempts by Mexican peasants and bandidos to win back the lands he expropriated from them.

d Aldo Florio   *p* Roberto Capitani, Aldo Ricci   *s* Alfonso Balcazar, Joe Antonio de la Loma Hernandez   *c* Victor Montreal   *lp* Guy Madison, Monica Randall, Vidal Molino, Molina Rojo, Vassili Karamesinis, Giovanni Cianfriglia

For a Dollar in the Teeth *orig* Un Dollaro Tra i Denti

(PRIMEX ITALIANA/TAKA PRODUCTIONS; IT, US)   96 (84) min

One of the many films closely modelled on Sergio Leone's **A Fistful of Dollars** (1964), this routine entry, like most of the others, outdoes Leone in violence but little else. Antony is the stranger who comes between a Mexican bandido and the gold he steals from a troop of American soldiers.

d Vance Lewis (Luigi Vanzi)   *p* Carlo Infascelli   *s* Jone Mang (Giuseppe Mangione), Warren Garfield   *c* Marcello Masciocchi   *lp* Tony Antony, Frank Wolff, Gia Sandri, Jolanda Modio, Raf Baldassarre, Aldo Berti

The Good, the Bad and the Ugly *orig* Il Buono, Il Brutto, Il Cattivo   (PRODUZIONI EUROPEE ASSOCIATE; IT)

scope   180 (148) min

For his third Western Leone added a third star, Wallach, to the team of Eastwood and Van Cleef and for the backdrop to their thievery he chose the Civil War. In his previous Dollar movies he had plundered the genre of its rituals and motifs and triumphantly re-assembled them to form a new and distinctly seedy, cynical and Catholic European view of a genre for so long dominated by the angular morality of American Puritanism. With *The Good, the Bad and the Ugly*, Leone began to re-examine the West itself. Hence his Civil War is photographed so as to suggest the trenches of the First

The Hellbenders *orig* **I Crudeli**

(ALBA CINEMATOGRAFICA/TECISA FILM; IT, SP)   95 (92) min

An excessive but impressive Italian Western that survives Corbucci's parodic direction thanks to producer Antonini's strong control over the filming of his own script. Cotten is the renegade Confederate resolved to win back the South for the Confederacy by continuing the war against the Union with the aid of his sons. In the course of his private vendetta he discovers that when, in the words of critic Chris Frayling, 'the ideals of Walter Scott can best be defended by means which owe more than a little to the mafia', then the ideals of Walter Scott are irrevocably lost.

d Sergio Corbucci   *p/co-s* Albert Band (Alfredo Antonini) *co-s* Ugo Liberatore   *c* Enzo Barboni   *lp* Joseph Cotten, Norma Bengell, Julian Mateos, Gino Pernice, Angel Aranda, Al Mulock

The Hills Run Red *orig* **Un Fiume di Dollari**

(DINO DE LAURENTIIS CINEMATOGRAFICA; IT)   scope   89 min

This is the first of veteran film-maker and former film critic Lizzani's pair of Westerns. Set against the backdrop of the Civil War, it stars Silva (who gives a marvellously excessive performance) and Duryea as the pair locked in a vendetta over a stolen payroll. Unlike so many Italian Westerns it is uncut, but the horrendous dubbing (which transforms the dialogue into a stream of cliches, Western-style) makes it very hard on the ear.

d Lee W. Beaver (Carlo Lizzani)   *p* Ermanno Donati, Luigi Carpentieri   *s* Mario Pierotti, Dean Craig   *lp* Thomas Hunter, Henry Silva, Dan Duryea, Nando Gazzolo, Nicoletta Machiavelli, Gianna Serra

Incident at Phantom Hill   (U)   scope   88 min

In this energetic but nonetheless indifferent Western Fuller leads a detachment of three soldiers to retrieve gold bullion stolen by Confederates at the close of the Civil War. Duryea is the treacherous prisoner offered a pardon if he'll lead them to the gold. The gold is recovered and after the inevitable shoot-out Fuller and dance-hall queen Lane ride into the sunset.

d Earl Bellamy   *p* Harry Tatelman   *s* Frank Nugent, Ken Pettus   *c* William Margulies   *lp* Robert Fuller, Jocelyn Lane, Dan Duryea, Claude Akins, Noah Beery Jnr, Paul Fix

Far left: *Clint Eastwood questions Eli Wallach in Sergio Leone's* The Good, the Bad and the Ugly, *the bitterest of the Dollar trilogy.*

World War. In contrast to the mixture of optimism and nostalgia that suffuse most American Westerns, Leone's arid depopulated West is the locale for a long-drawn-out dance of death. Accordingly, the central symbol of the film is death itself: the money Van Cleef, Wallach and Eastwood search for and attempt to double-cross each other over is hidden in a much-travelled coffin.

d/co-s Sergio Leone   *p* Alberto Grimaldi   *co-s* Luciano Vincenzoni   *c* Tonino Delli Colli   *lp* Clint Eastwood, Lee Van Cleef, Eli Wallach, Aldo Giuffre, Mario Brega, Luigi Pistilli

Gunpoint   (U)   86 min

In this serviceable low-budget film Murphy is the sheriff who leads a posse after Woodward and his gang when they rob a train and kidnap a dance-hall girl!, Staley. Pyle, as Murphy's deputy out for his job, and Buchanan, as comic support, give amiable performances while Murphy, as ever, is the easy-going figure of authority.

d Earl Bellamy   *p* Gordon Kay   *s* Mary Willingham, Willard Willingham   *c* William Margulies   *lp* Audie Murphy, Joan Staley, Morgan Woodward, Denver Pyle, Edgar Buchanan, Warren Stevens

He Who Shoots First *orig* **Django Spara per Primo**

(FIDA CINEMATOGRAFICA; IT)   scope   95 min

One of the thirty or so films devoted to the exploits of Django, here impersonated by Saxon. With the assistance of Sancho's Doc, a figure clearly modelled on Lee Van Cleef's Sabata persona, he sets out after Gazzolo's outlaw who's murdered his father. The plot is over complex and Martino directs slackly but Saxon and Sancho perform well together.

d Alberto De Martino   *p* Edmondo Amati   *s* Sandro Continenza, Massimiliano Capriccioli, Florenzo Carpi, Vincenzo Flamini, Alberto De Martino   *c* Riccardo Pallottini   *lp* Glenn Saxon, Fernando Sancho, Evelyn Stewart (Ida Galli), Nando Gazzolo, Lee Burton (Guido Lollobrigida), Erika Blanc

Henry Silva in mid gunfight in Carlo Lizzani's The Hills Run Red.

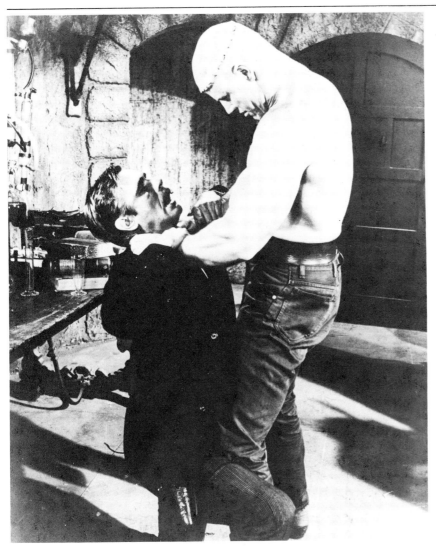

John Lupton in danger in Jesse James Meets Frankenstein's Daughter, *a film almost as ridiculous as* Carry On Cowboy *(1966).*

d R.G. Springsteen *p* A.C. Lyles *s* Steve Fisher *c* Hal Stine *lp* Dana Andrews, Jane Russell, Tom Drake, Lyle Bettger, Lon Chaney Jnr, John Agar

Kid Rodelo

(TRIDENT FILMS/FENIX; US, SP) b/w 91 min
An American Western made in Spain for the international market, *Kid Rodelo* demonstrates how different American and European conceptions of the genre were in the mid sixties. Despite its blood-splattered script, *Kid Rodelo* is aimed at a juvenile audience by actor-director Carlson. Italian Westerns were clearly aimed at adolescent audiences, the audience being wooed by American producers with Science Fiction and Horror movies.

Here, Murray is the ex-convict after the money Crawford and Carlson milked him of, as are Leigh and others. The Spanish landscapes are barren enough, but the script is too predictable. Even the principals seem unable to take their roles seriously.

d Richard Carlson *p* Jack O. Lamont, James J. Storrow *s* Jack Natteford *c* Manuel Merino *lp* Don Murray, Janet Leigh, Broderick Crawford, Richard Carlson, Jose Nieto, Julio Pena

My Name Is Pecos *orig* Mio Nome E Pecos

(ITALCINE; IT) scope 83 min
A routine Italian Western, efficiently directed by Lucidi (a director famous for his anti-clericism: in one of his films a priest makes love to a whore on the altar). Woods is Pecos, returning to the town he was brought up in to seek revenge on Carsten and his gang who murdered his parents. He overcomes every obstacle put in his way by, amongst others, the town's mercenary grave-digger, who stalks the streets collecting the corpses left behind by Woods and Carsten.

d/s Maurizio Lucidi *p* Franco Palombi *c* Franco Villa *lp* Robert Woods, Lucia Modugno, Peter Carsten, Peter Kapp, Louis Cassel, Christina Josani

Navajo Joe (DINO DE LAURENTIIS CINEMATOGRAFICA/

C.B. FILMS; IT, SP) scope 90 min
Though not one of Corbucci's best films, this is a superior Italian Western. Reynolds, in his first Western, is the mysterious stranger who repeatedly foils the plans of Sambrell and his men to steal a bank train and loot the township of Esperanza. Made immediately before **Django** (1966) the success of which gave Corbucci far larger budgets, *Navajo Joe* clearly lacks the production values of Corbucci's subsequent films. However, Reynolds' inscrutable acting style, which has the effect of almost suppressing his real motivation (revenge for the massacre of fellow Indians), and Ippoliti's fine cinematography give the film a distinctive edge.

The score is by Ennio Morricone.

d Sergio Corbucci *p* Ermanno Donati, Luigi Carpentieri *s* Dean Craig (Mario Pierotti), Fernando Di Leo *c* Silvano Ippoliti *lp* Burt Reynolds, Aldo Sambrell, Nicolleta Machiavelli, Tanya Lopert, Fernando Rey, Franca Polesello

Nevada Smith

(AVCO/SOLAR PRODUCTIONS) pv 131 (128) min
An overlong spin-off from *The Carpetbaggers* (1964) with McQueen in the role played by Alan Ladd in his last screen appearance. He's the man obsessed with tracking down the outlaws who murdered his parents before becoming a cowboy star in Hollywood. Kennedy and Landau are the villains and Keith the gunsmith who teaches McQueen there's more to guns than guns. Ballard's superior camerawork notwithstanding, Hathaway's direction is oddly laboured. Supposedly based on the early career of Ken Maynard, the film was an enormous box office hit, garnering rentals in excess of $5 million in North America alone.

Jesse James Meets Frankenstein's Daughter

(CIRCLE PRODUCTIONS) 82 min
This was the last film to be directed by Beaudine who entered the cinema as a property boy for D.W. Griffith in 1909 and is best remembered for his sex education film, *Mom and Dad* (1944), which, because it depicted the actual birth of a baby, was not released until 1957. From the forties on, Beaudine worked mostly on Poverty Row.

This, sadly, is an ineptly made gimmick Western. Onyx is the descendant of Baron Frankenstein who settles in Mexico and starts experimenting on kidnapped school children. When Lupton's Jesse James gets wise to her she transforms a wounded friend of his into a robot and sets it on him. Like its companion piece, **Billy the Kid vs. Dracula** (1965), this has achieved cult status in recent years.

d William Beaudine *p* Carroll Case *s* Carl K. Hittleman *c* Lothrop Worth *lp* John Lupton, Carl Bolder, Narda Onyx, Steven Geray, Raymond Barnes, Jim Davis

Johnny Reno (A.C. LYLES PRODUCTIONS) scope 83 min

An above-average Lyles Western that gently eases its ageing cast through an intriguing plot. Andrews is the marshal and Russell, as boisterous as ever, the owner of the gin palace he comes to visit. However, on his arrival with Drake, he discovers that law and order in Stone Junction is lynch law and that the town is ruled by Bettger. The film is well scripted – indeed this is the best screenplay of all Lyles' Westerns – and imaginatively directed by Springsteen, especially at the climax where a bunch of Indians all but tear down Stone Junction. This is a pleasant actioneer.

d/p Henry Hathaway   *s* John Michael Hayes   *c* Lucien
Ballard   *lp* Steve McQueen, Karl Malden, Brian Keith,
Suzanne Pleshette, Arthur Kennedy, Martin Landau

The Night of the Grizzly (PAR) scope 102 min
In this weak pioneering film Walker is the homesteader and
Hyer his wife in yet another American Western targeted at the
family audience, the audience that would make *Little House on
the Prairie* one of the most successful of teleseries and give rise
to the *Wilderness* series of Westerns of the seventies. Walker
and his family are menaced by a grizzly bear and Gordon.
These two finally eliminate each other in a decidedly
antiseptic fashion. Pevney directs aimlessly.

d Joseph Pevney   *p* Burt Dunne   *s* Warren Douglas
c Harold Lipstein, Loyal Griggs   *lp* Clint Walker, Martha
Hyer, Keenan Wynn, Leo Gordon, Jack Elam, Kevin Brodie

The Professionals
(COL/PAX PRODUCTIONS)   pv   123 (117) min
One of the most successful of recent Westerns, *The Professionals* is a more complex film than its adventure plot might
suggest. Lancaster, Marvin, Ryan and Strode are the mercenaries hired by Bellamy to rescue his wife, Cardinale, who has
been kidnapped by Palance's Mexican bandit. This they do,
only to discover that Cardinale prefers Palance to Bellamy.
Accordingly, having fulfilled their professional obligations by
returning Cardinale to Bellamy, they then restrain him when
Palance re-appears and once more claims his love. Woven
around this variant of *The Sheik* (1921) is a taut tale of
conflicting codes of loyalty that parallels, in a less bloody
fashion, contemporaneous developments in the Western in
Italy. Brooks' script is eloquent but it is his integration of the
action sequences into the flow of the film's perspective on the
fast-changing West that makes the movie so successful. The
themes, of the closing down of the West and the possibilities
for heroism it provided, are close to those broached by
Peckinpah in **The Wild Bunch** (1969) and **Pat Garrett and
Billy the Kid** (1973) but the spare style is Brooks' own.

d/p/s Richard Brooks   *c* Conrad Hall   *lp* Burt Lancaster,
Lee Marvin, Robert Ryan, Jack Palance, Ralph Bellamy,
Claudia Cardinale, Woody Strode

The Rare Breed (U) pv 97 min
A broad comedy Western from McLaglen that centres on the
attempts to introduce Hereford cattle into Texas, a plot device
that had done sterling work in films like **The Untamed Breed**
(1948) and **The Longhorn** (1951). McLaglen directs pleasant-
ly, letting Hardman's screenplay dictate the pace, but to no
purpose. Similarly Stewart, as the drifter who helps O'Hara
get the Hereford bull to Texas and keep it alive, O'Hara, as
the stubborn widow, and Keith as the hard-hearted cattle
baron, give strong performances but to little effect. Only

*Steve McQueen is
Nevada Smith.*

Carey and Elam as two would-be swindlers are able to make
anything special out of their characters.

d Andrew V. McLaglen   *p* William Alland   *s* Ric Hardman
c William H. Clothier   *lp* James Stewart, Maureen O'Hara,
Brian Keith, Jack Elam, Harry Carey Jnr, Ben Johnson

Return of the Seven (UA/MIRISCH) pv 95 min
Far better than most sequels, *Return of the Seven* is
intelligently scripted and efficiently directed by Kennedy, in
his bleak rather than his comic style. The plot is a virtual
inversion of that of **The Magnificent Seven** (1960) with
Brynner and his new band of gunmen rescuing kidnapped
Mexican farmers. Far more violent than the original, it
marked a perceptible shift in the American Western towards
the stylized violence of the Italian Western that would soon
overtake the genre.

d Burt Kennedy   *p* Ted Richmond   *s* Larry Cohen   *c* Paul
Vogel   *lp* Yul Brynner, Robert Fuller, Warren Oates,
Claude Akins, Julian Mateos, Virgilio Texeira

Ride Beyond Vengeance
(TIGER CO/SENTINAL FILMS/FENADY ASSOCS)   110 (100) min
Looking like a telefilm – it was made by the production team
of Connors' *Branded* teleseries – this is an ugly film. The
complex screenplay, with its double flashback structure,
features Connors returning home only to be branded by Akins
and sadist Bixby (who was eventually to achieve a fame of
sorts as the Incredible Hulk's better half). The rest of the film
sees him wreaking his vengeance on all concerned before
making it up with his wife, Hays, in her feature debut. The
violence, which won the film much condemnation at the time,
is the only notable feature of the film, marking as it does the
beginning of an American response to the Italian Western
which involved increasing the violence in the domestic
product.

d Bernard McEveety   *p/s* Andrew J. Fenady   *c* Lester
Shorr   *lp* Chuck Connors, Michael Rennie, Joan Blondell,
Kathryn Hays, Bill Bixby, Claude Akins

Ride in the Whirlwind (PROTEUS FILMS) 82 min
This superior Western is the companion piece to **The
Shooting** (1966). Nicholson wrote the script after reading the
diaries of old Westerners in the Los Angeles library. He drew
extensively from the diaries for the poetic language of his

*Far left: Burt Lancaster
(left), Claudia
Cardinale and Lee
Marvin in* The
Professionals, *the best
of Richard Brooks'
Westerns.*

Far right: *Jack Nicholson in the marvellous* Ride in the Whirlwind *which he also wrote for director Monte Hellman.*

characters and the sense of impending doom that surrounds their primitive existences.

Nicholson and Mitchell (who gives a superb performance) are the cowboys who give food and shelter to a band of outlaws and so are identified with them by the relentless band of vigilantes after the bandits. In a fight with the vigilantes the bandits all die and Nicholson and Mitchell flee. They are temporarily given shelter by homesteaders but are again forced to flee when the vigilantes reappear.

The endless chase gives the film a strong backbone from which Hellman hangs his cameos of frontier drudgery (the homesteaders hacking at a tree stump seemingly forever), that clearly makes the perilous life of outlawry so attractive.

d/co-p Monte Hellman   *co-p/s* Jack Nicholson   *c* Gregory Sandor   *lp* Cameron Mitchell, Jack Nicholson, Millie Perkins, Dean Stanton, George Mitchell, Tom Filer

Ringo and his Golden Pistol *orig* Johnny Oro
(SANSON FILM; IT)   88 min
The name of the character played by Damon, Johnny Oro in the original Italian version, was dubbed Ringo to cash in on the popularity of Duccio Tessari's Ringo films, for overseas markets. Corbucci handles the action with his usual invention, and surprisingly the script has fewer gimmicks and less violence than most Italian Westerns. Damon is the bounty hunter sought after by bandits who destroys most of the town of Coldstone in the course of defending himself with a seemingly endless supply of dynamite.

d Sergio Corbucci   *p* Joseph Fryd   *s* Adriano Bolzoni, Franco Rossetti   *c* Riccardo Pallotini   *lp* Mark Damon, Valeria Fabrizi, Ettore Manni, Giulia Rubini, Franco De Rosa, Andrea Aureli

The Shooting   (SANTA CLARA)   81 min
Shot back to back with the equally mysterious **Ride in the Whirlwind** (1966), *The Shooting* fully justifies its description as an existential Western. The pared-down, fragmented, storyline follows bounty hunter Oates who accepts the job of guiding a woman (Perkins), who refuses to explain her journey, through the desert. Just as previously Oates had

Below: Jack Nicholson as the killer and Will Hutchins as the puzzled cowboy in a scene from the enigmatic The Shooting, *which was shot back to back with* Ride in the Whirlwind *(1966).*

deliberately laid a trail in a successful attempt to trap the unseen pursuers who killed his friends, so Perkins leaves a trail for Nicholson's killer, whom she, Oates and the crazed Hutchins lead to her prey, Oates' twin brother, who is responsible for the death of her husband and child.

But, if like the children's puzzle Hutchins plays with, the real story can be constructed (as above) from the fragments, Hellman doesn't grant his characters that privilege. They remain forever on the brink of knowledge, only, like Oates, to die at the moment of revelation. Thus Oates, who has been trying to prevent Nicholson from killing his brother, having figured out the plan, dies, shot by his brother, as he guns down Nicholson. Equally significant is the world the characters inhabit, a parched, still, unchanging landscape which the characters, with their quirky, cryptic conversations, can never master. Hellman's calculated style, replete with disorienting close-ups and strange moments – at one point a character gives candy to a man dying of thirst in the middle of the desert – confirm the detached fatalism of his story. This is a marvellous film.

d/co-p Monte Hellman   *co-p* Jack Nicholson   *s* Adrien Joyce   *c* Gregory Sandor   *lp* Warren Oates, Will Hutchins, Millie Perkins, Jack Nicholson, B.J. Merholz, Guy El Tsosie

Stagecoach   (FOX)   scope   114 min
A lacklustre remake of Ford's classic 1939 film of the same title, this is notable only for being Crosby's last feature film. Cord, a far less charismatic actor than John Wayne, is the Ringo Kid, Crosby the alcoholic doctor and Ann-Margret (who turns in a worthy performance) the tart with the heart of gold.

d Gordon Douglas   *p* Martin Rackin   *s* Joseph Landon   *c* William H. Clothier   *lp* Ann-Margret, Alex Cord, Bing Crosby, Van Heflin, Slim Pickens, Red Buttons

10,000 Dollars Blood Money *orig* 10,000 Dollari per un Massacro
(ZENITH CINEMATOGRAFICA/FLORA FILM; IT)   scope   97 min
This is one of the early entries in the Django series with Garko in the role Franco Nero made famous. Now a bounty hunter,

Django at first refuses to rescue the daughter of a wealthy landowner for a fee, preferring to team up with the bandit (Camaso) who's kidnapped her, until he's double-crossed by Camaso.

A routine Italian Western, only of interest for the shift of the Django character from revenge hero to hired gun, in which role he was to remain for the rest of the thirty-or-so-strong series devoted to his exploits.

d Romolo Guerrieri   *co-p* Mino Loy   *co-p/co-s* Luciano Martino   *co-s* Franco Fogagnolo, Ernesto Gastaldi, Sauro Scavolini   *c* Frederico Zanni   *lp* Gary Hudson (Gianni Garko), Claudio Camaso, Adriana Ambesi, Fernando Sancho, Loredana Nuschiah, Pinuccio Ardia

Texas Across the River (U) scope 101 min

This is a spoof Western in the vein of Robert Aldrich's **Four for Texas** (1963). Martin and Delon, in the first of his failed attempts to establish himself as a Hollywood star, co-star as the loud-mouthed Texan and Spanish nobleman. The jokes come fast and furious – an Indian attack driven off by a herd of stampeding cattle and a chief's son who can't shoot a bow and arrow – but to little purpose. Gordon, once a director of real promise, here directs slackly, letting his cast do what they please.

d Michael Gordon   *p* Harry Keller   *s* Wells Root, Harold Green, Ben Starr   *c* Russell Metty   *lp* Dean Martin, Alain Delon, Joey Bishop, Rosemary Forsyth, Peter Graves, Roy Barcroft

The Texican (M.C.R./BALCAZARI; US, SP) scope 86 min

An aimless, low-budget Murphy Western shot entirely in Spain with a European crew but aimed solidly at the heartland of America. Murphy is the one-time lawman who returns from his Mexican hideout when he learns that his brother has been murdered. Needless to say, he avenges his brother's death, clears his own name and puts paid to Crawford, the man responsible. The film is a collection of tired cliches.

d Jose Luis Espinosa   *p/s* John C. Champion   *c* Francis Marin   *lp* Audie Murphy, Broderick Crawford, Diana Lorys, Luz Marquez, Antonio Casas, Molino Rojo

Thunder at the Border *orig* Winnetou und Sein Freund Old Firehand

(RIALTO FILM/PREBEN PHILIPSEN/JADRAN FILM; WG, YUG) scope 94 min

This indifferent, but significant entry in the Winnetou series sees Cameron replace Lex Barker and Stewart Granger as the white blood-brother to Brice's Apache chief. And, once again, he's old, this time 'Old Firehand'. More interestingly, the locale has been shifted from the mountains and forests of Karl May's original stories (which earlier entries in the series had kept to) to the dusty Mexican plains, a direct result of the phenomenal international success of the Italian Western that the Winnetou series created the cultural and commercial context for. Indeed the plot, which sees Brice and Cameron as a sort of Magnificent Two, defending a Mexican township against Leipnitz's bandit chief, even omits the obligatory May ending, with Winnetou and his braves riding to the rescue, in favour of dynamite and individual heroics.

d Alfred Vohrer   *p* Horst Wendlandt   *s* David Dereszke, C.B. Taylor, Harald G. Petersson   *c* Karl Lob   *lp* Rod Cameron, Pierre Brice, Todd Armstrong, Marie Versini, Harald Leipnitz, Nadia Gray

The Tramplers *orig* Gli Uomini del Passo Pessante

(A.M. CRETHIEN PRODUCTIONS; IT)   105 (99) min

Cotten is the Southern patriarch and Scott his rebellious son in this intriguing post-Civil War Western. Attempting to restore the family's fortunes, much depleted by the war, Cotten turns increasingly to violence until Scott is forced to act against him. Unusually for an Italian Western, the location scenes were shot in Argentina rather than the closer-to-home Spain.

d/co-s Albert Band (Alfredo Antonini)   *p* Joseph Levine, Alvaro Mancori   *co-s* Ugo Liberatore   *c* Alvaro Mancore   *lp* Gordon Scott, Joseph Cotten, James Mitchum, Franco Nero, Ilaria Occhini, Muriel Franklin

Waco (A.C. LYLES PRODUCTIONS) scope 85 min

In this sub-standard Lyles Western, Donlevy is the elderly all-in-black gunslinger and Keel the equally elderly gunman hired to clean up the town of Emporia after Arlen, the most regular of Lyles' informal stock company, is killed. Corey puts in a nice performance as a gunman-turned-preacher and Russell still sparkles but, despite an edge of violence unusual in Lyles' productions, Springsteen's direction is too sluggish to animate the players.

Far left: Extras eating lunch on the set of Gordon Douglas' inferior remake of Stagecoach.

Joey Bishop, Dean Martin and Alain Delon in Michael Gordon's insipid spoof Western Texas Across the River.

version), the film also features Mitchell as the bat-cloaked villain who is finally gunned down by Van Cleef when he tries to rob the mine of the payroll which is a replacement for the one Van Cleef helped him steal.

d Giorgio Stegani   *p* Alfonso Sansone, Enrico Chroscicki
s Warren Kiefer, Fernando Di Leo, Mino Roli, Giorgio Stegani   *c* Enzo Serafin   *lp* Lee Van Cleef, Antonio Sabato, Gordon Mitchell, Lionel Stander, Graziella Granata, Ann Smyrner

The Christmas Kid
(WESTSIDE INTERNATIONAL/L.M. FILMS; US, SP) 90 min
This is one of the best of the string of American-financed Westerns made in Spain. Hunter, in the title role, is the mixed-up kid who first turns hired gunman for gambler Hayward, brought to Jasper, Arizona, by the discovery of copper, and then turns to the side of law and order when Hayward starts to take over the town. As much a character study as an actioneer, the movie is neatly directed by producer Pink, though the post synchronization is ineptly done and the day for night scenes are laughably bright.

d/p Sidney Pink   *s* Jim Henaghan, Rodrigo Rivero
c Manuel Hernandez Sanjuan   *lp* Jeffrey Hunter, Louis Hayward, Perla Cristal, Gustavo Rojo, Luis Prendes, Reginald Gillam

Chuka   (RODLOR INC) 105 min
As efficiently directed collection of cliches as one's likely to see in a Western. Taylor is the wandering gunfighter, Paluzzi the loved one he's been parted from for so long, whom he meets again in the shadow of death, Mills the English commandant of a threatened frontier fort, Borgnine the tough sergeant and Whitmore the gruff scout. A further addition to the cast of cliches is Carson as the stagedriver who doesn't like war because horses get killed. More attractive are the Indians who for once behave sensibly and attack at night and massacre all the inhabitants of the fort, except, possibly, Taylor.

d Gordon Douglas   *p* Rod Taylor, Jack Jason   *s* Richard Jessup   *c* Harold Stine   *lp* Rod Taylor, Ernest Borgnine, John Mills, Luciana Paluzzi, James Whitmore, Lucky Carson

Day of Anger *orig* I Giorni dell'Ira
(SANCROSIAP/CORONA FILM/K.G. DIVINA FILM; IT, WG)
scope   109 (78) min
This routine, but cheerful, Italian Western is directed by Valerii, one-time assistant to Sergio Leone on **For a Few Dollars More** (1965), who was later to direct, under Leone's close supervision, **My Name Is Nobody** (1973).

Gemma is the social outcast who apprentices himself to Van Cleef's master gunman. The two of them take over a town, whereupon Van Cleef loses control and sets about killing virtually everyone in the town until Gemma takes on his tutor with Doc Holliday's guns. What is surprising is the complete absence of style, especially compared to Valerii's masterpiece, **The Price of Power** (1969).

d/co-s Tonino Valerii   *p* Alfonso Sansone, Enrico Chrosicki
co-s Ernesto Gestaldi, Renzo Genta   *c* Enzo Serafin
lp Giuliano Gemma, Lee Van Cleef, Walter Rilla, Yvonne Sanson, Andrea Bosic, Ennio Balbo

Dead or Alive *orig* Escondido
(DOCUMENTO FILM/SELMUR PRODUCTIONS; IT, US) 89 min
Cord is the gunman seeking an amnesty in this stylish, but otherwise only average, Italian Western. The plot is rambling, wasting the presence of Ryan and Kennedy, while the unusual attempt at realism fits badly with the parodic dialogue in which bounty hunters bewail amnesties and killers cross themselves after shooting priests.

Lee Van Cleef and Giuliano Gemma (centre), master and apprentice gunman in Day of Anger.

d R.G. Springsteen   *p* A.C. Lyles   *s* Steve Fisher
c Robert Pittack   *lp* Howard Keel, Jane Russell, Brian Donlevy, Richard Arlen, Wendell Corey, Fuzzy Knight

1967

The Ballad of Josie   (U) scope   102 min
Swanton's script is over-talkative and McLaglen's direction heavy handed but the film's central idea – Day as a feminist in turn-of-the-century Wyoming – and Day's performance transform the movie into a fascinating Western. First she's tried for manslaughter when her drunkard of a husband dies after she's defended herself with a billiard cue. Then, in need of money to support herself, she sheds her petticoats for denims and, to the consternation of her fellow townsfolk, makes a success of sheepfarming. One of the film's wittiest uses of the cliches of the genre is its transforming of the traditional sheepmen-v-cattlemen opposition into a battle of the sexes.

d Andrew V. McLaglen   *p* Norman Macdonnell   *s* Harold Swanton   *c* Milton Krasner   *lp* Doris Day, Peter Graves, George Kennedy, Andy Devine, William Talman, David Hartman

Bandidos *orig* Crepo Tue ... che Vivo
(EPIC FILM/HESPERIA FILMS; IT, SP) scope   94 min
A minor Italian Western, this stars Salerno (who dubbed Clint Eastwood in the Italian version of **A Fistful of Dollars,** 1964). He's the sharpshooter so viciously mutilated by outlaw Venatini that he has to earn a living as the promoter and publicist for a seedy Wild West Show. With the aid of Jenkins, whose education as a sharpshooter provides the film with its best sequences, he avenges himself on Venatini at the cost of his own life.

d Max Dillmann (Massimo Dallamano)   *p* Solly V. Bianco
s Romano Migliorini, Giambattista Mussetto, Juan Cobos
c Emilio Foriscot   *lp* Enrico Maria Salerno, Terry Jenkins, Venatino Venatini, Maria Martin, Marco Guglielmi, Chris Huerta

Beyond the Law *orig* Al di là della Legge
(SANCROSIAP/ROXY FILM; IT, WG) scope   110 (85) min
Van Cleef is the bandit turned sheriff in this routine Italian Western. Surprisingly non-violent (at least in its uncut

301

d Franco Giraldi *p/co-s* Albert Band (Alfredo Antonini)
co-s Ugo Liberatore, Luis Garfinkle *c* Alice Parolini
lp Alex Cord, Robert Ryan, Arthur Kennedy, Nicoletta
Machiavelli, Mario Brega, Renato Romano

Death Rides a Horse *orig* Da Uomo a Uomo

(P.E.C.; IT) scope 115 min
The often-seen duo of a youngster and a master guman is used
to good effect here. Law is the youth out for revenge on the
murderer of his parents who meets up with Van Cleef who is
seeking the bandits who jailed him. The two join up and find
that the bandits now occupy positions of authority in the new,
'civilized' West. More interestingly, when it transpires that
Van Cleef was present at the massacre of Law's parents, Law
decides not to draw on him; instead they part.

The film was remade in 1971 as *Viva Django* as part of the
long running Django series.

d Guilio Petroni *p* Alfonso Sansone, Henryk (Enrico)
Chrosicki *s* Luciano Vincenzoni *c* Carlo Carlini
lp Lee Van Cleef, John Phillip Law, Anthony Dawson
(Antonio Margheriti), Mario Brega, Luigi Pistilli, Jose
Torres

Death Sentence *orig* Sentenza di Morte

(B.L. VISION; IT) scope 90 (82) min
A routine Italian Western, full of the cliches (a gunslinger
priest, for example) and excesses (an epileptic albino outlaw!)
of the genre, but with little to set it apart. Clarke is the bandit,
hunting down the four men who killed his brother and
disposing of them one by one in spectacular fashion. Milian
clearly enjoys himself as the albino gunman.

d/p/s Mario Lanfranchi *c* Toni Secchi *lp* Robin Clarke,
Richard Conte, Enrico Maria Salerno, Adolfo Celi, Tomas
Milian, Lilli Lembo

Django Kill *orig* Sei Sei Vivo, Spara!

(G.I.A./HISPAMER FILM; IT, SP) 120 (101) min
The only Western made by Questi, *Django Kill* (even in its cut
version) is probably the most brutally violent Spaghetti
Western made. Milian is Django who rides into a town run by
two rival factions, Camardiel and his black-leather clad
homosexual muchachos (who ride about on white horses) and
a storekeeper (whose parrot comments on the action of the
final gunfight). The static plot simply has Milian (assisted by
two mysterious Indians) overcome bizarre obstacle after

bizarre obstacle while around him children are shot, outlaws
roasted on a spit, animals disembowelled and a man is
suffocated by molten gold.

The result is a surreal film – Questi had worked with Fellini
– which understandably was cut to ribbons outside Italy.

d/p/co-s Giulio Questi *co-s* Franco Arcalli *c* Franco Delli
Colli *lp* Tomas Milian, Pierro Lulli, Milo Quesada, Roberto
Camardiel, Marilu Tolu, Raymond Lovelock

*Sammy Jackson (left)
and rock'n'roll singer
Roy Orbison with The
Fastest Guitar Alive.*

El Dorado (LAUREL) 127 min

Virtually a remake of **Rio Bravo** (1959) with Mitchum, Caan,
Hunnicutt and Holt in the roles previously played by Dean
Martin, Rick Nelson, Walter Brennan and Angie Dickinson
respectively. For all its knockabout comedy – the treatment of
Mitchum's alcoholism for example – *El Dorado* is a bleak
movie. In the earlier film the characters' moral superiority to
their adversaries is translated into a physical superiority; in *El
Dorado* Wayne and Mitchum's aging gunmen, all too aware of
their failing capabilities – the final confrontation sees them
hobbling down the street on crutches – are all the time
struggling in their attempts to defend homesteaders against
Asner's cattle baron. In Caan and Carey, who are fighting for
a cause rather than merely self-esteem, Hawks for the first
time treats characters whose aspirations are higher than the
stoicism of his adventure-film heroes.

d/p Howard Hawks *s* Leigh Brackett *c* Harold Rosson
lp John Wayne, Robert Mitchum, James Caan, Charlene
Holt, Arthur Hunnicutt, Michele Carey, Edward Asner

*Far left: Lee Van Cleef,
by now a staple
ingredient of the Italian
Western, in Death
Rides a Horse.*

Face to Face *orig* Faccia a Faccia
(P.E.A./ARTURO GONZALES; IT, SP)   scope   110 (102) min
Like **The Big Gundown** (1966), Sollima's previous movie, this is an explicitly political allegory cast in Western form. Volonte is the tubercular professor of history convalescing in the South West who meets outlaw Milian and, fascinated by him, puts his intellect at the outlaw's disposal and finally usurps Milian's position as leader after the outlaw grows sick of the pointless violence that accompanies Volonte's descent into fascism. Berger, as the Pinkerton agent, is cast in the unlikely role of moral arbiter at the end when he lets the once-famous outlaw go free after he's killed the once-timid professor.

For all the film's cheapness and recourse to cliches, it has a freshness about it that few Hollywood Westerns of the period possess.

d/s Sergio Sollima   *p* Alberto Grimaldi   *c* Rafael Pacheco
lp Gian-Maria Volonte, Tomas Milian, William Berger, Jolanda Modio, Carole Andre, Gianni Rizzo

The Fastest Guitar Alive   (FOUR LEAF)   87 min
Orbison (minus his dark glasses) is the guitar toting Confederate spy who, with Jackson, hijacks the San Francisco mint of gold intended for Union coffers, in this lacklustre Katzman quickie. Orbison is no actor and the gimmick of a guitar that doubles as a rifle (the kind of gimmick the Italian Western would handle with so much more élan) is hardly enough to support a whole film.

d Michael Moore   *p* Sam Katzman   *s* Robert E. Kent
c W. Wallace Kelley   *lp* Roy Orbison, Sammy Jackson, Maggie Pierce, Lyle Bettger, John Doucette, Joan Freeman

Fort Utah   (A.C. LYLES PRODUCTIONS)   scope   83 min
A lacklustre film from Lyles this is directed by a tired Selander who clearly could do nothing with Craddock and Fisher's inept script. Lyles' low budget Westerns, virtually the only Westerns being regularly made in Hollywood in the sixties, reflected the near death of the genre. Certainly, in contrast to Italian Westerns, they reveal a tradition that had ossified and a limited imagination on behalf of their makers as they repeated the old cliches time and time again. Here John

Clint Eastwood in Hang 'Em High, the star's triumphant return to Hollywood.

Ireland valiantly battles against first Brady and his band of renegade cavalrymen, who have massacred an encampment of Indian women, and then the Indian braves seeking revenge, before he can claim Mayo.

d Lesley Selander   *p* A.C. Lyles   *s* Steve Fisher, Andrew Craddock   *c* Lothrop Worth   *lp* John Ireland, Virginia Mayo, Scott Brady, John Russell, Robert Strauss, Jim Davis

40 Guns to Apache Pass   (ADMIRAL FILMS)   95 min
The last Western of serial veteran Witney, this is a routine affair. Murphy is the Cavalry captain who single-handedly routs Cochise and his braves by first stemming a rebellion by his raw recruits, fermented by Tobey's scheming sergeant, and then retrieving the repeating rifles of the title. Unlike Murphy's Universal Westerns, which are at least exciting, his Columbia releases of the sixties are generally thin, cliche-ridden and lacklustre, like this one.

d William Witney   *p* Grant Whytock   *s* Willard Willingham, Mary Willingham   *c* Jacques Marquette
lp Audie Murphy, Michael Burns, Kenneth Tobey, Laraine Stephens, Kenneth MacDonald, Robert Brubaker

Gunfight in Abilene   (U)   scope   86 min
In this superior Western Darin (who also wrote the music and sang the title song) is the Confederate officer returning to find his home town run by cattle baron Nielsen. Nielsen appoints him sheriff, even though he's incapable of drawing his gun since accidentally killing Nielsen's brother. But, if the script is rambling, Hale, a graduate of television directing his first feature, is fully in control of his material and handles it stylishly. However, the film was received badly in America and Hale subsequently retreated to television, the telefilm and good reviews.

d William Hale   *p* Howard Christie   *s* Berne Giler, John D.F. Black   *c* Maury Gertsman   *lp* Bobby Darin, Leslie Nielsen, Emily Banks, Don Galloway, Michael Sarrazin, Donnelly Rhodes

Hang 'Em High
(MALPASO/LEONARD FREEMAN PRODUCTIONS)   114 min
Only nominally directed by Post whom Eastwood had known since his *Rawhide* days, *Hang 'Em High* represents Eastwood's triumphant return to Hollywood from Italy and the beginning of his directorial career. The first film made by Eastwood's own Malpaso company, it earned its star $400,000 and 25 percent of the take. Visually indebted to Leone, it is only partially successful as a film. Its most interesting feature, given the way Eastwood's career would subsequently develop, is the strong role given to the film's heroine, Stevens. Eastwood is the deputy sheriff (appointed by Hingle's hanging judge) who uses his job to search for the nine men who nearly hanged him and Stevens is the equally obsessed woman scouring the jails for information that might lead her to the murderers of her husband. Their uneasy relationship is the most successful part of the film.

d Ted Post   *p/co-s* Leonard Freeman   *co-s* Mel Goldberg
c Leonard South, Richard Kline   *lp* Clint Eastwood, Inger Stevens, Ed Begley, Pat Hingle, Ben Johnson

Hate for Hate *orig* Odio per Odio
(WEST FILM; IT)   scope   100 (79) min
For all its many faults, this is a fascinating Italian Western from Paolella, a one-time film critic who has worked as a director in nearly every section of the film industry, from peplums, through thrillers to working with the likes of Pasolini. Moreover, unlike most other Italian directors, Paolella's inspiration was clearly the classic American revenge Western. Thus, after the complicated opening in which Sabato and Ireland's friendship is established when Ireland

returns to Sabato the money he deposited in the bank Ireland's just robbed, Ireland then seeks out Sabato thinking he's responsible for the death of his wife. Finding him not responsible, the pair set out after Ellis, Sabato's one-time partner.

Though he directs efficiently enough, the attempt to unite the Italian and American strands of the Western is not really successful.

d/co-s Domenico Paolella *p* Italo Zingarelli *co-s* Bruno Corbucci, Fernando di Leo *c* Alejandro Ulloa *lp* Antonio Sabato, John Ireland, Fernando Sancho, Nadia Marconi, Mirko Ellis, Gloria Milland

Hombre (FOX) pv 111 min
A thoroughly pessimistic variant on the **Stagecoach** (1939) format with racism added to the catalogue of bourgeoise prejudices Dudley Nichols delineated for Ford. Newman (a superb mannered performance) is virtually silent playing the whiteman raised as a Indian who at first suffers at the hands of his fellow passengers and then reluctantly, under the taunts of Cilento's hard-bitten but soft-hearted working woman, sets about leading them to safety when Boone and his men ambush the stage. March, in one of his last roles, is the stagey corrupt Indian agent and Balsam the equivocating Mexican driver. Ritt's spare direction and Wong Howe's harsh photography are superb.

d/co-p Martin Ritt *co-p/co-s* Irving Ravetch *co-s* Harriet Frank Jnr *c* James Wong Howe *lp* Paul Newman, Fredric March, Richard Boone, Diane Cilento, Martin Balsam, Cameron Mitchell

Hour of the Gun (MIRISCH/KAPPA) pv 100 min
This impressive Western was much maligned at the time of its release for its cynical and bitter tone. It continues the story of Wyatt Earp (Garner) after **Gunfight at the O.K. Corral** (1957), which Sturges also directed. Where the earlier film saw Earp as a righteous lawman, Anhalt's script here treats Earp's moral decline from lawman to a person bent on nothing more than revenge after his brothers have been murdered by men in the pay of Ike Clanton (Ryan). The film is briskly mounted and emphatically directed by Sturges, who uses the moral growth of Robards, as Doc Halliday, as a counterweight to Earp's decline. In its attempts to demystify folk-hero Earp, the film is almost elegaic in tone. Anhalt wittily chooses for his cameo appearance the role of the medic who keeps the tubercular Robards alive.

d/p John Sturges *s* Edward Anhalt *c* Lucien Ballard *lp* James Garner, Jason Robards, Robert Ryan, Albert Salmi, Jon Voight, Edward Anhalt

The Last Challenge aka The Pistolero of Red River (MGM) pv 105 min
A slow, turgid B feature, this was the last film from Thorpe, who, in a little over 40 years, churned out nearly 200 feature films. Ford is the gunman turned marshal who wants to hang up his guns and settle down with Dickinson when Everett arrives in town looking for him. There follows a lengthy education process reminiscent of **The Tin Star** (1957) that ends with Everett dead and Ford finally throwing away his guns. The only memorable sequence comes when Ford gets his Indian attackers drunk (on the principle that a drunk Indian is better than a dead anybody) rather than fight it out with them, to Everett's evident disgust.

d/p Richard Thorpe *s* John Sherry, Robert Emmett Ginna *c* Ellsworth Fredericks *lp* Glenn Ford, Angie Dickinson, Chad Everett, Gary Merrill, Jack Elam, Delphi Lawrence

The Man Who Killed Billy the Kid orig El Hombre que Matao Billy el Nino
(AITOR FILMS/KINESIS FILM; SP, IT) scope 86 min
This is a lacklustre Italian Western that treats its subjects as romantically as a Hollywood B picture of the forties. Hirenbach is Billy and Tozzi Pat Garrett, the childhood friends who end up on different sides of the fence. The view presented of Billy the Kid, which is completely out of step with the post-Leone Italian Western, is a throwback to the early sixties, when Italian producers had no fixed idea of what an 'Italian Western' might be.

d/co-s Julio Buchs *p* Silvio Battistini *co-s* Federico de Urrutia *c* Miguel Mila *lp* Peter Lee Lawrence (Karl Hirenbach), Fausto Tozzi, Dianik Zurakowska, Gloria Milland, Luis Prendes, Barta Barry

Red Tomahawk (A.C. LYLES PRODUCTIONS) 82 min
An indifferent Lyles Western that quickly gets bogged down after an effective start in which Keel comes across the carnage that is the aftermath of the Battle of the Little Big Horn. As ever, Lyles and director Springsteen go for economy over everything else and the result is, despite contributions from the likes of Arlen, Crawford, Drake and Brady, the worse for it. Fisher's over-elaborate script (which features action by inference for reasons of economy) has Keel desperately trying to warn the troops headed to join Custer of the massacre. With a couple of gatling guns to help him, he does just that.

d R.G. Springsteen *p* A.C. Lyles *s* Steve Fisher *c* W. Wallace Kelley *lp* Howard Keel, Richard Arlen, Broderick Crawford, Scott Brady, Tom Drake, Joan Caulfield

James Garner (right) as Wyatt Earp in Hour of the Gun, *John Sturges' bitter sequel to his own* Gunfight at the O.K. Corral *(1957).*

Far left: Paul Newman as Hombre, *the white man reared as an Apache, reluctantly returning to the white man's world.*

The Ride to Hangman's Tree (U) 88 min

An unassuming, pleasing B Western, this opens with a delightfully staged bank robbery. Elegantly directed by Rafkin from a strong script by Bowers, Ward and Natteford, *The Ride to Hangman's Tree* is determinedly old fashioned with the one exception that its heroes are outlaws. Lord, Farentino and Galloway are the trio of outlaws – in many ways the descendants of the trios so prevalent in series Westerns of the thirties and forties, so firmly are they leader, young headstrong romantic and comic support – who rob their way through the West, often in amiable conflict with each other.

d Alan Rafkin *p* Howard Christie *s* Luci Ward, Jack Natteford, William Bowers *c* Gene Polito *lp* Jack Lord, James Farentino, Don Galloway, Melodie Johnson, Richard Anderson, Robert Yuro

Rough Night in Jerico

(MARTIN RACKIN PRODUCTIONS) scope 104 min

A morose, ponderous, violent Western in which Peppard is the former marshal turned gambler and Martin, in an unusual piece of casting, is the town tyrant intent on buying up Simmons' stagecoach line in Boehm and Albert's erratic but only too predictable screenplay. Pickens, equally unusually, is cast as a heavy and McIntire is the marshal who remembers the good times. Metty's high-key cinematography is the best thing about the film.

d Arnold Laven *p* Martin Rackin *s* Sydney Boehm, Marvin H. Albert *c* Russell Metty *lp* Dean Martin, Jean Simmons, George Peppard, John McIntire, Slim Pickens, Don Galloway

Savage Pampas *orig* Pampas Salvaje

(PRADES/COMET/DASA FILMS/SAMUEL BRONSTEIN INT; SP, ALGERIA, US, ARGENTINA) scope 112 (97) min

An Argentinian Western and Taylor's oddest film, *Savage Pampas* is a remake of the 1946 Argentinian film *Pampa Barbera*. Taylor is the guardian of a wagon train of women heading for a lonely outpost in the interior in 1870. The plot is reminiscent of his **Westward the Women** (1952) with the difference that this time the women are prostitutes, intended to be morale boosters to stop the men of the outpost from deserting. Shot in Spain by Hollywood veteran Fregonese who co-scripted it with a strong emphasis on realism, the film got lost in the flood of Spaghetti Westerns.

d/co-s Hugo Fregonese *p* Jaime Prades *co-s* John Melson *c* Manuel Berenguer *lp* Robert Taylor, Ron Randell, Ty Hardin, Rosenda Monteros

Jack Lord, James Farentino and Don Galloway as the engaging trio of outlaws in the elegant The Ride to Hangman's Tree.

Shoot First, Laugh Last *orig* Un Uomo, un Cavallo, una Pistola (PRIMEX ITALIANA/JUVENTUS/REVERSE PRODUCTIONS; IT, WG, US) 90 (79) min

A routine Italian Western that alternately mocks its macho hero (Antony) – he always spits out the cigarette he's just rolled in disgust after one drag, for example – and celebrates his invincibility. The main point of interest is the complex plot which has Antony's stranger as bewildered as anyone as he tracks down the bandit who robbed the stagecoach.

d Vance Lewis (Luigi Vanzi) *p* Roberto Infascelli, Massimo Gualdi *s* Jose Many (Giuseppe Mangione), Bob Enescelle Jnr *c* Marcello Masciocchi *lp* Tony Antony, Dan Vadis, Marco Gugliemi, Daniele Vargas, Marina Berti, Jill Banner

Stranger on the Run *aka* Death Dance at Banner

(NBC-TV) pv 97 min

Released theatrically in Europe, this telefilm was one of the several Siegel made during his five-year absence from making feature films. Scripted by Reisner, who was to become a regular collaborator of Siegel's, it features Fonda in the unlikely role of a bum and a drunkard who finally turns on his tormentors, who are bored gunmen/lawmen seeking excitement after subduing the township of Banner. The movie is structured like an elaborate formal game with the gunmen, Parks, Mineo and Duryea, chasing Fonda who they've 'decided' is guilty of murdering a local prostitute, catching him, letting him escape and then catching him again. This bleakness, intensified by the sun-parched desert scapes of cinematographer Thackery is akin to the mood of Boetticher's Westerns which are like floating poker games. Baxter is the rancher who persuades Fonda to fight rather than run and Parks the essentially decent gunman.

d Don Siegel *p* Richard Lyons *s* Dean Reisner *c* Bud Thackery *lp* Henry Fonda, Michael Parks, Dan Duryea, Anne Baxter, Sal Mineo

A Time for Killing *aka* The Long Ride Home

(COL/SAGE WESTERN PICTURES) pv 83 min

In this savage Western, Hamilton is the Confederate Major who escapes from a Union prison camp in Utah near the close of the Civil War with some of his men, and Ford is the Captain sent after him. Things become more personal for Ford when Hamilton takes hostage his wife, Stevens.

Karlson brings a real edge to the violence of the confrontations between Hamilton and Ford. Thus, although the script is far too talky and earnest, Karlson's fluent camera, seemingly just happening on the horrifying results of the events the characters are embroiled in, makes Ford's descent into violence only too understandable. A grotesque sequence early on in the film indicates just how bleak a vision Karlson has: a teenage Confederate is sentenced to death and as a final humiliation a squad of black orderlies is assembled as the firing squad. Not marksmen, they only wound him, leaving him screaming in agony; they fire again and still he doesn't die. After what seems an epoch, Ford lumbers into the frame and shoots him dead.

d Phil Karlson *p* Harry Joe Brown *s* Halsted Welles *c* Kenneth Peach *lp* Glenn Ford, George Hamilton, Inger Stevens, Paul Peterson, Max Baer, Todd Armstrong

The War Wagon

(U/BATJAC PRODUCTIONS) pv 101 (99) min

Like many of Kennedy's recent Westerns, *The War Wagon* is at its best in its comic moments. Wayne is the man wrongly jailed and determined to take his revenge on crooked mining contractor Cabot, who has stolen his land. Douglas is the gunfighter who teams up with him to rob Cabot's armour-plated war wagon of its half-million-dollar load of gold dust. Walker's drunken explosive expert, Keel's renegade Indian and Keenan Wynn's grizzling wagon driver complete the

gang. The action, which centres on the to-ing and fro-ing of the wagon with its revolving turret and gatling gun, is lethargic but the interplay between the cynical Douglas – he turns down Cabot's cash offer to kill Wayne because he thinks there's more money to be got robbing Cabot – and Wayne is always amusing.

d Burt Kennedy *p* Marvin Schwartz *s* Clair Huffaker *c* William H. Clothier *lp* John Wayne, Kirk Douglas, Howard Keel, Robert Walker, Bruce Cabot, Bruce Dern

Waterhole No. 3

(GEOFFREY PRODUCTIONS) scope 95 min

This uneven satirical Western was overseen by Blake Edwards who began his career as an actor in Westerns and later wrote and produced a fine pair of low-budget Westerns, **Panhandle** (1948) and **Stampede** (1949). The film's main failing is one-time attorney Steck's screenplay which is too imitative of **Cat Ballou** (1965). Coburn is the raffish gunman who seduces a sheriff's daughter and then sets off after Akins, Carey and Davis and their stolen loot with her and the sheriff in pursuit. The jokes are funny but have no resonance.

d William Graham *p/co-s* Joseph T. Steck *co-s* Robert R. Young *c* Robert Burks *lp* James Coburn, Carroll O'Connor, Claude Akins, Timothy Carey, Harry Davis, Bruce Dern

The Way West (UA) pv 122 min

Mitchum, in fine form as the trail scout with failing eyesight, Douglas, enjoying his role as the sadistic dreamer of a New Jerusalem, and superb cinematography from Clothier, are little compensation for McLaglen's wool-gathering direction in this dreary epic. McLaglen's most Fordian film, in the sense that virtually every frame sees him striving for 'Fordian effects' (as if Ford's images could be simply borrowed), *The Way West* reveals most clearly the limits of its director's vision. His celebration of the move Westward simply lacks the bittersweet complexity of Ford's, let alone Ford's ability to blend the personal and the mythic. Thus as Mitchum, Douglas and Widmark (as the farmer with 'Oregon fever') progress along the Oregon Trail in 1843, neither McLaglen nor writers Maddow and Lindemann are able to project any perspective on their journey and so they become mere

cyphers, pegs from which to hand a plot bizarre enough, as one critic cruelly put it, to sustain a full year of television soap operas.

d Andrew V. McLaglen *p* Harold Hecht *s* Ben Maddow, Mitch Lindemann *c* William Clothier *lp* Kirk Douglas, Robert Mitchum, Richard Widmark, Sally Field, Lola Albright, Stubby Kaye

Welcome to Hard Times *aka* Killer on a Horse

(MAX E. YOUNGSTEIN-DAVID KARR PRODUCTIONS)
103 (78) min

A bleak, cold, angry Western, this is scripted and directed by Kennedy, a man better known for his comic Westerns, like **Support Your Local Sheriff** (1968), and based on a novel by E.L. Doctorow, the author of *Ragtime*. Ray is the 'Man from Bodie', an evil-spirited gunman who returns to the town of Hard Times, rebuilt by its townsfolk after he and a sadistic accomplice have burnt it down. Once more he sets about destroying the town until a crazed Rule forces Hard Times' reluctant mayor, Fonda, into a desperate confrontation with Ray. The film has much of the feel, if not quite the power, of Clint Eastwood's mysterious and allegorical **High Plains Drifter** (1973).

d/s Burt Kennedy *p* Max E. Youngstein, David Karr *c* Harry Stradling Jnr *lp* Henry Fonda, Aldo Ray, Janice Rule, Keenan Wynn, Janis Paige, Warren Oates

Will Penny (PAR) 108 min

Tom Gries' best film, *Will Penny* is a decidedly domestic Western in which Heston (as the lonely cowboy) comes to terms with old age, his lack of education and a future of endless drifting when confronted by the seemingly weak and defenceless Hackett. Interestingly it stresses not the cowboy's individuality (in comparison to the blandness of modern life) like so many modern Westerns, but the hardships and loneliness of life on the cattle trail and ranch. The downbeat ending with Heston and Hackett separating – 'I'm a cowboy, I don't know nothing else' – though in love is rare in Westerns. Ballard's harsh yet poetic cinematography was another key element in the film's critical, but not commercial, success. Only the excesses of Pleasence as the crazy preacher Quint, one of whose sons Heston has killed, seems out of place.

d/s Tom Gries *p* Fred Engel, Walter Seltzer *c* Lucien Ballard *lp* Charlton Heston, Joan Hackett, Donald Pleasence, Bruce Dern, Lee Majors, Ben Johnson

Charlton Heston as Will Penny, *in one of the first Westerns to treat the cowboy as a labourer rather than a gunman.*

Gadgetry comes to the American Western: The War Wagon.

Above: *Henry Fonda, a baddie for the first time in his career, holds a gun on part-time sheriff James Stewart amidst the desolation of Firecreek.*

1968

Bandolero! (FOX) 106 min

An uneven film, influenced equally by the verities of Ford and the violence of the modern Western, *Bandolero!* is perhaps the oddest of McLaglen's films. Kennedy is the sheriff on the trail of badmen Stewart and Martin who have taken a reluctant Welch along with them as a hostage. The presence of Welch, attempting to consolidate her reputation as a Screen Goddess with a dramatic performance, and McLaglen's rumbustious comic direction seem contradictory. A further clue to writer Barrett and McLaglen's more traditional intentions lies in the appearance of Western favourites – 'Red' Barry, Harry Carey Jnr, Jock Mahoney and Roy Barcoft – in bit parts.

d Andrew V. McLaglen *p* Robert L. Jacks *s* James Lee Barrett *c* William H. Clothier *lp* James Stewart, Dean Martin, Raquel Welch, George Kennedy, Will Geer, Denver Pyle

Blue (PAR/KETTLEDRUM) pv 113 min

A beautifully photographed piece of silliness, *Blue* tells the unlikely story of the adopted son (Stamp) of a Mexican bandit (Montalban), who, after rescuing Pettet and her father (Malden) from the bandits, learns the confusing rules of civilization.

d Silvio Narizzano *p* Judd Bernard, Irwin Winkler *s* Meade Roberts, Ronald M. Cohen *c* Stanley Cortez *lp* Terence Stamp, Joanna Pettet, Karl Malden, Ricardo Montalban, Anthony Costello, Joe De Santis

Buckskin (A.C. LYLES/PAR) 97 (65) min

This is a competent, if unimaginative, actioneer from producer Lyles. Sullivan is the frontier marshal who leads the townspeople of Gloryhole against Corey's cattle baron who has cut off water supplies to the town: like its stars, the film's plot is old and tired. The film has the last screen appearance of MacLane, veteran of countless Westerns, usually as a bad guy. Here he plays the dependable town doctor.

d Michael Moore *p* A.C. Lyles *s* Michael Fisher *c* W. Wallace Kelley *lp* Barry Sullivan, Wendell Corey, Joan Caulfield, Lon Chaney, John Russell, Barton MacLane

Custer of the West *aka* A Good Day for Fighting
(SECURITY PICTURES) cinerama 146 (120) min

A carnival version of the Custer myth with stops along the way for cinerama sideshow effects – a runaway train, a soldier escaping down rapids – that is only partially redeemed by Shaw's convincing performance in the title role. The script's psychologizing which offers us Custer as a Peter Pan figure sits uneasily amidst the spectacular sequences. Ure is wooden as Custer's wife, while Ryan, as a gold-hungry deserter, steals the picture. Originally intended to have been directed by Akira Kurosawa, it was shot in Spain.

d Robert Siodmak (*Civil War sequences d* Irving Lerner) *p* Philip Yordon, Louis Dolivet *s* Bernard Gordon, Julian Halvey *c* Cecilio Paniagua *lp* Robert Shaw, Mary Ure, Jeffrey Hunter, Ty Hardin, Robert Ryan

Day of the Evil Gun (MGM) pv 93 min

Clearly cast in the mould of **The Searchers** (1956), this is an impressive minor Western. Warren's script is imaginative and Thorpe's direction assured, especially in the way it picks out telling details, and Ford and Kennedy give thoughtful performances. Ford is the would-be ex-gunman who joins up with neighbour Kennedy to search for his wife and two children stolen by the Apache. In the course of their search, helped by Jagger (whose mad Indian trader is a delicious homage to Hank Worden's performance of the same role in the John Ford film), the pair survive torture by bandits, an encounter with renegades and Indian raids. As this happens, slowly but surely the once peaceable Kennedy takes over more and more of the killing. On their safe return home with Ford's wife and children, Kennedy challenges Ford to a gunfight, only to die from a stranger's bullet when Ford refuses to draw.

The film was originally made for television but released first theatrically.

d/p Jerry Thorpe *s* Charles Marquis Warren, Eric Bercovici *c* W. Wallace Kelley *lp* Glenn Ford, Arthur Kennedy, Dean Jagger, John Anderson, Paul Fix, Nico Minardos

The Devil's Mistress (W.G.W. PICTURES) 66 min

A poorly mounted horror Western that is remarkably similar in theme and plot to **Shadow of Chikara** (1978). Set in the New Mexico of the 1870s it features Gregory and Westmoreland (who produced the picture under the pseudonym of Moreland) as two of a band of outlaws intent on raping their way to Mexico. They come upon Resley and his Indian wife, Stapleton, and murder him and rape her, only to die one by one, driven mad by her kisses.

d/s Orville Wanzer *p* Wes Moreland (Forest Westmoreland) *c* Teddy Gregory *lp* Joan Stapleton, Robert Gregory, Forest Westmoreland, Arthur Resley, Douglas Warren, Oren Williams

Firecreek (WB – 7 ARTS) pv 104 min

Despite the presence of both Stewart and Fonda, *Firecreek* is a routine film at best. Stewart is the part-time sheriff and Fonda the man who wrests control of the town from him. Once described as 'a geriatrics' *High Noon'*, because like that film it features a cowed community who refuse to assist the one man who feels it to be his duty to protect them, the script's interesting ideas are consistently betrayed by McEveety's melodramatic direction. **Welcome to Hard Times** (1967) which also stars Fonda treats the same subject far more interestingly.

d Vincent McEveety *p* Philip Leacock *s* Calvin Clements *c* William H. Clothier *lp* James Stewart, Henry Fonda, Gary Lockwood, Dean Jagger, Jack Elam, Jay C. Flippen

5 Card Stud (HAL WALLIS PRODUCTIONS/PAR) 103 min

This undistinguished Western wastes its cast and unusual mystery plot in regular bouts of pointless brutality. Mitchum, as the gun-toting preacher – 'elected by God and Mr Colt' – is a pale imitation of the vengeful incarnation of evil he played in

307

Night of the Hunter (1955), while Martin eases his way through the part of the laconic gambler with little conviction. Roberts' detective story of a plot has five members of a poker game, who lynched a cheat, gunned down one after the other by a mysterious assailant. Hathaway chooses the occasional odd camera angle to intensify his 'Who Dunnit' plot but the lack of commitment of all is there to see.

d Henry Hathaway *p* Hal B. Wallis *s* Marguerite Roberts
c Daniel L. Fapp *lp* Dean Martin, Robert Mitchum, Roddy McDowall, Inger Stevens, Katherine Justice, John Anderson

Guns of the Magnificent Seven (MIRISCH) pv 106 min

A second sequel to **The Magnificent Seven** (1960) with Kennedy in the Yul Brynner role. Surprisingly, though it was made in Spain where the influence of the Italian Western was high, it is closer to the original in feel than Burt Kennedy's violent **Return of the Seven** (1966). Set at the time of the Mexican Revolution, the plot has Kennedy lead his group of oddballs in a successful rescue of Rey as the revolutionary leader with Tony Davis tagging along in the role of the young Zapata no less!

d Paul Wendkos *p* Vincent M. Fennelly *s* Herman Hoffman *c* Antonio Macasoli *lp* George Kennedy, James Whitmore, Monte Markham, Bernie Casey, Joe Dan Baker, Fernando Rey

Heaven with a Gun

(KING BROS) pv 101 (98) min

Anderson is the cattle baron determined to stop sheepmen invading the range and Ford the gunman turned preacher who, though continually tempted to use his guns, finds a non-violent way to bring peace to the valley in this routine film. Hershey is the half-caste and Jones the saloon owner who vie for Ford's affections.

The film's producers, the King brothers, are best known for their continued use of blacklisted writers during the McCarthy era.

d Lee H. Katzin *p* Frank King, Maurice King *s* Richard Carr *c* Fred Koenekamp *lp* Glenn Ford, Carolyn Jones, Barbara Hershey, John Anderson, David Carradine, Noah Beery Jnr

Above: *Raquel Welch, the strangely mustachioed Burt Reynolds and Jim Brown form the unlikeliest of trios in* 100 Rifles.

Journey to Shiloh (U) scope 101 (81) min

An intriguing little film, this is sadly marred by extensive distributor and producer cuts. Caan and six other Texan youths leave home in pursuit of glory in the Confederate cause and discover instead the horrors of war. Episodically structured, with the group being prepared for the hell of the battle of Shiloh by stages as they edge closer to it, the film is remarkable for its pointed parallels with the Vietnam war. Hale directs his inexperienced cast of Universal juveniles with assurance.

d William Hale *p* Howard Christie *s* Gene Coon *c* Enzo A. Martinelli *lp* James Caan, Michael Sarrazin, Brenda Scott, Don Stroud, Paul Peterson, Michael Burns

Kill Them All and Come Back Alone *orig* **Ammazzali Tutti e Torno Solo** (FIDA CINEMATOGRAFICA/ CENTAURO FILM; IT, SP) scope 100 (98) min

A superior variant on *The Dirty Dozen* (1967) with Connors leading a successful assault on a Union fort to steal gold only to be captured after the gold has been hidden and imprisoned where Wolff's sadist tries to torture the hiding place out of the men. The stunt work is more realistic than usual and together with the film's fast pace helps paper over the gaping cracks in the script.

d/co-s Enzo G. Castellari (Enzo Girolami) *p* Edmondo Amati *co-s* Tito Carpi, Francesco Scardamaglia, Joaquin Romero Hernandez *c* Alejandro Ulloa *lp* Chuck Connors, Frank Wolff, Franco Citti, Leo Anchoriz, Ken Wood, Hercules Cortes

Lonesome Cowboys (FACTORY FILMS) 110 min

'A cowboy fantasy out on the range', *Lonesome Cowboys* is a key film in the Warhol canon. It sees the growing dominance of Morrisey who, as the film's editor, cinematographer and uncredited director, introduced the notion of direction and script to Warhol, although the 'plot' is decidedly slim by Hollywood standards. Viva and Mead, both desperate for male company, watch with delight when Waldon and his homosexual gang ride into the desert town they live in. Francine is the transvestite sheriff and Hompertz the boy

Michael Sarrazin (left) and James Caan re-united after their initiation into the horrors of war in the ambitious Journey to Shiloh.

everybody wants to bed. The improvised scenes, some of them hilarious, that follow are held together by the concept of the West to which in their different ways all the characters subscribe. The result is a quaint, parodic Western which, despite its many sexual couplings, is far more innocent than the sex Westerns that were to follow.

d/p/s Andy Warhol   *c* Paul Morrisey   *lp* Viva, Taylor Mead, Tom Hompertz, Joe d'Allesandro, Louis Waldon, Francis Francine

Mackenna's Gold

(HIGHROAD PRODUCTIONS/COL)   pv   136 min
This is a tedious film. Peck is the sheriff entrusted with a map to the legendary valley of gold who is forced to take it seriously when numerous gold-hungry bandits, prospectors, Indians and the like descend on him after he's burnt the map. Following a seemingly endless succession of gold-lust cliches, carefully shared between the film's numerous guest stars (Raymond Massey, Burgess Meredith, Lee J. Cobb, Edward G. Robinson, etc.) Sharif, the film's main villain, and Peck are left with Sparv and a sack of gold between them after an avalanche has permanently closed the canyon.

Although he co-produced it, his first move in that area, Tiomkin strangely didn't write the music; that's by Quincy Jones.

d J. Lee Thompson   *co-p/s* Carl Foreman   *co-p* Dimitri Tiomkin   *c* Joseph MacDonald   *lp* Gregory Peck, Omar Sharif, Telly Savalas, Camilla Sparv, Keenan Wynn, Julie Newmar

A Man Called Gannon   (U)   scope   105 min

A routine remake of **Man Without a Star** (1955) that lacks the passion and vitality of King Vidor's film. Goldstone opts for a more homely tone, stressing rootless cowpoke Franciosa's friendship with Sarrazin's innocent rather than his love-hate

Below: Claudia Cardinale, Lionel Stander (centre) and Charles Bronson in Sergio Leone's black fairytale of a Western, Once upon a Time in the West.

relationship with rancher West. The result is an efficient actioneer, and for the most part a non-violent film, that keeps closely to the storyline of the original.

d James Goldstone   *p* Howard Christie   *s* Gene Kearney, Borden Chase, D.D. Beauchamp   *c* William Margulies   *lp* Tony Franciosa, Michael Sarrazin, Judi West, Susan Oliver, John Anderson, David Sheiner

Once upon a Time in the West *orig* C'era una Volta il West   (RAFRAN CINEMATOGRAFICA/SAN MARCO; IT)
scope   168 (144) min
Leone's classic fairy tale of violence intertwines and gives a mythical edge to two classic Western themes, the revenge story and the arrival of civilization in the West (seen in the film as the coming of the railroad). The result is a bizarre cross between *The Iron Horse* (1924) and **The Big Trail** (1930), a film that examines the impact on the frontier of the colt 45, the dollar and the railroad's 'beautiful shiny rails'.

The complex script from an original outline by Bernardo Bertolucci (whose *1900*, 1976, was similarly epic in structure) tells the intersecting stories of Ferzetti, the dying railroad tycoon, determined to see the Pacific from a railroad car before he dies, who needs Cardinale's property, Fonda's gunman whom Ferzetti hires to facilitate matters, the mysterious Bronson who comes to her assistance and Robards' romantic bandit. Ferzetti represents the power of money, which Fonda, though he tries to become a business-man, never fully comprehends, so committed is he to the guns with which he had killed Bronson's brother in the past and Cardinale's husband in the film's opening. Similarly Robards' anarchic bandit is living on borrowed time, while Bronson is emotionally dead, living only to stage-manage his revenge on Fonda in the most elaborate fashion. Only Cardinale, who quits whoring for domesticity and becomes 'the mother of Sweetwater', like Ford's settlers, looks forward to the future.

The characters' compelling dance of death is made all the more rivetting by Leone's stylish bravura: the final confronta-tion between Fonda and Bronson is all eyes and ritual (like the sequence in Samuel Fuller's **Forty Guns,** 1957, where Barry Sullivan 'walks' down a man); the astonishing opening in which Leone kills off Elam and Strode; and perhaps most telling of all Leone's co-option of the American Western through quotation and even the annexation of John Ford's Monument Valley.

Sadly Leone's masterpiece had to wait some fifteen years before it was shown in its complete version outside Europe. Anticipating the even harsher treatment **Heaven's Gate** (1980) would suffer, it was drastically cut by its producers with the result that the film became largely unintelligible.

d/co-s Sergio Leone   *p* Fulvio Morsella   *co-s* Sergio Donati   *c* Tonino Delli Colli   *lp* Claudia Cardinale, Henry Fonda, Jason Robards, Charles Bronson, Jack Elam, Woody Strode, Gabriele Ferzetti

100 Rifles

(FOX/MARVIN SCHWARTZ PRODUCTIONS)   109 min
Sheriff Brown and half-breed prisoner Reynolds join Yaqui Indian Welch in her quest for vengeance against the Mexican army and O'Herlihy's railroad tycoon, who have shifted the Yaquis from their homeland in this routine Western. A violent film in which, in place of the leisurely, evocative style of his masterly **Will Penny** (1967), Gries opts for a punchy, even humorous, style but to little significant effect. For behind the characters lies a set of supporting cliches – the black Brown is sheriff because no one else would do the job and Lamas' Mexican army chief is given a boot-clicking German advisor, for example – that drains them of any real substance. Nonetheless, in Reynolds' engaging performance and in the occasional visual delight – the marvellous yellow car Lamas rides about in stranded in the desert, for example – the film has its moments.

d/co-s Tom Gries   *p* Marvin Schwartz   *co-s* Clair Huffaker
c Cecilio Paniagua   *lp* Jim Brown, Raquel Welch, Burt
Reynolds, Fernando Lamas, Don O'Herlihy, Hans Gudegast

A Professional Gun *orig Il Mercanario*

(P.E.A./DELPHOS/PROFILMS 21; IT, SP)   105 min
With **Companeros** (1970), this is Corbucci's best film. Like
so many of his movies it suffers from his lack of discipline and
his need to fit in jokes (like the revolutionaries dressed up as
angels) at any cost (the legacy of his days as a Cinecitta
gagman), but the strong performances of Musante as the rebel
and Nero as the mercenary who helps him, rescue the film.
Even Palance's homosexual gunman, who floridly dies in a
blood-splattered white suit in the middle of a circus ring,
cannot overbalance the film, so strong is the allegory in which
Musante is tutored in the practicalities of revolution by Nero,
and then grows used to riches only to rediscover his
revolutionary fervour at the end.

d/co-s Sergio Corbucci   *p* Alberto Grimaldi   *co-s* Luciano
Vincenzoni, Sergio Spina   *c* Alejandro Ulloa   *lp* Franco
Nero, Tony Masante, Jack Palance, Giovanna Ralli, Eduardo
Fajardo, Bruno Corazzari

Revenge at El Paso *orig Il Quattro dell' Ave Maria*

(CRONO CINEMATOGRAFICA; IT)   scope   137 (103) min
The first film to feature together Hill and Spencer who were
later to co-star in the successful Trinity series. The pair play a
cat and mouse game with Wallach, a condemned killer hired
by a bank president to recover the money they've stolen from
his bank. The best sequence, and also the most excessive, sees
a hotel orchestra playing a seemingly never-ending waltz as
Wallach faces McCarthy's gang and hotel residents dive to the
floor in fear.

d/co-p/s Giuseppe Colizzi   *co-p* Bino Cicogna   *c* Marcello
Masciocchi   *lp* Terence Hill (Mario Girotti), Bud Spencer
(Carlo Pedersoli), Eli Wallach, Brock Peters, Kevin
McCarthy, Livio Lorenzon

The Scalphunters   (BRISTOL/NORLAN)   pv   103 min

This is a shaggy-dog story of a Western with Lancaster as the
ill-educated trapper in a very uneasy alliance with a well-read
runaway slave, Davis. He is trying to get back a bunch of furs
stolen by Savalas' band of scalphunters. Directed rather too
heavy handedly – the climactic fistfight between Davis and
Lancaster, for example, goes on seemingly forever so that the
colour difference between the two disappears under a coating
of mud – by Pollack, the film nonetheless has an easygoing
charm about it. Winters, as the fading beauty who shrugs
with benign indifference when she is 'inherited' by Indians,
gives a marvellous performance, but it is Davis who steals the
film with his deeply subversive brand of humour.

d Sydney Pollack   *p* Jules Levy, Arthur Gardner, Arnold
Laven   *s* William Norton   *c* Duke Callaghan, Richard
Moore   *lp* Burt Lancaster, Ossie Davis, Telly Savalas,
Shelley Winters, Nick Cravat, Dan Vadis

The Shakiest Gun in the West   (U)   100 (87) min

A laboured remake of **The Paleface** (1948) with Knotts in the
Bob Hope role of the correspondent-school dentist who heads
out West to seek his fortune. Rhoades is a poor substitute for
Jane Russell as the girl who marries Knotts as a cover while
she sorts out Barry's gang of outlaws who are selling guns to
the Indians. Knotts' ineffectual weakling is equally inferior to
Hope's wisecracking interpretation of the role. Coogan as
Barry's henchman gives the best performance in the film.

d Alan Rafkin   *p* Edward J. Montague   *s* Jim Fritzell,
Everett Greenbaum, Frank Tashlin, Edmund Hartman
c Andrew Jackson   *lp* Don Knotts, Barbara Rhoades, Jackie
Coogan, Donald Barry, Ruth McDevitt, Dub Taylor

Shalako

(KINGSTON FILMS, A DIMITRI DE GRUNWALD PRODUCTION; GB)
scope   113 min
A 'British' Western, *Shalako* has too many of the flaws of the
international co-production genre for its beguiling casting and
interesting plot to succeed. Connery is the guide; Bardot, Van
Eyck, Boyd and Hawkins are amongst the company of
European aristocrats he leads in search of big game and has to
later rescue from Indians in the New Mexico of the 1880s.
The confrontation of Euopean civilization, complete with
crystal goblets and butlers, with bleak deserts and Indians
that lies at the centre of Louis L'Amour's original novel
quickly collapses into ridiculousness. Boyd is the amiable
villain.

d Edward Dmytryk   *p* Ewan Lloyd   *s* J.J. Griffith, Hal
Hopper, Scott Finch   *c* Ted Moore   *lp* Sean Connery,
Brigitte Bardot, Stephen Boyd, Jack Hawkins, Peter Van
Eyck, Honor Blackman

The Stalking Moon

(NATIONAL GENERAL PICTURES/STALKING MOON COMPANY.
A PAKULA-MULLIGAN PRODUCTION)   pv   109 min
This is an oddly static and talkative Western. Peck is the scout
who escorts a white woman, Saint, and her half-Indian son,
back home after she's been recovered from a ten-year
enforced stay with the Apache. Narciso is the renegade
Apache who wants his son back. Centring to such an extent on
the hidden menace of Narciso and on Peck and Forster's
attempts to capture him, the film needs a director more suited
to the outdoors than Mulligan, who seems happiest when his
characters are inside and talking. Even the lengthy set-piece
of the climactic duel between Narciso and Peck falls flat.

d Robert Mulligan   *p* Alan J. Pakula   *s* Alvin Sargent
c Charles Land   *lp* Gregory Peck, Eva Marie Saint, Robert
Forster, Noland Clay, Russell Thorson, Nathaniel Narciso

Support Your Local Sheriff

(CHEROKEE PRODUCTIONS)   93 min
An irreverent spoof Western with Garner accepting the job of
sheriff in a lawless town after gold is discovered in the local
cemetery. Garner's double-taking expressiveness and resour-
cefulness (honed to perfection on TV in first *Maverick* and later
The Rockford Files) make for some hilarious sending-up of the
usual humble-sheriff-cleans-up-the-town cliches. Brennan is
the father trying to spring son, Dern, from the town jail and
Elam is a wonderfully oafish deputy.

Unlike so many modern comedy Westerns which simply
poke fun at the genre, Kennedy neatly judges the difference
between sheer parody and affectionate teasing and situates his
movie slap bang in the middle.

*Brigitte Bardot shoots
her first Indian in
Shalako, one of several
international co-
productions that
followed in the wake of
the success of the Italian
Western.*

Rehearsing the prison break in Villa Rides, *written by Robert Towne and Sam Peckinpah and all but emasculated by director Buzz Kulik.*

Far right: Paul Newman and Robert Redford, *Butch Cassidy and the Sundance Kid.*

amongst the credits notwithstanding. Mitchum is the mercenary aviator press-ganged into becoming a one-man airforce for the revolution and Bronson (who gives a remarkably subtle performance) the sadistic aide to Brynner's bland but determined Pancho Villa. Kulik resolves the complex issues the script raises in 'heroic action' too often for the characters to remain credible, historical inaccuracies aside.

d Buzz Kulik *p* Ted Richmond *s* Robert Towne, Sam Peckinpah *c* Jack Hildyard *lp* Yul Brynner, Robert Mitchum, Grazia Buccella, Charles Bronson, Robert Viharo, Herbert Lom

Wanted (DOCUMENTO; IT) scope 104 min
Gemma and Marquand are the sheriff and villain respectively in this surprisingly traditional Western, its excessive violence notwithstanding. Gemma first has to clear his name and then catch up with Marquand's rustler and his collection of branding irons.

d Calvin Jackson Padget (Giorgio Ferroni) *p* Gianni Hecht Lucari *s* Fernando di Leo, Augusto Finocchi *c* Tony Secchi *lp* Giuliano Gemma, Teresa Gimpera, Serge Marquand, German Cobos, Gia Sandri, Daniele Vargas

1969

Today It's Me ... Tomorrow You! *orig* Oggi a Me ... Domani a Te! (P.A.C./SPLENDID; IT) 95 min
A stylish variant on **The Magnificent Seven** (1960) in which Halsey is the Indian who recruits a band of gunmen to help him capture Nakadai's brutal outlaw who framed him for the murder of his own wife. Less mannered than most Italian Westerns and looking beautiful with its autumnal colours, the film benefits from a collection of fine performances and a straightforward script.

d/co-s Tonino Cervi *p* Franco Cucca *co-s* Dario Argento *c* Sergio d'Offizi *lp* Montgomery Ford (Brett Halsey), Bud Spencer (Carlo Pedersoli), William Berger, Wayde Preston, Tatsuya Nakadai

Vengeance *orig* Joko, Invoco Dio ... e Muori
(SUPER INTERNATIONAL/TOP FILM; IT, WG) scope 100 (81) min
This is an interesting Gothic Italian Western that survives the inept acting of its macho hero, Harrison, imitating Clint Eastwood's every gesture, by centring on atmosphere rather than action. The simple plot has Harrison on the trail of the five men who tortured and killed his friend. The night scenes are particularly good, as one might expect from a director schooled in the horror genre.

d/co-s Anthony Dawson (Antonio Margheriti)
p/co-s Renato Savino *c* Riccardo Pallottini *lp* Richard Harrison, Claudio Camaso, Werner Pochat, Paolo Gozlino, Sheyla Rosia, Freddy Unger

Villa Rides (PAR) pv 124 min
Written by Peckinpah and Towne (author of the marvellous *Chinatown*, 1974) this brutal essay about the Mexican Revolution is transformed by director Kulik into an anodyne, if violent, adventure film, the dedication to Pancho Villa

d Burt Kennedy *p/s* William Bowers *c* Harry Stradling Jnr *lp* James Garner, Joan Hackett, Walter Brennan, Harry Morgan, Jack Elam, Bruce Dern

Butch Cassidy and the Sundance Kid
(TCF/CAMPANILE) pv 110 min
One of the top grossing Westerns of all time. Whereas in the forties, Western badmen had to be whitewashed and in the fifties 'explained' before they could become heroes, after the runaway success of *Bonnie and Clyde* (1967), in the sixties and seventies, the likes of Newman's Butch Cassidy and Redford's Sundance Kid were the stuff of heroes as they were. They didn't even have to die for the privilege; the film ends on a freeze frame of them as heroes blazing guns in hand.

Goldman's slick, joky script makes gestures in the direction of social concern, but a far more accurate summation of the film's stance is Newman's casual statement, 'I've got a vision, the rest of the world wears bifocals', made in defence of the string of robberies he and Redford embark on, first in America and then in Bolivia. Charming, rather than doomed by the contraction of the frontier, they are nonetheless traditional American heroes in one important respect: they are buddies showing their deep affection for each other through expressions of love for their girlfriend and accomplice, Ross. Hill's direction, which alternates between the exuberant and the poetic, is greatly helped by Hall's glorious cinematography.

d George Roy Hill *p* John Foreman *s* William Goldman *c* Conrad Hall *lp* Paul Newman, Robert Redford, Katharine Ross, Strother Martin, Henry Jones, Jeff Corey

Cain's Way (JC PRODUCTIONS) 88 (84) min
This tedious, extremely violent revenge Western is enlivened
by Carradine's hammy performance as the preacher turned
bounty hunter. Brady is the man whose family is murdered by
Confederate renegades and who sets out after them with help
from Carradine. The cinematography is murky and the
direction amateurish.

d/co-p Ken Osburne *co-p* Budd Dell *s* Will Denmark
c Ralph Waldo *lp* Scott Brady, John Carradine, Adair
Jamison, Robert Dix, Don Epperson, Bruce Kimbale

Charro (N.G.C.) pv 98 min
With **Flaming Star** (1960), this features Presley's only
straight dramatic performance. He's a reformed gunman
captured by his former colleagues and framed by them for the
theft of a jewel-encrusted cannon. Presley clearly tries but
Warren's static direction, the camera lingering on Presley's
bland expressions in close-up, as if a couple of days growth of
beard was acting personified, and the silly story, is too much.

Sturges, who plays the brother of French, the leader of the
outlaws, is the son of Preston Sturges.

d/p/s Charles Marquis Warren *c* Ellsworth Fredericks
lp Elvis Presley, Ina Balin, Barbara Werle, Lynn Kellogg,
Victor French, Solomon Sturges

Coogan's Bluff (U) pv 94 min
This, the first film Siegel made with Eastwood, established
one of the most productive director-star relationships in the
contemporary cinema. Eastwood is the laconic self-contained
Arizona deputy sent to New York, stetson, boots and all, to
escort a prisoner back home. Stroud is the prisoner who
escapes because Eastwood is unsure of New York ways, Clark
the liberal parole officer who teaches him about life in the city
and Cobb the tough city cop who mercilessly guys Eastwood's
cowboy, even calling him Tex in the film's running joke. But
it's Eastwood hunting Stroud through the concrete canyons of
New York and his confrontation with hippiedom that
occupies most of Siegel's interest, displacing the humorous
'cowboy comes to the big city' plot that seems to be the film's
centre.

d/p Don Siegel *s* Herman Miller, Dean Reisner, Howard
Rodman *c* Bud Thackery *lp* Clint Eastwood, Lee J. Cobb,
Susan Clark, Don Stroud, Tisha Sterling, Tom Tully

Death of a Gunfighter (U) 94 min
This film was begun by Totten and completed by Siegel after
Widmark and Totten fell out; hence the fictional credit to
Smithee. The result is a strangely compelling film that bears
enough of Siegel's stamp to be recognizably his. Widmark is
the gunslinger turned sheriff whose methods are deemed too
crude for the town burghers who are now seeking Eastern

Above: *One of the
numerous couplings in*
Five Bloody Graves, *a
testament to the arrival
of the sex Western.*

investment money and don't want to remind potential
investors of the town's frontier past. An appealing amalgam of
the gangster film and the Western, that looks forward to
Siegel's classic **The Shootist** (1976), in which the passing of
the West gives rise to a new era of corruption. Accordingly,
like John Wayne in the later film, Widmark prepares for his
own death, rejecting the future for the past.

d Allen Smithee (i.e. Robert Totten, Don Siegel)
p Richard E. Lyons *s* Joseph Calvelli *c* Andrew Jackson
lp Richard Widmark, Lena Horne, John Saxon, Michael
McGreevey, Darleen Carr, Carroll O'Connor

The Desperados (MEADWAY PRODUCTIONS) 90 min
This is an indifferent Western. Palance is the Confederate
fanatic of a parson whose guerilla band, which includes three
of his sons, continues raping and looting after the end of the
Civil War. Edwards escapes the family with his wife and
settles in Texas where, several years later, Palance and his
men arrive. There, as prophesied by an Indian soothsayer, the
family destroy one another in a bloody and gruesome fashion.

d Henry Levin *p* Irving Allen *s* Walter Brough *c* Sam
Leavitt *lp* Vince Edwards, Jack Palance, George Maharis,
Neville Brand, Sylvia Sims, Christian Roberts

Drop Them or I'll Shoot *orig* **Le Specialiste**
(LES FILMS MARCEAU/NEUE EMELKA/ADELPHIA COMPAGNIA
CINEMATOGRAFICA; FR, WG, SP) scope 98 (90) min
Elegantly staged by Corbucci, this Italian Western pits
French pop singer Hallyday against, amongst others, an
outlaw band composed of dope-smoking hippies, who, at one
point, force the population of Blackstone to crawl naked down
the main street. The film's unusual anti-hippie sentiments fit
oddly beside Corbucci's more overtly 'political' Westerns, **A
Professional Gun** (1968) and **Companeros** (1970).

Coogan's Bluff: *Clint
Eastwood as the
Arizona deputy sheriff
caught in the cold
canyons of New York.*

d/p/co-s Sergio Corbucci co-s Sabatine Gruffini c Dario Di Palma lp Johnny Hallyday, Sylvie Fennec, Gaston Moschin, Mario Adorf, Francoise Fabian, Serge Marquand

Five Bloody Graves

(DIX INTERNATIONAL PICTURES) scope 88 min

Despite its violence and sexual excesses, this is a surprisingly traditional Western. Dix is the brutal gunslinger, rather fetchingly called 'Messenger of Death' because he's so deadly, on the trail of renegades Brady and Young, who have been supplying guns to Yaqui Indian chief Cardos. With Brady, Carradine's lecherous preacher and Davis' cheat of a gambler, Dix fights off Indian attacks before settling matters in a hand-to-hand conflict with Cardos. The film is cheaply, but imaginatively, made.

d/p Al Adamson s Robert Dix c Vilmos (William) Zsigmond lp Robert Dix, Scott Brady, John Cardos, John Carradine, Jim Davis, Ray Young

The Five Man Army orig Un Esercito di 5 Uomini

(TIGER FILM; IT) 105 min

A Hollywood-backed Italian Western, this version of *The Dirty Dozen* (1967) sees a group of specialists (a samurai swordman, a dynamite expert, etc) set out first to rescue a revolutionary and then, with his knowledge, rob a train of its gold shipment. Taylor's direction is dour and the script predictable.

d Don Taylor s Dario Argento, Marc Richards c Enzo Barboni lp Peter Graves, Bud Spencer (Carlo Pedersoli), Nino Castelnuovo, James Daly, Tetsuro Tamba, Daniela Giordano

Four Rode Out

(SAGITTARIUS PRODUCTIONS/ADA FILMS; US, SP) 98 min

Despite its plethora of incident, including a forced marriage in the desert with the participants half dead from thirst, and the double rape of Lyon, this is a mediocre Western. Mateos is the Mexican outlaw sought after by his girlfriend Lyon, a marshal (Roberts) and a one-time accomplice, Nielsen.

Below: The bearded Elvis Presley as Charro.

Peyser's direction is a crude, not to say brutal, and his actors give the most rudimentary of performances.

d John Peyser p Pedro Vidal, Richard Landan s Don Balluck c Rafael Pacheco lp Sue Lyon, Pernell Roberts, Julian Mateos, Leslie Nielsen, Maria Martin, James Daly

The Good Guys and the Bad Guys

(RONDEN PRODUCTIONS) pv 90 min

With a script that makes more than just a bow in the direction of Sam Peckinpah's autumnal classic, **Ride the High Country** (1962), *The Good Guys and the Bad Guys* is the most openly nostalgic of Kennedy's Westerns, despite its avowedly comic tone. Mitchum is the sheriff of the aptly named town of Progress who is fearful of his glistening new office – he prefers to read old wanted posters and live in the past – and the new century that has just been ushered in. He grimly holds to his sense of duty and warns the mayor, Balsam, that his old enemy, Kennedy, is out for revenge and is retired for his troubles. Soon the plot resolves itself into Mitchum, Kennedy and the past against Carradine and his gang and the future. Accordingly, for once, Kennedy's farcical humour has a firm anchorage as his decrepit heroes overcome age and outlaws with an ease that is only surpassed by Balsam's effortless self-aggrandizement that is even able to turn being caught with his pants down by an angry husband to his own advantage.

d Burt Kennedy p/s Ronald M. Cohen, Dennis Shryack c Harry Stradling Jnr lp Robert Mitchum, George Kennedy, David Carradine, Tina Louise, Douglas V. Fowley, Martin Balsam

The Great Bank Robbery

(MALCOLM STUART PRODUCTIONS) pv 95 min

Though this slap-dash comic Western has its moments, it descends to speeded-up chases and the like too often to be successful. Moreover, Blatty's screenplay, which features an impregnable vault (so safe that Jesse James and assorted outlaws use it to bank their money) which several unlikely robbers attempt to break into, is too thin, and too coyly written, to support the elaborate series of jokes that is the plot. Mostel gives an unconvincing performance as the evangelist/robber while Novak, as his assistant, and Walker, as the Texas Ranger, are wooden. Akins, as a guilt-stricken gunman tormented by his abilities with the gun, and Anderson as the grasping banker have the best roles.

d Hy Averback p Malcolm Stuart s William Peter Blatty c Fred J. Koenekamp lp Zero Mostel, Kim Novak, Clint Walker, Claude Akins, Akim Tamiroff, John Anderson

The Gun Riders

(INDEPENDENT INTERNATIONAL) 98 min

One of the several violent Westerns made by Adamson on shoe-string budgets in the sixties and seventies when most independent directors and producers had deserted the genre. Sadly, he wastes his strong cast, Carradine's preacher (a role he often played in later life), Brady and Dix as the lawmen after gunrunner Davis whose guns, in the hands of Yaqui Indians, killed Dix's wife. The script solves the complexities it generates by killing off virtually everyone at the end of the film.

Although Adamson isn't an imaginative director – indeed his titles are often the best things about his films, notably *Blazing Stewardesses* (1975) about which little is known beyond the fact that it is a Western and co-stars Bob Livingston and Yvonne De Carlo – his commitment to the genre, at a time when Hollywood had such strong doubts about it, marks him out.

d/p Al Adamson s Robert Dix c Vilmos (William) Zsigmond lp Robert Dix, Jim Davis, Scott Brady, John Carradine

The Hanging of Jake Ellis *aka* The Calico Queen
(GREAT EMPIRE FILMS) 81 min
A softcore sex Western in which Napier is the drifter and Hall
his arch enemy. Hall plans to cheat the family of the girl
Napier seduces in a cattle deal. Several gunfights and sex
scenes later, in a rather traditional manner, hero and heroine
are triumphant. Unlike many sex films, *The Hanging of Jake
Ellis* is also a genre film. Thus director Hearn, a one-time
Dutch Navy officer, devotes as much time to sets and stunts
as he does to sex scenes. Nonetheless, this is a lacklustre film.

d/p/s J. Van Hearn   *c* John Koester   *lp* Charles Napier,
Deborah Downey, James Lemp, Bambi Allen, Louis Ojena,
John Hall

Land Raiders (MORNINGSIDE) 101 min
This is a mediocre Western from Juran, a one-time set
designer – he won an Oscar for *How Green Was My Valley*
(1941) – and workmanlike action director, mostly on Poverty
Row. Pettus' over-complicated screenplay is about feuding
brothers. Savalas is the Indian-hating boss of Fargo River
intent on driving Indians off rich land he wants for himself
and Maharis (who unwisely essays a Mexican accent), his
wandering brother who returns in time to save the Apache
and expose his treachery.

d Nathan H. Juran   *p* Charles H. Schneer   *s* Ken Pettus
c Wilkie Cooper   *lp* Telly Savalas, George Maharis, Arlene
Dahl, Janet Landgard, Jocelyn Lane, George Coulouris

Linda and Abilene
(UNITED PICTURES ORGANISATION) 93 min
Jones and Marsh are the incestuous pair in this hardcore sex
Western and Matt the girl left to comfort Jones after Marsh
has been killed defending her honour (!?). Crudely made and
amateurishly photographed, the film has the typical mathe-
matically precise plot of the sex film that attempts a storyline
to justify its various couplings. This film is only of curiosity
value.

d/s Mark Hansen   *p* J.H. Wells   *c* Lewis H. Gordon
lp Sharon Matt, Roxanne Jones, Kip Marsh, Tom Thorn,
William Varris, Audrey Cromm

The McMasters . . . Tougher than the West Itself
(JAYJEN) 90 (83) min
Much cutabout – it was even given alternative endings for
different markets – this is one of the earliest Westerns to treat
racial problems with any degree of seriousness. Peters is the
black Union soldier who has to fight the Civil War all over
again when he returns home to the South. Carradine is the
Indian who, after some hesitation, assists him in his fight
against the bigotry of town boss Palance, whose sneering
performance almost overtopples the film.

d Alf Kjellin   *p* Monroe Sachson   *s* Harold Jacob Smith
c Lester Shorr   *lp* Brock Peters, Burl Ives, David Carradine,
Nancy Kwan, Jack Palance, John Carradine

The Magnificent Bandits *orig* O Cangaceiro
(TRITONE/MEDUSA/D.I.A.; IT, SP) scope 102 (90) min
This political Italian 'Western', set in South America, sees
Milian as the peasant forming his own band of guerillas to
fight the Brazilian army and avenge the destruction of their
farms. Strangely, by literalizing the political allegories of
earlier political Westerns, Fago and his co-writers have
produced a less forceful work. Pagliani is the mercenary, here
a Dutch oil explorer, hired to capture Milian who changes
sides.

d/co-s Giovanni Fago   *co-s* Antonio Troisio, Bernardino
Zapponi, Jose Luis Jerez   *c* Alejandro Ulloa   *lp* Tomas
Milian, Ugo Pagliani, Eduardo Fajuardo, Howard Ross
(Renato Rossini), Alfredo Santa Cruz, Jesus Guzman

Above: *Jean Seberg
and Lee Marvin adrift
in* Paint Your Wagon.

More Dead than Alive
(AUBREY SCHENCK ENTERPRISES) 99 min
Walker is the gunman who, after an 18-year prison stretch, is
determined to stay out of trouble and away from guns, but can
only earn a living as a Wild West Show sharpshooter. As a
modernistic, ironic twist, he is eventually gunned down by a
relative of one of his many victims, just when all his troubles
seem over. Price, as the show's proprietor whose bizarre death
is the highlight of the film, adds a touch of class to the routine
proceedings.

d Robert Sparr   *p* Hal Klein   *s* George Schenck   *c* Jack
Marquette   *lp* Clint Walker, Vincent Price, Anne Francis,
Paul Hampton, Mike Henry, Craig Littler

No Room to Die *orig* Una Lunga Fila di Croci
(JUNIOR FILMS; IT) scope 93 (88) min
A silly but immensely enjoyable Italian Western thanks to the
wonderfully mannered performance of Berger as the bible-
thumping preacher and bounty hunter. He and De Teffe join
forces to collect the bounties due on Garrone's outlaw band
who are earning themselves a small fortune smuggling peons
across the border and then selling them as slave labour. A very
violent film, and with most of the violence in close-up, it
suffers from the slack direction of Carrone, who is unable to
orchestrate his effects to any purpose.

d/s Sergio Carrone   *p* Gabriele Crisanti   *c* Franco Villa
lp Anthony Steffen (Antonio De Teffe), William Berger,
Nicoletta Machiavelli, Mario Brega, Riccardo Garrone,
Mariangella Giordano

Paint Your Wagon (PAR) pv70 164 min

A disastrous film adaptation of Lerner and Frederic Loewe's Broadway musical. Eastwood and Marvin are the prospectors and Seberg the Mormon girl who 'marries' them both. Virtually a succession of sterile set-pieces, the slow pace of the movie and its static plot – Eastwood and Marvin deciding which one of them will stay with Seberg – make for an overlong film. Marvin beat Eastwood in the singing stakes because his version of 'Wandering Star' was a surprise No 1 chart hit when it was released in Britain as a single; Eastwood's rendition of 'I Talk to the Trees' was less successful. The only real point of interest in the film lies in watching its two stars attempt to extend their screen images in such a bizarre fashion.

d Joshua Logan *p* Alan Jay Lerner *s* Paddy Chayefsky *c* William A. Fraker *lp* Clint Eastwood, Lee Marvin, Jean Seberg, Harve Presnell, Ray Walston, Alan Dexter

The Price of Power *orig* Il Prezzo del Potere

(PATRY FILM/FILMS MONTANA; IT, SP) scope
122 (96) min

An amazing film which, though neither script nor performances live up to the promise of the original idea, shows the imaginative freedom possible in the Italian Western at a time when, with few exceptions, American directors were trapped in the most sterile of plots or deserting the genre. The central idea of the film is nothing less than a retelling of President Kennedy's Dallas assassination with Johnson as the Northern President Garfield assassinated in Dallas in 1890 by Southern fanatics out to rekindle the flames of the Civil War. The film even features the killing of the man accused of the crime as he's being transferred between jails.

Gemma is the lone gunman who both avenges his father's murder and foils the attempt of Southerners to raise the Confederate flag once more. The film uses many of the sets and some of the cast of Sergio Leone's **Once upon a Time in the West** (1968).

d Tonino Valerii *p* Bianco Manini *s* Massimo Patrizi *c* Stelvio Massi *lp* Giuliano Gemma, Van Johnson, Warren Vanders, Fernando Rey, Maria Jesus Cuadra, Ray Saunders

Ride a Northbound Horse (WALT DISNEY) 79 min

This is a nondescript children's Western from Totten, a director best known for being sacked during the making of **Death of a Gunfighter** (1969). Shea is the fifteen-year-old

orphan who travels to Texas determined to become a cattleman. However, sadly Groves' script leaves the clear narrative it has begun for a complex sub-plot concerning a confidence trickster and a pair of racehorses. Johnson, Elam and Harry Carey Jnr provide the sterling support.

d Robert Totten *p* Ron Miller *s* Herman Groves *c* Robert Hoffman *lp* Carroll O'Connor, Michael Shea, Ben Johnson, Andy Devine, Edith Atawer, Jack Elam

Sabata *orig* Ehi, Amico ... c'E Sabata, Hai Chiuso!

(P.E.A. CINEMATOGRAFICA/DELPHOS; IT) scope 106 min

Even the tired acrobatics that Parolini inserts in all his pictures can't diminish the appeal of this Italian Western that parades its baroque technology with such innocent glee. Berger is the cheerful gunman with a gun concealed in his banjo and Van Cleef is the taciturn bounty hunter with a bag of tricks that owes more to James Bond than the Western. Together they form a decidedly uneasy alliance to outwit and blackmail Ressel's bankrobber, who is hiding behind the mask of respectability. If the plot is closer to Hollywood than Cinecitta, Parolini's rhetorical orchestrating of the elements at hand represents the mainstream Italian Western at its best.

d/co-s Frank Kramer (Gianfranco Parolini) *p* Alberto Grimaldi *co-s* Renato Izzo *c* Sandro Mancori *lp* Lee Van Cleef, William Berger, Pedro Sanchez, Franco Ressel, Linda Veras, Gianni Rizzo

Sam Whiskey (BRIGHTON PICTURES) 97 min

An amiable comedy Western, this is badly let down by Laven's laboured direction. Reynolds takes the title role of the saddle tramp and gambler hired by Dickinson to replace the quarter of a million dollars' worth of gold bars lying at the bottom of the Platte River. Ossie Davis and Walker are on hand to provide suitable friendly complications while Davis is the outlaw out to hijack the gold. Reynolds and Dickinson make an appealing team.

Robert Redford (left) and Robert Blake at the climax of Tell Them Willie Boy Is Here.

d/co-p Arnold Laven   *co-p* Jules Levy, Arthur Gardner
s William W. Norton   *c* Robert Moreno   *lp* Burt Reynolds,
Clint Walker, Ossie Davis, Angie Dickinson, Rich Davis,
William Schallert

The Scavengers

(CRESSE-FROST PRODUCTIONS)   91 (87) min
An unpleasant sex Western, this tries to conceal its clear
titillatory nature – explicit in the frequent shots of nudity, the
lengthy mass rape sequence shown in close-up and the
extended sequences of violence – with much talk of the
'morality of war'. Bliss is the renegade Confederate who
captures a Union troop carrying a payroll and orders his men
to rape Lease and her black maid to 'persuade' Lease's Union
Officer husband to reveal the payroll's whereabouts. The
conclusion has Bliss meeting his just deserts when his men

and a band of freed slaves turn on him and leave him, not for
dead, but for the buzzards.

d Robert L. Frost   *p/s* R.W. Cresse   *c* Bob Maxwell
lp Jonathon Bliss, Maria Lease, Michael Dikova, Roda Spain,
John Riazzi, Wes Bishop

Smith!   (WALT DISNEY)   102 min

A handsomely mounted modern-day family Western with
Ford and Chief Dan George defending an Indian boy charged
with murder who's being trailed by an Indian-hating sheriff,
Wynn. All comes out well at the end after a lengthy court
scene that is much enlivened by Oates' performance as a
crooked Indian interpreter and a lengthy speech by Chief Dan
George about the changing relationship between the white
and redman. Nonetheless its attitudes to Indians seem very
demeaning, even if the Indians (members of the Indian Acting
Workshop) were directed by Jay Silverheels.

d Michael O'Herlihy   *p* Bill Anderson   *s* Louis Pelletier
c Robert Moreno   *lp* Glenn Ford, Nancy Olson, Chief Dan
George, Keenan Wynn, Warren Oates, Dean Jagger

Tell Them Willie Boy Is Here   (U)   pv   98 min

A misguided 'liberal' film, this, ironically, works best in its
celebration of Redford as star, in which guise it was
re-released in America to cash in on the Redford boom.
Indeed the credits are more interesting than the film itself. It's
directed and scripted by Polonsky, making his first film for
nearly a quarter of a century, after being blacklisted on
refusing, in April 1951, to either affirm or deny that he'd been
a member of the Communist Party. Equally interestingly, it
co-stars Blake who, as Bobby Blake, was a child star of the
forties. He was the Mexican boy in **The Treasure of the
Sierra Madre** (1948) and appeared regularly as the Indian
youth, Little Beaver, in Republic's Red Ryder Western
series. For him, at least, the title role of the Paiute Indian on
the run was a return to his origins.

Far left: *Chief Dan George (left) and Glenn Ford in the Walt Disney production* Smith!

Blake is the Indian cowboy who returns to the reservation to court Ross only to be rejected as unsuitable by her father. In a scuffle the old man is killed and Blake and Ross flee. To the Indians this is acceptable but local whites insist Redford's sheriff bring them back to justice. So, reluctantly, begins the lengthy chase, with Blake growing more determined (and more Indian) by the minute and a sense of doom invading Hall's (too perfectly) bleached images.

Individual sequences, notably the visit of President Taft, are neatly presented, but others (the orchestrated 'battle' in which Blake shoots the horses from beneath the posses and Ross' suicide when she knows that she's slowing Blake down and the final confrontation between Blake and Redford) are too pointed to work convincingly.

d/s Abraham Polonsky *p* Philip A. Waxman *c* Conrad Hall *lp* Robert Redford, Katharine Ross, Robert Blake, Susan Clark, Barry Sullivan, Charles McGraw

A Time for Dying (FIPCO PRODUCTIONS) 90 min
The most playful of Boetticher's series of games with the genre, its release was delayed for over a decade following the death of Murphy, its producer, whose last film it was. It is in direct contrast to the series of magnificent films he made with Randolph Scott in the fifties that culminated with **Ride Lonesome** (1959) and **Comanche Station** (1960). In those films, the hero is an old man whose life is in the past, someone going through the motions compared to the youngsters he meets along the way. Here the hero is an innocent youth whose immaturity guarantees him a quick death, his speed on the draw notwithstanding. Lapp is concerned to make

Below: Glen Campbell (left) and John Wayne (centre) in True Grit, *the film that finally got Duke his Oscar.*

something of his life, to 'amount to something' and since 'guns is all I know', he elects to become a bounty hunter. Married by Jory's Judge Roy Bean, purely for the licence fee, to the girl he rescues from the brothel (Randall) he still pursues this aim, only to be killed in a gunfight by Billy Pimple (Randon), of whom it is said, 'He ain't Billy the Kid, but he sure wants to be'.

Lapp, whose character's surname is Bunny and is identified by the rabbit he rescues from a rattlesnake at the beginning of the film, is a personable synthesis of the youngsters in *Ride Lonesome* and *Comanche Station,* people who need guidance. But, unlike them, Lapp has no father-figure of a Randolph Scott at hand so, despite his prowess with his gun and his good intentions (as seen by his attempted rescue of Randall from a life of shame), he is doomed because he's a boy trying to live in a man's world.

This is a marvellous film, full of wonderful details from Jory's monstrous irrational Judge Roy Bean to Lapp's jumping on his tethered horse only to immediately fall off in obedience to the rules of horsemanship rather than the accepted verities of the genre.

d/s Budd Boetticher *p* Audie Murphy *c* Lucien Ballard *lp* Richard Lapp, Anne Randall, Bob Randon, Victor Jory, Audie Murphy

True Grit (PAR) 128 min
A lively Western from Hathaway that in no way asked Wayne to do more than ease himself gracefully through the motions, *True Grit,* to everyone's surprise, secured vast praise both for itself and its star. In the fullness of time, and compared to

The Searchers (1956), **Red River** (1948), **Stagecoach** (1939) and **She Wore a Yellow Ribbon** (1949), all great films in their own right and wonderful examples of Wayne's capabilities as an actor, *True Grit* is a minor film. That said, it is hugely enjoyable and has the added dimension of being the one that got Duke his Oscar.

He's the cantankerous outlaw turned federal marshal who, in company with Campbell's uppity Texas Ranger and a prim but capable Darby, heads into the badlands in search of Duvall and Corey. Roberts' taut script makes marvellous use of vernacular and slang and has clever set pieces, ranging from Wayne's drunken tumble from his horse (which he attempts to camouflage with the suggestion of making camp at the place where he has fallen), to the almost medieval piece of jousting when he rides, reins between his teeth, a pistol in one hand and a blazing rifle in the other, at Duvall and his gang. The script gives Wayne the support necessary to pull off the role.

d Henry Hathaway   *p* Hal B. Wallis   *s* Marguerite Roberts   *c* Lucien Ballard   *lp* John Wayne, Glen Campbell, Kim Darby, Robert Duvall, Dennis Hopper, Jeff Corey

The Undefeated (FOX) pv 118 min

The least interesting of both Wayne's later Westerns and the many Western scripts by Barrett, a close friend of Wayne's and regular writer of his films. The plot has Wayne, accompanied by his adopted Indian son, Gabriel, driving a herd of horses to sell in Mexico and on the way joining forces with an embittered Confederate Colonel, Hudson (wearing an even more extravagant uniform than Errol Flynn in his introductory scenes in **They Died with Their Boots On,** 1941). Hudson is headed for exile in Mexico with his people. Once there, after several attempts to cheat the party, they turn right round and head for 'home'. With its theme of reconciliation between North and South and McLaglen's directorial homages to John Ford, the film is forever in Ford's shadow, which perhaps accounts for the ease implicit in the performances by Johnson, Agar and Harry Carey Jnr.

d Andrew V. McLaglen   *p* Robert L. Jacks   *s* James Lee Barrett   *c* William Clothier   *lp* John Wayne, Rock Hudson, Tony Aguilar, Roman Gabriel, Ben Johnson, John Agar

The Unholy Four *orig* Ciak Mull, l'Uomo della Vendetta
(B.R.C./ATLAS CINEMATOGRAFICA; IT)   96 min

This is a mediocre Italian Western populated with amnesiac gunmen and assorted lunatics on the trail of dyed-in-the-wool baddies, like the evil Montefiore. Strode and Mann do their best, but the direction of Barboni gives them no chance.

d E. B. Clucher (Enzo Barboni)   *p* Manolo Bolognini   *s* Franco Rossetti, Mario di Nardo   *c* Mario Mantuori   *lp* Leonard Mann, Woody Strode, Helmut Schneider, Evelyn Stewart, Luca Montefiore, Andrew Ray

The climactic, suicidal battle of The Wild Bunch, *another of Sam Peckinpah's mutilated masterpieces.*

Above: *Rock Hudson as the dandy of a Confederate officer in* The Undefeated.

do'. Holden is the outlaw (in 1912, almost the last outlaw) chased by Ryan, the man he betrayed and whose only way out is to hunt down Holden for Dekker's railroad magnate. Around these two congregate a bizarre collection of characters, the most notable of which are Borgnine's less honour-conscious outlaw and Sanchez's revolutionary (members of Holden's Wild Bunch) and Martin and Jones as the mercenary vultures who latch on to Ryan.

Ryan is left alive at the end, freed of his self-imposed task by Fernandez whose men mow down Holden and company when they decide to rescue Sanchez from him. This is less an act of heroism than a statement of their identity. But Peckinpah's heart is clearly with Holden and his bloody, but romantic, slow-motion death. The violence (and the many cut versions in circulation) has obscured its complex structure, making it for many merely Hollywood's response to the Italian Western. But its success in the market place produced numerous (inferior) imitations and helped establish the end of the West as the major theme of the Western in the seventies.

d/co-s Sam Peckinpah   *p* Phil Feldman   *co-s* Walon Green *c* Lucien Ballard   *lp* William Holden, Ernest Borgnine, Robert Ryan, Edmond O'Brien, Warren Oates, Ben Johnson, Strother Martin, L.Q. Jones, Jaime Sanchez, Emilio Fernandez, Albert Dekker
★ The running times given are of the longest and shortest versions in circulation; there exist several other versions of varying lengths between these.

Young Billy Young   (TALBOT-YOUNGSTEIN/UA)   89 min
An entertaining enough romp from writer/director Kennedy but a disappointment after the superior **Support Your Local Sheriff** (1968). Co-produced by Mitchum's Talbot company, the film stars him as the man intent on revenging the murder of his son by Anderson, educating Walker from his lawless ways and cleaning up Lordsburg into the bargain. The film has good comic moments – Mitchum amiably fixing the gun that has jammed after Walker has drawn on him and then giving it back – and boasts a nifty performance from Dickinson as the dance-hall queen who falls for Mitchum. It also fittingly features, for a plot so concerned with filial matters, a whole host of sons and daughters: Carradine, Deana Martin, Chris Mitchum and Jennifer Jones' son, Walker.

d/s Burt Kennedy   *p* Max Youngstein   *c* Harry Stradling Jnr   *lp* Robert Mitchum, Angie Dickinson, Robert Walker, David Carradine, Jack Kelly, John Anderson

Vengeance Is Mine *orig* Quei Disperati che Puzzano di Sudore et di Morte
(LEONE FILMS/DAIANO FILMS/ATLANTIDA FILMS; IT, SP) scope   100 (94) min
This is a dismal, cliched Italian Western. Hilton is the Confederate deserter who turns to banditry when his family die of cholera. Borgnine is the evil rancher who could have helped them, against whom Hilton takes his revenge before dying in a shoddily-photographed bloody ambush.

d/co-s Julio Buchs   *co-p* Elio Scardamaglia   *co-p/co-s* Ugo Guerra   *co-s* Jose Luis Martinez Mollo, Frederico de Urnutia   *c* Francisco Sempere   *lp* George Hilton, Ernest Borgnine, Alberto de Mendoza, Leo Anchoriz, Annabella Incontrera, Manuel Miranada

The Wild Bunch   (WB)   pv   145 (123) min★
Amongst the many baroque splendours that the Western has produced, *The Wild Bunch* stands out as one of the most extreme. The film's extraordinary opening images, of children grinning and laughing as they watch scorpions writhing in a sea of killer ants, anticipate the film's bloody climax with the Bunch making their last stand in the middle of the headquarters of Fernandez's bandit and announce that, in Peckinpah's world, innocence (children) and brutality exist side by side.

Based on an original idea by Lee Marvin, Peckinpah's richly romantic film reworks the story of the Joel McCrea and Randolph Scott characters from **Ride the High Country** (1962), with the difference that this time, though they are on different sides, they are virtually indistinguishable, as both live out the genre's greatest cliche and 'do what a man's gotta

Far right: *Robert Mitchum and Robert Walker in* Young Billy Young.

The
1970s

The Western in Transition

The Western of the seventies was marked by a degree of self-consciousness that many critics (especially those quick to pronounce the genre dead) found pretentious. In retrospect these modernist films represented a late flowering in the most traditional of American film genres. It was as if, spurred on by the radically different approach of the Italian Western, directors and writers were suddenly able to see the West and the Western through fresh eyes.

There were several strands to this new conception of the Western. A new emphasis on violence was the most obvious example of Hollywood's speedy assimilation of many of the features of the Italian Western. More interesting was Clint Eastwood's careful refining of his 'Man With No Name' persona throughout the decade until by the eighties he could parade as innocence personified in the charming **Bronco Billy** (1980). Another major theme that continued from the sixties was the death of the West. This theme, which appears as early as 1950 in **The Gunfighter** and was an underlying concern of many sixties Westerns, is given its most literal treatment in **The Ballad of Cable Hogue** (1970) which ends with its hero run over and killed by a motor car. But whereas until then the romantic cowboy 'doing what a man's gotta do' in the most difficult of circumstances had been simply contrasted to the anonymity of modern life, in the seventies things were more complex: when the image of the cowboy had been appropriated to help promote cigarettes (or breakfast cereal as in **The Electric Horseman,** 1979) the contrast between the last frontier and present times was seen to be more double-edged. Thus films like **Monte Walsh** (1970), **McCabe and Mrs Miller** (1971), **The Hired Hand** (1971) and **Heartland** (1979) showed the rigours of frontier life, allowing their heroes only moments of romantic rebellion, while films like **Dirty Little Billy** (1972) literally cut down their mythical heroes (here Billy the Kid) to size. In a similar fashion **The Missouri Breaks** (1976) resurrected one of the oldest of Western plots, rustling, only to leave it and the film's central characters floating in a world that seems to be alternately romantically and realistically conceived. Only in contemporary Westerns like **Rancho Deluxe** (1974), or those films set long after 1900 such as the charming **Hearts of the West** (1975), could the cowboy be romanticized, and even then only by imitation. The one exception to this rule was the decade's most resonant Western, **The Shootist** (1976), in which John Wayne's career and that of the Western were delicately played off against each other in Siegel's sombre elegy.

The other strands of the modernist Western were more particularized (and more limited): the Indian Western, the black Western and the wilderness film. This last trend, which surfaced most forcefully in the mainstream Western with **Jeremiah Johnson** (1972) and was clearly aimed at the disappearing family audience, was a reaction to the violence of other Westerns and a response to growing ecological concerns. Indian Westerns such as **Soldier Blue** and **Little Big Man** (both 1970) were displaced reactions to the Vietnam war. The crop of black Westerns (which were far more successful than their thirties forebears) were an extension of the 'blaxploitation' trend that reached its climax in the *Roots* teleseries.

The one Western that cheerfully stood apart from all the trends of the decade was the extraordinary, anarchic **Blazing Saddles** (1974), which remains to date the most successful Western ever.

The Animals *aka* **Five Savage Men**
(X.Y.Z. PRODUCTIONS) scope 86 min
A violent, sadistic Western with few redeeming features. Carey is the schoolteacher raped by Wynn and his gang who, after being nursed back to health and taught to shoot by Silva, sets out after them and one by one shoots them. When she catches up with Wynn she castrates him before going mad, whereupon, in a misjudged piece of irony, Silva is shot by the sheriff in mistake for Wynn. **Hannie Caulder** (1971) deals with the same subject more successfully.

d Ron Joy   *p/s* Richard Bakalyan   *c* Keith Smith
lp Henry Silva, Keenan Wynn, Michele Carey, John Anderson, Joseph Turkel, Pepper Martin

The Ballad of Cable Hogue (WB) 121 (119) min
A marvellous film. Robards' whimsical interpretation of his eccentric role as the man who finds success in the middle of the desert, only to die when his loved one returns, makes him the gentlest of Peckinpah's heroes who are confronted with the coming of modern times. Left to die by his partners (Martin and Jones giving their definitive performances as the personifications of irrational, petty greed) in the desert, Robards finds water and quickly turns his water hole into a profitable enterprise as a way station for the stagecoach. Committed to revenge, though why even he isn't sure, he refuses to leave his desert shack and so Stevens, the lively prostitute who loves him but wants to live in San Francisco, leaves him. However, when Jones and Martin return, Robards, though he shoots Jones justifiably, finds he can't take his revenge on the whining Martin. Free at last, he prepares to set out to find Stevens, only to die trying to save Martin, when the brakes of the car she's travelled to see him in fail.

Though its concerns are similar to those of **The Wild Bunch** (1969), the switch from tragedy to comedy, reflecting Robards' decision to adapt himself to the new West, is a deception for, in the end, like the William Holden character in *The Wild Bunch*, Robards can't change with the times: thus he dies trying to stop a car as he would stop a horse. In contrast to Warner's lecherous preacher (the film's most bewildering character), who is able to master any occasion (turning his collar to make him priest or mere man whichever will speed his seducing of women) and Stevens who is able to bury her past, Robards, like Martin and Jones, is a product of

Below: *Stella Stevens and Jason Robards, the gentlest of Sam Peckinpah's heroes, in* The Ballad of Cable Hogue.

Pedro Sanchez and Yul Brynner, as Indio Black, are The Bounty Hunters.

his times. Beautifully acted by all the principals, even if its romantic moments seem overly indulgent, its humour makes it, with the harsher *The Getaway* (1972), the most positive of Peckinpah's films.

d/p Sam Peckinpah   *s* John Crawford, Edmund Penney *c* Lucien Ballard   *lp* Jason Robards, Stella Stevens, David Warner, Strother Martin, Slim Pickens, L. Q. Jones

Barquero

(AUBREY SCHENK ENTERPRISES)   114 (109) min
This is an intriguing Western, far better than its lukewarm reception suggests. Van Cleef, the cruel hero of many an Italian Western, is the solitary man of the title who despises the townspeople he and his barge serve. He and Tucker first evade capture by an outlaw band awaiting the arrival of Oates and his wagon-load of plunder and then play a deadly game of hide-and-seek with Oates who wants to cross the river before the Federales catch him. Oates gives a wonderful performance as the psychopath of an outlaw who collapses into drugged Napoleonic reveries and Douglas directs extravagantly, which perfectly suits the material.

d Gordon Douglas   *p* Hal Klein   *s* George Schenk, William Marks   *c* Jerry Finnerman   *lp* Lee Van Cleef, Warren Oates, Forrest Tucker, Kerwin Mathews, Mariette Hartley, Maria Gomez

The Bounty Hunters *orig* Indio Black, Sai Che Ti Dico: Sei un Gran Figlio di . . .

(P.E.A. CINEMATOGRAFICA; IT)   scope   106 min
An entertaining Italian Western with Brynner impersonating Van Cleef's Sabata character courtesy of the dubbing which metamorphosed him from Indio Black to Sabata. Set against the backdrop of Maximillian's 1867 Mexican jaunt, it features Brynner leading an expedition to steal bullion from a sadistic Austrian commandant and being double-crossed by Herter. Parolini's direction is routine for the most part, but the occasional set-pieces (the death of Herter and 'the flamenco of death' torture sequence, for example) are wittily mounted.

James Stewart (left), Henry Fonda and, between them, their inheritance, The Cheyenne Social Club.

d Frank Kramer (Gianfranco Parolini)   *p* Alberto Grimaldi *s* Renato Izzo, Gianfranco Parolini   *c* Sandro Maniori *lp* Yul Brynner, Dean Reed, Pedro Sanchez (Ignazio Spalla), Gerard Herter, Sal Borgese, Franco Fantasia

Cannon for Cordoba   (MIRISCH)   pv   103 min

This is a workmanlike, anonymous Western. The complicated plot has army captain Peppard sent to retrieve cannons stolen by Vallone's bandit in the course of the Mexican Revolution. Ralli is the woman seeking revenge for Vallone's rape of her, who helps Peppard. Kandel's plot is stiffly orchestrated, the cast no more than adequate and Wendkos' direction efficient.

d Paul Wendkos   *p* Vincent M. Fennelly   *s* Stephen Kandel *c* Antonio Macasoli   *lp* George Peppard, Giovanna Ralli, Raf Vallone, Pete Duel, Don Gordon, Nico Minardos

The Cheyenne Social Club

(NATIONAL GENERAL)   pv   102 min
This would-be gentle, comic, shaggy-dog-tale of a Western quickly collapses into silliness, despite the presence of Fonda and Stewart as the elderly cowboys who inherit a brothel. Barrett's screenplay is soggy and Kelly's direction stagey and flat, lacking the wit and style that usually marks his work. Only Clothier's cinematography is as one expects.

d/p Gene Kelly   *s* James Lee Barrett   *c* William Clothier *lp* James Stewart, Henry Fonda, Shirley Jones, Sue Anne Langdon, Elaine Devry, Robert Middleton

Chisum   (BATJAC/WB)   pv   110 min

Although Fenady's script aspires to make a statement about the Lincoln County War that made a folk hero out of Billy the Kid (here Deuel) McLaglen seems content to film the letter of the script and let 'Big John' brawl to his heart's delight. He's the cattle baron of the title and Tucker is the corrupt businessman trying to do him down. Clothier's cinematography is superb.

d Andrew V. McLaglen   *p/s* Andrew J. Fenady   *c* William H. Clothier   *lp* John Wayne, Forrest Tucker, Christopher George, Ben Johnson, Bruce Cabot, Geoffrey Deuel

The Cockeyed Cowboys of Calico Country

(U)   100 min
Routine fare, this was made as a telefilm but shown theatrically first. MacDougall's script has the township of Calico intent on marrying off blacksmith Blocker, who is threatening to quit town because he can't find a bride. Their first plan fails when the Boston mail-order bride doesn't show, so they convince local saloon girl Fabray to stand in. Sixty minutes later, true love has developed between the odd

couple. The film is an example of what might be called bawdy family entertainment, enlivened by cameos from the likes of Beery, Kaye and Elam.

d Tony Leader *p/s* Ranald MacDougall *c* Richard L. Rawlings *lp* Dan Blocker, Nanette Fabray, Jack Elam, Stubby Kaye, Noah Beery Jnr, Mickey Rooney

Companeros *orig* **Vamos a Matar, Companeros!**
(TRITONE FILMINDUSTRIA/ATLANTIDA FILM/TERRA FILMKUNST; IT, SP, WG) scope 118 min
Corbucci is an unlikely director of 'political' Westerns. His love of excess – Palance here has a wooden hand because he was once nailed to a cross and was only freed when his pet hawk ate the pinned hand – and his undisciplined comic-strip directorial style, in which parody comes before anything else, make it hard to take the content of his films seriously. Yet, he is on record as claiming that both **A Professional Gun** (1968) and this, its sequel, are political films.

Nero is the mercenary who helps revolutionary Milian (dressed in the style of Che Guevara) to free a pacifist professor (Rey) and his students. However, Corbucci and Palance's need for excess completely undercuts the action. Accordingly, to take just one example, the symbolism of Palance's feeding his hawk (America) with chunks of meat from his Mexican victims (the Third World) is lost beneath the ludicrousness of its presentation.

d/co-s Sergio Corbucci *p* Alberto Grimaldi *co-s* Dino Maiuri, Massimo De Rita, Fritz Ebert *c* Alejandro Ulloa *lp* Franco Nero, Tomas Milian, Jack Palance, Fernando Rey, Iris Berben, Francisco Bodalo

Cry Blood Apache (GOLDEN EAGLE/GOLDSTONE) 82 min
One of the best of Starrett's low-budget action-pictures of the seventies, this intriguing Western was co-produced by its star, Jody (son of Joel) McCrea. Told in flashback by McCrea as an old man (played by Joel) as he reminisces about his past, MacGregor's screenplay has McCrea and a bunch of prospectors slaughtering a band of Indians until the last one left, Gahva, promises to tell them the whereabouts of a gold mine and lead them there. On the way they are pursued by Gahva's brother, who murders them one by one (including director Starrett), until Gahva kills him to save McCrea.

d Jack Starrett *p* Jody McCrea, Harold Roberts *s* Sean MacGregor *c* Bruce Scott *lp* Jody McCrea, Dan Kemp, Joel McCrea, Marie Gahva, Jack Starrett, Don Henley

The Deserter *orig* **La Spina Dorsale del Diavolo**
(DINO DE LAURENTIIS CINEMATOGRAFICA/JADRAN FILM/ HERITAGE; IT, YUG, US) pv 99 min
This disappointing movie was Kennedy and writer Huffaker's follow-up to **The War Wagon** (1967). The wooden Fehmiu leads his own dirty dozen to destroy the hideout of an Apache warchief. Huston, Crenna and especially Bannen (as the stiff-mannered British observer, noting down everything to report back to Queen Victoria) enjoy themselves, but neither Kennedy's direction nor Huffaker's script have any zest about them.

d Burt Kennedy *p* Norman Baer, Ralph Serpe *s* Clair Huffaker *c* Aldo Tonti *lp* Bekim Fehmiu, John Huston, Richard Crenna, Chuck Connors, Ricardo Montalban, Ian Bannen

Dirty Dingus Magee (MGM) pv 91 min
The highlight of this tawdry comic Western is Elam's performance as a swaggering John Wesley Hardin. The screenplay is co-authored by Heller but is far closer to a Carry On than *Catch 22*. Sinatra, in the title role, is the most underhand of outlaws, Kennedy, the sheriff he forever outsmarts, Carey the Indian maid who falls for Sinatra and

Frank Sinatra is Dirty Dingus Magee.

Jackson the madame/mayor intent on marrying Kennedy. Kennedy directs with a brusqueness that compares unfavourably to the affectionate wit of films like **Support Your Local Sheriff** (1968); but then, Sinatra is no James Garner.

d/p Burt Kennedy *s* Tom Waldman, Frank Waldman, Joseph Heller *c* Harry Stradling Jnr *lp* Frank Sinatra, George Kennedy, Anne Jackson, Lois Nettleton, Jack Elam, Michele Carey

El Condor
(NATIONAL GENERAL/CARTHAY CONTINENTAL) 102 min
This thin, pale imitation of an Italian Western features Brown and con-man Van Cleef joining forces to raid a gold-rich Mexican fort. After much butchery, which Guillermin forever tries to undercut with inept black humour, Brown is left with Hill.

The film was shot in Spain and marked the production debut of de Toth.

d John Guillermin *p* Andre de Toth *s* Larry Cohen, Steven Carabatsos *c* Henri Persin *lp* Jim Brown, Lee Van Cleef, Patrick O'Neal, Mariana Hill, Iron Eyes Cody, Imogen Hassall

The Emigrants *orig* **Utvandrana**
(SVENSK FILMINDUSTRI; SWEDEN) 191 (151) min
The first and least interesting of Troell's pair of films about the fortunes of a group of Swedes who leave famine-stricken Sweden, where most are bondsmen, to travel to the land of dreams, finally settling in Minnesota after a perilous journey. Troell manages the period detail well enough, but the characters, from bullying farmer to stubborn peasant, are stereotypes, the performances of von Sydow and Ullman notwithstanding. Accordingly the drama of the voyage to the New World is slow and solemn for the most part. The film was a surprise commercial success in America and both Troell and Ullman nominated for Oscars.

The second film is **The New Land** (1973).

d/co-s/c Jan Troell *p/co-s* Bengt Forslund *lp* Max von Sydow, Liv Ullman, Eddie Axberg, Svenolof Bern, Aina Alfredsson, Allan Edwall

Far right: *Dustin Hoffman as the perpetual adolescent in Arthur Penn's magnificent* Little Big Man.

Flap! *aka* **The Last Warrior** (WB) pv 106 min
For this feeble comedy, Quinn reprises his primitive savage. Here he's the drunken Indian who inaugurates a public relations war for Indian rights. Reed's leaden direction and the script's poetry-as-prose language trivializes every issue the film touches upon. Even the wonderful idea of lassoing a helicopter is thrown away. Akins and Winters (as Quinn's long-suffering mistress) do what they can with thankless parts.

d Carol Reed *p* Jerry Adler *s* Clair Huffaker *c* Fred J. Koenekamp *lp* Anthony Quinn, Shelley Winters, Claude Akins, Victor Jory, Rodolfo Acosta, Victor French

A Gunfight (HARVEST/THOROUGHBRED/BRYNA) 89 min
A laboured, if occasionally enjoyable, Western from Johnson, starring Douglas and Cash as a pair of tired gunfighters who transform their expected duel into a Barnum and Bailey affair, complete with paying customers and regulated gambling. Cash is the moody, all-in-black loner and Douglas the embittered family man, dreaming of buying a ranch with his winnings. The strong supporting cast includes Vallone as the breezy entrepreneur and Black as the saloon girl Cash takes up with.

The film was financed by the Jicarilla Apache tribe.

Shelley Winters and Anthony Quinn in Carol Reed's disappointing Flap!

d Lamont Johnson *co-p* Ronnie Lubin *co-p/s* Harold Jack Bloom *c* David M. Walsh *lp* Kirk Douglas, Johnny Cash, Jane Alexander, Raf Vallone, Karen Black, Eric Douglas

Joaquin Murrieta (FOX IN ASSOCIATION WITH V-R MONTALBAN ENTERPRISES) 83 min
Another, decidedly fictionalized, version of the life of Murrieta, a Mexican miner turned bandit, last filmed by George Sherman in 1965 under the title of *Murrieta*. The needlessly complicated plot features Montalban as Murrieta aiding Holliman's genial outlaw against Wilke's cold-blooded killer, only to have Holliman change sides when Montalban also tries to defend Mexican peons from Wilke.

The film was originally made for television.

d Earl Bellamy *p* David Silver *s* Jack Guss *c* George Stahl *lp* Ricardo Montalban, Slim Pickens, Jim McMullan, Roosevelt Grier, Earl Holliman, Robert Wilke

Little Big Man
(STOCKBRIDGE/HILLER) pv 147 (139) min
A major Western. Hoffman is the perpetual adolescent fathered by the heroes and villains of the West as they build their legends at the expense of others, notably the Indians, in this sprawling mock epic about the making of the myth of the West. Penn's direction, as ever, is analytic and reflective rather than visual but the broad panorama he takes of his subject gives the movie a strong emotional force. At the centre of the film is a horrifying re-creation of the Washita River Massacre of 1868 which Hoffman rightly remembers as 'an act of genocide'. A further mark of the shift in attitude to Indians represented by the film was the casting of an Indian actor, George, in a major role in a big budget movie, the first time this had been done. George's nonchalant performance perfectly complements Hoffman's edgy interpretation of the 121-year-old adolescent.

d Arthur Penn *p* Stuart Millar *s* Calder Willingham *c* Harry Stradling Jnr *lp* Dustin Hoffman, Faye Dunaway, Martin Balsam, Richard Mulligan, Chief Dan George, Jeff Corey

Machismo – 40 Graves for 40 Guns *aka* **Forty Graves for Forty Guns**
(PACIFIC INTERNATIONAL) 95 (82) min
A melodramatic, violent Western, this cross between **The Wild Bunch** (1969) and **The Magnificent Seven** (1960) is

directed with crude vigour by Hunt. Padilla makes an engaging enough bandit hired by the Federales, with the promise of a pardon, to bring back the notorious Harris brothers who've escaped to America with their loot. Much of the film concerns the beddings of Padilla and his men with various ladies throughout the South West.

d/co-s Paul Hunt *p* Ronald V. Garcia *co-s/c* Ronald Garcia
lp Robert Padilla, Dirk Peno, Frederico Gomez, Luis Ojena, Leslie York, Rita Rogers

Macho Callahan (FELICIDAD) pv 100 min
In this mediocre, ugly-looking Western Janssen is the imprisoned Union soldier who, on his escape, seeks out Cobb, whom he holds responsible for all his troubles. Along the way he carelessly kills Seberg's husband, thus incurring first her wrath, then her love and finally her sorrow when he is killed by one of the men she hired for the purpose.

d/co-p Bernard Kowalski *co-p* Martin C. Schute
s Clifford Newton Gould *c* Gerald Fisher *lp* David Janssen, Jean Seberg, Lee J. Cobb, James Booth, Pedro Armendariz Jnr, David Carradine

A Man Called Horse
(SANFORD HOWARD PRODUCTIONS) pv 114 min
The first of Harris' series of macho-masochistic Westerns that include **Man in the Wilderness** (1971), **The Deadly Trackers** (1973) and ends with **The Return of a Man Called Horse** (1976). All but *The Deadly Trackers* were produced by Howard and written by DeWitt who together clearly understood the appeal of Harris. Here he's an English lord captured by the Sioux. For the most part, the film is an anthropological and, by all accounts, accurate account of Sioux tribal life and customs with over 80 percent of the dialogue in Sioux. But, when it comes to the grisly Sun Vow Initiation ceremony, in which Harris is suspended in mid-air from ropes inserted in his chest – in a sequence supervised by Yakima Canutt – Silverstein's sense of melodrama, seen before partially in **Cat Ballou** (1965), takes over completely. The result is a film in which the audience's endurance is tested as well as Harris'.

d Elliot Silverstein *p* Sandy Howard *s* Jack DeWitt
c Robert Hauser *lp* Richard Harris, Dame Judith Anderson, Jean Gascon, Manu Tupou, Corinna Tsopei, Dub Taylor

Lee Marvin and the wonderful smile that lies at the heart of the delightful Monte Walsh.

A Man Called Sledge *aka* Sledge
(DINO DE LAURENTIIS CINEMATOGRAFICA; IT) scope 92 min
A magnificent Western, this was the second of a pair directed by actor Morrow, who subsequently was to work mostly in television. Garner, playing against type, takes the title role as a cold-blooded bandit who robs a gold shipment only to have the gold stolen from him. Morrow's West, like that of so many Italian Westerns, is of the 'mud and rags' school, but his visual style borrows more from directors like Samuel Fuller than Sergio Leone, even when the content of the images is the familiar Italian one of grotesque anti-clericism. An example of this is the climax with Garner, his arm broken, strapping on a crucifix so as to be able to use his gun in the final showdown which takes place during a religious festival.

d/co-s Vic Morrow *p* Dino De Laurentiis, Harry Bloom
co-s Frank Kowalsky *c* Luigi Kueveiller *lp* James Garner, Dennis Weaver, Claude Akins, John Marley

Monte Walsh (CINEMA CENTRE FILMS) 108 min
Fraker's magnificent elegaic Western is his directional debut. Only occasionally infected with the romantic mood of Charles B. Russell's Western paintings (over which the credits are played), script and direction combine to offer a bleak portrait of the end of the cowboy era. But Marvin, and Palance (a wonderful grin playing across his face for most of the film) give an example of the inarticulate but good-humoured friendship that alleviates the drudgery of a cowboy's life. As the plot leisurely unfolds, slowly taking over from the scenes of cowboys at work and play (many of which have the look of Frederick Remmington's realistic Western paintings) the sense of impending doom grows. The Eastern finance company closes down the ranch and Palance marries and quits cowboying while Marvin proposes to his tubercular mistress (Moreau), but to no effect. Palance is gunned down by an out-of-work cowboy and Moreau dies leaving Marvin to cold-bloodedly revenge his friend's murder. Fittingly, in the movie's one moment of unalloyed heroism, Marvin tames a wild stallion for his own satisfaction whereupon he is offered a job in a Wild West Show impersonating 'Texas Jack Barrat'. Much tempted by the prospect of a regular job he finally rejects the offer in his one articulate moment: 'I ain't spitting on my whole life'.

Far left: *The infamous Sun Vow initiation ceremony from* A Man Called Horse. *Richard Harris is the sufferer.*

d William A. Fraker   *p* Hal Landers, Bobby Roberts
s David Z. Goodman, Lukas Heller   *c* David M. Walsh
lp Lee Marvin, Jack Palance, Jeanne Moreau, Mitch Ryan,
Jim Davis, Roy Barcroft

Ned Kelly (WOODFALL; GB) 103 min

At the time, the casting of Jagger, a modern rebel, in the role of Ned Kelly, Australia's famous outlaw, was thought to be very clever. (Marianne Faithfull, Jagger's real life girlfriend was to have played his girlfriend in the film, but fell ill just before shooting began.) However, any excitement that might have been expected was lost in Richardson and Jones' script which has Jagger either proclaiming his innocence or declaring derring-do sentiments in *Boys' Own* cliches – 'Fearless, free and bold, that's how we'll live' – while Richardson's direction sets a completely false lyrical seal on the events.

Like so many 'Australian' films made before the seventies when the Australian film industry burst free of its collective sense of anonymity, Australia only really figures in the film as exotic scenery. By way of contrast, Philippe Mora's **Mad Dog Morgan** (1976), which recasts the Ned Kelly story, is a far more powerful film; but then it is also an Australian film in more than name.

d/co-s Tony Richardson   *p* Neil Hartley   *co-s* Ian Jones
c Gerry Fisher   *lp* Mick Jagger, Allen Bickford, Geoff
Gilmour, Serge Lazareff

Red White and Black *aka* Soul Soldiers
(HIRSCHMAN-NORTHERN) 103 (97) min

The first blaxploitation Western since the thirties, this is directed by Cardos, a regular as an actor in low-budget pictures. Romero is the sole whiteman in charge of a frontier outpost manned by the 10th Cavalry, a regiment of black troops. Doqui and Kilpatrick are the Cavalrymen who fight over seamstress Michelle but the real drama, its crudity of presentation notwithstanding, is the bloody battle the black cavalrymen must fight with the Indians for the benefit of the whiteman. On its re-release as *Soul Soldiers*, the film was so successful that it led to **The Legend of Nigger Charley** (1972).

d John Cardos   *p* James M. Northern, Stuart Z. Hirschman
s Marlene Weed   *c* Lewis J. Guinn   *lp* Robert Doqui,
Cesar Romero, Lincoln Kilpatrick, Issac Fields, Barbara
Hale, Janee Michelle

Rio Lobo (MALABAR) 114 min

Elegantly photographed by Clothier, *Rio Lobo* is Hawks' last film and the culmination of the loose trilogy that began with **Rio Bravo** (1959) and **El Dorado** (1967). Set in the years immediately after the Civil War, it features Wayne as an aging ex-Union officer in the company of a couple of youngsters tracking down the traitor who caused the death of Wayne's adopted son. They then end the traitor's attempted takeover of the township of Rio Lobo. Littered with references to the early films, it is, nonetheless, very different in tone and style from them. The rambling narrative moves from broad comedy, most of it at the expense of Wayne's age and hulking figure – at one point he's compared to a baby whale – to the dark mood of the final shoot-out which has none of the festival atmosphere of the similarly structured climax of *Rio Bravo*. In that film professionalism was all that Wayne and Hawks aspired to; in *El Dorado* a sense of mortality and filial loyalty undercuts the gunmens' professional ethics; in *Rio Lobo* Elam's manic gothic performance, as he restlessly fingers the trigger of his gun, suggests that revenge is the motor force of Wayne's assorted band of emotional cripples. Similarly, the scar on the cheek of Lansing (in one of her few films before moving to executive stardom at Twentieth Century Fox), shows pain as a reality whereas Hawks previously had tended to treat it metaphorically.

d/p Howard Hawks   *s* Leigh Brackett, Burton Wohl
c William Clothier   *lp* John Wayne, Jorge Rivero, Jennifer
O'Neill, Jack Elam, Chris Mitchum, Sherry Lansing

Soldier Blue (AVCO-EMBASSY) pv 114 min

Alternating between soft focus for Bergen's and Strauss' idyll in the cave and the goriest close-ups of hacked limbs as the Cavalry charge the Cheyenne in a re-creation of the Sand Creek Massacre of 1864, *Soldier Blue*, for all its unimpeachable good intentions, is sadly marred by its over-reliance on cliche, unlike **Little Big Man** (1970). A displaced reaction to the revelations of American atrocities in Vietnam, it features Bergen, whose strident performance is completely in keeping with the tone of the film, and Strauss as the sole survivors of a Cheyenne attack, slowly making their way back to civilization. Pleasence is the evil trader in guns and John Anderson the Cavalry officer concerned only with military matters.

d Ralph Nelson   *p* Gabriel Katzka, Harold Loeb   *s* John
Gay   *c* Robert Hauser   *lp* Candice Bergen, Peter Strauss,
Donald Pleasence, Bob Carraway, Jorge Rivero, Dana Elcar

There Was a Crooked Man (WB) pv 126 min

This is an enjoyably cynical, if erratic, comic Western from Mankiewicz. The plot's simple idea has Douglas trying to break out of jail to collect his buried loot and Fonda, as the essentially good man, trying to improve the conditions of the prisoners but finally unable to resist temptation when the money is his for the taking. The intelligent script is by Benton and Newman, the writers of *Bonnie and Clyde* (1967), and the strong support is provided by Oates, Randolph and Meredith (whose rheumy-eyed Missouri Kid is an outstanding creation). If the contrast between Fonda and Douglas is too pointed, making the film's development too mechanical by far, Douglas gives his best performance for some time as the charmer with the cold, cold heart.

Below: Candice Bergen in Soldier Blue.

d/p Joseph Mankiewicz   *s* David Newman, Robert Benton
c Harry Stradling Jnr   *lp* Kirk Douglas, Henry Fonda,
Hume Cronyn, Warren Oates, Burgess Meredith, John
Randolph

They Call Me Trinity *orig* Lo Chiamavano Trinita
(WEST FILM; IT)   scope   100 (93) min
This is the first of the slapstick comedies that made an
international star out of the blue-eyed Hill. He plays the lazy,
good-for-nothing who is always getting himself into trouble
and Spencer is his burly, dumb-witted brother. Interestingly,
the films are constructed more in the mould of Mack
Sennett's comedies – the opening sequence, for example, is
virtually a homage to that of Laurel and Hardy's **Way Out
West** (1937). Perhaps because the film (and later the series)
wasn't parodic like most other Italian Western comedies, it
seemed more original than it was.

Here the duo lead a group of Mormons against an outlaw
band.

d/s E.B. Clucher (Enzo Barboni)   *p* Italo Zingarelli   *c* Aldo
Giordani   *lp* Terence Hill (Mario Girotti), Bud Spencer
(Carlo Pedersoli), Farley Granger, Steffen Zacharias, Dan
Sturkie, Gisela Hahn

Two Mules for Sister Sara   (U/MALPASO)   116 (113) min
This is a failure. Yet in its broaching of the problems of sexual
attraction and aggression, *Two Mules for Sister Sara* is an
unsteady step for both Eastwood and Siegel towards the views
concretized in **The Beguiled** (1971) and *Play Misty for Me*
(1971). The film's greatest failing is the performance of
MacLaine as the nun/prostitute who is rescued by Eastwood's
drifter. Together, for money of course, they help Mexican
revolutionaries to overrun a French garrison.

Maltz's script is a rewrite of one by Budd Boetticher who
was originally slated to direct the film.

d Don Siegel   *p* Martin Rackin, Carroll Case   *s* Albert
Maltz   *c* Gabriel Figueroa   *lp* Shirley MacLaine, Clint
Eastwood, Manolo Fabregas, Alberto Morin, Armando
Silvestre, John Kelly

Valdez Is Coming
(NORLAN/IRA STEINER PRODUCTIONS)   90 min
Sherrin's directional debut, this is a promising, albeit flawed,
Western. Lancaster is the Mexican constable searching for
justice on behalf of the pregnant Apache wife of a blackman
killed by mistake by cattle baron Cypher. Cypher rejects
Lancaster's request for compensation, but, in a neat reversal
of the usual Mexican/American stereotypes, Lancaster proves
to be persistent, returning time and time again and finally gets
Cypher to pay up.

d Edwin Sherrin   *p* Ira Steiner   *s* Roland Kibbee, David
Rayfiel   *c* Gabor Pogany   *lp* Burt Lancaster, Susan Clark,
Jon Cypher, Barton Heyman, Richard Jordan, Frank Silvera

The Wild Country   (WALT DISNEY)   100 min
In this entertaining pioneer drama Forrest and Miles are the
would-be ranchers who, with assistance from Elam (in fine
comic form), take on Woodward's rancher, who denies them
the water they're due. Howard, later to be one of the stars of
television's *Happy Days* and who, even later, was to turn to
direction himself, is appealing as the adolescent son forced
into action.

d Robert Totten   *p* Ron Miller   *s* Calvin Clements Jnr, Paul
Savage   *c* Frank Phillips   *lp* Steve Forrest, Vera Miles, Jack
Elam, Ronny Howard, Frank de Kova, Morgan Woodward

Zachariah   (ABC PICTURES)   93 min
Zachariah was billed as the first 'electric Western', featuring
as it did music by Country Joe and the Fish and cameos from
various rock groups, including the aptly named James Gang.

Shirley MacLaine as the prostitute in nun's clothing and Clint Eastwood as the drifter she converts to the cause of revolution in the erratic Two Mules for Sister Sara.

The decidedly 'alternative culture' plot has the hero, Rubinstein, veering between the land and ecological/mystical
concerns and a career as a gunfighter. Johnson is his friend
and fellow gunfighter and Challee the old man of the desert
who awakens Rubinstein's love of the land. Probably the best
things in the film, the quirky details, derive from the Firesign
Theatre's involvement in the project. This is a curiosity, but
no more.

d/p George Englund   *s* Joe Massot, The Firesign Theatre
(Philip Austin, Peter Bergman, David Ossman, Philip
Proctor)   *c* Jorge Stahl   *lp* John Rubinstein, Pat Quinn,
Don Johnson, Country Joe and the Fish, Elvin Jones,
William Challee

1971

The Beguiled   (U)   pv   105 min
An extraordinary departure for Siegel and an almost elegaic
distillation of some of the key themes that he and Eastwood
have in common. Eastwood is the Union soldier whose
sanctuary – he finds refuge from the Civil War in a ladies'
seminary – becomes his nemesis. Wounded at the beginning,
he becomes a passive tabula rasa on which the women inscribe
their fantasies with predictably destructive results. The film,
which has a lot in common with John Ford's much underrated
Seven Women (1966), is central to Eastwood's development,
anticipating as it does *Play Misty For Me* (1971) in which he
also plays the imperilled male. A marvellous film.

d/p Don Siegel   *s* John B. Sherry, Grimes Grice (Albert
Maltz)   *c* Bruce Surtees   *lp* Clint Eastwood, Geraldine
Page, Elizabeth Hartman, Jo Ann Harris, Darlene Carr, Mae
Mercer

The Big and the Bad *orig* Si Puo Fare . . . Amigo
(SANCROSIAP-TERZAFILM/JACQUES ROITFELD PRODUCTIONS/
ATLANTIDA FILMS; IT, FR, SP)   84 min
This is an affectionate parody of Sergio Leone's Dollar films,
with slapstick taking the place of the violence of the originals.
Spencer is the Lothario pursued by Palance's evil-grinning,
but essentially soft-hearted, gunman whose sister Spencer
seduced. Although Palance overacts outrageously (as he was
asked to do in virtually every Italian Western he appeared in),
Lucidi handles the witty script well and Spencer (or Carlo
Pedersoli to give him his real name) ambles through the movie
quite charmingly.

d Maurizio Lucidi   *p* Alfonso Sasone, Enrico Chroscicki
s Rafael Azcona   *c* Aldo Tonti   *lp* Bud Spencer (Carlo
Pedersoli), Jack Palance, Francisco Rabal, Renato Cestie,
Dany Saval, Luciano Catenacci

Big Jake (BATJAC) pv 110 min

This routine movie sees Wayne re-united with Sherman, who had directed all his Three Mesquiteers series Westerns for Republic 30 years earlier. Sadly, Sherman's direction here lacks the economy of the earlier films. The result is an indifferent movie, all brawls but little purpose. Wayne agrees to deliver ransom money to Boone in exchange for his grandson and takes along Pat Wayne and Chris (son of Robert) Mitchum as help. Both Boone and Wayne clearly enjoy their larger-than-life roles, but the script, by the Finks, is simply too slight to carry them. As usual, Clothier's dusty cinematography is magnificent.

d George Sherman *p* Michael A. Wayne *s* Harry Julian Fink, R. M. Fink *c* William Clothier *lp* John Wayne, Richard Boone, Maureen O'Hara, Patrick Wayne, Chris Mitchum, Bruce Cabot

Billy Jack

(NATIONAL STUDENT FILM CORPORATION) 113 min
Made by the husband and wife team of Laughlin and Taylor under a variety of pseudonyms, *Billy Jack*, which cost a mere $800,000, was one of the biggest commercial successes of the seventies. The story of a half-breed Vietnam veteran (a sort of Lone Ranger in modern dress), the film's easy philosophizing struck a responsive chord with Americans tiring of the seemingly endless Vietnam War. Laughlin is the half-breed of the title who roams the desert protecting mustangs from hunters intent on transforming them into dog meat. He becomes the defender of young runaway Webb and takes her to Taylor's progressive school, which he eventually has to defend against the town's bully boys led by deputy sheriff Tobey. Schematically mounted and unadventurously photographed, the film's success was a considerable surprise.

Indeed, the most interesting thing about the movie was Laughlin's marketing strategy which made such a success of the film after Warners, who first handled its distribution, had declared it a box-office disaster. Securing the distribution rights for himself after a lengthy legal battle with Warners, Laughlin 'four walled' the film, promoting it extensively and naming the select cinemas it would be playing at exclusively, rather than relying on the block booking policy of the major studios. In this way Laughlin managed to transform *Billy Jack* from a mere film into an 'issue' in which the topics of the generation gap and hippies became an intrinsic part of the film.

Seen from a distance the film's crudeness and Laughlin's Hollywood radicalism are unappealing, but nonetheless the film remains a historical curiosity. Progressively less successful sequels followed: *The Trial of Billy Jack* (1974) and *Billy Jack Goes to Washington* (1977). In between these, Laughlin made the equally odd Zen Western, **The Master Gunfighter** (1975).

d T.C. Frank (Tom Laughlin) *p* Mary Rose Solti *s* Frank Cristina, Teresa Christina (Tom Laughlin, Dolores Taylor) *c* Fred Koenekamp, John Stephens *lp* Tom Laughlin, Dolores Taylor, Clark Howat, Bert Freed, Julie Webb, Ken Tobey

Blindman

(ABKCO/PRIMEX; US, IT) scope 105 (96) min
Intended as a parody of the Italian Western, *Blindman* looks too much like one to succeed. Moreover, despite the occasional visual delight, script, direction and acting, including the over-enthusiastic performance of ex-Beatle Starr, are far too mundane to keep one's attention. Anthony is the mysterious and all-powerful cracker-barrel philosopher determined to deliver a consignment of 50 girls to whoever will pay for them and Starr, Batistu and Baldassare are amongst those who steal the girls from him.

d Ferdinando Baldi *p/co-s* Tony Anthony, Saul Swimmer *co-s* Piero Anchisi, Vincenzo Cerami *c* Riccardo Pallottini *lp* Tony Anthony, Ringo Starr, Agneta Eckemyr, Lloyd Batistu, Magda Konopka, Raf Baldassare

The Boldest Job in the West

orig **El Mas Fabulosi Golpe del Far West** *aka* **Nevada**
(PROMOFILM/ACTION FILM/LES FILMS NUMBER ONE; SP, IT, FR) 101 min
This dull film lacks both the violence and the mannered style of the Italian Western; sadly it also lacks the wit that often accompanies these elements. The result is a lukewarm actioneer, a film stronger on atmosphere and detail than action. Edwards and Sancho lead a gang that plans a peaceful

Tony Anthony as the enigmatic hero of Blindman, *one of the first would-be parodies of the Italian Western.*

bank robbery that goes disastrously wrong when first there is a bloodbath outside the bank and then the money is stolen from the robbers, by one of their number. In a climactic shoot-out, Sancho recovers the money and, to his surprise, is given a hero's welcome by the townspeople who think he's recovered the money for them.

d/s Jose Antonio de la Loma   *p* Jose Maria Carcasona
c Hans Burmann, Antonio Millan   *lp* Mark Edwards, Carmen Sevilla, Fernando Sancho, Charly Bravo, Piero Lulli, Yvan Verella

Buck and the Preacher
(E & R PRODUCTIONS/BELAFONTE ENTERPRISES)   103 min
Memorable, if only for the delicious moment when the Indians ride to the rescue of the band of fleeing black slaves when all seems lost, *Buck and the Preacher* is an amiable black Western, even if it too often takes the easy (comic) way out. Poitier is Buck, a former Union Cavalryman turned wagon-master, who is leading a wagon train of freed slaves to the West and Belafonte (whose company co-produced the film) is the con-man of a preacher who helps him fend off Mitchell and his renegade Confederates determined to re-capture the slaves.

d Sidney Poitier   *p* Joel Glickman   *s* Ernest Kinoy
c Alex Phillips   *lp* Sidney Poitier, Harry Belafonte, Ruby Dee, Cameron Mitchell, Denny Miller, Nita Talbot

Captain Apache   (BENMAR; GB)   scope   94 min
A hybrid American-European Spaghetti Western produced in Britain, this is an unimpressive film. Singer directs with occasional flair but Sperling and Yordan's script is unsalvageable. Van Cleef is the Indian hired to track down the murderers of the Indian Commissioner. He puts an end to attempts to start an Indian war by landowner Whitman, whose men have been ordered to kill President Grant while in Indian disguise. Beneath the modern touches, which include drug-induced hallucinations, the plot is the old-fashioned one of trying to move the Indians on so as to get their oil- and gold-rich lands.

d Alexander Singer   *p/s* Milton Sperling, Philip Yordan
c John Cabrera   *lp* Lee Van Cleef, Carroll Baker, Stuart Whitman, Percy Herbert, Tony Vogel, Elisa Montes

John Wayne and one of the boys he makes a man of in the course of The Cowboys.

Catlow   (MGM; GB)   pv   101 min
A ridiculous European co-production of a Western in which Brynner is the carefree bandit repeatedly trying to steal $2 million from the Federales and being pursued by Crenna's amiable lawman and Nimoy's cruel gunman. Little of the humour of the original Louis L'Amour novel, on which the screenplay is based, remain. Of the principals only Lavi, as the rowdy lady bandit, makes anything substantial of her part.

d Sam Wanamaker   *p* Euan Lloyd   *s* Scot Finch, J. J. Griffith   *c* Ted Scaife   *lp* Yul Brynner, Richard Crenna, Leonard Nimoy, Daliah Lavi, Jo Ann Pflug, Jeff Corey

Chato's Land   (SCIMITAR; GB)   100 min
A posse is picked off one by one by the Indian they hunt (Bronson). Winner's direction, with its over-reliance on the zoom lens and its budget-paring ridiculous day-for-night cinematography, drains the film of any resonance. The film is written by Wilson, once a literate screenwriter who, after years of collaboration with Winner, seems content to produce cliches for characters, like the posse leader Palance who is a 'man of honour' and Oakland's Indian hater.

d/p Michael Winner   *s* Gerald Wilson   *c* Robert Paynter
lp Charles Bronson, Jack Palance, Richard Basehart, James Whitmore, Simon Oakland, Ralph Waite

The Cowboys   (SANFORD PRODUCTIONS/WB)   pv   127 min
This intriguing Western follows the futher education of a bunch of kids by Wayne who hires them to help drive his cattle to market after his regular hands have quit. Wayne is surprisingly at home with his youthful co-stars and director Rydell (who directs a touch flashily). The fact that he is not appearing in one of his usual broad action-packed pieces of fluff doesn't disturb him. The result is a better than average movie. Dern is the malevolent pursuer of the cowboys, intent on revenge for not being hired, who eventually kills Wayne, shooting him in the back, in a surprising scene, which in turn inspires the (literally) cow*boys* to avenge their 'father's' death. But if the end is needlessly melodramatic, for the most part Frank and Ravetch's script offers an accurate and engaging account of the travails of life on a cattle drive.

Far left: Harry Belafonte (left) and Sidney Poitier in Buck and the Preacher, *one of the first blaxploitation Westerns of the seventies.*

d/p Mark Rydell s Irving Ravetch, Harriet Frank Jnr, William Dale Jennings c Robert Surtees
lp John Wayne, Roscoe Lee Browne, Bruce Dern, Colleen Dewhurst, Slim Pickens, Lonny Chapman

Doc (FRANK PERRY FILMS) 96 min

This is yet another account of the infamous gunfight at the O.K. Corral. However, unlike John Sturges' 1957 film, this is a modern Western, more in keeping with Sturges' own further reflections of the subject, **Hour of the Gun** (1967). Like the later film, its hero is not Wyatt Earp (Yulin) but Keach's Doc Halliday. Seen in Hamill's screenplay as a morose loner unwilling to change with the times, he is contrasted to Yulin's scheming opportunist. More unusually, Perry seems to have little interest in the West, real or mythic. Thus the characters almost float in their own personal universe: Yulin seeking political advancement, Keach succumbing, against his better interests, to the claims and blandishments of friendship and Dunaway, his mistress, quitting Keach rather than compromising her beliefs. This is a minor, but engaging, bittersweet film that lacks the harder edge of the more successful *Hour of the Gun*.

d/p Frank Perry s Pete Hamill c Gerald Hirschfeld
lp Stacy Keach, Faye Dunaway, Harris Yulin, Mike Witney, Denver John Collins, Don Greenberg

A Fistful of Dynamite orig Giu La Testa
aka Duck You Sucker

(RAFRAN/SAN MARCO/MIURA; IT) scope 150 (138) min
This is the least interesting of Leone's Westerns, in part because it is the film he had the least to do with. He didn't want to make the film in the first place and only took over the project after Steiger and Coburn refused to be directed by Giancarlo Santi (Leone's regular assistant director) under Leone's supervision.

Steiger is the vulgar Mexican bandido and Coburn the cold expatriate IRA terrorist who tricks him into helping the Mexican Revolution and, in turn, learns from him a degree of humanity. In contrast to other political Westerns, which were directly geared towards the Third World, Leone's seems more academic and less felt. Certainly Coburn behaves very much as the paternalist towards Steiger and the professional revolutionary (Valli) is far more cynical than usual. In marked contrast to **Once upon a Time in the West** (1968), in which Leone shows how well he grasped the ambiguity of the arrival

James Coburn as the Irish revolutionary in Sergio Leone's A Fistful of Dynamite.

of civilization in the West, *A Fistful of Dynamite* shows how unsure he was of the intricacies of revolution.

d/co-s Sergio Leone p Fulvio Morsella co-s Luciano Vincenzoni, Sergio Donati c Giuseppe Ruzzolini lp Rod Steiger, James Coburn, Romolo Valli, Maria Monti, Rik Battaglia, Franco Graziosi

Fools' Parade aka Dynamite Man from Glory Jail
(STANMORE/PENBAR) 98 min

A surprisingly effective film, *Fools' Parade* stars Stewart as the man with a cheque that can only be cashed in the town that has outlawed him and Kennedy as the demented man determined to stop him. The resulting circular plot gives an added dimension to Stewart's cracker barrel philosophizing. Baxter, Russell and the marvellous Martin give fine support, while Barrett's screenplay gives McLaglen space to watch his characters rather than simply rush them through the plot.

d/p Andrew V. McLaglen s James Lee Barrett c Harry Stradling Jnr lp James Stewart, George Kennedy, Anne Baxter, Strother Martin, Kurt Russell, William Windom

The Gatling Gun
(WESTERN INTERNATIONAL) scope 91 min

Despite its fashionable modernisms – slow-motion footage and rapid cutting for example – this is no more than an indifferent traditional Western. Winkle and Hanna's screenplay follows the much thumbed plot of a Cavalry patrol and assorted fellow travellers being harrassed by hostile Indians. The only difference, and the film's major gimmick, is the powerful gun of the title which Stockwell and his men prevent from falling into the hands of the Indians. Fuller is the cardboard cut-out of a renegade and Luna the half-breed whose loyalties are predictably torn.

d Robert Gordon p Oscar Nichols s Joseph Van Winkle, Mark Hanna c Jacques Marquette lp Guy Stockwell, Woody Strode, Barbara Luna, Robert Fuller, Patrick Wayne, John Carradine

The Great Northfield Minnesota Raid
(U/ROBERTSON & ASSOCIATES) 90 min

The story of the James Gang's last bank robbery, this is a complex modern Western. In contrast to the heroic simplicities of Henry King's **Jesse James** (1939) or the view of the James brothers as adolescent rebels that characterized Nicholas Ray's **The True Story of Jesse James** (1957), Kaufman's film is clearly influenced by the 'mud and rags' view of the West. The movie traces the growing madness of Duvall's Jesse James who, when confronted with the arrival of civilization at the frontier (baseball for example) retreats into mysticism while Cole Younger (Robertson), his partner and loyal friend, attempts to adapt himself to the changing times. Accordingly, though the film shows them on the way to becoming folk-heroes as victims of the corrupting spread of capitalism, they do so by accident. The actual raid is particularly well staged.

d/s Philip Kaufman p Jennings Lang c Bruce Surtees
lp Cliff Robertson, Robert Duvall, Luke Askew, R. G. Armstrong, Dana Elcar, Donald Moffat

Hannie Caulder
(TIGON BRITISH/CURTWEL; GB) pv 85 min

A would-be parody of the revenge Western with Welch intent on killing the three men who raped her and murdered her husband, *Hannie Caulder*, like many of Kennedy's later films, uneasily mixes moments of gritty realism with light-hearted comedy. Nonetheless, the film is surprisingly successful, thanks to Welch, Martin and Elam as the near degenerates who rape her and Culp, as the enigmatic gunman who tutors her in the art of marksmanship. Lee is an unlikely, if amiable, gunsmith.

d Burt Kennedy p Patrick Curtis s Z. X. Jones (Burt Kennedy, David Haft) c Edward Scaife lp Raquel Welch, Robert Culp, Ernest Borgnine, Strother Martin, Jack Elam, Christopher Lee

Hard on the Trail *aka* Hard Trail

(BRENTWOOD INTERNATIONAL) 92 min
A hard-core pornographic Western. Forties star 'Lash' LaRue appears as the leader of a gang of bandits searching for a lost goldmine. He doesn't, however, appear in any of the sex scenes. Claiming he didn't know what kind of a movie he was involved with, he reportedly quit showbusiness to 'devote himself to missionary work' after the film's release. Bradley, Kemp and Romero provide the sultry action along the trail.

d/s Greg Corarito p Maurice Smith lp Al 'Lash' LaRue, Donna Bradley, Bruce Kemp, Bob Romero

The Hired Hand

(U/PANDO/BROWN, LIFTON AND WEISS) 90 min
Fonda's directorial debut, this tells the story of two drifters (Fonda and Oates) and their attempts to settle down to domesticity. Tersely scripted by Sharp and beautifully photgraphed by Zsigmond (though it occasionally slips into pretentiousness), the sense of period and the desultory ambitions of its characters are well caught. Bloom is particularly fine as the wife who comes between the two men. She listlessly takes her husband, Fonda, back, but only as a hired hand on the farm, with the words: 'It could as well have been either of you'. Whereupon, Fonda's sense of loyalty to his friend before his wife, sends him to rescue Oates, who in turn takes Fonda's place on the ranch when Fonda is killed in the rescue attempt. A superb evocation of the rigours and essential aimlessness of frontier life.

d Peter Fonda p William Hayward s Alan Sharp c Vilmos (William) Zsigmond lp Peter Fonda, Warren Oates, Verna Bloom, Robert Pratt, Severn Darden, Ted Markland

The Honkers (UA) 102 min

This is an accomplished directorial debut from actor Inhat (best remembered for his ferocious killer in Don Siegel's *Madigan*, 1968). Coburn is the fading rodeo star who loses all, his marriage, his son, his best friend (Pickens) because he can't control his quick temper. Coburn's easy-going perform-

ance makes the character he plays too charming to be believable. The film's best feature is the mosaic of rodeo life, built up detail by detail by Inhat, which is surprisingly realistic, especially when compared to films vaunted for their realism like **J. W. Coop** (1971).

d/co-s Steve Inhat p Jules Levy, Arthur Gardner co-s Stephan Lodge c John Crabbe lp James Coburn, Lois Nettleton, Slim Pickens, Richard Anderson, Jim Davis, Mitchell Ryan

The Hunting Party

(BRIGHTON PICTURES/LEVY-GARDNER-LAVEN; GB)
108 (102) min
Bergen is the estranged wife of sadistic rancher Hackman. She is kidnapped by outlaw Reed (who wants to learn to read!?) and falls for him. Whereupon, hunting fanatic Hackman, whose guns outdistance any in the territory, hunts the pair down as though they were big game. Reed's acting is atrocious and Norton's script a collection of violent cliches. The melodramatic end is laughable: in the desert Hackman (who gives the film's best performance) shoots Bergen and Reed before dying of thirst.

d Don Medford p/co-s Lou Morheim co-s William Norton, Gilbert Alexander c Cecilio Paniaqua lp Oliver Reed, Candice Bergen, Gene Hackman, Simon Oakland, Mitchell Ryan, L. Q. Jones

J. W. Coop (COL/ROBERTSON AND ASSOCIATES) 112 min

Despite its mass of self-indulgences, the mark of so many 'personal projects', *J. W. Coop* is redeemed by the easy charm of Robertson's performance in the crucial title role. He's the rodeo rider who sets out to win the national championship after a ten-year spell in jail. Though the film lacks the obsessional feel of *Cockfighter* (1974) and the sense of loss for the old rodeo ways that figures so strongly in Peckinpah's **Junior Bonner** (1972), Robertson suggests an effortless integrity that is not destroyed by either his success in the rodeo ring or by the relationship he forms with Ferrare's hippie. What is strange, however, considering the efforts made to ensure authenticity by all concerned, is the awkwardness of the rodeo scenes.

d/p/co-s Cliff Robertson co-s Gary Cartwright, Bud Shrake c Frank Stanley lp Cliff Robertson, Cristina Ferrare, Geraldine Page, R. G. Armstrong, John Crawford, Wode Crosby

Far left: A scene from The Great Northfield Minnesota Raid, *one from the 'mud and rags' school of Westerns of the seventies.*

Peter Fonda (left) and Warren Oates (right) as the drifters who try to settle down in The Hired Hand, *Fonda's assured directorial debut.*

Dennis Hopper, director and star of The Last Movie.

The Last Movie (ALTA-LIGHT/U) 108 min

Called by one critic a cross between Vincent Minnelli's *Two Weeks in Another Town* (1962) and Jean Luc Godard's *Weekend* (1968), and looking for all the world like missing footage from Werner Herzog's *Fitzcarraldo* (1982), *The Last Movie* is undeniably the most bizarre modern Western. Made by Hopper after the success of *Easy Rider* (1969) had opened all doors for him, the film was subsequently savaged by the critics on its brief release in 1972 despite winning the Golden Lion at the Venice Film Festival. Ten years later, in 1982, Hopper finally prised the film from Universal and re-released it himself to positive, if reverential, reviews and surprisingly good box office.

The movie's initial reception is easy to understand; even ten years on, the fragmented, interwoven narrative is hard to penetrate fully. The 'plot' (to force a story from the film) follows the wanderings of Hopper's wrangler who remains in a remote area of Peru after the film unit he's been with moves on. The unit, under the flamboyant direction of director Fuller, has just completed a bloodbath of a version of the story of Billy the Kid when the actor playing Billy (Stockwell) is killed doing a stunt. Though he is in no way to blame, Hopper feels responsible for Stockwell's death. Intending to make a fortune by encouraging film companies to make movies in the area, Hopper drifts into a destructive friendship with a pair of American tourists before joining Gordon in a search for gold. This jaunty episode ends with the pair discovering gold but being unable to exploit their find. They quarrel – 'I seriously doubt viewing *Treasure of the Sierra Madre* is sufficient preparation for a gold mining expedition' – and suddenly Gordon commits suicide, leaving Hopper once more feeling responsible. Whereupon, in one of the cinema's most intriguing and self-conscious sequences, Hopper gets caught up with the Peruvian Indians who have adapted and transformed the movie-making progress, complete with bamboo cameras and lights, to make it part of their religion. Their film-making is radically different from Hollywood's, however: they believe in doing things for real. Thus it seems that Hopper will die, which fits well with his quest for martyrdom, when he is cast by them as Billy the Kid. However, he is only wounded and the film ends with all the cast of *The Last Movie* reassuming their own identities and fooling about.

The film chronicles America's and Hollywood's continued abuse of power over the natives – it was to be shot in Mexico. But *The Last Movie* is neither simply an anti-colonial tract nor a massive 'in' joke (it is full of references to Hopper's career as an actor) about film-making. It certainly touches on both of these, but only as part of its exploration of the guilt clearly felt by Hopper and by all the other characters in varying degrees. The end, which is comparable in effect, if not tone, to that of Mel Brooks' **Blazing Saddles** (1974) is marvellous. Hopper is denied his martyrdom and the film an easy, dramatic resolution of the complex issues it raises.

d Dennis Hopper *p* Paul Lewis *s* Stewart Swern
c Laszlo Kovacs *lp* Dennis Hopper, Stella Garcia, Julie Adams, Tomas Milian, Don Gordon, Samuel Fuller, Dean Stockwell

The Last Rebel (LARRY G. SPANGLER) 90 min

This is a hit and miss Western made in Spain but with American rather than European audiences in mind. American football star Namath is the pool hustler who, with Elam (who finally turns on him) and Strode, charts an erratic course for himself through the bordellos of Missouri at the end of the Civil War. One-time television star Hardin is the sheriff on their trail. Kiefer's script, however, is impenetrable. Accordingly the film only works intermittently.

d Denys McCoy *p* Larry G. Spangler *s* Warren Kiefer
c Carlo Carlini *lp* Joe Namath, Jack Elam, Woody Strode, Ty Hardin, Victoria George, Renato Romano

Lawman (SCIMITAR) 99 min

Claimed by its maker to be 'one of the most authentic Westerns ever made', this unofficial remake of **Man with the Gun** (1955) with Lancaster in the Robert Mitchum role, is nothing of the sort. Rather it is a traditional Western deformed by Winner's excessive reliance on blood and gore in imitation of the Italian Western. Lancaster is the marshal who arrives at the town of Sabbath on the trail of seven killers, Cobb is the killers' protective boss and Ryan the pragmatic sheriff who watches from the sidelines as Lancaster takes on the town.

d/p Michael Winner *s* Gerald Wilson *c* Bob Paynter
lp Burt Lancaster, Robert Ryan, Lee J. Cobb, Sheree North, Joseph Wiseman, Robert Duvall

The Legend of Frenchie King *orig* Les Pétroleuses
(FRANCOS FILMS/VIDES/COPERCINES HEMDALE FILMS; FR, IT, SP, GB) 96 min

A tedious attempt to repeat the commercial success of *Viva Maria* (1965) in a Western setting, with Cardinale taking over the role of foil to Bardot from Jeanne Moreau in the earlier film. Here Bardot and her four half-sisters are the train robbers who lay claim to the Little P ranch in a French settlement in New Mexico, only to be threatened by Cardinale and her four brothers (who know the ranch is oil rich) and murderer Czarniak. The inevitable ending, after many dreary attempts at bawdy humour, has Czarniak killed and the two gangs united (in marriage, no less) while Bardot and Cardinale are chased by sheriff Pollard who clearly has notions of romance rather than justice on his mind. Oddly enough little is made of either the **Seven Brides for Seven Brothers** (1954) aspects of the plot or the idea of gun-toting women. The inept dubbing, which makes everybody speak in ze Engleesh, only makes the affair more wearing.

co-d/co-s Guy Casaril *co-d* Christine Jacques *p* Raymond Erger, Francis Cosne *co-s* Daniel Boulanger *c* Henri Persin *lp* Brigitte Bardot, Claudia Cardinale, Michael J. Pollard, Patty Shepard, Micheline Presle, Henri Czarniak

Lucky Luke
(DARGAUD FILMS/LES ARTISTES ASSOCIES; FR, BEL) 76 min

Based on Goscinny's popular European comic strip of the same name, this animated feature tells the story of a frontier town, Daisy Town. First it is cleaned up by a mild-mannered, chain-smoking, spindly cowboy, Lucky Luke, and then protected by him from the Daltons and then from marauding Indians. Little's (who narrates the film in rhyming couplets) vocal impersonations of James Stewart, Gary Cooper (as Lucky Luke) and James Cagney and Humphrey Bogart (as a couple of the Daltons) are the best thing in an otherwise slow-moving film that is only sporadically fun. Examples of this are Luke blowing smoke skulls as he faces down the Daltons, and the building of the town from prefabricated pieces each of which comes complete with its own cliche, the sleepy Mexican, the drunkard, etc.

d/co-p/co-s Rene Goscinny *co-p/co-s* Morris *co-s* Pierre Tchernia *c* Francois Leonard. With the voice of Rich Little

McCabe and Mrs Miller (WB) pv 121 min

This is possibly Altman's best film. Itinerant gambler turned saloon keeper Beatty and prostitute turned madame Christie are the drifters who settle in the bizarre town of Presbyterian Church. The ugly, half-built, mud-strewn (and later snow-bound) town that expands around them – so much so that others want to take over Beatty's small empire – is a testament to both their success and the precariousness of their endeavours. They are individualists, unable to commit themselves to each other or to deal with their successful enterprise. Thus Christie turns increasingly to drugs while the emotionally confused Beatty decides upon a suicidal gunfight against the gunmen sent by the mining company whose offer he grandly refused.

Squeezed between the frontier and the steady encroachment of companies owned by 'shareholders back East', Beatty is a temporary big man only too aware that his days are numbered but not sure of what to do. The result is an unheroic Western, rich in pathos and savage black humour. If Christie's role is predictable from the start, Beatty's imitation of running on the spot is simply marvellous. Similarly, Altman's jagged, edgy direction is greatly enhanced by Zsigmond's wintery cinematography. Only the score, a selection of songs by Leonard Cohen sung by their writer, seems out of place and too self-consciously arty. Against that it must be said that the songs help to clarify the issues.

d/co-s Robert Altman *p* David Foster, Mitchell Browser *co-s* Brian McKay *c* Vilmos (William) Zsigmond *lp* Warren Beatty, Julie Christie, Rene Auberjonois, Hugh Millais, Shelley Duvall, Michael Murphy

Man in the Wilderness

(WB/WILDERNESS FILM PRODUCTIONS) pv 105 min
Made by the producer, star and writer of **A Man Called Horse** (1970), this is another ecological/anthropological Western, a film about man's endurance in the face of the violent beauty of Nature. At least that was the view of the film's

Julie Christie and Warren Beatty as the uneasy bedfellows in McCabe and Mrs Miller.

publicists; less generous critics have described it as another excuse for sadism masquerading as ritual. Harris is Sam Bass, a scout left for dead by a party of explorers after being mauled by a grizzly in the Northwest territory in the 1820s. On his recovery, he vows revenge on them, only to forego it when he finally catches up with them. Huston, as the eccentric leader of the expedition, gives his usual grizzled performance.

d Richard C. Sarafian *p* Sanford Howard *s* Jack DeWitt *c* Gerry Fisher *lp* Richard Harris, John Huston, Henry Wilcoxon, Percy Herbert, Dennis Waterman, Prunella Ransome

One More Train to Rob (U) 108 min

This is an enjoyable romp from McLaglen who (with Burt Kennedy) was virtually the only American director regularly making Westerns in Hollywood in the seventies. Peppard and Vernon are the unrepentant villains, one a simple thief, the other a thief turned businessman, who try and double-cross each other and rob an old Chinaman of his gold. Muldaur is the girl they quarrel over. The film is lightweight but entertaining.

d Andrew V. McLaglen *p* Robert Arthur *s* Don Tait, Dick Nelson *c* Alric Edens *lp* George Peppard, Diana Muldaur, John Vernon, France Nuyen, Steve Sandor, Harry Carey Jnr

Pancho Villa (GRANADA FILMS; SP) 92 min

A dull, much fictionalized biography of Pancho Villa. Savalas is the enthusiastic revolutionary and Walker his lieutenant. They decide to invade the United States when double-crossed in an arms deal. They overrun a frontier fort run by an effete Connors before being repulsed by General Pershing. Sadly, the script's inventive narrative is not matched by either its dialogue or Martin's direction which is heavy-handed in the extreme.

d Gene Martin (Eugenio Martin) *p* Bernard Gordon *s* Julian Halevy *c* Alejandro Ulloa *lp* Telly Savalas, Clint Walker, Anne Francis, Chuck Connors, Angel Del Pozo, Jose Maria Prada

Red Sun *orig* Soleil Rouge

(CORONA FILMS/OCEANIA/BALCAZAR; FR, IT, SP) 108 min
This is a disaster of a would-be exotic international co-production of a Western. Bronson is the outlaw who joins up

Lee Van Cleef in Return of Sabata.

with Mifune's samurai warrior in search of loot, honour and Delon (horribly miscast as a gambling bandido). The film's one distinguishing feature is the non-appearance of Jill Ireland, normally a fixture in any film starring her husband, Bronson. Her place is taken by Andress and Capucine.

d Terence Young *p* Robert Dorfman *s* Laird Koenig, D.B. Petitclerc, W. Roberts, L. Roman *c* Henri Alekan *lp* Charles Bronson, Toshiro Mifune, Alain Delon, Ursula Andress, Capucine, Bart Barry

Return of Sabata *orig* E'Tornato Sabata ... Hai Chiuso un'Altro Volto

(P.E.A. CINEMATOGRAFICA/LES PRODUCTIONS ARTISTES ASSOCIES/ARTEMIS; IT, FR, WG) scope 107 (88) min
Full of the gadgetry that was central to the first Sabata film and the acrobatics that was a feature of all Parolini's films, be they sword and sandal epics or war films, this is a routine Italian Western. Much cut, and accordingly hard to follow, the story sees sharpshooter Van Cleef and Schone up against Albertini who controls the township of Hobsonville and extracts punishing taxes from the inhabitants. Energetically, if mechanically, put together, the film never quite matches the surreal grandeur of its opening sequence.

d/co-s Frank Kramer (Gianfranco Parolini) *p* Alberto Grimaldi *co-s* Renato Izza *c* Sandro Mancori *lp* Lee Van Cleef, Reiner Schone, Annabella Incontrera, Gianni Rizzo, Gianpiero Albertini, Pedro Sanchez (Ignazio Spalla)

Scandalous John (WALT DISNEY) pv 117 min
An interesting, if seriously flawed, transposition of *Don Quixote* to the Western. Keith, who gives a splendid, spirited performance, is the bewhiskered rancher threatened with bankruptcy by Oakland. With the assistance of his Sancho Panza, Arau, he resolves to drive his one skinny cow to market and so pay off the mortgage. In this he's aided by Oakland's son, Lenz, and his daughter, Carey, but it is Keith who dominates the movie with his serene performance. Only Rod McKuen's treacly songs and Butler's uneven direction let the film down.

d Robert Butler *p/co-s* Bill Walsh *co-s* Don DaGradi *c* Frank Phillips *lp* Brian Keith, Alfonso Arau, Michele Carey, Rick Lenz, Harry Morgan, Simon Oakland

Below: Alain Delon, Ursula Andress and Toshiro Mifune in Red Sun, *a hymn to the inanities that so often were the result of international co-productions.*

Shoot Out (U) 94 min
A weak revenge Western, this is made weaker by Hathaway's amiable, leisurely direction and the far too frequent nods in the direction of **True Grit** (1969) with which it shares director, producer and screenwriter. Peck is the jailbird who is saddled with the care of orphan Lynn out for revenge on his one-time partner Gregory and Lyons is the young gunman hired by Gregory. Peck is far too 'nice' a person for a revenge film and Hathaway too stagey a director to animate him.

d Henry Hathaway *p* Hal B. Wallis *s* Marguerite Roberts *c* Earl Rath *lp* Gregory Peck, Pat Quinn, Robert F. Lyons, Jeff Corey, James Gregory, Dawn Lynn

The Skin Game (CHEROKEE) pv 101 min
A stylish comedy featuring Garner and Gossett as the con-men scourges of the mid-West, Garner as the salesman and Gossett as the slave he rescues after he's been sold. Their easy money is stopped when Gossett and his love (Sykes) are 'liberated' by John Brown (a fine performance by Dano) and Garner finds his wallet stolen by Clark's nimble-fingered con-woman. When Gossett and Garner are re-united they are forced to play the 'skin game' again, only to be captured by someone they've tricked before and then rescued by Clark. Garner and Gossett work beautifully together and, if the narrative becomes a little too predictable in the second half, Bogart's direction never loses its light touch.

d Paul Bogart *p* Harry Keller *s* Pierre Marton (Peter Stone) *c* Fred Koenekamp *lp* James Garner, Lou Gossett, Susan Clark, Brenda Sykes, Edward Asner, Royal Dano

Smoke in the Wind (FRONTIER PRODUCTIONS) 94 min
The last film of both Brennan and director Kane (whose 163rd film it was), *Smoke in the Wind* is not the film either would like to be remembered for; indeed it's so bad that it wasn't released until some four years after being made. A family of mountain men, on their return from the Civil War, are attacked by Confederates who think they've been traitors to the Confederacy by taking the Union side. By the end, Ashley, the eldest son, has saved the family name but little else. Eminently forgettable, even the unusual Arkansas locations look flat and uninteresting. Brennan's role, as the benign storekeeper who comments on the action, is strictly of the guest-star variety, his star billing notwithstanding.

d Joseph Kane *p* Robert 'Whitey' Hughes, Bill Hughes *s* Eric Allen *c* Mario Tosi *lp* John Ashley, John Russell, Myron Healey, Walter Brennan, Susan Houston, Linda Weld

Something Big
(STANMORE & PENBAR PRODUCTIONS) 108 min
An enjoyable Western from the prolific team of Barrett, and McLaglen, who, with this film, begins to parody John Ford, the director he had previously slavishly imitated. Here the target is (mostly) **She Wore a Yellow Ribbon** (1949) with Keith and Johnson mercilessly guying the retirement scene from that film (played by John Wayne and McLaglen's father Victor). The rest of the film is an amiable rag-bag collection of jokes. Martin is the charming bandit attempting one last big job and Keith the bumbling colonel intent on stopping him, who finally comes to his aid in robbing Salmi's Mexican outlaw, under duress from his wife, Blackman.

d/p Andrew V. McLaglen *s* James Lee Barrett *c* Harry Stradling Jnr *lp* Dean Martin, Brian Keith, Honor Blackman, Carol White, Ben Johnson, Albert Salmi

Squares *aka* Riding Tall
(PLATEAU PRODUCTIONS) 92 (72) min
This is an amiable contemporary Western. Prine is the drifting no account rodeo rider and McCormick the New Yorker he falls in with. A casual affair ensues, but when he starts to lose in the rodeo ring, McCormick decides to move

on. At his next appearance, a bemused Prine wins. Rough-hewn and marvellously inconsequential, despite the occasional psychologizing of Saxon's script and the silly ending, Murphy's film has a rawness about it that is very appealing.

d/p Patrick J. Murphy   *s* Mary Ann Saxon   *c* John Koester   *lp* Andrew Prine, Gilmer McCormic, Robert Easton, William Wintersole, Dean Smith, Tom Hennesy

Support Your Local Gunfighter

(CHEROKEE/BRIGADE)   92 min

'I'm slow, but you're slower', mutters Garner to Elam as they wait to meet the gunfighter Elam has at first hesitantly and then gleefully impersonated in this hilarious, but surprisingly less commercially successful, sequel to **Support Your Local Sheriff** (1968). Once again Garner is the con man, this time on the run from marriage, who is mistaken for a famous gunman and sets out to milk the rival factions of the townspeople of Purgatory. Elam is superb as his oafish, shifting, side-kick, as is Pleshette as the girl who dreams of a Ladies Finishing School in upstate New York.

d Burt Kennedy   *p* Bill Finnegan   *s* James Edward Grant   *c* Harry Stradling Jnr   *lp* James Garner, Suzanne Pleshette, Jack Elam, Joan Blondell, Harry Morgan, Marie Windsor

El Topo   (PRODUCCIONES PANIC/ABKCO FILMS; MEXICO)

124 (120) min

In this bizarre Western writer/director Jodorowsky uses the classic storyline of the stranger with a gun who cleans up an isolated town as the peg from which to hang his hand-me-down surrealism. Rather in the manner of Frederico Fellini, whose self-conscious conflation of the roles of charlatan and ringmaster of the unconscious Jodorowsky apes, the film is a breathtaking concoction of often striking, but more often ludicrous, images. The result is a movie that, though it impressed many at the time of its original release, in retrospect is clearly a minor, albeit often very funny, work.

Jodorowsky takes the title role as the gunfighter and mystic whose path to self enlightenment involves 'out gunning' the four masters of the desert in the manner of the 'Man with No Name' before dying that he might be resurrected. The film doesn't hang together as the Biblical allegory it was clearly intended to be but decyphering the wide range of references

to directors as diverse as Buñuel and Ford provides hours of fun. Moreover, some of the sequences, such as the encounter of El Topo and the third master, whose colony of white rabbits die as the black clad gunfighter approaches, and the Russian roulette church service, are imaginatively staged.

d/p/s Alexandro Jodorowsky   *c* Raphael Corkidi
lp Alexandro Jodorowsky, Brontis Jodorowsky, Mara Lorenzio, David Silva, Paula Romo, Hector Martinez

A Town Called Bastard

(BENMAR/ZURBANO; GB, SP)   scope   97 min

One of a group of American Westerns that set out to rival the flood of Italian Westerns and ended up with all the violence but little of the wit of the films they imitated. A worthy cast, including Shaw, Savalas, Craig and the excellent Stevens, plod through a search for a Mexican revolutionary. Needless to say few end up alive, especially as the film features some 22 killings, not including the opening massacre.

d Robert Parrish   *p* S. Benjamin Fisz   *s* Richard Aubrey   *c* Manual Berenguer   *lp* Robert Shaw, Stella Stevens, Martin Landau, Telly Savalas, Michael Craig, Fernando Rey

Trinity Is Still My Name *orig* Continuavamo a Chiamarlo Trinity

(WEST FILM PRODUCTIONS; IT)   scope   121 (90) min

This is a sharper and better film than the first in the series, **They Call Me Trinity** (1970). This time out, the lazy, but quick on the draw when roused, Hill and his bumbling brother, Spencer, attempt to set up business as outlaws, only to end up helping those they try to rob. The main part of the episodic plot has them exposing a gunrunning racket that operates from a monastery.

d/s E. B. Clucher (Enzo Barboni)   *p* Italo Zingarelli   *c* Aldo Giordani   *lp* Terence Hill (Mario Girotti), Bud Spencer (Carlo Pedersoli), Harry Carey Jnr, Jessica Dublin, Yanti Somer, Enzo Tarascio

Wild Rovers   (GEOFFREY PRODUCTIONS)   pv70   132 min

A triumphant return to the genre by Edwards whose first scripts and sorties into production were Westerns, **Panhandle** (1948) and **Stampede** (1949). Holden is the aging cowboy and O'Neal (who gives his best performance ever) the naive youngster. Together they decide to try bank robbery in a futile attempt to amount to something. The tone of the film is admirably demonstrated by the bank robbery sequence: while waiting for the bank to open Holden shares a drink with the

Far left: William Holden and Ryan O'Neal as the aging cowboy and naive youngster who become the Wild Rovers.

James Garner and Lou Gossett in Paul Bogart's stylish comedy, The Skin Game.

Jeff Bridges, with Barry Brown as the youngster, falls in with Bad Company.

sheriff and O'Neal, supposedly holding a gun on the banker's family, romps with their pet dog in the living room. But if Holden and O'Neal come over as grizzled and clean-shaven innocents respectively, Edwards' West is no dusty Eden. Rather, like that of **Monte Walsh** (1970), it is a place of desperation. Thus behind the bland patriarchal front of Malden's rancher lies an adolescent obsessed with winning the favour of his father (Skerritt). Skerritt refuses to give up the chase after the bank robbers, even when his father is killed.

Because of their innocence, the harshness of the West and the qualities of strength needed to rise above it, Holden and O'Neal have no chance. Like the puppy O'Neal takes along, they are babes in arms. Edwards rams this point home in a bloody conclusion that sees Holden butchered by Skerritt. Then comes Edwards' one concession to the inner heroism he clearly feels his characters possess; he reprises in slow motion a sequence of Holden breaking a wild horse against a snowscape. The sequence echoes a similar one in *Monte Walsh*, like this, a glorious film of character and mood.

d/co-p/s Blake Edwards   *co-p* Ken Wales   *c* Philip Lathrop *lp* William Holden, Ryan O'Neal, Karl Malden, Lynn Carlin, Tom Skerritt, Jo Dan Baker

1972

Bad Company   (JAFFILMS)   92 min
Wildly overpraised for its realistic depiction of life in the West, *Bad Company* is, in fact, yet another grimly ironic tale of the West. Thus, for example, having said they'll live off the land, the band of adolescent would-be gunmen symbolically meet a wagon returning from the frontier having found that the West isn't the land of plenty, but the land of scarcity. Set against this disenchantment is the glowing cinematography of Willis and the screenplay's decidedly romantic view of its mock Horatio Alger heroes.

Bridges and Brown are the draft-dodging youngsters who become men when, in the company of fellow deserters, they head West intending to become outlaws. Slickly made, the film is much closer to **Butch Cassidy and the Sundance Kid** (1969) than *Bonnie and Clyde* (1967) which Benton and Newman wrote for Arthur Penn. Unlike **Dirty Little Billy** (1972) or **The Great Northfield Minnesota Raid** (1971), films which complemented their unheroic views of the West with muddy streets and the like, *Bad Company*, with its blending of the mythic and the comic, is full of quaint costumes and dusky, dusty skies.

d/co-s Robert Benton   *p* Stanley R. Jaffe   *co-s* David Newman   *c* Gordon Willis   *lp* Jeff Bridges, Barry Brown, Jim Davis, David Huddleston, John Savage, Jerry Houser

Charley-One-Eye
(DAVID PARADINE FILMS; GB)   107 (96) min
An awkward, allegorical Western; it's as though Stanley Kramer had made an Italian Western on a slim British budget, mused one critic. Roundtree is the black deserter who meets up with a crippled Indian, Thinnes. The unlikely couple set up home in a deserted Mexican church until Davenport's bounty hunter arrives and puts an end to their fragile security.

d Don Chaffey   *p* James Swann   *s* Keith Leonard *c* Kenneth Talbot   *lp* Richard Roundtree, Roy Thinnes, Nigel Davenport, Jill Pearson, Aldo Sambrell, Luis Aller

The Culpepper Cattle Company   (FOX)   92 min
The directorial debut of Richards (who also wrote the original story), this is a decidedly post **Wild Bunch** (1969) Western. A gritty, but nonetheless elegaic, account of the initiation of a romantic youth (Grimes) into the realities of life as a cowboy, it offers a view of the West in which boredom and random violence are ever-present. Grimes is fine as the would-be hero, but the script is a shade too mechanical, throwing Grimes first this way, then that with little reason. Thus his development from cook's assistant, to gunman, to the film's moral centre is hard to accept. Bush is equally good in the more considered role of the hard but honest trail boss, Culpepper, who hires Grimes.

d Dick Richards   *p* Paul A. Helmick   *s* Eric Bercovici, Gregory Prentiss   *c* Lawrence Edward Williams, Ralph Woolsey   *lp* Garry Grimes, Billy 'Green' Bush, Luke Askew, Bo Hopkins, Geoffrey Lewis, Wayne Sutherlin

Deaf Smith and Johnny Ears *orig* Los Amigos
(COMPAGNIA CINEMATOGRAFICA/IDEA FILM; IT)   92 min
A lacklustre Spaghetti Western. Quinn is the deaf mute gunfighter and Nero his companion. They are hired by Sam Houston to help protect the Republic of Texas during its passage into the Union in 1834. Graziosi is the villain of the piece planning, with German backing, to assume control of the Empire of Texas and whose plans are blown up with the much fortified secret garrison Quinn and Nero set blazing.

d/co-s Paolo Cavara   *p* Joseph Janni, Luciano Perugia *co-s* Harry Essex, Oscar Saul, Lucia Drudi, Augusto Finocchi   *c* Tonino Delli Colli   *lp* Anthony Quinn, Franco Nero, Pamela Tiffin, Ira Furstenberg, Franco Graziosi, Adolfo Lastretti

Dirty Little Billy   (WRG PRODUCTIONS)   92 min
A surrealistic account of the early days of Billy the Kid (a virtuoso performance by Pollard) that culminates in the first of his many killings. Dragoti's view of the West is truly unromantic. Accordingly, his Cofeyville, Kansas is little more than a mudbath with the saloon a womb that no one wants to leave and Billy the Kid is portrayed as being little more than a mentally retarded psychopath (which, by all accounts, he really was). Yet, at the same time, the visuals are breathtakingly beautiful, as one might expect from a former director of commercials.

1972

d/co-s Stan Dragoti p Jack L. Warner co-s Charles Moss
c Ralph Woolsey lp Michael J. Pollard, Lee Purcell,
Richard Evans, Charles Aidman, William Sage, Alex Wilson

Face to the Wind *aka* Naked Revenge *aka* Cry for Me Billy

(BURT PRODUCTIONS) 92 (87) min
A nondescript 'youth' Western in which the characters mouth
alternative society cliches while imprisoned in a predictable
and hackneyed plot. Potts is the gunfighter who drops out and
rescues an Indian girl (Xochitl) after being disgusted by the
Cavalry's treatment of Indians. After an idyll together, she is
recaptured by a group of Cavalrymen and raped by them,
whereupon Potts goes after them and kills them.

d William A. Graham p Harvey Matofsky s David
Markson c Jordan Cronenweth lp Cliff Potts, Xochitl,
Harry Dean Stanton, Don Wilbanks, Woodrow Chambliss,
James Gammon

High Plains Drifter

(MALPASO/U) pv 105 (102) min
One of the most exciting (and mysterious) Hollywood
Westerns of the seventies, *High Plains Drifter* is clearly, in
part at least, a private homage to the Sergio Leone Westerns
that made Eastwood a star. Here he takes a bizarre revenge on
a whole town. His motivation is explained in stylized
Leone-like flashbacks, while his invulnerability is of truly
magical proportions. But if Leone is the source of the film's
style, the inflections Eastwood gives his material are wholly
his own. Thus, in place of the nervous tics that are an essential
part of Leone's highly mannered style, Eastwood's (often
oddly angled) camera gazes impassively at the bewildering
demands Eastwood's stranger makes of the inhabitants of
Lago, whom he's been hired to defend against the three men
who've vowed vengeance on them. Similarly, Tidyman's
script, which finally reveals Eastwood to be literally a
re-incarnation, is a surreal version of an Italian Western
script, with Eastwood finally ordering the town be painted red
and renamed Hell before taking his revenge on first the three
gunmen and then the townspeople (who were responsible for

his death in a previous life). The result is a stunningly
confident, formalized, abstract work.

d Clint Eastwood p Robert Daley s Ernest Tidyman
c Bruce Surtees lp Clint Eastwood, Verna Bloom, Mariana
Hill, Mitchell Ryan, Jack Ging, Stefan Gierasch

Jeremiah Johnson (WB) pv 108 min

A magnificent-looking film, *Jeremiah Johnson* aims for the
mythic, with Redford as a latter-day Natty Bumpo, tired of
the ways of civilization and setting out to conquer the
wilderness. Yet, at the same time, Milius and Anhalt's script
is concerned to 'explain' the Redford character and thus
reduce him to the man behind the legend. Accordingly, the
film is somewhat broken-backed, a movie of moments, like
the eerie journey through the Crow burial ground, and of
characters, like Geer as the eccentric old trapper who teaches
Redford the ways of Nature.

d Sydney Pollack p Joe Wizan s John Milius, Edward
Anhalt c Andrew Callaghan lp Robert Redford, Will
Geer, Stefan Gierasch, Allyn Ann McLerie, Delle Bolton,
Charles Tyner

Jesse and Lester, Two Brothers in a Place Called Trinity *orig* Due Fratelli in un Posto Chiamato Trinita

(H.P. INTERNATIONAL FILM PRODUCTIONS; IT) scope 97 min
A knockabout farce of an Italian Western with producer
Harrison and O'Brien as warring brothers, one intent on
building a whorehouse, the other a Mormon tabernacle with
their windfall, if they can keep it from the numerous
would-be robbers who surround them. The parodic villains
are the best things in an otherwise routine outing.

d James London p Richard Harrison, Fernando Piazza
s Renzo Genta c Antonio Modica lp Richard Harrison,
Donald O'Brien, Anna Zinneman, George Wong, Gino
Maturano

Joe Kidd (U/MALPASO) pv 87 min

A confused Western in which Eastwood, as the gunman
caught in the middle of a range war between Duvall's
businessman and dispossessed Mexican-Americans, apes the
methods and manners of his previous 'Man With No Name'
persona to little purpose or effect under Sturges' anonymous,

Robert Redford and Will Geer, as the mountain man who teaches him the ways of nature, in Jeremiah Johnson; *this film's success helped further popularize the 'wilderness' sub-genre.*

Clint Eastwood and Verna Bloom in High Plains Drifter.

indifferent direction. Saxon is the guerilla Eastwood agrees to capture and Stroud the wonderfully gorilla-like heavy employed by Duvall to keep an eye on him.

The film's hilarious set-piece, albeit completely out of keeping with the rest of the film, features Eastwood driving a train into a saloon.

d John Sturges *p* Sidney Beckerman *s* Elmore Leonard *c* Bruce Surtees *lp* Clint Eastwood, Robert Duvall, John Saxon, Don Stroud, Stella Garcia, James Wainwright

Jory

(MINSKY-KIRSCHNER PRODUCTIONS/CINEMATOGRAFICA MARCO POLO) 97 min
A pretentious juvenile Western in which Benson's adolescent finds himself, in the course of a cattle drive to Texas, finally rejecting the career of a gunslinger for that of a rancher. The script's upbeat ending contrasts strangely with the series of killings in which Benson guns down anyone who hurts him. Marley provides the cracker-barrel philosophy that accompanies Benson's 'education'.

d Jorge Fons *p* Howard G. Minsky *s* Gerald Herman, Robert Irving *c* George Stahl *lp* John Marley, B. J. Thomas, Robby Benson, Brad Dexter, Todd Martin, Patricia Aspillaga

Journey Through Rosebud (G.S.F.) pv 93 min
A contemporary Indian Western, this offbeat film did disastrously at the box office when briefly released in America in early 1972. Tabori is the draft dodger who, while staying at the Sioux's Rosebud Reservation, gets a new perspective on Indian life through his complex relationship with the Indians' leader, a Vietnam veteran, Forster, and his ex-wife, Racimo. In its evocative detailing of their unusual relationship, it is the

Right: *Paul Newman as 'the law West of Tombstone' in a publicity picture for* The Life and Times of Judge Roy Bean.

closest Gries ever came to the simplicity of **Will Penny** (1967). The end is similarly tragic with Forster dead from a car crash and Racimo and Tabori once more set apart by the death.

d Tom Gries *p* David Gil *s* Albert Ruben *c* Minervino Rojas *lp* Robert Forster, Kristoffer Tabori, Victoria Racimo, Eddie Little Sky, Roy Jenson, Wright King

Junior Bonner
(JOE WIZAN – BOOTH GARDNER/SOLAR) Todd AO-35 103 min
With *Junior Bonner* Peckinpah returns to the world of **Ride the High Country** (1962) with the central difference that, whereas the earlier film was set in the mythic past, *Junior Bonner* is set squarely in the unheroic present. McQueen is the motel cowboy who hopes to leave the rat race of the rodeo circuit and settle down, only to discover that his home is being parcelled up and sold as lots for a 'Home on the Range' retirement plan by his go-getter of a brother (Baker). McQueen isn't given the freedom of a last gunfight, only the realization that urban life has no place for a would-be hero.

Preston and Lupino give fine performances as the parents, as dissipated as the children, living in their worlds of make-believe, but it is McQueen, winning only to discover that there's no point when there's no home to go to, who steals this gem of a film.

d Sam Peckinpah *p* Joe Wizan *s* Jeb Rosebrook *c* Lucien Ballard *lp* Steve McQueen, Robert Preston, Ida Lupino, Joe Dan Baker, Barbara Leigh, Ben Johnson

The Legend of Nigger Charley
(SPANGLER & SONS PICTURES) 98 (95) min
A lacklustre piece of blaxploitation. Williamson is the slave who heads Westward when his freedom is revoked and drifts from scrape to scrape. Several violent gunfights later, he and Martin are still heading West.

d Martin Goldman *p/co-s* Larry G. Spangler *co-s* Martin Goldman *c* Peter Eco *lp* Fred Williamson, D'Urville Martin, Don Pedro Colley, Gertrude Jeanette, Marcia McBroom, Alan Gifford

The Life and Times of Judge Roy Bean
(FIRST ARTIST PRODUCTIONS) pv 124 min
'He must have been some man' says Gardner, playing Lillie Langtry, at the end of *The Life and Times of Judge Roy Bean* after being shown around the museum devoted to the man who loved her passionately, but never met her. And, although Newman's performance in the title role is no match for Harry Carey's even more beguiling impersonation in **The Law West of Tombstone** (1938), the remark captures perfectly the flavour of Huston's impossibly romantic hero. The episodic plot has Newman as a brash drunkard first bringing law and order to Vinegroon, which he renames Langtry, and then returning some twenty years later to clean up the town once more in a glorious gun battle amidst the automobiles and oil derricks that mark the end of the West. Milius' script and Huston's rip-roaring direction occasionally clash but stand united in their commitment to a rowdy yet elegaic notion of heroism. The film, which was badly received at the time of its original release, is (like the marvellous *The Man Who Would Be King*, 1975) clearly one of Huston's most personal works and one of the best Westerns of the seventies.

d John Huston *p* John Foreman *s* John Milius *c* Richard Moore *lp* Paul Newman, Jacqueline Bisset, Ava Gardner, John Huston, Stacy Keach, Anthony Perkins

The Magnificent Seven Ride (MIRISCH) 100 min
Yet another encore for the Magnificent Seven. The film's start sees Chris, here Van Cleef in the Yul Brynner role, married and on the side of the law. But once he accepts the seemingly impossible task of defending the small Mexican town of Magdalena the plot soon falls into well-worn channels. The

characterization is brief but the elaborate final set-piece defence of the town is well conceived and worked out.

d George McCowan   *p* William A. Calihan   *s* Arthur Rowe
c Fred Koenekamp   *lp* Lee Van Cleef, Stefanie Powers, Mariette Hartley, Michael Callan, Luke Askew, Pedro Armendariz Jnr

Man and Boy (LEVITT-PICKMAN) 98 min

Notwithstanding the presence of Cosby in the lead and the interesting ideas of the screenplay which settles on the problems of a black family in the West, this is a very dull affair. Cosby and his son, Spell, journey through the South West in search of horses stolen by Ward and Kotto who play, in delightfully exaggerated fashion, a pair of fumbling outlaws. Swackhamer directs aimlessly.

d E. W. Swackhamer   *p* Marvin Miller   *s* Harry Essex, Oscar Saul   *c* Arnold Rich   *lp* Bill Cosby, Gloria Foster, Leif Erickson, George Spell, Turner Ward, Yaphet Kotto

Man of the East *orig* ... E Pri lo Chiamavono Il Magnifico

(P.E.A. CINEMATOGRAFICA/LES PRODUCTIONS ARTISTES ASSOCIES; IT, FR) scope 125 min
One of the lesser films of Barboni, best known for his Trinity movies, this comic Western sees a trio of happy-go-lucky outlaws teaching Hill's effete English gentleman the ways of the West. Jokily put together with parodies of **Butch Cassidy and the Sundance Kid** (1969) and other films abounding, it falls flat largely because Hill is unable to sustain his part. Carey, in his only Italian Western, adds a touch of class.

d/s E.B. Clucher (Enzo Barboni)   *p* Alberto Grimaldi
c Aldo Giordini   *lp* Terence Hill (Mario Girotti), Gregory Walcott, Harry Carey, Yanti Somer, Dominic Barto, Riccardo Pizzuti

Molly and Lawless John

(PRODUCERS DISTRIBUTING CORP) 98 min
This is routine fare, despite the odd storyline. Miles is the downtrodden wife of sheriff Anderson. She falls for Elliott's dashing young outlaw who wooes her by pretending to have a mother complex when Anderson jails him. She helps him break jail and they elope together. But after he starts to stray

she kills him and returns a liberated woman with a story about being kidnapped. Nelson directs stylishly, as he would again with the even bigger budget of the justly praised *Washington Behind Closed Doors* teleseries, but Kingsley-Smith's script is just too stiff to make the most of a promising situation.

d Gary Nelson   *p* Dennis Durney   *s* Terry Kingsley-Smith
c Charles Wheeler   *lp* Vera Miles, Sam Elliott, John Anderson, Clu Gulager, Cynthia Myers, Robert Westmoreland

Glenn Ford and Dana Wynter in Santee, *Gary Nelson's impressive directorial debut.*

Pocket Money

(FIRST ARTISTS/COLEYTOWN PRODUCTIONS) 100 min
A gentle, shaggy-dog story of a contemporary Western. Marvin and Newman are the cowboys who dream of big things while wily Mexicans and businessmen fleece them. Broke, Newman agrees to bring in some cattle from Mexico for a mean and devious Martin (a wonderful performance) and goes into partnership with Marvin, who claims to be able to deal with Mexicans. Eventually they get the cattle together and even go to America though they have no money, only to find that Martin won't pay them. Rosenberg directs well enough, but it is the screenplay, Kovacs' dusty cinematography and the central performances that are so enchanting. Accordingly, the film's best moments are those when character rather than story are centre frame: Marvin wondering about the possibilities of coloured salt, or explaining his way of doing business.

The film was the first to be produced by the short-lived company set up by Newman, Barbra Streisand, Sidney Poitier and Steve McQueen.

d Stuart Rosenberg   *p* John Foreman   *s* Terry Malick
c Laszlo Kovacs   *lp* Paul Newman, Lee Marvin, Strother Martin, Wayne Rogers, Christine Belford, Fred Graham

A Reason to Live, a Reason to Die *orig* Una Ragione per Vivere e una per Morire

(SANCROSIAP-TERZA/EUROPRODIS/ATLANTIDA/CORONA; IT, FR, SP, WG) scope 96 (91) min
A lacklustre Western from the erratic Valerii (who made the superb **The Price of Power,** 1969). This seems to be derived in equal proportions from **A Fistful of Dynamite** (1971) and *The Dirty Dozen* (1967), with Coburn as the bandit leader and Savalas as the mincing Confederate major (clearly modelled on Von Stroheim in *La Grande Illusion*, 1936) whose fort and bullion Coburn leads an assault upon.

Far left: Lee Marvin *and Paul Newman in* Pocket Money.

d/s Tonino Valerii *p* Michael Billingsley *lp* James Coburn, Telly Savalas, Bud Spencer (Carlo Pedersoli), Ralph Goodwin, Joseph Mitchell, Robert Burton

The Revengers (MARTIN RACKIN PRODUCTIONS/ ESTUDIOS CHURUBUSCO; US, MEX) pv 108 min

A formula Western in which Holden recruits a dirty half dozen to ride after Vanders, a renegade whiteman leading a band of Comanche who have massacred his family. Hayward, as the unlikely Irish nurse who nurses Holden back to life after one of his mercenaries has turned on him and replants the seed of care and concern in him, is just the most memorable of the film's many inanities as Mayes turns his characters first this way then that in search of more blood and gore.

d Daniel Mann *p* Martin Rackin *s* Wendell Mayes
c Gabriel Torres *lp* William Holden, Ernest Borgnine, Woody Strode, Susan Hayward, Roger Hanin, Warren Vanders

Santee (VAGABOND) 93 (91) min

The best film to date by Nelson, a regular television director since the early sixties, *Santee* is an impressive directorial debut. Influenced by films as diverse as Nicholas Ray's **Run for Cover** (1955), Budd Boetticher's **Comanche Station** (1960) and Sam Peckinpah's **Ride the High Country** (1962), it stars Ford as the horse breeder turned bounty hunter who befriends the son of an outlaw he kills, even though the youngster, Burns, vows to avenge his father. As the two become father and son to each other, it transpires that Ford's son was killed by outlaws long ago and that he subsequently turned obsessive bounty hunter. Momentarily satisfied, Ford quits bounty hunting and puts away his gun, whereupon the sheriff is shot and Burns blames him. Together they take on the gang, the same one that killed Ford's son, and wipe them out, but at the cost of Burns' death which once more leaves

Below: *Burt Lancaster and a mutilated Karl Swenson in Robert Aldrich's savage* Ulzana's Raid.

Ford a tormented man. The simple unadorned script has a classic feel, while Nelson's formal, spare direction gives the film an authority few modern Westerns have achieved.

d Gary Nelson *p* Deno Paoli, Edward Platt *s* Brand Bell
c Donald Morgan *lp* Glenn Ford, Michael Burns, Dana Wynter, Jay Silverheels, Henry Townes, John Larch

Showdown (U) Todd-AO 35 99 min

In this routine film Hudson and Martin are the old friends, sheriff and outlaw respectively, who, having chosen different sides of the fence, resolutely do what is expected of each other. Thus Martin commits a bank robbery and Hudson, married to Martin's ex-girlfriend, sets out after him. The film's major point of interest lies in its use of Todd-AO 35 which gives Laszlo's fine cinematography even greater clarity.

d/p George Seaton *s* Theodore Taylor *c* Ernest Laszlo
lp Rock Hudson, Dean Martin, Susan Clark, Donald Moffat, John McLiam, Charles Baca

To Hell You Preach *aka* Vengeance of a Gunfighter
(MODERN ART PRODUCTIONS) 90 (76) min

An indifferent Western of the 'mud and rags' school with an opportunist hero borrowed from the Italian Western. The only real point of interest is the circularity of Russell's screenplay which has gunfighter Smith impersonate a dead, snakebitten preacher he finds. He is accepted as a preacher and uses the disguise to milk the fashionably muddy town of what riches (sexual and monetary) it possesses, before leaving, only to die of a snakebite in the desert.

d/p Richard Robinson *s* David Allen Russell *c* David Worth *lp* Hagen Smith, Michael Christian, Tim Scott, Kitty Vallacher, Richard Hurst, Orville Sherman

Ulzana's Raid (U) 103 (100) min

Much cut about by its producers and distributors, with alternative versions (often comprising alternate takes of the same scenes) prepared for different markets, *Ulzana's Raid* is one of Aldrich's best films of the seventies and certainly his best Western since **Apache** (1954). Clearly intended as a commentary on both the Vietnam war and the liberalism of previous Indian films that had become so cliche-ridden, *Ulzana's Raid* treats its Indians as cultured savages. Under the leadership of Ulzana (Martinez) they rape and pillage with military precision. Lancaster and Davison are the cynical scout and idealist who quarrel over how best to deal with Ulzana. Sharp's script is savage in its indictment of Davison's liberalism, even if the end, where Davison proves his coming of age by leaving the older man to die, seems forced.

The film's undeserved reputation as a reactionary movie shows just how powerful it is.

d Robert Aldrich *p* Carter De Haven *s* Alan Sharp
c Joseph Biroc *lp* Burt Lancaster, Bruce Davison, Jorge Luke, Richard Jaeckel, Joaquin Martinez, Lloyd Bochner

When the Legends Die (SAGAPONACK FILMS) 105 min

An impressive contemporary Western, made even more so by the strong performances of Forrest as the Indian youth turned rodeo rider and Widmark as his drunken mentor who teaches him the ways of the world as well as of the rodeo ring. Dozier's articulate script carefully eschews any talk of the plight of Indians in modern America; instead Miller presents us with Forrest slowly learning that there is no way of avoiding the problems of life. The ending, in particular, with Forrest quitting the rodeo circuit for life on the reservation, is cleverly done.

d Stuart Millar *p* Gene Lasko *s* Robert Dozier *c* Richard H. Kline *lp* Richard Widmark, Frederic Forrest, Luana Anders, Vito Scotti, Herbert Nelson, John Gruber

Alien Thunder *aka* Dan Candy's Law

(ONYX FILMS INC) 90 min

This is a Canadian version of **Tell Them Willie Boy Is Here** (1969). Sutherland is the mountie who sets out after Chief Dan George, after the first mountie sent to apprehend him for the theft of a cow (taken to prevent Chief Dan George's family from starving) dies in mysterious circumstances.

The year-long chase through the boundless plains of Saskatchewan in the 1890s is beautifully photographed but too often the beauty is at the expense of the drama. It is only at the end when, to the embarrassment of the mounties, a platoon of policemen, complete with cannon, is needed to capture George that the film comes into its own.

d/c Claude Fournier *p* Marie Josee Raymond *s* George Malko *lp* Donald Sutherland, George Tootoosis, Chief Dan George, Kevin McCarthy, Jean Duceppe

Billy Two Hats (ALGONQUIN FILMS; GB) 99 min

An interesting Western, this is marred by Kotcheff's predictable direction. Sharp's script, like that for the more impressive **The Hired Hand** (1971), is concerned with the shifting relationship between two men. This time, however, one is old (Peck) and must learn to depend upon the younger (Arnez) for his safety. Warden is the racist sheriff on their trail.

The film was one of the first to be shot in Israel which, in the mid-seventies, temporarily replaced Spain as 'the cheap place' for budget-conscious Hollywood producers of action movies.

d Ted Kotcheff *p* Norman Jewison, Patrick Palmer *s* Alan Sharp *c* Brian West *lp* Gregory Peck, Desi Arnez Jnr, Jack Warden, Sian Barbara Allen, David Huddleston, John Pearce

Cahill, United States Marshal *aka* Cahill

(BATJAC/WB) pv 102 min

Though this Batjac production tries to make the most of the Wayne persona, it remains a resolutely minor film. Wayne is the marshal who through neglect turns his sons, Grimes and O'Brien, into robbers. Kennedy is the larger than life bandit and Brand, once remembered for his malevolent roles, his much-tamed accomplice. Indeed, the movie is more interesting for its cast, which includes such worthies as Paul Fix, Hank Worden, Jackie Coogan and Royal Dano, than for the performances of either its leads or director.

d Andrew V. McLaglen *p* Michael Wayne *s* Harry Julian Fink, Rita M. Fink *c* Joseph Biroc *lp* John Wayne, George Kennedy, Gary Grimes, Neville Brand, Clay O'Brien, Marie Windsor

The Con Men *orig* Te Deum

(F.P. CINEMATOGRAFICA CANARIA FILM/TECISA; IT, SP) scope 99 (91) min

A comic Italian Western, this variant on the *It's a Mad, Mad, Mad, Mad World* (1963) story, features Palance, Stander and others searching first for a fool gullible enough to buy what they think is a worthless gold mine and then trying to get it back, while all the while a growing number of people are after them, when they realize that the mine is far from worthless. The slim plot quickly breaks under the weight of the endless jokes Palance and company parade for our benefit.

d/co-s Enzo G. Castellari *p* Franco Palaggi, Virgilio De Blasi *co-s* Gianni Simonelli, Tito Carpi, J. Maesso *c* Manolo Rojas *lp* Jack Palance, Timothy Brent, Lionel Stander, F. Romana Coluzzi, Renzo Palmer, Maria Vico Villardo

The Deadly Trackers (CINE FILM) 105 min

A skeleton of two movies that might have been, *The Deadly Trackers* is the film that Sam Fuller was sacked from over irreconcilable differences between him and Harris. All

Richard Harris as the demented sheriff turned bounty hunter in The Deadly Trackers.

Fuller's footage (and his script) was scrapped and Shear hired to remake the film in Mexico (Fuller had been shooting in Spain). Shear's completed film was then savaged by Warners.

Heller's rewrite of Fuller's script features Harris as a once peaceable sheriff on the trail of a bunch of outlaws, led by Taylor, who've murdered his wife and son. Lettieri is the Mexican law officer who both helps and hinders Harris. Fullerian themes abound, the hero as renegade and the concern with nationality, for example. These are just two of the similarities to **Run of the Arrow** (1957), while at the same time the film has much of the look of Shear's earlier films, notably *The Todd Killings* (1970), but it is Harris' macho interpretation of his role – 'pastiche Brando' as one critic put it – that dominates and deforms the film.

As a mark of the economies of post production forced on the film by the costly abandonment of the original footage, the uncredited music is mostly Jerry Fielding's score for **The Wild Bunch** (1969).

d Barry Shear *p* Fouad Said *s* Lukas Heller *c* Gabriel Tomes *lp* Richard Harris, Rod Taylor, Al Lettieri, Neville Brand, William Smith, Paul Benjamin

Kid Blue (MARVIN SCHWARZ PRODUCTIONS) pv 100 min

From its hilarious opening with Hopper's outlaw jumping on the roof of a train as part of a would-be train robbery and promptly falling off, to his final attempted getaway on an 'aerocycle', this is a magical Western. Hopper is the failed minor desperado who turns solid citizen and fails at that too. Calmly orchestrated by Frawley, who turns even the smallest of parts into rounded characters and allows his story to develop out of such characters, *Kid Blue* never strains for meaning. Even the web of references to the Greece of mythology is never too pointed. Oates, as the seeker of manly friendships, Boyle, as the preacher, Johnson (cleverly cast against type), as the sheriff and Rule, offer solid support.

The conveyor belt full of Santa Claus ashtrays, in the factory where Hopper briefly works and then fails to rob, is surely the saddest and funniest image of the closing-in of the frontier in recent Westerns.

d James Frawley *p* Marvin Schwarz *s* Edwin Shrake *c* Billy Williams *lp* Dennis Hopper, Warren Oates, Peter Boyle, Janice Rule, Clifton James, Ben Johnson

Lovin' Molly *aka* The Wild and the Sweet

(STEPHEN FRIEDMAN PRODUCTIONS) 98 min

Based on a novel by Larry McMurtry, this is a peculiar cross between *Carnal Knowledge* (1971) and *The Last Picture Show*

Burt Reynolds and Sarah Miles in The Man Who Loved Cat Dancing.

(1971) which was also based on a McMurtry novel. Danner, who gives a superb performance, is the Texas woman who refuses to choose between the strait-laced Perkins and Bridges' drifter. Instead, after marrying someone else, she beds both of them in turn over a period of some 40 years. Lumet directs with little feeling for the rolling plains of Texas (for which he was publicly attacked by McMurtry).

d Sidney Lumet *p/s* Stephen Friedman *c* Edward Brown *lp* Blythe Danner, Anthony Perkins, Beau Bridges, Edward Binns, Susan Sarandon, Conrad Fowkes

The Man Who Loved Cat Dancing
(MGM) pv 114 (110) min
An inept Western, this is as gimmick-ridden as its title. Reynolds is the outlaw on the run for murder – he shot and killed the man who raped his Indian wife, Cat Dancing – and Miles the woman running away from her husband who slowly falls for him. Cobb is the bounty hunter with a heart of gold and Warden (as dependable as ever) and Hopkins, fellow outlaws of Reynolds. Sarafian anonymously directs the strangely vapid Perry script that was reportedly re-written by Miles' husband, writer Robert Bolt.

d Richard C. Sarafian *co-p* Martin Poll *s/co-p* Eleanor Perry *c* Harry Stradling Jnr *lp* Burt Reynolds, Sarah Miles, Lee J. Cobb, Jack Warden, George Hamilton, Bo Hopkins

My Name Is Nobody *orig* Il Mio Nome E Nessuno
(RAFRAN CINEMATOGRAFICA/LES FILMS JAQUES LEITIENNE/
LA SOCIETE ALCINTER/LA SOCIETE IMP. EX. CI./
RIALTO FILM PREBEN PHILIPSEN; IT, FR, WG) 116 min
This is a minor but enjoyable Western. Although it is officially directed by Valerii, its marked difference from Valerii's other films (such as the remarkable **The Price of Power,** 1969) and its close resemblance to those of Sergio Leone, who 'supervised' its making, make it clear that Leone's supervision was active rather than passive. As such it is a fitting 'last Western' by Leone.

The script follows Fonda as a famous gunfighter in 1899 planning to retire to Europe once he's avenged the death of his

Warren Oates, Dennis Hopper and a conveyor belt of Santa Claus ashtrays in James Frawley's magnificent Kid Blue.

brother. What makes the film so engaging, however, is Leone's delightful parodying of his earlier films and those of Sam Peckinpah. This last strand in the movie leads to an hilarious confrontation of Fonda and a 150-strong Wild Bunch (which betters even the performances of series characters such as Gene Autry and Hopalong Cassidy in taking on massive odds). This confrontation is engineered by Hill's admiring Nobody as part of his plan to remind people how great a gunfighter Fonda is before killing him and so becoming a Somebody.

A final ironic touch has Fonda warning Hill, in a letter written on board his ship to Europe, of the dangers that lie ahead for him now that their trick has worked.

d Tonino Valerii *p* Claudio Mancini *s* Ernesto Gastaldi *c* Giuseppe Ruzzolini, Armando Nannuzzi *lp* Henry Fonda, Terence Hill (Mario Girotti), Leo Gordon, R.G. Armstrong, Piero Lulli

The New Land *orig* Nybyggarna *aka* Unto a Good Land
(S.F. PRODUKTION; SWEDEN) 205 (191) min
A sequel to **The Emigrants** (1970), this film covers the first decade of the settlement the Swedish pioneers founded in Minnesota in the middle of the nineteenth century. It was less enthusiastically received than the first film, perhaps because its story of perseverance and endurance in the face of endless hardship seemed so static. Troell's direction, however, is far better, bringing the characters that play the Oskar family much more to life; before *The Emigrants*, Troell had been a documentary film-maker and, as such, was unused to working with actors.

d/co-s/c Jan Troell *co-s* Bengt Forslund *lp* Max von Sydow, Liv Ullman, Eddie Axberg, Pierre Lindstedt, Oscar Ljung, Per Oscarsson

One Little Indian (WALT DISNEY) 91 min
Even Garner's elegantly humorous performance as the deserter on the run from the army, whose heart of gold is touched by the plight of plucky runaway O'Brien, can't compensate for the blandness of this Disney production. Miles is the woman who makes a family of them and Rosebud the camel whose death, after outrunning the Cavalry, is the emotional climax of the film.

d Bernard McEveety *p* Winston Hibler *s* Harry Spalding *c* Charles F. Wheeler *lp* James Garner, Vera Miles, Pat Hingle, Morgan Woodward, John Doucette, Clay O'Brien

Pat Garrett and Billy the Kid (MGM) pv 106 min

A masterpiece, despite being mangled, like **Major Dundee** (1965), by its production company. Originally this static re-telling of the death of Billy the Kid (Kristofferson) at the hands of Pat Garrett (Coburn) was to have consisted of a long flashback from the murder of Coburn by his former allies. But even shorn of this structuring device, it remains the most impressive interpretation (as opposed to simple retelling) of the Billy the Kid myth. In place of the father-son relationship of Arthur Penn's **The Left Handed Gun** (1958) and the theme of the coming of civilization to the West (represented in part by law and order) that Ford articulates in **My Darling Clementine** (1946), Peckinpah offers what one critic has called 'a paralysed epic'. Coburn is on the side of law and order but a law and order that is depicted as little but legalized banditry and which he serves only to retain his freedom. Kristofferson just 'lights out for the territory', criss-crossing Peckinpah's dusty South-West aimlessly like a bewildered knight of yore looking for the Holy Grail to give his wanderings some purpose. The men are linked by Dylan's Alias, a mysterious child-like innocent observer whose songs (on the soundtrack) mythologize but never explain the travails of Billy and Garrett. Photographed in the burnished colours of a perpetual sunset by Coquillon and punctuated by virtuoso action-pieces and elegiac moments such as the prolonged death of Pickens during which, mortally wounded, he stumbles towards the river he had hoped to 'drift out of the territory on', which only intensify the static feel of the film, *Pat Garrett and Billy the Kid* is both the most beautiful looking and saddest of Peckinpah's films. Everything seems to take place in the past and lead inevitably to the moment where Coburn signals his betrayal of himself, by shooting his own dusty reflection after shooting Kristofferson. This film is essential viewing.

d Sam Peckinpah *p* Gordon Carroll *s* Rudolph Wurlitzer *c* John Coquillon *lp* James Coburn, Kris Kristofferson, Bob Dylan, Richard Jaeckel, Katy Jurado, Slim Pickens

The Soul of Nigger Charley (PAR) pv 109 min

A sequel to the phenomenally successful **The Legend of Nigger Charley** (1972), this is directed by Spangler, the producer of the earlier film. Williamson and Martin reprise their roles as the athletic but bumbling freed slaves. This time they're intent on freeing 71 slaves held by Hagen in a colony for former members of the Confederacy in Mexico. They are assisted by Mexican bandido Armendariz (as charming a bandit as the many impersonated by his late father). The extensive battle sequences are particularly bloody.

d/p Larry G. Spangler *s* Harold Stone *c* Richard C. Glonner *lp* Fred Williamson, D'Urville Martin, Kevin Hagen, Pedro Armendariz Jnr, Denise Nicholas, George Allen

To Kill or to Die orig Il Mio Nome E Shanghai Joe (CBA; IT) scope 98 min

A direct steal from David Carradine's successful *Kung Fu* teleseries and draining all resonance from the idea of a Buddhist monk in the West, this is a tedious, gimmicky film. Kinski's spectacular death, from knife wounds from the many knives he carries in the lining of his cloak, is the only moment of real excitement. The silly plot has Lee first suffer racism in his attempts to become a cowboy and then find himself herding peons across the border for sale as slaves before finally turning on his master.

d/co-s Mario Caiano *p* Renato Angiolini, Roberto Bessi *co-s* Fabrizio Trifone Trecca *c* Guglielmo Mancori *lp* Chen Lee, Carla Romanelli, Klaus Kinski, Katsutoshi Mikuriya, Giacomo Rossi Stuart, Gordon Mitchell

The Train Robbers (BATJAC) pv 92 min

Another minor Wayne Western. Kennedy's script has echoes of his earlier and superior scripts for Boetticher **Ride Lonesome** (1959) and **Comanche Station** (1960), but his direction neither gives any resonance to the desires for stability of Wayne, Johnson and Taylor, nor mocks their pretensions with the vigour he displays in his superb comic Westerns, **Support Your Local Sheriff** (1968) and **Support Your Local Gunfighter** (1971). Wayne and company are hired by Ann-Margret to recover gold supposedly stolen by her husband which she claims she intends to return using the reward to educate her daughter. But when, after recovering the gold and defeating the 'husband's' ex-partners who are also after the gold, the trio gallantly forego their finders' fee, a Pinkerton's agent pops up to tell them that she's just another con artist.

d/s Burt Kennedy *p* Michael Wayne *c* William H. Clothier *lp* John Wayne, Ann-Margret, Rod Tayor, Ben Johnson, Bobby Vinton, Christopher George

Westworld (MGM) pv 89 min

The classic Science Fiction theme of the robot as man's slave on the verge of self-emancipation is here neatly inserted into the thriller/Western format by Crichton. Benjamin is suitably wooden as the holiday-maker exploring the delights of the

Far left: R. G. Armstrong and Kris Kristofferson in Sam Peckinpah's Pat Garrett and Billy the Kid.

Cleavon Little eyes Madeline Kahn's suggestion with trepidation in Blazing Saddles, *the most successful Western of all time.*

Wild West who is suddenly confronted with a 'real' gunman to draw against rather than a slave robot to kill at will. Brynner – a marvellous piece of casting – is superb as the cold, cold robot who turns on its creators. The sequel, *Futureworld* (1976) is far less successful.

d/s Michael Crichton   *p* Paul N. Lazarus   *c* Gene Polito
lp Yul Brynner, Richard Benjamin, James Brolin, Norman Bartold, Allen Oppenheimer, Victoria Shaw

1974

The Apple Dumpling Gang   (WALT DISNEY)   100 min
This amiable Disney Western is less cloying and better plotted than usual. Bixby (soon to achieve a fame of sorts as the Incredible Hulk's better half) is the gambler tricked into becoming the guardian of three orphaned children who then just happen to stumble on a goldmine. Clark is the stagecoach driver who tames Bixby and turns him into a farmer after various baddies' plots to take over the guardianship of the children are stopped. A sequel followed in 1979, **The Apple Dumpling Gang Rides Again.**

d Norman Tokar   *p* Bill Anderson   *s* Don Tait   *c* Frank Phillips   *lp* Bill Bixby, Susan Clark, Don Knott, Tim Conway, Slim Pickens, Harry Morgan

Blazing Saddles   (CROSSBOW)   pv   93 min
A glorious celebration of 'bad taste', from farting cowboys to black sexual stereotypes and ending with an anarchic musical extravaganza, this is no simple parody Western but a marvellous collection of jokes, visual and verbal, strung together around the idea of the Western. Little is the blackman appointed sheriff of Rock Ridge to undermine the citizens' morale so they'll sell their land cheap to speculator Brooks who, in cahoots with the Governor (Brooks again), is planning to route a railroad through the town. When the town turns against Little, the jail's one prisoner, the once legendary gunman turned drunkard (Wilder) comes to his aid. Rather like a Marx Brothers film, the bits and pieces don't quite fit together, but Brooks' overkill methods produce more splendid sequences than one would expect: Kahn's irresistible parody of a Dietrich torch song (and her in between verses question 'Is that a ten-gallon hat or are you just enjoying yourself?'), the cardboard set the townspeople trick the soldiers with, Wilder's creative assembly, in the one role, of Western heroes from **Rio Bravo** (1959) to **Cat Ballou** (1965) and lastly, though it comes first, Frankie Laine's delicious portmanteau Western song celebrating a hero who 'rode a blazing saddle'.

Interestingly most Western critics dammed the film with faint praise, as though to parody the Western was to demean it. On the contrary, *Blazing Saddles* demonstrates both the flexibility of the genre and the tastes of the seventies: by 1983 it had become the top grossing Western of all time.

d/co-s Mel Brooks   *p* Michael Hertzberg   *co-s* Norman Steinberg, Andrew Bergman, Richard Pryor, Alan Unger   *c* Joseph Biroc   *lp* Cleavon Little, Gene Wilder, Slim Pickens, Mel Brooks, Madeline Kahn, Harvey Korman

Blood Money
(SHAW BROTHERS/COMPAGNIA CINEMATOGRAFICA CHAMPION/ MIDEGA FILM/HARBOR PRODUCTIONS; HONG KONG, IT, SP, US)
pv   100 min
The first Hong Kong-Italian Western, *Blood Money* is an awful movie, an inept mix of the delicate balletics of Kung Fu movies and the more brutal Spaghetti calisthenics. The plot is the oft-used one of a group of people each contributing bits of a map (here tattooes) detailing the whereabouts of a hidden fortune. Van Cleef stumbles bravely through to the end, his grin fixed as he pores over the various tattooes embossed on four ladies backsides before, with evident relief, taking out his usual motley collection of guns and shooting everyone in sight.

d Anthony M. Dawson (Antonio Margheriti)   *p* Run Run Shaw, Gustave Berne   *s* Barth Jules Sussman   *c* Alejandro Ulloa   *lp* Lee Van Cleef, Lo Lieh, Karen Yeh (Yeh Ling Chih), Julian Ugarte, Goyo Peralta, Al Tung

Boss Nigger *aka* The Black Bounty Killer
(BOSS PRODUCTIONS)   Todd-AO 35   92 (87) min
An interesting transitional black Western, this bridges the gap between Williamson's violent Nigger Charley films (**Legend of,** 1972 and **Soul of,** 1973) and the gentle comedy of his **Adios Amigo** (1975). The film sees writer/producer/star Williamson toning down the hysteria of his first outings. Thus, though the screenplay has Williamson and Martin terrorizing a frontier town that a band of outlaws take refuge in, the action is as much comic as violent. Arnold's jerky direction is confusing at times.

The film was the last one made by one-time series star Don 'Red' Barry.

d/co-p Jack Arnold   *co-p/s* Fred Williamson   *c* Bob Caramico   *lp* Fred Williamson, D'Urville Martin, R. G. Armstrong, William Smith, Carmen Hayworth, Barbara Leigh

The Castaway Cowboy   (WALT DISNEY)   91 min
A lacklustre companion piece to **One Little Indian** (1973), this Disney Western is set on a Hawaiian island. The locale isn't as novel as it might seem, having been used off and on since at least the time of **Hawaiian Buckaroo** (1938), and the plot is a well-used one. Culp is the baddie who lends money to Miles and then tries to disrupt her plans so she can't repay him and he'll get her property. Garner is the Texan of the title who takes on the daunting task of transforming Miles' potato farm into a cattle ranch and her native helpers into cowboys.

d Vincent McEveety   *p* Ron Miller, Winston Hibler   *s* Don Tait   *c* Andrew Jackson   *lp* James Garner, Vera Miles, Robert Culp, Eric Shea, Elizabeth Smith, Manu Tupou

Drummer of Vengeance   (TIMES FILM; GB)   scope   89 min
This is a prosaic Italian (in substance if not in country of origin) Western. Hardin is the 'stranger' hot on the heels of the six men who murdered his wife and child. The numerous killings that punctuate the film are handled mechanically with only Hardin masquerading as the grave digger and calling for vengeance against himself as an interesting departure from the predictable pattern of death. Brazzi, in his only Western, makes a suitably oily gangleader masquerading as the sheriff.

d/p/s Robert Paget   *c* Alvaro Lanzone   *lp* Ty Hardin, Rossano Brazzi, Craig Hill, Gordon Mitchell, Edda di Benedetta, Rosalda Neri

Rancho Deluxe (EK CORPORATION) 94 min

A highly self-conscious modern Western in which characters discuss the meaning of **Cheyenne Autumn** (1964) and the rock group Humble Pie, as they play at being 'the last of the plainsmen'. Written by McGuane (who also scripted the enigmatic **The Missouri Breaks,** 1976), it features Easterner Bridges and Waterston's Indian as latter-day rustlers who delight in stealing cattle from James' pompous Montana rancher and playing childish pranks all the while. Pickens is marvellous as the seemingly decrepit detective who, to everyone's surprise, catches them when his daughter, whom cowboy-turned-rustler Stanton has fallen for, betrays them.

A charming film, less for the script's quirkiness than for the wealth of incidental detail: a Navajo rug being vacuum-cleaned, a bull in a Holiday Inn bedroom and a Western flickering on an unwatched television screen that speaks oceans about the commercialization of the West.

d Frank Perry   *p* Elliott Kastner   *s* Thomas McGuane *c* William A. Fraker   *lp* Jeff Bridges, Sam Waterston, Elizabeth Ashley, Clifton James, Slim Pickens, Harry Dean Stanton

The Spikes Gang

(MIRISCH/DUO/SANDFORD PRODUCTIONS) 96 min

To all intents and purposes, this is a sequel to **Bad Company** (1972). Grimes and Howard are the youths who first shelter Marvin's wounded outlaw and then, inspired by his exciting descriptions of the outlaw life, are led by him into an ever-darkening world of banditry. Ravetch and Frank's script centres on the boys, but it is Marvin as Harry Spikes, a man acutely aware that his days are numbered – 'I'm on my way to meet my maker, but I ain't ready for him yet' – who steals the film. The result is a familiar-sounding film (but odd looking; it was shot in Spain).

Jeff Bridges and Sam Waterston as the would-be last of the rustlers in Frank Perry's gentle contemporary Western, Rancho Deluxe.

d Richard Fleischer   *p* Walter Mirisch   *s* Irving Ravetch, Harriet Frank   *c* Brian West   *lp* Lee Marvin, Gary Grimes, Ron Howard, Arthur Hunnicutt, Charles Martin Smith, Noah Beery Jnr

Zandy's Bride (WB) pv 116 min

Similar in theme to **Heartland** (1979), this beautiful-looking frontier romance stars Ullman as the mail-order bride and Hackman as the gruff Californian rancher she mellows. However, unlike *Heartland*, which allowed its characters space to breathe and so animate the slim story, Norman's screenplay is too mechanical, forever explaining why its characters behave as they do, and in the end the film becomes little but a string of frontier incidents.

Ullman, who also appeared in Troell's **The Emigrants** (1970) and **The New Land** (1973), copes best with Troell's unemphatic direction.

d Jan Troell   *p* Harvey Matofsky   *s* Marc Norman *c* Jordan Croneweth   *lp* Gene Hackman, Liv Ullman, Sam Bottoms, Eileen Heckart, Susan Tyrrell

Adios Amigo (ATLAS PRODUCTIONS) pv 87 min

A surprisingly gentle film, written, produced and directed by Williamson who first established himself with the far more violent Nigger Charley films, **Legend of** (1972) and **Soul of** (1973). In place of the violence and black-white animosity that was central to those, Williamson offers Pryor and his street jive who makes the wheeling, dealing con man he plays so irresistible. He and Williamson, always left holding the bag when Pryor's schemes backfire, as they always do, ease their way through a stagecoach robbery, a land swindle and a jailbreak.

Poorly mounted and indifferently directed, the film nonetheless marked a real shift in blaxploitation pictures, away from violence and towards humour.

d/p/s Fred Williamson   *c* Tony Palmieri   *lp* Fred Williamson, Richard Pryor, James Brown, Robert Phillips, Mike Henry, Suhaila Farhat

Bite the Bullet (PERSKY-BRIGHT/VISTA) pv 131 min

An attempt by writer/producer/director Brooks to recapture the success of **The Professionals** (1966), *Bite the Bullet* is an equally off-beat but less compelling movie. Structured around a 700-mile horse race at the turn of the century, its heroes, Hackman and Coburn, see the race as an endurance test against which they measure themselves. The other entrants in the race include Bergen and Johnson who, as usual, produces

Liv Ullman as the mail order bride and Gene Hackman as the gruff rancher who sends for her in Jan Troell's Zandy's Bride.

a splendid performance as the cowboy who just wants to amount to something. The plot, like the characters, stops and starts enough times for Brooks to indulge himself in vitriolic commentaries on mankind and its stupidity.

d/p/s Richard Brooks   *c* Harry Stradling Jnr   *lp* Gene Hackman, Candice Bergen, James Coburn, Ben Johnson, Ian Bannen, Jan Michael Vincent

Breakheart Pass (EK CORPORATION) 94 min
This is a misguided trainbound detective story cast in the form of a Western. MacLean's screenplay pays too much homage to the detective elements to give the characters a chance to do anything but hold in their stomachs as they pass each other in the corridors. Bronson is the undercover agent and Johnson the marshal involved in a conspiracy to relieve the train of its consignment of gold disguised as medicine.

d Tom Gries   *p* Jerry Gershwin   *s* Alistair MacLean
c Lucien Ballard   *lp* Charles Bronson, Ben Johnson, Jill Ireland, Richard Crenna, Charles Durning, Roy Jenson

From Noon Till Three (FRANKOVICH-SELF) 99 min
Despite its intriguing and novel idea, this is neither successful as a comic Western nor as a Bronson vehicle. He's the two-bit outlaw who, after his death is transformed into a legend by a one-time mistress, Ireland. She's so successful with her myth-building that she transforms her brief liaison into a vast sprawling commercial empire. Whereupon Bronson, who wasn't dead at all, returns only to be not recognized by all concerned, even Ireland. Fittingly, he ends up in a lunatic asylum where his claim to be the famous Graham Dorsey is accepted without comment. Sadly neither Gilroy's direction nor his cast do justice to his literate and, at times, very funny script.

d/s Frank D. Gilroy   *p* M. J. Frankovich, William Self
c Lucien Ballard   *lp* Charles Bronson, Jill Ireland, Douglas V. Fowley, Stan Haze, Damon Douglas, Hector Morales

Hearts of the West *aka* Hollywood Cowboy
(MGM) 103 min
A charming film that manages both to gently guy the wonderful world of Hollywood in which 'The Kid, a colt in

Jeff Bridges as the would-be Zane Grey and part-time stuntman leaps through a pane of sugar glass in the beguiling Hearts of the West.

either ham-like fist, scattered lead at the retreating dust' is quality prose, and to celebrate the cheap and nasty world of the series Western. Bridges is the would-be Zane Grey who travels to Hollywood to try and get work as a writer. With the help of Danner's magnificent Girl Friday, he supports himself doing stuntwork, even briefly becoming a series Western star, before, in a marvellously contrived double-edged ending, he both gets to be published and to be rescued by fading cowboy star Griffith who, dressed in full regalia, outshoots the gangsters who are after Bridges, even though he's only got blanks and they real bullets. Bridges and Danner are superb as the dreamers and idealists, gazing wistfully at the tawdry neon spires of Hollywood, but it is Griffith, as the over-the-hill cowboy star who still believes in himself, in the Western and in Hollywood, who is the emotional centre of the film. This is a magnificent film.

d Howard Zieff   *p* Tony Bill   *s* Rob Thompson   *c* Mario Tosi   *lp* Jeff Bridges, Blythe Danner, Andy Griffith, Donald Pleasence, Alan Arkin, Richard B. Shull

Jessie's Girls *aka* Wanted Women
(MANSON DISTRIBUTING CORPORATION) 84 min
This is a mediocre, down-market version of **Hannie Caulder** (1971) from Adamson, a director of exploitation quickies who briefly specialized in the Western in the seventies. Currie is the wife who, with the assistance of an unlikely trio of female prisoners (a gunslinger, a prostitute and an Indian maid) she has rescued, goes after the man who killed her husband and raped her. Currie's performance is undistinguished and Adamson's direction uninspired.

d/co-p Al Adamson   *co-p* Michael F. Goldman   *s* Budd Donnelly   *c* Gary Graver   *lp* Sondra Currie, Geoffrey Land, Ben Frank, Jennifer Bishop, Regina Carroll, Joe Cortese

Mackintosh and T. J. (PENLAND PRODUCTIONS) 96 min
Made nearly a quarter of a century after **Son of Paleface** (1952), his last starring role, this movie marked the return of Rogers to the silver screen. Shot in Texas, this is a family film with Rogers as a hard-working, bible-thumping cowboy, who plays father to O'Brien's drifter of a teenager. Chomsky directs his strong cast well, leaving Savage's script to make its points along the way, helped by Waylon Jennings' cycle of songs. But it is Rogers, plain denims replacing the gaudy costumes of old, who gives the movie its quiet dignity.

d Marvin M. Chomsky   *p* Tim Penland   *s* Paul Savage
c Terry Mead   *lp* Roy Rogers, Clay O'Brien, Billy 'Green' Bush, Joan Hackett, Andrew Robinson, Walter Barnes

The Master Gunfighter
(AVONDALE PRODUCTIONS) pv 121 (110) min
For this sterile revenge Western (based on the Samurai film, *Goyokin*, 1969), Laughlin retains the bland persona that served him so well in **Billy Jack** (1971) and *The Trial of Billy Jack* (1974), both of which were astoundingly successful at the box office. Here, he's the master gunman of the title, seeking revenge (with both a Samurai sword and a gun) on his father-in-law who he feels has sullied the family name. Angarda is the villainous patriarch.

The direction, officially credited to Laughlin's nine-year-old son, Frank, is so banal that even veteran Western cinematographer Marta can do little to enliven the film.

d Frank Laughlin (Tom Laughlin)   *p* Philip L. Parslow
s Harold Lapland   *c* Jack A. Marta   *lp* Tom Laughlin, Ron O'Neal, Lincoln Kilpatrick, Barbara Carrera, Victor Campos, Richard Angarda

Posse (BRYNA) pv 93 min
This quirky and enjoyable Western is certainly the best of Douglas' occasional forays into direction. It features Douglas as a marshal and would-be State Senator on the trail of Dern's

laconic outlaw in the middle of an election campaign. Douglas intends to make political capital out of the hunt, but quickly finds that he's met his match in Dern who is able to manipulate the increasingly weary posse far better than he. First, with Douglas as his hostage, Dern gets the posse to restore the $40,000 they found on him. Then, when they've looted a nearby town to get the money, he allows them to share it between themselves, so transforming them from a posse to replacements for the gang they decimated at the film's beginning. Cleverly and logically written, the film has the added advantage of a superb performance from Dern.

On Douglas' instructions, the part of the handicapped newspaper editor was specially written for Stacy who had just lost an arm and a leg in an accident.

d/p Kirk Douglas   *s* William Roberts, Christopher Knopf
c Fred Koenekamp   *lp* Kirk Douglas, Bruce Dern, Bo Hopkins, James Stacy, Luke Askew, David Canary

Rooster Cogburn   (U)   pv   108 min

A sequel to the phenomenally successful **True Grit** (1969). Wayne reprised his role as the gruff, one-eyed, paunchy marshal, here relieved of his badge at the film's beginning for being too willing to deal out death rather than make arrests. But he is given a chance of re-instatement if he apprehends Jordan and his gang who've hijacked a wagon-load of nitro-glycerine. Accompanied, much to his chagrin, by Hepburn (at her *African Queen* best as the strong-willed, bible-thumping daughter of one of the gang's victims), he accomplishes the task. The film is effectively, if anonymously, directed with Hepburn and Wayne (enthusiastically over-acting in the tradition of Robert Newton) obviously relishing their roles. Although the film overcame the jinx that seems to hang over sequels, its origins as an exploitable formula remain too visible for the movie to be wholly successful. In short, it's a film whose parts are decidedly better than its whole.

d Stuart Millar   *p* Hal B. Wallis   *s* Martin Julien
c Harry Stradling Jnr   *lp* John Wayne, Katharine Hepburn, Anthony Zerbe, Richard Jordan, John McIntire, Strother Martin

Take a Hard Ride

(FOX FANFARE MUSIC/EURO-GENERAL; US, IT)   103 (93) min
A Hollywood Spaghetti Western shot in the Canary Islands, *Take a Hard Ride* leavens its avalance of corpses with a deft, if surprising, touch of humour. Brown and Williamson, who gives a fine laconic performance as the black gambler, are the uneasy guardians of $86,000 and the target for an ever-growing band of would-be thieves led by Van Cleef's bounty hunter. The second unit direcion and stunt work is by Hal Needham who subsequently, alone and in partnership with Burt Reynolds, was to create a sub-division of the genre with his 'good ole boy' adventure films set in the modern south like *Smokey and the Bandit* (1977).

d Anthony M. Dawson (Antonio Margheriti)   *p* Harry Bernsen   *s* Eric Bercovici, Jerry Ludwig   *c* Riccardo Pallottini   *lp* Jim Brown, Lee Van Cleef, Fred Williamson, Catherine Spaak, Jim Kelly, Dana Andrews

Winterhawk

(CHARLES B. PIERCE PRODUCTIONS)   scope   98 (87) min
Clearly made with the best of intentions this routine film features Dante as the Blackfoot Indian who kidnaps a white woman and evades the posses of inflamed settlers who set out after him. The authentic feel of the film – it was shot on location with assistance from Indian organizations – is marred by the melodramatic plot – the fleeing couple fall in love – and Pierce's needless lionizing of his Indians (and over-reliance on slow motion). The result is a children's film that wastes its strong cast.

Left: *Bruce Dern as the outlaw who upsets Kirk Douglas' election plans in* Posse.

d/p/s Charles B. Pierce   *c* Jim Roberson   *lp* Michael Dante, Leif Erickson, Woody Strode, Denver Pyle, Elisha Cook Jnr, L. Q. Jones

Baker's Hawk   (DOTY-DAYTON)   105 min

Probably the best of the flood of 'Wilderness' pictures that were made by numerous independent companies in the seventies to capitalize on the middle American family audiences that Hollywood was no longer servicing, with Westerns at least. Most were crudely-made hymns to simple values; Dayton's (his directorial debut) is that much more carefully put together and the result is a noticeably superior film, reminiscent of **Shane** (1953) in some respects. Walker, Baker and young Montgomery are the family who take up arms in defence of hermit Ives when he's set upon by vigilantes. Even the end is less fluffy than most wilderness epics: Ives' life is saved but he's still forced to move on.

d/p Lyman D. Dayton   *s* Dan Greer, Hal Harrison Jnr
c Bernie Abrahamson   *lp* Clint Walker, Burl Ives, Diane Baker, Lee H. Montgomery, Alan Young, Taylor Lacher

Bobbi Jo and the Outlaw

(CALDWELL PRODUCTIONS)   89 min
The maniacal performance of Graham can't lift this silly youth-exploitation movie. Gortner is the quick-draw artist in contemporary New Mexico who believes himself to be the re-incarnation of Billy the Kid and goes on a killing spree. Even the car crashes are tame.

d/p Mark L. Lester   *s* Vernon Zimmerman   *c* Stanley Wright   *lp* Marjoe Gortner, Lynda Carter, Jesse Vint, Merrie Lynn Ross, Gerrit Graham, Peggie Stewart

Buffalo Bill and the Indians, or Sitting Bull's History Lesson

(DINO DE LAURENTIIS CORPORATION/LION'S GATE FILMS/TALENT ASSOCIATES-NORTON SIMON)   pv   123 min
Altman's most schematic and least interesting film, *Buffalo Bill* is far better at exposing the fakery and showbiz razzamataz of its title character than in giving its audience a history lesson of any sort. Newman is more than adequate in

the title role as the guilty creator of a showbiz legend yearning for authenticity in his show but aware that his audiences will not accept it, while Kaquitts is enigmatic as Sitting Bull, demanding nothing less than the truth, if not of Newman's Barnum and Baily world then of history. Lancaster is Buntline, Newman's mythologizer, Grey his callous promoter interested only in Kaquitts' box-office potential, and Keitel Newman's naive nephew.

d/p/co-s Robert Altman   *co-s* Alan Rudolph   *c* Paul Lohmann   *lp* Paul Newman, Joel Grey, Burt Lancaster, Harvey Keitel, Geraldine Chaplin, Frank Kaquitts

The Duchess and the Dirtwater Fox
(FOX)   pv   104 min

Segal once more parades his bruised smile as the bungling gambler who partners Hawn's whore-with-a-heart-of-gold in this fumbling comedy Western. Frank quickly runs out of ideas, but the occasional scene (Hawn and Segal hiding from a posse by posing as guests at a Jewish wedding for example) suggests that the film could have been far better, if Frank hadn't relied so much on the natural charm of his principals.

d/p/co-s Melvin Frank   *co-s* Barry Sandler, Jack Rose   *c* Joseph Biroc   *lp* George Segal, Goldie Hawn, Conrad Janis, Thayer David, Roy Jenson, Bob Hoy

The Great Scout and Cathouse Thursday
(KEEP FILMS/AMERICAN INTERNATIONAL PICTURES)   92 min

Reed as the Harvard-educated Indian just about sums up the level of humour in this wooden Western. Together with ex-scout and trapper Marvin and side-kick Martin (as crotchety as ever) he seeks to retrieve gold stolen from Marvin by Culp long ago. Lenz does well as the whore (the Thursday of the title) who falls for Marvin.

d Don Taylor   *p* Jules Buck, David Korda   *s* Richard Shapiro   *c* Alex Phillips Jnr   *lp* Lee Marvin, Oliver Reed, Robert Culp, Kay Lenz, Elizabeth Ashley, Strother Martin

The Last Hard Men   (FOX)   PV   97 min

Based on a novel by Western aficionado Brian Garfield, this is a slapdash Western. Constructed in the revenge mould with the evil Coburn out to get the good retired marshal who imprisoned him, Heston, it suffers from McLaglen's meandering direction. He tries too hard to give the film a contemporary relevance through insistence on details that signal the passing of the West, like automobiles, and leaves his principals too much to their own devices.

d Andrew V. McLaglen   *p* Russell Thacher, Walter Seltzer   *s* Guerdon Trueblood   *c* Duke Callaghan   *lp* Charlton Heston, James Coburn, Barbara Hershey, Christopher Mitchum, Jorge Rivero, Michael Parks

Mad Dog Morgan *aka* Mad Dog
(MAD DOG PTY FOR MOTION PICTURE PRODUCTIONS; AUSTRALIA)   pv   110 (95) min

A powerful Australian Western, this version of the Ned Kelly story is dominated by Hopper's marvellous performance in the title role. He's a prospector who falls on hard times during the Victorian Gold Rush of 1854 and turns to robbery. After his release from prison, where he's served a six-year sentence, he teams up with Gulpilil's half-caste Aborigine and becomes the Jesse James of New South Wales. However, increasingly his thoughts turn to revenge for his overlong imprisonment and so begins his slow journey to destruction, until, finally, knowing the house he takes refuge in to be surrounded, he walks into a fusillade of bullets.

Mora's direction neatly contrasts the beauty of the landscape with the petty brutalities of the humans who inhabit it, just as Hopper catches the inexorable shift from charming innocence to sheer desperation of his character. The result is a superior outback Western, especially when compared to the lacklustre **Ned Kelly** (1970).

d/s Philippe Mora   *p* Jeremy Thomas   *c* Mike Molloy   *lp* Dennis Hopper, Jack Thompson, David Gulpilil, Frank Thring, Michael Pate, Wallace Eaton

The Missouri Breaks   (EK)   126 min

It's instructive to compare *The Missouri Breaks* with Sergio Leone's masterpiece, **Once upon a Time in the West** (1968). Leone's film, for all its mysteries and complications, is a bleak and bitter, but straightforward, account of the corruption of the West by Eastern money. Penn's film, though it has an element of this in it (as do many Hollywood Westerns of the seventies), giving it the feel of an oft-told tale, is far more committed to the uniqueness of its characters and less to the

Marlon Brando (left) and Jack Nicholson as the odd couple in the magnificent The Missouri Breaks.

declining fortunes of the West. As such, the quaintness of McGuane's screenplay and the film's quirkily presented characters, simply cannot be unravelled; unlike Leone's characters, they just are. Such an approach is potentially dangerous, as the seriously flawed **Heaven's Gate** (1980) demonstrates, but, in the hand of Penn, the results are breathtaking. Indeed the film's only major failing was at the box office, which presumably further depressed the market for Western screenplays in Hollywood.

The film opens with what is apparently a Fourth of July celebration that turns out to be the hanging of a rustler (for the good of his soul) by McLiam's pompous and pious cattle baron. It sets the tone perfectly, defining the moment of the arrival of a patriarchal law and order. Nicholson is the rustler who, in imitation of McLiam and to better organize his rustling activities, buys a nearby ranch to use as a relay station, only to fall victim to the spirit of the land and become both a committed farmer, to his gang's disgust, and suitor of McLiam's daughter, Lloyd. At the same time, McLiam, obsessed with catching the rustlers who are literally disrupting the ordered life he needs, is slowly going mad.

Between Nicholson and McLiam, the rustler turned farmer and Victorian paterfamilias, struts the film's (and possibly the seventies Western's) strangest character, Brando's regulator, a self-appointed guardian of law and order, who is available for hire. Hired by McLiam to catch Nicholson, he represents an even more anarchic spirit than the rustlers. With his peculiar ways, that include wearing a bonnet and dress to hunt a man, he's so strange that Nicholson forgoes his first chance to kill him, so unnerved is he by the sight of him. Finally Brando's bravado, like McLiam's pious obstinacy, is the death of him, signalling his inability to move with the times as Nicholson and Lloyd do.

Penn and McGuane's achievement is to have created such a rich trio of characters and to have inserted them into such a resonant story.

d Arthur Penn   *p* Robert M. Sherman   *s* Thomas McGuane
c Michael Butler   *lp* Marlon Brando, Jack Nicholson, Randy Quaid, Kathleen Lloyd, Frederic Forrest, John McLiam

Mustang Country (U) 79 min
McCrea's last film, this is routine family fare. He plays the ex-rodeo rider turned rancher who, with the help of an Indian youth, Mina, succeeds in capturing the last wild mustang in Montana in the twenties. A pleasant enough 'wilderness' film, unlike McCrea's penultimate movie, the magnificent **Ride the High Country** (1962). Clips from McCrea's films are used for the flashbacks of his earlier life.

d/p/s John Champion   *c* J. Barry Herron   *lp* Joel McCrea, Nika Mina, Robert Fuller, Patrick Wayne

The Outlaw Josey Wales (MALPASO) pv 134 min
A magnificent Western, *The Outlaw Josey Wales* is Eastwood's best film to date. Like **High Plains Drifter** (1972), it has a circular structure, beginning and ending with Eastwood, as the farmer working the land. But whereas the earlier film saw Eastwood consumed by revenge, *Josey Wales* sees him freed from revenge and made human again. Indeed the script by Kaufman (who was originally slated to direct the film as well) and Chernus, even quotes the classic line from Anthony Mann's remarkably similar **The Naked Spur** (1952): 'Choosing a way to die, that's easy; it's choosing a way to live that's the difficult thing to do.'

The storyline is simple. After turning Confederate guerilla raider during the war to better seek McKinney who led the band that murdered his wife and children, Eastwood refuses to surrender at the close of the Civil War and as such is, reluctantly, hunted by his former leader, Vernon. In the course of his search for McKinney, he dispatches assorted

bounty hunters and soldiers and, to his surprise, assembles a growing band of outcasts and seeming losers. He leads them to an abandoned farm where they all find a new life with Eastwood, once the past is put aside, as their amiable patriarch. Accordingly, though Eastwood spends most of his time claiming to be seeking revenge, the outcasts, whom he unwillingly picks up when they simply refuse to take his talk seriously, turn him back into a farmer. If at first Eastwood seems to be merely playing games with his No Name persona, by the end of the film, when the outcasts have become a commune and brought life to a dying community, the idea of revenge has simply become ridiculous.

This transformation is presided over by Chief Dan George, who gives a performance that is both comic and marvellously

Above: *Clint Eastwood in* The Outlaw Josey Wales, *his best film as director to date.*

*Far right: Richard
Harris, once more
undergoing the Sun Vow
ceremony in the sequel
to* A Man Called
Horse *(1976),* The
Return of . . .

dignified as the Indian who, though he can't even sneak up on a white man, proudly claims 'I never surrendered' and whose gnomic pronouncements mask a rock-hard commitment to the future and life rather than to the past and its many sorrows. An added element of this slow unfurling of life, the return of spring to Eastwood's soul, is Surtees' glorious cinematography which invests the changing seasons and locations with a beauty that runs completely counter to Eastwood's talk of hate, murder and revenge.

d Clint Eastwood *p* Robert Daley *s* Phil Kaufman, Sonia Chernus *c* Bill Surtees *lp* Clint Eastwood, Chief Dan George, Sondra Locke, Bill McKinney, John Vernon, Paula Trueman

The Return of a Man Called Horse
(SANDY HOWARD PRODUCTIONS) pv 125 min
The inevitable sequel to the hugely successful **A Man Called Horse** (1970). Equally inevitably, since the (masochistic) appeal of that film was centred on Harris' being strung up by his chest as part of an initiation ceremony, the new film is less a sequel than a remake with Harris and the audience once more undergoing the agonizing Sun Vow ceremony, this time to restore the morale of the Lakota Indians. De Witt's schematic plot has English aristocrat Harris returning to his tribe when other Indians and fur traders join together to drive them from their lands. Kershner directs anonymously.

d Irvin Kershner *p* Terry Morse Jnr *s* Jack De Witt *c* Owen Roizman *lp* Richard Harris, Gale Sondergaard, Geoffrey Lewis, Bill Lucking, Jorge Luke, Claudio Brook

*Lauren Bacall and John
Wayne in Don Siegel's
marvellous elegy to the
Duke,* The Shootist.

The Shootist (DINO DE LAURENTIIS CORP) pv 100 min
Wayne's last film, *The Shootist* fittingly works best as a personal elegy rather than as an elegy for the Western its writers (presumably) intended. Its theme is a commonplace one of the modern Western, an out-of-time gunfighter (Wayne) meeting his end amongst the trolley cars and milk floats of the twentieth century while remaining true to his old-fashioned code of conduct. But what makes the film so successful is Siegel's pared-down direction which so assuredly uses Wayne's screen persona – the film is introduced by tinted clips from past Wayne Westerns and the central character is dying of cancer, as Wayne was – and at the same time uses his stoic facing-up to death to transform Wayne into the Siegel hero *par excellence*. Wayne's masterly, unfussy acting comes as a revelation (in the light of the mannered way he was usually directed in the seventies) as he and Bacall (his landlady for the week) prowl grandly around each other. However, it is Wayne's relationship with Bacall's son, Howard, that is the keynote of the film. As he faces up to his own death with a dignity and curiosity that is so characteristic of the Siegel hero, Wayne commences the education of Howard's would-be tearaway. Again this is a commonplace, but what gives it its bleak resonance is the magnificent denouement which has Howard learn, not self-control, but a desperate impulsiveness as he snatches the gun from the dying Wayne to kill his hero's killer and so become, like Wayne, a perpetual outsider. Accordingly, he runs not home, but past Bacall into the urban jungle of Carson City. A magnificent film.

d Don Siegel *p* M. J. Frankovich, William Self *s* Miles Hood Swarthout, Scott Hale *c* Bruce Surtees *lp* John Wayne, Lauren Bacall, Ron Howard, James Stewart, Harry Morgan, Richard Boone

1977

Another Man, Another Woman *orig* Un Autre Homme, Une Autre Chance *aka* Another Man, Another Chance
(LES FILMS ARIANE/LES FILMS/LES PRODUCTIONS ARTISTES ASSOCIES; FR) 128 min
As the title suggests this soft focus Western is an attempt by writer/director Lelouch to recapture the extraordinary success of his Oscar winning film, *A Man and a Woman* (1966). Bujold and Caan are the couple fated to become lovers despite the numerous impediments placed in their paths. The film commences with Bujold quitting France in the early 1870s and crossing America in the company of photographer Huster to settle in the West, only to have Huster die. Caan is the recently widowed vetinarian she meets and finally marries after he has avenged the murder of their partners.

Lelouch's West is decidedly romantic and the inevitability of the film's plot contrasts oddly with the clearly improvized central performances but, in contrast to **The Legend of Frenchie King** (1971), another French view of the Western, Lelouch's naivety is charming. Bujold gives a superior performance that momentarily gives some weight to this fluffiest of concoctions.

d/s Claude Lelouch *p* Alexandre Mnouchikine, Georges Dancigers *c* Jacques Lefrancois (Claude Lelouch), Stanley Cortez *lp* James Caan, Genevieve Bujold, Francie Huster, Jennifer Warren, Susan Tyrrell, Rossie Harris

Armed and Dangerous *orig* Wooruzhyon i Ochen Opasen
(SOVIET UNION) 123 min

In the Soviet Union, as in several other countries such as Australia and South Africa, there is a long tradition of making what can only be called 'pseudo-Westerns', films which adapt many of the conventions, situations and themes of the Western to local history and conditions. This, however, is a full-blooded Western. Subtitled 'The Time and Heroes of Francis Bret Harte' and set at the time of the discovery of oil in California and Texas, Vainstok's film is an old-fashioned celebration of things Western. Accordingly, the movie's episodic script has plenty of space for musical interludes, cameos of mining life and set pieces like a stagecoach robbery in the fashion of a De Mille epic, and in Martinson it has an evil villain who would not be out of place in a Mascot serial.

The film stars Banionis as a miner, Abdulov as a journalist (a role clearly based on Bret Harte) and Soviet pop star Senchina as a cabaret singer. They band together to save the claims of gold miners from Martinson and his heavies when oil is found. Vainstok, whose previous work includes adaptations of novels by Jules Verne and Robert Louis Stevenson, directs energetically with an eye to action. The result is a somewhat stilted, but nonetheless intriguing, would-be epic that can't hide its Europeanness behind its concern for authentic period detail.

d/p Vladimir Vainstok *s* Vladimir Vladimirov, Pavel Finn *c* Konstantin Ryzhov *lp* Donatas Banionis, Ludmila Senchina, Vsevolod Abdulov, Sergei Martinson, Leonid Bronevoy, Lev Durov

Grayeagle
(CHARLES B. PIERCE PRODUCTIONS) pv 104 (61) min

Even the presence of Johnson and Elam can do little to enliven this low-budget variant of **The Searchers** (1956). Director Pierce has a featured role as a madman Johnson comes across in the course of his search for his daughter kidnapped by the Indians. Intriguingly written from the point of view of the Indians rather than the pursuing whites, the film too often has recourse to cliches to convince one of the stated concern, to show the Indian way of life.

The cutting of some 40 minutes for most markets makes the film even more jerky and less about the Indian way of life.

d/p/s Charles B. Pierce *c* Jim Roberson *lp* Ben Johnson, Iron Eyes Cody, Lana Wood, Jack Elam, Paul Fix, Alex Cord

Sam Waterston as the Comanche chief in Eagle's Wing.

The Great Gundown (SUN PRODUCTIONS) pv 100 min

A listless crossing of **The Magnificent Seven** (1960) and **The Wild Bunch** (1969). Rust is the legendary outlaw against whom Padilla recruits a band of mercenaries. The banal slow-motion action sequences and lengthy flashbacks defuse any power Fisher's script intermittently has.

d Paul Hunt *p* Paul Nobert *s* Steve Fisher *c* Ronald V. Garcia *lp* Robert Padilla, Malila St Duval, Richard Rust, Steven Oliver, David Eastman, Stanley Adams

Kid Vengeance
(GOLAN-GLOBUS PRODUCTIONS) 94 (90) min

Teenage pop star Garrett is the son on the trail of the man who killed his parents in this violent but otherwise unremarkable Western. Van Cleef is the outlaw responsible and Brown the prospector, his gold stolen by Van Cleef, who joins Garrett in the search for vengeance. After the exploitatively filmed series of killings, the end is simply ridiculous: when everyone but Garrett and Van Cleef's half-caste son are killed, the pair throw down their guns in disgust and ride off their separate ways.

d Joe Manduke *p* Frank Johnson, Bob Burkhardt *s* Bud Robbins, Jay Telfer, Ken Globus *c* David Gurfinkel *lp* Lee Van Cleef, Jim Brown, John Marley, Leif Garrett, Glynnis O'Connor

Welcome to Blood City
(BLOOD CITY PRODUCTIONS/EMI IN COOPERATION WITH FAMOUS PLAYERS; CAN, GB) pv 96 min

Clearly influenced by **Westworld** (1973), this lacks the wit of that film and a central performance as compelling as Yul Brynner's. Winder and Schneck's plot has a group of individuals being tested by a team of researchers led by Eggar as to how well they survive in a Western 'environment' created especially for them. Palance is the heavy and Dullea the university professor, who, having proved himself to be more brutal than the next man, commits suicide by re-entering the programmed environment while defenceless. Sasdy's direction is surprisingly listless and unsure whether to concentrate on the Western action or the politicking of the computer men.

d Peter Sasdy *p* Marilyn Stonehouse *s* Stephen Schneck, Michael Winder *c* Reginald H. Morris *lp* Jack Palance, Keir Dullea, Samantha Eggar, Barry Morse, Hollis McLaren, Chris Wiggins

Far left: *Ben Johnson in* Grayeagle, *Charles B. Pierce's low budget version of* The Searchers *(1956).*

Far right: *A surprised Jack Nicholson in his own* Goin' South, *a leisurely and hugely enjoyable modernist Western.*

The White Buffalo

(DINO DE LAURENTIIS CORPORATION)   97 min

A silly Western variant on the *Moby Dick* story. Bronson is Wild Bill Hickok returning to the West under the pseudonym of James Otis to search for the white buffalo of his nightmares and Sampson is Crazy Horse who joins him in his mission. The film, produced by his agent, was the least successful at the box office of the star's movies in the seventies, making it more a white elephant than a buffalo.

The beast of the title represents one of the most unconvincing special effects of the decade.

d J. Lee Thompson   *p* Pancho Kohner   *s* Richard Sale
c Paul Lohmann   *lp* Charles Bronson, Jack Warden, Will Sampson, Kim Novak, Clint Walker, Slim Pickens

1978

Comes a Horseman   (UA) pv 118 min

A major Western, this is set in the cattle ranching West during the last months of the Second World War. Despite its celebration of the wide open spaces, it has much of the feel of Pakula's earlier films, *The Parallax View* (1974) and *All the President's Men* (1976). Fonda and Caan are the ranchers determined to resist the entreaties of Robards' declining cattle baron to buy them out, while Robards in turn attempts to resist the blandishments of an oil company wanting to move in. But, if the plot and feel are distinctly modern in their sense of unease, all the characters, with the sole exception of Farnsworth's ranch hand who holds to the external verities of loyalty and hard work, are focused on the past. Thus Robards wants to recreate the time of his grandfather, when the family

Below: *Jason Robards (right) seeks out James Caan at the climax of* Comes a Horseman.

really were cattle barons, Fonda longs for the innocent days of childhood while Caan wants to escape the horrors of modern warfare.

Gloriously photographed by Willis to look like a homage to the old West, the film's almost gothic concerns are at first suppressed by the traditional-seeming plot – big rancher tries to buy up little ranchers – until the pathological nature of Robards' needs emerge in the final third of the film as he sets about trying to recreate his own personal past at whatever expense to those around him.

d Alan J. Pakula   *p* Gene Kirkwood, Dan Paulson
s Dennis Lynton Clark   *c* Gordon Willis   *lp* James Caan, Jane Fonda, Jason Robards, George Grizzard, Richard Farnsworth, Jim Davis

Eagle's Wing

(EAGLE'S WING PRODUCTIONS) pv 111 min

An intriguing, and little-seen Western, *Eagle's Wing* is directed with real authority by Harvey. He marshals his impressive cast well and gives an ironic inflection to Briley's screenplay in which Waterston's Comanche chief and Sheen's trapper chase after each other and a beautiful, almost magical, white stallion that changes hands with almost clockwork regularity. A sub-plot has a posse of Spaniards also hunting Waterston after he's kidnapped Audran and stolen her dowry of jewels. Sheen gives a fine performance as the greenhorn trapper who slowly educates himself in the ways of the wilderness, but still fails to get the white stallion.

d Anthony Harvey   *p* Ben Arbeid   *s* John Briley   *c* Billy Williams   *lp* Martin Sheen, Sam Waterston, Harvey Keitel, Stephane Audran, Caroline Langrishe, John Castle

Goin' South   (PAR) 108 min

An infectiously enjoyable, off-beat Western, directed with real charm by Nicholson. Several critics have suggested that the film is an informal sequel to **The Missouri Breaks** (1976), with Nicholson reprising his role as the down-at-heel bandit. But though Nicholson plays both roles, the two are decidedly different: in *The Missouri Breaks,* Nicholson learns commitment to the land, in *Goin' South,* though he works the land, his aim from start to finish is to reach Mexico and drop out. Thus from the beginning, when his dream of safety across the Mexican border is rudely interrupted – he's still in Texas – to the end when he persuades his wife, Steenburgen, to head South, he's merely running on the spot.

Accordingly, much of the film's humour comes from the successive acts forced on Nicholson's would-be drop-out and failed applicant to the Younger gang, after he's saved from the gallows by an unlikely local law which gives him his life, if not his freedom, in exchange for marriage to Steenburgen to work her farm. The simple plot has Nicholson romance his prim wife while searching for gold which they need to find before the railway company can foreclose on the farm and Nicholson's old gang steal it from them.

But, if the plot is simple, the characters are far more complex, warily circling each other, aware of their own faults. Nicholson's direction is beautifully measured, as in the marvellously comic, meandering gunfight between the gang and the law at the end. The result is a hugely enjoyable film.

d Jack Nicholson   *p* Harry Gittes, Harold Schneider
s John Herman Shaner, Al Ranrus, Charles Shyer, Alan Mandel   *c* Nestor Almendros   *lp* Jack Nicholson, Mary Steenburgen, Christopher Lloyd, John Belushi, Veronica Cartwright, Richard Bradford

Shadow of Chikara *aka* Wishbone Cutter

(FAIRWINDS/HOWCO INTERNATIONAL)   pv   90 min
An unusual Western. Baker, and Houck, who plays an Irish-Indian called Half Moon O'Brien, are the disillusioned Confederates who set off in search of the diamonds the dying Pickens tells them he's left in a cave by a mysterious mountain deep in the wilderness. Sadly, after a promising opening, the film goes rapidly downhill, with the characters retreating into cliche – Neeley the romantic, Baker the swaggering realist, Houck the loyal Indian given to muttering that he knows they're being followed even though there're no traces and Locke the helpless girl watching her would-be protectors dying one by one. At the same time the plot slips into the supernatural – the diamonds are protected by a curse. Even odder though, is Smith's inability as a director to animate his script. An indication of the gap between imagination and achievement that runs through the movie comes early on when after the death of Pickens (called Virgil Cain in honour of the occasion), the Band's haunting 'The Night They Drove Ole Dixie Down' is played over images of the South's defeat. It's a wonderful idea, badly let down by the slightness of the images.

d/p/s Earl E. Smith   *co-p* Barbara Pryor   *c* Jim Roberson
lp Joe Don Baker, Sondra Locke, Ted Neeley, Slim Pickens, Joy Houck Jnr, Dennis Fimple

The Apple Dumpling Gang Rides Again

(WALT DISNEY PRODUCTIONS)   88 min
This is the sequel to Disney's immensely successful **The Apple Dumpling Gang** (1974) which grossed some $16 million at the box office in North America alone. The comedy is even more physical than before, with Conway and Knotts taking centre stage as the outlaw misfits while Elam and Mars (as a sheriff with revenge on his mind) offer only slightly more sophisticated interpretations of their roles. Matheson and Davalos are the romantic leads. If the end result is decidedly dull, it was also far more popular with family audiences than most Westerns of its time.

d Vincent McEveety   *p* Ron Miller   *s* Don Tait   *c* Frank Phillips   *lp* Tim Conway, Don Knotts, Tim Matheson, Kenneth Mars, Jack Elam, Elyssa Davalos

Butch and Sundance, the Early Days

(FOX/A PANTHEON – WILLIAM GOLDMAN PRODUCTION)
112 min
This is a 'prequel' to the phenomenally successful **Butch Cassidy and the Sundance Kid** (1969) with the title roles taken by Berenger (who in the course of the film develops an uncanny resemblance to Robert Redford) and Katt. In place

of the jaunty lyricism of George Roy Hill's film, Lester's has the witty, detached ironic feel that characterized his great success of the seventies, *The Three Musketeers* (1973). The result is a leisurely, inconsequential but hugely enjoyable Western, memorable more for its details, the visual delight of a main street covered by several feet of water, the wide armed-charm of its leads and a hilarious train robbery, than anything else. Burns' script is suitably episodic, considering the light-hearted nature of the material, but it is Lester's light, deft touch that rescues the project from the 'sequel' mentality that would have destroyed it.

d Richard Lester   *p* Gabriel Katzka   *s* Allan Burns
c Laszlo Kovacs   *lp* William Katt, Tom Berenger, Jeff Corey, John Schuck, Michael C. Gwynne, Jill Eikenberry

The Electric Horseman   (COL/U)   pv   120 min
A surprisingly weak contemporary Western in the vein of **Lonely Are the Brave** (1962) that manipulates the concerns of its principal actors, Redford's ecology and Fonda's crusading, with all the weary cynicism of its villains, Saxon and the Ampco Breakfast Cereal Corporation. The fact that it was probably made with the best of intentions, somehow makes it a far worse film.

Redford is the alcoholic rodeo star who quits the canyons of Las Vegas and his electronically lit costume for the wilds when he discovers that his horse is being fed drugs and Fonda is the newshound who trails him, bothers him and finally falls for his 'sincerity'. After them come representatives of Ampco, intent on stopping him freeing his horse which is the symbol

Above: *William Katt (right) and Tom Berenger in* Butch and Sundance, the Early Days.

Right: *Robert Redford as* The Electric Horseman.

of their 'Ranch' breakfast cereal. Country singer Nelson (who also performs the songs heard in the film) turns in a neat performance as Redford's cynical manager. Otherwise the weak script is simply too predictable to excite the emotions.

d Sydney Pollack *p* Ray Stark *s* Robert Garland *c* Owen Roizman *lp* Robert Redford, Jane Fonda, Valerie Perrine, Willie Nelson, John Saxon, Nicolas Coster

The Frisco Kid (WB) 119 min

A disastrous would-be comic Western, almost as bad as Aldrich's other comic Western, **Four for Texas** (1963). Wilder is the Polish rabbi and Ford the outlaw who form the 'odd couple' who cross America together. Ford's performance is leaden, Wilder's one-dimensional and the jokes few and far between.

d Robert Aldrich *p* Mace Neufeld *s* Michael Elias, Frank Shaw *c* Robert B. Hauser *lp* Gene Wilder, Harrison Ford, Ramon Bieri, Val Bisoglio, George Ralph DiCenzo

Heartland
(WILDERNESS WOMEN PRODUCTIONS/FILMHAUS) 96 min
A highly successful evocation of frontier life by former documentary film-maker Pearce, *Heartland* follows the slowly developing relationship between Torn and Ferrell as they struggle to survive and make a garden of the harsh wilderness that surrounds them. Adapted from the letters of Elinore Stewart, Ferris' script tells the story of Ferrell who, just before the First World War, travels to Wyoming with her daughter to become housekeeper to Torn's taciturn home-steader. After she has briefly sought her economic independence, they marry and, with great difficulty, including the loss of a child, survive the harshest of winters.

A moving film, as much for the rigours of pioneer life which are unemphatically detailed, as for the small but brightly shown joys that light their lives. Torn's performance is magisterial.

d Richard Pearce *co-p* Michael Hausman *co-p/s* Beth Ferris *c* Fred Murphy *lp* Rip Torn, Conchata Ferrell, Barry Primus, Lilia Skala, Megan Folsom, Amy Wright

The Mountain Men (COL) pv 105 min

This is an ineptly made saga of the fur trade. Heston (whose son wrote the script, after a spell of living with Alaskan Indians) and Keith are the trappers who first rescue an Indian woman (Racimo) and then protect her from her avenging husband (Macht). Heston, it is suggested, is the last of the fur trappers, a man who refuses to bend with the times. Accordingly, he is lionized by writer Heston and director Lang to such an extent that the film becomes embarrassing.

d Richard Lang *p* Martin Shafer, Andrew Scheinman *s* Fraser Clarke Heston *c* Michael Hugo *lp* Charlton Heston, Brian Keith, Victoria Racimo, Stephen Macht, John Glover, Seymour Cassel

The Villain *aka* Cactus Jack
(THE VILLAIN COMPANY) 89 min
Ill-served by Douglas' mechanical performance this is a live action 'Roadrunner' cartoon of a Western. Douglas is the villainous Cactus Jack, Schwarzenegger the hero called Handsome Stranger and Ann-Margret the heroine called Charming Jones whom Douglas is employed to kidnap, to no avail. Like the cartoon character of the coyote before him, all Douglas' schemes backfire until in a jokey end, Ann-Margret decides she prefers incompetence to honourable intentions. Sadly the timing necessary to bring off the stunts and jokes just isn't there.

d Hal Needham *p* Mort Engelberg *s* Robert G. Kane *c* Bobby Byrne *lp* Kirk Douglas, Ann-Margret, Arnold Schwarzenegger, Paul Lynde, Foster Brooks, Ruth Buzzi

The 1980s

Bronco Billy

(WB IN ASSOCIATION WITH SECOND STREET FILMS)   116 min

This is a charming, albeit lightweight, movie from Eastwood with the star as a failed shoe salesman turned Western hero and supporting his fantasies with an ailing Wild West Show. Eastwood is wonderful as the innocent hero whose belief in good food, education ('at least up to the eighth grade') and the American flag (or flags, which sewn together, provide him with a new tent when the old one burns down) is unshakeable. Locke is the flighty heiress on the run from her husband who takes refuge with the show and, despite her cynicism, soon falls under Eastwood's spell.

In effect a superior re-run of **The Cowboy and the Lady** (1938), without the Capraesque touches of that film (touches that would have given Hackin's script a greater density), the movie sees Eastwood coasting, playing games with the genre, just as he'd played games with his No Name persona earlier. It is this, its detached view of its characters, that contrasts so noticeably with the marvellous **The Outlaw Josey Wales** (1976).

d Clint Eastwood   *co-p/s* Dennis Hackin   *co-p* Neil Dobrofsky   *c* David Worth   *lp* Clint Eastwood, Sondra Locke, Geoffrey Lewis, Scatman Crothers, Bill McKinney, Sam Bottoms

Cattle Annie and the Little Britches

(HEMDALE/UA THEATRE CORPORATION)   98 min

Lane and Plummer are the adolescent girls in search of the adventures they've read about in too many dime novels in this predictable comic Western. They briefly join up with Lancaster's Bill Doolin until, tired of the girls' exhortations to be a proper outlaw, he lets lawman Steiger catch up with them. The film strains far too much for its effects and its jollity is accordingly short-lived.

d Lamont Johnson   *p* Rupert Hitzig, Alan King   *s* Robert Ward, David Eyre   *c* Larry Pizer   *lp* Burt Lancaster, John Savage, Rod Steiger, Diane Lane, Amanda Plummer, Scott Glenn

Heaven's Gate

(PARTISAN PRODUCTIONS)

pv   149 (first US release 205) min

An epic Western, *Heaven's Gate* celebrates America and Americanness far more equivocally than the same director's

Previous pages: Heaven's Gate, *the most ambitious Western of the eighties.*

Clint Eastwood as Bronco Billy.

The Western Is Dead – Long Live the Western!

Despite appearances, the fact that so few Westerns have been made in the eighties (a mere handful in three years compared to the 140 plus in 1940 alone!) does not signal the death of the genre. Rather it confirms a radical change in both the Western and Hollywood. Hollywood is quite simply making fewer movies. As to the Western, the genre is clearly out of fashion, as it has been in the past. This is largely because, since the seventies, the Western has been associated with questioning rather than celebrating those virtues of individual action that won the West. Put bluntly, at a time when box office receipts testified to the appeal of escapism and special effects, the message of the Western was either unfashionably sombre (**Heaven's Gate, The Long Riders** and **Tom Horn,** all 1980) or too gimmicky to be taken seriously (**Comin' at Ya, Zorro the Gay Blade** and **The Legend of the Lone Ranger,** all 1981).

The Western, for the first time in its long history, was simply irrelevant to Hollywood.

Above: *One of the several huge sets that consumed so much of the budget of* Heaven's Gate.

rapturously received *The Deer Hunter* (1978). Because of the controversy that surrounded its making and truncated release, and the villification the film was greeted with by American critics, *Heaven's Gate* remains to this day as much a *cause célèbre* as a film. Made by Cimino after the phenomenal commercial success of *The Deer Hunter* with a budget that eventually climbed to some $50 million ($36 million according to some sources) and complete artistic freedom, the movie was seen from the beginning as a test of nerve for Hollywood's money men. Accordingly its commercial failure was seen as a damning indictment of the trend to give young film-makers their head.

Equally important, the film treated a difficult and politically explosive subject. Cimino's script deals with the Johnson County Wars of 1892 in which the Wyoming Cattleman's Association waged bloody war on the homesteaders (mostly immigrants) and recruited a mercenary army to try and drive them out of the state. After a pitched battle, the mercenaries failed and the citizens of Johnson County captured them and their leaders, and the Federal authorities, who had passively stood by until then, had to intervene to prevent some of the leading cattlemen of the state from being lynched by the men they had intended to massacre. Much of the criticism of the film in America was devoted, not to the complex and far too elusive structure Cimino hangs his story on, but to the story's thrust – that a My Lai-type massacre was only just averted in America – which was roundly (and utterly incorrectly: the film's factual basis is clear) condemned as historically inaccurate. The film's problematic subject and its huge budget guaranteed that its release would be a fundamentally different kind of media event to that orchestrated for the release of, say, *Raiders of the Lost Ark* (1981). The one was willed to success by the American media, the other to resounding failure.

Turning from the event to the film, it is clear that both its attackers and (predominantly European) defenders have both exaggerated. Kristofferson is the son of a wealthy family who becomes a marshal and gets caught between the ranchers and the immigrants and Walken is the gunman who betrays his class to join the ranchers and lead their mercenaries. Their confrontation is inevitable, their sharing of Huppert as a mistress notwithstanding. The script has the characters frequently and awkwardly talking about their class position – itself an unusual thing in a Hollywood film – but Cimino, with the help of Zsigmond's masterly cinematography, is able to present their gropings and debates with a visual precision that is at times quite stunning. That said, the film's elliptical structure contrasts strongly with the intense (almost fetishistic) realism of its look and its re-creation of frontier life.

Cimino's major failing is his inability to balance the epic and the personal. Where John Ford is able to invest John Wayne and James Stewart in **The Man Who Shot Liberty Valance** (1962) with both a private and a mythical dimension, Cimino's characters are never fully integrated into the epic design of his film, and the movie accordingly seems strangely cold because of it. It is, nonetheless, a remarkable film.

d/s Michael Cimino *p* Joann Carelli *c* Vilmos (William) Zsigmond *lp* Kris Kristofferson, Christopher Walken, John Hurt, Sam Waterston, Isabelle Huppert, Joseph Cotten, Jeff Bridges

The Long Riders (HUKA FILMS) 99 min
This is one of the most idiosyncratic Westerns of recent years. Hill cast the Carradine brothers (plus Brophy) as the Youngers, the Keaches as the Jameses, the Quaids as the Millers and the Guests as the Ford brothers and then attempted to create a sense of period almost wholly through

the rich glowing cinematography of Waite. However, the lure of the Northfield, Minnesota bank raid proves too strong. Accordingly, though at the film's start Hill attempts to demystify the legend of the James and Younger gangs, by the end he is content to merely rework the myth and stage one of the most elaborate bank raids ever. But if the film's intentions are unclear and masked in the complicated storyline of deceit and betrayal, and the casting coup of having brothers as brothers is quickly lost, stylistically the film is a triumph. Hill, for the first time directing a script not written by himself, remoulds his material to produce an almost abstract film, beautiful looking, but very thin.

d Walter Hill   *p* Tim Zinnemann   *s* Bill Bryden, Steven Phillip Smith, Stacy Keach, James Keach   *c* Ric Waite *lp* David Carradine, Keith Carradine, Robert Carradine, James Keach, Stacy Keach, Dennis Quaid, Randy Quaid, Kevin Brophy, Christopher Guest, Nicholas Guest, Harry Carey Jnr

Tom Horn   (SOLAR/FIRST ARTISTS)   pv   97 min
Considering the talents on display and the possibilities inherent in the story of Tom Horn (which resulted in a magnificent two-part telefilm, *Mr Horn*, 1979, by Jack Starrett), this is a disappointing Western. McQueen, whose idea the film was, and who, by all accounts, must be held responsible for its unevenness, is Horn, the man who once caught Geronimo and who, at the film's beginning, is seen eking out a sad existence as a bounty hunter in 1901. Rancher Farnsworth press gangs him into service as a regulator to deal with troublesome rustlers and homesteaders, only to be revulsed by his violent efficiency. To end their association with him the embarrassed ranchers hire Bush to frame him, which he successfully does. The down-beat ending has McQueen facing his public execution with a dignity that comes from the knowledge that his West, like Geronimo's, is long gone.

On paper the script by McGuane (retreading the ground of **The Missouri Breaks,** 1976) and Shrake must have seemed impressive, just as Wiard's previous telefilms and work on the consistently excellent *Rockford Files* teleseries must have suggested that he was a good choice as director; on the screen and under the indifferent eye of a dying McQueen, only Alonzo's classical cinematography survives the constant platitudinizing that the movie is quickly reduced to.

d William Wiard   *p* Fred Weintraub   *s* Thomas McGuane, Bud Shrake   *c* John Alonzo   *lp* Steve McQueen, Linda Evans, Richard Farnsworth, Billy 'Green' Bush, Slim Pickens, Elisha Cook

Windwalker   (WINDWALKER PRODUCTIONS/ PACIFIC INTERNATIONAL ENTERPRISES)   108 min
This is a very ambitious and very odd Western. Although English actor Howard has the main role of the Indian patriarch who recounts the story of his youth while on his deathbed, the film, which is subtitled, is made almost entirely in the Cheyenne and Crow languages, apart from a voice-over narration, with Howard dubbed! As a result, much of the authentic feel of eighteenth-century America, before the white man came, and Indian life that director Merrill carefully builds up is lost by the simple presence of Howard, his brave performance notwithstanding.

Nonetheless the film remains impressive. The snowcapped Utah mountains are beautifully and starkly photographed by Smoot. Goldrup's similarly spare script has Remar (as Howard as a young man) searching for one of his twin sons (both played by Nick Ramus) who has been kidnapped by the Crow, the Cheyenne's traditional enemy, in a raid which also involves the death of his wife, Hedin. In the effective ending sequence the dead Howard returns to life to defend his family from the long lost twin when he returns as a Crow, before going peacefully to rest at last.

Director Merrill won an Oscar in 1973 for his documentary about rodeo riders, *The Great American Cowboy*.

d Keith Merrill   *p* Arthur R. Dubs, Thomas F. Ballard *s* Ray Goldrup   *c* Reed Smoot   *lp* Trevor Howard, Nick Ramus, James Remar, Serene Hedin, Dusty Iron Wing McCrea, Silvano Gallardo

Stacy Keach (right) and brother James (left) as Frank and Jesse James in Walter Hill's The Long Riders.

Above: *Steve McQueen is* Tom Horn.

The Lone Ranger, *as interpreted by Klinton Spilsbury.*

Comin' at Ya! (C/A/U PRODUCTIONS) 101 min
The first 3-D release in nearly twenty years, this silly film features its producer as the avenging hero on the trail of slave trader (and scriptwriter) Quintano, who has kidnapped Anthony's bride-to-be, Abril. The film's brutality and sex scenes are as unimaginatively directed as the 'pelt and burn' 3-D cliches Baldi resurrects from the heyday of the process.

On its release in America, it proved to be a surprise success on the drive-in circuit.

d Ferdinando Baldi   p Tony Anthony   s Wolf Lowenthal, Lloyd Battista, Gene Quintano   c Fernando Arribas lp Tony Anthony, Gene Quintano, Victoria Abril, Ricardo Palacios, Lewis Gordon

Death Hunt (GOLDEN HARVEST) pv 97 min
This is a mediocre Yukon Western. Set in 1931, Bronson is the trapper who first becomes the victim of fellow trappers when he upbraids them for their cruelty to animals and then the prey of Marvin's loutish mountie when he kills one of the trappers who attacks him. The hunt develops into a jamboree, with the press fuelling the chase with promises of rewards, the mounties taking to the air and even a mythical trapper who murders people for the gold in their teeth (Beckman) putting in an appearance, until in a 'surprise' ending, Marvin reveals that he understands Bronson and lets him go, even disfiguring Beckman's dead body so that it will be mistaken for Bronson's. Script, direction (which at one point was offered to Robert Aldrich) and acting are at best routine.

d Peter Hunt   p Murray Shostak   s Michael Grais, Mark Victor   c James Devis   lp Charles Bronson, Lee Marvin, Andrew Stevens, Angie Dickinson, Henry Beckman

The Legend of the Lone Ranger
(ITC/WRATHER PRODUCTIONS)   pv 98 (97) min
It's hard to believe that this dismal resurrection of the Lone Ranger (Spilsbury) was made by the director of the glorious **Monte Walsh** (1970). One key difference is the horrendous script which (presumably in imitation of *Superman*, 1978) devotes far too much space to the Lone Ranger's childhood. The action, when it comes, is equally tiresome with Spilsbury and his Tonto, Horse, rescuing a kidnapped President Grant (Robards) from a would-be dictator of Texas (Lloyd). A much used, traditional plot idea, it's one well suited to the Lone Ranger's serial origins, but is spoilt by the pointless violence that accompanies its unravelling. Unlike **The Lone Ranger** (1956) which breathed new life into the character without disturbing his essential innocence, Fraker's film makes the Lone Ranger into too contemporary and camp a hero.

d William A. Fraker   p Walter Coblenz   s Ivan Goff, Ben Roberts, Michael Kane, William Roberts   c Laszlo Kovacs lp Klinton Spilsbury, Michael Horse, Christopher Lloyd, Matt Clark, Juanin Clay, Jason Robards

Zorro the Gay Blade (MELVIN SIMON) 93 min
Conceived of by its producer and star as a sequel to his very successful Dracula parody, *Love at First Bite* (1979), this comic assault on the Zorro myth falls flat on its face, not least because Hamilton hogs the screen. The result is a few hilarious moments but a broken-backed film. Hamilton plays both Zorro's sons, one an ineffectual would-be defender of the poor and the other a mincing, but no less effective for that, homosexual who in the course of the film transforms the Zorro costume from sober black to glittering gold lamé. Sadly Dresner's script is not so colourful. Lieberman is the wooden villain, Vaccaro his vulgar consort and Hutton the heroine.

d Peter Medak   p George Hamilton   s Hal Dresner c John A. Alonzo   lp George Hamilton, Lauren Hutton, Brenda Vaccaro, Ron Leiberman, James Booth, Clive Revill

Gary Busey in trouble in Barbarosa.

1982

Barbarosa

(WITTLIFF, NELSON, BUSEY PRODUCTIONS/ITC FILMS) 90 min
This marvellous looking Western neatly illustrates the impasse in which the genre has found itself in the eighties. Outside the simple verities of the wilderness and juvenile films, there seems to be no substantial audience for Westerns at present, either on television or in the cinema. The genre has lost little of its appeal to writers, directors and actors, but whereas they, and critics, have been in the main interested in the quirks and complications that can be introduced into the Western, what audience there is for the Western seems to pine for the simplicities of action, action and yet more action, preferably performed by big stars. Accordingly, though *Barbarosa* was a critical success, it was a failure at the box office.

Country singer Nelson (who made his acting debut with great aplomb in **The Electric Horseman**, 1979) has the title role as an amiable outlaw roaming the Texas border country who has to be perpetually on his guard from assassination attempts by the family of his wife (Vega), that have their origins in the family feud that flared up on Nelson's wedding night some 30 years before. He takes Busey's soulful youngster (who's also on the run from a family feud) under his wing and in a series of set pieces and wry asides shows and teaches him the ways of the world. Australian director Schepisi has the knack of keeping the plot moving visually; moreover he's able to create the necessary space for Nelson's observations on life without in any way making the movie too talky. What makes the film doubly interesting is that the contrast between freedom and domesticity that underpins it also lies very much at the centre of the 'Outlaw' brand of modern country music of which Nelson is a founder member.

d Fred Schepisi *co-p/s* William D. Wittliff *co-p* Paul N. Lazarus III *c* Ian Baker *lp* Willie Nelson, Gary Busey, Isela Vega, Gilbert Roland, Danny De La Paz, Alma Martinez

The Grey Fox (MERCURY PICTURES; CAN) 90 min
This is a superb, elegaic Western. Ex-stuntman and veteran character actor Farnsworth (who was suggested for the role by Francis Ford Coppola) has the title role as Bill Miner. He's a notorious stagecoach robber who is sent to jail for 30 years and then released into the stagecoachless world at the turn of the century. Briskly, efficiently and, above all, charmingly, Farnsworth goes to work robbing trains and sets himself up as a Robin Hood/Don Quixote figure, taking the side of the miners, amongst whom he works, against greedy railroad tycoons and battling progress. Defeat is inevitable, but in a cleverly staged finale Farnsworth escapes from jail yet again and heads off to Chicago to join his lady love, Burroughs.

The directorial debut of one-time documentary film-maker Borsos, this movie has an air of confidence about it, in great part courtesy of cinematogapher Tidy who gives the film a lustrous look that belies its $3 million budget.

d Phillip Borsos *p* Peter O'Brian *s* John Hunter *c* Frank Tidy *lp* Richard Farnsworth, Jackie Burroughs, Wayne Robson, Ken Pogue, David Petersen

Harry Tracy – Desperado

(GUARDIAN TRUST CO; CAN) 100 min

Shot in Canada, with British Columbia standing in for Wyoming, this is a surprisingly anodyne attempt to resurrect yet another legendary outlaw whose life has relevance for our times. Dern, minus his facial tics, is the gentleman outlaw who pursues judge's daughter Shaver while still indulging his chosen profession of bank robbery. Gwynne is the failed painter and would-be recorder of the outlaw way of life Dern falls in with and who eventually betrays him, dying in a gun battle with Dern. More interesting is the casting of Canadian folksinger Lightfoot (in his acting debut) as the marshal relentless in his pursuit of Dern.

Oddly, however, Graham seems more concerned with making a comedy than either romanticizing or examining his chivalrous hero. The result is a disappointing movie, especially considering Graham's impressive telefilm career which includes *The Amazing Howard Hughes* (1977) and *Guyana Tragedy* (1981), in which even Dern's death is anticlimactic.

d William A. Graham *p* Ronald I. Cohen *s* David Lee Henry *c* Allen Daviau *lp* Bruce Dern, Helen Shaver, Michael G. Gwynne, Gordon Lightfoot

Plainsong (ED STABILE PRODUCTIONS) 88 (76) min

Clearly influenced by **Heartland** (1979), this Western sadly lacks both the style and economy of that film. Writer/director Stabile's attempt to marry a tale of range warfare to an account of pioneering life is awkwardly mounted and ill-conceived, even though the performances of Joseph, Nelson and Traverse catch well enough the sheer effort that pioneering demanded.

The film opens (in sepia) with the murder of Joseph by a mysterious gunman and then goes into flashback (and colour) to explain why. The reason is a range war in the 1880s in Kansas to which Joseph and a group of women have travelled in search of a new life. In the course of the bloody range war that erupts, Joseph kills Geiger's partner, who had murdered the husbands of Nelson and Traverse, and adopts the child of Nelson when she dies in childbirth, whereupon Geiger vows revenge on her and her family.

The film was shot over a period of years in and around a reconstructed Western town in New Jersey on a minuscule budget.

d/s Ed Stabile *p* Tiare Stack *c* Joe Ritter *lp* Teresanne Joseph, Jessica Nelson, Lyn Traverse, Steve Geiger, Sandon McCail, Carl Kielblock

Timerider *aka* The Adventures of Lyle Swann

(JENSEN-FARLEY PICTURES) 93 min

A silly but enjoyable action quickie, *Timerider* is directed with élan by Dear. Ward is the biker who rides his motorcycle through a time warp and ends up in the Wild West where outlaw Chief Coyote takes a fancy to his bike. The resulting tussle is enlivened by the performances of Masur and Walter as Coyote's ineffectual henchmen and Bauer as the woman who falls for Ward. The script by director Dear and executive producer Nesmith is witty, exploiting the bike versus horse cliches with evident delight; only Lauter's role seems ill-defined. Nesmith, whose first essay into independent production this is, was one of the original Monkees before he left the group to pursue a solo career as performer, record company executive, record producer, and now mini film mogul.

d/co-s William Dear *p* Harry Gittes *co-s* Michael Nesmith *c* Larry Pizer *lp* Fred Ward, Belinda Bauer, Peter Coyote, Ed Lauter, Richard Masur, Tracey Walter

Fred Ward and Belinda Bauer in Timerider.

Appendix 1

All-Time Western Rental Champs

This compilation is derived from *Variety's* 1983 list of All-Time Rental Champs and includes films which have secured rentals (ie distributor's receipts, not ticket sales) in America and Canada of $4 million and over. *Variety* suggests as a rough guide that foreign rentals 'sometimes equal or slightly surpass American and Canadian rentals'. Thus, doubling the figures listed here would give an indication of world-wide rentals. The figures relate, in the main, to the first release of a title. In the case of some older titles a successful release could well have significantly increased rental revenue. It is also worth pointing out that these figures do not include non-theatrical revenue, for example from television sales, which could be substantial. Needless to say the list is biased in favour of recent titles and their higher seat prices.

		in thousands of dollars
1	Blazing Saddles 1974	47,800
2	Butch Cassidy and the Sundance Kid 1969	46,039
3	Billy Jack 1971	32,500
4	The Electric Horseman 1979	31,116
5	Jeremiah Johnson 1972	21,900
6	The Apple Dumpling Gang 1974	16,580
7	Little Big Man 1970	15,000
	Bronco Billy 1980	15,000
9	Paint Your Wagon 1969	14,500
10	True Grit 1969	14,250
11	Giant 1956	14,000
12	The Outlaw Josey Wales 1976	13,500
13	How the West Was Won 1962	12,150

14	Duel in the Sun 1946	11,300
15	The Villain 1979	9,930
16	The Apple Dumpling Gang Rides Again 1979	9,468
17	Cat Ballou 1965	9,300
18	Windwalker 1980	9,059
19	Shane 1953	9,000
20	The Professionals 1966	8,800
21	Shenandoah 1965	8,120
22	The Life and Times of Judge Roy Bean 1972	8,100
23	Rooster Cogburn 1975	8,022
24	High Plains Drifter 1972	7,914
25	The Alamo 1960	7,910
26	Big Jake 1971	7,500
	The Cowboys 1971	7,500
28	The Legend of the Lone Ranger 1981	7,178
29	Oklahoma 1955	7,100
	The Trial of Billy Jack 1974	7,100
31	Westworld 1973	7,000
	The Missouri Breaks 1976	7,000
33	Hang 'Em High 1967	6,710
34	Joe Kidd 1972	6,675
35	A Man Called Horse 1970	6,500
36	Seven Brides for Seven Brothers 1954	6,298
37	The War Wagon 1967	6,079
38	The Long Riders 1980	6,070
39	The Good, the Bad and the Ugly 1966	6,030
40	The Sons of Katie Elder 1965	6,000
	El Dorado 1967	6,000
	Chisum 1970	6,000
43	The Shootist 1976	5,987
44	Rio Bravo 1959	5,750
45	Hombre 1967	5,610
46	Nevada Smith 1966	5,500
	Bandolero 1968	5,500
48	The Wild Bunch 1969	5,300
	The Frisco Kid 1979	5,300
50	Bite the Bullet 1975	5,274
51	Unconquered 1947	5,250
	The Cheyenne Social Club 1970	5,250
53	Support Your Local Sheriff 1968	5,135
54	Two Mules for Sister Sara 1970	5,108
55	The Outlaw 1943	5,075
56	Friendly Persuasion 1956	5,050
57	The Tall Men 1955	5,000
	North to Alaska 1960	5,000
	Hud 1963	5,000
	Comin' at Ya 1981	5,000
61	The Duchess and the Dirtwater Fox 1976	4,977
62	The Searchers 1956	4,900
63	Goin' South 1978	4,766
64	Gunfight at the O.K. Corral 1957	4,700
65	Annie Get Your Gun 1950	4,650
66	Vera Cruz 1954	4,565
67	McLintock! 1963	4,525
68	The Paleface 1948	4,500
69	Zorro, the Gay Blade 1981	4,490
70	Red River 1948	4,475
71	Tom Horn 1980	4,400
72	Texas Across the River 1966	4,354
73	Sergeants Three 1962	4,325
74	One-Eyed Jacks 1961	4,300
	For a Few Dollars More 1965	4,300
76	Saratoga Trunk 1945	4,250
	Five Card Stud 1968	4,250
	Rio Lobo 1970	4,250
79	A Fistful of Dollars 1964	4,200
80	Comes a Horseman 1978	4,185
81	Hondo 1953	4,100
	McCabe and Mrs Miller 1971	4,100
	Cahill 1973	4,100
	Stagecoach 1966	4,000
	The Undefeated 1969	4,000

Appendix 2

Most Successful Westerns: Inflation Adjusted

The list below provides a fascinating comparison with *Variety*'s All-Time Western Rental Champs (*see* Appendix 1). While the *Variety* list favours recent titles over earlier ones, Finler and Pirie's inflation-linked ranking redresses the balance. Thus, for example, by their figures, the Western's most commercially successful decade (seen in the number of titles in the list) is the forties, not the seventies as *Variety*'s figures suggest. Accordingly this list allows for more realistic comparisons between successful Westerns of different times.

Note: I include in this list the figures for *Blazing Saddles* which Finler and Pirie listed in their comedy section.

	Rental income from initial release period: $m.	Inflation factor	Adjusted total: $m.
1 *Duel in the Sun* 1946	10	x7	70
2 *Butch Cassidy and the Sundance Kid* 1969	29.2	x2	58.4
3 *Blazing Saddles* 1974	35.2	x1.4	49.2
4 *Shane* 1953	8	x5.5	44
5 *How the West Was Won* 1962	12.2	x3.5	42.7
6 *Unconquered* 1947	5.3	x7	37.1
7 *The Outlaw* 1943	5.1	x7	35.7
8 *The Covered Wagon* 1923	3.5	x10	35
9 *Jeremiah Johnson* 1972	21.6	x1.5	32.4
10 *The Alamo* 1960	7.9	x4	31.6
11 *Red River* 1948	4.5	x7	31.5
12 *Little Big Man* 1970	15	x2	30
13 *The Tall Men* 1955	5	x5	25
14 *True Grit* 1969	14.3	x2	28.6
15 *California* 1946	3.9	x7	27.3
16 *They Died with Their Boots On* 1941	2.55	x10	25.5
17 *The Searchers* 1956	4.9	x5	24.5
18 *The Virginian* 1946	3.35	x7	23.4
19 *Cat Ballou* 1965	9.3	x2.5	23.3
20 *Vera Cruz* 1954	4.6	x5	23
21 *The Professionals* 1966	8.8	x2.5	22
22 *Gunfight at the O.K.Corral* 1957	4.7	x4.5	21.2
23 *San Antonio* 1945	3	x7	21
Fort Apache 1948	3	x7	21
Broken Arrow 1950	3.5	x6	21
26 *Rio Bravo* 1959	5.2	x4	20.8
27 *Hondo* 1953	4.1	x5	20.5
28 *Pursued* 1947	2.9	x7	20.3
29 *Cimarron* 1931	2	x10	20
30 *Yellow Sky* 1948	2.8	x7	19.6
31 *Shenandoah* 1965	7.8	x2.5	19.5
32 *My Darling Clementine* 1946	2.75	x7	19.2
33 *She Wore a Yellow Ribbon* 1949	2.7	x7	18.9
34 *High Noon* 1952	3.4	x5.5	18.7
35 *Across the Wide Missouri* 1951	2.75	x6	16.5
Bend of the River 1952	3	x5.5	16.5
37 *The Iron Mistress* 1952	2.9	x5.5	16
38 *Distant Drums* 1951	2.85	x5.5	15.7
39 *The Outlaw Josey Wales* 1976	12.8	x1.2	15.4
40 *One-Eyed Jacks* 1961	4.3	x3.5	15.1
41 *Drums Along the Mohawk* 1939	1.5	x10	15
Jesse James 1939	1.5	x10	15
North West Mounted Police 1940	1.5	x10	15
Northwest Passage 1940	1.5	x10	15
Santa Fé Trail 1940	1.5	x10	15
The Sons of Katie Elder 1965	6	x2.5	15
Selected runners-up			
Winchester '73 1950	2.25	x6	13.5
Hang 'Em High 1967	6.7	x2	13.4
El Dorado 1967	6	x2	12
The Wild Bunch 1969	5.3	x2	10.6

Note: It was impossible to arrive at an accurate figure for John Ford's *Stagecoach* (1939), but research indicates that it was not quite as financially successful as its huge reputation suggests.

Compiled by Joel Finler and David Pirie and reprinted with thanks and permission from *Anatomy of the Movies*, Macmillan, New York, 1981.

Appendix 3
Biggest Money-Making Western Stars

Between the years 1936 and 1954, *Motion Picture Herald* listed Western stars separately in its Top Ten Money-Making Stars poll. Exhibitors were asked to 'name in order the ten players in Westerns whose pictures drew the greatest attendance to your theatres'. However, from the beginning when series Westerns were in full flight, to 1954 when the B Western died, the annual Top Tens were really only an indication of the popularity of series Western stars. This explains why John Wayne, who appeared in the list of Top Ten Box Office Stars every year, except 1956, from 1949 on, and was the Top Box Office Star on four occasions, only appears twice, in 1936 and 1939, in the Western list.

Note: The figures in brackets are the previous year's placings.

1936

1 Buck Jones
2 George O'Brien
3 Gene Autry
4 William Boyd
5 Ken Maynard
6 Dick Foran
7 John Wayne
8 Tim McCoy
9 Hoot Gibson
10 Buster Crabbe

1937

1 Gene Autry (3)
2 William Boyd (4)
3 Buck Jones (1)
4 Dick Foran (6)
5 George O'Brien (2)
6 Tex Ritter (-)
7 Three Mesquiteers (-)
8 Charles Starrett (-)
9 Ken Maynard (5)
10 Bob Steele (-)

1938

1 Gene Autry (1)
2 William Boyd (2)
3 Buck Jones (3)
4 George O'Brien (5)
5 Three Mesquiteers (7)
6 Charles Starrett (8)
7 Bob Steele (10)
8 Smith Ballew (-)
9 Tex Ritter (6)
10 Dick Foran (4)

1939

1 Gene Autry (1)
2 William Boyd (2)
3 Roy Rogers (-)
4 George O'Brien (4)
5 Charles Starrett (6)
6 Three Mesquiteers (5)
7 Tex Ritter (9)
8 Buck Jones (3)
9 John Wayne (-)
10 Bob Baker (-)

1940

1 Gene Autry (1)*
2 William Boyd (2)
3 Roy Rogers (3)
4 George O'Brien (4)
5 Charles Starrett (5)
6 Johnny Mack Brown (-)
7 Tex Ritter (7)
8 Three Mesquiteers (6)
9 Smiley Burnette (-)
10 Bill Elliott (-)
* Autry was also fourth in the Top Ten Money-Making Stars, 1940

1941

1 Gene Autry (1)*
2 William Boyd (2)
3 Roy Rogers (3)
4 Charles Starrett (5)
5 Smiley Burnette (9)
6 Tim Holt (-)
7 Johnny Mack Brown (6)
8 Three Mesquiteers (8)
9 Bill Elliott (10)
10 Tex Ritter (7)
* Autry was also sixth in the Top Ten Money-Making Stars, 1941

1942

1 Gene Autry (1)*
2 Roy Rogers (3)
3 William Boyd (2)
4 Smiley Burnette (5)
5 Charles Starrett (4)
6 Johnny Mack Brown (7)
7 Bill Elliott (9)
8 Tim Holt (6)
9 Don 'Red' Barry (-)
10 Three Mesquiteers (8)
* Autry was also seventh in the Top Ten Money-Making Stars, 1942

1943 *

1 Roy Rogers (2)

2 William Boyd (3)
3 Smiley Burnette (4)
4 Gabby Hayes (-)
5 Johnny Mack Brown (6)
6 Tim Holt (8)
7 Three Mesquiteers (10)
8 Don 'Red' Barry (9)
9 Bill Elliott (7)
10 Russell Hayden (-)
*Gene Autry serving in US Army Air Corps 1943-5

1944

1 Roy Rogers (1)
2 William Boyd (2)
3 Smiley Burnette (3)
4 Gabby Hayes (4)
5 Bill Elliott (9)
6 Johnny Mack Brown (5)
7 Don 'Red' Barry (8)
8 Charles Starrett (-)
9 Russell Hayden (10)
10 Tex Ritter (-)

1945

1 Roy Rogers (1)*
2 Gabby Hayes (4)
3 William Boyd (2)
4 Bill Elliott (5)
5 Smiley Burnette (3)
6 Johnny Mack Brown (6)
7 Charles Starrett (8)
8 Don 'Red' Barry (7)
9 Tex Ritter (10)
10 Rod Cameron (-)
* Roy Rogers was also tenth in the Top Ten Money-Making Stars, 1945

1946

1 Roy Rogers (1)
2 Bill Elliott (4)
3 Gene Autry (-)
4 Gabby Hayes (2)
5 Smiley Burnette (5)
6 Charles Starrett (7)
7 Johnny Mack Brown (6)
8 Sunset Carson (-)
9 Fuzzy Knight (-)
10 Eddie Dean (-)

1947

1 Roy Rogers (1)
2 Gene Autry (3)
3 William Boyd (-)
4 Bill Elliott (2)
5 Gabby Hayes (4)
6 Charles Starrett (6)
7 Smiley Burnette (5)
8 Johnny Mack Brown (7)
9 Dale Evans (-)
10 Eddie Dean (10)

1948

1 Roy Rogers (1)
2 Gene Autry (2)
3 Bill Elliott (4)
4 Gabby Hayes (5)
5 William Boyd (3)

6 Charles Starrett (6)
7 Tim Holt (-)
8 Johnny Mack Brown (8)
9 Smiley Burnette (7)
10 Andy Devine (-)

1949

1 Roy Rogers (1)
2 Gene Autry (2)
3 Gabby Hayes (4)
4 Tim Holt (7)
5 Bill Elliott (3)
6 Charles Starrett (6)
7 William Boyd (5)
8 Johnny Mack Brown (8)
9 Smiley Burnette (9)
10 Andy Devine (10)

1950

1 Roy Rogers (1)
2 Gene Autry (2)
3 Gabby Hayes (3)
4 Bill Elliott (5)
5 William Boyd (7)
6 Tim Holt (4)
7 Charles Starrett (6)
8 Johnny Mack Brown (8)
9 Smiley Burnette (9)
10 Dale Evans (-)

1951

1 Roy Rogers (1)
2 Gene Autry (2)
3 Tim Holt (6)
4 Charles Starrett (7)
5 Rex Allen (-)
6 Bill Elliott (4)
7 Smiley Burnette (9)
8 Allan Lane (-)
9 Dale Evans (10)
10 Gabby Hayes (3)

1952

1 Roy Rogers (1)
2 Gene Autry (2)
3 Rex Allen (5)
4 Bill Elliott (6)
5 Tim Holt (3)
6 Gabby Hayes (10)
7 Smiley Burnette (7)
8 Charles Starrett (4)
9 Dale Evans (9)
10 William Boyd (-)

1953 *

1 Roy Rogers (1)
2 Gene Autry (2)
3 Rex Allen (3)
4 Bill Elliott (4)
5 Allen Lane (-)
* Only five listed

1954 *

1 Roy Rogers (1)
2 Gene Autry (2)
3 Rex Allen (3)
4 Bill Elliott (4)
5 Gabby Hayes (-)
* Only five listed

Appendix 4
Critics' Top Tens

Ed Buscombe

Ed Buscombe has written extensively about genre and the Western.

The films are listed in order of preference.

The Searchers 1956
Rio Bravo 1959
Ride the High Country 1962
Duel in the Sun 1946
Heller in Pink Tights 1960
Comanche Station 1960
Man of the West 1958
Vera Cruz 1954
One-Eyed Jacks 1961
High Plains Drifter 1972

'This is a list not of the "most significant contributions" to the genre; simply of the ones I'd most like to see in an all-night screening if I were being hanged in the morning. They are chosen on an auteur principle in one sense, that I've only allowed myself one by each director.'

Allen Eyles

Allen Eyles is the author of *The Western* and the definitive book about the films of John Wayne.

The films are listed in alphabetical order.

Bend of the River 1952
The Hanging Tree 1959
The Man from Laramie 1955
Pursued 1947
Ride the High Country 1962
The Searchers 1956
Shane 1953
She Wore a Yellow Ribbon 1949
Support Your Local Sheriff 1968
The Tall T 1957

Christopher Frayling

Christopher Frayling, who is Professor of Cultural History at the Royal College of Art, is the author of *Spaghetti Westerns* and of numerous articles about the American Western and American society.

The films are listed in chronological order.

Rancho Notorious 1952
High Noon 1952
Shane 1953
Johnny Guitar 1954
Run of the Arrow 1957
Terror in a Texas Town 1958
Rio Bravo 1959
Comanche Station 1960
One-Eyed Jacks 1961
The Man Who Shot Liberty Valance 1962
The Professionals 1966
Once upon a Time in the West 1968

The Ballad of Cable Hogue 1970
McCabe and Mrs Miller 1971
Ulzana's Raid 1972
The Missouri Breaks 1976
The Shootist 1976

'Although this list is restricted to American Westerns of the sound era – films financed or shot in America – one film for each director (and omitting Eastwood, Hellman, Huston, King, Mann, McLaglen, Nelson, Pollack, Ritt, Sturges, and Walsh) I still could not prune it down to less than seventeen items.

'The list clearly shows a preference for "modernist" Westerns – films which aim to extend the basic rules of the genre, which re-mix the staple ingredients in an interesting way, which import ideas from other areas of film work, or which use other Westerns as reference points: it also shows a preference for the work of certain directors (hence the "one of each" look to it). *Top American Westerns* illustrates my strong belief that it was only when the cowboy stopped kissing his horse (or singing about his horse, or using him as an excuse for rodeo stunts) that the Western was able to grow up: as one of the cowhands says in *The Culpepper Cattle Company* (Dick Richards, 1972), "Son, you don't give a name to something you may have to *eat*."'

In view of the fact that Frayling's book *Spaghetti Westerns* is the seminal book on the Italian Western, it seemed appropriate to ask him for a separate list of Italian Westerns.

Django 1966
The Hills Run Red 1966
A Bullet for the General 1966
The Good, the Bad and the Ugly 1966
Face to Face 1967
A Professional Gun 1968
Django Kill 1969
They Call Me Trinity 1970
A Fistful of Dynamite 1971
My Name Is Nobody 1973

'Like my *Top American Westerns* list, this is in chronological order rather than order of preference: unlike that list, I've included more than one work by important directors (Corbucci, Leone) and several which were scored by the same composer – Ennio Morricone. Although William S. Hart originally coined the phrase "horse opera", it took the land of Puccini to show what the phrase really means...

'The reason these *Top Italian Westerns* were all made in the relatively brief time span of 1965-73, is that the "Spaghetti" phenomenon only lasted eleven years and took two years to get going. Nevertheless there were about 400 Italian Westerns made between 1963 and 1973 – and the choice was not as easy as some film critics might think.'

Phil Hardy

The films are listed in no particular order.

The Last Movie 1971
The Searchers 1956
Forty Guns 1957
Rancho Notorious 1952
Bend of the River 1952
The Shooting/Ride in the Whirlwind 1966★
A Time for Dying 1969
Fury at Showdown 1957
Johnny Guitar 1954
Ride the High Country 1962

★ I find it impossible to consider these movies, which were made back to back by the same group of people, separately.

'This is not a best Westerns' list; otherwise Hawks would figure in it. Rather, the films have been chosen to show what has been done with the genre and what can be done. Some of the films, the Mann and Ford for example, are traditional, movies made from the centre of the genre by directors working at their peak. Others show directors experimenting with the genre, twisting it this way and that to extend it (Hellman, Hopper) or overcome awesome production circumstances (Lang, Oswald). What all the films share, be they unassuming genre pieces (the Boetticher or Peckinpah, for example) or extravagant and excessive works like the Fuller and Ray, is a sense of re-inventing the Western as they go along.'

Colin McArthur

Colin McArthur has written extensively about genre. He has been film critic of *The Tribune* for several years in which capacity he has probably been the only regular newspaper critic to attempt to apply recent developments in film criticism in a consistent fashion.

The films are listed in chronological order.

The Covered Wagon 1923
Union Pacific 1939
The Westerner 1939
My Darling Clementine 1946
Run of the Arrow 1957
Lonely Are the Brave 1962
The Man Who Shot Liberty Valance 1962
Ride the High Country 1962
Cheyenne Autumn 1964
Once upon a Time in the West 1968

'The criteria on which my choice is based are neither the individual excellence of the films nor, still less, the sensibilities of their makers. The criteria are firmly *social*. The above films seem to me to pose most sharply the particular historical debates which underpin the Western: whether the West is garden or desert; whether industrialization or agrarianism carries the greater moral cachet; whether the Indian is a cruel savage or a noble primitive; whether Western energy is to be preferred to Eastern refinement; and how the traditional West (and Western) copes with the onset of modernity. The presence of these debates has the effect of troubling these films, of making them perform curious manoeuvres in an attempt to resolve incompatible ideological demands.'

Eric Mackenzie

Eric Mackenzie researched this book.
The films are listed in order of preference.

True Grit 1969
My Darling Clementine 1946
Fort Apache 1948
She Wore a Yellow Ribbon 1949
Winchester '73 1950
Bad Day at Black Rock 1955
J.W. Coop 1971
Lonely Are the Brave 1962
High Noon 1952
The Magnificent Seven 1960

'I have never had a particular preference for the Western genre above others nor seen a great number of Westerns. My research for this book has indicated those Westerns which are generally considered superior films and has also generated my interest in the films of people such as George O'Brien, and the desire to sample the many series Westerns. My list is compiled from those that have, for one reason or another, left a favourable impression.'

Tom Milne

Tom Milne is the author of *Mamoulian* and editor of *Godard on Godard*, amongst others.

The films are listed in chronological order.
Three Bad Men 1926
They Died With Their Boots On 1941
My Darling Clementine 1946
She Wore a Yellow Ribbon 1949
Wagonmaster 1950
Run of the Arrow 1957
Rio Bravo 1959
Little Big Man 1970
Ulzana's Raid 1972
Pat Garrett and Billy the Kid 1973

Ted Reinhart

Ted Reinhart reviews both A and series Westerns in several video magazines.

Top Ten A Westerns

High Noon 1952
Shane 1953
Stagecoach 1939
Ride the High Country 1962
Broken Arrow 1950
Red River 1948
The Gunfighter 1950
The Westerner 1940
The Three Godfathers 1948
Wagonmaster 1950

Western Series Stars and Their Career Best Movie

Rex Allen	*The Arizona Cowboy*
Gene Autry	*Blue Montana Skies*
Don Barry	*The Tulsa Kid*
William Boyd	*Three Men from Texas*
Johnny Mack Brown	*The Gentleman from Texas*
Buster Crabbe	*The Drifter*
Bill Elliott	*Beyond the Sacramento*
Monte Hale	*Home on the Range*
Tim Holt	*The Arizona Ranger*
George Houston	*Lone Rider Rides On*
Buck Jones	*White Eagle*
Allan Lane	*Sheriff of Wichita*
Tim McCoy	*The Westerner*
Ken Maynard	*The Strawberry Roan*
Tom Mix	*The Rider of Death Valley*
George O'Brien	*Gun Law*
Jack Randall	*Across the Plains*
Tex Ritter	*Oklahoma Raiders*
Roy Rogers	*My Pal Trigger*
Bob Steele	*Brand of the Outlaws*
Charles Starrett	*Outlaws of the Prairie*
John Wayne (as a 'B' star)	*Born to the West*
Range Busters	*Wranglers Roost*
Rough Riders	*Ghost Town Law*
Three Mesquiteers	*Wyoming Outlaw*
Trailblazers	*Arizona Whirlwind*

Richard Schickel

Richard Schickel is the film critic of *Time* magazine.
The films are listed in no particular order.

Stagecoach 1939
Fort Apache 1948
She Wore a Yellow Ribbon 1949
Red River 1948
My Darling Clementine 1946
The Searchers 1956
Rio Bravo 1959

The Wild Bunch 1969
Winchester '73 1950
Man of the West 1958

'Ten films, four directors. Not what you'd call a balanced list. Yet it seems to me to cover most of the classic genre themes – the search for lost kinsmen, the building of empires, the taming of towns (or anyway the ridding of bad influences in them), the cavalry and Indian conflict, or "civilization" versus "savagery" and even "the end of the west Western". If we were not confined to the apparently immutable dimensions of the ten best concept – has anyone ever traced that one back to its source? – I would want to add that great elegy, *Ride the High Country* (1962); the gloriously spacious and only half-specious *The Big Country* (1958); Clint Eastwood's neo-classic *The Outlaw Josey Wales* (1976); two successful Italianate coals-to-Newcastle efforts, *Once upon a Time in the West* (1968) and *My Name Is Nobody* (1973), and, for obscurity's sake, a forgotten Audie Murphy quickie that ought at least to have a cult following, *No Name on the Bullet* (1959).'

David Thomson

Amongst David Thomson's publications is the invaluable *A Biographical Dictionary of the Cinema*.

The films are listed in order of preference.

Red River 1948
Rio Bravo 1959
Man of the West 1958
The Searchers 1956
The Far Country 1955
Pursued 1947
Pat Garrett and Billy the Kid 1973
Run of the Arrow 1957
The Missouri Breaks 1976
The Shooting 1966

'You ask for ten top Westerns, on the assumption that we have a shared understanding of the range covered by the genre. So be it – these are my ten favourites of the moment. But for the last couple of years I have begun to live in the West, and so I feel more intrigued by the possibilities of twentieth-century Westerns about people who live in the real places of the legend. My second ten have a few cowboy hats and many of the themes, actors and situations familiar from the Western. I offer them in the hope that they may enrich our sense of our genre, and remind us how far the Western concerns a territory as well as a state of mind: *Greed* (1923); *White Heat* (1949); *The Lusty Men* (1952); *Touch of Evil* (1958); *The Birds* (1963); *Five Easy Pieces* (1970); *The Long Goodbye* (1973); *Bring Me the Head of Alfredo Garcia* (1974); *The Shining* (1980) and – on the strength of its script, the chance to see some of the shooting, and a few edited sequences – Phil Kaufman's 1983 release, *The Right Stuff*.'

Robin Wood

The films are listed in alphabetical order.

Drums Along the Mohawk 1939
Duel in the Sun 1946
Heaven's Gate 1980 *especially the original version*
Heller in Pink Tights 1960
Man of the West 1958
The Man Who Shot Liberty Valance 1962
McCabe and Mrs Miller 1971
Rancho Notorious 1952
Rio Bravo 1959
She Wore a Yellow Ribbon 1949

'Not a list of the ten "most important" Westerns (ie important to the development of the genre), and of course not "objective" (whatever that might mean). These are the ten films that seem to me particularly rich; they also happen to be Westerns. The richness is derived from a multiplicity of interacting factors (derived specifically from the interaction, rather than from the factors considered separately or in sum); among those factors, personal authorship, generic convention, complex relationship to "the dominant ideology", are especially important. Also important are the interactions of the films themselves: *Heaven's Gate* in relation to *Drums Along the Mohawk*, for example: the complex meanings produced by such (and innumerable other) interrelations.'

French Critics

A compilation of the movies mentioned in the 28 French critics' Ten Best Westerns lists, first published in *Le Western* (1966), based on the number of citations in the list. It is reprinted here to offer a comparison to the contemporary Ten Bests.

1 *Johnny Guitar* 1954

2 *Rio Bravo* 1959

3 *The Big Sky* 1952

4 *Man Without a Star* 1955
The Naked Spur 1953
Rancho Notorious 1952

5 *The Left-Handed Gun* 1958
My Darling Clementine 1946
Ride the High Country 1962
The Searchers 1956

6 *Duel in the Sun* 1946
The Hanging Tree 1959
Red River 1948
Run of the Arrow 1957
Seven Men from Now 1956
Silver Lode 1954

7 *Colorado Territory* 1949

The Far Country 1955
Heller in Pink Tights 1960
The Last Hunt 1956
Man of the West 1958
The Unforgiven 1960
Wagonmaster 1950

8 *The Last Frontier* 1955
The Last Wagon 1956
Man from Laramie 1955
The Plainsman 1936
River of No Return 1954
They Died with Their Boots On 1941
Warlock 1959
Western Union 1941
Winchester '73 1950

9 *Billy the Kid* 1930
Comanche Station 1960
Gunfight at the O.K. Corral 1957
The Magnificent Seven 1960

The Outlaw 1943
Stagecoach 1939
Tennessee's Partner 1955
3.10 to Yuma 1957
Wichita 1955
The Wonderful Country 1959

10 *Apache* 1954
Backlash 1956
Bend of the River 1952
Broken Arrow 1950
Buchanan Rides Alone 1958
Buffalo Bill 1944
The Covered Wagon 1923
Dallas 1950
The Devil's Doorway 1950
A Distant Trumpet 1964
Escape from Fort Bravo 1953
Forty Guns 1957
Go West 1925
The Gold Rush 1925
The Gunfighter 1950
The Horse Soldiers 1959
The Indian Fighter 1955
The Iron Horse 1924
Jesse James 1939
A King and Four Queens 1956

Last Train from Gun Hill 1959
The Law and Jake Wade 1958
The Lone Ranger 1956
Lonely Are the Brave 1962
Major Dundee 1965
The Misfits 1961
One-Eyed Jacks 1961
Pursued 1947
Rio Conchos 1964
Run for Cover 1955
Shane 1953
The Sheepman 1958
The Sheriff of Fractured Jaw 1959
Silver River 1948
The Singer Not the Song 1961
Taza, Son of Cochise 1954
The Tin Star 1957
The Treasure of the Sierra Madre 1948
The True Story of Jesse James 1957
Two Rode Together 1961
The Unconquered 1947
Union Pacific 1939
Westward the Women 1952
Yellow Sky 1948
Yellowstone Kelly 1959

Appendix 5

Western Oscars

The following is a list of all Oscars given to Western films since 1929 and of Western performances that were nominated for Oscars.

1929

Oscar: Best actor Warner Baxter, *In Old Arizona*
Nominations: Best picture *In Old Arizona*; Best director Irving Cummings, *In Old Arizona*; Writing Tom Barry, *In Old Arizona*; Cinematography Arthur Edeson, *In Old Arizona*

1931

Oscars: Best picture *Cimarron*; Writing (adaptation) Howard Estabrook, *Cimarron*; Interior decoration Max Ree, *Cimarron*
Nominations: Best director Wesley Ruggles, *Cimarron*; Best actor Richard Dix, *Cimarron*; Best actress Irene Dunne, *Cimarron*; Cinematography Edward Cronjager, *Cimarron*

1934

Nominations: Best picture *Viva Villa*; Writing (adaptation) Ben Hecht, *Viva Villa*; Cinematography George Folsey, *Operator 13*

1935

Nomination: Best picture *Ruggles of Red Gap*

1938

Oscar: Sound recording Thomas Moulton, *The Cowboy and the Lady*

1939

Oscar: Best supporting actor Thomas Mitchell, *Stagecoach*
Nominations: Best picture *Stagecoach*; Best director John Ford, *Stagecoach*; Cinematography (black and white) Bert Glennon, *Stagecoach*

1940

Oscar: Best supporting actor Walter Brennan, *The Westerner*
Nominations: Writing (original story) Stuart N. Lake, *The Westerner*; Cinematography (colour) Victor Milner, W. Howard Greene, *North West Mounted Police*; Sidney Wagner, William V. Skall, *Northwest Passage*

1943

Nomination: Best picture *The Ox-Bow Incident*

1946

Nominations: Best actress Jennifer Jones, *Duel in the Sun*; Best supporting actress Lillian Gish, *Duel in the Sun*

1948

Oscars: Best director John Huston, *The Treasure of the Sierra Madre*; Best supporting actor Walter Huston, *The Treasure of the Sierra Madre*; Writing (screenplay) John Huston, *The Treasure of the Sierra Madre*
Nomination: Best picture *The Treasure of the Sierra Madre*

1950

Nominations: Writing (motion picture story) William Bowers, André de Toth, *The Gunfighter*; Cinematography (colour) Charles Rosher, *Annie Get Your Gun*; Ernest Palmer, *Broken Arrow*; Music Adolph Deutsch, Roger Edens, *Annie Get Your Gun*

1952

Oscars: Best actor Gary Cooper, *High Noon*; Best supporting actor Anthony Quinn, *Viva Zapata!*; Best scoring of a dramatic or comedy picture Dimitri Tiomkin, *High Noon*; Best song Dimitri Tiomkin, Ned Washington, 'High Noon', *High Noon*; Film editing Elmo Williams, Harry Gerstad, *High Noon*
Nominations: Best picture *High Noon*; Best director Fred Zinnemann, *High Noon*; Best actor Marlon Brando, *Viva Zapata!*; Best supporting actor Arthur Hunnicutt, *The Big Sky*; Writing (screenplay) Carl Foreman, *High Noon*; Writing (story and screenplay) John Steinbeck, *Viva Zapata!*; Cinematography (black and white) Russell Harlan, *The Big Sky*; Virgil E. Miller, *Navajo*

1953

Nominations: Best picture *Shane*; Best director George Stevens, *Shane*; Best supporting actor Jack Palance, *Shane*; Writing (motion picture story) *Hondo* (writer not eligible under Academy laws, since story was not an original); Writing (screenplay) A.B. Guthrie Jnr, *Shane*; Writing (story and screenplay) Sam Rolfe, Harold Jack Bloom, *The Naked Spur*

1954

Oscar: Writing (motion picture story) Philip Yordan, *Broken Lance*

1955

Oscar: Best scoring of a musical picture Robert Russell Bennet, Jay Blackton, Adolph Deutsch, *Oklahoma!*
Nominations: Best director John Sturges, *Bad Day at Black Rock*; Best actor Spencer Tracy, *Bad Day at Black Rock*; Writing (screenplay) Millard Kaufman, *Bad Day at Black Rock*; Cinematography (colour) Robert Surtees, *Oklahoma!*; Sound recording Todd-AO Sound Dept, *Oklahoma!*

1956

Nominations: Writing (best screenplay) (adapted) *Friendly Persuasion* (writer not eligible for nomination under Academy bylaws which forbid any person who is a professed Communist or who refuses to deny such to receive an Academy Award; this bylaw was in effect from February 1957 to January 1959); Cinematography (black and white) Walter Strange, *Stagecoach to Fury*

1957

Nomination: Best story and screenplay (written directly for the screen) Barney Slater, Joel Kane, Dudley Nichols, *The Tin Star*

1958

Nomination: Best story and screenplay (written directly for the screen) James Edward Grant (story), William Bowers and James Edward Grant (screenplay), *The Sheepmen*

1960

Nominations: Best picture *The Alamo*; Best supporting actor Chill Wills, *The Alamo*; Cinematography (colour) William H. Clothier, *The Alamo*; Sound Samuel Goldwyn Studio Sound Dept and Todd-AO Sound Dept, *The Alamo*

1961

Nomination: Cinematography (colour) Charles Lang Jnr, *One-Eyed Jacks*

1963

Oscars: Best supporting actor Melvyn Douglas, *Hud*; Best actress Patricia Neal, *Hud*; Best story and screenplay (written directly for the screen) James R. Webb, *How the West Was Won*; Cinematography (black and white) James Wong Howe, *Hud*; Sound MGM Sound Dept, *How the West Was Won*; Film editing Harold F. Kress, *How the West Was Won*
Nominations: Best picture *How the West Was Won*; Best actor Paul Newman, *Hud*; Best screenplay (based on material from another medium) Irving Ravetch, Harriet Frank Jnr, *Hud*; Cinematography (colour) William H. Daniels, Milton Krasner, Charles Lang Jnr, Joseph LaShelle, *How the West Was Won*

1965

Oscar: Best actor Lee Marvin, *Cat Ballou*
Nomination: Best screenplay (based on material from another medium) Walter Newman, Frank R. Pierson, *Cat Ballou*

1966

Nominations: Best director Richard Brooks, *The Professionals*; Best screenplay (based on material from another medium)

Richard Brooks, *The Professionals*; Cinematography (colour) Conrad Hall, *The Professionals*

1969

Oscars: Best actor John Wayne, *True Grit*; Best story and screenplay (based on material not previously published or produced) William Goldman, *Butch Cassidy and the Sundance Kid*; Cinematography Conrad Hall, *Butch Cassidy and the Sundance Kid*; Best song Burt Bacharach, Hal David, 'Raindrops Keep Fallin' on My Head', *Butch Cassidy and the Sundance Kid*; Best original score of a nonmusical picture (for which only the composer shall be eligible) Burt Bacharach, *Butch Cassidy and the Sundance Kid*
Nominations: Best picture *Butch Cassidy and the Sundance Kid*; Best director George Roy Hill, *Butch Cassidy and the Sundance Kid*

1970

Nomination: Best supporting actor Chief Dan George, *Little Big Man*

1971

Nomination: Best actress Julie Christie, *McCabe and Mrs Miller*

1972

Nominations: Best picture *The Emigrants*; Best director Jan Troell, *The Emigrants*; Best actress Liv Ullman, *The Emigrants*; Best screenplay (based on material from another medium) Jan Troell, Bengt Forslund, *The Emigrants*; Foreign-language film *The New Land* (Sweden)

1973

Oscar: Documentary Keith Merrill, Rodeo Films, *The Great American Cowboy*

1974

Nomination: Best supporting actress Madeline Kahn, *Blazing Saddles*

1978

Nomination: Best supporting actor Richard Farnsworth, *Comes a Horseman*

Appendix 6

Selected Sound Westerns and Their Novel Sources

Compiled by Gerald Peary
(*st* = same title)

Abilene Town 1946 : *Trail Town*, Ernest Haycox
Albuquerque 1948 : *Dead Freight for Pilute*, Luke Short
Along Came Jones 1951 : *The Useless Cowboy*, Alan LeMay
Along the Great Divide 1951 : *st* Walter Doniger
Along the Navajo Trail 1945 : *st* William Colt MacDonald
Apache 1954 : *Bronco Apache*, Paul I. Wellman
Apache Drums 1951 : *Stand at Spanish Boot*, Harry Brown
Apache Territory 1958 : *The Last Stand at Papago Wells*, Louis L'Amour
Apache Uprising 1966 : *Way Station*, Harry Sanford, Max Steeber
The Appaloosa 1966 : *st* Walter McLeod
Arizona 1940 : *st* Clarence Boddington Kelland
Arizona Mahoney 1936 : *Stairs of Sand*, Zane Grey
Arizona Raiders 1936 : *Raiders of Spanish Peaks*, Zane Grey
Arrowhead 1953 : *Adobe Wells*, W.R. Burnett
The Avengers 1950 : *Don Careless*, Rex Beach
Backlash 1956 : *st* Frank Gruber
The Badlanders 1958 : *The Asphalt Jungle*, W.R. Burnett
The Big Country 1958 : *st* Donald Hamilton
The Big Land 1957 : *Buffalo Grass*, Frank Gruber
The Big Sky 1952 : *st* A.B. Guthrie Jnr
Billy the Kid 1930, 1941 : *The Saga of Billy the Kid*, Walter Noble Burns
Blood on the Moon 1948 : *Gunman's Choice*, Luke Short
The Border Legion 1930, 1940 : *st* Zane Grey
Branded 1951 : *Monta Rides Again*, Evan Evans (Max Brand)
The Bravados 1958 : *st* Frank O'Rourke
Broken Arrow 1950 : *Blood Brothers*, Elliott Arnold
Broken Lance 1954 : *House of Strangers*, Jerome Weidman
Buchanan Rides Alone 1958 : *The Name's Buchanan*, Jonas Ward
Bugles in the Afternoon 1952 : *st* Ernest Haycox
Bullet for a Badman 1964 : *Renegade Posse*, Marvin H. Albert
The Burning Hills 1956 : *st* Louis L'Amour
Call of the Yukon 1938 : *Swift Lightning*, James O. Curwood
Canyon Passage 1946 : *st* Ernest Haycox
Cat Ballou 1965 : *The Ballad of Cat Ballou*, Roy Chanslor
Cheyenne Autumn 1964 : *st* Mari Sandoz
Chuka 1967 : *st* Richard Jessup
Cimarron 1931, 1960 : *st* Edna Ferber
Colorado Territory 1949 : *High Sierra*, W.R. Burnett
The Comancheros 1961 : *st* Paul I. Wellman
Coroner Creek 1948 : *st* Luke Short
The Cowboys 1971 : *st* William Dale Jennings
Cow Country 1953 : *Shadow Range*, Curtis Bishop
Crashing Thru 1939 : *Renfrew Rides the Range*, Laurie York Ernskine

The Dark Command 1940 : *st* W.R. Burnett
The Deadly Companions 1961 : *Yellowleg*, A.S. Fleischman
Death of a Gunfighter 1969 : *st* Lewis B. Patten
Desert Gold 1936 : *st* Zane Grey
Destry 1955 : *Destry Rides Again*, Max Brand
Destry Rides Again 1932, 1939 : *st* Max Brand
The Devil's Party 1938 : *Trouble Wagon*, Borden Chase
A Distant Trumpet 1964 : *st* Paul Horgan
The Dude Ranger 1934 : *Novel*, Zane Grey
Duel at Diablo 1966 : *Apache Rising*, Marvin Albert
Duel in the Sun 1946 : *st* Niven Busch
El Dorado 1967 : *The Stars in Their Courses*, Harry Brown
Empty Holsters 1937 : *st* Earl Repp
Empty Saddles 1936 : *st* Cherry Wilson
End of the Trail 1936 : *Outlaws of Palouse*, Zane Grey
Five Card Stud 1968 : *Glory Gulch*, Ray Goulden
Flaming Star 1960 : *Flaming Lance*, Clair Huffaker
Four Faces West 1948 : *Paso Por Aqui*, Eugene M. Rhodes
Frontier Marshal 1939 : *Wyatt Earp, Frontier Marshal*, Stuart Lake
The Furies 1950 : *st* Niven Busch
Fury at Furnace Creek 1948 : *Four Men and a Prayer*, David Garth
Fury at Showdown 1957 : *Showdown Creek*, Lucas Todd
The Glory Guys 1965 : *Dice of God*, Hoffman Birney
God's Country 1946 : *st* James Oliver Curwood
Gold of the Seven Saints 1961 : *Desert Guns*, Steve Franzee
The Great Bank Robbery 1969 : *st* Frank O'Rourke
The Great Missouri Raid 1951 : *Broken Lance*, Frank Gruber
Gun Fury 1953 : *Ten Against Caesar*, George Granger and K. Roberts
Guns of the Timberland 1960 : *st* Louis L'Amour
Gunsmoke 1953 : *Roughshod*, Norman Fox
The Hallelujah Trail 1965 : *Hallelujah Train*, Bill Gulick
The Hanging Tree 1959 : *st* Dorothy Johnson
Heller in Pink Tights 1960 : *Heller with a Gun*, Louis L'Amour
Heritage of the Desert 1932, 1939 : *st* Zane Grey
Hit the Saddle 1937 : *st* William Colt MacDonald
Hombre 1967 : *st* Elmore Leonard
Hondo 1953 : *st* Louis L'Amour
The Iron Mistress 1952 : *st* Paul I. Wellman
Jeremiah Johnson 1972 : *Mountain Man*, Vardis Fisher
Johnny Guitar 1954 : *st* Roy Chanslor
Jubal 1956 : *Jubal Troop*, Paul I. Wellman
Jubilee Trail 1954 : *st* Glen Bristow
The Kansan 1943 : *Peace Marshal*, Frank Gruber
The Kentuckian 1955 : *The Gabriel Horn*, Felix Holt
The Last Frontier 1955 : *The Gilded Rooster*, Richard E. Roberts
The Last Hunt 1956 : *st* Milton Lott
Last of the Badmen 1957 : *st* Jay Monaghan
The Last Roundup 1934 : *The Border Legion*, Zane Grey
The Last Sunset 1961 : *Sundown at Crazy Horse*, Howard Rigsby
The Law and Jake Wade 1958 : *st* Marvin Albert
Law and Order 1932, 1940, 1953 : *Saint Johnson*, W.R. Burnett
Lawless Valley 1938 : *No Law in Shadow Valley*, W.C. Tuttle
The Light in the Forest 1958 : *st* Conrad Richter
The Light of the Western Stars 1930, 1940 : *st* Zane Grey
Little Big Man 1970 : *st* Thomas Berger
Lonely Are the Brave 1962 : *Brave Cowboy*, Edward Abbey
Lone Star Ranger 1930, 1942 : *st* Zane Grey
The Lone Texan 1959 : *st* James Landis
Lust for Gold 1949 : *Thunder God's Gold*, Barry Storm
Mackenna's Gold 1968 : st *Will Henry*
The Man from Dakota 1940 : *Arouse and Beware*, MacKinlay Kantor
The Man from Laramie 1955 : *st* Thomas T. Flynn
Man in the Saddle 1951 : *The Outcast*, Ernest Haycox

Man of the Forest 1933 : *st* Zane Grey
Man of the West 1958 : *The Border Jumpers*, Will C. Brown
Man without a Star 1955 : *st* Dee Linford
The Mark of Zorro 1940 : *The Curse of Capostrano*, Johnson McCully
McCabe and Mrs Miller 1971 : *McCabe*, Edmund Naughton
Medico of Painted Springs 1941 : *st* James L. Rubel
Mustang 1959 : *Capture of the Golden Stallion*, R. Montgomery
My Darling Clementine 1946 : *Wyatt Earp, Frontier Marshal*, Stuart Lake
My Outlaw Brother 1951 : *South of the Rio Grande*, Max Brand
North of the Rio Grande 1937 : *Cottonwood Gulch*, Clarence Mulford
Old Yeller 1957 : *st* Fred Gipson
Once Upon a Horse 1958 : *Why Rustlers Never Win*, Henry Gregor Felson
One-Eyed Jacks 1961 : *The Authentic Death of Hendry Jones*, C. Neiden
100 Rifles 1968 : *st* Robert McLeod
Oregon Passage 1957 : *st* Gordon D. Shirreffs
The Oregon Trail 1945 : *st* Frank Gruber
The Outcast 1954 : *Two-Edged Vengeance*, Todhunter Ballard
The Ox-Bow Incident 1943 : *st* Walter Van
The Plainsman 1936, 1966 : *Wild Bill Hickok*, Frank Wiltstach
Posse from Hell 1961 : *st* Clair Huffaker
Powder River 1953 : *st* Stuart Lake
Prairie Stranger 1941 : *The Medico Rides the Trail*, James Rubel
The Professionals 1966 : *A Mule for the Marquesa*, Frank O'Rourke
The Quiet Gun 1957 : *The Lawman*, Lauran Paine
Quincannon, Frontier Scout 1956 : *Frontier Feud*, Will Cook
Ramrod 1947 : *st* Luke Short
Red River 1948 : *The Blazing Guns on the Chisolm Trail*, B. Chase
Return of the Texan 1952 : *The Home Place*, Fred Gipson
The Reward 1965 : *st* Michael Barrett
Ride Beyond Vengeance 1966 : *The Night of the Tiger*, Al Dewlen
Riders of the Purple Sage 1931, 1941 : *st* Zane Grey
Rio Conchos 1964 : *Guns of Rio Conchos*, Clair Huffaker
The Road to Reno 1938 : *st* I.A.R. Wylie
Roarin' Lead 1936 : *st* William Colt MacDonald
Romance of the Rio Grande : *Conquistador*, Katherine Gerould
Santa Fé 1951 : *st* James Marshall
The Savage 1952 : *Renegade*, L.T. Foreman
Sea of Grass 1947 : *st* Conrad Richter
The Searchers 1956 : *st* Alan Le May
Seminole Uprising 1955 : *Bugle's Wake*, Curt Brandon
Seven Ways from Sundown 1960 : *st* Clair Huffaker
Shane 1953 : *st* Jack Schaefer
Shoot Out 1971 : *The Lone Cowboy*, Will James
Short Grass 1950 : *st* Tom Blackburn
Sierra 1950 : *st* Stuart Hardy
Sierra Baron 1958 : *st* Tom Blackburn
Silver City 1951 : *High Vermillion*, Luke Short
The Silver Whip 1953 : *First Blood*, Jack Schaefer
Singing Guns 1950 : *st* Max Brand
Smoky 1933, 1966 : *Smoky the Cowhorse*, Will James
Soldier Blue 1970 : *Arrow in the Sun*, Theodore V. Olson
Song of the Trail 1936 : *Playing with Fire*, James O. Curwood
The Spoilers 1930, 1942, 1956 : *st* Rex Beach
Stage to Tucson 1951 : *Lost Stage Valley*, Frank Bonham
Stallion Road 1947 : *st* Stephen Longstreet
Stampede 1949 : *st* Edward Beverly Mann
The Stand at Apache River 1953 : *Apache Landing*, Robert J. Hogan
Station West 1948 : *st* Luke Short
Sugarfoot 1951 : *st* Clarence B. Kelland
The Sundowners 1950 : *Thunder in the Dust*, Alan LeMay

Taggart 1964 : *st* Louis L'Amour
Tall in the Saddle 1951 : *st* Gordon Ray Young
Tall Man Riding 1955 : *st* Norman O. Fox
The Tall Men 1955 : *st* Clay Fisher
The Tall Stranger 1957 : *Showdown Trail*, Louis L'Amour
Tell Them Willie Boy Is Here 1969 : *Willie Boy*, Harry Lawton
Tension at Table Rock 1956 : *Bitter Sage*, Frank Gruber
The Texans 1938 : *North of '36*, Emerson Hough
The Texas Rangers 1936 : *st* Walter Prescott Webb
These Thousand Hills 1959 : *st* A.B. Guthrie Jnr
Three Godfathers 1936, 1948 : *st* Peter Kyne
Three Young Texans 1954 : *st* Wallace MacLeod Raine
Thunder Mountain 1947 : *To the Last Man*, Zane Grey
Thunder over the Prairie 1941 : *The Medico Rides*, James L. Rubel
Thunder Trail 1937 : *Arizona Ames*, Zane Grey
The Thundering Herd 1933 : *st* Zane Grey
Tonka 1958 : *Comanche*, David Appel
To the Last Man 1933 : *st* Zane Grey
Track of the Cat 1954 : *st* Walter Van Trilburg Clark
Trail of the Lonesome Pine 1936 : *st* John Fox Jnr
The Tramplers 1966 : *Guns of North Texas*, Will Cook
The Treasure of the Sierra Madre 1948 : *st* B. Taven
True Grit 1969 : *st* Charles Portis
Tumbleweed 1953 : *Three Were Renegades*, Kenneth Perkins
Two Rode Together 1961 : *Comache Captives*, Will Cook
Under the Tonto Rim 1933, 1947 : *st* Zane Grey
The Unforgiven 1960 : *st* Alan LeMay
Union Pacific 1939 : *Trouble Shooter*, Ernest Haycox
Utah Blaine 1957 : *st* Louis L'Amour
The Vanishing American 1955 : *st* Zane Grey
The Vanquished 1953 : *Decision to Kill*, Karl Brown
Vengeance Valley 1951 : *st* Luke Short
The Violent Men 1955 : *Smoky Valley*, Donald Hamilton
The Virginian 1929, 1946 : *st* Owen Wister
Viva Zapata! 1952 : *Zapata the Unconquerable*, Edgcumb Pinchon
Waco 1966 : *Emporia*, Harry Stanford, Max Lamb
Wanderer of the Wasteland 1935, 1945 : *st* Zane Grey
Warlock 1959 : *st* Oakley Hall
Warpath 1951 : *Broken Lance*, Frank Gruber
The Way West 1967 : *st* A.B. Guthrie Jnr
Welcome to Hard Times 1967 : *st* E.L. Doctorow
Western Union 1941 : *st* Zane Grey
Westward Ho, the Wagons 1956 : *Children of the Covered Wagon*, Mary J. Carr
The White Squaw 1956 : *The Gun Witch of Wyoming*, Larabie Sutter
Wild Horse Mesa 1932, 1947 : *st* Zane Grey
The Wonderful Country 1959 : *st* Tom Lea
Young Billy Young 1969 : *Who Rides with Wyatt*, Will Henry
Yukon Gold 1952 : *st* James Oliver Curwood
The Yukon Patrol 1942 : *King of the Royal Mounted*, Zane Grey

Reprinted by permission from *The Velvet Light Trap* No. 12, Spring 1974

Appendix 7
Select Bibliography

This bibliography lists only books about the Western. For brief descriptions of them and for details of books devoted to individual performers, directors of Westerns and the West, I would recommend Jack Nachbar's *Western Films*. A revision and updating of this very useful work would be welcomed by all Western scholars.

Agel, Henri (ed), *Le Western*, Lettres Modernes, Paris, 1961

Barbour, Alan G, *The Thrill of It All*, Collier Books, New York, 1971

Barbour, Alan G (ed), *The 'B' Western*, Screen Facts Press, New York, 1966

Bazin, Andre, *What Is Cinema? Vol II*, trans Hugh Gray, University of California Press, Berkeley, California, 1971 Contains Bazin's key essays on the Western.

Bellour, Raymond and Brion, Patrick (eds), *Le Western*, Union Générale d'Editions, Paris, 1966, revised 1969

Bichard, Robert S, *The Western in the 1920s* Only available for study at AFI, Centre for Advanced Film Studies, Beverly Hills, California.

Calder, Jenni, *There Must Be a Lone Ranger: The Myth and Reality of the American Wild West*, Sphere Books, London, 1976

Cawelti, John G, *The Six-Gun Mystique*, Bowling Green University Popular Press, Bowling Green, Ohio, 1971

Chiattone, Antonio, *Il Film Western*, Poligono Societa Editrice, Milan, 1949

Corneau, Ernest N, *The Hall of Fame of Western Stars*, Christopher Publishing House, North Quincy, Massachusetts, 1969

Eyles, Allen, *The Western: An Illustrated Guide*, Tantivy Press, London, 1967, revised and updated 1975

Fenin, George N and Everson, William K, *The Western: From Silents to the Seventies*, Grossman Publishers, New York, 1973

Frantz, Joe B and Choate, Julian Ernest, *The American Cowboy: The Myth and the Reality*, Thames and Hudson, London, 1956

Frayling, Christopher, *Spaghetti Westerns: Cowboys and Europeans from Karl May to Sergio Leone*, Routledge and Kegan Paul, London, 1981

French, Philip, *Westerns*, Secker & Warburg, London, 1973, revised 1977

Garfield, Brian, *Western Films*, Rawson Associates, New York, 1982

Hake, Theodore L and Cauler, Robert D, *Six Gun Heroes: A Price Guide to Movie Cowboy Collectibles*, Wallace Homestead Book Company, Des Moines, Iowa, 1976

Hembus, Joe, *Western-Lexikon*, Hanser Verlag, Munich, 1976

Horwitz, James, *They Went Thataway*, E.P. Dutton, New York, 1976

Kezich, Tullio (ed), *Il Western Maggiorenne: Saggi e Documenti sul Film Storico Americano*, F. Zigiotti, Trieste, 1953

Kitses, Jim, *Horizons West*, Secker & Warburg, London, 1969

Lahue, Kalton C, *Winners of the West: The Sagebrush Heroes of the Silent Screen*, A.S. Barnes and Co, New York, 1970

Lenihan, John H, *Showdown: Confronting Modern America in the Western Film*, University of Chicago Press, Urbana, Illinois, 1980

Manchel, Frank, *Cameras West*, Prentice-Hall Inc, Englewood Cliffs, New Jersey, 1971

McClure, Arthur and Jones, Ken D, *Heroes, Heavies and Sagebrush*, A.S. Barnes and Co, New York, 1972

Meyer, William R, *The Making of the Great Westerns*, Arlington House, New Rochelle, New York, 1979

Miller, Don, *Hollywood Corral*, Popular Library, New York, 1976

Nachbar, Jack, *Western Films: An Annotated Critical Bibliography*, Garland Publishing, New York, 1975

Nachbar, Jack (ed), *Focus On the Western*, Prentice-Hall Inc, Englewood Cliffs, New Jersey, 1974 Amongst the essays collected here is Robert Warshow's classic, 'Movie Chronicle: The Westerner'.

Parish, James Robert, *Great Western Stars*, Ace Books, New York, 1976

Parish, James Robert and Pitts, Michael R, *The Great Western Pictures*, New Jersey, Metuchen, 1976

Parkinson, Michael and Jeavons, Clyde, *A Pictorial History of Westerns*, Hamlyn, London, 1972

Rainey, Buck, *Saddle Aces of the Cinema*, A.S. Barnes and Co, New York, 1980

Rainey, Buck and Adams, Les, *Shoot Em Ups*, Arlington House, New Rochelle, New York, 1978

Riupeyrout, Jean-Louis, *La Grande Adventure du Western: du Far-West à Hollywood (1894-1963)*, Editions du Cerf, Paris, 1964

Rothel, David, *The Singing Cowboys*, A.S. Barnes and Co, New York, 1978

Staig, Laurence and Williams, Tony, *Italian Western, the Opera of Violence*, Lorrimer Press, London, 1975

Tuska, Jon, *The Filming of the West*, Doubleday & Co, Garden City, New York, 1976

Warman, Eric and Vallence, Tom, *Westerns*, Golden Pleasure Books, London, 1964

Wright, Will, *Six Guns and Society: A Structural Study of the Western*, University of California Press, Berkeley, California, 1975

Appendix 8
All Other Sound Westerns

The following is a list of all the Westerns which space dictated could not be covered in detail. Unless otherwise stated, the films were produced in America. The first name given is that of the director; this is followed by those of the two principal actors.

Note: The list excludes films constructed from TV episodes or telefilms unless they were theatrically released.

A Ghentar si Muore Facile 1967 (It)
Leon Klimowsky; George Hilton, T. Moore

Abilene Trail 1951 54 min
Lewis Collins; Whip Wilson, Andy Clyde

Ace High 1969 (Sp)
Giuseppe Colizzi; Eli Wallach, Terence Hill

Aces and Eights 1936 62 min
Sam Newfield; Tim McCoy, Luana Walters

Aces Wild 1936 57 min
Harry Fraser; Harry Carey, Gertrude Messinger

Across the Plains 1939 59 min
Spencer Bennet; Jack Randall, Frank Yaconelli

Across the Rio Grande 1949
Oliver Drake; Jimmy Wakely, Dub Taylor

Ad Uno ad Uno ... Spietatamente 1968 (It)
Rafael Romero Marchent; Peter Lee Lawrence, W. Bogart

Adios Gringo 1965 (It/Sp/Fr) 98 min
George Finlay (Giorgio Stegani); Giuliano Gemma, Evelyn Stewart (Ida Galli)

Adios Sabata 1971 (It/Sp)
Frank Kramer; Yul Brynner, Pedro Sanchez

The Adventures of Bullwhip Griffin 1967 110 min
James Neilson; Roddy McDowall, Karl Malden

The Adventures of Don Coyote 1947 65 min
Reginald LeBorg; Frances Rafferty, Richard Martin

Adventures of Frank and Jesse James 1948 13 chaps
Fred Brannon, Yakima Canutt; Clayton Moore, Steve Darrell

The Adventures of the Masked Phantom 1939 60 min
Charles Abbott; Monte Rawlins, Sonny LaMont

Alaska 1944 76 min
George Archainbaud; Kent Taylor, John Carradine

Alias Billy the Kid 1946 56 min
Thomas Carr; Sunset Carson, Roy Barcroft

Alias John Law 1935
Robert N. Bradbury; Bob Steele, Roberta Gale

Alias the Bad Man 1931 66 min
Phil Rosen; Ken Maynard, Charles King

Alive ... or Preferably Dead (Vivi o Preferibilimente Morti) 1969 (It/Sp) 90 min
Duccio Tessari; Giuliano Gemma, Cris Huerta

All Mine to Give 1957 102 min
Allen Reisner; Cameron Mitchell, Glynis Johns

All Out (Tutto per Tutto) 1968 (It/Sp) 89 min
Umberto Lenzi; Mark Damon, John Ireland

All 'Ovest di Sacramento 1971 (It)
R. Owens; P. Perret, R. Hossein

Alla Conquista dell 'Arkansas 1965 (It/Fr/WG)
Alberto Cardone, Paul Martin;

Alleluja e Sartana, Figli di . . . Dio 1972 (It)
Mario Siciliano; Richard Widmark, Ron Ely

Along the Navajo Trail 1945 66 min
Frank McDonald; Roy Rogers, George Hayes

Along the Rio Grande 1941 61 min
Edward Killy; Tim Holt, Robert Fiske

Along the Sundown Trail 1942
Sam Newfield; Bill Boyd, Charles King

Altrimenti ci Arrabbiamo 1974 (It)
M. Fondato; Terrence Hill, Bud Spencer

T'Ammazzo, Raccomandati a Dio 1968 (It)
Osvaldo Civirani; G. Hamilton, John Ireland

Ambush Trail 1946 60 min
Harry Fraser; Bob Steele, Syd Saylor

Ambush Valley 1936 57 min
B.B. Ray; Bob Custer, Wally Wales

The Americano 1955 85 min
William Castle; Glenn Ford, Frank Lovejoy

Amore Piombo e Furore 1979 (It/Sp)
Antonio Brandt; Warren Oates, Sam Peckinpah

An Eye for an Eye 1966 92 min
Michael Moore; Robert Lansing, Patrick Wayne

Anche gli Angeli Mangiano Fagioli 1973 (It)
E.B. Clucher (Enzo Barboni); Bud Spencer, Giuliano Gemma

Anche nel West, c'era una Volta Dio 1968 (It/Sp) 96 min
Mario Girolami; Richard Harrison, Gilbert Roland

Anche per Django la Carogne Hanno un Prezzo 1971 (It)
P. Solvay; J. Cameron, J. Desmont

Ancora Dollari per i McGregor 1970 (It)
J.L. Merino; Peter Lee Lawrence, Stan Cooper

And God Said to Cain (Dio Disse a Caino) 1970 (It/WG) 105 (100) min
Anthony Dawson; Klaus Kinski, Pater Carsten

. . .And Now Miguel 1966 95 min
James B. Carr; Guy Stockwell, Clu Gulager

Anda Muchacho, Spara 1971 (It)
A. Florio; Fabio Testi, C. Lopez

Any Gun Can Play 1968 (It)
Enzo Castellani; Gilbert Roland, Edd Byrnes

Apache 1970 (It)
Pasquale Squitieri;

Apache Chief 1949 60 min
Frank McDonald; Alan Curtis, Russell Hayden

Apache Country 1952 62 min
George Archainbaud; Gene Autry, Pat Buttram

The Apache Kid 1941 56 min
George Sherman; Donald Barry, Lynn Merick

The Apache Kid's Escape 1930 51 min
Robert J. Horner; Jack Perrin, Bud Osborne

Apache Rose 1947 75 min
William Witney; Roy Rogers, Dale Evans

Apache Territory 1958 75 min
Ray Nazarro; Rory Calhoun, John Dehner

Apache Uprising 1966 90 min
R.G. Springsteen; Rory Calhoun, Richard Arlen

Aquasanta Joe 1971 (It)
Mario Gariazzo; Lincoln Tate, Ty Hardin

Arizona Bad Man 1935 58 min
S. Roy Luby; Reb Russell, Edmund Cobb

Arizona Bushwackers 1968 86 min
Lesley Selander; Howard Keel, John Ireland

Arizona Colt si Scateno e li Fece 1970 (It/Sp)
Sergio Martino; Anthony Steffen, Erika Blank

Arizona Cyclone 1934
Robert Tansey; Wally Wales, Franklyn Farnum

Arizona Frontier 1940 60 min
Al Herman; Tex Ritter, Slim Andrews

Arizona Gangbusters 1940 57 min
Sam Newfield; Tim McCoy, Forrest Taylor

The Arizona Kid 1939 61 min
Joseph Kane; Roy Rogers, George Hayes

Arizona Nights 1934
Bernard B. Ray; Jack Perrin, Ben Corbett

The Arizona Raiders 1936 54 min
James Hogan; Larry 'Buster' Crabbe, Raymond Hatton

Arizona Roundup 1942 56 min
Robert Tansey; Tom Keene, Frank Yaconelli

Arizona Stagecoach 1942 58 min
S. Roy Luby; Ray Corrigan, John King

Arizona Territory 1950 56 min
Wallace Ford; Whip Wilson, Andy Clyde

The Arizona Terror 1931 64 min
Phil Rosen; Ken Maynard, Edmund Cobb

Arizona Trails 1935
Alan James; Bill Patton, Edna Aslin

Arkansas Judge 1941 72 min
Frank McDonald; Roy Rogers, Pauline Moore

Arm of the Law 1932 60 min
Louis King; Rex Bell, Robert Frazer

Arriva Durango, Paga o Muori 1971 (It)
Roberto Montero; B. Harris, Jose Torres

Arriva Sabata 1970 (It/Sp) 89 min
Tulio Demichele; Anthony Steffen, Peter Lee Lawrence

Arrivano Django e Sartana . . . e la Fine 1970 (It)
Anthony Ascott (Giuliano Carmineo); Antonio Vilar, Daniela Giordano

Attento Gringo . . . e Tornato Sabata 1972 (It)
A. Bragan; V.E. Richelmy, George Martin

Avenging Waters 1936 57 min
Spencer G. Bennet; Ken Maynard, Ward Bond

Back to God's Country 1953 78 min
Joseph Penney; Rock Hudson, Steve Cochran

Back to the Woods 1937
Preston Black; Moe Howard, Curley Howard

Back Trail 1948 57 min
Christy Cabanne; Johnny Mack Brown, Raymond Hatton

Bad Man from Red Butte 1940 58 min
Ray Taylor; Johnny Mack Brown, Fuzzy Knight

Badman of Deadwood 1941 61 min
Joseph Kane; Roy Rogers, George Hayes

Bad Man's River (E Continuano a Fregarsi il Milione di Dollari) 1971 (It/Fr/Sp) 90 min
Gene Martin (Eugenio Martin); Lee Van Cleef, Gina Lollobrigida

Bad Men of the Border 1945 56 min
Wallace Fox; Kirby Grant, Fuzzy Knight

Bad Men of the Hills 1942 58 min
William Berke; Charles Starrett, Russell Hayden

Bad Men of Thunder Gap 1943 57 min
Al Herman; Dave (Tex) O'Brien, Jim Newill

Bada Alla Tua Pelle Spirito Santo 1972 (It)
Roberto Mauri; V. Karis, Ray O'Connor

The Badge of Marshal Brennan 1957 74 min
Albert C. Gannaway; Jim Davis, Arleen Whelan

Badman's Gold 1951 56 min
Robert Tansey; Johnny Carpenter, Emmett Lynn

The Ballad of Ben and Charlie (Amico, Stammi Lontano Almeno un Palmo) 1972 (It) 118 min
Michele Lupo; Giuliano Gemma, G. Eastman

Ballata per un Pistolero 1967 (It/WG) 98 min
Alfio Caltabiano; Antony Ghidra, Angelo Infanti

The Bandit (O Cangaciero) 1953 (Brazil)
Lima Barreto; Marisa Prado, Alberto Ruschel

Bandit King of Texas 1949 60 min
Fred C. Brannon; Allan Lane, Eddy Waller

Bandit Ranger 1942
Lesley Selander; Tim Holt, Cliff Edwards

The Bandit Trail 1941 60 min
Edward Killy; Tim Holt, Ray Whitley

Die Banditen von Rio Grande 1965 (WG) 90 min
Helmuth M. Backhaus; Harald Leipniz, Maria Perschy

Bandits of Dark Canyon 1947 59 min
Phillip Ford; Allan Lane, Bob Steele

Bandits of Eldorado 1949 56 min
Ray Nazarro; Charles Starrett, Smiley Burnette

Bandits of the Badlands 1945 55 min
Thomas Carr; Sunset Carson, Peggy Stewart

Bandits of the West 1953 54 min
Harry Keller; Allan Lane, Eddy Waller

I Bandoleros della Dodicesima Ora 1972 (It)
A. Bragan; M. Forrest, F. Harrison

The Bang Bang Kid 1967 (It)
L. Lelli; Guy Madison, Tom Bosley

Bar L Ranch 1930 60 min
Harry S. Webb; Buffalo Bill Jnr, Wally Wales

Bar 20 Justice 1938 70 min
Lesley Selander; William Boyd, George Hayes

Bar Z Bad Men 1937 57 min
Sam Newfield; Johnny Mack Brown, Tom London

Una Bara per lo Sceriffo 1965 (It/Sp)
Mario Caiano;

Barbed Wire 1952 61 min
George Archainbaud; Gene Autry, Pat Buttram

The Barrier 1937 90 min
Lesley Selander; Leo Carillo, Jean Parker

Bastardo . . . Vamos a Matar 1971 (It)
L. Mangini; George Eastman, Lincoln Tate

La Battaglia di Fort Apache 1964 (It/Fr/Yug)
Hugo Fregonese;

Battle of Greed 1937 65 min
Harold Higgin; Tom Keene, Gwynne Shipman

The Battles of Chief Pontiac 1952 72 min
Felix Feist; Lex Barker, Lon Chaney

Battling Buckaroo 1932
Armand Schaefer; Lane Chandler, Yakima Canutt

Battling Marshal 1950 55 min
Oliver Drake; Sunset Carson, Forrest Mathews

The Beast of Hollow Mountain 1956 79 min
Edward Nassour; Guy Madison, Patricia Medina

Beau Bandit 1930 68 min
Lambert Hillyer; Rod LaRoque, George Duryea (Tom Keene)

Beauty and the Bandit 1946 77 min
William Nigh; Gilbert Roland, Frank Yaconelli

Belle Le Grande 1951 90 min
Allan Dwan; Vera Ralston, John Carroll

Belle of the Yukon 1944 84 min
William A. Seiter; Randolph Scott, Dinah Shore

Il Bello, il Brutto, il Cretino 1967 (It/WG)
Giovanni Grimaldi; Franco Franchi, Ciccio Ingrassia

The Bells of San Fernando 1947 74 min
Terry Morse; Donald Woods, Gloria Warren

Between Fighting Men 1932 62 min
Forrest Sheldon; Ken Maynard, Ruth Hall

Beyond the Law 1930 50 min
J.P. McGowan; Robert Frazer, Lane Chandler

Beyond the Law 1934 60 min
D. Ross Lederman; Tim McCoy, Lane Chandler

Beyond the Pecos 1945 58 min
Lambert Hillyer; Robert Cameron, Eddie Dew

Beyond the Rio Grande 1930 60 min
Harry Webb; Jack Perrin, Buffalo Bill Jnr

Beyond the Rockies 1932 60 min
Fred Allen; Tom Keene, Rochelle Hudson

Big Boy Rides Again 1935
Al Herman; Big Boy Williams, Lafe McKee

Big Calibre 1935
Robert N. Bradbury; Bob Steele, Peggy Campbell

Big Jack 1949 85 min
Richard Thorpe; Wallace Beery, Richard Conte

The Big Silence (Il Grande Silenzio) 1968 (It/Fr) 106 min
Sergio Corbucci; Jean-Louis Trintignant, Klaus Kinski

Bill il Taciturno 1967 (It) 97 min
Max Hunter; George Eastman, L. Orfei

Billy the Kid in Santa Fé 1941 66 min
Sherman Scott (Sam Newfield); Bob Steele, Al St John

Billy the Kid in Texas 1940 52 min
Peter Stewart (Sam Newfield); Bob Steele, Al St John

Billy the Kid Outlawed 1940 52 min
Peter Stewart (Sam Newfield); Bob Steele, Al St John

Billy the Kid Wanted 1941 64 min
Sherman Scott (Sam Newfield); Buster Crabbe, Al St John

Billy the Kid's Fighting Pals 1941 62 min
Sherman Scott (Sam Newfield); Bob Steele, Al St John

Billy the Kid's Gun Justice 1940 57 min
Peter Stewart (Sam Newfield); Bob Steele, Al St John

Billy the Kid's Range Law 1941 57 min
Peter Stewart (Sam Newfield); Bob Steele, Al St John

Billy the Kid's Roundup 1941 58 min
Sherman Scott (Sam Newfield); Buster Crabbe, Al St John

Billy the Kid's Smoking Guns 1942 58 min
Sherman Scott (Sam Newfield); Buster Crabbe, Al St John

Black Arrow 1944 15 chaps
Lew Landers; Robert Scott, Adele Jergens

Black Eagle 1948 76 min
Robert Gordon; William Bishop, Virginia Patton

Black Eagle of Santa Fé (Die Schwarzen Adler von Santa Fé) 1964 (WG/It/Fr) 93 (85) min
Ernst Hofbauer; Brad Harris, Joachim Hansen

Black Hills 1947 60 min
Ray Taylor; Eddie Dean, Roscoe Ates

Black Jack 1968 (It) 99 min
Gianfranco Baldanello; Robert Wood, Lucienne Bridou

The Black Lash 1952
Ron Ormond; Lash LaRue, Al St John

Black Market Rustlers 1943 58 min
S. Roy Luby; Ray Corrigan, John King

Black Spurs 1965 81 min
R.G. Springsteen; Rory Calhoun, Terry Moore

Blazing Across the Pecos 1948 56 min
Ray Nazarro; Charles Starrett, Smiley Burnette

Blazing Bullets 1951 51 min
Wallace Fox; Johnny Mack Brown, Lois Hall

Blazing Frontier 1943 59 min
Sam Newfield; Buster Crabbe, Al St John

Blazing Guns 1935
Ray Heinz; Reb Russell, Lafe McKee

Blazing Guns (Uomo Mezzo Ammazzato . . . Parola di Spirito Santo) 1972 (It/Sp) 89 min
Anthony Ascott (Giuliano Carmineo); Gianni Garko, Pilar Velasquez

Blazing Justice 1936
Al Herman; Bill Cody, Gertrude Messinger

Blazing Stewardesses 1975 85 min
Al Adamson; Yvonne De Carlo, Bob Livingston

The Blazing Sun 1950 70 min
John English; Gene Autry, Pat Buttram

Blazing the Western Trail 1945 60 min
Vernon Keays; Charles Starrett, Dub Taylor

The Blazing Trail 1949 56 min
Ray Nazarro; Charles Starrett, Smiley Burnette

The Blocked Trail 1943 58 min
Elmer Clifton; Bob Steele, Tom Tyler

Blood on the Arrow 1964 91 min
Sidney Salkow; Dale Robertson, Martha Hyer

Blood River (Dio Perdona . . . Io No!) 1967 (It/Sp) 115 (97) min
Giuseppe Colizzi; Terence Hill (Mario Girotti), Bud Spencer (Carlo Pedersoli)

Blu Gang (E Vissero per Sempre Felici e Ammazzati) 1973 (It)
Marc Meyer; Jack Palance, Antonio Falsi

Blue Canadian Rockies 1952 58 min
George Archainbaud; Gene Autry, Pat Buttram

Blue Montana Skies 1939 56 min
B. Reeves Eason; Gene Autry, Smiley Burnette

Die Blutigen Geier von Alaska 1973 (WG) 97 min
Harald Reinl; Doug McClure, Harald Leipnitz

Boiling Point 1932 70 min
George Melford; Hoot Gibson, George Hayes

Bonanza Town 1951 56 min
Fred F. Sears; Charles Starrett, Smiley Burnette

Boot Hill (La Collina degli Stivali) 1969 (It) 106 min
Giuseppe Colizzi; Terence Hill, Bud Spencer

Boot Hill Bandits 1942 58 min
S. Roy Luby; Ray Corrigan, John King

Boots and Saddles 1937 59 min
Joseph Kane; Gene Autry, Smiley Burnette

Boots of Destiny 1937 56 min
Arthur Rosson; Ken Maynard, Claudia Dell

Border Badmen 1945 59 min
Sam Newfield; Buster Crabbe, Al St John

Border Bandits 1946 58 min
Lambert Hillyer; Johnny Mack Brown, Raymond Hatton

Border Brigands 1935 56 min
Nick Grinde; Buck Jones, Fred Kohler

Border Caballero 1936 59 min
Sam Newfield; Tim McCoy, Lois January

Border Cafe 1937 69 min
Lew Landers; Harry Carey, Armida

Border Fence 1951 89 min
Norman Sheldo (Sheldon), H.W. Kier; Walt Wayne, Lee Morgan

Border Feud 1947 55 min
Ray Taylor; Lash LaRue, Al St John

Border G-Man 1938 60 min
David Howard; George O'Brien, Ray Whitley

Border Guns 1934
Jack Nelson; Bill Cody, Blanche Mehaffey

The Border Menace 1934
Jack Nelson; Bill Cody, Miriam Rice

The Border Patrolman 1936 60 min
David Howard; George O'Brien, Polly Ann Young

Border Rangers 1950 57 min
William Berke; Don Barry, Robert Lowery

Border Roundup 1942 57 min
Sam Newfield; George Houston, Al St John

Border Saddlemates 1952 67 min
William Witney; Rex Allen, Slim Pickens

Border Treasure 1950 60 min
George Archainbaud; Tim Holt, Jane Nigh

Border Vengeance 1935
Ray Heinz; Reb Russell, Mary Jane Carey

Bordertown Gunfighters 1943 55 min
Howard Bretherton; Bill Elliott, George Hayes

Bordertown Trail 1944 55 min
Lesley Selander; Smiley Burnette, Sunset Carson

Born Bad 1958 89 min
Richard L. Bare;

Born Reckless 1959 79 min
Howard Koch; Mamie Van Doren, Jeff Richards

Born to Battle 1935
Harry S. Webb; Tom Tyler, Earl Dwire

Born to the Saddle 1953 73 min
William Beaudine; Chuck Courtney, Donald Woods

Boss Cowboy 1934
Victor Adamson (Denver Dixon); Buddy Roosevelt, Frances Morris

Boss of Boomtown 1944 58 min
Ray Taylor; Rod Cameron, Fuzzy Knight

Boss of Bullion City 1941
Ray Taylor; Johnny Mack Brown, Fuzzy Knight

Boss of Rawhide 1943 57 min
Elmer Clifton; Dave O'Brien, Jim Newill

Both Barrels Blazing 1945 57 min
Derwin Abrahams; Charles Starrett, Dub Taylor

Un Bounty Killer a Trinita 1972 (It)
Oskar Faradine; Jeff Cameron, Paul McCren

The Bounty Killer 1966 (It/Sp)
Eugenio Martin; Richard Wyler, Tomas Milian

Boy's Ranch 1946 97 min
Roy Rowland; Jackie Jenkins, James Craig

Brand of Fear 1949 56 min
Oliver Drake; Jimmy Wakely, Dub Taylor

Brand of Hate 1934 63 min
Lew Collins; Bob Steele, William Farnum

Brand of Shame 1968 73 min
B. Ron Elliott;

Brand of the Devil 1944 57 min
Harry Fraser; Dave O'Brien, Jim Newill

Brand of the Outlaws 1936 60 min
Robert N. Bradbury; Bob Steele, Margaret Marquis

Branded 1931 61 min
D. Ross Lederman; Buck Jones, Ethel Kenton

Branded Men 1931 70 min
Phil Rosen; Ken Maynard, Charles King

Breed of the Border 1933 60 min
Robert N. Bradbury; Bob Steele, George Hayes

Breed of the West 1930 60 min
Alvin J. Neitz (Alan James); Wally Wales, Lafe McKee

The Broken Land 1962 60 min
John Bushelman; Kent Taylor, Jack Nicholson

The Broken Sabre 1965 89 min
Bernard McEveety; Chuck Connors, MacDonald Carey

Brothers of the West 1937 58 min
Sam Katzman; Tom Tyler, Lois Wilde

The Brute and the Beast (Tempo di Massacro) 1966 (It) 86 min
Lucio Fulci; Franco Nero, George Hilton

Buckaroo 1968 (It) 89 min
Adelchi Bianchi; Dean Reed, Monica Brugger

Buckaroo from Powder River 1947 55 min
Ray Nazarro; Charles Starrett, Smiley Burnette

Buckskin Frontier 1943 74 min
Lesley Selander; Richard Dix, Jane Wyatt

The Buckskin Lady 1957 66 min
Carl K. Hittleman; Patricia Medina, Richard Denning

Un Buco in Fronte 1968 (It) 100 (88) min
Joseph Warren (Giuseppe Vari); Antony Ghidra, Robert Hundar

Buffalo Bill 1964 (WG)
Mario Costa; Gordon Scott

Buffalo Gun 1961 72 min
Albert C. Gannaway; Webb Pierce, Marty Robbins

The Bull of the West 1971 99 min
Paul Stanley, Jerry Hopper;

Bulldog Courage 1935 60 min
Sam Newfield; Tim McCoy, Joan Woodbury

Bullet for a Stranger (Gli Fumavano le Colt . . . lo Chiamavano Camposanto) 1971 (It) 94 min
Anthony Ascott (Giuliano Carmineo); Gianni Garko, William Berger

Bullet for Billy the Kid 1963 61 min
Rafael Baledon; Gaston Sands, Steve Brodie

A Bullet for Sandoval 1969 (Sp)
Julio Buchs; Ernest Borgnine, G. Hilton

Bullets and Saddles 1943 54 min
Anthony Marshall; Ray Corrigan, Dennis Moore

Bullets for Bandits 1942 55 min
Wallace Fox; Bill Elliott, Tex Ritter

Bullets for Rustlers 1940 58 min
Sam Nelson; Charles Starrett, Bob Nolan

Buon Funerale Amigos, Paga Sartana 1970 (It) 91 min
Anthony Ascott (Giuliano Carmineo); Gianni Garko, Antonio Vicar

Bury Me Not on the Lone Prairie 1941 57 min
Ray Taylor; Johnny Mack Brown, Fuzzy Knight

Bury Them Deep (All'Ultimo Sangue) 1968 (It) 100 (91) min
John Byrd (Paolo Moffa); Craig Hill, Ken Wood

Bush Christmas 1947 (Australia)
Ralph Smart; Chips Rafferty, Helen Grieve

Buzzy and the Phantom Pinto 1941 55 min
Richard C. Kahn; Buzzy Henry, Dave O'Brien

Buzzy Rides the Range 1940 60 min
Richard C. Kahn; Dave O'Brien, Claire Rochelle

The Cactus Kid 1934
Harry S. Webb; Jack Perrin, Tom London

California 1963 86 min
Hamil Petroff; Jock Mahoney, Faith Domergue

California 1978 (It)
Michele Lupo; Giuliano Gemma, William Berger

California Firebrand 1948 63 min
Philip Ford; Monte Hale, Adrian Booth

California Gold Rush 1946 51 min
R.G. Springsteen; Bill Elliott, Peggy Stewart

California Joe 1943
Spencer Bennet; Don Barry, Helen Talbot

The California Trail 1933 67 min
Lambert Hillyer; Buck Jones, Helen Mack

Call of the Desert 1930 53 min
J.P. McGowan; Tom Tyler, Sheila LeGay

Call of the Forest 1949 74 min
John Link; Robert Lowery, Ken Curtis

Call of the Klondike 1950 67 min
Frank McDonald; Kirby Grant, Anne Gwynne

Call of the Prairie 1936 65 min
Howard Bretherton; William Boyd, Jimmy Ellison

Call of the Rockies 1931 60 min
Ray Johnston; Ben Lyon, Russell Simpson

Call of the Rockies 1938 54 min
Alan James; Charles Starrett, Donald Grayson

Call of the Rockies 1944
Lesley Selander; Smiley Burnette, Sunset Carson

Call of the West 1930 72 min
Albert Ray; Dorothy Revier, Matt Moore

The Call of the Wild 1972 (GB/WG/Sp/It/Fr) 105 min
Ken Annakin; Charlton Heston, Michele Mercier

Call of the Yukon 1938 70 min
B. Reeves Eason; Richard Arlen, Beverly Roberts

Campa Carogna - la Taglia Cresce 1973 (It/Sp)
Giuseppe Rosati; Gianni Garko, Stephen Boyd

Canadian Mounties vs Atomic Invaders 1953 12 chaps
Franklin Adreon; Bill Henry, Susan Morrow

Can't Help Singing 1944 90 min
Frank Ryan; Dianna Durbin, Robert Paige

Canyon Ambush 1952 53 min
Lewis Collins; Johnny Mack Brown, Phyllis Coates

Canyon City 1943
Spencer Bennet; Don Barry, Helen Talbot

Canyon Hawks 1930 60 min
J.P. McGowan, Alvin J. Neitz (Alan James); Wally Wales, Yakima Canutt

The Canyon of Missing Men 1930 53 min
J.P. McGowan; Tom Tyler, Bud Osborne

Canyon Raiders 1951 54 min
Lewis Collins; Whip Wilson, Fuzzy Knight

Captain John Smith and Pocahontas 1953 75 min
Lew Landers; Anthony Dexter, Alan Hale Jnr

Una Carabina per Schut 1966 (It)
R. Siodmak; Lex Barker, M. Versini

Carambola 1974 (It)
Fernando Baldi; P. Smith, M. Coppy

Carlos 1971 (WG) 107 min
Hans W. Geissendorfer;

Carogne si Nasce 1968 (It)
Al Bradley (A. Brescia); Glenn Saxson, Gordon Mitchell

Carolina Cannonball 1955 74 min
Charles Lamont; Judy Canova, Andy Clyde

Carolina Moon 1940 65 min
Frank McDonald; Gene Autry, Smiley Burnette

Carson City Cyclone 1943 55 min
Howard Bretherton; Don Barry, Lynn Merrick

The Carson City Kid 1940 57 min
Joseph Kane; Roy Rogers, George Hayes

Caryl of the Mountains 1936 68 min
Bernard B. Ray; Rin-Tin-Tin Jnr, Francis X. Bushman Jnr

Cast a Long Shadow 1959 82 min
Thomas Carr; Audie Murphy, John Dehner

Caught 1931 68 min
Edward Sloman; Richard Arlen, Syd Saylor

Cavalcade of the West 1936 59 min
Harry Fraser; Hoot Gibson, Rex Lease

Cavalry 1936 63 min
Robert N. Bradbury; Bob Steele, Frances Grant

Cavalry Charge (La Carga de la Policia Montada) 1965 (Sp) 103 min
Ramon Torrado;

C'e Sartana . . . Vendi la Pistola e Comprati la Bara 1970 (It) 93 min
Anthony Ascott (Giuliano Carnimeo); George Hilton, Charles Southwood

Centomila Dollari per Lassiter 1966 (It/Sp) 85 min
Joaquin Romero Marchent; Robert Hundar, Pamela Tudor

Centomila Dollari per Ringo 1965 (It/Sp) 100 min
Alberto De Martino;

The Challenge of Rin-Tin-Tin 1958 77 min
Robert G. Walker; Rin-Tin-Tin, Jim L. Brown

Challenge of the Mackennas (La Sfida dei Mackenna) 1969 (It/Sp)
Leon Klimowsky; John Ireland, Robert Wood

Challenge of the Range 1949 54 min
Ray Nazarro; Charles Starrett, Smiley Burnette

The Charge of the Seventh Cavalry (La Carica del 70 Cavallegeri) 1964 (It/Sp) 85 min
Herbert Martin (Alfredo De Martino); Edmund Purdom, Paul Piaget

Check Your Guns 1948 55 min
Ray Taylor; Eddie Dean, Roscoe Ates

Cherokee Strip 1940 86 min
Lesley Selander; Richard Dix, Victor Jory

Cherokee Uprising 1950 55 min
Lewis Collins; Whip Wilson, Andy Clyde

Chetan, Indian Boy (Tschetan der Indianerjunge) 1973 (WG) 94 min
Hark Bohm; Marquand Bohm, Willi Schultes

The Cheyenne Cyclone 1932 57 min
Armand Schaefer; Lane Chandler, Yakima Canutt

The Cheyenne Kid 1930
Jacques Jaccard; Buffalo Bill Jnr, Yakima Canutt

The Cheyenne Kid 1933 61 min
Robert Hill; Tom Keene, Mary Mason

The Cheyenne Kid 1940 50 min
Raymond K. Johnson; Jack Randall, Louise Stanley

Cheyenne Rides Again 1937 56 min
Robert Hill; Tom Tyler, Lucile Browne

Cheyenne Roundup 1943 59 min
Ray Taylor; Johnny Mack Brown, Tex Ritter

Cheyenne Tornado 1935
William O'Connor; Reb Russell, Edmund Cobb

Cheyenne Wildcat 1944 56 min
Lesley Selander; Bill Elliott, Peggy Stewart

Chiedi Perdono a Dio Non a Me 1968 (It) 88 min
Glenn Vincent Davis;

Ci Risiamo Vero Provvidenza 1973 (It/Sp/Fr)
Alberto De Martino; Tomas Milian, Gregg Palmer

Il Cieco 1971 (It) 102 min
Ferdinando Baldi;

Cinque Dollari per Ringo 1966 (It)
Ignacio F. Iquino; J.P. Tabarnero, V. Lagas

Cinque Pistole del Texas 1965 (It/Sp)
Ignacio F. Iquino; Anthony B. Taber, Vicky Lagos

Cipolla Colt 1976 (It)
Enzo G. Castellari; Franco Nero, Martin Balsam

Circle Canyon 1934
Victor Adamson (Denver Dixon); Buddy Roosevelt, June Mathews

Circle of Death 1935 60 min
J. Frank Glendon; Monte Montana, Yakima Canutt

City of Badmen 1953 82 min
Harmon Jones; Jeanne Crain, Dale Robertson

Cjamango 1967 (It) 90 min
Edward G. Muller; Sean Todd, Mikey Hargitay

Clancy of the Mounted 1933 12 chaps
Ray Taylor; Tom Tyler, William Desmond

Clint il Solitario 1967 (It)
A. Balcazar; George Martin, Marianne Koch

Code of Honor 1930 60 min
J.P. McGowan; Lafe McKee, Doris Hill

Code of the Cactus 1939 56 min
Sam Newfield; Tim McCoy, Ben Corbett

Code of the Fearless 1939 56 min
Raymond K. Johnson; Fred Scott, John Merton

Code of the Lawless 1945 57 min
Wallace Fox; Kirby Grant, Fuzzy Knight

Code of the Mounted 1935 60 min
Sam Newfield; Kermit Maynard, Robert Warwick

Code of the Outlaw 1942 57 min
John English; Bob Steele, Tom Tyler

Code of the Prairie 1944 56 min
Spencer Bennet; Smiley Burnette, Sunset Carson

Code of the Rangers 1938 56 min
Sam Newfield; Tim McCoy, Rex Lease

Code of the Saddle 1947 53 min
Thomas Carr; Johnny Mack Brown, Raymond Hatton

Code of the Silver Sage 1950 60 min
Fred Brannon; Allan Lane, Eddy Waller

Code of the West 1947 57 min
William Berke; James Warren, Steve Brodie

Cody of the Pony Express 1950 15 chaps
Spencer G. Bennet; Jock O'Mahoney, Peggy Stewart

Colorado 1940 57 min
Joseph Kane; Roy Rogers, George Hayes

Colorado Charlie 1965 (It)
Robert Johnson; Jack Berthier, Barbara Hudson

Colorado Kid 1937 56 min
Sam Newfield; Bob Steele, Karl Hackett

Colorado Pioneers 1945 57 min
R.G. Springsteen; Bill Elliott, Roy Barcroft

Colorado Ranger 1950 59 min
Thomas Carr; Jimmy Ellison, Russell Hayden

Colorado Sunset 1939 61 min
George Sherman; Gene Autry, Smiley Burnette

The Colorado Trail 1938 55 min
Sam Nelson; Charles Starrett, Iris Meredith

Le Colt Cantarano la Morte e Fu : Tempo di Massacro 1966 (It)
86 min
Lucio Fulci; Franco Nero, George Hilton

Una Colt in Pugno al Diavolo 1967 93 min
Sergio Bergonzelli; Bob Henry, George Wang

Column South 1953 84 min
Frederick de Cordova; Audie Murphy, Joan Evans

Comanche 1956 87 min
George Sherman; Dana Andrews, Kent Smith

Come On, Rangers 1938 57 min
Joseph Kane; Roy Rogers, Mary Hart

Come On, Tarzan 1932 61 min
Alan James; Ken Maynard, Roy Stewart

Comin' Round the Mountain 1936 55 min
Mack V. Wright; Gene Autry, Smiley Burnette

Con la Morte Alle Spalle 1967 (It)
Alfonso Balcazar; George Martin, V. Bach

Con Lui Cavalca la Morte 1967 (It)
Joseph Warren (Giuseppe Vari); Mike Marshall, H. Chanel

The Conquering Horde 1931 75 min
Edward Sloman; Richard Arlen, Fay Wray

Conquest of Cheyenne 1946 55 min
R.G. Springsteen; Bill Elliott, Peggy Stewart

Convict Stage 1965 71 min
Lesley Selander; Harry Lauter, Donald Barry

Une Corde, un Colt 1968 (Fr/It) 84 min
Robert Hossein;

Cornered 1932 58 min
B. Reeves Eason; Tim McCoy, Raymond Hatton

I Corni, Ti Scaveranno la Fossa 1971 (It)
Ignacio F. Iquino; Fernando Sancho, G. Hill

Corpus Christi Bandits 1945 55 min
Wallace Grissell; Allan Lane, Helen Talbot

Cosi Sia 1972 (It) 92 min
Alfio Caltabiano; Luc Merenda, Alf Thunder

The Cost of Dying (Quanto Costa Morire) 1968 (It/Fr) 92 min
Sergio Merolle; Andrea Giordana, John Ireland

Count Three and Pray 1955 102 min
George Sherman; Van Heflin, Joanne Woodward

The Country Beyond 1936 73 min
Eugene Forde; Paul Kelly, Rochelle Hudson

Courage of the North 1935
Robert Tansey; John Preston, Tom London

The Courageous Avenger 1935 58 min
Robert N. Bradbury; Johnny Mack Brown, Warner
Richmond

Courtin' Trouble 1948 56 min
Ford Beebe; Jimmy Wakely, Dub Taylor

Covered Wagon Raid 1950 60 min
R.G. Springsteen; Allan Lane, Eddy Waller

Covered Wagon Trails 1940 52 min
Raymond K. Johnson; Jack Randall, Lafe McKee

Cow Town 1950 70 min
John English; Gene Autry, Jock O'Mahoney

The Cowboy and the Bandit 1935 57 min
Al Herman; Rex Lease, Bobby Nelson

Cowboy and the Prizefighter 1949 59 min
Lewis D. Collins; Jim Bannon, Emmett Lynn

Cowboy Blues 1946 62 min
Ray Nazarro; Ken Curtis, Guy Kibbee

Cowboy Cavalier 1948 57 min
Derwin Abrahams; Jimmy Wakely, Dub Taylor

Cowboy from Lonesome River 1944 55 min
Ben Kline; Charles Starrett, Dub Taylor

The Cowboy from Sundown 1940 58 min
Spencer G. Bennet; Tex Ritter, Roscoe Ates

Cowboy Holiday 1934 56 min
Bob Hill; Big Boy Williams, Janet Chandler

The Cowboy Star 1936 56 min
David Selman; Charles Starrett, Iris Meredith

Cowboys from Texas 1939 57 min
George Sherman; Robert Livingston, Raymond Hatton

Coyote Trails 1935
B.B. Ray; Tom Tyler, Ben Corbett

Crashing Broadway 1933 55 min
John P. McCarthy; Rex Bell, Doris Hill

Crashing Thru 1949 58 min
Ray Taylor; Whip Wilson, Andy Clyde

The Crooked Trail 1936 60 min
S. Roy Luby; Johnny Mack Brown, John Merton

Crossed Trails 1948 53 min
Lambert Hillyer; Johnny Mack Brown, Raymond Hatton

La Cucharacha 1959 (Mex) 87 min
Ismael Rodriguez;

Custer's Last Stand 1936 15 chaps
Elmer Clifton; Rex Lease, William Farnum

Cut-Throat Nine 1973 (Sp)
; Robert Hundar

Cyclone Fury 1951 54 min
Ray Nazarro; Charles Starrett, Smiley Burnette

Cyclone Kid 1942 57 min
George Sherman; Don Barry, Lynn Merrick

The Cyclone Kid 1931 60 min
J.P. McGowan; Buzz Barton, Lafe McKee

Cyclone of the Saddle 1935
Elmer Clifton; Rex Lease, Yakima Canutt

Cyclone on Horseback 1941 60 min
Edward Killy; Tim Holt, Marjorie Reynolds

Cyclone Prairie Rangers 1944 56 min
Ben Kline; Charles Starrett, Dub Taylor

The Cyclone Ranger 1935 60 min
Bob Hill; Bill Cody, Donald Reed

Dai Nemici mi Guardo Io! 1968 (It) 97 min
Irving Jacobs (Mario Amendola);

The Dakota Kid 1951 60 min
Philip Ford; Michael Chapin, Roy Barcroft

The Dalton Gang 1949 58 min
Ford Beebe; Don Barry, Robert Lowery

Dalton That Got Away 1960 69 min
Jimmy Salvador; Michael Connors, Reed Howes

The Daltons' Women 1950 80 min
Thomas Carr; Lash LaRue, Al St John

Danger Ahead 1940 60 min
Ralph Staub; James Newill, Dave O'Brien

Danger on the River aka Mississippi Gambler 1942 64 min
John Rawlins; Kent Taylor, Frances Longford

Danger Trails 1935 55 min
Bob Hill; Big Boy Williams, Wally Wales

Danger Valley 1937 58 min
Robert N. Bradbury; Jack Randall, Charles King

Dangerous Venture 1947 59 min
George Archainbaud; William Boyd, Andy Clyde

Dangers of the Canadian Mounted 1948 12 chaps
Yakima Canutt, Fred Brannon; Jim Bannon, Virginia
Belmont

Daniel Boone – Frontier Trail Rider 1966 91 min
George Sherman; Fess Parker, Ed Ames

Daniel Boone, Trail Blazer 1956 76 min
Albert C. Gannaway, Ismael Rodriguez; Bruce Bennett, Lon
Chaney Jnr

The Daring Caballero 1949 60 min
Wallace Fox; Duncan Renaldo, Leo Carillo

Das War Buffalo Bill 1966 (WG/It/Fr) 89 min
J.W. Fordson; Gordon Scott, Jan Hendriks

Davy Crockett and the River Pirates 1956 81 min
Norman Foster; Fess Parker, Buddy Ebsen

Davy Crockett, Indian Scout 1950 71 min
Lew Landers; George Montgomery, Ellen Drew

Dawn at Socorro 1954 80 min
George Sherman; Rory Calhoun, Piper Laurie

Day of Fire (Quel Caldo Maledetto Giono di Fuoco) 1968
(It/Sp) 100 min
Paolo Bianchini; Robert Wood, John Ireland

A Day of Fury 1956 78 min
Harmon Jones; Dale Robertson, Jock Mahoney

Day of the Landgrabbber 1968 (GB) 101 min
Nathan Juran;

Days of Buffalo Bill 1946 56 min
Thomas Carr; Sunset Carson, Peggy Stewart

Days of Violence (I Giorni della Violenza) 1967 (It) 105 min
Al Bradley (Alfonso Brescia); Peter Lee Lawrence, Beba
Loncar

Dead Man's Gold 1948 60 min
Ray Taylor; Lash LaRue, Al St John

Dead Man's Trail 1952 59 min
Lewis Collins; Johnny Mack Brown, Jimmy Ellison

Dead Men Ride (Il Sole Sotta Terra) 1971 (It/Sp) 101 (94) min
Aldo Florio; Fabio Testi, Charo Lopez

Dead or Alive 1944 56 min
Elmer Clifton; Tex Ritter, Dave O'Brien

Deadline 1948 57 min
Oliver Drake; Sunset Carson, Lee Roberts

Deadlock 1970 (WG) 94 min
Roland Klick; Mario Adorf, Anthony Dawson

Deadwood Dick 1940 15 chaps
James W. Horne; Don Douglas, Lane Chandler

Deadwood Pass 1933 62 min
J.P. McGowan; Tom Tyler, Wally Wales

Death Goes North 1939 56 min
Frank McDonald; Edgar Edwards, Sheila Bromley

Death Rides the Range 1940 58 min
Sam Newfield; Ken Maynard, Charles King

Death Valley 1946 72 min
Lew Landers; Robert Lowery, Nat Pendleton

Death Valley Gunfighter 1949 60 min
R.G. Springsteen; Allan Lane, Eddy Waller

Death Valley Manhunt 1943 55 min
John English; Bill Elliott, George Hayes

Death Valley Outlaws 1941 56 min
George Sherman; Don Barry, Lynn Merrick

Deep West 1975 (It)
; George Hilton

Defying the Law 1935
Robert J. Horner; Ted Wells, George Chesebro

A Demon for Trouble 1934 58 min
Robert Hill; Bob Steele, Lafe McKee

The Denver Kid 1948 60 min
Philip Ford; Allan Lane, Eddy Waller

Deputy Marshal 1949 60 min
William Berke; Jon Hall, Dick Foran

Desert Guns 1936 70 min
Charles Hutchison; Conway Tearle, Budd Buster

The Desert Horseman 1946 57 min
Ray Nazarro; Charles Starrett, Smiley Burnette

Desert Justice 1936 58 min
Lester Williams (William Berke); Jack Perrin, David Sharpe

Desert Mesa 1935
Alan James; Tom Wynn (Wally West), Franklyn Farnum

Desert of Lost Men 1951 54 min
Harry Keller; Allan Lane, Irving Bacon

Desert Patrol 1938 56 min
Sam Newfield; Bob Steele, Rex Lease

Desert Pursuit 1952 71 min
George Blair; Wayne Morris, Virginia Grey

Desperadoes of Dodge City 1948 60 min
Philip Ford; Allan Lane, Eddy Waller

Desperadoes of the West 1950 12 chaps
Fred C. Brannon; Tom Keene, Roy Barcroft

Desperadoes' Outpost 1952 54 min
Philip Ford; Allan Lane, Eddy Waller

The Desperados Are in Town 1956 73 min
Kurt Neumann; Robert Arthur, Dave O'Brien

The Devil Horse 1932 12 chaps
Otto Brower, Richard Talmadge; Harry Carey, Noah Beery

Devil Riders 1943
Sam Newfield; Buster Crabbe, Al St John

Devil's Canyon 1935
Cliff Smith; Noah Beery Jnr, William Desmond

The Devil's Children 1962 75 min
James Sheldon; Doug McClure, James Drury

The Devil's Playground 1946 62 min
George Archainbaud; William Boyd, Andy Clyde

The Devil's Trail 1942 61 min
Lambert Hillyer; Bill Elliott, Tex Ritter

Uno Di Piu all'Inferno 1968 (It) 87 min
Giovanni Fago; George Hilton, P. Stevens

Di Tresette Ce N'e Uno Tutti gli Altri Son Nessuno 1974 (It)
Giuliano Carmineo; George Hilton

Los Diablos del Terror 1958 (Mex) 76 min
Fernando Mendez;

The Diamond Trail 1932 60 min
Harry Fraser; Rex Bell, Bud Osborne

Dig That Uranium 1956 61 min
Edward Bernds; Leo Gorcey, Huntz Hall

La Diligencia de los Condenados 1970 (Sp/It) 89 min
Juan Bosch;

Dinamite Jim 1966 (It)
Alfonso Balcazar; Fernando Sancho, L. Davila

Dio in Cielo ... Arizona in Terra 1972 (It)
Ignacio F. Iquino; Peter Lee Lawrence, M.P. Conte

Dio li Crea ... Io li Ammazzo 1968 (It) 100 min
Paolo Bianchini; Dean Read, Agnes Spaak

Dio Non Paga il Sabato 1967 (It/Sp) 95 min
Amerigo Anton (Tanio Boccia); Robert Mark, L. Ward

Dio Perdoni la Mia Pistola 1969 (It) 94 min
Mario Gariazzo, Leopoldo Savona; Wayde Preston,
Loredana Nusciak

The Dirty Outlaws (El Desperado) 1967 (It) 105 min
Franco Rossetti; Andrea Giordana, Rosemarie Dexter

Disciples of Death 1972 75 min
Frank Q. Dobbs; Josh Bryant, Irene Kelly

Django Challenges Sartana (Django Sfida Sartana) 1970 (It)
Pasquale Squitieri; Tony Kendall, G. Ardisson

Django – ein Sarg Voll Blut 1968 (WG/It) 95 min
Giuliano Carmineo; George Hilton, Walter Barnes

Django's Great Return 1977 (It)
Enzo Castellari; Franco Nero, Woody Strode

Djurado 1966 (It/Sp) 78 min
Gianni Narzisi; Montgomery Clark (Dante Posani), Scilla
Gabel

A Dollar of Fire (Un Dollaro di Fuoco) 1967 (It/Sp) 79 min
Nick Nostro; Michael Riva, Diana Garson

Un Dollaro per 7 Vigliacchi 1968 (It)
D. Ash; E. Martinelli, D. Hoffman

Dollars for a Fast Gun 1969
; Robert Hundar

Domani Passo a Salutare la Tua Vedova ... Parola di Epidemia
1972 (It/Sp) 92 min
John Wood (Ignacio F. Iquino); Craig Hill, Claude Lange

Don Daredevil Rides Again 1951 12 chaps
Fred D. Brannon; Ken Curtis, Roy Barcroft

Una Donna Chiamata Apache 1977 (It)
George McRoots; Al Cliver, Yara Kewa

Una Donna per Ringo 1966 (It/Sp) 84 min
Rafael Romero Marchent; S. Flynn, P. Milly

Donne Alla Frontiera 1966 (It/Sp/Austria)
Cechet Grooper; Annie Baxter, Rossella Como

Dont Fence Me In 1945 71 min
John English; Roy Rogers, Dale Evans

Don't Turn the Other Cheek (Viva la Muerte ... Tua!) 1971
(It/WG/Sp) 117 (98) min
Duccio Tessari; Franco Nero, Eli Wallach

Uno Dopo l'Altro 1968 (It/Sp) 105 (93) min
Nick Howard (N. Nostro); Richard Harrison, Pamela Tudor

Doppia Taglia per Minnesota Stinky 1971 (It)
Miles Deem (D. Fidani); Hunt Power, Gordon Mitchell

Dos Mil Dolares per Coyote 1966 (Sp) 87 min
Leon Klimovsky;

La Dove No Batte il Sole 1975 (It)
Anthony Dawson (Antonio Margheriti); Lee Van Cleef, Lo
Lieh

Dove si Spara di Piu 1967 (It/Sp) 84 min
Gianni Puccini; A Grant, C. Galbo

Down Laredo Way 1953 54 min
William Witney; Rex Allen, Slim Pickens

Drei Vaterunser fur Vier Halunken 1972 (WG/It/Fr) 98 min
Giancarlo Santi; Lee Van Kleef, Alberto Dentice

The Driftin' Kid 1941 57 min
Robert Tansey; Tom Keene, Frank Yaconelli

Driftin' River 1946 59 min
Robert Tansey; Eddie Dean, Roscoe Ates

Drifting Westward 1939 58 min
Robert Hill; Jack Randall, Frank Yaconelli

Drums of Destiny 1937 60 min
Ray Taylor; Tom Keene, Edna Lawrence

The Dude Bandit 1933 62 min
George Melford; Hoot Gibson, Gloria Shea

Dude Ranch 1931 67 min
Frank Tuttle; Jack Oakie, Stuart Erwin

The Dude Wrangler 1930 69 min
Richard Thorpe; Tom Keene, Francis X. Bushman

Due Croci a Danger Pass 1967 (It)
Rafael Romero Marchent; Peter Martell, A. Freeman

Il Due Facce del Dollaro 1967 (It/Fr) 95 min
Roberto Montero; Jacques Herlin, Maurice Poli

I Due Figli di Ringo 1966 (It) 105 min
Giorgio Simonelli; Franco Franchi, Ciccio Ingrassia

I Due Figli di Trinita 1972 (It) 94 min
Richard Kean (Osvaldo Civirani); Franco Franchi, Ciccio
Ingrassia

Due Gringos nel Texas 1967 (It) 90 min
Marino Girolami;

Due Mafiosi nel Far West 1964 (It/Sp)
Giorgio Simonelli; Franco Franchi, Fernando Sancho

Due Once di Piombo 1966 (It)
Maurizio Lucidi; Robert Wood, N. Clark

I Due Sergenti del Generale Custer 1965 (It/Sp)
Giorgio Simonelli; Franco Franchi, Fernando Sancho

Duel at Rio Bravo (Jennie Lees Ha una Nuova Pistola) 1964
(It/Sp/Fr) 100 (90) min
Tullio Demichelli; Guy Madison, Madeleine Lebeau

Duel at the Rio Grande (Il Segno di Zorro) 1962 (It/Sp/Fr)
93 min
Mario Caiano;

Duell vor Sonnenuntergang 1965 (WG/Yug) 101 min
Leopold Lahola; Peter von Eyck, Carole Gray

Dugan of the Badlands 1931 66 min
Robert N. Bradbury; Bill Cody, Andy Shuford

Duguejo 1966 (It)
Joseph Warren (Giuseppe Vari); Jack Stuart, Dan Vadis

Durango Valley Raiders 1938 55 min
Sam Newfield; Bob Steele, Louise Stanley

Dynamite Canyon 1941 58 min
Robert Tansey; Tom Keene, Slim Andrews

Dynamite Joe (Dinamite Joe) 1966 (It/Sp)
Antonio Margheriti; Ric Van Nutter, Halina Zalewska

Dynamite Pass 1950 61 min
Lew Landers; Tim Holt, Richard Martin

Dynamite Ranch 1932 59 min
Forrest Sheldon; Ken Maynard, Jack Perrin

E Alla Fine lo Chiamarono Jerusalemme l'Implacabile 1972 (It)
Toni Secchi; Scott Holden, D. Boccardo

E Continuavano a Chiamarlo Figlio Di 1972 (It)
Rafael Romero Marchent; Fabio Testi, S. Blondell

E Cosi Divennero i Tre Supermen del West 1973 (It)
I. Marinego; Fernando Sancho, C. Herta

E Divenne il Pio Spietato Bandito del Sud 1967 (It/Sp)
J. Buchs; Peter Lee Lawrence, Fausto Tozzi

... E Chiamavano Spirito Santo 1971 (It/Sp)
Anthony Ascott (Giuliano Carmineo); Dick Palmer, L. Karis

E per Tetto un Cielo di Stelle 1968 (It/Fr) 100 (86) min
Giulio Petroni; Giuliano Gemma, Mario Adorf

... E Venne il Tempo di Uccidere 1968 (It) 91 min
Vincent Eagle;

E Vennero in Quattro per Uccidere Sartana 1969 (It)
Miles Deem (D. Fidani); Jeff Cameron, Anthony G. Stenton

Ed Ora Raccomanda l'Anima a Dio 1968 (It)
Miles Deem (D. Fidani); Jeff Cameron

Ehi Amico, Sei Morto 1970 (It) 87 min
Paul Maxwell (Paolo Bianchini); Wayde Preston, R. Battaglia

El Cisco 1966 (It)
Sergio Bergonzelli; William Berger, George Wang

El Diablo Rides 1939 57 min
Ira Webb; Bob Steele, Claire Rochelle

El Dorado Pass 1948 56 min
Ray Nazarro; Charles Starrett, Smiley Burnette

El Macho 1977 (It)
Marcello Andrei; Carlos Monzon, Susanna Gimenez

El Paso 1949 91 min
Lewis R. Foster; John Payne, Sterling Hayden

The El Paso Kid 1946 54 min
Thomas Carr; Sunset Carson, Edmund Cobb

El Rancho de Los Implacables 1964 (Sp/WG/It) 79 min
Alfonso Balcazar;

El Rojo 1966 (It/Sp) 85 min
Leo Colman; Richard Harrison, Peter Carter

El Zorro Cabalga Otra Vez 1964 (Sp/It) 94 min
Riccardo Blasco;

Empty Holsters 1937 58 min
B. Reeves Eason; Dick Foran, Glenn Strange

Empty Saddles 1936 67 min
Lesley Selander; Buck Jones, Louise Brooks

Enemy of the Law 1945 59 min
Harry Fraser; Tex Ritter, Dave O'Brien

Era Sam Wallash 1971 (It)
Miles Deem (D. Fidani); Dean Strafford, Dennis Colt

The Erotic Adventures of Zorro 1972 (US/WG/Fr) 102 (70) min
Robert Freeman; Douglas Grey, Robyn Whitting

La Espada del Zorro 1961 (Sp/Fr/Mex) 90 min
Joaquin Luis Romero Marchent;

Everyman's Law 1936 62 min
Albert Ray; Johnny Mack Brown, Lloyd Ingraham

Execution 1968 (It) 100 min
Domenico Paolella; John Richardson, Dick Palmer

Face of a Fugitive 1959 81 min
Paul Wendkos; Fred MacMurray, James Coburn

Fair Warning 1931 74 min
Alfred Werker; George O'Brien, Louise Huntington

False Paradise 1948 60 min
George Archainbaud; William Boyd, Andy Clyde

Fangs of the Arctic 1953 62 min
Rex Bailey; Kirby Grant, Warren Douglas

Fangs of the Wild 1954 71 min
William Claxton; Charles Chaplin Jnr, Onslow Stevens

The Far Frontier 1948 67 min
William Witney; Roy Rogers, Gail Davis

Fargo 1952 69 min
Lewis Collins; Bill Elliott, Phyllis Coates

The Fargo Kid 1940 63 min
Edward Killy; Tim Holt, Emmett Lynn

Fast on the Draw 1950 55 min
Thomas Carr; Jimmy Ellison, Russell Hayden

Fence Riders 1950 57 min
Wallace Fox; Whip Wilson, Andy Clyde

The Ferocious Pal 1934
Spencer G. Bennet; Ruth Sullivan, Tom London

The Feud Maker 1938 55 min
Sam Newfield; Bob Steele, Karl Hackett

Feud of the Range 1939 56 min
Harry S. Webb; Bob Steele, Frank LaRue

The Feud of the Trail 1937 56 min
Robert Hill; Tom Tyler, Lafe McKee

Feud of the West 1936 62 min
Harry Fraser; Hoot Gibson, Joan Barclay

A Few Bullets More 1969 (It)
; Peter Lee Lawrence

A Few Dollars for Django (Pochi Dollari per Django) 1966
(Sp/It) 86 min
Leon Klimowsky; Anthony Steffen, G. Osuna

Few Dollars for Gypsy 1967 (It)
; Anthony Steffen

Fifteen Scaffolds for a Killer (Quindici Forche per un Assassino)
1968 (It/Sp) 95 min
Nunzio Malasomma; Craig Hill, Susy Andersen

The Fighter 1952 78 min
Herbert Kline; Richard Conte, Lee J. Cobb

Fightin' Thru 1930 61 min
William Nigh; Ken Maynard, Charles King

Fighting Bill Carson 1945 51 min
Sam Newfield; Buster Crabbe, Al St John

Fighting Bill Fargo 1941 57 min
Ray Taylor; Johnny Mack Brown, Fuzzy Knight

The Fighting Buckaroo 1943 58 min
William Berke; Charles Starrett, Arthur Hunnicutt

Fighting Caballero 1935
Elmer Clifton; Rex Lease, Dorothy Gulliver

The Fighting Champ 1932 59 min
J.P. McCarthy; Bob Steele, George Hayes

The Fighting Code 1933 65 min
Lambert Hillyer; Buck Jones, Ward Bond

The Fighting Cowboy 1933 58 min
Denver Dixon (Victor Adamson); Buffalo Bill Jnr, Maria
Sais

The Fighting Deputy 1937
Sam Newfield; Fred Scott, Al St John

The Fighting Fool 1932 58 min
Lambert Hillyer; Tim McCoy, Robert Ellis

Fighting for Justice 1932 61 min
Otto Brower; Tim McCoy, Walter Brennan

The Fighting Frontiersman 1946 61 min
Derwin Abrahams; Charles Starrett, Smiley Burnette

Fighting Hero 1934 59 min
Harry S. Webb; Tom Tyler, Renee Borden

The Fighting Lawman 1953 71 min
Thomas Carr; Wayne Morris, Virginia Grey

Fighting Mad 1939 60 min
Sam Newfield; James Newill, Dave O'Brien

The Fighting Marshal 1931 58 min
D. Ross Lederman; Tim McCoy, Dorothy Gulliver

Fighting Mustang 1948 56 min
Oliver Drake; Sunset Carson, Patricia Sterling

Fighting Pioneers 1935 60 min
Harry Fraser; Rex Bell, Ruth Mix

The Fighting Ranger 1948 57 min
Lambert Hillyer; Johnny Mack Brown, Raymond Hatton

The Fighting Renegade 1939 58 min
Sam Newfield; Tim McCoy, Dave O'Brien

Fighting Shadows 1935 58 min
David Selman; Tim McCoy, Ward Bond

The Fighting Sheriff 1931 67 min
Louis King; Buck Jones, Robert Ellis

The Fighting Stallion 1950 63 min
Robert Tansey; Bill Edwards, Forrest Taylor

The Fighting Texan 1937 59 min
Charles Abbott; Kermit Maynard, Frank LaRue

The Fighting Texans 1933 60 min
Armand Schaefer; Rex Bell, Luana Walters

Fighting Through 1934 55 min
Harry Fraser; Reb Russell, Yakima Canutt

Fighting to Live 1934 60 min
Edward F. Cline; Marion Shilling, Reb Russell

Fighting Valley 1943 58 min
Oliver Drake; Dave O'Brien, Jim Newill

The Fighting Vigilantes 1947 51 min
Ray Taylor; Lash LaRue, Al St John

Fighting with Kit Carson 1933 12 chaps
Armand Schaefer, Colbert Clark; John Mack Brown, Noah
Beery

The Final Hour 1962 74 min
Robert Douglas; Lee J. Cobb, Doug McClure

The Final Shot (Citta Violenta) 1970 (It/Fr) 109 (100) min
Sergio Sollima; Charles Bronson, Telly Savalas

Find a Place to Die (Joe, Cercati un Posto per Morire) 1968 (It)
90 min
Anthony Ascott (Giuliano Carmineo); Jeffrey Hunter,
Pascale Petit

Finger on the Trigger 1966 (US/Sp) 87 (74) min
Sidney Pink; Rory Calhoun, James Philbrook

The Firebrand 1962 63 min
Maury Dexter; Kent Taylor, Chubby Johnson

Firebrand Jordan 1930 60 min
Alvin J. Neitz (Alan James); Lane Chandler, Yakima Canutt

Firebrands of Arizona 1944 55 min
Lesley Selander; Smiley Burnette, Sunset Carson

Fistful of Rawhide 1970 65 min
W.G. Beggs;

Five Bad Men 1935
Cliff Smith; Noah Beery Jnr, Buffalo Bill Jnr

Five Bold Women 1960 82 min
Jorge Lopez-Portillo; Jeff Morrow, Merry Anders

Flaming Bullets 1945 55 min
Harry Fraser; Tex Ritter, Dave O'Brien

Flaming Frontier 1958 70 min
Sam Newfield; Bruce Bennett, Jim Davis

Flaming Frontiers 1938 15 chaps
Ray Taylor, Alan James; John Mack Brown, Charles
Middleton

Flaming Guns 1932 57 min
Arthur Rosson; Tom Mix, Ruth Hall

Flying Lariats 1931 60 min
Alvin J. Neitz (Alan James); Wally Wales, Buzz Barton

Fool's Gold 1946 63 min
George Archainbaud; William Boyd, Andy Clyde

For a Few Bullets More (Vado ... l'Ammazo e Torno) 1967 (It)
100 min
Enzo G. Castellari (Enzo Girolami); George Hilton, Edd
Byrnes

For a Few Dollars Less (Per Qualche Dollaro in Meno) 1966
(It)
Mario Mattoli; Lando Buzzanca, Elio Pandolfi

For 1,000 Dollars a Day (Per Mille Dollari al Giorno) 1966
(It/Sp) 77 min
Silvio Amadio; Zachary Hatcher, Dick Palmer

For the Service 1936 64 min
Buck Jones; Buck Jones, Fred Kohler

Forbidden Trail 1932 71 min
Lambert Hillyer; Buck Jones, Barbara Weeks

Forbidden Trails 1941 54 min
Robert N. Bradbury; Buck Jones, Tim McCoy

Una Forca per un Bastardo 1968 (It) 79 min
Amasi Daniani;

Fort Courageous 1965 72 min
Lesley Selander; Fred Beir, Donald Barry

Fort Dodge Stampede 1951 60 min
Harry Keller; Allan Lane, Chubby Johnson

Fort Osage 1952 72 min
Lesley Selander; Rod Cameron, Jane Nigh

Fort Yuma 1955 78 min
Lesley Selander; Peter Graves, Joan Taylor

Fort Yuma Gold (Per Pochi Dollari Ancora) 1966 (It/Fr/Sp)
100 min
Calvin Jackson Paget (Giorgio Ferroni); Montgomery Wood
(Giuliano Gemma), Dan Vadis

Forty-Five Calibre Echo 1932 60 min
Bruce Mitchell; Jack Perrin, Ben Corbett

The Forty-Niners 1932 59 min
John P. McCarthy; Tom Tyler, Betty Mack

Four Fast Guns 1960 72 min
William J. Hole Jnr; James Craig, Edgar Buchanan

Four Guns to the Border 1954 82 min
Richard Carlson; Rory Calhoun, Walter Brennan

Four Rode Out 1969 (US/Sp)
John Peyser; Pernell Roberts, Sue Lyon

The Fourth Horseman 1932 63 min
Hamilton McFadden; Tom Mix, Fred Kohler

Freddy und das Lied der Prarie 1964 (WG/Yug) 101 min
Sobey Martin; Freddy Quinn, Mamie van Doren

Freighters of Destiny 1931 60 min
Fred Allen; Tom Keene, Barbara Kent

Frenchie 1951 81 min
Louis King; Joel McCrea, Shelley Winters

Frisco Sal 1945 94 min
George Waggner; Susanna Foster, Andy Devine

Frisco Tornado 1950 60 min
R.G. Springsteen; Allan Lane, Eddy Waller

From Broadway to Cheyenne 1932 60 min
Harry Fraser; Rex Bell, Marceline Day

Frontier Agent 1948 56 min
Lambert Hillyer; Johnny Mack Brown, Raymond Hatton

Frontier Days 1934 61 min
Bob Hill; Bill Cody, Wheeler Oakman

Frontier Feud 1945 54 min
Lambert Hillyer; Johnny Mack Brown, Raymond Hatton

Frontier Fugitives 1945 53 min
Harry Fraser; Dave O'Brien, Tex Ritter

Frontier Fury 1943 55 min
William Berke; Charles Starrett, Arthur Hunnicutt

Frontier Gambler 1956 70 min
Sam Newfield; John Bromfield, Kent Taylor

Frontier Gun 1958 70 min
Paul Landres; John Agar, Joyce Meadows

Frontier Gunlaw 1946 60 min
Derwin Abrahams; Charles Starrett, Tex Harding

Frontier Hellcat 1966 (WG/Yug)
Alfred Vohrer; Stewart Granger, Elke Sommer

Frontier Justice 1936 58 min
Robert McGowan; Hoot Gibson, Richard Cramer

Frontier Law 1943 59 min
Elmer Clifton; Russell Hayden, Fuzzy Knight

Frontier Marshal 1949 59 min
Fred C. Brannon; Allan Lane, Eddy Waller

Frontier Outlaws 1944 56 min
Sam Newfield; Buster Crabbe, Al St John

Frontier Outpost 1950 55 min
Ray Nazarro; Charles Starrett, Smiley Burnette

The Frontier Phantom 1952 56 min
Ron Ormond; Lash LaRue, Al St John

Frontier Pony Express 1939 58 min
Joseph Kane; Roy Rogers, Raymond Hatton

Frontier Revenge 1948 55 min
Ray Taylor; Lash LaRue, Al St John

Frontier Town 1938 60 min
Ray Taylor; Tex Ritter, Charles King

Frontier Uprising 1961 60 min
Edward L. Cahn; Jim Davis, Nancy Hadley

Frontier Vengeance 1940 57 min
Nate Watt; Donald Barry, Yakima Canutt

Frontier Woman 1956 80 min
Ron Ormond; Cindy Carson, Lance Fuller

Fugitive from Sonara 1943 56 min
Howard Bretherton; Don Barry, Lynn Merrick

Fugitive of the Plains 1943 57 min
Sam Newfield; Buster Crabbe, Al St John

The Fugitive Sheriff 1936 58 min
Spencer G. Bennet; Ken Maynard, Beth Marion

Fugitive Valley 1941 61 min
S. Roy Luby; Ray Corrigan, Max Terhune

5000 Dollar fur den Kopf von Johnny R 1965 (WG/Sp) 91 min
Jose Luis Madrid; Lex Barker, Marianne Koch

Fury in Paradise 1955 77 min
George Bruce; Peter Thompson, Rea Iturbi

Fury of the Apaches (La Furia degli Apache) 1965 (It/Sp)
83 min
Jose Maria Ellorieta; Frank Latimore

Fuzzy Settles Down 1944 60 min
Sam Newfield; Buster Crabbe, Al St John

The Gallant Fool 1933 60 min
Robert N. Bradbury; Bob Steele, George Hayes

Galloping Dynamite 1937
Harry Fraser; Kermit Maynard, John Merton

The Galloping Kid 1932
Robert Tansey; Al Lane, Fred Parker

Galloping Thunder 1946 54 min
Ray Nazarro; Charles Starrett, Smiley Burnette

The Gambler from Natchez 1954 88 min
Henry Levin; Dale Robertson, Debra Paget

The Gambler Wore a Gun 1961 66 min
Edward L. Cahn; Jim Davis, Mark Allen

Gangs of Sonora 1941 56 min
John English; Robert Livingston, Bob Steele

Gangster's Den 1945 55 min
Sam Newfield; Buster Crabbe, Al St John

Gangsters of the Frontier 1944 56 min
Elmer Clifton; Tex Ritter, Dave O'Brien

Garringo 1969 (It/Sp) 84 min
Rafael Romero Marchent; Anthony Steffen, Peter Lee
Lawrence

Garter Colt (Giarrettiera Colt) 1967 (It)
Gian Andrea Rocco; Nicoletta Machiavelli, Marisa Solinas

Gas House Kids Go West 1947 61 min
William Beaudine; Carl Switzer, Bennie Bartlett

Gaucho Serenade 1940 66 min
Frank McDonald; Gene Autry, Smiley Burnette

Gauchos of Eldorado 1941 56 min
Les Orlebeck; Bob Steele, Tom Tyler

The Gay Amigo 1949 60 min
Wallace Fox; Duncan Renaldo, Leo Carillo

The Gay Buckaroo 1932 61 min
Phil Rosen; Hoot Gibson, Charles King

The Gay Cavalier 1946 65 min
William Nigh; Gilbert Roland, Martin Garralaga

The Gay Desperado 1936 86 min
Rouben Mamoulian; Ida Lupino, Leo Carrillo

Die Gejagten der Sierra Nevada 1965 (WG/Sp/It) 79 min
Alfonso Balcazar; Robert Wood, Maria Sebaldt

I Gemelli del Texas 1964 (It/Sp)
Steno; Walter Chiari, Raimondo Vianello

Gene Autry and the Mounties 1951 70 min
John English; Gene Autry, Pat Buttram

Un Genio, Due Compari e un Pollo 1976 (It/Fr/WG)
123 (92) min
Damiano Damiani; Terence Hill, Miou Miou

Gentle Annie 1944 80 min
Andrew Martin; James Craig, Donna Reed

The Gentleman from Arizona 1939 71 min
Earl Haley; J. Farrell MacDonald, Joan Barclay

The Gentleman from Texas 1946 55 min
Lambert Hillyer; Johnny Mack Brown, Raymond Hatton

Gentleman Joe . . . Uccidi 1967 (It/Sp) 97 min
George Finley; Anthony Steffen, E. Fajano

Gentlemen with Guns 1946 52 min
Sam Newfield; Buster Crabbe, Al St John

Geronimo's Revenge 1962 70 min
James Neilson, Harry Keller; Tom Tryon, Betty Lynn

Get a Coffin Ready (Preparati la Bara) 1968 (It) 90 min
Ferdinando Baldi; Terence Hill, Horst Frank

Ghost City 1932 60 min
Harry Fraser; Bill Cody, Charles King

Ghost Guns 1944 60 min
Lambert Hillyer; Johnny Mack Brown, Raymond Hatton

The Ghost of Crossbones Canyon 1952 56 min
Frank McDonald; Guy Madison, Andy Devine

Ghost of Hidden Valley 1946 56 min
Sam Newfield; Buster Crabbe, Al St John

Ghost of Zorro 1959 69 min
Fred C. Brannon; Clayton Moore, Roy Barcroft

The Ghost Rider 1943 58 min
Wallace Fox; Johnny Mack Brown, Raymond Hatton

Ghost Town 1956 75 min
Allen Miner; Kent Taylor, John Smith

Ghost Town Gold 1936 55 min
Joseph Kane; Bob Livingston, Ray Corrigan

Ghost Town Renegades 1947 57 min
Ray Taylor; Lash LaRue, Al St John

Ghost Town Riders 1938 54 min
George Waggner; Bob Baker, Fay Shannon

Ghost Valley 1932 54 min
Fred Allen; Tom Keene, Kate Campbell

Ghost Valley Raiders 1940 57 min
George Sherman; Donald Barry, LeRoy Mason

Giorni di Sangue 1968 (It)
Enzo Gicca; G. Hudson, Gianni Garko

The Girl and the Gambler 1939 63 min
Lew Landers; Leo Carrillo, Tim Holt

The Girl from Alaska 1942 75 min
Nick Grinde; Ray Middleton, Jean Parker

The Girl from San Lorenzo 1950 59 min
Derwin Abrahams; Duncan Renaldo, Leo Carrillo

Girl Trouble 1933
Bernard B. Ray; Jack Perrin, Ben Corbett

Git Along Little Dogies 1937 60 min
Joseph Kane; Gene Autry, Smiley Burnette

Giu le Mani . . . Carogna 1971 (It)
Lucky Dickinson; Hunt Powers, Gordon Mitchell

Giuro . . . e li Uccise ad Uno ad Uno 1968 (It)
Guido Celano; Edmund Purdom, Peter Holden

Gli Eroi del West 1963 (It/Sp)
Steno; Walter Chiari, Raimondo Vianello

Gli Eroi di Fort Worth 1964 (It) 96 min
Herbert Martin (Alberto De Martino);

Go For Broke 1972 (It)
; John Ireland

God's Country 1946 64 min
Robert Tansey; Robert Lowery, Buster Keaton

God's Country and the Woman 1937 85 min
William Keighley; George Brent, Barton MacLane

God's Gun 1976 (Israel) 94 min
Frank Kramer; Lee Van Cleef, Jack Palance

Gold 1932 58 min
Otto Brower; Jack Hoxie, Alice Day

Gold Fever 1952 63 min
Leslie Goodwins; John Calvert, Ralph Morgan

Gold, Glory and Custer 1963 95 min
George Waggner;

Gold Mine in the Sky 1938 60 min
Joseph Kane; Gene Autry, Smiley Burnette

Gold Raiders 1951 56 min
Edward Bernds; George O'Brien, The Three Stooges

Das Gold von Sam Cooper 1968 (WG/It) 106 min
George Halloway; Van Heflin, Klaus Kinski

Golden Girl 1951 108 min
Lloyd Bacon; Mitzi Gaynor, Dale Robertson

The Golden Trail 1940 52 min
Al Herman; Tex Ritter, Warner Richmond

The Golden West 1932 74 min
David Howard; George O'Brien, Janet Chandler

Good Day for a Hanging 1959 85 min
Nathan Juran; Fred MacMurray, Robert Vaughn

Gordon of Ghost Town 1933 12 chaps
Ray Taylor; Buck Jones, Madge Bellamy

Graf Bobby, der Schrecken des Wilden Westens 1965 (Austria/
Yug) 92 min
Paul Martin;

Il Grande Duello 1973 (It/Fr/WG)
Giancarlo Santi; Lee Van Cleef, Peter O'Brien

La Grande Notte di Ringo 1966 (It)
M. Maffei; William Berger, Adriona Ambesi

The Great Divide 1929 75 min
Reginald Barker; Dorothy Mackaill, Ian Keith

The Great Jesse James Raid 1953 73 min
Reginald Le Borg; Willard Parker, Barbara Payton

The Great Locomotive Chase 1956 85 min
Francis D. Lyon; Fess Parker, Jeffrey Hunter

The Great Meadow 1931 75 min
Charles Brabin; Johnny Mack Brown, Guinn Williams

The Great Sioux Massacre 1965 91 min
Sidney Salkow; Joseph Cotten, Philip Carey

The Great Sioux Uprising 1953 80 min
Lloyd Bacon; Jeff Chandler, Faith Domergue

Great Stagecoach Robbery 1945 56 min
Lesley Selander; Bill Elliott, Bobby Blake

The Great Train Robbery 1941
Joseph Kane; Bob Steele, Claire Carleton

*The Greatest Kidnapping in the West (La Piu Grande Rapina
del West)* 1967 (It) 115 (96) min
Maurizio Lucidi; George Hilton, Hunt Powers

Green Grass of Wyoming 1948 89 min
Louis King; Peggy Cummings, Charles Coburn

Gringo Getta il Fucile 1966 (It)
Joaquin Romero Marchent; John Richardson, Gloria Milland

Gringo's Pitiless Colt (La Spietate Colt del Gringo) 1966 (It/Sp)
84 min
Jose Luis Madrid; Jim Reed, Martha Dovan

I Gringos Non Perdonano 1965 (It/Fr/WG)
Albert Cardiff; Brad Harris, Tony Kendall

Guilty Trail 1938 57 min
George Waggner; Bob Baker, Marjorie Reynolds

Gun Battle at Monterey 1957 67 min
Carl K. Hittleman, Sidney A. Franklin Jnr; Sterling
Hayden, Lee Van Cleef

Gun Belt 1953 77 min
Ray Nazarro; George Montgomery, Tab Hunter

Gun Code 1940 54 min
Peter Stewart (Sam Newfield); Tim McCoy, Dave O'Brien

Gun Duel in Durango 1957 73 min
Sidney Salkow; George Montgomery, Steve Brodie

Gun Fight 1961 68 min
Edward L. Cahn; James Brown, Joan Staley

Gun Justice 1933 65 min
Alan James; Ken Maynard, Cecilia Parker

Gun Law 1933 59 min
Lew Collins; Jack Hoxie, Paul Fix

Gun Law Justice 1949 55 min
Lambert Hillyer; Jimmy Wakely, Dub Taylor

Gun Packer 1938 51 min
Wallace Fox; Jack Randall, Louise Stanley

Gun Runner 1949 54 min
Lambert Hillyer; Jimmy Wakely, Dub Taylor

Gun Smoke 1945 57 min
Howard Bretherton; Johnny Mack Brown, Raymond Hatton

Gun Smugglers 1948 61 min
Frank McDonald; Tim Holt, Richard Martin

Gun Talk 1957 57 min
Lambert Hillyer; Johnny Mack Brown, Raymond Hatton

Gun Town 1946 57 min
Wallace Fox; Kirby Grant, Fuzzy Knight

Gun Fight at High Noon (El Sabor de la Vengenza aka *I Tre Spietati)* 1963 (It/Sp) 88 min
J.L. Romero Marchent; Richard Harrison, Robert Hundar

Gunfight at Sandoval 1961 75 min
Harry Keller; Tom Tryon, Dan Duryea

Gunfighters of Casa Grande (Los Pistoleros de Casa Grande)
1964 (US/Sp) 92 (77) min
Roy Rowland;

Gunfighters of the Northwest 1954 15 chaps
Spencer G. Bennet; Jack (Jock) Mahoney, Clayton Moore

Gunfire 1935
Harry Fraser; Rex Bell, Ruth Mix

Gunfire 1950 59 min
William Berke; Don Barry, Robert Lowery

Gunfire at Indian Gap 1957 70 min
Joseph Kane; Vera Ralston, Anthony George

The Gunman 1952 52 min
Lewis Collins; Whip Wilson, Fuzzy Knight

Gunman in Town (Una Nuvola di Polvere . . . un Grido di Morte . . . Arriva Sartana) 1970 (It/Sp) 99 min
Anthony Ascott (Giuliano Carmineo); Gianni Garko, Susan Scott

Gunman's Code 1946 57 min
Wallace Fox; Kirby Grant, Fuzzy Knight

Gunmen from Laredo 1959 67 min
Wallace MacDonald; Robert Knapp, Jana Davi

Gunning for Justice 1948 55 min
Ray Taylor; Johnny Mack Brown, Raymond Hatton

Gunning for Vengeance 1946 56 min
Ray Nazarro; Charles Starrett, Smiley Burnette

Gunplay 1951 69 min
Lesley Selander; Tim Holt, Joan Dixon

Guns and Guitars 1936 56 min
Joseph Kane; Gene Autry, Smiley Burnette

Guns for Hire 1932 58 min
Lew Collins; Lane Chandler, Yakima Canutt

Guns in the Dark 1937 56 min
Sam Newfield; Johnny Mack Brown, Dick Curtis

Guns of a Stranger 1973 91 min
Robert Hinkle; Marty Robbins, Chill Wills

The Guns of San Sebastian (Los Canones de San Sebastian)
1967 (Fr/Mex/It) 111 min
Henri Verneuil;

Guns of the Law 1944 55 min
Elmer Clifton; Dave O'Brien, Jim Newill

Guns of the Pecos 1937 65 min
Noel Smith; Dick Foran, Bill Elliott

Gunslingers 1950 55 min
Wallace Fox; Whip Wilson, Andy Clyde

Gunsmoke 1947
Fred King; Nick Stuart, Carol Forman

Gunsmoke 1953 79 min
Nathan Juran; Audie Murphy, Susan Cabot

Gunsmoke in Tucson 1958 79 min
Thomas Carr; Mark Stevens, Forrest Tucker

Gunsmoke Mesa 1944 59 min
Harry Fraser; Dave O'Brien, Jim Newill

Gunsmoke on the Guadalupe 1935
Bartlett Carre; Henry Hall, Marion Shilling

Gunsmoke Trail 1938 57 min
Sam Newfield; Jack Randall, Louise Stanley

Gypsy Colt 1954 72 min
Andrew Marton; Donna Corcoran, Ward Bond

Hail to the Rangers 1943 57 min
William Berke; Charles Starrett, Arthur Hunnicutt

Hair-Trigger Casey 1936 59 min
Harry Fraser; Jack Perrin, Betty Mack

Half Breed 1973 (Yug)
; Lex Barker

Hands Across the Rockies 1941 58 min
Lambert Hillyer; Bill Elliott, Dub Taylor

Hands of a Gunman (Mani di Pistolero) 1965 (It/Sp) 77 min
Rafael Romero Marchent; Craig Hill, Gloria Milland

Harmony Trail 1944 57 min
Robert Tansey; Ken Maynard, Eddie Dean

The Haunted Mine 1946 51 min
Derwin Abrahams; Johnny Mack Brown, Raymond Hatton

Haunted Ranch 1943 57 min
Robert Tansey; John King, David Sharpe

Haunted Trails 1949 58 min
Lambert Hillyer; Whip Wilson, Andy Clyde

Haut fur Haut 1961 (WG/Fr) 89 min
Robert Hossein; Robert Hossein, Mario Adorf

The Hawk of Powder River 1948 54 min
Ray Taylor; Eddie Dean, Jennifer Holt

The Hawk of Wild River 1952 54 min
Fred F. Sears; Charles Starrett, Smiley Burnette

Hawmps 1976 126 min
Joe Camp; James Hampton, Slim Pickens

He Rides Tall 1964 84 min
R.G. Springsteen; Tony Young, Dan Duryea

Headin' for the Rio Grande 1936 60 min
Robert N. Bradbury; Tex Ritter, Eleanor Stewart

Headin' For Trouble 1931 60 min
J.P. McGowan; Bob Custer, Betty Mack

Heading West 1946 54 min
Ray Nazarro; Charles Starrett, Smiley Burnette

Heads I Kill You – Tails You Die (Testa t'Ammazzo, Croce Sei Morto . . . Mi Chiamano Alleluja) 1971 (It) 86 (79) min
Anthony Ascott (Giuliano Carmineo); George Hilton, Charles Southwood

Heads or Tails (Testa o Croce) 1969 (It) 95 min
Piero Pierotti; John Ericson, Sheyla Rosin

Heart of Arizona 1938 68 min
Lesley Selander; William Boyd, George Hayes

Heart of the North 1938 80 min
Lewis Seiler; Dick Foran, Gloria Dickson

Heart of the Rio Grande 1942 70 min
William Morgan; Gene Autry, Smiley Burnette

Heaven Only Knows 1947
Albert S. Rogell; Robert Cummings, Brian Donlevy

Heir to Trouble 1935 59 min
Spencer G. Bennet; Ken Maynard, Harry Woods

Heldorado 1946 70 min
William Witney; Roy Rogers, Dale Evans

Hell Canyon Outlaws 1957 72 min
Paul Landres, Dale Robertson, Brian Keith

Hellfire 1949 90 min
R.G. Springsteen; Bill Elliott, Marie Windsor

Hello Trouble 1932 67 min
Lambert Hillyer; Buck Jones, Ward Bond

Hell's Crossroads 1957 73 min
Franklin Adreon; Stephen McNally, Robert Vaughn

Hell's Outpost 1954 90 min
Joseph Kane; Rod Cameron, Joan Leslie

Hell's Valley 1931 60 min
Alvin J. Neitz; Wally Wales, Lafe McKee

Heroes of the Alamo 1937 75 min
Harry Fraser; Rex Lease, Lane Chandler

Heroes of the Range 1936 58 min
Spencer G. Bennet; Ken Maynard, Harry Woods

Heroes of the West 1932 12 chaps
Ray Taylor; Onslow Stevens, Noah Beery Jnr

Hiawatha 1952 80 min
Kurt Neumann; Vincent Edwards, Keith Larsen

Hidden Danger 1948 55 min
Ray Taylor; Johnny Mack Brown, Raymond Hatton

Hidden Gold 1940 61 min
Lesley Selander; William Boyd, Russell Hayden

Hidden Valley 1932 60 min
Robert N. Bradbury; Bob Steele, Gertrude Messinger

Hidden Valley Outlaws 1944
Howard Bretherton; Bill Elliott, George Hayes

The Hidden Woman (La Escondida) 1956 (Mex) 103 min
Roberto Gavaldon;

High Venture 1951 77 min
Lewis R. Foster; John Payne, Dennis O'Keefe

Hills of Oklahoma 1950 67 min
R.G. Springsteen; Rex Allen, Fuzzy Knight

Hills of Old Wyoming 1937 75 min
Nate Watt; William Boyd, George Hayes

Hills of Utah 1951 70 min
John English; Gene Autry, Pat Buttram

His Brother's Ghost 1945 54 min
Sam Newfield; Buster Crabbe, Al St John

His Fighting Blood 1935 60 min
John English; Kermit Maynard, Polly Ann Young

Hittin' the Trail 1937 58 min
Robert N. Bradbury; Tex Ritter, Earl Dwire

Hi-Yo Silver 1940 69 min
William Witney, John English; Lee Powell, Lynne Roberts

Die Holle von Manitoba 1964 (WG/Sp) 94 min
Sheldon Reynolds; Lex Barker, Paul Brice

Hollywood Barn Dance 1947 72 min
B.B. Ray; Ernest Tubb, Earle Hodgins

Hollywood Cowboy aka *Wings Over Wyoming* 1937 64 min
Ewing Scott; George O'Brien, Cecilia Parker

A Holster Full of Law 1961 84 min
James Neilson;

A Holy Terror 1931 63 min
Irving Cummings; George O'Brien, Humphrey Bogart

Home in Oklahoma 1946 72 min
William Witney; Roy Rogers, Dale Evans

Home in San Antone 1949 62 min
Ray Nazarro; Roy Acuff, Jacqueline Thomas

Home in Wyomin' 1942 67 min
William Morgan; Gene Autry, Smiley Burnette

Home on the Prairie 1939 58 min
Jack Townley; Gene Autry, Smiley Burnette

Home on the Range 1946 55 min
R.G. Springsteen; Monte Hale, Adrian Booth

The Homesteaders 1953 62 min
Lewis Collins; Bill Elliott, Robert Lowery

Homesteaders of Paradise Valley 1947 59 min
R.G. Springsteen; Allan Lane, Bobby Blake

Hondo and the Apaches 1967 85 min
Lee H. Katzin;

Honeychile 1951 90 min
R.G. Springsteen; Judy Canova, Eddie Foy Jnr

Honor of the Mounted 1932 62 min
Harry Fraser; Tom Tyler, Charles King

Honor of the West 1939 58 min
George Waggner; Bob Baker, Carleton Young

Hopalong Rides Again 1937 65 min
Lesley Selander; William Boyd, George Hayes

Hostile Guns 1967 91 min
R.G. Springsteen; George Montgomery, Yvonne De Carlo

Hot Lead 1951 60 min
Stuart Gilmore; Tim Holt, Richard Martin

Hot Spur 1970 86 min
R.L. Frost; James Arena, Virginia Gordon

Hudson's Bay 1941 93 min
Irving Pichel; Paul Muni, Gene Tierney

Human Targets 1932
J.P. McGowan; Rin-Tin-Tin, Buzz Barton

100 Fauste und ein Vaterunser 1972 (WG/It) 83 min
Mario Siciliano; Ron Ely, Robert Widmark

Hurricane Horseman 1931 50 min
Armand Schaefer; Lane Chandler, Yakima Canutt

Hurricane Smith 1941 69 min
Bernard Vorhaus; Ray Middleton, Jane Wyatt

I'll Go, I'll Kill Him, and Come Back (Vado … l'Ammazzo e Torno) 1967 (It)
Enzo G. Castellari; George Hilton, Gilbert Roland

I'll Sell My Skin Dearly (Vendo Cara la Pelle) 1968 (It)
100 (79) min
Ettore M. Fizzarotti; Mike Marshall, Michele Girardou

I'm From the City 1938 66 min
Ben Holmes; Joe Penner, Richard Lane

I'm Sartana … I'll Dig Your Grave (Sono Sartana, il Vostro Becchino) 1969 (It)
Anthony Ascott (Giuliano Carmineo); John Garko, Frank Wolff

If You Want to Live … Shoot (Se Vuoi Vivere … Spara) 1968 (It)
Willy S. Regan (S. Garrone); Sean Todd, Ken Wood

In a Colt's Shadow (All'Ombra di una Colt) 1965 (It/Sp)
85 (68) min
Gianni Grimaldi; Stephen Forsyth, Conrado Sammartin

In Old Amarillo 1951 67 min
William Witney; Roy Rogers, Estelita Rodriguez

In Old Caliente 1939 57 min
Joseph Kane; Roy Rogers, George Hayes

In Old California 1929 60 min
Burton King; Henry B. Wathall, George Duryea (Tom Keene)

In Old Cheyenne 1941 58 min
Joseph Kane; Roy Rogers, George Hayes

In Old Los Angeles 1948 88 min
Joseph Kane; Bill Elliott, John Carroll

In Old Montana 1939 61 min
Raymond K. Johnson; Fred Scott, John Merton

Indian Paint 1965 91 min
Norman Foster; Johnny Crawford, Jay Silverheels

Indian Uprising 1952 75 min
Ray Nazarro; George Montgomery, Audrey Long

Inginocchiati Straniero … I Cadaveri Non Fanno Ombra! 1970 (It) 83 min
Miles Deem (D. Fidani); Hunt Powers, Chet Davis

Inside Straight 1951 89 min
Gerald Mayer; Arlene Dahl, Barry Sullivan

Io Non Perdono … Uccido 1968 (It)
Rafael Romero Marchent; N. Bengell, J. Philbrook

The Irish Gringo 1935
William L. Thompson; Pat Carlyle, William Farnum

Iron Mountain Trail 1953 54 min
William Witney; Rex Allen, Slim Pickens

It Can Be Done, Amigo 1971 (It)
Maurizio Lucidi; Jack Palance, Bud Spencer

It Happened Out West 1937 56 min
Howard Bretherton; Paul Kelly, LeRoy Mason

J & S – Storia Criminale del Far West 1973 (It/Sp/WG) 97 min
Sergio Corbucci; Telly Savalas, Susan George

Jack McCall, Desperado 1953 76 min
Sidney Salkow; George Montgomery, Angela Stevens

Jack Slade 1953 90 min
Harold Schuster; Mark Stevens, Dorothy Malone

Jackass Mail 1942 80 min
Norman Z. McLeod; Wallace Beery, Marjorie Main

The James Brothers of Missouri 1950 12 chaps
Fred C. Brannon; Keith Richards, Robert Bice

Jaws of Justice 1933 58 min
Spencer G. Bennet; Richard Terry (Jack Perrin), Lafe McKee

Jesse James Jnr 1942 56 min
George Sherman; Don Barry, Lynn Merrick

Jesse James Rides Again 1947 13 chaps
Fred C. Brannon, Thomas Carr; Clayton Moore, Linda Stirling

Jiggs and Maggie West 1950 66 min
William Beaudine; Joe Yule, Tim Ryan

Joaquin Murrieta 1958 (Mex) 84 min
Miguel Contreras Torres;

Joe Dynamit 1969 (It) 90 min
Anthony Dawson (Giuliano Carmineo);

Joe l'Implacibale 1967 (It)
Antonio Margheriti; Van Nutter, J. Zalewska

John the Bastard (John il Bastardo) 1967 (It) 105 min
Armando Crispino; John Richardson, Claudio Comasco

Johnny Banco 1967 (It)
Y. Allegret; Horst Bucholz, Sylva Koscina

Johnny Hamlet 1972 (Sp)
Enzo G. Castellari; Gilbert Roland, Pedro Sanchez

Johnny West il Mancino 1965 (It/Fr/Sp) 94 (85) min
Frank Kramer (Gianfranco Parolini); Dick Palmer, Diana Garson

Johnny Yuma 1967 (It)
Romolo Guerrieri; Mark Damon, Lawrence Dobkin

Jonny Rettet Nebrador 1953 (WG) 95 min
Rudolf Jugerts;

Juana Gallo 1961 (Mex) 120 (85) min
Miguel Zacarias;

The Judgement Book 1935 63 min
Charles Hutchinson; Conway Tearle, Richard Cramer

Junction City 1952 54 min
Ray Nazarro; Charles Starrett, Smiley Burnette

K.O. Va e Uccidi 1966 (It)
G. Ferrero; M.N. Parenti, L. Love

Kentucky Rifle 1956 82 min
Carl K. Hittleman; Chill Wills, Lance Fuller

Kid Courageous 1935
Robert N. Bradbury; Bob Steele, Lafe McKee

The Kid from Amarillo 1951 56 min
Ray Nazarro; Charles Starrett, Smiley Burnette

The Kid from Arizona 1931 55 min
Robert J. Horner; Jack Perrin, Josephine Hill

The Kid from Gower Gulch 1950 56 min
Oliver Drake; Spade Cooley, Bob Gilbert

The Kid from Santa Fé 1940 57 min
Raymond K. Johnson; Jack Randall, Dave O'Brien

Kid il Monello del West 1973 (It)
T. Good; A. Balestri, F. Colombaioni

The Kid Ranger 1936 57 min
Robert N. Bradbury; Bob Steele, William Farnum

The Kid Rides Again 1943 60 min
Sherman Scott (Sam Newfield); Buster Crabbe, Al St John

The Kid's Last Ride 1941 55 min
S. Roy Luby; Ray Corrigan, John King

Kidnapped 1969 (It/Sp)
Albert Cardiff (Alberto Cardone); Brett Halsey, Fernando Sancho

Kill Johnny Ringo (Uccidete Jonny Ringo) 1966 (It) 100 min
Frank G. Carrol (Gianfranco Baldanello); Brett Halsey, Ray Scott

Kill or Be Killed (Uccidi o Muori) 1966 (It) 95 (92) min
Amerigo Anton; Robert Mark, Fabrizio Moroni

Killer, Adios 1968 (It/Sp) 95 min
Primo Zeglio; Peter Lee Lawrence, Marisa Solinas

Killer Calibre 32 (Killer Calibro 32) 1967 (It) 87 min
Al Bradley (Alfonso Brescia); Peter Lee Lawrence, Agnes Spaak

The Killer Kid (Chamaco) 1967 (It) 103 (88) min
Leopoldo Savona; Anthony Steffen, Liz Barret

King of the Arena 1933 59 min
Alan James; Ken Maynard, Lucile Brown

King of the Forest Rangers 1946 12 chaps
Spencer Bennet, Fred Brannon; Larry Thompson, Helen Talbot

King of the Royal Mounted 1940 12 chaps
William Witney, John English; Allan Lane, Robert Strange

King of the Stallions 1942 63 min
Edward Finney; Chief Thundercloud, Dave O'Brien

King of the Wild Horses 1933 62 min
Earl Haley; William Janney, Wallace MacDonald

King of the Wild Horses 1947 79 min
George Archainbaud; Preston Foster, Gail Patrick

Kino, the Padre on Horseback 1977 116 min
Ken Kennedy; Richard Egan, Ricardo Montalban

Kiss of Fire 1955 87 min
Joseph M. Newman; Jack Palance, Barbara Rush

Kitosch, l'Uomo Che Venna dal Nord 1967 (It/Sp)
Joseph Marvin; George Hilton, Krista Nell

Klondike 1932 68 min
Phil Rosen; Lyle Talbot, Thelma Todd

Klondike Kate 1943
William Castle; Ann Savage, Tom Neal

Konga, the Wild Stallion 1940 65 min
Sam Nelson; Fred Stone, Eddy Waller

Lady Godiva Rides 1969 89 min
A.C. Stephen; Marsha Jordan, Forman Shane

Land of Hunted Men 1943 58 min
S. Roy Luby; Ray Corrigan, Dennis Moore

The Land of Missing Men 1930 58 min
John P. McCarthy; Bob Steele, Al St John

Land of the Lawless 1947 54 min
Lambert Hillyer; Johnny Mack Brown, Raymond Hatton

Land of the Outlaws 1944 56 min
Lambert Hillyer; Johnny Mack Brown, Raymond Hatton

Land of the Six Guns 1940 54 min
Raymond K. Johnson; Jack Randall, Louise Stanley

Land of Wanted Men 1932 60 min
Harry Fraser; Bill Cody, Andy Shuford

Land Raiders aka Day of the Landgrabbers 1969 101 min
Nathan H. Juran; George Maharis, Telly Savalas

Landrush 1946 53 min
Vernon Keays; Charles Starrett, Smiley Burnette

Ein Langer Ritt nach Eden 1972 (WG) 80 min
Gunter Hendel; Mike Run, Karin Heske

Laramie 1949 55 min
Ray Nazarro; Charles Starrett, Smiley Burnette

The Laramie Kid 1935
Harry S. Webb; Tom Tyler, Al Ferguson

The Laramie Trail 1944 55 min
John English; Robert Livingston, Smiley Burnette

Lariats and Sixshooters 1931 65 min
Alvin J. Neitz (Alan James); Jack Perrin, George Chesebro

Lasca of the Rio Grande 1931 60 min
Edward Laemmle; Leo Carrillo, John Mack Brown

The Lash 1930 80 min
Frank Lloyd; Richard Barthelmess, Mary Astor

Lasst uns Toten, Companeros 1971 (WG/It/Sp)
Sergio Corbucci; Franco Nero, Tomas Milian

The Last Frontier 1932 12 chaps
Spencer G. Bennet, Thomas L. Story; Lon Chaney Jnr, Dorothy Gulliver

Last Frontier Uprising 1947 67 min
Lesley Selander; Monte Hale, Adrian Booth

The Last Gunfighter 1961 56 min
Lindsay Shonteff; Don Borisenko, Tass Tory

The Last Killer (L'Ultimo Killer) 1967 (It/Sp) 87 min
Joseph Warren (Giuseppe Vari);

The Last Musketeer 1952 67 min
William Witney; Rex Allen, Slim Pickens

The Last of the Mohicans 1932 12 chaps
B. Reeves Eason, Ford Beebe; Harry Carey, Bob Kortman

Last of the Redmen 1947 77 min
George Sherman; Jon Hall, Julie Bishop

Last of the Warrens 1936 60 min
Robert N. Bradbury; Bob Steele, Charles King

The Last Ride to Santa Cruz (Der Letzte Ritt nach Santa Cruz) 1963 (WG/Austria) 105 min
Rolf Olsen; Mario Adorf, Marianne Koch

Last Stagecoach West 1957 67 min
Joseph Kane; Jim Davis, Victor Jory

The Last Trail 1933 59 min
James Tinling; George O'Brien, Claire Trevor

Laughing Boy 1934 79 min
W.S. Van Dyke; Ramon Novarro, Lupe Velez

Law and Lawless 1932 59 min
Armand Schaefer; Jack Hoxie, Wally Wales

Law and Order 1942 56 min
Sherman Scott (Sam Newfield); Buster Crabbe, Al St John

Law Beyond the Range 1935 60 min
Ford Beebe; Tim McCoy, Billie Seward

The Law Comes to Gunsight 1947 56 min
Lambert Hillyer; Johnny Mack Brown, Raymond Hatton

The Law Commands 1937
William Nigh; Tom Keene, Bud Buster

Law Men 1944 58 min
Lambert Hillyer; Johnny Mack Brown, Raymond Hatton

Law of the Badlands 1951 60 min
Lesley Selander; Tim Holt, Richard Martin

Law of the Barbary Coast 1949 65 min
Lew Landers; Gloria Henry, Stephen Dunne

Law of the Canyon 1947 55 min
Ray Nazarro; Charles Starrett, Smiley Burnette

Law of the 45s 1935 57 min
John P. McCarthy; Big Boy Williams, Al St John

Law of the North 1932 55 min
Harry Fraser; Bill Cody, Andy Shuford

Law of the Panhandle 1950 55 min
Lewis Collins; Johnny Mack Brown, Jane Adams

Law of the Ranger 1937 57 min
Spencer G. Bennet; Bob Allen, Lafe McKee

Law of the Rio Grande 1931 57 min
Bennett Cohen, Forrest Sheldon; Bob Custer, Betty Mack

Law of the Saddle 1943 59 min
Melville De Lay; Bob Livingston, Al St John

Law of the Valley 1944 52 min
Howard Bretherton; Johnny Mack Brown, Raymond Hatton

Law of the West 1932 58 min
Robert N. Bradbury; Bob Steele, Earl Dwire

Law of the West 1949 54 min
Ray Taylor; Johnny Mack Brown, Max Terhune

The Law of the Wild 1934 12 chaps
B. Reeves Eason, Armand Schaefer; Rin-Tin-Tin Jnr, Bob Custer

Law of the Wolf 1941 55 min
Raymond K. Johnson; Dennis Moore, Luana Walters

The Law Rides 1936 57 min
Robert N. Bradbury; Bob Steele, Harley Wood

Lawless Borders 1935 58 min
John P. McCarthy; Bill Cody, Molly O'Day

Lawless Breed 1946 58 min
Wallace Fox; Kirby Grant, Fuzzy Knight

Lawless Code 1949 58 min
Oliver Drake; Jimmy Wakely, Dub Taylor

Lawless Cowboys 1951 58 min
Lewis Collins; Whip Wilson, Fuzzy Knight

The Lawless Eighties 1958 70 min
Joseph Kane; Buster Crabbe, John Smith

Lawless Empire 1945 58 min
Vernon Keays; Charles Starrett, Dub Taylor

Lawless Land 1937 55 min
Albert Ray; Johnny Mack Brown, Louise Stanley

Lawless Riders 1935 57 min
Spencer G. Bennet; Ken Maynard, Harry Woods

Lawless Valley 1932
J.P. McGowan; Lane Chandler, Gertrude Messinger

Lay That Rifle Down 1955 71 min
Charles Lamont; Judy Canova, Robert Lowery

Leadville Gunslinger 1952 54 min
Harry Keller; Allan Lane, Eddy Waller

The Legend of Custer 1967 94 min
Norman Foster;

The Legion of the Lawless 1940 59 min
David Howard; George O'Brien, Virginia Vale

Let Them Rest (Requiescant) 1967 (It/WG) 92 min
Carlo Lizzani; Lou Castel, Mark Damon

Die Letzte Kugel Traf den Besten 1965 (WG/It) 76 min
Joaquin Romero Marchent; Clyde Rodgers, Adrian Hoven

Die Letzte Rechnung Zahlst du Selbst 1968 (WG/It) 93 min
Giorgio Stegani; Lee Van Cleef, Antonio Sabato

Die Letzten Zwei vom Rio Bravo 1965 (WG/It/Sp) 93 min
Manfred Rieger; Rod Cameron, Horst Frank

Life in the Raw 1933 62 min
Louis King; George O'Brien, Claire Trevor

The Light in the Forest 1958 93 min
Herschel Daugherty; Fess Parker, Wendell Corey

Lightnin' Bill Carson 1936 75 min
Sam Newfield; Tim McCoy, Rex Lease

Lightnin' Smith Returns 1931 59 min
Jack Irwin; Buddy Roosevelt, Barbara Worth

Lightning Range 1934 53 min
Victor Adamson (Denver Dixon); Buddy Roosevelt, Patsy Bellamy

Lightning Strikes West 1940 56 min
Harry Fraser; Ken Maynard, Charles King

Lightning Triggers 1935
S. Roy Luby; Reb Russell, Fred Kohler

Lights of Old Santa Fé 1944 76 min
Frank McDonald; Roy Rogers, George Hayes

The Lion's Den 1936 59 min
Sam Newfield; Tim McCoy, Joan Woodbury

Little Rita in the West (Little Rita nel West) 1967 (It) 105 (86) min
Ferdinando Baldi; Rita Pavone, Terence Hill

The Littlest Outlaw 1955 75 min
Roberto Gavaldon; Andres Velasquez, Pedro Armendariz

Lo Chiamavano Tresette … Giocava Sempre col Morto 1973 (It) 100 (88) min
Anthony Ascott (Giuliano Carmineo); George Hilton, Chris Huerte

Lo Chiamavano Verita 1972 (It)
Luigi Perelli; Mark Damon, Pietro Nigro

Lo Credevano uno Stingo di Santo 1972 (It)
J. Bosch; A. Ascott, D. Martin

Lo Irritarono … e Sartana Fece Piazza Pulita 1970 (It)
Rafael Romero Marchent; John Garko, William Bogart

Lo Voglio Morto 1968 (It/Sp) 85 min
Paolo Bianchini; Craig Hill, Lea Massari

The Local Bad Man 1932 59 min
Otto Brower; Hoot Gibson, Sally Blaine

Lola Colt 1967 (It) 85 min
Siro Marcellini; Peter Martell, I.L. Falena

The Lone Avenger 1933 61 min
Alan James; Ken Maynard, Muriel Gordon

The Lone Bandit 1934
J.P. McGowan; Lane Chandler, Wally Wales

The Lone Cowboy 1934 64 min
Paul Sloane; Jackie Cooper, Barton MacLane

The Lone Defender 1930 12 chaps
Richard Thorpe; Rin-Tin-Tin, Walter Miller

The Lone Gun 1954 73 min
Ray Nazarro; George Montgomery, Dorothy Malone

The Lone Hand 1953 80 min
George Sherman; Joel McCrea, Barbara Hale

The Lone Prairie 1942 58 min
William Berke; Russell Hayden, Dub Taylor

The Lone Rider 1934
Robert Tansey; Wally Wales, Franklyn Farnum

The Lone Rider Ambushed 1941 67 min
Sam Newfield; George Houston, Al St John

The Lone Rider and the Bandit 1942 54 min
Sam Newfield; George Houston, Al St John

The Lone Rider Crosses the Rio 1941
Sam Newfield; George Houston, Al St John

The Lone Rider Fights Back 1941 64 min
Sam Newfield; George Houston, Al St John

The Lone Rider in Cheyenne 1942 59 min
Sam Newfield; George Houston, Al St John

The Lone Rider in Frontier Fury 1941
Sam Newfield; George Houston, Al St John

The Lone Rider in Ghost Town 1941 64 min
Sam Newfield; George Houston, Al St John

The Lone Rider in Texas Justice 1942 83 min
Sam Newfield; George Houston, Al St John

The Lone Rider Rides On 1941 61 min
Sam Newfield; George Houston, Al St John

Lone Star Law Men 1941 61 min
Robert Tansey; Tom Keene, Betty Miles

Lone Star Moonlight 1946 67 min
Ray Nazarro; Ken Curtis, Joan Barton

Lone Star Raiders 1940 57 min
George Sherman; Robert Livingston, Bob Steele

The Lone Star Vigilantes 1942 58 min
Wallace Fox; Bill Elliott, Tex Ritter

Lone Texas Ranger 1945 56 min
Spencer Bennet; Bill Elliott, Bobby Blake

The Lone Trail 1932
Forrest Sheldon, Harry S. Webb; Lane Chandler, Ben Corbett

Lonesome Trail 1945 57 min
Oliver Drake; Jimmy Wakely, Lee White

The Lonesome Trail 1955 73 min
Richard Bartlett; Wayne Morris, John Agar

A Long Ride from Hell (Vivo per la Tua Morte) 1968 (It) 90 min
Alex Burks (Camillo Bazzoni); Steve Reeves, Wayde Preston

The Long Rope 1961 61 min
William Witney; Hugh Marlowe, Alan Hale Jnr

The Longest Hunt (Spara, Gringo, Spara) 1968 (It) 100 (98) min
Frank B. Corlish (Bruno Corbucci); Brian Kelly, Frank Munroe (Fabrizio Maroni)

Loser's End 1934
Bernard B. Ray; Jack Perrin, Frank Rice

Lost Canyon 1943 61 min
Lesley Selander; William Boyd, Andy Clyde

Lost in Alaska 1952 76 min
Jean Yarbrough; Bud Abbott, Lou Costello

Love Me Tender 1956 89 min
Robert D. Webb; Richard Egan, Debra Paget

The Luck of Roaring Camp 1937 58 min
I.V. Willat; Owen Davis Jnr, Forrest Taylor

Lucky Cisco Kid 1940 68 min
H. Bruce Humberstone; Cesar Romero, Dana Andrews

Lucky Larrigan 1932 58 min
J.P. McCarthy; Rex Bell, Helen Foster

The Lucky Star 1980 (Can)
Max Fischer; Louise Fletcher, Rod Steiger

Lucky Terror 1936 61 min
Alan James; Hoot Gibson, Wally Wales

Lumberjack 1944 65 min
Lesley Selander; William Boyd, Andy Clyde

La Lunga Cavalcata della Vendetta 1972 (It)
T. Boccia; Richard Harrison, Anita Ekberg

La Lunga Notte di Tombstone 1968 (It)
J.J. Balcazar; Tomas Milian, Claudio Camaso

I Lunghi Giorni dell'Odio 1968 (It) 87 min
Gianfranco Baldanello; Guy Madison, Lucienne Bridou

I Lunghi Giorni della Vendetta 1966 (It/Sp) 120 (105) min
Stan Vance (Florestano Vancini); Giuliano Gemma, Francisco Rabal

Il Lungo Giorno del Massacro 1968 (It)
Alberto Cardone; Peter Martell, M. Serrano

Lure of the Wasteland 1939 55 min
Harry Fraser; Grant Withers, LeRoy Mason

Lust in the Dust (Dans la Poussière du Soleil) 1971 (Fr/Sp) 84 min
Richard Balducci;

Madron 1970 (Israel) 92 min
Jerry Hopper; Richard Boone, Leslie Caron

The Magnificent Four (I Quattro Inesorabili) 1965 (It/Fr)
92 min
Primo Zeglio; Adam West, Robert Hundar

The Magnificent Three (Tres Hombres Buenos aka *I Tre
Implacabili)* 1963 (It/Sp) 69 min
Joaquin L. Romero Marchent; Geoffrey Horne, Robert
Hundar

Il Magnifico Straniero 1965 (It/US) 94 min
Herschel Daugherty, Justus Addiss;

Il Magnifico Texano 1967 (It/Sp)
Lewis King (Luigi Capuano); Glenn Saxson, J. Barracuda

Il Magnifico West 1972 (It)
G. Crea; V. Karis, L. Fineschi

Le Maledette Pistole di Dallas 1964 (It/Sp/Fr) 92 min
Jose Maria Zabalza;

Mamma Mia e Arrivato Cosi Sia 1973 (It)
A. Calabiano; L. Merenda, Alf Thunder

The Man Called Gringo (Sie Nannten ihn Gringo) 1964
(WG/Sp/It) 89 min
Roy Rowland; Gotz George, Alexandra Stewart

The Man Called Noon 1973 (GB/Sp/It) 95 min
Peter Collinson; Richard Crenna, Stephen Boyd

The Man from Arizona 1932 58 min
Harry Fraser; Rex Bell, Charles King

The Man from Bitter Ridge 1955 80 min
Jack Arnold; Lex Barker, Stephen McNally

The Man from Button Willow 1965 84 min
David Detiege; animated cartoon

*The Man from Canyon City (L'Uomo che Viene da Canyon
City)* 1965 (It/Sp) 85 min
Alfonso Balcazar; Robert Wood, Fernando Sancho

The Man from Death Valley 1931 64 min
Lloyd Nosler; Tom Tyler, Betty Mack

Man from Hell's Edges 1932 61 min
Robert N. Bradbury; Bob Steele, George Hayes

Man from Montana 1941 56 min
Ray Taylor; Johnny Mack Brown, Fuzzy Knight

Man from Montreal 1940 60 min
Christy Cabanne; Richard Arlen, Andy Devine

Man from Music Mountain 1938 58 min
Joseph Kane; Gene Autry, Smiley Burnette

The Man from New Mexico 1932 60 min
J.P. McCarthy; Tom Tyler, Robert Walker

The Man from Nowhere 1968 (It)
; Giuliano Gemma

The Man from Oklahoma 1945 68 min
Frank McDonald; Roy Rogers, Dale Evans

Man from Oklahoma 1964 (WG)
Harald Reinl; Richard Horn

Man from Sonora 1951 54 min
Lewis Collins; Johnny Mack Brown, Phyllis Coates

The Man from Sundown 1939 58 min
Sam Nelson; Charles Starrett, Iris Meredith

The Man from Texas 1947 71 min
Leigh Jason; James Craig, Johnny Johnston

Man from the Black Hills 1952 51 min
Thomas Carr; Johnny Mack Brown, Jimmy Ellison

The Man from the Rio Grande 1943 57 min
Howard Bretherton; Don Barry, Wally Vernon

The Man from Thunder River 1943 57 min
John English; Bill Elliott, George Hayes

Man of Action 1933 57 min
George Melford; Tim McCoy, Wheeler Oakman

Man of Conquest 1939 97 min
George Nichols Jnr; Richard Dix, Joan Fontaine

Man or Gun 1958 79 min
Albert C. Gannaway; MacDonald Carey, James Gleason

Man with the Steel Whip 1954 12 chaps
Franklin Adreon; Richard Simmons, Roy Barcroft

Man's Country 1938 53 min
Robert Hill; Jack Randall, Marjorie Reynolds

A Man's Land 1932 65 min
Phil Rosen; Hoot Gibson, Marion Shilling

Mannaja 1978 (It)
Sergio Martino; Maurizio Merli, John Steiner

The Marauders 1955 80 min
Gerald Mayer; Dan Duryea, Keenan Wynn

Mark of the Spur 1932 58 min
J.P. McGowan; Bob Custer, Franklyn Farnum

Marked for Murder 1945 58 min
Elmer Clifton; Tex Ritter, Dave O'Brien

Marked Trails 1944 58 min
J.P. McCarthy; Hoot Gibson, Bob Steele

The Marksman 1953 62 min
Lewis Collins; Wayne Morris, Frank Ferguson

Marshal of Gunsmoke 1944 58 min
Vernon Keyes; Tex Ritter, Russell Hayden

Marshal of Heldorado 1950 53 min
Thomas Carr; Jimmy Ellison, Russell Hayden

Marshal of Laredo 1945 56 min
R.G. Springsteen; Bill Elliott, Bobby Blake

Marshal of Reno 1944 54 min
Wallace Grissell; Bill Elliott, George Hayes

Masked Raiders 1949 60 min
Lesley Selander; Tim Holt, Richard Martin

The Masked Rider 1941 58 min
Ford Beebe; Johnny Mack Brown, Fuzzy Knight

Mason of the Mounted 1932 58 min
Harry Fraser; Bill Cody, Andy Shuford

Massacre 1934
Alan Crossland; Richard Barthelmess, Ann Dvorak

Massacre at Fort Grant (Fuerte Perdido) 1965 (Sp) 92 (84) min
John Douglas (Jose Maria Elorrieta); Jerry Cobb (German
Cobos), Martha Hyier (Marta May)

Massacre at Marble City (Die Goldsucher von Arkansas) 1964
(WG/It/Fr) 107 (86) min
Paul Martin; Brad Harris, Mario Adorf

Massacre Canyon 1954 66 min
Fred F. Sears; Phil Carey, Guinn Williams

Massacro al Grande Canyon 1964 (It) 89 min
Stanley Corbett (Sergio Corbucci), Albert Band (Alfredo
Antonini);

Matalo! 1970 (It/Sp) 100 min
Cesare Canevari; Corrado Pani, Lou Castel

McKenna of the Mounted 1932 66 min
D. Ross Lederman; Buck Jones, James Glavin

Melody of the Plains 1937 55 min
Sam Newfield; Fred Scott, Al St John

Melody Trail 1935 60 min
Joseph Kane; Gene Autry, Smiley Burnette

Men of the North 1930 63 min
Hal Roach; Gilbert Roland, Robert Greaves

Men of the Plains 1936 62 min
Bob Hill; Rex Bill, Joan Barclay

Men of the Timberland 1941 61 min
Paul Jarrico; Richard Arlen, Andy Devine

Menace on the Mountain 1972 81 min
Vincent McEveety; Patricia Crowley, Albert Salmi

Mesquite Buckaroo 1939 55 min
Harry S. Webb; Bob Steele, Frank LaRue

Mexican Spitfire Out West 1940 76 min
Leslie Goodwins; Lupe Velez, Donald Woods

Midnight Canyon (Heiss Weht der Wind) 1964 (WG/Austria)
102 min
Rolf Olsen; Thomas Fritsch, Walter Giller

Mille Dollari sul Nero 1966 (It/WG) 92 min
Albert Cardiff (Alberto Cardone); Anthony Steffen, John
Garko

The Mine with the Iron Door 1936 66 min
David Howard; Richard Arlen, Cecilia Parker

A Minute to Pray, a Second to Die 1968 (It) 103 (97) min
Franco Giraldi; Alex Cord, Arthur Kennedy

Il Mio Corpo per un Poker 1968 (It) 99 min
Nathan Wich;

Il Mio Nome e Mallory : 'M' Come Morte 1971 (It)
M. Moroni; Robert Wood, Gabriella Giorgelli

The Mississippi Gambler 1953 98 min
Rudolph Mate; Tyrone Power, Piper Laurie

A Missouri Outlaw 1941 58 min
George Sherman; Don Barry, Lynn Merrick

The Missouri Traveller 1958 103 min
Jerry Hopper; Brandon de Wilde, Lee Marvin

The Missourians 1950 60 min
George Blair; Monte Hale, Paul Hurst

Mit Django Kam der Tod 1968 (WG/It) 91 min
Luigi Bazzoni; Franco Nero, Klaus Kinski

Mogen Sie in Frieden Runen 1967 (WG/It) 92 min
Carlo Lizzani; Lou Castel, Mark Damon

Mohawk 1956 79 min
Kurt Neumann; Scott Brady, Neville Brand

Mojave Firebrand 1944 55 min
Spencer G. Bennet; Bill Elliott, George Hayes

The Moment to Kill (Il Momento di Uccidere) 1968 (It/WG)
90 min
Anthony Ascott (Giuliano Carmineo); George Hilton, Walter
Barnes

Monta in Sella Figlio di 1972 (It)
T. Ricci; Mark Damon, R. Neri

Montana Desperado 1951 51 min
Wallace Fox; Johnny Mack Brown, Myron Healey

Montana Incident 1952 54 min
Lewis Collins; Whip Wilson, Peggy Stewart

Montana Territory 1952 64 min
Ray Nazarro; Lon McCallister, Preston Foster

Moon over Montana 1946 56 min
Oliver Drake; Jimmy Wakely, Jennifer Holt

Moonlight and Cactus 1944 60 min
Edward F. Cline; Andrews Sisters, Leo Carillo

La Morte Non Conta i Dollari 1967 (It)
R. Freda; Mark Damon, L. Gilli

La Morte sull'Alta Coclina 1969 (It/Sp)
Fred Ringoold; Peter Lee Lawrence, Louis Dawson

I Morti Non si Contano 1968 (It/Sp) 94 (81) min
Rafael Romero Marchent; Anthony Steffen, Mark Damon

Mosby's Marauders 1966 85 min
Michael O'Herlihy; James MacArthur, Nick Adams

Mountain Rhythm 1939 61 min
B. Reeves Eason; Gene Autry, Smiley Burnette

Mounted Fury 1931 63 min
Stuart Paton; John Bowers, Frank Rice

Mrs Mike 1949 99 min
Louis King; Dick Powell, Evelyn Keyes

Murder on the Yukon 1940 58 min
Louis Gasnier; James Newill, Polly Ann Young

Mustang 1959 73 min
Peter Stephens; Jack Buetel, Steve Keyes

My Friend Flicka 1943 90 min
Harold Shumate; Roddy McDowall, Preston Foster

My Name Is King (Lo Chiamavano King) 1971 (It)
Don Reynolds; Richard Harrison, Klaus Kinski

My Name Is Legend 1975 88 min
Duke Kelly; Duke Kelly, Tom Kirk

The Mysterious Desperado 1949 61 min
Lesley Selander; Tim Holt, Richard Martin

The Mysterious Rider 1942 56 min
Sam Newfield; Buster Crabbe, Al St John

Mystery Man 1944 58 min
George Archainbaud; William Boyd, Andy Clyde

Mystery Ranch 1934 56 min
Ray Bernard (Bernard B. Ray); Tom Tyler, Roberta Gale

Mystery Range 1937 56 min
Bob Hill; Tom Tyler, Lafe McKee

The Mystery Trooper 1931 10 chaps
Stuart Paton; Robert Frazer, Charles King

The Naked Gun 1956 69 min
Edward Dew; Willard Parker, Barton MacLane

The Naked Hills 1956 73 min
Josef Shaftel; David Wayne, Keenan Wynn

Naked in the Sun 1957 78 min
R. John Hugh; James Craig, Barton MacLane

Navajo Run 1964 75 min
Johnny Seven; Johnny Seven, Virginia Vincent

The Navajo Trail 1945 60 min
Howard Bretherton; Johnny Mack Brown, Raymond Hatton

Navajo Trail Raiders 1949 60 min
R.G. Springsteen; Allan Lane, Eddy Waller

'Neath Western Skies 1930 55 min
J.P. McGowan; Tom Tyler, Hank Bell

Nebraska – Jim (Nebraska il Pistolero) 1965 (It/Sp) 83 min
Antonio Roman; Ken Clark, Yvonne Bastien

Il Nero – Hass war Sein Gebet 1969 (WG/It) 95 min
Claudio Gora; Tony Kendall, Carlo Giordana

Nevada Badmen 1951 58 min
Lewis Collins; Whip Wilson, Fuzzy Knight

Nevada Buckaroo 1931 59 min
John P. McCarthy; Bob Steele, Dorothy Dix

Nevada City 1941 58 min
Joseph Kane; Roy Rogers, George Hayes

New Mexico 1951 76 min
Irving Reiss; Lew Ayres, Andy Devine

The Night of the Desperado (La Notte del Desperado) 1965 (It/Sp)
Mario Maffei; William Berger, Adriana Ambesi

The Night of the Snakes (La Notte del Serpenti) 1969 (It) 109 min
Giulio Petroni; Luke Askew, Luigi Pistilli

Night Stage to Galveston 1952 60 min
George Archainbaud; Gene Autry, Pat Buttram

Night Time in Nevada 1948 67 min
William Witney; Roy Rogers, Andy Devine

The Nine Lives of Elfego Baca 1959 79 min
Norman Foster; Robert Loggin, Lisa Montell

I Nipoti di Zorro 1969 (It)
Marcello Ciorciolini; Franco Franchi, Dean Reed

No Man's Range 1935
Robert N. Bradbury; Bob Steele, Roberta Gale

Non Aspettare Django Spara 1967 (It) 97 (88) min
Edward G. Muller; Sean Todd, P. Sanchez

North of Arizona 1935 60 min
Harry S. Webb; Jack Perrin, Lane Chandler

North of Nome 1936 63 min
William Nigh; Jack Holt, Guinn Williams

North of the Rio Grande 1937 70 min
Nate Watt; William Boyd, George Hayes

North of the Rockies 1942 60 min
Lambert Hillyer; Bill Elliott, Tex Ritter

North of the Yukon 1939 64 min
Sam Nelson; Charles Starrett, Lane Chandler

North to the Klondike 1942 58 min
Erle C. Kenton; Broderick Crawford, Andy Devine

Northern Lights 1978 97 min
John Hansson, Rob Nilsson;

Northern Patrol 1953 63 min
Rex Bailey; Kirby Grant, Emmett Lynn

Northwest Rangers 1942 64 min
Joe Newman; James Craig, John Carradine

Northwest Stampede 1948 79 min
Albert S. Rogell; James Craig, Joan Leslie

Northwest Territory 1951 61 min
Frank McDonald; Kirby Grant, Gloria Saunders

Northwest Trail 1945
Derwin Abrahams; Bob Steele, John Litel

Not Exactly Gentlemen 1931 70 min
Ben Stoloff; Victor McLaglen, Fay Wray

Oath of Vengeance 1944 57 min
Sam Newfield; Buster Crabbe, Al St John

Occhio per Occhio 1967 (It)
M. Iglesias; G. Rossi Stuart, L. Nicholas

Odia il Prossimo Tuo 1968 (It)
Ferdinando Baldi; C. Gamer, George Eastman

Oeste Nevada Joe 1965 (Sp/It) 92 min
Ignacio Iquino;

Oh, Susanna! 1936 59 min
Joseph Kane; Gene Autry, Smiley Burnette

Oh Susanna 1951 90 min
Joseph Kane; Rod Cameron, Adrian Booth

Oklahoma Annie 1952 90 min
R.G. Springsteen; Judy Canova, John Russell

Oklahoma Badlands 1948 59 min
Yakima Canutt; Allan Lane, Eddy Waller

Oklahoma Blues 1948 56 min
Lambert Hillyer; Jimmy Wakely, Dub Taylor

Oklahoma Cyclone 1930 66 min
John P. McCarthy; Bob Steele, Al St John

Oklahoma Jim 1931 61 min
Harry Fraser; Bill Cody, Marion Burns

Oklahoma John 1965 (WG/It/Sp) 86 min
Jesus Balcazar; Rick Horne, Sabine Bethmann

Oklahoma Justice 1951
Lewis Collins; Johnny Mack Brown, James Ellison

Oklahoma Renegades 1940 57 min
Nate Watt; Robert Livingston, Raymond Hatton

Oklahoma Terror 1939 50 min
Spencer Bennet; Jack Randall, Al St John

The Old Corral 1936 56 min
Joseph Kane; Gene Autry, Smiley Burnette

The Old Frontier 1950 60 min
Philip Ford; Monte Hale, Paul Hurst

Old Louisiana 1937 64 min
I.V. Willat; Tom Keene, Rita Cansino (Hayworth)

Old Overland Trail 1953 60 min
William Witney; Rex Allen, Slim Pickens

Old Surehand aka *Flaming Frontier* 1965 (WG/Yug) 93 min
Alfred Vohrer; Stewart Granger, Pierre Brice

The Old Texas Trail 1944 60 min
Lewis Collins; Rod Cameron, Fuzzy Knight

Old Yeller 1958 83 min
Robert Stevenson; Fess Parker, Dorothy McGuire

Ole Rex 1961 80 min
Robert Hinkle; Billy Hughes, William Foster

The Omaha Trail 1942 64 min
Edward Buzzell; James Craig, Dean Jagger

O'Malley of the Mounted 1936 59 min
David Howard; George O'Brien, Irene Ware

On the Great White Trail 1938 58 min
Al Herman; James Newill, Terry Walker

On Top of Old Smoky 1953 59 min
George Archainbaud; Gene Autry, Smiley Burnette

One Against All (Solo contro Tutti) 1965 (It/Sp) 90 min
Antonio del Amo; Robert Hundar, Mercedes Alonso

One Desire 1955 94 min
Jerry Hopper; Anne Baxter, Rock Hudson

One Man Law 1932 63 min
Lambert Hillyer; Buck Jones, Shirley Grey

One Silver Dollar (Un Dollaro Buccato) 1964 (It/Fr) 95 min
Kelvin Jackson Paget (Giorgio Ferroni); Montgomery Wood (Giuliano Gemma), Evelyn Stewart (Ida Galli)

Oregon Passage 1958 82 min
Paul Landres; John Ericson, Lola Albright

L'Oro dei Bravados 1970 (It/Fr)
Don Reynolds (Renato Savino); Linda Veras, George Ardisson

Orphan of the Pecos 1937 55 min
Sam Katzman; Tom Tyler, Lafe McKee

Out West with the Peppers 1940 63 min
Charles Barton; Edith Fellows, Dorothy Peterson

Outcasts of Black Mesa 1950 54 min
Ray Nazarro; Charles Starrett, Smiley Burnette

Outcasts of the Trail 1949 60 min
Philip Ford; Monte Hale, Paul Hurst

Outlaw Brand 1948 58 min
Lambert Hillyer; Jimmy Wakely, Dub Taylor

The Outlaw Deputy 1935 59 min
Otto Brower; Tim McCoy, Nora Lane

Outlaw Express 1938 56 min
George Waggner; Bob Baker, LeRoy Mason

Outlaw Gold 1950 56 min
Wallace Fox; Johnny Mack Brown, Jane Adams

Outlaw of the Plains 1946 56 min
Sam Newfield; Buster Crabbe, Al St John

Outlaw Queen 1957 70 min
Herbert Greene; Andrea King, Harry James

Outlaw Roundup 1944 55 min
Harry Fraser; Dave O'Brien, Jim Newill

Outlaw Rule 1935
S. Roy Luby; Reb Russell, Betty Mack

The Outlaw Stallion 1954 64 min
Fred F. Sears; Phil Carey, Dorothy Patrick

The Outlaw Tamer 1934
J.P. McGowan; Lane Chandler, George Hayes

Outlaw Treasure 1955 67 min
Oliver Drake; John Forbes (Carpenter), Adele Jergens

Outlawed Guns 1935
Ray Taylor; Buck Jones, Ruth Channing

The Outlaw's Daughter 1954 75 min
Wesley Barry; Jim Davis, Bill Williams

Outlaws' Highway 1934 61 min
Bob Hill; John King, Tom London

Outlaws of Boulder Pass 1942
Sam Newfield; George Houston, Al St John

Outlaws of Santa Fé 1944 56 min
Howard Bretherton; Donald Barry, Helen Talbot

Outlaws of Stampede Pass 1943 58 min
Wallace Fox; Johnny Mack Brown, Raymond Hatton

Outlaws of the Cherokee Trail 1941 56 min
Les Orlebeck; Bob Steele, Tom Tyler

Outlaws of the Plains 1944 84 min
Sam Newfield;

Outlaws of the Prairie 1937 59 min
Sam Nelson; Charles Starrett, Donald Grayson

Outlaws of the Range 1936 59 min
Al Herman; Bill Cody, Catherine Cotter

Outlaws of the Rio Grande 1941 63 min
Peter Stewart (Sam Newfield); Tim McCoy, Charles King

Outlaws of the Rockies 1945 55 min
Ray Nazarro; Charles Starrett, Dub Taylor

Outlaws' Paradise 1939 62 min
Sam Newfield; Tim McCoy, Ben Corbett

Outlaw's Son 1957 87 min
Lesley Selander; Dane Clark, Ben Cooper

Outpost of the Mounties 1939 63 min
C.C. Coleman Jnr; Charles Starrett, Iris Meredith

Over the Border 1950 58 min
Wallace Fox; Johnny Mack Brown, Myron Healey

Over the Santa Fé Trail 1947 63 min
Ray Nazarro; Ken Curtis, Jennifer Holt

The Overland Express 1938 55 min
Drew Eberson; Buck Jones, Marjorie Reynolds

Overland Mail 1939 51 min
Robert Hill; Jack Randall, Vince Barnett

Overland Mail 1942 15 chaps
Ford Beebe, John Rawlins; Lon Chaney Jnr, Helen Parrish

Overland Mail Robbery 1943 56 min
John English; Bill Elliott, Anne Jeffreys

Overland Riders 1946 55 min
Sam Newfield; Buster Crabbe, Al St John

Overland Stagecoach 1942
Sam Newfield; Bob Livingston, Al St John

Overland Telegraph 1951 60 min
Lesley Selander; Tim Holt, Gail Davis

Overland to Deadwood 1942 59 min
William Berke; Charles Starrett, Russell Hayden

Overland Trails 1948 58 min
Lambert Hillyer; Johnny Mack Brown, Raymond Hatton

Pack Train 1953 57 min
George Archainbaud; Gene Autry, Smiley Burnette

The Pal from Texas 1939 56 min
Harry S. Webb; Bob Steele, Jack Perrin

Palm Springs 1936 72 min
Aubrey Scotto; Guy Standing, Frances Langford

The Palomino 1950 73 min
Ray Nazarro; Jerome Courtland, Beverly Tyler

Pals of the Pecos 1941 56 min
Les Orlebeck; Robert Livingston, Bob Steele

Pals of the Range 1935 57 min
Elmer Clifton; Rex Lease, Yakima Canutt

Pals of the Silver Sage 1940 52 min
Al Herman; Tex Ritter, Slim Andrews

Pancho Villa Returns 1950 95 min
Miguel Contreras Torres; Leo Carillo, Esther Fernandez

Panhandle Calibre 38 (Padella Calibro 38) 1972 (It)
Tony Secchi; Scott Holden, Keenan Wynn

Un Par de Asesinos 1970 (Sp/It) 82 min
Rafael Romero Marchent;

Pardon My Gun 1930 63 min
Richard DeLacey; Tom Keene, Harry Woods

Pardon My Gun 1942 56 min
William Berke; Charles Starrett, Arthur Hunnicutt

Park Avenue Logger 1937 67 min
David Howard; George O'Brien, Ward Bond

La Parola di un Fuorilegge e Legge 1976 (It)
Anthony Dawson (Antonio Margheriti); Jim Brown, Lee Van Cleef

Paroled to Die 1938 55 min
Sam Newfield; Bob Steele, Karl Hackett

Partners 1932 58 min
Fred Allen; Tom Keene, Ben Corbett

Partners of the Sunset 1948 53 min
Lambert Hillyer; Jimmy Wakely, Dub Taylor

Partners of the Trail 1931 63 min
Wallace Fox; Tom Tyler, Betty Mack

Passa Sartana ... e l'Ombra della Tua Morte 1969 (It)
Sean O'Neal; Jeff Cameron, Frank Fargas

Paths of Hate (I Sentieri dell'Odio) 1964 (It/Sp) 90 min
Marino Girolami; Rod Cameron, Don Harrison

Payment in Blood 1968 (It) 89 min
E.G. Roland (Enzo Girolami);

Pecos Cleans Up (Pecos e Qui: Prega e Muori) 1967 (It) 88 min
Maurice A. Bright (Maurizio Lucidi); Robert Wood, E. Crisa

The Pecos Kid 1935
William Berke; Fred Kohler Jnr, Wally Wales

Pecos River 1951 54 min
Fred F. Sears; Charles Starrett, Smiley Burnette

Per Cento Mille Dollari t'Ammazzo 1967 (It) 95 min
Sidney Lean (G. Fago); G. Hudson, C. Camaso

Per un Bara Piena di Dollari 1971 (It)
Miles Deem (D. Fidani); Hunt Powers, Klaus Kinski

Per un Dollaro di Gloria 1966 (It)
F. Cerchio; Broderick Crawford, E. Montes

A Perilous Journey 1953 90 min
R.G. Springsteen; Vera Ralston, Scott Brady

Perils of the Royal Mounted 1942 15 chaps
James W. Horne; Kermit Maynard, Nell O'Day

Perils of the Wilderness 1956 15 chaps
Spencer G. Bennet; Dennis Moore, Richard Emory

The Phantom Cowboy 1935 55 min
Robert J. Horner; Ted Wells, Jimmy Aubrey

Phantom of Santa Fé 1937 75 min
Jacques Jaccard; Norman Kerry, Frank Mayo

Phantom of the Plains 1945 56 min
Lesley Selander; Bill Elliott, Bobby Blake

The Phantom of the Range 1936 57 min
Bob Hill; Tom Tyler, Beth Marion

The Phantom of the West 1931 10 chaps
Ross Lederman; Tom Tyler, William Desmond

The Phantom Plainsmen 1942 65 min
John English; Bob Steele, Tom Tyler

Phantom Rancher 1940 61 min
Harry Fraser; Ken Maynard, Dorothy Short

The Phantom Rider 1936 15 chaps
Ray Taylor; Buck Jones, Harry Woods

The Phantom Rider 1946 12 chaps
Spencer G. Bennet, Fred Brannon; Robert Kent, Peggy Stewart

The Phantom Stage 1939 57 min
George Waggner; Bob Baker, Marjorie Reynolds

The Phantom Stagecoach 1957 79 min
Ray Nazarro; William Bishop, Kathleen Crowley

The Phantom Stallion 1954 54 min
Harry Keller; Rex Allen, Slim Pickens

The Phantom Thunderbolt 1933 63 min
Alan James; Ken Maynard, Frank Rice

Pillars of the Sky 1956 95 min
George Marshall; Jeff Chandler, Dorothy Malone

Piluk 1968 (It) 97 min
Guido Celaro; Edmund Purdom, Peter Holden

The Pinto Bandit 1944 56 min
Elmer Clifton; Dave O'Brien, Jim Newill

Pinto Canyon 1940 55 min
Raymond Johnson; Bob Steele, Louise Stanley

The Pinto Kid 1941 61 min
Lambert Hillyer; Charles Starrett, Bob Nolan

Pinto Rustlers 1936 56 min
Henri Samuels (Harry S. Webb); Tom Tyler, Al St John

Il Piombo e la Carne 1965 (It/Fr/Sp)
Fred Wilson (Mario Girolami);

Pioneer Days 1940 51 min
Harry S. Webb; Jack Randall, Frank Yaconelli

Pioneer Trail 1938 59 min
Joseph Levering; Jack Luden, Joan Barclay

The Pioneers 1941 58 min
Al Herman; Tex Ritter, George Chesebro

Pioneers of the West 1940 56 min
Les Orlebeck; Robert Livingston, Raymond Hatton

Pirates of the Mississippi (Die Flusspiraten des Mississippi) 1963 (WG/It) 102 min
Jurgen Roland; Horst Frank, Brad Harris

Pirates of the Prairie 1942 57 min
Howard Bretherton; Tim Holt, Cliff Edwards

Pistol Harvest 1951 60 min
Lesley Selander; Tim Holt, Richard Martin

Las Pistolas no Discuten 1964 (Sp/It/WG) 93 min
Mike Perkins (Mario Caiano);

Le Pistolere 1972 (It)
Christian Jaque; Claudia Cardinale, Brigitte Bardot

Il Pistolero dell'Ave Maria 1969 (It) 96 min
Ferdinando Baldi; L. Mann, L. Paluzzi

Pistols Don't Say No (Le Pistole non Discutono) 1964 (It/Fr/WG)
Mike Perkins (Mario Caiano);

A Place Called Glory (Un Lugar Llamado Glory) 1966 (Sp/WG)
Ralph Gideon; Lex Barker, Pierre Brice

The Plainsman 1966 92 min
David Lowell; Don Murray, Guy Stockwell

Plunderers of Painted Flats 1959 77 min
Albert C. Gannaway; John Carroll, George Macready

The Pocatello Kid 1931 61 min
Phil Rosen; Ken Maynard, Marceline Day

The Poisoned Arrow (La Flecha Envenada) 1957 (Mex) 70 min
Rafael Baledon;

Poker with Pistols (Un Poker di Pistole) 1967 (It) 86 min
Joseph Warren (Giuseppe Vari); George Eastman (Luigi Montefiori), Annabella Incontrera

Pony Post 1940 59 min
Ray Taylor; Johnny Mack Brown, Fuzzy Knight

Por Que Seguir Matando 1966 (Sp/It) 86 min
Jose Antonio de la Loma;

Porno Erotico Western 1968 (It)
Gerald B. Lennox; Karin Well, Ray O'Connor

Posse from Heaven 1975 87 min
Philip Pine; Fanne Fox, Todd Compton

Potato Fritz 1976 (WG/Sp) 96 min
Peter Schamoni; Hardy Kruger, Stephen Boyd

Potluck Pards 1934
Bernard B. Ray; Walt Williams (Wally Wales), Ben Corbett

Praeriens Skrappe Drenge 1970 (Denmark) 83 min
Carl Ottosen;

Prairie Badmen 1946 55 min
Sam Newfield; Buster Crabbe, Al St John

Prairie Gunsmoke 1942 56 min
Lambert Hillyer; Bill Elliott, Tex Ritter

Prairie Justice 1938 57 min
George Waggner; Bob Baker, Hal Taliaferro

Prairie Law 1940 59 min
David Howard; George O'Brien, Virginia Vale

Prairie Pals 1942
Peter Stewart (Sam Newfield); Bill Boyd, Charles King

Prairie Pioneers 1941 58 min
Les Orlebeck; Robert Livingston, Bob Steele

Prairie Raiders 1947 54 min
Derwin Abrahams; Charles Starrett, Smiley Burnette

Prairie Rustlers 1945 56 min
Sam Newfield; Buster Crabbe, Al St John

Prairie Schooners 1940 58 min
Sam Nelson; Bill Elliott, Evelyn Young

La Preda e l'Avvoltoio 1971 (It/Sp)
Rafael Romero Marchent; Peter Lee Lawrence, Carlo Romero Marchent

Prega il Morto e Ammazza il Vivo 1971 (It)
Joseph Warren (Giuseppe Vari); Klaus Kinski, V. Zinny

The Prescott Kid 1934 60 min
David Selman; Tim McCoy, Sheila Mannors

The Price of Death (Il Vendicatore di Morte) 1971 (It)
Vincent Thomas (Enzo Gicca);

Pride of the Plains 1944 56 min
Wallace Fox; Robert Livingston, Smiley Burnette

Prima ti Perdono ... Poi t'Ammazzo 1970 (It)
Ignacio F. Iquino; Richard Harrison, Ferdinando Sancho

Prince of the Plains 1949 60 min
Philip Ford; Monte Hale, Paul Hurst

Professionisti per un Massacro 1967 (It/Sp) 95 min
Nado Cicero;

Providenza: Mauserfalle fur Zwei Schrage Vogel 1972 (WG/It/Fr) 100 min
Giulio Petroni; Tomas Milian, Gregg Palmer

Pueblo Terror 1931 59 min
Alvin J. Neitz (Alan James); Buffalo Bill Jnr, Yakima Canutt

The Purple Hills 1961 60 min
Maury Dexter; Gene Nelson, Kent Taylor

I Quattro dell'Apocalisse 1976 (It)
Lucio Fulci; Fabio Testi, Lynn Frederick

Quattro Dollari di Vendetta 1966 (It)
Alfonso Balcazar; Robert Wood, G. Arlen

I Quattro Pistoleri di Santa Trinita 1971 (It)
Geiorgio Cristallini; Peter Lee Lawrence, Evelyn Stewart

Queen of the Yukon 1940 73 min
Phil Rosen; Charles Bickford, George Cleveland

Quei Dannati Giorni dell'Odio e dell'Inferno 1971 (It)
S. Markson; P. Sullivan, Fernando Sancho

Quel Maledetto Giorno della Resa dei Conti 1971 (It)
W.S. Aegal; George Eastman, Ty Hardin

Quel Maledetto Giorno d'Inverno Django e Sartana all'Ultimo Sangue 1970 (It)
D. Fidani; Hunt Powers, S. Carson

Quelle Sporche Anime Dannate 1971 (It)
P. Solvay; Jeff Cameron, Donald O'Brien

The Quick Gun 1964 88 min
Sidney Salkow; Audie Murphy, Merry Anders

Quick on the Trigger 1948 55 min
Ray Nazarro; Charles Starrett, Smiley Burnette

Quick Trigger Lee 1931 59 min
J.P. Morgan; Bob Custer, Monte Montague

Quincannon, Frontier Scout 1956 83 min
Lesley Selander; Tony Martin, Peggie Castle

Quintana 1969 (It)
Glenn Vincent Davis; George Stevenson, Ferni Benussi

Racing Blood 1954 76 min
Wesley Barry; Bill Williams, Jimmy Boyd

Racketeer Round-Up 1934 50 min
Robert Hoyt; Edmund Cobb, Edna Aslin

The Raiders 1964 75 min
Herschel Daugherty; Brian Keith, Robert Culp

Raiders of Ghost City 1944 13 chaps
Ray Taylor, Lewis Collins; Dennis Moore, Lionel Atwill

Raiders of Old California 1957 72 min
Albert C. Gannaway; Jim Davis, Arleen Whelan

Raiders of Red Gap 1943
Sam Newfield; Bob Livingston, Al St John

Raiders of Sunset Pass 1943 57 min
John English; Eddie Dew, Smiley Burnette

Raiders of the Border 1944 58 min
John P. McCarthy; Johnny Mack Brown, Raymond Hatton

Raiders of the Range 1942 55 min
John English; Bob Steele, Tom Tyler

Raiders of the South 1947 55 min
Lambert Hillyer; Johnny Mack Brown, Raymond Hatton

Raiders of the West 1942 60 min
Peter Stewart (Sam Newfield); Bill Boyd, Rex Lease

The Rainbow Boys 1973
Gerald Potterton; Donald Pleasance, Kate Reid

Rainbow over Texas 1946 65 min
Frank McDonald; Roy Rogers, Dale Evans

Rainbow over the Range 1940 60 min
Al Herman; Tex Ritter, Warner Richmond

Rainbow over the Rockies 1947 54 min
Oliver Drake; Jimmy Wakely, Lee White

Rainbow Ranch 1933 55 min
Harry Fraser; Rex Bell, Bob Kortman

The Rainmaker 1957 121 min
Joseph Anthony; Burt Lancaster, Katharine Hepburn

Ramon the Mexican (Ramon il Messicano) 1966 (It)
Maurizio Pradeaux; Robert Hundar, Wilma Lindamar

Rampage at Apache Wells (Der Olprinz) 1965 (WG/Yug) 91 min
Harald Philipp; Stewart Granger, Pierre Brice

Ranch of the Rustlers (Il Ranch degli Spietati) 1965 (It/Sp/Wg)
Robert M. White; Rick Horn, Sabine Bethman

Rancho Grande 1940 68 min
Frank McDonald; Gene Autry, Smiley Burnette

Range Beyond the Blue 1947 53 min
Ray Taylor; Eddie Dean, Roscoe Ates

Range Justice 1948 57 min
Ray Taylor; Johnny Mack Brown, Max Terhune

Range Law 1931 63 min
Phil Rosen; Ken Maynard, Charles King

Range Renegades 1948 54 min
Lambert Hillyer; Jimmy Wakely, Dub Taylor

Range Riders 1934
Victor Adamson (Denver Dixon); Buddy Roosevelt, Denver Dixon

Range War 1939 66 min
Lesley Selander; William Boyd, Russell Hayden

Range Warfare 1935
S. Roy Luby; Reb Russell, Wally Wales

The Ranger and the Lady 1940 59 min
Joseph Kane; Roy Rogers, George Hayes

The Rangers Ride 1948 56 min
Derwin Abrahams; Jimmy Wakely, Dub Taylor

The Rangers Take Over 1942 60 min
Al Herman; Dave O'Brien, Jim Newill

Rattler Kid (Un Hombre Vino a Matar) 1968 (Sp/It) 87 min
Leon Klimovsky;

Raw Edge 1956 76 min
John Sherwood; Rory Calhoun, Yvonne De Carlo

Raw Timber 1937 63 min
Ray Taylor; Tom Keene, Budd Buster

Rawhide Mail 1934 59 min
Bernard B. Ray; Jack Perrin, Lafe McKee

Rawhide Rangers 1941 56 min
Ray Taylor; Johnny Mack Brown, Fuzzy Knight

Rawhide Romance 1934
Victor Adamson (Denver Dixon); Buffalo Bill Jnr, Lafe McKee

Rawhide Terror 1934 52 min
Bruce Mitchell; Art Mix, Edmund Cobb

The Rawhide Trail 1950
Robert Gordon; Rex (Rhodes) Reason, Nancy Gates

Rebel City 1953 62 min
Thomas Carr; Bill Elliott, Robert Kent

The Reckless Buckaroo 1935 57 min
Harry Fraser; Bill Cody, Bill Cody Jnr

The Reckless Rider 1932
Armand Schaefer; Lane Chandler, Ben Corbett

The Red Blood of Courage 1935 55 min
Charles English; Kermit Maynard, Ann Sheridan

Red Canyon 1949 82 min
George Sherman; Howard Duff, Ann Blyth

Red Garters 1954 90 min
George Marshall; Rosemary Clooney, Jack Carson

Red Pastures (I Pascoli Rossi) 1963 (It)
Alfredo Antonini; James Mitchum, Jill Powers

Red River Renegades 1946 55 min
Thomas Carr; Sunset Carson, Peggy Stewart

Red River Robin Hood 1943
Lesley Selander; Tim Holt, Cliff Edwards

Red River Shore 1953 54 min
Harry Keller; Rex Allen, Slim Pickens

Red Rock Outlaw 1950 56 min
Elmer Clifton; Bob Gilbert, Lee White

The Red Rope 1937 56 min
S. Roy Luby; Bob Steele, Charles King

The Red Stallion 1947 81 min
Lesley Selander; Robert Paige, Jane Darwell

Red Stallion in the Rockies 1949 85 min
Ralph Murphy; Arthur Franz, Jim Davis

Redwood Forest Trail 1950 67 min
Philip Ford; Rex Allen, Jane Darwell

Relentless 1948 93 min
George Sherman; Robert Young, Akim Tamiroff

The Relentless Four 1965 (It)
Prijo Zeglio; Adam West, Robert Hundar

The Renegade 1943
Sam Newfield; Buster Crabbe, Al St John

Renegade Girl 1946 65 min
William Berke; Alan Curtis, Ann Savage

Renegade Trail 1939 61 min
Lesley Selander; William Boyd, George Hayes

Renegades of Sonora 1948 60 min
R.G. Springsteen; Allan Lane, Eddy Waller

Renegades of the Rio Grande 1945 57 min
Howard Bretherton; Rod Cameron, Jennifer Holt

Renegades of the Sage 1949 56 min
Ray Nazarro; Charles Starrett, Smiley Burnette

Renegades of the West 1932 55 min
Casey Robinson; Rex Bell, Charles King

Reprisal 1956 74 min
George Sherman; Guy Madison, Felicia Farr

Requiem for a Gunfighter 1965 91 min
Spencer G. Bennet; Rod Cameron, Stephen McNally

The Return of Daniel Boone 1941 61 min
Lambert Hillyer; Bill Elliott, Dub Taylor

The Return of Jack Slade 1955 79 min
Harold Schuster; John Ericson, Mari Blanchard

Return of the Durango Kid 1945 58 min
Derwin Abrahams; Charles Starrett, Tex Harding

Return of the Gunfighter 1966 99 min
James Neilson; Robert Taylor, Chad Everett

Return of the Lash 1947 55 min
Ray Taylor; Lash LaRue, Al St John

The Return of the Rangers 1943 60 min
Elmer Clifton; Dave O'Brien, Jim Newill

The Revenge Rider 1935 60 min
David Selman; Tim McCoy, Billie Seward

Reverendo Colt 1970 (It/Sp)
Leon Klimowsky; Guy Madison, Richard Harrison

The Reward 1965 92 min
Serge Bourguignon; Max von Sydow, Yvette Mimieux

Rhythm of the Rio Grande 1940 53 min
Al Herman; Tex Ritter, Warner Richmond

Rhythm of the Saddle 1938 58 min
George Sherman; Gene Autry, Smiley Burnette

Rhythm Round-Up 1945 66 min
Vernon Keays; Ken Curtis, Raymond Hatton

Ric e Gian alla Conquista del West 1967 (It)
Osvaldo Civirani; Ricardo Miniggio, Gianfabio Bosco

Il Richiamo della Foresta 1973 (It/WG/Sp/Fr)
Ken Annakin; Charlton Heston, Michele Mercier

Ricochet Romance 1954 80 min
Charles Lamont; Marjorie Main, Chill Wills

Riddle Ranch 1936 63 min
Charles Hutchison; David Worth, June Marlowe

Ride a Crooked Mile 1958 87 min
Jesse Hibbs; Audie Murphy, Walter Matthau

Ride and Kill (Cavalco e Uccidi) 1963 (It/Sp) 70 min
J.L. Boraw; Alex Nicol, Margaret Grayson

Ride Bene chi Spara Ultimo 1967 (It/WG) 95 min
Vance Lewis (Luigi Vanzi);

Ride 'Em Cowboy 1936 59 min
Lesley Selander; Buck Jones, Luana Walters

Ride, Ranger, Ride 1936 59 min
Joseph Kane; Gene Autry, Smiley Burnette

Ride the Wind 1966 82 min
William Witney; Lorne Greene, Dan Blocker

The Rider of the Law 1935
Robert N. Bradbury; Bob Steele, Gertrude Messinger

Rider of the Plains 1931 57 min
J.P. McCarthy; Tom Tyler, Andy Shuford

Rider on a Dead Horse 1962 72 min
Herbert L. Strock; John Vivyan, Bruce Gordon

Riders from Nowhere 1940 55 min
Raymond K. Johnson; Jack Randall, Margaret Roach

Riders of Black Mountain 1940 57 min
Peter Stewart (Sam Newfield); Tim McCoy, Rex Lease

Riders of Black River 1939 59 min
Norman Deming; Charles Starrett, Iris Meredith

Riders of Pasco Basin 1940 56 min
Ray Taylor; Johnny Mack Brown, Fuzzy Knight

Riders of the Badlands 1941 57 min
Howard Bretherton; Charles Starrett, Russell Hayden

Riders of the Black Hills 1938 55 min
George Sherman; Bob Livingston, Ray Corrigan

Riders of the Cactus 1931 60 min
David Kirkland; Wally Wales, Buzz Barton

Riders of the Dawn 1945 58 min
Oliver Drake; Jimmy Wakely, Lee White

Riders of the Dusk 1949 57 min
Lambert Hillyer; Whip Wilson, Andy Clyde

Riders of the Golden Gulch 1932 52 min
Clifford Smith; Buffalo Bill Jnr, Yakima Canutt

Riders of the Lone Star 1947 55 min
Derwin Abrahams; Charles Starrett, Smiley Burnette

Riders of the North 1931 59 min
J.P. McGowan; Bob Custer, Frank Rice

Riders of the Northwest Mounted 1943
William Berke; Russell Hayden, Dub Taylor

Riders of the Pony Express 1949 60 min
Michael Salle; Ken Curtis, Shug Fisher

Riders of the Range 1950 60 min
Lesley Selander; Tim Holt, Richard Martin

Riders of the Rio 1931
Robert Tansey; Lane Chandler, Sheldon Lewis

Riders of the Rio Grande 1943 55 min
Howard Bretherton; Bob Steele, Tom Tyler

Riders of the Sage 1939 57 min
Harry S. Webb; Bob Steele, Claire Rochelle

Riders of the Santa Fé 1944 60 min
Wallace Fox; Rod Cameron, Eddie Dew

Riders of the Timberline 1941 59 min
Lesley Selander; William Boyd, Andy Clyde

Riders of the Whistling Pines 1949 70 min
John English; Gene Autry, Patricia White

Riders of Vengeance aka *The Raiders* 1952 80 min
Lesley Selander; Richard Conte, Viveca Lindfors

Ridin' Down the Canyon 1942 55 min
Joseph Kane; Roy Rogers, George Hayes

Ridin' Down the Trail 1947 53 min
Howard Bretherton; Jimmy Wakely, Dub Taylor

The Ridin' Fool 1931 58 min
J.P. McCarthy; Bob Steele, Frances Morris

Ridin' On 1936 56 min
Bernard B. Ray; Tom Tyler, Joan Barclay

Ridin' the Cherokee Trail 1941 62 min
Spencer G. Bennet; Tex Ritter, Slim Andrews

Ridin' the Lone Trail 1937 56 min
Sam Newfield; Bob Steele, Claire Rochelle

Ridin' the Trail 1940 57 min
Raymond K. Johnson; Fred Scott, Iris Lancaster

Ridin' Thru 1935
Harry S. Webb; Tom Tyler, Lafe McKee

The Riding Avenger 1936 58 min
Harry Fraser; Hoot Gibson, Ruth Mix

Riding Speed 1934
Jay Wilsey (Buffalo Bill Jnr); Buffalo Bill Jnr, Bud Osborne

Riding the California Trail 1947 59 min
William Nigh; Gilbert Roland, Martin Garralaga

Riding the Sunset Trail 1941 56 min
Robert Tansey; Tom Keene, Frank Yaconelli

Riding the Wind 1942 60 min
Edward Killy; Tim Holt, Ray Whitley

Riding through Nevada 1942
William Berke; Charles Starrett, Arthur Hunnicutt

Riding West 1944 58 min
William Berke; Charles Starrett, Arthur Hunnicutt

Riding Wild 1935 57 min
David Selman; Tim McCoy, Billie Seward

Riding with Buffalo Bill 1954 15 chaps
Spencer G. Bennet; Marshall Reed, Rick Vallin

Rimase uno Solo e Fu la Morte per Tutti 1971 (It)
K. Mulargia; Tony Kendall, J. Rogers

Rimfire 1949 64 min
B. Reeves Eason; James Millican, Mary Beth Hughes

Ringo del Nebraska 1966 (It/Sp)
Anthony Roman; Ken Clark, Yvonne Bastien

Ringo e Gringo contro Tutti 1966 (It/Sp) 83 min
Bruno Corbucci; Raimondo Vianello, Lando Buzzanca

Ringo, el Caballero Solitario 1968 (Sp/It) 85 min
Rafael Romero Marchent; Peter Martell, P. Lulli

Ringo, the Face of Revenge (Ringo:il Volto della Vendetta) 1966 (It/Sp) 98 min
Mario Caiano; Anthony Steffen, Frank Wolff

Rio Grande 1949 56 min
Norman Sheldon; Sunset Carson, Lee Morgan

Rio Grande Patrol 1950 60 min
Lesley Selander; Tim Holt, Richard Martin

Rio Grande Raiders 1946 56 min
Thomas Carr; Sunset Carson, Bob Steele

Rio Grande Ranger 1936 54 min
Spencer G. Bennet; Bob Allen, Iris Meredith

Rio Grande Romance 1936 60 min
Robert Hill; Eddie Nugent, Maxine Doyle

Rio Rattler 1935
Franklin Shamray (B.B. Ray); Tom Tyler, Marion Shilling

Rip Roarin' Buckaroo 1936 58 min
Robert Hill; Tom Tyler, Beth Marion

River Lady 1948 78 min
George Sherman; Yvonne De Carlo, Rod Cameron

The Road to Fort Alamo (La Strada per Fort Alamo) 1965 (It/Fr) 79 min
John Old (Mario Bava);

Road to Reno 1938 69 min
S. Sylvan Simon; Randolph Scott, Hope Hampton

Roamin' Wild 1936 58 min
Bernard B. Ray; Tom Tyler, Al Ferguson

Roar of the Iron Horse 1950 15 chaps
Spencer G. Bennet, Thomas Carr; Jock O'Mahoney, Virginia Herrick

Roarin' Guns 1936 59 min
Sam Newfield; Tim McCoy, Wheeler Oakman

Roaring Frontiers 1941 60 min
Lambert Hillyer; Bill Elliott, Tex Ritter

Roaring Rangers 1946 55 min
Ray Nazarro; Charles Starrett, Smiley Burnette

Roaring Timber 1937 65 min
Phil Rosen; Jack Holt, Raymond Hatton

The Roaring West 1935 15 chaps
Ray Taylor; Buck Jones, Muriel Evans

Roaring Westward 1949 58 min
Oliver Drake; Jimmy Wakely, Dub Taylor

Robber's Roost 1955 82 min
Sidney Salkow; George Montgomery, Richard Boone

Robin Hood of Monterey 1947 55 min
Christy Cabanne; Gilbert Roland, Evelyn Brent

Robin Hood of the Pecos 1941 59 min
Joseph Kane; Roy Rogers, George Hayes

Robin Hood of the Range 1943 57 min
William Berke; Charles Starrett, Arthur Hunnicutt

Rocco – der Einzelganger von Alamo 1967 (WG)
Alfio Caltabiano; Anthony Ghidra, Angelo Infanti

Rock River Renegades 1942 56 min
S. Roy Luby; Ray Corrigan, John King

Rockin' in the Rockies 1945 63 min
Vernon Keays; Mary Beth Hughes, Jay Kirby

Rocky Mountain Rangers 1940 58 min
George Sherman; Robert Livingston, Raymond Hatton

Rodeo Rhythm 1942 72 min
Fred Neymeyer; Fred Scott, Pat Dunn

Rogue of the Range 1936 58 min
S. Roy Luby; Johnny Mack Brown, Lois January

Rogue of the Rio Grande 1930 57 min
Spencer G. Bennet; Jose Bohr, Myrna Loy

Rogue River 1950 84 min
John Rawlins; Rory Calhoun, Peter Graves

Roll Along Cowboy 1937 55 min
Gus Meins; Smith Ballew, Cecilia Parker

Roll, Wagons, Roll 1940 52 min
Al Herman; Tex Ritter, Muriel Evans

Rollin' Home to Texas 1940 63 min
Al Herman; Tex Ritter, Eddie Dean

Rollin' Westward 1939 55 min
Al Herman; Tex Ritter, Dorothy Fay

Rolling Caravans 1938 55 min
Joseph Levering; John (Jack) Luden, Eleanor Stewart

Rolling Down the Great Divide 1942 59 min
Peter Stewart (Sam Newfield); Bill Boyd, Art Davis

The Romance of Rosy Ridge 1947 105 min
Roy Rowland; Van Johnson, Janet Leigh

Romance of the Rio Grande 1941 73 min
Herbert I. Leeds; Cesar Romero, Lynne Roberts

Romance on the Range 1942 63 min
Joseph Kane; Roy Rogers, George Hayes

Romance Rides the Range 1936 59 min
Harry Fraser; Fred Scott, Marion Shilling

Rootin' Tootin' Rhythm 1937 60 min
Mack Wright; Gene Autry, Smiley Burnette

Rose Marie 1954 104 min
Mervyn LeRoy; Ann Blyth, Howard Keel

Rose of the Rancho 1936
Marion Gering; John Boles, Charles Bickford

Rose of the Rio Grande 1938 60 min
William Nigh; John Carroll, Antonio Moreno

Rough Riders of Cheyenne 1945 56 min
Thomas Carr; Sunset Carson, Peggy Stewart

Rough Riders of Durango 1951 60 min
Fred C. Brannon; Allan Lane, Walter Baldwin

Rough Ridin' Justice 1945 58 min
Derwin Abrahams; Charles Starrett, Dub Taylor

Rough Riding Ranger 1935
Elmer Clifton; Rex Lease, Janet Chandler

Rough Riding Rhythm 1937 57 min
J.P. McGowan; Kermit Maynard, Dave O'Brien

Rough Romance 1930 54 min
A.F. Erickson; George O'Brien, Helen Chandler

The Rough, Tough West 1952 54 min
Ray Nazarro; Charles Starrett, Smiley Burnette

Round-Up Time in Texas 1937 58 min
Joseph Kane; Gene Autry, Smiley Burnette

Roy Colt and Winchester Jack 1970 (It) 96 min
Mario Bava; Brett Halsey, Charles Southwood

The Royal Mounted Rides Again 1945 13 chaps
Ray Taylor, Lewis D. Collins; Bill Kennedy, Milburn Stone

Run, Man, Run (Corri, Uomo, Corri) 1968 (It/Fr) 120 (90) min
Sergio Sollima; Tomas Milian, Donald O'Brien

Running Target 1956 82 min
Marvin R. Weinstein; Doris Dowling, Myron Healey

Rustlers' Hideout 1944 60 min
Sam Newfield; Buster Crabbe, Al St John

Rustlers of Red Dog 1935 12 chaps
Louis Friedlander (Lew Landers); Johnny Mack Brown, Raymond Hatton

Rustlers of the Badlands 1945 55 min
Derwin Abrahams; Charles Starrett, Dub Taylor

Rustlers on Horseback 1950 60 min
Fred C. Brannon; Allan Lane, Eddy Waller

Rustler's Roundup 1933 56 min
Henry MacRae; Tom Mix, Noah Beery Jnr

Rustler's Roundup 1946 57 min
Wallace Fox; Kirby Grant, Fuzzy Knight

Rusty Rides Alone 1933 58 min
D. Ross Lederman; Tim McCoy, Barbara Weeks

The Ruthless Four 1968 (It)
Giorgio Capitani; Van Heflin, Klaus Kinski

The Sad Horse 1959 78 min
James B. Clark; David Ladd, Chill Wills

Saddle Aces 1935 56 min
Harry Fraser; Rex Bell, Ruth Mix

Saddle Buster 1932 60 min
Fred Allen; Tom Keene, Helen Forest

Saddle Leather Law 1944
Ben Kline; Charles Starrett, Lloyd Bridges

Saddle Mountain Roundup 1941 55 min
S. Roy Luby; Ray Corrigan, John King

Saddle Pals 1947 72 min
Lesley Selander; Lynne Roberts

Saddle Serenade 1945 57 min
Oliver Drake; Jimmy Wakely, Lee White

Saddles and Sagebrush 1943
William Berke; Russell Hayden, Dub Taylor

Saga of Death Valley 1939 58 min
Joseph Kane; Roy Rogers, George Hayes

The Saga of Hemp Brown 1959 80 min
Richard Carlson; Rory Calhoun, Allan Lane

The Sagebrush Family Trails West 1940 60 min
Peter Stewart (Sam Newfield); Bobby Clark, Earle Hodgins

Sagebrush Law 1943
Sam Nelson; Tim Holt, Joan Barclay

The Sagebrush Troubador 1935 54 min
Joseph Kane; Gene Autry, Smiley Burnette

Saginaw Trail 1953 56 min
George Archainbaud; Gene Autry, Smiley Burnette

Salome, Where She Danced 1945 90 min
Charles Lamont; Yvonne De Carlo, Rod Cameron

Salt Lake Raiders 1950 60 min
Fred C. Brannon; Allan Lane, Eddy Waller

Sam Cooper's Gold (Ognuno per Se) 1968 (It/WG) 110 min
George Holloway (Lucio Giorgio Capitani); Van Heflin,
Gilbert Roland

Samson und der Schatz der Inkas 1965 (WG/It/Fr) 93 min
Piero Pierotti; Alan Steel, Toni Sailer

San Antone Ambush 1949 60 min
Philip Ford; Monte Hale, Paul Hurst

The San Francisco Story 1952 80 min
Robert Parrish; Joel McCrea, Yvonne De Carlo

Sand 1949 78 min
Louis King; Mark Stevens, Rory Calhoun

Sandflow 1937 58 min
Lesley Selander; Buck Jones, Bob Kortman

Sangue Chiama Sangue 1968 (It)
Luigi Capuano; Fernando Sancho, Stephen Forsyte

Santa Fé Bound 1936
Henri Samuels (Harry S. Webb); Tom Tyler, Richard
Cramer

Santa Fé Marshal 1940 65 min
Lesley Selander; William Boyd, Russell Hayden

Santa Fé Rides 1937 58 min
Raymond Samuels (B.B. Ray); Bob Custer, Eleanor Stewart

Santa Fé Scouts 1943 57 min
Howard Bretherton; Bob Steele, Tom Tyler

Santa Fé Trail 1930 65 min
Edwin Knopf, Otto Brower; Richard Arlen, Rosita Moreno

Santa Fé Uprising 1946 55 min
R.G. Springsteen; Allan Lane, Bobby Blake

Saranda 1970 (It/Sp)
Ted Mulligan (A. Mollica); Dean Reed, Patty Shepard

Sartana 1967 (It/WG) 92 min
Albert Cardiff (Alberto Cardone); Anthony Steffen, Johnny
Garko

Sartana – Bete um Deinen Tod 1969 (WG/It) 97 min
Frank Kramer; John Garko, William Berger

Sartana nella Valle degli Avvoltoi 1970 (It) 85 min
Roberto Mauri; William Berger, Wayde Preston

Sartana non Perdona 1968 (Sp/It) 84 min
Alfonso Balvazar; George Martin, Gilbert Roland

Satan's Cradle 1949 60 min
Ford Beebe; Duncan Renaldo, Leo Carrillo

Savage Frontier 1953 54 min
Harry Keller; Allan Lane, Eddy Waller

The Savage Guns 1961 (US/Sp) 83 min
Michael Carreras; Richard Basehart, Don Taylor

Savage Red – Outlaw White 1974
Paul Hunt; Robert Padilla, Richard Rust

Scansati . . . A Trinita Arriva Eldorado 1973 (It)
Dick Spitfire; Stan Cooper, Gordon Mitchell

Scarlet Brand 1932 58 min
Fred Allen; Bob Custer, Betty Mack

The Scarlet Horseman 1946 13 chaps
Ray Taylor, Lewis D. Collins; Peter Cookson, Janet Shaw

Lo Sceriffo di Rockspring 1971 (It)
A Green; Richard Harrison, C. Greco

Der Schrei der Schwarzen Wolfe 1972 (WG) 110 (85) min
Harald Reinl; Ron Ely, Gila von Weitershausen

Scorching Fury 1952 68 min
Rick Freers; Richard Devon, William Leslie

Scotty & Co 1979 (WG) 88 min
Peter Henkel; Joe Stewardson, Adrian Steed

Se Incontri, Sartana Prega per la Tua Morte 1968 (It)
Gianfranco Parolini; John Garko, William Berger

Se ti Incontrato t'Ammazzo 1971 (It)
G. Crea; Ferni Benussi, Gordon Mitchell

The Second Greatest Sex 1955 87 min
George Marshal; Jeanne Crain, George Nader

The Secret of Convict Lake 1951 83 min
Michael Gordon; Glenn Ford, Gene Tierney

Secret of Navajo Cave 1976 87 min
James T. Flocker; Rex Allen, Holger Kasper

Secret of Treasure Mountain 1956 68 min
Seymour Freidman; Valerie French, Raymond Burr

Secret Patrol 1936 60 min
David Selman; Charles Starrett, Finis Barton

Il Segno del Coyote 1963 (It/Sp) 81 min
Mario Caiano;

Sei Gia Cadavere Amigo ... Ti Cera Garringo 1971 (It)
Ignacio F. Iquino; Richard Harrison, Fernando Sancho

Sei Iellato Amico ... Hai Incontrato Sacramento 1972 (It)
Giorgio Cristallini; Ty Hardin, C. Hay

Sei una Carogna ... e t'Ammazzo 1972 (It)
M. Esteba; Fernando Sancho, Pierre Brice

Sella d'Argento 1978 (It)
Lucio Fulci; Giuliano Gemma, Sven Valsecchi

Semino Morte ... lo Chiamavano Castigo di Dio 1972 (It)
Roberto Mauri; Jose Torres, B. Harris

Seminole Uprising 1955 74 min
Earl Bellamy; George Montgomery, Karin Booth

Senor Jim 1936
Jacques Jaccard; Conway Tearle, Barbara Bedford

Senorita from the West 1945 63 min
Frank Strayer; Allan Jones, Fuzzy Knight

Sentivano ... uno Strano, Eccitante, Pericoloso Puzzo di Dollari
1973 (It)
Italo Alfaro; Robert Malcolm, Peter Landers

I Senzo Dio 1971 (It/Sp)
Roberto B. Montero; Antonio Sabato, Chris Avram

Serenade au Texas 1958 (Fr) 95 min
Richard Pottier;

Sette Dollari dul Rosso 1966 (It) 90 min
Albert Cardiff (Alberto Cardone); Anthony Steffen,
Fernando Sancho

Le Sette Magnifiche Pistole 1966 (It/Sp) 100 (85) min
Rod Gilbert; Fernando Sanchez, S. Flynn

Sette Winchester per un Massacro 1967 (It) 93 min
E.G. Rowland (Enzo Girolami); E. Byrnes, T. Moore

Seven Cities of Gold 1955 103 min
Robert D. Webb; Anthony Quinn, Michael Rennie

Seven From Texas (Camino del Sur) 1964 (It/Sp) 94 (91) min
Joaquin Romero Marchent; Paul Piaget, Robert Hundar
(Claudio Undari)

Seven Guns for Gringo (Sette Pistole per El Gringo) 1967 (It/Sp)
Juan Xiol Marchal; Gerard Landry, Dan Harrison

Seven Guns to Mesa 1958 69 min
Edward Dein; Charles Quinlivan, Lola Albright

Seven Hours of Gunfire (Adventuras del Oeste) 1964 (It/Sp/
WG) 96 (89) min
J.L. Romero Marchent; Clyde Rogers (Rick van Nutter),
Elga Sommerfeuld

Seven Hours Under Fire (Sette Ore di Fuoco) 1965 (It/Sp/WG)
76 min
Joaquin Romero Marchent; Clyde Rogers, Elga Sommerfeuld

Seven Ways from Sundown 1960 86 min
Harry Keller; Audie Murphy, Barry Sullivan

Seven Women for the MacGregors (Sette Donne per i Macgregor)
1967 (It/Sp) 100 min
Frank Garfield (Franco Giraldi); David Bailey, Agata Flori

Sfida a Rio Bravo 1965 (It/Fr/Sp) 100 min
Tulio Demicheli;

Sfida al Diavolo 1965 (It)
Giuseppe Veggezi;

La Sfida degli Implacabili 1965 (It/Sp)
Ignacio F. Iquino; George Martin, Audrey Amber

The Shadow of Zorro (l'Ombra di Zorro) 1962 (It/Sp) 88 min
Joaquin Romero Marchent; Frank Latimore, Maria Luz
Galicia

Shadow Ranch 1930 64 min
Louis King; Buck Jones, Frank Rice

Shadow Valley 1947 58 min
Ray Taylor; Eddie Dean, Roscoe Ates

Shadows of Death 1945 60 min
Sam Newfield; Buster Crabbe, Al St John

Shadows of the West 1949 59 min
Ray Taylor; Whip Wilson, Andy Clyde

Shadows of Tombstone 1953 54 min
William Witney; Rex Allen, Slim Pickens

Shadows on the Range 1946 58 min
Lambert Hillyer; Johnny Mack Brown, Raymond Hatton

Shadows on the Sage 1942 58 min
Les Orlebeck; Bob Steele, Tom Tyler

Shangoo la Pistola Infallibile 1970 (It)
Edward G. Muller (E. Mulargia); Anthony Steffen, Eduardo
Fajardo

Shark River 1953 80 min
John Rawlins; Steve Cochran, Carole Mathews

She Came to the Valley 1981
Albert Band; Ronnee Blakley, Dean Stockwell

Sheriff of Cimarron 1945 63 min
Yakima Canutt; Sunset Carson, Linda Stirling

Sheriff of Las Vegas 1944 55 min
Lesley Selander; Bill Elliott, Bobby Blake

The Sheriff of Medicine Bow 1948 55 min
Lambert Hillyer; Johnny Mack Brown, Raymond Hatton

Sheriff of Redwood Valley 1946 54 min
R.G. Springsteen; Bill Elliott, Bobby Blake

Sheriff of Sage Valley 1942 60 min
Sherman Scott (Sam Newfield); Buster Crabbe, Al St John

Sheriff of Sundown 1944
Lesley Selander; Allan Lane, Max Terhune

Sheriff of Tombstone 1941 56 min
Joseph Kane; Roy Rogers, George Hayes

The Sheriff Was a Lady 1964
Hugo Fregonese; Mamie Van Doren, Freddy Quinn

The Sheriff with the Gold (Uno Sceriffo Tutto d'Oro) 1966 (It)
Richard Kean; Bob Messenger, Kathleen Parker

The Sheriff's Secret 1931 58 min
James Hogan; Jack Perrin, George Chesebro

Shine On, Harvest Moon 1938 55 min
Joseph Kane; Roy Rogers, Mary Hart (Lynne Roberts)

Shoot 1964 (WG)
 ; Lex Barker, Rik Battaglia

Shoot Out at Big Sag 1962 64 min
Roger Kay; Walter Brennan, Leif Erickson

Shotgun Pass 1931 58 min
J.P. McGowan; Tim McCoy, Frank Rice

Shots Ring Out (Si Udirono Quattro Colpi di Fucile) 1963
(It/Sp)
Augustin Navarro; Paul Piaget, Fernando Casanova

Showdown 1963 79 min
R.G. Springsteen; Audie Murphy, Charles Drake

Showdown at Abilene 1956 80 min
Charles Haas; Jock Mahoney, Martha Hyer

Si Muore Solo una Volta 1967 (It)
G. Romitelli; R. Danton, Pamela Tudor

Sierra Passage 1951 81 min
Frank McDonald; Wayne Morris, Lola Albright

Sierra Sue 1941 64 min
William Morgan; Gene Autry, Smiley Burnette

The Sign of the Wolf 1931 10 chaps
Forrest Sheldon, Harry S. Webb; Rex Lease, Al Ferguson

The Sign of Zorro 1960 91 min
Norman Foster, Lewis R. Foster; Guy Williams, Henry
Calvin

Silent Barriers 1937
Milton Rosner; Richard Arlen, Lilli Palmer

The Silent Code 1935 60 min
Stuart Paton; Kane Richmond, Blanche Mehaffey

Silent Conflict 1948 51 min
George Archainbaud; William Boyd, Andy Clyde

Silent Men 1933 68 min
D. Ross Lederman; Tim McCoy, Wheeler Oakman

Silent Valley 1935
Bernard B. Ray; Tom Tyler, Wally Wales

The Silver Bullet 1935 58 min
Bernard B. Ray; Tom Tyler, Lafe McKee

Silver Canyon 1951 70 min
John English; Gene Autry, Pat Buttram

Silver City Kid 1944 55 min
John English; Allan Lane, Peggy Stewart

The Silver Horde 1930 75 min
George Archainbaud; Evelyn Brent, Joel McCrea

Silver on the Sage 1939 68 min
Lesley Selander; Charles Starrett, Lane Chandler

Silver Queen 1942 80 min
Lloyd Bacon; George Brent, Bruce Cabot

Silver Raiders 1950 55 min
Wallace Fox; Whip Wilson, Andy Clyde

Silver Range 1946 53 min
Lambert Hillyer; Johnny Mack Brown, Raymond Hatton

Silver Spurs 1936
Ray Taylor; Buck Jones, Muriel Evans

Silver Stallion 1941 57 min
Edward Finney; David Sharpe, LeRoy Mason

The Silver Whip 1953 73 min
Harmon Jones; Dale Robertson, Rory Calhoun

Sin Town 1942 75 min
Ray Enright; Constance Bennett, Broderick Crawford

Sing Me a Song of Texas 1945 66 min
Vernon Keays; Tom Tyler, Guinn Williams

Singin' in the Corn 1947 65 min
Del Lord; Judy Canova, Guinn Williams

The Singing Cowboy 1936 56 min
Mack V. Wright; Gene Autry, Smiley Burnette

Singing Guns 1950 91 min
R.G. Springsteen; Vaughn Monroe, Walter Brennan

The Singing Hill 1941 75 min
Lew Landers; Gene Autry, Smiley Burnette

Singing on the Trail 1946 60 min
Ray Nazarro; Ken Curtis, Guy Kibbee

Singing Spurs 1948 62 min
Ray Nazarro; Kirby Grant, Jay Silverheels

Single-Handed Sanders 1932 61 min
Lloyd Nosler; Tom Tyler, Margaret Morris

Sinister Journey 1948 59 min
George Archainbaud; William Boyd, Andy Clyde

Six Gun Gospel 1943 59 min
Lambert Hillyer; Johnny Mack Brown, Raymond Hatton

Six Gun Justice 1935 57 min
Robert Hill; Bill Cody, Wally Wales

Six Gun Man 1946 57 min
Harry Fraser; Bob Steele, Syd Saylor

Six Gun Serenade 1947 54 min
Ford Beebe; Jimmy Wakely, Lee White

Six-Gun Trail 1938 59 min
Sam Newfield; Tim McCoy, Nora Lane

Six-Shootin' Sheriff 1938 59 min
Harry Fraser; Ken Maynard, Marjorie Reynolds

Skipalong Rosenbloom 1951 72 min
Sam Newfield; Maxine Rosenbloom, Max Baer

Skull and Crown 1935
Elmer Clifton; Rin-Tin-Tin Jnr, Regis Toomey

Sky Bandits 1940 62 min
Ralph Staub; James Newill, Dave O'Brien

Slaughter Trail 1951 78 min
Irving Allen; Brian Donlevy, Gig Young

Smoke Lightning 1933 63 min
David Howard; George O'Brien, Virginia Sale

Smoke Tree Range 1937 59 min
Lesley Selander; Buck Jones, Muriel Evans

Smokey Smith 1935 57 min
Robert N. Bradbury; Bob Steele, George Hayes

Smoky 1933 69 min
Eugene Forde; Victor Jory, Irene Manning

Smoky 1966 103 min
George Sherman; Fess Parker, Katy Jurado

Smoky Canyon 1952 55 min
Fred F. Sears; Charles Starrett, Smiley Burnette

Smoky Mountain Melody 1948 61 min
Ray Nazarro; Roy Acuff, Guinn Williams

Smoky River Serenade 1947 67 min
Derwin Abrahams; Paul Campbell, Ruth Terry

Smoky Trails 1939 57 min
Bernard B. Ray; Bob Steele, Jean Carmen

Snake River Desperadoes 1951 54 min
Fred F. Sears; Charles Starrett, Smiley Burnette

Snow Dog 1950 63 min
Frank McDonald; Kirby Grant, Rick Vallin

Snowfire 1958 73 min
Dorrell & Stuart McGowan; Don Megowan, Molly
McGowan

Il Sogno di Zorro 1952 (It) 93 min
Mario Soldati;

Il Sogno di Zorro 1975 (It)
Mariano Laurenti;

The Sombrero Kid 1942 56 min
George Sherman; Don Barry, Lynn Merrick

Son of a Badman 1949 64 min
Ray Taylor; Lash LaRue, Al St John

Son of a Gunfighter 1964 (US/Sp) 90 min
Paul Landres; Russ Tamblyn, Fernando Rey

Son of Billy the Kid 1949 65 min
Ray Taylor; Lash LaRue, Al St John

Son of Django (Il Figlio di Django) 1967 (It) 79 min
Osvaldo Civirani; Guy Madison, Gabriele Tinti

Son of Geronimo 1952 15 chaps
Spencer G. Bennet; Clayton Moore, Rodd Redwing

Son of God's Country 1948 60 min
R.G. Springsteen; Monte Hale, Paul Hurst

Son of Oklahoma 1932 55 min
Robert N. Bradbury; Bob Steele, Carmen LaRoux

Son of Roaring Dan 1940 52 min
Ford Beebe; Johnny Mack Brown, Fuzzy Knight

Son of the Border 1933 60 min
Lloyd Nosler; Tom Keene, Edgar Kennedy

Son of the Renegade 1953 57 min
Reg Brown; John Carpenter, Jack Ingram

Song of Arizona 1946 68 min
Frank McDonald; Roy Rogers, Dale Evans

Song of Idaho 1948 69 min
Ray Nazarro; Kirby Grant, June Vincent

Song of Nevada 1944 75 min
Joseph Kane; Roy Rogers, Dale Evans

Song of Texas 1943 69 min
Joseph Kane; Roy Rogers, Sheila Ryan

Song of the Drifter 1948 53 min
Lambert Hillyer; Jimmy Wakely, Dub Taylor

Song of the Prairie 1945 62 min
Ray Nazarro; Ken Curtis, Guinn Williams

Song of the Range 1944 55 min
Wallace Fox; Jimmy Wakely, Dennis Moore

Song of the Sierras 1946 58 min
Oliver Drake; Jimmy Wakely, Lee White

Song of the Trail 1936 59 min
Russell Hopton; Kermit Maynard, Evelyn Brent

Song of the Wasteland 1947 56 min
Thomas Carr; Jimmy Wakely, Lee White

Song of the West 1930 80 min
Ray Enright; John Boles, Vivienne Segal

Songs and Saddles 1938 65 min
Harry Fraser; Gene Austin, Charles King

Sonora Stagecoach 1944 61 min
Robert Tansey; Hoot Gibson, Bob Steele

The Sons of Great Bear (Die Sohne der Grossen Barin) 1965
(EG) 98 (92) min
Josef Mach;

Sons of New Mexico 1950 71 min
John English; Gene Autry, Gail Davis

Sons of the Pioneers 1942 61 min
Joseph Kane; Roy Rogers, George Hayes

Sotto a Chi Tocca 1972 (It)
Gianfranco Parolini; Dean Reed, P. Sanchez

South of Arizona 1938 56 min
Sam Nelson; Charles Starrett, Iris Meredith

South of Caliente 1951 67 min
William Witney; Roy Rogers, Dale Evans

South of Death Valley 1949 54 min
Ray Nazarro; Charles Starrett, Gail Davis

South of Monterey 1946 63 min
William Nigh; Gilbert Roland, Martin Garralaga

South of Rio 1949 60 min
Philip Ford; Monte Hale, Paul Hurst

South of Santa Fé 1932 60 min
Bert Glennon; Bob Steele, Chris-Pin Martin

South of Santa Fé 1942 56 min
Joseph Kane; Roy Rogers, George Hayes

South Pacific Trail 1952 60 min
William Witney; Rex Allen, Slim Pickens

South of the Chisholm Trail 1947 58 min
Derwin Abrahams; Charles Starrett, Smiley Burnette

Southward Ho! 1939 57 min
Joseph Kane; Roy Rogers, George Hayes

Spara Joe ... e Cosi Sia 1972 (It)
Hal Brady (E. Miraglia); Richard Harrison, Jose Torres

Spirit of the West 1932 60 min
Otto Brower; Hoot Gibson, Doris Hill

Spoilers of the Plains 1951 68 min
William Witney; Roy Rogers, Penny Edwards

Spoilers of the Range 1939 57 min
C.C. Coleman Jnr; Charles Starrett, Iris Meredith

Spook Town 1944 59 min
Elmer Clifton; Dave O'Brien, Jim Newill

Springtime in the Rockies 1937 60 min
Joseph Kane; Gene Autry, Smiley Burnette

Springtime in Texas 1945 55 min
Oliver Drake; Jimmy Wakely, Dennis Moore

Square Dance Jubilee 1949 79 min
Paul Landres; Donald Barry, Wally Vernon

Square Shooter 1935 57 min
David Selman; Tim McCoy, Charles Middleton

Stage to Blue River 1951 55 min
Lewis Collins; Whip Wilson, Fuzzy Knight

Stage to Mesa City 1947 56 min
Ray Taylor; Lash LaRue, Al St John

Stagecoach Days 1938 58 min
Joseph Levering; Jack Luden, Eleanor Stewart

Stagecoach Driver 1951 52 min
Lewis Collins; Whip Wilson, Fuzzy Knight

Stagecoach Express 1942 57 min
George Sherman; Don Barry, Lynn Merrick

Stagecoach Kid 1949 60 min
Lew Landers; Tim Holt, Richard Martin

Stagecoach Outlaws 1945 55 min
Sam Newfield; Buster Crabbe, Al St John

Stagecoach to Dancer's Rock 1962 72 min
Earl Bellamy; Warren Stevens, Martin Landau

Stagecoach to Denver 1946 56 min
R.G. Springsteen; Allan Lane, Bobby Blake

Stagecoach to Monterey 1944 55 min
Lesley Selander; Allan Lane, Peggy Stewart

Stagecoach War 1940 63 min
Lesley Selander; William Boyd, Russell Hayden

Stairs of Sand 1929
Otto Brower; Wallace Beery, Jean Arthur

Stampede 1936 58 min
Ford Beebe; Charles Starrett, Finis Barton

Starblack 1966 (It)
Giovanni Grimaldi; Robert Woods, Elga Andersen

Stardust on the Sage 1942 65 min
William Morgan; Gene Autry, Smiley Burnette

Starlight over Texas 1938 58 min
Al Herman; Tex Ritter, Carmen LaRoux

Stars over Texas 1946 57 min
Robert Tansey; Eddie Dean, Roscoe Ates

Stick to Your Guns 1941 63 min
Lesley Selander; William Boyd, Andy Clyde

The Storm 1930 80 min
William Wyler; Lupe Velez, William Boyd

The Storm Rider 1957 70 min
Edward Bernds; Scott Brady, Mala Powers

Stormy 1935
Louis Friedlander (Lew Landers); Noah Beery Jnr,
Raymond Hatton

Stormy Trails 1936 58 min
Sam Newfield; Rex Bell, Lane Chandler

Straight Shooter 1939 54 min
Sam Newfield; Tim McCoy, Ben Corbett

Strange Gamble 1948 62 min
George Archainbaud; William Boyd, Andy Clyde

Stranger at My Door 1956 85 min
William Witney; McDonald Carey, Skip Homeier

Stranger at Sacramento (Uno Straniero a Sacramento) 1965 (It)
85 min
Serge Bergon (Sergio Bergonzelli); Mickey Hargitay,
Gabriella Giorgelli

The Stranger from Arizona 1938 54 min
Elmer Clifton; Buck Jones, Dorothy Fay

The Stranger from Pecos 1943 55 min
Lambert Hillyer; Johnny Mack Brown, Raymond Hatton

The Stranger from Ponca City 1947 56 min
Derwin Abrahams; Charles Starrett, Smiley Burnette

Stranger from Santa Fé 1945 57 min
Lambert Hillyer; Johnny Mack Brown, Raymond Hatton

The Stranger from Texas 1939 54 min
Sam Nelson; Charles Starrett, Dick Curtis

The Stranger's Gundown (Django il Bastardo) 1969 (It)
102 min
Sergio Garrone; Anthony Steffen, Paola Gozlino

Un Straniero a Paso Bravo 1968 (It/Sp) 96 min
Salvatore Rosso; Anthony Steffen, G. Rubin

Straniero Fatti il Segno della Croce 1968 (It)
Miles Deem (D. Fidani); Charles Southwood, Jeff Cameron

Streets of Ghost Town 1950 54 min
Ray Nazarro; Charles Starrett, Smiley Burnette

Su le Mani ... Cadaverei sei in Arresto 1971 (It/Sp)
Leon Klimowsky; Peter Lee Lawrence, Espartaco Santoni

Sudden Bill Dorn 1937 60 min
Ray Taylor; Buck Jones, Noel Francis

Sugar Colt 1966 (It/Sp) 100 min
Franco Giraldi; Hunt Powers, Soledad Miranda

Sun Valley Cyclone 1946 56 min
R.G. Springsteen; Bill Elliott, Bobby Blake

Sundown Kid 1942 57 min
Elmer Clifton; Don Barry, Ian Keith

Sundown in Santa Fé 1948 60 min
R.G. Springsteen; Allan Lane, Eddy Waller

Sundown Jim 1942 63 min
James Tinling; John Kimbrough, Paul Hurst

Sundown on the Prairie 1939 58 min
Al Herman; Tex Ritter, Dorothy Fay

The Sundown Rider 1933 65 min
Lambert Hillyer; Buck Jones, Barbara Weeks

The Sundown Trail 1934
Robert Tansey; Wally Wales, Fay McKenzie

Sunscorched (Vergeltung in Catano) 1965 (WG/Sp) 86 (78) min
Mark Stevens; Mario Adorf, Marianne Koch

Sunset Carson Rides Again 1948
Oliver Drake; Sunset Carson, Pat Starling

Sunset in the West 1950 67 min
William Witney; Roy Rogers, Penny Edwards

Sunset in Wyoming 1941 65 min
William Morgan; Gene Autry, Smiley Burnette

Sunset on the Desert 1942 54 min
Joseph Kane; Roy Rogers, George Hayes

Sunset Pass 1933 61 min
Henry Hathaway; Randolph Scott, Tom Keene

Sunset Serenade 1942 58 min
Joseph Kane; Roy Rogers, George Hayes

The Sunset Trail 1932 62 min
B. Reeves Eason; Ken Maynard, Frank Rice

Il Suo Nome Era Pot .. ma ... lo Chiamavano Allegria 1971 (It)
Dennis Ford; Peter Mitchell, Lincoln Tate

Il Suo Nome Gridava Vendetta 1968 (It) 94 min
William Hawkins (M. Caiano); Anthony Steffen, William
Berger

Susanna Pass 1949 67 min
William Witney; Roy Rogers, Dale Evans

Susannah of the Mounties 1939 78 min
William A. Seiter; Shirley Temple, Randolph Scott

Swifty 1935 58 min
Alan James; Hoot Gibson, June Gale

Swing, Cowboy, Swing 1944
Elmer Clifton; Cal Shrum, Max Terhune

Swing in the Saddle 1944
Lew Landers; Jane Frazee, Guinn Williams

Swordsmen Three (Las Tres Espadas del Zorro) 1963 (Sp/It)
90 min
Riccardo Blasco;

Taggart 1965 85 min
R.G. Springsteen; Tony Young, Dan Duryea

La Taglia e Tua e l'Ammazzo Io 1969 (It)
E. Mulargia; Robert Wood, M. Bonuglia

Take a Hard Ride 1975 (Us/It) 103 (93) min
Anthony Dawson (Antonio Margheriti); Lee Van Cleef, Jim
Brown

Take Me Back to Oklahoma 1940 57 min
Al Herman; Tex Ritter, Slim Andrews

The Tall Women (Frauen, die Durch die Holle Gehen) 1966
(Austria/It/Sp) 94 min
Sidney Pink (Rudolf Zehetgruber);

Tap Roots 1948 109 min
George Marshall; Van Heflin, Susan Hayward

A Taste for Killing (Per il Gusto di Uccidere) 1966 (It/Sp)
87 min
Tonino Valerii; Craig Hill, George Martin

The Taste of the Savage (El Sabor de la Venganza) 1970 (Mex)
86 (69) min
Alberto Mariscal;

Ten Days to Tulara 1958 77 min
George Sherman; Sterling Hayden, Grace Raynor

Ten Who Dared 1960 92 min
William Beaudine; Brian Keith, James Drury

A Tenderfoot Goes West 1937
Maurice O'Neill; Jack LaRue, Virginia Carroll

Tension at Table Rock 1956 93 min
Charles Marquis Warren; Richard Egan, Dorothy Malone

Terror at Black Falls 1962 72 min
Robert C. Sarafian; House Peters Jnr, Gary Gray

Terror of the Plains 1934 57 min
Harry S. Webb; Tom Tyler, Roberta Gale

Terror Trail 1933 57 min
Armand Schaefer; Tom Mix, Raymond Hatton

Terror Trail 1946 55 min
Ray Nazarro; Charles Starrett, Smiley Burnette

Il Terrore dell'Oklahoma 1960 (It) 86 min
Mario Amendola;

Tex Granger 1948 15 chaps
Derwin Abrahams; Robert Kellard, Peggy Stewart

Tex Takes a Holiday 1932 60 min
Alvin J. Neitz (Alan James); Wallace MacDonald, Ben
Corbett

The Texan 1932
Cliff Smith; Buffalo Bill Jnr, Lucile Browne

The Texan Meets Calamity Jane 1950 71 min
Ande Lamb; Evelyn Ankers, James Ellison

Texans Never Cry 1951 70 min
Frank McDonald; Gene Autry, Pat Buttram

Texas, Brooklyn and Heaven 1948 76 min
William Castle; Guy Madison, Diana Lynn

Texas Buddies 1932 59 min
Robert N. Bradbury; Bob Steele, George Hayes

Texas Carnival 1951 77 min
Charles Walters; Red Skelton, Esther Williams

Texas City 1952
Lewis Collins; Johnny Mack Brown, Jimmy Ellison

Texas Gun-Fighter 1932 63 min
Phil Rosen; Ken Maynard, Sheila Mannors

Texas Jack 1935 52 min
Bernard B. Ray; Jack Perrin, Budd Buster

Texas John Slaughter 1958 74 min
Harry Keller; Tom Tryon, Robert Middleton

Texas Justice 1942 58 min
Sam Newfield; George Houston, Al St John

The Texas Kid 1943 59 min
Lambert Hillyer; Johnny Mack Brown, Raymond Hatton

Texas Man Hunt 1942 60 min
Peter Stewart (Sam Newfield); Bill Boyd, Art Davis

The Texas Marshal 1941 58 min
Peter Stewart (Sam Newfield); Tim McCoy, Kay Leslie

Texas Masquerade 1944 59 min
George Archainbaud; William Boyd, Andy Clyde

Texas Panhandle 1945 57 min
Ray Nazarro; Charles Starrett, Tex Harding

Texas Pioneers 1932 58 min
Harry Fraser; Bill Cody, Andy Shuford

The Texas Gambler 1935 59 min
Bob Hill; Bill Cody, Earle Hodgins

Texas Renegades 1940 59 min
Peter Stewart (Sam Newfield); Tim McCoy, Nora Lane

Texas Terrors 1940 57 min
George Sherman; Donald Barry, Al St John

Texas Trouble Troubleshooters 1942 55 min
S. Roy Luby; Ray Corrigan, John King

Texas Wildcats 1939 57 min
Sam Newfield; Tim McCoy, Joan Barclay

That Dirty Story of the West (Quella Sporca Storia del West)
1968 (It) 90 min
Enzo G. Castellari; Andrea Giordana, Gilbert Roland

That Texas Jamboree 1946 59 min
Ray Nazarro; Ken Curtis, Guinn Williams

They Call Him Marcados (Los Marcados) 1972 (Mex) 82 min
Alberto Mariscal;

They Call Me Hallelujah 1972 (It)
Anthony Ascott; George Hilton, Agata Flory

They Came to Cordura 1959 123 min
Robert Rossen; Gary Cooper, Rita Hayworth

13 Fighting Men 1960 69 min
Harry Gerstad; Grant Williams, Brad Dexter

Thirty Winchester for El Diablo 1965 (It)
Frank G. Carrol; Karl Mohrer, John Heston

Thompson 1880 1966 (It/Sp) 85 min
Guido Zurli; George Martin, G. Sandri

Those Dirty Dogs 1974 (US/It/Sp) 89 min
Giuseppe Rosati; Stephen Boyd, Johnny Garko

Those Redheads from Seattle 1953 90 min
Lewis R. Foster; Rhonda Fleming, Gene Barry

The Three Avengers (Gli Invincibili Tre) 1964 (It) 97 min
Gianfranco Parolini; Alan Steel, Mimmo Palmara

Three Bullets for a Long Gun 1973 83 min
Peter Henkel;

Three Desperate Men 1951 71 min
Sam Newfield; Preston Foster, Jim Davis

Three Golden Boys (Tre Ragazzi d'Oro) 1966 (It)
Enzo Peri; Thomas Hunter, James Shigetano

Three in the Saddle 1945 61 min
Harry Fraser; Dave O'Brien, Tex Ritter

The Three Mesquiteers 1936 61 min
Ray Taylor; Bob Livingston, Ray Corrigan

Three on the Trail 1936 67 min
Howard Bretherton; William Boyd, Jimmy Ellison

The Three Outlaws 1956 74 min
Sam Newfield; Neville Brand, Alan Hale Jnr

Three Young Texans 1954 78 min
Henry Levin; Mitzi Gaynor, Jeffrey Hunter

Throw a Saddle on a Star 1946 60 min
Ray Nazarro; Ken Curtis, Jeff Donnell

The Throwback 1935 60 min
Ray Taylor; Buck Jones, Muriel Evans

Thunder in the Desert 1938 56 min
Sam Newfield; Bob Steele, Louise Stanley

Thunder in the Pines 1948 62 min
Robert Edwards; George Reeves, Ralph Byrd

Thunder Over Arizona 1956 70 min
Joseph Kane; Skip Homeier, Jack Elam

Thunder Pass 1954 76 min
Frank McDonald; Dane Clark, Andy Devine

Thunder River Feud 1942 51 min
S. Roy Luby; Ray Corrigan, John King

Thunder Town 1946 57 min
Harry Fraser; Bob Steele, Syd Saylor

Thunderbolt 1935
Stuart Paton; Kane Richmond, Bobby Nelson

Thundering Caravans 1952 54 min
Harry Keller; Allan Lane, Eddy Waller

Thundering Frontier 1940 57 min
D. Ross Lederman; Charles Starrett, Iris Meredith

Thundering Gun Slingers 1944 59 min
Sam Newfield; Buster Crabbe, Al St John

Thundering Hoofs 1942 61 min
Lesley Selander; Tim Holt, Luana Walters

The Thundering Trail 1951
Ron Ormond; Lash LaRue, Al St John

Thundering Trails 1943 56 min
John English; Bob Steele, Tom Tyler

The Thundering West 1939 57 min
Sam Nelson; Charles Starrett, Iris Meredith

Tiempo de Morir 1965 (Mex) 82 min
Arturo Ripstein;

Tiger Rose 1929
George Fitzmaurice; Monte Blue, Rin-Tin-Tin

Timber Stampede 1939 59 min
David Howard; George O'Brien, Chill Wills

Timber Terrors 1935 59 min
Robert Tansey; John Preston, Tom London

The Timber Trail 1948 67 min
Phillip Ford; Monte Hale, Lynne Roberts

Timber War 1935 60 min
Sam Newfield; Kermit Maynard, Lucille Lund

The Time of the Vultures (Il Tempo degli Avvoltoi) 1967 (It)
95 min
Nando Cicero; George Hilton, Frank Wolff

The Tioga Kid 1948 54 min
Ray Taylor; Eddie Dew, Roscoe Ates

To Trust Is Good ... but Shooting Is Better (Fidarsi E Bene, Sparare E Meglio) 1968 (It)
Osvaldo Civirani; George Hilton, John Ireland

Der Tod Ritt Dienstags 1968 (WG/It) 115 min
Tonino Valerii; Lee Van Cleef, Giuliano Gemma

Today We Kill, Tomorrow We Die 1972 (It)
Tonino Servi; Bud Spencer, Wayde Preston

Tomahawk Trail 1957 60 min
Robert Parry; Chuck Connors, John Smith

Tomboy and the Champ 1961 92 min
Francis D. Lyon; Candy Moore, Ben Johnson

Tombstone Terror 1935 58 min
Robert N. Bradbury; Bob Steele, George Hayes

Tonka 1958 97 min
Lewis Foster; Sal Mineo, Phil Carey

Tonto Basin Outlaws 1941 60 min
S. Roy Luby; Ray Corrigan, John King

The Tonto Kid 1935
Harry Fraser; Rex Bell, Ruth Mix

Too Much Beef 1936 60 min
Robert Hill; Rex Bell, Forrest Taylor

The Topeka Terror 1945 55 min
Howard Bretherton; Allan Lane, Linda Stirling

The Torch aka The Bandit General 1950 84 min
Emilio Fernandez; Paulette Godard, Pedro Armendariz

A Tornado in the Saddle 1942 59 min
William Berke; Russell Hayden, Dub Taylor

Tornado Range 1948 56 min
Ray Taylor; Eddie Dean, Roscoe Ates

Tough Assignment 1949 61 min
William Beaudine; Don Barry, Steve Brodie

Toughest Gun in Tombstone 1958 72 min
Earl Bellamy; George Montgomery, Don Beddoe

A Town Called Hell 1971 95 min
Robert Parrish; Robert Shaw, Stella Stevens

Track of the Falcon (Spur des Falken) 1968 (EG) 100 min
Gottfried Kolditz;

Tracy Rides 1935 60 min
Harry S. Webb; Tom Tyler, Edmund Cobb

The Trail Blazers 1940 58 min
George Sherman; Robert Livingston, Bob Steele

Trail Guide 1952 60 min
Lesley Selander; Tim Holt, Richard Martin

Trail of Kit Carson 1945 57 min
Lesley Selander; Allan Lane, Helen Talbot

Trail of Terror 1935
Robert N. Bradbury; Bob Steele, Beth Marion

Trail of the Hawk 1935 60 min
Edward Dmytryk; Yancie Lane, Dickie Jones

Trail of the Rustlers 1950 55 min
Ray Nazarro; Charles Starrett, Smiley Burnette

Trail of the Silver Spurs 1941 58 min
S. Roy Luby; Ray Corrigan, John King

Trail of the Yukon 1949 69 min
William X. Crowley; Kirby Grant, Suzanne Dalbert

Trail Riders 1942 55 min
Robert Tansey; John King, David Sharpe

Trail to Gunsight 1944 58 min
Vernon Keyes; Eddie Dew, Fuzzy Knight

Trail to Laredo 1948 54 min
Ray Nazarro; Charles Starrett, Smiley Burnette

Trail to Mexico 1946 56 min
Oliver Drake; Jimmy Wakely, Lee White

Trail to San Antone 1947 67 min
John English; Gene Autry, Peggy Stewart

Trail to Vengeance 1945 58 min
Wallace Fox; Kirby Grant, Fuzzy Knight

Trailing Danger 1947 58 min
Lambert Hillyer; Johnny Mack Brown, Raymond Hatton

Trailing North 1933 60 min
J.P. McCarthy; Bob Steele, Doris Hill

Trailing Trouble 1937 57 min
Arthur Rosson; Ken Maynard, Lona Andre

Trail's End 1935 61 min
Al Herman; Conway Tearle, Fred Kohler

Trails of Adventure 1935 57 min
Jay Wilsey (Buffalo Bill Jnr); Buffalo Bill Jnr, Edna Aslin

Trails of Danger aka Trails of Peril 1930 50 min
Alvin J. Neitz (Alan James); Wally Wales, Jack Perrin

Trails of the Golden West 1931 58 min
Leander De Cordova; Buffalo Bill Jnr, Tom London

Trails of the Wild 1935 60 min
Sam Newfield; Kermit Maynard, Billie Seward

Train to Durango (Un Treno per Durango) 1967 (It/Sp) 88 min
William Hawkins (Mario Caiano); Anthony Steffen, Mark Damon

Train to Tombstone 1950 56 min
William Berke; Don Barry, Robert Lowery

The Trap 1966 (GB) 106 min
Sidney Hayes; Oliver Reed, Rita Tushingham

I Tre che Sconvolsero il West 1968 (It)
Enzo G. Castellari; Antonio Sabato, J. Saxon

Tre Colpi di Winchester per Ringo 1966 (It) 91 min
Emimmo Salvi; Gordon Mitchell, Mikey Haritay

Tre Croci per Non Morire 1968 (It)
W.S. Regan (Sergio Garrone); Ken Wood, Craig Hill

I Tre del Colorado 1965 (It/Sp)
Amando De Ossorio; George Martin, Pamela Tudor

Tre Dollari di Piombo 1964 (It/Sp) 89 min
Joseph Trader;

Tre Pistole contro Cesare 1967 (It) 77 min
Enzo Peri;

Treason 1933 63 min
George B. Seitz; Buck Jones, Robert Ellis

Treasure of Ruby Hills 1955 71 min
Frank McDonald; Zachary Scott, Lee Van Cleef

Trigger Fingers 1939 60 min
Sam Newfield; Tim McCoy, Ben Corbett

Trigger Fingers 1946 56 min
Lambert Hillyer; Johnny Mack Brown, Raymond Hatton

Trigger Jnr 1950 68 min
William Witney; Roy Rogers, Dale Evans

Trigger Law 1944 56 min
Vernon Keyes; Hoot Gibson, Bob Steele

Trigger Smith 1939 59 min
Alan James; Jack Randall, Frank Yaconelli

Trigger Tom 1935
Henri Samuels (Harry S. Webb); Tom Tyler, Al St John

Trigger Trail 1944 59 min
Lewis Collins; Rod Cameron, Eddie Dew

Triggerman 1948 56 min
Howard Bretherton; Johnny Mack Brown, Raymond Hatton

Trinita e Sartana Figli Di ... 1972 (It) 93 min
Mario Siciliano; Richard Widmark, H. Baird

Trouble at Melody Mesa 1949 60 min
W.M. Connell; Brad King, Cal Shrum

Trouble Busters 1933 55 min
Lew Collins; Jack Hoxie, Lane Chandler

The Trusted Outlaw 1937 57 min
Robert N. Bradbury; Bob Steele, Lois January

Tucson Raiders 1944 55 min
Spencer G. Bennet; Bill Elliott, George Hayes

Tumbledown Ranch in Arizona 1941 60 min
S. Roy Luby; Ray Corrigan, John King

Tumbleweed 1953 80 min
Nathan Juran; Audie Murphy, Chill Wills

Tumbleweed Trail 1942 57 min
Peter Stewart (Sam Newfield); Bill Boyd, Art Davis

Tumbleweed Trail 1946 57 min
Robert Tansey; Eddie Dean, Roscoe Ates

Tutti Fratelli nel West ... per Parti di Padre 1972 (It)
Sergio Grieco; Antonio Sabato, Marisa Mell

Tutti per Uno, Botte per Tutti 1973 (It/Sp/WG) 86 min
Bruno Corbucci; Timothy Brent, George Eastman

The Twilight Avengers (I Vendicatori dell'Ave Maria) 1970 (It)
89 min
Al Albert (Adalberto Albertini); Tony Kendall, Alberto Dell'Acqua

Twilight in the Sierras 1950 67 min
William Witney; Roy Rogers, Dale Evans

Twilight on the Prairie 1944 62 min
Jean Yarbrough; Johnny Downs, Vivian Austin

Twilight on the Rio Grande 1947 71 min
Frank McDonald; Gene Autry, Bob Steele

Twilight on the Trail 1941 58 min
Howard Bretherton; William Boyd, Andy Clyde

The Twinkle in God's Eye 1955 73 min
George Blair; Mickey Rooney, Coleen Gray

Twisted Rails 1935
Al Herman; Jack Donovan, Alice Dahl

Two-Fisted Justice 1931 63 min
G. Arthur Durlam; Tom Tyler, Barbara Weeks

Two-Fisted Justice 1943 61 min
Robert Tansey; John King, David Sharpe

Two-Fisted Stranger 1946 50 min
Ray Nazarro; Charles Starrett, Smiley Burnette

Two Gun Caballero 1931 58 min
Jack Nelson; Robert Frazer, Bobby Nelson

Two Gun Justice 1938 58 min
Alan James; Tim McCoy, John Merton

Two Gun Law 1937 56 min
Leon Barsha; Charles Starrett, Charles Middleton

The Two Gun Man 1931 60 min
Phil Rosen; Ken Maynard, Lafe McKee

Two Gun Troubador 1939 58 min
Raymond K. Johnson; Fred Scott, John Merton

Two Gunmen (Los Rurales de Texas) 1964 (Sp/It) 95 min
Anthony Greepy (Primo Zeglio); Alan Scott, George Martin

Two Guns and a Coward (Due Pistole e un Vigliacco) 1967 (It)
Calvin Jackson Padget; Anthony Steffen, Richard Wiler

Two in Revolt 1936
Glenn Tyron; John Arledge, Louise Latimer

Uccidi Django ... Uccidi per Primo 1971 (It)
Sergio Garrone; G. Rossi Stuart, K. Doris

The Ugly Ones 1968 (It/Sp)
Eugenio Martin; Richard Wyler, Tomas Milian

Unconquered Bandit 1935 59 min
Harry S. Webb; Tom Tyler, Slim Whitaker

Under Arizona Skies 1946 59 min
Lambert Hillyer; Johnny Mack Brown, Raymond Hatton

Under California Stars 1948 70 min
William Witney; Roy Rogers, Jane Frazee

Under Fiesta Stars 1941 64 min
Frank McDonald; Gene Autry, Smiley Burnette

Under Montana Skies 1930 59 min
Richard Thorpe; Kenneth Harlan, Dorothy Gulliver

Under Nevada Skies 1946 69 min
Frank McDonald; Roy Rogers, Dale Evans

Undercover Man 1936 57 min
Albert Ray; Johnny Mack Brown, Ted Adams

Undercover Men 1935
Sam Newfield; Charles Starrett, Wheeler Oakman

Underground Rustlers 1941 56 min
S. Roy Luby; Ray Corrigan, John King

Unexpected Guest 1947 61 min
George Archainbaud; William Boyd, Rand Brooks

Unknown Valley 1933 69 min
Lambert Hillyer; Buck Jones, Cecilia Parker

Untamed Heiress 1954 70 min
Charles Lamont; Judy Canova, Donald Barry

Un Uome e una Colt 1967 (It/Sp) 84 min
Tulio Demicheli; Robert Hundar, Fernando Sancho

Un Uomo Chiamata Apocalisse Joe 1970 (It/Sp) 96 min
Leopoldo Savona; Anthony Steffen, Eduardo Faiardo

L'Uomo dal Lungo Facice 1969 (It/WG)
Harald Reinl; Pierre Brice, Lex Barker

L'Uomo della Pistola d'Oro 1967 (It/Sp) 85 min
Alfonso Balcazar;

L'Uomo della Valle Maledetta 1964 (It/Sp) 82 min
Omar Hopkins (Primo Zeglio); Ty Hardin, John Bartha

Urban Cowboy 1980 135 min
James Bridges; John Travolta, Debra Winger

The Utah Kid 1930
Richard Thorpe; Rex Lease, Boris Karloff

The Utah Kid 1944 55 min
Vernon Keyes; Hoot Gibson, Bob Steele

Utah Wagon Train 1951 67 min
Philip Ford; Rex Allen, Penny Edwards

Vado, Vedo e Sparo 1968 (It/Sp) 100 min
Enzo G. Castellari; Antonio Sabato, Frank Wolff

I Vagliacci non Pregano 1969 (It) 101 min
Marion Sirko;

Valdez, the Halfbreed (Valdez il Mezzosangue) 1973 (It/Fr/Sp)
97 min
Duilio Coletti; Charles Bronson, Jill Ireland

The Valiant Hombre 1948 60 min
Wallace Fox; Duncan Renaldo, Leo Carrillo

La Valle del'Eco Tonante 1965 (It)
Amerigo Anton (Tanio Boccia);

La Valle delle Ombre Rosse 1965 (It/Sp/WG)
Harald Reinl; Anthony Steffen, Karin Dor

Valley of Fear 1947 54 min
Lambert Hillyer; Johnny Mack Brown, Raymond Hatton

Valley of Fire 1951 70 min
John English; Gene Autry, Pat Buttram

Valley of Terror 1937 58 min
Al Herman; Kermit Maynard, John Merton

Valley of the Lawless 1936 56 min
Robert N. Bradbury; Johnny Mack Brown, George Hayes

Valley of the Widows (Das Tal der Tanzenden Witwen) 1974
(WG/Sp) 85 min
Volker Vogeler; Hugo Blanco, Harry Baer

The Valley of Vanishing Men 1942 15 chaps
Spencer G. Bennet; Bill Elliott, Jack Ingram

Valley of Vengeance 1944 56 min
Sam Newfield; Buster Crabbe, Al St John

Valley of Wanted Men 1935 62 min
Alan James; Frankie Darro, Grant Withers

Vamos a Matar Sartana 1971 (It)
M. Pinzauti; George Martin, I. Ravaioli

The Vanishing Legion 1931 12 chaps
B. Reeves Eason, Ford Beebe; Harry Carey, Edwina Booth

Vanishing Men 1932 62 min
Harry Fraser; Tom Tyler, Raymond Keane

The Vanishing Outpost 1951
Ron Ormond; Lash LaRue, Al St John

The Vanishing Riders 1935
Bob Hill; Bill Cody, Wally Wales

Vaya con Dios, Gringo 1966 (It)
Edward G. Muller (Eduardo Mulargia); Glenn Saxson,
Ignazio Spalla

La Vendetta E il Mio Perdono 1968 (It) 82 min
Roberto Mauri;

Vendetta per Vendetta 1968 (It) 99 min
Ray Calloway; John Ireland, J. Hamilton

Il Vendicatore di Kansas City 1964 (It/Sp) 79 min
Augustin Navarro;

Vengeance 1964 79 min
Dene Hilyard; William Thourlby, Melora Conway

The Vengeance of Pancho Villa 1967 (It)
Joe Lacy; John Ericson, James Philbrook

Vengeance of Rannah 1936 59 min
Franklyn Shamray (Bernard B. Ray); Bob Custer, Rin-Tin-
Tin Jnr

Vengeance of the West 1942 60 min
Lambert Hillyer; Tex Ritter, Bill Elliott

Vengeance Trail (La Vendetta E un Piatto che Si Serva Freddo)
1972 (It) 98 min
William Redford (Pasquale Squintieri); Klaus Kinski,
Leonard Mann

Verflucht dies Amerika 1973 (WG/Sp) 93 min
Volker Vogeler; Geraldine Chaplin, William Berger

Via Pony Express 1933 60 min
Lew Collins; Jack Hoxie, Marceline Day

The Vigilante 1947 15 chaps
Wallace Fox; Ralph Byrd, Ramsay Ames

Vigilante Hideout 1950 60 min
Fred C. Brannon; Allan Lane, Eddy Waller

Vigilante Terror 1953 70 min
Lewis Collins; Bill Elliott, Fuzzy Knight

The Vigilantes Are Coming 1936 12 chaps
Mack V. Wright, Ray Taylor; Robert Livingston, Guinn
Williams

Vigilantes of Dodge City 1944 54 min
Wallace Grissell; Bill Elliott, Bobby Blake

The Vigilantes Ride 1944 56 min
William Berke; Russell Hayden, Dub Taylor

I Vigliacchi non Pregano 1968 (It/Sp)
Marlon Sirko; John Garko, Sean Todd

The Violent Breed (Keoma) 1976 (It) 101 (85) min
Enzo G. Castellari (Enzo Girolami); Franco Nero, Woody
Strode

I Violenti di Rio Bravo 1967 (It)
Robert Siodmak; Lex Barker, G. Barray

La Vita, a Volte, e Molto Dura, Vero 'Providenza' 1972
(It/Fr/WG) 100 (78) min
Giulio Petroni; Tomas Milian, Gregg Palmer

Viva Gringo 1966 (It)
G. Marischka; Guy Madison, G. Nuni

Voltati ... Ti Uccido 1967 (It/Sp) 90 (77) min
Al Bradley (Alfonso Brescia); Richard Wyler, Fernando
Sancho

W. Django 1971 (It)
Edward G. Muller (E. Mulargia); Anthony Steffen,
Esmeralda Barros

The Wackiest Wagon Train in the West 1976 86 min
Morrie Parker; Bob Denver, Forrest Tucker

Wagon Team 1952 61 min
George Archainbaud; Gene Autry, Pat Buttram

Wagon Wheels Westward 1945 56 min
R.G. Springsteen; Bill Elliott, Bobby Blake

Wanderers of the West 1941 58 min
Robert Hill; Tom Keene, Betty Miles

Wanted Dead or Alive 1951 59 min
Thomas Carr; Whip Wilson, Fuzzy Knight

Wanted Johnny Texas 1967 (It)
Emimmo Salvi; Fernando Sancho, Monica Brugher

Wanted Sabata 1970 (It)
Roberto Mauri; B. Harris, V. Karis

War Arrow 1954 78 min
George Sherman; Jeff Chandler, Maureen O'Hara

War on the Range 1933 59 min
J.P. McGowan; Tom Tyler, Lane Chandler

War Party 1965 72 min
Lesley Selander; Michael T. Mikler, Donald Barry

The Way of the West 1934
Robert Tansey; Wally Wales, Bobby Nelson

Wells Fargo Gunmaster 1951 60 min
Philip Ford; Allan Lane, Chubby Johnson

Wer Kennt Johnny R 1966 (WG/Sp) 91 min
Jose Luis Madrid;

West and Soda 1965 (It) 81 min
Bruno Bozetto;

The West Is Still Wild/Mulefeathers 1977
Don Von Mizener; Rory Calhoun, Richard Webb

West of Carson City 1940 57 min
Ray Taylor; Johnny Mack Brown, Bob Baker

West of Cimarron 1941 56 min
Les Orlebeck; Bob Steele, Tom Tyler

West of Dodge City 1947 57 min
Ray Nazarro; Charles Starrett, Smiley Burnette

West of Eldorado 1949 56 min
Ray Taylor; Johnny Mack Brown, Max Terhune

West of Nevada 1936 57 min
Robert Hill; Rex Bell, Joan Barclay

West of Pinto Basin 1940 60 min
S. Roy Luby; Ray Corrigan, John King

West of Rainbow's End 1938 57 min
Alan James; Tim McCoy, Kathleen Eliot

West of Sonora 1948 52 min
Ray Nazarro; Charles Starrett, Smiley Burnette

West of Texas 1943
Oliver Drake; Dave O'Brien, Jim Newill

West of the Rio Grande 1944 57 min
Lambert Hillyer; Johnny Mack Brown, Raymond Hatton

West of the Rockies 1929
Horace B. Carpenter; Art Mix, Horace B. Carpenter

West of the Santa Fé 1938 57 min
Sam Nelson; Charles Starrett, Iris Meredith

West of Tombstone 1942 59 min
Howard Bretherton; Charles Starrett, Russell Hayden

West on Parade 1934
Bernard B. Ray; Denny Meadows (Dennis Moore), Ben
Corbett

Il West Ti Va Stretto, Amico … E Arrivato Alleluja 1972
(It/WG) 98 min
Anthony Ascott (Giuliano Carmineo); George Hilton, Agata
Flori

Westbound Mail 1937 54 min
Folmer Blansted; Charles Starrett, Rosalind Keith

Westbound Stage 1939 56 min
Spencer Bennet; Tex Ritter, Muriel Evans

Western Caravans 1939 58 min
Sam Nelson; Charles Starrett, Iris Meredith

The Western Code 1932 61 min
J.P. McCarthy; Tim McCoy, Nora Lane

Western Cyclone 1943 56 min
Sam Newfield; Buster Crabbe, Al St John

Western Frontier 1935 59 min
Al Herman; Ken Maynard, Lucile Browne

Western Heritage 1948 61 min
Wallace Grissell; Tim Holt, Nan Leslie

Western Jamboree 1938 56 min
Ralph Staub; Gene Autry, Smiley Burnette

Western Justice 1935
Robert N. Bradbury; Bob Steele, Lafe McKee

Western Mail 1942
Robert Tansey; Tom Keene, Frank Yaconelli

Western Racketeers 1935
Robert J. Horner; Bill Cody, Wally Wales

Western Trails 1938 57 min
George Waggner; Bob Baker, Marjorie Reynolds

The Westerner 1934 58 min
David Selman; Tim McCoy, Marion Shilling

Westward Ho 1942 56 min
John English; Bob Steele, Tom Tyler

The Westward Trail 1948 56 min
Ray Taylor; Eddie Dean, Roscoe Ates

Wheels of Destiny 1934 63 min
Alan James; Ken Maynard, Dorothy Dix

When a Man Rides Alone 1933 60 min
J.P. McGowan; Tom Tyler, Alan Bridge

When a Man Sees Red 1934 60 min
Alan James; Buck Jones, Syd Saylor

When a Man's a Man 1935
Edward Cline; George O'Brien, Harry Woods

When the Redskins Rode 1951 78 min
Lew Landers; Jon Hall, Mary Castle

Where the West Begins 1938 54 min
J.P. McGowan; Jack Randall, Luana Walters

Where Trails End 1942 58 min
Robert Tansey; Tom Keene, Frank Yaconelli

Whirlwind 1951 70 min
John English; Gene Autry, Smiley Burnette

Whirlwind Horseman 1938 58 min
Bob Hill; Ken Maynard, Joan Barclay

Whirlwind Raiders 1948 54 min
Vernon Keays; Charles Starrett, Smiley Burnette

The Whirlwind Rider 1935
Robert J. Horner; Buffalo Bill Jnr, Jack Long

The Whispering Skull 1944
Elmer Clifton; Dave O'Brien, Tex Ritter

Whistlin' Dan 1932 65 min
Phil Rosen; Ken Maynard, Jack Rockwell

Whistling Hills 1951 58 min
Derwin Abrahams; Johnny Mack Brown, Jimmy Ellison

White Comanche (Comanche Blanco) 1968 (US/Sp) 92 (83) min
Gilbert Lee Kay (Jose Briz); William Shatner, Joseph Cotten

White Eagle 1932 67 min
Lambert Hillyer; Buck Jones, Ward Bond

White Eagle 1941 15 chaps
James W. Horne; Buck Jones, Raymond Hatton

White Fang (Zanna Bianca) 1974 (It/Fr/Sp) 101 min
Lucio Fulci;

White Renegade 1931
Jack Irwin; Tom Santschi, Blanche Mehaffey

The White Squaw 1956 73 min
Ray Nazarro; David Brian, May Wynn

White, Yellow, Black (Il Bianco, il Giallo, il Nero) 1975
(It/Sp/Fr) 110 min
Sergio Corbucci;

The Wild and the Innocent 1959 84 min
Jack Shor; Audie Murphy, Joanne Dru

Wild Beauty 1946 61 min
Wallace Fox; Don Porter, Lois Collier

Wild Brian Ken 1936 60 min
Howard Bretherton; Ralph Bellamy, Mae Clark

Wild Country 1947 55 min
Ray Taylor; Eddie Dean, Roscoe Ates

Wild Dakotas 1956 73 min
Sam Newfield; Bill Williams, Coleen Gray

Wild Heritage 1958 78 min
Charles Haas; Will Rogers Jnr, Maureen O'Sullivan

Wild Horse Canyon 1938 56 min
Robert Hill; Jack Randall, Dorothy Short

Wild Horse Phantom 1944 56 min
Sam Newfield; Buster Crabbe, Al St John

Wild Horse Range 1940 58 min
Raymond K. Johnson; Jack Randall, Charles King

Wild Horse Stampede 1943 59 min
Alan James; Ken Maynard, Hoot Gibson

Wild Horse Valley 1940 57 min
Ira Webb; Bob Steele, Lafe McKee

Wild Mustang 1935 62 min
Harry Fraser; Harry Carey, Barbara Fritchie

Wild Stallion 1952 70 min
Lewis Collins; Ben Johnson, Edgar Buchanan

Wild West Days 1937 13 chaps
Ford Beebe, Cliff Smith; Johnny Mack Brown, Lynn Gilbert

Wild West Whoopee 1931 57 min
Robert J. Horner; Jack Perrin, Josephine Hill

The Wild Westerners 1962 70 min
Oscar Rudolph; James Philbrook, Nancy Kovack

Wildcat Saunders 1936 60 min
Harry Fraser; Jack Perrin, Blanche Mehaffey

Wilderness Mail 1935 65 min
Forrest Sheldon; Kermit Maynard, Fred Kohler

Wildfire 1945 57 min
Robert Tansey; Bob Steele, Sterling Holloway

The Winds of Autumn 1976
Charles B. Pierce; Jack Elam, Dub Taylor

Winners of the West 1940 13 chaps
Ford Beebe, Ray Taylor; Dick Foran, Anne Nagel

Winnetou und das Halbblut Apanatschi 1966 (WG/Yug) 90 min
Harald Philipp; Lex Barker, Pierre Brice

Winnetou und Old Shatterhand im Tal der Toten 1968
(WG/It/Yug) 90 min
Harald Reinl; Pierre Brice, Lex Barker

Winning of the West 1953 57 min
George Archainbaud; Gene Autry, Smiley Burnette

The Wistfull Widow of Wagon Gap 1947 78 min
Charles Barton; Bud Abbott, Lou Costello

Wolf Call 1939 62 min
George Waggner; John Carroll, Movita

Wolf Dog 1958 61 min
Sam Newfield; Jim Davis, Allison Hayes

The Wolf Hunters 1949 70 min
Oscar (Budd) Boetticher; Kirby Grant, Helen Parrish

Wolf Riders 1935
Harry S. Webb; Jack Perrin, Lafe McKee

Wolf Song 1929 76 min
Victor Fleming; Gary Cooper, Lupe Lupez

Wolves of the Range 1943
Sam Newfield; Bob Livingston, Al St John

Woman Hungry 1931
Sidney Blackmer; Sidney Blackmer, Fred Kohler

Woman of the North Country 1952 92 min
Joseph Kane; Ruth Hussey, Rod Cameron

The Woman of the Town 1943 90 min
George Archainbaud; Claire Trevor, Albert Dekker

Wrangler's Roost 1941 57 min
S. Roy Luby; Ray Corrigan, John King

The Wrath of God (I'Ira di Dio) 1968 (It) 100 min
Albert Cardiff (Alberto Cardone); Brett Halsey, Fernando
Sancho

A Wreath for the Bandits (Crisantemi per un Branco di Carogne)
1968 (It)
Serge Vidal (Sergio Pastore); Edmund Purdom

Wyoming Hurricane 1944 58 min
William Berke; Russell Hayden, Dub Taylor

Wyoming Roundup 1952 53 min
Thomas Carr; Whip Wilson, Phyllis Coates

Wyoming Whirlwind 1932
Armand Schaefer; Lane Chandler, Adele Tracy

Wyoming Wildcat 1941 56 min
George Sherman; Don Barry, Syd Saylor

Y Seguian Robandose el Milion de Dolares 1971 (Sp/Fr/It)
92 min
Gene Martin;

Yankee 1966 (It/Sp) 95 min
Tinto Brass; Adolfo Celli, P. Leroy

Yaqui Drums 1956 71 min
Jean Yarbrough; Rod Cameron, Mary Castle

The Yellow Mountain 1954 78 min
Jesse Hibbs; Lex Barker, Mala Powers

Yellow Rose of Texas 1944 69 min
Joseph Kane; Roy Rogers, Dale Evans

The Yellow Tomahawk 1954 82 min
Lesley Selander; Rory Calhoun, Peggie Castle

Yellowneck 1955 83 min
R. John Hugh; Lin McCarthy, Stephen Courtleigh

Yodelin' Kid from Pine Ridge 1937 60 min
Joseph Kane; Gene Autry, Smiley Burnette

Young Blood 1932 59 min
Phil Rosen; Bob Steele, Helen Foster

Young Buffalo Bill 1940 59 min
Joseph Kane; Roy Rogers, George Hayes

Young Daniel Boone 1950 71 min
Reginald LeBorg; David Bruce, Kristine Miller

The Young Guns 1956 84 min
Albert Band; Russ Tamblyn, Gloria Talbott

The Young in Heart 1943 77 min
George Archainbaud;

Yukon Flight 1940 57 min
Ralph Staub; James Newill, Louise Stanley

Yukon Gold 1952 62 min
Frank McDonald; Kirby Grant, Martha Hyer

Yukon Manhunt 1951 63 min
Frank McDonald; Kirby Grant, Gail Davis

Yukon Patrol 1942
William Witney, John English; Allan Lane, Robert Strange

Yukon Vengeance 1954 68 min
William Beaudine; Kirby Grant, Monte Hale

Zorro (La Espada del Zorro) 1961 (Sp) 90 min
Joaquin Romero Marchent; Frank Latimore, Maria Luz
Galicia

Zorro 1975 (Fr/It) 120 min
Duccio Tessari; Alain Delon, Stanley Baker

Zorro Rides Again 1959 68 min
William Witney, John English; John Carroll, Duncan
Renaldo

Zorro the Avenger 1960 97 min
Charles Barton; Guy Williams, Henry Calvin

Index

Abilene Town 1946
Above All Laws see Adventures in Silverado 1948
Across the Sierra 1941
Across the Wide Missouri 1951
Adios Amigo 1975
Advance to the Rear 1964
Adventures in Silverado 1948
Adventures of Red Ryder 1940
Al di la della Legge see Beyond the Law 1967
Al Jennings of Oklahoma 1951
Alamo, The 1960
Albuquerque 1948
Alias Jesse James 1959
Alien Thunder 1973
Allegheny Frontier see Allegheny Uprising 1939
Allegheny Uprising 1939
Along Came Jones 1945
Along the Great Divide 1951
Along the Oregon Trail 1947
Alvarez Kelly 1966
Ambush 1950
Ambush at Cimarron Pass 1958
Ambush at Tomahawk Gap 1953
American Empire 1942
Amigos, Los see Deaf Smith and Johnny Ears 1972
Ammazzali Tutti e Torno Solo see Kill Them All and Come Back Alone 1968
Among Vultures 1964
Anchor, The see Pioneers of the Frontier 1940
Angel and the Badman 1947
Animals, The 1970
Annie Get Your Gun 1950
Annie Oakley 1935
Another Man, Another Chance see Another Man, Another Woman 1977
Another Man, Another Woman 1977
Apache 1954
Apache Ambush 1955
Apache Drums 1951
Apache Gold see Winnetou the Warrior 1963
Apache Rifles 1964
Apache Trail 1943
Apache War Smoke 1952
Apache Warrior 1957
Apache Woman 1955
Apaches Last Battle see Old Shatterhand 1964
Appaloosa, The 1966
Apple Dumpling Gang, The 1974
Apple Dumpling Gang Rides Again, The 1979
Arena 1953
Arizona 1940
Arizona Bound 1941
Arizona Colt 1966
Arizona Cowboy 1950
Arizona Cyclone 1941
Arizona Days 1937
Arizona Gunfighter 1937
Arizona Kid, The 1930
Arizona Legion 1939
Arizona Mahoney 1936
Arizona Manhunt 1951
Arizona Raiders 1965
Arizona Rangers 1948
Arizona Terrors 1942
Arizona Trail 1943
Arizona Whirlwind 1944
Arizona Wildcat, The 1939
Arizonian, The 1935
Armed and Dangerous 1977
Arouse and Beware see The Man from Dakota 1940
Arrow in the Dust 1954
Arrowhead 1953
At Gunpoint 1955
Autre Homme, Une Autre Chance, Un see Another Man, Another Woman 1977
Avenger, The 1931
Avenger, The 1966
Avenging Rider 1943
Back in the Saddle 1941
Backlash 1956
Bad Bascomb 1946
Bad Company 1972
Bad Day at Black Rock 1955
Bad Lands 1939
Bad Man, The 1930
Bad Man, The 1941
Bad Man of Brimstone, The 1937
Bad Man of Harlem see Harlem on the Prairie 1937
Bad Man of Wyoming see Wyoming 1940
Bad Men of Missouri 1941
Bad Men of Tombstone 1949
Badlanders, The 1958

Badlands of Dakota, The 1941
Badlands of Montana 1957
Badman's Country 1958
Badman's Territory 1946
Baker's Hawk 1976
Ballad of a Gunfighter 1964
Ballad of Cable Hogue, The 1970
Ballad of Josie, The 1967
Bandido! 1956
Bandidos 1967
Bandit Queen 1950
Bandolero! 1968
Bar 20 1943
Bar 20 Rides Again 1935
Barbarosa 1982
Barbary Coast Gent 1944
Baron of Arizona, The 1950
Barquero 1970
Barricade 1950
Battle at Apache Pass, The 1951
Battle of Rogue River 1954
Battling with Buffalo Bill 1931
Beautiful Blonde from Bashful Bend, The 1949
Beguiled, The 1971
Belle of the Nineties 1934
Belle Starr 1941
Belle Starr's Daughter 1947
Bells of Capistrano 1942
Bells of Coronado 1950
Bells of Rosarita 1945
Bells of San Angelo 1947
Below the Border 1942
Bend of the River 1952
Beneath Western Skies 1944
Best of the Badmen 1951
Between Men 1935
Beyond the Last Frontier 1943
Beyond the Law 1967
Beyond the Purple Hills 1950
Beyond the Sacramento 1940
Big and the Bad, The 1971
Big Bonanza, The 1944
Big Country, The 1958
Big Deal at Dodge City see A Big Hand for the Little Lady 1966
Big Gundown, The 1966
Big Hand for the Little Lady, A 1966
Big Jake 1971
Big Land, The 1957
Big Show, The 1936
Big Sky, The 1952
Big Sombrero, The 1949
Big Stampede, The 1932
Big Trail, The 1930
Big Trees, The 1952
Billy Jack 1971
Billy the Kid 1930
Billy the Kid 1941
Billy the Kid Returns 1938
Billy the Kid Trapped 1942
Billy the Kid vs. Dracula 1965
Billy Two Hats 1973
Bite the Bullet 1975
Bitter Creek 1954
Black Aces 1937
Black Bandit 1938
Black Bart 1948
Black Bounty Killer, The see Boss Nigger 1974
Black Dakotas, The 1954
Black Hills Ambush 1952
Black Hills Express 1943
Black Horse Canyon 1954
Black Patch 1957
Black Whip, The 1956
Blackjack Ketchum, Desperado 1956
Blazing Arrows see Fighting Caravans 1931
Blazing Guns 1943
Blazing Saddles 1974
Blazing Six Shooters 1940
Blazing Sixes 1937
Blazing the Overland Trail 1956
Blindman 1971
Blood Arrow 1958
Blood Money 1974
Blood on the Moon 1948
Blue 1968
Blue Steel 1934
Bobbi Jo and the Outlaw 1976
Bold Caballero, The 1936
Bold Frontiersman, The 1948
Boldest Job in the West, The 1971
Boothill Brigade 1937
Border Buckaroos 1943
Border Devils 1932
Border Law 1931
Border Legion 1930
Border Legion, The 1940
Border Outlaws 1950
Border Patrol 1943
Border Phantom 1937
Border River 1954
Border Romance 1930
Border Vigilantes 1941
Border Wolves 1938

Borderland 1937
Born to the West 1937
Boss Nigger 1974
Boss of Hangtown Mesa 1942
Boss of Lonely Valley 1937
Boss Rider of Gun Creek, The 1936
Bounty Hunter, The 1954
Bounty Hunters, The 1970
Bounty Killer, The 1965
Bowery Buckaroos 1947
Boy from Oklahoma, The 1954
Branded 1951
Branded a Coward 1935
Brass Legend, The 1956
Bravados, The 1958
Brave Warrior 1952
Breakheart Pass 1975
Bride of the Desert 1929
Bride Wasn't Willing, The see Frontier Gal 1945
Brigham Young 1940
Brimstone 1949
Broadway to Cheyenne 1932
Broken Arrow 1950
Broken Lance 1954
Broken Star, The 1956
Bronco Billy 1980
Bronco Buster 1952
Bronze Buckaroo, The 1939
Brothers in the Saddle 1949
Buchanan Rides Alone 1958
Buck and the Preacher 1971
Buck Benny Rides Again 1940
Buckaroo Sheriff of Texas 1951
Buckskin 1968
Buffalo Bill 1944
Buffalo Bill and the Indians, Or Sitting Bull's History Lesson 1976
Buffalo Bill, Hero of the Far West 1964
Buffalo Bill in Tomahawk Territory 1952
Buffalo Bill, L'Eroe del Far West see Buffalo Bill, Hero of the Far West 1964
Buffalo Bill Rides Again 1947
Bugles in the Afternoon 1952
Bullet Code 1940
Bullet for a Badman 1964
Bullet for the General, A 1966
Bullwhip 1958
Buono, Il Brutto, Il Cattivo, Il see The Good, the Bad and the Ugly 1966
Burning Hills, The 1956
Bushwackers, The 1952
Butch and Sundance, the Early Days 1979
Butch Cassidy and the Sundance Kid 1969
Cactus Jack see The Villain 1979
Cahill see Cahill, United States Marshal 1973
Cahill, United States Marshal 1973
Cain's Way 1969
Calamity Jane 1953
Calamity Jane and Sam Bass 1949
Calico Queen, The see The Hanging of Jake Ellis 1969
California 1946
California Conquest 1952
California Frontier 1938
California Mail, The 1936
California Passage 1950
Californian, The 1937
Call of the Canyon 1942
Call of the Wild 1935
Call the Mesquiteers 1938
Callaway Went Thataway 1951
Calling Wild Bill Elliott 1943
Camels West see Southwest Passage 1954
Canadian Pacific 1949
Canadians, The 1961
Cannon for Cordoba 1970
Canyon Crossroads 1955
Canyon Passage 1946
Canyon Passage 1951 see Raton Pass 1951
Canyon River 1956
Captain Apache 1971
Captive of Billy the Kid 1952
Caravan Trail, The 1946
Cariboo Trail, The 1950
Carry on Cowboy 1966
Carson City 1952
Carson City Raiders 1948
Cassidy of Bar 20 1938
Castaway Cowboy, The 1974
Cat Ballou 1965
Catlow 1971
Cattle Annie and the Little Britches 1980
Cattle Drive 1951
Cattle Empire 1958
Cattle King 1963
Cattle Queen 1951
Cattle Queen of Montana 1954
Cattle Raiders 1938
Cattle Thief, The 1936
Cattle Town 1952
Cavalier of the West 1931
Cavalry Scout 1951
Cave of Outlaws 1951
C'Era una Volta il West see Once upon a Time in the West 1968

Charge of Feather River, The 1953
Charley-One-Eye 1972
Charro 1969
Chato's Land 1971
Cheat, The see The Lone Hand Texan 1947
Cherokee Flash, The 1945
Cherokee Strip 1937
Cheyenne 1947
Cheyenne Autumn 1964
Cheyenne Social Club, The 1970
Cheyenne Takes Over 1947
Chief Crazy Horse 1955
Chip of the Flying U 1939
Chisum 1970
Christmas Kid, The 1967
Chuka 1967
Cimarron 1931
Cimarron 1960
Cimarron Kid, The 1952
Cinque della Vendetta, I see Five Giants from Texas 1966
Cisco Kid, The 1931
Cisco Kid and the Lady, The 1940
Cisco Kid Returns, The 1945
Clearing the Range 1931
Cockeyed Cowboys of Calico County, The 1970
Code of the Range 1936
Cole Younger, Gunfighter 1958
Colorado Ambush 1951
Colorado Serenade 1946
Colorado Sundown 1952
Colorado Territory 1949
Colt Comrades 1943
Colt .45 1950
Comanche Station 1960
Comanche Territory 1950
Comancheros, The 1961
Come On Cowboy 1937
Come On Danger 1932
Come On Danger 1942
Comes a Horseman 1978
Comin' at Ya! 1981
Command, The 1954
Companeros 1970
Company of Cowards see Advance to the Rear 1964
Con Men, The 1973
Concentratin' Kid, The 1930
Conquerors, The 1932
Conquest of Cochise 1953
Continuavamo a Chiamarlo Trinity see Trinity Is Still My Name 1971
Coogan's Bluff 1969
Copper Canyon 1950
Copper Sky 1957
Coroner Creek 1948
Courage of the West 1937
Courtin' Wildcats 1929
Covered Wagon Days 1940
Cow Country 1953
Cowboy 1958
Cowboy and the Blonde, The 1941
Cowboy and the Indians, The 1949
Cowboy and the Kid, The 1936
Cowboy and the Lady, The 1938
Cowboy and the Senorita, The 1944
Cowboy Canteen 1944
Cowboy Commandos 1943
Cowboy Counsellor 1932
Cowboy from Brooklyn 1938
Cowboy in the Clouds 1943
Cowboy Millionaire, The 1935
Cowboy Serenade 1942
Cowboys, The 1972
Crashin' Thru 1939
Crepo Tue ... che Vivo see Bandidos 1967
Crimson Trail, The 1935
Cripple Creek 1952
Crooked River 1950
Crossfire 1933
Crudeli, I see The Hellbenders 1966
Cry Blood Apache 1970
Cry for Me Billy see Face to the Wind 1972
Culpepper Cattle Company, The 1972
Curse of the Undead 1959
Curtain Call at Cactus Creek 1950
Custer of the West 1968
Da Uomo a Uomo see Death Rides a Horse 1967
Dakota 1945
Dakota Incident 1956
Dakota Lil 1950
Dallas 1950
Dalton Girls, The 1957
Daltons Ride Again, The 1945
Dan Candy's Law see Alien Thunder 1973
Danger Rides the Range see Three Texas Steers 1939
Daniel Boone 1936
Daredevil Dick see Yankee Don 1931
Daredevils of the West 1943
Daring Danger 1932
Dark Command 1940
Daughter of the West 1949
David Crockett, King of the Wild

Frontier 1955
Dawn on the Great Divide 1942
Dawn Rider, The 1935
Day of Anger 1967
Day of the Bad Man 1958
Day of the Evil Gun 1968
Day of the Outlaw 1959
Days of Jesse James 1939
Days of Old Cheyenne 1943
Dead Don't Dream, The 1948
Dead Man's Gulch 1943
Dead or Alive 1967
Deadline 1931
Deadly Companions, The 1961
Deadly Peacemaker see Man with the Gun 1955
Deadly Trackers, The 1973
Deadwood '76 1965
Deaf Smith and Johnny Ears 1972
Death Dance at Banner see Stranger on the Run 1967
Death Hunt 1981
Death of a Gunfighter 1969
Death Rides a Horse 1967
Death Rides the Plains 1943
Death Sentence 1967
Death Valley Rangers 1943
Decision at Sundown 1957
Deep in the Heart of Texas 1942
Deerslayer, The 1943
Deerslayer, The 1957
Denver and Rio Grande 1952
Desert Bandit 1941
Desert Gold 1936
Desert Passage 1952
Desert Phantom 1936
Desert Trail, The 1935
Desert Vengeance 1931
Desert Vigilante 1949
Deserter, The 1970
Desperado, The 1954
Desperado Trail, The 1965
Desperadoes, The 1943
Desperados, The 1969
Desperate Siege see Rawhide 1951
Desperate Trails 1939
Destry 1955
Destry Rides Again 1932
Destry Rides Again 1939
Devil's Canyon 1953
Devil's Doorway, The 1950
Devil's Mistress, The 1968
Devil's Saddle Legion, The 1937
10,000 Dollari per un Massacro see 10,000 Dollars Blood Money 1966
Dirty Dingus Magee 1970
Dirty Little Billy 1972
Distant Drums 1951
Distant Trumpet, A 1964
Django 1966
Django Kill 1969
Django Spara per Primo see He Who Shoots First 1966
Doc 1971
Doctor's Alibi see The Medico of Painted Springs 1941
Dodge City 1939
Dodge City Trail 1936
Dollaro tra I Denti, Un see For a Dollar in the Teeth 1966
Domino Kid, The 1957
Doolins of Oklahoma, The 1949
Doomed at Sundown 1937
Doomed Caravan 1941
Down Dakota Way 1949
Down Mexico Way 1941
Down Rio Grande Way 1942
Down Texas Way 1942
Down the Wyoming Trail 1939
Dragoon Wells Massacre 1957
Drango 1957
Drift Fence 1936
Drifter, The 1944
Drifting Along 1946
Drop Them or I'll Shoot 1969
Drum Beat 1954
Drum Taps 1933
Drummer of Vengeance 1974
Drums Across the River 1954
Drums Along the Mohawk 1939
Drums in the Deep South 1951
Duchess and the Dirtwater Fox, The 1976
Duck You Sucker see A Fistful of Dynamite 1971
Dude Cowboy, The 1941
Dude Goes West, The 1948
Dude Ranger, The 1934
Due Fratelli in un Posto Chiamato Trinita see Jesse and Lester Two Brothers in a Place Called Trinity 1972
Duel at Apache Wells 1957
Duel at Diablo 1966
Duel at Silver Creek, The 1952
Duel in the Sun 1946
Duello nel Texas see Gringo 1963
Durango Kid, The 1940

Dynamite Man from Glory Jail see Fool's Parade 1971
E pri lo Chiamavono Il Magnifico see Man of the East 1972
Eagle and the Hawk, The 1950
Eagle's Brood, The 1935
Eagle's Wing 1978
Ehi, Amico … C'E Sabata, Hai Chiuso! see Sabata 1969
El Condor 1970
El Dorado 1967
El Paso Stampede 1953
El Topo 1971
Electric Horseman, The 1979
Emigrants, The 1970
Emperor of California, The 1936
End of the Trail 1932
End of the Trail 1936
Escape from Fort Bravo 1953
Escape from Red Rock 1958
Escondido see Dead or Alive 1967
Escort West 1959
Esercito di 5 Uomini, Un see The Five Man Army 1969
Eyes of Texas 1948
Fabulous Texan, The 1947
Faccia a Faccia see Face to Face 1967
Face to Face 1967
Face to the Wind 1972
False Colors 1943
Fanciullo Del West, Il 1943
Fancy Pants 1950
Far Country, The 1955
Far Horizons, The 1955
Fargo Express 1933
Fast Bullets 1936
Fastest Guitar Alive, The 1967
Fastest Gun Alive, The 1956
Fiddlin' Buckaroo, The 1933
Fiend Who Walked the West, The 1958
Fighting Caravans 1931
Fighting Frontier 1943
Fighting Gringo, The 1939
Fighting Kentuckian, The 1949
Fighting Legion, The 1930
Fighting Man of the Plains 1949
Fighting Parson, The 1933
Fighting Phantom, The see The Mysterious Rider 1933
Fighting Ranger, The 1934
Fighting Redhead, The 1949
Fighting Seventh, The see Little Big Horn 1951
Fighting Trooper, The 1934
Firecreek 1968
First Rebel, The see Allegheny Uprising 1939
First Texan, The 1956
First Travelling Saleslady, The 1956
Fistful of Dollars, A 1964
Fistful of Dynamite, A 1971
Fiume di Dollari, Un see The Hills Run Red 1966
Five Bloody Graves 1969
5 Card Stud 1968
Five Giants from Texas 1966
Five Guns to Tombstone 1961
Five Guns West 1955
Five Man Army, The 1969
Five Savage Men see The Animals 1970
Flame of Sacramento see In Old Sacramento 1946
Flame of the Barbary Coast 1945
Flame of the West see Flaming Frontier 1945
Flaming Feather 1952
Flaming Frontier 1945
Flaming Star 1960
Flap! 1970
Flesh and the Spur 1956
Fool's Parade 1971
For a Dollar in the Teeth 1966
For a Few Dollars More 1965
Forbidden Valley 1938
Forlorn River 1937
Fort Apache 1948
Fort Bowie 1958
Fort Defiance 1951
Fort Dobbs 1958
Fort Massacre 1958
Fort Savage Raiders 1951
Fort Ti 1953
Fort Utah 1967
Fort Worth 1951
Forty Graves for Forty Guns see Machismo - 40 Graves for 40 Guns 1970
Forty Guns 1957
Forty Guns to Apache Pass 1967
Forty-Niners, The 1954
Forty Thieves 1944
Four Faces West 1948
Four for Texas 1963
Four Rode Out 1969
Friendly Persuasion 1956
Frisco Kid, The 1979
From Hell to Texas 1958
From Noon Till Three 1975

Frontier Badman 1943
Frontier Crusader 1940
Frontier Gal 1945
Frontier Horizon see New Frontier 1939
Frontier Marshal 1934
Frontier Marshal 1939
Frontier Scout 1938
Frontiers of '49 1939
Frontiersman, The 1938
Fugitive, The 1933
Furies, The 1950
Fury at Furnace Creek 1948
Fury at Gunsight Pass 1956
Fury at Showdown 1957
Gal Who Took the West, The 1949
Gallant Defender 1935
Gallant Legion, The 1948
Galloping Romeo 1933
Galloping Thru 1932
Gambling Terror 1937
Garden of Evil 1954
Gatling Gun, The 1971
Gay Caballero, The 1932
Gay Caballero, The 1940
Gay Ranchero, The 1948
Gentleman from California, The see The Californian 1937
Geronimo 1940
Geronimo 1962
Ghost of Zorro 1949
Ghost Patrol 1936
Ghost Town 1936
Ghost Town Law 1942
Giant 1956
Giants A'Fire see The Royal Mounted Patrol 1941
Giorni Dell'Ira, I see Day of Anger 1967
Girl of the Golden West, The 1930
Girl of the Golden West, The 1938
Girl Rush 1944
Giu la Testa see A Fistful of Dynamite 1971
Glory Guys, The 1965
Glory Trail, The 1936
Go West 1940
Go West Young Lady 1941
God's Country and the Man 1931
God's Country and the Man 1937
Goin' South 1978
Gold Is Where You Find It 1938
Gold of the Seven Saints 1961
Golden Stallion, The 1949
Goldtown Ghost Raiders 1953
Good Day for Fighting, A see Custer of the West 1968
Good Guys and the Bad Guys, The 1969
Good, the Bad and the Ugly, The 1966
Grand Canyon Trail 1948
Grayeagle 1977
Great Adventures of Wild Bill Hickok, The 1938
Great Bank Robbery, The 1969
Great Day in the Morning 1956
Great Gundown, The 1977
Great Man's Lady, The 1942
Great Manhunt, The see The Doolins of Oklahoma 1949
Great Missouri Raid, The 1951
Great Northfield Minnesota Raid, The 1971
Great Scout and Cathouse Thursday, The 1976
Grey Fox, The 1982
Gringo 1963
Groom Wore Spurs, The 1951
Gun Brothers 1956
Gun Fever 1958
Gun for a Coward 1957
Gun Fury 1953
Gun Glory 1957
Gun Hawk, The 1963
Gun Law 1938
Gun Play 1935
Gun Ranger, The 1937
Gun Riders, The 1969
Gun Smoke 1931
Gun Street 1961
Gun that Won the West, The 1955
Gun the Man Down 1956
Gunfight, A 1970
Gunfight at Comanche Creek 1963
Gunfight at Dodge City 1959
Gunfight at Red Sands see Gringo 1963
Gunfight at the O.K. Corral 1957
Gunfight in Abilene 1967
Gunfighter, The 1950
Gunfighters, The 1947
Gunfighters of Casa Grande 1965
Gunlords of Stirrup Basin 1937
Gunman from Bodie 1941
Gunman's Walk 1958
Gunmen of Abilene 1950
Gunpoint 1966
Guns in the Afternoon see Ride the High Country 1962
Guns of Fort Petticoat, The 1957
Guns of Hate 1948
Guns of the Magnificent Seven 1968

Guns of the Timberland 1960
Gunsight Ridge 1957
Gunslinger, The 1956
Gunsmoke Ranch 1937
Half-Breed, The 1952
Hallelujah Trail, The 1965
Halliday Brand, The 1957
Hands Across the Border 1944
Hang 'Em High 1967
Hanging of Jake Ellis, The 1969
Hanging Tree, The 1959
Hangman, The 1959
Hangman's Knot 1952
Hannah Lee 1953
Hannie Caulder 1971
Hard Hombre 1931
Hard Man, The 1957
Hard on the Trail 1971
Hard Trail see Hard on the Trail 1971
Harlem on the Prairie 1937
Harlem Rides the Range 1939
Harmony Trail see White Stallion 1947
Harry Tracey - Desperado 1982
Harvey Girls, The 1946
Hate for Hate 1967
Haunted Gold 1932
Hawaiian Buckaroo 1938
Hawk, The see Ride Him Cowboy 1932
He Who Shoots First 1966
Headin' East 1937
Headin' North 1930
Heart of the Golden West 1942
Heart of the Rockies 1937
Heart of the Rockies 1951
Heart of the West 1936
Heartland 1979
Hearts of the West 1975
Heaven with a Gun 1968
Heaven's Gate 1980
Hell Bent for Leather 1960
Hell Fire Austin 1932
Hell Town see Born to the West 1937
Hell's Heroes 1930
Hellbenders, The 1966
Heller in Pink Tights 1960
Hellgate 1952
Heritage of the Desert 1932
Heritage of the Desert 1939
Heroes of the Hills 1938
Heroes of the Saddle 1940
Hidden Gold 1932
Hidden Guns 1956
High Lonesome 1950
High Noon 1952
High Plains Drifter 1972
High Venture see Passage West 1951
Highwayman Rides, The see Billy the Kid 1930
Hills Run Red, The 1966
Hired Gun, The 1957
Hired Hand, The 1971
Hit the Saddle 1937
Hoedown 1950
Hollywood Cowboy see Hearts of the West 1975
Hollywood Round Up 1937
Hombre 1967
Hombre Que Matao Billy El Nino, El see The Man Who Killed Billy the Kid 1967
Home on the Range 1935
Hondo 1953
Honkers, The 1971
Honky Tonk 1941
Honor of the Range 1934
Hop-A-Long Cassidy 1935
Hopalong Cassidy Enters see Hop-A-Long Cassidy 1935
Hopalong Cassidy Returns 1936
Hoppy Serves a Writ 1943
Hoppy's Holiday 1947
Horizons West 1952
Horse Soldiers, The 1959
Horsemen of the Sierras 1949
Hostile Country 1950
Hour of the Gun 1967
How the West Was Won 1962
Hud 1963
100 Rifles 1968
Hunting Party, The 1971
I Killed Geronimo 1950
I Killed Wild Bill Hickock 1956
I Shot Billy the Kid 1950
I Shot Jesse James 1949
I Take this Woman 1931
Idaho Kid 1936
In Early Arizona 1938
In Old Arizona 1929
In Old California 1942
In Old Cheyenne 1931
In Old Colorado 1941
In Old Mexico 1938
In Old Monterey 1939
In Old New Mexico 1945
In Old Oklahoma 1943
In Old Sacramento 1946
In Old Santa Fé 1934

Incident at Phantom Hill 1966
Indian Agent 1948
Indian Fighter, The 1955
Indian Love Call see Rose Marie 1936
Indian Territory 1950
Indians Are Coming, The 1930
Indio Black, sai che ti Dico : Sei un Gran
    Figlio di see The Bounty Hunters 1970
Invitation to a Gunfighter 1964
Iron Mistress, The 1952
Iron Sheriff, The 1957
Iroquois Trail 1950
Ivory-Handled Gun, The 1935
J.W. Coop 1971
Jayhawkers, The 1959
Jeremiah Johnson 1972
Jesse and Lester, Two Brothers in a Place
    Called Trinity 1972
Jésse James 1939
Jesse James at Bay 1941
Jesse James Meets Frankenstein's Daughter
    1966
Jesse James Versus the Daltons 1954
Jesse James' Women 1954
Jessie's Girls 1975
Joaquin Murrieta 1965 see Murrieta 1965
Joaquin Murrieta 1970
Joe Dakota 1957
Joe Kidd 1972
Johnny Concho 1956
Johnny Guitar 1954
Johnny Oro see Ringo and his Golden Pistol
    1966
Johnny Reno 1966
Joko, Invoco Dio ... E Muori see Vengeance
    1968
Jory 1972
Journey Through Rosebud 1972
Journey to Shiloh 1968
Jubal 1956
Jubilee Trail 1954
Junior Bonner 1972
Justice of the Range 1935
Justice Rides Again see Destry Rides Again
    1932
Kaiser von Kalifornien, Der see The
    Emperor of California 1936
Kangaroo 1952
Kangaroo Kid, The 1950
Kansan, The 1943
Kansas Cyclone 1941
Kansas Pacific 1953
Kansas Raiders 1950
Kansas Territory 1952
Kansas Terrors 1939
Kentuckian, The 1955
Kettle Creek see Mountain Justice 1930
Kid Blue 1973
Kid from Broken Gun, The 1952
Kid from Texas, The 1950
Kid Rodelo 1966
Kid Vengeance 1977
Kill Them All and Come Back Alone 1968
Killer, The see Mystery Ranch 1932
Killer on a Horse see Welcome to Hard
    Times 1967
King and Four Queens, The 1956
King of Dodge City, The 1941
King of the Bandits 1947
King of the Bullwhip 1951
King of the Cowboys 1943
King of the Mounties 1942
King of the Pecos 1936
King of the Royal Mounted 1936
King of the Texas Rangers 1941
King of the Wild Stallions 1959
Kissing Bandit, The 1948
Kit Carson 1940
Knight of the Plains 1938
Knights of the Range 1940
Lady from Cheyenne, The 1941
Lady from Texas, The 1951
Lady Takes a Chance, A 1943
Land Beyond the Law 1937
Land of the Fighting Men 1938
Land of the Open Range 1942
Land Raiders 1969
Laramie Mountains 1952
Last Bandit, The 1949
Last Challenge, The 1967
Last Command, The 1955
Last Days of Boot Hill, The 1947
Last Frontier, The 1955
Last Hard Men, The 1976
Last Horseman, The 1944
Last Hunt, The 1956
Last Movie, The 1971
Last of the Badmen 1957
Last of the Clintons, The 1935
Last of the Comanches 1953
Last of the Desperadoes 1955
Last of the Duanes 1930
Last of the Duanes 1941
Last of the Fast Guns, The 1958
Last of the Mohicans 1936
Last of the Pony Riders 1953

Last of the Renegades 1964
Last of the Wild Horses 1948
Last Outlaw, The 1936
Last Outpost, The 1951
Last Posse, The 1953
Last Rebel, The 1961
Last Rebel, The 1971
Last Round Up, The 1934
Last Round-Up, The 1947
Last Stand, The 1938
Last Sunset, The 1961
Last Tomahawk, The 1965
Last Train from Gun Hill, The 1959
Last Wagon, The 1956
Last Warrior, The see Flap! 1970
Law and Jake Wade, The 1958
Law and Lead 1936
Law and Order 1932
Law and Order 1940
Law and Order 1953
Law Comes to Texas, The 1939
Law for Tombstone 1937
Law of the Golden West 1949
Law of the Lash 1947
Law of the Lawless 1964
Law of the Northwest 1943
Law of the Pampas 1939
Law of the Plains 1938
Law of the Range 1941
Law of the Texan 1938
Law Rides Again, The 1943
Law Versus Billy the Kid, The 1954
Law West of Tombstone, The 1938
Lawless Breed, The 1952
Lawless Frontier 1934
Lawless Nineties, The 1936
Lawless Plainsmen 1942
Lawless Range, The 1935
Lawless Rider, The 1954
Lawless Street 1955
Lawless Valley 1938
Lawman 1971
Lawman is Born, A 1937
Leather Burners, The 1943
Left Handed Gun, The 1958
Left Handed Law 1937
Legend of Frenchie King, The 1971
Legend of Nigger Charley, The 1972
Legend of the Lone Ranger, The 1981
Legend of Tom Dooley, The 1959
Let Freedom Ring 1939
Letzte Mohikaner, Der see The Last
    Tomahawk 1965
Life and Times of Judge Roy Bean, The
    1972
Light of Western Stars 1930
Light of Western Stars, The 1940
Lightnin' Crandall 1937
Lightning Guns 1950
Lightning Raiders 1946
Lightning Warrior 1931
Linda and Abilene 1969
Lion and the Horse, The 1952
Little Big Horn 1951
Little Big Man 1970
Little Joe the Wrangler 1942
Llano Kid, The 1939
Lo Chiamavano Trinita see They Call Me
    Trinity 1970
Loaded Pistols 1949
Lone Hand Texan, The 1947
Lone Ranger, The 1938
Lone Ranger, The 1956
Lone Ranger and the Lost City of Gold, The
    1958
Lone Ranger Rides Again, The 1939
Lone Rider, The 1930
Lone Star 1952
Lone Star Pioneers 1939
Lone Star Ranger, The 1930
Lone Star Ranger 1942
Lone Star Trail, The 1943
Lone Texan 1959
Lonely Are the Brave 1962
Lonely Man, The 1957
Lonely Trail, The 1936
Lonesome Cowboys 1968
Lonesome Trail, The 1930
Long Ride Home, The see A Time for
    Killing 1967
Long Riders, The 1980
Longhorn, The 1951
Look Out Sister 1949
Lost Ranch, The 1937
Lost Stage Valley see Stage to Tucson 1951
Lost Trail, The 1945
Lovin' Molly 1973
Lucky Boots see Gun Play 1935
Lucky Luke 1971
Lucky Texan, The 1934
Lunga Fila di Croci, Una see No Room to
    Die 1969
Lust for Gold 1949
Lusty Men, The 1952
Machismo – 40 Graves for 40 Guns 1970
Macho Callahan 1970

Mackenna's Gold 1968
Mackintosh and T.J. 1975
Mad Dog see Mad Dog Morgan 1976
Mad Dog Morgan 1976
Magnificent Bandits, The 1969
Magnificent Seven, The 1960
Magnificent Seven Ride, The 1972
Mail Order Bride 1963
Major Dundee 1965
Man Alone, A 1955
Man and Boy 1972
Man Behind the Gun, The 1953
Man Called Gannon, A 1968
Man Called Horse, A 1970
Man Called Sledge, A 1970
Man from Bitter Ridge, The 1955
Man from Cheyenne 1942
Man from Colorado, The 1948
Man from Dakota, The 1940
Man from Del Rio, The 1956
Man from Galveston, The 1964
Man from God's Country 1958
Man from Guntown, The 1935
Man from Hell, The 1934
Man from Laramie, The 1955
Man from Monterey, The 1933
Man from Music Mountain 1943
Man from Nevada, The see The Nevadan
    1950
Man from Rainbow Valley, The 1946
Man from Texas, The 1938
Man from the Alamo, The 1953
Man from Tumbleweeds, The 1940
Man from Utah, The 1934
Man in the Saddle 1951
Man in the Shadow 1957
Man in the Wilderness 1971
Man of the East 1972
Man of the Forest 1933
Man of the West 1958
Man Trailer, The 1934
Man Who Killed Billy the Kid, The 1967
Man Who Loved Cat Dancing, The 1973
Man Who Shot Liberty Valance, The 1962
Man With the Gun 1955
Man Without a Star 1955
Manhunt see From Hell to Texas 1958
Many Rivers to Cross 1955
Marauders, The 1947
Mark of the Avenger see The Mysterious
    Rider 1938
Mark of the Lash 1948
Mark of the Renegades 1951
Mark of Zorro, The 1940
Marshal of Amarillo 1948
Marshal of Cedar Rock, The 1953
Marshal of Cripple Creek, The 1947
Marshal of Mesa City, The 1939
Marshal's Daughter, The 1953
Mas Fabulosi Golpe del Far West, El see The
    Boldest Job in the West 1971
Massacre 1956
Massacre River 1949
Master Gunfighter, The 1975
Masterson of Kansas 1955
Maverick, The 1952
Maverick Queen, The 1956
McCabe and Mrs Miller 1971
McLintock 1963
McMasters ... Tougher than the West Itself,
    The 1969
Medico of Painted Springs, The 1941
Melody Inn see Riding High 1943
Melody Ranch 1940
Men of Destiny see Men of Texas 1942
Men of Texas 1942
Men Without Law 1930
Mercanario, Il see A Professional Gun 1968
Mexicali Kid, The 1938
Mexicali Rose 1939
Michigan Kid 1947
Minnesota Clay 1964
Mio Nome E Nessuno, Il see My Name Is
    Nobody 1973
Mio Nome E Pecos see My Name Is Pecos
    1966
Mio Nome E Shanghai Joe, Il see To Kill or
    to Die 1969
Miracle in the Sand see Three Godfathers
    1936
Miracle of the Hills 1959
Miracle Rider, The 1935
Misfits, The 1961
Missouri Breaks, The 1976
Molly and Lawless John 1972
Money, Women and Guns 1959
Montana 1950
Montana Belle 1952
Montana Kid, The 1931
Montana Moon 1930
Monte Walsh 1970
Moonlight on the Prairie 1935
Moonlight on the Range 1937
Moonlighter, The 1953
More Dead Than Alive 1969
Mountain Justice 1930

Mountain Men, The 1979
Mounted Stranger, The 1930
Mule Train 1950
Murrieta 1965
Mustang Country 1976
My Brother the Outlaw 1951
My Darling Clementine 1946
My Hero see A Southern Yankee 1948
My Little Chickadee 1940
My Name Is Nobody 1973
My Name Is Pecos 1966
My Outlaw Brother see My Brother the
    Outlaw 1951
My Pal, the King 1932
My Pal Trigger 1946
My Son Alone see American Empire 1942
Mysterious Avenger, The 1936
Mysterious Rider, The 1933
Mysterious Rider, The 1938
Mystery Mountain 1934
Mystery of the Hooded Horsemen 1937
Mystery Ranch 1932
Naked Dawn, The 1955
Naked Revenge see Face to the Wind 1972
Naked Spur, The 1953
Navajo 1952
Navajo Joe 1966
Navajo Kid, The 1945
Near the Rainbow's End 1930
Near the Trail's End 1931
'Neath Arizona Skies 1934
Nebraskan, The 1953
Ned Kelly 1970
Nevada 1935
Nevada 1944
Nevada 1971 see The Boldest Job in the West
    1971
Nevada Smith 1966
Nevadan, The 1950
New Frontier, The 1935
New Frontier 1939
New Land, The 1973
Night of the Grizzly, The 1966
Night Passage 1957
Night Raiders 1952
Night Rider, The 1932
Night Riders, The 1939
Night Riders of Montana 1951
No Name on the Bullet 1959
No Room to Die 1969
Noose for a Gunman 1960
North from the Lone Star 1941
North of the Great Divide 1950
North to Alaska 1960
North West Mounted Police 1940
Northern Frontier 1935
Northwest Outpost 1947
Northwest Passage 1940
Nybyggarna see The New Land 1973
O Cangaceiro see The Magnificent Bandits
    1969
Odio per Odio see Hate for Hate 1967
Oggi a me ... Domani a te! see Today it's me
    ... Tomorrow you 1968
Oklahoma 1955
Oklahoma Frontier 1939
Oklahoma Kid, The 1939
Oklahoma Raiders 1944
Oklahoma Territory 1960
Oklahoma Woman 1956
Oklahoman, The 1957
Old Barn Dance, The 1938
Old Chisholm Trail, The 1942
Old Oklahoma Plains 1952
Old Shatterhand 1964
Old West, The 1952
Old Wyoming Trail, The 1937
On Secret Service see Trailin' West 1936
On the Old Spanish Trail 1947
Once upon a Horse 1958
Once upon a Time in the West 1968
One-Eyed Jacks 1961
One Foot in Hell 1960
One Little Indian 1973
One Man Justice 1937
One Man's Law 1940
One More Train to Rob 1971
One Way Trail, The 1931
Only the Brave 1930
Only the Valiant 1951
Operator 13 1933
Oregon Trail, The 1936
Oregon Trail, The 1939
Oregon Trail 1945
Oregon Trail, The 1959
Oregon Trail Scouts 1947
O'Rourke of the Royal Mounted see
    Saskatchewan 1954
Out California Way 1946
Out West with the Hardys 1938
Outcast, The 1954
Outcasts of Poker Flat, The 1937
Outcasts of Poker Flat, The 1952
Outlaw, The 1943
Outlaw Country 1949
Outlaw Josey Wales, The 1976

Outlaw Justice 1932
Outlaw Territory see Hannah Lee 1953
Outlaw Trail 1944
Outlaw Women 1952
Outlaws Is Coming, The 1965
Outlaws of Pine Ridge 1942
Outlaws of Sonora 1938
Outlaws of Texas 1950
Outlaws of the Desert 1941
Outlaws of the Panhandle 1941
Outrage, The 1964
Outriders, The 1950
Overland Bound 1929
Overland Pacific 1954
Overland Stage Raiders 1938
Overland with Kit Carson 1939
Ox-Bow Incident, The 1943
Paint Your Wagon 1969
Painted Desert, The 1931
Painted Desert, The 1938
Painted Stallion, The 1937
Painted Trail, The 1938
Paleface, The 1948
Pals of the Golden West 1951
Pals of the Saddle 1938
Pampas Salvaje see Savage Pampas 1967
Panamint's Bad Man 1938
Pancho Villa 1971
Panhandle 1948
Parade of the West 1930
Paradise Canyon 1935
Pardners 1956
Parson and the Outlaw, The 1957
Parson of Panamint, The 1941
Partners of the Plains 1938
Partners of the Trail 1944
Passage West 1951
Passion 1954
Pat Garrett and Billy the Kid 1973
Pathfinder, The 1953
Pawnee 1957
Pay the Devil see Man in the Shadow 1957
Peacemaker, The 1956
Per Qualche Dollari in Piu see For a Few
   Dollars More 1965
Per un Pugno di Dollari see A Fistful of
   Dollars 1964
Persuador, The 1957
Petroleuses, Les see The Legend of Frenchie
   King 1971
Phantom Cowboy, The 1941
Phantom Empire, The 1935
Phantom Gold 1938
Phantom Horseman, The see The Border
   Outlaws 1950
Phantom of the Desert 1930
Phantom Patrol 1936
Phantom Ranger, The 1938
Phantom Valley 1948
Pierre of the Plains 1942
Pioneer Justice 1947
Pioneer Marshal 1949
Pioneers of the Frontier 1940
Pirates of Monterey 1947
Pirates on Horseback 1941
Pistol for Ringo, A 1965
Pistola per Ringo, Una see A Pistol for Ringo
   1965
Pistolero of Red River, The see The Last
   Challenge 1967
Plainsman, The 1936
Plainsman and the Lady, The 1946
Plainsong 1982
Plunderers, The 1948
Plunderers, The 1960
Pocket Money 1972
Pony Express 1953
Pony Soldier 1952
Posse 1975
Posse from Hell 1961
Powder River 1953
Powder River Rustlers 1949
Powdersmoke Range 1935
Power of Justice see Beyond the Sacramento
   1940
Prairie, The 1947
Prairie Express 1947
Prairie Moon 1938
Prairie Round Up 1951
Prairie Stranger 1941
Prairie Thunder 1937
Prezzo del Potere, Il see The Price of Power
   1969
Price of Power, The 1969
Pride of the West 1938
Professional Gun, A 1968
Professionals, The 1966
Proud Ones, The 1956
Proud Rebel, The 1958
Public Cowboy No. 1 1937
Purple Vigilantes, The 1938
Pursued 1947
Quantez 1957
Quantrill's Raiders 1958
Quattro dell'Ave Maria, Il see Revenge at El
   Paso 1968

Queen of the West see Cattle Queen 1951
Quei Disperati che Puzzano di Sudore et di
   Morte see Vengeance Is Mine 1969
Quien Sabe see A Bullet for the General 1966
Quiet Gun, The 1957
Rachel and the Stranger 1948
Racketeers of the Range 1939
Rage at Dawn 1955
Ragione per Vivere e una per Morire, Una
   see A Reason to Live, a Reason to Die
   1972
Ragtime Cowboy Joe 1940
Raid, The 1954
Raiders, The 1952
Raiders of San Joaquin 1943
Raiders of Tomahawk Creek 1950
Rails into Laramie 1954
Rainbow Trail, The 1932
Rainbow Valley, 1935
Rainbow's End 1935
Ramona 1936
Ramrod 1947
Ramsbottom Rides Again 1956
Rancho Deluxe 1974
Rancho Notorious 1952
Randy Rides Alone 1934
Range Busters, The 1940
Range Defenders 1937
Range Feud 1931
Range Land 1949
Range Law 1944
Ranger Courage 1937
Ranger of Cherokee Strip 1949
Ranger's Code, The 1933
Rangers of Fortune 1940
Ranger's Roundup, The 1938
Rangers Step in, The 1937
Rare Breed, The 1966
Raton Pass 1951
Rawhide 1938
Rawhide 1951
Rawhide Years, The 1956
Reason to Live, A Reason to Die, A 1972
Rebel, The see The Bushwackers 1952
Rebel in Town 1956
Rebellion 1936
Reckless Ranger, The 1937
Red Badge of Courage, The 1951
Red Desert 1949
Red Fork Range 1931
Red Mountain 1951
Red Pony, The 1948
Red Rider, The 1934
Red River 1948
Red River Range 1938
Red River Valley 1936
Red River Valley 1941
Red Sun 1971
Red Sundown 1956
Red Tomahawk 1967
Red White and Black 1970
Redhead and the Cowboy, The 1951
Redhead from Wyoming, The 1953
Renegade Ranger, The 1938
Renegades 1946
Renfrew of the Royal Mounted 1937
Resa dei Conti, La see The Big Gundown
   1966
Restless Breed, The 1957
Return of a Man Called Horse, The 1976
Return of Frank James, The 1940
Return of Frontiersman 1950
Return of Jesse James, The 1950
Return of Ringo, The 1965
Return of Sabata 1971
Return of the Bad Men 1948
Return of the Cisco Kid, The 1939
Return of the Seven 1966
Return of the Texan 1952
Return of Wild Bill, The 1940
Return of Wildfire 1948
Revenge at El Paso 1968
Revengers, The 1972
Revolt at Fort Laramie 1957
Rhythm of the Range 1936
Ride a Northbound Horse 1969
Ride a Violent Mile 1957
Ride Back, The 1957
Ride Beyond Vengeance 1966
Ride Clear of Diablo 1954
Ride 'Em Cowboy 1942
Ride 'Em Cowgirl 1939
Ride Him Cowboy 1932
Ride in the Whirlwind 1966
Ride Lonesome 1959
Ride on Vaquero 1941
Ride Out for Revenge 1957
Ride, Tenderfoot, Ride 1940
Ride the High Country 1962
Ride the Man Down 1952
Ride to Hangman's Tree, The 1967
Ride Vaquero! 1953
Rider from Tucson 1950
Rider of Death Valley 1932
Riders in the Sky 1949
Riders of Death Valley 1941

Riders of Destiny 1933
Riders of the Dawn 1937
Riders of the Deadline 1943
Riders of the Desert 1932
Riders of the Frontier 1939
Riders of the Northland 1942
Riders of the Purple Sage 1931
Riders of the Purple Sage 1941
Riders of the Rockies 1937
Riders of the West 1942
Riders of the Whistling Skull 1937
Ridin' for Justice 1932
Ridin' Law 1930
Ridin' on a Rainbow 1941
Ridin' the Outlaw Trail 1951
Riding High 1943
Riding Shotgun 1954
Riding Tall see Squares 1971
Riding Tornado, The 1932
Rim of the Canyon 1949
Ringo and his Golden Pistol 1966
Rio Bravo 1959
Rio Conchos 1964
Rio Grande 1938
Rio Grande 1950
Rio Grande Stampede see Rio Grande 1938
Rio Lobo 1970
Ritorno di Ringo, Il see The Return of Ringo
   1965
River of no Return 1954
River's End 1930
River's End 1940
Road Agent 1941
Road Agent 1952
Road to Denver, The 1955
Roamin' Cowboy, The 1937
Roarin' Lead 1936
Roaring Ranch 1930
Roaring Six Guns 1937
Robbers of the Range 1941
Robbers Roost 1933
Robin Hood of El Dorado, The 1936
Robin Hood of Texas 1947
Rock Island Trail 1950
Rocky Mountain 1950
Rocky Mountain Mystery 1935
Rocky Rhodes 1934
Rodeo 1952
Rodeo King and the Senorita 1951
Roll on Texas Moon 1946
Roll Thunder Roll 1949
Rollin' Plains 1938
Romance of the Redwoods 1939
Romance of the Rio Grande 1929
Romance of the Rockies 1937
Romance of the West 1946
Rooster Cogburn 1975
Rose Marie 1936
Rose of Cimarron 1952
Rough Company see The Violent Men 1955
Rough Night in Jericho 1967
Rough Riders' Roundup 1939
Roughshod 1949
Round Up, The 1941
Rounders, The 1965
Rovin' Tumbleweeds 1939
Royal Mounted Patrol, The 1941
Ruggles of Red Gap 1935
Run for Cover 1955
Run Home Slow 1965
Run of the Arrow 1957
Rustlers 1949
Rustlers of Devils Canyon 1947
Rustler's Paradise 1935
Rustler's Valley 1937
Sabata 1969
Sabre and the Arrow, The see Last of the
   Comanches 1953
Saddle Legion 1951
Saddle the Wind 1958
Saddle Tramp 1950
Saddlemates 1941
Sagebrush Trail 1933
Sam Whiskey 1969
San Antone 1953
San Antonio 1945
San Antonio Kid, The 1944
San Fernando Valley 1944
Santa Fé 1951
Santa Fé Passage 1955
Santa Fé Saddlemates 1945
Santa Fé Stampede 1938
Santa Fé Trail 1940
Santee 1972
Saratoga Trunk 1945
Saskatchewan 1954
Savage, The 1952
Savage Pampas 1967
Savage Sam 1963
Scalphunters, The 1968
Scandalous John 1971
Scarlet River 1933
Scavengers, The 1969
Schatz im Silbersee, Der see The Treasure of
   Silver Lake 1962
Sea of Grass 1947

Searchers, The 1956
Second Time Around, The 1961
Secret Valley 1937
Secrets 1933
Secrets of the Wasteland 1941
Sei Sei Vivo, Spara! see Django Kill 1969
Seminole 1953
Senor Americano 1929
Sentenza di Morte see Death Sentence 1967
Sergeant Berry 1938
Sergeant Rutledge 1960
Sergeants Three 1962
7 Pistole per il MacGregor see Seven Guns
   for the MacGregors 1965
Seven Angry Men 1955
Seven Brides for Seven Brothers 1954
Seven Guns for the MacGregors 1965
Seven Men from Now 1956
Seventh Cavalry 1956
Shadow of Chikara 1978
Shakiest Gun in the West, The 1968
Shalako 1968
Shane 1953
Shatterhand see Old Shatterhand 1964
She Wore a Yellow Ribbon 1949
Sheepman, The 1958
Shenandoah 1965
Shepherd of the Hills, The 1941
Sheriff of Fractured Jaw, The 1959
Sheriff of Wichita 1949
Shoot First, Laugh Last 1967
Shoot Out 1971
Shoot Out at Medicine Bend 1957
Shooting, The 1966
Shooting High 1940
Shootist, The 1976
Short Grass 1950
Shotgun 1955
Showdown, The 1940
Showdown, The 1940 see West of Abilene 1940
Showdown, The 1950
Showdown 1972
Showdown at Boot Hill 1958
Shut My Big Mouth 1942
Si puo fare ... Amigo see The Big and the
   Bad 1971
Siege at Red River, The 1954
Sierra 1950
Sierra Baron 1958
Sierra Stranger 1957
Signora dell'Ovest, Una 1942
Silver Bandit, The 1950
Silver Bullet, The 1942
Silver City 1948 see Albuquerque 1948
Siliver City 1951
Silver City Bonanza 1951
Silver City Raiders 1943
Silver Lode 1954
Silver River 1948
Silver Spurs 1943
Silver Star, The 1955
Silver Trail, The 1937
Silver Trails 1948
Sing Cowboy Sing 1937
Singer not the Song, The 1961
Singing Buckaroo, The 1937
Singing Cowgirl, The 1939
Singing Outlaw, The 1938
Singing Sheriff, The 1944
Singing Vagabond, The 1935
Sioux City Sue 1946
Sitting Bull 1954
Six Black Horses 1962
Six Gun Gold 1941
Six Gun Law 1948
Six Gun Rhythm 1939
Skin Game, The 1971
Sky Full of Moon 1952
Sledge see A Man Called Sledge 1970
Slim Carter 1957
Smith! 1969
Smoke in the Wind 1971
Smoke Signal 1955
Smoking Guns 1934
Soldier Blue 1970
Soleil Rouge see Red Sun 1971
Something Big 1971
Somewhere in Sonora 1933
Son of Belle Starr 1953
Son of Davy Crockett, The 1941
Son of Paleface 1952
Son of the Plains 1931
Son of Zorro 1947
Song of Old Wyoming 1945
Song of the Buckaroo 1938
Song of the Caballero 1930
Song of the Gringo 1936
Song of the Saddle 1936
Songs and Bullets 1938
Sons of Adventure 1948
Sons of Katie Elder, The 1965
Sons of the Saddle 1930
Soul of Nigger Charley, The 1973
Soul Soldiers see Red White and Black 1970
South of St Louis 1949
South of the Border 1939

South of the Rio Grande 1932
South of the Rio Grande 1945
Southern Yankee, A 1948
Southwest Passage 1954
Southwest to Sonora see The Appaloosa 1966
Specialiste, Le see Drop Them or I'll Shoot 1969
Spikes Gang, The 1974
Spina Dorsale del Diavolo, La see The Deserter 1970
Spoilers, The 1930
Spoilers, The 1942
Spoilers, The 1956
Springfield Rifle 1952
Springtime in the Sierras 1947
Spurs 1930
Spy 13 see Operator 13 1933
Squares 1971
Squaw Man, The 1931
Stage to Chino 1940
Stage to Thunder Rock 1964
Stage to Tucson 1951
Stagecoach 1939
Stagecoach 1966
Stagecoach Buckaroo 1942
Stagecoach to Fury 1956
Stalking Moon, The 1968
Stallion Canyon 1949
Stampede 1949
Stampede 1960 see Guns of the Timberland 1960
Stampeded see The Big Land 1957
Stand at Apache River, The 1953
Stand Up and Fight 1939
Star in the Dust 1956
Star of Texas 1953
Star Packer, The 1934
Star Said No, The see Callaway Went Thataway 1951
Stars in My Crown 1950
Stars over Arizona 1937
Station West 1948
Stone of Silver Creek 1935
Storm over Wyoming 1950
Strange Incident see The Ox-Bow Incident 1943
Strange Lady in Town 1956
Strange Laws see Cherokee Strip 1937
Stranger on Horseback 1955
Stranger on the Run 1967
Stranger Wore a Gun, The 1953
Strawberry Roan 1933
Strawberry Roan, The 1948
Streets of Laredo 1949
Sugarfoot 1951
Sundown Riders 1948
Sundown Saunders 1936
Sundown Trail 1931
Sundown Valley 1944
Sundowners, The 1950
Sunrise Trail 1931
Sunset in El Dorado 1945
Sunset of Power 1936
Sunset Pass 1946
Sunset Range 1935
Sunset Trail 1939
Support Your Local Gunfighter 1971
Support Your Local Sheriff 1968
Sutter's Gold 1936
Swirl of Glory see Sugarfoot 1951
Take a Hard Ride 1975
Take Me to Town 1953
Taking Sides see Lightning Guns 1950
Tall in the Saddle 1944
Tall Man Riding 1955
Tall Men, The 1955
Tall Stranger, The 1957
Tall T, The 1957
Tall Texan, The 1953
Taming of the West 1939
Target 1952
Taza, Son of Cochise 1954
Te Deum see The Con Men 1973
Telegraph Trail, The 1933
Tell Them Willie Boy Is Here 1969
10,000 Dollars Blood Money 1966
Ten Wanted Men 1955
Tenderfoot, The 1932
Tennessee's Partner 1955
Tenting Tonight on the Old Camp Ground 1943
Terror in a Texas Town 1958
Terror of Tiny Town 1938
Terrors on Horseback 1946
Tex Rides with the Boy Scouts 1938
Texan, The 1930
Texans, The 1938
Texas 1941
Texas Across the River 1966
Texas Addio see The Avenger 1966
Texas Bad Man 1932
Texas Bad Man 1953
Texas Cyclone 1932
Texas Dynamo 1950
Texas Kid, Outlaw see The Kid from Texas 1950

Texas Lady 1955
Texas Lawmen 1951
Texas Ranger, The 1931
Texas Rangers, The 1936
Texas Rangers, The 1951
Texas Rangers Ride Again 1940
Texas Road Agent see Road Agent 1941
Texas Stagecoach 1940
Texas Stampede 1939
Texas Terror 1935
Texas to Bataan 1942
Texas Tornado 1932
Texas Trail 1937
Texican, The 1966
There Was a Crooked Man 1970
These Thousand Hills 1959
They Call Me Trinity 1970
They Died With Their Boots On 1941
They Passed This Way see Four Faces West 1948
They Rode West 1954
Three Godfathers 1936
Three Godfathers 1948
Three Hours to Kill 1954
Three Men from Texas 1940
Three Stooges Meet the Gunslinger see The Outlaws Is Coming 1965
3:10 to Yuma 1957
Three Texas Steers 1939
Three Violent People 1957
Thrill Hunter, The 1933
Thunder at the Border 1966
Thunder in God's Country 1951
Thunder in the Dust see The Sundowners 1950
Thunder in the Sun 1959
Thunder Mountain 1935
Thunder Mountain 1947
Thunder of Drums, A 1961
Thunder over Texas 1934
Thunder over the Plains 1953
Thunder over the Prairie 1941
Thunder Trail 1937
Thunderhoof 1948
Thundering Herd, The 1933
Ticket to Tomahawk, A 1950
Timberjack 1955
Time for Dying, A 1969
Time for Killing, A 1967
Timerider 1983
Tin Star, The 1957
To Hell You Preach 1972
To Kill or to Die 1973
To the Last Man 1933
Today It's Me ... Tomorrow You! 1968
Toll of the Desert 1935
Tom Horn 1980
Tomahawk 1951
Tomahawk Trail, The see Iroquois Trail 1950
Tombstone 1942
Tombstone Canyon 1932
Tombstone, the Town too Tough to Die see Tombstone 1942
Top Gun 1955
Topeka 1953
Tornado Sabata ... Hai Chiuso un Altro Volto, E' see Return of Sabata 1971
Toughest Man in Arizona 1952
Town Called Bastard, A 1971
Town Tamer 1965
Track of the Cat 1954
Trail Beyond, The 1934
Trail Drive, The 1933
Trail Dust 1936
Trail of Robin Hood 1950
Trail of the Lonesome Pine, The 1936
Trail of the Vigilantes 1940
Trail of Vengeance 1937
Trail Street 1947
Trailin' Double Trouble 1940
Trailin' Trouble 1930
Trailin' West 1936
Trail's End 1949
Train Robbers, The 1973
Traitor, The 1936
Tramplers, The 1966
Trapped 1937
Treachery Rides the Range 1936
Treasure of Lost Canyon, The 1952
Treasure of Pancho Villa, The 1955
Treasure of Silver Lake, The 1962
Treasure of the Sierra Madre, The 1948
Tribute to a Badman 1956
Trigger Pals 1939
Trigger Tricks 1930
Trigger Trio, The 1937
Trinity Is Still My Name 1971
Triple Justice 1940
Trooper Hook 1957
Trouble in Sundown 1939
Trouble in Texas 1937
True Grit 1969
True Story of Jesse James, The 1957
Tulsa Kid, The 1940
Tumbling Tumbleweeds 1935

Twenty Mule Train 1940
Two Fisted Law 1932
Two Fisted Rangers 1940
Two Fisted Sheriff 1937
Two Flags West 1950
Two Gun Lady 1956
Two Gun Sheriff 1941
Two Guns and a Badge 1954
Two Guns from Texas 1948
Two Mules for Sister Sara 1970
Two Rode Together 1961
Ultimo Rebelde, El see The Last Rebel 1961
Ulzana's Raid 1972
Unconquered 1947
Undefeated, The 1969
Under a Texas Moon 1930
Under Colorado Skies 1947
Under Mexicali Stars 1950
Under Strange Flags 1937
Under Texas Skies 1930
Under Texas Skies 1940
Under the Pampas Moon 1935
Under the Tonto Rim 1947
Under Western Stars 1938
Undercover Man 1942
Unforgiven, The 1960
Unholy Four, The 1969
Union Pacific 1939
Unknown Ranger, The 1936
Untamed Breed, The 1948
Untamed Frontier 1952
Unter Geiern see Among Vultures 1964
Unto a Good Land see The New Land 1973
Uomini del Passo Pessante, Gli see The Tramplers 1966
Uomo, un Cavallo, una Pistola, Un see Shoot First, Laugh Last 1967
Utah 1945
Utah Blaine 1957
Utah Trail 1938
Utvandrana see The Emigrants 1970
Valdez Is Coming 1970
Valley of Fury see Chief Crazy Horse 1955
Valley of Hunted, The 1942
Valley of the Giants 1938
Valley of the Sun 1942
Vamos a Matar, Companeros! see Companeros 1970
Vanishing American, The 1955
Vanishing Frontier, The 1932
Vanishing Westerner, The 1950
Vanquished 1953
Vendetta see Murrieta 1965
Vengeance 1968
Vengeance Is Mine 1969
Vengeance of a Gunfighter see To Hell You Preach 1972
Vengeance Valley 1951
Vera Cruz 1954
Vigilantes of Boomtown 1947
Vigilantes Return, The 1947
Villa! 1958
Villa Rides 1968
Villain, The 1979
Violent Men, The 1955
Virginia City 1940
Virginian, The 1929
Virginian, The 1946
Viva Cisco Kid 1940
Viva Villa 1934
Viva Zapata! 1952
Waco 1952
Waco 1966
Wagon Master, The 1929
Wagon Tracks West 1943
Wagon Trail 1935
Wagon Train 1940
Wagon Wheels 1934
Wagonmaster 1950
Wagons West 1952
Wagons Westward 1940
Walk Like a Dragon 1960
Walk Tall 1960
Walk the Proud Land 1956
Walking Hills, The 1949
Wall Street Cowboy 1939
Wanderer of the Wasteland 1935
Wanderer of the Wasteland 1945
Wanted 1968
Wanted Women see Jessie's Girls 1975
War Drums 1957
War of the Wildcats see In Old Oklahoma 1943
War Paint 1953
War Wagon, The 1967
Warlock 1959
Warpath 1951
Washington Cowboy see Rovin' Tumbleweeds 1939
Wasser für Canitoga see Water for Canitoga 1939
Water for Canitoga 1939
Water Rustlers 1939
Waterhole No. 3 1967
Way of a Goucho 1952
Way Out West 1930

Way Out West 1937
Way West, The 1967
Welcome to Blood City 1977
Welcome to Hard Times 1967
Wells Fargo 1937
West of Abilene 1940
West of Cheyenne 1931
West of Cheyenne 1938
West of Montana see Mail Order Bride 1963
West of Alamo 1954
West of the Badlands see The Border Legion 1940
West of the Brazos 1950
West of the Divide 1934
West of the Law 1942
West of the Pecos 1934
West of the Pecos 1945
West of Wyoming 1950
West to Glory 1947
Westbound 1959
Western Courage 1935
Western Gold 1937
Western Pacific Agent 1950
Western Renegades 1949
Western Union 1941
Westerner, The 1940
Westward Bound 1931
Westward Bound 1944
Westward Ho 1935
Westward Ho the Wagons 1956
Westward the Women 1952
Westworld 1973
When Legends Die 1972
When the Daltons Rode 1940
Where the Buffalo Roam 1938
Where the River Bends see Bend of the River 1952
Where Trails Divide 1937
Whispering Smith 1948
Whispering Smith Speaks 1935
Whistling Bullets 1937
White Buffalo, The 1977
White Feather 1955
White Man, The see The Squaw Man 1931
White Stallion 1947
Wichita 1955
Wide Open Town 1941
Wild and the Sweet, The see Lovin' Molly 1973
Wild and Woolly 1937
Wild Bill Hickok Rides 1942
Wild Bunch, The 1969
Wild Country, The 1970
Wild Frontier, The 1947
Wild Horse 1931
Wild Horse Ambush 1952
Wild Horse Mesa 1932
Wild Horse Mesa 1947
Wild Horse Rodeo 1937
Wild Horse Rustlers 1943
Wild North, The 1952
Wild Rovers 1971
Wild West, The 1946
Wildcat of Tucson 1940
Wildcat Trooper 1936
Will Penny 1967
Winchester '73 1950
Winds of the Wasteland 1936
Windwalker 1980
Wings of the Hawk 1953
Winnetou see Winnetou the Warrior 1963
Winnetou II see Last of the Renegades 1964
Winnetou III see The Desperado Trail 1965
Winnetou the Warrior 1963
Winnetou und sein Freund Old Firehand see Thunder at the Border 1966
Winterhawk 1975
Wishbone Cutter see Shadow of Chikara 1978
Without Honors 1932
Women They Almost Lynched, The 1953
Wonderful Country, The 1959
Wooruzhyon i Ochen Opasen see Armed and Dangerous 1977
Wyoming 1940
Wyoming 1947
Wyoming Bandit, The 1949
Wyoming Mail 1950
Wyoming Outlaw 1939
Wyoming Renegades 1955
Yankee Don 1931
Yellow Dust 1936
Yellow Sky 1948
Yellowstone Kelly 1959
Young Bill Hickok 1940
Young Billy Young 1969
Young Fury 1965
Young Guns of Texas 1962
Young Jesse James 1960
Young Land, The 1959
Younger Brothers, The 1949
Zachariah 1970
Zandy's Bride 1974
Zorro Rides Again 1937
Zorro the Gay Blade 1981
Zorro's Black Whip 1944
Zorro's Fighting Legion 1939

Ken Maynard in SMOKING GUNS

The GREATEST of all WESTERN STARS William S. HART in "TUMBLEWEEDS" His Greatest Epic

CLARENCE E. MULFORD'S TWILIGHT ON THE TRAIL featuring WILLIAM BOYD

THE GREAT TRAIN ROBBERY
SENSATIONAL AND STARTLING 'HOLD UP' OF THE 'GOLD EXPRESS' BY FAMOUS WESTERN OUTLAW

JOHN WAYNE Lawless Range

COOPER OBERON The Cowboy and the Lady — Released by FILM CLASSICS Inc.

TOM MIX AND TONY "DESTRY RIDES AGAIN"

ERROL FLYNN ANN SHERIDAN WARNER BROS "SILVER RIVER"

GARY COOPER Cecil B. DeMille's THE PL...

The MAN from DAKOTA — Wallace BEERY "These are my credentials!"

MAE WEST W.C. FIELDS My Little Chickadee — A NEW UNIVERSAL PICTURE

STAGECOACH

WITHERS AUTRY SHOOTING HIGH

Clark GABLE Lana TURNER HONKY TONK

"The VIRGINIAN" GARY COOPER, WALTER HUSTON, RICHARD ARLEN and MARY BRIAN — a Paramount Picture

ERROL FLYNN OLIVIA DE HAVILLAND ANN SHERIDAN DODGE CITY

ERROL FLYNN ☆ OLIVIA DeHAVILLAND "They Died with their Boots On" PRESENTED BY WARNER BROS PICTURES

TOM MIX TONY HORSEMAN of the PL... WILLIAM FOX Presents

GARY COOPER 'HIGH NOON'

"THE GIRL of the GOLDEN WEST"

MARLENE DIETRICH JAMES STEWART DESTRY RIDES AGAIN

EPIC FRONTIER DRAMA John Ford's New and Finest Picture of the Fighting Cavalry! JOHN WAYNE, JOANNE DRU, JOHN AGAR, BEN JOHNSON, HARRY CAREY, JR. "SHE WORE A YELLOW RIBBON" JOHN FORD

WITHERS AUTRY SHOOTING HIGH

CLARENCE E. MULFORD'S 'CASSIDY OF BAR 20' WILLIAM BOYD FRANK DARIEN, RUSSELL HAYDEN, NORA LANE, ROBERT FISKE, JOHN ELLIOTT — A Paramount Picture

CLARENCE E. MULFORD'S TWILIGHT ON THE TRAIL featuring WILLIAM BOYD

'JESSE JAMES AT BAY' Roy Rogers GEORGE GABBY HAYES REPUBLIC PICTURE

JOHN WAYNE Lawless Range

COOPER OBERON The Cowboy and the Lady — Released by FILM CLASSICS Inc.

TOM MIX AND TONY "DESTRY RIDES AGAIN"

ERROL FLYNN ANN SHERIDAN WARNER BROS "SILVER RIVER"

GARY COOPER Cecil B. DeMille's THE PL...